Management Information Systems

MANAGING THE DIGITAL FIRM

NINTH EDITION

Kenneth C. Laudon
New York University

Jane P. Laudon
Azimuth Information Systems

PEARSON

Prentice
Hall

Upper Saddle River • New Jersey 07458

Library of Congress Cataloging-in-Publication

Laudon, Kenneth C.
    Management information systems: managing the digital firm / Kenneth C. Laudon,
Jane P. Laudon.—9th ed.
        p. cm.
    Includes bibliographical references and index.
    ISBN 0-13-153841-1
    1. Management information systems.   I. Laudon, Jane Price.   II. Title.

T58.6.L376 2004
658.4'038'011—dc22   2004060202

Executive Editor/AVP: Bob Horan
VP/Editorial Director: Jeff Shelstad
Project Manager: Lori Cerreto
AVP/Executive Marketing Manager: Debbie Clare
Marketing Assistant: Joanna Sabella
Managing Editor: John Roberts
Production Editor: Renata Butera
Production Manager: Arnold Vila
Art Director: Pat Smythe
Interior and Cover Design: Pat Smythe
Cover Illustration: Tom White
Infographics & Line Art: Precision Graphics
Photo Researcher: Shirley Webster
Manager, Print Production: Christy Mahon
Composition/Full-Service Project Management: Sharon Anderson/BookMasters
Printer/Binder: Courier Kendallville Inc.

Credits and acknowledgments borrowed from other sources and reproduced, with permission, in this
textbook appear on appropriate page within text.

Pearson Education LTD.
Pearson Education Australia PTY, Limited
Pearson Education Singapore, Pte. Ltd
Pearson Education North Asia Ltd
Pearson Education, Canada, Ltd
Pearson Educación de Mexico, S.A. de C.V.
Pearson Education–Japan
Pearson Education Malaysia, Pte. Ltd

10 9 8 7 6 5 4 3 2
0-13-153841-1

For
Erica and Elisabeth

About the Authors

Kenneth C. Laudon is a Professor of Information Systems at New York University's Stern School of Business. He holds a B.A. in Economics from Stanford and a Ph.D. from Columbia University. He has authored twelve books dealing with electronic commerce, information systems, organizations, and society. Professor Laudon has also written over forty articles concerned with the social, organizational, and management impacts of information systems, privacy, ethics, and multimedia technology.

Professor Laudon's current research is on the planning and management of large-scale information systems and multimedia information technology. He has received grants from the National Science Foundation to study the evolution of national information systems at the Social Security Administration, the IRS, and the FBI. A part of this research is concerned with computer-related organizational and occupational changes in large organizations, changes in management ideology, changes in public policy, and understanding productivity change in the knowledge sector.

Ken Laudon has testified as an expert before the United States Congress. He has been a researcher and consultant to the Office of Technology Assessment (United States Congress) and to the Office of the President, several executive branch agencies, and Congressional Committees. Professor Laudon also acts as an in-house educator for several consulting firms and as a consultant on systems planning and strategy to several *Fortune 500* firms.

At NYU's Stern School of Business, Ken Laudon teaches courses on Managing the Digital Firm, Information Technology and Corporate Strategy, Professional Responsibility (Ethics), and Electronic Commerce and Digital Markets. Ken Laudon's hobby is sailing and he is a veteran Newport to Bermuda Race captain.

Jane Price Laudon is a management consultant in the information systems area and the author of seven books. Her special interests include systems analysis, data management, MIS auditing, software evaluation, and teaching business professionals how to design and use information systems.

Jane received her Ph.D. from Columbia University, her M.A. from Harvard University, and her B.A. from Barnard College. She has taught at Columbia University and the New York University Graduate School of Business. She maintains a lifelong interest in Oriental languages and civilizations.

The Laudons have two daughters, Erica and Elisabeth.

Brief Contents

Contents

Part Two   Information Technology Infrastructure   183

Chapter 6   IT Infrastructure and Platforms   184

Chapter 7   Managing Data Resources   228

Chapter 8   Telecommunications, Networks, and the Internet   260

Chapter 10 Security and Control 340

Part Two Project Creating a New Internet Business 375

Part Three   Organizational and Management Support Systems for the Digital Firm   377

Part Four   Building and Managing Information Systems   493

Chapter 14   Redesigning the Organization with Information Systems   494

Preface

Management Information Systems: Managing the Digital Firm, Ninth Edition, is based on the premise that information systems knowledge is essential for creating successful, competitive firms, managing global corporations, adding business value, and providing useful products and services to customers.

One of the central questions facing managers today is how to optimize their firms' returns on their information systems investments. In the United States alone, capital expenditures for computing and telecommunications equipment and services will amount to an estimated $1.8 trillion in 2005. Accordingly, one central focus of this book is to help managers make better decisions about technology and to achieve the maximum value from their information technology investments. We do this in part by describing how contemporary real-world managers and firms make these decisions, and in part by providing you with analytic concepts that you will find useful in making decisions in the future. This book provides an introduction to management information systems (MIS) that undergraduate and MBA students will find vital to their professional success regardless of their major area or concentration.

DIGITAL INTEGRATION OF THE ENTERPRISE: THE EMERGING DIGITAL FIRM

A continuing stream of information technology innovations, from the Internet to wireless networks to digital phone and cable systems, is continuing to transform the business world. This continuing stream of innovations is enabling entrepreneurs and innovative traditional firms to create new business models, destroy old business models, disrupt entire industries, build new business processes, and transform the day-to-day conduct of business.

Briefly, the growth of the Internet, the globalization of trade, and the rise of information economies have raised the importance of information technologies and systems in business and management. It is essential that business students understand how information technologies are changing business firms and markets today and how they will likely change in the near-term future as digital technologies continue to evolve.

For example, companies are relying on Internet and networking technology to conduct more of their work electronically, seamlessly linking factories, offices, and sales forces around the globe. Leading-edge firms, such as Cisco Systems, Dell Computer, and Procter & Gamble, are extending these networks to suppliers, customers, and other groups outside the organization so they can react instantly to customer demands and market shifts. Cisco Systems corporate managers can use information systems to "virtually close" their books at any time, generating consolidated financial statements based on up-to-the-minute figures on orders, discounts, revenue, product margins, and staffing expenses. Executives can constantly analyze performance at all levels of the organization. This digital integration both within the firm and without, from the warehouse to the executive suite, from suppliers to customers, is changing how we organize and manage a business firm.

Ultimately, these changes are leading to fully digital firms where all internal business processes and relationships with customers and suppliers are digitally enabled. In digital firms, information to support business decisions is available anytime and anywhere in the organization. Accordingly, we have changed the subtitle of this text to *Managing the Digital Firm.*

NEW TO THE NINTH EDITION

This edition has been totally rewritten to teach managers how to optimize the returns on investments in information technologies and systems. Throughout the text, chapter contents and case studies describe how information systems contribute to better management decisions, more efficient business processes, and higher firm profitability. Each chapter identifies the organizational and managerial factors that help the firm benefit from its information technology investments. This edition also highlights new opportunities for improving business performance from leading-edge technologies that are transforming computing and communications. The following features and content reflect this new direction.

New Chapter on IT Infrastructure and Platforms

A completely new chapter on information technology (IT) infrastructure and platforms (Chapter 6) replaces the chapter on hardware and software in previous editions. Instead of focusing on how hardware and software work, this new chapter provides an overview of the technology and service components of IT infrastructure and the most important trends in hardware and software platforms. The chapter examines the capabilities of major technology vendors as well as key technologies to help managers make intelligent choices about the appropriate technology platforms and services for their firms.

New Chapter on the Wireless Revolution

Wireless technology has created a whole new platform for delivering products and communicating with customers and suppliers. We believe wireless systems have become so pervasive and powerful that the topic merits its own chapter (Chapter 9). This chapter features in-depth discussion of technologies for wireless networking and wireless applications. Included in our coverage are cellular systems and network generations, wireless data networks and Internet access (Bluetooth, Wi-Fi, WiMax, and emerging broadband services), wireless networking standards, m-commerce, radio-frequency identification (RFID) systems, and other applications where wireless technology is having its greatest impact.

New Chapter on Enterprise Applications for Digital Integration

A new full chapter (Chapter 11) is dedicated to supply chain management, customer relationship management, enterprise systems, and new system platforms for delivering enterprise-wide services. It explains how these applications work, how they provide value for the business, and the challenges of building and using them successfully.

New Chapter on Information Systems Security and Control

In previous editions, security and control was one of the last chapters in the text. This topic has become so important that we've positioned it much earlier as Chapter 10 immediately following our chapters on information technology. The chapter has also been fully rewritten to provide in-depth coverage of Internet security; wireless security challenges; new legal obligations such as Sarbanes-Oxley and HIPAA for safeguarding the accuracy, security, and privacy of information systems; the organizational, management, and technical framework for an up-to-date security policy; and computer forensics.

New Chapter on Telecommunications, Networks, and the Internet

Earlier editions treated telecommunications and the Internet as separate topics. This is no longer possible. The Internet is becoming the dominant networking standard for voice as well as data communication, and the distinctions between providers of voice, cable, and Internet services are disappearing. We have created a new chapter on telecommunications, networks and the Internet that deals with the impact of the convergence of computing and communications technologies and the emergence of Internet technology for integrating voice, video, and data communication in a single network.

New Chapter on Knowledge Management Systems

Knowledge management systems are another core enterprise application and one of the fastest-growing software applications in business today. A new chapter (Chapter 12) provides in-depth coverage of leading-edge, enterprise-wide knowledge management systems for capturing, distributing, and applying organizational knowledge. The chapter shows how companies are using these enterprise-wide knowledge management systems along with knowledge work systems and intelligent techniques to improve organizational performance and management decision making.

New Management Opportunities, Challenges, and Solutions Section

We have replaced the "Management Challenges" section with a new section called "Management Opportunities, Challenges, and Solutions" at the end of each chapter to give more attention to relevant management issues. This section highlights opportunities as well as challenges and provides solution guidelines for addressing the challenges.

New Leading-Edge Topics

In addition to new chapters and features that we have already described, this edition includes up-to-date treatment of the following topics:

❑ Wi-Fi, WiMax, and EV-DO wireless networks (Chapter 9)

❑ Wi-Fi security issues (Chapter 10)

❑ Radio-frequency identification (RFID) systems (Chapter 9)

❑ Internet telephony (VoIP) (Chapter 8)

❑ Digital convergence (convergence of telecommunications and computing) (Chapters 6 and 8)

❑ Computer forensics (Chapter 10)

❑ Grid computing, edge computing, and autonomic computing (Chapter 6)

❑ Web services and service-oriented architecture (Chapter 6)

❑ Nanotechnology (Chapter 6)

❑ 3G cellular networks (Chapter 9)

❑ Wireless sensor networks (Chapter 9)

❑ Information systems implications of Sarbanes-Oxley, HIPAA, and other government regulations (Chapter 10)

❑ Business intelligence (Chapter 13)

❑ Strategic information systems for business ecosystems (Chapter 3)

Expanded Treatment of Outsourcing

Chapter 16, "Managing International Information Systems," features an expanded discussion of the challenges of managing international outsourcing and global teams. Chapter 6, "IT Infrastructure and Platforms," includes a detailed discussion of hardware and software outsourcing.

New Hands-On Guide to MIS

We have added a new appendix that provides students with hands-on knowledge they can apply in their MIS student projects and in the workplace. The "Hands-On Guide" includes helpful how-to instructions on how to solve a case study problem, how to design and normalize a relational database, how to use entity/relationship diagrams, and how to write structured query language (SQL) queries.

HALLMARK FEATURES OF THIS TEXT

Management Information Systems: Managing the Digital Firm, Ninth Edition, has many unique features designed to create an active, dynamic learning environment.

Integrated Framework for Describing and Analyzing Information Systems

An integrated framework portrays information systems as being composed of management, organization, and technology elements. This framework is used throughout the text to describe and analyze information systems and information system problems and is reinforced in the student projects and case studies.

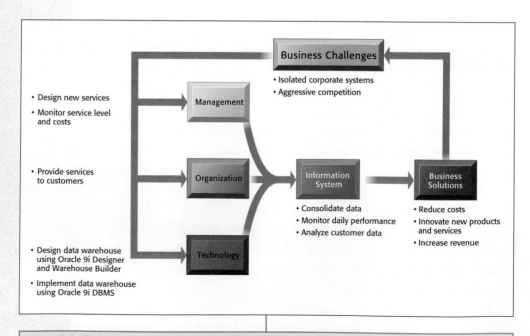

A special diagram accompanying each chapter-opening case graphically illustrates how management, organization, and technology elements work together to create an information systems solution to the business challenges discussed in the case.

Real-World Examples from Domestic and International Organizations

Real-world examples drawn from business and public organizations are used throughout the text to illustrate text concepts. More than 100 companies in the United States and nearly 100 organizations in Canada, Europe, Australia, Asia, Latin America, and the Middle East are discussed in long and short case studies and within the body of each chapter.

> *Content and products.* NTT DoCoMo, the wireless arm of Nippon Telegraph and Telephone Company, offers Internet-enabled cell phone users services for e-mail and for accessing Web sites formatted for tiny screens. Subscribers can check train schedules, obtain movie listings, browse restaurant guides, purchase tickets on Japan Airlines, trade stocks, view new cartoons, and read Japan's largest daily newspaper. Menus of services can be tailored to individual subscribers' interests. Some of these services are free. Those that aren't are bundled and charged to subscribers' monthly telephone bills.

Chapter concepts are illustrated with examples from real-world companies.

Variety of Case Studies

This text provides a variety of case studies to help students synthesize chapter concepts and apply their new knowledge to real-world problems and scenarios. Every chapter contains a short chapter-opening case, two short Window On cases, and a long chapter-ending case. At least one case study per chapter is based on a non-U.S. firm, and often there are more. Concluding the text are three long international case studies written by leading MIS scholars.

400 Part Three Organizational and Management Support Systems for the Digital Firm

WINDOW ON ORGANIZATIONS

CRM Drives Sales at Mercedes and Saab

Mercedes-Benz and Saab are both premium automobile brands, with large followings of loyal customers. However, both operate in a highly competitive market space with larger rivals launching aggressive marketing campaigns, price incentives, and inexpensive financing offers. Generating showroom traffic has proved a constant challenge. Instead of spending more on advertising, Mercedes-Benz Canada and Saab U.S.A. turned to customer relationship management to fight back.

Toronto-based Mercedes-Benz Canada, with a network of 55 dealers, believed it did not know enough about its customers. Dealers provided customer data to the automaker on an ad hoc basis. Mercedes did not force dealers to report this information, and its process for tracking dealers that failed to report was cumbersome.

Georgia-based Saab U.S.A., a subsidiary of the Swedish company Saab Automobile AB, imports and distributes more than 37,000 Saab sedans, wagons, and convertibles to 200 U.S. dealerships. Saab had been engaging customers through three channels: its dealer network, a customer assistance center dealing with service inquiries from Saab owners, and a lead management center handling marketing and information requests from prospective customers.

Each of these channels maintained customer data in its own database, leaving Saab with a splintered view of its customers. The customer assistance center relied on a SQL Server database to manage customer information; dealers kept customer data in their own lead management systems; and Saab stored lead data in other internal systems as well as in systems run by third-party vendors. The company had about 3 million records and 55 files at three different vendors.

Fragmentation of customer data meant that a prospective customer might receive a direct mail offer from Saab one week and an e-mail with an unrelated offer from a third-party marketing vendor the next week. The local dealer might not know about either of these offers and consequently delivered an ineffective pitch when the prospect visited the showroom.

Saab had no integrated lead management process. Saab salespeople received leads from Saab's lead management center by fax. The leads then had to be manually re-entered into the dealership's own lead management systems, a time-consuming and error-prone process. Lead quality was highly variable, so many dealers simply ignored the leads. Follow-up to leads was often slow and the company had no way of tracking leads faxed to its dealers.

Mercedes-Benz Canada sought a solution that would increase customer loyalty through personalized service and targeted marketing campaigns. The company chose Napoleon CRM software for automotive dealers sold by Strategic Connections.

Using its new CRM system, Mercedes-Benz Canada can determine, for example, which customers purchased earlier diesel cars and can send those buyers information about its new E Class diesel vehicle. The system helps salespeople at the dealerships create personalized brochures of vehicles for customers. If the customer does not want to purchase on the first showroom visit, that person can take home leasing, finance, and product specifications for the car that is of interest. The information is stored and made available on the Mercedes Web site for the prospective customer as well. The system also notifies salespeople to follow up with a potential customer in a set number of days or weeks.

Saab U.S.A. implemented three CRM applications from Siebel Systems' Automotive Dealer Integration Set. In January 2002 Saab implemented Siebel Call Center for 45 employees in a new Customer Interaction Center, which combines the former customer assistance center and lead management groups. This application provides Customer Interaction Center staff with a 360-degree view of each customer, including prior service-related questions and all the marketing communication they have received.

In July 2002 Saab rolled out Siebel Dealer to its 220 U.S. dealers. This application provides Saab dealers with a Web-based solution for coordinating sales and marketing activities. Sales leads generated by the Customer Interaction Center are delivered rapidly by this system to the right salespeople at the right dealerships. Saab salespeople now receive qualified leads through Siebel Dealer rather than from faxes.

The system provides detailed information to evaluate each lead more effectively. Saab can track the status of referred leads by monitoring events such as the salesperson's initial call to the customer and the scheduling and completion of a test drive. Saab can use this information to measure the sales results of specific leads, recommend better selling techniques, and target leads more precisely. Since the CRM system was implemented, Saab's follow-up rate on sales leads has increased from 38 to 50 percent and customer satisfaction has risen from 69 percent to 75 percent.

Sources: Lisa Picarille, "Planes, Trains, and Automobiles," *Customer Relationship Management Magazine*, February 2004; "Saab Cars USA Increases Lead Follow-Up from 38 Percent to 50 Percent with Siebel Automotive," www.siebel.com, accessed May 4, 2004; and Ginger Conlon, "Driving Sales," *Customer Relationship Management Magazine*, July 1, 2003.

To Think About: How did customer relationship management systems provide value for both of these companies? What management, organization, and technology issues had to be addressed when these companies implemented their CRM systems?

Each chapter contains two Window On boxes (Window on Management, Window on Organizations, or Window on Technology) that present real-world examples illustrating the management, organization, and technology issues in the chapter.

Electronic case studies on both U.S. and non-U.S. companies at www.prenhall.com/laudon provide additional opportunities for management problem solving.

Variety of Hands-On Projects

RUNNING CASE STUDY

A running case study at the end of each chapter provides students with opportunities for problem solving in an ongoing real-world business scenario. Students learn about a simulated company called Dirt Bikes U.S.A., and they can apply their information systems knowledge to problems facing this growing company. Examples of running case projects include the following:

❑ Analyzing Dirt Bikes's supply chain

❑ Identifying opportunities for knowledge management at Dirt Bikes

❑ Analyzing the return on investment for a new employee training system for Dirt Bikes

❑ Performing a competitive analysis for Dirt Bikes

❑ Redesigning Dirt Bikes's database for customer relationship management

> Each chapter contains a project requiring students to use application software, Web tools, or analytical skills to solve a problem that Dirt Bikes U.S.A. has encountered. Each assignment lists the software tools that students will need to use to solve the problem and the questions students need to answer.

The complete running case project and any required files are at www.prenhall.com/laudon and on the Laudon Interactive Multimedia CD-ROM.

HANDS-ON APPLICATION SOFTWARE EXERCISES

Each chapter features a hands-on application software exercise for which students can solve problems using spreadsheet, database, Web page development, or electronic presentation software. Some of these exercises require students to use these application software tools in conjunction with Web activities. The application software exercises include business problems dealing with supply chain management (Chapter 2), capital budgeting (Chapter 15), customer relationship management (Chapter 14), and product pricing (Chapter 13).

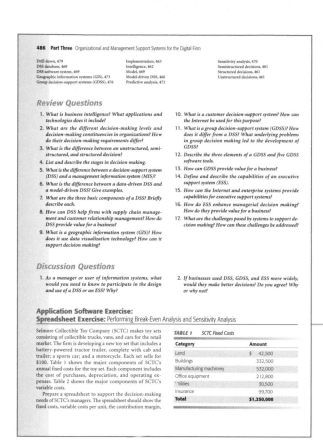

Review Questions

1. *What is business intelligence? What applications and technologies does it include?*

2. *What are the different decision-making levels and decision-making constituencies in organizations? How do their decision-making requirements differ?*

3. *What is the difference between an unstructured, semi-structured, and structured decision?*

4. *List and describe the stages in decision making.*

5. *What is the difference between a decision-support system (DSS) and a management information system (MIS)?*

6. *What is the difference between a data-driven DSS and a model-driven DSS? Give examples.*

7. *What are the three basic components of a DSS? Briefly describe each.*

8. *How can DSS help firms with supply chain management and customer relationship management? How do DSS provide value for a business?*

9. *What is a geographic information system (GIS)? How does it use data visualization technology? How can it support decision making?*

10. *What is a customer decision-support system? How can the Internet be used for this purpose?*

11. *What is a group decision-support system (GDSS)? How does it differ from a DSS? What underlying problems in group decision making led to the development of GDSS?*

12. *Describe the three elements of a GDSS and five GDSS software tools.*

13. *How can GDSS provide value for a business?*

14. *Define and describe the capabilities of an executive support system (ESS).*

15. *How can the Internet and enterprise systems provide capabilities for executive support systems?*

16. *How do ESS enhance managerial decision making? How do they provide value for a business?*

17. *What are the challenges posed by systems to support decision making? How can these challenges be addressed?*

Discussion Questions

1. *As a manager or user of information systems, what would you need to know to participate in the design and use of a DSS or an ESS? Why?*

2. *If businesses used DSS, GDSS, and ESS more widely, would they make better decisions? Do you agree? Why or why not?*

Application Software Exercise:
Spreadsheet Exercise: Performing Break-Even Analysis and Sensitivity Analysis

Selmore Collectible Toy Company (SCTC) makes toy sets consisting of collectible trucks, vans, and cars for the retail market. The firm is developing a new toy set that includes a battery-powered tractor trailer, complete with cab and trailer; a sports car; and a motorcycle. Each set sells for $100. Table 1 shows the major components of SCTC's annual fixed costs for the toy set. Each component includes the cost of purchases, depreciation, and operating expenses. Table 2 shows the major components of SCTC's variable costs.

Prepare a spreadsheet to support the decision-making needs of SCTC's managers. The spreadsheet should show the fixed costs, variable costs per unit, the contribution margin,

TABLE 1 *SCTC Fixed Costs*

Category	Amount
Land	$ 42,500
Buildings	332,500
Manufacturing machinery	532,000
Office equipment	212,800
Utilities	30,500
Insurance	99,700
Total	**$1,250,000**

> Students can use their application software skills to solve real-world business problems based on chapter concepts.

The application exercises are included in each chapter, at www.prenhall.com/laudon, and on the Laudon Interactive Multimedia CD-ROM along with the required data files and complete instructions.

E-COMMERCE AND E-BUSINESS PROJECTS

A hands-on electronic commerce or electronic business project concludes each chapter. Students can use interactive software at various company Web sites and Web research tools to solve specific business problems related to chapter concepts. These projects encourage critical-thinking skills as students explore business resources on the Internet.

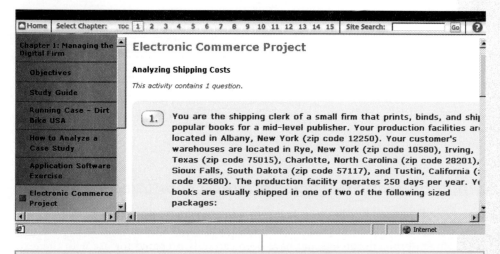

> Students are presented with a problem to develop a budget for annual shipping costs. To obtain the information required for the solution, they can input data online and use the interactive software at designated Web sites to perform the required calculations or analysis.

COMPREHENSIVE PROJECTS

A long comprehensive project concludes each major part of the text. These four projects require students to apply text concepts to demanding problems that they might encounter as firms become more digitally integrated and Internet enabled. The projects include the following:

❑ Analyzing business processes for an enterprise system (Part One project)

❑ Creating a new Internet business (Part Two project)

❑ Designing an enterprise information portal (Part Three project)

❑ Redesigning business processes (Part Four project)

Attention to Functional Business Applications of MIS

A "Make IT Your Business" section concluding every chapter shows how the topics in each chapter specifically relate to the major functional areas of business: finance and accounting, human resources, manufacturing and production, and sales and marketing. This section also directs students to pages in the chapter on which functional business examples can be found.

The Make IT Your Business section helps students identify functional business applications of chapter concepts within the body of the text. Students can immediately see how chapter material relates to business careers.

Companion Web Site (www.prenhall.com/laudon)

The text is supplemented by www.prenhall.com/laudon, which brings students a rich Web experience. The Laudon Web site provides a wide array of capabilities for interactive learning and management problem solving that have been carefully prepared for use with the text. They include the following:

Interactive Study Guide. Each chapter of the text features an Interactive Study Guide to help students review skills and test their mastery of chapter concepts with a series of multiple-choice, true-false, and essay questions.

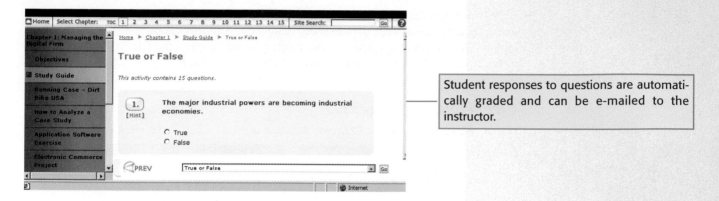

Student responses to questions are automatically graded and can be e-mailed to the instructor.

Internet Connections. Internet Connections identified by marginal notes in each chapter direct students to exercises and projects at www.prenhall.com/laudon that are related to organizations and concepts in the chapter.

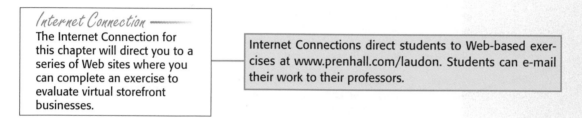

Internet Connection
The Internet Connection for this chapter will direct you to a series of Web sites where you can complete an exercise to evaluate virtual storefront businesses.

Internet Connections direct students to Web-based exercises at www.prenhall.com/laudon. Students can e-mail their work to their professors.

Additional Case Studies. The Web site contains additional case studies with hyperlinks to the Web sites of the organizations discussed.

International Resources. Links to Web sites of non-U.S. companies are provided for students interested in international material.

Interactive Multimedia CD-ROM

An interactive multimedia CD-ROM version of the text is available with the text. In addition to the full text and bullet text summaries by chapter, the CD-ROM features simulations,

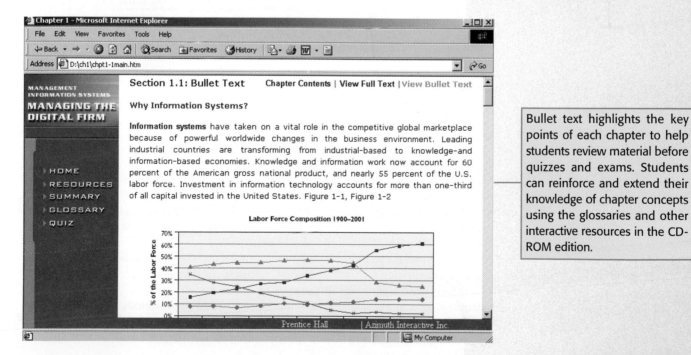

Bullet text highlights the key points of each chapter to help students review material before quizzes and exams. Students can reinforce and extend their knowledge of chapter concepts using the glossaries and other interactive resources in the CD-ROM edition.

audio/video overviews explaining key concepts, online quizzes, hyperlinks to the exercises at www.prenhall.com/laudon, the complete running case and application software exercises with required files, technology updates, and more. Students can use the CD-ROM edition as an interactive supplement or as an alternative to the traditional text.

Overview of the Text

Contents

Part One introduces students to the organizational and managerial foundations of systems, their strategic role, and the organizational and management changes driving electronic business and the emerging digital firm. Chapters in Part One provide an extensive introduction to real-world systems, focusing on their relationships to organizations, management, business processes, and important ethical and social issues.

Part Two provides the technical foundation for understanding information systems and for making wise information technology choices. Chapters in Part Two describe major components of information technology infrastructure: hardware and software platforms and services, data storage and management technology, and telecommunications services and technologies, including the Internet technology. Concluding this section are full chapters on wireless technology (Chapter 9) and on security and control (Chapter 10).

Part Three describes the role of information systems in enhancing business processes and management decision making across the enterprise. It devotes an entire chapter (Chapter 11) to enterprise applications because they have been so widely used for digital integration to improve organizational performance. Another full chapter (Chapter 12) deals with knowledge management systems because in an information economy much of a firm's value depends on its ability to create and manage knowledge. Part Three also describes decision-support and executive support systems that enhance firm performance by helping managers and employees make better decisions.

Part Four focuses on the process of building and managing systems in organizations. Chapter 14 describes how companies use new information systems to redesign their organizations and business processes and the role of new technologies such as Web services for rapid application development and digital integration. Chapter 15 explains how successful systems depend on understanding the business value of systems and managing system-related change. Chapter 16 deals with building and managing international information systems, including the special challenges and opportunities posed by offshore outsourcing.

Chapter Outline

Each chapter contains the following:

❑ An opening case describing a real-world organization to establish the theme and importance of the chapter

❑ A diagram analyzing the opening case in terms of the management, organization, and technology model used throughout the text

❑ A series of chapter objectives written in easy-to-understand language for students

❑ An Internet Connection margin note directing students to related material on the Internet

❑ A concluding section on management opportunities, challenges, and solutions related to the chapter theme

❑ A Make IT Your Business section directing students to portions of the chapter dealing with functional business applications of chapter concepts

❑ A chapter summary keyed to the learning objectives

❑ A list of key terms that students can use to review concepts

❑ Review questions for students to test their comprehension of chapter material

❑ Discussion questions raised by the broader themes of the chapter

❑ An application software exercise requiring students to use application software tools to develop solutions to real-world business problems based on chapter concepts

❑ A Dirt Bikes U.S.A. running case project

❑ An electronic commerce or electronic business project

❑ A group project to develop teamwork and presentation skills

❑ A chapter-ending long case study illustrating important themes

Instructor's Resource Center Online and on CD-ROM

The support materials described in the following sections are conveniently available for adopters both online and on CD within the Prentice Hall Instructor's Resource Center. The password-protected Instructor's Resource Center Online is accessible from www.prenhall.com/laudon. The Instructor's Resource Center on CD is available through your Prentice Hall representative. Both include the Instructor's Resource Manual, Test Item File, TestGen, TestGen conversions in WebCT and BlackBoard-ready files, PowerPoint slides, and the helpful lecture tool "Image Library." The CD features a new searchable format.

IMAGE LIBRARY

The Image Library is an impressive resource to help instructors create vibrant lecture presentations. Almost every figure and photo in the text is provided and organized by chapter for convenience. These images can be easily imported into Microsoft PowerPoint to create new presentations or to add to existing ones.

INSTRUCTOR'S MANUAL

The Instructor's Manual features not only answers to review, discussion, case study, and group project questions but also an in-depth lecture outline, teaching objectives, key terms, teaching suggestions, and Internet resources.

TEST ITEM FILE AND TESTGEN

The Test Item File is a comprehensive collection of true-false, multiple-choice, fill-in-the-blank, and essay questions. The questions are rated by difficulty level and the answers are referenced by section. It is available in Microsoft Word and in TestGen format. The TestGen is also available in WebCT and BlackBoard-ready format.

POWERPOINT SLIDES

Electronic color slides created by Azimuth Interactive, Inc., are available in Microsoft PowerPoint. The slides illuminate and build on key concepts in the text. Both students and faculty can download the PowerPoint slides from the Web site, and the slides are also provided on the Instructor's Resource CD-ROM.

COMPANION WEB SITE

Management Information Systems: Managing the Digital Firm, Ninth Edition, is supported by an excellent companion Web site at www.prenhall.com/laudon that truly reinforces and enhances text material with the complete Dirt Bikes U.S.A. running case, electronic commerce and electronic business projects, hands-on application software exercises, Internet connection exercises, an Interactive Study Guide, International Resources, additional case studies, and PowerPoint slides. The Web site links to a secure password-protected faculty area from which instructors can download the Instructor's Manual and suggested answers to the running case, Internet connections, and e-business/e-commerce projects. The site has an improved online syllabus tool to help professors add their own personal syllabi to the site in minutes. Please see the complete description earlier in this preface.

VIDEOS

Prentice Hall MIS Video, Volume I (0-13-027199-3)

The first video in the Prentice Hall MIS Video Library includes custom clips created exclusively for Prentice Hall, featuring real companies, such as Lands' End, Lotus Development Corporation, Oracle Corporation, and Pillsbury Company.

Prentice Hall MIS Video, Volume II (0-13-101500-1)

Video clips are provided to adopters to enhance class discussion and projects. These clips highlight real-world corporations and organizations and illustrate key concepts found in the text.

ONLINE COURSES

OneKey www.prenhall.com/onekey

OneKey gives you access to the best teaching and learning resources all in one place. OneKey for *Management Information Systems: Managing the Digital Firm,* Ninth Edition, is all your students need for anywhere, anytime access to your course materials conveniently organized by textbook chapter to reinforce and apply what they've learned in class. OneKey is all you need to plan and administer your course. All your instructor resources are in one place to maximize your effectiveness and minimize your time and effort spent.

OneKey for convenience, simplicity, and success . . . for you and your students. OneKey is available in WebCT, BlackBoard, and CourseCompass formats.

WebCT www.prenhall.com/webct

Gold Level customer support, available exclusively to adopters of Prentice Hall courses, is provided free of charge on adoption and provides priority assistance, training discounts, and dedicated technical support.

Blackboard www.prenhall.com/blackboard

Prentice Hall's abundant online content combined with Blackboard's popular tools and interface result in robust Web-based courses that are easy to implement, manage, and use—taking your courses to new heights in student interaction and learning.

CourseCompass www.prenhall.com/coursecompass

CourseCompass is a dynamic, interactive online course management tool powered exclusively for Pearson Education by Blackboard. This exciting product allows you to teach market-leading Pearson Education content in an easy-to-use customizable format.

TUTORIAL SOFTWARE

For instructors seeking application software support to use with this text, Prentice Hall is pleased to offer the PH Train IT CD-ROM for Microsoft Office 2003. This exciting tutorial product is fully certified up to the expert level of the Microsoft Office User Specialist (MOUS) Certification Program. This is not available as a stand-alone item but can be packaged with *Management Information Systems: Managing the Digital Firm,* Ninth Edition, at an additional charge. Please go to www.prenhall.com/phit for an online demonstration of this product, or contact your local Prentice Hall representative for more details.

SOFTWARE CASES

A series of optional management software cases, *Solve It! Management Problem Solving with PC Software,* has been developed to support the text. *Solve It!* consists of 10 spreadsheet cases, 10 database cases, and 6 Internet projects drawn from real-world businesses, plus the data files associated with the cases. The cases are graduated in difficulty. The case book contains complete tutorial documentation showing how to use spreadsheet, database, and Web browser software to solve the problems. A new version of *Solve It!* with all new cases is published every year. *Solve It!* must be adopted for an entire class. It can be purchased directly from the supplier, Azimuth Interactive Corporation, 23 North Division Street, Peekskill, New York, 10566 (**telephone: 800-416-6786; Web site: www.mysolveit.com**).

ACKNOWLEDGMENTS

The production of any book involves valued contributions from a number of persons. We would like to thank all of our editors for encouragement, insight, and strong support for many years. Bob Horan did a wonderful job guiding the development of this edition. We are grateful to Jeff Shelstad for his support of this project. We thank Debbie Clare, executive marketing manager, for her excellent marketing work.

We praise Lori Cerreto for her role in managing this project. Pat Smythe, Renata Butera, and Sharon Anderson must be commended for production/manufacturing of this text under an extraordinarily ambitious schedule. We thank Shirley Webster for her energetic photo research work.

Our special thanks go to our supplement authors for their work and to Lawrence Andrew for his recommendations for improving Chapter 7, "Managing Data Resources."

We are indebted to Kenneth Rosenblatt for his assistance in the preparation of the text and to Diana R. Craig for her help with the Hands-On Guide to MIS. Jiri Rodovsky and Todd Traver provided additional suggestions for improvements.

The Stern School of Business at New York University and the Information Systems Department provided a very special learning environment—one in which we and others could rethink the MIS field. Special thanks to Professors Vasant Dhar, Foster Provost, Roy Radner, and Alex Tuzhilin for providing critical feedback and support where deserved. Professor William H. Starbuck of the Management Department at New York University provided valuable comments and insights.

Professor Edward Stohr of Stevens Institute of Technology, Professors Al Croker and Michael Palley of Baruch College and New York University, Professor Thomas J. Housel of the Naval Postgraduate School, and Professor Donald Marchand of the International Institute for Management Development provided additional suggestions for improvement.

One of our goals was to write a book that was authoritative, synthesized diverse views in the MIS literature, and helped define a common academic field. A large number of leading scholars in the field were contacted and assisted us in this effort. Reviewers and consultants for *Management Information Systems: Managing the Digital Firm* are listed in the back endpapers of the book. We thank them for their contributions. Reviewers for the ninth edition include the following:

Rahul C. Basole, Georgia Institute of Technology

Timothy Kayworth, Baylor University

Robert Lee, Chapman University

Lannes L. Morris-Murphy, Troy State University

Peter J. Natale, Regent University

Alan Graham Peace, West Virginia University

Kala Chand Seal, Loyola Marymount University

Troy Strader, Drake University

David Teneyuca, Schreiner University

Jennifer Williams, University of Southern Indiana

It is our hope that this group endeavor contributes to a shared vision and understanding of the MIS field.

K.C.L.
J.P.L.

Organizations, Management, and the Networked Enterprise

Part One Project: Analyzing
Business Processes for an
Enterprise System

Part One describes the organizational and managerial foundations of information systems. This part describes the critical role played by various types of information systems in organizations, sweeping changes created by the Internet and digital integration of the enterprise, and the need to demonstrate the business value of information system investments. Chapters in this part provide an extensive introduction to real-world systems, focusing on their relationships to organizations, management, business processes, strategy, and important ethical and social issues.

Chapter 1

Managing the Digital Firm

OBJECTIVES

After reading this chapter, you will be able to:

1. Explain why information systems are so important today for business and management.

2. Evaluate the role of information systems in today's competitive business environment.

3. Assess the impact of the Internet and Internet technology on business and government.

4. Define an information system from both a technical and business perspective and distinguish between computer literacy and information systems literacy.

5. Identify the major management challenges to building and using information systems.

CHAPTER OUTLINE

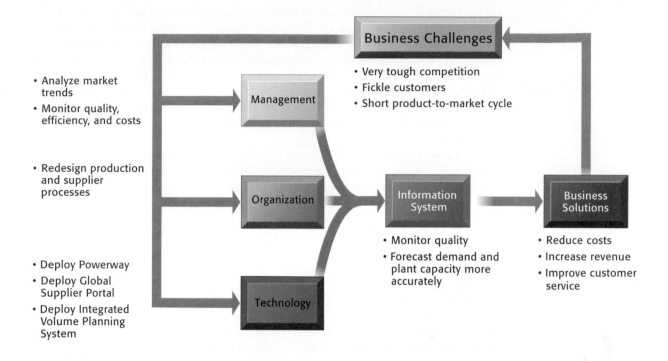

Opening Case: DaimlerChrysler's Agile Supply Chain

DaimlerChrysler includes the Chrysler Group, the Mercedes and Smart Passenger Car Group, and the Commercial Vehicles unit. It operates 104 plants in 37 countries, using 14,000 different suppliers and 13,000 sales outlets in 200 countries. The auto industry is known for tough competition and fickle customers. Survival depends on bringing new models rapidly to market as economically as possible.

DaimlerChrysler studied every step in the vehicle production and sales process, starting with the first stage of vehicle design and ending with its service and repair. It then built a series of information systems that automate and streamline all of its transactions with suppliers. An Integrated Volume Planning system gathers sales data and sends them back to production planning systems and from there to suppliers so that they can adjust deliveries of parts and production to make exactly the right amount of the vehicle models that are actually selling in dealer showrooms.

A Global Supplier Portal presents a common interface and system platform that handles every type of interaction between DaimlerChrysler and its suppliers. About 6,000 DaimlerChrysler suppliers registered for this portal use it to interact with DaimlerChrysler's various business groups. DaimlerChrysler also uses the portal internally to share information among different divisions and business units.

At the earliest stages of design, the Chrysler Group and 3,400 of its suppliers use a Web-enabled system called Powerway to track parts through nine quality control "gates" before they're certified for use on production lines. In the past, quality specialists used to store thousands of pieces of paper in hundreds of binders to deal with quality issues that surfaced with the thousands of companies that design Chrysler's parts. If a drive train was an eighth inch too short, it could take up to three weeks to notify the supplier, fix the problem, and incorporate the corrected part back into the design process.

Powerway replaces paper-based processes with digital links to supplier systems. It helps Chrysler identify potential design and engineering problems before physical parts are actually constructed, so that they can be more rapidly resolved. That in turn helps Chrysler design news cars much faster—and remain competitive.

Sources: Tracy Mayor, "The Supple Supply Chain," *CIO Magazine*, August 15, 2004; Larry Gould, "Effectively Managing Inventory in the Supply Chain," *Automotive Design & Production*, www.autofieldguide.com, accessed September 3, 2004; and www.daimlerchrysler.com, accessed September 3, 2004.

DaimlerChrysler's information systems use both technology and knowledge of the business to enable the company and its suppliers to respond instantly to changes in the marketplace or other events. These information systems give DaimlerChrysler the agility to monitor and react to data as events unfold, and they are intimately linked with systems of its suppliers and related companies. Managers can "see into" these systems and, when necessary, make adjustments on the fly to keep manufacturing and delivery processes aligned with customer needs.

The agility exhibited by DaimlerChrysler is part of the transformation of business firms throughout the world into fully digital firms. Such digital firms use the Internet and networking technology to make data flow seamlessly among different parts of the organization; streamline the flow of work; and create electronic links with customers, suppliers, and other organizations.

As a manager, you'll need to know how information systems can make your business more competitive, efficient, and profitable. In this chapter we begin our investigation of information systems and organizations by describing information systems from both technical and behavioral perspectives and by surveying the changes they are bringing to organizations and management.

1.1   WHY INFORMATION SYSTEMS?

We are in the midst of a swiftly moving river of technology and business innovations that is transforming the global business landscape. An entirely new Internet business culture is emerging with profound implications for the conduct of business. You can see this every day by observing how businesspeople work using high-speed Internet connections for e-mail and information gathering, portable computers connected to wireless networks, cellular telephones connected to the Internet, and hybrid handheld devices delivering phone, Internet, and computing power to an increasingly mobile and global workforce.

The emerging Internet business culture is a set of expectations that we all share. We have all come to expect online services for purchasing goods and services, we expect our business colleagues to be available by e-mail and cell phone, and we expect to be able to communicate with our vendors, customers, and employees any time of day or night over the Internet. We even expect our business partners around the world to be "fully connected." Internet culture is global.

In this text and in the business world, you'll often encounter the term *information technology*. **Information technology** (abbreviated **IT**) refers to all of the computer-based information systems used by organizations and their underlying technologies. Briefly, information technologies and systems are revolutionizing the operation of firms, industries, and markets. The main objective of this book is to describe the nature of this transformation and to help you as a future manager take advantage of the emerging opportunities.

Why Information Systems Matter

Let's start by examining why information systems and information technology (IT) are so important. There are four reasons why IT will make a difference to you as a manager throughout your career.

CAPITAL MANAGEMENT

Information technology has become the largest component of capital investment for firms in the United States and many industrialized societies. In 2005, U.S. firms alone will spend nearly $1.8 trillion on IT and telecommunications equipment and software. Investment in information technology has doubled as a percentage of total business investment since 1980, and now accounts for more than one-third of all capital invested in the United States and more than 50 percent of invested capital in information-intensive industries, such as finance, insurance, and real estate.

Figure 1-1 shows that between 1980 and 2003, private business investment in information technology (hardware, software, and telecommunications equipment) grew from 19 percent

FIGURE 1-1   *Information technology capital investment.*

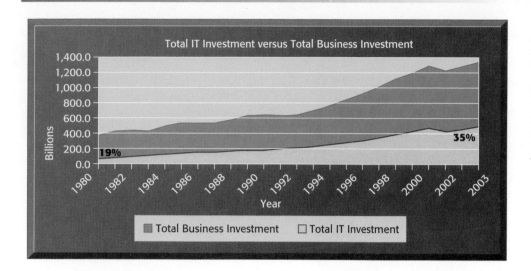

Information technology capital investment, defined as hardware, software, and telecommunications equipment, expanded from 19 percent of all business investment to 35 percent during the period from 1980 to 2003.

Source: Based on data in U.S. Department of Commerce, Bureau of Economic Analysis, *National Income and Product Accounts*, Tables 5.2 and 5.8, 2004.

to more than 35 percent of all domestic private business investment. If one included expenditures for managerial and organizational change programs and business and consulting services that are required to use this technology effectively, total information technology expenditures would rise above 50 percent of total private business investment.

As managers, many of you will work for firms that are intensively using information systems and making large investments in information technology. You will certainly want to know how to invest this money wisely. If you make wise choices, your firm can outperform competitors. If you make poor choices, you will be wasting valuable capital. This book is dedicated to helping you make wise decisions about IT and information systems.

FOUNDATION OF DOING BUSINESS

In the United States over 23 million managers and over 113 million workers in the labor force rely on information systems every day to conduct business (*Statistical Abstract*, 2003). In many industries, survival and even existence without extensive use of information systems is inconceivable. Obviously, all of e-commerce would be impossible without substantial IT investments, and firms such as Amazon, eBay, Google, E*Trade, or the world's largest online university, the University of Phoenix, simply would not exist. Today's service industries—finance, insurance, real estate as well as personal services such as travel, medicine, and education—could not operate without IT. Similarly, retail firms such as Wal-Mart and Sears and manufacturing firms such as General Motors and General Electric require IT to survive and prosper. Just like offices, telephones, filing cabinets, and efficient tall buildings with elevators were once of the foundations of business in the twentieth century, information technology is a foundation for business in the twenty-first century.

There is a growing interdependence between a firm's ability to use information technology and its ability to implement corporate strategies and achieve corporate goals (see Figure 1-2). What a business would like to do in five years often depends on what its systems will be able to do. Increasing market share, becoming the high-quality or low-cost producer, developing new products, and increasing employee productivity depend more and more on the kinds and quality of information systems in the organization. The more you understand about this relationship, the more valuable you will be as a manager.

PRODUCTIVITY

Today's managers have very few tools at their disposal for achieving significant gains in productivity. IT is one of the most important tools along with innovations in organization and management, and in fact, these innovations need to be linked together. A substantial and growing body of research reported throughout this book suggests investment in IT plays a critical role in increasing the productivity of firms, and entire nations (Zhu et al., 2004).

FIGURE 1-2 *The interdependence between organizations and information systems.*

In contemporary systems there is a growing interdependence between a firm's information systems and its business capabilities. Changes in strategy, rules, and business processes increasingly require changes in hardware, software, databases, and telecommunications. Often, what the organization would like to do depends on what its systems will permit it to do.

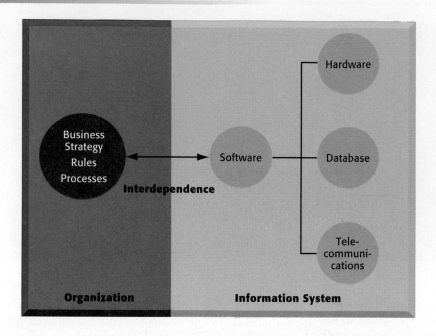

For instance, economists at the U.S. Federal Reserve Bank estimate that IT contributed to the lowering of inflation by 0.5 to 1 percentage point in the years from 1995 to 2000 (Greenspan, 2000). IT was a major factor in the resurgence in productivity growth in the United States, which began in 1995 and has continued until today at an average rate of 2.7 percent, up from 1.4 percent from 1973 to 1995 (Baily, 2002). Firms that invested wisely in information technology experienced continued growth in productivity and efficiency.

STRATEGIC OPPORTUNITY AND ADVANTAGE

If you want to take advantage of new opportunities in markets, develop new products, and create new services, chances are quite high you will need to make substantial investments in IT to realize these new business opportunities. If you want to achieve a strategic advantage over your rivals, to differentiate yourself from your competitors, IT is one avenue for achieving such advantages along with changes in business practices and management. We talk more about IT contributions to competitive strategy in Chapter 3. These advantages might not last forever, but then again most strategic advantages throughout history are short-lived. However, a string of short-lived competitive advantages is a foundation for long-term advantages in business, just as is true of any athletic sport or race.

How Much Does IT Matter?

In May 2003, Nicholas Carr, an editor at *Harvard Business Review*, wrote an article titled "IT Doesn't Matter," which stirred significant debate in the business community. Carr's argument in a nutshell is that because every firm can purchase IT in the marketplace, because any advantage obtained by one company can easily be copied by another company, and because IT is now a commodity based on standards (such as the Internet) that all companies can freely use, it is no longer a differentiating factor in organizational performance.

Carr argues that no firm can use IT to achieve a strategic edge over its competitors any more than it could with electricity, telephones, or other infrastructure. Therefore, Carr concludes, firms should reduce spending on IT, follow rather than lead IT in their industry, reduce risks by preparing for computer outages and security breaches, and avoid deploying IT in new ways.

Most management information system (MIS) experts disagree. As we discuss later in this chapter and subsequent chapters throughout the book, research demonstrates that there is considerable variation in firms' ability to use IT effectively. Many highly adept firms continually obtain superior returns on their investment in IT, whereas less adept firms do not.

Copying innovations of other firms can be devilishly difficult, with much being lost in the translation. There is only one Dell, one Wal-Mart, one Amazon, and one eBay, and each of these firms has achieved a competitive advantage in its industry based in large part on unique ways of organizing work enabled by IT that have been very difficult to copy. If copying were so easy, we would expect to find much more powerful competition for these market leaders.

Although falling prices for hardware and software and new computing and tele-communications standards such as the Internet have made the application of computers to business much easier than in the past, this does not signal the end of innovation or the end of firms developing strategic edges using IT. Far from the end of innovation, com-moditization often leads to an explosion in innovation and new markets and products. For example, the abundance and availability of materials such as wood, glass, and steel during the last century made possible a continuing stream of architectural innovation.

Likewise, the development of standards and lowering costs of computer hardware made possible new products and services such as the Apple iPod and iTunes, the Sony Walkman portable music player, RealMedia online streaming music, and the entire online content industry. Entirely new businesses and business models have emerged for the digi-tal distribution of music, books, journals, and Hollywood films.

Carr is surely correct in stating that not all investments in IT work out or have strategic value. Some are just needed to stay in business, to comply with government reporting requirements, and to satisfy the needs of customers and vendors. Perhaps the more important questions are how much does IT make a difference, and where can it best be deployed to make a competitive difference?

We make a major effort in this book to suggest ways you as a manager and potential entrepreneur can use information technology and systems to create differentiation from your competitors and strategic advantage in the marketplace. As we describe throughout, to achieve any measure of "success," investment in IT must be accompanied by significant changes in business operations and processes and changes in management culture, atti-tudes, and behavior. Absent these changes, investment in IT can be a waste of precious investor resources.

Why IT Now? Digital Convergence and the Changing Business Environment

A combination of information technology innovations and a changing domestic and global business environment makes the role of IT in business even more important for managers than just a few years ago. The Internet revolution is not something that hap-pened and then burst, but instead has turned out to be an ongoing, powerful source of new technologies with significant business implications for much of this century.

There are five factors to consider when assessing the growing impact of IT in business firms both today and over the next ten years.

- Internet growth and technology convergence
- Transformation of the business enterprise
- Growth of a globally connected economy
- Growth of knowledge and information-based economies
- Emergence of the digital firm

These changes in the business environment, summarized in Table 1-1, pose a number of new challenges and opportunities for business firms and their managements.

THE INTERNET AND TECHNOLOGY CONVERGENCE

One of the most frequently asked questions by Wall Street investors, journalists, and busi-ness entrepreneurs is, "What's the next big thing?" As it turns out, the next big thing is in front of us: We are in the midst of a networking and communications revolution driven

TABLE 1-1 *The Changing Contemporary Business Environment*

INTERNET GROWTH AND TECHNOLOGY CONVERGENCE

New business technologies with favorable costs

E-business, e-commerce, and e-government

Rapid changes in markets and market structure

Increased obsolescence of traditional business models

TRANSFORMATION OF THE BUSINESS ENTERPRISE

Flattening

Decentralization

Flexibility

Location independence

Low transaction and coordination costs

Empowerment

Collaborative work and teamwork

GLOBALIZATION

Management and control in a global marketplace

Competition in world markets

Global workgroups

Global delivery systems

RISE OF THE INFORMATION ECONOMY

Knowledge- and information-based economies

New products and services

Knowledge as a central productive and strategic asset

Time-based competition

Shorter product life

Turbulent environment

Limited employee knowledge base

EMERGENCE OF THE DIGITAL FIRM

Digitally enabled relationships with customers, suppliers, and employees

Core business processes accomplished using digital networks

Digital management of key corporate assets

Agile sensing and responding to environmental changes

by the growth of the Internet, Internet-based technologies, and new business models and processes that leverage the new technologies.

Although "digital convergence" was predicted a decade ago, it is now an undeniable reality. Four massive industries are moving toward a common platform: the $1 trillion computer hardware and software industry in the United States, the $250 billion consumer electronics industry, the $1.6 trillion communications industry (traditional and wireless telephone networks), and the $900 billion content industry (from Hollywood movies, to music, text, and research industries). Although each industry has its favored platform, the outlines of the future are clear: a world of near universal, online, on-demand, and personalized information services from text messaging on cell phones, to games, education, and entertainment.

The Internet is bringing about a convergence of technologies, roiling markets, entire industries, and firms in the process. Traditional boundaries and business relationships are breaking down, even as new ones spring up. Telephone networks are merging into the Internet, and cellular phones are becoming Internet access devices. Handheld storage devices such as iPods are emerging as potential portable game and entertainment centers. The Internet-connected personal computer is moving toward a role as home entertainment control center.

Traditional markets and distribution channels are weakening and new markets are being created. For instance, the markets for music CDs and video DVDs and the music and video store industries are undergoing rapid change. New markets for online streaming media and for music and video downloads have materialized.

Today, networking and the Internet are nearly synonymous with doing business. Firms' relationships with customers, employees, suppliers, and logistic partners are becoming digital relationships. As a supplier, you cannot do business with Wal-Mart, or Sears, or most national retailers unless you adopt their well-defined digital technologies. As a consumer, you will increasingly interact with sellers in a digital environment. As an employer, you'll be interacting more electronically with your employees and giving them new digital tools to accomplish their work.

So much business is now enabled by or based upon digital networks that we use the terms *electronic business* and *electronic commerce* frequently throughout this text. **Electronic business,** or **e-business,** designates the use of Internet and digital technology to execute all of the activities in the enterprise. E-business includes activities for the internal management of the firm and for coordination with suppliers and other business partners. It also includes **electronic commerce, or e-commerce.** E-commerce is the part of e-business that deals with the buying and selling of goods and services electronically with computerized business transactions using the Internet, networks, and other digital technologies. It also encompasses activities supporting those market transactions, such as advertising, marketing, customer support, delivery, and payment.

The technologies associated with e-commerce and e-business have also brought about similar changes in the public sector. Governments on all levels are using Internet technology to deliver information and services to citizens, employees, and businesses with which they work. **E-government** is the application of the Internet and related technologies to digitally enable government and public sector agencies' relationships with citizens, businesses, and other arms of government. In addition to improving delivery of government services, e-government can make government operations more efficient and also empower citizens by giving them easier access to information and the ability to network electronically with other citizens. For example, citizens in some states can renew their driver's licenses or apply for unemployment benefits online, and the Internet has become a powerful tool for instantly mobilizing interest groups for political action and fund-raising.

TRANSFORMATION OF THE BUSINESS ENTERPRISE

Along with rapid changes in markets and competitive advantage are changes in the firms themselves. The Internet and the new markets are changing the cost and revenue structure of traditional firms and are hastening the demise of traditional business models.

For instance, in the United States, 20 percent of travel sales are made online, and experts believe that 50 to 70 percent of travel sales will be online within a decade. Realtors have had to reduce commissions on home sales because of competition from Internet real estate sites. The business model of traditional local telephone companies, and the value of their copper-based networks, is rapidly declining as millions of consumers switch to cellular and Internet telephones. At current rates of decline in subscribers, about 15 percent per year, the value of traditional local phone networks will decline by 50 percent by 2010 (Brown and Latour, 2004).

The Internet and related technologies make it possible to conduct business across firm boundaries almost as efficiently and effectively as it is to conduct business within the firm. This means that firms are no longer limited by traditional organizational boundaries or physical locations in how they design, develop, and produce goods and services. It is possible to maintain close relationships with suppliers and other business partners at great distances and outsource work that firms formerly did themselves to other companies.

For example, Cisco Systems does not manufacture the networking products it sells; it uses other companies, such as Flextronics, for this purpose. Cisco uses the Internet to transmit orders to Flextronics and to monitor the status of orders as they are shipped.

At the Orbitz Web site, visitors can make online reservations for airlines, hotels, rental cars, cruises, and vacation packages and obtain information on travel and leisure topics. Such online travel services are supplanting traditional travel agencies.

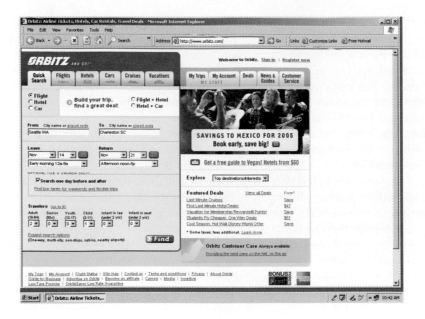

GKN Aerospace North America, which fabricates engine parts for aircraft and aerospace vehicles, uses a system called Sentinel with a Web interface to monitor key indicators of the production systems of Boeing Corporation, its main customer. Sentinel responds automatically to Boeing's need for parts by increasing, decreasing, or shutting down GKN's systems according to parts usage (Mayor, 2004).

In addition to these changes, there has also been a transformation in the management of the enterprise. The traditional business firm was—and still is—a hierarchical, centralized, structured arrangement of specialists who typically relied on a fixed set of standard operating procedures to deliver a mass-produced product (or service). The new style of business firm is a flattened (less hierarchical), decentralized, flexible arrangement of generalists who rely on nearly instant information to deliver mass-customized products and services uniquely suited to specific markets or customers.

The traditional management group relied— and still relies—on formal plans, a rigid division of labor, and formal rules. The new manager relies on informal commitments and networks to establish goals (rather than formal planning), a flexible arrangement of teams and individuals working in task forces, and a customer orientation to achieve coordination among employees. The new manager appeals to the knowledge, learning, and decision making of individual employees to ensure proper operation of the firm. Once again, information technology makes this style of management possible.

GLOBALIZATION

A growing percentage of the American economy—and other advanced industrial economies in Europe and Asia—depends on imports and exports. Foreign trade, both exports and imports, accounts for more than 25 percent of the goods and services produced in the United States, and even more in countries such as Japan and Germany. Companies are also distributing core business functions in product design, manufacturing, finance, and customer support to locations in other countries where the work can be performed more cost effectively. The success of firms today and in the future depends on their ability to operate globally.

Today, information systems provide the communication and analytic power that firms need to conduct trade and manage businesses on a global scale. Controlling the far-flung global corporation—communicating with distributors and suppliers, operating 24 hours a day in different national environments, coordinating global work teams, and servicing local and international reporting needs—is a major business challenge that requires powerful information system responses.

Globalization and information technology also bring new threats to domestic business firms: Because of global communication and management systems, customers now can shop in a worldwide marketplace, obtaining price and quality information reliably 24 hours a day. To become competitive participants in international markets, firms need powerful information and communication systems.

RISE OF THE INFORMATION ECONOMY

The United States, Japan, Germany, and other major industrial powers are being transformed from industrial economies to knowledge- and information-based service economies, whereas manufacturing has been moving to lower-wage countries. In a knowledge- and information-based economy, knowledge and information are key ingredients in creating wealth.

The knowledge and information revolution began at the turn of the twentieth century and has gradually accelerated. By 1976, the number of white-collar workers employed in offices surpassed the number of farm workers, service workers, and blue-collar workers employed in manufacturing (see Figure 1-3). Today, most people no longer work on farms or in factories but instead are found in sales, education, health care, banks, insurance firms, and law firms; they also provide business services, such as copying, computer programming, or making deliveries. These jobs primarily involve working with, distributing, or creating new knowledge and information. In fact, knowledge and information work now account for a significant 60 percent of the U.S. gross national product and nearly 55 percent of the labor force.

In knowledge- and information-based economies, the market value of many firms is based largely on intangible assets, such as proprietary knowledge, information, unique business methods, brands, and other "intellectual capital." Physical assets, such as buildings, machinery, tools, and inventory, now account for less than 20 percent of the market value of many public firms in the United States (Lev, 2001).

Knowledge and information provide the foundation for valuable new products and services, such as credit cards, overnight package delivery, or worldwide reservation systems. **Knowledge- and information-intense products**, such as computer games, require a great deal of knowledge to produce, and knowledge is used more intensively in the production of traditional products as well. In the automobile industry, for instance, both design and production now rely heavily on knowledge and information technology.

EMERGENCE OF THE DIGITAL FIRM

All of the changes we have just described, coupled with equally significant organizational redesign, have created the conditions for a fully digital firm. The **digital firm** can be defined along several dimensions. A digital firm is one in which nearly all of the organization's *significant business relationships* with customers, suppliers, and employees are digitally enabled

FIGURE 1-3   *The growth of the information economy.*

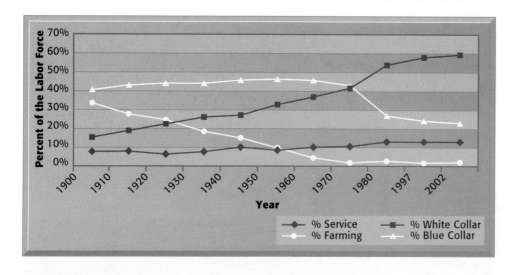

Since the beginning of the twentieth century, the United States has experienced a steady decline in the number of farm workers and blue-collar workers who are employed in factories. At the same time, the country is experiencing a rise in the number of white-collar workers who produce economic value using knowledge and information.

Sources: U.S. Department of Commerce, Bureau of the Census, *Statistical Abstract of the United States, 2003,* Table 615; and *Historical Statistics of the United States, Colonial Times to 1970,* Vol. 1, Series D, pp. 182–232.

and mediated. *Core business processes* are accomplished through digital networks spanning the entire organization or linking multiple organizations.

Business processes refer to the set of logically related tasks and behaviors that organizations develop over time to produce specific business results and the unique manner in which these activities are organized and coordinated. Developing a new product, generating and fulfilling an order, creating a marketing plan, and hiring an employee are examples of business processes, and the ways organizations accomplish their business processes can be a source of competitive strength. (A detailed discussion of business processes can be found in Chapter 2.)

Key corporate assets—intellectual property, core competencies, and financial and human assets—are managed through digital means. In a digital firm, any piece of information required to support key business decisions is available at any time and anywhere in the firm.

Digital firms sense and respond to their environments far more rapidly than traditional firms, giving them more flexibility to survive in turbulent times. Digital firms offer extraordinary opportunities for more global organization and management. By digitally enabling and streamlining their work, digital firms have the potential to achieve unprecedented levels of profitability and competitiveness. DaimlerChrysler, described earlier, illustrates some of these qualities. Electronically integrating key business processes with suppliers has made this company much more agile and adaptive to customer demands and changes in its supplier network.

Figure 1-4 illustrates a digital firm making intensive use of Internet and digital technology for electronic business. Information can flow seamlessly among different parts

---

FIGURE 1-4   *Electronic business and electronic commerce in the emerging digital firm.*

Companies can use Internet technology for e-commerce transactions with customers and suppliers, for managing internal business processes, and for coordinating with suppliers and other business partners. E-business includes e-commerce as well the management and coordination of the enterprise.

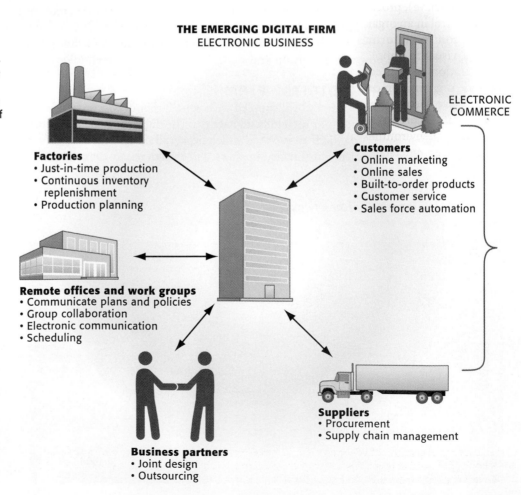

of the company and between the company and external entities—its customers, suppliers, and business partners. More and more organizations are moving toward this digital firm vision.

A few firms, such as Cisco Systems or Dell Computers, are close to becoming fully digital firms, using the Internet to drive every aspect of their business. In most other companies, a fully digital firm is still more vision than reality, but this vision is driving them toward digital integration. Firms are continuing to invest heavily in information systems that integrate internal business processes and build closer links with suppliers and customers.

The Window on Organizations describes such a digital firm in the making. Cemex, a world-leading global cement and construction materials firm, has achieved impressive results through ruthless focus on operational excellence. Management took an enterprise-wide view of its business processes and developed a series of information systems to turn the company into a lean, efficient, agile machine that could instantly respond to changes in customer orders, weather, and other last-minute events.

1.2 PERSPECTIVES ON INFORMATION SYSTEMS

Information systems can be best be understood by looking at them from both a technology and a business perspective.

What Is an Information System?

An **information system** can be defined technically as a set of interrelated components that collect (or retrieve), process, store, and distribute information to support decision making and control in an organization. In addition to supporting decision making, coordination, and control, information systems may also help managers and workers analyze problems, visualize complex subjects, and create new products.

Information systems contain information about significant people, places, and things within the organization or in the environment surrounding it. By **information** we mean data that have been shaped into a form that is meaningful and useful to human beings. **Data,** in contrast, are streams of raw facts representing events occurring in organizations or the physical environment before they have been organized and arranged into a form that people can understand and use.

Cemex uses a sophisticated scheduling system to expedite cement delivery. Cemex manages deliveries and all of its manufacturing and production processes from a highly computerized control room. The company is moving toward a digital firm organization.

WINDOW ON ORGANIZATIONS

CEMEX: A DIGITAL FIRM IN THE MAKING

Cemex, based in Monterrey, Mexico, is a 98-year-old company that sells cement and ready-mix concrete products. It has 53 plants around the globe in countries including the United States, Spain, Egypt, Colombia, and the Philippines, and is the world's third largest cement and concrete manufacturer.

The concrete business is an asset-intensive, low-efficiency business with unpredictable demand. Cemex dispatchers used to take orders for 8,000 grades of mixed concrete and forwarded them to six regional mixing plants, each with its own fleet of trucks. Customers routinely changed half of their orders, sometimes only hours before delivery, and these orders might have to be rerouted because of weather change, traffic jams, or problems with building permits. Cemex's phone lines were often jammed as customers, truckers, and dispatchers tried to get orders straight. Many orders were lost.

Until about 15 years ago, Cemex's Information Technology Division was viewed as a support department for the sales function. Cemex did not have an adequate computing or telecommunications infrastructure. Only a few executives had personal computers and integrated systems were a distant dream.

Lorenzo Zambrano, a grandson of the founder of the company, took over the business in 1985 and decided to apply information technology to these problems. He and Cemex chief information officer Gelacio Iniguez developed a series of systems that would enable Cemex to manage unforecastable demand better than its competitors.

Zambrano and Iniguez used ideas gleaned from visits to U.S. companies such as FedEx, Exxon, and Houston's 911 emergency dispatch system to see how other organizations anticipated demand for their services. They built a system linking Cemex delivery trucks to a Global Positioning System satellite to help dispatchers monitor the location, direction, and speed of every vehicle. This information helps Cemex send the right truck to deliver a specific grade of cement or redirect deliveries when prompted by last-minute changes.

The company has reduced average delivery time from three hours to 20 minutes, realizing huge savings in fuel, maintenance, and personnel costs. Cemex now uses 35 percent fewer trucks to deliver the same amount of cement. Customers are willing to pay premium prices to Cemex because they do not have to keep work crews idle waiting for cement deliveries to show up.

Cemex's production facilities previously operated independently, without precise knowledge of customer demand. A satellite communications system called CemexNet now electronically links all the firm's production facilities and coordinates them from a central clearinghouse. Dispatchers know the exact location, speed, and direction of all vehicles at all times and can quickly select the most optimal arrangement of trucks and mixing plant locations to fill an order.

Customers, distributors, and suppliers can use the Internet to place orders directly, check shipment delivery times, and review payment records without having to telephone a customer service representative. Zambrano and his managers now have access to almost every detail about Cemex operations within 24 hours, whereas competitors are working with month-old data.

Zambrano built a sophisticated executive information system that enables him to monitor closely from his laptop computer operations in the 35 countries where Cemex operates. If a region is colored green, it is doing well. Yellow signals a potential problem, and red indicates a real problem. Zambrano can then systematically dig down to find out the details of any area of interest. At that level of detail he can even read the e-mail exchanges about a production problem at an individual plant. Sometimes Zambrano will send an e-mail about production issues to plant workers to let them know he is watching.

Cemex's profit margins are higher than its bigger rivals, Zurich-based Holcim Limited and Paris-based Lafarge SA, even as the company has expanded from a provincial Mexican cement maker to an international powerhouse. In addition to maximizing operational efficiency, Cemex saves by using petroleum coke for half of its fuel needs. Petroleum coke, also known as pet coke, is the blackened leftover from the oil-refining process. In the cement industry, energy accounts for up to 40 percent of operating costs.

Cemex also designed software to make it easier for company executives and plant managers to keep tabs on power use. Managers use the software to plan each month's energy consumption, ensuring that conveyors, electric grinders, and other equipment run mainly during hours of off-peak electricity rates. As a result, Cemex cut its energy bills by 17 percent in the past four years.

Cemex's productivity has outpaced all of its major rivals in Mexico, and production output has grown sixfold since 1985. In an industry known for tough price competition and thin profit margins, Cemex revenue has grown at a rate of 9 percent over the past decade. As an agile, efficient e-business, Cemex appears to have the right ingredients for staying ahead of the pack.

Sources: Andrew Rowsell-Jones, "The Best of Both Worlds," *CIO Australia*, July 12, 2004; John Lyons, "Expensive Energy? Burn Other Stuff, One Firm Decides," *Wall Street Journal*, September 1, 2004; www.cemex.com, accessed September 2, 2004; John Lyons, "Cemex Cements Its Position with Agreement to Buy RMC," *Wall Street Journal*, September 28, 2004; and Melba Newsome, "The Cement Mixer," *Context*, December 2001/January 2002.

To Think About: How did digital technology transform the way Cemex ran its business? It has been said that Cemex has refocused efforts from managing assets to managing information. Explain. To what extent is Cemex a digital firm?

A brief example contrasting information and data may prove useful. Supermarket checkout counters ring up millions of pieces of data, such as product identification numbers or the cost of each item sold. Such pieces of data can be totaled and analyzed to provide meaningful information, such as the total number of bottles of dish detergent sold at a particular store, which brands of dish detergent were selling the most rapidly at that store or sales territory, or the total amount spent on that brand of dish detergent at that store or sales region (see Figure 1-5).

Three activities in an information system produce the information that organizations need to make decisions, control operations, analyze problems, and create new products or services. These activities are input, processing, and output (see Figure 1-6). **Input** captures or collects raw data from within the organization or from its external environment. **Processing** converts this raw input into a more meaningful form. **Output** transfers the processed information to the people who will use it or to the activities for which it will be used. Information systems also require **feedback**, which is output that is returned to appropriate members of the organization to help them evaluate or correct the input stage.

In DaimlerChrysler's Integrated Volume Planning system, raw input consists of dealer identification number, model, color, and optional features of cars ordered from dealers. DaimlerChrysler's computers store these data and process them to anticipate how many new vehicles to manufacture for each model, color, and option package. The output would consist of orders to suppliers specifying the quantity of each part or component that was needed and the exact date each part was to be delivered to DaimlerChrysler's production facilities to produce the vehicles that customers have ordered. The system provides meaningful information such as what models, colors, and options are selling in which locations; the most popular models and colors; and which dealers sell the most cars and trucks.

Our interest in this book is in formal, organizational computer-based information systems, such as those designed and used by DaimlerChrysler and its suppliers. **Formal systems** rest on accepted and fixed definitions of data and procedures for collecting, storing,

FIGURE 1-5   Data and information.

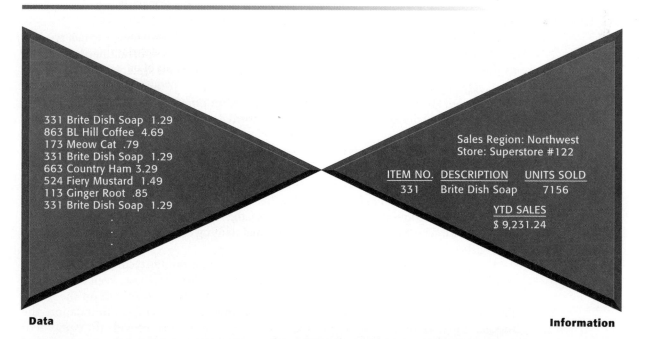

Data

331 Brite Dish Soap 1.29
863 BL Hill Coffee 4.69
173 Meow Cat .79
331 Brite Dish Soap 1.29
663 Country Ham 3.29
524 Fiery Mustard 1.49
113 Ginger Root .85
331 Brite Dish Soap 1.29

Information

Sales Region: Northwest
Store: Superstore #122

ITEM NO.	DESCRIPTION	UNITS SOLD
331	Brite Dish Soap	7156

YTD SALES
$ 9,231.24

Raw data from a supermarket checkout counter can be processed and organized to produce meaningful information such as the total unit sales of dish detergent or the total sales revenue from dish detergent for a specific store or sales territory.

FIGURE 1-6 *Functions of an information system.*

An information system contains information about an organization and its surrounding environment. Three basic activities—input, processing, and output—produce the information organizations need. Feedback is output returned to appropriate people or activities in the organization to evaluate and refine the input. Environmental actors such as customers, suppliers, competitors, stockholders, and regulatory agencies interact with the organization and its information systems.

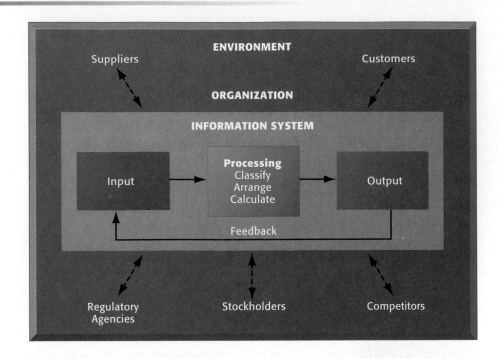

processing, disseminating, and using these data. The formal systems we describe in this text are structured; that is, they operate in conformity with predefined rules that are relatively fixed and not easily changed. For instance, DaimlerChrysler's Integrated Volume Planning system would require unique numbers or codes for identifying each vehicle part or component and each supplier.

Informal information systems (such as office gossip networks) rely, by contrast, on unstated rules of behavior. There is no agreement on what is information or on how it will be stored and processed. Such systems are essential for the life of an organization, but an analysis of their qualities is beyond the scope of this text.

Formal information systems can be either computer based or manual. Manual systems use paper-and-pencil technology. These manual systems serve important needs, but they too are not the subject of this text. **Computer-based information systems (CBIS)**, in contrast, rely on computer hardware and software technology to process and disseminate information. From this point on, when we use the term *information systems,* we are referring to computer-based information systems—formal organizational systems that rely on computer technology.

The Window on Technology describes some of the typical technologies used in computer-based information systems today. United Parcel Service (UPS) invests heavily in information systems technology to make its business more efficient and customer-oriented. It uses an array of information technologies including bar-code scanning systems, wireless networks, large mainframe computers, handheld computers, the Internet, and many different pieces of software for tracking packages, calculating fees, maintaining customer accounts, and managing logistics.

Although computer-based information systems use computer technology to process raw data into meaningful information, there is a sharp distinction between a computer and a computer program on the one hand, and an information system on the other. Electronic computers and related software programs are the technical foundation, the tools and materials, of modern information systems. Computers provide the equipment for storing and processing information. Computer programs, or software, are sets of operating instructions that direct and control computer processing. Knowing how computers and computer programs work is important in designing solutions to organizational problems, but computers are only part of an information system.

WINDOW ON TECHNOLOGY

UPS COMPETES GLOBALLY WITH INFORMATION TECHNOLOGY

United Parcel Service (UPS), the world's largest air and ground package-distribution company, started out in 1907 in a closet-sized basement office. Jim Casey and Claude Ryan—two teenagers from Seattle with two bicycles and one phone—promised the "best service and lowest rates." UPS has used this formula successfully for more than 90 years and is now the world's largest ground and air package-distribution company.

Today UPS delivers more than 13.6 million parcels and documents each day in the United States and more than 200 other countries and territories. The firm has been able to maintain leadership in small-package delivery services despite stiff competition from FedEx and Airborne Express by investing heavily in advanced information technology. During the past decade, UPS has poured billions of dollars into technology and systems to boost customer service while keeping costs low and streamlining its overall operations.

Using a handheld computer called a Delivery Information Acquisition Device (DIAD), a UPS driver can automatically capture customers' signatures along with pickup, delivery, and time-card information. The driver then places the DIAD into the UPS truck's vehicle adapter, an information-transmitting device that is connected to the cellular telephone network. Package tracking information is then transmitted to UPS's computer network for storage and processing in UPS's main computers in Mahwah, New Jersey, and Alpharetta, Georgia. From there, the information can be accessed worldwide to provide proof of delivery to customers or to respond to customer queries.

Through its automated package tracking system, UPS can monitor packages throughout the delivery process. At various points along the route from sender to receiver, bar-code devices scan shipping information on the package label; the information is then fed into the central computer. Customer service representatives can check the status of any package from desktop computers linked to the central computers and are able to respond immediately to inquiries from customers. UPS customers can also access this information from the company's Web site using their own computers or wireless devices such as pagers and cell phones.

Anyone with a package to ship can access the UPS Web site to track packages, check delivery routes, calculate shipping rates, determine time in transit, and schedule a pickup. Businesses anywhere can use the Web site to arrange UPS shipments and bill the shipments to the company's UPS account number or to a credit card. The data collected at the UPS Web site are transmitted to the UPS central computer and then back to the customer after processing. UPS also provides tools that enable customers such Cisco Systems to embed UPS functions, such as tracking and cost calculations, into their own Web sites so that they can track shipments without visiting the UPS site.

A capability called UPS Campus Ship allows employees in multiple offices of a business to process and ship from their computers and have shipping procedures controlled by a central administrator set up by the business. Morris, Schneider and Prior LLC, a top law firm serving the financial services industry, uses this capability to track and control shipping costs. This firm is constantly sending time-sensitive documents from three different locations to clients throughout the United States. UPS tools automate the allocation and reporting of this firm's shipping costs and even itemize and detail shipping expenses for each client.

Information technology helps UPS reinvent itself and keep growing. UPS is now leveraging its decades of expertise managing its own global delivery network to manage logistics and supply chain management for other companies. It created a UPS Supply Chain Solutions division that provides a complete bundle of standardized services to subscribing companies at a fraction of what it would cost to build their own systems and infrastructure. These services include supply chain design and management, freight forwarding, customs brokerage, mail services, multimodal transportation, and financial services, in addition to logistics services.

Birkenstock Footprint Sandals is one of many companies benefiting from these services. Birkenstock's German plants pack shoes in crates that are bar-coded with their U.S. destination. UPS contracts with ocean carriers in Rotterdam to transport the shoe crates across the Atlantic to New Jersey ports instead of routing them through the Panama Canal to Birkenstock's California warehouses. UPS trucks whisk each incoming shipment to a UPS distribution hub and, within hours, to 3,000 different retailers. By handing this work over to UPS, Birkenstock has cut the time to get its shoes to stores by half. Along the way, UPS uses bar-code scanning to keep track of every shipment until the merchant signs off on it. UPS also handles Internet orders for Jockey International, laptop repairs for Toshiba America, and X-ray machine installation in Europe for Philips Medical Systems.

Sources: Dean Foust, "Big Brown's New Bag," and "Online Extra: UPS's Eskew on 'the Next Logical Step,' " *BusinessWeek,* July 19, 2004; Galen Gruman, "UPS vs. FedEx: Head-to-Head on Wireless " and "New Technologies Hit Mainstream," *CIO Magazine,* June 1, 2004; "Paper Trail," *RoundUPS,* Fall 2004; and Todd R. Weiss, "UPS Delivers New Package Check-in System for Customers," *Computerworld,* April 9, 2003.

To Think About: What are the inputs, processing, and outputs of UPS's package tracking system? What technologies are used? How are these technologies related to UPS's business strategy? How do UPS's systems provide value for the company and its customers? What would happen if these technologies were not available?

Using a handheld computer called a Delivery Information Acquisition Device (DIAD), UPS drivers automatically capture customers' signatures along with pickup, delivery, and time-card information. UPS information systems use these data to track packages while they are being transported.

A house is an appropriate analogy. Houses are built with hammers, nails, and wood, but these do not make a house. The architecture, design, setting, landscaping, and all of the decisions that lead to the creation of these features are part of the house and are crucial for solving the problem of putting a roof over one's head. Computers and programs are the hammer, nails, and lumber of CBIS, but alone they cannot produce the information a particular organization needs. To understand information systems, you must understand the problems they are designed to solve, their architectural and design elements, and the organizational processes that lead to these solutions.

It Isn't Just Technology: A Business Perspective on Information Systems

Managers and business firms invest in information technology and systems because they provide real economic value to the business. The decision to build or maintain an information system assumes that the returns on this investment will be superior to other investments in buildings, machines, or other assets. These superior returns will be expressed as increases in productivity, as increases in revenues (which will increase the firm's stock market value), or perhaps as superior long-term strategic positioning of the firm in certain markets (which produce superior revenues in the future).

There are also situations in which firms invest in information systems to cope with governmental regulations or other environmental demands. For instance, one of the major ways firms can comply with the reporting requirements of the recent Sarbanes-Oxley Act or the Health Insurance Portability and Accountability Act (HIPAA) is to build a document management system that can trace the flow of virtually all material documents it uses (see Chapter 12).

In some cases, firms are required to invest in information systems simply because such investments are required to stay in business. For instance, some small banks may be forced to invest in automatic teller machine (ATM) networks or offer complex banking services requiring large technology investments simply because it is a "cost of doing business." Nevertheless, it is assumed that most information systems investments will be justified by favorable returns.

We can see that from a business perspective, an information system is an important instrument for creating value for the firm. Information systems enable the firm to increase its revenue or decrease its costs by providing information that helps managers make better decisions or that improves the execution of business processes. For example, the information system for analyzing supermarket checkout data illustrated in Figure 1-5 can increase firm profitability by helping managers make better decisions on which products to stock and promote in retail supermarkets and as a result increase business value.

Every business has an information value chain, illustrated in Figure 1-7, in which raw information is systematically acquired and then transformed through various stages that add value to that information. The value of an information system to a business, as well as the decision to invest in any new information system, is, in large part, determined by the extent to which the system will lead to better management decisions, more efficient business processes, and higher firm profitability. Although there are other reasons why systems are built, their primary purpose is to contribute to corporate value.

The business perspective calls attention to the organizational and managerial nature of information systems. An information system represents an organizational and management solution, based on information technology, to a challenge posed by the environment. Every chapter in this book begins with short case study that illustrates this concept. A diagram at the beginning of each chapter illustrates the relationship between a changing business environment and resulting management and organizational decisions to use IT as a solution to challenges generated by the business environment.

To fully understand information systems, a manager must understand the broader organization, management, and information technology dimensions of systems (see Figure 1-8) and their power to provide solutions to challenges and problems in the business environment. We refer to this broader understanding of information systems, which encompasses an understanding of the management and organizational dimensions of systems as well as the technical dimensions of systems, as **information systems literacy**. Information systems literacy includes a behavioral as well as a technical approach to studying information systems. **Computer literacy**, in contrast, focuses primarily on knowledge of information technology.

Review the diagram at the beginning of the chapter that reflects this expanded definition of an information system. The diagram shows how DaimlerChrysler's production and sup-

FIGURE 1-7   *The business information value chain.*

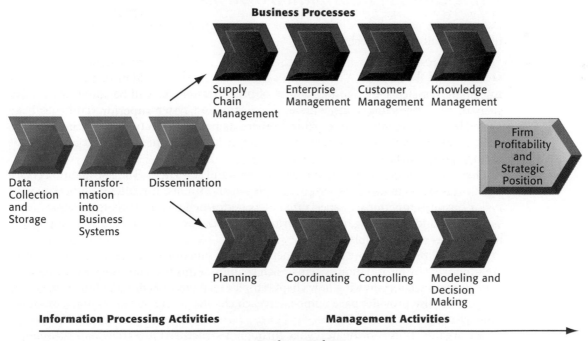

From a business perspective, information systems are part of a series of value-adding activities for acquiring, transforming, and distributing information that managers can use to improve decision making, enhance organizational performance, and, ultimately, increase firm profitability.

FIGURE 1-8   *Information systems are more than computers.*

Using information systems effectively requires an understanding of the organization, management, and information technology shaping the systems. An information system creates value for the firm as an organizational and management solution to challenges posed by the environment.

plier systems solve the business challenge presented by a fierce array of competitors and rapidly changing consumer preferences. These systems create value for DaimlerChrysler by making its production, supply chain, and quality control processes more efficient and cost effective. The diagram also illustrates how management, technology, and organizational elements work together to create the systems.

Each chapter of this text begins with a diagram similar to this one to help you analyze the chapter-opening case. You can use this diagram as a starting point for analyzing any information system or information system problem you encounter.

Dimensions of Information Systems

Let's examine each of the dimensions of information systems—organizations, management, and information technology.

ORGANIZATIONS

Information systems are an integral part of organizations. Indeed, for some companies, such as credit reporting firms, without an information system, there would be no business. The key elements of an organization are its people, structure, business processes, politics, and culture. We introduce these components of organizations here and describe them in greater detail in Chapters 2 and 3.

Organizations are composed of different levels and specialties. Their structures reveal a clear-cut division of labor. Experts are employed and trained for different functions. The major **business functions**, or specialized tasks performed by business organizations, consist of sales and marketing, manufacturing and production, finance and accounting, and human resources (see Table 1-2).

Chapter 2 provides more detail on these business functions and the ways in which they are supported by information systems. Each chapter of this text concludes with a *Make IT Your Business* section showing how chapter topics relate to each of these functional areas. The section also provides page numbers in each chapter where these functional examples can be found.

An organization coordinates work through a structured hierarchy and through its business processes, which we defined earlier. The hierarchy arranges people in a pyramid structure of rising authority and responsibility. The upper levels of the hierarchy consist of managerial, professional, and technical employees, whereas the lower levels consist of operational personnel.

TABLE 1-2 *Major Business Functions*

Function	Purpose
Sales and marketing	Selling the organization's products and services
Manufacturing and production	Producing products and services
Finance and accounting	Managing the organization's financial assets and maintaining the organization's financial records
Human resources	Attracting, developing, and maintaining the organization's labor force; maintaining employee records

Most organizations' business processes include formal rules that have been developed over a long time for accomplishing tasks. These rules guide employees in a variety of procedures, from writing an invoice to responding to customer complaints. Some of these procedures have been formalized and written down, but others are informal work practices, such as a requirement to return telephone calls from coworkers or customers, that are not formally documented. Many business processes are incorporated into information systems, such as how to pay a supplier or how to correct an erroneous bill.

Organizations require many different kinds of skills and people. In addition to managers, **knowledge workers** (such as engineers, architects, or scientists) design products or services and create new knowledge, and **data workers** (such as secretaries, bookkeepers, or clerks) process the organization's paperwork. **Production or service workers** (such as machinists, assemblers, or packers) actually produce the organization's products or services.

Each organization has a unique *culture*, or fundamental set of assumptions, values, and ways of doing things, that has been accepted by most of its members. Parts of an organization's culture can always be found embedded in its information systems. For instance, the United Parcel Service's concern with placing service to the customer first is an aspect of its organizational culture that can be found in the company's package tracking systems.

Different levels and specialties in an organization create different interests and points of view. These views often conflict. Conflict is the basis for organizational politics. Information systems come out of this cauldron of differing perspectives, conflicts, compromises, and agreements that are a natural part of all organizations. In Chapter 3 we examine these features of organizations and their role in the development of information systems in greater detail.

MANAGEMENT

Management's job is to make sense out of the many situations faced by organizations, make decisions, and formulate action plans to solve organizational problems. Managers perceive business challenges in the environment; they set the organizational strategy for responding to those challenges; and they allocate the human and financial resources to coordinate the work and achieve success. Throughout, they must exercise responsible leadership. The business information systems described in this book reflect the hopes, dreams, and realities of real-world managers.

But managers must do more than manage what already exists. They must also create new products and services and even re-create the organization from time to time. A substantial part of management responsibility is creative work driven by new knowledge and information. Information technology can play a powerful role in redirecting and redesigning the organization. Chapter 3 describes managerial activities, and Chapter 13 treats management decision making in detail.

It is important to note that managerial roles and decisions vary at different levels of the organization. **Senior managers** make long-range strategic decisions about what products and services to produce. **Middle managers** carry out the programs and plans of senior management. **Operational managers** are responsible for monitoring the firm's daily activities. All levels of management are expected to be creative, to develop novel solutions to a broad range of problems. Each level of management has different information needs and information system requirements.

TECHNOLOGY

Information technology is one of many tools managers use to cope with change. **Computer hardware** is the physical equipment used for input, processing, and output activities in an information system. It consists of the following: the computer processing unit; various input, output, and storage devices; and physical media to link these devices together.

Computer software consists of the detailed, preprogrammed instructions that control and coordinate the computer hardware components in an information system. Chapter 6 describes the contemporary software and hardware platforms used by firms today in greater detail.

Storage technology includes both the physical media for storing data, such as magnetic disk, optical disc, or tape, and the software governing the organization of data on these physical media. More detail on data organization and access methods can be found in Chapter 7.

Communications technology, consisting of both physical devices and software, links the various pieces of hardware and transfers data from one physical location to another. Computers and communications equipment can be connected in networks for sharing voice, data, images, sound, or even video. A **network** links two or more computers to share data or resources such as a printer.

The world's largest and most widely used network is the **Internet**. The Internet is an international network of networks that are both commercial and publicly owned. The Internet connects hundreds of thousands of different networks from more than 200 countries around the world. More than 900 million people working in science, education, government, and business use the Internet to exchange information or business transactions with other organizations around the globe. Chapter 8 provides more detail on networks and Internet technology.

The Internet is extremely elastic. If networks are added or removed, or if failures occur in parts of the system, the rest of the Internet continues to operate. Through special communication and technology standards, any computer can communicate with virtually any other computer linked to the Internet using ordinary telephone lines.

The Internet has created a new "universal" technology platform on which to build all sorts of new products, services, strategies, and business models. This same technology platform has internal uses, providing the connectivity to link different systems and networks within the firm. Internal corporate networks based on Internet technology are called **intranets**. Private intranets extended to authorized users outside the organization are called **extranets**, and firms use such networks to coordinate their activities with other firms for making purchases, collaborating on design, and other interorganizational work. Some of DaimlerChrysler's systems for coordinating with suppliers are based on extranets.

Because it offers so many new possibilities for doing business, the Internet service known as the **World Wide Web** is of special interest to organizations and managers. The World Wide Web is a system with universally accepted standards for storing, retrieving, formatting, and displaying information in a networked environment. Information is stored and displayed as electronic "pages" that can contain text, graphics, animations, sound, and video. These Web pages can be linked electronically to other Web pages, regardless of where they are located, and viewed by any type of computer. By clicking on highlighted words or buttons on a Web page, you can link to related pages to find additional information, software programs, or still more links to other points on the Web. The Web can serve as the foundation for new kinds of information systems such as UPS's Web-based package tracking system or Cemex's Web system for entering customer orders and checking shipments described in this chapter's Window on Organizations.

All of the Web pages maintained by an organization or individual are called a **Web site**. Businesses have created Web sites with stylish typography, colorful graphics, push-button interactivity, and sound and video to disseminate product information widely, to "broadcast" advertising and messages to customers, to collect electronic orders and cus-

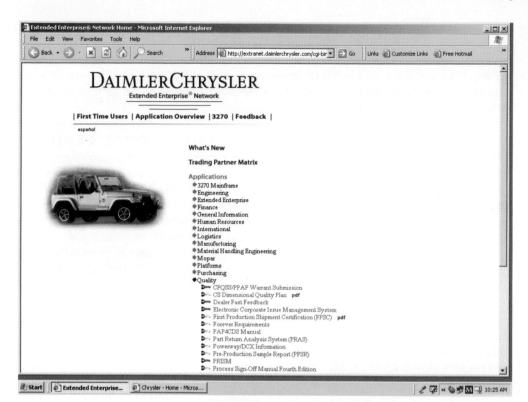

DaimlerChrysler's Extended Enterprise Network is an extranet for suppliers to access a series of internal company applications. Internet technology standards make it possible for DaimlerChrysler to link to the systems of many different companies.

tomer data, and, increasingly, to coordinate far-flung sales forces and organizations on a global scale.

In Chapters 4 and 8 we describe the Web and other Internet capabilities in greater detail. We also discuss relevant features of Internet technology throughout the text because it affects so many aspects of information systems in organizations.

All of these technologies represent resources that can be shared throughout the organization and constitute the firm's **information technology (IT) infrastructure**. The IT infrastructure provides the foundation, or *platform*, on which the firm can build its specific information systems. Each organization must carefully design and manage its information technology infrastructure so that it has the set of technology services it needs for the work it wants to accomplish with information systems. Chapters 6 through 10 of this text examine each major technology component of information technology infrastructure and show how they all work together to create the technology platform for the organization.

Let's look at the case about UPS's package tracking system in the Window on Technology and identify the organization, management, and technology elements. The organization element anchors the package tracking system in UPS's sales and production functions (the main product of UPS is a service—package delivery). It specifies the required procedures for identifying packages with both sender and recipient information, taking inventory, tracking the packages en route, and providing package status reports for UPS customers and customer service representatives. The system must also provide information to satisfy the needs of managers and workers. UPS drivers need to be trained in both package pickup and delivery procedures and in how to use the package tracking system so that they can work efficiently and effectively. UPS customers may need some training to use UPS in-house package tracking software or the UPS Web site.

UPS's management is responsible for monitoring service levels and costs and for promoting the company's strategy of combining low-cost and superior service. Management decided to use automation to increase the ease of sending a package using UPS and of checking its delivery status, thereby reducing delivery costs and increasing sales revenues.

Internet Connection —
The Internet Connection for this chapter will take you to the United Parcel Service Web site where you can complete an exercise to evaluate how UPS uses the Web and other information technology in its daily operations.

The technology supporting this system consists of handheld computers, bar-code scanners, wired and wireless communications networks, desktop computers, UPS's central computer, storage technology for the package delivery data, UPS in-house package tracking software, and software to access the World Wide Web. The result is an information system solution to the business challenge of providing a high level of service with low prices in the face of mounting competition.

COMPLEMENTARY ASSETS AND ORGANIZATIONAL CAPITAL

Awareness of the organizational and managerial dimensions of information systems can help us understand why some firms achieve better results from their information systems than others. Studies of returns from information technology investments show that there is considerable variation in the returns firms receive (see Figure 1-9). Some firms invest a great deal and receive a great deal (quadrant 2); others invest an equal amount and receive few returns (quadrant 4). Still other firms invest little and receive much (quadrant 1), whereas others invest little and receive little (quadrant 3). This suggests that investing in information technology does not by itself guarantee good returns. What accounts for this variation among firms?

The answer lies in the concept of complementary assets. Information technology investments alone cannot make organizations and managers more effective unless they are accompanied by supportive values, structures, and behavior patterns in the organization and other complementary assets. **Complementary assets** are those assets required to derive value from a primary investment (Teece, 1998). For instance, to realize value from automobiles requires substantial complementary investments in highways, roads, gasoline stations, repair facilities, and a legal regulatory structure to set standards and control drivers.

Recent research on business information technology investment indicates that firms that support their technology investments with investments in complementary assets, such as new business processes, management behavior, organizational culture, or training, receive superior returns, whereas those firms failing to make these complementary investments receive less or no returns on their information technology investments (Brynjolfsson, 2003; Brynjolfsson and Hitt, 2000; Davern and Kauffman, 2000; Laudon, 1974; Marchand, 2004). These investments in organization and management are also known as **organizational and management capital.**

Table 1-3 lists the major complementary investments that firms need to make to realize value from their information technology investments. Some of this investment involves tangible assets, such as buildings, machinery, and tools. However, the value of investments in information technology depends to a large extent on complementary investments in management and organization.

FIGURE 1-9   *Variation in returns on information technology investment.*

Although, on average, investments in information technology produce returns far above those returned by other investments, there is considerable variation across firms.

Source: Based on Erik Brynjolfsson and Lorin M. Hitt, "Beyond Computation: Information Technology, Organizational Transformation and Business Performance." *Journal of Economic Perspectives* 14, no. 4 (Fall 2000). Used with permission of the American Economic Association.

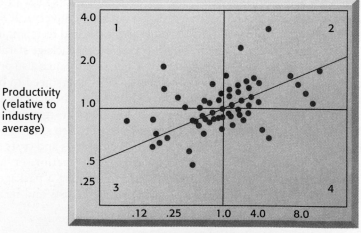

IT Capital Stock (relative to industry average)

TABLE 1-3 *Complementary Social, Managerial, and Organizational Assets Required to Optimize Returns from Information Technology Investments*

Organizational assets	Supportive organizational culture that values efficiency and effectiveness Efficient business processes Decentralized authority Distributed decision-making rights Strong IS development team
Managerial assets	Strong senior management support for technology investment and change Incentives for management innovation Teamwork and collaborative work environments Training programs to enhance management decision skills Management culture that values flexibility and knowledge-based decision making
Social assets	The Internet and telecommunications infrastructure IT-enriched educational programs raising labor force computer literacy Standards (both government and private sector) Laws and regulations creating fair, stable market environments Technology and service firms in adjacent markets to assist implementation

Key organizational complementary investments are a supportive business culture that values efficiency and effectiveness, efficient business processes, decentralization of authority, highly distributed decision rights, and a strong information system (IS) development team.

Important managerial complementary assets are strong senior management support for change, incentive systems that monitor and reward individual innovation, an emphasis on teamwork and collaboration, training programs, and a management culture that values flexibility and knowledge.

Important social investments (not made by the firm but by the society at large, other firms, governments, and other key market actors) are the Internet and the supporting Internet culture, educational systems, network and computing standards, regulations and laws, and the presence of technology and service firms.

Throughout the book we emphasize a framework of analysis that considers technology, management, and organizational assets and their interactions. Perhaps the single most important theme in the book, reflected in case studies, vignettes, and exercises, is that managers need to consider the broader organization and management dimensions of information systems to understand current problems as well as to derive substantial above-average returns from their information technology investments. As you will see throughout the text, firms that can address these related dimensions of the IT investment are, on average, richly rewarded.

1.3 CONTEMPORARY APPROACHES TO INFORMATION SYSTEMS

Multiple perspectives on information systems show that the study of information systems is a multidisciplinary field. No single theory or perspective dominates. Figure 1-10 illustrates the major disciplines that contribute problems, issues, and solutions in the study of information systems. In general, the field can be divided into technical and behavioral approaches. Information systems are sociotechnical systems. Though they are composed of machines, devices, and "hard" physical technology, they require substantial social, organizational, and intellectual investments to make them work properly.

Technical Approach

The technical approach to information systems emphasizes mathematically based models to study information systems, as well as the physical technology and formal capabilities of these systems. The disciplines that contribute to the technical approach are computer science, management science, and operations research.

Computer science is concerned with establishing theories of computability, methods of computation, and methods of efficient data storage and access. Management science emphasizes the development of models for decision-making and management practices. Operations research focuses on mathematical techniques for optimizing selected parameters of organizations, such as transportation, inventory control, and transaction costs.

Behavioral Approach

An important part of the information systems field is concerned with behavioral issues that arise in the development and long-term maintenance of information systems. Issues such as strategic business integration, design, implementation, utilization, and management cannot be explored usefully with the models used in the technical approach. Other behavioral disciplines contribute important concepts and methods.

For instance, sociologists study information systems with an eye toward how groups and organizations shape the development of systems and also how systems affect individuals, groups, and organizations. Psychologists study information systems with an interest in how human decision makers perceive and use formal information. Economists study information systems with an interest in what impact systems have on control and cost structures within the firm and within markets.

The behavioral approach does not ignore technology. Indeed, information systems technology is often the stimulus for a behavioral problem or issue. But the focus of this approach is generally not on technical solutions. Instead, it concentrates on changes in attitudes, management and organizational policy, and behavior.

FIGURE 1-10   *Contemporary approaches to information systems.*

The study of information systems deals with issues and insights contributed from technical and behavioral disciplines.

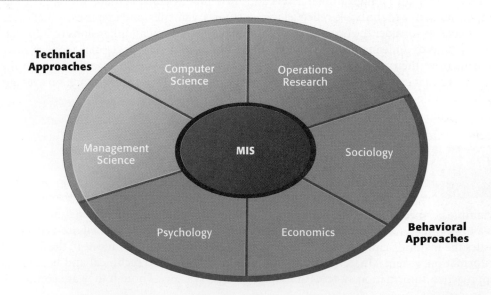

Approach of This Text: Sociotechnical Systems

Throughout this book you will find a rich story with four main actors: suppliers of hardware and software (the technologists); business firms making investments and seeking to obtain value from the technology; managers and employees seeking to achieve business value (and other goals); and the contemporary legal, social, and cultural context (the firm's environment). Together these actors produce what we call *management information systems*.

The study of **management information systems (MIS)** arose in the 1970s to focus on the use of computer-based information systems in business firms and government agencies (Laudon, 1974; Davis and Olson, 1985). MIS combines the work of computer science, management science, and operations research with a practical orientation toward developing system solutions to real-world problems and managing information technology resources. It is also concerned with behavioral issues surrounding the development, use, and impact of information systems, which are typically discussed in the fields of sociology, economics, and psychology. The study of information systems has just started to influence other disciplines (Baskerville and Myers, 2002) through concepts such as the information processing view of the firm.

Our experience as academics and practitioners leads us to believe that no single approach effectively captures the reality of information systems. The successes and failures of information systems are rarely all technical or all behavioral. Our best advice to students is to understand the perspectives of many disciplines. Indeed, the challenge and excitement of the information systems field is that it requires an appreciation and tolerance of many different approaches.

The view we adopt in this book is best characterized as the **sociotechnical view** of systems. In this view, optimal organizational performance is achieved by jointly optimizing both the social and technical systems used in production (Mumford, 2000 and 1997; Williams and Edge, 1996).

Adopting a sociotechnical systems perspective helps to avoid a purely technological approach to information systems. For instance, the fact that information technology is rapidly declining in cost and growing in power does not necessarily or easily translate into productivity enhancement or bottom-line profits. The fact that a firm has recently installed an enterprise-wide financial reporting system does not necessarily mean that it will be used, or used effectively. Likewise, the fact that a firm has recently introduced new business procedures and processes does not necessarily mean employees will be more productive in the absence of investments in new information systems to enable those processes.

In this book, we stress the need to optimize the firm's performance as a whole. Both the technical and behavioral components need attention. This means that technology must be changed and designed in such a way as to fit organizational and individual needs. At times, the technology may have to be "de-optimized" to accomplish this fit. For instance mobile phone users adapt this technology to their personal needs, and as a result manufacturers quickly seek to adjust the technology to conform with user expectations (Lee, 2003; Sawyer and Allen, 2003; Bautsch, 2001). Organizations and individuals must also be changed through training, learning, and planned organizational change to allow the technology to operate and prosper (Lamb et al., 2004; Orlikowski and Baroudi, 1991; Orlikowski, 1994). Figure 1-11 illustrates this process of mutual adjustment in a sociotechnical system.

1.4   LEARNING TO USE INFORMATION SYSTEMS: NEW OPPORTUNITIES WITH TECHNOLOGY

Although information systems are creating many exciting opportunities for both businesses and individuals, they are also a source of new problems, issues, and challenges for managers. In this course, you will learn about both the challenges and opportunities

FIGURE 1-11 *A sociotechnical perspective on information systems.*

In a sociotechnical perspective, the performance of a system is optimized when both the technology and the organization mutually adjust to one another until a satisfactory fit is obtained.

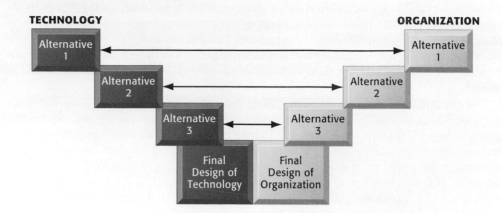

The Challenge of Information Systems: Key Management Issues

Although information technology is advancing at a blinding pace, there is nothing easy or mechanical about building and using information systems. There are five major challenges confronting managers:

1. *The information systems investment challenge: How can organizations obtain business value from their information systems?* Earlier in this chapter we described the importance of information systems as investments that produce value for the firm. We showed that not all companies realize good returns from information systems investments. It is obvious that one of the greatest challenges facing managers today is ensuring that their companies do indeed obtain meaningful returns on the money they spend on information systems. It's one thing to use information technology to design, produce, deliver, and maintain new products. It's another thing to make money doing it. How can organizations obtain a sizable payoff from their investment in information systems? How can management ensure that information systems contribute to corporate value?

   Senior management can be expected to ask these questions: How can we evaluate our information systems investments as we do other investments? Are we receiving the return on investment from our systems that we should? Do our competitors get more? Far too many firms still cannot answer these questions. Their executives are likely to have trouble determining how much they actually spend on technology or how to measure the returns on their technology investments. Most companies lack a clear-cut decision-making process for deciding which technology investments to pursue and for managing those investments (Hartman, 2002).

2. *The strategic business challenge: What complementary assets are needed to use information technology effectively?* Despite heavy information technology investments, many organizations are not realizing significant business value from their systems, because they lack—or fail to appreciate—the complementary assets required to make their technology assets work. The power of computer hardware and software has grown much more rapidly than the ability of organizations to apply and use this technology. To benefit fully from information technology, realize genuine productivity, and become competitive and effective, many organizations actually need to be redesigned. They will

have to make fundamental changes in employee and management behavior, develop new business models, retire obsolete work rules, and eliminate the inefficiencies of outmoded business processes and organizational structures. New technology alone will not produce meaningful business benefits.

3. *The globalization challenge: How can firms understand the business and system requirements of a global economic environment?* The rapid growth in international trade and the emergence of a global economy call for information systems that can support both producing and selling goods in many different countries. In the past, each regional office of a multinational corporation focused on solving its own unique information problems. Given language, cultural, and political differences among countries, this focus frequently resulted in chaos and the failure of central management controls. To develop integrated, multinational, information systems, businesses must develop global hardware, software, and communications standards; create cross-cultural accounting and reporting structures; and design transnational business processes.

4. *The information technology infrastructure challenge: How can organizations develop an information technology infrastructure that can support their goals when business conditions and technologies are changing so rapidly?* Many companies are saddled with expensive and unwieldy information technology platforms that cannot adapt to innovation and change. Their information systems are so complex and brittle that they act as constraints on business strategy and execution. Meeting new business and technology challenges may require redesigning the organization and building a new information technology (IT) infrastructure.

    Creating the IT infrastructure for a digital firm is an especially formidable task. Most companies are crippled by fragmented and incompatible computer hardware, software, telecommunications networks, and information systems that prevent information from flowing freely between different parts of the organization. Although Internet standards are solving some of these connectivity problems, creating data and computing platforms that span the enterprise—and, increasingly, link the enterprise to external business partners—is rarely as seamless as promised. Many organizations are still struggling to integrate their islands of information and technology. Chapters 6 through 10 provide more detail on IT infrastructure issues.

5. *Ethics and security: The responsibility and control challenge: How can organizations ensure that their information systems are used in an ethically and socially responsible manner?* How can we design information systems that people can control and understand? Although information systems have provided enormous benefits and efficiencies, they have also created new ethical and social problems and challenges. Chapter 5 is devoted entirely to ethical and social issues raised by information systems, such as threats to individual privacy and intellectual property rights, computer-related health problems, computer crimes, and elimination of jobs. A major management challenge is to make informed decisions that are sensitive to the negative consequences of information systems as well to the positive ones.

    Managers face an ongoing struggle to maintain security and control. Today, the threat of unauthorized penetration or disruption of information systems has never been greater. Information systems are so essential to business, government, and daily life that organizations must take special steps to ensure their security, accuracy, and reliability. A firm invites disaster if it uses systems that can be disrupted or accessed by outsiders, that do not work as intended, or that do not deliver information in a form that people can correctly use. Information systems must be designed so that they are secure, function as intended, and so that humans can control the process. Chapter 10 treats these issues in detail. Managers will need to ask: Can we apply high-quality assurance standards to our information systems, as well as to our products and services? Can we build systems with tight security that are still easy to use? Can we design information systems that respect people's rights of privacy while still pursuing our organization's goals? Should information systems monitor employees? What do we do when an information system designed to increase efficiency and productivity eliminates people's jobs?

This text is designed to provide future managers with the knowledge and understanding required to deal with these challenges. To further this objective, each succeeding chapter concludes with a Management Opportunities, Challenges, and Solutions section that outlines the key issues of which managers should be aware.

Integrating Text with Technology: New Opportunities for Learning

In addition to the changes in business and management that we have just described, we believe that information technology creates new opportunities for learning that can make the MIS course more meaningful and exciting. We have provided a series of hands-on projects, a student Web site, and an interactive multimedia CD-ROM for integrating the text with leading-edge technology.

Application software exercises require students to use spreadsheet, database, Web browser, and other application software in hands-on projects related to chapter concepts. Students can apply the application software skills they have learned in other courses to real-world business problems. You can find these exercises following the Discussion Questions at the end of each chapter, and both the exercises and their data files can be found at the Laudon Web site.

A running case study based on a simulated company called Dirt Bikes U.S.A. enables students to learn about a specific business and develop information system solutions for that business. Each chapter of the text contains a running case scenario and project where students can apply their analytical skills and chapter concepts. Many of these projects require extensive use of the Web or spreadsheet and database software. You can find a Dirt Bikes U.S.A. project following the Application Software Exercise at the end of every chapter. A complete description of each running case project and any data files required by the project can be found at the Laudon Web site and on the Laudon interactive multimedia CD-ROM.

For each chapter, you will also find an Electronic Commerce or Electronic Business project for which you can use Web research and interactive software at various company Web sites to solve specific business problems. The project is described at the end of each chapter after the running case and additional details can be found at the Laudon Web site for that chapter.

As you read each chapter of the text, you can visit the Prentice Hall Laudon Web site at **www.prenhall.com/laudon** and use the Internet for additional interactive learning and management problem solving. You will find an Internet Connection margin note in every chapter directing you to Web sites for which we have provided additional exercises and projects related to the concepts and organizations described in that particular chapter. A graded online Interactive Study Guide contains questions to help you review what you have learned and test your mastery of chapter concepts. Also at the Laudon Web site are links to additional online case studies and international resources.

The interactive CD-ROM multimedia version of the text features audio/video overviews explaining key concepts, bullet text summaries of key points in each chapter, full-color graphics and photos, Web links to the companion Web site, interactive quizzes, Dynamic Blackboard, a hyperlinked digital glossary, and the complete running case, along with any files or materials required by each running case project. You can use the CD-ROM as an interactive study guide or as an alternative to the traditional text.

Longer, comprehensive projects conclude each major section of the text. These projects require students to apply what they have learned to more demanding problems, such as analyzing enterprise system requirements, developing an Internet business model, designing a corporate knowledge intranet, and redesigning business processes for a new system. Some of these projects require use of the Web.

MAKE IT YOUR BUSINESS

Finance and Accounting

The Internet has created vast electronic marketplaces for the purchase and sale of stocks, bonds, and other financial products. Online trading and management of investment accounts are also available. Financial systems, some of the first systems to be computerized, are based today on high-speed computers and networks. Financial and accounting information can be obtained instantly from internal computer systems and can flow instantly across entire organizations. Financial information can also be obtained instantly on the Internet.

Human Resources

Human resources record keeping is now largely computer based, enabling companies to track their employee resources instantly. Networked communication systems and the Internet make it easy for managers to communicate with many employees simultaneously and manage distant task forces and worker teams. Work can be separated from location and managed from afar.

Manufacturing and Production

Internet and network technology have enhanced the precision and flexibility of the manufacturing and production function in both large and small companies. Companies can use these technologies to work collaboratively with other companies and coordinate their design, production and quality control processes more tightly with those of suppliers and distributors. You can find examples of manufacturing and production applications on pages 3, 14, 17, and 35–37.

Sales and Marketing

The Internet and the Web have opened up a powerful new sales and marketing channel to retail consumers and to other businesses. Companies can use the Internet for advertising, customer support, and even some forms of product testing, with customers ordering products and services over the Web from their desktop computers. The ubiquity of the Internet makes it possible for small businesses to sell their wares in many areas of the globe without a physical sales force or front offices. You can find examples of sales and marketing applications on pages 17 and 35–37.

Summary

1. **Explain why information systems are so important today for business and management.**

   Information systems are a foundation for conducting business today. In many industries, survival and even existence without extensive use of IT is inconceivable and IT plays a critical role in increasing productivity. Although information technology has become more of a commodity, when coupled with complementary changes in organization and management, it can provide the foundation for new products, services, and ways of conducting business that provide firms with a strategic advantage. Information technology has become the largest component of capital investment for firms in the United States and many industrialized societies.

2. **Evaluate the role of information systems in today's competitive business environment.**

   Information systems have become essential for helping organizations deal with changes in global economies and the business enterprise. Information systems provide firms with communication and analytic tools for conducting trade and managing businesses on a global scale. Information systems are the foundation of new knowledge-based products and services in knowledge economies and help firms manage their knowledge assets. Information systems make it possible for businesses to adopt more flexible arrangements of employees and management that can coordinate with other organizations across great distances. Organizations are trying to become more competitive and efficient by transforming themselves into digital firms where nearly all core business processes and relationships with customers, suppliers, and employees are digitally enabled. The Internet is bringing about a convergence of technologies that is further widening the use of information systems in business and transforming industries and business models.

3. **Assess the impact of the Internet and Internet technology on business and government.**

   The Internet provides global connectivity and a flexible platform for the seamless flow of information across the enterprise and between the firm and its customers and suppliers. It is the primary technology infrastructure for electronic commerce, electronic business, and the emerging digital firm. In electronic commerce (e-commerce), businesses can exchange electronic purchase and sale transactions with each other and with individual customers. Electronic business (e-business) uses Internet and other digital technology for organizational communication and coordination, collaboration with business partners, and the management of the firm, as well as for electronic commerce transactions. Digital firms use Internet technology intensively to manage their internal processes and relationships with customers, suppliers, and other external entities. E-government uses the Internet and intranets to improve delivery of government services, make internal operations more efficient, and empower citizens to network electronically with other citizens.

4. **Define an information system from both a technical and business perspective and distinguish between computer literacy and information systems literacy.**

An information system collects, stores, and disseminates information from an organization's environment and internal operations to support organizational functions and decision making, communication, coordination, control, analysis, and visualization. Information systems transform raw data into useful information through three basic activities: input, processing, and output. From a business perspective, an information system creates economic value for the firm as an organizational and management solution, based on information technology, to a challenge posed by the environment. The information system is part of a series of value-adding activities for acquiring, transforming, and distributing information to improve management decision making, enhance organizational performance, and, ultimately, increase firm profitability.

Information systems are rooted in organizations; they are an outcome of organizational structure, culture, politics, workflows, and business processes. They are instruments for organizational change and value creation, making it possible to recast these organizational elements into new business models and redraw organizational

boundaries. Managers are problem solvers who are responsible for analyzing the many challenges confronting organizations and for developing strategies and action plans. Information systems are one of their tools, delivering the information required for solutions. Information systems both reflect management decisions and serve as instruments for changing the management process. Information systems cannot make managers and organizations more effective unless they are accompanied by complementary assets such as new business processes, organizational culture, or management behavior.

Information systems literacy requires an understanding of the organizational and management dimensions of information systems as well as the technical dimensions addressed by computer literacy. Information systems literacy draws on both technical and behavioral approaches to studying information systems. Both perspectives can be combined into a sociotechnical approach to systems.

5. **Identify the major management challenges to building and using information systems.**

There are five key management challenges in building and using information systems: (a) obtaining business value from information systems; (b) providing appropriate complementary assets to use information technology effectively; (c) understanding the system requirements of a global business environment; (d) creating an information technology infrastructure that is flexible enough to support changing organizational goals; and (e) designing systems that people can control, understand, and use in a socially and ethically responsible manner.

Key Terms

Business functions, 20
Business processes, 12
Communications technology, 22
Complementary assets, 24
Computer-based information systems (CBIS), 16
Computer hardware, 22
Computer literacy, 19
Computer software, 22
Data, 15
Data workers, 21
Digital firm, 11
E-government, 9
Electronic business (e-business), 9

Electronic commerce (e-commerce), 9
Extranets, 22
Feedback, 15
Formal systems, 15
Information, 13
Information system, 13
Information systems literacy, 19
Information technology (IT), 4
Information technology (IT) infrastructure, 23
Input, 15
Internet, 22
Intranets, 22
Knowledge- and information-intense products, 11

Knowledge workers, 21
Management information systems (MIS), 27
Middle managers, 21
Network, 22
Operational managers, 21
Organizational and management capital, 24
Output, 15
Processing, 15
Production or service workers, 21
Senior managers, 21
Sociotechnical view, 27
Storage technology, 22
Web site, 22
World Wide Web, 22

Review Questions

1. **List and describe four reasons why information systems are so important for business today.**

2. **Describe five technology and business trends that have enhanced the role of information systems in today's competitive business environment.**

3. **Describe the capabilities of a digital firm. Why are digital firms so powerful?**

4. **What is an information system? Distinguish between a computer, a computer program, and an informa-**

tion system. What is the difference between data and information?

5. *What activities convert raw data to usable information in information systems? What is their relationship to feedback?*

6. *What is the purpose of an information system from a business perspective? What role does it play in the business information value chain?*

7. *What is information systems literacy? How does it differ from computer literacy?*

8. *What are the organizational, management, and technology dimensions of information systems?*

9. *What are the Internet and the World Wide Web? How have they changed the roles played by information systems in organizations?*

10. *Why do some firms obtain greater value from their information systems than others? What role do complementary assets and organizational and management capital play?*

11. *Distinguish between a behavioral and a technical approach to information systems in terms of the questions asked and the answers provided. What major disciplines contribute to an understanding of information systems?*

12. *What are the key management challenges involved in building, operating, and maintaining information systems today?*

Discussion Questions

1. *Information systems are too important to be left to computer specialists. Do you agree? Why or why not?*

2. *As computers become faster and cheaper and the Internet becomes more widely used, most of the prob-*

lems we have with information systems will disappear. Do you agree? Why or why not?

Application Software Exercise:
Database Exercise: Adding Value to Information for Management Decision Making

Effective information systems add value to data to create meaningful information for management decisions that improve business performance. At the Laudon Web site in the section for Chapter 1, you can find a Store and Regional Sales Database with raw data on weekly store sales of computer equipment in various sales regions. The database includes fields for store identification number, sales region number, item number, item description, unit price, units sold, and the weekly sales period when the sales were made. Develop some reports and queries to make this information more useful for management. Modify the database table, if necessary, to provide all of the information you require. Here are some questions you might consider:

1. Which are the best-performing stores and sales regions?

2. What are the best-selling products?

3. Which stores and sales regions sell the most of which products?

4. When are the strongest and weakest selling periods? For which stores? Which sales regions? Which products?

5. How can your company improve sales in the weakest store and sales region? (Answers will vary.)

Preparing a Management Overview of the Company

Software requirements: Word processing software

                         Electronic presentation software (optional)

Dirt Bikes's management has asked you to prepare a management analysis of the company to help it assess the firm's current situation and future plans. Review Dirt Bikes's company history, organization chart, prod-

ucts and services, sales and marketing, and selected financial data in the Introduction to Dirt Bikes, which can be found at the Laudon Web site in the section for Chapter 1. Then prepare a report that addresses these questions:

1. What are the company's goals and culture?

2. What products and services does Dirt Bikes U.S.A. provide? How many types of products and

services are available to customers? How does Dirt Bikes sell its products?

3. How many employees are managers, production workers, or knowledge or information workers? Are there levels of management?

4. What kinds of information systems and technologies would be the most important for a company such as Dirt Bikes?

5. (Optional) Use electronic presentation software to summarize your analysis for management.

Electronic Commerce Project: Analyzing Shipping Costs

You are the shipping clerk of a small firm that prints, binds, and ships popular books for a midlevel publisher. Your production facilities are located in Albany, New York (ZIP code 12250). Your customers' warehouses are located in Rye, New York (10580); Irving, Texas (75015); Charlotte, North Carolina (28201); Sioux Falls, South Dakota (57117); and Tustin, California (92680). The production facility operates 250 days per year. Your books are usually shipped in one of two sized packages:

(A) Height: 9 inches, Length: 13 inches, Width: 17 inches, Weight: 45 lbs.

(B) Height: 10 inches, Length: 6 inches, Width: 12 inches, Weight: 16 lbs.

The company ships about four of the A boxes to each of the warehouses on an average day and about eight B boxes daily.

Your task is to select the best shipper for your company. Compare three shippers, such as FedEx (www.fedex.com), UPS (www.ups.com), and the U.S. Postal Service (www.usps.gov). Consider not only costs but also such issues as delivery speed, pickup schedules, drop-off locations, tracking ability, and ease of use of the Web site. Which service did you select? Explain why.

Group Project: Analyzing a Business System

In a group with three or four classmates, find a description in a computer or business magazine of an information system used by an organization. Look for information about the company on the Web to gain further insight into the company, and prepare a brief description of the business.

Describe the system you have selected in terms of its inputs, processes, and outputs and in terms of its organization, management, and technology features and the importance of the system to the company. If possible, use electronic presentation software to present your analysis to the class.

CASE STUDY
Dollar General: Heavy on Organization, Light on Systems

Dollar General Corporation, headquartered in Goodlettsville, Tennessee, is an aggressive competitor in the deep discount retail industry, fighting for position with other dollar stores such as Family Dollar, Fred's, and Dollar Tree, as well as with retailers such as Wal-Mart, Kmart, CVS, and Rite Aid. Dollar General stores offer a product line of general merchandise that includes housewares and cleaning supplies, health and beauty aids, clothing, packaged food, stationery, seasonal offerings, and other household consumables. The company has been operating since 1939.

Dollar General's most recent annual sales figures total $6.9 billion, placing the chain at the top of the dollar store category of discount retailers. Somewhat surprisingly, the chain is not achieving its success by following the example set by other successful discount retailers. Whereas competitors such as 99 Cents Only stores consider middle- and high-income customers to be key contributors to their profits, Dollar General caters specifically to customers with low, middle, and fixed incomes.

Dollar General has kept away from the big box supercenter store model used by Wal-Mart and Kmart. This type of store is often located on the outskirts of cities or outside of particular towns to draw customers from a broad area. When placing new stores, Dollar General prefers to locate them within communities, often targeting municipalities that are home to fewer than 20,000 residents. In early 2004, over 4,000 Dollar General stores were in such communities. The company believes that filling the role of neighborhood store is a big part of its success. As such, stores follow a fixed, even-dollar pricing schedule with about one-third of all merchandise priced at $1 or lower. The maximum price for a Dollar General product is generally around $35.

When it comes to total revenue, the dollar store cannot really keep up with the superstore. Wal-Mart's most recent annual sales figures were over $250 billion. However, where Dollar General can make its mark is in getting the biggest bang for its buck. Many supermarkets struggle to keep up with Wal-Mart because the retail giant earns a higher percentage on each dollar of sales (3.5 cents last year) than most retailers are able to achieve. Last year Dollar General surpassed Wal-Mart's benchmark by earning 4.3 cents for every dollar of sales.

How Dollar General accomplishes this is by rapidly opening stores and running each store at the lowest operating cost possible. As of the middle of 2004, Dollar General operated 6,930 stores with 57,800 full- and part-time employees in 29 states, with an additional 695 new store openings in 2004 alone. Since 1999, when there were 3,687 stores, the chain has doubled in size. For every day that a new store is open, the company, on average, can expect to add $2,800 in sales and $124 in profit. Across a large scale, these numbers make quite a difference in the key columns of a profit and loss statement at the end of a year.

To take full advantage of this strategy, Dollar General has developed a system for opening new stores that whittles the procedure down to a scant eight days. Dollar General views this system as so vital to its business that it protects the details of the procedure in the same way that Coca-Cola protects the formula for its leading soft drink. However, *Baseline Magazine* has been able to reveal the basics of the typical Dollar General store opening, as well as how the operation fits in with the manner in which the store is run after opening. In both cases, a strict budget influences every step from hiring to implementing information systems.

The average Dollar General retail store occupies 6,800 square feet of space. The company views leasing space as the most favorable financial practice. The majority of stores are placed in either shopping centers (56%) or freestanding buildings (41%), with a handful housed in urban structures (3%). The opening of a new store is a chain reaction of events that begins with a district or area manager hiring a construction team to perform any work necessary for the site to serve as a Dollar General store. This can include putting in new floors or creating access for delivery trucks.

As this work begins to wind down, the Goodlettsville office authorizes the purchase of point-of-sale (POS) terminals from IBM, with the stipulation that IBM deliver the terminals on the second day of the upcoming store opening process. The POS purchase is the cue for Dollar General headquarters to notify its satellite link provider, Spacenet, to schedule an installation at the new store. The satellite link connects the IBM terminals to corporate headquarters so that the store can report sales data. Spacenet is contracted to perform the installation on the fourth or fifth day of the store opening process.

The opening of Dollar General stores falls under the direction of a store merchandiser, also known as a setter or an opener. Setters coordinate the entire process as it happens and their responsibilities include everything from managing employees and installing the IBM terminals to building shelves and stocking the shelves with products. They also test software and link up with headquarters. In a way, setters are like hired guns even though they work full-time for Dollar General. They spend most of their time on the road, traveling to different locations (wherever they are needed) to open, close, and reorganize stores. Once on-site, setters wield significant power because of their strong operational knowledge. Working beneath the setter, for the time being, is a store manager who will stay on to run the location once the setup process is complete.

A few weeks before a Dollar General store is scheduled to open, the store manager or the district manager solicits applicants to populate the crew for the eight-day opening effort. This crew normally consists of 10 to a maximum of 20 workers. Workers who apply themselves well during this period receive consideration for full- or part-time employment when the store opens. However, since the stores operate with a staff of no more than 6, continued employment is hardly a guarantee.

On the first day of setup, the crew unloads, constructs, and installs fixtures for the store including shelves, counters, display racks, and refrigerators. The workers also clean the floors and windows of the store. Dollar General outlines the proper positioning and placement for all fixtures and products in a guidebook known as a planogram, or pog, for short. Pogs are extremely detailed, right down to instructing employees that products must be positioned so that they are even with the front edge of a shelf. Corporate headquarters maintains close control over every aspect of operation. The company distributes handbooks to employees that direct them how to communicate with each other and with customers.

Over the next several days, the setter receives and sets up the IBM point-of-sale terminals, the crew sets up a stock room for surplus inventory, and a small manager's office is constructed. By the third day of the setup process, approximately 50 percent of the store's opening inventory arrives. On the fourth or fifth day, a Spacenet technician arrives to install the store's satellite dish on the roof and a satellite modem inside that connects to the IBM terminals. Spacenet is receiving $40 million over 10 years to fill this role for Dollar General.

Once the technician establishes a satellite link with corporate headquarters in Goodlettsville, corporate management begins to transmit pricing data and product codes to the IBM terminals. The store can begin sending payroll information back the other way. Spacenet also tests the point-of-sale software, called Triversity, which the store will need to run to authorize credit and debit card payments and transmit sales data. Meanwhile, the crew continues to unpack and shelve merchandise that has been delivered by the truckload.

As the second half of the eight-day opening process begins, the satellite network is up and running and the store manager can begin to train the store's assistant manager and candidates for cashier jobs on the IBM cash register terminals. Bar-code scanners that lay flat in the cashier counters are installed and connected to the registers. Training on the registers also provides the staff the opportunity to test the system, ensuring that products scan at the correct prices and that details about the store are properly entered in the fields of the sales application systems.

The last few days of setup involve additional product stocking, all the while taking advantage of every inch of space that the store has. The setter uses a map that was constructed specifically for this store to fit the thousands of standard items that Dollar General offers into the store. He or she also sets up the space that has been allotted to special or seasonal items. The final few days of the eight-day project are a flurry of activity as perishable goods arrive, the satellite network receives a final test, and the crew finally clears and mops the aisles to make the store bright and clean. If they can get the store ready for business in fewer than eight days, it could mean a bonus for the setter.

Once a Dollar General store is open for business, the use of information systems in the stores is rather thin. Systems are used to keep costs down and for very little else. According to Alinean, an Orlando, Florida, technology measurement firm, Dollar General spends less on technology per employee ($3,000 annually) than any of its dollar-store competitors.

Dollar General does use advanced satellite technology to communicate with headquarters, but it was chosen because dial-up and high-speed connections were unreliable in some areas and stores were not always able to complete their nightly sales reports. However, individual Dollar General stores do not use networks to facilitate operations. The IBM terminals include e-mail features, but the stores do not use them, relying on a private voice-mail system for communication instead. Managers, both during setup and operation, use paper on clipboards for tracking cash deposit logs, employee contact information, and the arrival of goods into the stores. Using handheld computerized devices for this purpose would add to the company's technology budget.

Individual Dollar General stores have no automated method for keeping track of their own inventory. Managers know approximately how many cases of a particular product they're supposed to receive when a delivery truck arrives. However, they do not scan the cartons or verify the item count inside the cases (the exception being perishable food items, which are generally supplied by local sources). Dollar General's distribution centers do use information systems, running Catalyst warehouse management software, to track the inventory they receive and subsequently ship to stores. However, recipients at the stores merely check to see whether the cases are sealed properly. Inventory management depends on the polling data that headquarters gathers from store cash registers each night, which indicates how many of a product were sold and at what price.

Dollar General has an increasing shrink rate, which refers to the percentage of total sales that the company writes off as losses resulting from theft of product or other mishap. Dollar General's shrink rate has grown steadily from 2.6 percent in 1998 to 3.05 percent in 2003. The company's goal is to keep shrink rates to no more than 1.75 percent to 2 percent. Store managers believe that most of the company's losses are caused by merchandise being stolen during shipping, which goes undetected because there is no scanning upon receipt, and to shoplifting in the stores.

Corporate headquarters has chosen to focus on the employees as the root of the problem. The measures that headquarters has taken to counter the shrink rate include deploying loss prevention software, which identifies unusual cash register transactions, and installing video cameras to monitor the registers, the stockroom, and even the store manager. These measures apparently have not made a dent in the shrink rate.

While Dollar General continues to watch the bottom line carefully, its business continues to grow. In 2003, the chain experimented with two larger, grocery-oriented stores under the Dollar General Market name. The company intends to open 20 more such stores in 2004. At the same time, the chain has continued to achieve growth through new stores and from increases in same-store sales. The question is, How long can this strategy work for Dollar General? Can the company keep ramping up its business without ramping up its technology budget?

Sources: Kim S. Nash, "Dollar General: 8 Days to Grow" and "Roadblock: 4,170 Newbies," *Baseline Magazine*, July 2004; A. Teymour Golsorkhi, "Sales Creep Higher at Dollar General, Fred's," TheStreet.com, August 5, 2004, www.thestreet.com/stocks/retail/10176678.html; "Dollar General Sales Continue Upward Trend," *Nashville Business Journal*, August 6, 2004, nashville.bizjournals.com/nashville/stories/2004/08/02/daily30.html; "Dollar General Reports Increased July Sales; Opens 61 New Stores; Announces Second Quarter Conference Call," *BusinessWire*, August 5, 2004, home.businesswire.com; "Dollar General Corporation Fact Sheet," Hoover's Online, www.hoovers.com; Dollar General Corporation 10-K Form, www.sec.gov, accessed September 10, 2004; and www.dollargeneral.com, accessed September 10, 2004.

CASE STUDY QUESTIONS

1. Describe Dollar General's business strategy. Why has the company been so successful?

2. Describe the role of management, organization, and technology in Dollar General's business strategy.

3. How well do information systems support Dollar General's business strategy? Explain your answer.

4. Does Dollar General miss out on any business opportunities as a result of its approach to information technology? If so, what are these opportunities?

5. Do you think Dollar General can continue growing at its current rate? Explain your answer.

Chapter 2

Information Systems in the Enterprise

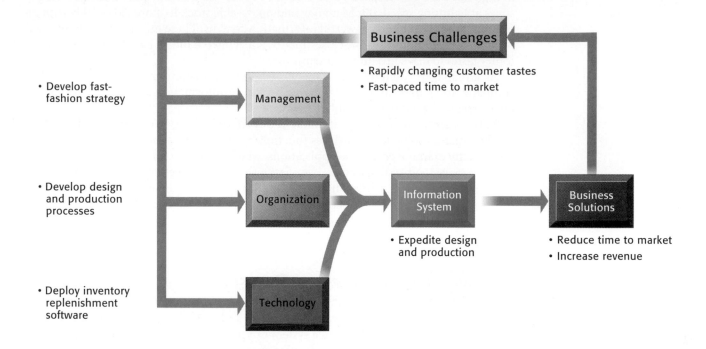

Business Challenges
• Rapidly changing customer tastes
• Fast-paced time to market

• Develop fast-fashion strategy → Management

• Develop design and production processes → Organization

• Deploy inventory replenishment software → Technology

Information System
• Expedite design and production

Business Solutions
• Reduce time to market
• Increase revenue

Opening Case: Fast Fashion, Hot Systems

In the fast-paced world of fashion retailing, nothing seems more important than time to market. Instead of the traditional four clothing fashion seasons (spring, summer, autumn, and winter), styles now change once a month or even faster. Some women's clothing store chains get a delivery of new styles twice a month. Welcome to the world of Speed Chic.

A number of companies have adopted this strategy, including Sweden's H &M, TopShop in the United Kingdom, and Spain's Zara and Mango. Mango/MNG Holding SL is based outside Barcelona, with more than 700 women's boutique stores in 72 countries. It's noted for an eclectic mix of body-hugging styles. Now it wants to break into the U.S. fashion market and it believes its approach to "fast fashion" will help.

Bringing out a steady stream of trendy new merchandise requires flexibility and speed from design through production and delivery to the store shelf. "We know how to improvise," says David Egea, Mango's merchandising director. "To react and have what people want, we have to break some rules. And here we keep breaking them." Once garments roll off production lines, Mango relies on a proprietary inventory replenishment system to determine exactly which pieces should be sent to which stores.

Four times each year, Mango's designers meet to discuss important new trends for each of its main collections. Each collection consists of five or six smaller collections. Design teams meet each week to adjust for changing trends. After clothing and accessories styles have been decided, Mango's product management and distribution team assigns them personalities, such as trendy, dressy, or suitable for hot weather.

Once items have been classified they are sent to one of Mango's 731 stores, each of which is classified by traits such as the climate where the shop is located or whether large or small sizes sell best. Mango's inventory replenishment system makes sure the merchandise is sent to compatible shops.

The system transmits order data to a large distribution machine on the ground floor of Mango headquarters, which is surrounded by a rotating ring of cardboard boxes on hooks. Bar-coded clothes that have just arrived from factories are scanned and placed into one of 466 store-specific slots. They then are boxed and shipped to retail stores. Mango can add new items to its stores once a week, about six times more frequently than the typical American clothing chain. Retail store managers can adjust store plans daily based on input from regional supervisors and headquarters.

Sources: Erin White, "For Retailer Mango, Frenzied 'Fast Fashion' Proves Sweet," *Wall Street Journal*, May 28, 2004; Kasra Ferdows, Michael A. Lewis, and Jose A. D. Machuca. "Rapid-Fire Fulfillment." *Harvard Business Review* (November 2004); and Cecilie Rohwedder, "Making Fashion Faster," *Wall Street Journal*, February 28, 2004.

Mango has a core of designers and production facilities that can churn out new fashion styles at lightning speed. But Mango would not be able stock its stores so quickly with hot fashion trends without its powerful information systems. These information systems support finely tuned business processes that organize merchandise based on style and customer tastes to drive inventory replenishment.

As a manager, you'll want to know exactly how information systems can help your company. You'll need to understand which types of information systems are available to businesses and what they can do for them.

In this chapter, we first look at different ways of classifying information systems based on the organizational level, business functions, and business processes they support. We then briefly examine enterprise applications, which consist of enterprise systems, supply chain management systems, customer relationship management systems, and knowledge management systems. These enterprise applications span the entire firm, integrating information from multiple functions and business processes to enhance the performance of the organization as a whole.

2.1   MAJOR TYPES OF SYSTEMS IN ORGANIZATIONS

Because there are different interests, specialties, and levels in an organization, there are different kinds of systems. No single system can provide all the information an organization needs. Figure 2-1 illustrates one way to depict the kinds of systems found in an organization. In the illustration, the organization is divided into strategic, management, and operational levels and then is further divided into functional areas such as sales and marketing, manufacturing and production, finance and accounting, and human resources. Systems are built to serve these different organizational interests (Anthony, 1965).

Different Kinds of Systems

Three main categories of information systems serve different organizational levels: operational-level systems, management-level systems, and strategic-level systems. **Operational-level systems** support operational managers by keeping track of the elementary activities and transactions of the organization, such as sales, receipts, cash deposits, payroll, credit decisions, and the flow of materials in a factory. The principal purpose of systems at this level is to answer routine questions and to track the flow of transactions through the organization. How many parts are in inventory? What happened to Mr. Williams's payment? To answer these kinds of questions, information generally must be easily available, current, and accurate. Examples of operational-level systems include a system to record bank deposits from automatic teller machines or one that tracks the number of hours worked each day by employees on a factory floor.

Management-level systems serve the monitoring, controlling, decision-making, and administrative activities of middle managers. The principal question addressed by such systems is this: Are things working well? Management-level systems typically provide periodic reports rather than instant information on operations. An example is a relocation control system that reports on the total moving, house-hunting, and home financing costs for employees in all company divisions, noting wherever actual costs exceed budgets.

Some management-level systems support nonroutine decision making. They tend to focus on less-structured decisions for which information requirements are not always clear. These systems often answer "what-if" questions: What would be the impact on production schedules if we were to double sales in the month of December? What would happen to our return on investment if a factory schedule were delayed for six months? Answers to these questions frequently require new data from outside the organization, as well as data from inside that cannot be easily drawn from existing operational-level systems.

FIGURE 2-1   *Types of information systems.*

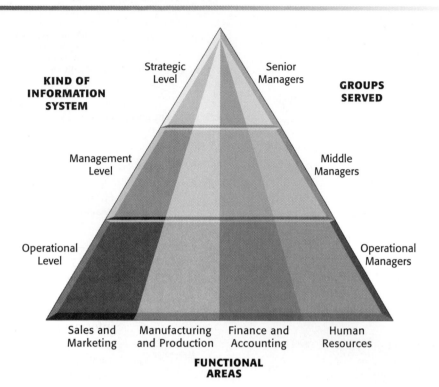

KIND OF INFORMATION SYSTEM

Strategic Level

Management Level

Operational Level

GROUPS SERVED

Senior Managers

Middle Managers

Operational Managers

Sales and Marketing

Manufacturing and Production

Finance and Accounting

Human Resources

FUNCTIONAL AREAS

Organizations can be divided into strategic, management, and operational levels and into four major functional areas: sales and marketing, manufacturing and production, finance and accounting, and human resources. Information systems serve each of these levels and functions.

Strategic-level systems help senior management tackle and address strategic issues and long-term trends, both in the firm and in the external environment. Their principal concern is matching changes in the external environment with existing organizational capability. What will employment levels be in five years? What are the long-term industry cost trends, and where does our firm fit in? What products should we be making in five years?

Information systems also serve the major business functions, such as sales and marketing, manufacturing and production, finance and accounting, and human resources. A typical organization has operational-, management-, and strategic-level systems for each functional area. For example, the sales function generally has a sales system on the operational level to record daily sales figures and to process orders. A management-level system tracks monthly sales figures by sales territory and reports on territories where sales exceed or fall below anticipated levels. A system to forecast sales trends over a five-year period serves the strategic level. We first describe the specific categories of systems serving each organizational level and their value to the organization. Then we show how organizations use these systems for each major business function.

Four Major Types of Systems

Figure 2-2 shows the specific types of information systems that correspond to each organizational level. The organization has executive support systems (ESS) at the strategic level; management information systems (MIS) and decision-support systems (DSS) at the management level; and transaction processing systems (TPS) at the operational level. Systems at each level in turn are specialized to serve each of the major functional areas. Thus, the typical systems found in organizations are designed to assist workers or managers at each level and in the functions of sales and marketing, manufacturing and production, finance and accounting, and human resources.

Table 2-1 summarizes the features of the four types of information systems. It should be noted that each of the different systems may have components that are used by organizational

FIGURE 2-2 *The four major types of information systems.*

This figure provides examples of TPS, DSS, MIS, and ESS, showing the level of the organization and business function that each supports.

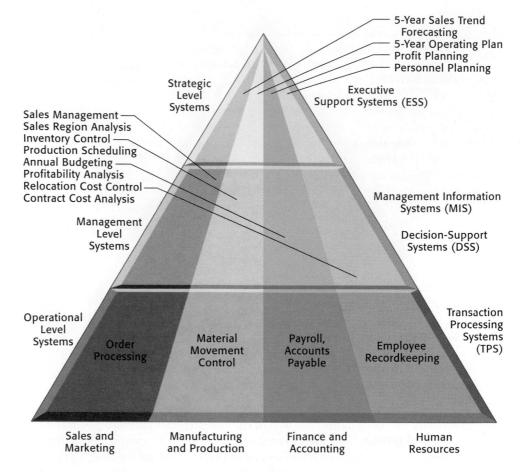

FUNCTIONAL AREAS

TABLE 2-1 *Characteristics of Information Processing Systems*

Type of System	Information Inputs	Processing	Information Outputs	Users
ESS	Aggregate data; external, internal	Graphics; simulations; interactive	Projections; responses to queries	Senior managers
DSS	Low-volume data or massive databases optimized for data analysis; analytic models and data analysis tools	Interactive; simulations; analysis	Special reports; decision analyses; responses to queries	Professionals; staff managers
MIS	Summary transaction data; high-volume data; simple models	Routine reports; simple models; low-level analysis	Summary and exception reports	Middle managers
TPS	Transactions; events	Sorting; listing; merging; updating	Detailed reports; lists; summaries	Operations personnel; supervisors

levels and groups other than its main constituencies. A secretary may find information on an MIS, or a middle manager may need to extract data from a TPS.

TRANSACTION PROCESSING SYSTEMS

Transaction processing systems (TPS) are the basic business systems that serve the operational level of the organization. A transaction processing system is a computerized system that performs and records the daily routine transactions necessary to conduct business. Examples are sales order entry, hotel reservation systems, payroll, employee record keeping, and shipping.

At the operational level, tasks, resources, and goals are predefined and highly structured. The decision to grant credit to a customer, for instance, is made by a lower-level supervisor according to predefined criteria. All that must be determined is whether the customer meets the criteria.

Figure 2-3 depicts a payroll TPS, which is a typical accounting transaction processing system found in most firms. A payroll system keeps track of the money paid to employees. The master file is composed of discrete pieces of information (such as a name, address, or employee number) called data elements. Data are keyed into the system, updating the data elements. The elements on the master file are combined in different ways to make up reports of interest to management and government agencies and to send paychecks to employees. These TPS can generate other report combinations of existing data elements.

Other typical TPS applications are identified in Figure 2-4. The figure shows that there are five functional categories of TPS: sales/marketing, manufacturing/production, finance/accounting, human resources, and other types of TPS that are unique to a particular industry. The United Parcel Service (UPS) package tracking system described in Chapter 1 is an example of a manufacturing TPS. UPS sells package delivery services; the TPS system keeps track of all of its package shipment transactions.

FIGURE 2-3   *A symbolic representation for a payroll TPS.*

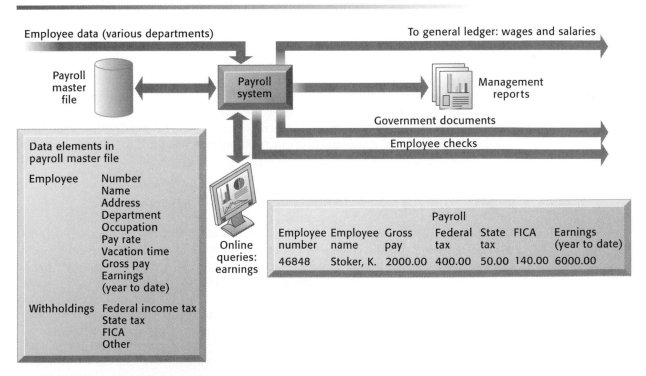

A payroll system is a typical accounting TPS that processes transactions such as employee time cards and changes in employee salaries and deductions. It keeps track of money paid to employees, withholding tax, and paychecks.

FIGURE 2-4   *Typical applications of TPS.*

		TYPE OF TPS SYSTEM			
	Sales/ marketing systems	Manufacturing/ production systems	Finance/ accounting systems	Human resources systems	Other types (e.g., university)
Major functions of system	Customer service Sales management Promotion tracking Price changes Dealer communications	Scheduling Purchasing Shipping/receiving Operations	General ledger Billing Cost accounting	Personnel records Benefits Compensation Labor relations Training	Admissions Grade records Course records Alumni records
Major application systems	Sales order information system Sales commission system Sales support system	Machine control systems Purchase order systems Quality control systems	General ledger Payroll Accounts receivable/payable Funds management systems	Employee records Benefit systems Employee skills inventory	Registration system Student transcript system Curriculum class control systems Alumni benefactor system

There are five functional categories of TPS: sales/marketing, manufacturing/production, finance/ accounting, human resources, and other types of systems specific to a particular industry. Within each of these major functions are subfunctions. For each of these subfunctions (e.g., sales management) there is a major application system.

Transaction processing systems are often so central to a business that TPS failure for a few hours can lead to a firm's demise and perhaps that of other firms linked to it. Imagine what would happen to UPS if its package tracking system were not working! What would the airlines do without their computerized reservation systems?

Managers need TPS to monitor the status of internal operations and the firm's relations with the external environment. TPS are also major producers of information for the other types of systems. (For example, the payroll system illustrated here, along with other accounting TPS, supplies data to the company's general ledger system, which is responsible for maintaining records of the firm's income and expenses and for producing reports such as income statements and balance sheets.)

MANAGEMENT INFORMATION SYSTEMS

In Chapter 1, we define management information systems as the study of information systems in business and management. The term *management information systems (MIS)* also designates a specific category of information systems serving management-level functions. **Management information systems (MIS)** serve the management level of the organization, providing managers with reports and often online access to the organization's current performance and historical records. Typically, MIS are oriented almost exclusively to internal, not environmental or external, events. MIS primarily serve the functions of planning, controlling, and decision making at the management level. Generally, they depend on underlying transaction processing systems for their data.

MIS summarize and report on the company's basic operations. The basic transaction data from TPS are compressed and are usually presented in long reports that are produced on a regular schedule. Figure 2-5 shows how a typical MIS transforms transaction-level data from inventory, production, and accounting into MIS files that are used to provide managers with reports. Figure 2-6 shows a sample report from this system.

FIGURE 2-5 *How management information systems obtain their data from the organization's TPS.*

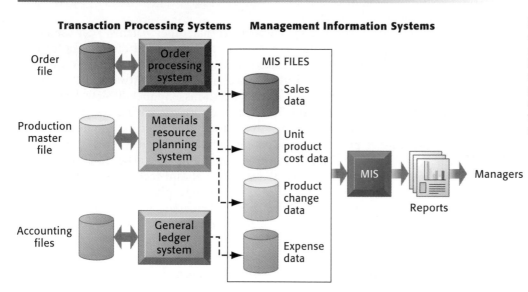

Transaction Processing Systems   Management Information Systems

In the system illustrated by this diagram, three TPS supply summarized transaction data to the MIS reporting system at the end of the time period. Managers gain access to the organizational data through the MIS, which provides them with the appropriate reports.

MIS usually serve managers primarily interested in weekly, monthly, and yearly results, although some MIS enable managers to drill down to see daily or hourly data if required. MIS generally provide answers to routine questions that have been specified in advance and have a predefined procedure for answering them. For instance, MIS reports might list the total pounds of lettuce used this quarter by a fast-food chain or, as illustrated in Figure 2-6, compare total annual sales figures for specific products to planned targets. These systems are generally not flexible and have little analytical capability. Most MIS use simple routines such as summaries and comparisons, as opposed to sophisticated mathematical models or statistical techniques.

DECISION-SUPPORT SYSTEMS

Decision-support systems (DSS) also serve the management level of the organization. DSS help managers make decisions that are unique, rapidly changing, and not easily specified in advance. They address problems where the procedure for arriving at a solution

FIGURE 2-6 *A sample MIS report.*

Consolidated Consumer Products Corporation Sales by Product and Sales Region: 2005

This report showing summarized annual sales data was produced by the MIS in Figure 2-5.

PRODUCT CODE	PRODUCT DESCRIPTION	SALES REGION	ACTUAL SALES	PLANNED	ACTUAL versus PLANNED
4469	Carpet Cleaner	Northeast	4,066,700	4,800,000	0.85
		South	3,778,112	3,750,000	1.01
		Midwest	4,867,001	4,600,000	1.06
		West	4,003,440	4,400,000	0.91
	TOTAL		16,715,253	17,550,000	0.95
5674	Room Freshener	Northeast	3,676,700	3,900,000	0.94
		South	5,608,112	4,700,000	1.19
		Midwest	4,711,001	4,200,000	1.12
		West	4,563,440	4,900,000	0.93
	TOTAL		18,559,253	17,700,000	1.05

may not be fully predefined in advance. Although DSS use internal information from TPS and MIS, they often bring in information from external sources, such as current stock prices or product prices of competitors.

Clearly, by design, DSS have more analytical power than other systems. They use a variety of models to analyze data, or they condense large amounts of data into a form in which they can be analyzed by decision makers. DSS are designed so that users can work with them directly; these systems explicitly include user-friendly software. DSS are interactive; the user can change assumptions, ask new questions, and include new data.

An interesting, small, but powerful DSS is the voyage-estimating system of a subsidiary of a large American metals company that exists primarily to carry bulk cargoes of coal, oil, ores, and finished products for its parent company. The firm owns some vessels, charters others, and bids for shipping contracts in the open market to carry general cargo. A voyage-estimating system calculates financial and technical voyage details. Financial calculations include ship/time costs (fuel, labor, capital), freight rates for various types of cargo, and port expenses. Technical details include a myriad of factors, such as ship cargo capacity, speed, port distances, fuel and water consumption, and loading patterns (location of cargo for different ports).

The system can answer questions such as the following: Given a customer delivery schedule and an offered freight rate, which vessel should be assigned at what rate to maximize profits? What is the optimal speed at which a particular vessel can optimize its profit and still meet its delivery schedule? What is the optimal loading pattern for a ship bound for the U.S. West Coast from Malaysia? Figure 2-7 illustrates the DSS built for this company. The system operates on a powerful desktop personal computer, providing a system of menus that makes it easy for users to enter data or obtain information.

This voyage-estimating DSS draws heavily on analytical models. Other types of DSS are less model-driven, focusing instead on extracting useful information to support decision making from massive quantities of data. For example, Intrawest—the largest ski operator in North America—collects and stores vast amounts of customer data from its Web site, call center, lodging reservations, ski schools, and ski equipment rental stores. It uses special software to analyze these data to determine the value, revenue potential, and loyalty of each customer so managers can make better decisions on how to target their marketing programs. The system segments customers into seven categories based on needs, attitudes, and behaviors, ranging from "passionate experts" to "value-minded family vacationers." The company then e-mails video clips that would appeal to each segment to encourage more visits to its resorts.

Sometimes you'll hear DSS systems referred to as *business intelligence systems* because they focus on helping users make better business decisions. You'll learn more about them in Chapter 13.

FIGURE 2-7   *Voyage-estimating decision-support system.*

This DSS operates on a powerful PC. It is used daily by managers who must develop bids on shipping contracts.

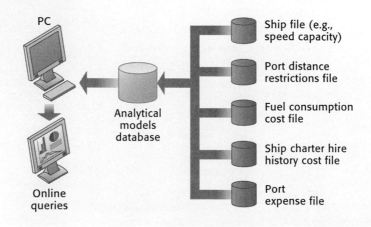

EXECUTIVE SUPPORT SYSTEMS

Senior managers use **executive support systems** (ESS) to help them make decisions. ESS serve the strategic level of the organization. They address nonroutine decisions requiring judgment, evaluation, and insight because there is no agreed-on procedure for arriving at a solution.

ESS are designed to incorporate data about external events, such as new tax laws or competitors, but they also draw summarized information from internal MIS and DSS. They filter, compress, and track critical data, displaying the data of greatest importance to senior managers. For example, the CEO of Leiner Health Products, the largest manufacturer of private-label vitamins and supplements in the United States, has an ESS that provides on his desktop a minute-to-minute view of the firm's financial performance as measured by working capital, accounts receivable, accounts payable, cash flow, and inventory.

ESS employ the most advanced graphics software and can present graphs and data from many sources. Often the information is delivered to senior executives through a **portal**, which uses a Web interface to present integrated personalized business content from a variety of sources. You will learn more about other applications of portals in Chapters 4, 11, and 12.

Unlike the other types of information systems, ESS are not designed primarily to solve specific problems. Instead, ESS provide a generalized computing and communications capacity that can be applied to a changing array of problems. Although many DSS are designed to be highly analytical, ESS tend to make less use of analytical models.

Questions ESS assist in answering include the following: In what business should we be? What are the competitors doing? What new acquisitions would protect us from cyclical business swings? Which units should we sell to raise cash for acquisitions? Figure 2-8 illustrates a model of an ESS. It consists of workstations with menus, interactive graphics, and communications capabilities that can be used to access historical and competitive data from internal corporate systems and external databases such as Dow Jones News/Retrieval or Standard & Poor's. Because ESS are designed to be used by senior managers who often have little, if any, direct contact or experience with computer-based information systems, they incorporate easy-to-use graphic interfaces. More details on leading-edge applications of DSS and ESS can be found in Chapter 13.

Relationship of Systems to One Another

Figure 2-9 illustrates how the systems serving different levels in the organization are related to one another. TPS are typically a major source of data for other systems, whereas

FIGURE 2-8 *Model of a typical executive support system.*

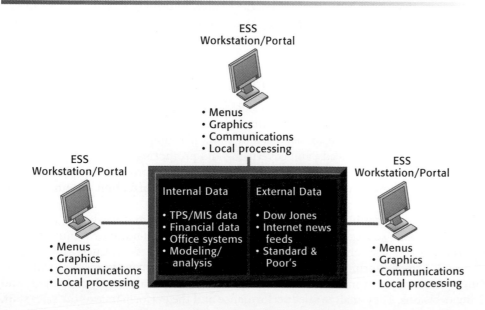

This system pools data from diverse internal and external sources and makes them available to executives in an easy-to-use form.

FIGURE 2-9   *Interrelationships among systems.*

The various types of systems in the organization have interdependencies. TPS are major producers of information that is required by the other systems, which, in turn, produce information for other systems. These different types of systems have been loosely coupled in most organizations.

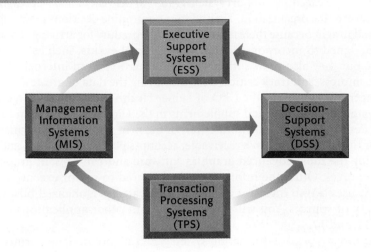

ESS are primarily a recipient of data from lower-level systems. The other types of systems may exchange data with each other as well. Data may also be exchanged among systems serving different functional areas. For example, an order captured by a sales system may be transmitted to a manufacturing system as a transaction for producing or delivering the product specified in the order or to a MIS for financial reporting.

It is definitely advantageous to integrate these systems so that information can flow easily between different parts of the organization and provide management with an enterprise-wide view of how the organization is performing as a whole. But integration costs money, and integrating many different systems is extremely time consuming and complex. This is a major challenge for large organizations, which are typically saddled with hundreds, even thousands of different applications serving different levels and business functions. Each organization must weigh its needs for integrating systems against the difficulties of mounting a large-scale systems integration effort. Section 2.3 and Chapter 11 treat this issue in greater detail.

2.2   SYSTEMS FROM A FUNCTIONAL PERSPECTIVE

Information systems can be classified by the specific organizational function they serve as well as by organizational level. We now describe typical information systems that support each of the major business functions and provide examples of functional applications for each organizational level.

Sales and Marketing Systems

The sales and marketing function is responsible for selling the organization's products or services. Marketing is concerned with identifying the customers for the firm's products or services, determining what customers need or want, planning and developing products and services to meet their needs, and advertising and promoting these products and services. Sales is concerned with contacting customers, selling the products and services, taking orders, and following up on sales. **Sales and marketing information systems** support these activities.

Table 2-2 shows that information systems are used in sales and marketing in a number of ways. At the strategic level, sales and marketing systems monitor trends affecting new products and sales opportunities, support planning for new products and services, and monitor the performance of competitors. At the management level, sales and marketing systems support market research, advertising and promotional campaigns, and pricing decisions. They analyze sales performance and the performance of the sales staff.

TABLE 2-2 *Examples of Sales and Marketing Information Systems*

System	Description	Organizational Level
Order processing	Enter, process, and track orders	Operational
Pricing analysis	Determine prices for products and services	Management
Sales trend forecasting	Prepare 5-year sales forecasts	Strategic

At the operational level, sales and marketing systems assist in locating and contacting prospective customers, tracking sales, processing orders, and providing customer service support.

Review Figure 2-6. It shows the output of a typical sales information system at the management level. The system consolidates data about each item sold (such as the product code, product description, and amount sold) for further management analysis. Company managers examine these sales data to monitor sales activity and buying trends.

Manufacturing and Production Systems

The manufacturing and production function is responsible for actually producing the firm's goods and services. Manufacturing and production systems deal with the planning, development, and maintenance of production facilities; the establishment of production goals; the acquisition, storage, and availability of production materials; and the scheduling of equipment, facilities, materials, and labor required to fashion finished products. **Manufacturing and production information systems** support these activities.

Table 2-3 shows some typical manufacturing and production information systems arranged by organizational level. Strategic-level manufacturing systems deal with the firm's long-term manufacturing goals, such as where to locate new plants or whether to invest in new manufacturing technology. At the management level, manufacturing and production systems analyze and monitor manufacturing and production costs and resources. Operational manufacturing and production systems deal with the status of production tasks.

Information systems can guide the actions of machines and equipment to help pharmaceutical and other types of firms monitor and control the manufacturing process.

TABLE 2-3   *Examples of Manufacturing and Production Information Systems*

System	Description	Organizational Level
Machine control	Control the actions of machines and equipment	Operational
Production planning	Decide when and how many products should be produced	Management
Facilities location	Decide where to locate new production facilities	Strategic

Most manufacturing and production systems use some sort of inventory system, as illustrated in Figure 2-10. Data about each item in inventory, such as the number of units depleted because of a shipment or purchase or the number of units replenished by reordering or returns, are either scanned or keyed into the system. The inventory master file contains basic data about each item, including the unique identification code for each item, a description of the item, the number of units on hand, the number of units on order, and the reorder point (the number of units in inventory that triggers a decision to reorder to prevent a stockout). Companies can estimate the number of items to reorder, or they can use a formula for calculating the least expensive quantity to reorder called the *economic order quantity*. The system produces reports that give information about such things as the number of each item available in inventory, the number of units of each item to reorder, or items in inventory that must be replenished.

Product life cycle management (PLM) systems are one type of manufacturing and production system that has become increasingly valuable in the automotive, aerospace, and consumer products industries. PLM systems are based on a data repository that organizes every piece of information that goes into making a particular product, such as formula cards, packaging information, shipping specifications, and patent data. Once all these data are available, companies can select and combine the data they need to serve specific functions. For, example, designers and engineers can use the data to determine which parts are needed for a new design, whereas retailers can use them to determine shelf height and how materials should be stored in warehouses.

For many years, engineering-intensive industries have used **computer-aided design (CAD)** systems to automate the modeling and design of their products. The software enables users to create a digital model of a part, a product, or a structure and make changes to the design on the computer without having to build physical prototypes. PLM software goes beyond CAD software to include not only automated modeling and design capabilities but also tools to help companies manage and automate materials sourcing, engineering change orders, and product documentation, such as test results, product packaging, and postsales data. The Window on Organizations describes how these systems are providing new sources of value.

FIGURE 2-10   *Overview of an inventory system.*

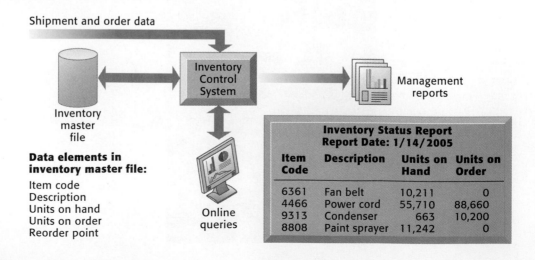

This system provides information about the number of items available in inventory to support manufacturing and production activities.

WINDOW ON ORGANIZATIONS

PRODUCT LIFE CYCLE MANAGEMENT SYSTEMS: FASTER PRODUCTS, FASTER PROCESSES

What if there were a way to determine automatically the feasibility of a new product's design? What if all the information related to that product—the marketing plan, design criteria, product specifications, testing data, and packaging data—were immediately available to make sure that design could be easily manufactured and sold? What if this information were instantly available to designers, engineers, suppliers, marketing staff, and anyone else involved in the development and rollout of a new product? Enter product life cycle management (PLM) systems.

Nissan Diesel Motor Company, established in 1950, manufactures trucks and buses. Its product line includes a wide range of light-, medium-, and heavy-duty vehicles, buses, and bus chassis, engines, vehicle components, and special-purpose engines. The company has distributors in nearly 60 countries around the world.

Developing a truck model involves more components and complex assembly combinations than developing passenger cars, generating vast amounts of data to manage. Like other truck manufacturers, Nissan Diesel Motor Company faced a challenge in keeping this complex product data organized. It turned to IBM and Dassault Systems' ENOVIA Product Life Cycle Management product for a solution

Nissan Diesel used ENOVIA's Digital Mock-Up (DMU) Navigator to manage and connect truck component data as a vehicle is developed from design to manufacturing. DMU simulates Nissan Diesel's manufacturing processes, so the company can detect errors during early stages of production planning. This tool also manages truck components so that engineers can easily search for and work on parts. ENOVIA links product data and processes so that each Nissan development team member can share comprehensive and up-to-date product information throughout the entire development cycle. This configuration management system has shortened Nissan's cycle time for creating a vehicle layout by 90 percent.

Waters Corporation is a leading supplier of high-performance liquid chromatography instrumentation, thermal analysis, and mass spectrometry products that provide fundamental data on the composition of natural products and synthetic chemical mixtures, as well as the physical properties of materials. The company introduces several new products each year. Waters implemented mySAP Product Lifecycle Management software to help those involved in designing, maintaining, and manufacturing a product share information more easily.

Waters had maintained data separately for product development and production, making it difficult to find out materials costs early in the development cycle. The company migrated 120,000 different files and pieces of data from its old systems to mySAP PLM to define the mechanical, electrical, and software components of its products.

Waters designers begin with a concept and move through the engineering design phases to a preliminary version of the product. After additional testing and design work, the product is moved to prerelease/preproduction status. The mySAP PLM software moves all supporting documents and bills of material for the product from one stage to another. It also introduces product data to manufacturing engineers and other specialists as product data and configurations are being created. As these configurations and data stabilize, marketing staff can view them to see what data and configurations will be introduced into the marketplace.

Jostens, known for its custom high school class rings, graduation announcements, and yearbooks, adopted UGS Corporation's PLM software to help it manage its vast array of product details. The company signs about 5,000 to 10,000 new agreements to produce class rings for schools each year. Each school has a specific mascot and other features that have to be designed into the rings. Once those parts of the rings are designed, students select additional features they want, such as an etching of an activity they participate in. That means many thousands of customized rings must be developed and tracked. The UGS PLM software reduces the time required to produce the molds for the rings.

Loewen, a Canadian specialty wood window manufacturer based in Steinbach, Manitoba, has standard products that, when combined with special features and designs, create more than 4.3 trillion potential options. To speed up design and production, the company needed to find a better way to manage this vast amount of product data. PLM software automatically determines the feasibility of a new product's design and enables multiple designers to work simultaneously on the same project and share design information with potential customers. The system enables engineers to know automatically which parts work together, while production groups can use the data to achieve savings by consolidating materials and orders. Loewen hopes that PLM will increase productivity by 30 percent while saving as much as $150,000 per year.

Sources: Debra D'Agostino, "PLM: The Means of Production," *eWeek*, February 7, 2004; Beth Bacheldor, "Deeper Than Designs," *Information Week*, August 9, 2004, and "Product Life-Cycle Management Market Ramps Up," *Information Week*, July 19, 2004; and Dassault Systems, "Nissan Diesel Develops Vehicle Configuration Management System with PLM Solutions from IBM and Dassault Systems," July 12, 2004.

To Think About: How do project life cycle management systems provide value for these companies? Should every company that manufactures products use this software? Explain your answer.

Finance and Accounting Systems

The finance function is responsible for managing the firm's financial assets, such as cash, stocks, bonds, and other investments, to maximize the return on these financial assets. The finance function is also in charge of managing the capitalization of the firm (finding new financial assets in stocks, bonds, or other forms of debt). To determine whether the firm is getting the best return on its investments, the finance function must obtain a considerable amount of information from sources external to the firm.

The accounting function is responsible for maintaining and managing the firm's financial records—receipts, disbursements, depreciation, payroll—to account for the flow of funds in a firm. Finance and accounting share related problems—how to keep track of a firm's financial assets and fund flows. They provide answers to questions such as these: What is the current inventory of financial assets? What records exist for disbursements, receipts, payroll, and other fund flows?

Table 2-4 shows some of the typical finance and accounting information systems found in large organizations. Strategic-level systems for the finance and accounting function establish long-term investment goals for the firm and provide long-range forecasts of the firm's financial performance. At the management level, information systems help managers oversee and control the firm's financial resources. Operational systems in finance and accounting track the flow of funds in the firm through transactions such as paychecks, payments to vendors, securities reports, and receipts.

Review Figure 2-3, which illustrates a payroll system, a typical accounting TPS found in all businesses with employees. You can find more examples of financial systems in the chapter-ending case study on Snyder's of Hanover.

Human Resources Systems

The human resources function is responsible for attracting, developing, and maintaining the firm's workforce. **Human resources information systems** support activities such as identifying potential employees, maintaining complete records on existing employees, and creating programs to develop employees' talents and skills.

Strategic-level human resources systems identify the manpower requirements (skills, educational level, types of positions, number of positions, and cost) for meeting the firm's long-term business plans. At the management level, human resources systems help managers monitor and analyze the recruitment, allocation, and compensation of employees. Human resources operational systems track the recruitment and placement of the firm's employees (see Table 2-5).

Figure 2-11 illustrates a typical human resources TPS for employee record keeping. It maintains basic employee data, such as the employee's name, age, sex, marital status, address, educational background, salary, job title, date of hire, and date of termination. The system can produce a variety of reports, such as lists of newly hired employees, employees who are terminated or on leaves of absence, employees classified by job type or educational level, or employee job performance evaluations. Such systems are typically designed to provide data that can satisfy federal and state record keeping requirements for Equal Employment Opportunity (EEO) and other purposes.

Internet Connection —
The Internet Connection for this chapter will take you to a series of Web sites where you can complete an exercise to evaluate the capabilities of human resources software.

TABLE 2-4 *Examples of Finance and Accounting Information Systems*

System	Description	Organizational Level
Accounts receivable	Tracks money owed the firm	Operational
Budgeting	Prepares short-term budgets	Management
Profit planning	Plans long-term profits	Strategic

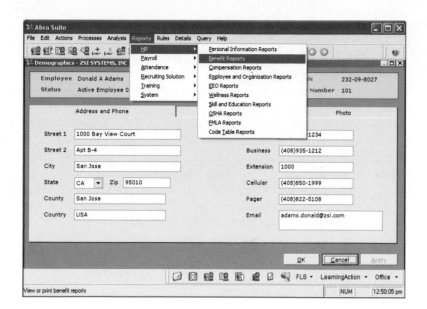

Best Software's ABRA Suite software for human resources and payroll management includes online tools to view and change employment and payroll information. Human resources information systems reduce administrative costs, provide faster service to employees, and help firms manage their workforce.

TABLE 2-5 *Examples of Human Resources Information Systems*

System	Description	Organizational Level
Training and development	Tracks employee training, skills, and performance appraisals	Operational
Compensation analysis	Monitors the range and distribution of employee wages, salaries, and benefits	Management
Human resources planning	Plans the long-term labor force needs of the organization	Strategic

FIGURE 2-11   *An employee record keeping system.*

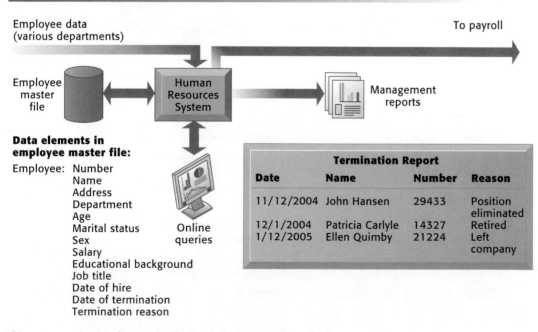

This system maintains data on the firm's employees to support the human resources function.

2.3 INTEGRATING FUNCTIONS AND BUSINESS PROCESSES: INTRODUCTION TO ENTERPRISE APPLICATIONS

One of the major challenges facing firms today is putting together data from the systems we have just described to make information flow across the enterprise. Electronic commerce, electronic business, and intensifying global competition are forcing firms to focus on speed to market, improving customer service, and more efficient execution. The flow of information and work needs to be orchestrated so that the organization can perform like a well-oiled machine. These changes require powerful new systems that can integrate information from many different functional areas and organizational units and coordinate firm activities with those of suppliers and other business partners.

Business Processes and Information Systems

The new digital firm business environment requires companies to think more strategically about their business processes, which we introduced in Chapter 1. Business processes refer to sets of logically related activities for accomplishing a specific business result. Business processes also refer to the unique ways in which organizations and management coordinate these activities. A company's business processes can be a source of competitive strength if they enable the company to innovate better or to execute better than its rivals. Business processes can also be liabilities if they are based on outdated ways of working that impede organizational responsiveness and efficiency.

Some business processes support the major functional areas of the firm, others are cross-functional. Table 2-6 describes some typical business processes for each of the functional areas.

Many business processes are cross-functional, transcending the boundaries between sales, marketing, manufacturing, and research and development. These cross-functional processes cut across the traditional organizational structure, grouping employees from different functional specialties to complete a piece of work. For example, the order fulfillment process at many companies requires cooperation among the sales function (receiving the order, entering the order), the accounting function (credit checking and billing for the order), and the manufacturing function (assembling and shipping the order). Figure 2-12 illustrates how this cross-functional process might work. Information systems support these cross-functional processes as well as processes for the separate business functions.

TABLE 2-6 *Examples of Functional Business Processes*

Functional Area	Business Process
Manufacturing and production	Assembling the product Checking for quality Producing bills of materials
Sales and marketing	Identifying customers Making customers aware of the product Selling the product
Finance and accounting	Paying creditors Creating financial statements Managing cash accounts
Human resources	Hiring employees Evaluating employees' job performance Enrolling employees in benefits plans

FIGURE 2-12   *The order fulfillment process.*

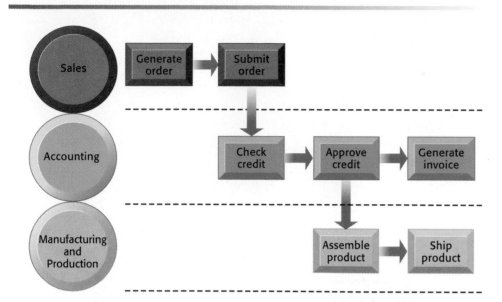

Generating and fulfilling an order is a multistep process involving activities performed by the sales, manufacturing and production, and accounting functions.

Systems for Enterprise-Wide Process Integration

Today's firms are finding that they can become more flexible and productive by coordinating their business processes more closely and, in some cases, integrating these processes so they focus on efficient management of resources and customer service. **Enterprise applications** are designed to support organization-wide process coordination and integration. These enterprise applications consist of enterprise systems, supply chain management systems, customer relationship management systems, and knowledge management systems. Each of these enterprise applications integrates a related set of functions and business processes to enhance the performance of the organization as a whole.

Generally, these more contemporary systems take advantage of corporate intranets and Web technologies that enable the efficient transfer of information within the firm and to partner firms. These systems are inherently cross-level, cross-functional, and business process oriented. Figure 2-13 shows that the architecture for these enterprise applications encompasses processes spanning the entire organization and, in some cases, extending beyond the organization to customers, suppliers, and other key business partners.

Enterprise systems create an integrated organization-wide platform to coordinate key internal processes of the firm. Information systems for supply chain management (SCM) and customer relationship management (CRM) help coordinate processes for managing the firm's relationship with its suppliers and customers. Knowledge management systems enable organizations to better manage processes for capturing and applying knowledge and expertise. Collectively, these four systems represent the areas in which corporations are digitally integrating their information flows and making major information system investments.

Overview of Enterprise Applications

Let's look briefly at each of the major enterprise applications to see how they fit into the overall information architecture of the enterprise. We examine enterprise systems and systems for supply chain management and customer relationship management in greater detail in Chapter 11 and cover knowledge management applications in Chapter 12.

OVERVIEW OF ENTERPRISE SYSTEMS

A large organization typically has many different kinds of information systems that support different functions, organizational levels, and business processes. Most of these systems were built around different functions, business units, and business processes that

FIGURE 2-13 *Enterprise application architecture.*

Enterprise applications automate processes that span multiple business functions and organizational levels and may extend outside the organization.

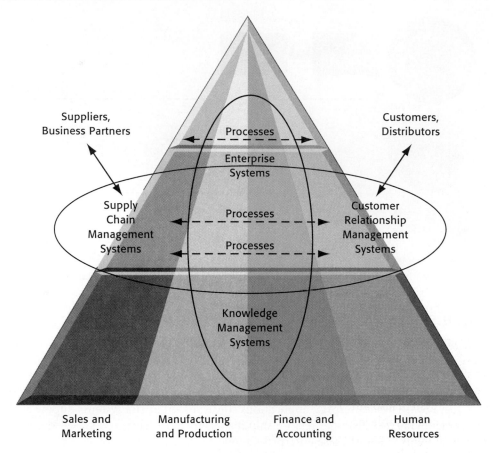

Suppliers, Business Partners

Customers, Distributors

Processes

Enterprise Systems

Supply Chain Management Systems

Processes

Customer Relationship Management Systems

Processes

Knowledge Management Systems

Sales and Marketing

Manufacturing and Production

Finance and Accounting

Human Resources

FUNCTIONAL AREAS

do not "talk" to each other and thus cannot automatically exchange information. Managers might have a hard time assembling the data they need for a comprehensive, overall picture of the organization's operations. For instance, sales personnel might not be able to tell at the time they place an order whether the items that were ordered were in inventory; customers could not track their orders; and manufacturing could not communicate easily with finance to plan for new production. This fragmentation of data in hundreds of separate systems could thus have a negative impact on organizational efficiency and business performance. Figure 2-14 illustrates the traditional arrangement of information systems.

Enterprise systems, also known as *enterprise resource planning (ERP) systems* solve this problem by providing a single information system for organization-wide coordination and integration of key business processes. Information that was previously fragmented in different systems can seamlessly flow throughout the firm so that it can be shared by business processes in manufacturing, accounting, human resources, and other areas. Discrete business processes from sales, production, finance, and logistics can be integrated into company-wide business processes that flow across organizational levels and functions. Figure 2-15 illustrates how enterprise systems work.

The enterprise system collects data from various key business processes in manufacturing and production, finance and accounting, sales and marketing, and human resources and stores the data in a single comprehensive data repository where they can be used by other parts of the business. Managers emerge with more precise and timely information for coordinating the daily operations of the business and a firmwide view of business processes and information flows.

FIGURE 2-14   *Traditional view of systems.*

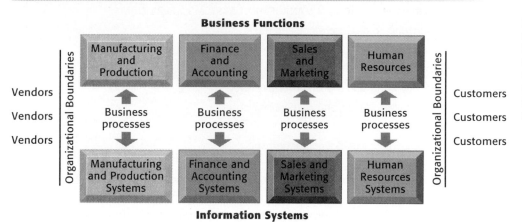

In most organizations today, separate systems built over a long period of time support discrete business processes and discrete segments of the business value chain. The organization's systems rarely include vendors and customers.

For instance, when a sales representative in Brussels enters a customer order, the data flow automatically to others in the company who need to see them. The factory in Hong Kong receives the order and begins production. The warehouse checks its progress online and schedules the shipment date. The warehouse can check its stock of parts and replenish whatever the factory has depleted. The enterprise system stores production information, where it can be accessed by customer service representatives to track the progress of the order through every step of the manufacturing process. Updated sales and production data automatically flow to the accounting department. The system transmits information for calculating the salesperson's commission to the payroll department. The system also automatically recalculates the company's balance sheets, accounts receivable and payable ledgers, cost-center accounts, and available cash. Corporate headquarters in London can view up-to-the-minute data on sales, inventory, and production at every step of the process, as well as updated sales and production forecasts and calculations of product cost and availability. Chapter 11 provides more detail on enterprise system capabilities.

OVERVIEW OF SUPPLY CHAIN MANAGEMENT SYSTEMS

Supply chain management (SCM) systems are more outward facing, focusing on helping the firm manage its relationship with suppliers to optimize the planning, sourcing, manufacturing, and delivery of products and services. These systems provide information to help suppliers, purchasing firms, distributors, and logistics companies coordinate,

FIGURE 2-15   *Enterprise systems.*

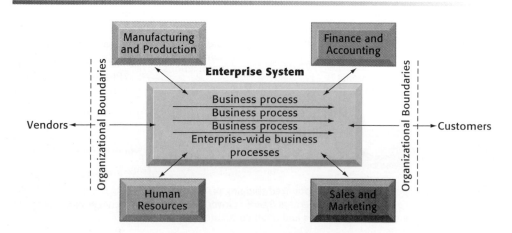

Enterprise systems integrate the key business processes of an entire firm into a single software system that enables information to flow seamlessly throughout the organization. These systems focus primarily on internal processes but may include transactions with customers and vendors.

TABLE 2-7 *How Information Systems Facilitate Supply Chain Management*

INFORMATION FROM SUPPLY CHAIN MANAGEMENT SYSTEMS HELPS FIRMS:
Decide when and what to produce, store, and move
Rapidly communicate orders
Track the status of orders
Check inventory availability and monitor inventory levels
Reduce inventory, transportation, and warehousing costs
Track shipments
Plan production based on actual customer demand
Rapidly communicate changes in product design

schedule, and control business processes for procurement, production, inventory management, and delivery of products and services.

Supply chain management systems are one type of **interorganizational system** because they automate the flow of information across organizational boundaries. A firm using a supply chain management system would exchange information with its suppliers about availability of materials and components, delivery dates for shipments of supplies, and production requirements. It might also use the system to exchange information with its distributors about inventory levels, the status of orders being fulfilled, or delivery dates for shipments of finished goods. You will find examples of other types of interorganizational information systems throughout this text because such systems make it possible for firms to link electronically to customers and to outsource their work to other companies.

Table 2-7 describes how firms can benefit from supply chain management systems. The ultimate objective is to get the right amount of their products from their source to their point of consumption with the least amount of time and with the lowest cost. Supply chain management systems can be built using intranets, extranets, or special supply chain management software.

Figure 2-16 illustrates the supply chain management systems used by Haworth, a world-leading manufacturer and designer of office furniture described in the Window on Technology. Haworth needed to synchronize manufacturing and distribution activities to cut costs and boost efficiency by having material flow continuously from multiple manufacturing centers to multiple distribution centers. It implemented new systems for warehouse management and transportation management. These systems enable Haworth to deliver multipart shipments requiring assembly in the correct sequence, accommodate shipping volumes that can vary by a factor of 10 from one day to the next, and handle last-minute changes in customer orders.

FIGURE 2-16 *Haworth's supply chain management systems.*

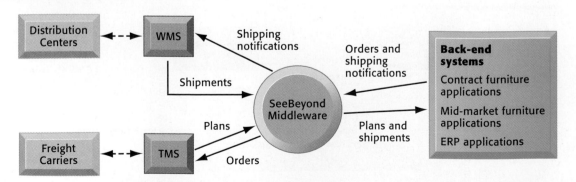

Customer orders, shipping notifications, optimized shipping plans, and other supply chain information flow among Haworth's Warehouse Management System (WMS), Transportation Management System (TMS), and its back-end enterprise systems and other corporate applications.

WINDOW ON TECHNOLOGY

HAWORTH OVERHAULS SUPPLY CHAIN MANAGEMENT

Haworth Incorporated, headquartered in Holland, Michigan, is the world's second largest designer and manufacturer of office furniture and workspaces. The company offers a full range of furniture known for its innovative design including desks, chairs, tables, partitions, and storage products. Haworth operates in more than 120 countries, with 9,000 employees, 40 manufacturing locations, 60 showrooms, and more than 600 independent dealers around the world.

Haworth was particularly successful during the booming economy of the late 1990s, which stimulated demand for new offices and office space. But the company was hit hard when many dot-coms went under because these companies glutted the market with their slightly used Haworth products.

To bring costs back in line with declining revenue, Haworth started an ambitious overhaul of its supply chain management systems in 2002. Haworth's 15 North American manufacturing facilities are located in North Carolina, Arkansas, Michigan, Mississippi, Texas, Ontario, Alberta, and Quebec. These facilities supply inventory to distribution centers in Michigan, Pennsylvania, Georgia, and Arkansas. Haworth needed to coordinate order fulfillment from multiple distribution centers with products received from all of its manufacturing facilities. The distribution centers needed to communicate more effectively with the manufacturing facilities to better plan the processing of customer orders.

Haworth's existing distribution system was an old-style mainframe locator application that could only handle inventory data for a single building and could not differentiate between facilities. Each distribution center used a different version of the system based on the computer system it interfaced with. The system did not provide a way to preplan shipments, so Haworth could not cross-dock material directly to an outbound shipment as efficiently as it desired, raising labor and freight costs. Cross-docking enables goods earmarked for a specific customer to move directly from the receiving dock to the shipping dock without being checked into the system and picked from inventory.

To solve these problems, Haworth implemented a new Warehouse Management System (WMS) based on IristaWarehouse software from Irista in Milwaukee. WMS tracks and controls the flow of finished goods from the receiving dock at any of Haworth's distribution centers to the customer site. The system has cross-docking capabilities to reduce labor costs in the warehouse. WMS interfaces with the various enterprise resource planning (ERP) applications running in the four distribution centers and with Haworth's Transportation Management System (TMS). Acting on shipping plans from TMS, WMS directs the movement of goods based on immediate conditions for space, equipment, inventory, and personnel.

The Transportation Management System (TMS) uses optimization and carrier communication software from Manugistics Group in Rockville, Maryland. The system examines customer orders, factory schedules, carrier rates and availability, and shipping costs to produce optimal lowest-cost delivery plans. These plans are generated daily and updated every 15 minutes. TMS has an automated interface that enables Haworth to negotiate deliveries with its carriers. To find the minimal freight cost for deliveries, TMS maps out more efficient routes that minimize "less-than-truckload" shipments and damage to goods.

TMS also electronically sends carriers "tenders," which are requests to bid on a shipment. These tenders are transmitted over a private network or the Web, and carriers transmit bids back automatically. In the past, that process required two phone calls. If a carrier doesn't reply within a specified time, the system automatically contacts another carrier.

Both TMS and WMS run on server computers from Hewlett-Packard using the Unix operating system. They interface with two sets of order entry, manufacturing planning, and shipping systems that service two different furniture markets. To tie these applications, Haworth uses special "middleware" software from SeeBeyond Technology in Monrovia, California. The middleware passes customer orders, shipping plans, and shipping notifications among the applications.

According to Jim Rohrer, a business applications process manager and key liaison between Haworth's information systems and supply chain operations, the new systems haven't merely optimized business processes—they've transformed them. Haworth used to have a "signpost" system where distribution centers received information on labels or on screens and then decided what to do with it. Now the system is more directed. TMS sets up a plan, feeds it to WMS, and WMS specifies the tasks that need to be accomplished.

The payoff from these systems was considerable: Warehouse worker productivity increased 35 percent, freight costs were reduced 16 percent, and "less-than-truckload" shipments and damaged goods in transit declined 50 percent. Haworth's investment in these supply chain management systems paid for itself in just nine months.

Sources: Gary H. Anthes, "Refurnishing the Supply Chain" and "Haworth's Supply Chain Project," *Computerworld*, June 7, 2004; Irista Inc., "Haworth: Synchronizing the Supply Chain," www.irista.com, accessed August 18, 2004; and www.haworth.com, accessed August 18, 2004.

To Think About: How did these supply chain management systems change the way Haworth worked? What value do they provide?

OVERVIEW OF CUSTOMER RELATIONSHIP MANAGEMENT SYSTEMS

Instead of treating customers as exploitable sources of income, businesses are now viewing them as long-term assets to be nurtured through customer relationship management. **Customer relationship management (CRM) systems** focus on coordinating all of the business processes surrounding the firm's interactions with its customers in sales, marketing, and service to optimize revenue, customer satisfaction, and customer retention. The ideal CRM system provides end-to-end customer care from receipt of an order through product delivery.

In the past, a firm's processes for sales, service, and marketing were highly compartmentalized, and these departments did not share much essential customer information. Some information on a specific customer might be stored and organized in terms of that person's account with the company. Other pieces of information about the same customer might be organized by products that were purchased. There was no way to consolidate all of this information to provide a unified view of a customer across the company. CRM systems try to solve this problem by integrating the firm's customer-related processes and consolidating customer information from multiple communication channels—telephone, e-mail, wireless devices, or the Web—so that the firm can present one coherent face to the customer (see Figure 2-17).

Good CRM systems provide data and analytical tools for answering questions such as these: What is the value of a particular customer to the firm over his or her lifetime? Who are our most loyal customers? (It can cost six times more to sell to a new customer than to an existing customer.) Who are our most profitable customers? What do these profitable customers want to buy? Firms can then use the answers to these questions to acquire new customers, provide better service and support to existing customers, customize their offerings more precisely to customer preferences, and provide ongoing value to retain profitable customers.

OVERVIEW OF KNOWLEDGE MANAGEMENT SYSTEMS

The value of a firm's products and services is based not only on its physical resources but also on intangible knowledge assets. Some firms perform better than others because they have better knowledge about how to create, produce, and deliver products and services. This firm knowledge is difficult to imitate, unique, and can be leveraged into long-term strategic benefit. **Knowledge management systems** collect all relevant knowledge and experience in the firm and make it available wherever and whenever it is needed to support

FIGURE 2-17 *Customer relationship management (CRM).*

Customer relationship management systems examine customers from a multifaceted perspective. These systems use a set of integrated applications to address all aspects of the customer relationship, including customer service, sales, and marketing.

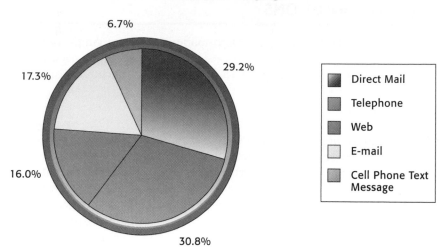

Responses by Channel for January 2005 Promotional Campaign

- 29.2% Direct Mail
- 30.8% Telephone
- 16.0% Web
- 17.3% E-mail
- 6.7% Cell Phone Text Message

Customer relationship management software provides a single point through which users can manage and evaluate marketing campaigns across multiple channels, including e-mail, direct mail, telephone, the Web, and wireless messages.

business processes and management decisions. They also link the firm to external sources of knowledge.

Knowledge management systems support processes for acquiring, storing, distributing, and applying knowledge, as well as processes for creating new knowledge and integrating it into the organization. They include enterprise-wide systems for managing and distributing documents, graphics, and other digital knowledge objects, systems for creating corporate knowledge directories of employees with special areas of expertise, office systems for distributing knowledge and information, and knowledge work systems to facilitate knowledge creation. Other knowledge management applications are expert systems that codify the knowledge of experts in information systems that can be used by other members of the organization and tools for knowledge discovery that recognize patterns and important relationships in large pools of data. Table 2-8 provides examples of knowledge management systems, and Chapter 12 describes these knowledge management applications in detail.

TABLE 2-8 *Knowledge Management Systems in the Organization*

Organizational Process	Role of Knowledge Management Systems
Acquiring knowledge	Knowledge discovery systems can find patterns or relationships in vast quantities of data, whereas other intelligent techniques can find solutions to problems that are too complex to be solved by humans. Knowledge work systems provide knowledge workers with graphics, analytical, communication, and document management tools, as well as access to internal and external sources of data to help them generate new ideas. Knowledge networks provide online directories of employees with special areas of expertise.
Storing knowledge	Knowledge repositories collect documents and digital media containing knowledge from internal and external sources in a single location. Expert systems elicit and incorporate expertise from human experts and embed it in software systems that can be accessed by other members of the organization.
Distributing knowledge	Office systems and communication tools distribute documents and other forms of information among information and knowledge workers and link offices to other business units inside and outside the firm. Group collaboration systems help employees access and work simultaneously on the same document from many different locations and coordinate their activities.
Applying knowledge	Organizational knowledge can be incorporated into management decision making through decision-support systems and incorporated into important business processes by being captured by key application systems, including enterprise applications.

2.4 MANAGEMENT OPPORTUNITIES, CHALLENGES, AND SOLUTIONS

Organizations still need different types of information systems serving various organizational levels, functions, and business processes, and they increasingly need systems providing enterprise-wide integration. These needs create both opportunities and challenges.

Opportunities

Businesses face extraordinary opportunities to apply information systems throughout the firm to achieve higher levels of productivity, earnings, and ultimately advance share prices. Today information systems support virtually all levels and functions in the firm. In addition they enhance decision making of both managers and employees, providing information where and when it is needed in a format that is easily integrated into everyday business life.

Management Challenges

There are challenges to achieving these objectives.

INTEGRATION AND THE WHOLE FIRM VIEW

In the past, information systems were built to serve the narrow interests of different business functions (such as marketing, finance, or operations) or to serve a specific group of decision makers (such as middle managers). The problem with this approach is that it results in the building of thousands of systems that cannot share information with one another and, worse, makes it difficult for managers to obtain the information they need to operate the whole firm. Building systems that both serve specific interests in the firm, but also can be integrated to provide firmwide information is a challenge.

MANAGEMENT AND EMPLOYEE TRAINING

With so many systems in a large business firm, and with fairly high employee turnover typical of the last few years, training people how to use the existing systems, and learn new systems, turns out to be a major challenge. Obviously, without training or when training is limited, employees and managers cannot use information systems to maximum advantage, and the result can be a low return on investment in systems.

ACCOUNTING FOR THE COST OF SYSTEMS AND MANAGING DEMAND FOR SYSTEMS

As the cost of information falls because of the power of information technology, demands for information and technology services proliferate throughout the firm. Unfortunately, if employees and managers believe information services are free, their demands will be infinite. One of the challenges facing business managers is understanding which systems are truly necessary, truly productive with high returns on investment, and which are merely conveniences that cost a great deal but deliver little.

Solution Guidelines

A number of solutions exist to the challenges we have just described.

INVENTORYING THE FIRM'S INFORMATION SYSTEMS FOR A 360-DEGREE VIEW OF INFORMATION

You should develop a list of firmwide information requirements to get a 360-degree view of the most important information needs for your company as a whole. Once you have this list developed, examine how your existing systems—most built to service specific groups and levels in the firm—provide this information to corporate-wide systems. You'll need to inventory your firm's existing information systems and those under construction. (Many firms have no idea of all the systems in their firm, or what information they contain.) Identify each system and understand which group or level in the firm benefits from the system.

EMPLOYEE AND MANAGEMENT EDUCATION

Systems are usually not obvious or self-taught for most people. You will need to ensure that you understand how much training is required to support new systems, and budget accordingly. Once you have an inventory of just the major systems in a firm that are used every day by thousands of employees, try to identify how they learn how to use the system, how effective their training is, and how well they use the systems. Do they exploit all the potential value built into the systems?

ACCOUNTING FOR THE COSTS AND BENEFITS OF INFORMATION SYSTEMS

To manage the demand for information services, you'll need an accounting system for information services. It is worthwhile to examine the methods used in your industry and by industry competitors to account for their information systems budgets. Your system should use some method for charging the budgets of various divisions, departments, and groups that directly benefit from a system. And there are other services that should not be charged to any group because they are a part of the firm's general information technology (IT) infrastructure (described in Chapter 6) and serve everyone. For instance, you would not want to charge various groups for Internet or intranet services because they are services provided to everyone in the firm, but you would want to charge the manufacturing division for a production control system because it benefits that division exclusively. Equally important, management should establish priorities on which systems most deserve funding and corporate attention.

MAKE IT YOUR BUSINESS

Finance and Accounting

Finance and accounting systems help firms keep track of their assets and fund flows. They can help firms maximize returns on their financial assets and investments and maintain financial records. Enterprise systems can integrate financial information with production and sales information so that the impact of sales and manufacturing transactions is immediately reflected on the firm's balance sheets, accounts receivable and payable ledgers, and reports of cash flows. Management can use enterprise systems to obtain up-to-the-minute reports of the firm's overall financial performance. You can find examples of finance and accounting applications on pages 68–69.

Human Resources

Human resources systems help businesses develop staffing requirements; identify potential new employees; maintain employee records; track employee training, skills, and job performance; and help managers develop appropriate plans for employee compensation and career development.

Enterprise systems can help businesses coordinate their staffing levels with sales and production activities and financial resources.

Manufacturing and Production

Manufacturing and production systems solve problems related to the planning, development, and delivery of products and services and control the flow of production. Supply chain management (SCM) systems provide information to coordinate sourcing and procurement, production scheduling, order fulfillment, inventory management, product development, warehousing, and customer service. When these processes are coordinated among supply chain members, goods can move smoothly and on time from suppliers to manufacturers to customers. Knowledge management systems provide tools and information to help engineers, designers, and product development staff innovate and design new products and manage the product life cycle. You can find examples of manufacturing and production applications on pages 39, 51, and 59.

Sales and Marketing

Information systems help businesses promote products, contact customers, track sales, and provide ongoing service and support. They can also be used to analyze the performance of the firm's sales staff. Today, customer relationship management (CRM) systems are especially useful for consolidating customer data from different sources so that the firm can coordinate its interactions with customers and provide better long-term customer relationships. You can find examples of sales and marketing applications on page 39.

Summary

1. **Evaluate the role played by the major types of systems in a business and their relationship to each other.**

   There are four major types of information systems in contemporary organizations. Operational-level systems are transaction processing systems (TPS), such as payroll or order processing, that track the flow of the daily routine transactions that are necessary to conduct business. Management-level systems (MIS and DSS) provide the management control level with reports and access to the organization's current performance and historical records. Most management information system (MIS) reports condense information from TPS and are not highly analytical. Decision-support systems (DSS) support management decisions when these decisions are unique, rapidly changing, and not specified easily in advance. They have more advanced analytical models and data analysis capabilities than MIS and often draw on information from external as well as internal sources. Executive support systems (ESS) support the strategic level by providing data of greatest importance to senior management decision makers, often in the form of graphs and charts delivered via portals. They have limited analytical capabilities but can draw on sophisticated graphics software and many sources of internal and external information.

   The various types of systems in the organization exchange data with one another. TPS are a major source of data for other systems, especially MIS and DSS. ESS primarily receive data from lower-level systems. Today's business environment calls for more integration among systems than in the past, but such integration is not easy to achieve.

2. **Describe the information systems supporting the major business functions: sales and marketing, manufacturing and production, finance and accounting, and human resources.**

   At each level of the organization information systems support the major functional areas of the business. Sales and marketing systems help the firm identify customers for the firm's products or services, develop products and services to meet customers' needs, promote the products and services, sell the products and services, and provide ongoing customer support. Manufacturing and production systems deal with the planning, development, and production of products and services, and controlling the flow of production. Finance and accounting systems keep track of the firm's financial assets and fund flows. Human resources systems maintain employee records; track employee skills, job performance, and training; and support planning for employee compensation and career development.

3. **Analyze the relationship between organizations, information systems, and business processes.**

   Business processes refer to the manner in which work activities are organized, coordinated, and focused to produce a specific business result. They also represent unique ways in which organizations coordinate work, information, and knowledge and the ways in which management chooses to coordinate work. Managers need to pay attention to business processes because they determine how well the organization can execute, and thus are a potential source of strategic success or failure. Although each of the major business functions has its own set of business processes, many other business processes are cross-functional, such as order fulfillment. Information systems can help organizations achieve great efficiencies by automating parts of these processes or by helping organizations rethink and streamline them. Firms can become more flexible and efficient by coordinating and integrating their business processes to improve management of resources and customer service.

4. **Explain how enterprise applications promote business process integration and improve organizational performance.**

   Enterprise applications, such as enterprise systems, supply chain management systems, customer relationship management systems, and knowledge management systems, are designed to support organization-wide process coordination and integration so that the organization can operate more efficiently. They span multiple functions and business processes and may be tied to the business processes of other organizations. Enterprise systems integrate the key internal business processes of a firm into a single software system so that information can flow throughout the organization, improving coordination, efficiency, and decision making. Supply chain management systems help the firm manage its relationship with suppliers to optimize the planning, sourcing, manufacturing, and delivery of products and services. Customer relationship management uses information systems to coordinate all of the business processes surrounding the firm's interactions with its customers to optimize firm revenue and customer satisfaction. Knowledge management systems enable firms to optimize the creation, sharing, distribution, and application of knowledge to improve business processes and management decisions.

5. **Assess the challenges posed by information systems in the enterprise and management solutions.**

The array of information systems available to businesses can help businesses achieve higher levels of productivity and financial worth. Management challenges include the tension between building systems that both serve specific interests in the firm but that also can be integrated to provide organization-wide information, the need for management and employee training to use systems properly, and the need to establish priorities on which systems most merit corporate attention and funding. Solutions include inventorying the firm's information systems to establish organization-wide information needs, employee and management training, and establishing a system for accounting for the costs of information systems and managing demand for them.

Key Terms

Computer-aided design (CAD), 50
Customer relationship management (CRM) systems, 60
Decision-support systems (DSS), 45
Enterprise applications, 55
Enterprise systems, 56
Executive support systems (ESS), 47
Finance and accounting information systems, 52

Human resources information systems, 52
Interorganizational system, 58
Knowledge management systems, 60
Management information systems (MIS), 44
Management-level systems, 40
Manufacturing and production information systems, 49
Operational-level systems, 40

Portal, 47
Product life cycle management (PLM) systems, 50
Sales and marketing information systems, 48
Strategic-level systems, 41
Supply chain management (SCM) systems, 57
Transaction processing systems (TPS), 43

Review Questions

1. *Identify and describe the three levels of the organizational hierarchy. Which types of information systems serve each level?*

2. *List and briefly describe the major types of systems in organizations.*

3. *What are the five types of TPS in business organizations? What functions do they perform? Give examples of each.*

4. *What are the characteristics of MIS? How do MIS differ from TPS? From DSS?*

5. *What are the characteristics of DSS? How do they differ from those of ESS?*

6. *Describe the relationship between TPS, MIS, DSS, and ESS.*

7. *List and describe the information systems serving each of the major functional areas of a business.*

8. *What is a business process? Give two examples of processes for functional areas of the business and one example of a cross-functional process.*

9. *Why are organizations trying to integrate their business processes? What are the four key enterprise applications for organization-wide process integration?*

10. *What are enterprise systems? How do they change the way an organization works?*

11. *What are supply chain management systems? How do they benefit businesses?*

12. *What are customer relationship management systems? How do they benefit businesses?*

14. *What is the role of knowledge management systems in the enterprise? What organizational processes are supported by knowledge management applications?*

15. *What are the challenges posed by the existence of various types of information systems in the enterprise? How can these challenges be addressed?*

Discussion Questions

1. *How could information systems be used to support the order fulfillment process illustrated in Figure 2-12? What are the most important pieces of information these systems should capture? Explain your answer.*

2. *Adopting an enterprise application is a key business decision as well as a technology decision. Do you agree? Why or why not? Who should make this decision?*

Application Software Exercise:
Spreadsheet Exercise: Improving Supply Chain Management

You run a company that manufactures aircraft components. You have many competitors who are trying to offer lower prices and better service to customers, and you are trying to determine if you can benefit from better supply chain management. At the Laudon Web site for Chapter 2, you can find a spreadsheet file that contains a list of all of the items that your firm has ordered from its suppliers during the past three months. The fields in the spreadsheet file include vendor name, vendor identification number, purchaser's order number, item identification number and item description (for each item ordered from the vendor), cost per item, number of units of the item ordered, total cost of each order, vendor's accounts payable terms, promised shipping date, promised transit time, and actual arrival date for each order.

Prepare a recommendation of how you can use the data in this spreadsheet database to improve your supply chain management. You may wish to consider ways to identify preferred suppliers or other ways of improving the movement and production of your products. Some criteria you might consider include the supplier's track record for on-time deliveries, suppliers offering the best accounts payable terms, and suppliers offering lower pricing when the same item can be provided by multiple suppliers. Use your spreadsheet software to prepare reports and, if appropriate, graphs to support your recommendations.

Analyzing Financial Performance

Software requirements: Spreadsheet software
Electronic presentation software (optional)

As part of your analysis of the company for management, you have been asked to analyze data on Dirt Bikes's financial performance. Review Dirt Bikes's selected financial data in the Introduction to Dirt Bikes, which can be found at the Laudon Web site. There you will find Dirt Bikes's income statement and summary balance sheet data from 2002–2004, annual sales of Dirt Bikes models between 2000 and 2004, and total domestic versus international sales between 2000 and 2004.

Use your spreadsheet software to create graphs of Dirt Bikes's sales history from 2000 to 2004 and its domestic versus international sales from 2000 to 2004. Select the type of graph that is most appropriate for presenting the data you are analyzing.

Use the instructions at the Laudon Web site and your spreadsheet software to calculate the gross and net margins in Dirt Bikes's income statements from 2002 to 2004. You can also create graphs showing trends in selected pieces of Dirt Bikes's income statement and balance sheet data if you wish. (You may want to rearrange the historical ordering of the data if you decide to do this.)

Prepare an addition to your management report that answers these questions:

1. What are Dirt Bikes's best- and worst-performing products? What is the proportion of domestic to international sales? Have international sales grown relative to domestic sales?

2. Are sales (revenues) growing steadily, and, if so, at what rate? What is the cost of goods sold compared to revenues? Is it increasing or decreasing? Are the firm's gross and net margins increasing or decreasing? Are the firm's operating expenses increasing or decreasing? Is the firm heavily in debt? Does it have assets to pay for expenses and to finance the development of new products and information systems?

3. (Optional) Use electronic presentation software to summarize your analysis of Dirt Bikes's performance for management.

Electronic Business Project: Planning Transportation Logistics

The MapQuest (www.mapquest.com) and Rand McNally (www.randmcnally.com) Web sites illustrate emerging capabilities of geographic software on the World Wide Web. They include interactive capabilities for planning a trip, as well as a service offering maps of 100 cities around the world, down to the street level. The software on the sites can calculate the distance between two points and provide itemized driving directions to any location. You can also click maps of your starting and ending locations to see detailed street maps and places of interest.

You have just started working as a dispatcher for Cross-Country Transport, a new trucking and delivery service based in Cleveland, Ohio. Your first assignment is to plan a delivery of office equipment and furniture from Omaha, Nebraska (at the corner of N. 17th and Howard Streets) to Easton, Pennsylvania (corner of Ferry and S. 12th Streets). To guide your trucker, you need to know the distance between the two cities and the most efficient route between them. The distance is too long to drive in one day, given the driver will drive for only 10 hours a day. Therefore, you also need to plan one or more stopovers. Use both sites to plan this trip, and select the one you would use in the future, considering ease of use, cost (if any), clarity of the maps, and the driving instructions.

Which service did you decide to use, and why? What changes would you suggest to the developers of that site? Consider all aspects of the site, including ease of viewing the route, help planning stopovers, time of route segments, and so forth.

Group Project: Describing Management Decisions and Systems

With a group of three or four other students, find a description of a senior manager of a corporation in *Business Week, Forbes, Fortune,* or other business magazines. Write a description of the kinds of decisions this manager has to make and suggest an executive support system or decision-support system that might be useful for this executive. Describe the data provided by the system and how that system would support decisions. If possible, use presentation software to present your findings to the class.

CASE STUDY
Snyder's of Hanover: New Systems for an Old Family Company

Harry V. Warehime began tempting the taste buds of southern Pennsylvanians with his Hanover Olde Tyme Pretzels in 1909. Since then, Snyder's of Hanover, as the company came to be known, has expanded its business beyond any scope that its founder might have dared to imagine. Snyder's of Hanover remains a family-owned and family-run company, but it has become the world's second largest pretzel maker, with 12.1 percent of the pretzel market. Snyder's pretzel and chip varieties include Old Tyme Pretzels, Jalapeno Pieces, Butter Snaps, and EatSmart All Natural Veggie Crisps, as well as other popular snacks. In 2002, Snyder's posted revenues of $164 million, trailing only Rold Gold, the reigning champion of the pretzel industry.

In addition to manufacturing its complete line of snack foods, Snyder's distributes its own products, as well as those of other snack food companies such as Tasty Baking Company's Tastykakes. With 40 distribution facilities all over the United States and Europe, over 4,500 products, and over 150 product lines, the home office in Hanover, Pennsylvania, has a considerable amount of data to manage.

If there was one last vestige of old-fashioned business left at Snyder's, it was the company's method of managing and analyzing data. Although Snyder's sells more than 78 million bags of pretzels, chips, and organic snack items each year, some of its core systems were still heavily manual and paper-based.

Snyder's financial department was using electronic spreadsheets for much of its data-gathering and reporting. Lois Stambaugh, Hanover's financial analyst, would spend the entire final week of each month collecting Excel spreadsheets from the heads of more than 50 departments worldwide. Then she would consolidate and reenter all the data into another Excel spreadsheet, which would serve as the company's monthly profit-and-loss statement. The financial data were harvested and consolidated the same way at the end of each fiscal quarter and the end of each year.

The overwhelming presence of the human factor made data-entry mistakes a concern. If a department needed to update its data with last-minute information after submitting its spreadsheet to the main office, the head analyst had to return the original spreadsheet, and then wait for the department to resubmit its data, before finally entering the updated data in the consolidated document.

Perhaps most important, this system of gathering the company's financial statistics at regular, but infrequent, intervals meant that important data simply were not available as often as they were needed. Snyder's lacked the ability to react to sudden trends and unpredictable events because the data were supplied too late to adjust shipping schedules, pricing schedules, or delivery counts.

CEO Michael Warehime and his management team could track the gross profits of business units but not the performance of each of Snyder's 4,500-plus products and over 150 product lines. For example, the spreadsheet-based system lacked the detail to show whether a specific snack product such as Sourdough Hard Pretzels or Pumpernickel & Onion Sticks was actually making or losing money. For a business focused on both production and distribution, this was a hindrance to growth.

Additionally, the spreadsheets could not reveal which distribution routes were worthwhile and which were cutting into the company's profit margin. Under these circumstances, Snyder's could only use the sales data it collected to make rough predictions about how much of a product should be manufactured and how quickly a product run should be repeated on a particular distribution route. Snyder's market share had been growing steadily until 2002, when it suddenly stalled; its annual sales growth, which had outpaced the industry's for years, was then no better than average. It was time to leap forward to a more modern approach in which the company could react to data immediately.

In late 2002, Snyder's of Hanover solicited the help of Satori Group, a provider of business performance management solutions to the consumer packaged goods industry that is headquartered in Conshohocken, Pennsylvania. Satori Group demonstrated how Snyder's could implement its proCube software to gather better sales and marketing data and, therefore, make better business decisions. ProCube would automate Snyder's budgeting processes, creating accurate forecasting facilities, improving financial reporting techniques, and refining Snyder's product marketing analysis so that Snyder's could evaluate the viability of each of its individual brands and products. Such analytical power was just what Snyder's would need to compete with Rold Gold, which is backed by the corporate powerhouses of Frito-Lay and PepsiCo.

What Snyder's found so appealing about proCube was the ease with which it could be integrated with the company's existing information systems. ProCube enables Snyder's department heads to continue using Microsoft Excel spreadsheets to collect sales and returns data. These data are collected in a large data repository, where they are consolidated and organized before being used by proCube reporting software for analysis. The proCube software also uses manufacturing data from Snyder's enterprise system.

Snyder's financial department now spends a couple of days preparing those same monthly, quarterly, and yearly statements that used to devour weeks' worth of productivity. This is only the first step in what Snyder's hopes is a chain of improvements that will result in new growth.

The next step is to add new levels of detail to the profit and loss data that Snyder's can collect and report so that the company can track and assess the profitability of individual products. Management could then use the proCube software to find out information such as how many bags of Honey BBQ Pretzel Pieces were sold in Michigan last week, or which stores and delivery routes are best servicing customers who like this product. The system will also enable managers to project sales for their unit for the next quarter or next year.

Such a system requires additional work to implement. Dave Thomas, Snyder's director of information technology, noted that to achieve the desired level of detail in its data analysis, the company must study all of its business processes. A comprehensive review will enable Snyder's to determine what types of data result from their business processes and which data they actually want to use.

These system enhancements will eventually provide information enabling Snyder's to increase production and distribution frequency of its most popular products almost immediately, rather than having to wait for an end-of-the-month report. Likewise, production and shipping of less popular products can be curbed. In other words, Snyder's will be able change its business model from one dependent on forecasts to one that's more demand-driven.

The first two phases of the proCube implementation carried a price tag of approximately a quarter-million dollars. The next phase introduced a corporate portal to provide Snyder's

department heads and executives with easier access to sales figures and distribution plans. The portal features a user-friendly Web interface through which managers can retrieve key data, as they require them. Upon completion, the cost of the entire venture should approach a half-million dollars.

Snyder's has also incorporated improved IT into other areas of its business. In 2003, Snyder's chose Gelco Trade Management Group's TMS Passport solution for its trade promotion funds management. Again, Snyder's found an IT solution that could be implemented quickly without sacrificing power. Gelco's TMS Passport promises a quick return on investment (ROI) for a competitively priced and scalable software package. The package features fund management, deduction management, payments, and analysis and reporting capabilities. In turn, Snyder's is confident that it can effectively plan and manage its trade promotion activities for years to come, even as the business continues to expand.

The American consumer has continued to increase its intake of pretzels over the last decade, and the snack food industry as a whole continues to boom. Snyder's faces stiff competition from rival Frito-Lay and other major players in the snack food industry such as Utz, Kellogg's, and Kraft Foods. At the very least, Snyder's has made a sincere attempt to transform its business practices with an

eye toward rocketing to the top of the boom. The question remains whether a family-owned organization can continue to compete with major corporate players in an industry that has yet to hit its ceiling.

Sources: Larry Barrett, "Twisted Logic," *Baseline Magazine*, January 2004; "Solutions for the Consumer Packaged Goods Industry," www.satorigroupinc.com, accessed March 31, 2004; "Snyder's of Hanover Selects Gelco's TMS Passport Solution," www.gelcotrade.com, accessed April 5, 2004; "Snyder's of Hanover Company Profile," biz.yahoo.com, accessed April 5, 2004; "Snacks: The Next Generation," www.consumerreports.org, March 2004; and www.snydersofhanover.com, accessed March 31, 2004.

CASE STUDY QUESTIONS

1. Assess Snyder's competitive standing in the pretzel and snack food industry.
2. What types of information systems are essential for this company?
3. How well did Snyder's information systems support its business? Explain.
4. How much did proCube improve Snyder's systems? Which management, organizational, and technology issues did it address? How does it provide value?
5. Assess the impact of Snyder's new systems on the way it runs its business and its business model. How much do these systems improve its competitive position?

Chapter 3

Information Systems, Organizations, Management, and Strategy

OBJECTIVES

After completing this chapter, you will be able to:

1. Identify and describe important features of organizations that managers need to know about in order to build and use information systems successfully.

2. Evaluate the impact of information systems on organizations.

3. Assess how information systems support the activities of managers in organizations.

4. Analyze how information systems support various business strategies for competitive advantage.

5. Assess the challenges posed by strategic information systems and management solutions.

CHAPTER OUTLINE

3.1 ORGANIZATIONS AND INFORMATION SYSTEMS
What Is an Organization?
Common Features of Organizations
Unique Features of Organizations
Organizing the IT Function

3.2 HOW INFORMATION SYSTEMS IMPACT ORGANIZATIONS AND BUSINESS FIRMS
Economic Impacts
Organizational and Behavioral Impacts
The Internet and Organizations

3.3 THE IMPACT OF IT ON MANAGEMENT DECISION MAKING
How IT Affects Management Decision Making
The Role of Managers in Organizations
Models of Decision Making
Implications for the Design and Understanding of Information Systems

3.4 INFORMATION SYSTEMS AND BUSINESS STRATEGY
Business-Level Strategy: The Value Chain Model
Firm-Level Strategy and Information Technology
Industry-Level Strategy and Information Systems: Competitive Forces and Network Economics

3.5 MANAGEMENT OPPORTUNITIES, CHALLENGES, AND SOLUTIONS
Opportunities
Management Challenges
Solution Guidelines

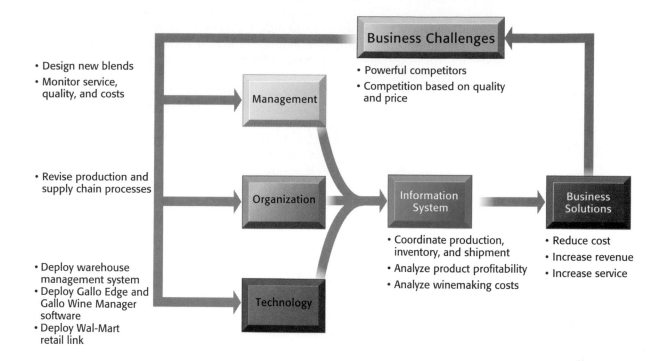

- Design new blends
- Monitor service, quality, and costs

- Revise production and supply chain processes

- Deploy warehouse management system
- Deploy Gallo Edge and Gallo Wine Manager software
- Deploy Wal-Mart retail link

Business Challenges

- Powerful competitors
- Competition based on quality and price

Management

Organization

Technology

Information System

- Coordinate production, inventory, and shipment
- Analyze product profitability
- Analyze winemaking costs

Business Solutions

- Reduce cost
- Increase revenue
- Increase service

Opening Case: Gallo Winery Leads by Blending Business with Technology

E.&J. Gallo Winery is the largest wine producer in the world, selling 65 million cases of wine in 2003. Despite its leadership position, Gallo must be concerned about how its wines taste and also about price and service. It has other large competitors, including Allied Domecq, Kendall Jackson, Beringer Blass, Robert Mondavi, and several Australian winemakers, all of whom offer good quality wines at low prices.

How does Gallo manage to maintain its market leadership? The answer is by continually finding new ways to master the art and science of winemaking and by paying close attention to the distribution and marketing of wine worldwide. Gallo very carefully manages its production processes and relationships with suppliers.

To make sure shoppers know exactly where to find its products, Gallo implemented a product accountability system at its regional distribution centers. A complex warehouse management system coordinates production, component replenishment, inventory, and shipment, integrating with Gallo's order and transportation management systems. This system helped shorten the order-to-door cycle by 10 days. All orders are electronic, and payment is received elec-

tronically. Gallo's distributors know exactly what they are going to get by eligibility, product, and place.

To further support close relationships with distributors and retailers, a system called Gallo Edge helps retail customers such as Albertsons and Wal-Mart manage wine placement and profitability in their stores. Gallo Edge analyzes Wal-Mart's data about Gallo sales to produce a by-bottle profitability analysis so that Wal-Mart buyers can see which products are selling quickly, which aren't, and whether they are making money on products. Gallo never sees the results—the data are Wal-Mart's, but Gallo clearly benefits from providing this service.

Gallo is updating a production control system called Gallo Wine Manager to help management evaluate the relationship between wine taste and costs. Because Gallo sells 95 different brands of wine in a variety of price ranges, from everyday table wine to very expensive wine, it wants to be able to understand the cost of each blend. This system lets winemakers see the cost impact of any winemaking recipe.

Sources: Thomas Claburn, "Recipe for a Better Winery," *Information Week*, September 20, 2004 and www.gallo.com, accessed September 26, 2004.

E.&J. Gallo Winery illustrates the interdependence of business environments, organizational culture, management strategy, and the development of information systems. Gallo developed a series of systems to increase service and operational efficiency in response to competitive pressures from its surrounding environment, but this systems effort could not succeed without a significant amount of organizational and management change. New information systems have changed the way Gallo and its customers run their businesses and make management decisions.

As a manager, you'll need to know how to use information systems strategically and how systems can help you make better decisions. This chapter explains some things you need to know about the relationship between organizations, management, information systems, and business strategy. First, we introduce the features of organizations that you will need to understand when you design, build, and operate information systems. Next, we survey the role of management in organizations and to see where information systems have had an impact. Finally, we examine the problems firms face from competition and the ways in which information systems can provide competitive advantage.

3.1   ORGANIZATIONS AND INFORMATION SYSTEMS

Information systems and organizations influence one another. Information systems are built by managers to serve the interests of the business firm. At the same time, the organization must be aware of and open to the influences of information systems to benefit from new technologies.

The interaction between information technology and organizations is complex and is influenced by many mediating factors, including the organization's structure, standard operating procedures, politics, culture, surrounding environment, and management decisions (see Figure 3-1). As a manager, you will need to understand how information systems can change social and work life in your firm. You will not be able to design new systems successfully or understand existing systems without understanding your own business organization.

As a manager, you will be the one to decide which systems will be built, what they will do, and how they will be implemented. You may not be able to anticipate all of the consequences of these decisions. Some of the changes that occur in business firms because of new information technology (IT) investments cannot be foreseen and have results that may or may not meet your expectations. Who would have imagined five years ago, for instance, that e-mail and instant messaging would become a dominant form of business communication and that many managers would be inundated with more than 200 e-mail messages each day (Walker, 2004)? A technology introduced to boost productivity may actually wind up lowering it.

FIGURE 3-1   *The two-way relationship between organizations and information technology.*

This complex two-way relationship is mediated by many factors, not the least of which are the decisions made—or not made—by managers. Other factors mediating the relationship include the organizational culture, structure, politics, business processes, and environment.

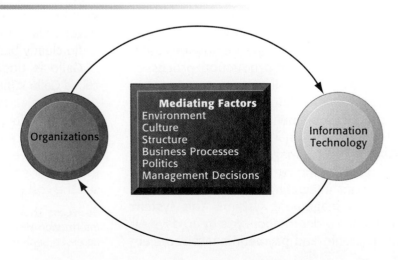

FIGURE 3-2   *The technical microeconomic definition of the organization.*

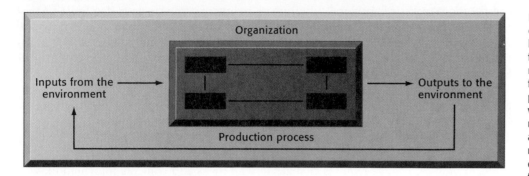

In the microeconomic definition of organizations, capital and labor (the primary production factors provided by the environment) are transformed by the firm through the production process into products and services (outputs to the environment). The products and services are consumed by the environment, which supplies additional capital and labor as inputs in the feedback loop.

What Is an Organization?

An **organization** is a stable, formal social structure that takes resources from the environment and processes them to produce outputs. This technical definition focuses on three elements of an organization. Capital and labor are primary production factors provided by the environment. The organization (the firm) transforms these inputs into products and services in a production function. The products and services are consumed by environments in return for supply inputs (see Figure 3-2).

An organization is more stable than an informal group (such as a group of friends that meets every Friday for lunch) in terms of longevity and routineness. Organizations are formal legal entities with internal rules and procedures, which must abide by laws. Organizations are also social structures because they are a collection of social elements, much as a machine has a structure—a particular arrangement of valves, cams, shafts, and other parts.

This definition of organizations is powerful and simple, but it is not very descriptive or even predictive of real-world organizations. A more realistic behavioral definition of an organization is that it is a collection of rights, privileges, obligations, and responsibilities that is delicately balanced over a period of time through conflict and conflict resolution (see Figure 3-3).

In this behavioral view of the firm, people who work in organizations develop customary ways of working; they gain attachments to existing relationships; and they make arrangements with subordinates and superiors about how work will be done, the amount of work that will be done, and under what conditions work will be done. Most of these arrangements and feelings are not discussed in any formal rulebook.

How do these definitions of organizations relate to information systems technology? A technical view of organizations encourages us to focus on how inputs are combined to

FIGURE 3-3   *The behavioral view of organizations.*

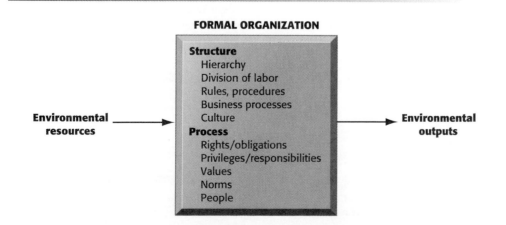

The behavioral view of organizations emphasizes group relationships, values, and structures.

create outputs when technology changes are introduced into the company. The firm is seen as infinitely malleable, with capital and labor substituting for each other quite easily. But the more realistic behavioral definition of an organization suggests that building new information systems, or rebuilding old ones, involves much more than a technical rearrangement of machines or workers. Some information systems change the organizational balance of rights, privileges, obligations, responsibilities, and feelings that have been established over a long period of time.

Changing these elements can take a long time, be very disruptive, and require more resources to support training and learning. For instance, the length of time required to implement effectively a new information system is much longer than usually anticipated simply because there is a lag between implementing a technical system and teaching employees and managers how to use the system.

Technological change requires changes in who owns and controls information; who has the right to access and update that information; and who makes decisions about whom, when, and how. This more complex view forces us to look at the way work is designed and the procedures used to achieve outputs.

The technical and behavioral definitions of organizations are not contradictory. Indeed, they complement each other: The technical definition tells us how thousands of firms in competitive markets combine capital, labor, and information technology, whereas the behavioral model takes us inside the individual firm to see how that technology affects the organization's inner workings. Section 3.2 describes how each of these definitions of organizations can help explain the relationships between information systems and organizations.

Some features of organizations are common to all organizations; others distinguish one organization from another. Let us look first at the features common to all organizations.

Common Features of Organizations

You might not think that Apple Computer, United Airlines, and the Aspen, Colorado, Police Department have much in common, but they do. In some respects, all modern organizations are alike because they share the characteristics that are listed in Table 3-1. German sociologist Max Weber was the first to describe these "ideal-typical" characteristics of organizations in 1911. He called organizations **bureaucracies** that have certain "structural" features.

According to Weber, all modern bureaucracies have clear-cut divisions of labor and specialization. Organizations arrange specialists in a hierarchy of authority in which everyone is accountable to someone and authority is limited to specific actions. Authority and action are further limited by abstract rules or procedures (standard operating procedures, or SOPs) that are interpreted and applied to specific cases. These rules create a system of impartial and universal decision making; everyone is treated equally. Organizations try to hire and promote employees on the basis of technical qualifications and professionalism (not personal connections). The organization is devoted to the principle of efficiency: maximizing output using limited inputs.

According to Weber, bureaucracies are prevalent because they are the most efficient form of organization. Other scholars have supplemented Weber, identifying additional

TABLE 3-1 *Structural Characteristics of All Organizations*

Clear division of labor
Hierarchy
Explicit rules and procedures
Impartial judgments
Technical qualifications for positions
Maximum organizational efficiency

features of organizations. All organizations develop business processes (routines), politics, and cultures.

ROUTINES AND BUSINESS PROCESSES

All organizations, including business firms, become very efficient over time because individuals in the firm develop **routines** for producing goods and services. Routines—sometimes called *standard operating procedures*—are precise rules, procedures, and practices that have been developed to cope with virtually all expected situations. As employees learn these routines, they become highly productive and efficient, and the firm is able to reduce its costs over time as efficiency increases. For instance, when you visit a doctor's office, receptionists have a well-developed set of routines for gathering basic information from you; nurses have a different set of routines for preparing you for an interview with a doctor; and the doctor has a well-developed set of routines for diagnosing you.

Business processes, which we describe in Chapters 1 and 2, are collections of such routines. A business firm in turn is a collection of business processes (Figure 3-4). By analyzing business processes and individual routines, you can achieve a very clear understanding of how a business actually works. Moreover, by conducting a business process analysis, you will also begin to understand how to change the business to make it more efficient or effective. Throughout this book we examine business processes with a view to understanding how they might be changed, or replaced, by using information technology to achieve greater efficiency and higher levels of customer service.

ORGANIZATIONAL POLITICS

People in organizations occupy different positions with different specialties, concerns, and perspectives. As a result, they naturally have divergent viewpoints about how resources, rewards, and punishments should be distributed. These differences matter to

FIGURE 3-4   *Routines, business processes, and firms.*

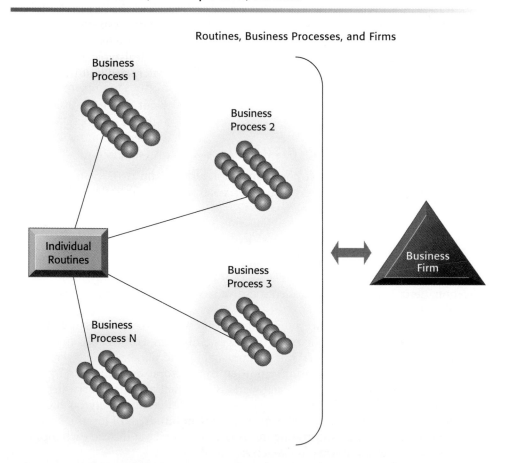

Routines, Business Processes, and Firms

Business Process 1

Business Process 2

Individual Routines

Business Process 3

Business Process N

Business Firm

All organizations are composed of individual routines and behaviors, a collection of which make up a business process. A collection of business processes make up the business firm. New information system applications require that individual routines and business processes change to achieve high levels of organizational performance.

both managers and employees, and they result in political struggle for resources, competition, and conflict within every organization. Political resistance is one of the great difficulties of bringing about organizational change—especially the development of new information systems. Virtually all large information systems investments by a firm that bring about significant changes in strategy, business objectives, business processes, and procedures become politically charged events. Managers who know how to work with the politics of an organization will be more successful than less skilled managers in implementing new information systems. Throughout this book you will find many examples of where internal politics defeated the best-laid plans for an information system.

ORGANIZATIONAL CULTURE

All organizations have bedrock, unassailable, unquestioned (by the members) assumptions that define their goals and products. **Organizational culture** is this set of fundamental assumptions about what products the organization should produce, how it should produce them, where, and for whom. Generally, these cultural assumptions are taken totally for granted and are rarely publicly announced or spoken about (Schein, 1985). Business processes—the actual way business firms produce value—are usually anchored in the organization's culture.

You can see organizational culture at work by looking around your university or college. Some bedrock assumptions of university life are that professors know more than students, the reason students attend college is to learn, and classes follow a regular schedule. Organizational culture is a powerful unifying force that restrains political conflict and promotes common understanding, agreement on procedures, and common practices. If we all share the same basic cultural assumptions, agreement on other matters is more likely.

At the same time, organizational culture is a powerful restraint on change, especially technological change. Most organizations will do almost anything to avoid making changes in basic assumptions. Any technological change that threatens commonly held cultural assumptions usually meets a great deal of resistance. However, there are times when the only sensible way for a firm to move forward is to employ a new technology that directly opposes an existing organizational culture. When this occurs, the technology is often stalled while the culture slowly adjusts. You will find many examples in later chapters that describe the difficulties of changing the culture of a business to implement a new information system.

Unique Features of Organizations

Although all organizations do have common characteristics, no two organizations are identical. Organizations have different structures, goals, constituencies, leadership styles, tasks, and surrounding environments.

DIFFERENT ORGANIZATIONAL TYPES

One important way in which organizations differ is in their structure or shape. The differences among organizational structures are characterized in many ways. Mintzberg's classification, described in Table 3-2, identifies five basic kinds of organizations (Mintzberg, 1979).

The kind of information systems you find in a business firm—and the nature of problems with these systems—often reflects the type of organization. For instance, in a professional bureaucracy such as a hospital it is not unusual to find parallel patient record systems operated by the administration, another by doctors, and another by other professional staff such as nurses and social workers. In small entrepreneurial firms you will often find poorly designed systems developed in a rush that often outgrow their usefulness quickly. In huge multidivisional firms operating in hundreds of locations you will often find there is not a single integrating information system, but instead each locale or each division has its set of information systems.

TABLE 3-2 *Organizational Structures*

Organizational Type	Description	Examples
Entrepreneurial structure	Young, small firm in a fast-changing environment. It has a simple structure and is managed by an entrepreneur serving as its single chief executive officer.	Small start-up business
Machine bureaucracy	Large bureaucracy existing in a slowly changing environment, producing standard products. It is dominated by a centralized management team and centralized decision making.	Midsize manufacturing firm
Divisionalized bureaucracy	Combination of multiple machine bureaucracies, each producing a different product or service, all topped by one central headquarters.	Fortune 500 firms, such as General Motors
Professional bureaucracy	Knowledge-based organization where goods and services depend on the expertise and knowledge of professionals. Dominated by department heads with weak centralized authority.	Law firms, school systems, hospitals
Adhocracy	Task force organization that must respond to rapidly changing environments. Consists of large groups of specialists organized into short-lived multidisciplinary teams and has weak central management.	Consulting firms, such as the Rand Corporation

ORGANIZATIONS AND ENVIRONMENTS

Organizations reside in environments from which they draw resources and to which they supply goods and services. Organizations and environments have a reciprocal relationship. On the one hand, organizations are open to, and dependent on, the social and physical environment that surrounds them. Without financial and human resources—people willing to work reliably and consistently for a set wage or revenue from customers—organizations could not exist. Organizations must respond to legislative and other requirements imposed by government, as well as the actions of customers and competitors. On the other hand, organizations can influence their environments. For example, business firms form alliances with other businesses to influence the political process; they advertise to influence customer acceptance of their products.

Figure 3-5 illustrates the role of information systems in helping organizations perceive changes in their environments and also in helping organizations act on their environments. Information systems are key instruments for environmental scanning, helping managers identify external changes that might require an organizational response.

Environments generally change much faster than organizations. The main reasons for organizational failure are an inability to adapt to a rapidly changing environment and a lack of resources—particularly among young firms—to sustain even short periods of troubled times. New technologies, new products, and changing public tastes and values (many of which result in new government regulations) put strains on any organization's culture, politics, and people. Most organizations do not cope well with large environmental shifts. The inertia built into an organization's standard operating procedures, the political conflict raised by changes to the existing order, and the threat to closely held cultural values typically inhibit organizations from making significant changes. It is not surprising that only 10 percent of the Fortune 500 companies in 1919 still exist today.

OTHER DIFFERENCES AMONG ORGANIZATIONS

Organizations have different shapes or structures for many other reasons also. They differ in their ultimate goals and the types of power used to achieve them. Some organizations have coercive goals (e.g., prisons); others have utilitarian goals (e.g., businesses). Still

Environments shape what organizations can do, but organizations can influence their environments and decide to change environments altogether. Information technology plays a critical role in helping organizations perceive environmental change and in helping organizations act on their environment.

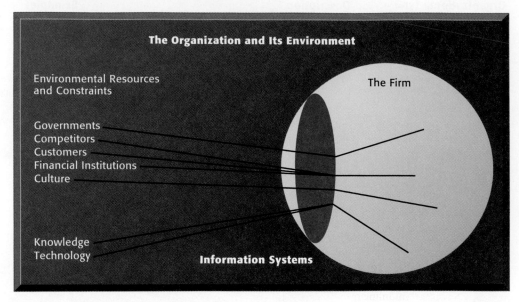

others have normative goals (universities, religious groups). Organizations also serve different groups or have different constituencies, some primarily benefiting their members, others benefiting clients, stockholders, or the public. The nature of leadership differs greatly from one organization to another—some organizations may be more democratic or authoritarian than others. Another way organizations differ is by the tasks they perform and the technology they use. Some organizations perform primarily routine tasks that could be reduced to formal rules that require little judgment (such as manufacturing auto parts), whereas others (such as consulting firms) work primarily with nonroutine tasks.

As you can see in Table 3-3, the list of unique features of organizations is longer than the common features list. It stands to reason that information systems will have different impacts on different types of organizations. Different organizations in different circumstances experience different effects from the same technology. Only by close analysis of a specific organization can a manager effectively design and manage information systems.

The Window on Organizations shows how unique environments, culture, and organizational characteristics have affected Internet use and electronic commerce in Canada and Mexico. Canada is more affluent than Mexico, with a high percentage of its population using the Internet. However, that does not necessarily translate into a high rate of online purchasing because consumers are heavily taxed and remain partial to bricks-and-mortar stores. Mexico's government is actively trying to promote Internet use, but a high percentage of citizens live below the poverty line and inexpensive telecommunications services are not widely available.

TABLE 3-3 *Summary of Salient Features of Organizations*

Common Features	Unique Features
Formal structure	Organizational type
Routines	Environments
Politics	Goals
Culture	Power
	Constituencies
	Function
	Leadership
	Tasks
	Technology

WINDOW ON ORGANIZATIONS

E-COMMERCE NORTH AND SOUTH OF THE BORDER

Internet shopping may be flourishing in the United States, but it is not equally popular in other countries. Let's look at e-commerce in the United States' closest neighbors—Canada to the north and Mexico to the south.

Canada is definitely a major user of the Internet, with more per capita users than the United States. About 71 percent of Canadian adults use the Internet, compared to 68 percent in the United States. About 35 percent of Canadian households using the Internet do so through high-speed connections. In addition 51 percent of Canadian Net users do their banking through the Internet, compared with only 33 percent of U.S. Internet users. About 3.2 million Canadian households engaged in e-commerce in 2003. Yet Canadians use the Internet much less than Americans for retail shopping, spending only $3 billion in online purchases in 2003. The reasons are unclear.

Canadian retail companies have responded accordingly, investing less in e-commerce Web sites than their U.S. counterparts. One famous department store organization, the Hudson's Bay Company, operates some of the most popular Canadian department store brands, including the Bay, Zellers, and Home Outfitters. However, its Web site (HBC.com) only offers less than 10 percent of its bricks-and-mortar products online. Moreover, consumers seem primarily interested in sale items, so HBC.com makes marked-down items its primary focus. Michael LeBlanc, HBC's coordinator of Web sites, does believe its online strategy is successful for increasing Hudson's Bay's store traffic. He points out, for example, that the company offers its Web customers the ability to pick up purchases at one of HBC's bricks-and-mortar stores.

Robert Sartor, the CEO of the Forzani Group, the owner of seven sporting goods brands, believes that one reason for Canadians' lower interest in online shopping is that Canadians are taxed more heavily than are Americans, leaving Canadians with less disposable income. Moreover, e-commerce shopping usually leaves the shopper "having to pay for shipping and handling online, and if you return it, you have to pay that again," according to Sartor. Forzani has successfully used the Internet to build an e-mail list to support its bricks-and-mortar stores. However, its attempt at online selling has failed. In 1999, Forzani built an e-commerce enterprise, but closed it after one and one-half years because it had generated too little growth. "At the rate of growth we were seeing," explains Sartor, "it'd be 12, 13, 14 years before we got the returns we're used to."

Nor are Canadian consumers doing their purchasing on foreign Web sites. In 2003, nearly 70 percent of Canadian purchases over the Internet were spent at domestic Web sites. "Canada is among the top countries worldwide in Internet usage . . . , but to date that has not translated into e-commerce

leadership," observes Jeffrey Grau, a senior analyst for eMarketer. Selling online in Canada is especially difficult for U.S. companies because of this slow adoption of e-commerce combined with regulatory complications when purchasing goods from foreign entities.

E-commerce challenges in Mexico stem from different sources. Per capita income is one-fourth that of the United States and distribution of that income is very uneven, with over 40 percent of the population below the poverty line. Mexico has an undeveloped telecommunications infrastructure, limited investment in information technology by small and medium-sized businesses, unreliable logistics and delivery systems, and limited online payment options. High-speed access to the Internet is very expensive.

A much smaller percentage of Mexicans (about 20 percent) use credit cards for purchases than in the United States, and they have less disposable income for shopping. About 9 million people in Mexico have PCs, and over half of them have Internet access. As of 2004, Mexico had over 13 million Internet users, most of whom are under 35 years old.

Nevertheless, interest in e-commerce and the Internet is high, and Internet use is increasing. According to Pyramid Research, close to $50 billion is being spent on Internet e-commerce in Mexico, making it one of the leading countries in Latin America for online business. Currently, more than 4 million Mexicans do their banking online. Local online retail sites and online Web sites for bricks-and-mortar retailers are being developed. One active Mexican online retailer is Sanborns, whose Web site is supported by more than 100 stores.

Mexico's business community strongly backs Internet business. Mexico's political and business leadership would like to use the Internet to catch up with more advanced countries. The government of Mexico wants to make Mexico a digital economy. It is actively trying to promote the development of an information technology industry in Mexico along with a regulatory framework for e-commerce. Mexico's e-Commerce Law legally recognizes electronic contracts and makes sure consumer protection laws apply to the online world.

Sources: Bob Tedeschi, "E-Commerce Report," *New York Times*, January 26, 2004; CBC Business News, "Shopping on the Web Up 25%: StatsCan," September 23, 2004; "eMarketer Report: Online Retailers Should Look to Canada for New Opportunities," December 9, 2004; "Internet Users in Select Countries in Latin America, 2002–2008," www.emarketer.com, accessed December 12, 2004; Eastern Michigan University, "Best Prospects in the ICT Market," revised April 24, 2004; and "The World Fact Book: Mexico," www.cia.gov, accessed September 25, 2004.

To Think About: What organizational factors explain why Canada and Mexico have had such different experiences adopting e-commerce?

Organizing the IT Function

Given that there are many types of business firms, there are many ways in which the IT function is organized within the firm. In the typical firm the formal organizational unit responsible for information technology services is called the **information systems department**. The information systems department is responsible for maintaining the hardware, software, data storage, and networks that comprise the firm's IT infrastructure. We describe IT infrastructure in detail in Chapter 6.

The information systems department consists of specialists, such as programmers, systems analysts, project leaders, and information systems managers (see Figure 3-6). **Programmers** are highly trained technical specialists who write the software instructions for computers. **Systems analysts** constitute the principal liaisons between the information systems groups and the rest of the organization. It is the systems analyst's job to translate business problems and requirements into information requirements and systems. **Information systems managers** are leaders of teams of programmers and analysts, project managers, physical facility managers, telecommunications managers, and heads of office system groups. They are also managers of computer operations and data entry staff. Also external specialists, such as hardware vendors and manufacturers, software firms, and consultants frequently participate in the day-to-day operations and long-term planning of information systems.

In many companies, the information systems department is headed by a **chief information officer (CIO)**. The role of CIO is a senior management position that oversees the use of information technology in the firm.

End users are representatives of departments outside of the information systems group for whom applications are developed. These users are playing an increasingly large role in the design and development of information systems.

In the early years of computing, the information systems group was composed mostly of programmers, who performed very highly specialized but limited technical functions. Today, a growing proportion of staff members are systems analysts and network specialists, with the information systems department acting as a powerful change agent in the organization. The information systems department suggests new business strategies and new information-based products and services and coordinates both the development of the technology and the planned changes in the organization.

In the past, firms generally built their own software and managed their own computing facilities. Today, many firms are turning to external vendors to provide these services (see Chapters 6, 8, and 14) and are using their information systems departments to manage these service providers.

FIGURE 3-6   *Information technology services.*

Many types of specialists and groups are responsible for the design and management of the organization's information technology infrastructure.

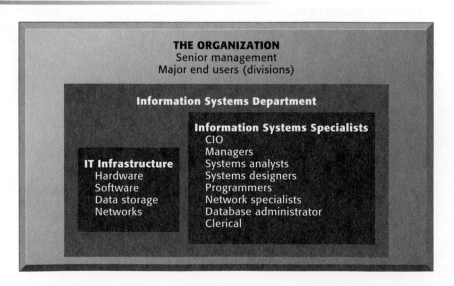

3.2　HOW INFORMATION SYSTEMS IMPACT ORGANIZATIONS AND BUSINESS FIRMS

Information systems have become integral, online, interactive tools deeply involved in the minute-to-minute operations and decision making of large organizations. Over the last decade, information systems have fundamentally altered the economics of organizations and greatly increased the possibilities for organizing work. Theories and concepts from economics and sociology help us understand the changes brought about by IT.

Economic Impacts

From the point of view of economics, IT changes both the relative costs of capital and the costs of information. Information systems technology can be viewed as a factor of production that can be substituted for traditional capital and labor. As the cost of information technology decreases, it is substituted for labor, which historically has been a rising cost. Hence, information technology should result in a relative decline in the number of middle managers and clerical workers as information technology substitutes for their labor (Laudon, 1990).

As the cost of information technology decreases, it also substitutes for other forms of capital such as buildings and machinery, which remain relatively expensive. Hence, over time we should expect managers to increase their investments in IT because of its declining cost relative to other capital investments.

IT also obviously affects the cost and quality of information and changes the economics of information. Information technology helps firms contract in size because it can reduce transaction costs—the costs incurred when a firm buys on the marketplace what it cannot make itself. According to **transaction cost theory**, firms and individuals seek to economize on transaction costs, much as they do on production costs. Using markets is expensive (Coase, 1937; Williamson, 1985) because of costs such as locating and communicating with distant suppliers, monitoring contract compliance, buying insurance, obtaining information on products, and so forth. Traditionally, firms have tried to reduce transaction costs through vertical integration, by getting bigger, hiring more employees, and buying their own suppliers and distributors, as both General Motors and Ford used to do.

Information technology, especially the use of networks, can help firms lower the cost of market participation (transaction costs), making it worthwhile for firms to contract with external suppliers instead of using internal sources. For instance, by using computer links to external suppliers, the Chrysler Corporation can achieve economies by obtaining more than 70 percent of its parts from other companies. Information systems make it possible for companies such as Cisco Systems and Dell Computer to outsource their production to contract manufacturers such as Flextronics instead of making their products themselves.

Figure 3-7 shows that as transaction costs decrease, firm size (the number of employees) should shrink because it becomes easier and cheaper for the firm to contract for the purchase of goods and services in the marketplace rather than to make the product or offer the service itself. Firm size can stay constant or contract even if the company increases its revenues. For example, when Eastman Chemical Company split off from Kodak in 1994, it had $3.3 billion in revenue and 24,000 full-time employees. By 2003, it generated $5.8 billion in revenue with only 15,000 employees.

Information technology also can reduce internal management costs. According to **agency theory**, the firm is viewed as a "nexus of contracts" among self-interested individuals rather than as a unified, profit-maximizing entity (Jensen and Meckling, 1976). A principal (owner) employs "agents" (employees) to perform work on his or her behalf. However, agents need constant supervision and management; otherwise, they will tend to pursue their own interests rather than those of the owners. As firms grow in size and scope, agency costs or coordination costs rise because owners must expend more and more effort supervising and managing employees.

Information technology, by reducing the costs of acquiring and analyzing information, permits organizations to reduce agency costs because it becomes easier for managers to

FIGURE 3-7   *The transaction cost theory of the impact of information technology on the organization.*

Firms traditionally grew in size to reduce transaction costs. IT potentially reduces the costs for a given size, shifting the transaction cost curve inward, opening up the possibility of revenue growth without increasing size, or even revenue growth accompanied by shrinking size.

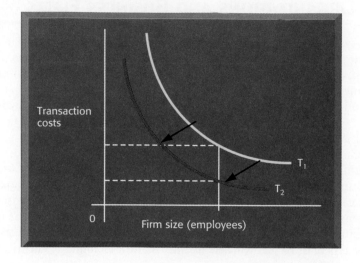

oversee a greater number of employees. Figure 3-8 shows that by reducing overall management costs, information technology enables firms to increase revenues while shrinking the number of middle managers and clerical workers. We have seen examples in earlier chapters where information technology expanded the power and scope of small organizations by enabling them to perform coordinating activities such as processing orders or keeping track of inventory with very few clerks and managers.

Organizational and Behavioral Impacts

Theories based in the sociology of complex organizations also provide some understanding about how and why firms change with the implementation of new IT applications.

IT FLATTENS ORGANIZATIONS

Large, bureaucratic organizations, which primarily developed before the computer age, are often inefficient, slow to change, and less competitive than newly created organizations. Some of these large organizations have downsized, reducing the number of employees and the number of levels in their organizational hierarchies.

FIGURE 3-8   *The agency cost theory of the impact of information technology on the organization.*

As firms grow in size and complexity, traditionally they experience rising agency costs. IT shifts the agency cost curve down and to the right, enabling firms to increase size while lowering agency costs.

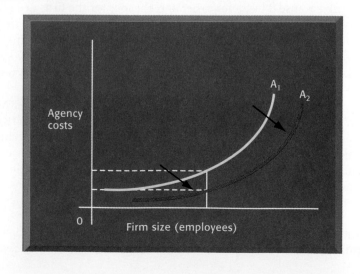

Behavioral researchers have theorized that information technology facilitates flattening of hierarchies by broadening the distribution of information to empower lower-level employees and increase management efficiency (see Figure 3-9). IT pushes decision-making rights lower in the organization because lower-level employees receive the information they need to make decisions without supervision. (This empowerment is also possible because of higher educational levels among the workforce, which give employees the capabilities to make intelligent decisions.) Second, because managers can now receive so much more accurate information on time, they become much faster at making decisions, so fewer managers are required. Management costs decline as a percentage of revenues, and the hierarchy becomes much more efficient (Drucker, 1988; Bresnahan, Brynjolffson, and Hitt, 2000; Laudon and Marr, 1995; Malone, 1997).

These changes mean that the management span of control has also been broadened, enabling high-level managers to manage and control more employees spread over greater distances. Many companies have eliminated thousands of middle managers as a result of these changes.

POSTINDUSTRIAL ORGANIZATIONS AND VIRTUAL FIRMS

Postindustrial theories based more on history and sociology than economics also support the notion that IT should flatten hierarchies. In postindustrial societies, authority increasingly relies on knowledge and competence, and not merely on formal positions. Hence, the shape of organizations should flatten because professional workers tend to be self-managing, and decision making should become more decentralized as knowledge and information become more widespread throughout the firm (Drucker, 1988). Information technology may encourage task force–networked organizations in which groups of professionals come together—face to face or electronically—for short periods of time to accomplish a specific task (e.g., designing a new automobile); once the task is accomplished, the individuals join other task forces.

More firms may operate as **virtual organizations** in which work no longer is tied to geographic location. Virtual organizations use networks to link people, assets, and ideas. They can ally with suppliers, customers, and, sometimes, even competitors to create and distribute new products and services without being limited by traditional organizational boundaries or physical locations. For example, Calyx and Corolla is a networked virtual organization selling fresh flowers directly to customers, bypassing traditional florists. The

FIGURE 3-9   *Flattening organizations.*

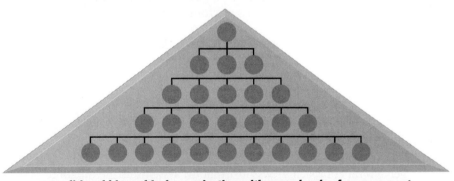

A traditional hierarchical organization with many levels of management

Information systems can reduce the number of levels in an organization by providing managers with information to supervise larger numbers of workers and by giving lower-level employees more decision-making authority.

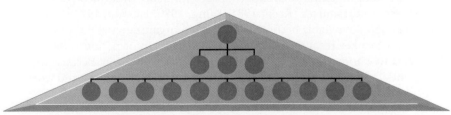

An organization that has been "flattened" by removing layers of management

firm takes orders over the telephone or from its Web site and transmits them to grower farms, which ship flowers using FedEx directly to customers.

Who makes sure that self-managed teams do not head off in the wrong direction? Who decides which person works on which team and for how long? How can managers evaluate the performance of someone who is constantly rotating from team to team? How do people know where their careers are headed? New approaches for evaluating, organizing, and informing workers are required, and not all companies can make virtual work effective.

INCREASING FLEXIBILITY OF ORGANIZATIONS

Information technology helps companies organize in more flexible ways, increasing their ability to sense and respond to changes in the marketplace and to take advantage of new opportunities. Information systems can give both large and small organizations additional flexibility to overcome some of the limitations posed by their size.

Small organizations can use information systems to acquire some of the muscle and reach of larger organizations. They can perform coordinating activities, such as processing bids or keeping track of inventory, and many manufacturing tasks with very few managers, clerks, or production workers.

Large organizations can use information technology to achieve some of the agility and responsiveness of small organizations. One aspect of this phenomenon is **mass customization**, which is the ability to offer individually tailored products or services using the same production resources as mass production. Information systems can make the production process more flexible so that products can be tailored to each customer's unique set of requirements (Zipkin, 2001). Software and computer networks can be used to link the plant floor tightly with orders, design, and purchasing and to control production machines finely so products can be produced in greater variety and easily customized with no added cost for small production runs.

For example, the Lands' End Web site enables users to order jeans, dress pants, chino pants, and shirts custom-tailored to their own specifications. Customers enter their measurements into a form on the Web site, which then transmits each customer's specifications over a network to a computer that develops an electronic made-to-measure pattern for that customer. The individual patterns are then transmitted electronically to a manufacturing plant, where they are used to drive fabric-cutting equipment (Ives and Piccoli, 2003). There are almost no extra production costs because the process does not require additional warehousing, production overruns, and inventories, and the cost to the customer is only slightly higher than that of a mass-produced garment.

A related trend is micromarketing, in which information systems can help companies pinpoint tiny target markets for these finely customized products and services—as small as individualized "markets of one." We discuss micromarketing in more detail in Section 3.4.

UNDERSTANDING ORGANIZATIONAL RESISTANCE TO CHANGE

Throughout this book you will find many case studies that describe resistance to new systems in the organization and the difficulties that managers face in getting their firms to change rapidly. Our previous discussion of business processes suggests one powerful reason why there is resistance to IT applications: Many IT investments require changes in personal, individual routines that can be painful for those involved and require retraining and additional effort on the part of the employee who may or may not be compensated.

Another behavioral approach views information systems as the outcome of political competition between organizational subgroups for influence over the organization's policies, procedures, and resources (Keen, 1981; Kling, 1980; Laudon, 1974; Laudon, 1986). Information systems inevitably become bound up in organizational politics because they influence access to a key resource—namely, information. Information systems can affect who does what to whom, when, where, and how in an organization. Because information systems potentially change an organization's structure, culture, politics, and work, there is often considerable resistance to them when they are introduced.

Because organizational resistance to change is so powerful, many information technology investments flounder and do not increase productivity. Indeed, research on project

FIGURE 3-10   *Organizational resistance and the mutually adjusting relationship between technology and the organization.*

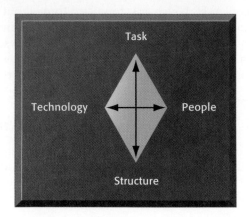

Implementing information systems has consequences for task arrangements, structures, and people. According to this model, to implement change, all four components must be changed simultaneously.

Source: Reprinted by permission of James G. March.

implementation failures demonstrates that the most common reason for failure of large projects to reach their objectives is not the failure of the technology, but organizational and political resistance to change. Chapter 15 treats this issue in detail. Therefore, as a manger involved in future IT investments, your ability to work with people and organizations is just as important as your technical awareness and knowledge.

The Internet and Organizations

The Internet, especially the World Wide Web, is beginning to have an important impact on the relationships between firms and external entities, and even on the organization of business processes inside a firm. The Internet increases the accessibility, storage, and distribution of information and knowledge for organizations. In essence, the Internet is capable of dramatically lowering the transaction and agency costs facing most organizations. For instance, brokerage firms and banks in New York can now deliver their internal-operations procedures manuals to their employees at distant locations by posting them on the corporate Web site, saving millions of dollars in distribution costs. A global sales force can receive nearly instant price product information updates using the Web or instructions from management sent by e-mail. Vendors of some large retailers can access retailers' internal Web sites directly for up-to-the-minute sales information and to initiate replenishment orders instantly.

Businesses are rapidly rebuilding some of their key business processes based on Internet technology and making this technology a key component of their IT infrastructures. One result will be simpler business processes, fewer employees, and much flatter organizations than in the past.

3.3   THE IMPACT OF IT ON MANAGEMENT DECISION MAKING

One of the most important contributions of information technology and systems to business firms is the reduction in information uncertainty and the resulting improvement in decision making. Over the last decade, IT has directly contributed to an improvement in the quality of information flowing to management and employee decision makers.

Prior to the development of the Internet and corporate-wide enterprise information systems (described in Chapters 2, 11, and 13), business decision makers had limited, delayed, and inaccurate knowledge of customers, sales, inventories, and business processes such as delivery, order fulfillment times, and order entry. This meant decisions were made using information that was at best approximate, and often wrong. In this environment, as a reaction to the information uncertainty, the solution was to double up people, increase production buffers of spare parts, and build very large warehouses to store excess production.

Significant investments in IT, which are chronicled throughout this book, have lifted the fog of uncertainty and replaced it with a much more precise, timely, and accurate level of decision making that was unimaginable a few years ago. These trends toward more real-time information and decision making will accelerate as new wireless communications technologies and mobile computing platforms extend their reach.

How IT Affects Management Decision Making

Although almost everyone believes IT has contributed to better management decision making, there have actually been few large-scale quantitative studies on this topic. The positive impact of IT on management decision making is typically inferred from productivity measures and the overall performance of the firm (profitability), along with its stock market share price.

The role of manager is very complex and involves a great deal more than simply decision making. In Chapter 13 we review in detail the process of decision making, the types of decisions managers make and the stages of the decision-making process. In this chapter it is important to understand the breadth of the management role and the various approaches to understanding exactly how IT supports managers.

The Role of Managers in Organizations

Managers play key roles in organizations. Their responsibilities range from making decisions, to writing reports, to attending meetings, to arranging birthday parties. We can better understand managerial functions and roles by examining classical and contemporary models of managerial behavior.

CLASSICAL DESCRIPTIONS OF MANAGEMENT

The **classical model of management**, which describes what managers do, was largely unquestioned for the more than 70 years since the 1920s. Henri Fayol and other early writers first described the five classical functions of managers as planning, organizing, coordinating, deciding, and controlling. This description of management activities dominated management thought for a long time, and it is still popular today.

But these terms actually describe formal managerial functions and are unsatisfactory as a description of what managers actually do. The terms do not address what managers do when they plan, decide things, and control the work of others. We need a more fine-grained understanding of how managers actually behave.

BEHAVIORAL MODELS

Contemporary behavioral scientists have observed that managers do not behave as the classical model of management led us to believe. Kotter (1982), for example, describes the morning activities of the president of an investment management firm.

> 7:35 A.M. Richardson arrives at work, unpacks her briefcase, gets some coffee, and begins making a list of activities for the day.

> 7:45 A.M. Bradshaw (a subordinate) and Richardson converse about a number of topics and exchange pictures recently taken on summer vacations.

> 8:00 A.M. They talk about a schedule of priorities for the day.

> 8:20 A.M. Wilson (a subordinate) and Richardson talk about some personnel problems, cracking jokes in the process.

> 8:45 A.M. Richardson's secretary arrives, and they discuss her new apartment and arrangements for a meeting later in the morning.

8:55 A.M. Richardson goes to a morning meeting run by one of her subordinates. Thirty people are there, and Richardson reads during the meeting.

11:05 A.M. Richardson and her subordinates return to the office and discuss a difficult problem. They try to define the problem and outline possible alternatives. She lets the discussion roam away from and back to the topic again and again. Finally, they agree on a next step.

In this example, it is difficult to determine which activities constitute Richardson's planning, coordinating, and decision making. **Behavioral models** state that the actual behavior of managers appears to be less systematic, more informal, less reflective, more reactive, less well organized, and much more frivolous than students of information systems and decision making generally expect it to be.

Observers find that managerial behavior actually has five attributes that differ greatly from the classical description: First, managers perform a great deal of work at an unrelenting pace—studies have found that managers engage in more than 600 different activities each day, with no break in their pace. Second, managerial activities are fragmented; most activities last for less than nine minutes, and only 10 percent of the activities exceed one hour in duration. Third, managers prefer speculation, hearsay, gossip—they want current, specific, and ad hoc information (printed information often will be too old). Fourth, they prefer oral forms of communication to written forms because oral media provide greater flexibility, require less effort, and bring a faster response. Fifth, managers give high priority to maintaining a diverse and complex web of contacts that acts as an informal information system and helps them execute their personal agendas and short- and long-term goals.

Analyzing managers' day-to-day behavior, Mintzberg found that it could be classified into 10 managerial roles. **Managerial roles** are expectations of the activities that managers should perform in an organization. Mintzberg found that these managerial roles fell into three categories: interpersonal, informational, and decisional.

Interpersonal Roles   Managers act as figureheads for the organization when they represent their companies to the outside world and perform symbolic duties, such as giving out employee awards, in their **interpersonal role**. Managers act as leaders, attempting to motivate, counsel, and support subordinates. Managers also act as liaisons between various organizational levels; within each of these levels, they serve as liaisons among the members of the management team. Managers provide time and favors, which they expect to be returned.

Informational Roles   In their **informational role**, managers act as the nerve centers of their organizations, receiving the most concrete, up-to-date information and redistributing it to those who need to be aware of it. Managers are therefore information disseminators and spokespersons for their organizations.

A corporate chief executive learns how to use a computer. Senior managers' time is very limited, so they require systems that are extremely easy to use.

Decisional Roles Managers make decisions. In their **decisional role**, they act as entrepreneurs by initiating new kinds of activities; they handle disturbances arising in the organization; they allocate resources to staff members who need them; and they negotiate conflicts and mediate between conflicting groups in the organization.

Table 3-4, based on Mintzberg's role classifications, is one look at where systems can and cannot help managers. The table shows that information systems do not yet contribute to some important areas of management life. These areas will provide great opportunities for future systems efforts.

Models of Decision Making

It is simplistic to think that organizations are composed of individual managers acting as rational decision makers and making decisions in a vacuum. The real business world is rarely like this. In fact most managers are members of a team of decision makers, working in a specific firm with a specific culture and set of political alliances and conflicts. The decisions that come out of an organization are the result of these many different forces and influences. A number of models attempt to describe how business people in firms make decisions. Some of these models focus on individual decision making, whereas others focus on decision making in groups.

One place to start thinking about decision making is to consider the rational individual model. Individual models of decision making assume that human beings are in some sense rational. The **rational model** of human behavior is built on the idea that people engage in basically consistent, rational, value-maximizing calculations. According to this model, an individual identifies goals, ranks all possible alternative actions by their contributions to those goals, and chooses the alternative that contributes most to those goals.

Critics of this model show that in fact people cannot specify all of the alternatives and that most individuals do not have singular goals and so are unable to rank all alternatives and consequences. Many decisions are so complex that calculating the choice (even if done by computer) is virtually impossible. Instead of searching through all alternatives, people tend to choose the first available alternative that moves them toward their ultimate goal. In making policy decisions, people choose policies most like the previous policy (Lindblom, 1959). Finally, some scholars point out that decision making is a continuous process in which final decisions are always being modified.

Other research has found that humans differ in how they maximize their values and in the frames of reference they use to interpret information and make choices. Tversky and

TABLE 3-4 *Managerial Roles and Supporting Information Systems*

Role	Behavior	Support Systems
Interpersonal Roles		
Figurehead - →		None exist
Leader - - - - - - - - - - - - - - - - - Interpersonal - - - - - - - - →		None exist
Liaison - →		Electronic communication systems
Informational Roles		
Nerve center- →		Management information systems, ESS
Disseminator - - - - - - - - - - - - - - Information- - - - - - - - - - →		Mail, office systems
Spokesperson- - - - - - - - - - - - - - processing - - - - - - - - - - →		Office and professional systems, workstations
Decisional Roles		
Entrepreneur - - - - - - - - - - - - - - Decision- - - - - - - - - - - →		None exist
Disturbance handler- - - - - - - - - - making - - - - - - - - - - - →		None exist
Resource allocator- →		DSS systems
Negotiator - →		None exist

Sources: Kenneth C. Laudon and Jane P. Laudon; and Mintzberg, 1971.

Kahneman (1981) show that humans have built-in biases that can distort decision making. They show that humans are very poor at assessing risk, almost always overestimating the probability of unlikely events and underestimating the likelihood of probable events. For instance, people are much more likely to fear shark attacks at the beach and much less likely to fear having a car accident driving to the beach. People can be manipulated into choosing alternatives that they might otherwise reject simply by changing the frame of reference (Tversky and Kahneman, 1981). These biases can affect the way information systems are designed and used for management decision making.

Decision making often is not performed by a single individual but by entire groups or organizations. **Organizational models of decision making** take into account the structural and political characteristics of an organization. Bureaucratic, political, and even "garbage can" models have been proposed to describe how decision making takes place in organizations.

According to **bureaucratic models of decision making** an organization's most important goal is the preservation of the organization. The reduction of uncertainty is another major goal. Policy tends to be incremental, only marginally different from the past, because radical policy departures involve too much uncertainty. These models depict organizations generally as not choosing or deciding in a rational sense. Rather, according to bureaucratic models, whatever organizations do is the result of routines and existing business processes honed over years of active use.

Organizations rarely change these routines and business processes because they may have to change personnel and incur risks (who knows if the new techniques work better than the old ones?). Although senior management and leaders are hired to coordinate and lead the organization, they are effectively trapped by the organization's standard business processes and existing solutions. Some organizations do, of course, change; they learn new ways of behaving, and they can be led. But all of these changes require a long time. Look around and you will find many organizations doing pretty much what they did 10, 20, or even 30 years ago. Most business firms that you know about now and do business with every day will not exist in 10 years. About half of all new firms fail in five years, and only 17 percent of the Fortune 500 of 1955 still exists (Starbuck, 1983).

In **political models of decision making,** what an organization does is a result of political bargains struck among key leaders and interest groups. Organizations do not come up with solutions that are chosen to solve some problem. Instead they reach compromises that reflect the conflicts, the major stakeholders, the diverse interests, the unequal power, and the confusion that constitute organizational politics.

Implications for the Design and Understanding of Information Systems

To deliver genuine benefits, information systems must be built with a clear understanding of the organization in which they will be used and of exactly how they can contribute to managerial decision making. In our experience, the central organizational factors to consider when planning a new system are the following:

- The environment in which the organization must function
- The structure of the organization: hierarchy, specialization, routines, and business processes
- The organization's culture and politics
- The type of organization and its style of leadership
- The principal interest groups affected by the system and the attitudes of workers who will be using the system
- The kinds of tasks, decisions, and business processes that the information system is designed to assist

Systems should be built to support individual, group, and organizational decision making. Information systems builders should design systems that have the following characteristics:

- They are flexible and provide many options for handling data and evaluating information.
- They are capable of supporting a variety of styles, skills, and knowledge as well as keeping track of many alternatives and consequences.
- They are sensitive to the organization's bureaucratic and political requirements.

3.4 INFORMATION SYSTEMS AND BUSINESS STRATEGY

Business strategy is a set of activities and decisions firms make that determine the following:

- Products and services the firm produces
- Industries in which the firm competes
- Competitors, suppliers, and customers of the firm
- Long-term goals of the firm

Strategies often result from a conscious strategic planning process in which nearly all small to large firms engage at least once a year. This process produces a document called the strategic plan, and the managers of the firm are given the task of achieving the goals of the strategic plan. But firms have to adapt these plans to changing environments. Where firms end up is not necessarily where they planned to be. Nevertheless, strategic plans are useful interim tools for defining what the firm will do until the business environment changes.

Thinking about strategy usually takes place at three different levels:

- **Business.** A single firm producing a set of related products and services
- **Firm.** A collection of businesses that make up a single, multidivisional firm
- **Industry.** A collection of firms that make up an industrial environment or ecosystem

Information systems and technologies play a crucial role in corporate strategy and strategic planning at each of these three different levels. Just about any substantial information system—a supply chain system, customer relationship system, or enterprise management system—can have strategic implications for a firm. As we point out in Chapter 1, and again in Chapter 6, what the firm wants to do in the next five years will be shaped in large part by what its information systems enable it to do. IT and the ability to use IT effectively will shape what the firm makes or provides customers, how it makes the product/ service, how it competes with others in its industry, and how it cooperates with other firms and logistic partners.

To understand how IT fits into the strategic thinking process, it is useful to consider the three levels of business strategy (the business, the firm, and the industry level). At each level of strategy IT plays an important role.

Business-Level Strategy: The Value Chain Model

At the business level of strategy, the key question is, "How can we compete effectively in this particular market?" The market might be light bulbs, utility vehicles, or cable television, or the business may be a service firm providing travel or financial services. The most common generic strategies at this level are (1) to become the low-cost producer, (2) to differentiate your product or service, and/or (3) to change the scope of competition by either enlarging the market to include global markets or narrowing the market by focusing on small niches not well served by your competitors. Digital firms provide new capabilities for supporting business-level strategy by managing the supply chain, building efficient customer "sense and respond" systems, and participating in value webs to deliver new products and services to market.

LEVERAGING TECHNOLOGY IN THE VALUE CHAIN

At the business level the most common analytical tool is value chain analysis. The **value chain model** highlights specific activities in the business where competitive strategies can best be applied (Porter, 1985) and where information systems are most likely to have a strategic impact. The value chain model identifies specific, critical leverage points where a firm can use information technology most effectively to enhance its competitive position. This model views the firm as a series or chain of basic activities that add a margin of value to a firm's products or services. These activities can be categorized as either primary activities or support activities.

Primary activities are most directly related to the production and distribution of the firm's products and services that create value for the customer. Primary activities include inbound logistics, operations, outbound logistics, sales and marketing, and service. Inbound logistics includes receiving and storing materials for distribution to production. Operations transforms inputs into finished products. Outbound logistics entails storing and distributing finished products. Sales and marketing includes promoting and selling the firm's products. The service activity includes maintenance and repair of the firm's goods and services.

Support activities make the delivery of the primary activities possible and consist of organization infrastructure (administration and management), human resources (employee recruiting, hiring, and training), technology (improving products and the production process), and procurement (purchasing input).

Firms achieve competitive advantage when they provide more value to their customers or when they provide the same value to customers at a lower price. An information system could have a strategic impact if it helps the firm provide products or services at a lower cost than competitors or if it provides products and services at the same cost as competitors but with greater value. The value activities that add the most value to products and services depend on the features of each particular firm.

The firm's value chain can be linked to the value chains of its other partners, including suppliers, distributors, and customers. Figure 3-11 illustrates the activities of the firm value chain and the industry value chain, showing examples of information systems that could be developed to make each of the value activities more cost-effective. A firm can achieve a strategic advantage over competitors using information systems not only by improving its internal value chain, but also by developing highly efficient ties to its industry partners—such as suppliers, logistics firms, and distributors—and their value chains.

Digitally enabled networks can be used not only to purchase supplies but also to closely coordinate production of many independent firms. For instance, the Italian casual wear company Benetton uses subcontractors and independent firms for labor-intensive production processes, such as tailoring, finishing, and ironing, while maintaining control of design, procurement, marketing, and distribution. Benetton uses computer networks to provide independent businesses and foreign production centers with production specifications so that they can efficiently produce the items needed by Benetton retail outlets (Camuffo, Romano, and Vinelli, 2001).

Internet technology has made it possible to extend the value chain so that it ties together all the firm's suppliers, business partners, and customers into a value web. A **value web** is a collection of independent firms that use information technology to coordinate their value chains to produce a product or service for a market collectively. It is more customer driven and operates in a less linear fashion than the traditional value chain.

Figure 3-12 shows that this value web synchronizes the business processes of customers, suppliers, and trading partners among different companies in an industry or related industries. These value webs are flexible and adaptive to changes in supply and demand. Relationships can be bundled or unbundled in response to changing market conditions. A company can use this value web to maintain long-standing relationships

FIGURE 3-11 *The firm value chain and the industry value chain.*

Illustrated are various examples of strategic information systems for the primary and support activities of a firm and of its value partners that would add a margin of value to a firm's products or services.

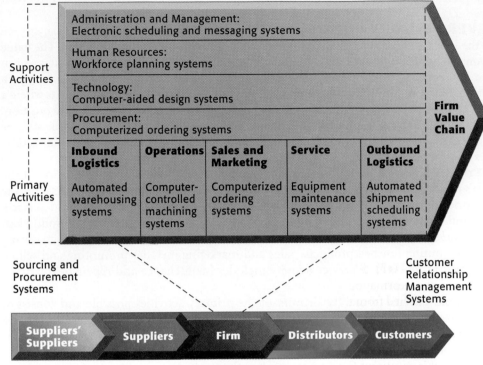

FIGURE 3-12 *The value web.*

The value web is a networked system that can synchronize the value chains of business partners within an industry to respond rapidly to changes in supply and demand.

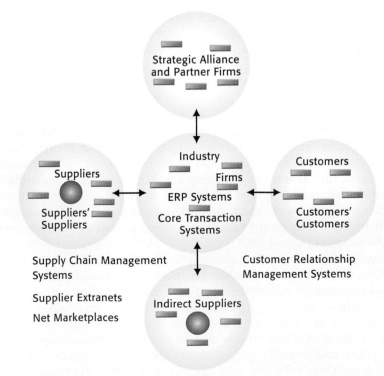

with many customers over long periods or to respond immediately to individual customer transactions. Firms can accelerate time to market and to customers by optimizing their value web relationships to make quick decisions on who can deliver the required products or services at the right price and location.

Businesses should try to develop strategic information systems for both the internal value chain activities and the external value activities that add the most value. A strategic analysis might, for example, identify sales and marketing activities for which information systems could provide the greatest boost. The analysis might recommend a system to reduce marketing costs by targeting marketing campaigns more efficiently or by providing information for developing products more finely attuned to a firm's target market. A series of systems, including some linked to systems of other value partners, might be required to create a strategic advantage.

Value chains and value webs are not static. From time to time they may have to be redesigned to keep pace with changes in the competitive landscape (Fine et al., 2002). Companies may need to reorganize and reshape their structural, financial, and human assets and recast systems to tap new sources of value.

We now show how information technology at the business level helps the firm reduce costs, differentiate products, and serve new markets.

INFORMATION SYSTEMS PRODUCTS AND SERVICES

Firms can use information systems to create unique new products and services that can be easily distinguished from those of competitors. Strategic information systems for **product differentiation** can prevent the competition from responding in kind so that firms with these differentiated products and services no longer have to compete on the basis of cost.

Many of these information technology–based products and services have been created by financial institutions. Citibank developed automatic teller machines (ATMs) and bank debit cards in 1977. Citibank is one of the largest banks in the United States. Citibank ATMs were so successful that Citibank's competitors were forced to counterstrike with their own ATM systems. Citibank, Wells Fargo Bank, and others have continued to innovate by providing online electronic banking services so that customers can do most of their banking transactions using home computers linked to the Internet. These banks have recently launched new account aggregation services that enable customers to view all of their accounts, including their credit cards, investments, online travel rewards, and even accounts from competing banks, from a single online source. Some companies, such as NetBank, have used the Web to set up virtual banks offering a full array of banking services without any physical branches. (Customers mail in their deposits and use designated ATMs to obtain cash.)

Computerized reservation systems such as American Airlines's SABRE system started out as a powerful source of product differentiation for the airline and travel industries. These traditional reservation systems are now being challenged by new travel services with which consumers can make their own airline, hotel, and car reservations directly on the Web, bypassing travel agents and other intermediaries.

Manufacturers and retailers are starting to use information systems to create products and services that are custom-tailored to fit the precise specifications of individual customers. Dell Computer Corporation sells directly to customers using assemble-to-order manufacturing. Individuals, businesses, and government agencies can buy computers directly from Dell, customized with the exact features and components they need. They can place their orders directly using a toll-free telephone number or Dell's Web site. Once Dell's production control receives an order, it directs an assembly plant to assemble the computer using components from an on-site warehouse based on the configuration specified by the customer.

SYSTEMS TO FOCUS ON MARKET NICHE

A business can create new market niches by identifying a specific target for a product or service that it can serve in a superior manner. Through **focused differentiation**, the firm can provide a specialized product or service for this narrow target market better than competitors.

Internet Connection —
The Internet Connection for this chapter will take you to the NetBank Web site where you can see how one company used the Internet to create an entirely new type of business. You can complete an exercise for analyzing this Web site's capabilities and its strategic benefits.

An information system can give companies a competitive advantage by producing data for finely tuned sales and marketing techniques. Such systems treat existing information as a resource that the organization can mine to increase profitability and market penetration. Information systems enable companies to analyze customer buying patterns, tastes, and preferences closely so that they efficiently pitch advertising and marketing campaigns to smaller and smaller target markets.

The data come from a range of sources—credit card transactions, demographic data, purchase data from checkout counter scanners at supermarkets and retail stores, and data collected when people access and interact with Web sites. Sophisticated software tools can find patterns in these large pools of data and infer rules from them that can be used to guide decision making. Analysis of such data can drive one-to-one marketing where personal messages can be created based on individualized preferences. Contemporary customer relationship management (CRM) systems feature analytical capabilities for this type of intensive data analysis (see Chapters 2 and 11).

For example, Sears Roebuck continually analyzes purchase data from its 60 million past and present credit card users to target appliance buyers, gardening enthusiasts, and mothers-to-be with special promotions. The company might mail customers who purchase a washer and dryer a maintenance contract and annual contract renewal forms.

The Window on Technology shows how the hotel industry is trying to wring more value out of its customer data. Hotel chains are aggressively recruiting business travelers to sign up with their customer loyalty programs to capture more detailed data about their repeat customers. The customer data they had been collecting through their reservation systems was not sufficiently reliable or detailed for them to develop targeted customer profiles for marketing. The hotels believe such data is key to their growth. More examples of customer data analysis can be found in Chapters 7, 11, and 13.

The cost of acquiring a new customer has been estimated to be five times that of retaining an existing customer. By carefully examining transactions of customer purchases and activities, firms can identify profitable customers and win more of their business. Likewise, companies can use these data to identify nonprofitable customers. Companies that skillfully use customer data focus on identifying their most valued customers and use data from a variety of sources to understand these customers' needs (Reinartz and Kumar, 2002; Davenport, Harris, and Kohli, 2001; Clemons and Weber, 1994).

SUPPLY CHAIN MANAGEMENT AND EFFICIENT CUSTOMER RESPONSE SYSTEMS

A powerful business-level strategy available to digital firms involves linking the value chains of vendors and suppliers to the firm's value chain (Kopczak and Johnson, 2003). Digital firms can carry integration of value chains further by linking the customer's value chain to the firm's value chain in an efficient customer response system. Firms using systems to link with customers and suppliers are able to reduce their inventory costs while responding rapidly to customer demands.

By keeping prices low and shelves well stocked using a legendary inventory replenishment system, Wal-Mart has become the leading retail business in the United States. Wal-Mart's continuous replenishment system sends orders for new merchandise directly to suppliers as soon as consumers pay for their purchases at the cash register. Point-of-sale terminals record the bar code of each item passing the checkout counter and send a purchase transaction directly to a central computer at Wal-Mart headquarters. The computer collects the orders from all Wal-Mart stores and transmits them to suppliers. Suppliers can also access Wal-Mart's sales and inventory data using Web technology.

Because the system can replenish inventory with lightning speed, Wal-Mart does not need to spend much money on maintaining large inventories of goods in its own warehouses. The system also enables Wal-Mart to adjust purchases of store items to meet customer demands. Competitors, such as Sears, have been spending 24.9 percent of sales on overhead. But by using systems to keep operating costs low, Wal-Mart pays only 16.6 percent of sales revenue for overhead. (Operating costs average 20.7 percent of sales in the retail industry.)

WINDOW ON TECHNOLOGY

HOTEL LOYALTY PROGRAMS BECOME COMPETITIVE WEAPONS

Hotels have traditionally used customer loyalty programs to provide incentives for repeat customers. Now they are promoting them even more aggressively, especially for business travelers. Why? The answer lies in the data.

Growing awareness of customer relationship management techniques has made hotels realize they can profit even more than in the past by collecting and analyzing detailed data about their guests. According to Robert Mandelbaum, a hotel analyst with PKF Consulting in Atlanta, the hotel chains are "desperate for data. . . . Hotels need information about their guests and especially about business travelers." Encouraging guests to sign up for customer loyalty programs is "the easiest way to get that information."

Guests signing up for Wyndham Hotels' frequent-guest program provide information about their choice of bed, whether they prefer to relax with a soda or a glass of wine after checking in, the airline frequent flyer program to which they belong, as well as their addresses, e-mail addresses, and phone numbers. Those who sign up online are automatically registered for a monthly "Wyndham News ByRequest" e-mail notice of special members-only offers and program updates.

Guests who refuse to sign up for such programs do not receive as much preferential treatment as those who do. For example, those who do not sign up for Wyndham's ByRequest loyalty program have to pay extra for high-speed Internet access and phone calls. Similarly, Hilton HHonors loyalty program members are allowed to check out late, whereas nonmembers who check out late have to pay for an additional day.

The hotels use such detailed data to better serve their guests, and they also use it to develop targeted sales and marketing campaigns for enlarging their market share. Until recently, these data collection efforts have been woefully inadequate. According to Robert Burke, of Egroup Communications of Miami, which manages e-mail databases for the lodging industry, the U.S. hotel industry had collected data on only about 10 percent of its business travelers. The databases were incomplete or disorganized so that the hotels really knew very little about their guests.

One exception is the Hilton Hotel chain. It spent $50 million on a customer information system called OnQ, which contains 7.5 million profiles of active guests in every property across the eight hotel brands owned by Hilton, including Hilton, Doubletree, Conrad, Embassy Suites, Hampton Inn, Hilton Garden Inn, Hilton Grand Vacations, and Homewood Suites. In combination with Hilton's HHonors frequent-guest program, the system can recognize the same customer whether that person is checking into a $79 room at Hampton Inn or a $540 suite at the Hilton Hawaiian Village in Honolulu.

OnQ was largely custom-developed for Hilton. It includes a property management system and a hotel-owner reporting module, as well as Hilton's customer relationship management applications. All the pieces are integrated with a central reservation system, a sales force automation tool, an older revenue management system, a financial and human resources application from PeopleSoft enterprise software, and Hilton's e-commerce site. The system is delivered as an information technology service to the 52 hotels directly owned by Hilton and hotels that are operated as Hilton franchises. The franchisees license the software for about three-fourths of a percent of their annual revenue.

"TheName, OnQ (pronounced 'On Cue'), supports the Hilton Hotels Corporation Customer Really Matters (CRM) strategy and represents information that is available to team members on demand, prompting them to act on guest 'cues'—preferences and service-recovery alerts—that will delight customers and create a bond of loyalty to the Hilton Family of Hotels," said Tim Harvey, chief information officer for Hilton Hotels Corporation. "OnQ also represents an integrated suite of tools that 'cue' hotel operators to respond decisively to current market conditions and make informed business decisions based on historical trends and competitive data."

OnQ makes it easier to match customer reservations with records of customer profiles in the Hilton database. Employees at the front desk tapping into the system can instantly search through 180 million records to find out the preferences of customers checking in and their past experiences with Hilton so they can give these guests exactly what they want. Before this system was implemented, only 2 out of every 10 guest reservations could be matched to an existing customer profile. OnQ is matching 4.7 and will eventually be able to match 6 out of 10.

One of the main ways OnQ provides value is by establishing the value of each customer to Hilton, based on personal history and on predictions about the value of that person's future business with Hilton. OnQ can also identify customers that are clearly not profitable. Extra attention to profitable customers appears to be paying off. The rate of staying at Hilton Hotels instead of the hotels of rivals has soared to 61 percent from 41 percent two years ago. OnQ will be further put to the test as Hilton opens an additional 125 hotels in 2004 and 150 in 2005.

Sources: Tony Kontzer, "Data-Driven," *Information Week*, August 2, 2004; Hilton Hotels, "Hilton's Customer-Information System, Called OnQ, Rolling Out Across 8 Hotel Brands; Seeking Guest Loyalty and Competitive Advantage with Proprietary Technology," August 31, 2004; and Christopher Elliott, "Hotels Get Pushy About Their Loyalty Programs," *New York Times*, June 1, 2004.

To Think About: Why are frequent-guest programs so important for the hotel industry? How do they provide value? To what extent can OnQ provide the Hilton chain with a competitive advantage? Explain your answer.

Wal-Mart's continuous inventory replenishment system uses sales data captured at the checkout counter to transmit orders to restock merchandise directly to its suppliers. The system enables Wal-Mart to keep costs low while fine-tuning its merchandise to meet customer demands.

Wal-Mart's continuous replenishment system is an example of efficient supply chain management, which we introduced in Chapter 2. Supply chain management systems can not only lower inventory costs, but they also can deliver the product or service more rapidly to the customer. Supply chain management plays an important role in **efficient customer response systems** that respond to customer demands more efficiently. An efficient customer response system directly links consumer behavior to distribution and production and supply chains. Production begins after the customer purchases or orders a product. Wal-Mart's continuous replenishment system provides such an efficient customer response. Dell Computer Corporation's assemble-to-order system, described earlier, is another example of an efficient customer response system.

The convenience and ease of using these information systems raise **switching costs** (the cost of switching from one product to a competing product), which discourages customers from going to competitors. Another example is Baxter International's stockless inventory and ordering system, which uses supply chain management to create an efficient customer response system. Participating hospitals become unwilling to switch to another supplier because of the system's convenience and low cost. Baxter supplies nearly two-thirds of all products used by U.S. hospitals. When hospitals want to place an order, they do not need to call a salesperson or send a purchase order—they simply use a desktop computer that links electronically to Baxter's supply catalog either through proprietary software or through the Web. The system generates shipping, billing, invoicing, and inventory information, providing customers with an estimated delivery date. With more than 80 distribution centers in the United States, Baxter can make daily deliveries of its products, often within hours of receiving an order.

Baxter delivery personnel no longer drop off their cartons at loading docks to be placed in hospital storerooms. Instead, they deliver orders directly to the hospital corridors, dropping them at nursing stations, operating rooms, and supply closets. This has created in effect a "stockless inventory," with Baxter serving as the hospitals' warehouse.

Figure 3-13 compares stockless inventory with the just-in-time supply method and traditional inventory practices. Whereas just-in-time inventory enables customers to reduce their inventories by ordering only enough material for a few days' inventory, stockless inventory enables them to eliminate their inventories entirely. All inventory responsibilities shift to the distributor, which manages the supply flow. The stockless inventory is a powerful instrument for locking in customers, thus giving the supplier a decided competitive advantage. Information systems can also raise switching costs by making product support, service, and other interactions with customers more convenient and reliable (Vandenbosch and Dawar, 2002).

Supply chain management and efficient customer response systems are two examples of how emerging digital firms engage in business strategies not available to traditional firms. Both types of systems require network-based information technology infrastructure investment and software competence to make customer and supply chain data flow

FIGURE 3-13 *Stockless inventory compared to traditional and just-in-time supply methods.*

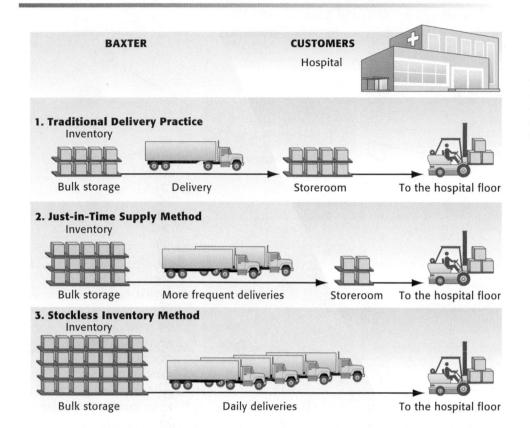

The just-in-time supply method reduces inventory requirements of the customer, whereas stockless inventory enables the customer to eliminate inventories entirely. Deliveries are made daily, sometimes directly to the departments that need the supplies.

seamlessly among different organizations. Both types of strategies have greatly enhanced the efficiency of individual firms and the U.S. economy as a whole by moving toward a demand-pull production system and away from the traditional supply-push economic system in which factories were managed on the basis of 12-month official plans rather than on near-instantaneous customer purchase information. Chapter 10 provides more detail on this topic. Figure 3-14 illustrates the relationships between supply chain management, efficient customer response, and the various business-level strategies.

Firm-Level Strategy and Information Technology

A business firm is typically a collection of businesses. Often, the firm is organized financially as a collection of strategic business units, and the returns to the firm are directly tied to strategic business unit performance. Information systems can improve the overall performance of these business units by promoting synergies and core competencies. The idea driving synergies is that when the output of some units can be used as inputs to other units, or two organizations can pool markets and expertise, these relationships can lower costs and generate profits. Recent bank and financial firm mergers, such as the merger of J. P. Morgan Chase and Bank One Corporation, Bank of America and FleetBoston Financial Corporation, Deutsche Bank and Bankers Trust, and Citicorp and Travelers Insurance, occurred precisely for this purpose.

One use of information technology in these synergy situations is to tie together the operations of disparate business units so that they can act as a whole. For example, merging with Bank One provides JP Morgan Chase with a massive network of retail branches in the Midwest and Southwest. Information systems would help the merged banks lower retailing costs and increase cross-marketing of financial products.

ENHANCING CORE COMPETENCIES

A second concept for firm-level strategy involves the notion of core competency. The argument is that the performance of all business units can increase insofar as these

FIGURE 3-14 *Business-level strategy.*

Efficient customer response and supply chain management systems are often inter-related, helping firms lock in customers and suppliers while lowering operating costs. Other types of systems can be used to support product differentiation, focused differentiation, and low-cost producer strategies.

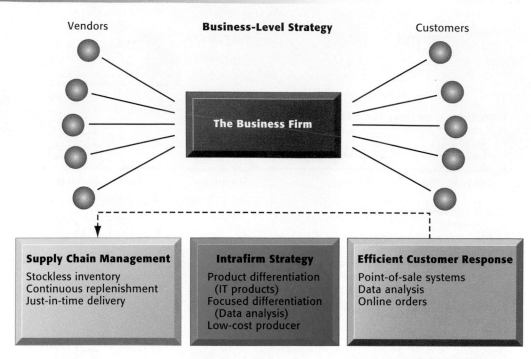

business units develop, or create, a central core of competencies. A **core competency** is an activity for which a firm is a world-class leader. Core competencies may involve being the world's best miniature parts designer, the best package delivery service, or the best thin-film manufacturer. In general, a core competency relies on knowledge that is gained over many years of experience and a first-class research organization or simply key people who follow the literature and stay abreast of new external knowledge.

Any information system that encourages the sharing of knowledge across business units enhances competency. Such systems might encourage or enhance existing competencies and help employees become aware of new external knowledge; such systems might also help a business leverage existing competencies to related markets.

Industry-Level Strategy and Information Systems: Competitive Forces and Network Economics

Firms together comprise an industry, such as the automotive industry, telephone, television broadcasting, and forest products industries, to name a few. The key strategic question at this level of analysis is, "How and when should we compete with as opposed to cooperate with others in the industry?" Whereas most strategic analyses emphasize competition, a great deal of money can be made by cooperating with other firms in the same industry or firms in related industries. For instance, firms can cooperate to develop industry standards in a number of areas; they can cooperate by working together to build customer awareness and by working collectively with suppliers to lower costs. The principal concepts for analyzing strategy at the industry level are information partnerships, the competitive forces model, business ecosystems, and network economics.

INFORMATION PARTNERSHIPS

Firms can form information partnerships and even link their information systems to achieve unique synergies. In an **information partnership**, both companies can join forces without actually merging by sharing information. American Airlines has an arrangement with Citibank to award one mile in its frequent flier program for every dollar spent using Citibank credit cards. American benefits from increased customer loyalty, and Citibank gains new credit card subscribers and a highly creditworthy customer base for cross-marketing. Northwest Airlines has a similar arrangement with U.S. Bank. American and Northwest have also allied with MCI, awarding frequent flier miles for each dollar of long-distance billing.

Such partnerships help firms gain access to new customers, creating new opportunities for cross-selling and targeting products. Companies that have been traditional competitors may find such alliances to be mutually advantageous. Baxter Healthcare International offers its customers medical supplies from competitors and office supplies through its electronic ordering channel.

THE COMPETITIVE FORCES MODEL

In Porter's **competitive forces model**, which is illustrated in Figure 3-15, a firm faces a number of external threats and opportunities: the threat of new entrants into its market, the pressure from substitute products or services, the bargaining power of customers, the bargaining power of suppliers, and the positioning of traditional industry competitors (Porter 1985). The nature of the players in an industry and their relative bargaining power determine **industry structure** and the overall profitability of doing business in the industry's specific environment.

Competitive advantage can be achieved by enhancing the firm's ability to deal with customers, suppliers, substitute products and services, and new entrants to its market, which in turn may change the balance of power between a firm and other competitors in the industry in the firm's favor.

How can information systems be used to achieve strategic advantage at the industry level? By working with other firms, industry participants can use information technology to develop industry-wide standards for exchanging information or business transactions electronically (see Chapters 6, 8, and 9), which force all market participants to subscribe to similar standards. Earlier we described how firms can benefit from value webs with complementary firms in the industry. Such efforts increase efficiency at the industry level as well as at the business level—making product substitution less likely and perhaps raising entry costs—thus discouraging new entrants. Also, industry members can build industry-wide, IT-supported consortia, symposia, and communications networks to coordinate activities concerning government agencies, foreign competition, and competing industries.

An example of such industry-level cooperation can be found in Exostar, an electronic marketplace shared by major aerospace and defense firms for procurement and for cooperation on joint development projects. These companies can raise the industry's productivity by working together to create an integrated supply chain.

In the age of the Internet, the traditional competitive forces are still at work, but competitive rivalry has become much more intense (Porter, 2001). Internet technology is

FIGURE 3-15   *Porter's competitive forces model.*

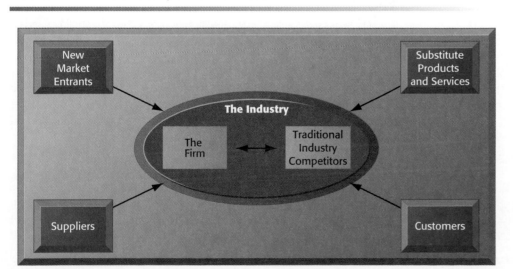

Various forces affect an organization's ability to compete and therefore greatly influence a firm's business strategy. There are threats from new market entrants and from substitute products and services. Customers and suppliers wield bargaining power. Traditional competitors constantly adapt their strategies to maintain their market positioning.

based on universal standards that any company can use, making it easy for rivals to compete on price alone and for new competitors to enter the market. Because information is available to everyone, the Internet raises the bargaining power of customers, who can quickly find the lowest-cost provider on the Web. Profits have been dampened. Some industries, such as the travel industry and the financial services industry, have been more impacted than others. Table 3-5 summarizes some of the potentially negative impacts of the Internet for business firms.

However, contrary to Porter's somewhat negative assessment, the Internet also creates new opportunities for building brands and building very large and loyal customer bases that are willing to pay a premium for the brand, for example, Yahoo!, eBay, Amazon, Google, and many others. In addition, as with all IT-enabled business initiatives, some firms are far better at using the Internet than other firms are, which creates new strategic opportunities for the successful firms.

BUSINESS ECOSYSTEMS: KEYSTONE AND NICHE FIRMS

The Internet and the emergence of digital firms call for some modification of the industry competitive forces model. The traditional Porter model assumes a relatively static industry environment; relatively clear-cut industry boundaries; and a relatively stable set of suppliers, substitutes, and customers, with the focus on industry players in a market environment. Instead of participating in a single industry, some of today's firms are much more aware that they participate in industry sets—collections of industries that provide related services and products (see Figure 3-16). **Business ecosystem** is another term for these loosely coupled but interdependent networks of suppliers, distributors, outsourcing firms, transportation service firms, and technology manufacturers (Iansiti and Levien, 2004).

The concept of a business ecosystem builds on the idea of the value web described earlier, the main difference being that cooperation takes place across many industries rather than many firms. For instance, both Microsoft and Wal-Mart provide platforms composed of information systems, technologies, and services that thousands of other firms in different industries use to enhance their own capabilities. Microsoft has estimated that more than 40,000 firms use its Windows platform to deliver their own products, support Microsoft products, and extend the value of Microsoft's own firm. Wal-Mart's order entry and inventory management system is a platform used by thousands of suppliers to obtain real-time access to customer demand, track shipments, and control inventories (as described in the chapter-opening case).

Business ecosystems can be characterized as having one or a few keystone firms that dominate the ecosystem and create the platforms used by other niche firms. Keystone

TABLE 3-5 *Impact of the Internet on Competitive Forces and Industry Structure*

Competitive Force	Impact of the Internet
Substitute products or services	Enables new substitutes to emerge with new approaches to meeting needs and performing functions.
Customers' bargaining power	Availability of global price and product information shifts bargaining power to customers.
Suppliers' bargaining power	Procurement over the Internet tends to raise bargaining power over suppliers. Suppliers can also benefit from reduced barriers to entry and from the elimination of distributors and other intermediaries standing between them and their users.
Threat of new entrants	The Internet reduces barriers to entry, such as the need for a sales force, access to channels, and physical assets. It provides a technology for driving business processes that makes other things easier to do.
Positioning and rivalry among existing competitors	Widens the geographic market, increasing the number of competitors, and reduces differences among competitors. Makes it more difficult to sustain operational advantages. Puts pressure to compete on price.

FIGURE 3-16   An ecosystem strategic model.

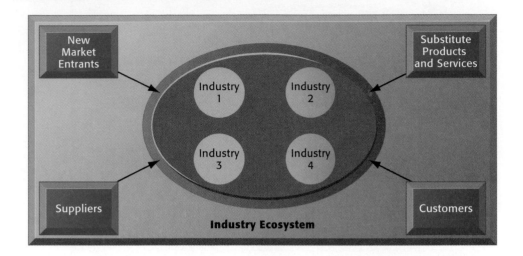

The digital firm era requires a more dynamic view of the boundaries among industries, firms, customers, and suppliers, with competition occurring among industry sets in a business ecosystem. In the ecosystem model, multiple industries work together to deliver value to the customer. IT plays an important role in enabling a dense network of interactions among the participating firms.

firms in the Microsoft ecosystem would include Microsoft and technology producers such as Intel and IBM. Niche firms include thousands of software application firms, software developers, service firms, networking firms, and consulting firms that both support and rely on the Microsoft products.

Alternatively, it is equally possible to think of ecosystems at the industry level. The computer chip, automobile, aircraft, and medical device industries can be usefully seen as industrial sets or ecosystems that involve the cooperation of multiple other industries to function efficiently or even survive. For instance, the medical device industry relies on a university research community for innovative designs and research, on the microprocessor industry for sensors and controls, and on the precision machining industry for production.

Information technology plays a powerful role in establishing business ecosystems. Obviously, many firms use information systems to develop into keystone firms by building IT-based platforms that other firms can use. For instance, eBay has created a platform for auctions and online stores used by over 400,000 small businesses every day. Amazon.com and portals such as Yahoo! have created online store business platforms used by Fortune 500 firms such as Dell (and thousands of smaller firms) to sell directly to the public. In the digital firm era, we can expect greater emphasis on the use of IT to build industry ecosystems because the costs of participating in such ecosystems will fall and the benefits to all firms will increase rapidly as the platform grows (see the following discussion of network economics).

Individual firms should consider how their investments in IT will enable them to become profitable niche players in larger ecosystems created by keystone firms. For instance, in making decisions about which products to build or which services to offer, a firm should consider the existing business ecosystems these products are related to and how it might use IT to enable participation in these larger ecosystems.

NETWORK ECONOMICS

A final strategic concept useful at the industry level is **network economics**. In traditional economics—the economics of factories and agriculture—production experiences diminishing returns. After a certain point, the more any given resource is applied to production, the lower the marginal gain in output, until a point is reached where the additional inputs produce no additional outputs. This is the law of diminishing returns, and it is the foundation for most of modern economics.

In some situations the law of diminishing returns does not work. For instance, in a network, the marginal costs of adding another participant are about zero, whereas the marginal gain is much larger. The larger the number of subscribers in a telephone system, or the Internet, the greater the value to all participants because each user can interact with more people (see Chapters 6 and 8 for more detailed discussions of network economics). It is no more expensive to operate a television station with 1,000 subscribers than with 10 million eBay provides a platform for over 400,000 small and large businesses to operate online storefronts and auctions. A massive information system powers this business ecosystem.

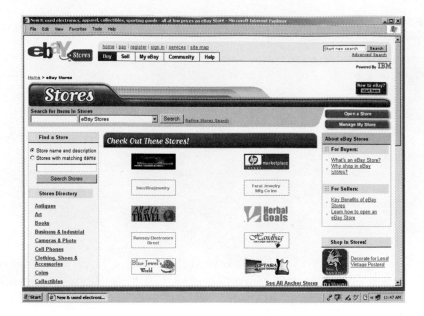

subscribers. And the value of a community of people grows exponentially with size, whereas the cost of adding new members is inconsequential.

Network economics plays an underlying role in the ecosystem model described earlier insofar as participants in the ecosystem gain value as the ecosystem grows in power. From this network economics perspective, information technology can be strategically useful. Internet sites can be used by firms to build communities of users—like-minded customers who want to share their experiences. This can build customer loyalty and enjoyment and build unique ties to customers. eBay, the giant online auction site, and iVillage, an online community for women, are examples. Both businesses are based on networks of millions of users, and both companies have used the Web and Internet communication tools to build communities. The more people offering products on eBay, the more valuable is the eBay site to everyone because more products arc listed and more competition among suppliers lowers prices. Network economics can also provide strategic benefits to commercial software vendors. The value of their software and complementary software products increases as more people use them, and there is a larger installed base to justify continued use of the product and vendor support (Gallaugher and Wang, 2002).

3.5   MANAGEMENT OPPORTUNITIES, CHALLENGES, AND SOLUTIONS

We have seen that the relationship between information systems and organizational performance is very complex, providing managers with both opportunities and challenges.

Opportunities

Business firms face a continuing stream of IT-enabled opportunities to lower their transaction and agency costs and to harness the power of the new information technologies that appear regularly to develop unique products, services, and processes. Clearly, some firms will excel in learning how to use the technology, and because of this fact there are opportunities for strategic competitive advantages at all three levels—business, firm, and industry.

Management Challenges

Some firms achieve better organizational performance and strategic advantage with systems, often after overcoming significant hurdles.

DIFFICULTIES OF SUSTAINING COMPETITIVE ADVANTAGE

Competitive advantages, regardless of their origin, do not last forever. Competitors will always attempt to copy the information systems a firm uses if they provide competitive advantage. Markets, customer expectations, and technology are also continually changing and providing competitors with new opportunities to achieve their own advantages. Nevertheless, information systems do provide many large and small firms with strategic advantages for significant periods of time. Wal-Mart's efficient customer response and supply chain systems are not easily imitated, although many have tried (and failed). Even if a firm's systems can be copied, the business processes and industry relationships underlying those systems often cannot be replicated. Moreover, firms that achieve a strategic advantage by making early investments in information technology can often apply their experience and knowledge to new investments that confer new strategic advantages later on.

DIFFICULTIES OF MANAGING SYSTEM-RELATED CHANGE

Bringing about change through new information technology and systems is slowed considerably by the natural inertia of organizations. Of course, organizations can and do change, but the process is more complicated and much slower than is typically anticipated.

Solution Guidelines

Strategic information systems often change the organization as well as its products, services, and business processes, driving the organization into new behavioral patterns. Using technology for strategic benefit requires careful planning and management.

PERFORMING A STRATEGIC SYSTEMS ANALYSIS

Managers interested in using information systems for competitive advantage will need to perform a strategic systems analysis. To identify the types of systems that would provide a strategic advantage to their firms, managers should ask the following questions:

1. What is the structure of the industry in which the firm is located?
   - What are some of the competitive forces at work in the industry? Are there new entrants to the industry? What is the relative power of suppliers, customers, and substitute products and services over prices?
   - Is the basis of competition quality, price, or brand?
   - What are the direction and nature of change within the industry? From where are the momentum and change coming?
   - How is the industry currently using information technology? Is the organization behind or ahead of the industry in its application of information systems?

2. What are the business, firm, and industry value chains for this particular firm?
   - How is the company creating value for the customer—through lower prices and transaction costs or higher quality? Are there any places in the value chain where the business could create more value for the customer and additional profit for the company?
   - Does the firm understand and manage its business processes using the best practices available? Is it taking maximum advantage of supply chain management, customer relationship management, and enterprise systems?
   - Does the firm leverage its core competencies?
   - Is the industry supply chain and customer base changing in ways that benefit or harm the firm?
   - Could the firm benefit from strategic partnerships and value webs?
   - Where in the value chain would information systems provide the greatest value to the firm?

MANAGING STRATEGIC TRANSITIONS

Adopting the kinds of strategic systems described in this chapter generally requires changes in business goals, relationships with customers and suppliers, internal operations, and information architecture. These sociotechnical changes, affecting both social and technical elements of the organization, can be considered **strategic transitions**—a movement between levels of sociotechnical systems.

Such changes often entail blurring of organizational boundaries, both external and internal. Suppliers and customers must become intimately linked and may share each other's responsibilities. For instance, in Baxter International's stockless inventory system, Baxter has assumed responsibility for managing its customers' inventories (Johnston and Vitale, 1988). Managers will need to devise new business processes for coordinating their firms' activities with those of customers, suppliers, and other organizations. The organizational change requirements surrounding new information systems are so important that they merit attention throughout this text. Chapters 14 and 15 examine organizational change issues in greater detail.

MAKE IT YOUR BUSINESS

Finance and Accounting

Information systems promote better management of the firm's assets and cash flows that can increase revenues and reduce operating costs, thereby enhancing its competitive position. Online systems provide more immediate tracking and identification of the firm's assets and the return on the firm's investments. The accounting function can monitor transaction flows and keep track of costs and revenues more precisely in real time. Tracking and identifying changes in assets and fund flows that previously took weeks can now be accomplished in hours or days. New financial products and services based on information systems have been a source of strategic advantage.

Human Resources

Information systems lower agency costs, enabling the firm to manage more employees with fewer resources. Networked systems also make it possible to create work groups outside traditional places of work. Employees from many different locations can use information systems to work together on virtual teams. Understanding human resources issues is essential for successful system implementation because people need to adjust to the organizational change created by introducing a new information system.

Manufacturing and Production

Information systems can be used to streamline manufacturing and production processes so that they require fewer steps and less human intervention. By taking advantage of more precise flows of information, firms can tighten coordination of production and distribution, lowering transaction and agency costs. You can find examples of manufacturing and production applications on pages 71 and 109–111.

Sales and Marketing

Information systems provide a rich new set of capabilities for fine-tuning sales and marketing that are often a source of competitive advantage. Systems can be used to analyze vast pools of data for highly targeted marketing campaigns, and they can also generate unique new products and services that the organization can sell. Efficient customer response systems can improve sales by tightly coordinating production and distribution with customer orders. You can find examples of sales and marketing applications on pages 71, 79, 95 and 109–111.

Summary

1. *Identify and describe important features of organizations that managers need to know about in order to build and use information systems successfully.*

    Managers need to understand certain essential features of organizations to build and use information systems successfully. All modern organizations are hierarchical, specialized, and impartial. They use explicit routines to maximize efficiency. All organizations have their own cultures and politics arising from differences in interest groups. Organizations differ in goals, groups served, social roles, leadership styles, incentives, surrounding environments, and types of tasks performed. These differences create varying types of organizational structures, and they also help explain differences in organizations' use of information systems.

2. *Evaluate the impact of information systems on organizations.*

Information systems and the organizations in which they are used interact with and influence each other. The introduction of a new information system will affect organizational structure, goals, work design, values, competition between interest groups, decision making, and day-to-day behavior. At the same time, information systems must be designed to serve the needs of important organizational groups and will be shaped by the organization's structure, tasks, goals, culture, politics, and management. Information technology can reduce transaction and agency costs, and such changes have been accentuated in organizations using the Internet. The information systems department is the formal organizational unit that is responsible for the organization's information systems function. Organizational characteristics and managerial decisions determine the role this group will actually play.

3. *Assess how information systems support the activities of managers in organizations.*

Several different models of what managers actually do in organizations show how information systems can be used for managerial support. Early classical models of managerial activities stress the functions of planning, organizing, coordinating, deciding, and controlling. Contemporary research looking at the actual behavior of managers has found that managers' real activities are highly fragmented, variegated, and brief in duration, with managers moving rapidly and intensely from one issue to another. Managers spend considerable time pursuing personal agendas and goals, and contemporary managers shy away from making grand, sweeping policy decisions.

Decision making can also take place at the individual or group level. Individual models of decision making assume that human beings can rationally choose alternatives and consequences based on the priority of their objectives and goals. Organizational models of decision making illustrate that real decision making in organizations takes place in arenas where many psychological, political, and bureaucratic forces are at work.

Information technology provides new tools for managers to carry out both their traditional and newer roles, enabling them to monitor, plan, and forecast with more precision and speed than ever before and to respond more rapidly to the changing business environment. Information systems have been most helpful to managers by providing support for their roles in disseminating information, providing liaisons between organizational levels, and allocating resources. However, some managerial roles cannot be supported by information systems, and information systems are less successful at supporting unstructured decisions.

4. *Analyze how information systems support various business strategies for competitive advantage.*

Businesses can use strategic information systems to gain an edge over competitors. Such systems change organizations' goals, business processes, products, services, or environmental relationships, driving them into new forms of behavior.

Information systems can be used to support strategy at the business, firm, and industry levels. At the business level of strategy, information systems can be used to help firms become the low-cost producers, differentiate products and services, or serve new markets. Information systems can also be used to lock in customers and suppliers using efficient customer response and supply chain management applications. Value chain analysis is useful at the business level to highlight specific activities in the business where information systems are most likely to have a strategic impact.

At the firm level, information systems can be used to achieve new efficiencies or to enhance services by tying together the operations of disparate business units so that they can function as a whole or promote the sharing of knowledge across business units.

At the industry level, systems can promote competitive advantage by facilitating cooperation with other firms in the industry, creating consortiums or communities for sharing information, exchanging transactions, or coordinating activities. The competitive forces model, information partnerships, business ecosystems, and network economics are useful concepts for identifying strategic opportunities for systems at the industry level.

5. *Assess the challenges posed by strategic information systems and management solutions.*

Information systems are closely intertwined with an organization's structure, culture, and business processes. New systems disrupt established patterns of work and power relationships, so there is often considerable resistance to them when they are introduced.

Implementing strategic systems often requires extensive organizational change and a transition from one sociotechnical level to another. Such changes are called *strategic transitions* and are often difficult and painful to achieve. Moreover, not all strategic systems are profitable, and they can be expensive to build. Many strategic information systems are easily copied by other firms so that strategic advantage is not always sustainable. The complex relationship between information systems, organizational performance, and decision making must be carefully managed. A strategic system analysis is helpful.

Key Terms

Review Questions

1. *What is an organization? Compare the technical definition of organizations with the behavioral definition.*

2. *What features do all organizations have in common? In which ways can organizations differ?*

3. *How are information technology services delivered in organizations? Describe the role played by programmers, systems analysts, information systems managers, and the chief information officer (CIO).*

4. *Describe the major economic theories that help explain how information systems affect organizations.*

5. *Describe the major behavioral theories that help explain how information systems affect organizations.*

6. *Why is there considerable organizational resistance to the introduction of information systems?*

7. *Compare the descriptions of managerial behavior in the classical and behavioral models.*

8. *Which specific managerial roles can information systems support? Where are information systems particularly strong in supporting managers, and where are they weak?*

9. *Compare individual and organizational models of decision making.*

10. *What is the impact of the Internet on organizations and the process of management?*

11. *Describe appropriate models for analyzing strategy at the business level and the types of strategies and information systems that can be used to compete at this level.*

12. *Describe appropriate strategies for the firm level and how information systems can help companies compete at this level.*

13. *How can the competitive forces model, information partnerships, business ecosystems, and network economics be used to identify strategies at the industry level?*

14. *How have the value chain and competitive forces models changed as a result of the Internet and the emergence of digital firms?*

15. *Describe the management challenges posed by the role of information systems in organizations and suggest some solutions.*

Discussion Questions

1. *It has been said that there is no such thing as a sustainable strategic advantage. Do you agree? Why or why not?*

2. *It has been said that the advantage that leading-edge retailers such as Dell and Wal-Mart have over their* competition isn't technology; it's their management. *Do you agree? Why or why not?*

Application Software Exercise:
Database Exercise: Using a Database for Strategic Business Development

The Presidents' Inn is a small three-story hotel on the Atlantic Ocean in Cape May, New Jersey, a popular northeastern U.S. resort. Ten rooms overlook side streets, 10 rooms have bay windows that offer limited views of the ocean, and the remaining 10 rooms in the front of the hotel face the ocean. Room rates are based on room choice, length of stay, and number of guests per room. Room rates are the same for one to four guests. Fifth and sixth guests must pay an additional $20 charge each per day. Guests staying for seven days or more receive a 10 percent discount on their daily room rates.

Business has grown steadily during the past 10 years. Now totally renovated, the hotel uses a romantic weekend package to attract couples, a vacation package to attract young families, and a weekday discount package to attract business travelers. The owners currently use a manual reservation and bookkeeping system, which has caused many problems. Sometimes two families have been booked in the same room at the same time. Management does not have immediate data about the hotel's daily operations and income.

Use the information provided in this description and in the database tables at www.prenhall.com/Laudon in the Chapter 3 area to develop reports that would provide information to help management make the business more competitive and profitable. The database and related queries should be designed to make it easy to identify information, such as the average length of stay per room type, the average number of visitors per room type, and the base income per room (i.e., length of visit multiplied by the daily rate) during a specified period of time.

After identifying the preceding information, write a brief report describing what the database information reveals about the current business situation. For example, what is the strongest customer base? Which specific business strategies might be pursued to increase room occupancy and revenue? How could the database be improved to provide better information for strategic decisions?

Performing a Competitive Analysis for Dirt Bikes

Software requirements:　Web browser software
　　　　　　　　　　　Word processing software
　　　　　　　　　　　Electronic presentation software (optional)

Dirt Bikes's management would like to be sure it is pursuing the right competitive strategy. You have been asked to perform a competitive analysis of the company using the Web to find the information you need. Prepare a report that analyzes Dirt Bikes using the value chain and competitive forces models. Your report should include the following:

1. Which activities at Dirt Bikes create the most value?

2. How does Dirt Bikes provide value to its customers?

3. What other companies are Dirt Bikes's major competitors? How do their products compare in price to those of Dirt Bikes? What are some of the product features they emphasize?

4. What are the competitive forces that can affect the industry?

5. What competitive strategy should Dirt Bikes pursue?

6. (Optional) Use electronic presentation software to summarize your findings for management.

Electronic Commerce Project: Configuring and Pricing an Automobile

Your current seven-year-old car has tried your patience one too many times and you decide to purchase a new automobile. You have been interested in a Ford family car and want to investigate the Ford Taurus (if you are personally interested in another car, domestic or foreign, investigate that one instead). Go to the Web site of CarsDirect (www.carsdirect.com) and begin your investigation. Locate the Ford Taurus. Research the various specific automobiles available in that model and determine which you would prefer. Explore full details about the specific car, including pricing, standard features, and options. Locate and read at least two reviews if possible. Also investigate the safety of that model based on the U.S. government crash tests performed by the National Highway Traffic Safety Administration if those test results are available. Explore the features for locating a vehicle in inventory and purchasing directly. Finally, explore the other capabilities of the CarsDirect site for financing.

Having recorded or printed the information you need from CarsDirect for your purchase decision, surf to the Web site of the manufacturer, in this case Ford (www.ford.com). Compare the information available on this Web site for the Ford Taurus. Be sure to check the price and any incentives being offered (which may disagree with what you found at CarsDirect). Next, find a dealer on the Ford site so that you can view the car before making your purchase decision. Explore the other features of this Web site.

Finally, visit a third site, Edmunds (www.edmunds.com) and research the car you have selected as you did on CarsDirect. Compare the information you found at this site with the information provided by CarsDirect and the auto manufacturer site and try to locate the lowest price for the car you want in a local dealer's inventory. Which site would you use to purchase your car? Why? Also, suggest improvements for the sites of CarsDirect, Ford, and Edmunds.

Group Project: Identifying Opportunities for Strategic Information Systems

With a group of three or four students, select a company described in the *Wall Street Journal*, *Fortune*, *Forbes*, or another business publication. Visit the company's Web site to find additional information about that company and to see how the firm is using the Web. On the basis of this information, analyze the business. Include a description of the organization's features, such as important business processes, culture, structure, and environment, as well as its business strategy. Suggest strategic information systems appropriate for that particular business, including those based on Internet technology, if appropriate. If possible, use electronic presentation software to present your findings to the class.

CASE STUDY
Can Albertsons Trounce Wal-Mart with Advanced Information Technology?

With 2,305 retail stores in 31 states, Albertsons is one of the largest retail food and drug chains in the world. Among these retail stores are 1,351 combination food-drug stores, 707 standalone drugstores, and 247 conventional and warehouse stores. Stores flying the Albertsons flag include Albertsons, Albertsons Express, Albertsons-Osco, Albertsons-Sav-on, Jewel, Jewel-Osco, Acme, Sav-on Drugs, Osco Drug, Max Foods, and Super Saver Foods.

Albertsons' marketing vow is to "Make Life Easier for Our Customers." This credo plays a large part in another of the company's priorities, which is to make Albertsons the number one grocer in the United States. Wal-Mart currently holds that distinction with $56 million in annual revenue from its grocery departments. Albertsons stands in third place, $20 million behind Wal-Mart in revenue.

Wal-Mart has been selling groceries for a mere 16 years, making it a relative newcomer in the industry compared to most of its competitors. Of course, Wal-Mart does have vast retail experience, massive purchasing power, and leading-edge systems to apply to its grocery business to catapult it ahead of the competition. Wal-Mart's supply chain management systems are extremely quick and efficient. They keep inventory down to the necessary minimums and operating costs low so that overhead takes a much smaller chunk out of the company's sales revenue. Wal-Mart's Retail Link network pulls in point-of-sale data from its retail stores every 15 minutes, giving suppliers incredibly up-to-date information on how their products are selling. Other retailers capture sales data only once or twice each day.

To move up to the top rung of the ladder, Albertsons has borrowed a page from Wal-Mart's book and written a few new pages of its own. The author of these efforts is CEO and president Larry Johnston. Johnston came to Albertsons from a highly suc-

cessful corporate environment, having worked under Jack Welch during the peak of his tenure at General Electric. Johnston wants to use information technology to keep prices competitive while making the shopping experience more compelling. He also wants to bolster the company's leadership with the best minds available and use motivational techniques to invigorate his employees. By approaching business strategy on these two fronts, Johnston hopes to distance Albertsons from competitors such as Kroger and Safeway and catch up to industry leader Wal-Mart.

Albertsons earmarked half a billion dollars for technology advancements in 2004. One goal of this investment is to improve the company's profit margin. Profit margins are razor-thin in the supermarket business, averaging around one cent per dollar of sales. Currently, Albertsons earns 1.4 cents for every dollar of merchandise that it sells. Wal-Mart is famous for keeping the prices of its merchandise low, but still manages to earn more than 3 cents for every dollar of sales. Albertsons must close that margin if it is to become the number one grocer in the United States. Working against Albertsons is the fact that its merchandise sells for 20 to 25 percent more on average than Wal-Mart's product offerings. Albertsons has a wide gap to overcome.

The technology strategies put forth by Larry Johnston cover a wide range of the company's operations. Albertsons has begun to install self-service checkout stations in some of its stores. These stations enable customers to scan the items they are buying to create a sales bill and pay for the items by swiping a credit or debit card, all without the intervention of a cashier. Using a handheld scanner, customers may scan their purchases as they place them in their shopping cart, resulting in a checkout process that may take only a few seconds. Not having to wait in line to pay at the supermarket can be a major

draw for customers. Albertsons views this improvement to the shopping experience as exactly the type of change it wants to implement to keep its current customers happy, bring in new customers, and thereby increase sales revenue.

Of course, self-service checkout stations provide Albertsons with another benefit: They cut personnel costs. The stations enable Albertsons to replace human cashiers with machines that do not earn wages. Cutting payroll is a critical aspect of the company's repositioning, especially when you compare wage numbers with Wal-Mart. The average Wal-Mart worker earns about $8.50 per hour. Albertsons pays its average worker in the neighborhood of $13 per hour. In addition, Albertsons extends benefits to its employees, including health insurance and retirement packages that, in some cases, nearly double the value of the employee's total compensation. The company line says that installing self-service checkout facilities is intended solely to create a better shopping experience for the customer. Retail analysts seem to think otherwise, saying that such claims are transparent; eliminating cashier positions could produce savings in excess of $100 million for Albertsons.

Larry Johnston's plans for technology-enabled grocery stores include a completely digital shopping experience that begins in the home and involves the Internet and Global Positioning System satellite technology. Customers would be able to set up their shopping lists from home through an Internet portal that is connected to their local Albertsons store. They could also add information to their accounts such as allergies and dietary restrictions. When customers arrive at the store, they would use a customer loyalty card to obtain a handheld device. The device would download the shopping list and any other important information, and then sync up with the store's inventory. The device would guide customers through the store on the most efficient path to gather and scan all of their items. In addition, customers could receive text messages notifying them about special offers, photos and prescriptions ready for pickup, and conflicts between scanned items and the customer's preset dietary or allergy restrictions. Under such a system, a customer account could be linked to a credit card and checkout would be reduced to passing through an electronic gate.

Introducing such a radical change in shopping habits will not be easy. For now, Albertsons has deployed handheld scanning devices in only a few stores. To roll out widespread use of the scanners and self-service checkout, as well as Johnston's grander vision of a wired supermarket, Albertsons will have to persuade two important groups of people that such changes are a good idea. The company will have to convince its store employees that a more independent customer is good for business. At the same time, the employees know that some of their services will be rendered unnecessary, thousands of their colleagues have lost their jobs already, and they have run into strong resistance in their pursuit of higher salaries and better benefits. The attitude of the employees is critical to the success of the company and there are no assurances of cooperation with a vision that could reduce their role.

As if that weren't enough of a concern, Albertsons' customers also would have to buy into Johnston's vision for high-tech shopping. Michael Lenz, a retail supply-chain analyst for the Canadian firm Thinking Group, notes, "You're going to the store for bread, milk, and eggs. It might be a little overwhelming for some folks." Wal-Mart explicitly tries to keep technology in the background to keep customer shopping experiences simple. On the other hand, if Johnston's futuristic store proves to be successful, Albertsons would gain a significant edge over Wal-Mart.

Another Albertsons goal is simply to have current customers buy more when they visit the store. The key to

such a goal is cataloging and analyzing purchase data. Albertsons invested $50 million in an NCR Teradata warehouse to examine customer buying habits. By providing customer loyalty cards, Albertsons can give loyal customers special offers and track exactly what they buy and when they buy it.

Analytics software from KhiMetrics of Scottsdale, Arizona, enables Albertsons to determine, for example, whether lowering the price of a box of Wheaties by 15 cents will bring in more profits by increasing sales than would increasing the price by 15 cents. The software will also tell Albertsons which products, such as milk and bread, need lower prices to prevent shoppers from defecting to Wal-Mart and which items aren't so critical.

Albertsons is working to reduce costs in its supply chain so that its stores can offer prices that are more competitive with Wal-Mart's prices. Johnston has consolidated distribution centers and is using the Web to coordinate shipments and to reduce billing and invoicing costs. The company has also upgraded its core corporate systems, moving financial applications to software from Oracle and its human resources management to PeopleSoft software.

Chief Technology Officer Bob Dunst intends to overhaul 90 percent of the company's applications by 2007. In addition to the Oracle and PeopleSoft adoptions, he has also upgraded the company's high-speed network infrastructure. Albertsons had already added electronic data interchange (EDI) capabilities, which enable better processing of transactions with suppliers. However, Albertsons does not yet have a system comparable to Wal-Mart for sharing sales data with suppliers and for automatically placing orders in reaction to sales that are taking place in the field.

Albertsons will not be relying solely on computing power in its pursuit of Wal-Mart. CEO Johnston believes that brain power is just as critical to the success of his company as technology is. Johnston scoured corporate America for the most talented and respected executives in retail and

other industries. He hired CTO Dunst away from competitor Safeway, where Dunst had 25 years of experience developing applications, working with loyalty card systems, and using advanced technology to analyze data. The supply chain management team has been stocked with technology pioneers and top guns who bring their expertise from such companies as PepsiCo, Dell, and even Wal-Mart.

Analysts are impressed with the crew that Johnston has assembled and believe that he is taking the right approach to competing with Wal-Mart, but the benefits of a first-rate staff have been slow to materialize. The question remains whether a massive investment in technology and intellect will be enough for Albertsons to reach the top of the industry. Wal-Mart is a moving target and it continues to move faster and farther. Johnston has saved Albertsons approximately $500 million already, but sales haven't increased significantly. Meanwhile, Wal-Mart's grocery sales continue to grow steadily.

Also worrisome is the introduction of Wal-Mart's Neighborhood Markets. Wal-Mart is traditionally known for its Supercenters, big-box stores that cover expansive square footage and offer extensive product selection. The Neighborhood Markets are significantly smaller and are intended to reach the local markets that aren't always covered by a Wal-Mart big-box store. In many cases, these markets contain the customers that Albertsons has targeted as crucial to its success.

Albertsons has already lost significant market shares to Wal-Mart Supercenters in various parts of the country, including Boise, where Albertsons headquarters are located. Between 2000, when Wal-Mart came to Boise, and 2004, Albertsons saw its market share drop from 65 to 39 percent, with nearly all of the loss benefiting Wal-Mart. Wal-Mart's Neighborhood Markets are strengthened by the same low prices and powerful supply chain that make the company's Supercenters a seemingly unstoppable force. Other than self-service checkout stations, the Neighborhood Markets are decidedly no-frills in comparison to the average

Albertsons store, which often has its own butcher, baker, and gourmet coffee bar. Albertsons is betting that a specialized, customized, and technologically advanced shopping experience will be appealing enough to keep customers from the allure of Wal-Mart's lower prices and simple presentation. It is not a sure bet.

Albertsons may not be able to beat Wal-Mart consistently on price but it must come closer than in the past. Albertsons can also use its loyalty card program to obtain more precise information about individual customers and offer products that they might not find on Wal-Mart shelves. Albertsons has the financial backing to continue investing heavily in advanced information technology, and it is fortified by strong chains of drug stores, which tend to see greater profit margins than grocery stores. The company has recently joined Wal-

Mart in requiring (by April 2005) its suppliers to use radio-frequency identification (RFID) tags on all product shipments. The use of RFID will increase Albertsons' ability to manage its supply chain more precisely. Additionally, Albertsons stores have fared well in urban markets where Wal-Mart has struggled. Overall, however, Wal-Mart has set the bar very high. Albertsons remains convinced that it can soar to greater heights.

Sources: Mel Duvall and Kim S. Nash, "Albertson's: A Shot at the Crown," Mel Duvall, "Roadblock: Internal Resistance," David F. Carr, "Gotcha! The Problems with Self-Service Checkout Systems," and Todd Spangler, "Teradata: Too Rich for Your Blood?" *Baseline Magazine*, February 1, 2004; Jonathan Collins, "Albertsons Announces Mandate," *RFID Journal*, March 5, 2004; Associated Press, "Albertsons to Test Handheld Grocery Scanners," *USA Today*, March 29, 2004.

CASE STUDY QUESTIONS

1. Analyze Albertsons using the value chain and competitive forces models.
2. What role do information systems play in Albertsons' business strategy? How do systems provide value for Albertsons?
3. Compare Albertsons to Wal-Mart in terms of business strategy, current success, and future success.
4. Which management, organization, and technology factors hinder Albertsons from achieving the goals of its business strategy? Which management, organization, and technology factors help Albertsons achieve its goals?
5. Do you think Albertsons' business strategy will work? Why or why not?

Chapter 4

The Digital Firm: Electronic Business and Electronic Commerce

OBJECTIVES

After completing this chapter, you will be able to:

1. Analyze how Internet technology has changed value propositions and business models.

2. Define electronic commerce and describe how it has changed consumer retailing and business-to-business transactions.

3. Compare the principal payment systems for electronic commerce.

4. Evaluate the role of Internet technology in facilitating management and coordination of internal and interorganizational business processes.

5. Assess the challenges posed by electronic business and electronic commerce and management solutions.

CHAPTER OUTLINE

4.1 ELECTRONIC BUSINESS, ELECTRONIC COMMERCE, AND THE EMERGING DIGITAL FIRM
Internet Technology and the Digital Firm
New Business Models and Value Propositions

4.2 ELECTRONIC COMMERCE
Categories of Electronic Commerce
Customer-Centered Retailing
Business-to-Business Electronic Commerce:
    New Efficiencies and Relationships
Electronic Commerce Payment Systems

4.3 ELECTRONIC BUSINESS AND THE DIGITAL FIRM
How Intranets Support Electronic Business
Intranet Applications for Electronic Business
Business Process Integration

4.4 MANAGEMENT OPPORTUNITIES, CHALLENGES, AND SOLUTIONS
Opportunities
Management Challenges
Solution Guidelines

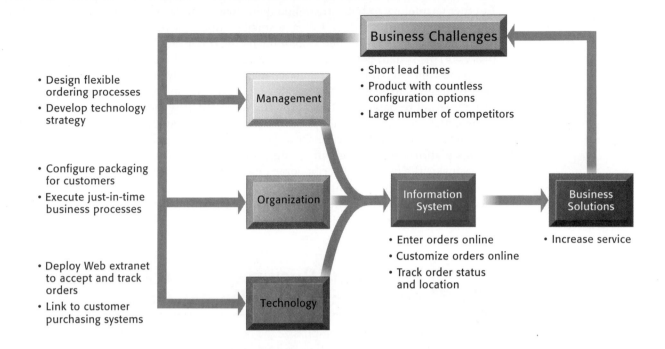

- Design flexible ordering processes
- Develop technology strategy

- Configure packaging for customers
- Execute just-in-time business processes

- Deploy Web extranet to accept and track orders
- Link to customer purchasing systems

Management

Organization

Technology

Business Challenges
- Short lead times
- Product with countless configuration options
- Large number of competitors

Information System
- Enter orders online
- Customize orders online
- Track order status and location

Business Solutions
- Increase service

Opening Case: Corrugated Supplies: The Internet Helps a Small Company Act Big

Corrugated Supplies Corporation (CSC) is a small Bedford Park, Illinois, manufacturer of made-to-order corrugated cardboard sheets for boxes, displays, and other custom packaging. CSC management has always been very forward-looking and the firm was an early leader in providing e-commerce services and customer access to its internal corporate systems to track their orders.

CSC's business does not involve multiple components and products but rather a product that has many, many different configurations—trillions of product variations are theoretically possible. As a result, many CSC orders come with special instructions, such as requests for deep scores, customized logos to be printed, or specific shipping requirements. The orders are usually small with very short lead times, and more than half needing delivery within 24 hours. Moreover, the business is very competitive: There are approximately 700 corrugators in the United States alone.

CSC uses a Web extranet for roughly 85 percent of the 600 orders it processes daily. Customers can either enter their order information into an online order form, or their purchase order systems can transmit the orders electronically to CSC without customers having to retype them into the Web site. CSC sends the customer an e-mail confirming the transaction.

CSC's Web site provides capabilities for customizing orders. If a customer wants its corrugated sheets stamped with a company logo instead of CSC's, it can specify these requirements. Customers can use the Web to transmit changes to orders before completion by clicking on an "edit" icon next to the order, even if it's in the queue for a machine. Because this ordering system is integrated with CSC's inventory system, customers can immediately see whether an order can be fulfilled. Most orders can be turned around within 24 hours.

The Web site incorporates shipping information, enabling the company to track all products as they come off the manufacturing line and are loaded into trailers or placed in a temporary inventory area. Customers can not only view the contents of the trailer but also the sequence in which items were loaded. This information helps customers direct the corrugated paper to the designated packaging machinery more quickly once it has been delivered, so they don't have to put the delivered paper in inventory and later try to locate it.

Sources: Howard Baldwin, "Thinking Big," *Cisco IQ Magazine*, First Quarter 2004; Wes Iversen, "Real-Time for Real Savings," *Automation World*, April 2004; and www.csclive.com, accessed August 26, 2004.

Corrugated Supply Company's extranet is an example of how companies are using Internet technology to both streamline their own business processes and integrate them with customers and suppliers. CSC is a small company, with only 100 employees. Yet it's able to produce a sophisticated system for taking orders and fine-tuning the production process. This system is both an e-commerce site for selling corrugated paper to other companies and an e-business system for managing the flow of manufacturing raw materials through Corrugated's Web site. It's an innovative example of how companies are using Internet technology to transform the way business is conducted.

As a manager, you will want to know how your firm can benefit from e-business and e-commerce. In this chapter we show you how the Internet is creating a universal technology platform for buying and selling goods and for driving important business processes inside the firm. We describe some new ways of organizing and managing based on Internet technology. In addition to describing new benefits and opportunities, we also identify the management challenges raised by electronic business and electronic commerce and suggest strategies for dealing with them.

4.1 ELECTRONIC BUSINESS, ELECTRONIC COMMERCE, AND THE EMERGING DIGITAL FIRM

Throughout this edition, we emphasize the benefits of integrating information across the enterprise, creating an information technology infrastructure in which information flows seamlessly from one part of the organization to another and from the organization to its customers, suppliers, and business partners. The emerging digital firm requires this level of information integration, and companies increasingly depend on such an infrastructure today to remain efficient and competitive. Internet technology has emerged as the key enabling technology for this digital integration.

Internet Technology and the Digital Firm

For a number of years, companies used proprietary systems to integrate information from their internal systems and to link to their customers and trading partners. Such systems were expensive and based on technology standards that only a few companies could follow.

The Internet is rapidly becoming the infrastructure of choice for electronic commerce because it offers businesses an even easier way to link with other businesses and individuals at a very low cost. It provides a universal and easy-to-use set of technologies and technology standards for all organizations, no matter which computer system or information technology platform the organizations are using.

Trading partners can directly communicate with each other, bypassing intermediaries and inefficient multilayered procedures. Web sites are available to consumers 24 hours a day. Some information-based products, such as software, music, and videos, can actually be physically distributed over the Internet. Vendors of other types of products and services use the Internet to distribute the information surrounding their wares, such as product pricing, options, availability, and delivery time. The Internet can replace existing distribution channels or extend them, creating outlets for attracting and serving customers who otherwise would not patronize the company. For example, Web-based discount brokerages have attracted new customers who could not afford paying the high commissions and fees charged by conventional brokerage and financial services firms.

Internet technology is helping companies radically reduce their transaction costs. Chapter 3 introduced the concept of transaction costs, which include the costs of searching for buyers and sellers, collecting information on products, negotiating terms, writing and enforcing contracts, and transporting merchandise. Information on buyers, sellers, and prices for many products is immediately available on the Web. For example, manually processing a single customer order costs $15. Using a Web-based system, the cost drops to 80 cents per transaction.

TABLE 4-1 *How the Internet Reduces Transaction Costs*

Transaction	Traditional	Internet
Checking a bank account balance	$1.08	$0.13
Answering a customer question	$10–$45	Answering an e-mail query: $1–$5 Web self-service: $0.10–$0.20
Trading 100 shares of stock	$100	$9.95
Correcting an employee record	$128	$2.32
Processing an expense report	$36, 22 days	$4–$8, 72 hours
Sending an advertising brochure	$0.75–$10.00	$0–$0.25
Paying a bill	$2.22–$3.32	$0.65–$1.10

Table 4-1 provides other examples of transaction cost reductions from the Internet or Internet technology. Handling transactions electronically reduces transaction costs and delivery time for some goods, especially those that are purely digital (such as software, text products, images, or videos) because these products can be distributed over the Internet as electronic versions.

What's more, Internet technology is providing the infrastructure for running the entire business because its technology and standards enable information to flow seamlessly from one part of the organization to another. Internet technology provides a much less expensive and easier to use alternative for coordination activities than proprietary networks.

Managers are using e-mail and other Internet communication capabilities to oversee larger numbers of employees, to manage many tasks and subtasks in projects, and to coordinate the work of multiple teams working in different parts of the world. Internet standards can link disparate systems, such as those for order processing and logistics tracking, which previously could not communicate with each other. The Internet also reduces other agency costs, such as the cost to coordinate activities of the firm with suppliers and other external business partners. The low-cost connectivity and universal standards provided by Internet technology are the driving force behind the explosion of electronic business and the emergence of the digital firm.

New Business Models and Value Propositions

The Internet has introduced major changes in the way companies conduct business. It has created a dramatic decline in the cost of developing, sending, and storing information while making that information more widely available. Millions of people are able to exchange massive amounts of information directly, instantly, and for free.

In the past, information about products and services was usually tightly bundled with the physical value chain for those products and services. If a consumer wanted to find out about the features, price, and availability of a refrigerator or an automobile, for instance, that person had to visit a retail store that sold those products. The cost of comparison shopping was very high because people had to physically travel from store to store.

The Internet has changed that relationship. Once everyone is connected electronically, information about products and services flows on its own directly and instantly to consumers. The traditional link between the flow of the product and the flow of product-related information is broken. Information is not limited to traditional physical methods of delivery. Customers can find out about products on their own on the Web and buy directly from product suppliers instead of using intermediaries, such as retail stores.

This unbundling of information from traditional value chain channels is having a disruptive effect on old business models and is creating new business models as well. A **business model** describes how the enterprise produces, delivers, and sells a product or service, showing how the enterprise delivers value to customers and how it creates wealth (Magretta, 2002). Some of the traditional channels for exchanging product information have become unnecessary or uneconomical, and business models based on the coupling of information with products and services may no longer be necessary.

For example, in pre-Internet retailing days, people who wanted to purchase books had to go to a physical bookstore to learn which titles were available, the books' contents, and prices. The bookstore had a monopoly on this information. When Amazon.com opened as an online bookstore, it provided visitors to its Web site with a vast electronic catalog containing close to 3 million titles, along with tables of contents, reviews, and other information about those titles. People could order books directly from their desktop computers. Amazon.com was able to sell books at lower cost because it did not have to pay rent, employee salaries, warehousing, and other overhead to maintain physical retail bookstores. Selling books and other goods directly to consumers online without using physical storefronts represents a new business model.

THE CHANGING ECONOMICS OF INFORMATION

The Internet and the Web have vastly increased the total amount and quality of information available to all market participants, consumers and merchants alike. Customers benefit from lower **search costs**—the effort to find suitable products and to find all the suppliers, prices, and delivery terms of a specific product anywhere in the world (Bakos, 1998). Merchants benefit from using the same technology to find out much more about consumers than they previously could and to provide more accurate and detailed information to target their marketing and sales efforts.

The Internet shrinks information asymmetry, making it easy for consumers to find out the variety of prices in a market and to discover the actual costs merchants pay for products. An **information asymmetry** exists when one party in a transaction has more information that is important for the transaction than the other party. That information helps determine their relative bargaining power.

For example, until auto retailing sites appeared on the Web, there was a pronounced information asymmetry between auto dealers and customers. Only the auto dealers knew the manufacturers' prices, and it was difficult for consumers to shop around for the best price. Auto dealers' profit margins depended on this asymmetry of information.

Today's consumers have access to a legion of Web sites providing competitive pricing information, and three-fourths of U.S. auto buyers use the Internet to shop around for the best deal (Markillie, 2004). Thus, the Web has reduced the information asymmetry surrounding an auto purchase. The Internet has also helped businesses seeking to purchase from other businesses reduce information asymmetries and locate better prices and terms.

Before the Internet, businesses had to make trade-offs between the richness and reach of their information. **Richness** refers to the depth and detail of information—the amount

Visitors to CarsDirect.com can research the price, availability, and features of most models of new and used cars and find the best prices and terms for auto purchases. The Internet can reduce search costs and information asymmetry.

of information the business can supply to the customer, as well as information the business collects about the customer. **Reach** refers to how many people a business can connect with and how many products it can offer those people. Rich communication occurs, for example, when a sales representative meets with a customer, sharing information that is very specific to that interaction. Such an interaction is very expensive for a business because it can take place only with a small audience.

Newspaper and television ads could reach millions of people quite inexpensively, but the information they provide is much more limited. It used to be prohibitively expensive for traditional businesses to have both richness and reach. Few, if any, companies could afford to provide highly detailed, customized information to a large mass audience. The Internet has transformed the richness and reach relationships (see Figure 4-1). Using the Internet and Web multimedia capabilities, companies are able to provide detailed product information quickly and inexpensively and detailed information specific to each customer to very large numbers of people simultaneously (Evans and Wurster, 2000).

INTERNET BUSINESS MODELS

The Internet helps companies create and capture profit in new ways by adding extra value to existing products and services or by providing the foundation for new products and services. Table 4-2 describes some of the most important Internet business models that have emerged. All in one way or another add value: They provide the customer with a new product or service; they provide additional information or service along with a traditional product or service; or they provide a product or service at a lower cost than traditional means.

Some of these new business models take advantage of the Internet's rich communication capabilities. eBay is an online auction forum that uses e-mail and other interactive features of the Web. People can make online bids for items, such as computer equipment, antiques and collectibles, wine, jewelry, rock-concert tickets, and electronics, which are posted by sellers from around the world. The system accepts bids for items entered on the Internet, evaluates the bids, and notifies the highest bidder. eBay collects a small commission on each listing and sale. (eBay has become so popular that its site serves as a huge trading platform for other companies, hosting around 225,000 "virtual storefronts.")

Business-to-business auctions are proliferating as well. GoIndustry, for instance, features Web-based auction services for business-to-business sales of industrial equipment and machinery. Online bidding, also known as **dynamic pricing**, is expected to grow rapidly because buyers and sellers can interact so easily through the Internet to determine what an item is worth at any particular moment.

The Internet has created online communities, where people with similar interests exchange ideas from many different locations. Some of these virtual communities are providing the foundation for new businesses. iVillage.com provides an online community for women sharing similar interests, such as diet and fitness, pregnancy, parenting, home and garden, and food. Members post their own personal Web pages, participate in online discussion groups, and join online "clubs" with other like-minded people.

FIGURE 4-1   *The changing economics of information.*

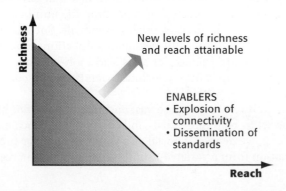

New levels of richness and reach attainable

ENABLERS
• Explosion of connectivity
• Dissemination of standards

In the past, companies have had to trade off between the richness and reach of their information. Internet connectivity and universal standards for information sharing radically lower the cost of providing rich, detailed information to large numbers of people, reducing the trade-off.

TABLE 4-2 *Internet Business Models*

Category	Description	Examples
Virtual storefront	Sells physical products directly to consumers or to individual businesses.	Amazon.com EPM.com
Information broker	Provides product, pricing, and availability information to individuals and businesses. Generates revenue from advertising or from directing buyers to sellers.	Edmunds.com Kbb.com Insweb.com Realtor.com
Transaction broker	Saves users money and time by processing online sales transactions, generating a fee each time a transaction occurs. Also provides information on rates and terms.	E*TRADE.com Expedia.com
Online marketplace	Provides a digital environment where buyers and sellers can meet, search for products, display products, and establish prices for those products. Can provide online auctions or reverse auctions in which buyers submit bids to multiple sellers to purchase at a buyer-specified price as well as negotiated or fixed pricing. Can serve consumers or B2B e-commerce, generating revenue from transaction fees.	eBay.com Priceline.com ChemConnect.com Pantellos.com
Content provider	Creates revenue by providing digital content, such as digital news, music, photos, or video, over the Web. The customer may pay to access the content, or revenue may be generated by selling advertising space.	WSJ.com CNN.com TheStreet.com GettyImages.com MP3.com
Online service provider	Provides online service for individuals and businesses. Generates revenue from subscription or transaction fees, from advertising, or from collecting marketing information from users.	@Backup.com Xdrive.com Employease.com Salesforce.com
Virtual community	Provides an online meeting place where people with similar interests can communicate and find useful information.	Motocross.com Friendster.com iVillage.com Sailnet.com
Portal	Provides initial point of entry to the Web along with specialized content and other services.	Yahoo.com MSN.com StarMedia.com

A major source of revenue for these communities involves providing ways for corporate clients to target customers, including the placement of banner ads and pop-up ads on their Web sites. A **banner ad** is a graphic display on a Web page used for advertising. The banner is linked to the advertiser's Web site so that a person clicking the banner is transported to a Web page with more information about the advertiser. **Pop-up ads** work in the opposite manner. They automatically open up when a user accesses a specific Web site, and the user must click on the ad to make it disappear.

Social networking sites are a type of online community that have become increasingly popular. Social networking is the practice of expanding the number of one's business or social contacts by making connections through individuals. Social networking sites link people through their mutual business or personal connections, enabling them to mine their friends (and their friends' friends) for sales leads, job-hunting tips, or new friends. Web sites dedicated to social networking include Friendster, Linkedin, Spoke, Tribe, and ZeroDegrees.

The Web's information resources are so vast and rich that *portals* have emerged as an Internet business model to help individuals and organizations locate information more efficiently. In Chapter 2, we defined a portal as a Web interface for presenting integrated personalized information from a variety of sources. As an e-commerce business model, a

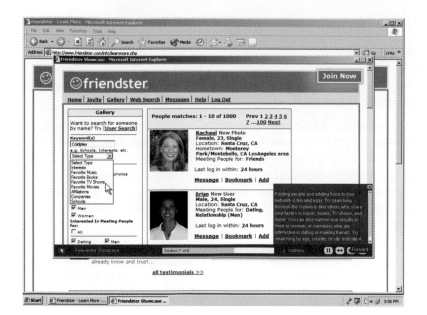

Friendster.com is an Internet business based on creating an online community for social networking. The company generates revenue from advertising sponsors.

portal is a "supersite" that provides a comprehensive entry point for a huge array of resources and services on the Internet.

Yahoo! is an example. It provides capabilities for locating information on the Internet along with news, sports, weather, telephone directories, maps, games, shopping, e-mail, chat, discussion boards, and links to other sites. Also, specialized portals help users with specific interests. For example, StarMedia is a portal customized for Latin American Internet users and the portal Sina.com is customized for Chinese users.

Yahoo! and other portals and Web content sites often combine content and applications from many different sources and service providers. Other Internet business models use syndication as well to provide additional value. For example, E*TRADE, the discount Web trading site, purchases most of its content from outside sources, such as Reuters (news), Bridge Information Systems (quotes), and BigCharts.com (charts). Online **syndicators**, who aggregate content or applications from multiple sources, package them for distribution, and resell them to third-party Web sites, have emerged as another variant of the online content provider business model (Werbach, 2000). The Web makes it much easier for companies to aggregate, repackage, and distribute information and information-based services.

Chapter 6 describes application service providers, such as Employease.com or Salesforce.com, which feature software that runs over the Web. They provide online services to subscribing businesses. Other online service providers offer services to individual consumers, such as remote storage of data at Xdrive.com. Service providers generate revenue through subscription fees or from advertising.

Most of the business models described in Table 4-2 are called **pure-play** business models because they are based purely on the Internet. These firms did not have an existing bricks-and-mortar business when they designed their Internet business. However, many existing firms such as L.L. Bean, Office Depot, REI, and the *Wall Street Journal* have developed Web sites as extensions of their traditional bricks-and-mortar businesses. Such businesses represent a hybrid **clicks-and-mortar** business model.

4.2 ELECTRONIC COMMERCE

Although most commercial transactions still take place through conventional channels, rising numbers of consumers and businesses are using the Internet for electronic commerce. Projections show that by 2006, total e-commerce spending by consumers and businesses could surpass $5 trillion (eMarketer, 2004 and 2003).

Categories of Electronic Commerce

There are many ways to classify electronic commerce transactions. One is by looking at the nature of the participants in the electronic commerce transaction. The three major electronic commerce categories are business-to-consumer (B2C) e-commerce, business-to-business (B2B) e-commerce, and consumer-to-consumer (C2C) e-commerce.

- **Business-to-consumer (B2C) electronic commerce** involves retailing products and services to individual shoppers. BarnesandNoble.com, which sells books, software, and music to individual consumers, is an example of B2C e-commerce.

- **Business-to-business (B2B) electronic commerce** involves sales of goods and services among businesses. Milacron's Web site for selling machinery, mold bases, and related tooling, supplies, and services to companies engaged in plastics processing is an example of B2B e-commerce.

- **Consumer-to-consumer (C2C) electronic commerce** involves consumers selling directly to consumers. For example, eBay, the giant Web auction site, enables people to sell their goods to other consumers by auctioning the merchandise off to the highest bidder.

Another way of classifying electronic commerce transactions is in terms of the participants' physical connection to the Web. Until recently, almost all e-commerce transactions took place over wired networks. Now mobile phones and other wireless handheld digital appliances are Internet enabled to send text messages, access Web sites, and make purchases. Companies are offering new types of Web-based products and services that can be accessed by these wireless devices. The use of handheld wireless devices for purchasing goods and services from any location has been termed **mobile commerce** or **m-commerce**. Both business-to-business and business-to-consumer e-commerce transactions can take place using m-commerce technology. Chapter 9 discusses m-commerce and wireless technology in detail.

Customer-Centered Retailing

Despite the many failures of early dot-com retail companies, online retailing continues to grow at a brisk pace. The Internet provides companies with new channels of communication and interaction that can create closer yet more cost-effective relationships with customers in sales, marketing, and customer support. Companies can use the Web to provide ongoing information, service, and support, creating positive interactions with customers that can serve as the foundations for long-term relationships and repeat purchases.

DIRECT SALES OVER THE WEB

Manufacturers can sell their products and services directly to retail customers, bypassing intermediaries such as distributors or retail outlets. Eliminating intermediaries in the distribution channel can significantly lower purchase transaction costs. Operators of virtual storefronts, such as Amazon.com or EPM.com, do not have large expenditures for rent, sales staff, and the other operations associated with a traditional retail store. Airlines can sell tickets directly to passengers through their own Web sites or through travel sites such as Travelocity without paying commissions to travel agents.

To pay for all the steps in a traditional distribution channel, a product may have to be priced as high as 135 percent of its original cost to manufacture (Mougayar, 1998). Figure 4-2 illustrates how much savings can result from eliminating each of these layers in the distribution process. By selling directly to consumers or reducing the number of intermediaries, companies can achieve higher profits while charging lower prices. The removal of organizations or business process layers responsible for intermediary steps in a value chain is called **disintermediation**.

The Internet is accelerating disintermediation in some industries and creating opportunities for new types of intermediaries in others. In certain industries, distributors with warehouses of goods, or intermediaries such as real estate agents may be replaced by new

Internet Connection ——
The Internet Connection for this chapter will direct you to a series of Web sites where you can complete an exercise to evaluate virtual storefront businesses.

FIGURE 4-2   *The benefits of disintermediation to the consumer.*

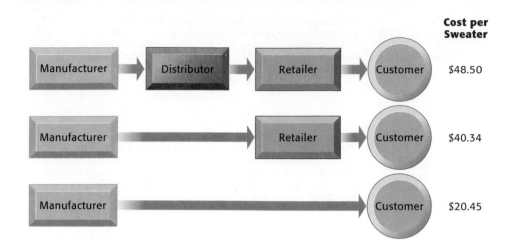

The typical distribution channel has several intermediary layers, each of which adds to the final cost of a product, such as a sweater. Removing layers lowers the final cost to the consumer.

intermediary services that specialize in helping Internet business and retail users reduce search costs, tailor offerings more precisely to their needs, obtain assurances about quality and reliability, handle product complexity, or preserve anonymity while conducting online transactions (Bhargava and Choudhary, 2004; Andal-Ancion, Cartwright, and Yip, 2003; Anderson and Anderson, 2002; Gallaugher, 2002; Hagel III and Singer, 1999). The information brokers listed in Table 4-2 are examples of one type of service for which such intermediaries can provide value. The process of shifting the intermediary function in a value chain to a new source is called **reintermediation**.

INTERACTIVE MARKETING AND PERSONALIZATION

Marketers are using the interactive features of Web pages to hold consumers' attention or to capture detailed information about consumer tastes and interests for one-to-one marketing (see Chapter 3). Web sites have become a bountiful source of detailed information about customer behavior, preferences, needs, and buying patterns that companies can use to tailor promotions, products, services, and pricing.

Some customer information may be obtained by asking visitors to "register" online and provide information about themselves, but many companies also collect customer information using software tools that track the activities of Web site visitors.

Clickstream tracking tools collect data on customer activities at Web sites and store them in a log. The tools record the site that users visited prior to coming to a particular Web site and where these users go when they leave that site. They also record the specific pages visited on the particular site, the time spent on each page of the site, the types of pages visited, and what the visitors purchased (see Figure 4-3). Firms can analyze this information about customer interests and behavior to develop precise profiles of existing and potential customers.

Communications and product offerings can be tailored precisely to individual customers. Firms can create unique personalized Web pages that display content or ads for products or services of special interest to each user, improving the customer's experience and creating additional value (see Figure 4-4). By using **Web personalization** technology to modify the Web pages presented to each customer, marketers achieve the benefits of using individual salespeople at dramatically lower costs. Personalization can also help firms form lasting relationships with customers by providing individualized content, information, and services.

One technique for Web personalization is **collaborative filtering**, which compares information gathered about a specific user's behavior at a Web site to data about other customers with similar interests to predict what the user would like to see next. The software then makes recommendations to users based on their assumed interests. For example,

FIGURE 4-3 *Web site visitor tracking.*

E-commerce Web sites have tools to track a shopper's every step through an online store. Close examination of customer behavior at a Web site selling women's clothing shows what the store might learn at each step and what actions it could take to increase sales.

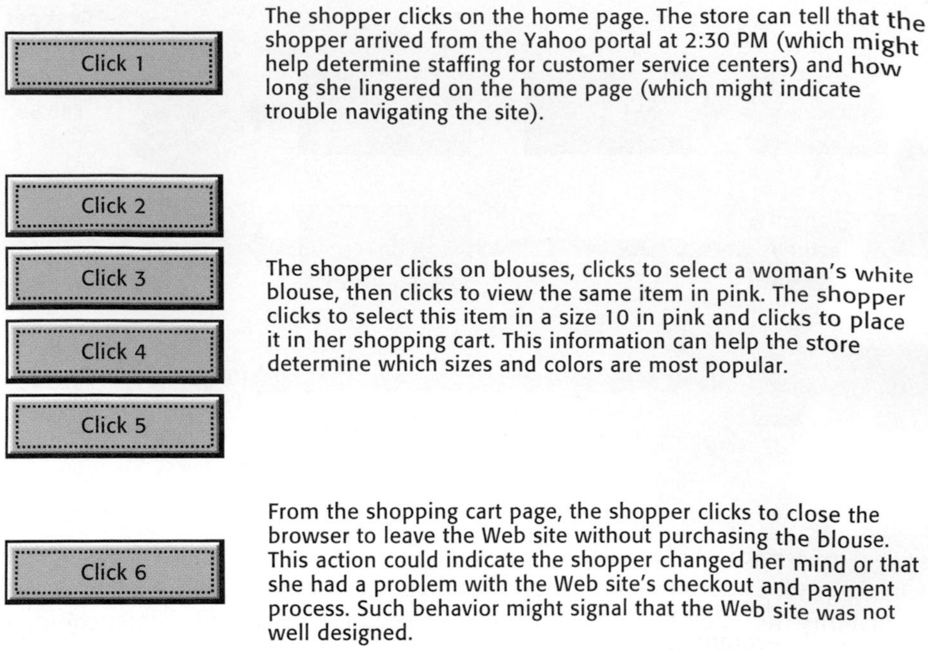

Click 1
The shopper clicks on the home page. The store can tell that the shopper arrived from the Yahoo portal at 2:30 PM (which might help determine staffing for customer service centers) and how long she lingered on the home page (which might indicate trouble navigating the site).
Click 2
Click 3
Click 4
Click 5
The shopper clicks on blouses, clicks to select a woman's white blouse, then clicks to view the same item in pink. The shopper clicks to select this item in a size 10 in pink and clicks to place it in her shopping cart. This information can help the store determine which sizes and colors are most popular.
Click 6
From the shopping cart page, the shopper clicks to close the browser to leave the Web site without purchasing the blouse. This action could indicate the shopper changed her mind or that she had a problem with the Web site's checkout and payment process. Such behavior might signal that the Web site was not well designed.

FIGURE 4-4 *Web site personalization.*

Firms can create unique personalized Web pages that display content or ads for products or services of special interest to individual users, improving the customer experience and creating additional value.

User
Web site
Based on your portfolio and recent market trends, here are some recommendations.
Welcome back, Steve P. Munson. Check out these recommended titles: One Minute Manager Leading Change Results-Based Leadership
Sarah, Here are the items you want to bid on: Iron Scroll Lamp Sparkle Beach Barbie Beatles Silk Tie

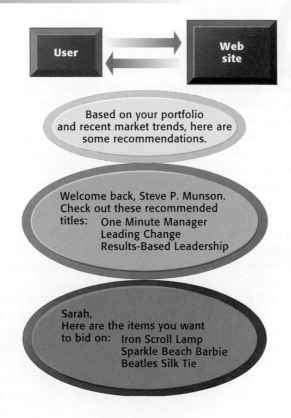

Web sites can tailor their content to the specific interests of individual visitors. The Subaru Web site will create personalized Web pages for individual Subaru auto owners where they can access their vehicle's service history, request parts, schedule appointments with Subaru dealers, view the Owner's Manual, and find other valuable information about their cars.

Amazon.com and BarnesandNoble.com use collaborative filtering software to prepare personalized book recommendations: "Customers who bought this book also bought . . ."

Blogs have emerged as another promising Web-based tool for marketing. A **blog**, the popular term for Weblog, is an informal yet structured Web site where individuals can publish stories, opinions, and links to other Web sites of interest. Many users subscribe to a blog site, post their views and opinions, and create links to and from other blogs or Web sites. Most blogs are published by individuals, but corporate blogs have emerged as useful marketing tools.

Blogs provide a more personal way of presenting information to the public and prospective customers about new products and services. For example, Macromedia, which makes Flash, Dreamweaver, Fireworks and Cold Fusion software for multimedia applications, uses weblogs to nurture ties with customers and introduce them to new features in its software. The blogs provide a forum where managers can discuss the new products, show developers how to use the new features, answer questions, and obtain customer feedback. Some companies also use blogs internally to communicate and exchange ideas about projects and company news.

The cost of customer surveys and focus groups is very high. Learning how customers feel or what they think about products or services by examining customer visits to Web sites and online feedback is much cheaper. Customer information that can be acquired over the Internet has become so useful that new third-party services have arisen to provide businesses with customer-generated information that cannot be obtained by directly interacting with customers on the company Web site. Such services monitor customer discussions about products that are taking place through online communities and message boards, conduct online market research surveys, or monitor the online surfing and buying behavior of large numbers of customers at many different Web sites (Sawhney, Prandelli, and Veroa, 2003).

CUSTOMER SELF-SERVICE

The Web and other network technologies are inspiring new approaches to customer service and support. Many companies are using their Web sites and e-mail to answer customer questions or to provide customers with helpful information. The Web provides a medium for customers to interact with the company, at the customers' convenience, and find information that previously required a human customer-support expert. Automated self-service or other Web-based responses to customer questions cost only a fraction of what a live customer service representative on the telephone costs.

Companies are realizing substantial cost savings from Web-based customer self-service applications. For instance, American, Northwest, and other major airlines have created Web sites where customers can review flight departure and arrival times, seating charts, and airport logistics; check frequent-flyer miles; and purchase tickets online. Chapter 1 describes how customers of UPS can use its Web site to track shipments, calculate shipping costs, determine time in transit, and arrange for a package pickup. FedEx and other package delivery firms provide similar Web-based services.

New software products are even integrating the Web with customer call centers, where customer service problems have been traditionally handled over the telephone. A **call center** is an organizational department responsible for handling customer service issues by telephone and other channels. For example, visitors can click on a "push to talk" link on the Lands' End Web site that lets a user request a phone call. The user enters his or her telephone number and a call-center system directs a customer service representative to place a voice telephone call to the user's phone. Some systems also let the customer interact with a service representative on the Web while talking on the phone at the same time.

Business-to-Business Electronic Commerce: New Efficiencies and Relationships

Today, about 80 percent of B2B e-commerce is based on proprietary systems for electronic data interchange (EDI). **Electronic data interchange (EDI)** enables the computer-to-computer exchange between two organizations of standard transactions, such as invoices, bills of lading, shipment schedules, or purchase orders. Transactions are automatically transmitted from one information system to another through a network, eliminating the printing and handling of paper at one end and the inputting of data at the other. Each major industry in the United States and much of the rest of the world has EDI standards that define the structure and information fields of electronic documents for that industry.

EDI originally automated the exchange of documents such as purchase orders, invoices, and shipping notices. Although some companies still use EDI for document automation, firms engaged in just-in-time inventory replenishment and continuous production use EDI as a system for continuous replenishment. Suppliers have online access to selected parts of the purchasing firm's production and delivery schedules and automatically ship materials and goods to meet prespecified targets without intervention by firm purchasing agents (see Figure 4-5).

Visitors to the Web sites of KLM and its partner Northwest Airlines can find flight schedules and gates, select seats, print boarding passes, and check themselves in for flights. Web sites for customer self-service are convenient for customers and help firms lower their customer service and support costs.

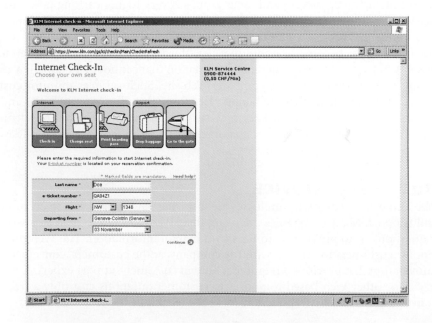

FIGURE 4-5   *Electronic data interchange (EDI).*

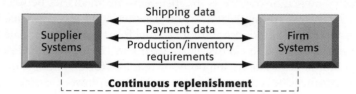

Companies use EDI to automate transactions for B2B e-commerce and continuous inventory replenishment. Suppliers can automatically send data about shipments to purchasing firms. The purchasing firms can use EDI to provide production and inventory requirements and payment data to suppliers.

Although many organizations still use private networks for EDI, companies are increasingly turning to the Internet for this purpose because it provides a much more flexible and low-cost platform for linking to other firms. Using the Internet, businesses can extend digital technology to a wider range of activities and broaden their circle of trading partners.

Take procurement, for example. **Procurement** involves not only purchasing goods and materials but also sourcing, negotiating with suppliers, paying for goods, and making delivery arrangements. Businesses can now use the Internet to locate the most low-cost supplier, search online catalogs of supplier products, negotiate with suppliers, place orders, make payments, and arrange transportation. They are not limited to partners linked by traditional EDI networks but use the Web to work with any other business that is linked to the Internet. *E-procurement* over the Internet provides new opportunities for lowering costs and improving service because Internet technology enables businesses to cast their nets more widely.

The Internet and Web technology enable businesses to create new electronic storefronts for selling to other businesses with multimedia graphic displays and interactive features similar to those for B2C commerce. Alternatively, businesses can use Internet technology to create extranets or electronic marketplaces for linking to other businesses for purchase and sale transactions. *Extranets*, which we introduced in Chapter 1, are private intranets extended to authorized users outside the company.

Private industrial networks are B2B extranets that focus on continuous business process coordination between companies for collaboration and supply chain management. A private industrial network typically consists of a large firm using an extranet to link to its suppliers and other key business partners (see Figure 4-6). The network is owned by the buyer, and it permits the firm and designated suppliers, distributors, and other business partners to share product design and development, marketing, production scheduling, inventory management, and unstructured communication, including graphics and e-mail. Another term for a private industrial network is a **private exchange**. Private exchanges are currently the fastest-growing type of B2B commerce.

FIGURE 4-6   *A private industrial network.*

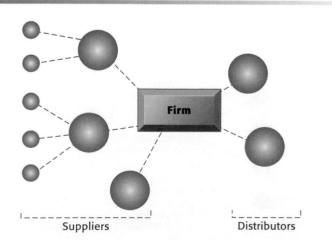

A private industrial network, also known as a private exchange, links a firm to its suppliers, distributors, and other key business partners for efficient supply chain management and other collaborative activities.

Net marketplaces, which are sometimes called *e-hubs*, provide a single digital market-place based on Internet technology for many different buyers and sellers (see Figure 4-7). They are industry-owned or operate as independent intermediaries between buyers and sellers. Net marketplaces are more transaction oriented (and less relationship oriented) than private industrial networks, generating revenue from purchase and sale transactions and other services provided to clients. Participants in Net marketplaces can establish prices through online negotiations, auctions, or requests for quotations, or they can use fixed prices. Customers benefit from lower search costs, lower transaction costs, and wider selection.

There are many different types of Net marketplaces and ways of classifying them. Some Net marketplaces sell direct goods and some sell indirect goods. *Direct goods* are goods used in a production process, such as sheet steel for auto body production. *Indirect goods* are all other goods not directly involved in the production process, such as office supplies or products for maintenance and repair. Some Net marketplaces support contractual purchasing based on long-term relationships with designated suppliers, and others support short-term spot purchasing, where goods are purchased based on immediate needs, often from many different suppliers. Some Net marketplaces serve vertical markets for specific industries, such as automobiles, telecommunications, or machine tools, whereas others serve horizontal markets for goods and services that can be found in many different industries, such as office equipment or transportation.

Ariba bundles extensive e-commerce services with a Net marketplace for long-term contractual purchasing of both indirect and direct goods. It provides both buyers and sellers with software systems and Net marketplace services, aggregating hundreds of catalogs into a single marketplace and customizing procurement and sales processes to work with their systems. For buyers, Ariba automates sourcing, contract management, purchase orders, requisitions, business rules enforcement, and payment. For sellers, Ariba provides services for catalog creation and content management, order management, invoicing, and settlement.

FedEx uses Ariba's e-procurement system for $8 million in purchases. Employees use Ariba to order from more than 32 MRO (maintenance, repair, and operations) suppliers and catalogs. The system automatically invokes FedEx's business rules for purchasing to route, review, and approve requisitions electronically. By using this Net marketplace, FedEx has reduced the cost of processing purchases by 75 percent and the prices paid for MRO supplies by 12 percent, and it has cut parts delivery time from an average of seven days to two days.

Industry-owned Net marketplaces focus on long-term contract purchasing relationships and on providing common networks and computing platforms for reducing supply chain inefficiencies. Buyer firms benefit from competitive pricing among alternative suppliers, and suppliers benefit from stable long-term selling relationships with large firms.

Exostar is an example. This aerospace and defense industry-sponsored Net market-place was founded jointly by BAE Systems, Boeing, Lockheed Martin, Raytheon, and

---

FIGURE 4-7   *A Net marketplace.*

Net marketplaces are online marketplaces where multiple buyers can purchase from multiple sellers.

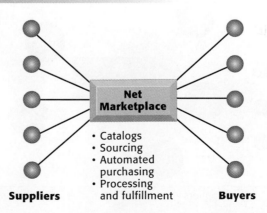

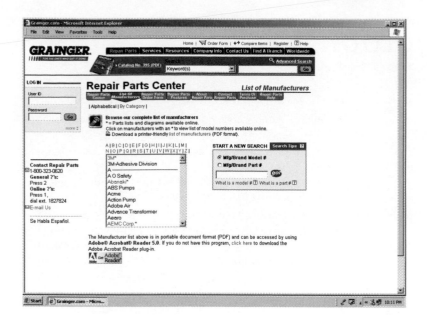

Grainger.com provides a single online source from which customers can make spot purchases of maintenance, repair, and operations products from many different companies.

Rolls-Royce PLC to connect these companies to their suppliers and facilitate collaboration on major projects. More than 16,000 trading partners in the commercial, military, and government sectors use Exostar's sourcing, e-procurement, and collaboration tools for both direct and indirect goods. Exostar includes capabilities for auctioning, purchase forecasting, issuing electronic payments and receipts, and linking to participants' internal corporate systems. Also featured are capabilities for collaboration on joint development projects and sharing engineering product data.

Other industry-owned Net marketplaces include ChemConnect.com, for the chemical industry, Transora.com, for the food industry, and Pantellos.com for the energy services and utilities industries.

Exchanges are independently owned third-party Net marketplaces that can connect thousands of suppliers and buyers for spot purchasing. Many exchanges provide vertical markets for a single industry, such as food, electronics, or industrial equipment, and they primarily deal with direct inputs. For example, FoodTrader.com automates spot purchases among buyers and sellers from over 180 countries in the food and agriculture industry.

Exchanges proliferated during the early years of e-commerce, but many have failed. Suppliers were reluctant to participate because the exchanges encouraged competitive bidding that drove prices down and did not offer any long-term relationships with buyers or services to make lowering prices worthwhile. Many essential direct purchases are not conducted on a spot basis because they require contracts and consideration of issues such as delivery timing, customization, and quality of products (Laudon, 2003; Wise and Morrison, 2000).

The Window on Technology sheds light on these issues. The Volkswagen Group opted for a private industrial network (private exchange) instead of an industry-sponsored Net marketplace or exchange precisely because it wanted to preserve its control over supplier relationships and its unique business processes for supply chain management. VWGroupSupply.com has become one of Europe's most successful B2B sites and a model for the global automobile industry.

Electronic Commerce Payment Systems

Special **electronic payment systems** have been developed to pay for goods electronically on the Internet. Electronic payment systems for the Internet include systems for credit card payments, digital cash, digital wallets, accumulated balance digital payment systems, stored value payment systems, peer-to-peer payment systems, electronic checks, and electronic billing presentment and payment systems.

WINDOW ON TECHNOLOGY

VOLKSWAGEN REVS UP ITS B2B NETWORK

Volkswagen AG is Europe's largest car manufacturer, producing 5 million cars, trucks, and vans each year. VW owns luxury car makers such as Audi, Lamborghini, and Bentley and family car makers such as SEAT in Spain and Skoda in the Czech Republic. The company has 300,000 employees and operates plants in Europe, Africa, the Asia/Pacific Rim, and the Americas. Vehicles produced by Volkswagen Group account for over 12 percent of the world market.

VW companies purchase annually 60 billion euros worth, or about US$73 billion, in components, automotive parts, and indirect materials, and these purchases represent more than 70 percent of VW's annual revenue. Obviously, the procurement process and relationships with suppliers are absolutely critical for Volkswagen's success.

The VW Group was looking for ways to create more efficient relationships with its suppliers and reduce the cost of paper-based procurement processes. However, the company did not want to automate procurement using a public exchange or an industry-sponsored Net marketplace because it would have had to adapt its own business processes to a common framework that could be used by many different organizations. It decided not to participate in Covisint, the giant industry consortium Net marketplace set up by Ford, General Motors, and DaimlerChrysler, which provides procurement and other supply chain services for these companies, other automotive manufacturers, and their suppliers.

Instead, VW opted for a private platform that would enable it to integrate its suppliers more tightly with its own business processes. Operating as a private industrial network, VWGroupSupply.com enabled the VW Group to design a system that optimized its own business processes.

During the early summer of 2002 the company began implementing a massive private B2B extranet for the Volkswagen Group and its suppliers called VWGroupSupply.com. VWGroupSupply.com handles 90 percent of all global purchasing for VW, including all automotive and parts components. It is one of the most comprehensive private exchanges in the global automotive industry.

The online Web-based platform can handle requests for quotations (RFQs), contract negotiations, catalog purchases, purchase order management, engineering change management, vehicle program management, and payments. This B2B private industrial network was developed using technology from a number of vendors, including Ariba, IBM, and i2 Technologies.

Suppliers of all sizes can access VWGroupSupply.com with standard Web browser software. The Web site is limited to suppliers that have done business with one or several companies in the Volkswagen Group and potential new suppliers that go through an authorization process. The system maintains a common data repository with details on each supplier concerning procurement, logistics, production, quality, technical design, and finance.

It also features an online catalog with 1.37 million items from 750 global suppliers. The catalog uses the eCl@ss standard for classifying its contents. All suppliers who participate in the catalog ordering process classify their products using this standard.

Online negotiations involve multiple bids by suppliers for various purchasing contracts. VWGroupSupply.com ensures that all participants meet its technical and commercial qualifications. Before an online solicitation begins, the system informs vendors about the data and precise rules governing the negotiations.

Shifts in market demand have a drastic impact on VW's production activities and affect the ability of suppliers to deliver. Production bottlenecks can result if suppliers are unprepared for a sudden upsurge in demand. If suppliers stock too much inventory, they may incur excess costs from running at overcapacity. VWGroupSupply.com has an application called Electronic Capacity Management (eCAP) to alert both VW and its suppliers to changes in trends in advance.

eCAP enables suppliers to track VW's continually updated production plans and materials requirements in real time online. This capability captures information about participating suppliers' planned maximum and minimum capacities. If VW production requirements go beyond these limits, the system sets off an alarm so both parties can react quickly. eCAP maintains information on over 200 suppliers and 4,000 critical parts.

During its first three years of operation, the material cost reductions and productivity gains from VWGroupSupply.com produced more than 100 million euros (US$122 million) in cost reductions.

As of mid-2004, VWGroupSupply.com had handled over 500,000 transactions with more than 5,500 suppliers. More than 4,200 online contract negotiations involving 26,000 suppliers were conducted online, with a value of 42 billion euros (US$51 billion). Over 13,200 people used the online catalog and placed orders totaling 150 million euros (US$182 million).

Sources: Martin Hoffman, "Best Practices: VW Revs Up Its B2B Engine," *Optimize Magazine*, March 2004; www.vwgroupsupply.com, accessed August 23, 2004; and www.hoovers.com, accessed August 24, 2004.

To Think About: What are the benefits to Volkswagen from using a private industrial network instead of a more open exchange? How does this system change how VW and it suppliers do business? What value does VWGroupSupply.com provide to Volkswagen and to its suppliers?

Credit cards account for 80 percent of online payments in the United States and about 50 percent of online purchases outside the United States. The more sophisticated electronic commerce software has capabilities for processing credit card purchases on the Web. Businesses can also contract with services that extend the functionality of existing credit card payment systems. **Digital credit card payment systems** extend the functionality of credit cards so they can be used for online shopping payments. They make credit cards safer and more convenient for online merchants and consumers by providing mechanisms for authenticating the purchaser's credit card to make sure it is valid and arranging for the bank that issued the credit card to deposit money for the amount of the purchase in the seller's bank account.

Digital wallets make paying for purchases over the Web more efficient by eliminating the need for shoppers to enter their address and credit card information repeatedly each time they buy something. A **digital wallet** securely stores credit card and owner identification information and provides that information at an electronic commerce site's "checkout counter." The digital wallet enters the shopper's name, credit card number, and shipping information automatically when invoked to complete the purchase. Amazon.com's 1-Click Shopping, which enables a consumer to fill in shipping and credit card information automatically by clicking one button, uses electronic wallet technology. MSN Wallet, MasterCard Wallet, and America Online's Quick Checkout are other digital wallet systems.

Micropayment systems have been developed for purchases of less than $10, such as downloads of individual articles or music clips, that would be too small for conventional credit card payments. Accumulated balance payment systems or stored value payment systems are useful for such purposes.

Accumulated balance digital payment systems enable users to make micropayments and purchases on the Web, accumulating a debit balance that they must pay periodically on their credit card or telephone bills. IPIN has been widely adopted by online music sites that sell music tracks for 99 cents. It invoices customers through existing consumer billing services such as telephone and wireless service companies, Internet service providers, and banks. PaymentOne and Trivnet enable consumers to charge small purchases to their monthly telephone bill.

Stored value payment systems enable consumers to make instant online payments to merchants and other individuals based on value stored in a digital account. Online value systems rely on the value stored in a consumer's bank, checking, or credit card account, and some of these systems require the use of a digital wallet. Ecount offers a prepaid debit account for online purchases, and RocketCash is a new online stored value system aimed at teenagers.

Smart cards are another type of stored value system used for micropayments. A **smart card** is a plastic card the size of a credit card that stores digital information. The smart card can store health records, identification data, or telephone numbers, or it can serve as an "electronic purse" in place of cash. The Mondex and American Express Blue smart cards contain electronic cash and can be used to transfer funds to merchants in physical storefronts and to merchants on the Internet. Both are contact smart cards that require use of special card-reading devices whenever the cards need to transfer cash to either an online or offline merchant. (Internet users must attach a smart card reader to their PCs to use the card. To pay for a Web purchase, the user would swipe the smart card through the card reader.)

Digital cash (also known as electronic cash or e-cash) can also be used for micropayments or larger purchases. **Digital cash** is currency represented in electronic form that moves outside the normal network of money (paper currency, coins, checks, credit cards). Users are supplied with client software and can exchange money with another e-cash user over the Internet or with a retailer accepting e-cash. eCoin.net is an example of a digital cash service. In addition to facilitating micropayments, digital cash can be useful for people who do not have credit cards and wish to make Web purchases.

New Web-based **peer-to-peer payment systems** have sprung up to serve people who want to send money to vendors or individuals who are not set up to accept credit card payments. The party sending money uses his or her credit card to create an account with the designated payment at a Web site dedicated to peer-to-peer payments. The recipient "picks up" the payment by visiting the Web site and supplying information about where to send the payment (a bank account or a physical address). PayPal has become a popular peer-to-peer payment system.

Digital checking payment systems, such as Western Union MoneyZap and eCheck, extend the functionality of existing checking accounts so they can be used for online shopping payments. Digital checks are less expensive than credit cards and much faster than traditional paper-based checking. These checks are encrypted with a digital signature that can be verified and used for payments in electronic commerce. Electronic check systems are useful in business-to-business electronic commerce.

Electronic billing presentment and payment systems are used for paying routine monthly bills. They enable users to view their bills electronically and pay them through electronic fund transfers from bank or credit card accounts. These services support payment for online and physical store purchases of goods or services after the purchase has taken place. They notify purchasers about bills that are due, present the bills, and process the payments. Some of these services, such as CheckFree, consolidate subscribers' bills from various sources so that they can all be paid at one time. Table 4-3 summarizes the features of some of these payment systems.

The process of paying for products and services purchased on the Internet is complex and merits additional discussion. We discuss electronic commerce security in detail in Chapter 10.

4.3   ELECTRONIC BUSINESS AND THE DIGITAL FIRM

Businesses are finding that some of the greatest benefits of Internet technology come from applications that lower agency and coordination costs. Although companies have used internal networks for many years to manage and coordinate their business processes, intranets quickly are becoming the technology of choice for electronic business.

TABLE 4-3   *Examples of Electronic Payment Systems for E-Commerce*

Payment System	Description	Commercial Example
Digital credit card payment systems	Secure services for credit card payments on the Internet that protect information transmitted among users, merchant sites, and processing banks	eCharge
Digital wallet	Software that stores credit card and other information to facilitate payment for goods on the Web	MSN Wallet MasterCard Wallet AOL Quick Checkout
Accumulated balance payment systems	Accumulates micropayment purchases as a debit balance that must be paid periodically on credit card or telephone bills	Trivnet PaymentOne
Stored value payment systems	Enables consumers to make instant payments to merchants based on value stored in a digital account	Ecount American Express Blue smart card
Digital cash	Digital currency that can be used for micropayments or larger purchases	eCoin.net
Peer-to-peer payment systems	Sends money using the Web to individuals or vendors who are not set up to accept credit card payments	PayPal Yahoo PayDirect
Digital checking	Electronic check with a secure digital signature	Western Union MoneyZap ECheck
Electronic billing presentment and payment systems	Supports electronic payment for online and physical store purchases of goods or services after the purchase has taken place	CheckFree Yahoo Bill Pay, MSN Bill Pay

An intranet typically centers around a portal to provide a single point of access to internal systems and documents using a Web interface. Such corporate portals provide a single, consolidated view of the information resources on the intranet and can be customized to suit the information needs of specific business groups and individual users if required. They may also feature e-mail, collaboration tools, and tools for searching internal corporate systems and documents.

The Window on Organizations describes two intranets used by CARE, the global humanitarian relief organization. CARE has a global staff of 12,000 operating in over 70 different countries that can benefit from immediate access to other staff members and to critical information. These intranets feature portals to provide access to information from many different sources and group collaboration tools. Portions of these intranets have been extended to authorized outsiders.

How Intranets Support Electronic Business

Whereas most companies, particularly larger ones, must support a multiplicity of computer platforms that cannot communicate with each other, intranets provide instant connectivity, uniting all computers into a single, virtually seamless, network system. Web software presents a uniform interface, which can be used to integrate many different processes and systems throughout the company. Companies can connect their intranets to internal company transaction systems, enabling employees to take actions central to a company's operations.

Internal corporate applications based on the Web page model can be made interactive using a variety of media, text, audio, and video. A principal use of intranets has been to create online repositories of information that can be updated as often as required. Product catalogs, employee handbooks, telephone directories, or benefits information can be revised immediately as changes occur. This event-driven publishing enables organizations to respond more rapidly to changing conditions than traditional paper-based publishing while eliminating paper, printing, and distribution costs.

For instance, Sun Healthcare, a chain of nursing and long-term care facilities headquartered in Albuquerque, New Mexico, saved $400,000 in printing and mailing costs when it put its corporate newsletter on an intranet. The newsletter is distributed to 69,000 employees in 49 states.

INTRANETS AND GROUP COLLABORATION

Intranets provide a rich set of tools for creating collaborative environments in which members of an organization can exchange ideas, share information, and work together on common projects and assignments regardless of their physical location. Information from many different sources and media, including text, graphics, video, audio, and even digital slides can be displayed, shared, and accessed across an enterprise through a simple common interface. The intranet for CARE Canada, described in the Window on Organizations, has some of these capabilities.

The Mitre Corporation, which conducts research and development work for the U.S. federal government, set up a collaborative environment called Mitre Information Infrastructure for sharing personnel, planning, and project information. This intranet includes a corporate directory with names, telephone numbers, and résumés of Mitre employees; a Lessons Learned Library with best practices and lessons learned from 10 years of Mitre projects; and capabilities for filing human resources reports, such as time sheets, service requests, and property inventory and tracking forms. Chapter 12 provides additional detail about intranets in knowledge-sharing and collaborative work.

Intranet Applications for Electronic Business

Intranets are springing up in all the major functional areas of businesses, enabling organizations to manage more business processes electronically. Figure 4-8 illustrates some of the intranet applications that have been developed for finance and accounting, human resources, sales and marketing, and manufacturing and production.

WINDOW ON ORGANIZATIONS

CARE's Humanitarian Intranets

CARE International is a nonprofit and nonsectarian charitable agency that manages both disaster relief and long-term development programs in more than 70 countries. Ensuring its global staff of 12,000 can communicate and access the information they need on the spot is absolutely critical to its success. In times of disaster, access to accurate, relevant information can literally mean the difference between life and death.

CARE is actually a federation of 12 relief agencies, the largest being CARE Canada, CARE Australia, and CARE US. This decentralized structure makes CARE's communication problems somewhat greater than those of other large organizations. Additionally, about 80 percent of the staff works in the field providing assistance to local communities, and most CARE workers are in the field in Latin America, Asia, and Africa, which lack robust communication infrastructures.

Much of the information and knowledge used by CARE is housed in disparate systems in over 70 different locations around the world. Critical information was often difficult to access when it was urgently needed.

CARE is trying to cope with supplying its workers with the information and communication capabilities they need by using two closely linked intranet portals. CARE Canada implemented an intranet for collaboration and storing documents that has evolved into a global portal with more than 1,000 users throughout the entire CARE federation.

This intranet uses OpenText Livelink groupware software for streamlined collaboration. It is accessible directly from the Web using standard Web browser software, so relief teams can use this tool wherever they are located without installing any special software on their computers.

OpenText Livelink provides more than 380 project teams from multiple organizations with access to information and tools for analyzing data. Livelink captures and indexes data entered by users in memos, online discussions, and project log reports, providing users with tools to help them retrieve specific information and view it in report format.

Integrated with Livelink is a data-gathering application from MODEL Technologies called MERlite. MERlite provides a set of tools for monitoring and evaluating project results so that users can perform sophisticated analyses such as comparing emergency needs to available global materials and resources.

This is how the intranet helps. A CARE staff member working on a water and sanitation project in Indonesia, for example, might put a note into a Livelink shared workspace where it could be immediately accessed by other CARE staff in the Indonesian country office, in the Ottawa office, and in the field. CARE Canada's water and sanitation specialist could access the documents and make comments while traveling in Ghana. The ability to access documents and the threads of a discussion and make comments immediately is much more efficient than using e-mail. As Carl Frappaolo, executive vice president of the Delphi Group Consultants, points out, "The more geographically dispersed the community is, the greater value you're going to find from the portal."

CARE's second intranet portal, called GYST, was rolled out in 2002 to provide better federation-wide data gathering and reporting. GYST collects and reports on performance management data for over 800 global relief projects run by CARE and its agencies. Field workers around the globe supply the performance management system with data collected through surveys, evaluations, and informal means. These data are centralized and consolidated so that CARE management can evaluate performance on an organization-wide level and also by country or individual project.

When CARE analyzes performance, it tries to measure intangible benefits related to social change as well as hard-core numbers about how many wells were dug or how many tons of food were distributed. For example, it will try to determine if its programs enabled X number of people to attend school and how that might relate to better health care.

GYST also links to the Livelink intranet and other internal finance and human resources applications. Today GYST has over 800 management-level users and is available in multiple language versions—French, English, and Spanish.

With the exception of human resources data, the data and documents on CARE portals are accessible to all CARE users. Some portions of the CARE intranets have been made accessible to members of other humanitarian and relief organizations, such as an e-library with final evaluations of programs and lessons learned.

Because CARE operates in many remote areas, pages are designed so that people with low-capacity Internet access can access information. Network connections have improved considerably in Asia and Latin America, but those in Africa are still problematic.

Sources: Kathleen Reidy, "Global Relief," *Portals Magazine*, February 1, 2004; "CARE Canada—Tackling World Problems" and "CARE Canada—CAREing Enough to Manage World Problems," Open Text Corporation, 2003; www.opentext.com, accessed August 25, 2004.

To Think About: Why are intranets useful for a global organization such as CARE? How do they provide value?

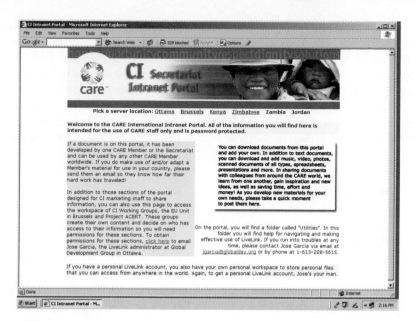

Care Canada's Intranet Portal provides access to documents from many different sources for authorized CARE staff members throughout the world.

FINANCE AND ACCOUNTING

Many organizations have extensive transaction processing systems (TPS) that collect operational data on financial and accounting activities, but their traditional management reporting systems, such as general ledger systems and spreadsheets, often cannot bring this detailed information together for decision making and performance measurement. Intranets are very valuable for finance and accounting because they can provide an integrated view of financial and accounting information online in an easy-to-use format. For example, Charles Schwab's SMART reporting system provides managers with a comprehensive view of Schwab's financial activities, including a template to help them evaluate nine categories of risk. The Schwab intranet also delivers General Ledger reporting in an easy-to-digest format.

HUMAN RESOURCES

Principal responsibilities of human resources departments include keeping employees informed of company issues and providing information about employees' personnel records and benefits. The human resources function often uses intranets for online pub-

FIGURE 4-8   *Functional applications of intranets.*

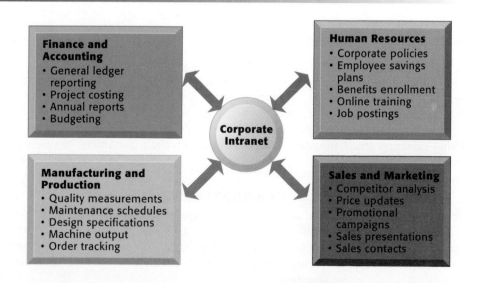

Intranet applications have been developed for each of the major functional areas of business.

lishing of corporate policy manuals, job postings and internal job transfers, company telephone directories, and training classes. Employees can use an intranet to enroll in health care, employee savings, and other benefits plans if the intranet is linked to the firm's human resources or benefits database, or employees can use it to take online competency tests. Human resources departments are able to deliver information about upcoming events or company developments to employees rapidly using newsgroups or e-mail broadcasts. For example, TransCanada Pipeline employees use the company intranet to process timesheets and expense reports as well as manage their own pension and benefit accounts.

SALES AND MARKETING

Earlier we described how the Internet and the Web are used for selling to individual customers and to other businesses. Internet technology is also useful for the internal management of the sales and marketing function. One of the most popular applications for corporate intranets involves overseeing and coordinating the activities of the sales force. Sales staff consult the intranet for updates on pricing, promotions, rebates, or customers or to obtain information about competitors. They could access presentations and sales documents and customize them for customers. For example, e-mail marketing company Yesmail.com uses a sales intranet for sharing tools and documents about contacts, sales leads, and prospects. The application includes tools for measuring the company's progress in different stages of the sales process.

MANUFACTURING AND PRODUCTION

In manufacturing, information management issues are highly complex, involving massive inventories, capturing and integrating real-time production data flows, changing relationships with suppliers, and volatile costs. The manufacturing function typically uses multiple types of data, including graphics as well as text, which are scattered in many disparate systems. Manufacturing information is often very time sensitive and difficult to retrieve because files must be continuously updated. Developing intranets that integrate manufacturing data under a uniform user interface is more complicated than in other functional areas.

Despite these difficulties, companies are launching intranet applications for manufacturing. Intranets coordinating the flow of information between lathes, controllers, inventory systems, and other components of a production system make manufacturing information more accessible to different parts of the organization, increasing precision and lowering costs. For example, Sony Corporation operates an intranet that provides data on production quality measurements, such as defects and rejects, along with maintenance and training schedules.

Business Process Integration

In the pre-Internet environment, business process integration was hampered by the difficulties of making information flow smoothly among many different kinds of systems servicing different functional areas and parts of the organization. Some of this integration can be supplied relatively inexpensively using Internet technology. Firms are using intranets to improve coordination among their internal business processes, and they are deploying extranets to coordinate processes shared with their customers, business partners, and other organizations.

THE INTERNET AND COLLABORATIVE COMMERCE

In some industries, Internet technology is helping companies collaborate more closely with customers, suppliers, and other firms to improve planning, production, and distribution of goods and services. The use of digital technologies to enable multiple organizations to design, develop, move, and manage products collaboratively through their life cycles is called **collaborative commerce**.

The development of a new product usually involves collaboration among different departments in a single firm and, increasingly, among several different firms. Internet technology provides communication and collaboration tools to connect designers, engineers, and marketing and manufacturing staff in different locations or even different organizations. Internet-based tools help companies coordinate work with suppliers or contract manufacturers as they build and deliver their products.

Firms are using the customer feedback from Web sites or online communities to improve product design. Equipped with appropriate software tools, customers can actually help companies design and develop some types of products. For example, GE Plastics provides its customers with Web-based tools to help them design better plastic products (Thomke and von Hippel, 2002). A firm engaged in collaborative commerce with its suppliers and customers can achieve new levels of efficiency in reducing product design cycles, minimizing excess inventory, forecasting demand, and keeping partners and customers informed (see Figure 4-9).

Table 4-4 provides examples of how companies are using Internet technology for collaborative commerce.

4.4   MANAGEMENT OPPORTUNITIES, CHALLENGES, AND SOLUTIONS

Internet technology has provided businesses with powerful new tools to innovate and to execute much more efficiently, and it has also created a new series of management challenges.

Opportunities

The Internet and Internet technology have created extraordinary opportunities for new and traditional businesses to exploit digital technology. Firms are using these technologies to create new products and services, new channels for sales and marketing, and even entirely new businesses. These technologies have also strengthened traditional business models by helping firms reduce supply chain costs, increase production efficiency, and

FIGURE 4-9   *Collaborative commerce.*

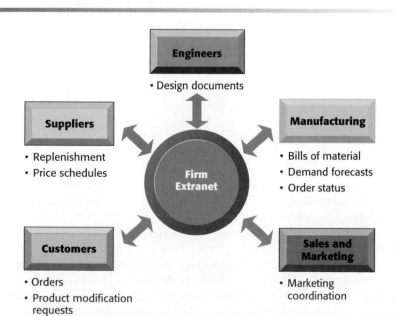

Collaborative commerce is a set of digitally enabled collaborative interactions between an enterprise and its business partners and customers. Internet technology helps the collaborative community share data and processes that were once considered internal.

TABLE 4-4 *How the Internet Facilitates Collaborative Commerce*

Application	Example
Product service and support	American Axle and Manufacturing, which produces automobile driveline systems, chassis components, and forged products, uses the Web to share with suppliers photos of defective parts that stall its assembly line and to discuss the problem so they can solve it on the spot.
Collaborative product design across multiple locations	Engineers at Johnson Controls and DaimlerChrysler used a Web-based design and collaboration system to design part of the Jeep Liberty interior together.
Customer service	Packaging company Menasha lets customers use the Web to proof products, change colors and specifications, and check scheduling directly in its enterprise resource planning (ERP) system.
Supply chain coordination	Hewlett-Packard (HP) Laserjet Imaging Systems uses a Web-based workgroup collaboration system to share information with its contract manufacturers, distribution centers, and resellers. The application makes parts plans from HP's internal production system available on a shared electronic workspace where they can be accessed by suppliers. Suppliers can then adjust their plans to coordinate their inventory with that of HP.
Collaborative sourcing	B2B Net marketplace Exostar provides a collaboration tool for multiple suppliers to collaborate on the design and performance of products they jointly develop and sell to companies in the aerospace and defense industries.

tighten relationships with customers. No company can afford to ignore the Internet and Internet technology, even if it does not do business online.

Management Challenges

Although digitally enabling business processes and relationships with other organizations can help companies achieve new levels of competitiveness and efficiency, it does pose challenges for managers. Many new Internet business models have yet to prove enduring sources of profit. Web-enabling business processes for electronic commerce and electronic business requires changing the way the organization works. The legal environment for electronic commerce has not yet solidified, and companies pursuing electronic commerce must be vigilant about establishing trust, security, and consumer privacy.

FINDING A SUCCESSFUL INTERNET BUSINESS MODEL

The Internet has clearly changed business models in a number of key industries, including the media (books and music), financial services, travel, and automobile retailing. But not all Internet business models have been successful. Hundreds of retail dot-com firms, including Kozmo.com, Webvan, Garden.com, Chinese Books Cyberstore, Productopia.com, and Pets.com, have closed their doors. Only a fraction of the independent exchanges that were operating in the spring of 2000 survive today.

Doing business over the Internet is not necessarily more efficient or cost effective than traditional business methods. Virtual retailers may not need to pay for costly storefronts and retail workers, but they require heavy outlays for warehousing, customer service call centers, and customer acquisition.

Challenges also confront businesses that are trying to use the Web to supplement or enhance traditional business models. Businesses that are unclear about their online strategy—and its relationship to their overall business strategy—can waste thousands and even millions of dollars building and maintaining Web sites that fail to deliver the desired results (Pinker, Seidmann, and Foster, 2002). Introducing a Web site with self-service technology may undermine the business model—and competitive advantage—of a firm that relies on traditional sales representatives to provide unique personalized services to customers (Schultze and Orlikowski, 2004). And even if a company has a viable Internet business model, it can fail if that business model is poorly executed.

ORGANIZATIONAL CHANGE CHALLENGES

E-business and e-commerce often require new organizational designs and management processes to take advantage of Internet technology. Companies may need to redesign entire business processes rather than trying to graft new technology on existing business practices. Companies must consider a different organizational structure, changes in organizational culture, a different support structure for information systems, different procedures for managing employees and networked processing functions, and, perhaps, a different business strategy.

Traditional boundaries between departments and divisions, and companies and distributors may be impediments to collaboration and relationship building. Companies with traditional retail outlets or sales forces can expect **channel conflict** if they use the Web for online sales and marketing. Their sales force and distributors may fear that their revenues will drop as customers make purchases directly from the Web or that they will be displaced by this new channel.

TRUST, SECURITY, AND PRIVACY

Electronic commerce cannot flourish unless there is an atmosphere of trust among buyers, sellers, and other partners involved in online transactions. Because online relationships are more impersonal perhaps than those in bricks-and-mortar commerce, some consumers remain hesitant to make purchases over the Web from unfamiliar vendors. Consumers also worry about the security and confidentiality of the credit card number and other personal data that they supply over the Internet. Internet-based systems are even more vulnerable to penetration by outsiders than private networks because the Internet was designed to be open to everyone.

The Web provides an unprecedented ability to learn about and target customers. But the same capability can also undermine individual privacy. Using Web site monitoring software and other technology for tracking Web visitors, companies can gather detailed information about individuals without their knowledge. In other instances, Web site visitors knowingly supply personal information, such as their names, addresses, e-mail addresses, and special interests, in exchange for access to the site without realizing how the organization owning the Web site may use the information. For companies collecting detailed customer information over the Web, the challenge is balancing the desire to profit from such information with the need to safeguard individual privacy.

Solution Guidelines

Digitally enabling the enterprise with Internet technology requires attention to these issues and careful management planning.

DETERMINING HOW INTERNET TECHNOLOGY CAN PROVIDE VALUE FOR THE BUSINESS

Managers need to understand precisely how Internet technology can provide value for their company.

Companies need to think carefully about whether they can create a genuinely workable business model on the Internet and how the Internet relates to their overall business strategy. Internet technology alone is not a substitute for an effective business strategy (Rangan and Adner, 2001; Willcocks and Plant, 2001).

MANAGING BUSINESS PROCESS CHANGES

Before embarking on e-commerce or e-business initiatives, managers will need to identify carefully the organizational changes required to make them work. They should then put in place a change management plan for dealing with impacted groups within the firm as well as with suppliers and other business partners in the company's network of value creation. Also essential are well-defined policies and procedures for sharing data with other organizations, including specifications for the type, format, level of precision, and security of the data to be exchanged (Barua, Konana, Whinston, and Yin, 2001).

Channel conflict merits special attention. One way to deal with this problem is to compensate sales representatives for online sales in their territories even if they do not work on the sale or meet the buyer. Another solution is to offer only a portion of the company's full product line on the Web. The importance of traditional channels and the level of resistance to Web sales will help determine the appropriate response.

SAFEGUARDING SECURITY AND PRIVACY

Both electronic commerce and electronic business require companies to be both more open and more closed at the same time. Companies need to be open to outsiders such as customers, suppliers, and trading partners, yet these systems also must be closed to hackers and other intruders and protective of customers. Firms engaging in e-commerce and e-business need a new security culture and infrastructure that enable them to straddle this fine line. They also need to reexamine corporate privacy policies to make sure they are properly respecting the privacy of customers and Web site visitors. Chapters 5 and 10 provide more detail on how Internet privacy and security can be safeguarded.

MAKE IT YOUR BUSINESS

Finance and Accounting

Internet technology facilitates access to and integration of financial data from sources inside and outside the firm. Firms that have embarked on ambitious programs to integrate their systems can use corporate intranets to obtain company-wide views of their firm's financial performance. The Internet has opened up new avenues for businesses to make and receive payments electronically and has provided the financial industry with new products and channels to customers.

Human Resources

Internet technology has led to efficiencies and cost savings in employee communication and training as well as the processing of basic human resources (HR) transactions. Many companies are installing self-service HR systems on intranets to deliver HR-related services, such as enrolling in insurance and medical plans, maintaining employee savings plans, and applying for company jobs. Companies can use Web technology to deliver interactive employee training and HR policy manuals and company directories. Human resources staff members can use intranets to access employee records from the firm's basic human resources transaction systems. You can find examples of human resources applications on page 132.

Manufacturing and Production

Internet technology creates a common platform for communication and data exchange that can be used to integrate manufacturing and production data from disparate systems inside the firm and to coordinate manufacturing and production processes with those of suppliers and distributors. Internet technology can help companies bring products to market more quickly and, in some cases, outsource most and even all of their production or order fulfillment. Public B2B commerce systems and private industrial networks can help reduce procurement costs and make other supply chain processes more efficient. The Internet can play a role in every step of the manufacturing and production process, from gauging demand and taking orders to scheduling production jobs, managing inventory, and handling shipping and logistics. You can find examples of manufacturing and production applications on pages 113 and 128.

Sales and Marketing

Although the Internet may not have overwhelmed traditional retailing, it has spawned powerful new channels for reaching consumers and providing new digital products and services. A significant percentage of financial products and services, books, computers, music, video, and travel services is now purchased on the Web. Internet technologies can help differentiate products by using personalization, customization techniques, and community marketing techniques.

The Internet has broadened the scope of marketing communications by making it much easier for firms to reach large numbers of people. The Internet has also increased the richness of marketing communications by combining text, video, and audio content into rich interactive messages. Personalized messages can be delivered at very low cost to individuals and groups. Finally, the Internet provides marketers with unparalleled, fine-grained, detailed real-time information about consumers as they transact on the Web. You can find examples of sales and marketing applications on pages 113 and 143–145.

Summary

1. *Analyze how Internet technology has changed value propositions and business models.*

   The Internet is rapidly becoming the infrastructure of choice for electronic commerce and electronic business because it provides a universal and easy-to-use set of technologies and technology standards that can be adopted by all organizations, no matter which computer system or information technology platform they use. Internet technology provides a much lower cost and easier to use alternative for coordination activities than proprietary networks. Companies can use Internet technology to radically reduce their transaction and agency costs.

   The Internet radically reduces the cost of creating, sending, and storing information while making that information more widely available. Information is not limited to traditional physical methods of delivery. Customers can find out about products on their own on the Web and buy directly from product suppliers instead of using intermediaries such as retail stores. This unbundling of information from traditional value chain channels is having a disruptive effect on old business models, and it is creating new business models as well. Some of the traditional channels for exchanging product information have become unnecessary or uneconomical, and business models based on the coupling of information with products and services may no longer be necessary. By using the Internet and other networks for electronic commerce, organizations in some industries can exchange purchase and sale transactions directly with customers and suppliers, eliminating inefficient intermediaries.

   The Internet shrinks information asymmetry and has transformed the relationship between information richness and reach. Using the Internet and Web multimedia capabilities, companies can quickly and inexpensively provide detailed product information and detailed information specific to each customer to very large numbers of people simultaneously. The Internet can help companies create and capture profit in new ways by adding extra value to existing products and services or by providing the foundation for new products and services. Many different business models for electronic commerce on the Internet have emerged, including virtual storefronts, information brokers, transaction brokers, Net marketplaces, content providers, online service providers, virtual communities, and portals.

2. *Define electronic commerce and describe how it has changed consumer retailing and business-to-business transactions.*

   Electronic commerce is the process of buying and selling goods electronically with computerized business transactions using the Internet or other digital network technology. It includes marketing, customer support, delivery, and payment. The three major types of electronic commerce are business-to-consumer (B2C), business-to-business (B2B), and consumer-to-consumer (C2C). Another way of classifying electronic commerce transactions is in terms of the participants' physical connection to the Web. Conventional e-commerce transactions, which take place over wired networks, can be distinguished from mobile commerce, or m-commerce, which is the purchase of goods and services using hand-held wireless devices.

   The Internet provides a universally available set of technologies for electronic commerce that can be used to create new channels for marketing, sales, and customer support and to eliminate intermediaries in buy-and-sell transactions. Interactive capabilities on the Web can be used to build closer relationships with customers in marketing and customer support. Firms can use various Web personalization technologies to deliver Web pages with content geared to the specific interests of each user, including technologies to deliver personalized information and ads through m-commerce channels. Companies can also reduce costs and improve customer service by using Web sites, as well as e-mail and telephone access to customer service representatives, to provide helpful information.

   B2B e-commerce generates efficiencies by enabling companies to locate suppliers, solicit bids, place orders, and track shipments in transit electronically. Businesses can use their own Web sites to sell to other businesses or use Net marketplaces or private industrial networks. Net marketplaces provide a single digital marketplace based on Internet technology for many buyers and sellers. Net marketplaces can be differentiated by whether they sell direct or indirect goods, support spot or long-term purchasing, or serve vertical or horizontal markets. Private industrial networks link a firm with its suppliers and other strategic business partners to develop highly efficient supply chains and to respond quickly to customer demands.

3. *Compare the principal payment systems for electronic commerce.*

   The principal electronic payment systems for electronic commerce are digital credit card systems, digital wallets, accumulated balance digital payment systems, stored value payment systems, digital cash, peer-to-peer payment systems, digital checking, and electronic billing presentment and payment systems. Accumulated balance systems, stored value systems (including smart cards), and digital cash are useful for small micropayments.

4. *Evaluate the role of Internet technology in facilitating management and coordination of internal and inter-organizational business processes.*

Private, internal corporate networks called intranets can be created using Internet connectivity standards. Extranets are private intranets that are extended to selected organizations or individuals outside the firm. Intranets and extranets are forming the underpinnings of electronic business by providing a low-cost technology that can run on almost any computing platform. Organizations can use intranets to create collaboration environments for coordinating work and information sharing, and to make information flow between different functional areas of the firm. Intranets also provide a low-cost alternative for improving coordination of cross-functional business processes within the organization.

Extranets help coordinate business processes shared with customers, suppliers, and other external organizations. Collaborative commerce builds on extranets to enable multiple organizations to collaboratively design, develop, build, move, and manage products through their life cycles. A firm engaged in collaborative commerce with its suppliers and customers can achieve new efficiencies by reducing product design cycles, minimiz-

ing excess inventory, forecasting demand, and keeping partners and customers informed.

5. *Assess the challenges posed by electronic business and electronic commerce and management solutions.*

Many new business models based on the Internet have not yet found proven ways to generate profits or reduce costs. Digitally enabling a firm for electronic commerce and electronic business requires far-reaching organizational change, including redesign of business processes; recasting relationships with customers, suppliers, and other business partners; and new roles for employees. Channel conflicts may erupt as the firm turns to the Internet as an alternative outlet for sales. Security, privacy, and legal issues pose additional electronic commerce challenges. Before embracing e-commerce and e-business, firms should understand exactly how Internet technology provides value to the business and relates to their overall business strategy. They should also should anticipate making organizational changes, including changing business processes and developing a plan for managing channel conflict. Finally, they will need corporate policies and tools for promoting security and privacy within an e-business environment.

Key Terms

Accumulated balance digital payment systems, 129
Banner ad, 118
Blog, 123
Business model, 115
Business-to-business (B2B) electronic commerce, 120
Business-to-consumer (B2C) electronic commerce, 120
Call center, 124
Channel conflict, 137
Clicks-and-mortar, 119
Clickstream tracking, 121
Collaborative commerce, 134
Collaborative filtering, 121
Consumer-to-consumer (C2C) electronic commerce, 120

Digital cash, 129
Digital checking, 130
Digital credit card payment systems, 129
Digital wallet, 129
Disintermediation, 120
Dynamic pricing, 117
Electronic billing presentment and payment systems, 130
Electronic data interchange (EDI), 124
Electronic payment systems, 127
Exchanges, 127
Information asymmetry, 116
Micropayment, 129
Mobile commerce (m-commerce), 120
Net marketplaces, 126

Peer-to-peer payment systems, 129
Pop-up ads, 118
Private exchange, 125
Private industrial networks, 125
Procurement, 125
Pure-play, 119
Reach, 117
Reintermediation, 121
Richness, 116
Search costs, 116
Smart card, 129
Social networking sites, 118
Stored value payment systems, 129
Syndicators, 119
Web personalization, 121

Review Questions

1. *What are the advantages of using the Internet as the infrastructure for electronic commerce and electronic business?*

2. *How is the Internet changing the economics of information and business models?*

3. *Name and describe six Internet business models for electronic commerce. Distinguish between a pure-play Internet business model and a clicks-and-mortar business model.*

4. *Name and describe the various categories of electronic commerce.*

5. *How can the Internet facilitate sales and marketing to individual customers? Describe the role played by Web personalization.*

6. *How can the Internet help provide customer service?*

7. *How can Internet technology support business-to-business electronic commerce?*

8. *What are Net marketplaces? Why do they represent an important business model for B2B e-commerce? How do they differ from private industrial networks?*

9. *Name and describe the principal electronic payment systems used on the Internet.*

10. *Why are intranets so useful for electronic business?*

11. *How can intranets support organizational collaboration?*

12. *Describe the uses of intranets for electronic business in sales and marketing, human resources, finance and accounting, and manufacturing.*

13. *How can companies use Internet technology for integrating business processes? How does Internet technology facilitate collaborative commerce?*

14. *What is channel conflict? Why is it becoming a growing problem in electronic commerce?*

15. *Describe the management challenges posed by electronic commerce and electronic business and suggest some solutions.*

Discussion Questions

1. *How does the Internet change firm's consumer and supplier relationships?*

2. *The Internet may not make corporations obsolete, but they will have to change their business models. Do you agree? Why or why not?*

Application Software Exercise:
Spreadsheet Exercise: Analyzing a Dot-Com Business

Pick one e-commerce company on the Internet, for example, Ashford.com, Buy.com, Yahoo.com, or Priceline.com. Study the Web pages that describe the company and explain its purpose and structure. Look for articles at Web sites such as Bigcharts.com or Hoovers.com that comment on the company. Then visit the Securities and Exchange Commission's Web site at www.sec.gov and access the company's 10-K (annual report) forms showing income statements and balance sheets. Select only the sections of the 10-K form containing the desired portions of financial statements that you need to examine, and download them into your spreadsheet. (*Hint*: When you find the page that lists specific forms, select the text version. Do not select the HTML version. The Laudon Web site for Chapter 4 provides more detailed instructions on how to download 10-K data into a spreadsheet.) Create simplified spread-sheets of the company's balance sheets and income statements for the past three years.

Is the company a dot-com success, borderline business, or failure? What information forms the basis of your decision? Why? When answering these questions, pay special attention to the company's three-year trends in revenues, costs of sales, gross margins, operating expenses, and net margins. See the Laudon Web site for Chapter 4 for definitions of these terms and how they are calculated. Prepare an overhead presentation (minimum of five slides), including appropriate spreadsheets or charts, and present your work to your professor and/or classmates. If the company is successful, which additional business strategies could it pursue to become even more successful? If the company is a borderline or failing business, which specific business strategies (if any) could make it more successful?

Developing an E-Commerce Strategy

Software requirements: Web browser software
Word processing software
Web page development tool (optional)

Dirt Bikes's management believes that the company could benefit from e-commerce. The company has sold motorcycles and parts primarily through authorized dealers. Dirt Bikes advertises in various magazines catering to dirt bike enthusiasts and maintains booths at important off-road motorcycle racing events. You have been asked to explore how Dirt Bikes could benefit from e-commerce and a Dirt Bikes Web site. Prepare a report for management that answers the following questions:

1. How could Dirt Bikes benefit from e-commerce? Should it sell motorcycles or parts over the Web? Should it use its Web site primarily to advertise its products and services? Should it use the Web for customer service?

2. How would a Web site provide value to Dirt Bikes? Use the Web to research the cost of an

e-commerce site for a small to medium-sized company. How much revenue or cost savings would the Web site have to produce to make it a worthwhile investment for Dirt Bikes?

3. Prepare specifications describing the functions that should be performed by Dirt Bikes's Web site. Include links to other Web sites or other systems in your specifications.

4. (Optional) Design the home page and an important secondary page linked to the home page using the capabilities of word processing software or a Web page development tool of your choice.

Electronic Commerce Project: Comparing Online Storefront Hosting Services

You would like to set up a Web site to sell towels, linens, pottery and tableware from Portugal and are examining services for hosting small business Internet storefronts. Your Web site should be able to take secure credit card payments and to calculate shipping costs and taxes. Initially you would like to display photos and descriptions of 40 different products. Visit Yahoo! Store and Freemerchant.com and compare the range of e-commerce hosting services they offer to small business, their capabilities and costs. Also examine the tools they provide for creating an e-commerce site. Compare both of these services and decide which of the two you would use if you were actually establishing a Web store. Write a small report indicating your choice and explaining the strengths and weaknesses of both.

Group Project: Performing a Competitive Analysis of E-Commerce Sites

Form a group with three or four of your classmates. Select two businesses that are competitors in the same industry that use their Web sites for electronic commerce. Visit their Web sites. You might compare, for example, the Web sites for virtual banking created by Citibank and Wells Fargo Bank, or the Internet trading Web sites of E*TRADE and Scottrade. Prepare an evaluation of each business's Web site in terms of its functions, user friendliness, and ability to support the company's business strategy. Which Web site does a better job? Why? Can you make some recommendations to improve these Web sites?

CASE STUDY
Can the Music Industry Change Its Tune?

Would you pay $15.99 for a CD of your favorite recording artist if you could get it for free on the Web? This question has shaken the music industry to its foundations. A tremendous number of Internet users have taken advantage of online file-sharing services where they can download digitized music files from other users free of charge.

The first such service to be widely used was Napster. Its Web site provided software and services that enabled users to locate any of the 1 billion digitized MP3 music files on the computers of other online Napster members and copy them onto their own computers for free. Napster's own computers did not store any music files, but instead acted as a matchmaker. To obtain a specific music file, you would sign on to the Napster Web site and type in the name of the desired song. Napster's central title index would display the connected computers with that specific song. Napster then established a direct connection between the requesting computer and the one storing the desired music file. Your Napster software then would download that file onto your computer. You could play the song on your computer and copy it onto CDs. If you stored it on your computer, others could copy it from you. Napster quickly became so popular that when it was shut down in 2001, it had more than 80 million users worldwide.

Napster users could legally copy and trade uncopyrighted material, but reproducing copyrighted files without permission is illegal because the recipient does not compensate the owner for the use of the intellectual property. In December 1999, the Recording Industry Association of America (RIAA), representing the five major music recording companies (Universal Music, Sony Music, Warner Music, BMG, and EMI), which together were responsible for 80 percent of recorded music, sued Napster for violating copyright laws. U.S.

courts ordered Napster to stop allowing users to share copyrighted music files, and the site closed down in July 2002 when it declared bankruptcy. It has since been transformed into a legal fee-based online digital music service.

Napster was held liable for the illegal copying of copyrighted songs because it maintained a central index of members' music on its own central computer. Its closure did not stop widespread illegal music file sharing. Alternative "peer-to-peer" approaches to free downloading were developed that did not require a centralized computer to manage the file swapping. Services using this approach include Kazaa (KaZaA), Morpheus, and Grokster. Many of the estimated 37 million Americans who have downloaded music have done so using Kazaa. According to research firm BigChampagne LLC, users download more than 1 billion songs per week from Kazaa, Morpheus, and other file-sharing programs.

Kazaa's corporate headquarters are located in Vanatu, a tiny independent island near Australia. Kazaa's software is stored on individual computers, enabling anyone to locate servers where individuals have stored music files available to be copied. Once the software locates the desired song, it establishes a direct peer-to-peer link between the two computers and downloads the desired song file, with no one paying any fees. Distributors of the software claim that their software has valuable legal uses, and they are not responsible if millions of people use it illegally.

To profit from its software, Kazaa allows pop-up advertisements and unsolicited e-mail from vendors who pay for the service. Because the free trading of digitized materials does not go through a centralized computer, no one knows what or how many songs are being downloaded or by whom. But Kazaa reported that, by June 2003, its Media Desktop software for computer-to-

computer file sharing had been downloaded 270 million times.

The courts have been unable to shut down sites that only make the peer-to-peer software available. On October 2, 2001, through RIAA, the major record label firms filed suit against Kazaa, Morpheus, and other peer-to-peer services, alleging copyright infringement against all firms who use Media Desktop and similar software to swap copyrighted materials. However, because the exchange of music files is strictly between two individuals, Kazaa claims it is breaking no laws and so cannot be shut down. Instead, individual users of Kazaa's software are breaking laws and can be punished.

A big blow against the recording companies came on April 25, 2003, when a suit brought by the major record labels, movie studios, and music publishers against Grokster Ltd. (Grokster software) and StreamCast Networks Inc. (Morpheus software) was decided in favor of the file-sharing services. The U.S. District Court in Los Angeles ruled that the two companies could not be held responsible for illegal music swapping using their software because they cannot monitor or control how users of their software exchange files, and so they were not breaking any laws by making their software available. A subsequent ruling on August 19, 2004, by the U.S. Court of Appeals, Ninth District in San Francisco upheld this earlier ruling.

RIAA started to prosecute first students and then other individuals use the Internet for illegal music downloading. The effort began in the autumn of 2002 with 2,300 "cease and desist" letters to colleges, warning them to stop their students from downloading music. RIAA then filed a suit against four individual students in an attempt to stop students from downloading free popular songs illegally and then making them available for other students to copy. In an out-of-court settlement on April 30, 2003, the students agreed to cease their music downloading activities and pay RIAA more than $10,000 each. Immediately after the agreement, a number of similar file-sharing networks on other campuses were pulled down.

In the spring of 2003 RIAA started sending Kazaa and Grokster users millions of instant messages which said, "When you break the law, you risk legal penalties. There is a simple way to avoid that risk: DON'T STEAL MUSIC." Then on September 8, 2003, RIAA filed lawsuits against 261 American computer users whom it believed were using Internet file-sharing services to distribute and download large amounts of copyrighted music illegally. RIAA launched additional suits against users of online file-sharing networks, targeting 532 people in January 2004 and 744 people in August 2004. Legal experts expect most of these lawsuits to be settled in favor of RIAA, but these suits are unlikely to halt illegal music file sharing.

Although RIAA's legal campaign has frightened some illegal music downloaders, many individuals continue to believe that there is nothing wrong with downloading and distributing copyrighted music. This widespread attitude cannot be easily changed. The music industry believes that widespread music file sharing on the Internet has caused music CD sales to plummet and that Internet downloading is costing them billions of dollars in lost sales each year.

In 2000, CD sales were about $35.5 billion; in 2001, sales fell to $33.7 billion, a decrease of 5 percent. According to Nielsen SoundScan, CD music sales fell another 8.8 percent in 2002. In 2003, U.S. recorded music sales only fell 0.8 percent from 2002, but worldwide, sales fell around 10 percent.

Critics of the recording industry claimed that sales slipped only a little in the falling economy. A Jupiter Research report of May 2002 and a report by Professor Felix Oberholzer-Gee of Harvard Business School and Koleman Strumpf of University of North Carolina found that those who use such free Internet file-sharing networks as Kazaa to download songs are more likely to increase their

spending on music than other music CD purchasers. These reports concluded that free downloading increases music CD sales by getting people enthusiastic about new and catalog music.

Critics pointed out that the number of industry releases has fallen sharply, from a record 38,900 titles in 1999 to 31,734 in 2001, a 20.3 percent drop. Nielsen also reported that although the 2002 releases rose to 33,443, that was still a 14 percent drop. "The music industry's [approach] is to throw things against the wall and see what sticks," said Nathan Brackett, *Rolling Stone*'s senior editor. "If they're throwing 20 percent less stuff out there, there's less chance something will stick." Also, the average CD price rose 7.2 percent between 1999 and 2001 from $13.04 to $14.19, whereas consumer prices rose barely at all.

Critics believe that new forms of competition for entertainment dollars have also contributed to the drop in CD sales. For example, 35 percent of U.S. homes had DVD players in 2002 versus none in 1999. DVDs, video games, and the Internet are becoming strong competitors for entertainment dollars.

Observers emphasize that those who continue to download songs for free actually do face costs. First, users must spend time downloading the music. Then, to play it anywhere but on their computers, they must "burn" it onto compact discs. Moreover, specific songs can be hard to locate. And users have to endure technological problems, including pop-up advertising to pay for the "free" services. Also, prior to downloading, users cannot tell if the song contains a computer virus, is only a virus, or is otherwise a phony or incomplete song. The quality may even be poor, including scratching and popping sounds. Students may have time to experiment, but most people with full-time jobs do not.

The recording industry now realizes that it must change the way it does business if it is to survive. Some industry analysts believe it must find ways to cut costs. Michael Nathanson, the music analyst for Sanford C. Bernstein, said the biggest costs (about 36 percent) were talent and marketing.

Some analysts recommend that recording companies consider signing fewer artists. According to Michael Wolff of McKinsey & Company, "The revenues today can't support such a broad number of releases." Others believe the only way to cut these costs is through consolidation, perhaps cutting the major recording companies from five to three. However, because overhead amounts to only one-third of recorded music costs, the savings would be limited and inadequate. Some claim the underlying problem is that entertainment executives compete with each other for a limited pool of talent. Nathanson suggests the companies need to rely on other sources of revenue. For example, he believes they should get a portion of artists' earnings for concerts, sponsorships, and merchandise sales, all of which are currently kept by the artists themselves.

For years, the recording companies balked at licensing their songs for legal sale online. Most of them burdened the music with unwieldy technical safeguards that prevented consumers from recording songs onto CDs or transferring them to portable music players. These services often required monthly subscription fees, offering too few songs and at too high a price per song. They were not very successful.

In 2002, the major labels did a turnaround and started to embrace online music sales. They began experimenting with alternative pricing structures for music delivered legally over the Internet. Some executives believed that the industry should not sell songs individually (as over the Net) because people will purchase a whole CD to get one or two songs. However, with the proper price, individual songs could be effectively sold. Tests showed that above $1 per song, sales fell off rather quickly. John Rose, executive vice president of EMI, concluded, "If all consumers who pirate tracks today bought them for a buck, that would be a $5 billion a month business."

On April 29, 2003, Apple Computer announced a new Web site for downloading music named the iTunes Music

Store. It was an immediate success, selling 1.4 million songs in its first week, and 100 million by August 2004. It stunned the industry. The site charges 99 cents per song and at first offered more than 200,000 songs. Apple has a licensing agreement with all five of the big recording companies and now has available all the songs in their catalogs.

Users do not subscribe to this site, making it less expensive than the other sites. The person purchasing the songs can burn as many as 10 compact discs with the same list of songs so the whole family can use them. The site is easy to use. Songs can be located by genre, artist, or album, and they can be downloaded at the click of a single button. Album covers are downloaded with each song or album. Moreover, users can play a 30-second preview of each song for free. Most complete albums cost between $8 and $11, with the majority priced at $10. The songs belong to the purchaser who is able to copy them to as many as three computers (a restriction demanded by the big labels).

iTunes has inspired a new wave of similar online music services, including Napster 2.0 (a legal version owned by Roxio Inc.), Sony Connect, RealNetworks, and BuyMusic.com. Microsoft and Yahoo! have entered this market and Viacom's MTV and Virgin Group have similar plans. As in many other industries, this intense competition is commoditizing the digital music market. Outside of sales or limited promotions there is very little variation among the major music sites in price or tune selection.

Online distribution of individual songs is still an unproven business model, and profits are very thin—usually about 10 percent at best. Some believe that these sites are useful more as loss leaders to help companies sell other related products, such as portable music players or subscription services.

Will reduced CD prices and Apple's model be the solution for which the music industry as been searching? Or will the illegal downloading of copyrighted music continue to grow? The motion picture industry is anxiously watching because, as high-speed Internet connections become more popular, it may face the same fate as the recording industry. Will the living room become a war zone for digital entertainment or a thriving marketplace shared by the creators of content and the makers of the machines that deliver it?

Sources: Nick Wingfield and Sarah McBride, "Green Light for Grokster," *Wall Street Journal*, August 20, 2004; Nick Wingfield, "Price War in Online Music," *Wall Street Journal*, August 17, 2004, and "Online Music's Latest Tune," *Wall Street Journal*, August 27, 2004; Sarah McBride, "Stop the Music!" *Wall Street Journal*, August 23, 2004; Thomas Claburn, "Feds Target Scofflaws and Spammers," *Information Week*, August 30, 2004; Alex Veiga, "Recording Industry Sues 532 Over Swapping," Associated Press, March 23, 2004; David McGuire, "Study: File-Sharing No Threat to Music Sales," *Washington Post*, March 30, 2004; Sue Zeidler, "Sony Unveils Music Service, Mulls iPod Killer," Reuters, May 4, 2004; John Schwartz and John Markoff, "Power Players: Big Names Are Jumping into the Crowded Online Music Field," *New York Times*, January 12, 2004; Martin Peers, "Buddy Can You Spare Some Time?" *Wall Street Journal*, January 26, 2004; Ethan Smith, "Music Industry Sounds Upbeat as Losses Slow," *Wall Street Journal*, January 2, 2004; Nick Wingfield and Ethan Smith, "With the Web Shaking Up Music, a Free-for-All in Online Songs," *Wall Street Journal*, November 19, 2003, and "New Ways to Pay 99 Cents for Music," *Wall Street Journal*, October 9, 2003; Cade Metz, "The Changing Face of Online Music," *PC Magazine*, September 24, 2003; Mike France, "Music Pirates, You're Sunk," *Business Week*, August 29, 2003; Amy Harmon, "Despite Suits, Music File Sharers Shrug Off Guilt and Keep Sharing," *New York Times*, September 19, 2003; Amy Harmon, "Industry Offers a Carrot in Online Music Fight," *New York Times*, June 8, 2003; "Kazaa Stays on Track to Be Most Downloaded Program," news.yahoo.com, May 25, 2003; Amy Harmon, "Music Swappers Get a Message on PC Screens: Stop It Now," *New York Times*, May 19, 2003; Jane Black, "Big Music: Win Some, Lose a Lot More?" *Business Week Online*, May 5, 2003; Amy Harmon, "Suit Settled for Students Downloading Music Online," *New York Times*, May 2, 2003; Pui-Wing Tam, "Apple Launches Online Store Offering Downloadable Music," *Wall Street Journal*, April 29, 2003; Anna Wilde Mathews and Nick Wingfield, "Entertainment Industry Loses Important File-Sharing Battle," *Wall Street Journal*, April 28, 2003; Jane Black, "Digital Music: Still Scores Left to Settle," *Business Week Online*, April 22, 2003; Jane Black, "Web Music Gets Its Act Together," *Business Week Online*, April 22, 2003; Sarah D. Scalet, "The Pirates Among Us," *CIO Magazine*, April 15, 2003; David Pogue, "The Internet as Jukebox, at a Price," *New York Times Circuits*, March 6, 2003; Saul Hansell, "E-Music Settle on Prices. It's a Start," *New York Times*, March 3, 2003; Julia Angwin and Nick Wingfield, "AOL Brings Online Music to the Masses, for a Price," *Wall Street Journal*, February 26, 2003; Anne Wilde Mathews and Charles Goldsmith, "Music Industry Faces New Threats on Web," *Wall Street Journal*, February 21, 2003; Jane Black, "Big Music's Broken Record," *Business Week Online*, February 13, 2003; Laura M. Holson and Geraldine Fabrikant, "Music Industry Braces for a Shift," *New York Times*, January 13, 2003; and Matt Richtel, "Access to Free Online Music Is Seen as a Boost to Sales," *New York Times*, May 6, 2002.

CASE STUDY QUESTIONS

1. Apply the value chain and competitive forces models to the music recording industry.

2. What role did the Internet play in changing value propositions and the competitive environment? To what extent has it been responsible for declining CD sales? Explain your answer.

3. Analyze the response of the music recording industry to these changes. What management, organization, and technology issues affected this response?

4. What is the current business strategy of the music industry? Do you think it is viable? Explain your answer.

Chapter 5

Ethical and Social Issues in the Digital Firm

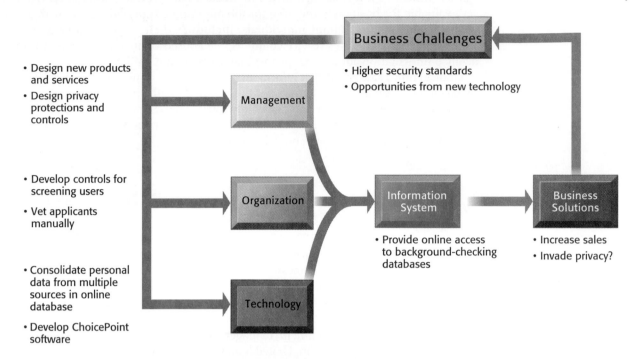

- Design new products and services
- Design privacy protections and controls

- Develop controls for screening users
- Vet applicants manually

- Consolidate personal data from multiple sources in online database
- Develop ChoicePoint software

Business Challenges
- Higher security standards
- Opportunities from new technology

Management

Organization

Technology

Information System
- Provide online access to background-checking databases

Business Solutions
- Increase sales
- Invade privacy?

Opening Case: "Attention Shoppers: Background Checks for Sale"

Many companies today require background checks of job applicants and hired employees to make sure they do not have criminal records or other problems. Commercial services are now available to help employers with this task. ChoicePoint, based in Alpharetta, Georgia, one of the largest U.S. vendors of financial, personal, and legal data, provides an array of services for employee background checks.

A new ChoicePoint product called check-in-a-box sells in stores such as Sam's Club along with other software for home and small business users. It features a CD-ROM that enables users to tap into ChoicePoint's online databases, giving small business users access to data that previously were beyond their reach.

Although easy access to data for background checking is very useful for employers, it has privacy advocates very worried. Selling background checks over-the-counter could place personal information in the wrong hands. Private investigators are concerned as well, fearing that inexpensive background-checking systems could compete with their businesses. They also complain that ChoicePoint's requirement that users have a business license is not a sufficiently strong control for preventing personal information from falling into the wrong hands. "There are tons of people who have a business license who don't have a business," notes

Chris Appelby, president of the Georgia Association of Professional Private Investigators.

James Lee, ChoicePoint's chief marketing officer, notes that the data provided by check-in-the-box is public information that can be found at courthouses and other government offices if individuals really wanted to find it. The system includes safeguards, including the requirement that a user supply the Social Security number and name of the person they are checking. Federal law requires employers to obtain the signed permission of job applicants before they run background checks on them. However, ChoicePoint users only need to click on a box—it does not require that a form be presented to check to see whether it has been signed by an applicant.

ChoicePoint imposes tighter controls on users who want to search motor vehicle records and personal credit reports. Users are required to fill out and fax in a number of forms. Each application is than hand-vetted by a ChoicePoint employee, who calls the user to verify that there is a business license. The process usually takes 24 to 48 hours, with users notified by e-mail if access has been approved or denied.

Sources: Adam Geller, "High-Tech Background Checks Hit Stores," Associated Press, March 8, 2004; "Background Checks in a Box," CBSNews.com, March 8, 2004; and www.choicepoint.net, accessed May 15, 2004.

ChoicePoint uses information systems to create a background checking service that is very valuable for businesses and even for job applicants. It provides users with access to massive pools of data about individuals, including their credit history and driving records. But ChoicePoint's service could also be abused by making it easier to find out detailed information about other people that users are not entitled to see.

ChoicePoint's case shows that information systems raise new and often perplexing ethical challenges. You'll want to know what these ethical challenges are and how you should deal with them as a manager and as an individual. This chapter helps you by describing the major ethical and social issues raised by information systems and by providing guidelines for analyzing ethical issues on your own.

5.1 UNDERSTANDING ETHICAL AND SOCIAL ISSUES RELATED TO SYSTEMS

In the last five years we have witnessed arguably one of the most ethically challenging periods for U.S. and global business. Table 5-1 provides a small sample of cases demonstrating failed ethical judgment by senior and middle managers in the past few years. These lapses in management ethical and business judgment occurred across a broad spectrum of industries.

In today's new legal environment, managers who violate the law and are convicted will most likely spend time in prison. United States Federal Sentencing Guidelines adopted in 1987 mandate that federal judges impose stiff sentences on business executives based on the monetary value of the crime, the presence of a conspiracy to prevent discovery of the crime, the use of structured financial transactions to hide the crime, and failure to cooperate with prosecutors (U.S. Sentencing Commission, 2004).

Although in the past business firms would often pay for the legal defense of their employees enmeshed in civil charges and criminal investigations, now firms are encouraged to cooperate with prosecutors to reduce charges against the entire firm for obstructing investigations. These developments mean that, more than ever, managers and employees will have to judge for themselves what constitutes proper legal and ethical conduct.

Although these major instances of failed ethical and legal judgment were not masterminded by information systems departments, financial reporting information systems were instrumental in many of these frauds. In many cases, the perpetrators of these crimes artfully used financial reporting information systems to bury their decisions from public scrutiny in the vain hope they would never be caught. We deal with the issue of control in financial reporting and other information systems in Chapter 10. In this chapter we talk about the ethical dimensions of these and other actions based on the use of information systems.

Ethics refers to the principles of right and wrong that individuals, acting as free moral agents, use to make choices to guide their behaviors. Information systems raise new ethical questions for both individuals and societies because they create opportunities for intense social change, and thus threaten existing distributions of power, money, rights, and obligations. Like other technologies, such as steam engines, electricity, telephone, and radio, information technology can be used to achieve social progress, but it can also be used to commit crimes and threaten cherished social values. The development of information technology will produce benefits for many and costs for others.

Ethical issues in information systems have been given new urgency by the rise of the Internet and electronic commerce. Internet and digital firm technologies make it easier than ever to assemble, integrate, and distribute information, unleashing new concerns about the appropriate use of customer information, the protection of personal privacy, and the protection of intellectual property.

Other pressing ethical issues raised by information systems include establishing accountability for the consequences of information systems, setting standards to safeguard system quality that protect the safety of the individual and society, and preserving values and institutions considered essential to the quality of life in an information society.

TABLE 5-1 *Recent Examples of Failed Ethical Judgment by Managers*

Enron	Top three executives, and several middle managers, criminally indicted for misstating earnings using illegal accounting schemes. Bankruptcy declared in 2001
WorldCom	Second largest U.S. telecommunications firm. Chief executives indicted for improperly inflating revenue by billions using illegal accounting methods. Bankruptcy declared in July 2002 with $41 billion in debts
Merrill Lynch	Indicted for assisting Enron in the creation of financial vehicles that had no business purpose, enabling Enron to misstate its earnings
Parmalat	Italy's eighth largest industrial group indicted for misstating over $5 billion in revenues, earnings, and assets over several years; senior executives indicted for embezzlement
Bristol-Myers Squibb	Pharmaceutical firm agreed to pay a fine of $150 million for misstating its revenues by $1.5 billion, and inflating its stock value

When using information systems, it is essential to ask, What is the ethical and socially responsible course of action?

A Model for Thinking About Ethical, Social, and Political Issues

Ethical, social, and political issues are closely linked. The ethical dilemma you may face as a manager of information systems typically is reflected in social and political debate. One way to think about these relationships is given in Figure 5-1. Imagine society as a more or less calm pond on a summer day, a delicate ecosystem in partial equilibrium with individuals and with social and political institutions. Individuals know how to act in this pond because social institutions (family, education, organizations) have developed well-honed rules of behavior, and these are backed by laws developed in the political sector that prescribe behavior and promise sanctions for violations. Now toss a rock into the

FIGURE 5-1 *The relationship between ethical, social, and political issues in an information society.*

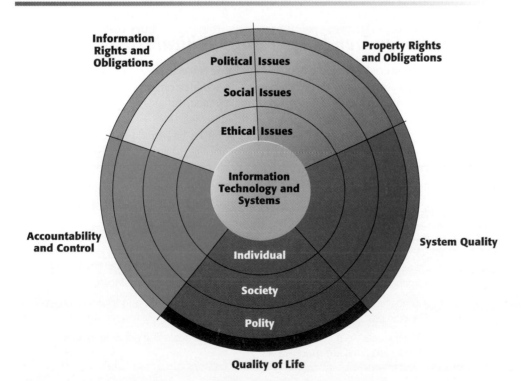

The introduction of new information technology has a ripple effect, raising new ethical, social, and political issues that must be dealt with on the individual, social, and political levels. These issues have five moral dimensions: information rights and obligations, property rights and obligations, system quality, quality of life, and accountability and control.

center of the pond. But imagine instead of a rock that the disturbing force is a powerful shock of new information technology and systems hitting a society more or less at rest. What happens? Ripples, of course.

Suddenly individual actors are confronted with new situations often not covered by the old rules. Social institutions cannot respond overnight to these ripples—it may take years to develop etiquette, expectations, social responsibility, politically correct attitudes, or approved rules. Political institutions also require time before developing new laws and often require the demonstration of real harm before they act. In the meantime, you may have to act. You may be forced to act in a legal gray area.

We can use this model to illustrate the dynamics that connect ethical, social, and political issues. This model is also useful for identifying the main moral dimensions of the information society, which cut across various levels of action—individual, social, and political.

Five Moral Dimensions of the Information Age

The major ethical, social, and political issues raised by information systems include the following moral dimensions:

- *Information rights and obligations.* What **information rights** do individuals and organizations possess with respect to information about themselves? What can they protect? What obligations do individuals and organizations have concerning this information?

- *Property rights and obligations.* How will traditional intellectual property rights be protected in a digital society in which tracing and accounting for ownership are difficult and ignoring such property rights is so easy?

- *Accountability and control.* Who can and will be held accountable and liable for the harm done to individual and collective information and property rights?

- *System quality.* What standards of data and system quality should we demand to protect individual rights and the safety of society?

- *Quality of life.* What values should be preserved in an information- and knowledge-based society? Which institutions should we protect from violation? Which cultural values and practices are supported by the new information technology?

We explore these moral dimensions in detail in section 5.3.

Key Technology Trends That Raise Ethical Issues

Ethical issues long preceded information technology. Nevertheless, information technology has heightened ethical concerns, taxed existing social arrangements, and made some laws obsolete or severely crippled. There are four key technological trends responsible for these ethical stresses and they are summarized in Table 5-2.

The doubling of computing power every 18 months has made it possible for most organizations to use information systems for their core production processes. As a result, our dependence on systems and our vulnerability to system errors and poor data quality

TABLE 5-2 *Technology Trends That Raise Ethical Issues*

Trend	Impact
Computing power doubles every 18 months	More organizations depend on computer systems for critical operations.
Rapidly declining data storage costs	Organizations can easily maintain detailed databases on individuals.
Data analysis advances	Companies can analyze vast quantities of data gathered on individuals to develop detailed profiles of individual behavior.
Networking advances and the Internet	Copying data from one location to another and accessing personal data from remote locations are much easier.

have increased. Social rules and laws have not yet adjusted to this dependence. Standards for ensuring the accuracy and reliability of information systems (see Chapter 10) are not universally accepted or enforced.

Advances in data storage techniques and rapidly declining storage costs have been responsible for the multiplying databases on individuals—employees, customers, and potential customers—maintained by private and public organizations. These advances in data storage have made the routine violation of individual privacy both cheap and effective. Already massive data storage systems are cheap enough for regional and even local retailing firms to use in identifying customers.

Advances in data analysis techniques for large pools of data are a third technological trend that heightens ethical concerns because companies and government agencies are able to find out much detailed personal information about individuals. With contemporary data management tools (see Chapter 7) companies can assemble and combine the myriad pieces of information about you stored on computers much more easily than in the past.

Think of all the ways you generate computer information about yourself—credit card purchases, telephone calls, magazine subscriptions, video rentals, mail-order purchases, banking records, and local, state, and federal government records (including court and police records). Put together and mined properly, this information could reveal not only your credit information but also your driving habits, your tastes, your associations, and your political interests.

Companies with products to sell purchase relevant information from these sources to help them more finely target their marketing campaigns. Chapters 3 and 7 describe how companies can analyze large pools of data from multiple sources to rapidly identify buying patterns of customers and suggest individual responses. The use of computers to combine data from multiple sources and create electronic dossiers of detailed information on individuals is called **profiling**.

For example, hundreds of Web sites allow DoubleClick (**www.doubleclick.net**), an Internet advertising broker, to track the activities of their visitors in exchange for revenue from advertisements based on visitor information DoubleClick gathers. DoubleClick uses this information to create a profile of each online visitor, adding more detail to the profile as the visitor accesses an associated DoubleClick site. Over time, DoubleClick can create a detailed dossier of a person's spending and computing habits on the Web that can be sold to companies to help them target their Web ads more precisely.

A new data analysis technology called **nonobvious relationship awareness (NORA)** has given both government and the private sector even more powerful profiling capabilities. NORA can take information about people from many disparate sources, such as employment applications, telephone records, customer listings, and "wanted" lists, and

Credit card purchases can make personal information available to market researchers, telemarketers, and direct-mail companies. Advances in information technology facilitate the invasion of privacy.

correlate relationships to find obscure hidden connections that might help identify criminals or terrorists (see Figure 5-2).

NORA technology scans data and extracts information as the data are being generated so that it could, for example, instantly discover a man at an airline ticket counter who shares a phone number with a known terrorist before that person boards an airplane. The technology is considered a valuable tool for homeland security but does have privacy implications because it can provide such a detailed picture of the activities and associations of a single individual (Barrett and Gallagher, 2004).

Last, advances in networking, including the Internet, promise to reduce greatly the costs of moving and accessing large quantities of data and open the possibility of mining large pools of data remotely using small desktop machines, permitting an invasion of privacy on a scale and with a precision heretofore unimaginable. If computing and networking technologies continue to advance at the same pace as in the past, by 2023 large organizations will be able to devote the equivalent of a contemporary desktop personal computer to monitoring each of the 350 million individuals who will then be living in the United States (Farmer and Mann, 2003).

The development of global digital superhighway communication networks widely available to individuals and businesses poses many ethical and social concerns. Who will account for the flow of information over these networks? Will you be able to trace information collected about you? What will these networks do to the traditional relationships between family, work, and leisure? How will traditional job designs be altered when millions of "employees" become subcontractors using mobile offices for which they themselves must pay?

In the next section we consider some ethical principles and analytical techniques for dealing with these kinds of ethical and social concerns.

FIGURE 5-2   *Nonobvious relationship awareness (NORA).*

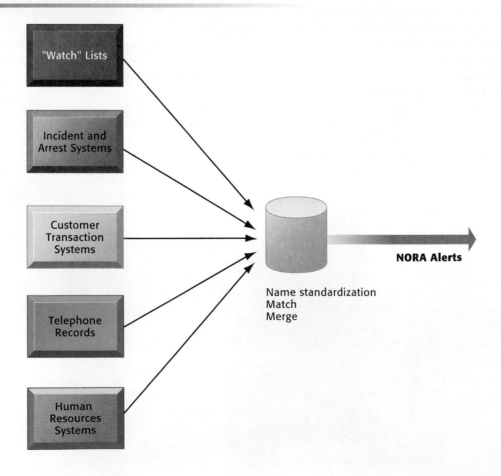

NORA technology can take information about people from disparate sources and find obscure, nonobvious relationships. It might discover, for example, that an applicant for a job at a casino shares a telephone number with a known criminal and issue an alert to the hiring manager.

5.2   ETHICS IN AN INFORMATION SOCIETY

Ethics is a concern of humans who have freedom of choice. Ethics is about individual choice: When faced with alternative courses of action, what is the correct moral choice? What are the main features of ethical choice?

Basic Concepts: Responsibility, Accountability, and Liability

Ethical choices are decisions made by individuals who are responsible for the consequences of their actions. **Responsibility** is a key element of ethical action. Responsibility means that you accept the potential costs, duties, and obligations for the decisions you make. **Accountability** is a feature of systems and social institutions: It means that mechanisms are in place to determine who took responsible action, who is responsible. Systems and institutions in which it is impossible to find out who took what action are inherently incapable of ethical analysis or ethical action. Liability extends the concept of responsibility further to the area of laws. **Liability** is a feature of political systems in which a body of laws is in place that permits individuals to recover the damages done to them by other actors, systems, or organizations. **Due process** is a related feature of law-governed societies and is a process in which laws are known and understood and there is an ability to appeal to higher authorities to ensure that the laws are applied correctly.

These basic concepts form the underpinning of an ethical analysis of information systems and those who manage them. First, as discussed in Chapter 3, information technologies are filtered through social institutions, organizations, and individuals. Systems do not have impacts by themselves. Whatever information system impacts exist are products of institutional, organizational, and individual actions and behaviors. Second, responsibility for the consequences of technology falls clearly on the institutions, organizations, and individual managers who choose to use the technology. Using information technology in a socially responsible manner means that you can and will be held accountable for the consequences of your actions. Third, in an ethical, political society, individuals and others can recover damages done to them through a set of laws characterized by due process.

Ethical Analysis

When confronted with a situation that seems to present ethical issues, how should you analyze it? The following five-step process should help.

1. *Identify and describe clearly the facts.* Find out who did what to whom, and where, when, and how. In many instances, you will be surprised at the errors in the initially reported facts, and often you will find that simply getting the facts straight helps define the solution. It also helps to get the opposing parties involved in an ethical dilemma to agree on the facts.

2. *Define the conflict or dilemma and identify the higher-order values involved.* Ethical, social, and political issues always reference higher values. The parties to a dispute all claim to be pursuing higher values (e.g., freedom, privacy, protection of property, and the free enterprise system). Typically, an ethical issue involves a dilemma: two diametrically opposed courses of action that support worthwhile values. For example, the chapter-ending case study illustrates two competing values: the need to protect citizens from terrorist acts and the need to protect individual privacy.

3. *Identify the stakeholders.* Every ethical, social, and political issue has stakeholders: players in the game who have an interest in the outcome, who have invested in the situation, and usually who have vocal opinions (Smith, 2003). Find out the identity of these groups and what they want. This will be useful later when designing a solution.

4. *Identify the options that you can reasonably take.* You may find that none of the options satisfy all the interests involved, but that some options do a better job than others.

Sometimes arriving at a good or ethical solution may not always be a balancing of consequences to stakeholders.

5. *Identify the potential consequences of your options.* Some options may be ethically correct but disastrous from other points of view. Other options may work in one instance but not in other similar instances. Always ask yourself, "What if I choose this option consistently over time?"

CANDIDATE ETHICAL PRINCIPLES

Once your analysis is complete, what ethical principles or rules should you use to make a decision? What higher-order values should inform your judgment? Although you are the only one who can decide which among many ethical principles you will follow, and how you will prioritize them, it is helpful to consider some ethical principles with deep roots in many cultures that have survived throughout recorded history.

1. Do unto others as you would have them do unto you (the Golden Rule). Putting yourself into the place of others, and thinking of yourself as the object of the decision, can help you think about fairness in decision making.

2. If an action is not right for everyone to take, it is not right for anyone (**Immanuel Kant's Categorical Imperative**). Ask yourself, "If everyone did this, could the organization, or society, survive?"

3. If an action cannot be taken repeatedly, it is not right to take at all (**Descartes' rule of change**). This is the slippery-slope rule: An action may bring about a small change now that is acceptable, but if repeated would bring unacceptable changes in the long run. In the vernacular, it might be stated as "once started down a slippery path you may not be able to stop."

4. Take the action that achieves the higher or greater value (the **Utilitarian Principle**). This rule assumes you can prioritize values in a rank order and understand the consequences of various courses of action.

5. Take the action that produces the least harm, or the least potential cost (**Risk Aversion Principle**). Some actions have extremely high failure costs of very low probability (e.g., building a nuclear generating facility in an urban area) or extremely high failure costs of moderate probability (speeding and automobile accidents). Avoid these high-failure-cost actions, paying greater attention obviously to high-failure-cost potential of moderate to high probability.

6. Assume that virtually all tangible and intangible objects are owned by someone else unless there is a specific declaration otherwise. (This is the ethical "**no free lunch**" **rule**.) If something someone else has created is useful to you, it has value, and you should assume the creator wants compensation for this work.

Although these ethical rules cannot always be guides to action, actions that do not easily pass these rules deserve some very close attention and a great deal of caution. The appearance of unethical behavior may do as much harm to you and your company as actual unethical behavior.

Professional Codes of Conduct

When groups of people claim to be professionals, they take on special rights and obligations because of their special claims to knowledge, wisdom, and respect. Professional codes of conduct are promulgated by associations of professionals such as the American Medical Association (AMA), the American Bar Association (ABA), the Association of Information Technology Professionals (AITP), and the Association of Computing Machinery (ACM). These professional groups take responsibility for the partial regulation of their professions by determining entrance qualifications and competence. Codes of ethics are promises by professions to regulate themselves in the general interest of society. For example, avoiding harm to others, honoring property rights (including intellectual property), and respecting privacy are among the General Moral Imperatives of the ACM's Code of Ethics and Professional Conduct (ACM, 1993).

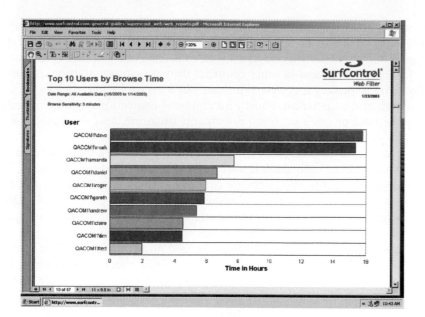

SurfControl offers tools for tracking Web and e-mail activity and for filtering unauthorized e-mail and Web site content. The benefits of monitoring employee e-mail and Internet use should be balanced with the need to respect employee privacy.

Some Real-World Ethical Dilemmas

Information systems have created new ethical dilemmas in which one set of interests is pitted against another. For example, many of the large telephone companies in the United States are using information technology to reduce the sizes of their workforces. Voice recognition software reduces the need for human operators by enabling computers to recognize a customer's responses to a series of computerized questions. Many companies monitor what their employees are doing on the Internet to prevent them from wasting company resources on nonbusiness activities (see the Chapter 8 Window on Management).

In each instance, you can find competing values at work, with groups lined on either side of a debate. A company may argue, for example, that it has a right to use information systems to increase productivity and reduce the size of its workforce to lower costs and stay in business. Employees displaced by information systems may argue that employers have some responsibility for their welfare. Business owners might feel obligated to monitor employee e-mail and Internet use to minimize drains on productivity (Jackson, Dawson, and Wilson, 2003; Urbaczewski and Jessup, 2002). Employees might believe they should be able to use the Internet for short personal tasks in place of the telephone. A close analysis of the facts can sometimes produce compromised solutions that give each side "half a loaf." Try to apply some of the principles of ethical analysis described to each of these cases. What is the right thing to do?

5.3 THE MORAL DIMENSIONS OF INFORMATION SYSTEMS

In this section, we take a closer look at the five moral dimensions of information systems first described in Figure 5-1. In each dimension we identify the ethical, social, and political levels of analysis and use real-world examples to illustrate the values involved, the stakeholders, and the options chosen.

Information Rights: Privacy and Freedom in the Internet Age

Privacy is the claim of individuals to be left alone, free from surveillance or interference from other individuals or organizations, including the state. Claims to privacy are also involved at the workplace: Millions of employees are subject to electronic and other forms of high-tech surveillance (Ball, 2001). Information technology and systems threaten individual claims to privacy by making the invasion of privacy cheap, profitable, and effective.

The claim to privacy is protected in the U.S., Canadian, and German constitutions in a variety of different ways and in other countries through various statutes. In the United States, the claim to privacy is protected primarily by First Amendment guarantees of freedom of speech and association, Fourth Amendment protections against unreasonable search and seizure of one's personal documents or home, and the guarantee of due process.

Table 5-3 describes the major U.S. federal statutes that set forth the conditions for handling information about individuals in such areas as credit reporting, education, financial records, newspaper records, and electronic communications. The Privacy Act of 1974 has been the most important of these laws, regulating the federal government's collection, use, and disclosure of information. At present, most U.S. federal privacy laws apply only to the federal government and regulate very few areas of the private sector.

Most American and European privacy law is based on a regime called Fair Information Practices (FIP) first set forth in a report written in 1973 by a federal government advisory committee (U.S. Department of Health, Education, and Welfare, 1973). **Fair Information Practices (FIP)** are a set of principles governing the collection and use of information about individuals. FIP principles are based on the notion of a mutuality of interest between the record holder and the individual. The individual has an interest in engaging in a transaction, and the record keeper—usually a business or government agency—requires information about the individual to support the transaction. Once information is gathered, the individual maintains an interest in the record, and the record may not be used to support other activities without the individual's consent. In 1998, the Federal Trade Commission (FTC) restated and extended the original FIP to provide guidelines for protecting online privacy. Table 5-4 describes the FTC's Fair Information Practices principles.

The FTC's FIP are being used as guidelines to drive changes in privacy legislation. In July 1998, the U.S. Congress passed the Children's Online Privacy Protection Act (COPPA), requiring Web sites to obtain parental permission before collecting information on children under the age of 13. (This law is in danger of being overturned.) The FTC

TABLE 5-3 *Federal Privacy Laws in the United States*

GENERAL FEDERAL PRIVACY LAWS

Freedom of Information Act of 1966 as Amended (5 USC 552)

Privacy Act of 1974 as Amended (5 USC 552a)

Electronic Communications Privacy Act of 1986

Computer Matching and Privacy Protection Act of 1988

Computer Security Act of 1987

Federal Managers Financial Integrity Act of 1982

PRIVACY LAWS AFFECTING PRIVATE INSTITUTIONS

Fair Credit Reporting Act of 1970

Family Educational Rights and Privacy Act of 1974

Right to Financial Privacy Act of 1978

Privacy Protection Act of 1980

Cable Communications Policy Act of 1984

Electronic Communications Privacy Act of 1986

Video Privacy Protection Act of 1988

Health Insurance Portability and Accountability Act of 1996 (HIPAA)

Children's Online Privacy Protection Act of 1998 (COPPA)

Financial Modernization Act (Gramm-Leach-Bliley Act) of 1999

TABLE 5-4   *Federal Trade Commission Fair Information Practices Principles*

1. *Notice/Awareness (core principle)*: Web sites must disclose their information practices before collecting data. Includes identification of collector; uses of data; other recipients of data; nature of collection (active/inactive); voluntary or required status; consequences of refusal; and steps taken to protect confidentiality, integrity, and quality of the data.

2. *Choice/Consent (core principle):* There must be a choice regime in place allowing consumers to choose how their information will be used for secondary purposes other than supporting the transaction, including internal use and transfer to third parties.

3. *Access/Participation:* Consumers should be able to review and contest the accuracy and completeness of data collected about them in a timely, inexpensive process.

4. *Security:* Data collectors must take responsible steps to assure that consumer information is accurate and secure from unauthorized use.

5. *Enforcement:* There must be in place a mechanism to enforce FIP principles. This can involve self-regulation, legislation giving consumers legal remedies for violations, or federal statutes and regulations.

has recommended additional legislation to protect online consumer privacy in advertising networks that collect records of consumer Web activity to develop detailed profiles that are then used by other companies to target online ads. Other proposed Internet privacy legislation focuses on protecting the online use of personal identification numbers such as Social Security numbers, protecting personal information collected on the Internet that deals with individuals not covered by the Children's Online Privacy Protection Act of 1998, and limiting the use of data mining for homeland security (see the chapter-ending case study).

Privacy protections have also been added to recent laws deregulating financial services and safeguarding the maintenance and transmission of health information about individuals. The Gramm-Leach-Bliley Act of 1999, which repeals earlier restrictions on affiliations among banks, securities firms, and insurance companies, includes some privacy protection for consumers of financial services. All financial institutions are required to disclose their policies and practices for protecting the privacy of nonpublic personal information and to allow customers to opt out of information-sharing arrangements with nonaffiliated third parties.

The Health Insurance Portability and Accountability Act of 1996 (HIPAA), which took effect on April 14, 2003, includes privacy protection for medical records. The law gives patients access to their personal medical records maintained by health care providers, hospitals, and health insurers and the right to authorize how protected information about themselves can be used or disclosed. Doctors, hospitals, and other health care providers must limit the disclosure of personal information about patients to the minimum necessary to achieve a given purpose.

THE EUROPEAN DIRECTIVE ON DATA PROTECTION

In Europe, privacy protection is much more stringent than in the United States. Unlike the United States, European countries do not allow businesses to use personally identifiable information without consumers' prior consent. On October 25, 1998, the European Commission's Directive on Data Protection went into effect, broadening privacy protection in the European Union (EU) nations. The directive requires companies to inform people when they collect information about them and disclose how it will be stored and used. Customers must provide their informed consent before any company can legally use data about them, and they have the right to access that information, correct it, and request that no further data be collected. **Informed consent** can be defined as consent given with knowledge of all the facts needed to make a rational decision. EU member nations must translate these principles into their own laws and cannot transfer personal data to countries such as the United States that do not have similar privacy protection regulations.

Working with the European Commission, the U.S. Department of Commerce developed a safe harbor framework for U.S. firms. A **safe harbor** is a private self-regulating policy and enforcement mechanism that meets the objectives of government regulators and legislation but does not involve government regulation or enforcement. U.S. businesses would be allowed to use personal data from EU countries if they develop privacy protection policies that meet EU standards. Enforcement would occur in the United States, using self-policing, regulation, and government enforcement of fair trade statutes.

INTERNET CHALLENGES TO PRIVACY

Internet technology has posed new challenges for the protection of individual privacy. Information sent over this vast network of networks may pass through many different computer systems before it reaches its final destination. Each of these systems is capable of monitoring, capturing, and storing communications that pass through it.

It is possible to record many online activities, including which online newsgroups or files a person has accessed, which Web sites and Web pages he or she has visited, and what items that person has inspected or purchased over the Web. Much of this monitoring and tracking of Web site visitors occurs in the background without the visitor's knowledge. Tools to monitor visits to the World Wide Web have become popular because they help organizations determine who is visiting their Web sites and how to better target their offerings. (Some firms also monitor the Internet usage of their employees to see how they are using company network resources.) Web retailers now have access to software that lets them "watch" the online shopping behavior of individuals and groups while they are visiting a Web site and making purchases. The commercial demand for this personal information is virtually insatiable.

Web sites can learn the identities of their visitors if the visitors voluntarily register at the site to purchase a product or service or to obtain a free service, such as information. Web sites can also capture information about visitors without their knowledge using cookie technology.

Cookies are tiny files deposited on a computer hard drive when a user visits certain Web sites. Cookies identify the visitor's Web browser software and track visits to the Web site. When the visitor returns to a site that has stored a cookie, the Web site software will search the visitor's computer, find the cookie, and know what that person has done in the past. It may also update the cookie, depending on the activity during the visit. In this way, the site can customize its contents for each visitor's interests. For example, if you purchase a book on the Amazon.com Web site and return later from the same browser, the site will welcome you by name and recommend other books of interest based on your past purchases. DoubleClick, introduced earlier in this chapter, uses cookies to build its dossiers with details of online purchases and to examine the behavior of Web site visitors. Figure 5-3 illustrates how cookies work.

FIGURE 5-3   *How cookies identify Web visitors.*

Cookies are written by a Web site on a visitor's hard drive. When the visitor returns to that Web site, the Web server requests the ID number from the cookie and uses it to access the data stored by that server on that visitor. The Web site can then use these data to display personalized information.

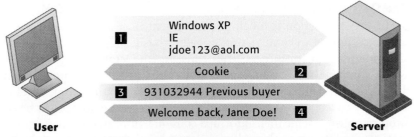

1. The Web server reads the user's Web browser and determines the operating system, browser name, version number, Internet address, and other information.
2. The server transmits a tiny text file with user identification information called a cookie, which the user's browser receives and stores on the user's computer hard drive.
3. When the user returns to the Web site, the server requests the contents of any cookie it deposited previously in the user's computer.
4. The Web server reads the cookie, identifies the visitor, and calls up data on the user.

Web sites using cookie technology cannot directly obtain visitors' names and addresses. However, if a person has registered at a site, that information can be combined with cookie data to identify the visitor. Web site owners can also combine the data they have gathered from cookies and other Web site monitoring tools with personal data from other sources such as offline data collected from surveys or paper catalog purchases to develop very detailed profiles of their visitors.

There are now even more subtle and surreptitious tools for surveillance of Internet users. Marketers use Web bugs as another tool to monitor online behavior. **Web bugs** are tiny graphic files embedded in e-mail messages and Web pages that are designed to monitor who is reading the e-mail message or Web page and transmit that information to another computer. Other **spyware** can secretly install itself on an Internet user's computer by piggybacking on larger applications. Once installed, the spyware calls out to Web sites to send banner ads and other unsolicited material to the user, and it can also report the user's movements on the Internet to other computers. You will learn more about Web bugs, spyware, and other intrusive software in Chapter 10.

Google has been using tools to scan the contents of messages received by users of its free Web-based e-mail service called Gmail. Ads that users see when they read their e-mail are related to the subjects of these messages. Google's service offers users 1 gigabyte of storage space—far more than any of its competitors—but privacy advocates find the practice offensive (Hansell, 2004).

The United States has allowed businesses to gather transaction information generated in the marketplace and then use that information for other marketing purposes without obtaining the informed consent of the individual whose information is being used. U.S. e-commerce sites are largely content to publish statements on their Web sites informing visitors about how their information will be used. Some have added *opt-out* selection boxes to these information policy statements. An **opt-out** model of informed consent permits the collection of personal information until the consumer specifically requests that the data not be collected. Privacy advocates would like to see wider use of an **opt-in** model of informed consent in which a business is prohibited from collecting any personal information unless the consumer specifically takes action to approve information collection and use.

The online industry has preferred self-regulation to privacy legislation for protecting consumers. In 1998, the online industry formed the Online Privacy Alliance to encourage self-regulation to develop a set of privacy guidelines for its members. The group promotes the use of online seals, such as that of TRUSTe, certifying Web sites adhering to certain privacy principles. Members of the advertising network industry, including DoubleClick, Atlas DMT, ValueClick, and 24/7 Real Media, have created an additional industry association called the Network Advertising Initiative (NAI) to develop its own privacy policies to help consumers opt out of advertising network programs and provide consumers redress from abuses.

In general, however, most Internet businesses do little to protect the privacy of their customers, and consumers do not do as much as they should to protect themselves. Many companies with Web sites do not have privacy policies. Of the companies that do post privacy polices on their Web sites, about half do not monitor their sites to ensure they adhere to these policies. The vast majority of online customers claim they are concerned about online privacy, but less than half read the privacy statements on Web sites (Laudon and Traver, 2004).

TECHNICAL SOLUTIONS

In addition to legislation, new technologies are available to protect user privacy during interactions with Web sites. Many of these tools are used for encrypting e-mail, for making e-mail or surfing activities appear anonymous, for preventing client computers from accepting cookies, or for detecting and eliminating spyware.

There are now tools to help users determine the kind of personal data that can be extracted by Web sites. The Platform for Privacy Preferences, known as P3P, enables automatic communication of privacy policies between an e-commerce site and its visitors. P3P provides a standard for communicating a Web site's privacy policy to Internet users and

Internet Connection ———
The Internet Connection for this chapter will direct you to a series of Web sites where you can learn about the privacy issues raised by the Internet and the Web. You can complete an exercise to analyze the privacy implications of existing technologies for tracking Web site visitors.

Web sites are starting to post their privacy policies for visitors to review. The TRUSTe seal designates Web sites that have agreed to adhere to TRUSTe's established privacy principles of disclosure, choice, access, and security.

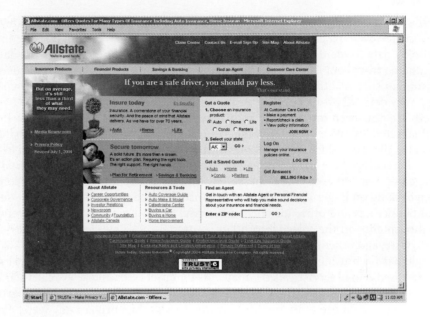

for comparing that policy to the user's preferences or to other standards such as the FTC's new FIP guidelines or the European Directive on Data Protection. Users can use P3P to select the level of privacy they wish to maintain when interacting with the Web site.

The P3P standard allows Web sites to publish privacy policies in a form that computers can understand. Once it is codified according to P3P rules, the privacy policy becomes part of the software for individual Web pages (see Figure 5-4). Users of recent versions of Microsoft Internet Explorer Web browsing software can access and read the P3P site's privacy policy and a list of all cookies coming from the site. Internet Explorer enables users to adjust their computers to screen out all cookies or let in selected cookies based on specific levels of privacy. For example, the "medium" level accepts cookies from first-party host sites that have opt-in or opt-out policies but rejects third-party cookies that use personally identifiable information without an opt-in policy.

However, P3P only works with Web sites of members of the World Wide Web Consortium who have translated their Web site privacy policies into P3P format. The technology will display cookies from Web sites that are not part of the consortium, but users will not be able to obtain sender information or privacy statements. Many users

FIGURE 5-4 *The P3P standard.*

P3P enables Web sites to translate their privacy policies into a standard format that can be read by the user's Web browser software. The user's Web browser software evaluates the Web site's privacy policy to determine whether it is compatible with the user's privacy preferences.

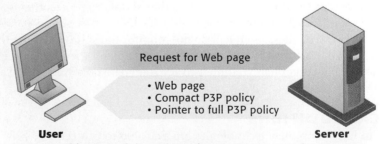

1. The user with P3P Web browsing software requests a Web page.
2. The Web server returns the Web page along with a compact version of the Web site's policy and a pointer to the full P3P policy. If the Web site is not P3P compliant, no P3P data are returned.
3. The user's Web browsing software compares the response from the Web site with the user's privacy preferences. If the Web site does not have a P3P policy or the policy does not match the privacy levels established by the user, it warns the user or rejects the cookies from the Web site. Otherwise, the Web page loads normally.

may also need to be educated about interpreting company privacy statements and P3P levels of privacy.

ETHICAL ISSUES

The ethical privacy issue in this information age is as follows: Under what conditions should I (you) invade the privacy of others? What legitimates intruding into others' lives through unobtrusive surveillance, through market research, or by whatever means? Do we have to inform people that we are eavesdropping? Do we have to inform people that we are using credit history information for employment screening purposes?

SOCIAL ISSUES

The social issue of privacy concerns the development of expectations of privacy, or privacy norms, as well as public attitudes. In what areas of life should we as a society encourage people to think they are in private territory as opposed to public view? For instance, should we as a society encourage people to develop expectations of privacy when using electronic mail, cellular telephones, bulletin boards, the postal system, the workplace, or the street? Should expectations of privacy be extended to criminal conspirators?

POLITICAL ISSUES

The political issue of privacy concerns the development of statutes that govern the relations between record keepers and individuals. Should we permit the FBI to monitor e-mail at will to apprehend suspected criminals and terrorists (see the chapter-ending case study). To what extent should e-commerce sites and other businesses be allowed to maintain personal data about individuals?

Property Rights: Intellectual Property

Contemporary information systems have severely challenged existing law and social practices that protect private intellectual property. **Intellectual property** is considered to be intangible property created by individuals or corporations. Information technology has made it difficult to protect intellectual property because computerized information can be so easily copied or distributed on networks. Intellectual property is subject to a variety of protections under three different legal traditions: trade secret, copyright, and patent law.

TRADE SECRETS

Any intellectual work product—a formula, device, pattern, or compilation of data—used for a business purpose can be classified as a **trade secret**, provided it is not based on information in the public domain. Protections for trade secrets vary from state to state. In general, trade secret laws grant a monopoly on the ideas behind a work product, but it can be a very tenuous monopoly.

Software that contains novel or unique elements, procedures, or compilations can be included as a trade secret. Trade secret law protects the actual ideas in a work product, not only their manifestation. To make this claim, the creator or owner must take care to bind employees and customers with nondisclosure agreements and to prevent the secret from falling into the public domain.

The limitation of trade secret protection is that although virtually all software programs of any complexity contain unique elements of some sort, it is difficult to prevent the ideas in the work from falling into the public domain when the software is widely distributed.

COPYRIGHT

Copyright is a statutory grant that protects creators of intellectual property from having their work copied by others for any purpose during the life of the author plus an additional 70 years after the author's death. For corporate-owned works, copyright protection lasts for 95 years after their initial creation. Congress has extended copyright protection to books, periodicals, lectures, dramas, musical compositions, maps, drawings, artwork of any kind, and motion pictures. The intent behind copyright laws has been to encourage creativity and authorship by ensuring that creative people receive the financial and other benefits of their work. Most industrial nations have their own copyright laws, and there are several international conventions and bilateral agreements through which nations coordinate and enforce their laws.

In the mid-1960s, the Copyright Office began registering software programs, and in 1980 Congress passed the Computer Software Copyright Act, which clearly provides protection for software program code and for copies of the original sold in commerce, and sets forth the rights of the purchaser to use the software while the creator retains legal title.

Copyright protects against copying of entire programs or their parts. Damages and relief are readily obtained for infringement. The drawback to copyright protection is that the underlying ideas behind a work are not protected, only their manifestation in a work. A competitor can use your software, understand how it works, and build new software that follows the same concepts without infringing on a copyright.

"Look and feel" copyright infringement lawsuits are precisely about the distinction between an idea and its expression. For instance, in the early 1990s Apple Computer sued Microsoft Corporation and Hewlett-Packard for infringement of the expression of Apple's Macintosh interface, claiming that the defendants copied the expression of overlapping windows. The defendants countered that the idea of overlapping windows can be expressed only in a single way and, therefore, was not protectable under the merger doctrine of copyright law. When ideas and their expression merge, the expression cannot be copyrighted.

In general, courts appear to be following the reasoning of a 1989 case—*Brown Bag Software v. Symantec Corp.*—in which the court dissected the elements of software alleged to be infringing. The court found that similar concept, function, general functional features (e.g., drop-down menus), and colors are not protectable by copyright law (*Brown Bag v. Symantec Corp.*, 1992).

PATENTS

A **patent** grants the owner an exclusive monopoly on the ideas behind an invention for 20 years. The congressional intent behind patent law was to ensure that inventors of new machines, devices, or methods receive the full financial and other rewards of their labor and yet still make widespread use of the invention possible by providing detailed diagrams for those wishing to use the idea under license from the patent's owner. The granting of a patent is determined by the Patent Office and relies on court rulings.

The key concepts in patent law are originality, novelty, and invention. The Patent Office did not accept applications for software patents routinely until a 1981 Supreme Court decision that held that computer programs could be a part of a patentable process. Since that time, hundreds of patents have been granted and thousands await consideration.

The strength of patent protection is that it grants a monopoly on the underlying concepts and ideas of software. The difficulty is passing stringent criteria of nonobviousness (e.g., the work must reflect some special understanding and contribution), originality, and novelty, as well as years of waiting to receive protection.

CHALLENGES TO INTELLECTUAL PROPERTY RIGHTS

Contemporary information technologies, especially software, pose severe challenges to existing intellectual property regimes and, therefore, create significant ethical, social, and political issues. Digital media differ from books, periodicals, and other media in terms of ease of replication; ease of transmission; ease of alteration; difficulty classifying a software work as a program, book, or even music; compactness—making theft easy; and difficulties in establishing uniqueness.

The proliferation of electronic networks, including the Internet, has made it even more difficult to protect intellectual property. Before widespread use of networks, copies of software, books, magazine articles, or films had to be stored on physical media, such as paper, computer disks, or videotape, creating some hurdles to distribution. Using networks, information can be more widely reproduced and distributed. A study conducted by the International Data Corporation for the Business Software Alliance found more than one-third of the software worldwide was counterfeit or pirated and the Business Software Alliance reported $29 billion in yearly losses from software piracy (Geitner 2004; Lohr, 2004).

The Internet was designed to transmit information freely around the world, including copyrighted information. With the World Wide Web in particular, you can easily copy and distribute virtually anything to thousands and even millions of people around the world, even if they are using different types of computer systems. Information can be illicitly copied from one place and distributed through other systems and networks even though these parties do not willingly participate in the infringement.

Individuals have been illegally copying and distributing digitized MP3 music files on the Internet. Napster provided software and services that enabled users to locate and share digital music files, including those protected by copyright. In February 2001, a U.S. federal district court ruled that Napster had to stop listing all copyrighted files without permission on its central index and the company was forced to declare bankruptcy. (It eventually became a Web site selling only legal music downloads.)

Major entertainment industry groups subsequently filed suit to block illegal file sharing on other Web sites, such as Madster, Grokster, Kazaa, and Morpheus. However, these sites, as well as software and services for file trading over the Web, such as Gnutella, cannot be so easily regulated, so copyrighted music continues to be traded for free. Illegal file sharing is so widespread that it is threatening the viability of the music recording industry. (More detail on this topic can be found in the case study concluding Chapter 4.) As more and more homes adopt high-speed Internet access, illegal file sharing of videos will pose similar threats to the motion picture industry.

The manner in which information is obtained and presented on the Web further challenges intellectual property protections. Web pages can be constructed from bits of text, graphics, sound, or video that may come from many different sources. Each item may belong to a different entity, creating complicated issues of ownership and compensation (see Figure 5-5). Web sites use a capability called **framing** to let one site construct an on-screen border around content obtained by linking to another Web site. The first site's border and logo stay on-screen, making the content of the new Web site appear to be offered by the previous Web site.

Mechanisms are being developed to sell and distribute books, articles, and other intellectual property on the Internet, and the **Digital Millennium Copyright Act (DMCA)** of 1998

FIGURE 5-5   *Who owns the pieces? Anatomy of a Web page.*

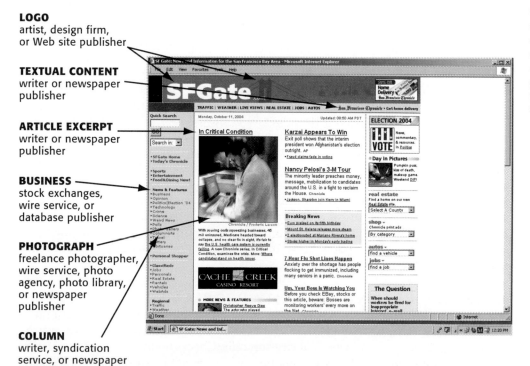

LOGO
artist, design firm,
or Web site publisher

TEXTUAL CONTENT
writer or newspaper
publisher

ARTICLE EXCERPT
writer or newspaper
publisher

BUSINESS
stock exchanges,
wire service, or
database publisher

PHOTOGRAPH
freelance photographer,
wire service, photo
agency, photo library,
or newspaper
publisher

COLUMN
writer, syndication
service, or newspaper
publisher

Web pages are often constructed with elements from many different sources, clouding issues of ownership and intellectual property protection.

Source: ©2005 Hearst Communications Inc. All rights reserved. Used with permission of the *San Francisco Chronicle*.

is providing some copyright protection. The DMCA implemented a World Intellectual Property Organization treaty that makes it illegal to circumvent technology-based protections of copyrighted materials. Internet service providers (ISPs) are required to take down sites of copyright infringers that they are hosting once they are notified of the problem.

ETHICAL ISSUES

The central ethical issue concerns the protection of intellectual property such as software, digital books, digital music, or digitized video. Should I (you) copy for my own use a piece of software or other digital content material protected by trade secret, copyright, and/or patent law? Is there continued value in protecting intellectual property when it can be so easily copied and distributed over the Internet?

SOCIAL ISSUES

There are several property-related social issues raised by new information technology. Most experts agree that the current intellectual property laws are breaking down in the information age. The vast majority of Americans report in surveys that they routinely violate some minor laws—everything from speeding to taking paper clips from work to copying books and software. The ease with which software and digital content can be copied contributes to making us a society of lawbreakers. These routine thefts threaten significantly to reduce the speed with which new information technologies can and will be introduced and, therefore, threaten further advances in productivity and social well-being.

POLITICAL ISSUES

The main property-related political issue concerns the creation of new property protection measures to protect investments made by creators of new software, digital books, and digital entertainment. Microsoft and 1,400 other software and information content firms are represented by the Software and Information Industry Association (SIIA), which lobbies for new laws and enforcement of existing laws to protect intellectual property around the world. (SIIA was formed on January 1, 1999, from the merger of the Software Publishers Association [SPA] and the Information Industry Association [IIA].) The SIIA runs an antipiracy hotline for individuals to report piracy activities and educational programs to help organizations combat software piracy and has published guidelines for employee use of software.

Allied against SIIA are a host of groups and millions of individuals who believe that antipiracy laws cannot be enforced in the digital age and that software should be free or be paid for on a voluntary basis (shareware software). According to these groups, the greater social benefit results from the free distribution of software.

Accountability, Liability, and Control

Along with privacy and property laws, new information technologies are challenging existing liability law and social practices for holding individuals and institutions accountable. If a person is injured by a machine controlled, in part, by software, who should be held accountable and, therefore, held liable? Should a public bulletin board or an electronic service such as America Online permit the transmission of pornographic or offensive material (as broadcasters), or should they be held harmless against any liability for what users transmit (as is true of common carriers such as the telephone system)? What about the Internet? If you outsource your information processing, can you hold the external vendor liable for injuries done to your customers? Some real-world examples may shed light on these questions.

COMPUTER-RELATED LIABILITY PROBLEMS

During the weekend of March 15, 2002, tens of thousands of Bank of America customers in California, Arizona, and Nevada were unable to use their paychecks and social security payments that had just been deposited electronically. Checks bounced. Withdrawals were blocked because of insufficient funds. Because of an operating error at the bank's computer center in Nevada, a batch of direct deposit transactions was not processed. The bank lost track of money that should have been credited to customers' accounts, and it took days to rectify the problem (Carr and Gallagher, 2002). Who is liable for any economic harm caused to individuals or businesses that could not access their full account balances in this period?

This case reveals the difficulties faced by information systems executives who ultimately are responsible for any harm done by systems developed by their staffs. In general, insofar as computer software is part of a machine, and the machine injures someone physically or economically, the producer of the software and the operator can be held liable for damages. Insofar as the software acts like a book, storing and displaying information, courts have been reluctant to hold authors, publishers, and booksellers liable for contents (the exception being instances of fraud or defamation), and hence courts have been wary of holding software authors liable for booklike software.

In general, it is very difficult (if not impossible) to hold software producers liable for their software products when those products are considered like books, regardless of the physical or economic harm that results. Historically, print publishers, books, and periodicals have not been held liable because of fears that liability claims would interfere with First Amendment rights guaranteeing freedom of expression.

What about software as service? ATM machines are a service provided to bank customers. Should this service fail, customers will be inconvenienced and perhaps harmed economically if they cannot access their funds in a timely manner. Should liability protections be extended to software publishers and operators of defective financial, accounting, simulation, or marketing systems?

Software is very different from books. Software users may develop expectations of infallibility about software; software is less easily inspected than a book, and it is more difficult to compare with other software products for quality; software claims actually to perform a task rather than describe a task like a book; and people come to depend on services essentially based on software. Given the centrality of software to everyday life, the chances are excellent that liability law will extend its reach to include software even when the software merely provides an information service.

Telephone systems have not been held liable for the messages transmitted because they are regulated common carriers. In return for their right to provide telephone service, they must provide access to all, at reasonable rates, and achieve acceptable reliability. But broadcasters and cable television systems are subject to a wide variety of federal and local constraints on content and facilities. Organizations can be held liable for offensive content on their Web sites; and online services, such as America Online, might be held liable for postings by their users. Although U.S. courts have increasingly exonerated Web sites and ISPs for posting material by third parties, the threat of legal action still has a chilling effect on small companies or individuals who cannot afford to take their cases to trial (Kapner, 2003).

ETHICAL ISSUES

The central liability-related ethical issue raised by new information technologies is whether individuals and organizations that create, produce, and sell systems (both hardware and software) are morally responsible for the consequences of their use (see Johnson and Mulvey, 1995). If so, under what conditions? What liabilities (and responsibilities) should the user assume, and what should the provider assume?

SOCIAL ISSUES

The central liability-related social issue concerns the expectations that society should allow to develop around service-providing information systems. Should individuals (and organizations) be encouraged to develop their own backup devices to cover likely or easily anticipated system failures, or should organizations be held strictly liable for system services they provide? If organizations are held strictly liable, what impact will this have on the development of new system services? Can society permit networks and bulletin boards to post libelous, inaccurate, and misleading information that will harm many persons? Or should information service companies become self-regulating and self-censoring?

POLITICAL ISSUES

The leading liability-related political issue is the debate between information providers of all kinds (from software developers to network service providers), who want to be relieved of liability as much as possible (thereby maximizing their profits), and service users (individuals, organizations, and communities), who want organizations to be held responsible for providing high-quality system services (thereby maximizing the quality of service). Service providers argue they will withdraw from the marketplace if they are held liable, whereas service users argue that only by holding providers liable can they guarantee a high level of service and compensate injured parties. Should legislation impose liability or restrict liability on service providers? This fundamental cleavage is at the heart of numerous political and judicial conflicts.

System Quality: Data Quality and System Errors

The debate over liability and accountability for unintentional consequences of system use raises a related but independent moral dimension: What is an acceptable, technologically feasible level of system quality? At what point should system managers say, "Stop testing, we've done all we can to perfect this software. Ship it!" Individuals and organizations may be held responsible for avoidable and foreseeable consequences, which they have a duty to perceive and correct. And the gray area is that some system errors are foreseeable and correctable only at very great expense, an expense so great that pursuing this level of perfection is not feasible economically—no one could afford the product.

For example, although software companies try to debug their products before releasing them to the marketplace, they knowingly ship buggy products because the time and cost of fixing all minor errors would prevent these products from ever being released (Rigdon, 1995). What if the product was not offered on the marketplace, would social welfare as a whole not advance and perhaps even decline? Carrying this further, just what is the responsibility of a producer of computer services—should it withdraw the product that can never be perfect, warn the user, or forget about the risk (let the buyer beware)?

Three principal sources of poor system performance are (1) software bugs and errors, (2) hardware or facility failures caused by natural or other causes, and (3) poor input data quality. Chapter 10 discusses why zero defects in software code of any complexity cannot be achieved and why the seriousness of remaining bugs cannot be estimated. Hence, there is a technological barrier to perfect software, and users must be aware of the potential for catastrophic failure. The software industry has not yet arrived at testing standards for producing software of acceptable but not perfect performance (Collins et al., 1994).

This topic is explored in the Window on Technology, which describes how software contributed to the radiation poisoning of 28 patients at Panama's National Cancer Institute. As you read this case, try to determine what factors allowed this terrible tragedy to occur. How much was the software responsible? How much were "people" factors responsible? Whom should be assigned blame?

Although software bugs and facility catastrophe are likely to be widely reported in the press, by far the most common source of business system failure is data quality. Few companies routinely measure the quality of their data, but studies of individual organizations report data error rates ranging from 0.5 to 30 percent (Redman, 1998).

ETHICAL ISSUES

The central quality-related ethical issue that information systems raise is at what point should I (you) release software or services for consumption by others? At what point can you conclude that your software or service achieves an economically and technologically adequate level of quality? What are you obliged to know about the quality of your software, its procedures for testing, and its operational characteristics?

SOCIAL ISSUES

The leading quality-related social issue once again deals with expectations: As a society, do we want to encourage people to believe that systems are infallible, that data errors are impossible? Do we instead want a society where people are openly skeptical and questioning

WINDOW ON TECHNOLOGY

WHEN SOFTWARE KILLS: WHAT HAPPENED AT PANAMA'S NATIONAL CANCER INSTITUTE

Victor Garcia feels lucky to be alive. He was one of 28 patients at the National Cancer Institute of Panama who received excessive doses of gamma ray radiation for cancer treatments in November 2000. Since then, 21 of these patients have died, and the International Atomic Energy Agency (IAEA) believes at least five of these deaths were caused by radiation poisoning.

The three Panamanian medical physicists who used the software to figure out the dose of radiation for these patients were charged with second-degree murder. Under Panamanian law, they may be held responsible because they introduced changes in the software that guided the radiation therapy machine used on these patients. How could this tragedy have happened?

Before administering radiation treatment, a physician devises a treatment plan that determines what dose of radiation can be safely targeted at a cancerous tumor. The plan also specifies where to place metal shields known as "blocks" to protect noncancerous areas. Using this plan, a medical physicist inputs information on the size, shape, and location of the blocks into software for guiding radiation machines. The software creates a three-dimensional picture of how the dose will be distributed and calculates how long the radiation treatment should last.

The Panamanian medical physicists were following a doctor's instructions to be more protective of pelvic organs by adding a fifth block to the four blocks ordinarily used on cancer patients. However, the radiation machine software, which was created by Multidata Systems International of St. Louis, Missouri, was designed for treatments only when four or fewer blocks are prescribed.

Olivia Saldana, one of the Panamanian physicists, tried to make the software work for a fifth block. She entered the dimensions of all five blocks as a single composite shape. Although it looked like the system could work with this composite shape, the software miscalculated appropriate doses. Patients were subjected to 20 to 50 percent more radiation than they should have received.

Multidata insists that it did nothing wrong. Multidata's software manual stated it is "the responsibility of the user" to verify the results of the software's calculations. Had the hospital verified the radiation doses by manually checking the software's calculations or by testing the dosages in water before radiating patients, the staff would have found out about the overdoses before they were administered.

Unfortunately, National Cancer Institute physicists did not always manually verify the results of the software calculations. Three radiation physicists were working overtime to treat more

than 100 patients per day because the hospital was understaffed. The IAEA found that the hospital examined only the functioning of the hardware. It had no quality assurance program for the software or for its results. Consequently, physicists were not required to tell anyone they had changed the way they entered data into the system and no one questioned the software's results.

By 1997, the hospital staff was so worried about radiation overdoses that it reported to the Panamanian Ministry of Health that "overexposure of radiation therapy patients due to human error" would be a risk unless conditions at the hospital improved.

Independent experts not associated with the case assert that the software that controls medical equipment and other life-critical devices should be designed to pause or shut down if told to execute a task it is not programmed to perform. When the IAEA investigated the National Cancer Institute incident in May 2001, it found other ways to get the software to miscalculate treatment times. Every time investigators treated one, two, or four blocks of varying shapes as a single block, the software miscalculated the treatment times.

The IAEA investigating team and a team from the M. D. Anderson Cancer Center in Houston found Multidata's manual did not describe precisely how to digitize coordinates of shielding blocks. The report also noted that the manual did not provide specific warnings against data entry approaches that are different from the standard procedure described.

Examiners from the U.S. Food and Drug Administration (FDA) who inspected Multidata in May 2001 found that Multidata had received at least six complaints about calculation errors related to the software's inability to handle certain types of blocks correctly. The examiners reported that Multidata had been aware of this failure since at least September 1992, but had not taken any corrective action. In 2003, Multidata signed a consent decree with the FDA that it would not make or sell software for radiation therapy devices in the United States, although it can sell its products abroad.

Sources: Deborah Gage and John McCormick, "We Did Nothing Wrong," *Baseline Magazine*, March 2004; and "FDA Seeks Injunction against Multidata Systems Intl.," *FDA News*, May 7, 2003.

To Think About: What management, organization, and technology factors were responsible for the excess radiation doses at Panama's National Cancer Institute? Who was responsible for the malfunctioning of the system? Was an adequate solution developed for this problem? Explain your answer.

of the output of machines, where people are at least informed of the risk? By heightening awareness of system failure, do we inhibit the development of all systems, which in the end contributes to social well-being?

POLITICAL ISSUES

The leading quality-related political issue concerns the laws of responsibility and account-ability. Should Congress establish or direct the National Institute of Science and Technology (NIST) to develop quality standards (software, hardware, and data quality) and impose those standards on industry? Or should industry associations be encouraged to develop industry-wide standards of quality? Or should Congress wait for the marketplace to punish poor system quality, recognizing that in some instances this will not work (e.g., if all retail grocers maintain poor quality systems, customers will have no alternatives)?

Quality of Life: Equity, Access, and Boundaries

The negative social costs of introducing information technologies and systems are begin-ning to mount along with the power of the technology. Many of these negative social con-sequences are not violations of individual rights or property crimes. Nevertheless, these negative consequences can be extremely harmful to individuals, societies, and political institutions. Computers and information technologies potentially can destroy valuable elements of our culture and society even while they bring us benefits. If there is a balance of good and bad consequences of using information systems, who do we hold responsible for the bad consequences? Next, we briefly examine some of the negative social conse-quences of systems, considering individual, social, and political responses.

BALANCING POWER: CENTER VERSUS PERIPHERY

An early fear of the computer age was that huge, centralized mainframe computers would centralize power at corporate headquarters and in the nation's capital, resulting in a Big Brother society, as was suggested in George Orwell's novel *1984*. The shift toward highly decentralized computing, coupled with an ideology of empowerment of thousands of work-ers, and the decentralization of decision making to lower organizational levels have reduced fears of power centralization in institutions. Yet much of the empowerment described in popular business magazines is trivial. Lower-level employees may be empowered to make minor decisions, but the key policy decisions may be as centralized as in the past.

RAPIDITY OF CHANGE: REDUCED RESPONSE TIME TO COMPETITION

Information systems have helped to create much more efficient national and interna-tional markets. The now-more-efficient global marketplace has reduced the normal social buffers that permitted businesses many years to adjust to competition. Time-based com-petition has an ugly side: The business you work for may not have enough time to respond to global competitors and may be wiped out in a year, along with your job. We stand the risk of developing a "just-in-time society" with "just-in-time jobs" and "just-in-time" workplaces, families, and vacations.

MAINTAINING BOUNDARIES: FAMILY, WORK, AND LEISURE

Parts of this book were produced on trains, planes, as well as on family vacations and dur-ing what otherwise might have been "family" time. The danger of ubiquitous computing, telecommuting, nomadic computing, and the "do anything anywhere" computing envi-ronment is that it might actually come true. If so, the traditional boundaries that separate work from family and just plain leisure will be weakened. Although authors have tradi-tionally worked just about anywhere (typewriters have been portable for nearly a cen-tury), the advent of information systems, coupled with the growth of knowledge-work occupations, means that more and more people will be working when traditionally they would have been playing or communicating with family and friends. The work umbrella now extends far beyond the eight-hour day.

Although some people enjoy the convenience of working at home, the do anything anywhere computing environment can blur the traditional boundaries between work and family time.

Weakening these institutions poses clear-cut risks. Family and friends historically have provided powerful support mechanisms for individuals, and they act as balance points in a society by preserving private life, providing a place for people to collect their thoughts, think in ways contrary to their employer, and dream.

DEPENDENCE AND VULNERABILITY

Today, our businesses, governments, schools, and private associations, such as churches, are incredibly dependent on information systems and are, therefore, highly vulnerable if these systems should fail. With systems now as ubiquitous as the telephone system, it is startling to remember that there are no regulatory or standard-setting forces in place similar to telephone, electrical, radio, television, or other public-utility technologies. The absence of standards and the criticality of some system applications will probably call forth demands for national standards and perhaps regulatory oversight.

COMPUTER CRIME AND ABUSE

New technologies, including computers, create new opportunities for committing crime by creating new valuable items to steal, new ways to steal them, and new ways to harm others. **Computer crime** is the commission of illegal acts through the use of a computer or against a computer system. Computers or computer systems can be the object of the crime (destroying a company's computer center or a company's computer files), as well as the instrument of a crime (stealing valuable financial data by illegally gaining access to a computer system using a home computer). Simply accessing a computer system without authorization or with intent to do harm, even by accident, is now a federal crime. Chapter 10 provides more detail on this topic.

Computer abuse is the commission of acts involving a computer that may not be illegal but that are considered unethical. One widespread form of abuse is *spamming*, in which thousands and even hundreds of thousands of unsolicited e-mail and electronic messages are sent out. **Spam** is junk e-mail sent by an organization or individual to a mass audience of Internet users who have expressed no interest in the product or service being marketed. Spammers tend to market pornography, fraudulent deals and services, outright scams, and other products not widely approved in most civilized societies. Some countries have passed laws to outlaw spamming or to restrict its use. In the United States, it is still legal if it does not involve fraud and the sender and subject of the e-mail are properly identified.

Spamming has been growing because it only costs a few cents to send thousands of messages advertising wares to Internet users. Hundreds of CDs can be purchased on the Web that offer spammers millions of e-mail addresses harvested by software robots that read message boards, chat rooms, and Web sites, or spammers can use their own harvesting

Spam consists of unsolicited e-mail messages, which can be bothersome, offensive, and even a drain on office worker productivity. Spam filtering software such as McAfee's SpamKiller blocks suspicious e-mail.

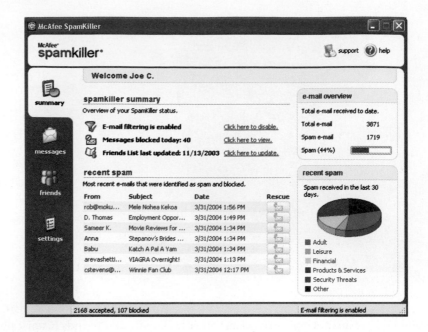

tools for this purpose. These minuscule costs make spamming worthwhile if only one recipient in 100,000 e-mail messages sent makes a purchase.

Spamming is more tightly regulated in Europe than in the United States. On May 30, 2002, the European Parliament passed a ban on unsolicited commercial messaging. Electronic marketing can be targeted only to people who have given prior consent.

Although 33 states in the United States have passed laws to restrict spamming, the Window on Management shows that the practice is to control through legislation and through technical means. Members of the Direct Marketing Association and other companies believe that regulating spam, rather than banning it altogether, would still allow legitimate businesses to use e-mail for direct-marketing purposes. Other major interest groups, however, have lobbied against antispam legislation, believing it would harm legitimate e-mail marketing and put e-commerce at a disadvantage. The spamming problem is a serious one because spam messages clog the Internet and because of its impact on business productivity.

EMPLOYMENT: TRICKLE-DOWN TECHNOLOGY AND REENGINEERING JOB LOSS

Reengineering work (see Chapter 14) is typically hailed in the information systems community as a major benefit of new information technology. It is much less frequently noted that redesigning business processes could potentially cause millions of middle-level managers and clerical workers to lose their jobs. One economist has raised the possibility that we will create a society run by a small "high tech elite of corporate professionals . . . in a nation of the permanently unemployed" (Rifkin, 1993).

Other economists are much more sanguine about the potential job losses. They believe relieving bright, educated workers from reengineered jobs will result in these workers moving to better jobs in fast-growth industries. Missing from this equation are unskilled, blue-collar workers and older, less well educated middle managers. It is not clear that these groups can be retrained easily for high-quality (high-paying) jobs. Careful planning and sensitivity to employee needs can help companies redesign work to minimize job losses.

EQUITY AND ACCESS: INCREASING RACIAL AND SOCIAL CLASS CLEAVAGES

Does everyone have an equal opportunity to participate in the digital age? Will the social, economic, and cultural gaps that exist in the United States and other societies be reduced by information systems technology? Or will the cleavages be increased, permitting the better off to become even more better off relative to others?

WINDOW ON MANAGEMENT

CAN THE SPAMMING MONSTER BE TAMED?

E-mail may have made the Internet the most socially inter-active medium in history, but spam is turning it into the most cluttered. Spam now accounts for 65 percent of e-mail traffic worldwide, and that percentage is even higher in some countries (80 percent in Korea). According to International Data Center research, spam volume jumped to 8.5 billion messages daily in 2004. If spam keeps growing at its current rate, the Internet will soon become unusable.

Spam costs for businesses are very high because of the computing and network resources consumed by billions of unwanted e-mail messages and the time consumed in trying to deal with them. The Gartner Group estimated that 35 percent of all business e-mail messages received are spam, and this figure is likely to reach 50 percent by 2005. A great deal of spam e-mail uses subject lines that conceal the real purpose of the messages. Most messages take only a few seconds for the recipient to delete, but some messages use subject headings that require recipients to read the messages quickly to see if they are worthwhile.

According to Nucleus Research, the average worker receives 13.3 spam messages per day, which take six and one half minutes to review and process, amounting to 1.4 percent of each worker's productive time. Assuming an hourly pay rate of $30 and 2,080 hours of work a year, Nucleus calculates spam costs businesses $874 each year in lost productivity for every office worker with an e-mail account. Multiplying that number by 100 million workers amounts to $87 billion in wasted productivity in the United States alone. According to consulting firm mi2g Limited, which focuses on risk management, worldwide spam caused more damage than the worldwide losses from computer viruses and worms ($8.5 billion).

Spam continues to defy most legal and technical efforts to eliminate it. Spammers can easily switch back and forth among free e-mail accounts to broadcast their messages, disguising their true e-mail addresses. Many spam messages are sent from one country, while another country hosts the spam Web site. There are legitimate business and personal uses for e-mail, and many businesses using direct marketing do not wish to see e-mail regulated.

Most corporate networks use spam filters, as do many Internet service providers. Individuals can purchase filtering software from companies such as Brightmail, MailFrontier, or Sendmail or use the filtering capabilities of major e-mail software. These tools block suspicious e-mail before it enters a recipient's e-mail inbox. Another technique for avoiding spam is to block any messages sent from computers or e-mail addresses known to be used by spammers.

However, spam filters can block legitimate messages, and many spammers skirt around filters by continually changing

their accounts, creating false return addresses, or using cryptic phrases that most filters won't catch. Nevertheless, antispam systems appear to be a good investment. An International Data Center study found that antispam systems in a typical company with 5,000 e-mail users halved the amount of time employees spent on e-mail, saving the company $783,000.

The U.S. CAN-SPAM Act of 2003, which went into effect on January 1, 2004, does not outlaw spamming but does ban deceptive e-mail practices by requiring commercial e-mail messages to display an accurate subject line, identify the true sender, and offer recipients an easy way to remove their names from e-mail lists. Experts believe the CAN-SPAM Act will have little impact. Although it makes it easier to know who is sending spam, it overrides stronger state statutes, some of which outlaw spam, and it has little impact on spammers based abroad. According to John Mozena, vice president of the anti-spam advocacy group Coalition Against Unsolicited Commercial E-Mail, unsolicited e-mail can't be regulated in the same manner as regular postal service mail or telemarketing because there is no additional cost to the marketer to send e-mails to people who haven't opted out.

So far, this has been the case. A few people have been prosecuted under the law, but the flow of unsolicited junk e-mail is as strong as ever, with spammers turning to instant messaging as a new channel for their activities. A Consumer Reports study surveying more than 2,000 e-mail users found that 47 percent were receiving more spam three months after the law went into effect than before.

The question is, What will it take to stop spamming abuses, or will Internet users remain prey to the spamming monster?

Sources: Sudhir Chowdhary, "Festival Blues: India Inc. Grapples with Spam," *ZDNet India*, December 20, 2004; Daniel Nasaw, "Federal Law Fails to Lessen Flow of Junk E-Mail," *Wall Street Journal*, August 10, 2004; Saul Hansell, "Junk E-Mail and Fraud Are Focus of Crackdown," *New York Times*, August 25, 2004, "4 Rivals Near Agreement on Ways to Fight Spam," *New York Times*, June 23, 2004; Laurie J. Flynn, "Internet Giants File 7 Suits Aimed at Stopping Spam," *New York Times*, October 29, 2004; Brent Staples, "The Battle Against Junk Mail and Spyware on the Web," *New York Times*, January 3, 2004; Thomas Claburn, "Anti-Spam Technologies Prove Their Value," *Information Week*, April 26, 2004; G. Patrick Pawling "Turning Drains into Gains," *Cisco IQ Magazine*, First Quarter 2004; Pui-Wing Tam, "Fruitcake Debutantes Defined by O, and Other Spam Tricks," *Wall Street Journal*, May 28, 2004; and Saul Hansell, "Totaling Up the Bill for Spam," *New York Times*, July 28, 2003.

To Think About: Is spamming an important management issue? Why or why not? How should this problem be handled?

These questions have not yet been fully answered because the impact of systems technology on various groups in society has not been thoroughly studied. What is known is that information, knowledge, computers, and access to these resources through educational institutions and public libraries are inequitably distributed along ethnic and social class lines, as are many other information resources. Several studies have found that certain ethnic and income groups in the United States are less likely to have computers or online Internet access even though computer ownership and Internet access have soared in the past five years. Although the gap is narrowing, higher-income families in each ethnic group are still more likely to have home computers and Internet access than lower-income families in the same group (Lenhart et al., 2003).

A similar **digital divide** exists in U.S. schools, with schools in high-poverty areas less likely to have computers, high-quality educational technology programs, or Internet access available for their students. Left uncorrected, the digital divide could lead to a society of information haves, computer literate and skilled, versus a large group of information have-nots, computer illiterate and unskilled. Public interest groups want to narrow this digital divide by making digital information services—including the Internet—available to virtually everyone just as basic telephone service is now.

HEALTH RISKS: RSI, CVS, AND TECHNOSTRESS

The most important occupational disease today is **repetitive stress injury** (RSI). RSI occurs when muscle groups are forced through repetitive actions often with high-impact loads (such as tennis) or tens of thousands of repetitions under low-impact loads (such as working at a computer keyboard).

The single largest source of RSI is computer keyboards. The most common kind of computer-related RSI is **carpal tunnel syndrome** (CTS), in which pressure on the median nerve through the wrist's bony structure, called a carpal tunnel, produces pain. The pressure is caused by constant repetition of keystrokes: In a single shift, a word processor may perform 23,000 keystrokes. Symptoms of carpal tunnel syndrome include numbness, shooting pain, inability to grasp objects, and tingling. Millions of workers have been diagnosed with carpal tunnel syndrome.

RSI is avoidable. Designing workstations for a neutral wrist position (using a wrist rest to support the wrist), proper monitor stands, and footrests all contribute to proper posture and reduced RSI. New, ergonomically correct keyboards are also an option. These measures should be backed by frequent rest breaks and rotation of employees to different jobs.

Repetitive stress injury (RSI) is the leading occupational disease today. The single largest cause of RSI is computer keyboard work.

RSI is not the only occupational illness computers cause. Back and neck pain, leg stress, and foot pain also result from poor ergonomic designs of workstations. **Computer vision syndrome (CVS)** refers to any eyestrain condition related to computer display screen use. Its symptoms, which are usually temporary, include headaches, blurred vision, and dry and irritated eyes.

The newest computer-related malady is **technostress**, which is stress induced by computer use. Its symptoms include aggravation, hostility toward humans, impatience, and fatigue. According to experts, humans working continuously with computers come to expect other humans and human institutions to behave like computers, providing instant response, attentiveness, and an absence of emotion. Technostress is thought to be related to high levels of job turnover in the computer industry, high levels of early retirement from computer-intense occupations, and elevated levels of drug and alcohol abuse.

The incidence of technostress is not known but is thought to be in the millions and growing rapidly in the United States. Computer-related jobs now top the list of stressful occupations based on health statistics in several industrialized countries.

To date, the role of radiation from computer display screens in occupational disease has not been proved. Video display terminals (VDTs) emit nonionizing electric and magnetic fields at low frequencies. These rays enter the body and have unknown effects on enzymes, molecules, chromosomes, and cell membranes. Long-term studies are investigating low-level electromagnetic fields and birth defects, stress, low birth weight, and other diseases. All manufacturers have reduced display screen emissions since the early 1980s, and European countries such as Sweden have adopted stiff radiation emission standards.

The computer has become a part of our lives—personally as well as socially, culturally, and politically. It is unlikely that the issues and our choices will become easier as information technology continues to transform our world. The growth of the Internet and the information economy suggests that all the ethical and social issues we have described will be heightened further as we move into the first digital century.

5.4 MANAGEMENT OPPORTUNITIES, CHALLENGES, AND SOLUTIONS

The ethical and social implications of information systems are now more far-reaching than ever, affecting individuals who use information systems as well as managers and employees in business firms.

Opportunities

Managers have the opportunity to create an ethical business environment that is within the law, and it is their responsibility to do so. Doing the right thing with information systems in the long term will always lead to a stronger, more reliable organization. This may not mean that management actions will always make employees, shareholders, or customers happy, but these actions should be the result of a careful ethical analysis using the principles we have outlined in this chapter.

Management Challenges

Technology can be a double-edged sword. It has been the source of many benefits, but it also has created new opportunities for breaking the law or taking benefits away from others, raising the following management challenges.

UNDERSTANDING THE MORAL RISKS OF NEW TECHNOLOGY
Rapid technological change means that the choices facing individuals also rapidly change, and the balance of risk and reward and the probabilities of apprehension for wrongful acts change as well. In this environment it is important for management to conduct an ethical

and social impact analysis of new technologies as they emerge. Managers might take each of the moral dimensions described in this chapter and briefly speculate on how a new technology impacts each dimension. There may not always be right answers for how to behave, but there should be management awareness of the moral risks of new technology.

ESTABLISHING CORPORATE ETHICS POLICIES THAT INCLUDE INFORMATION SYSTEMS ISSUES

As a manager, you will be responsible for developing, enforcing, and explaining corporate ethics policies. Historically, corporate management has paid much more attention to financial integrity and personnel policies than to the information systems area. But based on what you will have learned after reading this chapter, it will be clear your corporation should have an ethics policy in the information systems (IS) area covering such issues as privacy, property, accountability, system quality, and quality of life. The challenge will be in educating non-IS managers about the need for these policies, as well as educating your workforce.

Solution Guidelines

Some corporations have developed far-reaching corporate IS codes of ethics, including FedEx, IBM, American Express, and Merck & Co. Most firms, however, have not developed these codes of ethics, leaving their employees unsure about expected correct behavior. There is some dispute concerning a general code of ethics versus a specific information systems code of ethics. As managers, you should strive to develop an IS-specific set of ethical standards for each of the five moral dimensions:

- *Information rights and obligations.* A code should cover topics such as employee e-mail and Internet privacy, workplace monitoring, treatment of corporate information, and policies on customer information.

- *Property rights and obligations.* A code should cover topics such as software licenses, ownership of firm data and facilities, ownership of software created by employees on company hardware, and software copyrights. Specific guidelines for contractual relationships with third parties should be covered as well.

- *System quality.* The code should describe the general levels of data quality and system error that can be tolerated, with detailed specifications left to specific projects. The code should require that all systems attempt to estimate data quality and system error probabilities.

- *Quality of life.* The code should state that the purpose of systems is to improve the quality of life for customers and for employees by achieving high levels of product quality, customer service, and employee satisfaction and human dignity through proper ergonomics, job and workflow design, and human resources development.

- *Accountability and control.* The code should specify a single individual responsible for all information systems, and reporting to this individual should be others who are responsible for individual rights, the protection of property rights, system quality, and quality of life (e.g., job design, ergonomics, and employee satisfaction). Responsibilities for control of systems, audits, and management should be clearly defined. The potential liabilities of systems officers and the corporation should be detailed in a separate document.

MAKE **IT** YOUR BUSINESS

Finance and Accounting

Poor data quality and software errors can have a devastating impact on the firm's financial and accounting systems because errors in these systems can easily lead to huge losses. Financial and accounting systems are prime targets for fraud and computer crime, as are the specialized financial systems of financial and banking institutions. One growing area of computer crime is securities fraud over the Internet.

Human Resources

Developing and enforcing a corporate ethics policy and procedures that balance the need to run the business responsibly and efficiently with the need to safeguard employee privacy, health, and well-being has become an important responsibility of the human resources function. Employees and their managers may need special training to sensitize them to the new ethical issues surrounding information systems, such as personal use of the Internet or corporate systems or copying digital material and software. You can find examples of human resources applications and issues on pages 147, 171, and 179–181.

Manufacturing and Production

Economic prosperity and the quality of daily life are highly dependent on the smooth and accurate flow of information among disparate manufacturing and production systems. Data quality problems and software errors in one system can affect the performance of other systems inside the firm and the performance of suppliers, distributors, and logistics services that depend on information from these systems.

Sales and Marketing

The Internet has provided powerful new ways of reaching customers and gathering information about them to provide more targeted marketing and products. Information about consumers' activities is marketing gold—and often a critical success factor—for companies doing business online. However, the customer information that is required to create a personalized Web experience raises serious privacy concerns because contemporary information technology makes it so easy for businesses to monitor online behavior and assemble highly detailed profiles of individual consumers. You can find examples of sales and marketing applications on page 171.

Summary

1. *Analyze the relationship among ethical, social, and political issues that are raised by information systems.*

   Information technology has raised new possibilities for behavior for which laws and rules of acceptable conduct have not yet been developed. Information technology is introducing changes that create new ethical issues for societies to debate and resolve. Increasing computing power, storage, and networking capabilities—including the Internet—can expand the reach of individual and organizational actions and magnify their impact. The ease and anonymity with which information can be communicated, copied, and manipulated in online environments are challenging traditional rules of right and wrong behavior. Ethical, social, and political issues are closely related. Ethical issues confront individuals who must choose a course of action, often in a situation in which two or more ethical principles are in conflict (a dilemma). Social issues spring from ethical issues as societies develop expectations in individuals about the correct course of action. Political issues spring from social conflict and are mainly concerned with using laws that prescribe behavior to create situations in which individuals behave correctly.

2. *Identify the main moral dimensions of an information society and specific principles for conduct that can be used to guide ethical decisions.*

   The moral dimensions of information systems center around information rights and obligations, property rights and obligations, accountability and control, system quality, and quality of life. Six ethical principles are available to judge conduct. These principles are derived independently from several cultural, religious, and intellectual traditions and include the Golden Rule, Immanuel Kant's Categorical Imperative, Descartes' rule of change, the Utilitarian Principle, the Risk Aversion Principle, and the ethical "no free lunch" rule. These principles should be used in conjunction with an ethical analysis to guide decision making. The ethical analysis involves identifying the facts, values, stakeholders, options, and consequences of actions. Once completed, you can consider which ethical principle to apply to a situation to arrive at a judgment.

3. *Evaluate the impact of contemporary information systems and the Internet on the protection of individual privacy and intellectual property.*

   Contemporary information systems technology, including Internet technology, challenges traditional regimens for protecting individual privacy and intellectual property. Data storage and data analysis technology enables companies to easily gather personal data about individuals from many different sources and analyze these data to create detailed electronic profiles about individuals and their behaviors. Data flowing over the Internet can be monitored at many points. The activities of Web site visitors can be closely tracked using cookies and other Web monitoring tools. Not all Web sites have strong privacy protection policies, and they do not always allow for informed consent regarding the use of personal information. The online industry prefers self-regulation to the U.S. government tightening privacy protection legislation.

   Traditional copyright laws are insufficient to protect against software piracy because digital material can be copied so easily. Internet technology also makes other intellectual property even more difficult to protect because digital material can be copied easily and transmitted to many different locations simultaneously over the Net. Web pages can be constructed easily using pieces of content from other Web sites without permission.

4. Assess how information systems have affected everyday life.

Although computer systems have been sources of efficiency and wealth, they have some negative impacts. Errors in large computer systems are impossible to eradicate totally. Computer errors can cause serious harm to individuals and organizations, and existing laws and social practices are often unable to establish liability and accountability for these problems. Less serious errors are often attributable to poor data quality, which can cause disruptions and losses for businesses. Jobs can be lost when computers replace workers or tasks become unnecessary in reengineered business processes. The ability to own and use a computer may be exacerbating socioeconomic disparities among different racial groups and social classes. Widespread use of computers increases opportunities for computer crime and computer abuse. Computers can also create health problems such as repetitive stress injury, computer vision syndrome, and technostress.

5. Identify the principal management challenges posed by the ethical and social impact of information systems and management solutions.

The main management challenges posed by the ethical and social impact of information systems are the need to understand the moral risks of new technology and the difficulty of establishing corporate ethics policies that address information systems issues. For each of the five moral dimensions of information systems, corporations should develop a corporate ethics policy statement to guide individuals and to encourage appropriate decision making. The policy areas are as follows:

- *Individual information rights.* Spell out corporate privacy and due process policies.
- *Property rights.* Clarify how the corporation will treat property rights of software owners.
- *System quality.* Identify methodologies and quality standards to be achieved.
- *Quality of life.* Identify corporate policies on family, computer crime, decision making, vulnerability, job loss, and health risks.
- *Accountability and control.* Clarify who is responsible and accountable for corporate information.

Key Terms

Accountability, 153	Fair Information Practices (FIP), 156	Privacy, 155
Carpal tunnel syndrome (CTS), 172	Framing, 163	Profiling, 151
Computer abuse, 169	Immanuel Kant's Categorical Imperative, 154	Repetitive stress injury (RSI), 172
Computer crime, 169	Information rights, 150	Responsibility, 153
Computer vision syndrome (CVS), 173	Informed consent, 157	Risk Aversion Principle, 154
Cookies, 158	Intellectual property, 161	Safe harbor, 157
Copyright, 161	Liability, 153	Spam, 169
Descartes' rule of change, 154	Nonobvious relationship awareness (NORA), 151	Spyware, 159
Digital divide, 172	Opt-in, 159	Technostress, 173
Digital Millennium Copyright Act (DMCA), 163	Opt-out, 159	Trade secret, 161
Due process, 153	P3P, 159	Utilitarian Principle, 154
Ethical "no free lunch" rule, 154	Patent, 162	Web bugs, 159
Ethics, 148		

Review Questions

1. In what ways are ethical, social, and political issues connected? Give some examples.
2. What are the key technological trends that heighten ethical concerns?
3. What are the differences between responsibility, accountability, and liability?
4. What are the five steps in an ethical analysis?
5. Identify and describe six ethical principles.
6. What is a professional code of conduct?
7. What are meant by privacy and fair information practices?
8. How is the Internet challenging the protection of individual privacy?
9. What role can informed consent, legislation, industry self-regulation, and technology tools play in protecting individual privacy of Internet users?

10. *What are the three different regimes that protect intellectual property rights? What challenges to intellectual property rights does the Internet pose?*

11. *Why is it so difficult to hold software services liable for failure or injury?*

12. *What is the most common cause of system quality problems?*

13. *Name and describe four quality of life impacts of computers and information systems.*

14. *What is technostress, and how would you identify it?*

15. *Name three management actions that could reduce RSI injuries.*

Discussion Questions

1. *Should producers of software-based services, such as ATMs, be held liable for economic injuries suffered when their systems fail?*

2. *Should companies be responsible for unemployment caused by their information systems? Why or why not?*

Application Software Exercise:
Word Processing and Web Page Development Tool Exercise: Creating a Simple Web Site

Build a simple Web site of your own design for a business using the Web page creation function of Microsoft Word, Microsoft FrontPage, or a Web page development tool of your choice. Your Web site should include a home page with a description of your business and at least one picture or graphic. From the home page, you must be able to link to a second Web page and, from there, link to a third Web page. Make the home page long enough so that when you arrive at the bottom of the page, you can no longer see the top. There, include a link back to the top. Also include a link to one of the secondary Web pages. On the secondary page, include a link

to the top of that page and a link back to the top of the home page. Also include a link to the third page, which should contain a link to its own top and a link back to the top of the home page. Finally, on one of the secondary pages, include another picture or graphic, and on the other page include an object that you create using Microsoft Excel or other spreadsheet software. The Laudon Web site for Chapter 5 includes instructions for completing this project. If you have tested every function and all work to your satisfaction, save the pages you have created for submission to your instructor.

 **Developing a Web Site Privacy Policy**

Software requirements: Web browser software
Word processing software
Electronic presentation software (optional)

Dirt Bikes's management wants to make sure it has policies and procedures in place to protect the privacy of visitors to its Web site. You have been asked to develop Dirt Bikes's Web site privacy policy. The TRUSTe Web site (www.truste.org) has Model Privacy Policy Disclosures in its Resources for businesses that you can download and review to help you draft Dirt Bikes's privacy policy. You can also examine specific companies' privacy policies by searching for Web site privacy policy on Yahoo! or using another search engine.

Prepare a report for management that addresses the following issues:

1. How much data should Dirt Bikes collect on visitors to its Web site? What information could it discover by tracking visitors' activities at its Web site? What value would this information provide the company? What are the privacy problems raised by collecting such data?

2. Should Dirt Bikes use cookies? What are the advantages of using cookies for both Dirt Bikes and its Web site visitors? What privacy issues do they create for Dirt Bikes?

3. Should Dirt Bikes join an organization such as TRUSTe to certify it has adopted approved privacy practices? Why or why not?

4. Should Dirt Bikes design its site so that it conforms to P3P standards? Why or why not?

5. Should Dirt Bikes adopt an opt-in or opt-out model of informed consent?

6. Include in your report a short (two to three pages) privacy statement for the Dirt Bikes Web site. You can use the TRUSTe Model Privacy Disclosures as a guideline if you wish.

7. (Optional) Use electronic presentation software to summarize your recommendations for management.

Electronic Commerce Project: Using Internet Newsgroups for Online Market Research

You are producing hiking boots that you are selling through a few stores at this time. You think your boots are more comfortable than those of your competition. You believe you can undersell many of your competitors if you can significantly increase your production and sales. You would like to use the Internet discussion groups interested in hiking, climbing, and camping to both sell your boots and to make them well known. Visit Google's Usenet archives (groups.google.com), which store discussion postings from many thousands of newsgroups. Through this site you can locate all relevant newsgroups and search them by keyword, author's name, forum, date, and subject. Choose a message and examine it carefully, noting all the information you can obtain, including information about the author.

1. How could you use these newsgroups to market your boots?

2. What ethical principles might you be violating if you use these messages to sell your boots? Do you think there are ethical problems in this type of use of the newsgroups? Explain your answer.

3. Decide whether you want to use the newsgroups to locate Web sites on the topic being searched for the hiking boots industry. Examine the various sites to determine whether there are other ways to draw potential buyers to the Web site you may decide to establish.

4. Next go to Yahoo.com to search for the hiking boots industry and locate sites that will help you develop other new ideas for contacting potential customers.

5. Given what you have learned in this and previous chapters, prepare a plan to use newsgroups and other alternative methods to begin attracting visitors to your site.

Group Project: Developing a Corporate Ethics Code

With three or four of your classmates, develop a corporate ethics code on privacy that addresses both employee privacy and the privacy of customers and users of the corporate Web site. Be sure to consider e-mail privacy and employer monitoring of worksites, as well as corporate use of information about employees concerning their off-job behavior (e.g., lifestyle, marital arrangements, and so forth). If possible, use electronic presentation software to present your ethics code to the class.

CASE STUDY
Security Versus Privacy: Does Terrorism Change the Debate?

Discussions on many levels are underway in the United States about the kind of country in which its citizens want to live and the nation's balance between public safety and private freedom. Is the government's collection of so much information on each of us more dangerous than the possible benefits? Are we willing to give up some of our freedom and privacy if we believe our safety depends on it?

People want technology both for convenience and for protection, and so most are now tolerant of increasingly prevalent surveillance cameras and collection of personal data by the government and private corporations. There are around 300 million cameras in use around the world. Such cameras are already being used in the United States to monitor bridges, tunnels, airports, and border crossings, as well as activities in stores, banks, and garages. In Great Britain, an estimated 2.5 million closed-circuit television cameras are being used so that the average Londoner is probably photographed 300 times a day. London systems record every vehicle that enters the city to better control traffic and so police can plan emergency routes when needed. This information is also shared with intelligence agencies to help protect citizens and solve crimes.

Computers record immigration and visa applications—the U.S. database for visa applications already contains 50 million records, most with photographs. Law enforcement organizations are also now using this database. According to Miles Matthews, a senior Justice Department official, "It's not just useful for terrorism. It's drug trafficking, money laundering, a variety of frauds, not to mention domestic crimes."

Large databases of medical records are being created so that "if you're brought to an emergency room anywhere in the world, your medical records pop up in 30 seconds," explains Ben Schneiderman, a University of Maryland expert on new computing techniques. The U.S. federal government's Centers for Disease Control and Prevention is creating a computerized network to collect and analyze health data from eight major cities, including doctors' reports, emergency room visits, and medication sales to watch out for clusters of symptoms associated with both terrorist attacks and major natural disease outbreaks.

These surveillance activities generate massive amounts of data, and information systems technology is now capable of storing and transmitting them. Jeffrey Ullman, a former Stanford University database researcher, claims that, if all of these data were collected, a digital dossier of every person in the United States would require only "a couple terabytes (trillion characters) of well-defined information." One estimate projects that by 2023 a corporation will be able to devote one PC to monitoring every U.S. citizen in the population, estimated to be at more than 325 million people by then.

In May 2003, President George W. Bush ordered U.S. intelligence agencies to purchase as much satellite imagery as possible from private companies because satellite photos from all over the world are so high-quality that they can be used for domestic and foreign surveillance. The United States is also planning to increase its own surveillance satellites under a program called Future Imagery Architecture. The United States is coming closer to being able to monitor all movements of people everywhere. The Central Intelligence Agency (CIA) has been spending about $35 million annually since 1999 to improve its own technology in its enormous electronic archives. For example, it is improving face-recognition software to help track specific people through photographs and videos.

After the 9/11 terrorist attacks, we have been asked to place more trust in law enforcement and intelligence agencies. The Bush administration argues that we can even trust these agencies to exercise broad new powers. Congress overwhelmingly approved an extension of such powers when it passed the USA Patriot Act in October 2001 with almost no opposition. This law automatically expires in October 2005, but the president is asking Congress to make it permanent.

This 342-page act gave law enforcement officials broader authority to conduct electronic surveillance and wiretaps and tightened oversight of financial activities to prevent money laundering that might benefit terrorists. It changed provisions of the Foreign Intelligence Surveillance Act passed in 1978 by allowing the Federal Bureau of Investigation (FBI) to share information gathered in terrorism investigations with local law enforcement agencies so that it could potentially be used for criminal prosecution. The Patriot Act enabled federal prosecutors to seek wiretap and surveillance authority and to obtain client records from financial institutions without evidence of criminal activity. (A federal judge ruled this part of the act unconstitutional in late September 2004.) Civil liberties groups and hundreds of communities have objected to this legislation.

On December 13, 2003, President Bush granted the FBI additional powers by signing into law the Intelligence Authorization Act, which funds all the intelligence activities of the federal government. This statute defines financial institutions to include travel agencies, car dealers, real estate and insurance agents, casinos, hotels, and even the U.S. Postal Service. Under its provisions, the FBI can obtain personal data from all of these organizations without obtaining court approval and without their knowledge.

The FBI has been using a tool called Carnivore to eavesdrop on communication flowing through the Internet. Carnivore software, stored on the computers of Internet service providers (ISPs), inspects all the headers of the millions of e-mail messages passing through an ISP's computer system to identify those of criminal or terrorist suspects falling under court orders. Carnivore then selects those messages and contents for FBI agents to review.

Privacy watchdogs view the system as "the electronic equivalent of listening to everybody's phone calls to see if it's the phone call you should be monitoring." FBI Director Robert Mueller defended the practice at a June 2003 American Civil Liberties Union (ACLU) meeting. "In our free and exceptionally open society, there is no guarantee that there will never be another terrorist attack. And therefore we must thoroughly investigate every threat, whether at home or abroad, carefully—carefully—observing the constitutional rights of all," he said.

On March 12, 2004, the FBI, the Department of Justice, and the Drug Enforcement Administration filed a proposal to require major Internet service providers to modify their networks to facilitate further electronic eavesdropping by law enforcement officials. The proposal gives law enforcement agencies easy access to all forms of switched Internet communications, including new Internet-based telephone services, instant messaging systems, and high-capacity Internet communications provided by cable systems and the telephone network.

The U.S. government is combining surveillance data from multiple sources into massive databases. The Transportation Security Administration (TSA) had been using a computer system implemented in 1996 called Computer Assisted Passenger Prescreening System (CAPPS) to profile airline passengers to identify those who are high risk. It tags unusual behavior such as purchasing one-way airline tickets with cash.

CAPPS problems included inaccurate or out-of-date data and mix-ups as to the people on the high-risk list. Names written in alphabets other than the Roman alphabet, such as Japanese, Russian, or Arabic, could be written in English in many different ways. Moreover, the same name could be written differently, for example, by omitting a middle initial. Senator Edward Kennedy of Massachusetts was stopped from boarding airplanes five times between March 1 and April 6, 2004 because his name resembled an alias used by a suspected terrorist who had been barred from flying on airlines in the United States.

TSA developed a more sophisticated approach called CAPPS II. In addition to evaluating such travel-related behavior and looking for passenger names on watch lists, CAPPS II gave transportation agencies access to numerous public and private databases when a passenger books a flight. It matched passenger names, addresses, phone numbers, dates of birth, and photo IDs from airline passenger lists against data from credit-reporting agencies, and then it scanned law enforcement and intelligence files to determine whether the person was a security risk.

In June 2004 TSA dropped CAPPS II in response to criticism from Congress and privacy advocates. In its place TSA proposed a system called Secure Flight, which has many of the same features as CAPPS II. Secure Flight also matches passenger data against commercial databases, but it does not use the computer routines developed for CAPPS II that tried to determine if passengers not on watch lists should be singled out for scrutiny.

The Defense Advanced Research Projects Agency (DARPA) has been working on a number of projects that would create massive databases that capture transactional data from many different sources. A project called Combat Zones That See (CTS) would record and analyze the movement of every vehicle in a foreign city using software to identify vehicles by size, color, shape, license plate, or drivers' and passengers' faces. Its goal is to help the U.S. military protect its troops overseas. Its founding document states that the program "aspires to build the world's first multi-camera surveillance system that uses automatic . . . analysis of live video" to study vehicle movement "and significant events across an extremely large area."

MATRIX, which stands for Multistate Anti-Terrorism Information Exchange, is a massive database developed by a private company called Seisint and funded and managed by the Department of Homeland Security and several state governments. MATRIX was launched in 2002 to help investigators establish patterns and links for profiling crime and terrorism suspects. The database includes 4 billion records with data

on criminal histories, federal terrorist watch lists, drivers' licenses, vehicle registrations, and incarcerations as well as credit histories, pilot licenses, aircraft ownership, boat ownership, property ownership, and other public and commercial data. So far, only five states have signed on to MATRIX— Florida, Connecticut, Michigan, Ohio, and Pennsylvania. Eleven others have withdrawn from the project.

The construction of massive databases of personal information has alarmed both government officials and privacy watchdogs. Marc Rotenberg, the executive director of the Electronic Privacy Information Center (EPIC), describes the problem: "What seems to be small-scale, discrete systems end up being combined into large databases." Although the public has no problem with the collection of most of this "small" data independently, weaving it all together can become a massive invasion of privacy he believes. A June 2004 report by a bipartisan Technology and Privacy Advisory Committee appointed by Secretary of Defense Donald Rumsfeld to evaluate Pentagon programs for data mining called for restrictions on federal agency searches of personally identifiable information to safeguard privacy when fighting terrorism.

There are also technical problems with assembling and analyzing gigantic pools of data. Although information technology enables the creation of such massive databases, it has not solved the problems of integrating disparate sources of information and of arriving at valid conclusions. Massive databases can produce very unreliable results because they become very difficult to examine. Piotr Indyk, a Massachusetts Institute of Technology (MIT) database researcher, points out that as the amount of data collected rapidly increases, the number of chance correlations also increases so that the number of logically valid but actually useless solutions grows just as rapidly.

Data in very large data repositories can be very unreliable. Information systems specialists often use the term GIGO, meaning "garbage in, garbage out." Think of the problems in your own financial records, from misspellings to digital transposition to misidentification to outdated records. According to Larry English of Information Impact, a database consulting firm, "It is routine to find in large customer databases defective records—records with at least one major error or omission—at a rate of at least 20 to 35 percent." Moreover, researching using a massive database requires both an "unusually smart analyst," Ullman points out, as well as an accurate model of what that analyst is looking for.

Only a 1 percent error rate in searching for terrorists using so much data would produce millions of false alarms, requiring an immense amount of waste of investigators' time while wrongly labeling and greatly disturbing many innocent people. "A 99 percent hit rate is great for advertising, but terrible for spotting terrorism" is the explanation given by Gene Spafford, the director of Purdue University's Center for Education and Research in Information Assurance and Security. In addition, further tightening identification criteria would result in many terrorists and criminals being missed, including, for example, many of those who hijacked the 9/11 planes but who had previously lived quiet, seemingly normal lives.

So far, thousands of intercepted phone calls, e-mail messages, documents, and other messages collected for terror surveillance have proved too massive to analyze. Three years after the September 11 attacks, more than 120,000 hours of potentially valuable terrorism-related recordings had not yet been translated by the FBI because the agency did not have enough linguists trained in Arabic and other languages.

Although consumers balk at businesses intruding on their privacy, they are more supportive of government agencies collecting personal information to fight terrorism. A Harris Poll conducted in February 2003 revealed that 84 percent of those polled favored stronger document and physical security for travelers, and 44 percent supported expanded government monitoring of cell phones and e-mail. According to Columbia University professor Alan Westin, who conducted the poll, "How to put a system in place to protect us from [both] terrorism and invasions of privacy is something we are just barely beginning to understand."

Sources: Eric Lichtblau, "F.B.I. Said to Lag on Translations of Terror Tapes," *New York Times*, September 28, 2004; Reuters, "Judge Rules Against Patriot Act Provision," September 29, 2004; Matthew L. Wald, "U.S. Wants Air Traveler Files for Security Test," *New York Times*, September 22, 2004; Rachel L. Swarns, "Senator? Terrorist? A Watch List Stops Kennedy at Airport," *The New York Times*, August 20, 2004; Ryan Singel, "Secure Flight Gets Wary Welcome," *Wired News*, August 27, 2004; Sebastian Rupley, "FBI Petitions for Broad Wiretapping Rights," *PC Magazine*, March 15, 2004; Robert Pear, "Panel Urges New Protection on Federal 'Data Mining,' " *New York Times*, May 17, 2004; Brian Bergstein, "Terrorist Scoring System Sparked Investigations and Arrests," *Information Week*, May 20, 2004; Brian Gail Repsher Emery, "Patriot Games," and Andy Sullivan, "U.S. to Force Airlines to Provide Traveler Data," Yahoo! News, March 17, 2004; Sara Kehaulani Goo, "Northwest Gave U.S. Data on Passengers," *Washington Post*, January 18, 2004; Matthew L. Wald, "Privacy Issues Slow Updated Airlines Security," *New York Times*, May 11, 2004; Heather Mac Donald, "The 'Privacy' Jihad," *Wall Street Journal*, April 1, 2004; Larry Greenemeier, "Lawmakers Want Info," *Information Week*, February 25, 2004; Joe Sharkey, "When Flying Is Truly the Only Way to Go," *New York Times*, May 25, 2004; Matthew L. Wald, "Privacy Issue Delays Change in Airport Screening System," *New York Times*, February 13, 2004; Meg Mitchell Moore, "Serving Up Your Customers," *CSO Magazine*, January 2004; Jeffrey Rosen, "How to Protect America, and Your Rights," *New York Times*, February 6, 2004; Ethan Bronner, "Collateral Damage," *New York Times*, February 22, 2004; Andrew P. Napolitano, "Repeal the Patriot Act," *Wall Street Journal*, March 5, 2004; David E. Sanger, "President Urging Wider U.S. Powers in Terrorism Law," *New York Times*, September 11, 2003; Adam Clymer, "In Fight for Privacy, States Set Off Sparks," *New York Times*, July 6, 2003; Sean Marciniak, "Web Privacy Services Complicate Work of Federal Investigators," *Wall Street Journal*, July 3, 2003; Michael J. Sniffen, "Pentagon Developing System to Track Every Vehicle in a City," www.security-focus.com, July 1, 2003; "Pentagon Tool Records Every Breath," australianit.news.com.au, June 3, 2003; Jeff Milchen, "Fighting Terror Without Losing Our Freedom," *Baltimore Sun*, June 22, 2003; Randall Edwards, "CAPPS II Faces Scrutiny Before Funding," www.fce.com, June 19, 2003; Jane Black, "Privacy: For Every Attack, a Defense," *Business Week*, July 22, 2003; "Putting the Blinders Back on Big Brother," *BusinessWeek Online*, March 27, 2003; "Mueller Defends FBI at Civil Liberties Meeting," www.cnn.com, June 13, 2003; Eric Lichtblau, "Administration Plans Defense of Terror Law," *New York Times*, August 19, 2003; Jesse J. Holland, "Ashcroft Pushes Anti-Terror Law Expansion," Associated Press, June 5, 2003; Dan Farmer and Charles C. Mann, "Give Me Duquesne Minus 7, for a Nickel," *Technology Review*, May 2003; "Surveillance Nation," *Technology Review*, April 2003; James Bamford, "Big Brother Is Tracking You, Without a Warrant," *New York Times*, May 18, 2003; Jane Black, "At Justice, NSEERS Spells Data Chaos," *BusinessWeek Online*, May 2, 2003; Ann Davis, "Why a 'No Fly List' Aimed at Terrorists Delays Others," *Wall Street Journal*, April 22, 2003; Charles Lewis and Adam Mayle, "Justice Department Drafts Sweeping Expansion of Anti-Terrorism Act," www.publicintegrity.org, February 7, 2003; Farhad Manjoo, "Please Step to the Side, Sir," www.salon.com, April 10, 2003; Matt Welch, "Get Ready for PATRIOT II," www.alternet.org, April 2, 2003; Kevin Poulsen, "FBI Seeks Internet Telephony Surveillance," *BusinessWeek Online*, March 28, 2003; T. C. Webster, "Government to 'Save' Digital History," www.worldnetdaily.com, March 4, 2003; Matthew Brezezinski, "Fortress American," *New York Times*, February 23, 2003; Jennifer 8. Lee, "State Department Link Will Open Visa Database to Police Officers," *New York Times*, January 31, 2003; and William J. Broad and Judith Miller, "Health Data Monitored for Bioterror Warning," *New York Times*, January 27, 2003.

CASE STUDY QUESTIONS

1. Do the increased surveillance power and capability of the U.S. government present an ethical dilemma? Explain your answer.

2. Apply an ethical analysis to the issue of the U.S. government's use of information technology to ensure public safety and U.S. citizens' privacy rights.

3. What are the ethical, social, and political issues raised by the U.S. government creating massive databases to collect personal data on individuals and profile them?

4. How effective are electronic eavesdropping and massive databases as terrorism and crime-prevention tools? Explain your answer.

5. State your views on ways to solve the problems of collecting the key data the U.S. government needs to combat terrorism without interfering with individual privacy.

PART ONE PROJECT

Analyzing Business Processes for an Enterprise System

Your firm manufactures specialty chemicals and dyestuffs used in plastics, fibers, and coatings. It operates five different production facilities in the southeastern United States, with corporate headquarters in Memphis, Tennessee.

Rapid time-to-market of new products, strong customer service, and low costs are essential for remaining competitive in the chemical industry. Management is looking for ways to make the company operate more efficiently and would like to start by examining order processing.

This is how the firm's order processing currently operates: A customer can call, fax, or mail in an order. A customer service representative writes down order information on an order pad. This information includes the customer name, identification number, shipping address, billing address, product number, product description, quantity, and shipping instructions (such as to call the receiving manager to make an appointment for delivery). After gathering all the relevant information, the representative confirms the entire order with the customer.

While taking down the order information, the customer service representative accesses the company's order entry system and checks the inventory for each product ordered. The customer service representative first checks the warehouse closest to the customer's shipping address. If the product is not available there, the representative checks another warehouse. If the order is placed on the telephone, the customer service representative suggests a delivery date, which is four to five business days away. If the customer needs the order sooner, the customer service representative queries the existing order entry system to see which warehouse might have the inventory to fulfill the order. Generally the warehouse closest to the customer's shipping address will fill the order.

All current orders are collected manually and entered into the firm's order entry system. The order will not be accepted by the system unless it includes the customer's identification number, shipping address, and billing address. (If the order is from a new customer, the system can assign a new customer number.) If the order has a delivery date of 8 to 10 business days in the future, the order form will be held manually for several days and then input into the system. If an order is for more than 10 days in the future, it will be treated as a back order when it is input into the system. The system generates a back-order report daily to remind customer service representatives of orders that they have on back order.

When each order has been entered, the system performs a credit check on the customer. Some customers are assigned "credit hold" status and are not shipped their orders until payment has been received for the purchase. Other customer orders are processed immediately and the customer pays for the purchase after receiving the shipment and an invoice. A report on credit hold is forwarded to the credit department and the customer service representatives receive a daily report on orders placed on credit hold.

Different business units at your company use different identification codes for the same products. In other words, corporate headquarters might use a different product number for a product such as Purple Dye #211 than the product identification number used at the plant where it was manufactured.

1. Diagram the order process. What are the outputs of this process?

2. What other major business processes outside of the order process are likely to be impacted by the order process? Explain.

3. How could this process be made more efficient? Draw a diagram of your proposed process and information changes.

4. Prepare descriptions of two reports from this system, one that would be important to the order entry staff and one that would be important to corporate management.

5. Your company is thinking about installing enterprise software. You would like to learn more about enterprise software and how it could handle your order entry process. Explore the Solutions Map for the chemical industry in the SAP Business Maps on the SAP Web site (**www.mysap.com**). Which SAP processes are likely to address the activities in order processing that we have described? What questions would you ask to see if SAP's software could handle your order process?

6. You have heard that enterprise software might not be able to handle the following situations:

   ■ When the system checks for available inventory, it treats material (batches of chemicals) that is still undergoing quality control inspection as available inventory as well as material in inventory that has already passed quality control inspection.

   ■ There is no way to automatically check customer records to see which qualify for sales tax exemptions.

   ■ The system assigns a different date for back-ordered items that are currently out of stock rather than the original requested date on the customer order.

What impact might this lack of functionality have on order processing and other parts of the company? How could you determine how serious a problem this creates? What questions would you ask?

Information Technology Infrastructure

Part Two Project: Creating a
New Internet Business

Part Two provides the technical foundation for understanding information systems by examining technologies and managerial issues in the firm's information technology (IT) infrastructure. Chapters 6–9 describe contemporary hardware and software platforms along with technologies for data management and communications, highlighting the Internet, wireless networking technologies, and the convergence of computing and communications. Chapter 10 is devoted to security and control, reflecting new urgency of this topic for e-business and for meeting higher standards of control and accountability in the firm.

Chapter 6

IT Infrastructure and Platforms

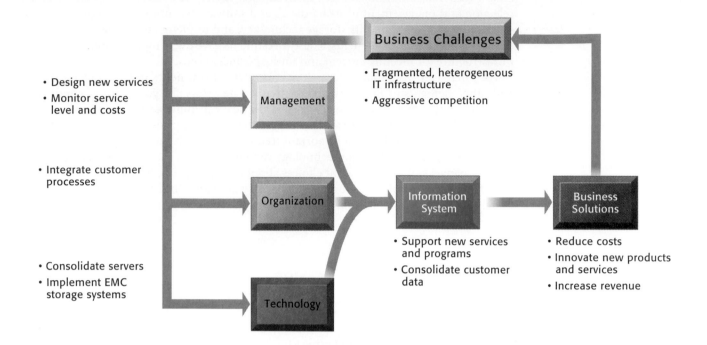

- Design new services
- Monitor service level and costs

- Integrate customer processes

- Consolidate servers
- Implement EMC storage systems

Management

Organization

Technology

Business Challenges

- Fragmented, heterogeneous IT infrastructure
- Aggressive competition

Information System

- Support new services and programs
- Consolidate customer data

Business Solutions

- Reduce costs
- Innovate new products and services
- Increase revenue

Opening Case: Hong Kong's New World Telecommunications Prospers with a New IT Infrastructure

New World Telecommunications is a Hong Kong–based telecommunications company that offers international calling services to 1.1 million subscribers. It also provides telecommunications services to businesses, such as private leased lines, Internet telephone, Internet-based virtual private networks, high-speed frame-relay data transmission, and online data centers.

New World's market is one of cutthroat competition. Its ability to deliver its services competitively depends on a flexible information technology (IT) infrastructure that can provide uninterrupted and smooth access to data and the ability to support new services in a very short time. New World had been storing its data on different servers, which required license fees for each and some fragmentation of data. To keep its business running and reduce maintenance costs, New World needed to integrate its storage and servers. The company also needed to integrate its customer relationship management, billing, and operational support systems so that, for example, a corporate customer could log on to a Web portal to view service usage, maintain account information, and monitor network performance.

New World Telecommunications enlisted storage vendor EMC to manage its 400-gigabyte production

and billing data as well as 80 gigabytes of customer data that were residing on six Sun Solaris servers and a Hewlett-Packard (HP) Unix server. EMC updated New World's storage infrastructure to an automated storage area network (SAN) to make it easier to access data from many different servers across the enterprise.

New World was using different brands of servers: Sun, HP, and Compaq Tru64. EMC helped the company centralize its data across all these different brands of servers. New World also consolidated servers so that processing work was transferred from 107 to 70 machines.

By adopting this new infrastructure, New World has reduced system administration costs by 25 percent and has considerably enhanced its flexibility in providing new products and services. In the past, it would take the company nearly three weeks to roll out new market programs. In Hong Kong's fiercely competitive telecommunications business, three weeks seems like an eternity. According to Samuel Poon, New World's director of information technology, "Now we're able to launch a new program within two or three days."

Sources: Raoul LeBlond and Ben Worthen, "Taking IT to the Next Level," *CIO Asia*, January 2004; and www.nwt-009.com, accessed September 10, 2004.

New World Telecommunications enhanced its efficiency and competitiveness by better selection and management of its hardware and software technology. The company consolidated servers, updated its storage technology, and implemented software that could integrate its key business systems. These investments gave the company a more flexible IT infrastructure for meeting current and future business needs.

As a manager, you'll face many decisions about investments in hardware, software, and other elements of IT infrastructure that are necessary for your firm to conduct its business—and which may even give your firm new capabilities to surge ahead of competitors. This chapter provides an overview of the technology and service components of IT infrastructure and the most important trends in hardware and software platforms. We look at the capabilities of major technology vendors as well as the technologies themselves to help managers make intelligent choices about the appropriate technology platform for their firm. If you would like a more introductory discussion of hardware and software or a review of basic hardware and software concepts, you can find this information at the Laudon Web site for Chapter 6.

6.1   IT INFRASTRUCTURE

In Chapter 1, we defined *information technology (IT) infrastructure* as the shared technology resources that provide the platform for the firm's specific information system applications. IT infrastructure includes investment in hardware, software, and services—such as consulting, education, and training—that are shared across the entire firm or across entire business units in the firm. For instance, a firm's investment in thousands of new desktop computers networked together and linked to the Internet is an infrastructure investment because it serves many groups, goals, and business initiatives.

Supplying U.S. firms with IT infrastructure is a $1.8 trillion dollar industry when telecommunications, networking equipment and telecommunications services (Internet, telephone, and data transmission) are included. Investments in infrastructure account for between 25 and 35 percent of information technology expenditures in large firms (Weill et al., 2002).

A firm's IT infrastructure provides the foundation for serving customers, working with vendors, and managing internal firm business processes (see Figure 6-1). In this sense, IT infrastructure defines the capabilities of the firm today and in the near term of, say, three to five years (the length of time it takes to make a significant change in the firm's IT infrastructure). For instance, if you want to provide customers with a daily balance of cell phone charges on a Web site, and if you plan to use this capability as a strategic differentiating feature of your firm, this implies certain infrastructure capabilities. If you are a bank and want to sell banking services anywhere in the United States or the world to all your customers, whether they have car loans, home loans, brokerage accounts, or just checking accounts, you will need an infrastructure that crosses these different lines of business and operates on a global enterprise-wide basis.

Defining IT Infrastructure

There are two ways of defining IT infrastructure: as *technology* or as *services clusters*. In one sense IT infrastructure is like the plumbing or electrical systems in a building: a set of physical devices and software applications that are required to operate the entire enterprise. But an even more useful *service-based* definition focuses on the services provided by all this hardware and software. In this definition, IT infrastructure is a set of firmwide services budgeted by management and comprising both human and technical capabilities (Weill et al., 2002). These services include the following:

- Computing platforms used to provide computing services that connect employees, customers, and suppliers into a coherent digital environment, including large mainframes, desktop and laptop computers, and personal digital assistants (PDAs) and Internet appliances.

FIGURE 6-1   *The connection between the firm, IT infrastructure, and business capabilities.*

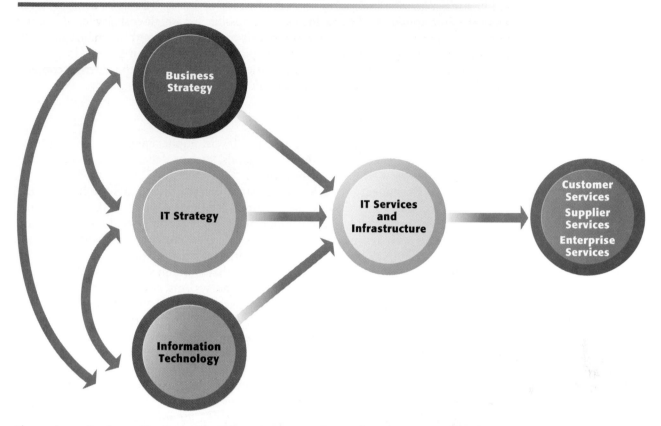

The services a firm is capable of providing to its customers, suppliers, and employees are a direct function of its IT infrastructure. Ideally, this infrastructure should support the firm's business and information systems strategy. New information technologies have a powerful impact on business and IT strategies, as well as the services that can be provided to customers.

- Telecommunications services that provide data, voice, and video connectivity to employees, customers, and suppliers.

- Data management services that store and manage corporate data and provide capabilities for analyzing the data.

- Application software services that provide enterprise-wide capabilities such as enterprise resource planning, customer relationship management, supply chain management, and knowledge management systems that are shared by all business units.

- Physical facilities management services that develop and manage the physical installations required for computing, telecommunications, and data management services.

- IT management services that plan and develop the infrastructure, coordinate with the business units for IT services, manage accounting for the IT expenditure, and provide project management services.

- IT standards services that provide the firm and its business units with policies that determine which information technology will be used, when, and how.

- IT education services that provide training in system use to employees and offer managers training in how to plan for and manage IT investments.

- IT research and development services that provide the firm with research on potential future IT projects and investments that could help the firm differentiate itself in the marketplace.

This "service platform" perspective makes it easier to understand the business value provided by infrastructure investments. For instance, the real business value of a fully loaded Pentium 4 PC operating at 2 gigahertz that costs about $1,500 with a high-speed

Internet connection is hard to understand without knowing who will use it and how it will be used. When we look at the services provided by these tools, however, their value becomes more apparent: The new PC makes it possible for a high-cost employee making $100,000 a year to connect to all the company's major systems and the public Internet. The high-speed Internet service saves this employee about one hour per day in reduced wait time for corporate and Internet information. Without this PC and Internet connection, the value of this one employee to the firm might be cut in half.

Levels of IT Infrastructure

Firm infrastructure is organized at three major levels: public, enterprise, and business unit (Figure 6-2). There may be other lower levels, such as departments or individual employees, but for now we focus on these three.

All firms are dependent on public IT infrastructure, which includes the Internet, the public switched telephone network, industry-operated networks, and other IT support facilities such as cable systems and cellular networks. Enterprise-wide infrastructure includes services such as e-mail, a central corporate Web site, corporate-wide intranets, and an increasing array of enterprise-wide software applications (see Chapter 11). Business units also have their own infrastructure that is uniquely suited to their line of business such as specialized production software and systems, customer and vendor systems, and local order entry and other transaction systems.

In multiunit businesses, typical of most large firms, a central corporate infrastructure is also used to manage the entire enterprise, receive reports from business units, and exercise central oversight.

FIGURE 6-2   *Levels of IT infrastructure.*

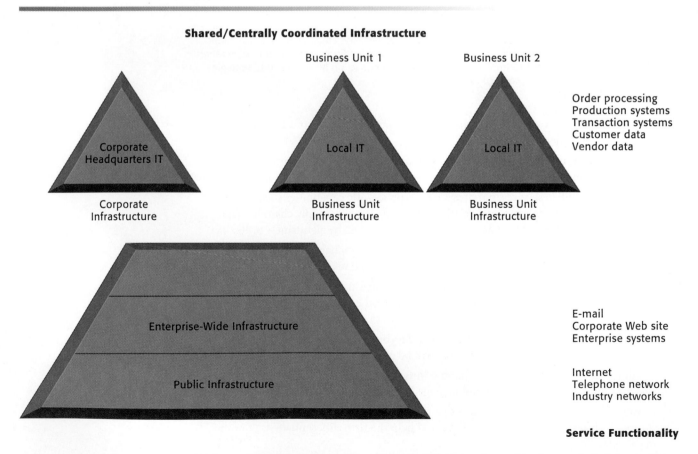

IT infrastructure exists at three different levels: public, enterprise, and business unit. Each level of infrastructure provides a set of IT services and capabilities.

Source: Adapted from "Building IT Infrastructure for Strategic Agility" by Peter Weill et. al, *Sloan Management Review* (Fall 2002), by permission of publisher. Copyright © 2005 by Massachusetts Institute of Technology. All rights reserved.

Figure 6-2 raises some interesting questions: What, for instance, should be handled by enterprise infrastructure and what by local business units? How much should local business units be charged (and on what basis) for use of enterprise architecture? Local business units may have unique demands that an enterprise-wide infrastructure may not address.

Evolution of IT Infrastructure: 1950–2005

The IT infrastructure in organizations today is an outgrowth of over 50 years of evolution in computing platforms. We have identified five stages in this evolution, each representing a different configuration of computing power and infrastructure elements (see Figure 6-3). The five eras are automated special-purpose machines, general-purpose mainframe and minicomputer computing, personal computers, client/server networks, and enterprise and Internet computing.

These eras do not necessarily end for all organizations at the same time, and the technologies that characterize one era may also be used in another time period for other purposes. For example, some companies still run traditional mainframe or minicomputer systems. Mainframe computers today are used as massive servers supporting large Web sites and corporate enterprise applications. More detail on infrastructure history can be found on the Laudon Web site for Chapter 6.

ELECTRONIC ACCOUNTING MACHINE ERA: 1930–1950

The first era of business computing used specialized machines that could sort computer cards into bins, accumulate totals, and print reports (DaCruz, 2004). Although the electronic accounting machine was an efficient processor of accounting tasks, the machines were large and cumbersome. Software programs were hardwired into circuit boards, and they could be changed by altering the wired connections on a patch board. There were no programmers, and a human machine operator was the operating system, controlling all system resources.

GENERAL-PURPOSE MAINFRAME AND MINICOMPUTER ERA: 1959 TO PRESENT

The first commercial all-electronic vacuum tube computers appeared in the early 1950s with the introduction of the UNIVAC computers and the IBM 700 Series. Not until 1959 with the introduction of the IBM 1401 and 7090 transistorized machines did widespread commercial use of **mainframe** computers begin in earnest. In 1965, the general-purpose commercial mainframe computer truly came into its own with the introduction of the IBM 360 series. The 360 was the first commercial computer with a powerful operating system that could provide time sharing, multitasking, and virtual memory in more advanced models.

Mainframe computers eventually became powerful enough to support thousands of online remote terminals connected to a centralized mainframe using proprietary communication protocols and proprietary data lines. The first airline reservation systems appeared in 1959 and became the prototypical online, real-time interactive computing system that could scale to the size of an entire nation.

IBM dominated mainframe computing from 1965 onward and still dominates this $27 billion global market in 2004. Today IBM mainframe systems can work with a wide variety of different manufacturers' computers and multiple operating systems on client/ server networks and networks based on Internet technology standards.

The mainframe era was a period of highly centralized computing under the control of professional programmers and systems operators (usually in a corporate data center), with most elements of infrastructure provided by a single vendor, the manufacturer of the hardware and the software. This pattern began to change with the introduction of **minicomputers** produced by Digital Equipment Corporation (DEC) in 1965. DEC minicomputers (PDP-11 and later the VAX machines) offered powerful machines at far lower prices than IBM mainframes, making possible decentralized computing, customized to

FIGURE 6-3 *Eras in IT infrastructure evolution.*

Illustrated here are the typical computing configurations characterizing each of the five eras of IT infrastructure evolution.

Stages in IT Infrastructure Evolution

Electronic
Accounting
Machine
(1930–1950)

Mainframe/
Minicomputer
(1959–present)

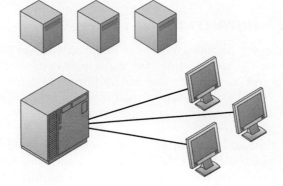

Personal
Computer
(1981–present)

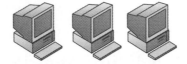

Client Server
(1983–present)

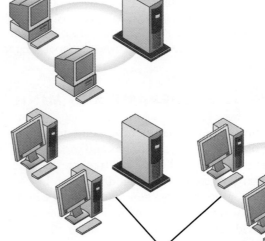

Enterprise
Internet
(1992–present)

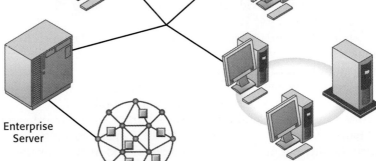

Enterprise
Server

Internet

the specific needs of individual departments or business units rather than time sharing on a single huge mainframe.

PERSONAL COMPUTER ERA: (1981 TO PRESENT)

Although the first truly personal computers (PCs) appeared in the 1970s (the Xerox Alto, MIT's Altair, and the Apple I and II, to name a few), these machines had only limited distribution to computer enthusiasts. The appearance of the IBM PC in 1981 is usually credited as the beginning of the PC era because this machine was the first to become widely adopted in American businesses. At first using the DOS operating system, a text-based command language, and later the Microsoft Windows operating system, the **Wintel PC** computer (Windows operating system software on a computer with an Intel microprocessor) became the standard desktop personal computer. Today, 95 percent of the world's estimated 1 billion computers use the Wintel standard.

Proliferation of PCs in the 1980s and early 1990s launched a spate of personal desktop productivity software tools—word processors, spreadsheets, electronic presentation software, and small data management programs—that were very valuable to both home and corporate users. These PCs were standalone systems until PC operating system software in the 1990s made it possible to link them into networks.

CLIENT/SERVER ERA (1983 TO PRESENT)

In **client/server computing**, desktop or laptop computers called **clients** are networked to **server** computers that provide the client computers with a variety of services and capabilities. Computer processing work is split between these two types of machines. The client is the user point of entry, whereas the server provides communication among the clients, processes and stores shared data, serves up Web pages, or manages network activities. The term *server* refers to both the software application and the physical computer on which the network software runs. The server could be a mainframe, but today server computers typically are more powerful versions of personal computers, based on inexpensive Intel chips and often using multiple processors in a single computer box.

The simplest client/server network consists of a client computer networked to a server computer, with processing split between the two types of machines. This is called a *two-tiered client/server architecture*. Whereas simple client/server networks can be found in small businesses, most corporations have more complex, **multitiered** (often called **N-tier**) **client/server architectures** in which the work of the entire network is balanced over several different levels of servers, depending on the kind of service being requested (see Figure 6-4).

FIGURE 6-4   *A multitiered client/server network (N-tier).*

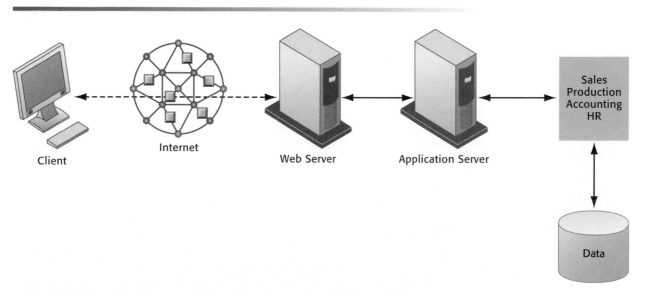

In a multitiered client/server network, client requests for service are handled by different levels of servers.

For instance, at the first level a **Web server** will serve a Web page to a client in response for a request for service. Web server software is responsible for locating and managing stored Web pages. If the client requests access to a corporate system (a product list or price information, for instance), the request is passed along to an **application server**. Application server software handles all application operations between a user and an organization's back-end business systems. The application server may reside on the same computer as the Web server or on its own dedicated computer. Chapters 7 and 8 provide more detail on other pieces of software that are used in multitiered client/server architectures for e-commerce and e-business.

Client/server computing enables businesses to distribute computing work across a number of smaller, inexpensive machines that cost much less than minicomputers or centralized mainframe systems. The result is an explosion in computing power and applications throughout the firm.

Novell Netware was the leading technology for client/server networking at the beginning of the client/server era. Today Microsoft is the market leader, with its **Windows** operating systems (Windows Server, Windows XP, Windows 2000), controlling 78 percent of the local area network market.

ENTERPRISE INTERNET COMPUTING ERA (1992 TO PRESENT)

The success of the client/server model posed a new set of problems for corporations. Many large firms found it difficult to integrate all of their local area networks (LANs) into a single, coherent corporate computing environment. Applications developed by local departments and divisions in a firm, or in different geographic areas, could not communicate easily with one another and share data.

In the early 1990s, firms turned to networking standards and software tools that could integrate disparate networks and applications throughout the firm into an enterprise-wide infrastructure. As the Internet developed into a trusted communications environment after 1995, business firms began using the *Transmission Control Protocol/ Internet Protocol (TCP/IP)* networking standard to tie their disparate networks together. We discuss TCP/IP in detail in Chapter 8.

The resulting IT infrastructure links different types and brands of computer hardware and smaller networks into an enterprise-wide network so that information can flow freely across the organization and between the firm and other organizations. Enterprise networks link mainframes, servers, PCs, mobile phones, and other handheld devices, and connect to public infrastructures such as the telephone system, the Internet, and public network services.

The enterprise infrastructure employs software that can link disparate applications and enable data to flow freely among different parts of the business. Chapter 2 describes how enterprise applications perform this function. Other solutions for enterprise integration include enterprise application integration software, Web services, and outsourcing to external vendors that provide hardware and software for a comprehensive enterprise infrastructure. We discuss these solutions in detail in section 6.4 and in Chapter 11.

The enterprise era promises to bring about a truly integrated computing and IT services platform for the management of global enterprises. The hope is to deliver critical business information painlessly and seamlessly to decision makers when and where they need it to create customer value. This could be everything from getting inventory data to the mobile salesperson in the customer's office, to helping a customer at a call center with a problem customer, or providing managers with precise up-to-the-minute information on company performance.

That is the promise, but the reality is wrenchingly difficult and awesomely expensive. Most large firms have a huge, tangled web of hardware systems and software applications inherited from the past. This makes achieving this level of enterprise integration a difficult, long-term process that can last perhaps as long as a decade and cost large companies hundreds of millions of dollars. Table 6-1 compares each era on the infrastructure dimensions discussed above.

TABLE 6-1 *Stages in the IT Infrastructure Evolution*

Infrastructure Dimension	Electronic Accounting Machine Era (1930–1950)	Mainframe Era (1959 to Present)	PC Era (1981 to Present)	Client/Server Era (1983 to Present)	Enterprise Era (1992 to Present)
Signature Firm(s)	IBM Burroughs NCR	IBM	Microsoft/Intel Dell HP IBM	Novell Microsoft	SAP Oracle PeopleSoft
Hardware Platform	Programmable card sorters	Centralized mainframe	Wintel computers	Wintel computers	Multiple: • Mainframe • Server • Client
Operating System	Human operators	IBM 360 IBM 370 Unix	DOS/Windows Linux IBM 390	Windows 3.1 Windows Server Linux	Multiple: • Unix/Linux • OS 390 • Windows Server
Application and Enterprise Software	None; application software created by technicians	Few enterprise-wide applications; departmental applications created by in-house programmers	No enterprise connectivity; boxed software	Few enterprise-wide applications; boxed software applications for workgroups and departments	Enterprise-wide applications linked to desktop and departmental applications: • mySAP • Oracle E-Business Suite • PeopleSoft Enterprise One
Networking/ Telecommunications	None	Vendor-provided: • Systems Network Architecture (IBM) • DECNET (Digital) • AT&T voice	None or limited	Novell NetWare Windows 2003 Linux AT&T voice	LAN Enterprise-wide area network (WAN) TCP/IP Internet standards-enabled
System Integration	Vendor-provided	Vendor-provided	None	Accounting and consulting firms Service firms	Software manufacturer Accounting and consulting firms System integration firms Service firms
Data Storage and Database Management	Physical card management	Magnetic storage Flat files Relational databases	DBase II and III Access	Multiple database servers with optical and magnetic storage	Enterprise database servers
Internet Platforms	None	Poor to none	None at first Later browser-enabled clients	None at first Later: • Apache server • Microsoft IIS	None in the early years Later: • Intranet- and Internet-delivered enterprise services • Large server farms

Technology Drivers of Infrastructure Evolution

The changes in IT infrastructure we have just described have resulted from developments in computer processing, memory chips, storage devices, telecommunications and networking hardware and software, and software design that have exponentially increased computing power while exponentially reducing costs. Let's look at the most important developments.

MOORE'S LAW AND MICROPROCESSING POWER

In 1965, Gordon Moore, the director of Fairchild Semiconductor's Research and Development Laboratories, an early manufacturer of integrated circuits, wrote in *Electronics* magazine that since the first microprocessor chip was introduced in 1959, the number of components on a chip with the smallest manufacturer costs per component (generally transistors) had doubled each year. This assertion became the foundation of **Moore's Law**. Moore later reduced the rate of growth to a doubling every two years (Tuomi, 2002).

This law would later be interpreted in multiple ways. There are at least three variations of Moore's Law, none of which Moore ever stated: (1) the power of microprocessors doubles every 18 months (Tuomi, 2002); (2) computing power doubles every 18 months; and (3) the price of computing falls by half every 18 months.

Figure 6-5 illustrates the relationship between number of transistors on a microprocessor and millions of instructions per second (MIPS), a common measure of processor power. Figure 6-6 shows the exponential decline in the cost of transistors and rise in computing power.

There is reason to believe the exponential growth in the number of transistors and the power of processors coupled with an exponential decline in computing costs will continue into the future. Chip manufacturers continue to miniaturize components. Intel has recently changed its manufacturing process from 0.13-micron component size (a micron is a millionth of a meter), introduced in 2002, to a newer 90-nanometer process in 2004 (a nanometer is a billionth of a meter). With a size of about 50 nanometers, today's transistors should no longer be compared to the size of a human hair but rather to the size of a virus, the smallest form of organic life.

By using nanotechnology, Intel believes it can shrink the size of transistors down to the width of several atoms. **Nanotechnology** uses individual atoms and molecules to create computer chips and other devices that are thousands of times smaller than current technologies permit. IBM and other research labs have created transistors from nanotubes and other electrical devices (IBM, 2004) and have developed a manufacturing process that could produce nanotube processors economically (Figure 6-7). Other new technologies

---

FIGURE 6-5 *Moore's Law and microprocessor performance.*

Packing more transistors into a tiny microprocessor has exponentially increased processing power.

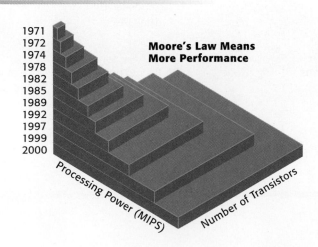

FIGURE 6-6   *Falling cost of chips.*

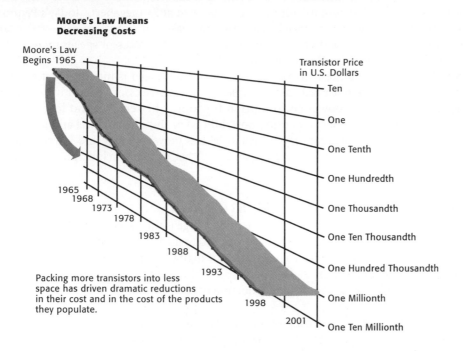

Moore's Law Means Decreasing Costs

Moore's Law Begins 1965

1965
1968
1973
1978
1983
1988
1993
1998
2001

Packing more transistors into less space has driven dramatic reductions in their cost and in the cost of the products they populate.

Transistor Price in U.S. Dollars

Ten
One
One Tenth
One Hundredth
One Thousandth
One Ten Thousandth
One Hundred Thousandth
One Millionth
One Ten Millionth

Packing more transistors into less space has driven down transistor cost dramatically as well as the cost of the products in which they are used.

FIGURE 6-7   *Examples of nanotubes.*

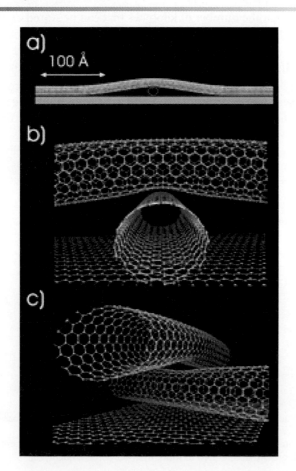

a)
100 Å
b)
c)

Nanotubes are tiny tubes about 10,000 times thinner than a human hair. They consist of rolled up sheets of carbon hexagons. Discovered in 1991 by researchers at NEC, they have the potential uses as minuscule wires or in ultrasmall electronic devices and are very powerful conductors of electrical current.

include strained silicon, 300-millimeter production wafers (which decrease the costs of production), and denser interconnections among components.

Whereas the first Pentium microprocessors operated at 75 megahertz, today's Pentiums are available with 3-gigahertz speeds. However, increasing processor speeds at the same exponential rate as in the past may no longer be possible. As processor speeds increase, heat is generated that cannot be dissipated with air fans.

Another brake on future increases in microprocessor speed is more market-oriented: Most consumers may not need vast increases in microprocessor speed but instead are more interested in low power consumption for longer battery life and low weight to increase laptop and handheld computer portability. For this reason, Intel and other firms are designing the next generation of chips to be less power hungry and lower in weight even if they are the same or even slower speeds. Other options include putting multiple processors on a single chip.

THE LAW OF MASS DIGITAL STORAGE

A second technology driver of IT infrastructure change is the Law of Mass Digital Storage. The world produces as much as 5 exabytes of unique information per year (an exabyte is a billion gigabytes, or 10^{18} bytes). The amount of digital information is roughly doubling every year (Lyman and Varian, 2003). Almost all of this information growth involves magnetic storage of digital data, and printed documents account for only 0.003 percent of the annual growth.

Fortunately, the cost of storing digital information is falling at an exponential rate. Figure 6-8 shows that PC hard drive capacity—beginning with a Seagate 506 in 1980 that had 5 megabytes of memory—has grown at a compound annual growth rate of 25 percent in the early years to over 60 percent a year since 1990. Today's PC hard drives have storage densities approaching 1 gigabyte per square inch and total capacities of over 200 gigabytes (IBM, Seagate).

Figure 6-9 shows that the number of kilobytes that can be stored on magnetic disks for one dollar from 1950 to 2004 roughly doubled every 15 months.

METCALFE'S LAW AND NETWORK ECONOMICS

Moore's Law and the Law of Mass Storage help us understand why computing resources are now so readily available. But why do people want more computing and storage power? The economics of networks and the growth of the Internet provide some answers.

FIGURE 6-8 *The capacity of hard disk drives grows exponentially, 1980–2004.*

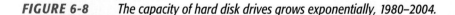

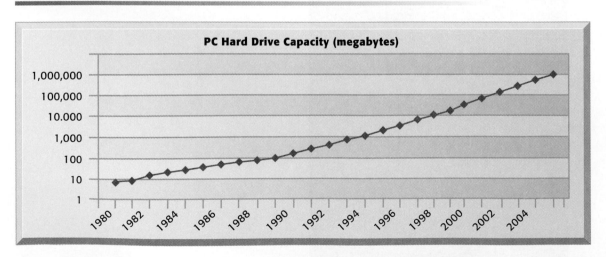

From 1980 to 1990, hard disk drive capacities for PCs grew at the rate of 25 percent annual compound growth, but after 1990 growth accelerated to more than 65 percent each year.
Source: Authors.

FIGURE 6-9   *The cost of storing data declines exponentially, 1950–2004.*

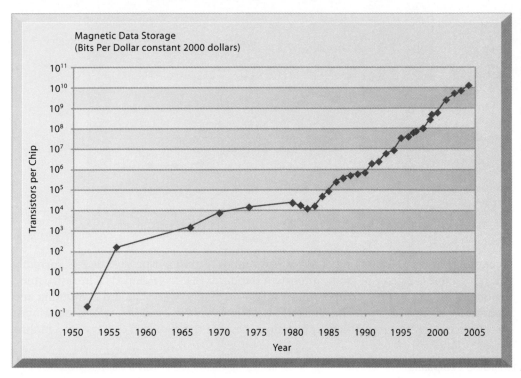

Since the first magnetic storage device was used in 1955, the cost of storing a kilobyte of data has fallen exponentially, doubling the amount of digital storage for each dollar expended every 15 months on average.

Source: "Exponential Growth an Illusion?: Response to Ilkka Tuomi," by Ray Kurzweil, KurzweilAI.net, September 23, 2003. Used with permission.

Robert Metcalfe—inventor of Ethernet local area network technology—claimed in 1970 that the value or power of a network grows exponentially as a function of the number of network members. Metcalfe and others point to the *increasing returns to scale* that network members receive as more and more people join the network. As the number of members in a network grows linearly, the value of the entire system grows exponentially and theoretically continues to grow forever as members increase. Demand for information technology has been driven by the social and business value of digital networks, which rapidly multiply the number of actual and potential links among network members. We discuss Metcalfe's Law in greater detail in Chapter 8.

DECLINING COMMUNICATIONS COSTS AND THE INTERNET

A fourth technology driver transforming IT infrastructure is the rapid decline in the costs of communication and the exponential growth in the size of the Internet. An estimated 1 billion people worldwide now have Internet access, and over 250 million Web host computers exist in the United States. Figure 6-10 illustrates the exponentially declining cost of communication both over the Internet and over telephone networks (which increasingly are based on the Internet). As communication costs fall toward a very small number and approach 0, utilization of communication and computing facilities explodes.

To take advantage of the business value associated with the Internet, firms must greatly expand their Internet connections, including wireless connectivity, and greatly expand the power of their client/server networks, desktop clients, and mobile computing devices. There is every reason to believe these trends will continue.

STANDARDS AND NETWORK EFFECTS

Today's enterprise infrastructure and Internet computing would be impossible—both now and in the future—without agreements among manufacturers and widespread consumer acceptance of **technology standards**. Technology standards are specifications that establish the compatibility of products and the ability to communicate in a network (Stango, 2004).

Technology standards unleash powerful economies of scale and result in price declines as manufacturers focus on the products built to a single standard. Without these

FIGURE 6-10   *Exponential declines in Internet communications costs.*

One reason for the growth in the Internet population is the rapid decline in Internet connection and overall communication costs. The cost per kilobit of Internet access has fallen exponentially since 1995. Digital Subscriber Line (DSL) and cable modems now deliver a kilobit of communication for a retail price of around 2 cents.

Source: Authors.

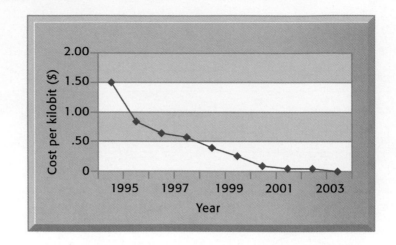

economies of scale, computing of any sort would be far more expensive than is currently the case. Table 6-2 describes some important standards that have shaped IT infrastructure.

Beginning in the 1990s, corporations started moving toward standard computing and communications platforms. The Wintel PC with the Windows operating system and Microsoft Office desktop productivity applications became the standard desktop and mobile

TABLE 6-2   Some Important Standards in Computing

Standard	Significance
American Standard Code for Information Interchange (ASCII)(1958)	Made it possible for computer machines from different manufacturers to exchange data; later used as the universal language linking input and output devices such as keyboards and mice to computers. Adopted by the American National Standards Institute in 1963.
Common Business Oriented Language (COBOL) (1959)	An easy-to-use software language that greatly expanded the ability of programmers to write business-related programs and reduced the cost of software. Sponsored by the Defense Department in 1959.
Unix (1969–1975)	A powerful multitasking, multiuser, portable operating system initially developed at Bell Labs (1969) and later released for use by others (1975). It operates on a wide variety of computers from different manufacturers. Adopted by Sun, IBM, HP, and others in the 1980s and became the most widely used enterprise-level operating system.
Transmission Control Protocol/Internet Protocol (TCP/IP) (1974)	Suite of communications protocols and a common addressing scheme that enables millions of computers to connect together in one giant global network (the Internet). Later, it was used as the default networking protocol suite for local area networks and intranets. Developed in the early 1970s for the U.S. Department of Defense.
Ethernet (1973)	A network standard for connecting desktop computers into local area networks that enabled the widespread adoption of client/server computing and local area networks and further stimulated the adoption of personal computers.
IBM/Microsoft/Intel Personal Computer (1981)	The standard Wintel design for personal desktop computing based on standard Intel processors and other standard devices, Microsoft DOS, and later Windows software. The emergence of this standard, low-cost product laid the foundation for a 25-year period of explosive growth in computing throughout all organizations around the globe. Today, more than 1 billion PCs power business and government activities every day.
World Wide Web (1989–1993)	Standards for storing, retrieving, formatting, and displaying information as a worldwide web of electronic pages incorporating text, graphics, audio, and video enables the creation of a global repository of billions of Web pages by 2004.

client computing platform. Widespread adoption of Unix as the enterprise server operating system of choice made possible the replacement of proprietary and expensive mainframe infrastructure. In telecommunications, the Ethernet standard enabled PCs to connect together in small local area networks (LANs; see Chapter 8), and the TCP/IP standard enabled these LANs to be connected into firmwide networks, and ultimately, to the Internet.

6.2   INFRASTRUCTURE COMPONENTS

IT infrastructure today is composed of seven major components. Figure 6-11 illustrates these different but related infrastructure components and the major vendors within each component category. Table 6-3 describes the overall spending on each component in the United States estimated for 2005. From the point of view of the firm, these components constitute investments that must be coordinated with one another to provide the firm with a coherent infrastructure.

In the past, technology vendors were often in competition with one another, offering purchasing firms a mixture of incompatible, proprietary, partial solutions. But increasingly the vendor firms have been forced by large customers to cooperate in strategic partnerships with one another. For instance, a hardware and services provider such as IBM

FIGURE 6-11   *The IT infrastructure ecosystem.*

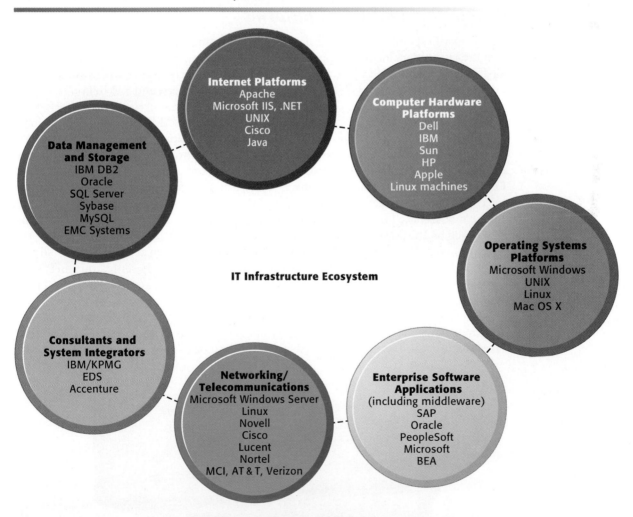

There are seven major components that must be coordinated to provide the firm with a coherent IT infrastructure. Listed here are major technologies and suppliers for each component.

TABLE 6-3 *Estimated Size of U.S. Infrastructure Marketplace Components*

Infrastructure Component	Expenditure ($ billions)	Percentage of Total
Computer hardware platforms	109	13
Operating system platforms	100	12
Enterprise software applications	165	20
Database management	70	9
Networking and telecommunications hardware	155	19
Internet platforms	32	4
Consulting services and system integrators	180	22
Total	811	

Sources: Industry sources, author estimates; SEC Form 10K annual reports for large firms.

cooperates with all the major enterprise software providers, has strategic relationships with system integrators (often accounting firms), and promises to work with whichever database products its client firms wish to use (even though it sells its own database management software called DB2). Let's examine the size and dynamics of each these infrastructure components and their markets.

Computer Hardware Platforms

U.S. firms will spend about $109 billion in 2005 on computer hardware. This component includes client machines (desktop PCs, mobile computing devices such as PDAs and laptops) and server machines. The client machines use primarily Intel or AMD microprocessors. In 2004, 150 million PCs were shipped to U.S. customers, and $30 billion was spent on clients (eMarketer, 2004).

The server market is more complex, using mostly Intel or AMD processors in the form of blade servers in racks, but also includes Sun SPARC microprocessors and IBM PowerPC chips specially designed for server use. **Blade servers** are ultrathin computers consisting of a circuit board with processors, memory, and network connections that are stored in racks. They take up less space than traditional box-based servers. Secondary storage may be provided by a hard drive in each blade server or by external mass-storage drives.

Internet Connection

The Internet Connection for this chapter will direct you to a series of Web sites where you can complete an exercise to survey the products and services of major computer hardware vendors and the use of Web sites in the computer hardware industry.

The marketplace for computer hardware has increasingly become concentrated in top firms such as IBM, HP, Dell, and Sun Microsystems, which produce 90 percent of the machines, and three chip producers, Intel, AMD, and IBM, which account for over 90 percent of the processors sold in 2004. The industry has collectively settled on Intel as the standard processor, with major exceptions in the server market for Unix and Linux machines, which might use SUN or IBM Unix processors.

Mainframes have not disappeared. The mainframe market has actually grown steadily over the last decade, although the number of providers has dwindled to one: IBM. IBM has also repurposed its mainframe systems so they can be used as giant servers for massive

A blade server is a thin, modular processing device that is intended for a single dedicated application (such as serving Web pages) and that can be easily inserted into a space-saving rack with many similar servers.

enterprise networks and corporate Web sites. A single IBM mainframe can run up to 17,000 instances of Linux or Windows server software and is capable of replacing thousands of smaller blade servers.

Operating System Platforms

In 2005, the U.S. market for **operating systems**, which manage the resources and activities of the computer, is expected to amount to $100 billion. At the client level, 95 percent of PCs and 45 percent of handheld devices use some form of Microsoft Windows operating system (such as Windows XP, Windows 2000, or Windows CE). In contrast, in the server marketplace, more than 85 percent of the corporate servers in the United States use some form of the **Unix** operating system or **Linux**, an inexpensive and robust open-source relative of Unix. Although Microsoft Windows Server 2003 is capable of providing enterprise-wide operating system and network services, it is generally not used when there are more than 3,000 client computers in a network.

Unix and Linux constitute the backbone of corporate infrastructure throughout much of the world because they are scalable, reliable, and much less expensive than mainframe operating systems. They can also run on many different types of processors. The major providers of Unix operating systems are IBM, HP, and Sun, each with slightly different and partially incompatible versions.

Although Windows continues to dominate the client marketplace, many corporations have begun to explore Linux as a low-cost desktop operating system provided by commercial vendors such as RedHat Linux and Linux-based desktop productivity suites such as Sun's StarOffice.

Linux is also available in free versions downloadable from the Internet as **open-source software**. Open-source software is described more fully later, but in essence it is software created and updated by a worldwide community of programmers and available for free.

Enterprise Software Applications

In addition to software for applications used by specific groups or business units, U.S. firms will spend about $165 billion in 2005 on software for enterprise applications that are treated as components of IT infrastructure. The largest providers of enterprise application software are SAP, followed by Oracle and PeopleSoft. In December 2004 Oracle purchased PeopleSoft. SAP and PeopleSoft promise to provide software that works with any hardware or operating system; Oracle applications run only on Oracle databases (although they are compatible with all operating systems and hardware platforms). Also included in this category is middleware software supplied by vendors such as BEA for achieving firmwide integration by linking the firm's existing application systems. We describe both types of software in detail in section 6.4.

Microsoft is attempting to move into the lower ends of this market by focusing on small and medium-sized businesses. (There are over 35 million such businesses in the United States, and most have not yet developed enterprise applications.) In general, most large firms already have implemented enterprise applications and have developed long-term relationships with their providers. Once a firm decides to work with an enterprise vendor, switching can be difficult and costly, though not impossible.

Data Management and Storage

There are few choices for enterprise database management software, which is responsible for organizing and managing the firm's data so that it can be efficiently accessed and used. Chapter 7 describes this software in detail. The leading database software providers are IBM (DB2), Oracle, Microsoft (SQL Server), and Sybase (Adaptive Server Enterprise), which supply more than 90 percent of the estimated $70 billion U.S. database software marketplace. A growing new entrant is MySQL, a Linux open-source relational database product available for free on the Internet and increasingly supported by HP and others in a move designed to prevent Microsoft from monopolizing the small and medium-sized firm database market with its SQL Server product.

The physical data storage market (about $35 billion in 2004) is dominated by EMC Corporation for large-scale systems, and a small number of PC hard disk manufacturers led by Seagate, Maxtor, and Western Digital. In addition to traditional disk arrays and tape libraries, large firms are turning to network-based storage technologies. **Storage area networks (SANs)** connect multiple storage devices on a separate high-speed network dedicated to storage. The SAN creates a large central pool of storage that can be rapidly accessed and shared by multiple servers.

The amount of new digital information in the world is doubling every three years, driven in part by e-commerce and e-business and by statutes and regulations requiring firms to invest in extensive data storage and management facilities (such as the Sarbanes-Oxley Act of 2002 and the Health Insurance Portability and Accountability Act, or HIPAA). Consequently, the market for digital data storage devices has been growing at more than 15 percent annually over the last five years.

Networking/Telecommunications Platforms

U.S. firms spend about $150 billon a year on networking and telecommunications hardware and nearly $700 billion on networking services (consisting mainly of telecommunications and telephone company charges for voice lines and Internet access; these are not included in this discussion). Chapter 8 is devoted to an in-depth description of the enterprise networking environment, including the Internet. Windows Server 2003, Windows 2000 Server, and Windows NT are predominantly used as local area network operating systems, followed by Novell, Linux, and Unix. Large enterprise wide area networks primarily use some variant of Unix. Nearly all local area networks, as well as wide area enterprise networks, use the TCP/IP protocol suite as a standard (see Chapter 8).

The leading networking hardware providers are Cisco, Lucent, Nortel, and Juniper Networks. Telecommunications platforms are typically provided by telecommunications/telephone services companies that offer voice and data connectivity, wide area networking, and Internet access. Leading telecommunications service vendors include MCI, AT&T, and regional telephone companies such as Verizon. As noted in Chapter 8, this market is exploding with new providers of cellular wireless, Wi-Fi, and Internet telephone services.

Internet Platforms

Internet platforms overlap with, and must relate to, the firm's general networking infrastructure and hardware and software platforms. Nevertheless, in most corporations, Internet expenditures are separated out from general IT infrastructure expenditures.

U.S. firms spent an estimated $32 billion annually on Internet-related infrastructure. These expenditures were for hardware, software, and management services to support a firm's Web site, including Web hosting services, and for intranets and extranets. A **Web hosting service** maintains a large Web server, or series of servers, and provides fee-paying subscribers with space to maintain their Web sites. This category of technology expenditures is growing by approximately10 percent per year.

The Internet revolution of the late 1990s led to a veritable explosion in server computers, with many firms collecting thousands of small servers to run their Internet operations. Since then there has been a steady push toward server consolidation, reducing the number of server computers by increasing the size and power of each. The Internet hardware server market has become increasingly concentrated in the hands of Dell, HP/Compaq, and IBM as prices have fallen dramatically.

The major Web software application development tools and suites are supplied by Microsoft (FrontPage and the Microsoft .NET family of development tools used to create Web sites using Active Server Pages for dynamic content), Sun (Sun's Java is the most widely used tool for developing interactive Web applications on both the server and client sides), and a host of independent software developers, including Macromedia (Flash), media software (Real Media), and text tools (Adobe Acrobat). Chapter 8 describes the components of the firm's Internet platform in greater detail.

Consulting and System Integration Services

Although 20 years ago it might have been possible for a large firm to implement all its own IT infrastructure, today this is far less common simply because even large firms do not have the staff, the skills, the budget, or the necessary experience to do so. Implementing new infrastructure requires (as noted in Chapters 1 through 3) significant changes in business processes and procedures, training and education, and software integration.

Software integration means ensuring the new infrastructure works with the firm's older, so-called legacy systems and ensuring the new elements of the infrastructure work with one another. **Legacy systems** are generally older transaction processing systems created for mainframe computers that continue to be used to avoid the high cost of replacing or redesigning them. Replacing these systems is cost prohibitive and generally not necessary if these older systems can be integrated into a contemporary infrastructure.

Most companies in the past relied on their accounting firms to provide consulting and system integration services simply because the accounting firms were the only ones that truly understood a company's business processes and had the expertise to change its software. However, in the United States accounting firms have been prohibited by law from providing these services and as a result have split off consulting services into separate entities, such as Accenture (formerly part of Arthur Andersen) and KPMG Consulting (split off from the KPMG accounting firm and now part of IBM).

Consulting and system integration have become a lucrative market that can greatly expand the revenues of computer hardware and enterprise software vendors. IBM's consulting services revenues now equal its hardware revenues, and for enterprise software firms such as Oracle and SAP, consulting, integration, and maintenance revenue exceed the revenues from software sales.

6.3 CONTEMPORARY HARDWARE PLATFORM TRENDS

Although the cost of computing per se has fallen exponentially, the cost of the IT infrastructure has not followed suit, but rather has expanded as a percentage of corporate revenues and budgets. Why? The cost of computing services (consulting, systems integration) has risen dramatically, the cost of software remains high, and the intensity of computing and communicating has increased as other costs have declined. For instance, employees now use much more sophisticated applications, requiring more powerful and expensive hardware of many different types (laptop, desktop, handheld, and tablet computers).

Firms also face a number of other challenges. They need to integrate information stored in different applications, on different platforms (telephone, legacy systems, intranet, Internet sites, desktop, and mobile devices). Firms also need to build resilient infrastructure that can withstand huge increases in peak loads and routine assaults from hackers and viruses. Because customer and employee expectations for service are increasing, firms need to increase their service levels to meet customer demands.

Each of the trends in hardware and software platforms we now describe seeks to address some or all of these challenges.

The Integration of Computing and Telecommunications Platforms

Arguably the most dominant theme in hardware platforms today is the convergence of telecommunications and computing platforms to the point where, increasingly, computing takes place over the network. You can see this convergence at several levels.

At the client level, communication devices such as cell phones are taking on functions of handheld computers, whereas handheld personal digital assistants (PDAs) are taking on cell phone functions. For instance, the Palm Treo 600 digital handheld integrates phone, camera, and handheld computer in one device. Soon full-length films and short commercials

The Palm Treo 600 combines a mobile phone, e-mail, personal organizer, Web access, and camera all in one device. The convergence of computing and communications technologies has turned cell phones into mobile computing platforms.

will be distributed over cell-phone-like devices. Television, radio, and video are moving toward all-digital production and distribution. There is little doubt that personal computers of some sort will be the core of the home entertainment center and the mobile personal entertainment center of the next five years as a storage device and operating system.

At the server and network level, the growing success of Internet telephone systems (now the fastest-growing type of telephone service) demonstrates how historically separate telecommunications and computing platforms are converging toward a single network—the Internet. Chapter 8 describes the convergence of computing and telecommunications in greater depth.

Other major trends in hardware platforms described here are based in large part on computing over high-capacity networks. The network in many respects is becoming the source of computing power, enabling business firms to expand their computing power greatly at very little cost.

Grid Computing

Grid computing involves connecting geographically remote computers into a single network to create a virtual supercomputer by combining the computational power of all computers on the grid. Grid computing takes advantage of the fact that most computers in the United States use their central processing units on average only 25 percent of the time for the work they have been assigned, leaving these idle resources available for other processing tasks. Grid computing was impossible until high-speed Internet connections enabled firms to connect remote machines economically and move enormous quantities of data.

Grid computing requires software programs to control and allocate resources on the grid, such as open-source software provided by Globus Alliance (**www.globus.org**) or other private providers. Client software communicates with a server software application. The server software breaks data and application code into chunks that are then parceled out to the grid's machines. The client machines can perform their traditional tasks while running grid applications in the background.

The business case for using grid computing involves cost savings, speed of computation, and agility. For example, Royal Dutch/Shell Group is using a scalable grid computing platform that improves the accuracy and speed of its scientific modeling applications to find the best oil reservoirs. This platform, which links 1,024 IBM servers running Linux, in effect creates one of the largest commercial Linux supercomputers in the world. The grid adjusts to accommodate the fluctuating data volumes that are typical in this seasonal business. Royal Dutch/Shell Group claims the grid has enabled the company to cut processing time for seismic data, while improving output quality and helping its scientists pinpoint problems in finding new oil supplies.

In another example, the University of Pennsylvania is using grid computing to promote early detection of breast cancer, a disease that affects one out of every eight women today. The grid captures, manages, stores, and analyzes patient files from multiple locations throughout North America for fast retrieval and diagnostic evaluation. The system is being commercialized as the National Digital Mammography Archive (NDMA). The NDMA can now deliver images and physician notes in less than 90 seconds to remote grid users. This improved access to patient records enables physicians to make rapid and well-informed diagnoses in breast cancer screening, potentially saving numerous lives through early detection (IBM, 2004).

On-Demand Computing (Utility Computing)

On-demand computing refers to firms off-loading peak demand for computing power to remote, large-scale data processing centers. In this manner, firms can reduce their investment in IT infrastructure by investing just enough to handle average processing loads and paying for only as much additional computing power as the market demands. Another term for on-demand computing is **utility computing**, which suggests that firms purchase computing power from central computing utilities and pay only for the amount of computing power they use, much as they would pay for electricity.

IBM is investing $10 billion to bring this vision to reality and has created four on-demand computing centers around the United States where businesses can experiment with the concepts. HP's Adaptive Enterprise offers similar capabilities.

In addition to lowering the cost of owning hardware resources, on-demand computing gives firms greater agility to use technology. On-demand computing shifts firms from having a fixed infrastructure capacity toward a highly flexible infrastructure, some of it owned by the firm, and some of it rented from giant computer centers owned by IBM and HP. This arrangement frees firms to launch entirely new business processes that they would never attempt with a fixed infrastructure.

For example, the Canadian Imperial Bank of Commerce (CIBC) outsources a significant portion of its infrastructure to Hewlett-Packard's Adaptive Computing Center. HP provides support for 28,000 CIBC e-mail users, 41,000 desktop PCs, 4,500 automatic teller machines (ATMs), and 10,000 point-of-sale terminals. CIBC management believed that it was more cost-effective to outsource this portion of its infrastructure and focus on banking rather than operating its own IT infrastructure for these functions (HP, 2004).

In another example, specialty food and gift specialist Harry and David uses IBM's On Demand services to deal with an annual traffic surge before the gift-giving season. About 65 percent of annual sales takes place between mid-November and late December. Rather than purchase enough infrastructure to handle this peak load, Harry and David rents this capacity when they need it (Shankland, 2003; IBM, 2004b).

Additional examples of value from on-demand computing can be found in the Window on Management. Qantas Airways contracted with IBM for a flexible on-demand computing arrangement and as a way of lowering operational costs, helping it remain competitive against other carriers. Ford Motor Company Europe switched to an IBM on-demand service for its help desk. Both companies pay IBM a basic fee for an anticipated level of service and then pay IBM additional fees for any spikes if they use more computing resources than planned.

Autonomic Computing

Computer systems have become so complex today that some experts believe they may not be manageable in the near future. With operating systems, enterprise, and database software weighing in at millions of lines of code, and large systems encompassing many thousands of networked devices, the problem of managing these systems looms very large (Kephardt and Chess, 2003).

It is estimated that one-third to one-half of a company's total IT budget is spent preventing or recovering from system crashes. About 40 percent of these crashes are caused

WINDOW ON MANAGEMENT

ON-DEMAND COMPUTING AT QANTAS AIRWAYS AND FORD MOTOR COMPANY EUROPE

Qantas Airways is the leading airline in Australia, flying to about 140 destinations in Australia and 33 other countries. Although recent profits have been strong, the company faces cost pressures from high fuel prices and lower levels of global airline traffic since 2000. Moreover, two-thirds of the international airlines flying to Australia are owned or subsidized by their governments and Qantas must try to keep prices in line with its competition. Keeping costs low and service to customers high are very big priorities.

When Qantas decided to replace its 30-year-old data center, it had a choice: It could build a new one to be maintained in-house or it could outsource its IT infrastructure. IBM Global Services offered an arrangement for on-demand computing with flexible pricing that was too good to pass up. In May 2004, Qantas signed a 10-year contract with IBM worth more than $450 million for these services.

Qantas CIO Fiona Balfour believes that airlines no longer obtain a competitive advantage because they possess information technology. The advantage lies in "how they use it. Running IT at a low unit cost becomes a competitive advantage," says Balfour. On-demand computing with IBM enables Qantas to better match its IT infrastructure to actual business needs and to "get out of the capital investment cycle." Qantas is able to predict its computing requirements by looking at how it is filling aircraft seats.

Qantas's arrangement with IBM covers primarily the infrastructure and systems that support its core applications. Most of Qantas's 450 Unix servers, which had been running at less than 50 percent of capacity, will be replaced by Linux servers at IBM's hosting center in Sydney, Australia. The contract established a baseline usage of computing resources that is less than half of what Qantas was paying for fixed IT costs. Qantas can adjust its usage upward or downward, depending on business conditions, and should be ensured fast response times for its processing.

Qantas will continue to develop its own software applications, while IBM will handle change management for application development and maintenance and the migration of applications from testing to production status. IBM will also provide Qantas with services for information system procurement and security and a service desk for resolving issues with all the providers of its IT services.

According to Brendon Riley, General Manager for IBM Global Services Australia and New Zealand, "It is not only IBM's data center infrastructure and variable cost model that will provide increased flexibility and efficiency to Qantas. IBM gives Qantas access to thousands of professionals with an extensive range of skills as well."

Qantas awarded a $500 million outsourcing contract to Telstra Corporation to convert its telecommunications infra-structure into a network based on the Internet Protocol (IP) and to provide data, voice, and desktop services.

Outsourcing much of Qantas's IT infrastructure to IBM has not only reduced fixed costs for information technology but also has freed its new employees to pursue technology-modernization projects that may have higher value. By outsourcing to IBM and Telstra, Qantas was able to cut down its information systems staff from 900 to 700 people.

IBM believes the travel industry is especially well suited for on-demand computing because travel companies are looking for ways to shift their focus from IT operations to core business issues.

Another company that has benefited from IBM's on-demand computing is Ford Motor Company Europe. Ford Motor Company is the world's second largest car and truck manufacturer, with 350,000 employees across the globe. Ford Motor Company Europe has a Company to Dealer Systems Division that is responsible for infrastructure and application support to its European Dealer network.

Ford's lines of business, which are the "customers" of Ford's Company to Dealer Systems (CDS), wanted more variable and immediate support. CDS maintained an automated help desk service that was fixed in price and capabilities, with little flexibility to address constantly changing dealer application needs.

Ford worked with IBM Business Consulting Services/AMS to design a "pay-as-you-go" help desk solution hosted and staffed by IBM. Computing resources for the help desk are allocated based on a quarterly computer capacity plan reflecting estimated volume of calls, user registrations, and application launches. IBM bills Ford for usage over the capacity plan at a premium to encourage efficient planning.

This on-demand arrangement has made Ford's CDS a more responsive provider of IT services, adding to retail customer satisfaction and to Ford Europe's brand reputation. By using efficient demand forecasting and capacity planning, combined with on-demand computing services, Ford Europe is saving 10 percent per help desk call.

Sources: Tony Kontzer, "Airline Taps IBM for Flexible Pricing Deal," *Information Week*, May 24, 2004 and "Qantas Airways Hands over IT Management to IBM, *Information Week*, May 17, 2004; "Case Studies: Ford Motor Company Europe—Company to Dealer Systems," www.ibm.com, accessed September 10, 2004; IBM Media Relations, "Qantas Awards IBM Global Services a $650 million IT Services Contract," May 17, 2004; and Qantas Corporate Communication, "Qantas Faces Significant Challenges," August 19, 2004.

To Think About: What are the management benefits of on-demand computing for these companies? How do IBM's on-demand services provide value for them?

by operator error. The reason is not because operators are not well trained or do not have the right capabilities. Rather, it is because the complexities of today's computer systems are too difficult to understand, and IT operators and managers are under pressure to make decisions about problems in seconds.

Today, the consequences of an outage are far more serious than in the past. For example, energy firms stand to lose close to $3 million in revenue for every hour systems are not operational. Therefore, firms must spend extraordinary resources to ensure systems do not fail. You can find out more about the impact of system outages and preventive measures in Chapter 10.

One approach to dealing with this problem from a computer hardware perspective is to employ autonomic computing. **Autonomic computing** is an industry-wide effort to develop systems that can configure themselves, optimize and tune themselves, heal themselves when broken, and protect themselves from outside intruders and self-destruction. Imagine, for instance, a desktop PC that could know it was invaded by a computer virus. Instead of blindly allowing the virus to invade, the PC would identify and eradicate the virus or, alternatively, turn its workload over to another processor and shut itself down before the virus destroyed any files.

By choosing the word *autonomic*, computer firms such as HP and IBM are making an analogy with the autonomic nervous system. The autonomic nervous system controls lower-level but vital functions of the human body without raising them to a conscious level. The vision of autonomic computing is that it will free system administrators from many of today's routine system management and operational tasks so administrators can devote more of their IT skills to fulfilling the needs of their core businesses (Ganek and Corbi 2003).

Table 6-4 describes the four dimensions of autonomic computing. Currently, the bare outlines of some of these capabilities are already present in desktop operating systems. For instance, virus and firewall protection software can detect viruses on PCs, automatically defeat the viruses, and alert operators. These programs can be updated automatically as the need arises by connecting to an online virus protection service such as McAfee. Other key elements of autonomic computing are still missing but are sure to be on the agenda of research centers in the next decade. Without progress toward self-managing systems, the management resources required to operate a large-scale computing environment may be cost prohibitive.

Edge Computing

Edge computing is a multitier, load-balancing scheme for Web-based applications in which significant parts of Web site content, logic, and processing are performed by smaller, less expensive servers located nearby the user. In this sense, edge computing is another technique like grid computing and on-demand computing for using the Internet

TABLE 6-4   *Four Aspects of Self-Management as They Are Now and Would Be with Autonomic Computing*

Concept	Current Computing	Autonomic Computing
Self-configuration	Corporate data centers have multiple vendors and and platforms. Installing, configuring, and integrating systems is time consuming and error prone.	Automated configuration of components and systems follows high-level policies. Rest of system adjusts automatically and seamlessly.
Self-optimization	Systems have hundreds of manually set, nonlinear tuning parameters, and their number increases with each release.	Components and systems continually seek opportunities to improve their own performance and efficiency.
Self-healing	Problem determination in large, complex systems can take a team of programmers weeks.	System automatically detects, diagnoses, and repairs localized software and hardware problems.
Self-protection	Detection of and recovery from attacks and cascading failures is manual.	System automatically defends against malicious attacks or cascading failures. It uses early warning to anticipate and prevent systemwide failures.

to share the workload experienced by a firm across many computers located remotely on the network.

Figure 6-12 illustrates the components of edge computing. There are three tiers in edge computing: the local client; the nearby edge computing platform, which consists of servers positioned at any of the 5,000-plus Internet service providers in the United States; and enterprise computers located at the firm's main data center. The edge computing platform is owned by a service firm such as Akamai, which employs about 15,000 edge servers around the United States.

In an edge platform application, requests from the user client computer are initially processed by the edge servers. Presentation components such as static Web page content, reusable code fragments, and interactive elements gathered on forms are delivered by the edge server to the client. Database and business logic elements are delivered by the enterprise computing platform.

There are four main business benefits to edge computing:

- Technology costs are lowered because the firm does not need to purchase infrastructure at its own data center to handle all of the requests from customers and can instead focus on building infrastructure to contain corporate databases and business logic.

- Service levels are enhanced because response time of Web-based applications is reduced. Local client computers can be served with most static and dynamic content immediately, and customer response time is dramatically reduced.

- Flexibility of the firm is enhanced because it can respond to business opportunities quickly without going through a lengthy infrastructure acquisition cycle by making use of service provider platforms that already exist.

- Resilience is increased because seasonal or even daily spikes in the workload can be shared across the Web, and failure in edge nodes will not disable the entire system.

FIGURE 6-12   *Edge computing platform.*

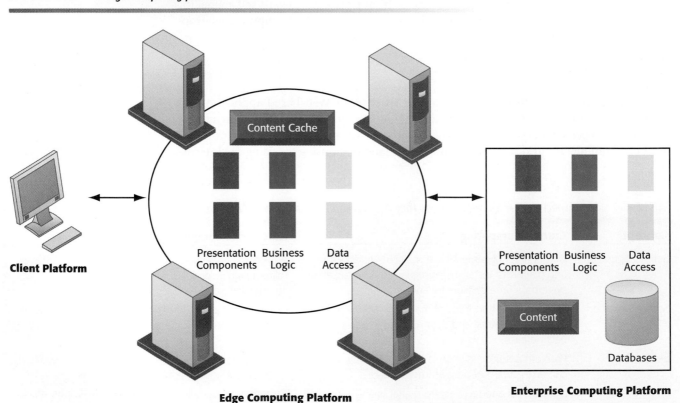

Client Platform

Content Cache

Presentation Components   Business Logic   Data Access

Edge Computing Platform

Presentation Components   Business Logic   Data Access

Content

Databases

Enterprise Computing Platform

Edge computing involves the use of the Internet to balance the processing load of enterprise platforms across the client and edge computing platform.

6.4 CONTEMPORARY SOFTWARE PLATFORM TRENDS

There are four major themes in contemporary software platform evolution:

- Linux and open-source software
- Java
- Web services and service-oriented architecture
- Software outsourcing

The Rise of Linux and Open-Source Software

Open-source software is software produced by a community of several hundred thousand programmers around the world. According to the leading open-source professional association, OpenSource.org, open-source software is free and can be modified by users. Works derived from the original code must also be free, and the software can be redistributed by the user without additional licensing. Open-source software is by definition not restricted to any specific operating system or hardware technology, although most open-source software is currently based on a Linux or Unix operating system (opensource.org, 2004). A related free software movement supported by the Free Software Foundation supports similar goals of making software freely available without the restrictions of copyright or patent law (which we explain in Chapter 5).

Open-source software is based on the premise that it is superior to commercially produced proprietary software because thousands of programmers around the world working for no pay can read, perfect, distribute, and modify the source code much faster, and with more reliable results, than small teams of programmers working for a single software company.

Although it may seem that contributors to open-source software receive nothing in return, in fact they receive respect, prestige, and access to a network of knowledgeable programmers (who in turn can be tapped for solutions, or even employment). And although it may seem the process of software improvement is chaotic or unorganized, in fact these are self-organizing communities of dedicated professionals who have a well-defined organizational structure and a set of business processes (or procedures) for getting the work done. The open-source movement has been evolving for more than 30 years and has demonstrated after many years of effort that it can produce commercially acceptable, high-quality software.

Now thousands of open-source programs are available from hundreds of Web sites. The range of open-source software extends from operating systems to office suites, browsers such as Mozilla's Firefox, and games. Several large software companies are converting some of their commercial programs to open source. IBM, for instance, is handing over its Java-based database program called Cloudscape to the Apache Software Foundation, an open-source group. Novell is investing heavily in open-source companies that sell versions of open-source server software.

Few complain about the cost of open-source software, which can result in the savings of millions of dollars for large corporations (see Table 6-5).

You can find out more about the Open Source Definition from the Open Source Initiative and the history of open-source software at the Laudon Web site for Chapter 6.

TABLE 6-5 *Proprietary and Open-Source Software Pricing Comparison*

Proprietary Software	Open-Source Software Equivalent
Microsoft Windows XP Pro $299	Linux free
Microsoft Office $399	Open Office $3.99 StarOffice 7 $79.95
Microsoft Outlook $109	Mozilla browser with e-mail free
Microsoft Access $229	MySQL $69.95

LINUX

Perhaps the most well known open-source software is Linux, an operating system related to Unix. Linux was created by the Finnish programmer Linus Torvalds and was first posted on the Internet in August 1991. Linux is now the world's fastest-growing client and server operating system. Linux was installed in nearly 3 percent of new shipments of PCs in 2004, and this number is expected to grow to over 20 percent of new PC shipments by 2010 (Bulkeley, 2004).

Applications for the Linux operating system are rapidly growing also. Many of these applications are embedded in cell phones, PDAs, and other handheld devices (Open Source Development Lab, 2004). Although Linux is currently a small but rapidly growing presence on the desktop, it plays a major role in the back office running Web servers and local area networks. In the $50.9 billion U.S. server market, Linux is the most rapidly growing LAN server, with a current 23 percent market share, up from 1 percent in 1998.

IBM, HP, Intel, Dell, and Sun have made Linux a central part of their offerings to corporations. More than two dozen countries in Asia, Europe, and Latin America have adopted open-source software and Linux (Lohr, 2002). Cost is a major driver. For example, Morgan Stanley is replacing 4,000 servers running Windows NT with much cheaper machines running Linux for an estimated five-year cost saving of $100 million (Kerstetter, 2003).

Cost played an important role in the decisions to adopt Linux in the Canadian cities of Calgary and Toronto. Both cities, described in the Window on Technology, have very low technology budgets and are under pressure to seek out no-frills solutions. The city of Calgary found that adopting Linux not only reduced software purchase costs, but it also created additional savings by cutting down on computer processing time.

The rise of open-source software, particularly Linux and the applications it supports at the client and server level, has profound implications for corporate software platforms: cost reduction, reliability and resilience, and integration, because Linux works on all the major hardware platforms from mainframes to servers to clients. Linux has the potential to break Microsoft's monopoly of the desktop. Sun's StarOffice has an inexpensive Linux-based version that competes with Microsoft's Office productivity suite. However, this transition will take many years because of the sunk costs of billions of spreadsheets, Word documents, and PowerPoint presentations, many of which will not be easily converted to Linux office suites.

Java Is Everywhere

Java is an operating system–independent, processor-independent, object-oriented programming language that has become the leading interactive programming environment for the Web. If an object moves on the Web or takes input from the user, a Java applet is likely behind it.

Java was created by James Gosling and the Green Team at Sun Microsystems in 1992 as a programming environment to support interactive cable television content delivery. Widespread use of Java did not occur until 1995 when large numbers of people started using the World Wide Web and Internet. Nearly all Web browsers come with a Java platform built in. More recently, the Java platform has migrated into cellular phones, automobiles, music players, game machines, and finally, into set-top cable television systems serving interactive content and pay-per-view services.

Java software is designed to run on any computer or computing device, regardless of the specific microprocessor or operating system the device uses. A Macintosh PC, an IBM PC running Windows, a Sun server running Unix, and even a smart cellular phone or personal digital assistant can share the same Java application. For each of the computing environments in which Java is used, Sun has created a Java Virtual Machine that interprets Java programming code for that machine. In this manner, the code is written once and can be used on any machine for which there exists a Java Virtual Machine.

Java is particularly useful in network environments such as the Internet. Here, Java is used to create miniature programs called *applets* that are designed to reside on centralized network servers. The network delivers to client computers only the applets required for a specific function. With Java applets residing on a network, a user can download only

WINDOW ON TECHNOLOGY

Two Canadian Cities Go for Linux

"Downward budget pressure" convinced the Canadian city of Calgary to take a hard look at Linux. Like other municipal governments, Calgary was on the receiving end of budget cuts that left it searching for low-cost technology solutions.

In the fall of 2002 Calgary had about 140 Unix servers, with 60 percent running the Sun Solaris version of Unix, 25 percent running HP's Tru64 Unix, and the rest running other operating systems. According to Dan Ryan, Calgary's manager of infrastructure and desktop management, "Unix was so expensive because everything was proprietary—both the hardware and the software." As these servers aged and required replacement, Calgary found it did not have the money to upgrade to another expensive environment.

Ryan and his team started investigating Linux. They found out that both HP and IBM had invested heavily in making sure their products could support Linux and that Oracle had become certified on commercial Red Hat Linux. Calgary uses Oracle database products extensively. Ryan was further sold on Linux when he learned that many other large organizations, including DaimlerChrysler, the U.S. Department of Defense, and the U.S. Postal Service, had started using Linux.

To test Linux capabilities, Calgary ran four pilot projects over a three-month period in 2003. The first two were led by HP, and Calgary's information systems staff who were versed in Unix learned enough Linux to take over the remaining two tests.

One application tested Calgary's tax installment plan running on Linux. This application has about 175,000 records in its file for residents who pay property taxes once a month. Running on a Unix computer, this application took about 73 minutes to process. In the test, the same application took only 31 minutes running on an Intel computer with two CPUs and the Linux operating system.

Another test used the application for Calgary's annual tax account balance, which handles 330,000 property tax records. This application took about 60 hours to process on an 8-CPU computer running Unix. Running on a Linux-based Intel computer with 2 CPUs, the application took only 13.5 hours.

From these tests Ryan learned that Linux could improve computer performance as well as lower costs. As a result of adopting Linux, Calgary's capital and operating costs for information technology have dropped by 75 percent. Calgary used to pay over $650,000 for equipment maintenance on its Unix servers. By the end of 2004, it will pay less than $150,000 to maintain its Linux computers. These savings mean that Ryan does not have to wait as long as before to replace Calgary's computer systems.

Toronto's Children's Services Division (CSD) is reporting similar benefits from Linux. CSD has 62 branches, a main office, and remote locations, including 58 day care centers. This organization has a small information technology budget of approximately $2 million per year, which is tiny compared to other city departments. CSD, as well as other Toronto departments, has some autonomy in technology decisions, and it is allowed to purchase the hardware and software that it believes is best for its purposes.

CSD's service and support costs were escalating as old PCs neared the end of their useful life cycle. The division investigated purchasing new PCs running Microsoft Windows XP, but the cost was prohibitive—about $1,600 to purchase each PC plus an additional hundred dollars per machine to license Windows XP. The Children's Services Division instead installed Red Hat Linux version 7.3 on about 450 desktop computers at a cost of about $250 per machine.

The transition to Linux was not difficult for the division because it uses inexpensive desktop machines with no floppy disk drives or hard drives. All data and software are stored on a central server networked to these desktop clients, so users have no opportunity to install unauthorized software. Everything is centrally maintained.

By installing Linux, the division does not need to worry about licensing operating systems—Linux is almost free. If there is a problem, CSD's information systems staff can turn to the open-source community supporting Linux. To help them, CSD staff typically find many other users that have already dealt with the problem. Hardware and software are so easy to maintain that the division needs only six information systems staff members to support 450 users.

On the negative side, the Children's Services Division did have to spend some time and money training its staff on Linux, and not all software is yet compatible with Linux.

By reducing maintenance at the desktop, CSD saves in human resources and can use its technology budget for other purposes, including new Sun servers and data storage services.

Sources: Patricia Pickett, "City of Calgary Moves to Linux," *ComputerWorld Canada*, March 5, 2004; Kathleen Sibley, "A Tale of Two Open Source Cities," www.itbusiness.ca, accessed April 30, 2004; Ryan B. Patrick, "City Rolls Out Desktop Linux," www.opencitygov.org, accessed September 10, 2004.

To Think About: Is Linux a good choice for these government organizations? Why or why not? How does Linux provide value? Would private business firms obtain similar benefits? What are the business as well as the technology issues that should be addressed when making that decision?

the software functions and data that he or she needs to perform a particular task, such as analyzing the revenue from one sales territory. The user does not need to maintain large software programs or data files on his or her desktop machine.

Java is also a very robust language that can handle text, data, graphics, sound, and video, all within one program if needed. Java enables PC users to manipulate data on networked systems using Web browsers, reducing the need to write specialized software. A **Web browser** is an easy-to-use software tool with a graphical user interface for displaying Web pages and for accessing the Web and other Internet resources. Microsoft's Internet Explorer, Mozilla and Netscape Navigator are examples. At the enterprise level, Java is being used for more complex e-commerce and e-business applications that require communication with an organization's back-end transaction processing systems.

The rapid deployment of Java was hindered in the past because of disagreements between Sun Microsystems and Microsoft over Java standards. In an effort to promote widespread adoption of the Java technology, Sun had embarked on an open licensing program. Beginning in August 1995, Sun entered into license and distribution agreements with major platform manufacturers, including Apple, DEC, Fujitsu, Hewlett-Packard, IBM, Microsoft, Netscape, Novell, SCO, Siemens, and Silicon Graphics.

Shortly thereafter, Microsoft began introducing variations to the standard Java Virtual Machine and created its own proprietary version of Java that was incompatible with standard Java. Sun filed a series of antitrust lawsuits against Microsoft to halt these actions. In April 2004, under pressure from major customers such as General Motors, Microsoft and Sun entered into a 10-year-long agreement that settled Sun's antitrust lawsuits. Microsoft agreed to stop distributing the Microsoft Java Virtual Machine (MSJVM) it had developed for its proprietary version of Java and to cooperate with Sun in the development of new technologies, including Java.

Software for Enterprise Integration

Without doubt the single most urgent software priority for U.S. firms is integration of existing legacy software applications with newer Web-based applications into a coherent single system that can be rationally managed. In the past business firms typically built their own custom software and made their own choices about their software platform (all of the various pieces of software that need to work together). This strategy produced hundreds of thousands of computer programs that frequently could not communicate with other software programs, were difficult and expensive to maintain, and were nearly impossible to change quickly as business models changed.

One solution is to replace isolated systems that cannot communicate with enterprise applications for customer relationship management, supply chain management, knowledge management, and enterprise systems, which integrate multiple business processes. Chapters 11 and 12 provides a detailed description of these enterprise applications and their roles in digitally integrating the enterprise.

Not all firms can jettison all of their legacy systems to convert to enterprise-wide platforms. These existing legacy mainframe applications are essential to daily operations and are very risky to change, but they can become more useful if their information and business logic can be integrated with other applications.

Some integration of legacy applications can be achieved by using special software called **middleware** to create an interface or bridge between two different systems. Middleware is software that connects two otherwise separate applications, enabling them to communicate with each other and to exchange data.

Firms may choose to write their own software to connect one application to another, but increasingly they are purchasing **enterprise application integration (EAI) software** packages for this purpose to connect disparate applications or application clusters. This software enables multiple systems to exchange data through a single software hub rather than building countless custom software interfaces to link each system (see Figure 6-13). WebMethods, Tibco, CrossWorlds, SeeBeyond, BEA, and Vitria are leading enterprise application software vendors.

FIGURE 6-13   *Enterprise application integration (EAI) software versus traditional integration.*

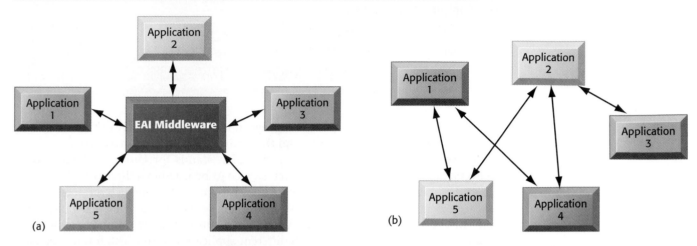

EAI software (a) creates a common platform through which all applications can freely communicate with each other. EAI requires much less programming than traditional point-to-point integration (b).

WEB SERVICES AND SERVICE-ORIENTED ARCHITECTURE

Enterprise application integration software tools are product specific, meaning that they can work only with certain pieces of application software and operating systems. For example, one EAI tool to connect a specific piece of sales order entry software to manufacturing, shipping, and billing applications might not work with another vendor's order entry software. Web services provide a standardized alternative for dealing with integration.

Web services refer to a set of loosely coupled software components that exchange information with each other using standard Web communication standards and languages. They can exchange information between two different systems regardless of the operating systems or programming languages on which the systems are based. They can be used to build open standard Web-based applications linking systems of two different organizations, and they can also be used to create applications that link disparate systems within a single company. Web services are not tied to any one operating system or programming language, and different applications can use them to communicate with each other in a standard way without time-consuming custom coding.

The foundation technology for Web services is **XML**, which stands for **Extensible Markup Language**. This language was developed in 1996 by the World Wide Web Consortium (W3C, the international body that oversees the development of the Web) as a more powerful and flexible markup language than hypertext markup language (HTML) for Web pages. **Hypertext markup language (HTML)** is a page description language for specifying how text, graphics, video, and sound are placed on a Web page document. Whereas HTML is limited to describing how data should be presented in the form of Web pages, XML can perform presentation, communication, and storage of data. In XML, a number is not simply a number; the XML tag specifies whether the number represents a price, a date, or a ZIP code. Table 6-6 illustrates some sample XML statements.

By tagging selected elements of the content of documents for their meanings, XML makes it possible for computers to manipulate and interpret their data automatically and perform operations on the data without human intervention. Web browsers and computer programs, such as order processing or enterprise resource planning (ERP) software, can follow programmed rules for applying and displaying the data. XML provides a standard format for data exchange, enabling Web services to pass data from one process to another.

Web services communicate through XML messages over standard Web protocols. **SOAP**, which stands for **Simple Object Access Protocol**, is a set of rules for structuring messages that enables applications to pass data and instructions to one another. **WSDL**

TABLE 6-6 *Examples of XML*

Plain English	XML
Subcompact	<AUTOMOBILETYPE="Subcompact">
4 passenger	<PASSENGERUNIT="PASS">4</PASSENGER>
$16,800	<PRICE CURRENCY="USD">$16,800</PRICE>

stands for **Web Services Description Language**; it is a common framework for describing the tasks performed by a Web service and the commands and data it will accept so that it can be used by other applications. **UDDI**, which stands for **Universal Description, Discovery, and Integration**, enables a Web service to be listed in a directory of Web services so that it can be easily located. Companies discover and locate Web services through this directory much as they would locate services in the yellow pages of a telephone book. Using these protocols, a software application can connect freely to other applications without custom programming for each different application with which it wants to communicate. Everyone shares the same standards.

The collection of Web services that are used to build a firm's software systems constitutes what is known as a service-oriented architecture. A **service-oriented architecture (SOA)** is set of self-contained services that communicate with each other to create a working software application. Business tasks are accomplished by executing a series of these services. Software developers reuse these services in other combinations to assemble other applications as needed.

Dollar Rent A Car's systems use Web services to link its online booking system with Southwest Airlines' Web site. Although both companies' systems are based on different technology platforms, a person booking a flight on SouthwestAir.com can reserve a car from Dollar without leaving the airline's Web site. Instead of struggling to get Dollar's reservation system to share data with Southwest's information systems, Dollar used Microsoft .NET Web services technology as an intermediary. Reservations from Southwest are translated into Web services protocols, which are then translated into formats that can be understood by Dollar's computers.

Other car rental companies have linked their information systems to airline companies' Web sites before. But without Web services, these connections had to be built one at a time. Web services provide a standard way for Dollar's computers to "talk" to other companies' information systems without having to build special links to each one. Dollar is now expanding its use of Web services to link directly to the systems of a small tour operator and a large travel reservation system as well as a Wireless Web site for mobile phones and PDAs. It does not have to write new software code for each new partner's information systems or each new wireless device (see Figure 6-14).

Virtually all major software vendors such as IBM, Microsoft, Sun, and HP provide tools and entire platforms for building and integrating software applications using Web services. IBM includes Web service tools in its WebSphere e-business software platform, and Microsoft has incorporated Web services tools in its Microsoft .NET platform.

Businesses such as FedEx publish the Web services they offer to customers, describing each service using Web Service Description Language (WSDL). FedEx customers, such as JCPenney, can then incorporate these Web services into their own systems such as a Web site.

Software Outsourcing

Today most business firms continue to operate their legacy systems that continue to meet a business need and that would be extremely costly to replace. But they will purchase most of their new software applications from external sources. Figure 6-15 illustrates the rapid growth in external sources of software for U.S. firms.

There are three external sources for software: software packages from a commercial software vendor, software services from an application service provider, and outsourcing

FIGURE 6-14 How Dollar Rent A Car uses Web services.

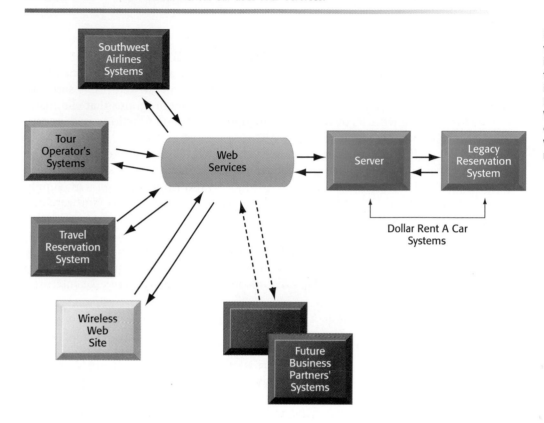

Dollar Rent A Car uses Web services to provide a standard intermediate layer of software to "talk" to other companies' information systems. Dollar Rent A Car can use this set of Web services to link to other companies' information systems without having to build a separate link to each firm's systems.

FIGURE 6-15 Changing sources of firm software.

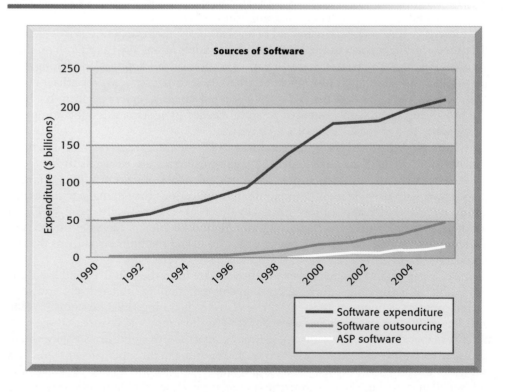

U.S. firms spend a little over $200 billion each year on software. In 2005, about 25 percent of that software will originate outside the firm, either from enterprise software vendors selling firmwide applications or individual application service providers selling software modules.

Sources: BEA National Income and Product Accounts, Forrester Research, December 2003; eMarketer Inc., "IT Spending 2004," www.emarketer.com; and author estimates.

custom application development to an outside software firm, often offshore firms in low-wage areas of the world.

SOFTWARE PACKAGES AND ENTERPRISE SOFTWARE

We have already described software packages for enterprise applications as one of the major types of software components in contemporary IT infrastructures. A **software package** is a prewritten commercially available set of software programs that eliminates the need for a firm to write its own software programs for certain functions, such as payroll processing or order handling.

Enterprise application software vendors such as SAP, PeopleSoft, and Oracle have developed powerful software packages that can support the primary business processes of a firm worldwide from warehousing, customer relationship management, supply chain management, and finance to human resources. Somewhat like the "software in a box" purchased with a personal computer, these large-scale enterprise software systems provide a single, integrated, worldwide software system for firms at a cost much less than they would pay if they developed it themselves. These systems are so complex, and require so much experience, that very few corporations have the expertise required to develop these packages. Chapter 11 is devoted to a discussion of the benefits and risks of enterprise systems.

APPLICATION SERVICE PROVIDERS

A second external source of software is online application service providers (ASPs). An **application service provider (ASP)** is a business that delivers and manages applications and computer services from remote computer centers to multiple users using the Internet or a private network. Instead of buying and installing software programs, subscribing companies can rent the same functions from these services. Users pay for the use of this software either on a subscription or per-transaction basis.

The ASP's solution combines package software applications and all of the related hardware, system software, network, and other infrastructure services that the customer otherwise would have to purchase, integrate, and manage independently. The ASP customer interacts with a single entity instead of an array of technologies and service vendors.

The time-sharing services of the 1970s, which ran applications such as payroll on their computers for other companies, were an earlier version of this application hosting. But today's ASPs run a wider array of applications than these earlier services and deliver many of these software services over the Web. At Web-based services, servers perform the bulk of the processing and the only essential program needed by users is a desktop computer running either thin client software or a Web browser.

Large and medium-sized businesses are using ASPs for enterprise systems, sales force automation, or financial management, and small businesses are using them for functions such as invoicing, tax calculations, electronic calendars, and accounting. ASP vendors are starting to provide tools to integrate the applications they manage with clients' internal systems or with applications hosted by different vendors (McDougall, 2003). In addition, enterprise software vendors such as SAP and PeopleSoft have developed ASP versions of their enterprise software packages for small and medium-sized firms that do not want to run this enterprise software on their own servers.

Some companies find it much easier to rent software from the ASP firm and avoid the expense and difficulty of installing, operating, and maintaining the hardware and software for complex systems, such as enterprise resource planning (ERP) systems (Walsh, 2003). The ASP contracts guarantee a level of service and support to ensure that the software is available and working at all times. Today's Internet-driven business environment is changing so rapidly that getting a system up and running in three months instead of six could mean the difference between success and failure. Application service providers also enable small and medium-sized companies to use applications that they otherwise could not afford.

SOFTWARE OUTSOURCING

A third external source of software is **outsourcing**, in which a firm contracts custom software development or maintenance of existing legacy programs to outside firms, frequently firms that operate offshore in low-wage areas of the world. Outsourcing is expected to total over $50 billion in 2005. The largest expenditure here is paid to domestic U.S. firms providing middleware, integration services, and other software support that is often required to operate larger enterprise systems.

For example, in 2004 Dow Chemical hired IBM for $1.1 billion to create an integrated communication system based on Internet standards to handle text, video, and voice communications for more than 50,000 Dow employees in 63 countries. The contract extends to other infrastructure management services, such as LAN, e-mail, and application support. The system will be run from IBM data centers in Boulder, Colorado, as well as Brazil, Singapore, and the Netherlands (McDougall, 2004).

Offshore firms provided about $8 billion in software services to the United States in 2004, which is about 2 percent of the combined U.S. software plus software services budget (around $400 billion). Up until recently, this type of software development involved lower-level maintenance, data entry, and call center operations, but with the growing sophistication and experience of offshore firms, particularly in India, more and more new-program development is taking place offshore. Chapter 16 discusses offshore software outsourcing in greater detail.

6.5 MANAGEMENT OPPORTUNITIES, CHALLENGES, AND SOLUTIONS

The objective of infrastructure management is to provide a coherent and balanced set of computer-based services to customers, employees, and suppliers. To attain this objective, firms must deal with a series of issues:

- Cost of IT infrastructure
- Integration of information, applications, and platforms
- Flexibility to respond to business environments
- Resilience
- Service levels

Let's look more closely at infrastructure opportunities and challenges.

Opportunities

There is a continuous increase in the power of information technology. This means that new business models and processes can be invented around new technologies as they appear. Firms that have the capability and knowledge to manage their IT infrastructures to take advantage of these opportunities will reap important benefits.

Management Challenges

Creating and managing a coherent IT infrastructure raises multiple challenges: making wise infrastructure investments, coordinating infrastructure components, dealing with scalability and technology change, and management and governance.

MAKING WISE INFRASTRUCTURE INVESTMENTS

IT Infrastructure is a major capital investment for the firm. If too much is spent on infrastructure, it lies idle and constitutes a drag on firm financial performance. If too little is spent, important business services cannot be delivered and the firm's competitors (who spent just the right amount) will outperform the underinvesting firm. How much should the firm spend on infrastructure? This question is not easy to answer.

A related question is whether a firm should purchase its own IT infrastructure components or rent them from external suppliers. As we discussed earlier, a major trend in computing platforms—both hardware and software—is to outsource to external providers. The decision either to purchase your own IT assets or rent them from external providers is typically called the *rent versus buy* decision.

CHOOSING AND COORDINATING INFRASTRUCTURE COMPONENTS

Firms today create IT infrastructures by choosing combinations of vendors, people, and technology services and fitting them together so they function as a coherent whole. When each element of infrastructure is driven by somewhat different forces, accomplishing this is a major management job. For instance, changes in law may mandate vast increases in data storage and retrieval, but the existing hardware platform may be incapable of supporting the addition computing demand.

DEALING WITH INFRASTRUCTURE CHANGE

As firms grow, they can quickly outgrow their infrastructure. As firms shrink, they can get stuck with excessive infrastructure purchased in better times. How can a firm remain flexible when most of the investments in IT infrastructure are fixed cost purchases and licenses? How well does the infrastructure scale? **Scalability** refers to the ability of a computer, product, or system to expand to serve a larger number of users without breaking down.

How can the infrastructure be changed, and over what time frame? Because the firm's digital infrastructure permeates every nook and cranny of the firm, and therefore directly affects how employees perform on a daily basis, any change in this infrastructure would seem to have to occur slowly, guided by some vision (business or technology based) or understanding of the future requirements for infrastructure. Left to constituent business units, or a single chief information officer and his or her staff, chaos could reign or, alternatively, bold technologically advanced plans may come and go without any real change. Who will supply this vision or understanding needed for long-term, stable evolution?

MANAGEMENT AND GOVERNANCE

A long-standing issue among information system managers and CEOs has been the question of who will control and manage the firm's IT infrastructure. Should departments and divisions have the responsibility of making their own information technology decisions or should IT infrastructure be centrally controlled and managed? What is the relationship between central information systems management and business unit information systems management? How will infrastructure costs be allocated among business units? Each organization will need to arrive at answers based on its own needs.

Solution Guidelines

There are no formulas or easy answers to these questions, and each firm arrives at a different set of decisions based on the firm's history, current financial condition, and its strategy. The following guidelines will be helpful.

Perhaps the single most frequent question that CIOs ask (often prodded by their boards of directors) is, "Are we spending too much on IT infrastructure?" In some companies the opposite question is more common: "Are we spending enough on IT to keep up with our competitors?" As it turns out, there is no single, simple answer, no formula for getting it right. But there are several ways to approach the issue and several rules of thumb.

COMPETITIVE FORCES MODEL FOR IT INFRASTRUCTURE

Figure 6-16 illustrates a competitive forces model you can use to address the question of how much your firm should spend on IT infrastructure.

FIGURE 6-16 *Competitive forces model for IT infrastructure.*

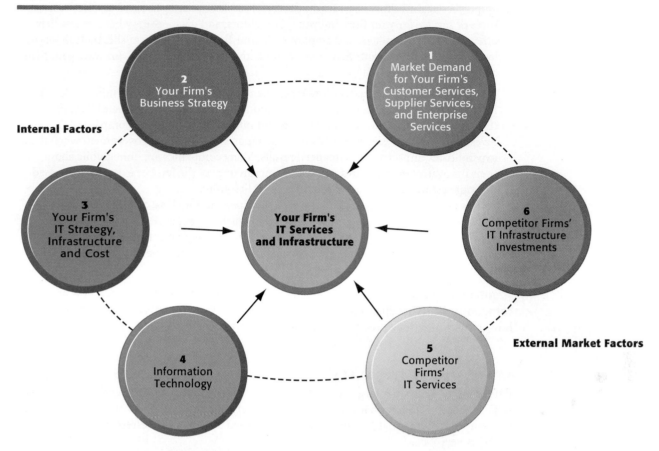

There are six factors you can use to answer the question, "How much should our firm spend on IT infrastructure?"

Market demand for your firm's services. Make an inventory of the services you currently provide to customers, suppliers, and employees. Most firms do not have such an inventory. Survey each group, or hold focus groups to find out if the services you currently offer are meeting the needs of each group. For example, are customers complaining of slow responses to their queries about price and availability? Are employees complaining about the difficulty of finding the right information for their jobs? Are suppliers complaining about the difficulties of discovering your production requirements?

Your firm's business strategy. Analyze your firm's five-year business strategy and try to assess what new services and capabilities will be required to achieve strategic goals.

Your firm's information technology (IT) strategy, infrastructure, and cost. Examine your firm's information technology plans for the next five years and assess its alignment with the firm's business plans. Make an inventory of existing IT infrastructure cost. Many firms do not know the total cost of their existing IT infrastructure. You will want to perform a total cost of ownership analysis (see the discussion later). If your firm has no IT strategy, you will need to devise one that takes into account the firm's five-year strategic plan.

Information technology assessment. Is your firm behind the technology curve or at the bleeding edge of information technology? Both situations are to be avoided. Clearly, you do not want to spend resources on advanced technologies that are still experimental, often expensive, and sometimes unreliable. You want to spend on technologies for which standards have been established and suppliers of IT are competing on cost, not design, and where there are multiple suppliers. On the other hand, you do not want to put off investment in new technologies, allowing your competitors time to develop new business models and capabilities and experience using the new technologies.

Competitor firm services. Benchmark your service levels to customers, suppliers, and employees against those of your competitors. Establish quantitative and qualitative measures of service for your firm and your competitors, and try to assess what services they offer customers, suppliers, and employees. If your firm has significant shortfalls in service levels to either group, your firm is at a competitive disadvantage. Look for ways your firm can excel at service levels.

Competitor firm IT infrastructure investments. Benchmark your expenditures for IT infrastructure against your competitors. Although some firms regard their IT expenditures as a competitive secret, you can find out information on public companies' IT investments in their SEC Form 10-K annual reports to the federal government when those expenditures impact a firm's financial results. Many companies are quite public about their innovative expenditures on IT, and you can impute the level of expenditures based on your research in the trade and professional literature.

It is not necessarily the case that you should spend as much as, or more than, your competitors. Perhaps your firm has discovered much less expensive ways of providing services, and this can lead to a cost advantage. Alternatively, your firm may be spending far less than competitors and experiencing commensurate poor performance and losing market share.

After completing this analysis, you will have a good idea of how much you and your competitor firms are spending on IT infrastructure, what you are receiving in return, and how your competitive position might be improved.

STARTING OUT SMALL

Before embarking on a large-scale infrastructure project, it may be useful to experiment with new technologies on a smaller scale. Such projects should concentrate on infrastructure improvements that can be easily implemented and where the return on investment (ROI) is very clear.

TOTAL COST OF OWNERSHIP OF TECHNOLOGY ASSETS

In benchmarking your firm's expenditures on IT infrastructure with that of your competitors, you will need to consider a wide range of costs. The actual cost of owning technology resources includes the original cost of acquiring and installing hardware and software, as well as ongoing administration costs for hardware and software upgrades, maintenance, technical support, training, and even utility and real estate costs for running and housing the technology. The **total cost of ownership (TCO)** model can be used to analyze these direct and indirect costs to help firms determine the actual cost of specific technology implementations.

Table 6-7 describes the most important TCO components to consider in a TCO analysis. When all these cost components are considered, the TCO for a PC might run up to three times the original purchase price of the equipment. Hidden costs for support staff, downtime, and additional network management can make distributed client/server architectures—especially those incorporating handheld computers and wireless devices—more expensive than centralized mainframe architectures.

Hardware and software acquisition costs account for only about 20 percent of TCO, so managers must pay close attention to administration costs to understand the full cost of the firm's hardware and software. It is possible to reduce some of these administration costs through better management. Many large firms are saddled with redundant, incompatible hardware and software because their departments and divisions have been allowed to make their own technology purchases. Such information technology infrastructures are excessively unwieldy and expensive to administer.

These firms could reduce their TCO through greater centralization and standardization of their hardware and software resources. Companies could reduce the size of the information

TABLE 6-7   *Total Cost of Ownership (TCO) Cost Components*

Infrastructure Component	Cost Components
Hardware acquisition	Purchase price of computer hardware equipment, including computers, terminals, storage, and printers
Software acquisition	Purchase or license of software for each user
Installation	Cost to install computers and software
Training	Cost to provide training for information systems specialists and end users
Support	Cost to provide ongoing technical support, help desks, and so forth
Maintenance	Cost to upgrade the hardware and software
Infrastructure	Cost to acquire, maintain, and support related infrastructure, such as networks and specialized equipment (including storage backup units)
Downtime	Cost of lost productivity if hardware or software failures cause the system to be unavailable for processing and user tasks
Space and energy	Real estate and utility costs for housing and providing power for the technology

systems staff required to support their infrastructure if the firm minimizes the number of different computer models and pieces of software that employees are allowed to use. In a centralized infrastructure, systems can be administered from a central location and troubleshooting can be performed from that location (David, Schuff, and St. Louis, 2002).

MAKE **IT** YOUR BUSINESS

Finance and Accounting
One of the earliest tasks assigned to computers was automating calculations for finance and accounting, and these functions have remained high-priority targets for computerization. Many application software packages for individuals as well as for large businesses support financial processes, such as corporate accounting, tax calculations, payroll processing, or investment planning. Calculating the total cost of ownership (TCO) of technology assets usually requires models and expertise supplied by finance and accounting. You can find examples of finance and accounting applications on pages 206 and 226–227.

Human Resources
Hardware and software technologies are changing very rapidly, providing many new productivity tools to employees and powerful software packages and services for the human resources department. Employees will need frequent retraining to use these tools effectively. You can find examples of human resources applications on page 211.

Manufacturing and Production
Many manufacturing applications are based on client/server networks, which use networked computers to control the flow of work on the factory floor. Handheld computers and bar-code scanners are widely used to track items in inventory and to track package shipments. XML provides a set of standards through which all systems of participants in an industry supply chain can exchange data with each other without high expenditures for specialized translation programs and middleware. You can find examples of manufacturing and production applications on pages 226–227.

Sales and Marketing
Sales and marketing has benefited from hardware and software technologies that provide customers and sales staff with rapid access to information, responses to customer questions, and order taking. Web browser software provides an easy-to-use interface for accessing product information or placing orders over the Web, whereas e-mail software is a quick and inexpensive tool for answering customer queries. Web sites can be enhanced with Java applets that enable users to perform calculations or view interactive product demonstrations using standard Web browser software. You can find examples of sales and marketing applications on page 185.

Summary

1. *Define IT infrastructure and describe the components and levels of IT infrastructure.*

IT infrastructure is the shared technology resources that provide the platform for the firm's specific information system applications. IT infrastructure includes hardware, software, and services that are shared across the entire firm. Major IT infrastructure components include computer hardware platforms, operating system platforms, enterprise software platforms, networking and telecommunications platforms, database management software, Internet platforms, and consulting services and systems integrators. There are three different levels of IT infrastructure: public, enterprise, and business unit.

You can better understand the business value of IT infrastructure investments by viewing IT infrastructure as a platform of services as well as a set of technologies.

2. *Identify and describe the stages of IT infrastructure evolution.*

There are five stages of IT infrastructure evolution. IT infrastructure in the earliest stage consisted of specialized "electronic accounting machines" that were primitive computers used for accounting tasks. IT infrastructure in the mainframe era (1959 to present) consists of a mainframe performing centralized processing that could be networked to thousands of terminals and eventually some decentralized and departmental computing using networked minicomputers. The personal computer era (1981 to present) in IT infrastructure has been dominated by the widespread use of standalone desktop computers with office productivity tools. The predominant infrastructure in the client/server era (1983 to present) consists of desktop or laptop clients networked to more powerful server computers that handle most of the data management and processing. The enterprise Internet computing era (1992 to present) is defined by large numbers of PCs linked into local area networks and growing use of standards and software to link disparate networks and devices into an enterprise-wide network so that information can flow freely across the organization.

3. *Identify and describe the technology drivers of IT infrastructure evolution.*

A series of technology developments has driven the continuing transformation of IT infrastructure. Moore's Law deals with the exponential increase in processing power and decline in the cost of computer technology, stating that every 18 months the power of microprocessors doubles and the price of computing falls in half. The Law of Mass Digital Storage deals with the exponential decrease in the cost of storing data, stating that the number of kilobytes of data that can be stored on magnetic media for $1 roughly doubles every 15 months. Metcalfe's Law helps explain the mushrooming use of computers by showing that a network's value to participants grows exponentially as the network takes on more members. Also driving exploding computer use is the rapid decline in costs of communication and growing agreement in the technology industry to use computing and communications standards.

4. *Assess contemporary computer hardware platform trends.*

Contemporary hardware and software platform trends address the overwhelming need to reduce IT infrastructure costs, to integrate information across platforms, and to provide a higher level of flexibility and service to the firm and its customers. The integration of computing and telecommunications platforms, grid computing, edge computing, and on-demand computing demonstrate that, increasingly, computing is taking place over a network. Grid computing involves connecting geographically remote computers into a single network to create a computational grid that combines the computing power of all the computers on the network to attack large computing problems. Edge computing balances the processing load for Web-based applications by distributing parts of the Web content, logic, and processing among multiple servers. On-demand computing also depends on networks for firms to purchase additional processing power from large computer service firms and to have that power delivered when they need it over a network. In autonomic computing, computer systems have capabilities for automatically configuring and repairing themselves.

5. *Assess contemporary software platform trends.*

Contemporary software platform trends include the growing use of Linux, open-source software, and Java, software for enterprise integration, and software outsourcing. Open-source software is produced and maintained by a global community of programmers and is downloadable for free. Linux is a powerful, resilient open-source operating system that can run on multiple hardware platforms and is used widely to run Web servers. Java is an operating-system–and hardware-independent programming language that is the leading interactive programming environment for the Web.

Software for enterprise integration includes enterprise applications and middleware such as enterprise application integration (EAI) software and Web services. Unlike EAI software, Web services are loosely coupled software components based on open Web standards that are not product-specific and can work with any application software and operating system. They can be used as components of Web-based applications linking the systems of two different organizations or to link disparate systems of a single company. Companies are purchasing their new software applications from outside sources, including application software packages, outsourcing custom application development to an external vendor (that may be offshore), or renting software services from an application service provider.

6. *Evaluate the challenges of managing IT infrastructure and management solutions.*

Major infrastructure challenges include making wise infrastructure investments, choosing and coordinating infrastructure components, dealing with infrastructure change, and agreeing on infrastructure management and governance. Solution guidelines include using a competitive forces model to determine how much to spend on IT infrastructure and where to make strategic infrastructure investments, starting out new infrastructure initiatives with small experimental pilot projects, and establishing the total cost of ownership (TCO) of information technology assets. The total cost of owning technology resources includes not only the original cost of computer hardware and software but also costs for hardware and software upgrades, maintenance, technical support, and training.

Key Terms

Application server, 192
Application service provider (ASP), 216
Autonomic computing, 206
Blade servers, 199
Clients, 191
Client/server computing, 191
Edge computing, 206
Enterprise application integration (EAI) software, 213
Extensible Markup Language (XML), 213
Grid computing, 204
Hypertext Markup Language (HTML), 214
Java, 210
Legacy systems, 203
Linux, 201

Mainframe, 189
Middleware, 213
Minicomputers, 189
Moore's Law, 194
Multitiered (N-tier) client/server architecture, 191
Nanotechnology, 194
On-demand computing, 205
Open-source software, 201
Operating systems, 201
Outsourcing, 217
Scalability, 218
Server, 191
Server farms, 194
Service-oriented architecture (SOA), 214
Simple Object Access Protocol (SOAP), 214

Software package, 215
Storage area network (SAN), 202
Technology standards, 198
Total cost of ownership (TCO), 220
Universal Description, Discovery, and Integration (UDDI), 214
Unix, 201
Utility computing, 205
Web browser, 212
Web hosting service, 203
Web server, 192
Web services, 213
Web Services Description Language (WSDL), 214
Windows, 192
Wintel PC, 191

Review Questions

1. *Define IT infrastructure from both a technology and a services perspective. Which services does IT infrastructure comprise?*

2. *Name and describe the different levels of IT infrastructure.*

3. *List each of the eras in IT infrastructure evolution and describe their distinguishing characteristics.*

4. *Define and describe the following: Web server, application server, multitiered client/server architecture.*

5. *What are Moore's Law and the Law of Mass Digital Storage? What aspects of infrastructure change do they help explain?*

6. *How do network economics, declining communications costs, and technology standards affect IT infrastructure and the use of computers?*

7. *List and describe the components of IT infrastructure that firms need to manage.*

8. *Compare grid computing and edge computing.*

9. *How can businesses benefit from on-demand computing and autonomic computing?*

10. *Define and describe open-source software and Linux. How can they benefit businesses?*

11. *What is Java? Why is it important today?*

12. *What is the difference between enterprise application integration software and Web services? What role is played by XML in Web services?*

13. *Name and describe the three external sources for software.*

14. *Name and describe the management challenges posed by IT infrastructure.*

15. *How would using a competitive forces model help firms with infrastructure investments?*

16. *How would calculating the total cost of ownership (TCO) of technology assets help firms make infrastructure investments?*

Discussion Questions

1. *Why is selecting computer hardware and software for the organization an important management decision? What management, organization, and technology issues should be considered when selecting computer hardware and software?*

2. *Should organizations use application service providers (ASPs) for all their software needs? Why or why not? What management, organization, and technology factors should be considered when making this decision?*

Application Software Exercise:
Spreadsheet Exercise: Evaluating Computer Hardware and Software Options

You have been asked to obtain pricing information on hardware and software for an office of 30 people. Using the Internet, get pricing for 30 PC desktop systems (monitors, computers, and keyboards) manufactured by IBM, Dell, and Compaq as listed at their respective corporate Web sites. (For the purposes of this exercise, ignore the fact that desktop systems usually come with preloaded software packages.) Also obtain pricing on 15 monochrome desktop printers manufactured by Hewlett-Packard and by Xerox. Each desktop system must satisfy the minimum specifications shown in the following table:

Minimum Desktop Specifications

Processor speed	2 GHz
Hard drive	60 GB
RAM	512 MB
CD-ROM speed	48 speed
Monitor (diagonal measurement)	17 inches

Each desktop printer must satisfy the minimum specifications shown in the following table:

Minimum Monochrome Printer Specifications

Print speed	12 pages per minute
Print resolution	600 × 600
Network ready?	Yes
Maximum price/unit	$1,000

After pricing the desktop systems and printers, obtain pricing on 30 copies of Microsoft's Office XP or Office 2003, the most recent versions of Corel's WordPerfect Office and IBM's Lotus SmartSuite application packages, and on 30 copies of Microsoft Windows XP Professional Edition. The application software suite packages come in various versions, so be sure that each package contains programs for word processing, spreadsheet analysis, database analysis, graphics preparation, and e-mail.

Prepare a spreadsheet showing your research results for the desktop systems, for the printers, and for the software. Use your spreadsheet software to determine the desktop system, printer, and software combination that will offer both the best performance and pricing per worker. Because every two workers will share one printer (15 printers/30 systems), assume only half a printer cost per worker in the spreadsheet. Assume that your company will take the standard warranty and service contract offered by each product's manufacturer.

Analyzing the Total Cost of Ownership (TCO) of Desktop Software Assets

Software requirements: Spreadsheet software

Web browser software

Electronic presentation software (optional)

Dirt Bikes would like to replace the desktop office productivity software used by its corporate administrative staff, including the controller, accountant, administrative assistant, two human resources specialists, and three secretaries—a total of eight users. These employees need a suite that has word processing, spreadsheet, database, electronic presentation, and e-mail software tools. Occasionally, they would like to use these software tools to publish Web pages or to access data from the Internet. Use the Web to research and compare the pricing and capabilities of either Microsoft Office 2003 or Office XP versus Sun StarOffice.

1. Use your spreadsheet software to create a matrix comparing the prices of each software suite as well as their functionality. Identify the lowest-price system that meets Dirt Bikes's requirements.

2. You have learned that hardware and software purchase costs represent only part of the total cost of ownership (TCO) of technology assets and that there are additional cost components to consider. For this particular software system, assume that one-time installation costs $25 per user, one-time training costs $100 per user, annual technical support costs 30 percent of initial purchase costs, and annual downtime costs another 15 percent of purchase costs. What is the total cost of ownership of Dirt Bikes's new desktop productivity systems over a three-year period?

3. (Optional) If possible, use electronic presentation software to summarize your findings for management.

Electronic Business Project: Planning and Budgeting for a Sales Conference

The Foremost Composite Materials Company is planning a two-day sales conference for October 15–16, starting with a reception on the evening of October 14. The conference consists of all-day meetings that the entire sales force, numbering 125 sales representatives and their 16 managers, must attend. Each sales representative requires his or her own room, and the company needs two common meeting rooms, one large enough to hold the entire sales force plus a few visitors (200) and the other able to hold half the force. Management has set a budget of $80,000 for the representatives' room rentals. The hotel must also have such services as overhead and computer projectors as well as business center and banquet facilities. It also should have facilities for the company reps to be able to do work in their rooms and to enjoy themselves in a swimming pool or gym facility. The company would like to hold the conference in either Miami or New Orleans.

Foremost usually likes to hold such meetings in Hilton- or Marriott-owned hotels. Use the Hilton (www.hilton.com) and Marriott (www.marriott.com) sites to select a hotel in whichever of these cities that would enable the company to hold its sales conference within its budget. Other features you should use to help select a hotel include convenience to the airport and to areas of interest to tourists (such as New Orleans' French Quarter or Miami's South Beach) in case some employees would like to take an extra day or two to vacation.

Link to the two sites' home pages, and search them to find a hotel that meets Foremost's sales conference requirements. Once you have selected the hotel, locate flights arriving the afternoon prior to the conference because the attendees will need to check in the day before and attend your reception the evening prior to the conference. Your attendees will be coming from Los Angeles (54), San Francisco (32), Seattle (22), Chicago (19), and Pittsburgh (14). Determine costs of each airline ticket from these cities. When you are finished, draw up a budget for the conference. The budget will include the cost of each airline ticket, the room cost, and $40 per attendee per day for food.

What was your final budget? Which did you select as the best hotel for the sales conference and why?

Group Project: Evaluating Server Operating Systems

Form a group with three or four of your classmates. One group should research and compare the capabilities and costs of Linux versus the most recent version of the Windows operating system for servers. Another group should research and compare the capabilities and costs of Linux versus Unix. Each group should present its findings to the class, using electronic presentation software if possible.

CASE STUDY
99 Cents Only Stores: IT Infrastructure on a Budget

99 Cents Only Stores is one of the leading retailers in the deep-discount sales industry. The first 99 Cents Only Store opened in 1982, and the company now operates 194 retail locations, including 150 in California, 19 in Texas, 15 in Arizona, and 10 in Nevada. The stores carry mostly name-brand general merchandise, including food and beverages, health and beauty aids, cleaning supplies, house wares, hardware, stationery, toys, gifts, pet products, and clothing.

The chain makes purchases from over a thousand suppliers, including such notables as General Electric, Colgate-Palmolive, General Mills, Johnson & Johnson, Procter & Gamble, Kraft, Nabisco, and Unilever. Stores cover an average of 21,500 square feet, and those stores that were open for the entire year in 2003 averaged $4.9 million in net sales per store. Overall, 99 Cents Only Stores experienced a 21 percent company-wide increase in sales in 2003, totaling $863 million.

The majority of products can be restocked regularly. 99 Cents Only Stores also feature close-out merchandise, which is not available for reorder. The deep-discount industry is characterized by the purchase of close-out and special opportunity merchandise at costs below wholesale. Deep-discount retailers pass the savings on wholesale from these purchases to customers, who are able to buy products at prices that are well below retail. There is increasing competition with other deep-discount retailers for this special-situation merchandise, and some competitors have more financial resources and buying power than 99 Cents Only.

99 Cents Only Stores' recipe for continued growth is to open more stores while expanding same-store sales and trying to wring more out of each dollar to keep profit margins higher than competitors. The company has set a target of expanding its store square footage by 25 percent every year and believes that the states in which it already operates have the potential to support over 400 stores. Approximately half of the new stores launched in 2004 are in Texas. These stores will be serviced by a 741,000-square-foot distribution center near Houston that the company purchased for $23 million in 2003.

How does 99 Cents Only Stores manage its widespread chain of stores while keeping down costs? The answer is, with information technology, but on a budget. In 2003, despite opening 38 new stores and beginning operations in the new distribution center in Texas, the company's IT budget did not surpass $5 million. Although David Gold, 99 Cents Only's founder, chairman, and CEO, resists computer technology in his own office, he knows that computers have played a large role in enabling his company to grow. Gold introduced Radio Shack TRS-80 personal computers to the business in the 1980s. Gold's son, Jeff, now a senior vice president, programmed the company's first order-entry and warehouse inventory systems on those computers.

Today the company obviously requires far more computing power. The task of choosing and implementing that power without breaking the bank falls to Robert Adams, vice president of information services for 99 Cents Only Stores. 99 Cents Only Stores is not a typical single price point business. The average 99 Cents Only Store is about five times larger than the industry standard and generates approximately five times more in sales than its competitors ($4.8 million to $1 million). 99 Cents Only Stores also differs from its competitors in its target customer demographic, even pursuing locations in high-income areas. David Gold says, "Rich people like to save money too, and they do it in higher volumes."

With these factors in mind, Robert Adams continues to improve and expand the company while keeping the clientele satisfied and not spending too much money. For example, he saved the company tens of thousands of dollars on database management software licenses by searching the Web for the best price available rather than simply defaulting to the usual vendor. Adams acknowledges that he is able to make such decisions because the company is family-owned and -run, which concentrates the power among only a few people. In fact, most projects that the company takes on are implemented rapidly because there are fewer people involved in the decision-making process.

At every step of the way, Adams evaluates actual cost versus business value to the company of every initiative, whether it involves technology, real estate, or the melding of the two. Because Adams has a programming background, when it comes time for the company to deploy a new system, he can effectively weigh the cost of purchasing software off the shelf against the cost of writing the software code himself or with his IT team. Since 40 percent of 99 Cents Only Stores' products flow through the inventory only once because they are close-out items, the company's systems need to be very flexible to deal with unique nonrepeating items in inventory. Given these parameters, Adams often finds that the cost of buying prepackaged software combined with the time and cost required to customize such software for the deep-discount business makes programming the company's systems in-house the better option.

One of Adams's greatest challenges was launching the company's new distribution center in Texas. The sale of the facility, which David Gold purchased for $23 million from Albertsons, included over 200,000 square feet of refrigerated storage, approximately 500,000 square feet of dry storage, forklifts, cabling, and furniture. Working with a tight time constraint, Adams had to decide between revising the warehouse management system he had designed for the company's distribution center in City of Commerce, California, so that it could be used in Texas and purchasing a system from a developer or vendor. Adams already knew that his own system would have to be replaced in California to keep up with the company's aggressive growth plans, so he set about finding a warehouse management system that allowed for the degree and ease of customization that his company would require.

In addition to carrying close-out merchandise that only goes through inventory once, 99 Cents Only Stores sometimes receives shipments of products that aren't exactly what the company ordered. However, as Adams says, "We have to accept it, get it to our stores, and turn it fast." A system that would lock out such shipments because of inflexible rules would be a hindrance to the business.

Adams found the flexibility he needed in HighJump Software's Supply Chain Advantage software. The HighJump package addressed all of the major concerns related to the operation of the new distribution center: quick implementation, high functionality (particularly in regard to receiving), adaptability, and interoperability with the advanced automation technology of the new distribution center. One of the most attractive aspects of the package was that it didn't force 99 Cents Only Stores to change its business processes to conform to the structure of the system.

Christopher Heim, president and CEO of HighJump, explains that his company has basically developed a set of tools that enables users to build their own sets of functions according to the needs of their particular businesses, "almost akin to an Excel spreadsheet." The Supply Chain Advantage system is designed in such a way that users can make changes themselves instead of relying on IT specialists, the vendor, or outside sources to upgrade and manage the system. This is especially important to Adams, who likes to avoid recurring costs that can drain a company's budget.

HighJump developers worked with Adams and his staff to integrate the system with the specific needs of 99 Cents Only Stores, including a radio frequency identification (RFID) system and a voice-based inventory picking system. The Supply Chain Advantage package includes a warehouse management system, Warehouse Advantage, that tracks the status of every product during its time in the warehouse. Warehouse Advantage works closely with a Voxware voice-based picking system, which instructs warehouse employees known as "pickers" to retrieve products that need to be released from the warehouse for shipment to stores. The Voxware system also informs pickers when storage bins need to be refilled and where to find replenishments.

The Supply Chain Advantage software module called Yard Advantage manages the company's delivery trucks, directing them to the proper locations for loading or unloading and monitoring the inventory that each truck is carrying. Customer Service Advantage creates a portal that employees at 99 Cents Only Stores retail locations can use to check on scheduled shipments. Managers use Advantage Dashboard to monitor the performance of both facilities and workers using charts and graphs that update in real time. Event Advantage alerts warehouse managers to unforeseen problems in the supply chain before they can have a negative effect on profit margin.

Adams has been sufficiently satisfied with HighJump's solutions to plan for implementation of the Supply Chain Advantage systems at his company's City of Commerce distribution center. The process of installing the systems in this California center could be more complex because the center operates three shifts and employees need retraining. Furthermore, the City of Commerce center already serves 150 of 99 Cents Only Stores' retail locations. When the Texas center went online, it was responsible for far fewer stores. Adams has also decided that the receiving process in City of Commerce should undergo the conversion to the HighJump system first. Once that process functions smooth, other functions will be added.

99 Cents Only Stores planned to have the City of Commerce distribution center running on HighJump technology beginning in the fall of 2004. In the meantime, the need for improved systems has become very apparent. In mid-2004, the company's stock price had fallen around 50 percent. One factor contributing to the falloff was that the California distribution center was working beyond its means, which decreased productivity, affected delivery schedules, and left stores unable to replenish their shelves. Overall the chain experienced lower same-store sales and increased sales of products with lower profit margins.

99 Cents Only Stores has to reevaluate its inventory control procedures and to expand its warehouse capacity. Robert Adams will continue to explore advanced information technology using what he calls the "low-hanging fruit" method. He gives the highest priority to technology initiatives that promise the best return on investment (ROI). If a new project comes along that offers a better opportunity to improve the business, Adams will shift gears even if the previous project has not been deployed fully. The company still receives most of the benefit of the first project, and doesn't miss out on a new opportunity. Can 99 Cents Only Stores continue to rely on the uneasy relationship between leading-edge technology and a bottom-line-oriented business to rebound from its recent struggles?

Sources: "Case Study: 99 Cents Only Stores' Efficient IT Infrastructure," *CIO Insight*, January 1, 2004 (www.cioinsight.com); Janet Rae-Dupree, "Thinking Out Loud: Robert Adams," *CIO Insight*, January 1, 2004 (www.cioinsight.com); "Big Problems at 99 Cents Only," TheStreet.com, June 14, 2004; "Supply Chain Advantage: 99 Cents Only Stores Drives Expansion with Solutions from HighJump Software, a 3M Company," HighJump Software, www.highjumpsoftware. com, accessed September 15, 2004; Merrill Douglas, "Flex Time: Finding Adaptable Software," InboundLogistics.com, July 2003; Mike Cianciolo, "99 Cents? That May Be Too Much," Motley Fool via Yahoo! Finance, biz.yahoo.com, accessed June 15, 2004; and 99 Cents Only 10-K Report.

CASE STUDY QUESTIONS

1. Analyze 99 Cents Only Stores using the value chain and competitive forces models.

2. Evaluate the current business strategy of 99 Cents Only Stores in response to its competitive environment. What is the role of information technology infrastructure in that strategy? How does it provide value for 99 Cents Only Stores?

3. How effective is 99 Cents Only Stores' strategy for IT infrastructure investments? Explain your answer.

4. How successful have 99 Cents Only Stores' strategy and use of information systems been in addressing the company's problems? What kind of problems can they solve? What are some of the problems that they cannot address?

Chapter 7

Managing Data Resources

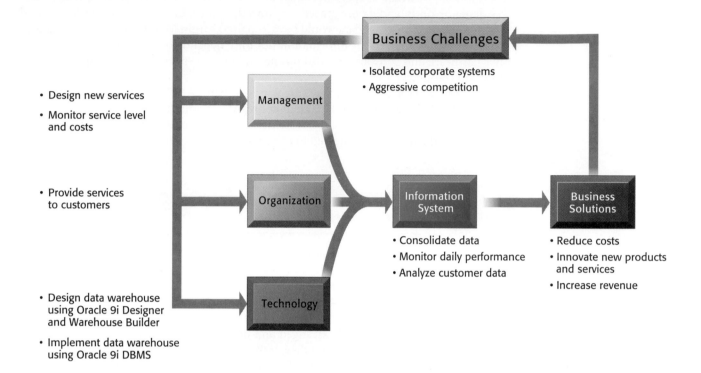

Opening Case: Better Data Help Virgin Mobile Australia Win the Customer Wars

Virgin Mobile Australia is a major player in the Australian mobile phone industry. It had grown aggressively by pioneering new products and services, including a prepaid service that did not require a contract, free voice mail, and billing all calls by the second. Other competitors followed suit, leaving Virgin Mobile Australia wondering how it could maintain its competitive lead. The answer lay in making better use of the company's data.

Senior management wanted a better picture of the Virgin Mobile's customer base and how well the company was operating. This was no easy task. Virgin Mobile Australia had many different systems, each with different pieces of data that could solve only part of the puzzle. It had an enterprise system, a customer relationship management system, and systems for prepaid cell phone service as well as service that was billed to the customer each month. The company needed to develop a single enterprise-wide view of the data in all of these systems to produce "one version of the truth."

The company created a data warehouse that reorganized the data from all of these systems in a massive database to produce the company-wide information management required. The data warehouse runs on Oracle 9i database management software and was developed using Oracle 9i Designer to define the system's data model and Oracle 9i Warehouse Builder to design the data warehouse.

With the data warehouse, Virgin Mobile Australia can pull data from multiple systems together to obtain an integrated view of its customers and services. Every morning Virgin Mobile executives can check indicators such as the number of new connections made the previous day, the demographic profile of new customers, and the handsets they purchased. Management can also find out the performance of each store and point-of-sale campaign, consumer reaction to new products and services, and customer attrition rates.

Most important, the warehouse provides data for monitoring customer usage in terms of the total minutes used each month and the revenue generated by each customer. Average revenue-per-user (ARPU) is a key performance indicator for this company to measure its success. All of this information helps Virgin Mobile react quickly to changes in a very dynamic market and improve its profitability.

Sources: Lynn Tryba, "Winning with a Warehouse," *Profit Magazine,* February 2004; and "Virgin Mobile Uses Business Intelligence to Achieve Rapid Expansion," www.oracle.com, accessed May 17, 2004.

Virgin Mobile Australia's experience illustrates how much information system effectiveness depends on how data are stored, organized, and accessed. Inability to locate and assemble essential business data would have impaired Virgin Mobile's organizational performance. Proper delivery of information not only depends on the capabilities of computer hardware and software but also on the organization's ability to manage data as an important resource.

As a manager, you'll want to make sure your company's data are organized so that they can be easily accessed and used. This chapter introduces you to the technologies for managing data as a resource. We also describe the managerial and organizational issues and key decisions that must be addressed to use data resources effectively

7.1 ORGANIZING DATA IN A TRADITIONAL FILE ENVIRONMENT

An effective information system provides users with accurate, timely, and relevant information. Accurate information is free of errors. Information is timely when it is available to decision makers when it is needed. Information is relevant when it is useful and appropriate for the types of work and decisions that require it.

Contemporary systems store data that can provide useful information in computer files. When the files are properly arranged and maintained, users can easily store, access, modify, and retrieve the information they need. Despite the use of excellent hardware and software, many organizations have inefficient information systems because of poor file management. Let's start by looking at the traditional methods organizations have used to arrange data in computer files and the problems they pose.

File Organization Terms and Concepts

A computer system organizes data in a hierarchy that starts with bits and bytes and progresses to fields, records, files, and databases (see Figure 7-1). A bit represents the smallest unit of data a computer can handle. A group of bits, called a byte, represents a single character, which can be a letter, a number, or another symbol. A grouping of characters into a word, a group of words, or a complete number (such as a person's name or age) is called a **field**. A group of related fields, such as the student's name, the course taken, the date, and the grade, comprises a **record**; a group of records of the same type is called a **file**.

For example, the student records in Figure 7-1 could constitute a course file. A group of related files makes up a **database**. The student course file illustrated in Figure 7-1 could be grouped with files on students' personal histories and financial backgrounds to create a student database.

A record describes an entity. An **entity** is a person, place, thing, or event on which we store and maintain information. An order is a typical entity in a sales order file, which maintains information on a firm's sales orders. Each characteristic or quality describing a particular entity is called an **attribute**. For example, order number, order date, item number, and item quantity would each be an attribute of the entity order. The specific values that these attributes can have can be found in the fields of the record describing the entity order (see Figure 7-2). In this illustration ORDER represents an *entity class* or *entity type*, a group of similar entities about which we collect information (attributes). The particular set of values for Order number, Order date, Item number, and Quantity shown in Figure 7-2 are for a single occurrence of that entity type and this is called an *instance* of that entity.

Every record in a file should contain at least one field that uniquely identifies that record so that the record can be retrieved, updated, or sorted. This identifier field is called a **key field**. An example of a key field is the order number for the order record illustrated in Figure 7-2 or an employee number or social security number for a personnel record (containing employee data, such as the employee's name, age, address, job title, and so forth).

WINDOW ON ORGANIZATIONS

A DATABASE HELPS P&G MANAGE PRODUCT INFORMATION

Procter & Gamble (P&G) is one of the largest consumer goods companies in the world, with more than $43 billion in annual sales. P&G sells more than 300 brands worldwide, including major brands such as Tide, Mr. Clean, Ivory Soap, Crest, Pringles, Pampers, Clairol, and Prell. P&G has five global business units in more than 80 countries, including research and development and contract manufacturing operations. This dispersed business deals with 100,000 suppliers.

The fundamental product development process at P&G begins with the creation of a set of technical specifications for a product, raw material, packaging material, piece of artwork, or analytical and process standards. Each P&G product has its own set of technical standards and specifications. For example, the formula card (equivalent to a list of ingredients or instructions) for a single size and fragrance of one Olay product defines technical standards for 30 raw material specifications, 20 test methods, 3 packaging standards, 8 packaging material standards, 4 artwork standards, manufacturing instructions, a set of quality acceptance criteria, 1 process standard, 2 additional formula cards tied to the same packaging standard, and 15 substitute ingredient standards for producing a product in a different location.

Because P&G is a global company with some products tailored to regional markets and consumer tastes, P&G has many functionally similar products with significant variations in actual specifications for different regions. There were no global data standards or "pick lists" across all P&G divisions. Consequently, P&G has more than 600,000 specifications and a mountain of product data to manage.

These massive quantities of technical standards data used to be stored in 30 separate data repositories, preventing information sharing among researchers. Difficulties integrating and accessing this information made material acquisition more inefficient and expensive. For example, P&G had perhaps 12 different sets of specifications for blue dye, and it was placing 12 different orders for the same blue dye to the same supplier at 12 different prices. One large P&G business unit was using more than 50 different types of adhesives around the world with scores of suppliers, even though the specifications for several adhesives were identical with different commercial names and only three adhesive types were needed to meet all global needs.

P&G made the management of product information easier by cataloging the technical standards for all of its products and organizing them in a single global database called the Corporate Standards System (CSS). The system is based on eMatrix from MatrixOne, a provider of product life cycle management software. This database is now available to 8,200 P&G employees and will be made available to some suppliers and contract manufacturers.

The database organizes any and every piece of information that goes into making a particular product. Once this informa-

tion is in the database, data can be analyzed from many different perspectives to deliver information to serve specific functions. For instance, designers and engineers can use the data to design a new product or improve an old one. Purchasing can use the data to consolidate materials orders. The data even help retailers determine the proper shelf height for storing an item.

P&G's investment in the database is producing returns. With all product data in one place, P&G can obtain a unified company-wide picture of what materials it needs and use this information to consolidate purchases to secure better prices. This information helped P&G cut down on total adhesive use and develop new processes for applying adhesives more economically.

The database also enables P&G researchers who need constant access to standards to work more efficiently and facilitates reuse of technical standards that have already been defined. A researcher in one facility may have already defined a technical standard for a hair-coloring gel, while another researcher may be working on a similar product or a product that may interact with that brand of hair color. The second researcher will be able to reuse the coloring product's technical standards and know precisely how an ingredient in that product might react with other ingredients. In heavily regulated industries such as health and beauty products, ingredients and their proportions must be exact. Precision and consistency among technical standards are critical.

When P&G's research and development group is working on new products, it can use this information without repeating a study to show that there is no problem with using that color in a new product. The database helped P&G achieve a tenfold reduction in the number of colorants and a reduction in colorant suppliers to one for colors and one for whites, which enables new package development teams to select from this pre-approved palette.

CSS is being enhanced to create more structured data from technical standards that can be easily shared with more groups in the company. Specification data will be delivered to users through specialized interfaces that are tailored for specific business needs. CSS will define and catalog technical standards for any new product, whether that product was developed internally or through an acquisition.

Sources: Lafe Low, "They Got It Together," *CIO Magazine*, February 15, 2004; Deborah D'Agostino, "PLM: The Means of Production," *eWeek*, February 27, 2004; "Procter & Gamble Awarded Enterprise Value Award by *CIO Magazine* for Work with MatrixOne on Innovative Product Lifecycle Management Application," *MatrixOne*, February 23, 2004; and "Procter & Gamble," www.matrixone.com, accessed May 20, 2004.

To Think About: How does P&G's CSS database provide value for the company? What management, organization, and technology issues had to be addressed when developing this database?

FIGURE 7-6   *The relational data model.*

Each table is a relation, each row is a tuple representing a record, and each column is an attribute representing a field. These relations can easily be combined and extracted to access data and produce reports, provided that any two share a common data element. In this example, the PART and SUPPLIER files share the data element Supplier_Number.

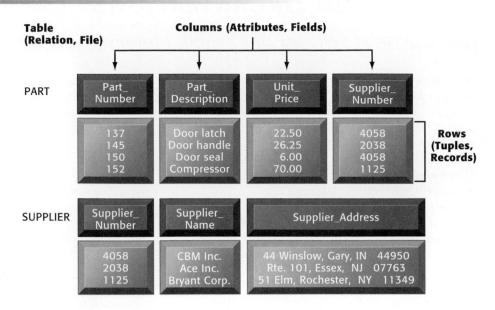

FIGURE 7-7   *The three basic operations of a relational DBMS.*

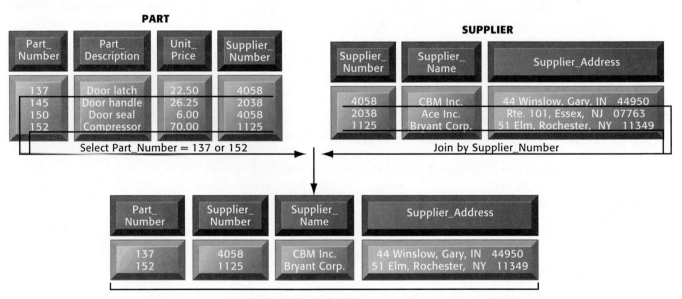

Project selected columns

The select, project, and join operations enable data from two different tables to be combined and only selected attributes to be displayed.

The SQL statements for producing the new resultant table in Figure 7-7 would be as follows:

SELECT PART.Part_Number, SUPPLIER.Supplier_Number, SUPPLIER.Supplier_Name, SUPPLIER.Supplier_Address

FROM PART, SUPPLIER

WHERE PART.Supplier_Number = SUPPLIER.Supplier_Number AND Part_Number = 137 OR Part_Number = 152;

You can learn more about SQL and how to create a SQL query in the Hands-On Guide to MIS at the end of this text.

Internet Connection ———
The Internet Connection for this chapter directs you to a series of Web sites where you can complete an exercise to evaluate various commercial database management system products.

FIGURE 7-8   *A hierarchical database for a human resources system.*

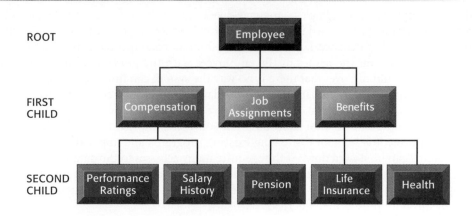

The hierarchical database model looks like an organizational chart or a family tree. It has a single root segment (Employee) connected to lower level segments (Compensation, Job Assignments, and Benefits). Each subordinate segment, in turn, may connect to other subordinate segments. Here, Compensation connects to Performance Ratings and Salary History. Benefits connects to Pension, Life Insurance, and Health. Each subordinate segment is the child of the segment directly above it.

Leading mainframe relational database management systems include IBM's DB2 and Oracle from the Oracle Corporation. DB2, Oracle, and Microsoft SQL Server are used as DBMS for midrange computers. Microsoft Access is a PC relational database management system, and Oracle Lite is a DBMS for small handheld computing devices.

HIERARCHICAL AND NETWORK DBMS

You can still find older systems that are based on a hierarchical or network data model. The **hierarchical DBMS** is used to model one-to-many relationships, presenting data to users in a treelike structure. Within each record, data elements are organized into pieces of records called segments. To the user, each record looks like an organizational chart with one top-level segment called the root. An upper segment is connected logically to a lower segment in a parent–child relationship. A parent segment can have more than one child, but a child can have only one parent.

Figure 7-8 shows a hierarchical structure that might be used for a human resources database. The root segment is Employee, which contains basic employee information such as name, address, and identification number. Immediately below it are three child segments: Compensation (containing salary and promotion data), Job Assignments (containing data about job positions and departments), and Benefits (containing data about beneficiaries and benefit options). The Compensation segment has two children below it: Performance Ratings (containing data about employees' job performance evaluations) and Salary History (containing historical data about employees' past salaries). Below the Benefits segment are child segments for Pension, Life Insurance, and Health, containing data about these benefit plans.

Whereas hierarchical structures depict one-to-many relationships, **network DBMS** depict data logically as many-to-many relationships. In other words, parents can have multiple children, and a child can have more than one parent. A typical many-to-many relationship for a network DBMS is the student–course relationship (see Figure 7-9). There are many courses in a university and many students. A student takes many courses, and a course has many students.

FIGURE 7-9   *The network data model.*

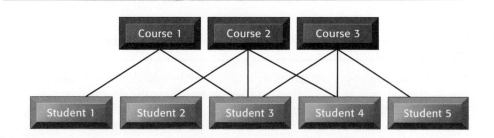

This illustration of a network data model showing the relationship the students in a university have to the courses they take represents an example of logical many-to-many relationships.

Hierarchical and network DBMS are considered outdated and are no longer used for building new database applications. They are much less flexible than relational DBMS and do not support ad hoc, English language–like inquiries for information. All paths for accessing data must be specified in advance and cannot be changed without a major programming effort. For instance, if you queried the human resources database illustrated in Figure 7-8 to find out the names of the employees with the job title of administrative assistant, you would discover that there is no way the system can find the answer in a reasonable amount of time. This path through the data was not specified in advance.

Relational DBMS, in contrast, have much more flexibility in providing data for ad hoc queries, combining information from different sources, and providing capability to add new data and records without disturbing existing programs and applications. However, these systems can be slowed down if they require many accesses to the data stored on disk to carry out the select, join, and project commands. Selecting one part number from among millions, one record at a time, can take a long time. Of course, the database can be tuned to speed up prespecified queries.

Hierarchical DBMS can still be found in large legacy systems that require intensive high-volume transaction processing. Banks, insurance companies, and other high-volume users continue to use reliable hierarchical databases, such as IBM's Information Management System (IMS) developed in 1969. As relational products acquire more muscle, firms will shift away completely from hierarchical DBMS, but this will happen over a long period of time.

OBJECT-ORIENTED DATABASES

Conventional database management systems were designed for homogeneous data that can be easily structured into predefined data fields and records organized in rows and columns. But many applications today and in the future will require databases that can store and retrieve not only structured numbers and characters but also drawings, images, photographs, voice, and full-motion video. Conventional DBMS are not well suited to handling graphics-based or multimedia applications. For instance, design data in a computer-aided design (CAD) database consist of complex relationships among many types of data. Manipulating these kinds of data in a relational system requires extensive programming to translate complex data structures into tables and rows. An **object-oriented DBMS**, however, stores the data and procedures that act on those data as objects that can be automatically retrieved and shared.

Object-oriented database management systems (OODBMS) are becoming popular because they can be used to manage the various multimedia components or Java applets used in Web applications, which typically integrate pieces of information from a variety of sources. OODBMS also are useful for storing data types such as recursive data. (An example would be parts within parts as found in manufacturing applications.) Finance and trading applications often use OODBMS because they require data models that must be easy to change to respond to new economic conditions.

Although object-oriented databases can store more complex types of information than relational DBMS, they are relatively slow compared with relational DBMS for processing large numbers of transactions. Hybrid **object-relational DBMS** are now available to provide capabilities of both object-oriented and relational DBMS. A hybrid approach can be accomplished in three different ways: by using tools that offer object-oriented access to relational DBMS, by using object-oriented extensions to existing relational DBMS, or by using a hybrid object-relational database management system.

7.3 CREATING A DATABASE ENVIRONMENT

To create a database environment, you must understand the relationships among the data, the type of data that will be maintained in the database, how the data will be used, and how the organization may need to change to manage data from a company-wide perspective. Increasingly, database design will also have to consider how the organization can share some of its data with its business partners (Jukic, Jukic, and Parameswaran, 2002). We now describe important database design principles and the management and organizational requirements of a database environment.

Designing Databases

To create a database, you must go through two design exercises: a conceptual design and a physical design. The conceptual, or logical, design of a database is an abstract model of the database from a business perspective, whereas the physical design shows how the database is actually arranged on direct-access storage devices. Logical design requires a detailed description of the business information needs of the actual end users of the database. Ideally, database design will be part of an overall organizational data-planning effort (see Chapter 14).

The conceptual database design describes how the data elements in the database are to be grouped. The design process identifies relationships among data elements and the most efficient way of grouping data elements to meet information requirements. The process also identifies redundant data elements and the groupings of data elements required for specific application programs. Groups of data are organized and refined until an overall logical view of the relationships among all the data elements in the database emerges.

To use a relational database model effectively, complex groupings of data must be streamlined to minimize redundant data elements and awkward many-to-many relationships. The process of creating small, stable, yet flexible and adaptive data structures from complex groups of data is called **normalization**. Figures 7-10 and 7-11 illustrate this process.

FIGURE 7-10   *An unnormalized relation for ORDER.*

An unnormalized relation contains repeating groups. For example, there can be many parts and suppliers for each order. There is only a one-to-one correspondence between Order_Number, Order_Date, and Delivery_Date.

FIGURE 7-11   *Normalized tables created from ORDER.*

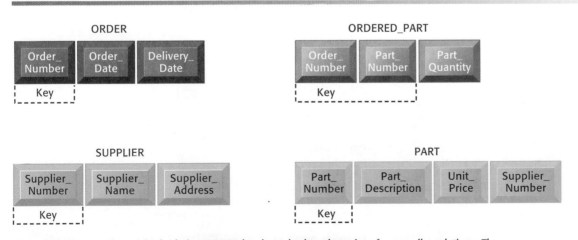

After normalization, the original relation ORDER has been broken down into four smaller relations. The relation ORDER is left with only three attributes and the relation ORDERED_PART has a combined, or concatenated, key consisting of Order_Number and Part_Number.

In the particular business modeled here, an order can have more than one part but each part is provided by only one supplier. If we build a relation called ORDER with all the fields included here, we would have to repeat the name and address of the supplier for every part on the order, even though the order is for parts from a single supplier. This relationship contains what are called *repeating data groups* because there can be many parts on a single order to a given supplier. A more efficient way to arrange the data is to break down ORDER into smaller relations, each of which describes a single entity. If we go step by step and normalize the relation ORDER, we emerge with the relations illustrated in Figure 7-11. You can find out more about normalization, entity-relationship diagramming, and database design in the Hands-On Guide to MIS at the end of this text.

If a database has been carefully considered, with a clear understanding of business information needs and usage, the database model will be in a normalized form. Many real-world databases are not fully normalized because this may not be the most efficient or cost-effective way to meet business requirements.

Database designers document their data model with an **entity-relationship diagram**, illustrated in Figure 7-12. This diagram illustrates the relationship between the entities ORDER, ORDERED_PART, PART, and SUPPLIER. The boxes represent entities. The lines connecting the boxes represent relationships. A line connecting two entities that ends in two short marks designates a one-to-one relationship. A line connecting two entities that ends with a crow's foot topped by a short mark indicates a one-to-many relationship. Figure 7-12 shows that one ORDER can contain many ORDERED_PARTs. Each PART can be ordered many times and can appear many times in a single order. Each PART can have only one SUPPLIER, but many PARTs can be provided by the same SUPPLIER.

Distributing Databases

Database design also considers how the data are to be distributed. Information systems can be designed with a centralized database that is used by a single central processor or by multiple processors in a client/server network. Alternatively, the database can be distributed. A **distributed database** is one that is stored in more than one physical location.

There are two main methods of distributing a database (see Figure 7-13). In a *partitioned* database, parts of the database are stored and maintained physically in one location and other parts are stored and maintained in other locations (see Figure 7-13a)

FIGURE 7-12 *An entity-relationship diagram.*

This diagram shows the relationships between the entities ORDER, ORDERED_PART, PART, and SUPPLIER that might be used to model the database in Figure 7-11.

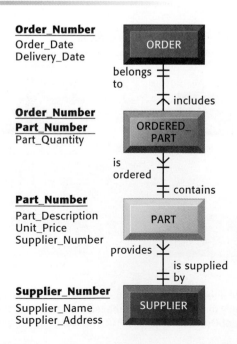

FIGURE 7-13   *Distributed databases.*

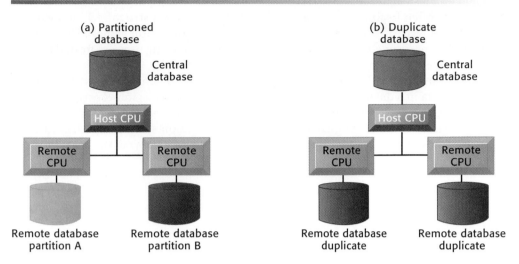

There are alternative ways of distributing a database. The central database can be partitioned (a) so that each remote processor has the necessary data to serve its own local needs. The central database also can be replicated (b) at all remote locations.

so that each remote processor has the necessary data to serve its local area. Changes in local files can be justified with the central database on a batch basis, often at night. Another strategy is to *replicate* (that is, duplicate in its entirety) the central database (Figure 7-13b) at all remote locations. For example, Lufthansa Airlines replaced its centralized mainframe database with a replicated database to make information more immediately available to flight dispatchers. Any change made to Lufthansa's Frankfort DBMS is automatically replicated in New York and Hong Kong. This strategy also requires updating the central database during off-hours.

Distributed systems reduce the vulnerability of a single, massive central site. They increase service and responsiveness to local users and often can run on smaller, less expensive computers. Distributed systems, however, depend on high-quality telecommunications lines, which themselves are vulnerable. Moreover, local databases can sometimes depart from central data standards and definitions, and they pose security problems by widely distributing access to sensitive data. Database designers need to weigh these factors in their decisions.

Ensuring Data Quality

A good database design and data model is not enough to guarantee that the database will deliver the information the organization needs. Data that are inaccurate, untimely, or inconsistent with other sources of information can create serious operational and financial problems for businesses. When faulty data go unnoticed, they can lead to incorrect decisions, product recalls, and even financial losses. According to the Data Warehousing Institute in Seattle, inaccurate and low-quality data cost U.S. businesses $611 billion each year in bad mailings and staff overhead. The Gartner Group believes that customer data degrades at a rate of 2 percent per month, making poor data quality a major obstacle to successful customer relationship management implementation (Klau, 2003).

Some of these data quality problems are caused by redundant and inconsistent data produced by a traditional file environment. During the database design effort, data describing entities such as a customer, product, or order should be named and defined consistently for all business areas using the database. If a database is properly designed and enterprise-wide data standards established, duplicate or inconsistent data elements should be minimal.

Most data quality problems, however, such as misspelled names, transposed numbers, or incorrect or missing codes, stem from errors during data input. The incidence of such errors is rising as companies move their businesses to the Web and allow customers and suppliers to enter data into their Web sites that directly update internal systems.

Before a new database is in place, organizations need to identify and correct their faulty data and establish better routines for editing once the database is in operation. Analysis of data quality often begins with a **data quality audit**, which is a structured survey of the accuracy and level of completeness of the data in an information system. Data quality audits can be performed by surveying entire data files, surveying samples from data files, or surveying end users for their perceptions of data quality.

Data cleansing, also known as *data scrubbing*, consists of activities for detecting and correcting data in a database or file that are incorrect, incomplete, improperly formatted, or redundant. Data cleansing not only corrects data but also enforces consistency among different sets of data that originated in separate information systems. Specialized data-cleansing software can automatically survey data files, correct errors in the data, and integrate the data in a consistent company-wide format.

7.4   DATABASE TRENDS

Organizations are installing powerful data analysis tools and data warehouses to make better use of the information stored in their databases and are taking advantage of database technology linked to the World Wide Web. Let's explore these developments.

Multidimensional Data Analysis

Sometimes managers need to analyze data in ways that traditional database models cannot represent. For example, a company selling four different products—nuts, bolts, washers, and screws—in the East, West, and Central regions might want to know actual sales by product for each region and might also want to compare them with projected sales. This analysis requires a multidimensional view of data.

To provide this type of information, organizations can use either a specialized multidimensional database or a tool that creates multidimensional views of data in relational databases. Multidimensional analysis enables users to view the same data in different ways using multiple dimensions. Each aspect of information—product, pricing, cost, region, or time period—represents a different dimension. So, a product manager could use a multidimensional data analysis tool to learn how many washers were sold in the East in June, how that compares with the previous month and the previous June, and how it compares with the sales forecast. Another term for multidimensional data analysis is **online analytical processing (OLAP)**.

Figure 7-14 shows a multidimensional model that could be created to represent products, regions, actual sales, and projected sales. A matrix of actual sales can be stacked on top of a matrix of projected sales to form a cube with six faces. If you rotate the cube 90 degrees one way, the face showing will be product versus actual and projected sales. If you rotate the cube 90 degrees again, you can see region versus actual and projected sales. If you rotate 180 degrees from the original view, you can see projected sales and product versus region. Cubes can be nested within cubes to build complex views of data.

Data Warehouses and Data Mining

Decision makers need concise, reliable information about current operations, trends, and changes. What has been immediately available at most firms is current data only (historical data were available through special information system reports that took a long time to produce). Data often are fragmented in separate operational systems, such as sales or payroll, so that different managers make decisions from incomplete knowledge bases. Users and information systems specialists may have to spend inordinate amounts of time locating and gathering data (Watson and Haley, 1998). Data warehousing addresses this problem by integrating key operational data from around the company in a form that is consistent, reliable, and easily available for reporting.

FIGURE 7-14   *Multidimensional data model.*

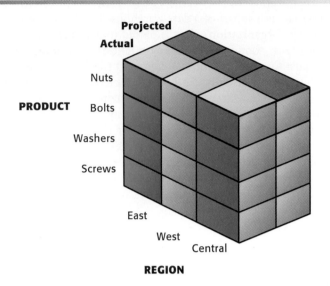

The view that is showing is product versus region. If you rotate the cube 90 degrees, the face that will be showing is product versus actual and projected sales. If you rotate the cube 90 degrees again, you can see region versus actual and projected sales. Other views are possible. The ability to rotate the data cube is the main technique for multidimensional reporting. It is sometimes called "slice and dice."

WHAT IS A DATA WAREHOUSE?

A **data warehouse** is a database that stores current and historical data of potential interest to managers throughout the company. The data originate in many core operational systems and external sources, including Web site transactions, each with different data models. They may include legacy systems, relational or object-oriented DBMS applications, and systems based on Hypertext Markup Language (HTML) or Extensible Markup Language (XML) documents. The data from these diverse applications are copied into the data warehouse database as often as needed—hourly, daily, weekly, monthly. The data are standardized into a common data model and consolidated so that they can be used across the enterprise for management analysis and decision making. The data are available for anyone to access as needed but cannot be altered.

Figure 7-15 illustrates the data warehouse concept. The data warehouse must be carefully designed by both business and technical specialists to ensure it can provide the right information for critical business decisions. The firm may need to change its business processes to benefit from the information in the warehouse (Cooper, Watson, Wixom, and Goodhue, 2000).

FIGURE 7-15   *Components of a data warehouse.*

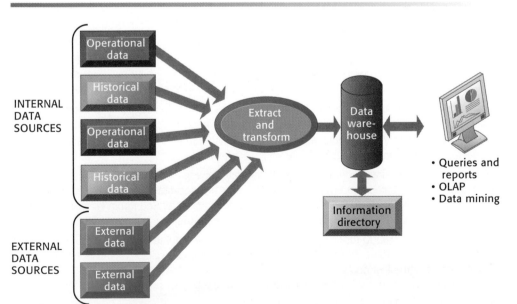

A data warehouse extracts current and historical data from operational systems inside the organization. These data are combined with data from external sources and reorganized into a central database designed for management reporting and analysis. The information directory provides users with information about the data available in the warehouse.

Companies can build enterprise-wide data warehouses where a central data warehouse serves the entire organization, or they can create smaller, decentralized warehouses called data marts. A **data mart** is a subset of a data warehouse in which a summarized or highly focused portion of the organization's data is placed in a separate database for a specific population of users. For example, a company might develop marketing and sales data marts to deal with customer information. A data mart typically focuses on a single subject area or line of business, so it usually can be constructed more rapidly and at lower cost than an enterprise-wide data warehouse. However, complexity, costs, and management problems will arise if an organization creates too many data marts.

The Window on Technology describes some of the technical issues that must be addressed when creating a data warehouse. Both AT&T and Axfood had collected massive amounts of customer data that they wanted to analyze immediately to make better marketing, pricing, and inventory decisions. As you read this case, pay attention to the benefits that can be provided by large data warehouses and the technology issues that need to be addressed to make them effective.

DATA MINING

A data warehouse system provides a range of ad hoc and standardized query tools, analytical tools, and graphical reporting facilities, including tools for OLAP and data mining. **Data mining** uses a variety of techniques to find hidden patterns and relationships in large pools of data and infer rules from them that can be used to predict future behavior and guide decision making (Fayyad et al., 2002; Hirji, 2001). Data mining is often used to provide information for targeted marketing in which personalized or individualized messages can be created based on individual preferences, and there are many other data-mining applications in both business and scientific work. These systems can perform high-level analyses of patterns or trends, but they can also drill down to provide more detail when needed. Table 7-1 describes how some organizations are benefiting from data mining, and Chapter 13 provides more detail on how data mining is being used to guide business decision making.

Data mining is both a powerful and profitable tool, but it poses challenges to the protection of individual privacy. Data-mining technology can combine information from many diverse sources to create a detailed "data image" about each of us—our income, our driving habits, our hobbies, our families, and our political interests. The question of whether companies should be allowed to collect such detailed information about individuals is explored in Chapter 5.

TABLE 7-1 *How Businesses Are Using Data Mining*

Organization	Data-Mining Application
Disco S.A.	Argentine supermarket chain uses data mining to analyze purchasing patterns of more than 1.5 million customers who participate in a frequent-buyer program in more than 200 stores.
Lillian Vernon Corporation	Catalog company mines data from its Web site as well as from its catalog sales to determine which products sell best. By analyzing its Web visitor data, it found that men were more likely to visit its Web site than to flip through a paper catalog. Lillian Vernon now places products that appeal to men prominently on its Web site.
Red Robin Restaurants	Greenwood, Colorado-based chain uses OLAP and data mining to analyze the menus for its 87 corporate restaurants and more than 100 franchise locations. By analyzing the price, cost, and quality of each item in all the meals the restaurants serve, Red Robin can identify the menu items that offer both high volume and high profit margin.
Samsung Electronics America	Analyzes data from 10,000 resellers to identify orders that went to competitors. It found that for its computer monitors sold to the health care industry, one competitor was responsible for 40 percent of the lost deals.

WINDOW ON TECHNOLOGY

LARGE DATA WAREHOUSES: WHEN BIGGER IS BETTER

Until a few years ago, a data warehouse or transactional database that held 1 terabyte (TB) of data was considered big. Today a "big" database holds tens of terabytes. The data warehouses used by AT&T and Axfood are examples, and they provide special benefits.

AT&T Labs maintains a 26-TB data warehouse, which holds two years of detailed records of local and long-distance telephone calls on the AT&T network. The data in the warehouse are split between computers in two different locations, and the warehouse runs on Sun Microsystems Enterprise 10000 servers, with 2,670 disk drives for storage. AT&T stores data over two years old offline. About 3,000 AT&T employees routinely tap into the warehouse to check billing errors, to analyze call volumes to plan network expansions and upgrades, and to calculate prices to pitch new services to customers.

One of the most important benefits of the warehouse is the ability to analyze data shortly after they are captured by the system. Data from AT&T's operational billing and network management systems enter the warehouse directly so that the warehouse can provide answers to queries almost instantly. For example, the warehouse enables AT&T to analyze consumer calls in response to AT&T television ads an hour after they run. An analyst can query the warehouse for all calls made to a country from a specific area code during a specific month and obtain an answer in less than a minute. Before AT&T built this warehouse, marketing personnel had to wait four to six weeks for billing reports to determine whether an ad produced sales.

Axfood, a major grocery chain with hundreds of retail stores throughout Scandinavia, also wanted instant analysis of its customer data. It already held a 20 percent market share, but the retail food industry is fiercely competitive, with razor-thin profit margins and many perishable goods with a limited shelf life. Axfood management believed its company could strengthen its leadership position in the Nordic retail food market by offering unique products combined with superior convenience and service. Axfood is based in Stockholm, Sweden, has 8,000 employees, and generates about US$4 billion in annual revenue.

Like many other retail chains, Axfood had been gathering point-of-sale data about customer purchases and analyzing the data to make decisions about what items to stock in its stores. But its data-warehousing technology was not up to the task. The company was using two data warehouses for this purpose, one running on an Oracle DBMS and the other on Microsoft SQL Server. These warehouses could support only weekly analyses of all the point-of-sale data and could not scale to handle Axfood's growing volume of data. Axfood's management had determined that by 2005 it would need 10 terabytes of storage.

Axfood's management wanted to know about which products customers decided to buy within an hour of the actual purchase. If its hundreds of retail outlets experienced a sudden run on a particular brand of paper towels, for example, Axfood could replenish store shelves by the next day. Accurate and up-to-date customer purchase data would also help Axfood minimize excess inventory by enabling it to stock its shelves with items customers were sure to buy. "This level of responsiveness is the only way to maintain customer loyalty," states Axfood's data architect. "By having a better grasp on customer buying activities, we could make more targeted purchasing decisions, which would ultimately save us money and generate more revenue."

Axfood management determined that it could reduce the total cost of ownership of its technology assets for data management if it consolidated on a single platform for its data warehousing. It selected IBM's DB2 Universal Database Enterprise Server Edition for AIX, Version 8.1 running on an IBM pSeries 670 server, with 2.3 terabytes of storage in an IBM TotalStorage Enterprise Storage Server. The pSeries 670 server met Axfood's requirements for a high level of performance and availability. It is large enough to host other applications besides the data warehouse, enabling Axfood to get a higher return on its hardware investment. This platform is more scalable, cost-effective, and easier to manage than the Oracle and Microsoft systems and can easily support Axfood's data management and storage needs.

Axfood's DB2 data warehouse uses DataStage from Ascential Software to extract, transform, and load sales data into the DB2 database, which stores and consolidates all the merchandise, stock, and purchase data.

Once the Axfood data warehouse is at full capacity, the company should recoup all the costs of its investment within two to three years. Axfood also expects the cost of maintaining the data warehouse to decrease significantly in its third year of operation because of the declining need for information systems staff to administer it. The company can then allocate more information systems staff to more critical areas.

The data warehouse has helped transform Axfood into a much more agile and proactive company where the products customers want are instantly available on store shelves when and where they need them. The DB2 data warehouse will provide Axfood with a crystal-clear view of its customers' shopping habits well into the future. Never again will rapid business changes take it by surprise.

Sources: Marianne Kolbasuk McGee, "Bigger and Better," *Information Week*, March 22, 2004) and "Axfood Transforms Inventory Management Process with DB2 Data Warehouse," www.ibm.com, accessed May 17, 2004.

To Think About: How do large data warehouses provide value for a business? What special technology challenges do they pose?

BENEFITS OF DATA WAREHOUSES

Data warehouses not only offer improved information, they also make it easy for decision makers to obtain this information. They even include the ability to model and remodel the data. It has been estimated that 70 percent of the world's business information resides on mainframe databases, many of which support older legacy systems. Many of these legacy systems are critical production applications that support the company's core business processes. As long as these systems can efficiently process the necessary volume of transactions to keep the company running, firms are reluctant to replace them, thereby avoiding disrupting critical business functions and high system replacement costs. Many of these legacy systems use hierarchical DBMS or even older nondatabase files in which information is difficult for users to access. Data warehouses enable decision makers to access data as often as they need without affecting the performance of the underlying operational systems. Many organizations are making access to their data warehouses even easier by using Web technology.

Databases and the Web

Database technology plays an important role in making organizations' information resources available on the World Wide Web. We now explore the role of hypermedia databases on the Web and the growing use of Web sites to access information stored in conventional databases inside the firm.

THE WEB AND HYPERMEDIA DATABASES

Web sites store information as interconnected pages that contain text, sound, video, and graphics by using a hypermedia database. The **hypermedia database** approach to information management stores chunks of information in the form of nodes connected by links the user specifies (see Figure 7-16). The nodes can contain text, graphics, sound, full-motion video, or executable computer programs. Searching for information does not have to follow a predetermined organization scheme. Instead, a user can branch instantly to related information in any kind of relationship the author establishes. The relationship between records is less structured than in a traditional DBMS. The hypermedia database approach enables users to access topics on a Web site in whichever order they wish.

LINKING INTERNAL DATABASES TO THE WEB

A series of middleware and other software products has been developed to help users gain access to organizations' legacy data through the Web. For example, a customer with a Web browser might want to search an online retailer's database for pricing information. Figure 7-17 illustrates how that customer might access the retailer's internal database over

---

FIGURE 7-16   *A hypermedia database.*

In a hypermedia database, users can choose their own paths to move from node to node. Each node can contain text, graphics, sound, full-motion video, or executable programs.

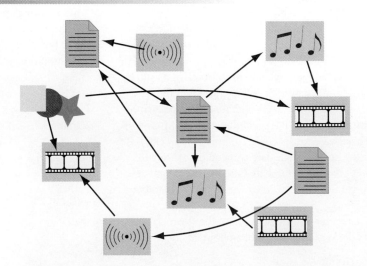

FIGURE 7-17   *Linking internal databases to the Web.*

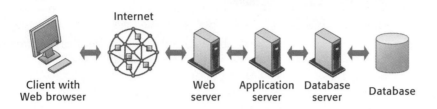

Users can access an organization's internal database through the Web using their desktop PCs and Web browser software.

the Web. The user would access the retailer's Web site over the Internet using Web browser software on his or her client PC. The user's Web browser software would request data from the organization's database, using HTML commands to communicate with the Web server. Because many back-end databases cannot interpret commands written in HTML, the Web server would pass these requests for data to special software that would translate HTML commands into SQL so that they could be processed by the DBMS working with the database. In a client/server environment, the DBMS resides on a special dedicated computer called a **database server**. The DBMS receives the SQL requests and provides the required data. The middleware transfers information from the organization's internal database back to the Web server for delivery in the form of a Web page to the user.

Figure 7-17 shows that the middleware working between the Web server and the DBMS could be an application server running on its own dedicated computer (see Chapter 6). The application server software handles all application operations, including transaction processing and data access, between browser-based computers and a company's back-end business applications or databases. The application server takes requests from the Web server, runs the business logic to process transactions based on those requests, and provides connectivity to the organization's back-end systems or databases. Alternatively, the software for handling these operations could be a custom program or a series of software scripts. *Common Gateway Interface (CGI)* is a specification for transferring information between a Web server and a program designed to accept and return data. The program could be written in any programming language, including C, C++, Perl, Java, or Visual Basic.

There are a number of advantages to using the Web to access an organization's internal databases. Web browser software is extremely easy to use, requiring much less training than even user-friendly database query tools. The Web interface requires no changes to the internal database. Companies leverage their investments in older systems because it costs much less to add a Web interface in front of a legacy system than to redesign and rebuild the system to improve user access.

The ThomasNet.com Web site links to a database of more than 170,000 companies, 400,000 products, thousands of online catalogs, and millions of CAD drawings searchable by product. More organizations are using the Web to provide an interface to internal databases.

TABLE 7-2 *Examples of Web-Enabled Databases*

Organization	Use of Web-Enabled Database
Domania.com	Home price database of 27 million past real estate sales.
Internet Movie Database	Web site linked to a massive database that includes summaries, cast information, and actor biographies for almost every film ever released.
iGo.com	Web site linked to a giant relational database housing information about batteries and peripherals for computers and other portable electronic devices. Visitors can immediately find online information about each electronic device and the batteries and parts it uses and can place orders for these parts over the Web.
St. Luke's Hospital in Chesterfield, Missouri	Web-enabled Patient Information Network System (WebPINS) uses a Web interface to enable physicians to obtain a unified view of patient information, which has been consolidated in a Sybase database.

Accessing corporate databases through the Web is creating new efficiencies and opportunities, and, in some cases, it is even changing the way business is being done. Some companies have created new businesses based on access to large databases through the Web. Others are using Web technology to provide employees with integrated firmwide views of information. Table 7-2 describes some of these applications of Web-enabled databases.

7.5 MANAGEMENT OPPORTUNITIES, CHALLENGES, AND SOLUTIONS

Effectively managing the organization's data resources requires much more than simply selecting a logical database model. The database is an organizational discipline, a method, not just a tool or technology. It requires organizational and conceptual change. Management commitment and understanding are essential.

Opportunities

Firms have become acutely aware of how much organizational performance can be improved by making better use of their data, as the examples in this chapter and other chapters of the text so clearly illustrate. This is why so many companies are investing in data mining and customer relationship management technology.

Management Challenges

It has been very difficult for organizations to manage their data effectively. A true database environment requires an organization to change the way it defines and uses data and typically represents a very large investment.

ORGANIZATIONAL OBSTACLES TO A DATABASE ENVIRONMENT

Implementing a database requires widespread organizational change in the role of information (and information managers), the allocation of power at senior levels, the ownership and sharing of information, and patterns of organizational agreement. A database management system (DBMS) challenges the existing power arrangements in an organization and for that reason often generates political resistance. In a traditional file environment, each department constructed files and programs to fulfill its specific needs. Now, with a database, files and programs must be built that take into account the whole organization's interest in data. Although the organization has spent the money on hardware and software for a database environment, it may not reap the benefits it should if it is unwilling to make the requisite organizational changes.

COST/BENEFIT CONSIDERATIONS

Designing a database to serve the enterprise can be a lengthy and costly process. In addition to the cost of DBMS software, related hardware, and data modeling, organizations should anticipate heavy expenditures for integrating, merging, and standardizing data from different systems and functional areas. Despite the clear advantages of the DBMS, the short-term costs of developing a DBMS often appear to be as great as the benefits. It may take time for the database to provide value.

Solution Guidelines

The critical elements for creating a database environment are (1) data administration, (2) data-planning and modeling methodology, (3) database technology and management, and (4) users. This environment is depicted in Figure 7-18.

DATA ADMINISTRATION

Database systems require that the organization recognize the strategic role of information and begin actively to manage and plan for information as a corporate resource. This means that the organization must develop a **data administration** function with the power to define information requirements for the entire company and with direct access to senior management. The chief information officer (CIO) or vice president of information becomes the primary advocate in the organization for database systems.

Data administration is responsible for the specific policies and procedures through which data can be managed as an organizational resource. These responsibilities include developing information policy, planning for data, overseeing logical database design and data dictionary development, and monitoring how information systems specialists and end-user groups use data.

The fundamental principle of data administration is that all data are the property of the organization as a whole. Data cannot belong exclusively to any one business area or organizational unit. All data should be available to any group that requires them to fulfill its mission. An organization needs to formulate an **information policy** that specifies its rules for sharing, disseminating, acquiring, standardizing, classifying, and inventorying information throughout the organization. Information policy lays out specific procedures

FIGURE 7-18   *Key organizational elements in the database environment.*

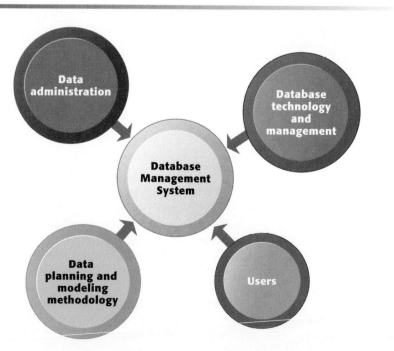

For a database management system to flourish in any organization, data administration functions and data-planning and modeling methodologies must be coordinated with database technology and management. Resources must be devoted to train end users to use databases properly.

and accountabilities, specifying which organizational units share information, where information can be distributed, and who is responsible for updating and maintaining the information. Although data administration is a very important organizational function, it has proved very challenging to implement.

DATA-PLANNING AND MODELING METHODOLOGY

The organizational interests served by the DBMS are much broader than those in the traditional file environment; therefore, the organization requires enterprise-wide planning for data. Enterprise analysis, which addresses the information requirements of the entire organization (as opposed to the requirements of individual applications), is needed to develop databases. The purpose of enterprise analysis is to identify the key entities, attributes, and relationships that constitute the organization's data. These techniques are described in greater detail in Chapter 14.

DATABASE TECHNOLOGY, MANAGEMENT, AND USERS

Databases require new software and a new staff specially trained in DBMS techniques, as well as new data management structures. Most corporations develop a database design and management group within the corporate information systems division that is responsible for defining and organizing the structure and content of the database and maintaining the database. In close cooperation with users, the design group establishes the physical database, the logical relations among elements, and the access rules and procedures. The functions it performs are called **database administration**.

A database serves a wider community of users than traditional systems. Relational systems with user-friendly query languages permit employees who are not computer specialists to access large databases. In addition, users include trained computer specialists. To optimize access for nonspecialists, more resources must be devoted to training end users.

MAKE IT YOUR BUSINESS

Finance and Accounting

Banks and financial services have benefited from a database approach to information management. Much of their data were traditionally organized along product lines in a number of different systems where it was difficult to provide a complete picture of a customer's transactions with the organization. Database management software and data warehouses have enabled these firms to organize their data more flexibly so that they can view information by customer, financial product, or other criteria. Financial firms are also intensive users of data mining for analyzing credit risk or for identifying profitable customers. You can find examples of finance and accounting applications on page 247.

Human Resources

Companies typically maintain human resources databases, enabling them to maintain data on employees, benefits plans, and training programs and to provide reports to the government concerning compliance with health, safety, and equal employment opportunity regulations. Because these human resources databases contain sensitive information, such as salaries, job performance evaluations, and medical history, companies must be very careful about distributing this information. The security and data access rules for DBMS can help protect confidentiality and privacy. You can find examples of human resources applications on pages 257–259.

Manufacturing and Production

Many manufacturing and production processes rely on database technology. Companies maintain large databases of finished goods, raw materials in inventory, and goods in transit that can be used for supply chain management. The manufacturing process makes use of numerous databases on suppliers, jobs in progress, product components, product quality, and costs. You can find examples of manufacturing and production applications on page 237.

Sales and Marketing

Database, data warehouse, and data-mining technologies have been powerful tools for marketers because they enable firms to assemble and analyze vast quantities of data about customers from many different sources. By querying these customer databases, analysts can identify customers most interested in specific products or highly profitable customers. They can target specialized products and promotions based on these detailed customer profiles. The sales function can benefit by allowing customers to access corporate databases linked to the Web to place orders or to find out product information. You can find examples of sales and marketing applications on pages 229 and 247.

Summary

1. **Describe basic file organization concepts and the problems of managing data resources in a traditional file environment.**

   A computer system organizes data in a hierarchy that starts with bits and bytes and progresses to fields, records, files, and databases. Traditional file management techniques make it difficult for organizations to keep track of all of the pieces of data they use in a systematic way and to organize these data so that they can be easily accessed. Different functional areas and groups were allowed to develop their own files independently. Over time, this traditional file management environment creates problems such as data redundancy and inconsistency, program-data dependence, inflexibility, poor security, and lack of data sharing and availability.

2. **Describe how a database management system organizes information and compare the principal database models.**

   A database management system (DBMS) consists of software that permits centralization of data and data management so that businesses have a single consistent source for all their data needs. A single database services multiple applications. A DBMS includes a data definition language, a data manipulation language, and a data dictionary capability. The most important feature of the DBMS is its ability to separate the logical and physical views of data. The user works with a logical view of data. The DBMS retrieves information so that the user does not have to be concerned with its physical location.

   The principal types of databases today are relational DBMS and object-oriented DBMS. Relational systems are very flexible for supporting ad hoc requests for information and for combining information from different sources. They support many-to-many relationships among entities. Relational DBMS are efficient for storing alphanumeric data that can be organized into structured fields and records, which are represented by attributes and tuples in two-dimensional tabular models. This flexibility was not possible with the older hierarchical and network database models. Object-oriented DBMS can store graphics and other types of data in addition to conventional text data to support multimedia applications. Organizations should use the DBMS that is best suited for their data model.

3. **Apply important database design principles.**

   Designing a database requires both a logical design and a physical design. The logical design models the database from a business perspective. The organization's data model should reflect its key business

   processes and decision-making requirements. The process of creating small, stable, flexible, and adaptive data structures from complex groups of data when designing a relational database is termed *normalization*. Database design also considers whether a complete database or portions of the database can be distributed to more than one location to increase responsiveness and reduce vulnerability and costs. There are two major types of distributed databases: replicated databases and partitioned databases.

4. **Evaluate new database trends.**

   Powerful tools are available to analyze the information in databases and to take advantage of the information resources on the World Wide Web. Multidimensional data analysis, also known as online analytical processing (OLAP), can represent relationships among data as a multidimensional structure, which can be visualized as cubes of data and cubes within cubes of data, enabling more sophisticated data analysis. Data can be more conveniently analyzed across the enterprise by using a data warehouse, in which current and historical data are extracted from many different operational systems and consolidated for management decision making. Data mining analyzes large pools of data, including the contents of data warehouses, to find patterns and rules that can be used to predict future behavior and guide decision making. Hypermedia databases enable data to be stored in nodes linked together in any pattern the user establishes and are used for storing information at Web sites. Conventional databases can be linked to the Web to facilitate user access to an organization's internal data.

5. **Identify the challenges posed by data resource management and management solutions.**

   Developing a database environment requires much more than selecting database technology. It requires a formal information policy governing the maintenance, distribution, and use of information in the organization. The organization must also develop a data administration function and a data-planning methodology. Data planning may need to be performed to make sure that the organization's data model delivers information efficiently for its business processes and enhances organizational performance. There is political resistance in organizations to many key database concepts, especially the sharing of information that has been controlled exclusively by one organizational group. Creating a database environment is a long-term endeavor requiring large up-front investments and organizational change.

Key Terms

Attribute, 230
Conceptual schema, 233
Data administration, 251
Data cleansing, 244
Data definition language, 234
Data dictionary, 234
Data element, 235
Data inconsistency, 232
Data manipulation language, 234
Data mart, 246
Data mining, 246
Data quality audit, 244
Data redundancy, 232

Data warehouse, 245
Database, 230
Database (rigorous definition), 233
Database administration, 252
Database management system (DBMS), 233
Database server, 249
Distributed database, 242
Entity, 230
Entity-relationship diagram, 242
Field, 230
File, 230
Hierarchical DBMS, 239
Hypermedia database, 248

Information policy, 251
Key field, 230
Network DBMS, 239
Normalization, 241
Object-oriented DBMS, 240
Object-relational DBMS, 240
Online analytical processing (OLAP), 244
Program-data dependence, 232
Record, 230
Relational DBMS, 236
Structured query language (SQL), 234
Subschema, 234
Tuple, 236

Review Questions

1. Why is file management important for overall system performance?

2. List and describe each of the components in the data hierarchy.

3. Define and explain the significance of entities, attributes, and key fields.

4. List and describe the problems of the traditional file environment.

5. Define a database and a database management system.

6. Name and briefly describe the three components of a DBMS.

7. What is the difference between a logical and a physical view of data?

8. List some benefits of a DBMS and the solutions it provides for the problems of a traditional file environment.

9. Describe the principal types of databases and the advantages and disadvantages of each.

10. What is normalization? How is it related to the features of a well-designed relational database?

11. What is a distributed database, and what are the two main ways of distributing data?

12. Why are data quality audits and data cleansing essential?

13. Describe the capabilities of online analytical processing (OLAP) and data mining.

14. What is a data warehouse? How can it benefit organizations?

15. What is a hypermedia database? How does it differ from a traditional database? How is it used for the Web?

16. How can users access information from a company's internal databases through the Web?

17. What are the challenges of a database environment? What are the four key organizational elements for creating a database environment?

Discussion Questions

1. It has been said that you do not need database management software to create a database environment. Discuss.

2. To what extent should end users be involved in the selection of a database management system and database design?

Application Software Exercise:
Database Exercise: Building a Relational Database for a Small Business

Sylvester's Bike Shop, located in San Francisco, California, sells road, mountain, hybrid, leisure, and children's bicycles. Currently, Sylvester's purchases bikes from three suppliers, but plans to add new suppliers in the near future. This rapidly growing business needs a database system to manage this information.

Initially, the database should house information about suppliers and products. The database will contain two tables: a supplier table and a product table. The reorder level refers to the number of items in inventory that triggers a decision to order more items to prevent a stockout. (In other words, if the number of units of a particular item in inventory falls below the reorder level, the item should be reordered.) The user should be able to perform several queries and produce several managerial reports based on the data contained in the two tables.

Using the information found in the tables on the Laudon Web site for Chapter 7, build a simple relational database for Sylvester's. Once you have built the database, perform the following activities.

1. Prepare a report that identifies the five most expensive bicycles. The report should list the bicycles in descending order from most expensive to least expensive, the quantity on hand for each, and the markup percentage for each.

2. Prepare a report that lists each supplier, its products, the quantities on hand, and associated reorder levels. The report should be sorted alphabetically by supplier. Within each supplier category, the products should be sorted alphabetically.

3. Prepare a report listing only the bicycles that are low in stock and need to be reordered. The report should provide supplier information for the items identified.

4. Write a brief description of how the database could be enhanced to further improve management of the business. What tables or fields should be added? What additional reports would be useful?

Redesigning the Customer Database

Required software: Database software

Dirt Bikes sells primarily through its distributors. It maintains a small customer database with the following data: customer name, address, telephone number, model purchased, date of purchase, and distributor. You can find this database on the Laudon Web site for Chapter 7. These data are collected by its distributors when they make a sale and are then forwarded to Dirt Bikes. Dirt Bikes would like to be able to market more aggressively to its customers. It would like to be able to send customers e-mail notices of special racing events and of sales on parts. It would also like to learn more about customer interests and tastes: their ages, years of schooling, another sport in which they are interested, and whether they attend dirt bike racing events. Additionally, Dirt Bikes would like to know whether they own more than one motorcycle. (Some Dirt Bikes customers own two or three motorcycles purchased from Dirt Bikes USA or other manufacturers.) If a motorcycle was purchased from Dirt Bikes, the company would like to know the date of purchase,

model purchased, and distributor. If the customer owns a non–Dirt Bikes motorcycle, the company would like to know the manufacturer and model of the other motorcycle (or motorcycles) and the distributor from whom the customer purchased that motorcycle.

1. Redesign Dirt Bikes's customer database so that it can store and provide the information needed for marketing. You will need to develop a design for the new customer database and then implement that design using database software. Consider using multiple tables in your new design. Populate each new table with 10 records.

2. Develop several reports that would be of great interest to Dirt Bikes's marketing and sales department (for example, lists of repeat Dirt Bikes customers, Dirt Bikes customers who attend racing events, or the average ages and years of schooling of Dirt Bikes customers) and print them out.

Electronic Commerce Project: Searching Online Databases

The Internet is a valuable source of databases where users can search for services and products in areas or countries that are far from their own locations. Your company is located in Greensboro, North Carolina, and manufacturers office furniture of various types. You have recently acquired several new customers in Australia, and a study you commissioned indicates that with a presence there you could greatly increase your sales. Moreover, your study indicates that you could do even better if you actually manufactured many of your products locally (in Australia). First, you need to set up an office in Melbourne to establish a presence, and then you

need to begin importing from the United States. You then can plan to start producing locally.

You will soon be traveling to the area to make plans to actually set up an office, and you want to meet with organizations that can help you with your operation. You will need to engage people or organizations that offer many services necessary for you to open your office, including lawyers, accountants, import-export experts, telecommunications equipment and support, and even trainers who can help you to prepare your future employees to work for you. List the companies you would contact to interview on your trip to determine if they can help you with these and any other functions you think vital to establishing your office. Start by searching for U.S. Department of Commerce advice on doing business in Australia. Then try the following online databases to locate companies that you would like to meet with during your coming trip: Australian Business Register (abr.business.gov.au/), Australia Trade Now (australiatradenow.com/), and the Nationwide Business Directory of Australia (www.nationwide.com.au). If necessary, you should also try search engines such as Yahoo! (www.yahoo.com) and Google (www.google.com).

Rate the databases you used for accuracy, completeness, ease of use, and general helpfulness. What does this exercise tell you about the design of databases?

Group Project: Creating Company-Wide Data Standards

An industrial supply company wants to create a data warehouse from which management can obtain a single corporate-wide view of critical sales information to identify best-selling products in specific geographic areas, key customers, and sales trends. The company's sales and product information are stored in two different systems: a divisional sales system running on a UNIX server, and a corporate sales system running on an IBM mainframe. Management would like to create a single standard format that consolidates these data from both systems in the data warehouse. The following format has been proposed.

Product_ID	Product_Description	Cost_Per_Unit	Units_Sold	Sales_Region	Division	Customer_ID

Following are sample reports from the two systems that would supply the data for the data warehouse.

Mechanical Parts Division Sales System

Prod._No.	Product_Description	Cost_Per_Unit	Units_Sold	Sales_Region	Customer_ID
60231	4" steel bearing	5.28	900,245	N.E.	Anderson
85773	SS assembly unit	12.45	992,111	M.W.	Kelly Industries

Corporate Sales System

Product_ID	Product_Description	Unit_Cost	Units_Sold	Sales_Territory	Division
60231	Bearing, 4"	5.28	900,245	Northeast	Parts
85773	SS assembly unit	12.02	992,111	Midwest	Parts

1. What business problems are created by not having these data in a single standard format?

2. How easy would it be to create a database with a single standard format that could store the data from both systems? Identify the problems that would have to be addressed.

3. Should the problems be solved by database specialists or general business managers? Who should have the authority to finalize a single company-wide format for this information in the data warehouse? Explain your position.

4. If possible, use electronic presentation software to present your findings to the class.

CASE STUDY
Database Woes Plague Homeland Security and Law Enforcement

The World Trade Center and Pentagon terrorist attacks on September 11, 2001, have focused attention on the need for accurate information about terrorist activities to prevent similar catastrophes in the future. Much of the information necessary to combat future terrorist attacks, as well as to fight domestic crime, is stored in databases of literally thousands of federal, state, and local organizations. Bringing together these data to make them useful for fighting terrorism and crime is proving to be an immense task.

To begin with, the new U.S. Department of Homeland Security (DHS) comprises 22 agencies, each with its own computer systems and hardware. One major reason for creating this new department was to bring together the data stored in agency systems to collect, analyze, and distribute information about suspected terrorist activities. But the task is actually much larger than that because these 22 agencies represent only a few of the federal government's 146 agencies with law enforcement responsibilities.

Each of these agencies in turn has numerous databases, most of which are incompatible and technically archaic. They have different computing platforms, data names, data definitions, data sizes, and data files. They do not share their data with state and local agencies, which are vital for tracking potential terrorists and their activities. Ben Gianni, the vice president for homeland security of Computer Sciences Corporation, estimates that a project to connect the data from all of these agencies would take at least five years and cost a minimum of $15 billion.

When the FBI tried to create the huge Integrated Automated Fingerprint Identification System (IAFIS) in the late 1990s, for example, it had to integrate two already-existing but dissimilar systems, the FBI's IAFIS and the Immigration and Naturalization Service's Automated Biometric Identification (IDENT) System. Whereas the IAFIS stored 10 rolled prints for each person, IDENT stored only two flat prints. For an interim solution, the FBI had to develop custom software to exchange fingerprinting data from the two systems. Two fingerprints from IAFIS were added to IDENT, while workstations for using 10 rolled prints were also being designed. Second, a study had to be undertaken to determine how to capture the 10 prints more rapidly. Ultimately, the FBI developed a fast transaction type that retrieves an individual's criminal history without displaying the fingerprints. Fingerprint matching could be done later if needed.

The same data in different systems, even within the same organization, usually have different names, codes, and formats. So, for example, over the years the FBI had created five critical but independent investigative application systems, each storing its data differently. These databases are considered the backbone of the FBI systems. The FBI was not made part of the DHS, remaining part of the Department of Justice (DOJ), but it needs to collect and analyze accurate and timely criminal information to deal with terrorism and criminal activity.

The FBI is buried under an immense amount of paperwork and continues to rely on paper as its chief information management tool. Its computer systems are antiquated. For example, the FBI has five investigative application systems, but these systems could be viewed only using very old-fashioned green IBM 3270 terminals. Many agents could not access the Internet from their desks because of security concerns. Moreover, although the agents need to search these data, the technology allowed only single-word searches. So, for example, after the terrorist attacks of September 11, agents could search on such words as *flight* or *school* but could not search for phrases such as *flight school*. In fact, the FBI has no enterprise-wide architecture but rather has separate databases for more than 50 applications, which are written in various languages and running on disparate systems.

Agents required security clearances to access much of the data, but security clearance often took up to eight months to obtain. Because of the secretive FBI culture, it has had a mind-set to keep information to itself, a problem highlighted by and after September 11. In the past, when the FBI had to store its own information, it often overlooked key areas. For example, after September 11, the FBI needed data on foreign students, including obvious information such as their current schools and locations, but it had not collected it. So, it turned to the Immigration and Naturalization Service (INS), but this agency did not even have a computer system to collect such data. Ultimately, the FBI had to contact all U.S. colleges and universities to ask them for the required information.

In November 2000, Congress allocated $379 million to update the FBI's systems. The FBI has already installed 21,000 desktop computers, more than 3,000 printers, and nearly 1,500 scanners. In addition, it has linked 622 FBI offices with high-speed data connections. Perhaps the single most important software project involves creating the Virtual Case File (VCF) system linking 31 FBI databases through a single Web portal. "We are now focused on implementing a data warehousing capability that can bring together our information into databases that can be accessed by agents throughout the world," observes FBI director Robert Mueller. FBI field agents can access the VCF system using a standard Web browser to search the entire FBI data warehouse. Instead of faxing or mailing pertinent information about a suspected terrorist from one office to another, FBI agents have electronic access to the files, which could also be shared with the CIA, the National Security Agency, and local police departments. A system is being built to automate and scan all paper-based information into a relational database that can be mined.

In May 2002, the FBI's investigative guidelines were updated to allow agents to surf the Web and to use commercial data services and e-mail. (Formerly, agents could not receive e-mails directly; the e-mail messages were received elsewhere and were printed out then handed to the agents, creating serious delays.)

The FBI is also working to communicate more openly with state and local law enforcement agencies. It is opening its National Law Enforcement Online (LEO) system to other law enforcement agencies to distribute information on terrorism. The FBI is also now improving its National Crime Information Center (NCIC), its repository of 17 criminal records databases that contains mug shots and thumbprints.

The INS is another federal organization with serious database problems. The INS estimates that there are about 500 million people entering the United States each year, an immense volume that requires a huge system to track. However, aside from its lack of information on foreign students, after September 11, the INS could not even locate 45 percent of the aliens the FBI wanted to question about terrorism, according to a General Accounting Office (GAO) assessment report of November 2002. The report said the INS had even lost track of 4,334 aliens from countries where al-Qaeda is known to operate.

The primary reason for the problems is the failure of the INS to maintain a database system that is both integrated and current. It has more than 16 separate database systems to capture data on aliens, including a Non-Immigrant Information System, an Asylum Prescreening System, a Student Exchange Visitor Information System, an Arrival Departure Information System, a Student and Schools System, a Deportable Alien Control System, and a Refugees,

Asylum and Parole System. According to the GAO report, "INS does not update all databases that contain alien address information [recorded when they entered the country] and does not have the ability to update address information in NIIS [the Non-Immigrant Information System]." Its databases do not even distinguish between aliens with the same names. Late in 2002, the INS formed a task force to find ways to centralize and improve its alien address systems.

The United States still lacks an accurate, up-to-date watch list of suspected terrorists and their supporters that is the most essential tool for combating international terrorism. In September 2003, the White House, Central Intelligence Agency, FBI, and Department of Homeland Security agreed to set up a Terrorist Screening Center (TSC) as an interagency body to create, maintain, and control a master terrorist database. The TSC would be run by the FBI using the State Department's watch list, known as TIPOFF, as the backbone of a new database that would integrate all other existing databases on terrorism into a new state-of-the-art system.

To create the master watch list, TSC staff members would cleanse the data, weeding out duplications, obsolete records, and people who in the past had been wrongfully identified as terrorists or who shared the same last name as suspected terrorists. Data on fingerprints, distinguishing scars, birthmarks, credit card accounts, and other details would be employed to help distinguish harmless namesakes from serious suspects.

The TSC opened in Crystal City, Virginia, on December 1, 2003. The FBI Counterintelligence Division had announced to law enforcement agencies across the United States that the TSC was open for business as the single point of contact for assistance in identifying people with possible terrorist connections. The FBI cautioned, however, that TSC's initial capabilities were "limited."

On December 22, 2003, The FBI attaché to the American embassy

in Paris informed French police that al-Qaeda planned to hijack an Air France jet and crash it somewhere in the United States. The French government grounded three flights and detained six passengers whose names matched the FBI watch list. All were mistaken identities, including a child whose name matched that of a Tunisian terrorist leader. The TSC was never consulted when U.S. intelligence picked up the information about the potential Air France hijacking, including the names of the suspected terrorists.

An October 1, 2004 report by Clark Kent Ervin, inspector general for the Department of Homeland Security (DHS), pointed out that the U.S. government had failed to consolidate all of its terrorist watch lists as of that date, partly because the DHS did not play a sufficiently strong leadership role in the project. The report further noted that although TSC had started integrating the various watch lists, it had trouble hiring enough analysts with high security clearances. The integrated terrorist database that was envisioned is still months and possibly years away.

Sources: John Mintz, "DHS Blamed for Failure to Combine Watch Lists," *The Washington Post*, October 2, 2004; Robert Black, Gary Fields, and Jo Wrighton, "U.S. 'Terror' List Still Lacking," *Wall Street Journal,* January 2, 2004; Ted Bridis, "Review: FBI Computer Upgrades Inadequate," Associated Press, May 10, 2004; Christopher Whitcomb, "The Needle in the Database," *New York Times*, May 14, 2004; Larry Dignan, "A Fort Knox for Data," *Baseline*, January 16, 2004; Alex Salkever, "Spooks, Sleuths, and Data Sharing," *Business Week*, May 25, 2004; Larry Barrett, "FBI: Under the Gun," *Baseline*, September 10, 2003; Dan Verton, "FBI Has Made Major Progress, Former IT Chief Says," *Computerworld*, April 21, 2003, "FBI Begins Knowledge Management Face-Lift," *Computerworld*, April 21, 2003, and "Database Woes Thwart Counterterrorism Work," *Computerworld*, December 2, 2002; Judith Lamont, "Law Enforcement Gains Ground in Data Integration and Analysis," *KMWorld*, March 2003; Jennifer 8. Lee, "Threats and Responses: Law Enforcement; State Department Link Will

Open Visa Database to Police Officers," *New York Times,* January 31, 2003; Debbie Gage, "FBI Bureaucracy Hobbies Tech Adoption," *Baseline*, September 11, 2002; Debbie Gage and John McCormick, "The Disconnected Cop," *Baseline*, September 10, 2002; "NYPD Base Case," *Baseline*, September 10, 2002; Sean Gallagher, "Gotcha! Extending Existing Systems," *Baseline*, September 10, 2002; Doug Brown, "How Homeland Security Budgets Technology," *Baseline*, September 9, 2002.

CASE STUDY QUESTIONS

1. Briefly summarize the problems and major issues in this case.

2. Describe the major data management problems involved in bringing together the data needed to combat terrorism.

3. What management, organization, and technology issues need to be addressed to solve this problem?

4. Suppose you are a consultant to the U.S. federal government. Based on what you have read in this chapter, suggest and describe several approaches you might recommend for solving this problem.

Chapter 8

Telecommunications, Networks, and the Internet

OBJECTIVES

After reading this chapter, you will be able to:

1. Describe the features of a contemporary corporate network infrastructure and key networking technologies.

2. Evaluate alternative transmission media, types of networks, and network services.

3. Assess the role of the Internet and the World Wide Web in a firm's information technology infrastructure.

4. Identify and describe the most important tools for communication and e-business.

5. Identify and describe the challenges posed by networking and the Internet and management solutions.

CHAPTER OUTLINE

8.1 ***TELECOMMUNICATIONS AND NETWORKING IN TODAY'S BUSINESS WORLD***
The Business Telecommunications Environment
Networking and Communications Trends
The Business Value of Telecommunications and Networking

8.2 ***CONTEMPORARY NETWORKING INFRASTRUCTURE***
Networks and Corporate Infrastructure
Key Digital Networking Technologies
Physical Transmission Media
Types of Networks
Broadband Network Services and Technologies

8.3 ***THE INTERNET***
Internet Addressing, Architecture, and Governance
Internet Services
The Internet and Business Value
The World Wide Web
Intranets and Extranets
Next-Generation Networks and Internet2

8.4 ***TECHNOLOGIES AND TOOLS FOR COMMUNICATION AND E-BUSINESS***
E-Mail, Chat, Instant Messaging, and Electronic Discussions
Groupware, Teamware, and Electronic Conferencing
Internet Telephony
Virtual Private Networks

8.5 ***MANAGEMENT OPPORTUNITIES, CHALLENGES, AND SOLUTIONS***
Opportunities
Management Challenges
Solution Guidelines

- Develop network-based business processes
- Develop technology strategy and standards

- Revise teaching methods
- Develop new collaboration processes among teachers, students, and parents

- Develop Web site
- Install IP telephony
- Install multiservice network

Business Challenges
- Declining revenue
- Increasing demand for services

Management

Organization

Technology

Information System
- Consolidate voice and data communication
- Provide online learning

Business Solutions
- Increase service
- Reduce cost

Opening Case: Okanagan-Skaha School District Does More with Less Using Networking and the Internet

The Okanagan-Skaha School District in Penticon, British Columbia, is in an area blessed with "beaches, peaches, and wine." It is also an area where tax revenues and school budgets have been declining for several years while demand for information access and support services continue to grow. School administrators realized that the district's 19 schools serving more than 8,000 students had to do more with less. How could this be done? The answer: Use networking and the Internet to cut operational costs while expanding programs to schools and the wider community.

The school district had been using an expensive public telephone network and an aging data network that had cobbled together many different hardware and operating system platforms. Working with Cisco Systems and Boardwalk Communications, the school district standardized desktop hardware and operating system software and replaced its outdated data and telephone networks with a multiservice network that can run voice, data, and video applications using the Internet Protocol (IP).

The network supports Voice over IP (VoIP) technology which converts each teacher's classroom computer into a telephone that can transmit voice data in the form of packets over a data network based on the Internet Protocol. Using just a handset

and a microphone, teachers can make calls from their computers without having to make a special trip to the administration office. This IP telephony system reduces the number of phone lines needed by the district from 150 to 25 and provides a uniform system for voice mail and systems administration, saving the district about $60,000 per year.

Teachers have developed Web sites for collaborating with students and parents. For example, physics instructor Dan Bergstrom uses software to demonstrate difficult scientific concepts so that students can make observations, take measurements, and manipulate the data to understand what is actually going on. Lecture notes are linked to lab notes, homework questions, and test questions. Students and teachers can access the district's network and all of its applications wherever they are working using a Web browser program.

The new learning environment helps students learn responsibility and time management. Each class has a Web site with its course schedule, rules and expectations, and dates for tests and assignments.

Sources: Howard Baldwin, "Thinking Big," *Cisco IQ Magazine*, First Quarter 2004 and "Okanagan-Skaha School District and Cisco Solutions Empower Teachers, Students and Parents," www. cisco.com, accessed April 27, 2004.

The Okanagan-Skaha School District had been hampered by outdated networking technology, which prevented it from operating efficiently. By installing a multiservice network based on Internet technology that could handle voice, data, and video, the district realized multiple benefits. The network was simpler to administer, reduced communication costs, and provided a platform for multimedia Web sites where students could learn more effectively.

As more and more companies rely on telecommunications and the Internet to run their business, it is important for you to understand exactly how this technology can improve business performance and provide value. This chapter introduces the most important networking concepts and technologies used in business. We identify the key decisions and challenges you will face as a manager in implementing and using networking and the Internet.

8.1   TELECOMMUNICATIONS AND NETWORKING IN TODAY'S BUSINESS WORLD

We are in the midst of a networking and communications revolution driven by new Internet-based technologies and new business models and processes that leverage the new technologies. This networking revolution shows no sign of abating. Until about 1990, all business communication was accomplished primarily through the postal system or telephone system as voice or fax traffic. Today a great deal of this communication takes place using computers and e-mail, the Internet, cellular telephones, and mobile computers connected to wireless networks.

In 2004 there were an estimated 1 billion instant messages sent every day in the United States, 4 billion e-mails, and millions of spreadsheets and database files. On average, people in the United States transmitted about 4 billion digital photos to each other over the Internet and downloaded about 65 million music files (Madden and Rainie, 2004; Telecommunications Industry Association, 2004).

In 2004, businesses in the United States invested $149 billion in telecommunications and networking equipment and spent an additional $620 billion on telecommunications services, for a combined $769 billion spent on telecommunications of (Figure 8-1). This is nearly as much as U.S. business spent on computing hardware, software, and services (about $1 trillion in 2004). Worldwide, telecommunications equipment and services spending hit $2.2 trillion in 2004 and will expand to over $3 trillion by 2007.

Today, networking and the Internet are now nearly synonymous with doing business. To this extent, nearly all business has become "e-business" insofar as the business is enabled by or based upon digital networks.

The Business Telecommunications Environment

Understanding the telecommunications environment for business turns out to be a very complicated task (Figure 8-2). The purpose of business telecommunications is to make it possible for employees, customers, and suppliers to communicate whenever necessary to accomplish their work. A telecommunications environment provides *connectivity on demand* by providing communication channels for text, voice, and video images. In practice this is not so simple. Figure 8-2 illustrates the complexity of providing text, voice, and video connectivity to business firms.

The network infrastructure for a large corporation consists of many different kinds of networks for both data and voice communication. At the center of the corporate networking infrastructure is a collection of local area networks (LANs) linked to other local area networks and to firmwide corporate networks. A series of servers supports a corporate Web site, a corporate intranet, and perhaps an extranet. Some of these servers link to other large computers supporting backend systems. The infrastructure also supports a mobile sales force using cell phones; mobile employees linking to the company Web site or internal company networks using mobile wireless local area networks (Wi-Fi networks); and a videoconferencing system to support managers across the world. In addition to these computer networks, the firm's infrastructure includes a totally separate telephone network that handles most voice data.

FIGURE 8-1   *Telecommunications spending in the United States, 2002–2007.*

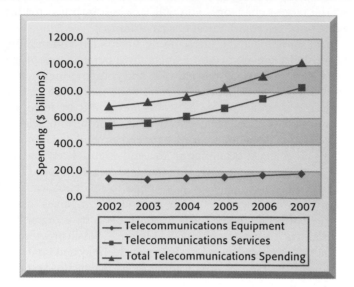

Whereas investment in telecommunications equipment has increased slowly since 2002, spending on telecommunication services has advanced at more than 10 percent a year. Telecommunication services include transport services (wireless and local exchange), specialized services (Internet backbone and local connections), and support services (wireless, cable, and high-speed broadband services; wireless public networks; enterprise networks).

Sources: Bureau of Economic Analysis, National Income and Product Accounts, 2004; and eMarketer and the Telecommunications Industry Association, 2004.

FIGURE 8-2   *Corporate network infrastructure.*

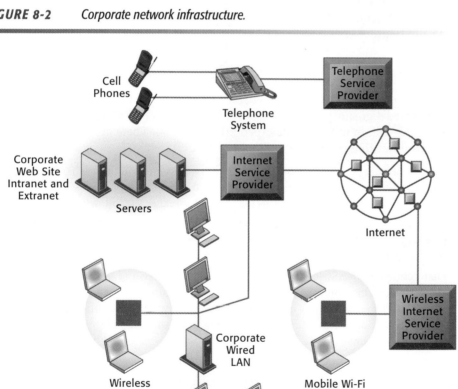

Today's corporate network infrastructure is a collection of many different networks from the public switched telephone network; to the Internet; to corporate local area networks linking workgroups, departments, or office floors.

Most of these disparate networks are moving toward a single common foundation based on Internet technologies. One of the major problems facing corporations today is how to integrate all the different communication networks and channels into a coherent system that enables information to flow from one part of the corporation to another, from one system to another. As more and more communication systems become digital, it is easier to integrate them into a coherent telecommunications system.

Today many different vendors provide some or all of the required **connectivity**. However, very few can provide all the different types of connectivity needed—text, video, and voice. A wide variety of technologies is required, everything from ordinary telephone service to Internet service, **broadband** Internet service, wireless Internet, and wireless cell phones. One of the largest challenges you will face as a business manager is making choices about your firm's telecommunications environment.

One way to start examining and understanding a firm's telecommunications environment is to consider that there are two fundamentally different types of telecommunications networks that firms use: telephone networks and computer networks.

Telephone networks historically handled voice communication, and computer networks handled data traffic. Telephone networks were built by telephone companies throughout the twentieth century using voice transmission technologies (hardware and software), and these companies almost always operated as regulated monopolies throughout the world. This all changed beginning in the mid-1980s. Telephone networks today offer much more than voice service, including standard and high-speed Internet, wireless telephone, and even video on demand services similar to residential cable systems.

Computer networks were originally built by computer companies seeking to transmit data between distributed workstations. Today these networks have largely been replaced by the Internet and local area networks in offices and buildings, which provide mostly data connectivity but which have expanded to include Internet telephony and limited video services.

These historically different telecommunications networks are slowly merging into a single digital network using shared Internet-based standards and equipment. Business managers like you will need to navigate this very complex environment, make the right decisions and investments, and choose the right vendors. This chapter can help clarify your thinking and improve your decision making.

Networking and Communications Trends

The telecommunications revolution is enabled by new digital technologies, facilitated by market-oriented regulatory policies worldwide, and financed by global capital investment exceeding $2.2 trillion in worldwide expenditures in 2004. There are seven major trends in telecommunications of which you should be aware:

- Rapid technological innovation has resulted in a proliferation of new hardware devices and new alternatives for business communications, from cell phones with Internet access to Wi-Fi wireless local area networks (described in the following chapter).
- Continuing telecommunications deregulation has encouraged competition, lowered prices in long-distance telephone service, and created many alternatives for local phone service such as wireless, cable, and Internet telephones.
- Distinctions between telephone, cable television, Internet, and satellite telecommunication providers have blurred as each type of network supplier seeks to provide video, voice, and data connectivity in a single network. For instance, telephone companies are moving into video delivery and programming using their digital subscriber lines into the house and small businesses.
- Growing dominance of Internet technologies in voice, video, and data communications.
- Rapid growth in "last-mile" high-speed broadband connections to homes and businesses. Today, more than half of U.S. Internet users have broadband access provided by telephone and cable TV companies. In Korea, more than 90 percent of the Internet population has broadband access (Vara, 2004).
- Rapid growth in wireless telephone, wireless computer networks, and mobile Internet devices.
- Growing scope of communication-intense services and products, such as Internet telephone and telephone photography.

DEREGULATION OF THE TELECOMMUNICATIONS INDUSTRY

This revolution in telecommunications technology and services was facilitated by a regulatory environment that sought to break up old monopolies, encourage new market entrants, and reduce barriers to competition. Until about 20 years ago, the American Telephone and

Telegraph (AT&T) Company provided virtually all telecommunications services in the United States, with monopoly status granted by the Communications Act of 1934. In return for the right to provide a single national telephone and telegraph network, Congress regulated the prices that AT&T could charge and required universal service to be extended to all regions of the country, including rural America, at a "reasonable price."

Starting in the mid-1950s , the U.S. Department of Justice started antitrust action to end the AT&T monopoly and promote more competition in telecommunications. A 1982 court order, implemented in 1984, broke up AT&T into a long-distance company and seven independent, regional telephone companies (Regional Bell Operating Companies, known as RBOCs) that were ordered to permit long-distance competitors such as Sprint and MCI to offer service to local customers. The court order stimulated competition in manufacturing, long-distance, and information services, while retaining regulated monopoly in local telephony.

The Telecommunications Act of 1996 unleashed even more competition in telecommunications by permitting long-distance companies to offer local service and by requiring RBOCs to lease local last-mile lines to competitors at a deeply discounted rate. The act also allowed RBOCs to enter the long-distance market.

The combined impact of technological change and deregulation was to create a much more complex, diverse, and competitive telecommunications environment. Table 8-1 illustrates the complexity of today's telecommunications environment and the options available to business firms and individuals as a result of deregulation and new technologies. New entrants have poured into local communications markets—from wireless cell phones and networks for wireless Internet access to long-distance carriers, VoIP Internet telephone service providers, and cable companies.

Prior to deregulation and new technologies, telecommunications decisions were comparatively simple. AT&T was the only choice for telephone service, and for data communication, managers chose IBM, Digital Equipment, or another networking/computer firm. Now managers must make decisions that involve comparing many competitors and many different technologies, all of which promise to provide effortless connectivity.

The Business Value of Telecommunications and Networking

The reason behind the explosion in e-mail, instant messages, wireless computing, wireless Internet, and cell phones is very clear: businesses and managers derive extraordinary business value from participating in communications networks. According to Metcalfe's Law, the more people participating in a network, the greater its value.

Robert Metcalfe was founder of Netscape Communications in 1992, which produced one of the first commercial Web browsers. Metcalfe argued that the Internet would grow exponentially because the value of the network to individuals grows exponentially as the network adds members (see Figure 8-3). In a simple two-person (two-node) network, each person can talk to one other and there are two communication paths (Person A→Person B and Person B→Person A). With three nodes, there are six communication links (AB, BA, AC, CA, BC, and CB). Each communication link can be thought of as adding value. In the case of business use of the Internet, millions of businesspeople are available nearly instantly online, and the value of participating in high-speed digital networks for every participant has grown exponentially as the cost of joining the Internet has plummeted.

Other business value impacts of the telecommunications revolution are as follows:

- Declining transaction costs. It becomes less and less expensive to purchase, sell, and bargain in both digital and traditional markets as networking becomes less expensive and more powerful.

- Declining agency costs. The costs of managing falls as managers are able to monitor the performance of employees and markets remotely over networks.

- Increased agility. Managers and firms can respond more rapidly to changing business environment conditions.

- Higher quality management decisions. Managers are more likely to make the right decisions based on correct and timely information.

TABLE 8-1 *Telephone Industry Firms*

LONG DISTANCE CARRIERS	SERVICES PROVIDED
AT&T	Local, long distance, Internet access, Internet telephone, business continuity and transaction-based voice and data services
MCI	Local, long distance, high-speed Internet access, dedicated Web hosting, managed network services
Sprint	Local, long distance, wireless, high-speed Internet access, Internet telephone, high-speed data networks, Internet data networks, online conferencing services, managed network services, business continuity services
BABY BELLS (LOCAL NETWORKS)	
Verizon Communications Inc.	Local, long distance, wireless, high-capacity data networks, Internet telephone and Internet data networks, Internet access, network security
SBC	Local, long distance, wireless, Internet access, digital satellite television, wireless Internet access, Web hosting, network management services, videoconferencing services
Bell South	Local, long distance, Internet access, digital satellite television, managed network services, shared Web hosting, managed network services
Qwest	Local, long distance, wireless, Internet access, digital satellite television, digital TV programming through phone lines, satellite TV, Internet telephone, dedicated Web hosting, integrated voice, data and Internet services
CABLE TELEPHONE PROVIDERS	
Comcast, CableVision TimeWarner Cable (AOL for Internet)	Cable TV, digital cable TV, high-speed Internet access, Internet telephone
PURE WIRELESS PROVIDERS	
Virgin Mobile	Wireless voice service, text messaging, downloaded music and movie clips on mobile phones
T-Mobile	Wireless voice service, picture and video messaging, instant messaging, e-mail, mobile Web access, downloadable games, wireless Internet access
Nextel	Walkie-talkie services, wireless voice service, e-mail, wireless Internet access, wireless data services, wireless e-mail, instant messaging and multimedia messaging
ATT Wireless (acquired by SBC)	Wireless voice service, music downloads, text messaging, wireless mobile phone Internet access, e-mail, text messaging, instant messaging
INTERNET TELEPHONY (VoIP) PROVIDERS	
Vonage (Private)	Internet telephone voice and Fax services

- Declining geographical barriers. Coffee growers in Central America now use the Internet to obtain the best prices from large wholesale buyers in the United States, eliminating local intermediaries and brokers.

- Declining temporal barriers. Some goods such as software can be produced around the clock, seven days a week. For instance, software production workers in India come to work in the morning to work on software projects handed off by U.S. software workers who have just finished their day.

8.2 CONTEMPORARY NETWORKING INFRASTRUCTURE

Now that we have sketched the outlines of the broad business telecommunications environment, let's examine more closely computer networks and networking technologies.

FIGURE 8-3   *Metcalfe's Law.*

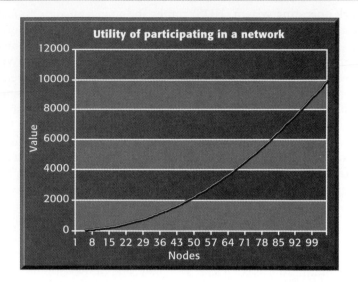

According to Metcalfe's Law, the value of participating in a network grows exponentially as the network adds more members.

Networks and Corporate Infrastructure

In its simplest form, a network consists of two or more connected computers. Figure 8-4 illustrates the major hardware, software, and transmission components used in a simple network: computers, network interfaces, a connection medium, network operating system software, and either a hub or a switch. Each computer on the network contains a network interface device called a **network interface card** (**NIC**). Most personal computers today have this card built into the motherboard. The connection medium for linking

FIGURE 8-4   *Components of a simple network.*

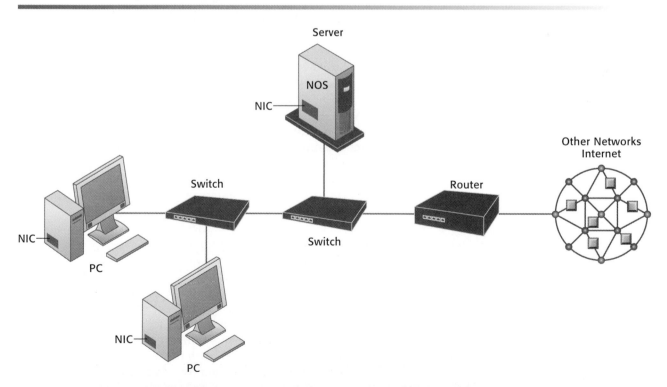

Illustrated here is a very simple network, consisting of computers, network operating system software, cable (wiring) to connect the devices, network interface cards, switches, and a router. In this illustration, the network operating system (NOS) resides on a dedicated server.

network components can be a telephone wire, coaxial cable, or radio signal in the case of cell phone and wireless local area networks (Wi-Fi networks).

The **network operating system (NOS)** routes and manages communications on the network and coordinates network resources. It can reside on every computer in the network, or it can reside primarily on a dedicated server for all the applications on the network. Microsoft Windows Server 2003, along with the server versions of Windows 2000, Linux, and Novell NetWare, is the most widely used local area network operating system.

Most networks also contain a switch or a hub acting as a connection point between the computers. **Hubs** are very simple devices that connect network components, sending a packet of data to all other connected devices. A **switch** has more intelligence than a hub and can filter and forward data to a specified destination. Switches are used within individual networks. To communicate with another network, the network would use a device called a router. A **router** is a special communications processor used to route packets of data through different networks, ensuring that the message sent gets to the correct address.

Key Digital Networking Technologies

Contemporary digital networks and the Internet are based on three key technologies: client/server computing, the use of packet switching, and the development of widely used communications standards (the most important of which is Transmission Control Protocol/Internet Protocol [TCP/IP]) for linking disparate networks and computers.

CLIENT/SERVER COMPUTING

In Chapter 6, we introduce client/server computing in which client computers are connected in a network with one or more server computers. Client/server computing is a distributed computing model in which much of the processing power is located within small, inexpensive client computers under user control and resides on desktops, laptops, or in handheld devices. These powerful clients are linked to one another through a network that is controlled by a network server computer. The server sets the rules of communication for the network and provides every client with an address so it can be found by others on the network.

Client/server computing has largely replaced centralized mainframe computing in which most or all of the processing takes place on a central large mainframe computer. Client/server computing has extended computing to departments, workgroups, factory floors, and other parts of the business that could not be served by a centralized architecture. The Internet is the largest implementation of client/server computing.

PACKET SWITCHING

Packet switching is a method of slicing digital messages into parcels called packets, sending the packets along different communication paths as they become available, and then reassembling the packets once they arrive at their destinations (see Figure 8-5). Prior to the development of packet switching, computer networks used leased, dedicated telephone circuits to communicate with other computers in remote locations. In circuit-switched networks, such as the telephone system, a complete point-to-point circuit is assembled, and then communication can proceed. These dedicated circuit-switching techniques were expensive and wasted available communications capacity—the circuit was maintained regardless of whether any data were being sent.

Packet switching makes much more efficient use of the communications capacity of a network. In packet-switched networks, messages are first broken down into small bundles of data called packets. There are many different packet sizes, depending on the communications standard being used. The packets include information for directing the packet to the right address and for checking transmission errors along with the data.

Data are gathered from many users, divided into small packets, and transmitted over available communications channels using routers. Each packet travels independently through these networks. Packets of data originating at one source can be routed through many different paths and networks before being reassembled into the original message when they reach their destinations.

FIGURE 8-5 *Packed-switched networks and packet communications.*

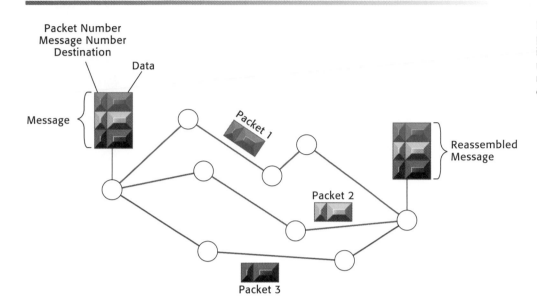

Packet Number
Message Number
Destination
Data
Message
Packet 1
Packet 2
Packet 3
Reassembled Message

Data are grouped into small packets, which are transmitted independently over various communications channels and reassembled at their final destination.

Packet switching does not require a dedicated circuit but can make use of any spare capacity that is available. If some lines are disabled or too busy, the packets can be sent over any available line that eventually leads to the destination point.

TCP/IP AND CONNECTIVITY

A typical telecommunications network consists of diverse hardware and software components that need to work together to transmit information. Different components in a network can communicate with each other only by adhering to a common set of rules called protocols. A **protocol** is a set of rules and procedures governing transmission of information between two points in a network. In the past many diverse proprietary and incompatible protocols often forced business firms to purchase computing and communications equipment from a single vendor. But today corporate networks are increasingly using a single, common, worldwide standard called **Transmission Control Protocol/Internet Protocol (TCP/IP)**.

TCP/IP provides a universally agreed-on method for breaking up digital messages into packets, routing them to the proper addresses, and then reassembling them into coherent messages. TCP/IP was developed during the early 1970s to support U.S. Department of Defense Advanced Research Projects Agency (DARPA) efforts to help scientists transmit data among different types of computers over long distances.

TCP/IP uses a suite of protocols, the main ones being TCP and IP. *TCP* refers to the Transmission Control Protocol (TCP), which handles the movement of data between computers. TCP establishes a connection between the computers, sequences the transfer of packets, and acknowledges the packets sent. *IP* refers to the Internet Protocol (IP), which is responsible for the delivery of packets and includes the disassembling and reassembling of packets during transmission. Figure 8-6 illustrates the four-layered Department of Defense reference model for TCP/IP.

1. Application layer. Enables client application programs to access the other layers and defines the protocols that applications use to exchange data. One of these application protocols is the Hypertext Transfer Protocol (HTTP) that is used to transfer Web page files.

2. Transport layer. Responsible for providing the application layer with communication and packet services. This layer includes TCP and other protocols.

3. Internet layer. Responsible for addressing, routing, and packaging data packets called IP datagrams. The Internet Protocol (IP) is one of the protocols used in this layer.

4. Network interface layer. At the bottom of the reference model, the network interface layer is responsible for placing packets on and receiving them from the physical network medium, which could be any networking technology.

FIGURE 8-6 *The Transmission Control Protocol/Internet Protocol (TCP/IP) reference model.*

This figure illustrates the four layers of the TCP/IP reference model for communications.

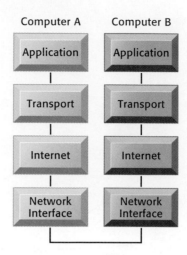

Two computers using TCP/IP can communicate even if they are based on different hardware and software platforms. Data sent from one computer to the other passes downward through all four layers, starting with the sending computer's application layer and passing through the network interface layer. After the data reach the recipient host computer, they travel up the layers and are reassembled into a format the receiving computer can use. If the receiving computer finds a damaged packet, it asks the sending computer to retransmit it. This process is reversed when the receiving computer responds.

Open Systems Interconnect (OSI) is another network connectivity model developed by the International Standards Organization for linking different types of computers and networks. Like TCP/IP, OSI enables a computer connected to a network to communicate with any other computer on the same network or a different network, regardless of the manufacturer. OSI divides the telecommunications process into seven layers.

Physical Transmission Media

Networks can use different kinds of physical transmission media, including twisted wire, coaxial cable, fiber optics, and media for wireless transmission. Each has advantages and limitations. A wide range of speeds is possible for any given medium depending on the software and hardware configuration.

TWISTED WIRE

Twisted wire consists of strands of copper wire twisted in pairs and is the oldest electronic transmission medium. Nearly all of the telephone systems in buildings used twisted wires for analog communication, and these same wires can be used for digital communication as well.

An *analog signal* is represented by a continuous waveform that passes through a communications medium and has been used for voice communication. A *digital signal* is a discrete, rather than a continuous, waveform. It transmits data coded into two discrete states: 1 bits and 0 bits, which are represented as on–off electrical pulses. Computers use digital signals, so if one wants to use the analog telephone system to send digital data, a device called a **modem** is required to translate digital signals into analog form (see Figure 8-7). *Modem* stands for modulation/demodulation.

Although twisted wire is low in cost and usually is already in place, it can be relatively slow and noisy for transmitting data. There are limits to the amount of data that ordinary twisted wire can carry, but new software and hardware used by local telephone companies have raised twisted-wire transmission capacity to make it useful for high-speed connectivity to the Internet at speeds up to 1 megabits per second (Mbps), or 1 million bits per second.

FIGURE 8-7   *Functions of the modem.*

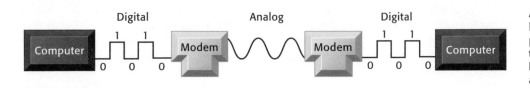

A modem is a device that translates digital signals from a computer into analog form so that they can be transmitted over analog telephone lines. The modem also is used to translate analog signals back into digital form for the receiving computer.

COAXIAL CABLE

Coaxial cable, similar to that used for cable television, consists of thickly insulated and shielded copper wire, which can transmit a larger volume of data than twisted wire. Cable is commonly used for local area networks because it is a faster, more interference-free transmission medium, typically operating at 10 Mbps at the desktop and 100 Mbps and 1 Gbps in network backbones.

FIBER OPTICS AND OPTICAL NETWORKS

Fiber-optic cable consists of strands of clear glass fiber, each the thickness of a human hair, which are bound into cables. Data are transformed into pulses of light, which are sent through the fiber-optic cable by a laser device at rates varying from 500 kilobits to several trillion bits per second in experimental settings. Fiber-optic cable is considerably faster, lighter, and more durable than wire media and is well suited to systems requiring transfers of large volumes of data. However, fiber-optic cable is more difficult to work with, more expensive, and harder to install.

Until recently, fiber-optic cable had been used primarily as the high-speed network backbone, whereas twisted wire and coaxial cable were used to connect the backbone to individual businesses and households. A **backbone** is the part of a network that handles the major traffic. It acts as the primary path for traffic flowing to or from other networks. Now, local cable companies and telephone companies are bringing fiber optic cable to homes and small businesses.

These **optical networks** can transmit all types of traffic—voice, data, and video—over fiber cables and provide the massive bandwidth for new types of services and software. Using optical networks, on-demand video, software downloads, and high-quality digital audio can be accessed using set-top boxes and other information appliances without severe degradation in quality or delays.

Optical networks can boost capacity by using **dense wavelength division multiplexing (DWDM)**. **Multiplexing** enables a single communications channel to carry simultaneous data transmissions from multiple sources. (This can be accomplished by dividing a high-speed channel into multiple channels of slower speeds or by assigning each transmission source a very small slice of time for using a high-speed channel.) DWDM boosts transmission capacity by using many different colors of light, or different wavelengths, to carry separate streams of data over the same fiber strand at the same time. DWDM combines up to 160 wavelengths per strand and can transmit up to 6.4 terabits per second (Tbps) over a single fiber. This technology will enable communications service providers to add transmission capacity to an existing fiber-optic network without having to lay more fiber-optic cable. Before wavelength division multiplexing, optical networks could use only a single wavelength per strand.

WIRELESS TRANSMISSION

Much of the recent growth in communications and networking services is based on wireless technologies that use radio frequencies or infrared signals to send data between communications devices without using wires. Common technologies for wireless data transmission include microwave transmission, communication satellites, pagers, cellular telephones, personal digital assistants (PDAs), and smart phones. Personal computers using wireless Wi-Fi network interface cards can connect to corporate networks and the Internet in locations where a Wi-Fi transmitter has been installed. Wireless transmission has become so important to corporations that we devote the following chapter to this topic.

TRANSMISSION SPEED

The total amount of digital information that can be transmitted through any telecommunications medium is measured in bits per second (bps). One signal change, or cycle, is required to transmit one or several bits; therefore, the transmission capacity of each type of telecommunications medium is a function of its frequency. The number of cycles per second that can be sent through that medium is measured in **hertz**—one hertz is equal to one cycle of the medium.

The range of frequencies that can be accommodated on a particular telecommunications channel is called its **bandwidth**. The bandwidth is the difference between the highest and lowest frequencies that can be accommodated on a single channel. The greater the range of frequencies, the greater the bandwidth and the greater the channel's transmission capacity. Table 8-2 compares the transmission speeds of the major types of transmissions media.

Types of Networks

There are many different kinds of networks and ways of classifying them. One way of looking at networks is in terms of their geographic scope (see Table 8-3).

LOCAL AREA NETWORKS

The first computer networks appeared in the early 1960s and consisted of display terminals linked to a mainframe computer within the same building. Researchers at Xerox Palo Alto Research Center (PARC) invented the first local area network in the early 1970s to connect desktop machines into a coherent computing facility. These networks enabled desktop machines to share printers, communicate with one another, and store files on a central desktop machine called a server.

Today most people in corporations connect to other employees and groups using local area networks. A **local area network (LAN)** is designed to connect personal computers and other digital devices within a half mile or 500-meter radius. LANs typically connect a few computers in a small office, all the computers in one building, or all the computers in several buildings in close proximity. LANs interconnected within multiple buildings or a geographic area such as a school campus or military base create a **campus area network (CAN)**. LANs can link to long-distance wide area networks (WANs, described later in this section) and other networks around the world by using the Internet.

Review Figure 8-4, which could serve as a model for a small LAN that might be used in an office. One computer is a dedicated network file server, providing users with access to shared computing resources in the network, including software programs and data files. The server determines who gets access to what and in which sequence. The router connects the LAN to other networks, which could be the Internet or another corporate network, so that the LAN can exchange information with networks external to it. The most common LAN operating systems are Windows, Linux, and Novell. Each of these network operating systems supports TCP/IP as its default networking protocol.

TABLE 8-2 *Typical Speeds and Costs of Telecommunications Transmission Media*

Medium	Speed
Twisted wire	Up to 100 Mbps
Microwave	Up to 600+ Mbps
Satellite	Up to 600+ Mbps
Coaxial cable	Up to 1 Gbps
Fiber-optic cable	Up to 6+ Tbps

Mbps = megabits per second
Gbps = gigabits per second
Tbps = terabits per second

TABLE 8-3 *Types of Networks*

Type	Area
Local area network (LAN)	Up to 500 meters (half a mile); an office or floor of a building
Campus area network (CAN)	Up to 1,000 meters (a mile); a college campus or corporate facility
Metropolitan area network (MAN)	A city or metropolitan area
Wide area network (WAN)	Transcontinental or global area

Ethernet is the dominant LAN standard at the physical network level, specifying the physical medium to carry signals between computers, access control rules, and a standardized frame, or set of bits used to carry data over the system. Originally, Ethernet supported a data transfer rate of 10 Mbps. Newer versions, such as Fast Ethernet and Gigabit Ethernet, support data transfer rates of 100 Mbps and 1 Gbps, respectively, and are used in network backbones.

The LAN illustrated in Figure 8-4 uses a client/server architecture where the network operating system resides primarily on a single file server and the server provides much of the control and resources for the network. Alternatively, LANs may use a **peer-to-peer** architecture. A peer-to-peer network treats all processors equally and is used primarily in small networks with 10 or fewer users. The various computers on the network can exchange data by direct access and can share peripheral devices without going through a separate server.

In LANs using the Windows Server 2003 family of operating systems, the peer-to-peer architecture is called the *workgroup network model* in which a small group of computers can share resources, such as files, folders, and printers over the network without a dedicated server. The Windows *domain network model*, in contrast, uses a dedicated server to manage the computers in the network.

Larger LANs have many clients and multiple servers, with separate servers for specific services, such as storing and managing files and databases (file servers or database servers), managing printers (print servers), storing and managing e-mail (mail servers), or storing and managing Web pages (Web servers).

Sometimes LANs are described in terms of the way their components are connected together, or their **topology**. There are three major LAN topologies: star, bus, and ring (see Figure 8-8).

In a star topology, all devices on the network connect to a single hub. Figure 8-8 illustrates a simple **star network** in which all network components connect to a single hub. All network traffic flows through the hub. In an *extended star*, multiple layers or hubs are organized into a hierarchy.

In a bus topology, one station transmits signals, which travel in both directions along a single transmission segment. All of the signals are broadcast in both directions to the entire network. All machines on the network receive the same signals, and software installed on the clients enables each client to listen for messages addressed specifically to it. **Bus networks** are the most common Ethernet topology.

A ring topology connects network components in a closed loop. Messages pass from computer to computer in only one direction around the loop, and only one station at a time may transmit. **Ring networks** are used primarily in older LANs using Token Ring networking software.

METROPOLITAN AND WIDE AREA NETWORKS

Wide area networks (WANs) span broad geographical distances—entire regions, states, continents, or the entire globe. The most universal and powerful WAN is the Internet. Computers connect to a WAN through public networks such as the telephone system, private cable systems, or through leased lines or satellites. A **metropolitan area network** (**MAN**) is a network that spans a metropolitan area, usually a city and its major suburbs. Its geographic scope falls between a WAN and a LAN. MANs sometimes provide Internet connectivity for local area networks in a metropolitan region.

FIGURE 8-8   *Network topologies.*

The three basic network topologies are the bus, star, and ring.

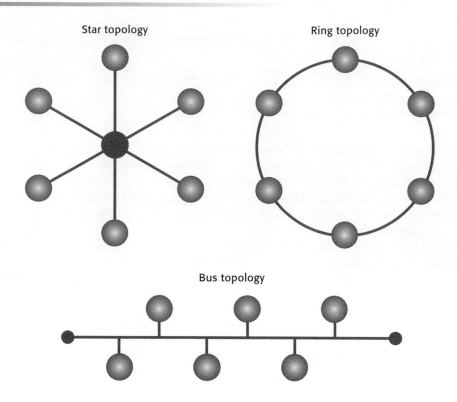

Star topology

Ring topology

Bus topology

Broadband Network Services and Technologies

A number of network services and technologies are available to companies that need high-speed transmission or access to the Internet.

Frame relay is a shared network service that is faster and less expensive than packet switching and can achieve transmission speeds ranging from 56 kilobits per second (Kbps) to more than 40 Mbps. Frame relay packages data into frames similar to packets but takes advantage of higher-speed, more reliable digital circuits that require less error checking than packet

The Texas Health and Human Services Consolidated Network HHSCN) provides wide-area network (WAN) services to Texas state agencies and certain private sector partners.

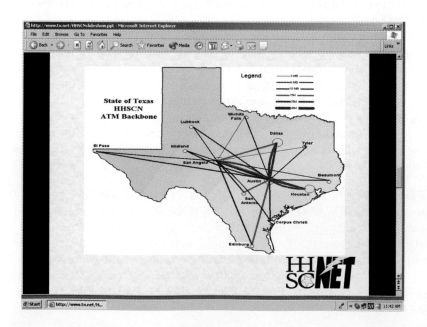

switching. The major telecommunications carriers provide frame relay services. Many organizations use frame relay services in their international data communication networks.

A technology called **Asynchronous Transfer Mode (ATM)** can handle many types of network traffic and provides transmission speeds ranging from 1.5 Mbps up to more than 9 Gbps. Like frame relay, ATM takes advantage of high-bandwidth digital circuits, parceling information into fixed 53-byte cells, of which 48 bytes are for data and 5 are for header information. ATM can pass data between computers from different vendors and is popular for transmitting data, video, and audio over the same network. Many telecommunications carrier and large enterprise backbone networks use ATM.

Integrated Services Digital Network (ISDN) is an international standard for dial-up network access that integrates voice, data, image, and video services in a single link. There are two levels of ISDN service: basic rate ISDN (which can transmit 128 Kbps) and primary rate ISDN (which can transmit at 1.5 Mbps).

ISDN is being replaced by Digital Subscriber Line (DSL). Like ISDN, **Digital Subscriber Line (DSL)** technologies also operate over existing copper telephone lines to carry voice, data, and video, but they have higher transmission speeds than ISDN. There are several categories of DSL. Asymmetric digital subscriber lines (ADSLs) support a transmission rate of 1.5 to 9 Mbps when receiving data and up to 640 Kbps when sending data. Symmetric digital subscriber lines (SDSLs) support the same transmission rate for sending and receiving data of up to 3 Mbps.

Other high-capacity services include cable modems and T lines. **Cable modems** are modems designed to operate over cable TV lines. They can provide high-speed access to the Web or corporate intranets of up to 4 Mbps. However, cable modems use a shared line so that transmission slows down if there are a large number of local users sharing the cable line, although this problem can be solved by increasing the capacity of the local cable.

Firms that have large amounts of data to move across the continent, or around the world, or which have high security or guaranteed service level requirements, often lease high-speed data lines from communication providers, typically long-distance telephone companies. These lines are designated as **T lines**, which range from T-1 to T-4. A T-1 line offers up to twenty-four 64-Kbps channels that can support a total data transmission rate of 1.544 Mbps. Each of these 64-Kbps channels can be configured to carry voice or data traffic. A T-3 line offers delivery at 45 Mbps, and a T-4 line (although rarely used) can deliver up to 274 Gbps. Leasing a T-1 line costs about $1,000 to $2,000 per month, whereas a T-3 line costs around $10,000 to $30,000 per month. Table 8-4 summarizes these network services.

TABLE 8-4 *Broadband Network Services*

Service	Description	Bandwidth
Frame relay	Packages data into frames for high-speed transmission over reliable circuits that require less error checking than packet switching	56 Kbps to 40+ Mbps
Asynchronous Transfer Mode (ATM)	Parcels data into uniform 53-byte cells for high-speed transmission; can transmit data, video, and audio over the same network	1.5 Mbps to 9+ Gbps
Integrated Services Digital Network (ISDN)	Dial-up network access standard that can integrate voice, data, and video services	Basic rate ISDN: 128 Kbps Primary rate ISDN: 1.5 Mbps
Digital Subscriber Line (DSL)	Series of technologies for high-capacity transmission over copper wire	ADSL: Up to 9 Mbps for receiving and up to 640 Kbps for sending data SDSL: Up to 3 Mbps for both sending and receiving
Cable modem	Service for high-speed transmission of data over cable TV lines that are shared by many users	Up to 4 Mbps
T lines	Dedicated lines for high-speed secure data transmission and Internet connection	T-1: 1.544 Mbps T-3: 45 Mbps

8.3 THE INTERNET

The Internet is the most well known and largest implementation of client/server computing and internetworking, linking hundreds of thousands of individual networks all over the world, which in turn service over 600 million individual PCs or host computers. The word *Internet* derives from the word **internetworking** or the linking of separate networks, each of which retains its own identity, into an interconnected network. In the United States, about 160 million people access the Internet at home or work. The World Wide Web is the most popular service provided by the Internet, providing users access to over 500 billion Web pages containing text, graphics, audio, video, and other objects (Brandt, 2004).

Technically, the Internet is a global information system defined by three characteristics (Federal Networking Council, 1995):

- A network composed of computers and other devices that are logically linked together by a unique address space based on the Internet Protocol

- A network where network devices (computers, routers, hubs, and other equipment) are able to support communications using TCP/IP or other compatible protocols

- A network that provides high-level services layered on a communication and network infrastructure

The incredible success of the Internet as the world's most extensive, public communication system that rivals the global telephone system in reach and range results from a number of design factors. Table 8-5 describes four design factors that have made the Internet a nearly universal communications system.

This gigantic network of networks began in the early 1970s as a U.S. Department of Defense network to link scientists and university professors around the world. Individuals connect to the Internet in two ways. Most homes connect to the Internet by subscribing to an Internet service provider. An **Internet service provider (ISP)** is a commercial organization with a permanent connection to the Internet that sells temporary connections to retail subscribers. These connections can be provided by telephone lines, cable lines, or wireless connections. America Online, Yahoo!, and Microsoft Network (MSN) are ISPs in addition to being content portals. There are over 4,000 independent ISPs in the United States. Individuals also connect to the Internet through their business firms, universities, or research centers that have designated Internet domains, such as **www.ibm.com**.

TABLE 8-5 *Internet Success Design Factors*

Design Factor	Significance
Hourglass layered architecture	The Internet can be viewed as an hourglass in which the network technology and higher-level user services such as the Web are separated. Users do not have to be concerned with the details of network hardware or configurations; developers are not restricted in evolving new technologies by fears of interrupting user services.
End-to-end architecture	The network provides a very basic level of message transport to computers at the edge or end of the network, whereas intelligence and processing power is located in or close to the devices attached at the edge of the network.
Scalability	The Internet's design enables it to support a growing volume of communications per device and growing numbers of devices without changes in network principles or design.
Distributed design and decentralized control	Except for the allocation of address blocks and top-level domain management, control of the network—such as how data packets are routed through the Internet—is distributed among thousands of local network operations and hundreds of other participants (such as local ISPs, campus and metropolitan network operators).

Source: Based on "The Internet's Coming of Age," National Research Council, Washington, D.C., 2000.

Internet Addressing, Architecture, and Governance

The Internet is based on the TCP/IP networking protocol suite described earlier in this chapter. Every computer on the Internet is assigned a unique **Internet Protocol (IP) address**, which currently is a 32-bit number represented by four strings of numbers and ranging from 0 to 255. For instance, the IP address of **www.microsoft.com** is 207.46.250.119.

When a user sends a message to another user on the Internet, the message is first decomposed into packets using the TCP protocol. Each packet contains its destination address. The packets are then sent from the client to the network server, and from there onto as many other servers as necessary to arrive at a specific computer with a known address. At the destination address, the packets are reassembled into the original message.

THE DOMAIN NAME SYSTEM

Because it would be incredibly difficult for Internet users to remember strings of 12 numbers, a **Domain Name System (DNS)** converts IP addresses to domain names. The **domain name** is the English-like name that corresponds to the unique 32-bit numeric Internet Protocol (IP) address for each computer connected to the Internet. DNS servers maintain a database containing IP addresses mapped to their corresponding domain names. To access a computer on the Internet, users need only specify its domain name.

DNS has a hierarchical structure (see Figure 8-9). At the top of the DNS hierarchy is the root domain. The child domain of the root is called a top-level domain, and the child domain of a top-level domain is called a second-level domain. Top-level domains are two- and three-character names you are familiar with from surfing the Web, such as .com, .edu, .gov, and the various country codes such as .ca for Canada or .it for Italy. Second-level domains have two parts, designating a top-level name and a second-level name—such as buy.com, nyu.edu, or amazon.ca. A host name at the bottom of the hierarchy designates a specific computer on either the Internet or a private network.

The most common domain extensions currently available and officially sanctioned are shown in the following list. Countries also have domain names such as .uk, .au, and .fr (United Kingdom, Australia, and France, respectively). Also shown in the following list are recently approved top-level domains .biz and .info, as well as new domains under

FIGURE 8-9   *The Domain Name System.*

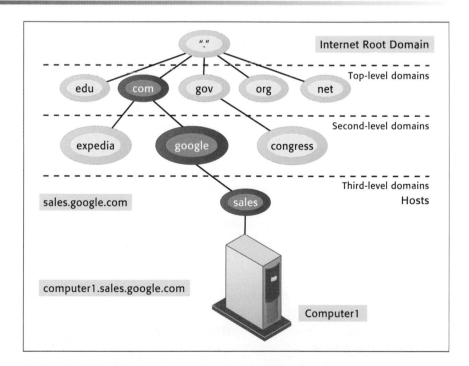

The Domain Name System is a hierarchical system with a root domain, top-level domains, second-level domains, and host computers at the third level.

consideration. In the near future, this list will expand to include many more types of organizations and industries.

.com	Commercial organizations/businesses
.edu	Educational institutions
.gov	U.S. government agencies
.mil	U.S. military
.net	Network computers
.org	Nonprofit organizations and foundations

New top-level domains approved May 15, 2001:

.biz	Business firms
.info	Information providers

Proposed top-level domains:

.aero	Air transport industry
.coop	Cooperatives
.museum	Museums
.name	Individuals
.pro	Professionals

LIMITATIONS ON IP ADDRESSES: IPV4 AND IPV6

How many unique addresses are there on the Internet if over 600 million people are connected? The Internet addressing convention described earlier is called Internet Protocol version 4 (IPv4). This "dotted quad" addressing scheme (a 32-bit string of numbers organized into four sets of numbers ranging from 0 to 255) contains up to 4 billion addresses (2 to the 32nd power).

Because many corporations and governments have been given large blocks of millions of IP addresses to accommodate current and future workforces, and because of sheer Internet population growth, the world is running out of available IP addresses using this scheme. A new version of the IP addressing scheme being developed is called Internet Protocol version 6 (IPv6) and contains 128-bit addresses (2 to the power of 128), or over a quadrillion possible unique addresses (National Research Council, 2000).

INTERNET ARCHITECTURE

Internet data traffic courses over transcontinental high-speed backbone networks that generally operate today in the range of 45 Mbps to 2.5 Gbps (Figure 8-10). These trunk lines are typically owned by long-distance telephone companies (called network service providers) or by national governments. Local connection lines are owned by regional telephone and cable television companies in the United States that connect retail users in homes and businesses to the Internet. The regional networks lease access to ISPs, private companies, and government institutions.

INTERNET GOVERNANCE

No one "owns" the Internet, and it has no formal management organization per se. However, worldwide Internet policies are established by a number of different organizations and government bodies including the following:

- The Internet Architecture Board (IAB), which helps define the overall structure of the Internet
- The Internet Corporation for Assigned Names and Numbers (ICANN), which assigns IP addresses
- The Internet Network Information Center (InterNIC), which was created by the U.S. Department of Commerce, and assigns domain names
- The Internet Engineering Steering Group (IESG), which oversees standards setting with respect to the Internet

FIGURE 8-10   *Internet network architecture.*

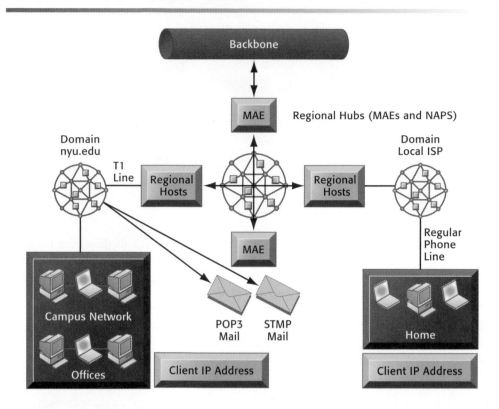

The Internet backbone connects to regional networks, which in turn provide access to Internet service providers, large firms, and government institutions. Network access points (NAPs) and metropolitan area exchanges (MAEs) are hubs where the backbone intersects regional and local networks and where backbone owners connect with one another.

- The Internet Engineering Task Force (IETF), which forecasts the next step in the growth of the Internet, keeping watch over its evolution and operation
- The Internet Society (ISOC), which is a consortium of corporations, government agencies, and nonprofit organizations that monitors Internet policies and practices
- The World Wide Web Consortium (W3C), which sets Hypertext Markup Language (HTML) and other programming standards for the Web

Although none of these organizations has actual control over the Internet and how it functions, they can and do influence government agencies, major network owners, and ISPs. In addition to these professional bodies, the Internet must also conform to the laws of the sovereign nation-states in which it operates, as well as the technical infrastructures that exist within the nation-state. Although in the early years of the Internet and the Web very little legislative or executive interference occurred, this situation is changing as the Internet plays a growing role in the distribution of information and knowledge, including content that some find objectionable.

Each organization pays for its own networks and its own local Internet connection services, a part of which is paid to the long-distance trunk line owners through monthly charges for telephone and Internet services. Consequently, the costs of e-mail and other Internet connections tend to be far lower than equivalent voice, postal, or overnight delivery, making the Internet a very inexpensive communications medium. It is also a very fast method of communication, with messages arriving anywhere in the world in a matter of seconds, or after a minute or two at most.

Internet Services

The Internet is based on client/server technology. Individuals using the Internet control what they do through client applications on their computers, such as Web browser software. All the data, including e-mail messages and Web pages, are stored on servers. A client uses the Internet to request information from a particular Web server on a distant

TABLE 8-6 *Major Internet Services*

Capability	Functions Supported
E-mail	Person-to-person messaging; document sharing
Usenet newsgroups	Discussion groups on electronic bulletin boards
LISTSERVs	Discussion groups using e-mail mailing list servers
Chatting and instant messaging	Interactive conversations
Telnet	Logging on to one computer system and doing work on another
FTP	Transferring files from computer to computer
World Wide Web	Retrieving, formatting, and displaying information (including text, audio, graphics, and video) using hypertext links

computer, and that server sends the requested information back to the client over the Internet. Chapters 6 and 7 describe how Web servers can also work with application servers and database servers to access information from an organization's internal information systems applications and their associated databases.

Client platforms today include not only PCs and other computers but also cell phones, small handheld digital devices, and other information appliances. An **information appliance** is a device, such as an Internet-enabled cell phone or a TV Internet receiver for Web access and e-mail, that has been customized to perform a few specialized computing tasks well with minimal user effort. People are increasingly relying on these easy-to-use specialized information appliances to connect to the Internet.

A client computer connecting to the Internet has access to a variety of services. These services include e-mail, electronic discussion groups (Usenet newsgroups and LISTSERVs), chatting and instant messaging, **Telnet**, **File Transfer Protocol (FTP)**, and the World Wide Web. Table 8-6 provides a brief description of these services.

Each Internet service is implemented by one or more software programs. All of the services may run on a single server computer, or different services may be allocated to different machines. Only one disk drive may store the data for these services, or multiple disks may store data for each type, depending on the amount of information being stored. Figure 8-11 illustrates one way that these services might be arranged in a multitiered client/server architecture.

FIGURE 8-11 *Client/server computing on the Internet.*

Client computers running Web browser and other software can access an array of services on servers over the Internet. These services may all run on a single server or on multiple specialized servers.

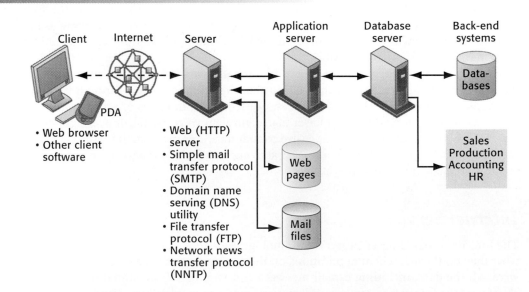

The Internet and Business Value

The Internet is unique and very different from any other networking technology developed in the past (Table 8-7). These unique features translate directly into business value for all businesses, worldwide, whether they are small or large.

In addition to lowering transaction and agency costs, the Internet creates value for businesses by enabling digital markets that are more efficient than traditional markets. In digital markets firms can interact directly with consumers, creating the possibility for developing new products and services and customizing existing products. Companies can use e-mail, chat, instant messaging, and electronic discussion groups to create ongoing dialogues with their customers and use the information they have gathered to tailor communication and products precisely to the needs of each individual (see Chapter 4). For all of these reasons, the Internet and Internet technology have become the primary infrastructure for electronic business, electronic commerce, and the digital firm.

The World Wide Web

The World Wide Web (the Web) is the most popular Internet service. It is a system with universally accepted standards for storing, retrieving, formatting, and displaying information using a client/server architecture. Web pages are formatted using hypertext with embedded links that connect documents to one another and that also link pages to other objects such as sound, video, or animation files. When you click a graphic and a video clip plays, you have clicked a hyperlink.

The Web was invented in the period from 1989 to 1991 by Dr. Tim Berners-Lee and his associates at the European Particle Physics Laboratory, better known as CERN. Information shared on the Web remained text-based until 1993, when Marc Andreessen and others at the National Center for Supercomputing Applications (NCSA) at the University of Illinois created a Web browser with a graphical user interface (GUI) called Mosaic that made it possible to view documents on the Web graphically—using colored backgrounds,

TABLE 8-7 *Seven Unique Features of Internet Technology*

Technology Feature	Business Significance
Ubiquity—Internet/Web technology is available everywhere: at work, at home, and elsewhere by using mobile devices, anytime.	The marketplace is extended beyond traditional boundaries and is removed from a temporal and geographic location. Shopping can take place anywhere in a marketspace. Customer convenience is enhanced, shopping costs reduced.
Global reach—The technology reaches across national boundaries, around the earth.	Commerce is enabled across cultural and national boundaries seamlessly and without modification. The marketspace includes potentially billions of consumers and millions of businesses worldwide.
Universal standards—There is one set of technology standards, namely Internet standards.	One set of technical media standards exists across the globe.
Richness—It is possible to transmit video, audio, and text messages.	Video, audio, and text marketing messages can be integrated into a single marketing message and consumer experience.
Interactivity—The technology works through interaction with the user.	Businesses can engage consumers in a dialogue that dynamically adjusts the experience for each individual consumer and makes the consumer a co-participant in process of delivering goods to market.
Information density—The technology reduces information costs and raises quality.	Information processing, information storage, and communication costs drop dramatically, while currency, accuracy, and timeliness improve greatly. Information becomes plentiful, cheap, and accurate.
Personalization/Customization—The technology enables personalized messages to be delivered to individuals as well as groups.	Businesses can personalize marketing messages and customize products and services based on individual consumer characteristics and preferences.

images, and even primitive animations. In 1994, Andreessen and Jim Clark founded Netscape, which created the first commercial browser, Netscape Navigator. In August 1995, Microsoft Corporation released its own browser, called Internet Explorer (IE), which became the dominant Web browser.

HYPERTEXT

Web pages are based on a standard Hypertext Markup Language (HTML), which formats documents and incorporates dynamic links to other documents and pictures stored in the same or remote computers (see Chapter 6). Web pages are accessible through the Internet because Web browser software on your computer can request Web pages stored on an Internet host server using the **Hypertext Transfer Protocol (HTTP)**. HTTP is the communications standard used to transfer pages on the Web. For example, when you type a Web address in your browser such as **www.sec.gov**, your browser sends an HTTP request to the sec.gov server requesting the home page of sec.gov.

HTTP is the first set of letters at the start of every Web address, followed by the domain name, which specifies the organization's server computer that is storing the document. Most companies have a domain name that is the same as or closely related to their official corporate name. The directory path and document name are two more pieces of information within the Web address that help the browser track down the requested page. Together, the address is called a **Uniform Resource Locator (URL)**. When typed into a browser, a URL tells the browser software exactly where to look for the information. For example, in the following URL:

http://www.megacorp.com/content/features/082602.html

http names the protocol used to display Web pages, **www.megacorp.com** is the domain name, **content/features** is the directory path that identifies where on the domain Web server the page is stored, and **082602.html** is a document name and the format of the document (it is an HTML page).

WEB SERVERS

A Web server is software for locating and managing stored Web pages. It locates the Web pages requested by a user client on the computer where they are stored and delivers the Web pages to the user's computer. The most common Web server in use today is Apache HTTP Server, which controls 67 percent of the market. Apache is an open source product that is free of charge and can be downloaded from the Web (Figure 8-12). Microsoft's Internet Information Services is the second most commonly used Web server with a 22 percent market share.

Server applications usually run on dedicated computers, although they can all reside on a single computer in small organizations. Chapters 6 and 7 describe how Web servers can also work with application servers and database servers to access information from an organization's internal information systems applications and their associated databases.

FIGURE 8-12 *Major Web server providers.*

This figure illustrates the market share of each of the major Web server software providers.

Source: Based on data from Netcraft Web Server Survey, July 2004, www.serverwatch.internet.com/netcraft.

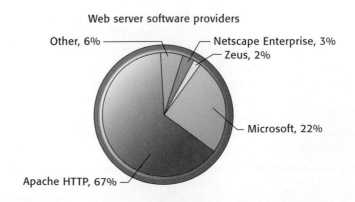

Web server software providers

Other, 6% — Netscape Enterprise, 3%
Zeus, 2%
Microsoft, 22%
Apache HTTP, 67%

A typical Web site is a collection of Web pages linked to a **home page**—a text and graphical screen display that usually welcomes the user and provides a brief description of the organization that has established the Web site. Most home pages offer a way to contact the organization or individual. The person in charge of an organization's Web site is called a **Webmaster**.

SEARCHING FOR INFORMATION ON THE WEB

Locating information on the Web is a critical function. Billions of Web pages exist, and this number will quickly double. No comprehensive catalog of Web sites is available. The principal methods of locating information on the Web are Web site directories, search engines, intelligent agents, and broadcast or "push" technology.

Search Engines and Web Site Directories   Several companies have created directories of Web sites and their addresses, providing search tools for finding information. Yahoo! is an example. People or organizations submit sites of interest, which then are classified and ranked by human experts. To search the Yahoo! directory, you enter one or more keywords and then see displayed a list of categories and sites with those keywords in the title.

Other search tools do not require Web sites to be preclassified and will search Web pages automatically. Such tools, called **search engines**, can find Web sites that may be little known. Search engines contain software that looks for Web pages containing one or more of the search terms, then they display matches ranked by a method that usually involves the location and frequency of the search terms. These search engines create indexes of the Web pages they visit. The search engine software then locates Web pages of interest by searching through these indexes.

Some search engines are more comprehensive or current than others, depending on how their components are tuned, and some also classify Web sites by subject categories. Some search engines, such as AltaVista, seek to visit every Web site in existence, read the contents of the home page, identify the most common words or keywords, and create a huge database of domain names with keywords. Sometimes the search engines will only read the metatags and other keyword sections of the home page. The program that search engines unleash on the Web to perform this indexing function is called a *spider* or *crawler*. Because search engines do not always overlap, users may miss a page on one engine but pick it up on another.

Google has become overwhelmingly the most popular Web search tool and is used for about 55 percent of all searches on the Web through its own site. Google works by sending "crawlers" across the Internet and using its 10,000 computers to update its index

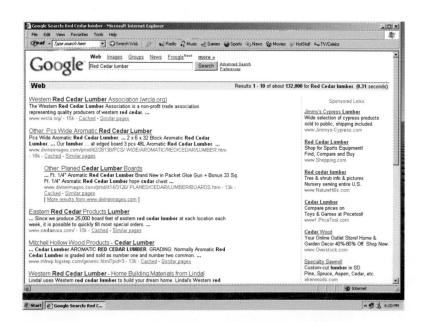

Google is the most popular Web search engine. It offers search-based advertising. The listings displayed under "Sponsored Links" are links paid by advertisers. The unbiased results of the search are displayed under "Web".

of about 8 billion Web pages. Google software indexes and ranks sites based on relevance measured by how prominently the user's search terms appear on the pages that include them, the number of users who access these pages, and the number of outside links to a particular page.

Specialized search engines are also available to help users locate specific types of information easily. For example, PubMed specializes in searches for articles in medical journals. Some Web sites for locating information such as Yahoo! and Google have become so popular and easy to use that they also serve as portals for the Internet (see Chapter 4).

Search engines are no longer simply search engines but instead have transformed themselves into major shopping tools by offering search-related advertising. When users enter a search term at Google, MSN Search, Yahoo!, or any of the other sites serviced by these search engines, they receive two types of listings: sponsored links, for which advertisers have paid to be listed (usually at the top of the search results page) and unsponsored search results. For firms who pay the search engine companies $2 billion a year for sponsored links, this feature represents a powerful new marketing tool called **search-based advertising** that precisely matches consumer interest and timing with an advertising message.

Although the major search engines are used for locating general information of interest to users, they have also become a crucial tool within e-commerce sites. Customers can more easily search for the product information they want with the help of an internal search program; the difference is that within Web sites, the search engine is limited to finding matches from that one site.

Intelligent Agent Shopping Bots   Chapter 12 details the capabilities of software agents with built-in intelligence that can gather or filter information and perform other tasks to assist users. The Web crawler and spider software for searching the Web that we mentioned earlier is one type of intelligent software agent. **Shopping bots** are another type of intelligent agent software for searching the Internet for shopping information. Shopping bots can help people interested in making a purchase filter and retrieve information about products of interest, evaluate competing products according to criteria the users have established, and negotiate with vendors for price and delivery terms (Kocas, 2002–2003; Maes, Guttman, and Moukas, 1999). Many of these shopping agents search the Web for pricing and availability of products specified by the user and return a list of sites that sell the item along with pricing information and a purchase link. Table 8-8 compares various types of electronic commerce agents.

Broadcast and Push Technology   Instead of spending hours surfing the Web, users can have the information in which they are interested delivered automatically to their desktops through **push technology**. This technology enables a computer to broadcast information of interest directly to the user, rather than having the user "pull" content from Web sites.

Special client software enables the user to specify the categories of information he or she wants to receive, such as news, sports, financial data, and so forth, and how often this information should be updated. After finding the kind of information requested, push server programs serve it to the push client. The streams of information distributed

TABLE 8-8   *Examples of Electronic Commerce Agents*

Agent	Description
MySimon	Real-time shopping bot that searches more than 1,000 affiliated and unaffiliated merchants in 90 categories
Froogle	Shopping bot service powered by Google that looks for the lowest prices of products for sale on the Web
BizRate	Provides comparison shopping information, including customer reviews, for millions of products and thousands of online stores
BestBookBuys.com	Shopping bot that searches 26 online bookstores to help users find the lowest prices for titles they specify
PricingCentral.com	Price comparison shopping portal that indexes price search engines and shopping bots into a comprehensive directory
Valuefind	Searches for the best deal from retail vendors and auctions; users can limit the search to a specific Web site

Froogle features a shopping bot that can search Internet retailers for price and availability of products specified by the user.

through push technology are known as channels. Using push technology to transmit information to a select group of individuals is one example of **multicasting**. (LISTSERVs sending e-mail to members of specific mailing lists is another.)

Push technology is the foundation of new content services for both computers and mobile devices. New online content services, such as the LATimes.com's NewsDirect, are using push technology to provide paid subscribers with news articles customized to their interests. Online marketplaces and exchanges can use push services to alert buyers about price changes and special deals. Companies are using internal push channels to broadcast important information, such as price updates or new competitor products, on their own private networks.

The Semantic Web   Most of the Web's content today is designed for humans to read and for computers to display, not for computer programs to analyze and manipulate. Search engines can discover when a particular term or keyword appears in a Web document, but they do not really understand its meaning or how it relates to other information on the Web. The **Semantic Web** is a collaborative effort led by the World Wide Web Consortium to make Web searching more efficient by reducing the amount of human involvement in searching for and processing Web information. Tim Berners-Lee wrote the road map for the Semantic Web in 1998.

Although the Semantic Web is still in its infancy, it could eventually bring additional structure to the meaningful content of Web pages so that machines could make more sense of the Web and data in Web pages could be processed automatically. Two important technologies for developing the Semantic Web are Extensible Markup Language (XML), which we introduced in Chapter 6, and the Resource Description Framework (RDF). RDF goes beyond XML to describe data in terms of objects and their interrelationships. Once data on the Web have specific meanings and rules for reasoning about them, agent technology could be harnessed to unleash software agents roaming from page to page to automatically carry out sophisticated tasks for users.

One prototype application is the Semantic Web Environmental Directory (SWED) in the United Kingdom. Instead of centralizing the storage, management, and ownership of information about environmental organizations and projects, SWED continually harvests data and uses these data to create the directory (Frauenfelder, 2004).

Intranets and Extranets

Organizations can use Internet networking standards and Web technology to create private networks called intranets. We introduced intranets in Chapter 1, explaining that an intranet is an internal organizational network that provides access to data across the enterprise. It uses the existing company network infrastructure along with Internet connectivity standards and software developed for the World Wide Web. Intranets can create networked applications that can run on many different kinds of computers throughout the organization, including mobile handheld computers and wireless remote access devices.

Whereas the Web is available to anyone, an intranet is private and is protected from public visits by **firewalls**—security systems with specialized software to prevent outsiders from entering private networks. Intranet software technology is the same as that of the World Wide Web. Intranets use HTML to program Web pages and to establish dynamic, point-and-click hypertext links to other pages. The Web browser and Web server software used for intranets are the same as those on the Web. A simple intranet can be created by linking a client computer with a Web browser to a computer with Web server software using a TCP/IP network with software to keep unwanted visitors out.

EXTRANETS

A firm can create an extranet to allow authorized vendors and customers to have limited access to its internal intranet. For example, authorized buyers could link to a portion of a company's intranet from the public Internet to obtain information about the costs and features of the company's products. The company can use firewalls to ensure that access to its internal data is limited and remains secure; firewalls can also authenticate users, making sure that only authorized users can access the site.

Both intranets and extranets reduce transaction and agency costs by providing additional connectivity for coordinating disparate business processes within the firm and for linking electronically to customers and suppliers. Private industrial networks (introduced in Chapter 4) are based on extranets because they are so useful for linking organizations with suppliers, customers, or business partners. Extranets often are employed for collaborating with other companies for supply chain management, product design and development, and training efforts.

Next-Generation Networks and Internet2

The public Internet was not designed to handle massive numbers of very large files flowing to and from hundreds of millions of host computers. Today's Internet often has delays and does not guarantee any specific level of service. Experimental national research networks (NRNs) are developing high-speed, next-generation networks to address this problem. These private networks do not replace the public Internet, but they do provide test beds for leading-edge technology for research institutions, universities, and corporations that may eventually migrate to the public Internet. These national research networks include 6NET in Europe, the Asia Pacific Advanced Network (APAN), and CANARIE in Canada.

In the United States, **Internet2** and Next-Generation Internet (NGI) are NRN consortia representing 200 universities, private businesses, and government agencies that are working on a new, robust, high-bandwidth version of the Internet. The advanced networks provide an environment in which new technologies can be tested and enhanced. Several new networks have been established, including Abilene and vBNS (a WorldCom/National Science Foundation partnership).

Abilene and vBNS (short for very high performance backbone network service) are high-performance backbone networks with bandwidths ranging from 2.5 Gbps to 9.6 Gbps that interconnect the gigaPoPs used by Internet2 members to access the network. A *gigaPoP* is a regional gigabit Point of Presence, or point of access, to the Internet2 network that supports data transfers at the rate of 1 Gbps or higher. In February 2003, Internet2 announced it had successfully tested the Abilene network at more than 8 Gbps in a cross-country test that lasted 5 hours (**www.internet2.edu**, 2003).

Internet2 research groups are developing and implementing new quality of service technologies that will enable the Internet to provide different levels of service, depending on the type and importance of the data being transmitted. Today's Internet transmissions are considered "best effort"—packets of data arrive without any regard to the priority of their contents. Different types of packets could be assigned different levels of priority as they travel over the network. For example, packets for applications such as videoconferencing, which must arrive simultaneously without any break in service, would receive higher priority than e-mail messages, which do not have to be delivered instantaneously.

Other Internet2 projects include the development of more effective routing practices; standardized middleware that incorporates identification, authentication, and security services that today are often handled as a part of applications running on the Internet; and advanced applications for distributed computation, virtual laboratories, digital libraries, distributed learning, and tele-immersion.

The most recent effort to revitalize the Internet is called PlanetLab. It is a grassroots group of nearly 100 computer scientists at academic institutions backed by leading high-tech companies such as Intel and Hewlett-Packard. PlanetLab researchers are building an experimental overlay network on top of the Internet using computers called smart nodes attached to traditional Internet routers. Each smart node runs software that divides the machine's resources among many users, vastly increasing processing power, data storage capacity, and the ability to track data and programs flowing over the Internet. The smart nodes could be used to create a much smarter and more flexible network than today's Internet that could potentially monitor itself for damaging computer viruses, relieve bottlenecks automatically, and make users' personal computer programs and files portable to any Internet-connected terminal (Roush, 2003).

8.4 TECHNOLOGIES AND TOOLS FOR COMMUNICATION AND E-BUSINESS

Internet technology provides many tools used today in business for communication and coordination.

E-Mail, Chat, Instant Messaging, and Electronic Discussions

E-mail enables messages to be exchanged from computer to computer, eliminating costly long-distance telephone charges while expediting communication between different parts of the organization. In addition to providing electronic messaging, e-mail software has capabilities for routing messages to multiple recipients, forwarding messages, and attaching text documents or multimedia files to messages. Although some organizations operate their own internal electronic mail systems, a great deal of e-mail today is sent through the Internet.

CHATTING AND INSTANT MESSAGING

Over 80 percent of employees in U.S. companies now communicate interactively using **chat** or instant messaging tools. Chatting enables two or more people who are simultaneously connected to the Internet to hold live, interactive conversations. Chat groups are divided into channels, and each is assigned its own topic of conversation. The first generation of chat tools was for written conversations in which participants typed their remarks using their keyboard and read responses on their computer screen. Chat systems now feature voice and even video chat capabilities.

Instant messaging is a type of chat service that enables participants to create their own private chat channels. The instant messaging system alerts the user whenever someone on his or her private list is online so that the user can initiate a chat session with other individuals. A number of competing instant messaging systems exist for consumers, including Yahoo! Messenger, MSN Messenger, and AOL Instant Messenger. Some of these systems can provide voice-based instant messages so that a user can click a Talk button and have an online conversation with another person. Companies concerned with security are building proprietary instant messaging systems using tools such as Lotus Sametime. Many online retail businesses offer chat services on their Web sites to attract visitors, to encourage repeat purchases, and to improve customer service.

ELECTRONIC DISCUSSION GROUPS

Usenet newsgroups are worldwide discussion groups posted on Internet electronic bulletin boards on which people share information and ideas on a defined topic, such as

The L.L.Bean Web site provides on-line chat capabilities to answer visitors' questions and to help them find items for which they are looking.

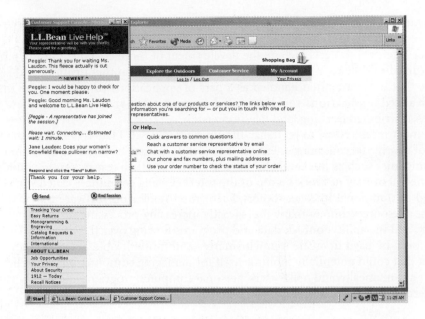

radiology or rock bands. Anyone can post messages on these bulletin boards for others to read. Many thousands of groups exist that discuss almost all conceivable topics.

Another type of forum, **LISTSERV**, enables discussions to be conducted through predefined groups but uses e-mail mailing list servers instead of bulletin boards for communications. If you find a LISTSERV topic you are interested in, you can subscribe. From then on, through e-mail, you will receive all messages sent by other subscribers concerning that topic. You can, in turn, send a message to your LISTSERV and it will automatically be broadcast to the other subscribers.

Groupware, Teamware, and Electronic Conferencing

Groupware provides capabilities for supporting enterprise-wide communication and collaborative work. Individuals, teams, and workgroups at different locations in the organization can use groupware for writing and commenting on group projects, sharing ideas and documents, conducting electronic meetings, tracking the status of tasks and projects, scheduling, and sending e-mail. Any group member can review the ideas of other group members at any time and add to them, or individuals can post a document for others to comment on or edit. Commercial groupware products such as Lotus Notes and OpenText's LiveLink, which were originally based on proprietary networks, have been enhanced to integrate with the Internet or private intranets. Groove is a new groupware tool based on peer-to-peer technology, which enables people to work directly with other people over the Internet without going through a central server.

Teamware is similar to groupware, but features simpler Internet tools for building and managing work teams. Although teamware application development capabilities are not as powerful as those provided by sophisticated groupware products, teamware enables companies to implement collaboration applications easily that can be accessed using Web browser software. Documentum eRoom and Lotus Team Workplace are examples of commercial teamware products.

ELECTRONIC CONFERENCING TOOLS

Internet Connection —

The Internet Connection for this chapter will direct you to a series of Web sites where you can complete an exercise to evaluate various Internet conferencing systems.

A growing number of companies are using Internet conferencing tools to stage meetings, conferences, and presentations online. Web conferencing and collaboration software provides a virtual conference table where participants can view and modify documents and slides or share their thoughts and comments using chat, audio, or video. The current generation of such tools from Lotus, Microsoft, and WebEx work through a standard Web browser. These forms of electronic conferencing are growing in popularity because they reduce the need for face-to-face meetings, saving travel time and cost.

Internet Telephony

Hardware and software have been developed for **Internet telephony**, enabling companies to use Internet technology for telephone voice transmission over the Internet or private networks. (Internet telephony products sometimes are called IP telephony products.) **Voice over IP (VoIP)** technology uses the Internet Protocol (IP) to deliver voice information in digital form using packet switching, avoiding the tolls charged by local and long-distance telephone networks (see Figure 8-13). Calls that would ordinarily be transmitted over public telephone networks would travel over the corporate network based on the Internet Protocol or the public Internet. IP telephony calls can be made and received with a desktop computer equipped with a microphone and speakers or with a VoIP-enabled telephone.

Early VoIP systems would drop voice packets or deliver them late, causing voice conversations to be choppy or garbled. As the technology matures, these performance problems are being resolved. VoIP networks pose some additional security issues, which are described in Chapter 10.

Although there are up-front investments required for an IP phone system, VoIP can reduce communication and network management costs by 20 to 30 percent. In addition to lowering long-distance costs and eliminating monthly fees for private lines, an IP network provides a single infrastructure for running voice, data, and video applications. Companies no longer have to maintain separate networks for each or provide support services and personnel for each different type of network. Businesses can use this technology for applications such as Internet conference calls using video, for Web sites that enable users to reach a live customer service representative by clicking a link on a Web page, or for unified messaging. **Unified messaging** systems combine voice mail, e-mail, and faxes so they can all be obtained from one system.

Another advantage of VoIP is its flexibility. Phones can be added or moved to different offices without rewiring or reconfiguring the network. If a phone needs to be added or moved in a traditional telephone network, some additional cabling might be required and the firm would have to pay the telecommunications vendor to do the installation. With VoIP, users merely plug their VoIP-enabled phones into the IP network at the new locations. Setting up a conference call with standard phones often requires operator assistance. With VoIP, a conference call can be arranged by a simple click and drag operation on the computer screen to select the names of the conferees. Voice and e-mail can be combined into a single directory. The Window on Organizations details why more and more businesses are adopting this technology.

FIGURE 8-13   How IP telephony works.

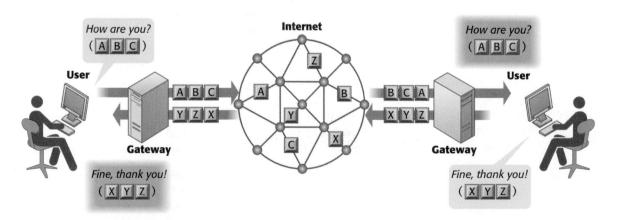

An IP phone call digitizes and breaks up a voice message into data packets that may travel along different routes before being reassembled at their final destination. A processor nearest the call's destination, called a gateway, arranges the packets in the proper order and directs them to the telephone number of the receiver or the IP address of the receiving computer.

WINDOW ON ORGANIZATIONS

INTERNET TELEPHONES: WHY NOT?

Allied Domecq is the world's second largest publicly traded company for international spirits, wine, and quick-service restaurants, with nearly 12,000 employees and 50 businesses worldwide. Its brands include Courvoisier, Kahlua, Beefeater Gin, and the Dunkin' Donuts and Baskin-Robbins food chains.

Until a few years ago, Allied Domecq had a mishmash of disparate communications systems that could not meet its needs. Mark Whittle, senior manager for global communications at Domecq's Windsor, Canada, unit, used to say, "We had trouble getting data across our computer room, let alone North America." While modernizing its network infrastructure, the company decided to start using VoIP. Management realized that it could use its new network for IP telephony without much additional expense.

Domecq's Windsor computer center supports IP telephony services for six smaller sites in sales and marketing, which include California, Florida, Chicago, and New York. Consolidating each site's individual contracts for network maintenance and telephone systems produced savings. Besides reducing long-distance fees, the VoIP network eliminated service and travel fees that telecommunications companies typically charge to add lines, create new extensions, or change the phone system. Domecq's various North American business units realized time savings for their own employees responsible for administering the traditional telephone networks. Some of these employees spent 15 to 20 percent of their time on this task. The VoIP network freed up their time so they could focus on more important business initiatives.

Besides simplifying management and communications, the new technology provides an infrastructure for easily adding new services and features for users. When 100 executives moved after Domecq's spirits division was reorganized, very few changes had to be made to provide them with telephone service. No new wiring was required. They merely picked up their phones and moved to a new desk.

Bruce Cumming, the vice president of National Money Mart Co., a financial-services firm based in Victoria, British Columbia, uses VoIP to manage his voice calls from his computer. When he wants to call someone, he clicks on the name in the contact list in his computer's Microsoft Outlook program. When the number rings and someone answers, he talks to them on his speaker phone. Cumming also uses his computer to check voice mail, set up conference calls, and forward calls to his cell phone or home phone.

Canada's Maritime Steel and Foundries Ltd. has used a VoIP system from 3Com for more than four years. Maritime Steel has five divisions in three cities: Alberton on Prince Edward Island and New Glasgow and Dartmouth in Nova Scotia. Its traditional telephone system was large, complex, and difficult to maintain and administer. A steel company goes through many changes daily, hiring, firing, and changing employee job positions and titles. The communications system has to mirror these changes. It might cost $200 for a telecommunications specialist to visit each site to make such changes.

Sean Green, Maritime's manager of information systems, wanted a system that is easy to administer. By using VoIP, he now spends very little time taking care of Maritime's telephone needs. The system can be administered from a Web page, which Green can access anywhere he is working. Creating a new extension for an employee, for example, only takes about ten seconds. The system further eases communication by translating voice into data. Voice messages can be turned into Wav files (Windows' digital audio format) and accessed by the recipient as audible e-mail. That means that Maritime's executives can bring up a Web page anywhere in the world and access all their messages, including voice. Maritime's system paid for itself within two years.

Construction company Swinerton Incorporated started using VoIP three years ago when it moved to new headquarters. Swinerton had been building more cubicles and spending money for the telephone provider to add more lines and move telephones around. Swinerton lacked sufficient internal staff to support a conventional phone system, so it purchased a system for $230,000 from NEC Corporation that included a server, 220 phones, two operator consoles, a voice mail system, management software, and training. Managers can control the system and make changes to phones and user accounts in many different locations from a single console.

Swinerton's VoIP service isn't quite as reliable as the conventional telephone system. Now and then a NEC handset fails. Larry Mathews, Swinerton's director of information technology (IT), observes that a VoIP system is "only going to be as reliable as your data network," and users are accustomed to conventional telephones that always work. VoIP telephones may perform more like computers, which need to be rebooted from time to time, and are vulnerable to hackers, computer viruses, and other security risks. If IP voice traffic isn't properly secured, it could be intercepted, copied, or redirected. Nevertheless, Swinerton is so pleased with the system that it installed 700 VoIP lines in offices from Houston to Oakland, California, and Seattle.

Sources: Susan Maclean, "Dialing IP for Increased Productivity," ItWorld Canada.com, accessed January 1, 2004; "Ready for Prime Time," *Wall Street Journal*, January 12, 2004; and David M. Ewalt, "The New Voice Choice," *Information Week*, March 1, 2004.

To Think About: How does VoIP technology provide value for businesses? What management, organization, and technology issues would have to be addressed to convert from a conventional telephone system to one using VoIP?

FIGURE 8-14   *The growth of Internet telephony.*

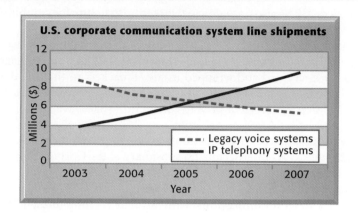

Internet telephony systems are rapidly replacing traditional legacy voice systems for business communication.

Sources: Infotech and authors.

Today about 10 to 12 percent of all calls in the United States run over VoIP networks. Telecommunications and cable companies such as AT&T, Verizon, and Cablevision are starting to offer Internet calling services for consumers. Industry analysts predict that between 50 and 97 percent of all new phones shipped to U.S. businesses will use VoIP by 2007 and that cable companies offering Internet phone service will grab nearly 20 percent of residential phone lines from regional telephone companies over the next decade (see Figure 8-14). The majority of long-distance phone calls in China use VoIP, and China's new local phone systems are also being built with this infrastructure (Ewalt, 2004; Grant, 2004; Ramstad and Brown, 2004).

Virtual Private Networks

Internet technology can also reduce communication costs by enabling companies to create virtual private networks as low-cost alternatives to private WANs. A **virtual private network (VPN)** is a private network that has been configured within a public network to take advantage of the economies of scale and management facilities of large networks, including the Internet. The VPN provides the organization with the same capabilities at a much lower cost than owned or leased lines that can be used only by one organization. Although some VPNs run over proprietary networks open only to subscribers, many companies are turning to VPNs based on the Internet Protocol (IP) that run over the public Internet.

A virtual private network based on the Internet Protocol provides a secure connection between two points across the Internet, enabling private communications to travel securely over the public infrastructure (see Figure 8-15). VPNs based on the Internet

FIGURE 8-15   *A virtual private network using the Internet.*

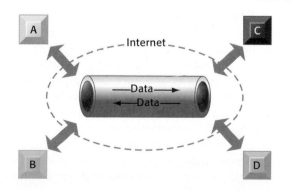

This VPN is a private network of computers linked using a secure "tunnel" connection over the Internet. It protects data transmitted over the public Internet by encoding the data and "wrapping" them within the Internet Protocol (IP). By adding a wrapper around a network message to hide its content, organizations can create a private connection that travels through the public Internet.

Protocol provide substantial savings over non-IP networks while providing more bandwidth, more flexible network designs, and the ability to link more easily to remote and international offices. VPNs also provide a network infrastructure for combining voice and data networks.

Several competing protocols are used to protect data transmitted over the public Internet, including Point-to-Point Tunneling Protocol (PPTP). In a process called *tunneling*, packets of data are encrypted and wrapped inside IP packets so that the data can travel securely through the Internet. By adding this wrapper around a network message to hide its content, organizations can create a private connection that travels through the public Internet.

Internet-based VPNs can be used in countries where private networks are not easily available. For example, CVG Internacional, a subsidiary of the Corporation Venezolana de Guayana that markets products from Guyana, uses an Internet VPN from Equant to link offices in Miami, Venezuela, and Rotterdam. By using this VPN service for interoffice communications and communications with affiliated companies, CVG is cutting telecommunications costs. VPNs are also useful for building extranets because businesses can operate their own IP VPNs and give partners access over the public Internet. ISPs provide VPN services, or companies can create and manage their own VPNs.

8.5	**MANAGEMENT OPPORTUNITIES, CHALLENGES, AND SOLUTIONS**

Throughout your managerial career, you will face decisions on how to use networking technology and services to enhance the performance of your firm. You should be aware of the challenges in trying to implement these decisions and how they can be addressed.

Opportunities

Firms have an opportunity to bring about radical reductions in the cost of data and voice communication and to use networking and Internet technology in new ways as parts of new business models. The business value of these technologies cannot be underestimated.

Management Challenges

Telecommunications and networking technologies present challenges as well as opportunities for organizations. Three challenges stand out: loss of management control over information systems, the need for organizational change, and the difficulty of ensuring infrastructure scalability and reliability.

LOSS OF MANAGEMENT CONTROL
Managing information systems technology and corporate data is more difficult in a distributed networked environment because of the lack of a single, central point where needed management can occur. Distributed client/server networks, peer-to-peer computing networks, mobile wireless networks, and Internet computing have created new independent sources of computing power. End users may be collecting, storing, and disseminating data and software that do not meet corporate standards.

Another consequence of placing computing power and networking resources in the hands of employees is the surging use of the Web and e-mail for nonbusiness purposes. This practice is draining productivity and business performance, prompting many organizations to monitor employee use of networks and the Internet. The Window on

Management explores the ethical implications of employee monitoring. When you read this case, pay attention to both sides of the issue in the ethical dilemma raised by workplace monitoring.

ORGANIZATIONAL CHANGE REQUIREMENTS

Leading-edge telecommunications technology and the Internet cannot make organizations more effective unless underlying organizational issues are fully addressed. Old ways of doing business must also be changed to work effectively with the Internet and related network technologies. Such changes in corporate culture and organizational structure are not easy to make. It took several years of hard work and large financial investments for IBM to make its business processes Web enabled and to convince disparate business units to adopt a "one IBM" mind-set in which everyone uses common tools (Kanter, 2001).

SCALABILITY, RELIABILITY, AND SECURITY

Companies that intensively use communications technology require plentiful bandwidth and storage capacity for transmitting and maintaining all of the data generated by electronic commerce and electronic business transactions. Network infrastructures must be able to handle current e-commerce demands and scale rapidly to meet future demands while providing high levels of performance and availability for mission-critical applications.

Today's business firms are incredibly dependent on the Internet and World Wide Web to conduct business. Whereas telephone, television broadcasting, and cable TV systems rarely suffer security breaches, the Internet is rife with rogue software in the form of worms and viruses that can bring down corporate networks and millions of PCs in a few hours. The Internet's "open architecture" design gives hackers and other criminals extraordinary opportunities for mischief. Chapter 10 discusses Internet security issues in greater depth.

Solution Guidelines

Careful planning and change management are essential for meeting these challenges.

DEVELOPING A STRATEGIC NETWORKING PLAN

A strategic networking plan is a good first step. The plan should describe how communications services and technology could enhance your firm's competitive position. Your analysis should identify the most critical areas where new network-based applications could make a large difference in performance. What areas need improvement? What communications services does your firm need? Do these services need to be integrated? How many different locations and users in the organization require access to communications services and networks? What is the anticipated frequency and volume of communications? What types of networks does your firm need to accomplish its business goals? Does the firm need long-distance networks, local area networks, or public networks such as the Internet? What level of availability and reliability do networks have to maintain? How much is your firm willing to spend to achieve this level of service?

MANAGING THE CHANGE

To gain the full benefit of any new technology, organizations must carefully plan for and manage the changes. Business processes may need to be reengineered to accompany infrastructure changes (see Chapter 14). Management must address the organizational issues that arise from shifts in staffing, function, power, and the organizational culture that result when a new information technology infrastructure is implemented. Data administration (see Chapter 7) becomes even more important when networks link many different applications, business areas, and computing devices.

WINDOW ON MANAGEMENT

MONITORING EMPLOYEES ON NETWORKS: UNETHICAL OR GOOD BUSINESS?

E-mail use has exploded as hundreds of millions of people the world over turn to it for speedy, convenient, and inexpensive business and personal communications. Not surprisingly, the use of e-mail for personal reasons at the workplace has also grown, as has use of the Web for personal business at work. A number of studies have concluded that at least 25 percent of employee online time is spent on non-work-related Web surfing, and perhaps as many as 90 percent of employees receive or send personal e-mail at work.

Many companies have begun monitoring their employees' use of e-mail and the Internet. A study by the American Management Association concluded that more than 75 percent of large U.S. companies are recording and reviewing employee communications and activities on the job, including e-mail, Internet connections, and computer files. Although U.S. companies have the legal right to monitor employee Internet and e-mail activity, is such monitoring unethical, or is it simply good business?

Managers worry about the loss of time and employee productivity when employees are focusing on personal rather than company business. If personal traffic on company networks is too high, it can also clog the company's network so that business work cannot be performed. Some employees at Xerox had sent so much junk and pornographic e-mail while on the job that the company's e-mail system shut down. Too much time on personal business, on the Internet or not, can mean lost revenue or overcharges to clients. Some employees may be charging time they spend trading their personal stocks online or pursuing other personal business to clients, thus overcharging the clients.

When employees use e-mail or the Web at employer facilities or with employer equipment, anything they do, including anything illegal, carries the company's name. Therefore, the employer can be traced and held liable. Management in many firms fear that racist, sexually explicit, or other potentially offensive material accessed or traded by their employees could result in adverse publicity and even lawsuits for the firm. Even if the company is found not to be liable, responding to lawsuits could cost the company tens of thousands of dollars. Companies also fear e-mail leakage of trade secrets.

Companies have the legal right to monitor what employees are doing with company equipment during business hours. The question is whether electronic surveillance is an appropriate tool for maintaining an efficient and positive workplace. Some companies try to ban all personal activities on corporate networks—zero tolerance. Others block employee access to specific Web sites or limit personal time on the Web using software that enables IT departments to track the Web sites employees visit, the amount of time employees spend at these

sites, and the files they download. Some firms have fired employees who have stepped out of bounds.

According to Steve Purdham, chief executive of Surf Control PLC, Congleton, England, a maker of content-filtering software, most companies primarily block access to sites dealing with pornography or illegal drugs. But a number also block access to Web sites dealing with sports, shopping, entertainment, and other distractions or limit access to certain times of the day, such as during lunch or after work hours.

Chaparral Energy, an Oklahoma City oil and gas producer, uses Websense software to block employee access to religious, political, and sexually oriented Web sites. It also bars Web-based e-mail sites and restricts online shopping to lunchtime and off-hours. After employees were informed their Internet use was being monitored, their time online fell from about an hour a day to less than 15 minutes per day.

Employee Web use for personal activities also fell at Comtech Telecommunications Corporation in Melville, New York after employees were informed they were being monitored. This satellite-communications company installed software that tracks individual users' surfing habits and provides managers with daily reports.

No solution is problem free, but many consultants believe companies should write corporate policies on employee e-mail and Internet use. The policies should include explicit ground rules that state, by position or level, under what circumstances employees can use company facilities for e-mail or Internet activities. The policies should also inform employees whether these activities are monitored and explain why.

The rules should be tailored to specific business needs and organizational cultures. For example, although some companies may exclude all employees from visiting sites that have explicit sexual material, law firm or hospital employees may require access to these sites. Investment firms will need to allow many of their employees access to other investment sites. A company dependent on widespread information sharing, innovation, and independence could very well find that monitoring creates more problems than it solves.

Sources: Riva Richmond, "It's 10 A.M. Do You Know Where Your Workers Are?" *Wall Street Journal,* January 12, 2004; Eric Zoeckler, "Issues to Ponder Before E-Monitoring Workers," *Snohomish County Business Journal,* July 2004; Olga Kharif, "Ever-Sharper Eyes Watch You Work," *Business Week,* July 22, 2003; Jason Gertzen, "Company Spy," *Milwaukee Journal Sentinel,* May 17, 2003; and Laurie Willis, "More Companies Keeping Tabs on Employees," *San Francisco Chronicle,* May 13, 2003.

To Think About: Should managers monitor employee e-mail and Internet usage? Why or why not? Describe an effective e-mail and Web use policy for a company.

MAKE IT YOUR BUSINESS

Finance and Accounting

Telecommunications systems are widely used in specialized financial services firms and in other businesses to expedite funds transfer. Many nonfinancial companies use Electronic Data Interchange (EDI) and extranets to transfer payments to suppliers and invoices to large corporate customers. Banks maintain networks to link their automated teller machines (ATMs) and branch offices to central computers that monitor deposits, withdrawals, and fund transfer transactions occurring at remote locations. Financial services firms today depend on networked systems to provide their managers and clients with instant access to account information. These firms are heavy users of online digital information services, such as Dow Jones, to obtain data on firms' financial positions and on financial markets.

Human Resources

Contemporary human resources systems have realized great efficiencies by using communications technology and the Internet to provide authorized human resources professionals and employees with direct online access to employee information. Employees can use telephone-based systems, the Web, or private corporate networks to review their employment records or to make changes to their benefits plans. Managers can use e-mail, instant messaging, chat, and videoconferencing to communicate with employees and work teams in many different locations. You can find examples of human resources applications on pages 261, 290 and 294.

Manufacturing and Production

The manufacturing and production function has become highly networked and communications driven. Computers and computer-controlled machines on the factory floor are often linked by LANs. In companies with advanced manufacturing systems, each step in the manufacturing or production process uses networks to transmit data to the next step. Data from orders trigger transactions that can be transmitted by networks directly to scheduling systems, to supply chain management systems, to the assembly line, and to systems for warehousing and delivery. Extranets are especially useful for collaborative commerce and supply chain management. You can find examples of manufacturing and production applications on pages 300–301.

Sales and Marketing

Many sales transactions today use point-of-sale systems that capture sales transaction data at the checkout counter and transmit them over networks to the firm's central computer, where they update the firm's order processing and inventory systems. Once consolidated in corporate systems, these data can be analyzed to identify high-performing and low-performing items, buying trends, and items needing rapid replenishment from suppliers. E-mail and call centers where customers' telephone calls are directed to service representatives have become popular technologies for customer service and support. The Web is an especially powerful medium for sales and marketing because it provides capabilities for personalization and interacting with customers that cannot be found through other channels. Companies can engage in ongoing dialogues with customers using e-mail, chat, and electronic discussion groups to solidify their customer relationships. You can find examples of sales and marketing applications on pages 300–301.

Summary

1. *Describe the features of a contemporary corporate network infrastructure and key networking technologies.*

   A contemporary corporate network infrastructure relies on both public and private infrastructures to support the movement of information across diverse technological platforms. It includes the traditional telephone system, mobile cellular communication, wireless local area networks, videoconferencing systems, a corporate Web site, intranets, extranets, and an array of local and wide area networks, including the Internet. This collection of networks evolved from two fundamentally different types of networks: telephone networks and computer networks.

   A simple network consists of two or more connected computers. Basic network components include computers, network interfaces, a connection medium, network operating system software, and either a hub or a switch.

   Contemporary networks have been shaped by the rise of client/server computing, the use of packet switching, and the adoption of TCP/IP as a universal communications standard for linking disparate networks and computers. Client/server networks have distributed much of the organization's computing power to the desktop and factory floor. Packet switching makes more efficient use of network communications capacity by breaking messages into small packets that are sent independently along different paths in a network and then reassembled at their destination. Protocols provide a common set of rules that enable communication among diverse components in a telecommunications network. TCP/IP is a suite of protocols that has become the dominant model of achieving connectivity among different networks and computers. It is the connectivity model used in the Internet.

2. *Evaluate alternative transmission media, types of networks, and network services.*

The principal physical transmission media are twisted copper telephone wire; coaxial copper cable; fiber-optic cable; and wireless transmission using microwave, satellite, low-frequency radio waves, or infrared waves. The choice of transmission medium depends on the distance and volume of communication required by the organization and its financial resources. Twisted wire enables companies to use existing wiring for telephone systems for digital communication, although it is relatively slow. Fiber-optic and coaxial cable are used for high-volume transmission but are expensive to install. Microwave and satellite are used for wireless communication over long distances. The transmission capacity of a medium, known as the bandwidth, is determined by the range of frequencies it can accommodate.

There are different types of networks and network services available to organizations. Network selection and design should be based on the organization's information requirements and the distance required for transmission. Local area networks (LANs) connect PCs and other digital devices together within a 500-meter radius and are used today for many corporate computing tasks. Network components may be connected together using a star, bus, or ring topology. Wide area networks (WANs) span broad geographical distances, ranging as far as entire continents or across the globe, and are private networks that are independently managed. Metropolitan area networks (MANs) span a single urban area, whereas campus area networks (CANs) span a campus of buildings or a military base.

A number of network services are available to organizations requiring high-bandwidth transmission. Frame relay is a shared network service with transmission speeds ranging from 56 Kbps to more than 40 Mbps; it relies on digital circuits that require less error checking than packet switching. Asynchronous Transfer Mode (ATM) provides transmission speeds of 1.5 Mbps to more than 9 Gbps, parceling data into fixed 53-byte cells. ATM can pass data between computers from different vendors and is popular for transmitting data, video, and audio over the same network. Integrated Services Digital Network (ISDN) is an international standard for dial-up network access that uses existing local telephone lines to integrate voice, data, image, and video services. Basic rate ISDN can transmit data at a rate of 128 Kbps.

Digital Subscriber Line (DSL) technologies, cable modems, and T lines are often used for high-capacity Internet connections. Like ISDN, DSL technologies also operate over existing copper telephone lines to carry voice, data, and video, but they have higher transmission capacities than ISDN. Asymmetric Digital Subscriber Line (ADSL) supports a transmission rate of 1.5 to 9 Mbps when receiving data and up to 640 Kbps when sending data. Symmetric Digital Subscriber Line (SDSL) supports the same transmission rate for sending and receiving data of up to 3 Mbps.

Cable modems, which operate over cable TV lines, can provide high-speed access to the Web or corporate intranets at speeds of up to 4 Mbps. T lines are high-speed data lines leased from communications providers. A T-1 line supports a data transmission rate of 1.544 Mbps.

3. *Assess the role of the Internet and the World Wide Web in a firm's information technology infrastructure.*

The Internet is a worldwide network of networks that uses the client/server model of computing and the TCP/IP network reference model. Every computer on the Internet is assigned a unique numeric IP address. The Domain Name System (DNS) converts IP addresses to domain names so that users only need to specify a domain name to access a computer on the Internet instead of typing in the numeric IP address. No one owns the Internet and it has no formal management organization. However, worldwide Internet policies are established by organizations and government bodies such as the Internet Architecture Board and the World Wide Web Consortium. The Internet must also conform to the laws of the sovereign nation-states in which it operates, as well as the technical infrastructures that exist within the nation-state.

The Internet's global reach and connectivity, scalability, distributed design, universal standards, richness, and interactivity have made it the primary infrastructure for electronic business and electronic commerce. Major Internet services include e-mail, Usenet, LISTSERV, chatting, instant messaging, Telnet, FTP, and the World Wide Web.

The World Wide Web provides a universal set of standards for storing, retrieving, and displaying information in a client/server environment, enabling users to link to information resources housed on many different computer systems around the world. Web pages are based on Hypertext Markup Language (HTML) and can display text, graphics, video, and audio. Web site directories, search engines, and push technology can help users locate the information they need on the Web. Web technology and Internet networking standards provide the connectivity and interfaces for internal private intranets and private extranets that can be accessed by many different kinds of computers inside and outside the organization.

4. *Identify and describe the most important tools for communication and e-business.*

The principal applications for communication are e-mail, chatting, instant messaging, Usenet newsgroups, and LISTSERV services. These tools reduce time and cost when firms must manage organizational activities and communicate with many employees. Groupware, teamware, and electronic conferencing software provide tools to support communication and collaboration when people work together in groups or work teams, often in different locations. Firms are also starting to realize economies by using Internet telephony, which enables Internet technology to be used for telephone voice transmission. Internet technology can also reduce communication costs by enabling companies to create virtual private networks (VPNs) as low-cost alternatives to private WANs.

5. *Identify and describe the challenges posed by networking and the Internet and management solutions.*

Challenges posed by networking and the Internet include loss of management control over information systems; the need for organizational change; and the difficulty of ensuring infrastructure scalability and reliability. Solutions include developing a strategic networking plan and carefully managing the business and organizational changes associated with intensive networking and the Internet.

Key Terms

Asynchronous Transfer Mode (ATM), 275
Backbone, 271
Bandwidth, 272
Broadband, 264
Bus networks, 273
Cable modems, 275
Campus area network (CAN), 272
Chat, 287
Coaxial cable, 271
Connectivity, 263
Dense wavelength division multiplexing (DWDM), 271
Digital Subscriber Line (DSL), 275
Domain name, 277
Domain Name System (DNS), 277
E-mail, 287
Fiber-optic cable, 271
File Transfer Protocol (FTP), 280
Firewalls, 286
Frame relay, 274
Groupware, 288
Hertz, 272
Home page, 283
Hubs, 268

Hypertext Transfer Protocol (HTTP), 282
Information appliance, 280
Instant messaging, 287
Integrated Services Digital Network (ISDN), 275
Internet Protocol (IP) address, 277
Internet service provider (ISP), 278
Internet telephony, 289
Internet2, 286
Internetworking, 278
LISTSERV, 288
Local area network (LAN), 272
Metropolitan area network (MAN), 273
Modem, 270
Multicasting, 285
Multiplexing, 271
Network interface card (NIC), 267
Network operating system (NOS), 268
Open Systems Interconnect (OSI), 270
Optical networks, 271
Packet switching, 268
Peer-to-peer, 273
Protocol, 269
Push technology, 284

Ring networks, 273
Router, 268
Search engines, 283
Search-based advertising, 284
Semantic Web, 285
Shopping bots, 284
Star network, 273
Switch, 268
T lines, 275
Teamware, 288
Telnet, 280
Topology, 273
Transmission Control Protocol/Internet Protocol (TCP/IP), 269
Twisted wire, 270
Unified messaging, 289
Uniform Resource Locator (URL), 282
Usenet, 287
Virtual private network (VPN), 291
Voice over IP (VoIP), 289
Webmaster, 283
Wide area networks (WANs), 273

Review Questions

1. *Describe the features of a contemporary corporate telecommunications infrastructure and a simple network.*

2. *Describe seven major trends in telecommunications.*

3. *What is the business value of telecommunications and networking? What role is played by Metcalfe's Law?*

4. *Name and describe the three technologies that have shaped contemporary telecommunications systems.*

5. *Name the different types of physical transmission media and compare them in terms of speed and cost.*

6. *What is a local area network (LAN)? What are the components of a typical LAN? What are the functions of each component?*

7. *Name and describe the principal network topologies.*

8. *Define the following: WAN, MAN, modem, protocol, optical network, and bandwidth.*

9. *List and describe the various broadband network services.*

10. *What are the features that define the Internet? How is the Internet governed? How does it provide business value?*

11. *Explain how the domain name and IP addressing system works.*

12. *List and describe the principal Internet services.*

13. *List and describe alternative ways of locating information on the Web.*

14. *What are intranets and extranets? How do they provide value to businesses?*

15. *Describe the capabilities of next-generation networks, including Internet2? How do they differ from those of*

the existing public Internet? What benefits can they provide?

16. *Name and describe the principal technologies and tools that support communication and electronic business.*

17. *What are Internet telephony and virtual private networks? How do they provide value to businesses?*

18. *Describe the challenges posed by networking and the Internet and some ways to address them.*

Discussion Questions

1. *Network design is a key business decision as well as a technology decision. Why?*

2. *A fully integrated IT infrastructure is essential for business success. Do you agree? Why or why not?*

Application Software Exercise:
Spreadsheet Exercise: Analyzing Web Site Visitors

Your firm, Marina Clothiers, makes casual pants, shirts, and other clothes for both men and women. Your firm has been attempting to increase the number of online customers by placing advertising banners for your Web site at other Web sites. When users click on these banner ads, they automatically are transported to your Web site. Data from your advertising campaign are summarized in the weekly Marketing Trends Reports (MTR) produced by your Web site analysis software, which appears on the Laudon Web site for Chapter 8.

- Visitors are the number of people who visited your Web site by clicking on a banner ad for your site that was placed on an affiliated Web site.

- Shoppers are the number of visitors referred by banner ads who reached a page in your Web site designated as a shopping page.

- Attempted buyers are the number of potential buyers referred by banner ads who reached a page at your Web site designated for summarizing and paying for purchases.

- Buyers are the number of buyers referred by banner ads who actually placed an order from your Web site.

- Source indicates the specific Web site from which visitors came to your Web site.

In trying to increase the number of online customers, you must determine your Web site's success in converting visitors to actual buyers. You must also look at the abandonment rate—the percentage of attempted buyers who abandon your Web site just as they were about to make a purchase. Low conversion rates and high abandonment rates are indicators that a Web site is not very effective. You also must identify likely Web site partners for a new advertising campaign. Use the MTR with your spreadsheet software to help you answer the following questions. Include a graphics presentation to support your findings:

1. What are the total number of visitors, shoppers, attempted buyers, and buyers at your Web site?

2. Which sources provided the highest conversion rate to buyers at your Web site—that is, the percentage of visitors from a previous site who become buyers on your site? What is the average conversion rate for your Web site?

3. Which sources provided the highest abandonment rate at your Web site—that is, the percentage of attempted buyers who abandoned their shopping cart at your Web site before completing a purchase. What is the average abandonment rate for your Web site?

4. On which Web sites (or types of Web sites) should your firm purchase more banner ads?

Using Internet Tools to Increase Efficiency and Productivity

Software requirements: Web browser software
Word processing software
Electronic presentation software (optional)

Dirt Bikes's management is concerned about how much money is being spent communicating with people inside and outside the company and on obtaining information about developments in the motorcycle industry and the global economy. You have been asked to investigate how Internet tools and technology

could be used to help Dirt Bikes employees communicate and obtain information more efficiently. Dirt Bikes provides Internet access to all its employees who use desktop computers.

1. How could the various Internet tools help employees at Dirt Bikes? Create a matrix showing what types of employees and business functions would benefit from using each type of tool and why.

2. How could Dirt Bikes benefit from intranets for its sales and marketing, human resources, and manu-

facturing and production departments? Select one of these departments and describe the kind of information that could be provided by an intranet for that department. How could this intranet increase efficiency and productivity for that department?

3. (Optional) If possible, use electronic presentation software to summarize your findings for management.

Electronic Commerce Project: *Using Web Search Engines for Business Research*

You have heard that fuel cells are new and might be an inexpensive way to provide electricity for your house, but you do not know anything about fuel cells. You decide that you want to research the topic to learn what fuel cells are and how they can be used for generating electricity for your house. Use the following four search engines to obtain that information:

Yahoo!, AltaVista, Google, and Ask Jeeves. If you wish, try some other search engines as well. Compare the volume and quality of information you find with each search tool. Which tool is the easiest to use? Which produced the best results for your research? Why?

Group Project: Identifying Strategic Opportunities for Networking Technology

With a group of two or three of your fellow students, describe in detail the ways that telecommunications technology can provide a firm with competitive advantage. Use the companies described in the chapters you have read so far to

illustrate the points you make, or select from business or computer magazines examples of other companies using telecommunications. If possible, use electronic presentation software to present your findings to the class.

CASE STUDY
Can REI Climb Higher with Networking and the Internet?

With an old-fashioned sensibility and a forward-looking embrace of networking and Internet technology, Recreational Equipment, Inc. (REI), occupies a distinctive position in the retail market. Selling gear and clothing for outdoor recreational activities, REI operates 70 stores throughout the United States, as well as 2 stores on the Web and an adventure-themed travel service. Together, these entities recorded over $800 million in sales during 2003.

The company was started in 1938 as a cooperative by mountain climbers Lloyd and Mary Anderson and a group of associates to acquire quality climbing gear and other outdoor recreational equipment at affordable prices. Despite the significant expansion and modernization, REI remains a cooperative, with more than 2 million members. REI pays out approximately 85 percent of its total income to cover rebates to cooperative members equaling 10 percent of their purchases. Because REI is not a publicly traded company, it does not have to base its performance on meeting short-term earnings targets and can take a longer-term view of its technology investments.

REI was one of the first retailers to investigate the potential of e-commerce, and by 1996, REI was already doing business on the Web. Two years later, the company's Web store had become a profitable venture. Now, REI.com and REI-OUTLET.com combine with REI's catalog phone sales to account for 17 percent of the company's total annual sales revenue. More important, REI has successfully integrated an e-commerce channel into its business without hurting the traditional channels, retail stores and catalog sales.

REI does not attempt to compete on price. Its business strategy emphasizes product selection, staff expertise, extensive product information, and multiple channels working together to provide consumers with the best shopping experience possible. According to Brian Unmacht, REI's senior vice president of retail, "The

key for REI is to be the place to come for information. We're always working on ways to tie information to the shopping path in a relevant way."

For example, REI was one of the first retailers to employ kiosks in its stores. From these kiosks customers can view products, accessories, styles, and information that may not be available in the physical store in which they are shopping. REI has over 40,000 pages of product information on its Web site, which traditional shoppers can also view from the kiosks when they are in an REI store. The content goes beyond simple choices such as sizes and colors to include detailed advice from experts on everything from how to choose a sleeping bag to how to measure yourself properly to fit a piece of equipment. Stores get credit for online sales made through the kiosks.

As the company grew, REI graduated from low-speed dial-up connections to a wide area network (WAN) and then to a state-of-the-art high-availability network based on Cisco Systems networking technology. In 2002, REI installed a Cisco Aironet wireless local area network (LAN) in every store to provide a platform for applications such as barcode scanning, shipping, receiving, pricing, and inventory. The wireless implementation resulted from the company's decision to use technology to eliminate inefficiencies that were cutting into profits. Specifically, the company wanted to reduce the amount of time employees needed to spend receiving shipments, integrate shelf stocking with supply chain management operations to reduce errors, and introduce a system by which vendors would ship products directly to stores rather than to distribution centers.

Before implementing the wireless LAN, employees in each store spent an average of 48 hours per week in shipping and receiving. After implementing the wireless system, the same work can be performed in 25 to 28 hours. Multiply that by 70 stores and you have major cost savings.

REI is now experimenting with new ways to deliver information to the store floor. It is testing wireless handheld devices that give employees instant access to product information on the Web, wireless cash registers and point-of-sale devices to facilitate quick changes to store layouts, and live two-way videoconferencing based on IP/TV technology that would enable shoppers or sales associates at kiosks to talk to call center agents or product specialists at REI headquarters or other stores. REI has rolled out wireless IP telephony phones in its flagship Seattle store, and it is considering using its network to deliver on-demand videos to kiosks to supplement employee training.

REI has remained determined to use its multiple channels to support each other. The company's philosophy is that it doesn't matter which segment of the company is responsible for a sale occurring; the sale benefits the company as a whole. Jeff Schueler, a usability consultant and founder and CEO of Usability Sciences, views a sale as the final step in the multistep process of shopping. According to Schueler, the vast majority of people who visit e-commerce Web sites do so for purposes such as fact finding, price comparisons, obtaining special discount coupons, and account maintenance and bill paying. Most do not actually visit Web sites to make their purchases. Therefore, any business that is open to encouraging its customers to flow from one channel to another has a competitive advantage. So, although the end product of consumerism still takes place mostly by traditional means at REI, it is heavily influenced by Internet technology.

In mid-2003, the company introduced a new service that enables customers to order products from home over the Web and then pick up their orders at their local REI store. According to Joan Broughton, REI's vice president of multichannel programs, approximately one-third of all customers who make purchases online will spend about $100 more simply as a result of being in the physical store to retrieve their online orders. The benefit to in-store pickup for the customer is that it eliminates shipping costs. The company does not incur additional costs either. It saves money by shipping a number of items in bulk to one store rather than to the individual addresses of multiple customers. Furthermore, items that are shipped to an REI store for in-store pickup travel on the same trucks that are already en route to the store with inventory replenishments.

Combining these two distinct forms of order fulfillment required a technology solution. REI was able to integrate orders from its Web site with restocking orders from its stores by using IBM's WebSphere business platform running on an RS/6000 server linked to an Oracle database. The database feeds an order-processing system running on a midrange IBM AS/400 computer. Brad Brown, REI's vice president of information services, explains that integrating the two types of data wasn't as challenging as synchronizing the fulfillment of the two types of orders. When a customer purchases a product online, the item leaves the warehouse, cued by the order, and waits for the appropriate truck to be loaded. Inventory replenishment orders, on the other hand, are generated by an automated system that prompts items to leave the warehouse at regularly scheduled intervals.

To ensure that integration runs smoothly from the customer's point of view, the information services team developed an algorithm to inform customers when the products they have ordered online will be available for pickup. The algorithm takes into account the possibility that an order is placed too close to the departure day of the delivery truck to be met and promises a more conservative delivery estimate. REI still attempts to complete the order before the promised date.

REI took a major step in unifying its technology infrastructure by adopting IBM's WebSphere Web-development environment in 2002. Using this environment and an integrated database, REI is able to develop technology sys-

tems for each of its business channels simultaneously, rather than having to devote resources individually to Web or store-based applications. REI has implemented a content management system from Documentum to help centralize information for its various business channels. REI is also working toward establishing matching keywords and item numbers for products on its Web site, in its mail-order catalog, and in its retail stores so that shoppers can roam seamlessly from one channel to another, viewing products in person and retrieving their specifications from the Web. REI publicizes discount incentives for online purchases in its mail-order catalog because the company can process orders from the Web more cheaply than orders placed by phone or mail.

The main purpose behind all of this effort at integration is to create a perception that REI doesn't have distinct channels at all, that customers don't see channels at REI, they see only REI. The company hopes that its customers simply view REI as providing every convenience that it can while still offering high-quality merchandise and service.

REI continues to be progressive both in adopting technology and in shaping its product line for maximum appeal. Around the same time that REI implemented WebSphere, it also installed a data warehouse to improve the company's ability to perform customer transaction analysis. Output from data mining enables REI to refine its buying, marketing, and sales initiatives according to trends and customers' buying habits.

In 2004, REI announced that its use of SeaTab Software's PivotLink surpassed the expectations that REI's director of inventory and logistics, John Strother, had for a business intelligence solution. PivotLink integrates enterprise-wide data so that key decision makers can access the bottom-line results of company processes more easily. REI uses PivotLink to expand the availability of internal data economically, lending greater support to the decision-making process, as well as to communicate critical data to vendors, who require them to maintain their own

business processes properly. According to Strother, PivotLink enables REI to increase profits and performance; increases employees' and partners' ability to do their jobs effectively; and offers an information access solution that is easy to implement, affordable, and scalable.

Can REI continue to thrive on all fronts of its multichannel business? Brian Unmacht actually downplays his company's role as an innovator of Internet and telecommunications business strategies. He states, "From a technology perspective, we're not very adventurous. We like to find the most effective and reliable way to meet all of our goals." For REI, that way is to build a powerful and flexible network that can house all of its applications and use the Internet as the medium through which all of its business processes flow together.

Sources: Eric J. Adams, "Retail Trailblazing," *Cisco IQ Magazine*, Second Quarter 2004; Megan Santosus, "How REI Scaled E-Commerce Mountain," *CIO Magazine*, www.cio.com, May 15, 2004; "Recreational Equipment Inc. Presents Success Story with SeaTab's PivotLink Business Intelligence Solution at Retail Systems 2004," PRNewswire press release, May 13, 2004; Bill Becher, "Feminine Side Is Coming Out," *Los Angeles Daily News*, www.dailynews.com, June 2, 2004; Ian Mylchreest, "Competition Gets Tough in the Sporting Goods Stores," *Las Vegas Business Press*, www.lvbusinesspress.com, May 21, 2004; and www.rei.com, accessed June 10, 2004.

CASE STUDY QUESTIONS

1. Evaluate REI using the competitive forces and value chain models.

2. What is REI's business strategy? What role do networking and Internet technology play in this strategy?

3. What management, organization, and technology issues does REI face in running its business? What role do telecommunications and the Internet play in solving these challenges?

4. How effectively has REI used information systems and the Internet to meet its business strategy goals and maintain a competitive edge?

Chapter 9

The Wireless Revolution

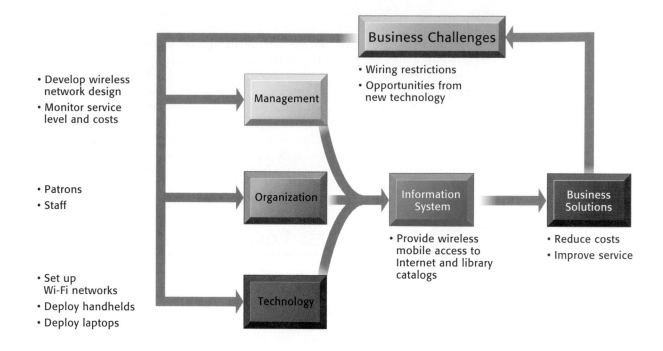

Develop wireless network design
- Develop wireless network design
- Monitor service level and costs

Management

Business Challenges
- Wiring restrictions
- Opportunities from new technology

- Patrons
- Staff

Organization

Information System
- Provide wireless mobile access to Internet and library catalogs

Business Solutions
- Reduce costs
- Improve service

- Set up Wi-Fi networks
- Deploy handhelds
- Deploy laptops

Technology

Opening Case: The Boston Public Library Goes Wireless

Founded in 1848, the Boston Public Library (BPL) was the first free municipal library in the United States, the first to have a branch library, and the first to have a children's room. In recent years, BPL made history as one of the first large public libraries to offer Internet access. Now BPL is in the forefront again as an early library adopter of high-speed wireless networking.

BPL's landmark Copley Square facility and 27 other branches in Boston house 7.5 million books and serve over 2 million patrons each year. When BPL was renovating the Copley Square location, it became interested in installing a wireless network. A wireless network would not require extensive wiring, which could prove very difficult in a registered historic building that has federal restrictions on alterations. The library had a limited number of wired PCs with Internet access. A local area network (LAN) with 802.11b (Wi-Fi) wireless networking technology would provide convenient Internet access for library patrons with Wi-Fi-enabled computing devices, easing the demand on the wired PCs and also on the library's network switches. The wireless network would enable patrons and staff to access the network from anywhere within the library.

BPL enlisted Dimension Data and Cisco Systems for technical assistance with its wireless network. Working with the library staff, these companies developed a system to provide different levels of network access for staff, patrons, and children. Children logging on are automatically routed to a filtered server to prevent them from accessing inappropriate Web sites.

Dimension Data developed a plan for 70 strategically positioned wireless access points throughout the 1-million-square-foot-library site so there were no forgotten areas or spots with weak wireless signals. This created savings by eliminating the need to move or replace equipment.

Wireless network access is available throughout virtually all publicly accessible areas inside the main library. Patrons were so enthusiastic that the library extended the wireless network outside the building to include the building's exterior perimeter adjacent to the Copley Square park.

Since going wireless BPL has seen a significant jump in library membership. The number of Internet sessions is growing every month. The library is now planning to extend the wireless network into its reserve stacks so library assistants with handheld wireless devices can receive requests directly from patrons instead of requests on paper.

Sources: Amy Glynn Hornick, "Modern History," *Cisco IQ Magazine*, Second Quarter 2004 and www.bpl.org, accessed July 29, 2004.

Wireless networking helped the Boston Public Library increase its service to the public while keeping down costs and preserving its historic setting. The library was able to use Wi-Fi technology to create wireless local area networks (LANs) that could provide wireless access to library catalogs and the Internet as well as platforms for new services without disrupting the library's existing networking infrastructure.

Wireless networking is changing the way the Boston Public Library serves its patrons and it's changing the way that other organizations and businesses work. So, it's important for you to understand how this technology works, its benefits and challenges, and how it can provide business value. In this chapter you'll learn about the technologies for wireless networking, different types of wireless networks and networking standards, and m-commerce and other applications where wireless is having its greatest impact. We also identify the key decisions and challenges you will face as a manager in implementing and using this technology.

9.1 THE WIRELESS COMPUTING LANDSCAPE

We are at the edge of a wireless revolution that is transforming computing and information systems. Until very recently, using a computer meant going to where the computer was located and logging on. If the computer was networked to another computer or the Internet, that connection was wired and our ability to use computers was limited to those wired locations.

We still use tethered computer systems, but increasingly we are turning to wireless devices—cell phones, wireless handhelds, laptops with wireless Internet connections—to communicate and to obtain information and data. In the future, it is even more likely that we'll be using some form of wireless technology.

The Wireless Revolution

By most accounts, the wireless revolution is still in its beginning stages. But already, it is changing the way businesses produce and communicate their products, how they sell them, and even how they define them.

Mobile phones are cheaper, more powerful, and nearly ubiquitous. Usage has exploded, with an average of 186 million new subscribers added every year. In 2002, the number of mobile phones worldwide surpassed the number of fixed-line phones (see Figure 9-1), and 1.8 billion or more global users are anticipated by 2007. Today over 55 percent of U.S. inhabitants have cell phones, with even higher percentages in Western Europe (85% of the population) and some Asian nations (62% in Japan, 75% in Korea). China is emerging as a mobile giant, counting over 300 million subscribers today and 575 million predicted by 2010 (Evans, 2004; eMarketer, 2002).

Today's mobile phones are not just for voice communication—they have become mobile platforms for delivering digital data. By 2006, two-thirds of the 180 million mobile phone users in the United States will be using them for data services such as e-mail. With faster computer chips, compression technology, and wireless networks, cell phones are finding new uses as mobile information appliances for recording and downloading photos, video, music, and games and for accessing the Internet. Already cell phones have screens that display 65,000 colors, compared to 256 colors just a few years ago. Mobile phones are also emerging as alternatives to cash or credit cards as people use them to transmit payments to scanners on cash registers and vending machines.

Anytime, anywhere Internet access will soon be within reach. An array of technologies has emerged to provide high-speed wireless access to the Internet for PCs and other wireless handheld devices as well as for cell phones. These new high-speed services have extended Internet access to numerous locations that could not be covered by traditional wired Internet services. Even more powerful wireless transmission technologies are under development.

FIGURE 9-1   *Mobile versus fixed-line subscribers worldwide.*

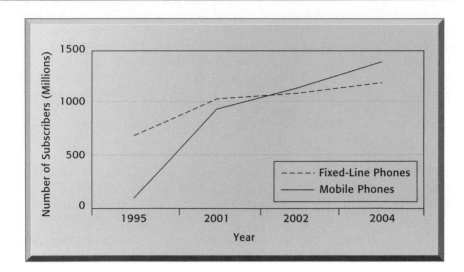

Mobile phone use is surpassing fixed-line use and will continue to grow very rapidly.

Sources: International Telecommunications Union, 2002 and 2003, and authors.

As they become woven together, wireless technologies will create a foundation for other innovations. Consequently, businesses of all sizes are devoting more of their resources to wireless devices, services, and applications. According to International Data Corporation, worldwide wireless infrastructure and mobile network spending will grow from $38.8 billion in 2002 to $49 billion by 2007 (IDC, 2003).

Businesses will increasingly use wireless networks and applications to cut costs, increase flexibility, and create new products and services. Ford Motor Company has a totally wireless body shop and staging area for truck assembly in Dearborn, Michigan, with a customized materials-replenishment system and wireless tracking of each vehicle as it moves through assembly. Doctors are prescribing medications using wireless handhelds as they walk down hospital halls. Real estate agents use Palm smart phones to access all the available data on a house as they are showing it to prospective buyers. Sprint provides a wireless service for insurance adjusters to access data from corporate systems to process claims on site, find local repair shops, and even issue checks to customers on the spot. The implications for organizational productivity and performance are truly astounding.

Business Value of Wireless Networking

Exactly how do the wireless innovations we have just described provide value for businesses? Chapter 8 described the business value provided by telecommunications and networking. Wireless networks for voice and data further amplify that value by providing anytime, anywhere communication and access to information, including the information resources of the Internet.

Wireless communication helps businesses stay more easily in touch with customers, suppliers, and employees and provides more flexible arrangements for organizing work. Companies can save on wiring offices and conference rooms by using wireless networks because they do not have to pull cables through walls. Wireless networks also make additions, moves, and changes much easier.

A number of studies have shown that wireless networking increases worker productivity and output. If important data and people are accessible anywhere and anytime, workers spend less time trying to establish contact with these people or to access information (Intel, 2004; Sandsmark, 2002).

For example, Intel studied the work habits and productivity of more than 100 of its employees who were upgraded to notebook computers that could access wireless LANs and the Internet. By taking advantage of wireless connectivity for tasks such as searching for files, copying documents, sending e-mail, or scheduling meetings, these employees realized a productivity gain of more than two hours per week, representing 5 percent of a typical 40-hour work week and nearly 100 hours of additional productivity per employee per year. If the average cost per employee was $100,000 per year, the annual benefit per employee would be $5,000. The cost savings from using this technology more than paid for Intel's first-year cost of the new mobile devices.

Continuously connected wireless mobile systems actually changed the way Intel employees worked in the following ways:

- Employees made productive use of formerly wasted slices of time between larger tasks. Without a wireless notebook, an extra five minutes would have been insufficient to allow an employee to plug in, start up the system, connect to a remote network, and do useful work.

- Work locations became more flexible, with mobile employees believing they had more control over their work locations. They were able to select workplaces and times optimized to the task at hand—for example, working outside normal hours to support employees or partners in other parts of the world or finishing a piece of work while commuting.

- Wireless mobility allowed workers to reallocate their working time around professional and personal obligations.

Wireless technology has also been the source of new products, services, and sales channels in a variety of industries:

- Automotive manufacturers offer telematics as a value-added technology with their luxury cars. **Telematics** services combine wireless communication with tracking capabilities from the **global positioning system (GPS)**, a worldwide satellite navigational system. OnStar is an example. This optional telematics service is available in cars from General Motors (GM), Subaru, Volkswagen, Audi, and Isuzu. It has capabilities for on-board navigation, e-mail, stolen vehicle tracking, accident assistance, and information services such as news, stock quotes, and local traffic and road condition reports, using GPS to track the exact location of the vehicle on the road.

- Airlines, hotels, restaurants, and coffee shops such as Starbucks are equipping their lounges with hotspots for wireless Internet access to provide additional services and value to their customers.

- Safeway in the United Kingdom gave customers wireless Palm handheld devices and software to order products, increasing customer service. The wireless system also created a new low-cost channel to deliver coupons and special offers.

Inexpensive mobile devices make communication and Internet access available to groups that cannot afford conventional telephone or Internet service. For example, in China over 300 million people use mobile phones, which is more than the number of fixed telephone lines in that country. In Africa, there are twice as many cellular telephones as fixed lines, and by 2008 mobile phones will outnumber fixed phones by four to one. Rapidly declining costs promise to make high-speed wireless communication even more affordable, with tremendous benefits for business, education, medicine, government, and social services.

Wireless Transmission Media and Devices

Wireless transmission sends signals through air or space without being tied to a physical line. All wireless media rely on various parts of the electromagnetic spectrum, as illustrated in Figure 9-2. Some types of wireless transmission, such as **microwave** or infrared,

Mobile phones provide an inexpensive way of communicating and accessing information for people in Africa and other countries without extensive fixed phone lines or high PC usage and ownership.

by nature occupy specific spectrum frequency ranges (measured in megahertz [MHz]). Other types of wireless transmissions, such as cellular telephones and paging devices, have been assigned a specific range of frequencies by national regulatory agencies and international agreements. Each frequency range has characteristics that have helped determine the specific function or data communications niche assigned to it.

Microwave systems, both terrestrial and celestial, transmit high-frequency radio signals through the atmosphere and are widely used for high-volume, long-distance, point-to-point communication. Microwave signals follow a straight line and do not bend with the curvature of the earth; therefore, long-distance terrestrial transmission systems

FIGURE 9-2   *Frequency ranges for communications media and devices.*

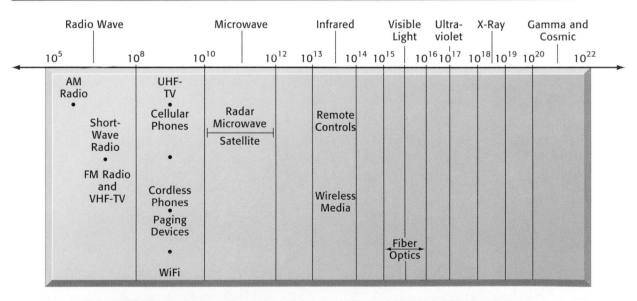

Each telecommunications transmission medium or device occupies a different frequency range, measured in megahertz, on the electromagnetic spectrum.

require that transmission stations be positioned about 37 miles apart, adding to the expense of microwave.

This problem can be solved by bouncing microwave signals off communication **satellites**, enabling them to serve as relay stations for microwave signals transmitted from terrestrial stations. Communication satellites are cost-effective for transmitting large quantities of data over very long distances. Satellites are typically used for communications in large, geographically dispersed organizations that would be difficult to tie together through wired media or terrestrial microwave transmission.

For instance, Amoco uses satellites for real-time data transfer of oil field exploration data gathered from searches of the ocean floor. Using geosynchronous satellites, exploration ships transfer these data to central computing centers in the United States for use by researchers in Houston, Tulsa, and suburban Chicago. Figure 9-3 illustrates how this system works.

Conventional communication satellites move in stationary orbits approximately 22,000 miles above the earth. A newer satellite system, the low-orbit satellite, travels much closer to the earth and is able to pick up signals from weak transmitters. Low-orbit satellites also consume less power and cost less to launch than conventional satellites.

DEVICES FOR WIRELESS TRANSMISSION

A range of alternative wireless devices is available for individuals requiring remote access to corporate systems and mobile communication and computing power. These devices include pagers, e-mail handhelds, personal digital assistants (PDAs), cellular telephones, and smart phones. Personal computers are also starting to be used in wireless transmission, and Section 9.2 provides a detailed description of the technology for wireless computing.

Paging systems, which beep when the user receives a short alphanumeric message, have been used for communicating with mobile workers. A more popular method of wireless text messaging is through **e-mail handhelds**, such as the BlackBerry Handheld, which operate on a variety of wireless data network services. These devices include a small display screen and a keypad for typing short messages. Newer versions of these devices have an organizer, Web and voice transmission features, and the ability to integrate with corporate applications. E-mail wireless handhelds are popular in the legal, financial, real estate, and other industries where there is a need to keep in constant touch with clients and the office.

Cellular telephones (cell phones) work by using radio waves to communicate with radio antennas (towers) placed within adjacent geographic areas called cells. A telephone message is transmitted to the local cell by the cellular telephone and then is passed from antenna to antenna—cell to cell—until it reaches the cell of its destination, where it is

FIGURE 9-3   *Amoco's satellite transmission system.*

Satellites help Amoco transfer seismic data between oil exploration ships and research centers in the United States.

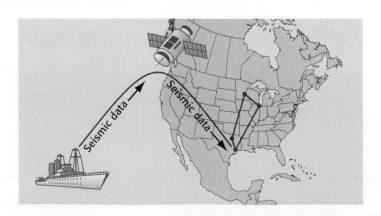

transmitted to the receiving telephone. As a cellular signal travels from one cell into another, a computer that monitors signals from the cells switches the conversation to a radio channel assigned to the next cell. The radio antenna cells normally cover eight-mile hexagonal cells, although their radius is smaller in densely populated localities.

Older cellular systems are analog and newer cellular systems are digital. These digital cellular systems are capable of sending and receiving short text messages. **Short message service (SMS)** is a text message service used by a number of digital cell phone systems to send and receive short alphanumeric messages less than 160 characters in length. Like e-mail, SMS messages can be forwarded and stored for later retrieval.

Personal digital assistants (PDAs) are small, handheld computers capable of entirely digital communications transmission. The handheld device includes applications such as an electronic scheduler, address book, memo pad, and expense tracker. More advanced models display, compose, send, and receive e-mail messages and provide wireless access to the Internet. Some have built-in digital cameras and voice communication capabilities.

Higher-speed cellular networks and the Internet have spawned a new class of digital communication appliances that combine the functionality of a PDA with that of a digital cell phone and require a cellular phone service connection. These **smart phones** can handle voice transmission and e-mail; save addresses; store schedules; access a private corporate network; and access information from the Internet. Some have embedded digital cameras. Smart phones include Web browser software that enables digital cellular phones to access Web pages formatted to send text or other information that is suitable for tiny screens.

Cellular Network Standards and Generations

Digital cellular service uses several different competing standards that do not interoperate with each other. This means that digital cellular handsets cannot work on networks that use another wireless standard.

In Europe and much of the rest of the world outside the United Sates, the standard is **GSM**, short for **Global System for Mobile Communication**. Three out of four of the world's estimated 2 billion cell phones are GSM, including most of China, the world's largest cell phone market. The system's strength is its international roaming capability. Users have seamless same-number roaming in more than 170 countries. Most GSM systems outside North America operate in the 900-MHz and 1.8-GHz frequency bands. (In North America they operate in the 1.9-GHz band.) The bandwidth is divided among users based on *time division multiple access (TDMA)* in which each user is allocated a portion of time on the frequency.

In the United States, GSM is not the standard because the Federal Communications Commission (FCC) permitted open competition in cell phone technology, resulting in multiple incompatible standards. This situation limits roaming and contributes to the high prices of U.S. cell phones.

There are GSM cell phone systems in the United States, including T-Mobile, VoiceStream, Cingular, and AT&T. However, the major standard in the United States is **Code Division Multiple Access (CDMA)**, which is the system used by Verizon, MCI, and Sprint. CDMA was developed by the military during World War II. It transmits over several frequencies, occupies the entire spectrum, and randomly assigns users to a range of frequencies over time. In general, CDMA is cheaper to implement, is more efficient in use of spectrum, and provides higher quality throughput of voice and data than GSM. Because of its inherent efficiency, implementing CDMA and a standard called wide-band CDMA (WCDMA) is the long-term objective even of existing GSM systems.

CELLULAR GENERATIONS

Wireless phone systems throughout the world are gradually moving toward much higher speeds and capacities. This transition involves over $200 billion in worldwide investment in what are called **3G networks** (third-generation cellular networks).

The first generation (1G) of cellular networks originating in the early 1980s were analog based. They supported voice communication and could only be used for data transfer with a proper modem. Second-generation (2G) cellular networks appeared about 10 years later using digital networks. 2G systems provide better voice quality and global roaming capabilities and can support simple data services such as SMS. Although 2G systems are used primarily for voice, they can support data transmission at rates ranging from 9.6 to 14.4 kilobits per second (Kbps). This transmission speed is still too slow for comfortable Internet access.

Third-generation (3G) cellular networks are based on packet-switched technology that achieves greater efficiencies and higher transmission speeds. 3G networks have speeds ranging from 144 Kbps for mobile users in, say, a car, to over 2 Mbps for stationary users. This is sufficient transmission capacity for video, graphics, and other rich media, in addition to voice, making 3G networks suitable for wireless broadband Internet access and always-on data transmission. If 3G networks live up to their promise, they will be able to handle e-mail, instant messaging, and Web browsing as effortlessly as current wired technologies.

Although wireless carriers have invested in 3G technology, it is still not in wide use. In the meantime, those interested in high-speed Internet access and data transmission are turning to an interim solution called **2.5G networks**. These networks are packet-switched, use many existing infrastructure elements, and have data transmission rates ranging from 50 to 144 Kbps. A 2.5G service called **General Packet Radio Service (GPRS)** transports data over GSM wireless networks and improves wireless Internet access. 2.5G also improves data transmission rates for CDMA. Table 9-1 summarizes these cellular generations.

Mobile Wireless Standards for Web Access

There are also competing standards governing the way wireless mobile devices access the Internet and the World Wide Web. **Wireless Application Protocol (WAP)** is a system of protocols and technologies that enables cell phones and other wireless devices with tiny display screens, low-bandwidth connections, and minimal memory to access Web-based information and services. WAP uses **Wireless Markup Language (WML)**, which is based on Extensible Markup Language (XML; see Chapter 6) and is optimized for tiny displays.

A person with a WAP-compliant phone uses the built-in microbrowser to make a request in WML. A **microbrowser** is an Internet browser with a small file size that can work with the low-memory constraints of handheld wireless devices and the low bandwidth of wireless networks. The request is passed to a WAP gateway, which retrieves the information from an Internet server in either standard Hypertext Markup Language (HTML) format or WML. The gateway translates HTML content back into WML so that the WAP client can receive it. The complexity of the translation process can affect the speed of information delivery. WAP supports most wireless network standards and operating systems for handheld computing devices.

TABLE 9-1 *Wireless Cellular Generations*

Generation	Capacity	Description
1G	Low	Analog cellular networks for voice communication
2G	10–14 Kbps	Digital wireless networks, primarily for voice communication; limited data transmission capability
2.5G	50–144 Kbps	Interim step toward 3G in the United States
3G	144 Kbps–2+ Mbps fixed	High-speed, mobile, supports video and other rich media, always-on for e-mail, Web browsing, instant messaging

FIGURE 9-4   Wireless Application Protocol (WAP) versus I-mode.

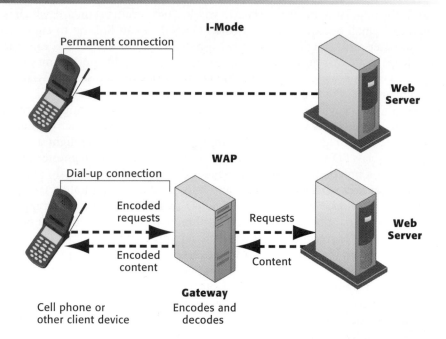

WAP and I-mode use alternative standards for accessing information from the wireless Web.

I-mode is a wireless service offered by Japan's NTT DoCoMo mobile phone network that uses a different set of standards. Instead of using WAP, I-mode uses compact HTML to deliver content, making it easier for businesses to convert their HTML Web sites to mobile service. I-mode uses packet switching, which enables users to be connected constantly to the network and content providers to broadcast relevant information to users. (WAP users have to dial in to see if a site has changed.) I-mode can handle color graphics not available on WAP handsets as well as video, although WAP is being modified to handle color graphics (see Figure 9-4).

9.2 WIRELESS COMPUTER NETWORKS AND INTERNET ACCESS

The Institute of Electrical and Electronics Engineers (IEEE) has established a hierarchy of complementary standards for wireless computer networks. These standards include IEEE 802.15 for the Personal Area Network (Bluetooth), IEEE 802.11 for the Local Area Network (LAN) (Wi-Fi), 802.16 for the Metropolitan Area Network (MAN) (WiMax), and the proposed 802.20 standard for the Wide Area Network (WAN). Table 9-2 summarizes these standards.

TABLE 9-2   Global Wireless Network Standards

Type of Network	Standard
Personal area network (PAN)	IEEE 802.15 (Bluetooth)
Local area network (LAN)	IEEE 802.11 (Wi-Fi)
Metropolitan area network (MAN)	IEEE 802.16 (WiMax)
Wide area network (WAN)	IEEE 802.20 (proposed)

Bluetooth

Bluetooth is the popular name for the 802.15 wireless networking standard, which is useful for creating small **personal area networks** (**PANs**). It can link up to eight devices within a 10-meter area using low-power, radio-based communication and can transmit up to 722 Kbps in the 2.4-gigahertz (GHz) band. The name Bluetooth comes from the 10th-century Danish King Harald Blatan (Bluetooth). Ericsson, the Scandinavian mobile handset company, was the first to develop this specification.

Wireless phones, keyboards, computers, printers, and computing devices using Bluetooth can communicate with each other and even operate each other without direct user intervention (see Figure 9-5). For example, a person could highlight a telephone number on a wireless PDA and automatically activate a call on a digital phone or that person could direct a notebook computer to send a document file wirelessly to a printer. Bluetooth can connect wireless keyboards and mice to PCs or cell phone ear pieces to a cell phone without wires. Bluetooth has low power requirements, making it appropriate for battery-powered handheld computers, cell phones, or PDAs. By 2006, 80 percent of mobile phones and 70 percent of PDAs will be Bluetooth-enabled.

Although Bluetooth lends itself to home networking, it has uses in large corporations. A Coca-Cola bottling company in Australia equipped field sales and marketing staff with Bluetooth-enabled laptop computers and Bluetooth-enabled phones. Bluetooth enabled the laptop to connect to the mobile phone's data network so that employees could be connected to the Internet, company network, e-mail, and client information anywhere and any time. Both United Parcel Service (UPS) and FedEx equipped their delivery drivers with Bluetooth-enabled handhelds to expedite their work. You can find out more about these companies' use of Bluetooth in the chapter-ending case study.

Wi-Fi

The IEEE set of standards for wireless LANs is the 802.11 family, also known as **Wi-Fi** (for Wireless Fidelity). There are three standards in this family: 802.11a, 802.11b, and 802.11g.

FIGURE 9-5   *A Bluetooth network (PAN).*

Bluetooth enables a variety of devices, including cell phones, PDAs, wireless keyboards and mice, PCs, and printers, to interact wirelessly with each other within a small 30-foot (10-meter) area. In addition to the links shown, Bluetooth can be used to network similar devices to send data from one PC to another, for example.

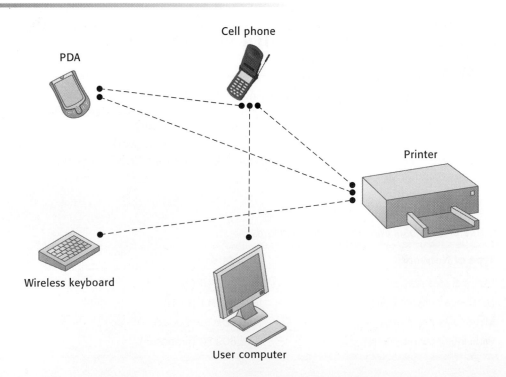

The 802.11a standard can transmit up to 54 Mbps in the unlicensed 5-GHz frequency range and has an effective distance of 10 to 30 meters. The **802.11b** standard can transmit up to 11 Mbps in the unlicensed 2.4-GHz band and has an effective distance of 30 to 50 meters, although this range can be extended outdoors by using tower-mounted antennas. The 802.11g standard, which was recently finalized, can transmit up to 54 Mbps in the 2.4-GHz range.

Because 802.11b and 802.11g operate in the 2.4-GHz frequency, products built for either of these two standards are compatible. Products designed for the 802.11a specification won't work with either 802.11b or 802.11g because 802.11a uses a different frequency band.

The 802.11b standard has been the most widely used standard for creating wireless LANs and providing wireless Internet access. However, 802.11g may become more popular in the next few years, and dual-band systems capable of handling 802.11b and 802.11g are expected to proliferate.

A Wi-Fi system can operate in two different modes. In *infrastructure mode,* wireless devices communicate with a wired LAN using access points. An **access point** is a box consisting of a radio receiver/transmitter and antennas that links to a wired network, router, or hub. Each access point and its wireless devices are known as a Basic Service Set (BSS).

In *ad-hoc mode,* also known as peer-to-peer mode, wireless devices communicate with each other directly and do not use an access point. Most Wi-Fi communication uses infrastructure mode. (Ad-hoc mode is used for very small LANs in the home or small business offices.)

Figure 9-6 illustrates an 802.11 wireless LAN operating in infrastructure mode that connects a small number of mobile devices to a larger wired LAN. Most wireless devices are client machines. The servers that the mobile client stations need to use are on the wired LAN. The access point controls the wireless stations and acts as a bridge between the main wired LAN and the wireless LAN. (A *bridge* connects two LANs based on different technologies.)

Mobile wireless stations often need an add-in card called a wireless network interface card (NIC) that has a built-in radio and antenna. **Wireless NICs** can be credit-card-size

FIGURE 9-6   *An 802.11 wireless LAN.*

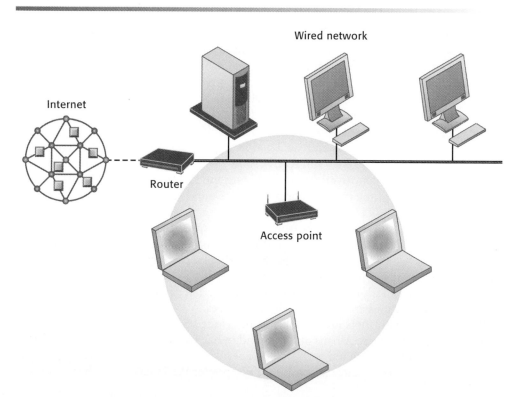

Mobile laptop computers equipped with wireless network interface cards link to the wired LAN by communicating with the access point. The access point uses radio waves to transmit network signals from the wired network to the client adapters, which convert them into data that the mobile device can understand. The client adapter then transmits the data from the mobile device back to the access point, which forwards the data to the wired network.

cards that snap into the PCMCIA card slot on a PC or external adapters that plug into the PC's universal serial bus (USB) port. Newer laptop PCs come equipped with chips that can send and receive Wi-Fi signals.

WI-FI AND WIRELESS INTERNET ACCESS

The 802.11 standard can also be used to provide wireless access to the Internet using a broadband connection. In this instance, an access point plugs into an Internet connection, which could come from a cable Internet line or Digital Subscriber Line (DSL) telephone service. Computers within a range of the access point would be able to use it to link wirelessly to the Internet.

Wi-Fi networking costs have declined so that a simple wireless Wi-Fi network can be set up for a few hundred dollars. Computer makers are making wireless capability a standard feature of their hardware. Intel now sells Centrino microprocessor and accessory chips for notebook computers that have specialized Wi-Fi capabilities (the accessory chips include a Wi-Fi transmitter) and smaller power consumption requirements.

BENEFITS OF WI-FI

Large corporations and small businesses are using Wi-Fi networks to create low-cost wireless LANs and to provide Internet access from conference rooms and temporary workstations. Wi-Fi hotspots are springing up in hotels, airport lounges, libraries, and college campuses to provide mobile access to the Internet.

Hotspots typically consist of one or more access points positioned on a ceiling, wall, or other strategic spot in a public place to provide maximum wireless coverage for a specific area. Users in range of a hotspot can then access the Internet from their laptops. Some hotspots are free or do not require any additional software to use; others may require activation and the establishment of a user account by providing a credit card number over the Web.

American Airlines has installed Wi-Fi in its Admiral's Clubs and is partnering with T-Mobile, along with Delta Air Lines and United Airlines, to install Wi-Fi services at the gates of several major airports. American Airlines also uses Wi-Fi for curbside check-in, baggage handling, and cargo package racking. Because 75 percent of its employees do not have a fixed workplace, American sees many other opportunities for integrating mobile computing into its business.

Passengers will also be able to use Wi-Fi services during their airline flights. Lufthansa Airlines and other airlines are starting to equip their jet airplanes with a Wi-Fi service called Connexion supplied by Boeing so that passengers with laptop computers can log on to the Internet while they are in flight.

Wi-Fi is very popular in South Korea. Hotels, restaurants, universities, and other public facilities have Wi-Fi hotspots, and thousands of college students use Wi-Fi on campus for research, course work, and downloading and listening to music.

Companies such as Starbucks and McDonald's are offering customers Wi-Fi services in many of their retail outlets. They will receive some revenue from their fees for Wi-Fi services, but their primary motivation for deploying the technology is to encourage customers to spend more time in their stores, purchase more food, or select their establishments over competitors'.

For Starbucks, providing Wi-Fi hotspots provides special management benefits. The Window on Management shows how Starbucks managers use the Wi-Fi networks in stores under their supervision to link to the Starbucks corporate network. This setup enables them to work with corporate systems on-site instead of having to travel to Starbucks' regional headquarters to use a computer. The time savings enable them to focus on store operations and working with employees.

Many free public hotspots are available in the United States and other countries. For example, Wialess.com in St. Albans outside London has set up hotspots in pubs and bars. Café chain Beugo has partnered with Broadscape to offer free Wi-Fi service to compete with Starbucks and Costa Coffee, where users must pay for Wi-Fi services. Other businesses

Over 3600 Starbucks cafes have Wi-Fi networks providing customers with wireless Internet access. These networks also provide managers with wireless access to Starbucks' private corporate network.

around Europe are wiring numerous public gathering places where professionals and students are likely to congregate.

WI-FI CHALLENGES

Wi-Fi is clearly helping individual companies extend their networking to new areas and obtain Internet services at a very low cost. The challenge facing the technology industry as a whole, however, is how to transform Wi-Fi from a wireless hit-or-miss phenomenon into a sustainable business.

Right now, users cannot freely roam from hotspot to hotspot if these hotspots use different Wi-Fi network services. Unless the service is free, users would need to log on to separate accounts for each service, each with its own fees. All of the hotspots, some public, some private, need to be transformed into interoperable, dependable networks with billing systems, roaming agreements, and technical standards that will enable users to plug into hotspots at will. Some question whether commercial Wi-Fi services can flourish when so many free hotspots are available to mobile users.

One of the major drawbacks of Wi-Fi is its weak security features, which make these wireless networks vulnerable to intruders. Because the range of a Wi-Fi network can extend beyond the confines of the building where it is being used, an outsider may be able to penetrate the network, obtain a free Internet connection, and even gain access to the resources on the computers of legitimate network users. We provide more detail about Wi-Fi security issues in Chapter 10.

Another drawback of Wi-Fi networks is susceptibility to interference from nearby systems operating in the same spectrum. There is no way to control additional new devices in the same area that might cause interference, such as wireless phones, microwave ovens, or other wireless LANs.

WiMax and EV-DO

A surprisingly large number of areas in the United States and throughout the world do not have access to Wi-Fi or fixed broadband connectivity. Traditional DSL can reach only about 3 miles from the central telephone office switch, leaving many urban and suburban areas without DSL connections. Many older cable networks cannot handle high-speed broadband. The range of Wi-Fi systems is typically not more than 300 feet from the base station, making it difficult for rural groups that don't have cable or DSL service to find high speed access to the Internet.

WINDOW ON MANAGEMENT

WI-FI: STARBUCKS'S SOLUTION TO GO

From one Seattle coffee bean store in 1971 Starbucks has grown into the world's number one specialty coffee chain, with about 6,500 outlets in 25 countries. Starbucks shops can be found on street corners, in airport terminals, in supermarkets, and in office buildings. In 2001, the company started to provide wireless Internet access in stores that it owns. Of the company's 3,645 stores in the United States, about 60 percent have Wi-Fi hotspots.

Deutsche Telekom's T-Mobile USA unit is footing much of the cost of building these Wi-Fi wireless networks in the hope of acquiring subscribing Starbucks customers. To use the T-Mobile HotSpot service at Starbucks, customers need to activate a T-Mobile HotSpot account. Then using a Wi-Fi-enabled laptop computer, Tablet PC, Pocket PC, or other Wi-Fi-enabled PDA, customers can launch their Web browsers from a participating Starbucks store and log on to the Internet.

The T-Mobile HotSpot account can be used for wireless Internet access at other locations, such as Borders Books & Music stores, FedEx Kinko's stores, airports, lounges for American, Delta, United, and US Airways, and selected Hyatt hotel locations throughout the United States.

Starbucks benefits in several ways. According to Ken Lombard, Starbucks president of Music and Entertainment, "The convenience and reliability of T-Mobile HotSpot is bringing customers in frequently and keeping them in the stores longer." Internal research shows that T-Mobile HotSpot subscribers visit Starbucks more often, an average of eight times per month, and spend more time in the stores than non-Wi-Fi customers. (On average, 70 percent of Starbucks customers stay in a store five minutes or less.) The average time spent on the Internet at a Starbucks store lasts approximately one hour. Nearly 90 percent of T-Mobile Internet use at Starbucks occurs after 9 A.M., increasing business during nonpeak hours.

The Wi-Fi networks could add to Starbucks's profits by enabling more sales per minute, reducing the time for clearing credit card sales at the cash register, and delivering interactive training to local stores from a central server. The networks may even generate new sources of revenue, such as selling music downloads and even entertainment videos in Starbucks cafés. Starbucks is marketing its Wi-Fi service at real estate trade shows to entice agents into making its stores their remote offices, where they can show clients houses online.

In addition to boosting revenue, Starbucks's Wi-Fi networks are helping Starbucks improve the internal management of the business. Starbucks managers are using the service to create wireless local area networks (WLANs) to help run store operations and to give them wireless access to the company's private corporate network and systems. Starbucks has started equip-

ping its district managers with Wi-Fi-enabled laptop computers to take advantage of these networks.

Lisa Jansen, who oversees 10 Starbucks stores in the Willamette Valley area near Portland, Oregon, previously had to go to a store, review its operations, develop a list of items on which to follow up, and drive as far as 23 miles to Starbucks regional headquarters to file reports and send e-mail. Then she would head out to another store and do the same thing again. Now, instead of running her business from a cubicle in regional headquarters, Jansen can do her work sitting at a table in one of the stores she oversees. She saves 45 minutes of driving time twice a day, or up to 10 hours per week.

With the newfound time, Jansen can spend more time in stores to observe customers being served and their reactions to the service. She can see whether employees are following Starbucks's cash-handling policies and procedures and can determine whether each customer transaction is completed within the company's three-minute benchmark. If a store needs a new umbrella, she can order it on the spot. If a particular type of coffee been has been selling well, she can send an electronic message to restock before the store's inventory runs out.

Artie Dohler, a manager for several Starbucks stores in the New York Times Square district, has been able to increase the number of employees he manages from 100 to 115 and to improve their training. He uses the time he saves with wireless networking to interact more frequently with his employees. He works with them to taste and evaluate the coffees they serve and watches them introduce themselves or the store's products to customers. In 2001, Dohler's employee turnover rate was 117 percent, meaning he had to train a whole new staff each year. Since then he has been able to reduce that turnover rate to two-thirds.

By implementing Wi-Fi, Starbucks has been able to increase the presence of district managers by 25 percent without adding any extra managers. With productivity gains such as these, one can see why Lovina McMurchy, director of Starbucks New Ventures Group, calls Starbucks's Wi-Fi networks a "great strategic asset."

Sources: Susan Rush, "Starbucks Brews Up More Wi-Fi," *Wireless Week,* July 7, 2004; "More than 3100 Wi-Fi Hotspots in Starbucks Stores," www.geekzone. com, accessed July 19, 2004; Tom Steinert-Threlkeld, "Mine Mine 'To Stay,'" *Baseline Magazine,* April 2003; Tischelle George, "Starbucks' Data to Go," *Information Week,* January 20, 2003; Dan Richman, "Starbucks on Top of the Wi-Fi World," *Seattle Post-Intelligencer,* March 31, 2003, www.starbucks.com, accessed December 10, 2004; and Rick Anderson, "Business: Starbucks: Just Getting Started," *Seattle Weekly,* April 30–May 6, 2003.

To Think About: How does Wi-Fi provide value for Starbucks? What management, organization, and technology issues did it have to address in installing Wi-Fi networks in its stores?

The IEEE developed a new family of standards known as WiMax to deal with these problems. **WiMax**, which stands for Worldwide Interoperability for Microwave Access, is the popular term for IEEE Standard 802.16, known as the "Air Interface for Fixed Broadband Wireless Access Systems." WiMax has a wireless access range of up to 31 miles, compared to 300 feet for Wi-Fi and 30 feet for Bluetooth, and a data transfer rate of up to 75 Mbps. The 802.16 specification also has robust security and quality of service features to support voice and video.

WiMax antennas will be able to beam high-speed Internet connections to rooftop antennas of homes and businesses that are miles away. The technology can thus provide long-distance broadband wireless access to rural areas and other locations that are not currently served while avoiding the steep installation costs of the traditional wired infrastructure. The 802.16 standard supports use of frequencies ranging from 2 to 11 GHz, which include both licensed and unregulated bands.

Intel is bringing out WiMax-enabled versions of its Centrino chip, and Nokia will have a WiMax cell phone in 2005. WiMax technology should be broadly available in 2006.

EV-DO AND WIRELESS CELLULAR ACCESS

In addition to 3G networks for mobile phones, major cellular carriers are upgrading their networks to provide anytime, anywhere broadband access for PCs and other devices. Verizon's service, called BroadBand Access, uses a technology called **EV-DO**, which stands for Evolution Data Optimized. EV-DO provides wireless access to the Internet over a cellular network at an average speed of 300 to 500 Kbps. Although it has a wider range of coverage than Wi-Fi, it won't work in "dead spots" where regular cell phone systems have weak signals, including deep inside buildings.

To use this service, Verizon subscribers install specific software and insert a special card into their laptops. The card has a mini antenna that connects the laptop to the Verizon Wireless network and establishes an Internet connection. Verizon is also starting to extend EV-DO service to PDAs and cell phones and expects the service to be available in every major U.S. metropolitan area by the end of 2005.

Over time, cell phones, wireless PDAs, and laptops will be able to switch from one type of network to another, moving from Wi-Fi to WiMax to cellular networks. Cell phone makers Nokia, LG Electronics, and Samsung are adding Wi-Fi capabilities to their phones. Motorola's CN620 clamshell mobile device combines Wi-Fi and GSM cellular technology. Hewlett-Packard's iPaq H6315 Pocket PC handheld supports Wi-Fi, Bluetooth, and GSM/GPRS cellular service. It will automatically connect to the fastest-available network and allows voice and data services to be used simultaneously.

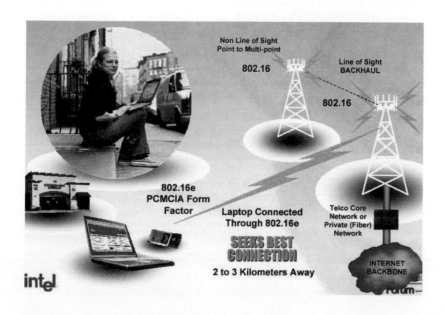

WiMax is a standards-based technology that provides high-speed wireless communication for metropolitan area networks (MANs). It can be used for "last mile" broadband connections to the home or office, for creating wireless hotspots, and for providing high-speed enterprise connectivity for businesses.

Hewlett-Packard's HP6315 PocketPC handheld supports Wi-Fi, Bluetooth, and cellular service. Users will be able to switch from one type of network to another to find the fastest service as they move from place to place.

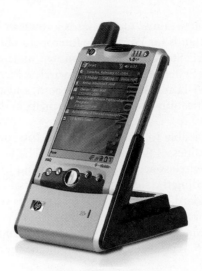

9.3 M-COMMERCE AND MOBILE COMPUTING

We have already described how Wi-Fi wireless network technology can be used to access the Internet from an untethered PC or handheld computing device. Wi-Fi offers some mobility for Internet access, but users can access the Web only if they are in range of their wireless networks. This type of wireless computing, in which users move from wireless hotspot to wireless hotspot to gain network or Internet access, is sometimes referred to as **nomadic computing**.

Mobile computing, in contrast, enables Internet-enabled cell phones, PDAs, and other wireless computing devices to access digital information on the Internet from any location. Truly mobile computing will support a new kind of mobile commerce. Chapter 4 introduced m-commerce—the use of the Internet for purchasing goods and services as well as for transmitting messages using wireless mobile devices. Although m-commerce represents a small fraction of total e-commerce transactions, revenue has been steadily growing (see Figure 9-7).

M-Commerce Services and Applications

Table 9-3 describes the most popular categories of m-commerce services and applications for mobile computing. Location-based applications are of special interest because they take advantage of the unique capabilities of mobile technology. Whenever a user is connected to the Internet by a wireless device (cell phone, PDA, handheld), the transmission technology can be leveraged to determine that person's location and beam location-specific services or product information. For example, drivers could use this capability to obtain local weather data and traffic information along with alternate route suggestions and descriptions of nearby restaurants.

Instead of focusing on how to bring a customer to a Web site, marketing strategies will shift to finding ways of bringing the message directly to the customer at the point of need (Kenny and Marshall, 2000). Figure 9-8 illustrates how personalization can be extended by the ubiquitous Internet and m-commerce.

M-commerce applications have taken off for services that are time-critical, that appeal to people on the move, or that accomplish a task more efficiently than other methods. They are especially popular in Europe, Japan, South Korea, and other countries where fees for conventional Internet usage are very expensive. Here are some examples:

Mobile bill payment. Sumit Mobile Systems, working with mobile providers, banks, and utility companies, provides a service for people in Shanghai, China, to pay their utility

FIGURE 9-7   *Global m-commerce revenue, 2000–2005.*

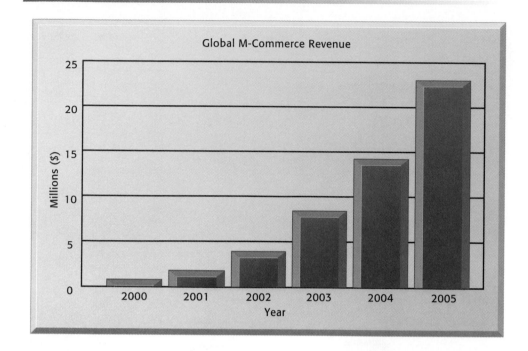

M-commerce sales represent a small fraction of total e-commerce sales, but that percentage is steadily growing.

Source: Copyright 2005 Jupitermedia Corporation. All rights reserved.

bills by cell phone. Most people in China do not have checking accounts and very few have credit cards, so bills must be paid by standing in a long line at a bank. The Sumit Smartpay system flashes a message on a subscriber's cell phone when a payment is due. The user then types in a secret number to authorize the payment from his or her bank account.

Content and products. NTT DoCoMo, the wireless arm of Nippon Telegraph and Telephone Company, offers Internet-enabled cell phone users services for e-mail and for accessing Web sites formatted for tiny screens. Subscribers can check train schedules, obtain movie listings, browse restaurant guides, purchase tickets on Japan Airlines, trade stocks, view new cartoons, and read Japan's largest daily newspaper. Menus of services can be tailored to individual subscribers' interests. Some of these services are free. Those that aren't are bundled and charged to subscribers' monthly telephone bills.

Banking and financial services. Citibank offers wireless alerts about changes in account information on digital cell phones that support text messaging. Thailand's Bank of Asia offers a mobile service called ASIA M-Banking. Enrolled customers can check account

TABLE 9-3   *M-Commerce Services and Applications for Mobile Computing*

M-Commerce Service	Applications
Information-based services	Instant messaging, e-mail, searching for a movie or restaurant using a cell phone or handheld PDA
Transaction-based services	Purchasing stocks, concert tickets, music, or games; searching for the best price for an item using a cell phone and buying it in a physical store or on the Web
Personalized services	Services that anticipate what a customer wants based on that person's location or data profile, such as updated airline flight information or beaming coupons for nearby restaurants

FIGURE 9-8   *Customer personalization with the ubiquitous Internet.*

Companies can use mobile wireless devices to deliver new value-added services directly to customers at any time and in any place, extending personalization and deepening their relationships.

Target	Platform	When	Content and Service
Traveler	Computer-equipped car 	Whenever car is moving	Provide maps, driving directions, weather reports, ads for nearby restaurants and hotels.
Parent	Cell phone 	During school days	Notify about school-related closings: Hello, Caroline. Your children's school is closing early. Press 1 for closure reason Press 2 for weather reports Press 3 for traffic reports
Stockbroker	Pager 	During trading days. Notify if unusually high trading volume.	Summary portfolio analysis showing changes in positions for each holding.

balances, transfer funds between savings and other accounts, and pay their mobile phone and Internet usage charges using a Web-enabled mobile phone. They can complete these banking transactions anywhere at any time without having to visit a bank branch. Seoul-based Infobank offers a secure wireless platform for mobile phone users interested in securities trading.

Wireless advertising. The cable television History Channel worked with Enpocket, a mobile marketing technology provider, to send selected wireless users 100,000 text messages promoting its special "Barbarians" show. An Enpocket survey of message recipients found that 88 percent received the message, 18 percent watched "Barbarians," and 12 percent forwarded the message to a friend. The History Channel decided to use wireless text messaging to promote more shows (Cho, 2004).

Location-based services. Vodafone Italy, which has offered mobile services since 1995 to 19 million customers, started offering location-based services in mid-2002. Vodafone customers can access relevant traffic information, calculate itineraries, and search for nearby gas stations, hotels, restaurants, and health care centers. In London, Zingo offers a service for using a mobile phone to hail nearby taxicabs. A mobile phone call to a specified telephone number connects to the closest available taxi driver. The caller speaks directly to the driver to confirm the details of the trip.

Games and entertainment. AT&T Wireless and Sprint offer services for viewing video clips from CNBC and College Sports Television and for listening to radio broadcasts of Major League Baseball games and National Public Radio reports. Korean mobile phone users can view an array of TV programs, store hours of digital music on their phones, and download video clips. Many mobile phone services offer downloadable digital games and ringtones (digitized melodies that play on mobile phones).

Accessing Information from the Wireless Web

Although cell phones, PDAs, and other handheld mobile devices can access the Web at any time and from any place, the amount of information that they can actually handle at one time is very limited. Until 3G broadband service comes into widespread use, these devices will not be able to transmit or receive large amounts of data. The information must fit onto small display screens.

Some Web sites have been specifically designed for m-commerce. They feature Web pages with very few graphics and just enough information to fit on a small mobile handheld screen. Special **wireless portals** (also known as mobile portals) feature content and services optimized for mobile devices to steer users to the information they are most likely to need. They typically offer a variety of features, links to other wireless sites, and the ability to select content to be pushed to the user's device, as well as providing a point of entry for anyone to send the user a message.

For example, Microsoft's wireless portal provides access to news from MSNBC, sports from ESPN, movie times, local traffic reports, restaurant listings, yellow pages, and stock market reports, as well as capabilities for managing e-mail messages and instant messaging. The Wireless Portal of the Canadian government provides access to selected government information and services, such as Canadian government news releases, estimated waiting times for crossing the Canadian–U.S. land border, currency exchange rates and a currency converter, passport office locations and phone numbers, economic statistics, contact information for Canadian members of Parliament, and Canadian government employee phone numbers.

Voice portals accept voice commands for accessing Web content, e-mail, and other electronic applications from a cell phone or standard telephone. Sophisticated voice recognition software processes the requests, and responses are translated back into speech for the customer. For example, AOLbyPhone provides voice access to weather forecasts, movie show times, sports scores, top news stories, stock prices, financial news, and business and residential directories. Users can also listen and reply to any e-mail using their own voice.

Digital Payment Systems and M-Commerce

With a Wi-Fi connection, you can take advantage of all existing forms of Internet payment—the fact that you are connected wirelessly should have no impact. However, m-commerce requires special digital payment systems geared to the types of transactions that are taking place using cell phones, PDAs, and other small handheld devices. These transactions are mainly small and frequent purchases for items such as soft drinks, sports scores, newspapers, mobile games, or concert tickets amounting to $10 or less that are not well-suited to credit card billing. (For purchases below this amount, the charges levied by payment processors and banks make credit cards too expensive.)

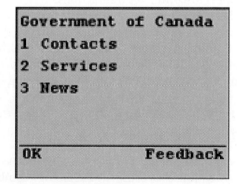

The government of Canada's Wireless Portal is a quick and easy single point of access to selected government information and services for mobile users.

Micropayment systems are working well in Europe and Asia, where mobile operators and Internet service providers (ISPs) handle small payments by adding them up and presenting them on a single bill such as the mobile telephone bill. Examples are Vodafone's mPay bill in Europe and mONEPayment in Austria. Mobile phone bills can be used to pay for ring tones, logs, java games, and car parking. In London, you can buy Virgin Cola using a Virgin Mobile phone by simply dialing a number on the vending machine (the cost of the drink is charged to your cell phone account). A mobile micropayment system from Finland's Sonera enables users in Helsinki to pay for parking using their mobile phones and have the payment amount invoiced on their mobile phone bills. In Japan, NTT DoCoMo handles the billing for millions of small purchases made by its I-mode subscribers.

NTT DoCoMo customers can also use a new stored payment system for their purchases. Special cell phones are equipped with a smart card computer chip that can store electronic cash. To pay, a person merely needs to wave the cell phone within a few inches of a special display in stores, restaurants, and near vending machines. There is no need to dial any special numbers. When the smart card chip runs out of cash, it can be recharged by slipping the phone into a slot of a machine found in offices and convenience stores and inserting money into the machine.

In both the United States and Europe, the micropayment services just described are based on a "walled garden" model in which individual service providers run their own separate payment systems. What is needed to help m-commerce take off is more interoperability achieved by having all the players agree on a common, secure platform for wireless m-commerce payments. To become widely adopted, a universal m-commerce payment system requires the backing of most of the major stakeholders in payment systems—consumers, vendors, phone equipment manufacturers, wireless service providers, and financial industry participants.

Several noteworthy interoperability initiatives have appeared. In March 2003, a consortium called Mobile Payment Services Association (MPSA) was founded by leading global wireless service providers Vodafone PLC, T-Mobile, Orange SA, and Telefonica Moviles SA to offer a single, simple way of paying for goods and services by mobile phone across the European continent. MPSA rebranded itself under the name Simpay in June 2003, and other wireless service providers are likely to join. Simpay works with a number of mobile phone systems, enabling customers to make purchases through mobile operator– managed payment accounts either online or in physical stores. Along similar lines, four of Austria's top five national communications operators, including T-Mobile, Hutchinson, One, and Telering, offer a single m-payment interface to merchants.

MOBILE WALLETS

In Chapter 4 we described the value of digital wallets that store online shoppers' personal information and credit card numbers to expedite the purchase process. A few companies have started offering **mobile wallets (m-wallets)** that perform the same functions for wireless m-commerce transactions.

Deutsche Telecom's wireless service users in Germany and the United Kingdom can use the T-Mobile mobile wallet to enter all their personal data just once. Then when they make purchases from vendors in the Deutsche Telecom network, the mobile wallet automatically fills in the blanks on the order form. Some Nokia cell phone models include a mobile wallet capability for securely storing sensitive information.

M-Commerce Challenges

The number of Wi-Fi hotspots for wireless Internet access has been mushrooming in many countries because the technology combines high-speed Internet access with a measure of flexibility and mobility. Rollout of mobile m-commerce services, however, has proved more problematic. Keyboards and screens on cell phones are still tiny and awkward to use. The data transfer speeds on second-generation cellular networks are very slow compared to dial-up and high-speed Internet connections for PCs. Each second waiting for data to download costs the customer money. Most Internet-enabled phones have limited memory and power supplies.

Web content for wireless devices is primarily in the form of text with very little graphics. For mobile commerce to become popular and successful, more Web sites need to be designed specifically for small wireless devices, and these wireless devices need to be more Web-friendly. M-commerce will benefit from 3G networks and other cellular broadband services and from interoperable payment systems.

9.4 WIRELESS TECHNOLOGY IN THE ENTERPRISE

In addition to m-commerce, mobile applications have permeated many other areas of business, creating new efficiencies and ways of working. In this section we present examples of where mobile and wireless technologies are having their greatest impact.

Wireless Applications for Customer Relationship Management

Major customer relationship management (CRM) vendors have enhanced their products to provide mobile support for sales and service activities. A growing number of sales professionals work outside the office and require up-to-date customer records and account information to help them close deals. The ability to deliver this information on the spot helps mobile sales staff act decisively at the point of customer interaction.

For example, Siebel Systems' Siebel Sales Wireless enables sales professionals to access customer account records and related information such as order status or recent service issues at any time or location. They can also enter the most current account and deal information data into their wireless devices to update the Siebel corporate customer database. The system will alert representatives to important events using wireless messaging.

Field service workers benefit from wireless applications that provide real-time access to critical information while they are servicing customers. Wireless CRM applications provide access to critical customer and service information while service representatives are working with clients. For example, a field service technician might use a wireless handheld to obtain information about the service history for a piece of equipment that must be fixed or whether parts required to fix the equipment are available. Some wireless CRM tools include capabilities for reporting field service staff time, expenses, parts availability, and details for follow-on work.

Pitney Bowes, a large vendor of postage meters and mailing systems, uses a wireless customer relationship management application for its Global Mailing Systems Division, in which 1,500 employees service its machines designed for low-volume distribution of mail. This system links Pitney Bowes field service representatives to the company's call center and service applications and enables them to access data from multiple back-end systems.

Figure 9-9 illustrates how this system works. When a customer calls to place a field service request, Siebel CRM software identifies the product needing repair, selects the field service representative to dispatch, and messages that technician's wireless device with the service request. The technician then acknowledges receipt of the order. Messages from

FIGURE 9-9   *Pitney Bowes's wireless CRM system.*

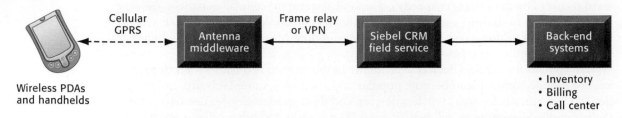

The application uses Pocket PC PDAs, RIM 957s wireless e-mail handhelds and other wireless hand-helds, field service software from CRM vendor Siebel Systems, cellular wireless data service from Cingular Wireless, and Antenna SmartClient and Antenna A3 middleware to link field workers using wireless handhelds to Siebel CRM software and Pitney Bowes's back-end systems.

the technicians' handhelds are routed to Antenna's wireless gateways, which translate the data into XML format and forward them over a frame relay or virtual private network (VPN) to Pitney Bowes's computer center for use by Siebel Systems' CRM field service software, which automatically updates inventory, billing, call center, and other back-end applications.

The system delivers customer and service history data instantly to the field service technician's handheld. It also tells the technician whether the work is covered by contract or is billable and feeds data for billable work into Pitney Bowes's billing system. If parts are required, the Siebel field service application determines if the part is in stock and sends information on these parts to a legacy inventory application that is linked to the company's SAP supply chain management system. Information from this system has enabled Pitney Bowes's field service staff to solve problems faster and complete more service calls per day (Songini, 2004).

Wireless Supply Chain Management and Radio Frequency Identification (RFID)

Contemporary supply chain management (SCM) systems are a fertile area for mobile wireless technology because of the need to provide simultaneous, accurate information about demand, supply, production, and logistics as goods move among supply chain partners. SCM software vendors include capabilities for mobile support and wireless capture of data on movements of goods and other events.

mySAP Supply Chain Management software offers a number of mobile capabilities. Manufacturing employees can view work instructions on wireless handheld devices anywhere on the factory floor. Supervisors can use wireless handhelds to call up data from process control systems to monitor production-line behavior.

A firm that needs to ship out goods can use mySAP SCM to create a shipment order and tender it to a selected freight forwarder. The forwarder can access this tendering application from a mobile device and accept, reject, or modify the planned order. If the forwarder rejects the tender or does not reply within an anticipated time frame, the supply chain management software triggers a text message alert to the logistics manager's mobile phone to expedite the search for another forwarder.

mySAP SCM also uses mobile technology for warehouse management tasks such as picking, packing, unpacking, freight loading and unloading checks, and inventory queries. Some of these activities use radio frequency identification technology (RFID) technology. Because RFID technology is such a powerful tool for supply chain management, let's take a closer look.

RADIO FREQUENCY IDENTIFICATION (RFID)

Radio frequency identification (RFID) systems provide a powerful technology for tracking the movement of goods throughout the supply chain. RFID systems use tiny tags with embedded microchips containing data about an item and its location to transmit radio signals over a short distance to special RFID readers. The RFID readers then pass the data over a network to a computer for processing. Unlike bar codes, RFID tags do not need line-of-sight contact to be read.

Internet Connection ——
The Internet Connection for this chapter will direct you to a series of Web sites where you can complete an exercise to evaluate RFID systems.

The transponder, or RFID tag, is electronically programmed with information that can uniquely identify an item, such as an electronic identification code, plus other information about the item, such as its location, where and when it was made, or its status during production. Embedded in the tag is a microchip for storing the data. The rest of the tag is an antenna that transmits data to the reader.

The reader unit consists of an antenna and radio transmitter with a decoding capability attached to a stationary or handheld device. The reader emits radio waves in ranges anywhere from 1 inch to 100 feet, depending on its power output, the radio frequency employed, and surrounding environmental conditions. When a RFID tag comes within the range of the reader, the tag is activated and starts sending data. The reader captures these data, decodes them, and sends them back over a wired or wireless network to a host computer for further processing (see Figure 9-10). Both RFID tags and antennas come in a variety of shapes and sizes.

RFID tags are categorized as either active or passive. Active RFID tags are powered by an internal battery and typically enable tag data to be rewritten and modified. Such tags might be used, for example, when manufacturing a part to give a machine a set of instructions and have the machine report its performance to the tag. The tag would capture these data so that they are added to the history of the tagged part. Active tags generally have a longer read range, but they are larger in size, cost more, and have a shorter operational life (up to 10 years) than passive tags. Automated toll-collection systems such as EZ Pass use active RFID tags.

Passive RFID tags do not have a separate power source and obtain their operating power from the radio frequency energy transmitted by the RFID reader. They are smaller, lighter, and less expensive than active tags with a virtually unlimited operational lifetime.

FIGURE 9-10   *How RFID works.*

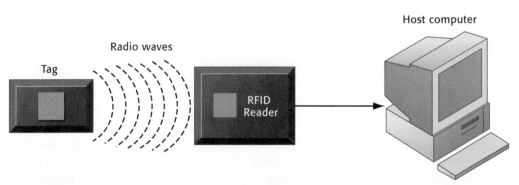

A microchip holds data including an identification number. The rest of the tag is an antenna that transmits data to a reader.

Has an antenna that constantly transmits. When it senses a tag, it wakes it up, interrogates it, and decodes the data. Then it transmits the data to a host system over wired or wireless connections.

Processes the data from the tag that have been transmitted by the reader.

RFID uses low-powered radio transmitters to read data stored in a tag at distances ranging from 1 inch to 100 feet. The reader captures the data from the tag and sends them over a network to a host computer for processing.

They also have shorter read ranges than active tags and require a higher-powered reader. Passive tags are usually read-only and are programmed with data that cannot be modified.

RFID systems operate in a number of unlicensed frequency bands worldwide. Low-frequency systems (30 kilohertz to 500 kilohertz) have short reading ranges (inches to a few feet) and lower system costs. Low-frequency systems are often used in security, asset tracking, or animal identification applications. High-frequency RFID systems (850 MHz to 950 MHz and 2.4 GHz to 2.5 GHz) offer reading ranges that can extend beyond 90 feet and have high reading speeds. High-frequency RFID applications include railroad car tracking or automated toll collection for highways or bridges.

A RFID tag with an integrated circuit will never be as inexpensive as a bar code label, and RFID systems will not supplant bar codes entirely. However, RFID systems will become popular where bar codes or other optical technologies are not effective.

In inventory control and supply chain management, RFID can capture and manage more detailed information about items in warehouses or in production than bar-coding systems. If a large number of items are shipped together, RFID can track each pallet, lot, or even unit item in the shipment. Manufacturers using RFID will be able to track the production history of each product for better understanding of product defects and successes.

The real savings from RFID come from the way it can improve an entire business process. Data from suppliers can be carried on tags and uploaded into the receiving company's enterprise system or supply chain management system the moment a component is delivered. RFID systems can give suppliers, manufacturers, distributors, and retailers much more detailed and real-time data for control over inventory, shipping, and other logistics. RFID could even change the way invoices are paid by triggering an electronic payment to the shipper once a tagged pallet enters a retailer's warehouse.

RFID has been available for decades, but widespread use was held back by the expense of the tags, which ranged from just under $1.00 to $20.00 each. Now the cost of a tag has dropped to about 19 cents and could drop to 5 cents within a few years. At these prices for tags, RFID becomes cost-effective for many companies, including Wal-Mart, Home Depot, Delta Airlines, FedEx, and Unilever.

The top 100 suppliers to Wal-Mart stores and thousands of suppliers to the U.S. Department of Defense are required to use passive RFID tags on cases and pallets they ship to these organizations. Wal-Mart expects RFID-tagged shipments will help it track and record inventory flow.

Coors UK, Scottish & Newcastle, and other large British brewing companies are using RFID to improve tracking of kegs that are shipped out and returned. Breweries lose on average 5 to 6 percent of their kegs each year, and RFID tracking has cut those losses in half (Hellweg, 2004).

Boeing Company and Airbus S.A.S., the world's largest airplane makers, are requiring more than 2,000 of their suppliers to begin RFID tagging of aircraft and engine parts. Seventy percent of the purchase orders that Airbus receives from its customers contain incorrect part numbers and pricing data. If parts for Airbus planes had RFID tags, they could be scanned to generate accurate replacement orders, saving Airbus as much as $400 million per year. RFID tagging of Boeing airplane parts would provide more accurate information than what mechanics enter manually, preventing unapproved parts from being used in finished products. This application of RFID could save Boeing $100 million per year in Federal Aviation Administration fines and part replacement time (Kontzer, 2004).

Steep costs and extensive planning and preparation are required for successful deployment of RFID. A Forrester Research study estimated that a supplier that was required by Wal-Mart to implement RFID technology might spend $9.1 million in startup and maintenance fees for one year (Overby, 2004). In addition to installing RFID readers and tagging systems, these companies may need to upgrade their hardware and software to process the massive amounts of data produced by RFID systems—transactions that could add up to tens or hundreds of terabytes.

Special middleware is required to filter, aggregate, and prevent RFID data from overloading business networks and system applications. The middleware translates RFID data into formats that applications can use. Applications will need to be redesigned to accept massive volumes of RFID-generated data frequently and to share those data with other applications. Major enterprise software vendors, including SAP, Oracle, and PeopleSoft, now offer RFID-ready versions of their supply chain management applications.

Privacy activists have objected to RFID technology applications that could lead to more tracking and monitoring of individual behavior. They fear it could someday enable marketers, the government, or insurers to compile details about individuals' shopping habits or even enable people's movements to be tracked. The Window on Organizations explores this topic.

Wireless in Health Care

Another area in which wireless technology is having a major impact is health care. Health care systems have been hampered by inefficiencies from paper-based processes and gaps between information systems. Many hospitals have wired networks but still have problems getting essential information to the right place at the right time because most physicians and nurses are rarely in one place for long.

Mobile technology can provide some solutions. Hospitals are installing wireless LANs in emergency rooms and treatment areas, and are equipping staff with Wi-Fi-enabled laptop computers or wireless PDAs and smart phones. According to a study by consulting firm A. T. Kearney, about 50 percent of U.S. hospitals have adopted wireless technology, and that number will exceed 90 percent by 2010 (A. T. Kearney, 2004).

Table 9-4 provides examples of the efficiencies and improvements in patient care that result from using wireless technology.

Wireless Sensor Networks and Pervasive Computing

Innovations in wireless technology are pushing computing into every facet of life, including cars, homes, office buildings, tools, and factories. A mesh of these technologies will provide connections anywhere and any time, making computing devices an even more integral part of our everyday lives. Computers will become increasingly embedded in our natural movements and interactions with our environments. This phenomenon is known as **pervasive computing**.

One example is the use of wireless sensor networks. **Wireless sensor networks** (WSNs) are networks of interconnected wireless devices that are embedded into the physical environment to provide measurements of many points over large spaces. They are based on devices with built-in processing, storage, and radio frequency sensors and antennas. The devices are linked into an interconnected network where data are routed seamlessly among all the nodes and forwarded to a computer for analysis.

These networks require no external infrastructure and can range from hundreds to thousands of nodes. Because wireless sensor devices are placed in the field for years at a time without any maintenance or human intervention, they must have very low power requirements and batteries capable of lasting for long periods of time—years.

Sensor networks typically have a tiered architecture such as that used by the wireless security system illustrated in Figure 9-11. This particular wireless sensor network consists of a hierarchy of nodes, starting with low-level sensors and progressing toward nodes for high-level data aggregation, analysis, and storage. Lower-level sensors for monitoring events such as doors opening and closing, motion, and breakage of windows and doors are complemented by a small group of more advanced sensors placed in key locations, such as cameras and acoustic and chemical detectors. Both simple and complex data are

WINDOW ON ORGANIZATIONS

Does RFID Threaten Privacy?

German retailer Metro AG has been an early and vigorous adopter of radio frequency identification (RFID) technology. It is implementing a wireless inventory tracking system for 250 stores, 10 central warehouses, and 300 of its biggest suppliers, representing 65 percent of its sales in Germany. Metro expects to bring all of its approximately 800 German stores onto the system by the end of 2007. Gerd Wofram, Metro's project manager, believes the cost of this system will be offset by the savings it produces for both Metro and its suppliers, including Procter & Gamble, Gillette Company, and Kraft Foods.

Under Metro's system, suppliers will attach RFID tags to pallets and cases of goods supplied to certain stores and warehouses. As these tagged containers move in and out of Metro warehouses and stores, they will be tracked by RFID readers. By tracking supply and inventory more precisely, the RFID system will enable Metro to cut down on lost, stolen, or damaged products, ensure shelves are stocked, and eventually reduce staff. If all goes well, Metro could reduce its inventory carrying costs by up to 20 percent.

So far, so good. But when Metro tried to bring RFID closer to the customer, it unleashed a storm of controversy. Metro also uses RFID microchips in its Payback customer loyalty cards and RFID tags on CDs and DVDs for theft protection and for controlling customer previews of age-restricted DVDs. (Without a loyalty card as a key, customers can preview only the equivalent of G-rated films.) No RFID readers are in the stores tracking customers.

Nevertheless, Metro's move into RFID technology alarmed privacy activists. Katherine Albrecht, founder and director of Consumers Against Supermarket Privacy Invasion and Numbering (CASPIAN), which opposes marketing data collection, questioned the use of RFID in Metro loyalty cards. She warned that the identifying serial numbers in the store's RFID tags could not be deleted, so that the tags could be used to track customer whereabouts after they have taken their purchases home. Metro claimed the technology to erase the serial number from RFID tags would soon be available.

Privacy advocates in the United States are worried about RFID tagging as well. According to Barry Steinhardt, director of the Technology and Liberty Project for the American Civil Liberties Union, growing use of RFID will give government officials "tremendous new power to track and control the movement of citizens." If such tags were embedded in identification documents such as a passport or driver's license, government agents could potentially follow an individual.

For many companies, privacy is still not an issue because they are not using RFID to track individual items—only pallets or shipping containers containing items. It is only when stores start RFID tagging individual items that privacy issues come into play. Once the price of RFID tags drops to 5 cents or less, companies will use them on individual consumer items, but that remains several years away.

If these companies want to please their customers, however, they will need to start thinking about how they will handle the privacy issue once RFID becomes cost-effective at the package level. Mark Roberti, editor of *RFID Journal*, recommends that businesses develop RFID privacy policies as they are gradually implementing this powerful technology.

Some organizations are already looking for positive ways of dealing with the RFID privacy issue. U.K. department store Marks & Spencer tested RFID tagging of in-store merchandise. It used throwaway paper RFID tags called Intelligent Labels that were attached to, but not embedded in, men's suits, shirts, and ties. Each tag contained a unique number that pointed to an entry in a database detailing product characteristics such as style, size, and color. The tag numbers were not scanned when customers purchased the items, so no personal information was associated with them.

Before implementing this system, Marks & Spencer discussed the project with Katherine Albrecht of CASPIAN and with the United Kingdom's National Consumer Council. When Marks & Spencer heard the concerns of members of these organizations about RFID tags embedded in products that customers would take home, it decided to use removable tags.

Such a measure would find support from privacy advocates in the United States, who are urging Congress to enact legislation limiting government use of tags and requiring retailers to provide easily removable tags for consumers who want to jettison their tags after completing their purchases.

In Singapore, the Alexander Hospital's Department of Emergency Medicine is running a pilot program in which emergency room (ER) patients are tracked using RFID tags. This system must manage a situation in which patients are admitted and discharged very quickly and move in unpredictable patterns around the ER. The RFID system was designed to reduce the time staff spend tracking down people. To maintain privacy, all personally identifiable information (patient names and contact numbers) can be accessed only by designated staff using individual passwords. The department keeps the patient tracking data only for 21 days, as required by the Ministry of Health.

Sources: Thomas Claburn, "Watching Out," *Information Week*, February 16, 2004; Karen J. Delaney, "Inventory Tool to Launch in Germany," *Wall Street Journal*, January 12, 2004; Marilyn Geewax, "Privacy Advocates Assail Radio-ID Tags," *Atlanta Journal-Constitution*, July 16, 2004; Erika Morphy, "Metro Gives RFID 'Future Stores' Green Light," *CRM Daily*, July 7, 2004; and Steve Ulfelder, "Raising an RFID Ruckus," *NewsFactor Top Tech News*, October 7, 2003.

To Think About: How does RFID technology threaten individual privacy? Should retailers have a RFID privacy policy? Why or why not? What issues should the privacy policy address?

TABLE 9-4 *Examples of Wireless Health Care Applications*

Wireless Application	Description
Electronic medical record (EMR) retrieval	Health care professionals can use wireless handhelds to enter and view medical records, including diagnostic information in real time. They can review data immediately and update patient records while making their rounds.
Wireless note taking for patient charts	Doctors and nurses can enter data electronically into wireless PDAs, smart phones, or laptops.
Lab test results	Doctors can immediately obtain data about lab tests from a wireless PDA, smart phone, or laptop.
Prescription generation	Health care professionals can use a mobile phone, wireless laptop, or handheld to send a prescription to a pharmacy, reducing delays and errors.
Medical databases	Health care professionals can check drug references and other medical information wherever they are working by connecting wirelessly to medical databases.

routed over a network to an automated facility that provides continuous building monitoring and control.

Wireless sensor networks are valuable in areas such as monitoring environmental changes, monitoring traffic or military activity, protecting property, efficiently operating and managing machinery and vehicles, establishing security perimeters, monitoring supply chain management, or detecting chemical, biological, or radiological material.

WIRELESS SENSOR NETWORK STANDARDS AND ZIGBEE

Standards are being developed for this form of wireless computing. The 802.15.4 standard provides a specification of the radio frequency channel and signaling protocol to be used. Atop 802.15.4 is the **ZigBee** protocol that handles application-level communication between devices. Standard 802.15.4 determines which radio hardware to use, whereas ZigBee determines the content of messages transmitted by each node in the network.

Andover Controls Corporation, which has installed 100,000 building-control systems worldwide, is working with Goodman Manufacturing to use ZigBee sensors to cut energy consumption. The sensors monitor motion and temperature in rooms, tracking whether an air conditioner is on, whether someone is in the room, and the temperature. The data are passed from sensor to sensor to a computer that monitors the temperature or equipment. If air-conditioning has made a room too cold, the system could turn off that air conditioner.

The U.S. Department of Energy hired Honeywell International to use ZigBee sensors to reduce energy costs by up to 15 percent in steel, aluminum, and six other industries. Honeywell installed sensors at companies such as ExxonMobil, Alcoa, and Dow Chemical to track energy loss from piping systems and to monitor the use of gases in production processes. The network of sensors monitors the amount of gas constantly, enabling companies to eliminate leaks or wasted energy almost immediately. This application could save up to 256 trillion BTUs per year, more than the amount of natural gas used by Washington state in 2003.

9.5 MANAGEMENT OPPORTUNITIES, CHALLENGES, AND SOLUTIONS

Some businesses will benefit from incorporating wireless technology into their business strategy; others may not. Before investing heavily in wireless technology, firms must address a series of technology and organizational issues.

FIGURE 9-11   *A wireless sensor network.*

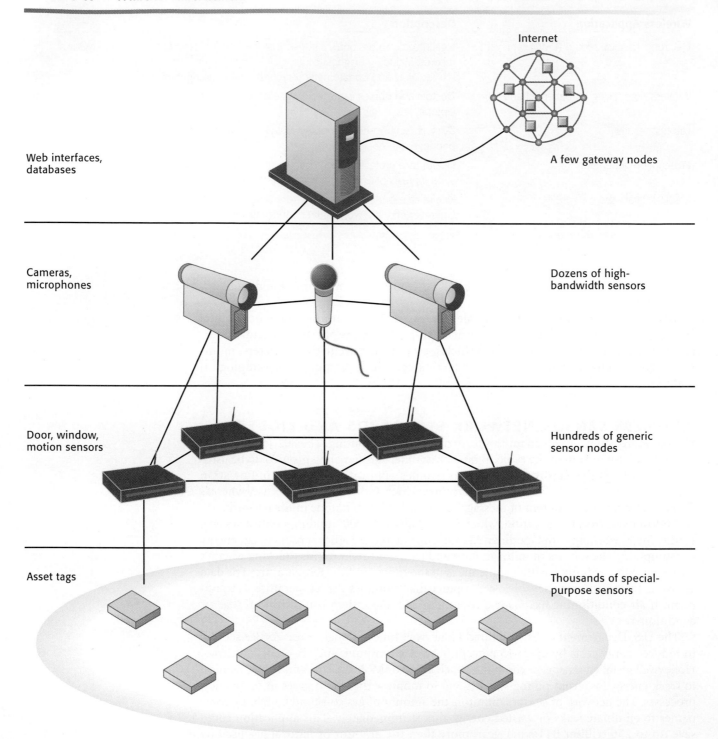

This wireless sensor network for a security system illustrates the hierarchical organization of wireless sensor networks. Each level handles different types of sensing.

Source: From Jason Hill, Mike Horton, Ralph Kling, and Lakshman Krishnamurthy, "The Platforms Enabling Wireless Sensor Networks," *Communications of the ACM* 47, no. 6 (June 2004).

Opportunities

Wireless technology gives firms more flexibility and the ability to innovate in unexpected ways. Wireless systems support business processes that are not limited by time or location, extending the company's reach and saving employees and customers substantial amounts of time. The technology provides a new channel for connecting with customers. It can be a source of exciting new products and services.

Management Challenges

The main challenges posed by wireless technology deal with managing this technology, integrating it into the firm's information technology (IT) infrastructure, and maintaining security and privacy.

INTEGRATING WIRELESS TECHNOLOGY INTO THE FIRM'S IT INFRASTRUCTURE

A large enterprise may have hundreds of wireless access points and many thousands of wireless devices to configure and monitor, similar to a desktop environment. It will be a challenge to integrate this new network infrastructure with the firm's existing infrastructure and applications, and central coordination and oversight are required.

Some companies have found that the savings they expected from using wireless did not materialize because of unexpected costs. Gains in productivity and efficiency from equipping employees with wireless mobile computing devices must be balanced against increased costs associated with integrating these devices into the firm's IT infrastructure and providing technical support. Other cost components include fees for wireless air time, end-user training, help-desk support, and software for special applications.

Although the cost per wireless PDA for a corporate employee is around $300, the total cost of ownership (TCO) for each device is much higher, running from $1,000 to $3,000, according to various consultant estimates. Costs are higher if a mobile device has extra processing power and runs many different applications and if mobile devices need to be integrated into back-end systems such as enterprise applications.

MAINTAINING SECURITY AND PRIVACY

Maintaining security and privacy poses special challenges for users of wireless technology. Wi-Fi security is not well-developed, making such systems especially vulnerable to penetration from outsiders (see Chapter 10). Wireless systems are easily susceptible to interference from other devices in the same bandwidth.

One of the unique benefits of wireless technology is its location-tracking capability. However, this same capability worries privacy advocates who fear the technology could be abused to monitor where users are going and what they are doing every minute. We have already described some of these privacy issues in our discussion of RFID technology. Wireless PDAs, mobile phones, or automobiles with telematics features raise similar concerns.

Solution Guidelines

Here are some guidelines for managing mobile technology in the enterprise.

- *Identifying areas in which wireless can provide value.* Once the value of wireless technology has been established, management should rank the areas where mobile connectivity will provide the greatest value to the company, quantifying likely benefits, costs, and risks. The areas where net benefits are highest and risks lowest or least likely to occur would be the first for wireless technology investments.

- *Creating a management framework for wireless technology.* Firms need to establish a framework for managing their mobile technology and integrating it into their IT infrastructure. Special corporate policies are necessary for wireless usage, including security, end-user responsibilities, and wireless standards for hardware, software, and networking infrastructure. Limiting the number of different mobile hardware, software, and network vendors will help reduce the total cost of ownership (TCO). Management of wireless technology can also be improved by using special system management tools for downloading software, monitoring usage, and controlling security (see Chapter 10).

- *Using a pilot program before full-scale rollout of wireless systems.* It is very important to test wireless systems on a small scale before launching them throughout the organization. A pilot program enables employees to gain experience while providing feedback to improve the program. Once the wireless system has been fully launched, the firm should monitor progress using the indicators it has established to measure productivity and innovation.

MAKE IT YOUR BUSINESS

Finance and Accounting

Wireless technology has been the source of new financial services. Individual investors and investment professionals can use their mobile phones to obtain stock quotes and financial market news, to make stock trades, and to review their portfolios. Wireless Web and Internet technology are also making it possible to speed up fund flows by providing capabilities for immediate billing and invoicing.

Human Resources

Wireless devices can be used to broadcast messages to employees working offsite and to provide access to human resources information in corporate systems. Wireless technology facilitates teamwork by making it possible for employees to communicate with each other anytime and anyplace. Wireless technology is improving health care by providing more rapid access to and transmittal of patient data and medical information. You can find examples of human resources applications on page 303.

Manufacturing and Production

Wireless technology is making many contributions to manufacturing and production efficiency and flexibility. Wireless networks on factory floors support more flexible and efficient

arrangements of production equipment. Wireless applications provide field service workers with instant access to critical information while they are servicing customers' equipment. RFID systems have powerful capabilities for providing detailed information about the movement of goods throughout the supply chain. You can find examples of manufacturing and production applications on pages 328 and 337–339.

Sales and Marketing

Mobile devices are being used for purchasing movie tickets, soft drinks, and music clips; for obtaining news and sports scores; or for participating in online auctions. Both mobile handhelds and wireless-enabled laptops have been very helpful to mobile sales professionals who need on-the-spot information while working with customers or other sales and marketing staff. Wireless technology is also inspiring new information and location-based services. You can find examples of sales and marketing applications on pages 316 and 328.

Summary

1. *Identify the principal wireless transmission media and devices, cellular network standards and generations, and standards for mobile Web access.*

   Devices for wireless transmission include pagers, e-mail handhelds, personal digital assistants (PDAs),

cellular telephones, and smart phones. Personal computers are also starting to be used in wireless transmission.

   Microwave systems, both terrestrial and celestial, transmit high-frequency radio signals through the atmosphere and are widely used for high-volume, long-distance, point-to-point communication. Communication satellites serve as relay stations for microwave signals transmitted from terrestrial stations.

Major cellular standards include Code Division Multiple Access (CDMA), which is used primarily in the United States, and Global System for Mobile Communication (GSM), which is the standard in Europe and much of the rest of the world.

Cellular networks have evolved from slow-speed (1G) analog networks to high-speed high-bandwidth digital packet-switched third-generation (3G) networks with speeds ranging from 144 Kbps to over 2 Mbps for data transmission. Second-generation (2G) cellular networks are digital networks used primarily for voice transmission, but they can also transmit data at rates ranging from 9.6 to 14.4 Kbps. 2.5G networks are packet-switched, use many existing infrastructure elements, and have data transmission rates ranging from 50 to 144 Kbps.

Alternative standards governing the way wireless mobile devices access the Internet and the World Wide Web include Wireless Application Protocol (WAP) and I-mode.

2. Describe the major standards for wireless networks and for wireless Internet access.

The Institute of Electrical and Electronics Engineers (IEEE) has established a hierarchy of complementary standards for wireless computer networks. These include Bluetooth (802.15) for small personal area networks (PANs), Wi-Fi (802.11) for local area networks (LANs), and WiMax (802.16) for metropolitan area networks (MANs).

Bluetooth can link up to eight devices within a 10-meter area using low-power, radio-based communication and can transmit up to 722 Kbps in the 2.4-GHz band. Wireless phones, keyboards, computers, printers, and PDAs using Bluetooth can communicate with each other and even operate each other without direct user intervention.

The most popular of the 802.11 standards is currently 802.11b, which can transmit up to 11 Mbps in the unlicensed 2.4-GHz band and has an effective distance of 30 to 50 meters, although this range can be extended outdoors by using tower-mounted antennas. The 802.11b standard has been the most widely used standard for creating wireless LANs and providing broadband wireless Internet access. However, 802.11b is vulnerable to penetration by outsiders and interference from other wireless devices in the same frequency spectrum.

WiMax has a wireless access range of up to 31 miles and a data transfer rate of up to 75 Mbps, making it suitable for providing broadband Internet access in areas lacking DSL and cable lines. The 802.16 specification also has robust security and quality of service features to support voice and video.

Major cellular carriers are also upgrading their networks to provide wireless broadband access to the Internet

at an average speed of 300 to 500 Kbps. Verizon's service, called BroadBand Access, uses a technology called EV-DO to provide Internet access over a cellular network.

3. Evaluate the role of m-commerce in business and describe the most important m-commerce applications.

M-commerce uses the Internet for purchasing goods and services as well as for transmitting messages using wireless mobile devices. It is especially well-suited for location-based applications, such as finding local hotels and restaurants, monitoring local traffic and weather, and providing personalized location-based marketing. Mobile phones and handhelds are being used for mobile bill payment, banking, securities trading, transportation schedule updates, and digital music and game downloads.

Wireless portals (mobile portals) feature content and services optimized for mobile devices to steer users to the information they are most likely to need. Voice portals accept voice commands for accessing Web content, e-mail, and other electronic applications from a cell phone or standard telephone.

M-commerce requires special digital payment systems that can handle micropayments, because most m-commerce purchases today are for very small amounts. Mobile wallets (m-wallets) expedite purchases by storing online shoppers' personal information and credit card numbers.

M-commerce represents a tiny fraction of all online purchases because wireless mobile devices can't display merchandise very well. Mobile phones have tiny keyboards, small screens, and slow data transfer speeds (9.6 to 14.4 Kbps). M-commerce will benefit from interoperable payment systems for wireless devices and faster wireless networks to support more data-rich communication.

4. Assess the business value of wireless technology and describe important wireless applications in business.

Wireless technology increases productivity and worker output by providing anytime, anywhere communication and access to information, including the information resources of the Internet. Wireless communication helps businesses stay more easily in touch with customers, suppliers, and employees and provides more flexible arrangements for organizing work.

Mobile applications are having a significant impact on customer relationship management (CRM), supply chain management (SCM), and health care. Mobile CRM applications provide additional support for sales and service activities at the point of customer interaction.

Mobile wireless technology facilitates supply chain management by capturing data on the movement of goods as these events take place and by providing detailed, immediate information as goods move among supply chain partners. Radio frequency identification (RFID) systems provide a powerful technology for this purpose. These systems use tiny tags that have embedded microchips that contain data about an item and its location. The tags transmit radio signals over a short distance to special RFID readers. The RFID readers then pass the data over a network to a computer for processing.

Mobile technology is improving health care by delivering essential information to physicians and nurses who constantly move from place to place and capturing patient information for electronic record systems at the point of creation.

Wireless sensor networks (WSNs) are networks of interconnected wireless devices with some processing and radio-transmitting capability that are embedded into the physical environment to provide measurements of many points over large spaces. Wireless sensor networks are valuable for monitoring environmental changes, traffic patterns, security incidents, or supply chain events.

5. *Identify and describe the challenges posed by wireless technology and management solutions.*

The principal challenges posed by wireless technology are maintaining security and privacy and integrating this technology into the firm's IT infrastructure.

Solutions include identifying the areas in which wireless can provide the greatest value, creating an appropriate framework for managing wireless technology, and using a pilot program before full-scale rollout of wireless systems. Key management decisions deal with establishing the business value of wireless technology, selecting appropriate wireless technologies and standards, and identifying the necessary changes in business processes to make wireless technology work.

Key Terms

2.5G networks, 310
3G networks, 309
802.11b, 313
Access point, 313
Bluetooth, 312
Cellular telephones (cell phones), 308
Code Division Multiple Access (CDMA), 309
E-mail handhelds, 308
EV-DO, 317
General Packet Radio Service (GPRS), 310
Global Positioning System (GPS), 306
Global System for Mobile Communication (GSM), 309

Hotspot, 314
I-mode, 311
Microbrowser, 310
Microwave, 306
Mobile computing, 318
Mobile wallets (m-wallets), 322
Nomadic computing, 318
Paging systems, 308
Personal area networks (PANs), 312
Personal digital assistants (PDAs), 309
Pervasive computing, 327
Radio frequency identification (RFID), 325
Satellites, 308

Short message service (SMS), 309
Smart phones, 309
Telematics, 306
Voice portals, 321
Wi-Fi, 312
WiMax, 317
Wireless Application Protocol (WAP), 310
Wireless Markup Language (WML), 310
Wireless NICs, 313
Wireless portals, 321
Wireless sensor networks (WSNs), 327
ZigBee, 329

Review Questions

1. *How does wireless technology provide business value?*

2. *Name and describe the principal wireless transmission media and devices.*

3. *List and describe the major cellular network standards and cellular network generations.*

4. *What is Bluetooth? Describe its capabilities. For what types of applications is it best suited?*

5. *What is Wi-Fi? Describe the 802.11b standard for wireless networking. How does it work?*

6. *What are the benefits and challenges of using Wi-Fi?*

7. *What is WiMax? How does it differ from Wi-Fi?*

8. *What is EV-DO? How does it differ from WiMax and Wi-Fi?*

9. *Compare the WAP and I-mode standards for wireless access to the Web.*

10. *What is the difference between nomadic computing and mobile computing?*

11. *List and describe the most important types of m-commerce services and applications.*

12. *How do wireless portals and voice portals help users access information on the Web?*

13. *Describe the payment systems for m-commerce. What role is played by mobile wallets?*

14. *What are some of the barriers to m-commerce?*

15. *How can wireless technology support customer relationship management and supply chain management?*

16. *What is RFID? How does it work? How does it provide value to businesses?*

17. *What are wireless sensor networks? How do they work? What applications use them?*

18. *Describe the challenges posed by wireless technology and some ways to address them.*

Discussion Questions

1. *Should all major retailing and manufacturing companies switch to RFID? Why or why not?*

2. *Is wireless technology a threat to privacy? Explain your answer.*

Application Software Exercise:
Spreadsheet Exercise: Comparing Wireless Services

You would like to equip your sales force of 35 based in Cincinnati, Ohio, with mobile phones that have capabilities for voice transmission, text messaging, and taking and sending photos. Use the Web to select a wireless service provider that provides nationwide service as well as good service in your home area. Examine the features of the mobile handsets offered by each of these vendors. Assume that each of

the 35 salespeople will need to spend 3 hours per day during business hours (8 AM to 6 PM) on mobile voice communication, send 30 text messages per day, and 5 photos per week. Use your spreadsheet software to determine the wireless service and handset that will offer both the best pricing per user over a two-year period. For the purposes of this exercise, you do not need to consider corporate discounts.

Determining the Cost of RFID Systems

Software requirements: Web browser software
Word processing software
Electronic presentation software (optional)

Some of Dirt Bikes's suppliers are starting to use radio frequency identification (RFID) tags on their parts and components. Dirt Bikes's management wants to find out if the company should adopt RFID technology for managing these parts in its warehouses and its finished products. You have been asked to gather some preliminary information on the costs, benefits, and organizational impact for a company such as Dirt Bikes. Your report should answer the following questions:

1. Describe the specific activities for which RFID could be used in Dirt Bikes's warehouse and its shipments of parts and motorcycles to dealers.

2. How would using RFID change these business processes? How would RFID provide business value?

3. How much would it cost initially to implement RFID systems in the processes you have identified? Use the Web to identify the hardware, software, and networking components of a RFID system for a company such as Dirt Bikes and their costs. Your calculations should include the cost of hiring at least one RFID warehouse specialist and estimated costs for retraining existing information systems staff and employees to use the new system.

4. (Optional) Use electronic presentation software to summarize your findings for management.

Electronic Business Project: Identifying Wi-Fi Hotspots for Nomadic Computing

Your company has a sales force of 15 representatives, and customers are concentrated in Seattle, Washington; Vancouver, British Columbia; and Portland, Oregon. Your sales reps are constantly on the road, and you are looking for a way to provide them with Internet e-mail and Web access so that they can easily communicate throughout the day with corporate headquarters as they meet with clients and travel from one meeting to another. Use Web sites such as www.wifinder.com, www.hotspot-locations.com, and www.wi-fizone.org to determine which commercial hotspots

would be the most appropriate for your sales force and the commercial network services that these hotspots use. Then, research the Web sites of two or three commercial networks that seem most appropriate to discover more about their pricing and services. Finally, use www.wifinder.com and www.wififreespot.com to determine how many free public hotspots are available in these cities. Are there enough for your company to rely on them, or should you use a commercial Wi-Fi system? If so, which one?

Group Project: Comparing Mobile Internet Access Systems

Form a group with three or four of your classmates. Select mobile devices with Internet access from two different vendors, such as Palm, BlackBerry, Nokia, and Motorola. Your analysis should consider the purchase cost of each device, any additional software required to make it Internet enabled, the cost of wireless Internet services, and what Internet services are available for each device. You should also consider other capabilities of each device, including the ability to integrate with existing corporate or PC applications. Which device would you select? What criteria would you use to guide your selection? If possible, use electronic presentation software to present your findings to the class.

CASE STUDY
UPS versus FedEx: Two Competitors, Two Wireless Strategies

FedEx Corporation (FedEx) and United Parcel Service, Incorporated (UPS) are industry leaders in air and ground package distribution and specialized transportation and logistics services. The companies compete on a global scale and have established strongholds on particular aspects of the shipping business. UPS achieved its status primarily on the strength of its time-definite ground delivery of packages and documents. FedEx traditionally attributes its success and reputation to its unmatched performance in overnight deliveries. UPS delivers an average of over 13 million packages each day. FedEx averages approximately 5 million daily deliveries, but surpasses UPS in air deliveries, 3.1 million to 2 million. The two rivals have grown out of very different beginnings to occupy their current standings in the marketplace. As technological advances enable UPS and FedEx to carry their respective businesses to greater heights, the evolution of the technology has them walking a fine line between fanning the flames of competition and growing side by side.

Nearly a century old, UPS has grown from a two-man, two-bicycle operation in Seattle that promised the "best service and lowest rates" into a 355,000-employee corporate giant with a delivery fleet of 88,000 ground vehicles and nearly 600 airplanes. The fleet services 1.8 million shipping customers daily, bringing deliveries to 6.1 million consignees. UPS first expanded to Europe in 1975. In 2003, UPS revealed a $600 million improvement initiative for its package sorting and delivery systems. By 2007, UPS expects this initiative to result in a $600 million annual reduction in operating costs, mostly as a result of productivity improvements and more efficient driving routes.

UPS counts global reach, technology systems, customer relationships, brand equity, and e-commerce capabilities among its competitive strengths. The company's growth strategies include building on its status as the leader in domestic package operations, continuing to expand internationally, offering comprehensive supply chain solutions to businesses that seek to outsource such a complicated business component, and backing up the core delivery service with a strong portfolio of e-commerce solutions. UPS.com fields more than 9 million requests for package tracking each day, and the Web site receives 115 million daily hits overall.

FedEx Corporation is the parent company of the various operating companies under the FedEx name, which include FedEx Express, FedEx Ground, FedEx Freight, FedEx Trade Networks, and FedEx Services. FedEx Express, the corporation's time-certain express delivery service, was founded in 1971. The corporation as a whole employs 216,500 workers and contractors, and 134,000 of those employees serve FedEx Express as it provides delivery services to 214 countries using 53,500 drop-off locations, 643 aircraft, and 48,000 road vehicles. FedEx Ground recently began a six-year, $1.8 billion expansion initiative that by 2009 will double the company's capacity to process ground packages, currently at 2.5 million daily.

The growth strategies of FedEx include increasing high-tech and high-value-added business goods, globalization, acceleration of the supply chain, and continued expansion of Internet and e-commerce solutions. The corporation views its brand as a strong business asset and uses it to provide customers with an integrated set of business solutions, including those available from FedEx.com.

As UPS and FedEx continue to jockey for position in each other's strongest market domains, it is clear that the two companies take different approaches to the same goal. Both, like any company that is seeking to grow, look to increase the efficiency of their operations. Improved efficiency generally results from cut-ting costs of business processes and extending the usefulness and capabilities of resources beyond current expectations. One of the most important ways that UPS and FedEx have improved their businesses since the late 1980s is through the use of wireless technologies. The companies take on contrasting personalities in their implementations of such technologies.

FedEx acts more like a startup business, jumping at the chance to adopt the latest and greatest applications as soon as they prove to be economical and effective for both the company and its customers. UPS, on the other hand, adheres to a more measured schedule of new technology rollouts, generally waiting from 5 to 7 years between major initiatives. This approach enables UPS to revamp its systems with uniform upgrades that can replace segments of the old systems in phases.

Their approaches, however, are not diametrically opposite. UPS is willing to make intermediate technology changes to take advantage of opportunities, whereas FedEx tries to makes sure its adoptions have long-term viability and support its critical priorities. And regardless of approach, FedEx and UPS have determined that wireless technologies have a major impact on their key business processes, especially package pickup and delivery transactions and the physical packaging and sorting of packages.

Fifteen years ago, deploying wireless technology generally required contracting with a technology vendor to develop proprietary systems. Such systems were costly because they had to be developed from the ground up and neither company had the existing infrastructure or bandwidth to support wireless technology at the outset. These days, UPS and FedEx have taken advantage of wireless solutions based on global standards. Both companies use the Bluetooth short-range wireless specification, 802.11b wireless

LANs, and general packet radio service (GPRS) cellular networks to varying degrees. The fact that these technologies are available off the shelf translates to greatly reduced development costs, easier maintenance, better capacity and security, and lower implementation costs.

For companies such as FedEx and UPS, reducing the time required to make every delivery by even one second can have an enormous impact on the cost of doing business across the board. Wireless technology has become the driving force behind making such improvements in efficiency possible. Not surprisingly, both companies have devoted sums in excess of $100 million to wireless initiatives. Wireless technology brings UPS and FedEx as close as they can come to having real-time data available for their operations. Putting wireless handheld devices in the hands of delivery personnel enables these workers to complete their tasks more quickly and provide an elevated level of customer service.

At UPS, drivers carry a handheld unit called a Delivery Information Acquisition Device (DIAD). The current version of the device is the DIAD IV, which, like its predecessor, the DIAD III, can connect to UPS operations centers directly using cellular transmitters in the delivery trucks. Therefore, information from pickup and delivery transactions that is gathered by personnel in the field can be transmitted to the company's global network almost immediately.

UPS plans to augment the power of its handheld units by adding Bluetooth capabilities to them. The upgrade will enable the devices to connect the handhelds to the trucks and to run applications, such as credit card transaction processing, in areas where an adequate GPRS cellular signal is not available. John Killeen, the director of global network services for UPS, admits that the full scope of Bluetooth's usefulness to the new DIADs is not apparent yet, but the reasonable cost and potential of the implementation make it worthwhile. UPS is also looking to improve customer service by adding Global Positioning System (GPS) tracking

technology to the DIAD IV units. This type of tracking would facilitate services such as rerouting packages that are already in transit by the most economical route.

The FedEx equivalent of UPS's DIAD is the PowerPad. Like their counterparts at UPS, FedEx drivers use the handheld PowerPad to scan packages for pickup and delivery information. The method that FedEx uses to transmit these data to headquarters differs slightly, however. FedEx had previously equipped its vehicles with cellular transmitters for this purpose. When the company rolled out the PowerPad handhelds, it decided to keep the cellular transmitters and have the handhelds upload their data to the transmitters using Bluetooth. Because drivers previously had to dock their handheld units physically in the transmitters to transmit data to home base, the PowerPad with Bluetooth still provides FedEx with significant time and cost savings ($20 million per year) even though it does not provide a direct connection to the company's central systems.

The PowerPad units have other time-saving features as well. For example, FedEx drivers can lock and unlock drop boxes using an infrared signal from the PowerPad instead of a key. Because infrared signals require that the communicating devices line up to each other's apertures unimpeded, FedEx would like to improve this time-saving measure further by using a Bluetooth signal instead of the infrared signal. First, FedEx must address issues related to how much it would cost to deploy and maintain Bluetooth in the drop boxes. Taking the technology another step further, FedEx hopes that using Bluetooth in its drop boxes will eventually permit drivers to pass by empty drop boxes without having to check them.

Again, there are technology challenges to overcome: a drop box could be "silent" because it is empty or because the battery in its Bluetooth transmitter is dead. Other plans for the future of the PowerPad include making it 802.11b-enabled to maintain compatibility with Microsoft operating systems and adding information look-up and retrieval features so that

delivery personnel can provide customers with better and more detailed information on topics such as packaging rules and regulations, supplies, and rates.

FedEx and UPS are also seeing the benefits of wireless technology in their sorting facilities and distribution centers. The main hubs for FedEx, in Memphis, Tennessee, and UPS, in Louisville, Kentucky, are huge facilities that process millions of packages every day. For both companies, lowering the cost of sorting these packages at their main hubs and smaller centers is an important business consideration. To collect package data during sorting, UPS and FedEx both use a portable ring scanner, which consists of a finger-mounted bar code reader that is connected to a terminal. The user wears the terminal on his or her forearm.

UPS will soon complete the rollout of a new scanning unit that places the terminal on the user's waist. Employees prefer this location because it results in less physical stress over the course of a workday. Additionally, the new scanners will use Bluetooth for communication between the finger-mounted bar code scanner and the waist-mounted terminal. Workers at UPS sorting facilities scan packages as they load them onto trucks. It was not unusual for the cables connecting the two pieces of the old scanners to get caught and break during the loading process. The new scanners will reduce UPS maintenance costs by 30 percent, spare parts costs by 35 percent, and downtime by 35 percent. Also, once turned on, the scanners are in an always-on mode and do not have to be triggered for each bar code read, as the old ring scanners did. The scanners can also transmit data to the company system in real time, so UPS inventory systems can flag issues and report more quickly to customers. (The old systems stored the data and transmitted them in periodic batches.) During the next four years, 55,000 scanners will be rolled out to about 1,700 facilities.

FedEx has not yet found the need to replace its current ring scanner model. Despite the company's interest in increasing its volume of ground package shipping, smaller packages such as envelopes still account for the majority of the business. Therefore, FedEx requires fewer people to handle boxes, uses fewer ring scanners than UPS, and is not adversely affected by the costs associated with the equipment. FedEx also has found a problem with implementing Bluetooth because its signals interfere with the operation of the 802.11b network that the company installed only three years ago. UPS avoided this problem by upgrading its new scanning system all at once and designing devices and access points to use time-division multiplexing to alternate between 802.11b and Bluetooth so that signals don't conflict.

Other wireless technology areas that UPS and FedEx are considering include radio frequency identification (RFID) and Global Positioning System (GPS) applications. RFID tags would replace bar code scanning entirely, whereas GPS would enable precise tracking of drivers, vehicles, and packages in the field. Even though several industries have begun using RFID for shipping and supply chain

management, for now, it remains cost-prohibitive for such companies as UPS and FedEx. They have many customers who operate on small budgets. Although having these customers print their own bar codes is quite reasonable, asking them to create RFID tags requires a much heavier investment. However, according to Winn Stephenson, FedEx Services' senior vice president of IT for technology services, adoption of RFID seems inevitable; it's just a matter of timing.

One significant challenge that remains for UPS and FedEx is designing applications that conform to the narrower bandwidth that is characteristic of wireless networks and that provide fault tolerance for disconnects. Despite these issues, both companies would insist that the dynamic transfer of data that wireless connectivity provides has them poised to continue as industry leaders.

Sources: Galen Gruman, "UPS vs. FedEx: Head-to-Head on Wireless" and "New Technologies Hit Mainstream," *CIO Magazine*, June 1, 2004; "RFID Adoption Survey: Current and Future Plans," *CIO*

Magazine, June 30, 2004; Dean Foust, "Big Brown's New Bag," *Business Week*, July 19, 2004; Robert Carter, "Six Degrees of Preparation," *Optimize Magazine* 22 (January 2004); Mark Samuels, "UPS Wireless Plan Reaches Europe," VNU, www.vnunet.com, June 30, 2004; United Parcel Service, Inc., 10-K Report, www.ups.com; FedEx Corporation 10-K Report, www.fedex.com.

CASE STUDY QUESTIONS

1. Analyze UPS and FedEx using the competitive forces and value chain models.

2. How are wireless technologies related to the core information systems and business strategies of UPS and FedEx? How do these technologies provide value to these companies?

3. How do the implementations of wireless technology reflect the organizational differences between UPS and FedEx? Which wireless strategy is more effective? Explain your answer.

4. How will wireless technologies help UPS and FedEx in the future?

Chapter 10

Security and Control

OBJECTIVES

After completing this chapter, you will be able to:

1. Explain why information systems need special protection from destruction, error, and abuse.

2. Assess the business value of security and control.

3. Evaluate elements of an organizational and managerial framework for security and control.

4. Evaluate the most important tools and technologies for safeguarding information resources.

5. Identify the challenges posed by information systems security and control and management solutions.

CHAPTER OUTLINE

10.1 SYSTEM VULNERABILITY AND ABUSE
Why Systems Are Vulnerable
Malicious Software: Viruses, Worms, Trojan Horses, and Spyware
Hackers and Cybervandalism
Computer Crime and Cyberterrorism
Internal Threats: Employees
Software Vulnerability

10.2 BUSINESS VALUE OF SECURITY AND CONTROL
Legal and Regulatory Requirements for Electronic Records Management
Electronic Evidence and Computer Forensics

10.3 ESTABLISHING A MANAGEMENT FRAMEWORK FOR SECURITY AND CONTROL
Types of Information Systems Controls
Risk Assessment
Security Policy
Ensuring Business Continuity
The Role of Auditing in the Control Process

10.4 TECHNOLOGIES AND TOOLS FOR SECURITY AND CONTROL
Access Control
Firewalls, Intrusion Detection Systems, and Antivirus Software
Securing Wireless Networks
Encryption and Public Key Infrastructure
Ensuring Software Reliability

10.5 MANAGEMENT OPPORTUNITIES, CHALLENGES, AND SOLUTIONS
Opportunities
Management Challenges
Solution Guidelines

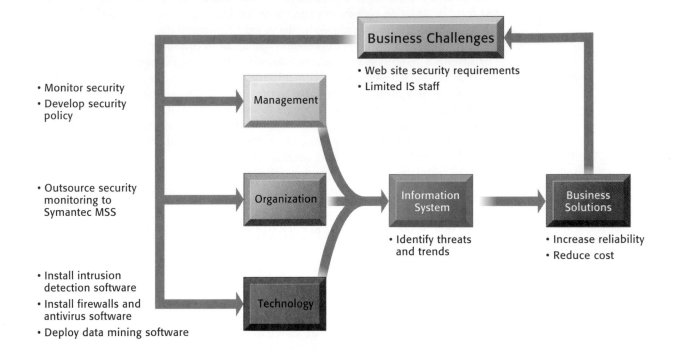

- Monitor security
- Develop security policy

- Outsource security monitoring to Symantec MSS

- Install intrusion detection software
- Install firewalls and antivirus software
- Deploy data mining software

Management

Organization

Technology

Business Challenges
- Web site security requirements
- Limited IS staff

Information System
- Identify threats and trends

Business Solutions
- Increase reliability
- Reduce cost

Opening Case: Wesfarmers Outsources to a Managed Security Service

Wesfarmers Limited is a diversified Australian holding company for businesses in home improvement retailing, chemical and fertilizer production, building materials, industrial and safety product distribution, rail transport, and forest products harvesting, milling, and processing. Its subsidiaries include companies such as Bunnings, Blackwoods, and Kleenheat Gas.

Wesfarmers had to pay more attention to the security of its information systems when it set up an Internet banking site in early 2003 for its Landmark division supplying financial services and products for agribusinesses. People were accessing the Wesfarmers Landmark Web site 24 hours a day, seven days a week. Wesfarmers had already invested heavily in firewalls, intrusion detection systems, antivirus, and other security software, but it did not have sufficient information systems staff and resources for round-the-clock monitoring of infrastructure security.

Wesfarmers decided to outsource the management of its information systems security to Symantec's Managed Security Services, which now manages Wesfarmers's security environment remotely from an operations center in North Ryde, Australia. The service provides real-time security monitoring, enhanced reporting, and complete management of Wesfarmers's network using intrusion detection software, and it monitors Wesfarmers's firewalls. Symantec identified ways to improve Wesfarmers's security and to better manage vulnerabilities that could potentially threaten its network.

Symantec demonstrated a unique and highly cost-effective solution that uses best-practice processes and procedures. A key feature is the ability to log on to an online security portal and retrieve real-time reports that can immediately alert the company to potential risks.

Wesfarmers subsequently sold Landmark, but it decided to keep the Symantec monitoring service because it provides so many benefits. Symantec can analyze the data the system collects while it is monitoring Wesfarmers's network to identify trends and threats over time.

Data from Symantec's security monitoring logs for Wesfarmers are put in a data-mining process to identify intruders who keep coming back. And because Symantec constantly tracks new security threats around the world, it can take protective action on vulnerabilities to head off trouble.

Sources: Karen Dearne, "Wesfarmers Trusts Security to Specialists," *Australian IT News*, February 10, 2004; "Wesfarmers Limited Protects Its Resources with Symantec Managed Security Services," www.riptech.com/region/au_nz, accessed June 19, 2004; and www. symantec.com, accessed October 4, 2004.

Wesfarmers's experience illustrates the need for organizations to take special measures to protect their information systems to ensure their continued operation. Network disruptions, unauthorized users, software failures, hardware failures, natural disasters, employee errors—and terrorist attacks—can prevent information systems from running properly or running at all.

Computer systems play such a critical role in business, government, and daily life that firms need to make security and control a top priority. **Security** refers to the policies, procedures, and technical measures used to prevent unauthorized access, alteration, theft, or physical damage to information systems. **Controls** consist of all the methods, policies, and organizational procedures that ensure the safety of the organization's assets, the accuracy and reliability of its accounting records, and operational adherence to management standards. Let's see how information systems can be controlled and made secure so that they serve the purposes for which they are intended.

10.1 SYSTEM VULNERABILITY AND ABUSE

Before computer automation, data about individuals or organizations were maintained and secured as paper records dispersed in separate business or organizational units. Information systems concentrate data in computer files that can potentially be accessed by large numbers of people and by groups outside of the organization.

When large amounts of data are stored in electronic form they are vulnerable to many more kinds of threats than when they exist in manual form. Through communications networks, information systems in different locations can be interconnected. The potential for unauthorized access, abuse, or fraud is not limited to a single location but can occur at any access point in the network.

Why Systems Are Vulnerable

Figure 10-1 illustrates the most common threats against contemporary information systems. They can stem from technical, organizational, and environmental factors compounded by poor management decisions. In the multitier client/server computing environment illustrated here, vulnerabilities exist at each layer and in the communications between the layers. Users at the client layer can cause harm by introducing errors or by accessing systems without authorization. It is possible to access data flowing over networks, steal valuable data during transmission, or alter messages without authorization. Radiation can disrupt a network at various points as well. Intruders can launch denial of service attacks or malicious software to disrupt the operation of Web sites. Those capable of penetrating corporate systems can destroy or alter corporate data stored in databases or files.

Systems malfunction if computer hardware breaks down, is not configured properly, or is damaged by improper use or criminal acts. Errors in programming, improper installation, or unauthorized changes cause computer software to fail. Computer systems can also be disrupted by power failures, floods, fires, or other natural disasters.

Domestic or offshore outsourcing to another company adds to system vulnerability because valuable information will reside on networks and computers outside the organization's control. Without strong safeguards, valuable data could be lost, destroyed, or could fall into the wrong hands, revealing important trade secrets or information that violates personal privacy. Some worry that outsourcing application development to offshore companies might provide opportunities for programmers to insert hidden code that would later enable someone to gain control over an application or its data (Schmerken and Fitzgerald, 2004).

INTERNET VULNERABILITIES

Large public networks such as the Internet are more vulnerable than internal networks because they are virtually open to anyone. The Internet is so huge that when abuses do occur, they can have an enormously widespread impact. When the Internet becomes part of the corporate network, the organization's information systems are even more vulnerable to actions from outsiders.

FIGURE 10-1 *Contemporary security challenges and vulnerabilities.*

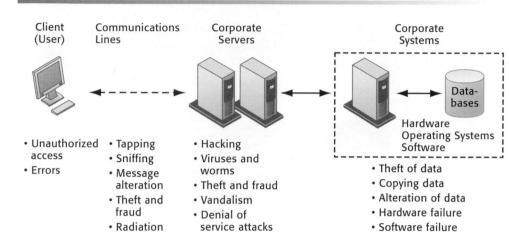

Client (User)	Communications Lines	Corporate Servers	Corporate Systems

Hardware
Operating Systems
Software

- Unauthorized access
- Errors

- Tapping
- Sniffing
- Message alteration
- Theft and fraud
- Radiation

- Hacking
- Viruses and worms
- Theft and fraud
- Vandalism
- Denial of service attacks

- Theft of data
- Copying data
- Alteration of data
- Hardware failure
- Software failure

The architecture of a Web-based application typically includes a Web client, a server, and corporate information systems linked to databases. Each of these components presents security challenges and vulnerabilities. Floods, fires, power failures, and other electrical problems can cause disruptions at any point in the network.

Computers that are constantly connected to the Internet by cable modems or Digital Subscriber Line (DSL) are more open to penetration by outsiders because they use fixed Internet addresses where they can be easily identified. (With dial-up service, a temporary Internet address is assigned for each session.) A fixed Internet address creates a fixed target for hackers.

Telephone service based on Internet technology (see Chapter 8) can be more vulnerable than the switched voice network if it does not run over a secure private network. Most Voice over IP (VoIP) traffic over the public Internet is not encrypted, so anyone linked to a network can listen in on conversations. Hackers can intercept conversations to obtain credit card and other confidential personal information or shut down voice service by flooding servers supporting VoIP with bogus traffic.

Vulnerability has also increased from widespread use of e-mail and instant messaging (IM). E-mail can contain attachments that serve as springboards for malicious software or unauthorized access to internal corporate systems. Employees may use e-mail messages to transmit valuable trade secrets, financial data, or confidential customer information to unauthorized recipients. Popular instant messaging applications for consumers do not use a secure layer for text messages, so they can be intercepted and read by outsiders during transmission over the public Internet. IM activity over the Internet can in some cases be used as a back door to an otherwise secure network. (IM systems designed for corporations, such as IBM's SameTime, include security features.)

WIRELESS SECURITY CHALLENGES

Wireless networks using radio-based technology are even more vulnerable to penetration because radio frequency bands are easy to scan. Although the range of Wireless Fidelity (Wi-Fi) networks is only several hundred feet, it can be extended up to one-fourth of a mile using external antennae. Local area networks (LANs) that use the 802.11b (Wi-Fi) standard can be easily penetrated by outsiders armed with laptops, wireless cards, external antennae, and freeware hacking software. Hackers use these tools to detect unprotected networks, monitor network traffic, and, in some cases, gain access to the Internet or to corporate networks.

Wi-Fi transmission technology uses spread spectrum transmission in which a signal is spread over a wide range of frequencies, and the particular version of spread spectrum transmission used in the 802.11 standard was designed to make it easier for stations to find and hear one another. The *service set identifiers (SSID)* identifying the access points in a Wi-Fi network are broadcast multiple times and can be picked up fairly easily by intruders' sniffer programs (see Figure 10-2). Wireless networks in many locations do not have basic protections against **war driving**, in which eavesdroppers drive by buildings or park outside and try to intercept wireless network traffic.

The 802.11 standard specifies the SSID as a form of password for a user's radio network interface card (NIC) to join a particular wireless network. The user's radio NIC must have the same SSID as the access point to enable association and communication. Most access points

FIGURE 10-2 *Wi-Fi security challenges.*

Many Wi-Fi networks can be penetrated easily by intruders using sniffer programs to obtain an address to access the resources of a network without authorization.

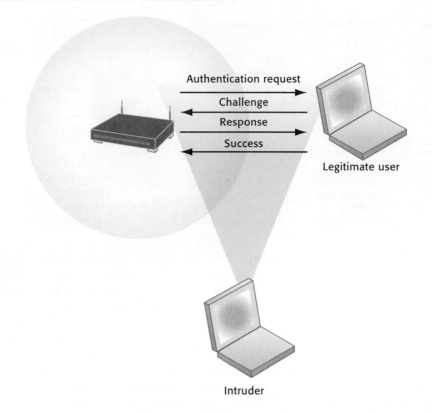

broadcast the SSID multiple times per second. A hacker can employ an 802.11 analysis tool to identify the SSID. (Windows XP has capabilities for detecting the SSID used in a network and automatically configuring the radio NIC within the user's device.) An intruder that has associated with an access point by using the correct SSID can then obtain a legitimate IP address to access other resources on the network because many wireless LANs automatically assign IP addresses to users as they become active. This enables an intruder who has illicitly associated with a wireless LAN to use the Windows operating system to determine which other users are connected to the network, and even to click on other users' devices, locate their documents folders, and open or copy their files. This is a serious problem many end users overlook when connecting to access points at airports or other public locations.

Intruders can also use the information they have gleaned about Internet Protocol (IP) addresses and SSIDs to set up rogue access points on a different radio channel in physical locations close to users to force a user's radio NIC to associate with the rogue access point. Once this association occurs, hackers using the rogue access point can capture the names and passwords of unsuspecting users.

The initial security standard developed for Wi-Fi, called *Wired Equivalent Privacy (WEP),* is not very effective. WEP is built into all standard 802.11 products, but its use is optional. Users must turn it on, and many neglect to do so, leaving many access points unprotected. The basic WEP specification calls for an access point and all of its users to share the same 40-bit encrypted password, which can be easily decrypted by hackers from a small amount of traffic. Manufacturers of wireless networking products are now beefing up their security by offering stronger encryption and authentication systems.

Malicious Software: Viruses, Worms, Trojan Horses, and Spyware

Malicious software programs referred to as **malware** include a variety of threats such as computer viruses, worms, and Trojan horses. A **computer virus** is a rogue software program that attaches itself to other software programs or data files in order to be executed, usually without user knowledge or permission. Most computer viruses deliver a "payload." The payload may be relatively benign, such as the instructions to display a message or image, or it may be highly destructive—destroying programs or data, clogging computer memory, reformatting a computer's hard drive, or causing programs to run improperly. Viruses typically spread from computer to computer when humans take an action such as sending an e-mail attachment or copying an infected file.

Many recent attacks have come from **worms**, which are independent computer programs that copy themselves from one computer to others over a network. (Unlike viruses, they can operate on their own without attaching to other computer program files and rely less on human behavior in order to spread from computer to computer. This explains why computer worms spread much more rapidly than computer viruses.) Worms can destroy data and programs as well as disrupt or even halt the operation of computer networks.

Worms and viruses are often spread over the Internet from files of downloaded software, from files attached to e-mail transmissions, or from compromised e-mail messages. Viruses have also invaded computerized information systems from "infected" disks or infected machines. Today e-mail attachments are the most frequent source of infection, followed by Internet downloads and Web browsing.

Now viruses and worms are spreading to wireless computing devices (Bank, 2004). Mobile device viruses could pose serious threats to enterprise computing because so many wireless devices are now linked to corporate information systems. Table 10-1 describes the characteristics of the some of the most harmful worms and viruses that have appeared.

Over 80,000 viruses and worms are known to exist, with about 25 new ones detected each day. Over the past decade, worms and viruses have caused billions of dollars of damage to corporate networks, e-mail systems, and data. According to the research firm Computer Economics, viruses and worms caused an estimated $12.5 billion in damage worldwide in 2003 (Hulme, 2004).

A **Trojan horse** is a software program that appears to be benign, but then does something other than expected. The Trojan horse is not itself a virus because it does not replicate, but is

TABLE 10-1 *Examples of Malicious Code*

Name	Type	Description
Sasser.ftp	Worm	First appeared May 11, 2004. Spreads over the Internet by attacking random IP addresses. Runs a script that downloads the worm by using File Transfer Protocol (FTP).
Klez	E-mail worm	Most prolific virus of 2002. Delivered in an e-mail containing a random subject line and message body targeting all addresses in the Windows address book, the database of instant messaging program ICQ, and local files. A file from the user's system is randomly selected and sent along with the worm. Klez also attempts to disable antivirus software and drops another virus in the user's system that tries to infect executable files there and across network filing systems.
StartPage.FH	Trojan Horse	First appeared June 15, 2004. Transmitted through infected floppy disks, CD-ROMs, Internet downloads, or peer-to-peer (P2P) file sharing. Changes Microsoft Internet Explorer's homepage to display fake messages warning users of spyware infection. Attempts to entice users to visit a Web site where additional malware can be installed.
Netsky.P	Worm	First appeared March 21, 2004. Spreads through e-mail and through P2P file sharing. Deletes entries belonging to several other worms, including MyDoom and Bagle. Activated when the message is viewed in Microsoft Outlook's preview pane.
Sobig.F	Worm	First detected on August 19, 2003. Sends massive amounts of mail with forged sender information. Payload activates on Fridays or Sundays, when it downloads a program and runs it on the infected computer.
Melissa	Macro virus/worm	First appeared in March 1999. At the time, it was the fastest-spreading infectious program ever discovered. Attacked Microsoft Word's Normal.dot global template, ensuring infection of all newly created documents. Mailed infected Word file to first 50 entries in user's Microsoft Outlook address book.

often a way for viruses or other malicious code to be introduced into a computer system. The term *Trojan horse* is based on the huge wooden horse used by the Greeks to trick the Trojans into opening the gates to their fortified city during the Trojan War. Once inside the city walls, Greek soldiers hidden in the horse revealed themselves and captured the city.

An example of a modern-day Trojan horse is Trojan.Xombe, which was detected on the Internet in early 2004. It masqueraded as an e-mail message from Microsoft, directing recipients to open an attached file that purportedly carried an update to the Windows XP operating system. When the attached file was opened, it downloaded and installed malicious code on the compromised computer. Once this Trojan horse was installed, hackers could access the computer undetected, steal passwords, and take over the machine to launch denial of service attacks on other computers (Keizer, 2004).

Some types of *spyware*, which we introduced in Chapter 5, can also act as malicious software. These small programs install themselves on computers to monitor user Web surfing activity and serve up advertising. Some Web advertisers use spyware to obtain information about users' buying habits and to serve tailored advertisements. Many users find such spyware annoying and some critics worry about its infringement on computer users' privacy.

Other forms of spyware, however, are much more nefarious. *Key loggers* record every keystroke made on a computer to steal serial numbers for software, to launch Internet attacks, to gain access to e-mail accounts, to obtain passwords to protected computer systems, or to pick up personal information such as credit card numbers. Other spyware programs reset Web browser home pages, redirect search requests, or slow computer performance by taking up too much memory. Nearly 1,000 forms of spyware have been documented.

Hackers and Cybervandalism

A **hacker** is an individual who intends to gain unauthorized access to a computer system. Within the hacking community, the term **cracker** is typically used to denote a hacker with criminal intent, although in the public press, the terms *hacker* and *cracker* are used interchangeably. Hackers and crackers gain unauthorized access by finding weaknesses in the security protections employed by Web sites and computer systems, often taking advantage of various features of the Internet that make it an open system that is easy to use.

Hacker activities have broadened beyond mere system intrusion to include theft of goods and information, as well as system damage and **cybervandalism**, the intentional disruption, defacement, or even destruction of a Web site or corporate information system. Early in 2003, hackers introduced the Slammer worm, which targeted a known vulnerability in Microsoft SQL Server database software. Slammer struck thousands of companies; crashed Bank of America cash machines, especially in the southwestern part of the

These three charts show the regional distribution of computer viruses and worms worldwide reported by Trend Micro during the past 24 hours, 7 days, and 30 days as of October 5, 2004. The virus count represents the number of infected files and the percentage shows the relative prevalence in each region compared to worldwide statistics for each measuring period.

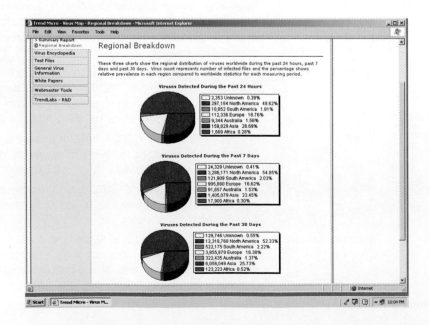

United States; affected cash registers at supermarkets such as the Publix chain in Atlanta, where staff could not dispense cash to frustrated buyers; and took down most Internet connections in South Korea, causing a dip in the stock market there (CNN, 2003). Some hackers, motivated by "hacktivism," launch politically motivated attacks with the same effect. For instance, after the October 12, 2002, terrorist nightclub bombings in Bali, Indonesian hackers hacked or defaced more than 200 Australian Web sites to protest security raids targeting Indonesian families in Australia.

SPOOFING AND SNIFFING

Hackers attempting to hide their true identity often spoof, or misrepresent themselves by using fake e-mail addresses or masquerading as someone else. **Spoofing** also can involve redirecting a Web link to an address different from the intended one, with the site masquerading as the intended destination. Links that are designed to lead to one site can be reset to send users to a totally unrelated site, one that benefits the hacker. For example, if hackers redirect customers to a fake Web site that looks almost exactly like the true site, they can then collect and process orders, effectively stealing business as well as sensitive customer information from the true site. We provide more detail on other forms of spoofing in our discussion of computer crime.

A **sniffer** is a type of eavesdropping program that monitors information traveling over a network. When used legitimately, sniffers can help identify potential network trouble-spots or criminal activity on networks, but when used for criminal purposes, they can be damaging and very difficult to detect. Sniffers enable hackers to steal proprietary information from anywhere on a network, including e-mail messages, company files, and confidential reports.

DENIAL OF SERVICE ATTACKS

In a **denial of service (DoS) attack**, hackers flood a network server or Web server with many thousands of false communications or requests for services to crash the network. The network receives so many queries that it cannot keep up with them and is thus unavailable to service legitimate requests. A **distributed denial of service (DDoS) attack** uses numerous computers to inundate and overwhelm the network from numerous launch points. For example, on June 15, 2004, Web infrastructure provider Akamai Technology was hit by a distributed denial of service attack that slowed some of its customers' Web sites for over two hours. The attack used thousands of "zombie" PCs, which had been infected by malicious software without their owners' knowledge (Thomson, 2004). Microsoft, Apple, and Yahoo! were among the sites affected.

Although DoS attacks do not destroy information or access restricted areas of a company's information systems, they can cause a Web site to shut down, making it impossible for legitimate users to access the site. For busy e-commerce sites such as eBay and Buy.com, these attacks are costly; while the site is shut down, customers cannot make purchases.

Figure 10-3 illustrates the estimated worldwide damage from all forms of digital attack, including hacking, malware, and spam between 1997 and 2004.

Computer Crime and Cyberterrorism

Most hacker activities are criminal offenses, and the vulnerabilities of systems we have just described make them targets for other types of computer crime as well. We introduced the topic of computer crime and abuse in Chapter 5. The U.S. Department of Justice defines *computer crime* as "any violations of criminal law that involve a knowledge of computer technology for their perpetration, investigation, or prosecution." The computer can be a target of a crime or an instrument of a crime. Table 10-2 provides examples of both categories of computer crime.

No one knows the magnitude of the computer crime problem—how many systems are invaded, how many people engage in the practice, or the total economic damage. According to one study by the Computer Crime Research Center, U.S. companies lose approximately $14 billion annually to cybercrimes. Many companies are reluctant to report computer crimes because the crimes may involve employees or the company fears that publicizing its vulnerability will hurt its reputation.

FIGURE 10-3   *Worldwide damage from digital attacks.*

This chart shows estimates of the average annual worldwide damage from hacking, malware, and spam since 1997. Figures for 2004 are estimates based on the historical rate of growth according to data from mi2G and the authors.

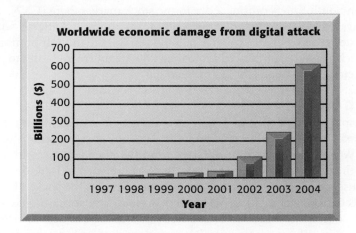

The most economically damaging kinds of computer crime are DoS attacks, introducing viruses, theft of services, and disruption of computer systems. Traditionally, employees—insiders—have been the source of the most injurious computer crimes because they have the knowledge, access, and, frequently, job-related motives to commit such crimes. However, the Internet's ease of use and accessibility have created new opportunities for computer crime and abuse by outsiders.

IDENTITY THEFT

With the growth of the Internet and electronic commerce, identity theft has become especially troubling. **Identity theft** is a crime in which an imposter obtains key pieces of personal information, such as social security identification numbers, driver's license numbers, or credit card numbers, to impersonate someone else. The information may be used to obtain credit, merchandise, or services in the name of the victim or to provide the thief with false credentials. According to a 2003 U.S. Federal Trade Commission report, 9.9 million cases of identity theft were reported in the United States in the 12 months ending in April 2003, causing consumer losses of about $5 million (Chipman, 2004).

The Internet has made it easy for identity thieves to use stolen information because goods can be purchased online without any personal interaction. Credit card files are a

TABLE 10-2 *Examples of Computer Crime*

COMPUTERS AS TARGETS OF CRIME

Breaching the confidentiality of protected computerized data

Accessing a computer system without authority

Knowingly accessing a protected computer to commit fraud

Intentionally accessing a protected computer and causing damage, negligently or deliberately

Knowingly transmitting a program, program code, or command that intentionally causes damage to a protected computer

Threatening to cause damage to a protected computer

COMPUTERS AS INSTRUMENTS OF CRIME

Theft of trade secrets

Unauthorized copying of software or copyrighted intellectual property, such as articles, books, music, and video

Schemes to defraud

Using e-mail for threats or harassment

Intentionally attempting to intercept electronic communication

Illegally accessing stored electronic communications, including e-mail and voice mail

Transmitting or possessing child pornography using a computer

major target of Web site hackers. Moreover, e-commerce sites are wonderful sources of customer personal information—name, address, and phone number. Armed with this information, criminals can assume a new identity and establish new credit for their own purposes.

One increasingly popular tactic is a form of spoofing called **phishing**. It involves setting up fake Web sites or sending e-mail messages that look like those of legitimate businesses to ask users for confidential personal data. The e-mail message instructs recipients to update or confirm records by providing social security numbers, bank and credit card information, and other confidential data either by responding to the e-mail message or by entering the information at a bogus Web site.

For example, Dan Marius Stefan was convicted of stealing nearly $500,000 by sending e-mail messages that appeared to come from the online auction site eBay to people who were unsuccessful auction bidders. The message described similar merchandise for sale at even better prices. To purchase these goods, recipients had to provide bank account numbers and passwords and wire the money to a fraudulent "escrow site" that Stefan had set up.

Phishing appears to be escalating. Brightmail of San Francisco, a company that filters e-mail for spam, identified 2.3 billion phishing messages in February 2004, representing 4 percent of the e-mail it processed; this figure is up from only 1 percent in September 2003 (Hansell, 2004). Phishing scams have posed as PayPal, the online payment service, online service provider America Online (AOL), Citibank, Fleet Bank, American Express, the Federal Deposit Insurance Corporation, the Bank of England, and other banks around the world. British security firm mi2g estimates the worldwide economic damage from phishing scams exceeded $13.5 billion in customer and productivity losses, business interruptions, and efforts to repair damage to brand reputation (Barrett, 2004).

The U.S. Congress responded to the threat of computer crime in 1986 with the Computer Fraud and Abuse Act. This act makes it illegal to access a computer system without authorization. Most states have similar laws, and nations in Europe have similar legislation. Congress also passed the National Information Infrastructure Protection Act in 1996 to make virus distribution and hacker attacks to disable Web sites federal crimes. U.S. legislation such as the Wiretap Act, Wire Fraud Act, Economic Espionage Act, Electronic Communications Privacy Act, E-Mail Threats and Harassment Act, and Child Pornography Act covers computer crimes involving intercepting electronic communication, using

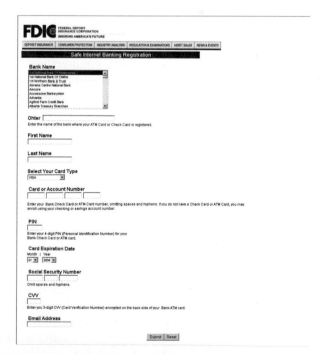

The Anti-Phishing Working Group Web site displays a phishing message pretending to come from the U.S. Federal Deposit Insurance Corporation (FDIC). The message requests recipients to provide their credit card and social security numbers on a bogus Web site set up by identity thieves. Phishing and identity theft have become serious problems on the Internet.

electronic communication to defraud, stealing trade secrets, illegally accessing stored electronic communications, using e-mail for threats or harassment, and transmitting or possessing child pornography.

CYBERTERRORISM AND CYBERWARFARE

Concern is mounting that the vulnerabilities of the Internet or other networks could be exploited by terrorists, foreign intelligence services, or other groups to create widespread disruption and harm. Such cyberattacks might target the software that runs electrical power grids, air traffic control systems, or networks of major banks and financial institutions. Groups from a number of countries, including China, have been probing and mapping U.S. networks, and at least 20 countries are believed to be developing offensive and defensive cyberwarfare capabilities. U.S. military networks and U.S. government agencies suffer hundreds of hacker attacks each year.

The U.S. government has taken some steps to deal with the potential threat. The Department of Homeland Security has an Information Analysis and Infrastructure Protection Directorate to coordinate cybersecurity. The directorate's National Cyber Security Division is responsible for protecting critical infrastructure. It conducts cyberspace analysis, promotes information sharing, issues alerts, and aids in national recovery efforts. The U.S. Department of Defense has joint task forces for computer network defense and for managing computer network attacks. Congress has approved a Cybersecurity Research and Development Act to fund universities that are researching ways to protect computer systems.

Internal Threats: Employees

We tend to think the security threats to a business originate outside the organization. In fact, the largest financial threats to business institutions come from insiders. Some of the largest disruptions to service, destruction of e-commerce sites, and diversion of customer credit data and personal information have come from insiders—once trusted employees. Employees have access to privileged information, and in the presence of sloppy internal security procedures, they are often able to roam throughout an organization's systems without leaving a trace.

Studies have found that users' lack of knowledge is the single greatest cause of network security breaches. Many employees forget their passwords to access computer systems or allow other coworkers to use them, which compromises the system. Malicious intruders seeking system access sometimes trick employees into revealing their passwords by pretending to be legitimate members of the company in need of information. This practice is called **social engineering**.

Employees—both end users and information systems specialists—are also a major source of errors introduced into an information system. Employees can introduce errors by entering faulty data or by not following the proper instructions for processing data and using computer equipment. Information systems specialists can also create software errors as they design and develop new software or maintain existing programs.

Software Vulnerability

Software errors also pose a constant threat to information systems, causing untold losses in productivity. The U.S. Department of Commerce National Institute of Standards and Technology (NIST) reports that software flaws (including vulnerabilities to hackers and malware) cost the U.S. economy $59.6 billion each year (Hulme, 2004).

A major problem with software is the presence of hidden **bugs**, or program code defects. Studies have shown that it is virtually impossible to eliminate all bugs from large programs. The main source of bugs is the complexity of decision-making code. Important programs within most corporations may contain tens of thousands or even millions of lines of code, each with many alternative decision paths. Such complexity is difficult to document and design—designers may document some reactions incorrectly or may fail to consider some possibilities. Even after rigorous testing, developers do not know for sure that a piece of software is dependable until the product proves itself after much operational use.

Commercial software often contains flaws that create not only performance issues but also security vulnerabilities that open networks to intruders. These vulnerabilities and bugs can enable malware to slip past antivirus defenses. A great deal of malware has been trying to exploit vulnerabilities in the Microsoft Windows operating system and other Microsoft products, but malware targeting the Linux operating system is on the rise as well.

To correct software flaws once they are identified, the software vendor creates lines of code called *patches* to repair the flaw without disturbing proper operation of the software. An example is Microsoft's XP Service Pack 2 (SP2) introduced in 2004, which features added firewall protection against viruses and intruders, capabilities for automatic security updates, and an easy-to-use interface for managing the security applications on the user's computer. It is up to users of the software to track these vulnerabilities, test, and apply all patches. This process is called *patch management*.

Because a company's information technology (IT) infrastructure is typically laden with multiple business applications, operating system installations, and other system services, the process of maintaining patches on all devices and services used by a company can be very time consuming and costly. The Yankee Group consulting firm estimates that a firm with more than 500 PCs spends up to 120 staff hours testing and installing every patch (Foley and Hulme, 2004).

The Window on Technology illustrates some of the problems faced by companies trying to practice patch management. Companies are now besieged with numerous malevolent viruses and worms that regularly bring down systems that fail to implement applicable patches. This malevolent software is being created so rapidly that companies have very little time to respond between the time a vulnerability and a patch are announced and the time malicious software appears to exploit the vulnerability. This is one reason why Sasser, SQL Slammer, Blaster, SoBig.F, and other worms and viruses have been able to infect so many computer systems so rapidly.

10.2 BUSINESS VALUE OF SECURITY AND CONTROL

Security and control have become a critical, although perhaps unappreciated, area of information systems investment. When computer systems fail to run or work as required, firms that depend heavily on computers experience a serious loss of business function. The longer computer systems are down, the more serious the consequences for the firm. Some firms relying on computers to process their critical business transactions might experience a total loss of business function if they lose computer capability for more than a few days. And with so much business now dependent on the Internet and networked systems, firms are more vulnerable than ever to disruption and harm. Security incidents have been growing at a phenomenal rate (see Figure 10-4).

For example, during the summer of 2003 corporate networks and home computer systems were overwhelmed by attacks from the SoBig.F worm. SoBig.F disguises itself in e-mail, which, once opened, scans a computer for e-mail addresses and then sends scores of messages to the addresses it has collected using its own built-in sending program. SoBig caused an estimated $50 million in damage in the United States alone during that period, temporarily disabling freight and computer traffic in Washington, D.C., and overwhelming computer systems with the sheer volume of e-mail. The 2004 joint Computer Security Institute and FBI (CSI/FBI) "Computer Crime and Security Survey" found that losses attributable to security problems and cybercrimes accounted for $141,496,560 among the 486 companies that quantified their damages that year (Gordon et al., 2004).

Companies have very valuable information assets to protect. Systems often house confidential information about individuals' taxes, financial assets, medical records, and job performance reviews. They also may contain information on corporate operations, including trade secrets, new product development plans, and marketing strategies. Government systems may store information on weapons systems, intelligence operations, and military targets. These information assets have tremendous value, and the repercussions can be devastating if they are lost, destroyed, or placed in the wrong hands. A recent

WINDOW ON TECHNOLOGY

THE RUSH TO PATCH

Computer viruses and worms appear to be growing smarter and more numerous every day. Fast-spreading worms such as Sasser, SQL Slammer, and Blaster have been able to proliferate rapidly because companies cannot update their software quickly enough to deter them.

A new vulnerability in a software product is not announced until a patch is available. At that point hackers rush to exploit the vulnerability before the patch has been widely applied. These malicious hackers have become so efficient that they are churning out these powerful new worms faster than corporate security experts can patch their systems. According to Foundstone, Inc., a technology risk-management firm in Mission Viejo, California, the average time between the announcement of a security flaw and the appearance of malicious code to exploit it has declined from 281 days in 1999 to merely 10 days. That means that patch management—tracking and applying updates to fix security flaws—is more challenging today than ever.

The course of the Sasser worm illustrates some of these challenges. A small security firm called eEye Digital Security had informed Microsoft about a vulnerability in the networking feature of the Windows operating system in October 2003. eEye agreed with Microsoft not to disclose vulnerabilities it found until Microsoft evaluated the risk and created a software patch. It took six months for Microsoft to release a protective patch. In the meantime, eEye waited, knowing that its network was wide open to being attacked and there was nothing it could do.

Microsoft finally announced the vulnerability and the availability of a patch in April 2003. Within hours, snippets of "exploitable code" appeared on Internet discussion boards. Sasser's authors then quickly went to work. Only 17 days passed between the time Microsoft announced the flaw and the Sasser worm was released, on April 30, 2004.

Patches can be very time consuming to apply, especially if security updates are needed for client machines as well as servers and larger computers. A large corporation might have hundreds of servers and thousands of desktop client PCs that need to be secured against each virus or worm outbreak, and a separate software patch might need to be installed on each of these machines. For example, Motorola, headquartered in Schaumburg, Illinois, must patch as many as 100,000 computers running the Windows operating system if such updates are required. Station Casinos in Las Vegas has 220 Windows servers running slot machine accounting, player tracking, and restaurant cash register systems that must be patched if necessary.

Moreover, some of these patches are incompatible with the software in some computer systems. Research from AssetMetrix, a Canadian asset-monitoring service provider, found that upgrading to Windows XP Service Pack 2 causes problems in about one in every 10 PCs running the operating system.

Difficulties applying patches explain how the SQL Slammer worm could infect so many computers in such a short period of time. In less than 10 minutes in January 2003 the worm infected tens of thousands of servers running Microsoft SQL Server 2000 database management software, including those supporting the Finnish telephone system, the Davis-Beese nuclear power station outside Toledo, Ohio, and 13,000 Bank of America automatic teller machines (ATMs). Microsoft had developed a patch for SQL Server software to deal with this vulnerability six months earlier, but many organizations had been reluctant to apply it, citing concerns that the patch needed more testing and time required to apply it.

If a new vulnerability appears, "anything less than near-perfection in patching puts you at risk of substantial downtime," says William Boni, chief information security officer for Motorola. And achieving 100 percent perfection is also difficult because employees are traveling or working remotely. If a system has not been patched, Boni's team removes it from Motorola's network. But that means the system must be updated manually by a technician.

In 2003, Boni was satisfied if his team completed all the patching work for 100,000 computers within 30 days. But the Sasser worm hit the Internet only 17 days after Microsoft disclosed the vulnerability the worm targeted. So, Motorola must respond immediately to new vulnerabilities as if it is already under attack.

System administrators must scramble whenever a new vulnerability is announced. Microsoft, Oracle, SAP, Computer Associates, and other software vendors are trying to make the process more predictable by scheduling disclosure of vulnerabilities and release of patches on a routine monthly basis.

Even with better scheduling of patch release, many organizations don't have the time or resources to keep up with tracking security flaws and installing patches. For example, a U.S. General Accounting Office report in June 2004 stated that half of the 24 government agencies surveyed lacked the staff and money to keep up with the security flaws that have been discovered in commercial software. Station Casinos was recently still testing one patch when Microsoft issued the next one.

Sources: David Bank, "Computer Worm Is Turning Faster," *Wall Street Journal*, May 27, 2004; "Editorial: Time to Apply a Patch," *Federal Computer Week*, June 22, 2004; Gregg Keizer, "Windows XP Service Pack 2: The 10% Problem," *Information Week*, August 31, 2004; and Jaikumar Vijayan, "Unprepared Firms Slammed," *Computerworld*, February 3, 2003.

To Think About: What management, organization, and technology factors explain why companies have so much difficulty protecting themselves from worms and other malicious software? What steps should they take to deal with this problem more effectively?

FIGURE 10-4   *Security incidents continue to rise.*

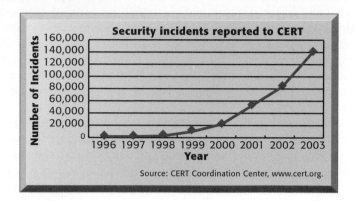

This chart shows the growth in the number of security incidents reported to the Computer Emergency Response Team (CERT) between 1996 and 2003.

Source: CERT Coordination Center, www.cert.org, accessed July 6, 2004.

study estimates that when the security of a large firm is compromised, the company loses approximately 2.1 percent of its market value within two days of the security breach, which translates into an average loss of $1.65 billion in stock market value per incident (Cavusoglu, Mishra, and Raghunathan, 2004).

Inadequate security and control may also create serious legal liability. Businesses must protect not only their own information assets but also those of customers, employees, and business partners. Failure to do so can open the firm to costly litigation for data exposure or theft. An organization can be held liable for needless risk and harm created if it fails to take appropriate protective action to prevent loss of confidential information, data corruption, or breach of privacy. A sound security and control framework that protects business information assets can thus produce a high return on investment.

Legal and Regulatory Requirements for Electronic Records Management

Recent U.S. government regulations are forcing companies to take security and control more seriously by mandating the protection of data from abuse, exposure, and unauthorized access. Firms face new legal obligations for electronic records management and document retention as well as for privacy protection. **Electronic records management** (ERM) consists of policies, procedures, and tools for managing the retention, destruction, and storage of electronic records. Following is a list of laws related to data security and control.

HIPAA. The Health Insurance Portability and Accountability Act (HIPAA) of 1996 outlines medical security and privacy rules and procedures for simplifying the administration of health care billing and automating the transfer of health care data between health care providers, payers, and plans. It requires members of the health care industry to retain patient information for six years and ensure the confidentiality of those records. It specifies privacy, security, and electronic transaction standards for health care providers handling patient information, providing penalties for breaches of medical privacy, disclosure of patient records by e-mail, or unauthorized network access.

Gramm-Leach-Bliley Act. The Financial Services Modernization Act of 1999, better known as the Gramm-Leach-Bliley Act after its Congressional sponsors, requires financial institutions to ensure the security and confidentiality of customer data. Data must be stored on a secure medium. Special security measures must be enforced to protect such data on storage media and during transmittal.

Sarbanes-Oxley Act of 2002. The Public Company Accounting Reform and Investor Protection Act of 2002, better known as Sarbanes-Oxley after its sponsors Senator Paul Sarbanes of Maryland and Representative Michael Oxley of Ohio, was designed to protect investors after the financial scandals at Enron, WorldCom, and other public companies. It imposes responsibility on companies and their management to safeguard the integrity of the information that is used internally and released externally.

Sarbanes-Oxley requires chief executives and chief financial officers at all publicly traded companies in the United States to certify the accuracy of their organizations' quarterly and annual financial reports and to establish adequate internal controls over their reporting systems. All documents and communications related to these reports and their data must be retained for seven years following an audit. Companies must institute procedures for keeping track of all financial information from the moment it is created, to final submission in annual reports to the Securities and Exchange Commission (SEC). These senior managers face up to 20 years in jail if the firm's financial statements have been falsified.

Sarbanes-Oxley is fundamentally about ensuring that internal controls are in place to govern the creation and documentation of information in financial statements. Because information systems are used to generate, store, and transport such data, the legislation requires firms to consider information systems security and other controls required to ensure the integrity, confidentiality, and accuracy of their data. Each system application that deals with critical financial reporting data requires controls to make sure the data are accurate. Controls to secure the corporate network, prevent unauthorized access to systems and data, and ensure data integrity and availability in the event of disaster or other disruption of service are essential as well.

Electronic Evidence and Computer Forensics

Security, control, and electronic records management have become essential for responding to legal actions. Much of the evidence today for stock fraud, embezzlement, theft of company trade secrets, computer crime, and many civil cases is in digital form. In addition to information from printed or typewritten pages, legal cases today increasingly rely on evidence represented as computer data stored on portable floppy disks, CDs, and computer hard disk drives, as well as in e-mail, instant messages, and e-commerce transactions over the Internet. E-mail is currently the most common type of electronic evidence.

In a legal action, a firm may have to submit to a discovery request for access to information that may be used as evidence, and the company is required by law to produce those data. The cost of responding to a discovery request can be enormous if the company has trouble assembling the required data or the data have been corrupted or destroyed. Courts now impose severe financial and even criminal penalties for improper destruction of electronic documents.

An effective electronic document retention policy ensures that electronic documents, e-mail, and other records are well organized, accessible, and neither retained too long nor discarded too soon. It also reflects an awareness of how to preserve potential evidence for computer forensics. **Computer forensics** is the scientific collection, examination, authentication, preservation, and analysis of data held on or retrieved from computer storage media in such a way that the information can be used as evidence in a court of law. It deals with the following problems:

- Recovering data from computers while preserving evidential integrity
- Securely storing and handling recovered electronic data
- Finding significant information in a large volume of electronic data
- Presenting the information to a court of law

Electronic evidence can reside on computer storage media in the form of computer files and as *ambient data,* which are not visible to the average user. An example might be a file that has been deleted on a PC hard drive. Data that a computer user may have deleted on computer storage media can be recovered through various techniques. Computer forensics experts try to recover such hidden data for presentation as evidence.

An awareness of the need for computer forensics should be incorporated into a firm's contingency planning process. The CIO, security specialists, information systems staff, and corporate legal counsel should all work together to have a plan in place that can be executed if a legal need arises.

10.3 ESTABLISHING A MANAGEMENT FRAMEWORK FOR SECURITY AND CONTROL

Technology is not the key issue in information systems security and control. The technology provides a foundation, but in the absence of intelligent management policies, even the best technology can be easily defeated. For instance, experts believe that over 90 percent of successful cyberattacks could have been prevented by technology available at the time. Inadequate human attention made these attacks so prevalent.

Protection of information resources requires a sound security policy and set of controls. **ISO 17799**, an international set of standards for security and control, provides helpful guidelines. It specifies best practices in information systems security and control, including security policy, business continuity planning, physical security, access control, compliance, and creating a security function within the organization.

Types of Information Systems Controls

Protection of information resources requires a well-designed set of controls. Computer systems are controlled by a combination of general controls and application controls. **General controls** govern the design, security, and use of computer programs and the security of data files in general throughout the organization's information technology infrastructure. On the whole, general controls apply to all computerized applications and consist of a combination of hardware, software, and manual procedures that create an overall control environment. **Application controls** are specific controls unique to each computerized application, such as payroll or order processing. They consist of controls applied from the business functional area of a particular system and from programmed procedures.

GENERAL CONTROLS

General controls include software controls, physical hardware controls, computer operations controls, data security controls, controls over the systems implementation process, and **administrative controls**. Table 10-3 describes the functions of each type of control.

APPLICATION CONTROLS

Application controls include both automated and manual procedures that ensure that only authorized data are completely and accurately processed by that application. Application controls can be classified as (1) input controls, (2) processing controls, and (3) output controls.

Input controls check data for accuracy and completeness when they enter the system. There are specific input controls for input authorization, data conversion, data editing, and error handling. **Processing controls** establish that data are complete and accurate during updating. Run control totals, computer matching, and programmed edit checks are used as processing controls. **Output controls** ensure that the results of computer processing are accurate, complete, and properly distributed. Table 10-4 provides more detailed examples of each type of application control.

Not all of the application controls discussed here are used in every information system. Some systems require more of these controls than others, depending on the importance of the data and the nature of the application.

Risk Assessment

Before an organization commits resources to controls, it must know which assets require protection and the extent to which these assets are vulnerable. A risk assessment helps answer these questions and also helps the firm determine the most cost-effective set of controls for protecting assets.

A **risk assessment** determines the level of risk to the firm if a specific activity or process is not properly controlled. Business managers working with information systems specialists can determine the value of information assets, points of vulnerability, the likely frequency of a problem, and the potential for damage. For example, if an event is likely to occur no more

TABLE 10-3 General Controls

Type of General Control	Description
Software controls	Monitor the use of system software and prevent unauthorized access of software programs, system software, and computer programs. System software is an important control area because it performs overall control functions for the programs that directly process data and data files.
Hardware controls	Ensure that computer hardware is physically secure and check for equipment malfunction. Computer equipment should be specially protected against fires and extremes of temperature and humidity. Organizations that are dependent on their computers also must make provisions for backup or continued operation to maintain constant service.
Computer operations controls	Oversee the work of the computer department to ensure that programmed procedures are consistently and correctly applied to the storage and processing of data. They include controls over the setup of computer processing jobs and computer operations and backup and recovery procedures for processing that ends abnormally.
Data security controls	Ensure that valuable business data files on either disk or tape are not subject to unauthorized access, change, or destruction while they are in use or in storage.
Implementation controls	Audit the systems development process at various points to ensure that the process is properly controlled and managed. The systems development audit looks for the presence of formal reviews by users and management at various stages of development; the level of user involvement at each stage of implementation; and the use of a formal cost-benefit methodology in establishing system feasibility. The audit should look for the use of controls and quality assurance techniques for program development, conversion, and testing and for complete and thorough system, user, and operations documentation.
Administrative controls	Formalize standards, rules, procedures, and control disciplines to ensure that the organization's general and application controls are properly executed and enforced.

than once a year, with a maximum of a $1,000 loss to the organization, it would not be feasible to spend $20,000 on the design and maintenance of a control to protect against that event. However, if that same event could occur at least once a day, with a potential loss of more than $300,000 a year, $100,000 spent on a control might be entirely appropriate.

Table 10-5 illustrates sample results of a risk assessment for an online order processing system that processes 30,000 orders per day. The likelihood of each exposure occurring

TABLE 10-4 Application Controls

Name of Control	Type of Application Control	Description
Control totals	Input, processing	Totals established beforehand for input and processing transactions. These totals can range from a simple document count to totals for quantity fields, such as total sales amount (for a batch of transactions). Computer programs count the totals from transactions input or processed.
Edit checks	Input	Programmed routines that can be performed to edit input data for errors before they are processed. Transactions that do not meet edit criteria are rejected. For example, data might be checked to make sure they are in the right format (for instance, a nine-digit social security number should not contain any alphabetic characters).
Computer matching	Input, processing	Matches input data with information held on master or suspense files and notes unmatched items for investigation. For example, a matching program might match employee time cards with a payroll master file and report missing or duplicate time cards.
Run control totals	Processing, output	Balance the total of transactions processed with total number of transactions input or output.
Report distribution logs	Output	Documentation specifying that authorized recipients have received their reports, checks, or other critical documents.

TABLE 10-5 Online Order Processing Risk Assessment

Exposure	Probability of Occurrence (%)	Loss Range/Average ($)	Expected Annual Loss ($)
Power failure	30	5,000–200,000 (102,500)	30,750
Embezzlement	5	1,000–50,000 (25,500)	1,275
User error	98	200–40,000 (20,100)	19,698

over a one-year period is expressed as a percentage. The next column shows the highest and lowest possible loss that could be expected each time the exposure occurred and an average loss calculated by adding the highest and lowest figures together and dividing by 2. The expected annual loss for each exposure can be determined by multiplying the average loss by its probability of occurrence.

This risk assessment shows that the probability of a power failure occurring in a one-year period is 30 percent. Loss of order transactions while power is down could range from $5,000 to $200,000 (averaging $102,500) for each occurrence, depending on how long processing is halted. The probability of embezzlement occurring over a yearly period is about 5 percent, with potential losses ranging from $1,000 to $50,000 (and averaging $25,500) for each occurrence. User errors have a 98 percent chance of occurring over a yearly period, with losses ranging from $200 to $40,000 (and averaging $20,100) for each occurrence. Once the risks have been assessed, system builders can concentrate on the control points with the greatest vulnerability and potential for loss. In this case, controls should focus on ways to minimize the risk of power failures and user errors because anticipated annual losses are highest for these areas.

One problem with risk assessment and other methods for quantifying security costs and benefits is that organizations do not always know the precise probability of threats occurring to their information systems, and they may not be able to quantify the impact of such events accurately. Nevertheless, some effort to anticipate, budget for, and control direct and indirect security costs will be appreciated by management (Mercuri, 2003).

The end product of risk assessment is a plan to minimize overall cost and maximize defenses. To decide which controls to use, information systems builders must examine various control techniques in relation to each other and to their relative cost-effectiveness. A control weakness at one point may be offset by a strong control at another. It may not be cost-effective to build tight controls at every point in the processing cycle if the areas of greatest risk are secure or if compensating controls exist elsewhere. The combination of all of the controls developed for a particular application determines the application's overall level of control.

Security Policy

Firms must develop a coherent corporate policy that takes into account the nature of the risks, the information assets that need protecting, and the procedures and technologies required to address the risks, as well as implementation and auditing mechanisms.

A growing number of firms have established a formal corporate security function headed by a **chief security officer** (CSO). The security group educates and trains users, keeps management aware of security threats and breakdowns, and maintains the tools chosen to implement security. The chief security officer is responsible for enforcing the firm's security policy.

A **security policy** consists of statements ranking information risks, identifying acceptable security goals, and identifying the mechanisms for achieving these goals. What are the firm's most important information assets? Who generates and controls this information in the firm? What existing security policies are in place to protect the information? What level of risk is management willing to accept for each of these assets? Is it willing, for instance, to lose customer credit data once every 10 years? Or will it build a security edifice for credit card data that can withstand the once-in-a-hundred-year disaster? Management must estimate how much it will cost to achieve this level of acceptable risk.

The security organization typically administers acceptable use policies and authorization policies. An **acceptable use policy (AUP)** defines acceptable uses of the firm's information resources and computing equipment, including desktop and laptop computers, wireless devices, telephones, and the Internet. The policy should clarify company policy regarding privacy, user responsibility, and personal use of company equipment and networks. A good AUP defines unacceptable and acceptable actions for every user and specifies consequences for noncompliance.

Authorization policies determine differing levels of access to information assets for different levels of users. **Authorization management systems** establish where and when a user is permitted to access certain parts of a Web site or a corporate database. Such systems allow each user access only to those portions of a system that person is permitted to enter, based on information established by a set of access rules.

The authorization management system knows exactly what information each user is permitted to access as shown in Figure 10-5. This figure illustrates the security allowed for two sets of users of an online personnel database containing sensitive information, such as employees' salaries, benefits, and medical histories. One set of users consists of all employees who perform clerical functions, such as inputting employee data into the system. All individuals with this type of profile can update the system but can neither read nor update sensitive fields, such as salary, medical history, or earnings data. Another profile applies to a divisional manager, who cannot update the system but who can read all employee data fields for his or her division, including medical history and salary. These profiles are based on access rules supplied by business groups. The system illustrated in Figure 10-5 provides very fine grained security restrictions, such as allowing authorized personnel users to inquire about all employee information except that in confidential fields, such as salary or medical history.

Ensuring Business Continuity

As companies increasingly rely on digital networks for their revenue and operations, they need to take additional steps to ensure that their systems and applications are always available. Many factors can disrupt the performance of a Web site, including denial of ser-

FIGURE 10-5 *Security profiles for a personnel system.*

These two examples represent two security profiles or data security patterns that might be found in a personnel system. Depending on the security profile, a user would have certain restrictions on access to various systems, locations, or data in an organization.

SECURITY PROFILE 1

User: Personnel Dept. Clerk

Location: Division 1

Employee Identification
Codes with This Profile: 00753, 27834, 37665, 44116

Data Field Restrictions	Type of Access
All employee data for Division 1 only	Read and Update
• Medical history data	None
• Salary	None
• Pensionable earnings	None

SECURITY PROFILE 2

User: Divisional Personnel Manager

Location: Division 1

Employee Identification
Codes with This Profile: 27321

Data Field Restrictions	Type of Access
All employee data for Division 1 only	Read Only

vice attacks, network failure, heavy Internet traffic, and exhausted server resources. Computer failures, interruptions, and downtime translate into disgruntled customers, millions of dollars in lost sales, and the inability to perform critical internal transactions. **Downtime** refers to periods of time in which a system is not operational.

Firms such as those in the airline and financial services industries with critical applications requiring online transaction processing have traditionally used fault-tolerant computer systems for many years to ensure 100 percent availability. In **online transaction processing**, transactions entered online are immediately processed by the computer. Multitudinous changes to databases, reporting, and requests for information occur each instant.

Fault-tolerant computer systems contain redundant hardware, software, and power supply components that create an environment that provides continuous, uninterrupted service. Fault-tolerant computers contain extra memory chips, processors, and disk storage devices to back up a system and keep it running to prevent failure. They use special software routines or self-checking logic built into their circuitry to detect hardware failures and automatically switch to a backup device. Parts from these computers can be removed and repaired without disruption to the computer system.

Fault tolerance should be distinguished from **high-availability computing**. Both fault tolerance and high-availability computing are designed to maximize application and system availability. Both use backup hardware resources. However, high-availability computing helps firms recover quickly from a crash, whereas fault tolerance promises continuous availability and the elimination of recovery time altogether. High-availability computing environments are a minimum requirement for firms with heavy electronic commerce processing or for firms that depend on digital networks for their internal operations.

High-availability computing requires an assortment of tools and technologies to ensure maximum performance of computer systems and networks, including redundant servers, mirroring, load balancing, clustering, high-capacity storage, and good disaster recovery and business continuity plans. The firm's computing platform must be extremely robust with scalable processing power, storage, and bandwidth.

Load balancing distributes large numbers of access requests across multiple servers. The requests are directed to the most available server so that no single device is overwhelmed. If one server starts to get swamped, requests are forwarded to another server with more capacity.

Mirroring uses a backup server that duplicates all the processes and transactions of the primary server. If the primary server fails, the backup server can immediately take its place without any interruption in service. However, server mirroring is very expensive because each server must be mirrored by an identical server whose only purpose is to be available in the event of a failure.

High-availability **clustering** links two computers together so that the second computer can act as a backup to the primary computer. If the primary computer fails, the second computer picks up its processing without any pause in the system. (Computers can also be clustered together as a single computing resource to speed up processing.)

Researchers are exploring ways to make computing systems recover even more rapidly when mishaps occur, an approach called **recovery-oriented computing**. This work includes designing systems that can recover quickly and implementing capabilities and tools to help operators pinpoint the sources of faults in multicomponent systems and easily correct their mistakes (Fox and Patterson, 2003).

BUSINESS CONTINUITY AND DISASTER RECOVERY PLANNING

Disaster recovery planning devises plans for the restoration of computing and communications services after they have been disrupted by an event such as an earthquake, flood, or terrorist attack. Disaster recovery plans focus primarily on the technical issues involved in keeping systems up and running, such as which files to back up and the maintenance of backup computer systems or disaster recovery services.

For example, MasterCard maintains a duplicate computer center in Kansas City, Missouri, to serve as an emergency backup to its primary computer center in St. Louis. Rather than build their own backup facilities, many firms contract with disaster recovery firms, such as Comdisco Disaster Recovery Services in Rosemont, Illinois, and SunGard Recovery Services, headquartered in Wayne, Pennsylvania. These disaster recovery firms provide hot sites housing spare computers at locations around the country where subscribing firms can run their critical applications in an emergency.

Business continuity planning focuses on how the company can restore business operations after a disaster strikes. The business continuity plan identifies critical business processes and determines action plans for handling mission-critical functions if systems go down.

Business managers and information technology specialists need to work together on both types of plans to determine which systems and business processes are most critical to the company. They must conduct a business impact analysis to identify the firm's most critical systems and the impact a systems outage would have on the business. Management must determine the maximum amount of time the business can survive with its systems down and which parts of the business must be restored first.

The Window on Management describes how business continuity planning is conducted at Deutsche Bank. This global financial institution cannot afford to have critical operations disrupted by computer failures. It has both disaster recovery facilities and a business continuity plan in place and prepares employees for its execution.

SECURITY OUTSOURCING

Many companies such as Wesfarmers, described in the chapter-opening case, lack the resources or expertise to provide a secure high-availability computing environment on their own. They can outsource many security functions to **managed security service providers (MSSPs)** that monitor network activity and perform vulnerability testing and intrusion detection. Guardent, Counterpane, VeriSign, and Symantec are leading providers of MSSP services.

The Role of Auditing in the Control Process

How does management know that information systems security and controls are effective? To answer this question, organizations must conduct comprehensive and systematic audits. An **MIS audit** identifies all of the controls that govern individual information systems and assesses their effectiveness. To accomplish this, the auditor must acquire a thorough understanding of operations, physical facilities, telecommunications, security systems, security objectives, organizational structure, personnel, manual procedures, and individual applications.

The auditor usually interviews key individuals who use and operate a specific information system concerning their activities and procedures. Security, application controls, overall integrity controls, and control disciplines are examined. The auditor should trace the flow of sample transactions through the system and perform tests, using, if appropriate, automated audit software.

Security audits should review technologies, procedures, documentation, training, and personnel. A very thorough audit will even simulate an attack or disaster to test the response of the technology, information systems staff, and business employees.

The audit lists and ranks all control weaknesses and estimates the probability of their occurrence. It then assesses the financial and organizational impact of each threat. Figure 10-6 is a sample auditor's listing of control weaknesses for a loan system. It includes a section for notifying management of such weaknesses and for management's response. Management is expected to devise a plan for countering significant weaknesses in controls.

10.4 TECHNOLOGIES AND TOOLS FOR SECURITY AND CONTROL

An array of tools and technologies can help firms protect against or monitor intrusion. They include tools for authentication, firewalls, intrusion detection systems, antivirus software, and encryption. Tools and methodologies are also available to help firms make their software more reliable.

WINDOW ON MANAGEMENT

DEUTSCHE BANK TIES BUSINESS CONTINUITY PLANNING TO THE BUSINESS

Deutsche Bank AG is one of the world's largest banks, with 65,700 employees serving 21 million customers in 74 different countries. It has investment banking and asset management businesses throughout Europe, the Pacific Rim, and the Americas. Management is dedicated to protecting the interests of customers, employees, partners, regulators, and shareholders against loss of revenue and reputation, and the company has always treated business continuity planning very seriously.

The bank has a global business continuity and disaster recovery program which addresses data backup and recovery and procedures for minimizing changes in operational, financial, and credit risk exposures. Operational risk focuses on the firm's ability to maintain communications with customers and keep mission-critical systems up and running. Financial risk deals with the firm's ability to continue generating revenue and obtaining adequate financing. Credit risk occurs when investments erode from lack of liquidity in the broader market.

Every six months Deutsche Bank New York offices test their disaster recovery plan, practicing what they would do if their computer centers in the World Trade Center and in neighboring New Jersey went down. The company's data are always backed up on tape. Tragically, Deutsche Bank lost two employees and its New York offices in the September 11 World Trade Center terrorist attacks, but the remaining employees were back working within a few days because the company is so well prepared.

Deutsche Bank has a permanent structure to manage and govern business continuity management. Deutsche Bank's Asia Pacific headquarters in Singapore and its bigger locations in Hong Kong, Japan, India, and Australia have full-time teams for this purpose. The bank's business continuity planning (BCP) function brings together various internal units and experts dealing with all aspects of risk—information risk, physical risk, or business risk—to coordinate plans addressing loss of facilities, personnel, or critical systems.

A team headed by Kenny Seow, head of Business Continuity Management for Deutsche Bank's Asia Pacific Region, maintains a 12,000-square-foot Disaster Recovery Center (DRC) outside the Singapore Central Business District. The DRC is a "lights-out facility," meaning that it contains no staff during normal business operations. It does contain, however, work space to support critical business functions for over 200 staff and all backup computer and network equipment for disaster recovery, including a generator with a 10-hour refillable fuel tank and smoke detection and sprinkler systems.

The computer center in the DRC also acts as a backup regional processing hub for Deutsche Bank Asia Pacific so that the Asia Pacific Region will not be affected if there is an outage at its production data center. Its systems are monitored and controlled remotely from Deutsche Bank's main production computer center or from bank offices where information systems staff work.

Seow's team organizes and conducts interviews with heads of Deutsche Bank businesses to identify what is most critical to

them—revenue loss, loss of reputation, loss of customer confidence, or violations of government regulations. Each business then identifies the processes required to minimize the identified risks.

Deutsche Bank has classified critical processes into two major categories: processes for business survival and processes critical to crisis support. Business survival processes are those required for Deutsche Bank to meet its business objectives. An example might be ensuring that traders in money markets and foreign exchange can work continuously because their business is a major revenue stream for the bank. (Deutsche Bank trading amounts to billions of dollars every day.) Deutsche Bank has a trading room in its disaster recovery site for this purpose, along with backup back office operations to support the trading activity.

An example of processes critical to crisis support is human resources because it looks after staff welfare and staff counseling. Corporate communications are also important in the event of a crisis, but marketing, for instance, would receive less priority at that time.

Seow's group is responsible for ensuring that appropriate processes and resources are in place so that the bank can respond effectively if a catastrophic event occurs. Deutsche Bank's business continuity planning revolves around planning for various scenarios that could affect its operations to make sure business can continue. Worst-case events could be a bomb, an earthquake, or an epidemic such as SARS.

Deutsche Bank communicates its business continuity plan, rehearses it, and keeps it updated to make sure the organization is always prepared. Staff are educated about safety measures, whom to contact in event of emergency, and who is responsible at different stages of an incident. The bank performs power tests on generators to make sure it can switch to backup power at any time. Finally, the bank tests the actual plan. It tests calling trees to make sure that contact numbers are working. It verbally walks employees through the plans so they understand exactly what they should do. Then it brings people to the disaster recovery site to use the systems at this facility to make sure they can work at that location. The bank conducts tests once a year, but some business units test more often if they feel their work is especially critical.

Sources: Ann Toh, "The Business of Security," *CIO Asia*, January 2004; Kate Pritchard, "Banking on Technology," *EMC Corporation*, 2004; George Hulme and Jennifer Zaino, "Spring Conference: Leave Complacency Out of Business Plans," *InformationWeek*, March 19, 2002; and Deutsche Bank, "Business Continuity Program," www.deutsche-bank.de, accessed November 24, 2004.

To Think About: Why is business continuity planning so important for a firm such as Deutsche Bank? What management, organization, and technology issues need to be addressed by a business continuity plan?

An auditor often traces the flow of sample transactions through an information system and may perform tests using automated audit software. MIS audits help management identify security vulnerabilities and determine whether information system controls are effective.

Access Control

Access control consists of all the policies and procedures a company uses to prevent improper access to systems by unauthorized insiders and outsiders. To gain access a user must be authorized and authenticated. **Authentication** refers to the ability to know that a person is who he or she claims to be. Access control software is designed to allow only authorized persons to use systems or to access data using some method for authentication.

Authentication is often established by using passwords known only to authorized users. An end user uses a password to log on to a computer system and may also use passwords for accessing specific systems and files. However, users often forget passwords, share them, or choose poor passwords that are easy to guess, which compromises security. Passwords can also be "sniffed" if transmitted over a network or stolen through social engineering.

FIGURE 10-6   *Sample auditor's list of control weaknesses.*

Function: Loans Location: Peoria, IL	Prepared by: J. Ericson Preparation date: June 16, 2005		Received by: T. Benson Review date: June 28, 2005	
Nature of Weakness and Impact	**Chance for Error/Abuse**		**Notification to Management**	
	Yes/ No	Justification	Report Date	Management Response
User accounts with missing passwords	Yes	Leaves system open to unauthorized outsiders or attackers	5/10/05	Eliminate accounts without passwords.
Network configured to allow some sharing of system files	Yes	Exposes critical system files to hostile parties connected to the network	5/10/05	Ensure only required directories are shared and that they are protected with strong passwords.
Programs can be put in production libraries to meet critical deadlines without final approval from the Standards and Controls group.	No	All production programs require management authorization. Standards and Controls group assigns such cases to a temporary production status.		

This chart is a sample page from a list of control weaknesses that an auditor might find in a loan system in a local commercial bank. This form helps auditors record and evaluate control weaknesses and shows the results of discussing those weaknesses with management, as well as any corrective actions taken by management.

Securing Wireless Networks

Despite its flaws, WEP provides some margin of security if Wi-Fi users remember to activate it. Corporations can further improve WEP security by using it in conjunction with virtual private network (VPN) technology when a wireless network has access to internal corporate data.

Vendors of Wi-Fi equipment have developed new and stronger security standards. The Wi-Fi Alliance industry trade group issued a Wi-Fi Protected Access (WPA) specification that will work with future wireless LAN products and that can update equipment that uses 802.11b. WPA improves data encryption by replacing the static encryption keys used in WEP with longer, 128-bit keys that continually change, making them harder to crack. To strengthen user authentication, WPA provides a mechanism based on the Extensible Authentication Protocol (EAP) that works with a central authentication server to authenticate each user on the network before the user can join it. It also employs mutual authentication so that a wireless user does not get pulled into a rogue network that might steal the user's network credentials. Data packets can be checked to make sure they are part of a current network session and not repeated by hackers to fool network users.

Encryption and Public Key Infrastructure

Many organizations rely on encryption to protect sensitive information transmitted over the Internet and other networks. **Encryption** is the coding and scrambling of messages to prevent unauthorized access to or understanding of the data being transmitted. A message can be encrypted by applying a secret numerical code, called an encryption key, so that the data are transmitted as a scrambled set of characters. (The key consists of a large group of letters, numbers, and symbols.) To be read, the message must be decrypted (unscrambled) with a matching key.

There are several alternative methods of encryption, but public key encryption is becoming popular. Public key encryption as shown in Figure 10-8 uses two different keys, one private and one public. The keys are mathematically related so that data encrypted with one key can be decrypted using only the other key. To send and receive messages, communicators first create separate pairs of private and public keys. The public key is kept in a directory and the private key must be kept secret. The sender encrypts a message with the recipient's public key. On receiving the message, the recipient uses his or her private key to decrypt it.

Encryption is especially useful to shield messages on the Internet and other public networks because they are less secure than private networks. Encryption helps protect transmission of payment data, such as credit card information, and addresses the problems of message integrity and authentication. **Message integrity** is the ability to be certain that the message being sent arrives at the proper destination without being copied or changed.

Digital signatures and digital certificates help with authentication. The Electronic Signatures in Global and National Commerce Act of 2000 has given digital signatures the same legal status as those written with ink on paper. A **digital signature** is a digital code attached to an electronically transmitted message that is used to verify the origin and contents of a message. It provides a way to associate a message with a sender, performing a function similar to a written signature. For an electronic signature to be legally binding in

A public key encryption system can be viewed as a series of public and private keys that lock data when they are transmitted and unlock the data when they are received. The sender locates the recipient's public key in a directory and uses it to encrypt a message. The message is sent in encrypted form over the Internet or a private network. When the encrypted message arrives, the recipient uses his or her private key to decrypt the data and read the message.

FIGURE 10-8   *Public key encryption.*

Sender → Encrypt with public key → Scrambled Message → Decrypt with private key → Recipient

court, someone must be able to verify that the signature actually belongs to whoever sent the data and that the data were not altered after being digitally signed.

Digital certificates are data files used to establish the identity of users and electronic assets for protection of online transactions (see Figure 10-9). A digital certificate system uses a trusted third party known as a certificate authority (CA) to validate a user's identity. The CA system can be run as a function inside an organization or by an outside company such as VeriSign. The CA verifies a digital certificate user's identity offline. This information is put into a CA server, which generates an encrypted digital certificate containing owner identification information and a copy of the owner's public key. The certificate authenticates that the public key belongs to the designated owner. The CA makes its own public key available publicly either in print or perhaps on the Internet. The recipient of an encrypted message uses the CA's public key to decode the digital certificate attached to the message, verifies it was issued by the CA, and then obtains the sender's public key and identification information contained in the certificate. Using this information, the recipient can send an encrypted reply. The digital certificate system would enable, for example, a credit card user and a merchant to validate that their digital certificates were issued by an authorized and trusted third party before they exchange data. **Public key infrastructure (PKI)**, the use of public key cryptography working with a certificate authority, is becoming the principal technology for providing secure authentication of identity online (Backhouse, Hsu, and McDonnell, 2003).

Two primary methods for encrypting network traffic on the Web are SSL and S-HTTP. **Secure Sockets Layer (SSL)** and its successor **Transport Layer Security (TLS)** are protocols used for secure information transfer over the Internet. They enable client and server computers to manage encryption and decryption activities as they communicate with each other during a secure Web session. **Secure Hypertext Transfer Protocol (S-HTTP)** is another protocol used for encrypting data flowing over the Internet, but it is limited to Web documents, whereas SSL and TLS encrypt all data being passed between client and server.

Internet Connection ———

The Internet Connection for this chapter will direct you to a series of Web sites where you can complete an exercise to evaluate various secure electronic payment systems for the Internet.

FIGURE 10-9   *Digital certificates.*

Digital certificates can be used to establish the identity of people or electronic assets.

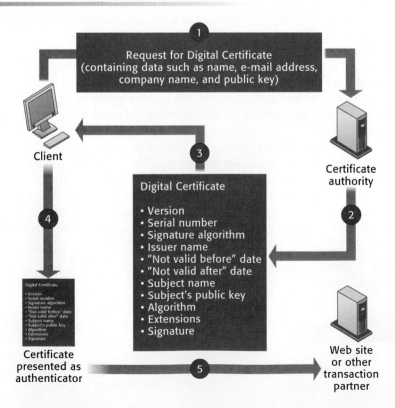

Ensuring Software Reliability

In addition to implementing effective security measures, firms can make systems more reliable by devoting more attention to software reliability and quality. Chapter 14 describes various tools and methodologies that can be used to enforce quality standards as software is being designed and programmed.

Software quality can be improved by expending more resources during the early stages of software design when it is possible to correct errors before the software is actually programmed. Thorough testing further reduces software errors, even though it may be impossible to eliminate them completely. Before software is written, the test normally used is a **walkthrough**—a review of a specification or design document by a small group of carefully selected people. Once programming begins, code must be tested by computer runs. When errors are discovered, the source is found and eliminated through a process called **debugging**.

Electronic commerce and electronic business applications introduce new levels of complexity for testing to ensure high-quality performance and functionality. Behind each large Web site, such as Amazon.com, eBay, or E*TRADE, are hundreds of servers and software programs, creating numerous points of vulnerability. These Web sites must be built and tested to make sure they are secure and that they can withstand unexpected spikes in traffic

Testing wireless applications poses additional challenges. Many wireless and conventional Web applications are linked to the same back-end systems so the total load on those systems increases dramatically as wireless users are added. Automated load-testing tools that simulate thousands of simultaneous wireless Web and conventional Web browser sessions can help companies measure the impact on system performance.

10.5 MANAGEMENT, OPPORTUNITIES, CHALLENGES, AND SOLUTIONS

Information systems security needs organizational and management resources as well as technologies. Establishing a good framework for security and control requires skillful balancing of risks, rewards, and the firm's operational capabilities.

Opportunities

Information system security and control are more crucial than ever. Firms today have opportunities to create marvellously secure, reliable Web sites and systems that can support their e-commerce and e-business strategies. On the downside, revenue, liability, reputation, brand image—and even a company's ability to survive—will suffer if a firm is found to be insecure or unreliable. The stakes have never been higher.

Management Challenges

There are many alternative technologies to help firms achieve security and control, but organizational discipline is required to use these technologies effectively.

DESIGNING SYSTEMS THAT ARE NEITHER OVERCONTROLLED NOR UNDERCONTROLLED

Although security breaches and damage to information systems still come from organizational insiders, security breaches from outside the organization are increasing because firms pursuing electronic commerce are open to outsiders through the Internet. It is difficult for organizations to determine how open or closed their networks should be to protect themselves. If a system requires too many passwords, authorizations, or levels of security to access information, the system will go unused and therefore is ineffective. Controls that are effective but that do not discourage authorized individuals from using a system are difficult to design.

IMPLEMENTING AN EFFECTIVE SECURITY POLICY

Despite increased awareness of worms, denial of service attacks, and computer crime, far too many firms do not pay sufficient attention to security. Controls and security programs are often treated as an afterthought rather than incorporated into the design of key business processes and systems. Research has shown that 75 percent of companies with information security policies do not keep them up-to-date and that only 9 percent of employees understand these security policies. Many firms lack disaster recovery and business continuity plans or fail to patch their software routinely against security vulnerabilities. Managers do not appreciate the value of a sound security strategy. Security threats abound, but they are neither predictable nor finite, making it more difficult to calculate returns on security investments. Unless managers change their thinking about security, security budgets will be inadequate.

Solution Guidelines

One thing is clear: Security and control must become a more visible and explicit priority and area of information systems investment, with greater emphasis on the overall organizational planning process. Coordinating the firm's security plan with its overall business plan shows that security is just as essential to the success of the business as any other business function. Larger firms may merit a formal security function with a chief security officer (CSO). To develop sound security and controls, users may need to change the way they work. Support and commitment from top management is required to show that security is indeed a corporate priority and vital to all aspects of the business.

Security and control will never be a high priority unless there is *security awareness* throughout the firm. Security and control should be the responsibility of everyone in the organization. Users may need special training on how to protect equipment and passwords and how to work with antivirus and other protective software. Key management decisions include determining an appropriate level of control for the organization and establishing standards for system accuracy and reliability. Managers should ask the following questions:

- What firm resources are the most critical to control and secure? How much would it cost to replace these critical assets if they were destroyed or compromised? What would be the legal and business impact if they were accessed by unauthorized parties?

- What level of system downtime is acceptable? How much disruption in business function or financial loss is the business willing to tolerate?

- What is the minimum acceptable level of performance for software and systems? If zero defects are impossible to achieve in large complex pieces of software, what constitutes acceptable, if not perfect, software performance?

- How much is the business willing to invest to protect its information assets?

MAKE IT YOUR BUSINESS

Finance and Accounting

Security and reliability are absolutely critical in systems for banking and financial services because errors, fraud, and disruption of service can lead to large monetary losses and the erosion of consumer confidence in these companies and even in the entire financial industry. Prevention of fraud, errors, and manipulation of assets in financial and accounting systems is a key objective of application and general controls. The accounting function is often involved in information systems audits and in the design of information systems controls. You can find examples of finance and accounting applications on pages 341, 361, and 373–374.

Human Resources

"People factors" are as important as technology in establishing the security and reliability of the firm's information systems. Many security breaches and system errors are caused by legitimate company insiders. Software quality depends on the commitment to quality of the people designing the software. Establishing quality and security consciousness among employees has become an important human resources function because human resources data include pieces of confidential information, such as salary figures and health records, which require tight data security safeguards. You can find examples of human resources applications on page 352.

Manufacturing and Production

Manufacturing systems today are more vulnerable than in the past to security breaches because they have become increasingly networked and integrated with each other as well as with the manufacturing systems of other firms. Supply chain management systems can be deeply affected by network outages or software quality problems because interrupted flows of information can adversely impact so many members of the supply chain. Security and reliability are thus very high priorities in the design of intranets and extranets for manufacturing and production.

Sales and Marketing

Electronic commerce requires secure payment systems for online purchases as well as fault-tolerant or high-availability systems that prevent interruptions of service. Encryption, digital signatures, digital certificates, and technologies for scalability and high-availability computing are important technologies for creating such systems. Data quality standards must be high so that the company can immediately process accurate customer data.

Summary

1. *Explain why information systems need special protection from destruction, error, and abuse.*

    With data concentrated into electronic form and many procedures invisible through automation, computerized information systems are vulnerable to destruction, misuse, error, fraud, and hardware or software failures. Corporate systems using the Internet are especially vulnerable because the Internet is designed to be an open system and makes internal corporate systems more vulnerable to actions from outsiders. Hackers can unleash denial of service (DoS) attacks or penetrate corporate networks to cause serious system disruptions. Wi-Fi networks can easily be penetrated by intruders using sniffer programs to obtain an address to access the resources of the network. Computer viruses and worms can spread rampantly from system to system, clogging computer memory or destroying programs and data. Software presents problems because software bugs may be impossible to eliminate and because software vulnerabilities can be exploited by hackers and malicious software. End users can introduce errors.

2. *Assess the business value of security and control.*

    Security and control are important but often neglected areas for information systems investment. Firms relying on computer systems for their core business functions can lose sales and productivity. Information assets such as confidential employee records, trade secrets, or business plans lose much of their value if they are revealed to outsiders or if they expose the firm to legal liability. New laws such as HIPAA, the Sarbanes-Oxley Act, and the Gramm-Leach-Bliley Act require companies to practice stringent electronic records management and adhere to strict standards for security, privacy, and control. Legal actions requiring electronic evidence and computer forensics also require firms to pay more attention to security and electronic records management.

3. *Evaluate elements of an organizational and managerial framework for security and control.*

    Firms need to establish an appropriate organizational and managerial framework for security and control to use technologies effectively to protect their information resources. They must establish a well-designed set of general and application controls. General controls handle the overall design, security, and use of computers, programs, and files for the organization's information technology infrastructure. Application controls are those unique to specific computerized applications. They focus on the completeness and accuracy of input, updating and maintenance, and the validity of the information in the system. Application controls consist of (1) input controls, (2) processing controls, and (3) output controls.

    To determine which controls are required, designers and users of systems must identify the most important assets requiring protection and the extent to which these assets are vulnerable. A risk assessment evaluates information assets, identifies control points and control weaknesses, and determines the most cost-effective set of controls.

    Firms must also develop a coherent corporate security policy and plans for continuing business operations in the event of disaster or disruption. The security policy includes policies for acceptable use and authorization. A disaster recovery plan provides procedures and facilities for restoring computing and communication services after they have been disrupted, whereas a business continuity plan focuses on how the company can restore business operations.

    Comprehensive and systematic MIS auditing can help organizations determine the effectiveness of security and controls for their information systems.

4. *Evaluate the most important tools and technologies for safeguarding information resources.*

    Companies require special measures to support electronic commerce and digital business processes. They can use fault-tolerant computer systems or create high-availability computing environments to make sure that their information systems are always available and performing without interruptions. Firewalls are placed between an organization's private network and external networks such as the Internet to prevent unauthorized users from accessing the private network. Intrusion detection systems monitor private networks for suspicious network traffic and attempts to access corporate systems. Passwords, tokens, and biometric authentication can be used for authenticating system users. Antivirus software can check computer systems for infection by viruses and worms and often eliminate the malicious software. Encryption, the coding and scrambling of messages, is a widely used technology for securing electronic transmissions over the Internet and over Wi-Fi networks. Digital certificates combined with public key encryption provide further protection of electronic transactions by authenticating a user's identity.

The quality and reliability of software can be improved by thorough testing procedures and by allocating resources to put more emphasis on secure software design.

5. *Identify the challenges posed by information systems security and control and management solutions.*

Establishing a good framework for security and control requires skillful balancing of risks, rewards, and the firm's operational capabilities. Designing systems that are neither overcontrolled nor undercontrolled and implementing an effective security policy are major management challenges. Solutions include making security and control a higher management priority and instilling security awareness throughout the firm. Key management decisions include determining an appropriate level of control for the organization and establishing standards for system accuracy and reliability.

Key Terms

Acceptable use policy (AUP), 358
Access control, 362
Administrative controls, 355
Antivirus software, 364
Application controls, 355
Application proxy filtering, 364
Authentication, 362
Authorization policies, 358
Authorization management systems, 358
Biometric authentication, 363
Bugs, 350
Business continuity planning, 360
Chief security officer (CSO), 357
Clustering, 359
Computer forensics, 354
Computer virus, 344
Controls, 342
Cracker, 346
Cybervandalism, 346
Debugging, 367
Digital certificates, 366
Digital signature, 365

Disaster recovery planning, 359
Distributed denial of service (DDoS) attack, 347
Downtime, 359
Electronic records management (ERM), 353
Encryption, 365
Fault-tolerant computer systems, 359
General controls, 355
Gramm-Leach-Bliley Act, 353
Hacker, 346
High-availability computing, 359
HIPAA, 353
Identity theft, 348
Input controls, 355
Intrusion detection systems, 364
ISO 17799, 355
Load balancing, 359
Malware, 344
Managed security service providers (MSSPs), 360
Message integrity, 365
Mirroring, 359
MIS audit, 360
Network Address Translation (NAT), 364
Online transaction processing, 359

Output controls, 355
Packet filtering, 364
Phishing, 349
Processing controls, 355
Public key infrastructure (PKI), 366
Recovery-oriented computing, 359
Risk assessment, 355
Sarbanes-Oxley Act of 2002, 353
Secure Hypertext Transfer Protocol (S-HTTP), 366
Secure Sockets Layer (SSL), 366
Security, 342
Security policy, 357
Sniffer, 347
Social engineering, 350
Spoofing, 347
Stateful inspection, 364
Token, 363
Transport Layer Security (TLS), 366
Trojan horse, 345
Walkthrough, 367
War driving, 343
Worms, 345

Review Questions

1. *Why are computer systems so vulnerable? Describe the most common threats against contemporary information systems.*

2. *Why are the Internet and Wi-Fi networks so difficult to secure?*

3. *What is malware? Distinguish between a virus, a worm, and a Trojan horse.*

4. *What is a hacker? How do hackers create security problems and damage systems?*

5. *How can software affect system performance and security?*

6. *What is computer crime? Provide two examples of crime in which computers are a target and two examples in which computers are used as instruments of crime.*

7. *What is identity theft? Why is it such a big problem today? How does phishing promote identity theft?*

8. *How can computer systems and networks be used for cyberterrorism and cyberwarfare?*

9. *What security problems are created by employees?*

10. *Define security and control. How do they provide business value? How are security and control related to*

recent U.S. government regulatory requirements and to computer forensics?

11. *Distinguish between general controls and application controls.*

12. *What is the function of risk assessment? How is it conducted for information systems?*

13. *Define and describe the following: security policy, acceptable use policy, authorization policy.*

14. *Distinguish between fault-tolerant and high-availability computing and between disaster recovery planning and business continuity planning.*

15. *How does MIS auditing enhance the control process?*

16. *Name and describe three authentication methods.*

17. *Describe the roles of firewalls, intrusion detection systems, and antivirus software in promoting security.*

18. *How can encryption be used to protect information? Describe the role of encryption and digital certificates in a public key infrastructure.*

19. *What management challenges are raised by information systems security and control? How can these challenges be addressed?*

Discussion Questions

1. *Security isn't just a technology issue, it's business issue. Discuss.*

2. *If you were developing a business continuity plan for your company, where would you start? What aspects of the business would the plan address?*

Application Software Exercise:
Spreadsheet Exercise: Performing a Security Risk Assessment

Mercer Paints is a small but highly regarded paint manufacturing company located in Alabama. The company has a network in place linking many of its business operations. Although the firm believes that its security is adequate, the recent addition of a Web site has become an open invitation to hackers. Management requested a risk assessment. The risk assessment identified a number of potential exposures. These exposures, their associated probabilities, and average losses are summarized in the following table.

Mercer Paints Risk Assessment

EXPOSURE	PROBABILITY OF OCCURRENCE (%)	AVERAGE LOSS ($)
Virus attack	60	75,000
Data loss	12	70,000
Embezzlement	3	30,000
User errors	95	25,000
Threats from hackers	95	90,000
Improper use by employees	5	5,000
Power failure	15	300,000

In addition to the potential exposures listed, you should identify at least three other potential threats to Mercer Paints, assign probabilities, and estimate a loss range. Using spreadsheet software and the risk assessment data, calculate the expected annual loss for each exposure. Which control points have the greatest vulnerability? What recommendations would you make to Mercer Paints? Prepare a written report that summarizes your findings and recommendations.

Developing a Disaster Recovery Plan

Required software: Web browser software

Electronic presentation software (optional)

Management is concerned that Dirt Bikes's computer systems could be vulnerable to power outages, vandalism, computer viruses, natural disasters, or telecommunications disruptions. You have been asked to perform an analysis of system vulnerabilities and disaster recovery planning for the company. Your report should answer the following questions:

1. What are the most likely threats to the continued operation of Dirt Bikes's systems?

2. What would you identify as Dirt Bikes's most critical systems? What is the impact on the company if these systems cannot operate? How long could the company survive if these systems were down? Which systems are the most important to back up and restore in the event of a disaster?

3. Use the Web to locate two disaster recovery services that could be used by a small business such as Dirt Bikes. Compare them in terms of the services they offer. Which should Dirt Bikes use? Exactly how could these services help Dirt Bikes recover from a disaster?

4. (Optional) If possible use electronic presentation software to summarize your findings for management.

Electronic Business Project: Evaluating Security Outsourcing Services

Data and network security are major challenges, and many companies have taken some action to protect their equipment and access to their data. Some of those companies have chosen to outsource the security function rather than train their own staff or hire specialists from outside the company. Finding security outsourcing services can be difficult, although finding sources that help you decide whether to outsource is much easier. In both cases, use several search engines to find sources that can help you decide whether to outsource and to locate companies that offer outsourcing of computer security.

As an information systems expert in your firm, you have been assigned the following tasks. First, present a brief summary of the arguments for and against outsourcing computer security. Second, select two firms that offer computer security outsourcing services, and compare them and their services. Third, prepare a written recommendation to management on whether you believe they should opt for outsourcing computer security and on which of the two firms you believe they should select if they do decide to outsource.

Group Project: Analyzing Security Vulnerabilities

A survey of your firm's information technology infrastructure has produced the following security analysis statistics:

Security Vulnerabilities by Type of Computing Platform

PLATFORM	NUMBER OF COMPUTERS	HIGH RISK	MEDIUM RISK	LOW RISK	TOTAL VULNERABILITIES
Windows Server 2003 (corporate applications)	1	11	37	19	
Linux (e-mail and printing services)	1	3	154	98	
Sun Solaris (UNIX) (e-commerce and Web servers)	2	12	299	78	
Windows XP Professional Edition (desktops and laptops with office productivity tools that can also be linked to the corporate network running corporate applications and the intranet)	195	14	16	1237	

High-risk vulnerabilities include nonauthorized users accessing applications, guessable passwords, matching of user names and passwords, active user accounts with missing passwords, and unauthorized programs in application systems.

Medium-risk vulnerabilities include users' ability to shut down the system without being logged on, passwords and screen saver settings that were not established for PCs, and outdated versions of software stored on hard drives.

Low-risk vulnerabilities include the inability of users to change their passwords, user passwords not being changed periodically, and passwords smaller than the minimum size specified by the company.

With a group of your classmates, use this information to perform an analysis of this firm's security vulnerabilities that answers the following questions:

1. What is the total number of vulnerabilities for each platform? What is the potential impact of the security problems for each computing platform in the organization?

2. If you have only one information systems specialist in charge of security, which platforms should you address first in trying to eliminate these vulnerabilities? Second? Third? Last? Why?

3. Identify the types of control problems illustrated by these vulnerabilities and explain the measures that should be taken to solve them.

4. What does your firm risk by ignoring the security vulnerabilities identified?

If possible, use electronic presentation software to present your findings to the class.

CASE STUDY
Royal Bank of Canada's Software Woes

Founded in 1864 and chartered in 1869 as the Merchants' Bank of Halifax, Royal Bank of Canada (RBC) took its current name in 1901. In 1941, based on its total assets of $1 billion, RBC became Canada's largest bank. Twenty years later, RBC installed its first computer, making it the first bank in Canada to employ such technology. In October 2003, the organization had 60,000 employees, totaled $413 billion in assets, and served 12 million customers. Including worldwide operations, RBC has spent $1.6 billion on technology.

On Monday, May 31, 2004, the RBC information technology staff made a programming upgrade to what has been described as "key banking software." According to Martin Lippert, RBC's vice chairman and CIO, a glitch in the bank's computer systems "was most likely caused by a single worker entering 'a relatively small number' of incorrect pieces of code during the update." The glitch resulted in a massive computer failure that affected millions of banking customers around the country. Lippert specified that the incorrect code was related to "transit numbers or field identifiers in a table." The mistakes worked their way through the bank's systems quickly, but conspicuously. RBC had already discovered the problem by six o'clock the next morning. Unfortunately, recognition of the error wasn't even half the battle.

In fact, RBC fixed the programming error that had been made on May 31 early on Tuesday, June 1. Still, several days later, millions of RBC customers were still unable to check their account balances, had not received their paychecks, or had automatic payments or transfers delayed. The reactions of customers, as could be expected, were tinged with displeasure. Some customers merely suffered the inconvenience of not having access to information that they were accustomed to having at their fingertips all of the time. Other customers, those who count on their paychecks

to get by, had their lives affected more seriously. One such person, a law firm executive assistant named Andrea Mitchell, was forced to ask her employer for a cash advance to make up for her temporarily lost paycheck and to meet her personal expenses.

So, if the human programming error was corrected so swiftly, why did RBC continue to experience problems related to the glitch over the course of a work week? The glitch put into motion a chain of management and control procedures that exacerbated the problem. Procedures that were intended to fix the problem instead caused a logjam of activity from which the bank could not recover immediately.

The first question that most people asked was, Why weren't backup systems used to keep business flowing while the main systems were being fixed? As stated on the bank's Web site, "Back up facilities exist in case our primary facility is disabled. As a matter of policy, therefore, all program changes are implemented simultaneously to both the primary and backup facilities." Therefore, the same error that compromised the main system also affected the backup system.

According to Lippert, in addition to the programming code update being entered incorrectly, the new code was not tested properly before it was deployed. RBC policy calls for all new pieces of software to be tested thoroughly before they are used in production systems.

On Tuesday, June 1, with the knowledge that random duplications of transactions were occurring in its systems, RBC decided to suspend its end-of-day processing rather than let it run with incomplete or inaccurate data. When verifying the health of its systems took longer than expected, RBC was left with a backlog of transactions to process. All the while, new transactions were pouring in, as they would on a normal business day, and these added to the logjam. On

Wednesday, June 2, the IT department was confident that it could make up the ground lost on Tuesday and remain current with Wednesday's transactions. The newer transactions were placed at the end of queue because of a sequential numbering system, so the backlog had to be cleared before RBC could process any new transactions. Also slowing down the effort was the bank's decision to monitor data processing manually following the glitch to make sure that no coding errors persisted. Trying to process two days of transactions at once proved to be more difficult than the bank imagined it would be.

As if the event itself were not bad enough for business, RBC came under criticism for the way in which it handled the public relations end of the problem. First, RBC made assurance that all systems and accounts would be normalized by Thursday, June 3. Confident in this assessment, the bank's CEO, Gordon Nixon, left for Europe on Wednesday, June 2. When customers were still experiencing difficulties with their accounts later in the week, the bank appeared weak by not having its leader available to address customers' concerns. As a possible reason for Nixon's untimely exit from the scene, John Layne, of the crisis management company Contingency Management Consultants, surmises the common organizational flaw in which lower-level employees are loathe to pass bad news up the corporate ladder. In Nixon's absence, other RBC executives took turns addressing the media and the public, though the first public comments on the glitch did not come forth until late Wednesday afternoon. Having a single representative of the bank to interface with the public would have inspired more confidence in customers.

Unfortunately for RBC, the cumulative effect of its errors was widespread. About 62,000 government workers in Ontario and 10,000 in New Brunswick didn't receive their automatic deposits even if they didn't do their personal banking at RBC. Their provincial governments did use RBC to route the payroll, so the deposits didn't reach the workers' own banks. Hundreds of thousands of other workers around Canada ran into similar delays or difficulties accessing their deposits. The government of Ontario indicated that it would issue physical checks to employees who still had not received their deposits by the Monday following the initial computer glitch.

RBC's service disruption had one particularly dangerous side effect, over which the bank had little control. Opportunistic scam artists seized on the glitch to unleash a phishing scam that targeted RBC customers, taking advantage of the customers' frustrations, security fears, or simply their naïveté. An e-mail message with the subject line "Official information from RBC Royal Bank" stated that "due to the increased fraudulent activity within our site we are undertaking a review of member accounts." The e-mail linked to a page that looked like RBC's official Web site that instructed customers "be sure to enter both client card number or business card number & password otherwise your account will not be verified and your access to the account will be blocked." Once RBC customers entered the requested information at that bogus site, hackers could access their accounts.

RBC announced that it had resumed normal business practices during the week beginning June 8, 2004. The bank continued to resolve discrepancies from service charges and overdraft interest that resulted

from the disruption and indicated that all accounts should be reflected accurately in customers' next statements, by June 30. On June 18, RBC announced that it had hired Crawford Adjusters Canada as its "administrator for non-banking-related costs and losses in the bank's processing disruption." The bank made claim forms available, by phone and on the Internet and set a deadline of September 30, 2004 for customers to file claims. RBC was to handle all claims under $100 itself, leaving larger claims to Crawford. The total loss to RBC was contingent on the number of claims filed. However, that cost could rise significantly based on a class-action suit filed in Quebec that requested damages of $500 for each customer that was affected.

In hindsight, analysts agree that RBC handled the technology portion of its problem effectively. The bank erred mostly in its estimates of how long the recovery period would be. In addition to issuing a formal apology, RBC created an area of its Web site that was devoted to detailed explanations of the problem and updates on the progress of restoring its records. The bank also enlisted IBM Corporation as a consultant to investigate the causes of the problem and provide guidance on how to avoid such problems going forward. RBC offered refunds to its customers for any banking fees that they incurred as a result of the computer problems and agreed to reimburse other financial institutions and their customers for certain expenses that may have resulted from RBC's errors. These moves could go a long way toward restoring faith in customers of the

bank, who, in the immediate aftermath, were understandably concerned about the security of their finances. One client said that she didn't intend to leave RBC just then, but, "If it happened again, I may not be so loyal."

Sources: Ian Austen, "Bank Software Woes Leave Many Canadians Without Money," *New York Times*, June 7, 2004; "RBC Admits Human Error, Scam Artists Act," *Ottawa Business Journal*, June 10, 2004; Lindsay Bruce, "RBC Glitch Still Not Ironed Out," ITWorldCanada.com, June 7, 2004; Chris Conrath, "Anatomy of a Snafu," ITWorldCanada.com, June 11, 2004; Paul Waldie, "RBC Calls in Help," *Globe and Mail*, www.theglobeandmail.com, accessed June 19, 2004; Mel Duvall, "RBC's Account Imbalance," *Baseline Magazine*, July 1, 2004; and CP, "RBC Still Making Up for Glitch," *London Free Press*, www.canoe.ca, accessed June 19, 2004.

CASE STUDY QUESTIONS

1. Provide a summary of the security and control problems experienced by the Royal Bank of Canada. How did this problem impact the organization and its clients?

2. What management, organization, and technology factors contributed to the control problems at RBC?

3. What was the most critical flaw in the security and control systems in place at RBC? Explain your answer.

4. How well did RBC respond to its computer problem? What do you think the bank might have done differently to prevent the problem and to handle it once it did occur?

5. If you were a manager at RBC, how would you prevent a problem like this from happening?

PART TWO PROJECT
Creating a New Internet Business

We have prepared a list of new businesses that could benefit from going on the Web. Select one of the businesses from the list and develop an Internet strategy for that business. You will need to identify the Internet business model to be pursued, use the Internet to research and analyze markets and competitors, and design part of the Web site for that business.

Virtual Tour of Electronic Commerce Sites

To prepare for this project, review Internet business models by taking the virtual tour of the electronic commerce sites described in the following table. To take the tour, visit the Web site representing each business model. Explore the Web site so that you have a clear idea of how that business uses the Web for electronic commerce.

Selecting an Internet Business Model and Designing a Web Strategy

The five businesses we describe are fictitious but are based on real-world scenarios. Review each of them. Then select one business and answer the following questions:

1. What Internet business model would be appropriate for the company to follow in creating a Web site?

2. In what ways can the company benefit from a Web site? How would it provide value to the firm? What functions should it perform for the company (marketing, sales, customer support, internal communications, etc.)?

3. In what other ways might the company use the Internet for its own benefit?

4. Prepare functional specifications for the company's use of the Web and the Internet. Include links to and from other sites in your design.

5. Prepare a cost-benefit analysis of a proposal to implement the company's use of the Internet.

For each of the five businesses, we list a Web site of a real-world company in the same or a related business to help you understand that type of business. Visit the Web site related to the business you have selected and review it carefully.

Business 1: InfoInc

InfoInc is a start-up company that would like to provide a service by offering easy access to needed information in specialized fields such as accounting, finance, or medicine. Although its business plan calls for moving into a number of fields, InfoInc would like to begin by addressing the

Virtual Tour of Electronic Commerce Sites

Business Model	Description	Organization	URL
Virtual Storefront	Sells physical goods online instead of through a physical storefront or retail outlet. The goods are then shipped to the customer.	Amazon.com	www.amazon.com
Information Broker	Provides primarily product, pricing, and availability information. The final purchase transaction is usually conducted elsewhere.	Edmunds.com	www.edmunds.com
Transaction Broker	Provides services that allow people to complete transactions, such as buying and selling securities.	E*TRADE	www.etrade.com
Online Marketplace	Provides digital environment where buyers and sellers can meet, search for products, display products, and establish prices for those products. Can provide online auctions or reverse auctions as well as negotiated or fixed pricing.	eBay	www.ebay.com
Content Provider	Creates revenue by providing digital content, such as digital news, music, photos, or video, over the Web.	Wall Street Journal Interactive	www.wsj.com
Online Service Provider	Provides online hardware and software services for individuals and businesses.	Xdrive	www.xdrive.com
Portal	Provides an initial point of entry to the Web along with specialized content and other services.	Yahoo!	www.yahoo.com
Virtual Community	Provides an online meeting place where people with similar interests can communicate and find useful information.	iVillage	www.ivillage.com

needs of people in the accounting and tax fields. Its first two target groups are accounting professionals and the general public. For the general public, the plan is to provide a Web site with advice on various issues such as tax laws and IRA savings rules. The site would also contain links to other sites where visitors will be able to obtain advice on such issues as how to establish a new business. For accounting professionals, such as certified public accountants (CPAs) and corporate financial officers, InfoInc would like to offer more detailed information services. In addition, the company wants to provide capabilities that might help the CPAs and financial officers manage their e-mail, voice mail, and fax.

Web reference: WebMD Inc. <http://webmd.com/>

Business 2: Aerospace Metal Alloys

Aerospace Metal is a distributor of exotic steel, aluminum, and titanium alloys to the aerospace industry and to other specialty industries. These metals, such as kovar and inconel, must meet exceptionally exacting standards because they become parts in airplanes, rockets, industrial furnaces, and other high-performance products. Aerospace sells raw materials produced in the form of bars, sheets, rings, and forgings. In turn, Aerospace customers use these materials to fabricate their final products. Many Aerospace customers are actually parts suppliers to end-product assemblers such as Boeing Aircraft. Aerospace Metal maintains a sales staff to sell these metals, and the company stores its products in seven warehouses throughout the country. They obtain their products from steel and metal manufacturers throughout North America. If a customer requests a product not carried by Aerospace, the company will special-order it from an appropriate supplier.

Web reference: Specialty Steel and Storage <www.steelforge.com>

Business 3: Columbiana

Columbiana is a small, independent island in the Caribbean. It is underdeveloped and is also off the tourist path for most visitors to that area despite its many attractions. The island has a unique history, with Indian ruins dating back 800 years and with many historical buildings, forts, and other sites built during its centuries as a British colony. A few first-class hotels have been built along some of its beautiful white beaches, and less expensive accommodations are also available along beaches, in several towns, and near several fishing villages. Its rain forests, rivers, striking mountains, and volcano cone all could be of interest to tourists. In addition, it has many restaurants that specialize in native dishes and fresh fish. The government not only wants to increase

tourism but it also wants to increase trade by developing new markets for its tropical agricultural products. In addition, leaders hope to attract investment capital so that many of the unemployed residents can find jobs. Two major airlines have regular flights to Columbiana, as do several small Caribbean airlines. The island is on the tourist itinerary of only one cruise ship company. The Web site will not transact any business, but it will offer information and links to other appropriate sites.

Web reference: Dominica <www.dominica.dm>

Business 4: Home Do-It-Yourself Tools Inc.

As more and more people are turning to do-it-yourself home repairs, the market for tools of all kinds for home use has grown rapidly. The buyer has thousands of tools to choose from, and so the search can be time consuming and the prices paid can be very high. Home Do-It-Yourself Tools Inc. (Home Tools) was founded to capitalize on this trend. The founder initially opened a small store in Atlanta, Georgia, and soon thereafter established a catalog to try to expand the business. Home Tools uses a toll-free 800 telephone number to take orders and to answer potential customers' technical and product questions. It solicits new customers through advertisements in magazines read by home repair enthusiasts. The owners now wants to make better use of the Internet to reach out to new customers, reduce Home Tools' cost per sale, and improve service quality. The heart of the business is a database listing several thousand tools and the tasks for which they are commonly used.

Web reference: iGo.com <www.igo.com>

Business 5: Low Cost Tires Inc.

Low Cost Tires Inc. (Tires Inc.) began as a small auto repair and tire shop in a small city outside of Chicago. While the original goal of the shop was to gain a reputation for quality repair, the owner also stressed meeting customer needs on the sale of tires. Tires Inc. carries a very wide selection of tires so that customers can always be served on the spot. Its staff is highly trained and very knowledgeable about tires. Selling tires has turned out to be more profitable than auto repairs. Although the owner plans to maintain the auto repair business, he wants to use the Internet to expand tire sales and to capitalize on his staff's understanding of customer needs. Management believes the correct Web strategy could help Tires Inc. improve customer service locally, increase its customer base, and help it create retail outlets in new locations.

Web reference: The Luggage Factory <www.luggagefactoryoutlet.com>

Organizational and Management Support Systems for the Digital Firm

Part Three Project: Designing
an Enterprise Information Portal

Part Three describes the role of information systems in enhancing business processes and decision making across the enterprise. Chapters 11 and 12 are devoted to the major enterprise applications for digital integration: enterprise systems and systems for supply chain management, customer relationship management, and knowledge management. This part also describes business intelligence, decision-support and executive support systems that improve firm performance and business value by helping managers and employees make better decisions.

Chapter 11

Enterprise Applications and Business Process Integration

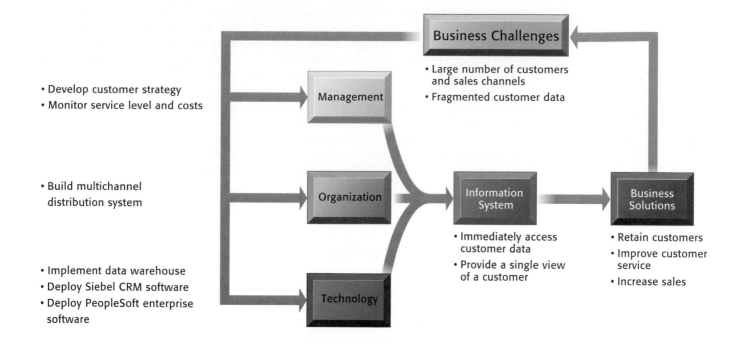

- Develop customer strategy
- Monitor service level and costs

- Build multichannel distribution system

- Implement data warehouse
- Deploy Siebel CRM software
- Deploy PeopleSoft enterprise software

Management

Organization

Technology

Business Challenges

- Large number of customers and sales channels
- Fragmented customer data

Information System

- Immediately access customer data
- Provide a single view of a customer

Business Solutions

- Retain customers
- Improve customer service
- Increase sales

Opening Case: PNC Banks on Enterprise Applications

PNC Bank is the largest business unit of Pittsburgh-based PNC Financial Services Group, a diversified financial services company with more than $60 billion in assets. It operates bank branches in Pennsylvania, New Jersey, Ohio, and Delaware as well as maintains a Web site for online banking. In addition to consumer banking services, PNC provides corporate banking, real estate finance, asset management, wealth management, and global fund services. PNC manages a broad array of customers and channels, and the bank wants to improve the service and value it provides to all of them.

The bank instituted a "Segment of 1" concept to guarantee its customers maximum personalization and information access, regardless of how they conducted business with the bank. It built a multichannel distribution system for its retail banking sector based on Siebel Systems customer relationship management (CRM) software and a data warehouse. To make sure the system worked properly, PNC carefully cleansed its customer data to eliminate incorrect addresses and multiple accounts opened by the same individual under slightly different names.

The system makes it possible to access and update customer information from any customer touch point, whether it is a bank branch, automated teller machine (ATM), telephone, or the Web. A customer transaction from any of these channels immediately enters the system and updates the customer's account data, which are maintained in a legacy mainframe hierarchical database and in Siebel's relational database. If a customer needs help, PNC service representatives can access up-to-the-minute information on that person's account, making it easier for customers to deal with the bank.

Extending the customer relationship management system to PNC's corporate customers proved more challenging. Each client company might appear as multiple clients because different groups within the same company use different financial products and services, such as cash management and corporate finance. Each product and service has its own information system and set of sales and service specialists. This situation made it even more difficult to obtain a single view of the customer for optimal customer service. The Siebel CRM system nevertheless is able to integrate multiple account information to produce this holistic view of the customer.

Since making these changes, PNC has improved its retail customer retention rate from 91 to 94 percent, which is well above the banking industry's average retention rate of 85 percent for checking account customers.

Sources: Timothy Shack, "Banking on Customer Care," *Optimize Magazine* 22 (March 2004) and David F. Carr, "Bank Rolls," *Baseline Magazine*, March 1, 2004).

PNC Bank found it could improve customer service and expand its product offerings by implementing a customer relationship management system. It had been storing customer data in multiple systems based on the financial product or service the customer was using, which made it difficult to know all the customer's interactions with the company. The system enabled the bank to integrate customer data from multiple accounts and analyze that data to provide customers with additional service and financial products.

As a manager, you will need to know how customer relationship management and the other major enterprise applications can provide value for your organization. You will also want to know how these systems can create enterprise-wide platforms for the delivery of new services. This chapter helps you learn about customer relationship management, supply chain management, and enterprise systems, identifying the key decisions and challenges you will face in implementing and using them. We discuss knowledge management systems in the following chapter.

11.1 ENTERPRISE SYSTEMS

Around the globe, companies are increasingly becoming more connected, both internally and with other companies. They want to be able to react instantaneously when a customer places a large order or when a shipment from a supplier is delayed. Managers want to know the impact of these events on every part of the business and how the business is performing at any point in time. Enterprise systems provide the integration to make this possible. Let's look at how they work and what they can do for the firm.

What Are Enterprise Systems?

Chapter 2 introduced enterprise systems, which focus on integrating the key internal business processes of the firm. These systems, which are known as *enterprise resource planning (ERP)* systems, are based on a suite of integrated software modules and a common central database. The database collects data from and feeds the data into numerous applications that can support nearly all of an organization's internal business activities. When new information is entered by one process, the information is made immediately available to other business processes (see Figure 11-1).

If a sales representative places an order for tire rims, for example, the system would verify the customer's credit limit, schedule the shipment, identify the best route, and reserve the necessary items from inventory. If inventory stock was insufficient to fill the order, the system would schedule the manufacture of more rims, ordering the needed materials and components from suppliers. Sales and production forecasts would be immediately updated. General ledger and corporate cash levels would be automatically updated with the revenue and cost information from the order. Users could tap into the system and find out where that particular order was at any minute. Management could obtain information at any point in time about how the business was operating. The system could also generate enterprise-wide data for management analyses of product cost and profitability.

How Enterprise Systems Work

Both the value—and the challenge—of enterprise systems can be found in the integration they force on firms' information and business processes. **Enterprise software** consists of a set of interdependent software modules that support basic internal business processes for finance and accounting, human resources, manufacturing and production (including logistics and distribution), and sales and marketing. The software enables data to be used by multiple functions and business processes for precise organizational coordination and control. Table 11-1 describes some of the business processes supported by enterprise software.

tied to such strategic issues as the ability to create and deliver new products or to create and implement new business models (Kopczak and Johnson, 2003).

The Supply Chain

Supply chain management refers to the close linkage and coordination of activities involved in buying, making, and moving a product. It integrates business processes to speed information, product, and fund flows up and down a supply chain to reduce time, redundant effort, and inventory costs.

The **supply chain** is a network of organizations and business processes for procuring raw materials, transforming these materials into intermediate and finished products, and distributing the finished products to customers. It links suppliers, manufacturing plants, distribution centers, retail outlets, and customers to supply goods and services from source through consumption. Materials, information, and payments flow through the supply chain in both directions. Goods start out as raw materials and move through logistics and production systems until they reach customers. Returned items flow in the reverse direction from the buyer back to the seller.

Figure 11-3 provides a simplified illustration of a supply chain, showing the flow of information and material among suppliers, manufacturers, distributors, retailers, and

FIGURE 11-3   *A supply chain.*

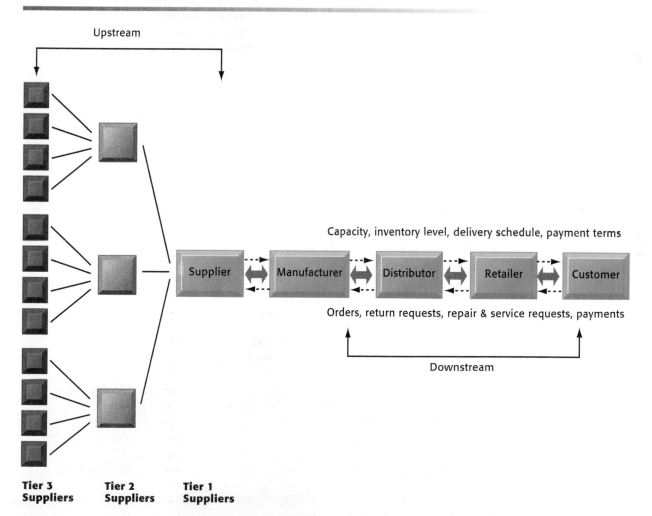

This figure illustrates the major entities in the supply chain and the flow of information upstream and downstream to coordinate the activities involved in buying, making, and moving a product. The wide arrows show the flow of materials between supply chain members, and the dotted line and arrows show the flow of information. Suppliers transform raw materials into intermediate products or components, and then manufacturers turn them into finished products. The products are shipped to distribution centers and from there to retailers and customers.

customers. The *upstream* portion of the supply chain includes the organization's suppliers and their suppliers and the processes for managing relationships with them. The *downstream* portion consists of the organizations and processes for distributing and delivering products to the final customers. The manufacturer also manages *internal supply chain* processes for transforming the materials, components, and services furnished by suppliers into finished goods and for managing materials and inventory.

Materials flow downstream from raw material sources through manufacturing facilities that transform the raw materials into intermediate products (also referred to as components or parts). These are assembled on the next level to form finished products. The products are shipped to distribution centers and from there to retailers and customers.

The supply chain illustrated in Figure 11-3 has been simplified. Most supply chains, especially those for large manufacturers such as automakers, are multitiered, with many thousands of primary (Tier 1), secondary (Tier 2), and tertiary (Tier 3) suppliers. DaimlerChrysler, for instance, has more than 20,000 suppliers of parts, packaging, and technology. Its primary suppliers are its principal suppliers, which furnish chassis, engines, and other major automotive components. These suppliers have their own suppliers (secondary suppliers), who in turn may have their own set of suppliers (tertiary suppliers.)

SUPPLY CHAIN PROCESSES

Many processes and subprocesses are involved in managing the supply chain to expedite this flow of information and materials. The Supply Chain Council (SCC) developed a Supply Chain Operations Reference Model (SCOR) as a cross-industry process reference model for supply chain management. (SCC members are organizations interested in applying and advancing state-of-the-art supply chain management systems and practices.) SCOR defines a common set of supply chain processes to help companies better understand supply chain management issues and set goals for supply chain improvement. SCOR identifies five major supply chain processes: plan, source, make, deliver, and return (see Figure 11-4).

Plan: Consists of processes that balance aggregate demand and supply to develop a course of action to meet sourcing, production, and delivery requirements

Source: Consists of processes that procure goods and services needed to create a specific product or service

Make: Consists of processes that transform a product into a finished state to meet planned or actual demand

FIGURE 11-4   *Key supply chain management processes.*

The five supply chain management processes consist of many subprocesses performed by members of the supply chain.

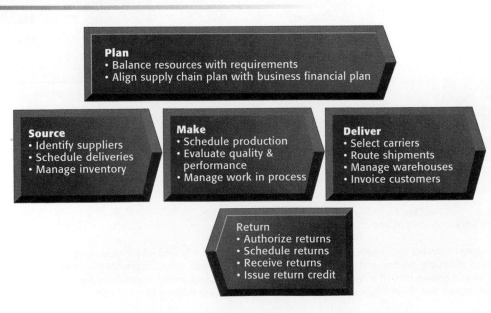

Deliver: Consists of processes that provide finished goods and services to meet actual or planned demand, including order management, transportation management, and distribution management

Return: Consists of processes associated with returning products or receiving returned products, including postdelivery customer support

Logistics plays an important role in these processes, dealing with the planning and control of all factors that will have an impact on transporting the correct product or service to where it is needed on time and at the least cost. (Logistics accounts for 12 to 14 percent of a typical manufacturer's cost of goods sold.) Supply chain management provides an opportunity to optimize the movement of materials and goods among different members of the supply chain.

To manage the supply chain, a company tries to eliminate redundant steps, delays, and the amount of resources tied up along the way as it manages relationships with other supply chain members. Information systems make supply chain management more efficient by providing information to help companies coordinate, schedule, and control procurement, production, inventory management, and delivery of products and services.

Information and Supply Chain Management

Inefficiencies in the supply chain, such as parts shortages, underutilized plant capacity, excessive finished goods inventory, or runaway transportation costs, are caused by inaccurate or untimely information. For example, manufacturers may keep too many parts in inventory because they do not know exactly when they will receive their next shipment from their suppliers. Suppliers may order too few raw materials because they do not have precise information on demand. These supply chain inefficiencies can waste as much as 25 percent of a company's operating costs.

If a manufacturer had perfect information about exactly how many units of product customers wanted, when they wanted them, and when they could be produced, it would be possible to implement a highly efficient **just-in-time** strategy. Components would arrive exactly at the moment they were needed and finished goods would be shipped as they left the assembly line.

In a supply chain, however, uncertainties arise because many events cannot be foreseen—uncertain product demand, late shipments from suppliers, defective parts or raw material, or production process breakdowns. To satisfy customers, manufacturers often deal with such uncertainties and unforeseen events by keeping more material or products in inventory than what they think they may actually need. The safety stock acts as a buffer for the lack of flexibility in the supply chain. Although excess inventory is expensive, low fill rates are also costly because business may be lost from canceled orders.

One recurring problem in supply chain management is the **bullwhip effect**, in which information about the demand for a product gets distorted as it passes from one entity to the next across the supply chain (Lee, Padmanabhan, and Wang, 1997). A slight rise in demand for an item might cause different members in the supply chain—distributors, manufacturers, suppliers, secondary suppliers (suppliers' suppliers), and tertiary suppliers (suppliers' suppliers' suppliers)—to stockpile inventory so each has enough "just in case." These changes ripple throughout the supply chain, magnifying what started out as a small change from planned orders, creating excess inventory, production, warehousing, and shipping costs (see Figure 11-5).

For example, Procter & Gamble (P&G) found it had excessively high inventories of its Pampers disposable diapers at various points along its supply chain because of such distorted information. Although customer purchases in stores were fairly stable, orders from distributors would spike when P&G offered aggressive price promotions. Pampers and Pampers' components accumulated in warehouses along the supply chain to meet demand that did not actually exist. To eliminate this problem, P&G revised its marketing, sales, and supply chain processes and used more accurate demand forecasting.

The bullwhip can be tamed by reducing uncertainties about demand and supply when all members of the supply chain have accurate and up-to-date information. If all

FIGURE 11-5 *The bullwhip effect.*

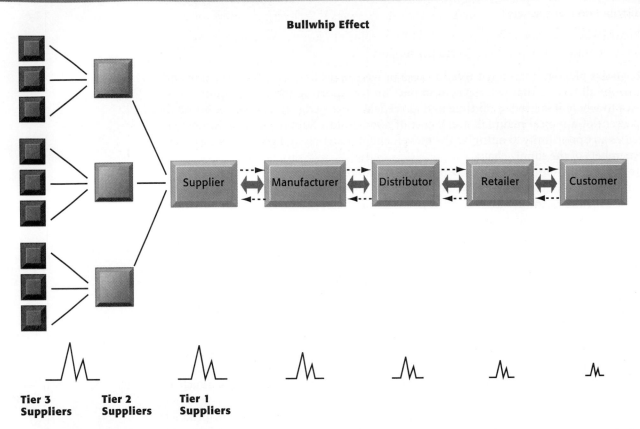

Inaccurate information can cause minor fluctuations in demand for a product to be amplified as one moves further back in the supply chain. Minor fluctuations in retail sales for a product can create excess inventory for distributors, manufacturers, and suppliers.

members of the supply chain could share dynamic information about inventory levels, schedules, forecasts, and shipments, they would have a more precise idea of how to adjust their sourcing, manufacturing, and distribution plans. Supply chain management systems provide the kind of information that can help members of the supply chain make better purchasing and scheduling decisions.

Supply Chain Management Applications

The central objective of supply chain management systems is information visibility—open and rapid communication and information sharing between members of the supply chain. Correct movement of accurate information makes it possible to time orders, shipments, and production properly to minimize stocking levels and expedite deliveries to customers. Supply chain management systems automate the flow of information between a company and its supply chain partners so they can make better decisions to optimize their performance.

In essence, supply chain software can be classified as either software to help businesses plan their supply chains (supply chain planning) or software to help them execute the supply chain steps (supply chain execution). **Supply chain planning systems** enable the firm to generate demand forecasts for a product and to develop sourcing and manufacturing plans for that product. Such systems help companies make better operating decisions, such as determining how much of a specific product to manufacture in a given time period; establishing inventory levels for raw materials, intermediate products, and finished goods; determining where to store finished goods; and identifying the transportation mode to use for product delivery.

For example, if a large customer places a larger order than usual or changes that order on short notice, it can have a widespread impact throughout the supply chain. Additional

Internet Connection —
The Internet Connection for this chapter will take you to a series of Web sites where you can complete an exercise to evaluate supply chain management software.

raw materials or a different mix of raw materials may need to be ordered from suppliers. Manufacturing may have to change job scheduling. A transportation carrier may have to reschedule deliveries. Supply chain planning software makes the necessary adjustments to production and distribution plans. Information about changes is shared among the relevant supply chain members so that their work can be coordinated. One of the most important—and complex—supply chain planning functions is **demand planning**, which determines how much product a business needs to make to satisfy all of its customers' demands.

Supply chain execution systems manage the flow of products through distribution centers and warehouses to ensure that products are delivered to the right locations in the most efficient manner. They track the physical status of goods, the management of materials, warehouse and transportation operations, and financial information involving all parties. Table 11-2 provides more details on supply chain planning and execution systems.

SUPPLY CHAIN PERFORMANCE MEASUREMENT

Companies need to be able to measure the performance of their supply chain management efforts using objective performance information. A number of metrics can be used to evaluate the performance of supply chain processes, and supply chain management systems can provide the data for them. A **metric** is a standard measurement of performance. Important metrics for measuring supply chain performance include the fill rate (the ability to fill orders by the due date), the average time from order to delivery, the number of days of supply in inventory, forecast accuracy, and the cycle time for sourcing and making a product. (Cycle time is the total elapsed time to complete a business process.)

Companies may not necessarily excel in all these areas, but management should choose the operations that are most critical for the success of the firm and focus on metrics that measure their performance. Although large software vendors have tools for automating many of the most important supply chain processes, no software package or set of tools does everything. The specific supply chain management objectives for each company should determine which supply chain management package or set of software tools to use.

Supply Chain Management and the Internet

In the pre-Internet environment, supply chain coordination was hampered by the difficulties of making information flow smoothly among disparate internal supply chain systems for purchasing, materials management, manufacturing, and distribution. It was also difficult to share information with external supply chain partners because the systems of

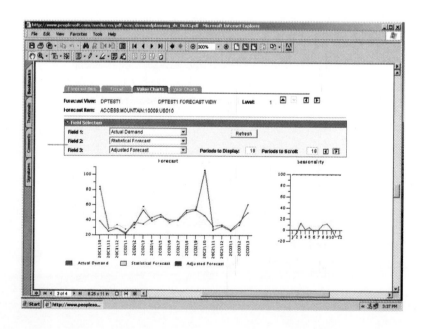

PeopleSoft Demand Forecasting software enables users to create forecasts based on statistical analyses of demand history, causal factors such as promotional events and new product introductions, and input from other members of the organization or trading partners.

TABLE 11-2 *Supply Chain Planning and Execution Systems*

CAPABILITIES OF SUPPLY CHAIN PLANNING SYSTEMS

Order planning: Select an order fulfillment plan that best meets the desired level of service to the customer given existing transportation and manufacturing constraints.

Advanced scheduling and manufacturing planning: Provide detailed coordination of scheduling based on analysis of changing factors, such as customer orders, equipment outages, or supply interruptions. Scheduling modules create job schedules for the manufacturing process and supplier logistics.

Demand planning: Generate demand forecasts from all business units using statistical tools and business forecasting techniques.

Distribution planning: Create operating plans for logistics managers for order fulfillment, based on input from demand and manufacturing planning modules.

Transportation planning: Track and analyze inbound, outbound, and intracompany movement of materials and products to ensure that materials and finished goods are delivered at the right time and place at the minimum cost.

CAPABILITIES OF SUPPLY CHAIN EXECUTION SYSTEMS

Order commitments: Enable vendors to quote accurate delivery dates to customers by providing more real-time detailed information on the status of orders from availability of raw materials and inventory to production and shipment status.

Final production: Organize and schedule final subassemblies required to make each final product.

Replenishment: Coordinate component replenishment work so that warehouses remain stocked with the minimum amount of inventory in the pipeline.

Distribution management: Coordinate the process of transporting goods from the manufacturer to distribution centers to the final customer. Provide online customer access to shipment and delivery data.

Reverse distribution: Track the shipment and accounting for returned goods or remanufactured products.

suppliers, distributors, or logistics providers were based on incompatible technology platforms and standards. Enterprise systems could supply some integration of internal supply chain processes but they were not designed to deal with external supply chain processes.

Some supply chain integration can be supplied inexpensively using Internet technology. Firms can use *intranets* to improve coordination among their internal supply chain processes, and they can use *extranets* to coordinate supply chain processes shared with their business partners (see Figure 11-6).

Using intranets and extranets, all members of the supply chain can instantly communicate with each other, using up-to-date information to adjust purchasing, logistics, manufacturing, packaging, and schedules. A manager can use a Web interface to tap into suppliers' systems to

PeopleSoft Supply Planning software enables users to view ongoing material requirements and available capacity data to help quickly identify potential shortages or capacity issues and respond in a timely manner.

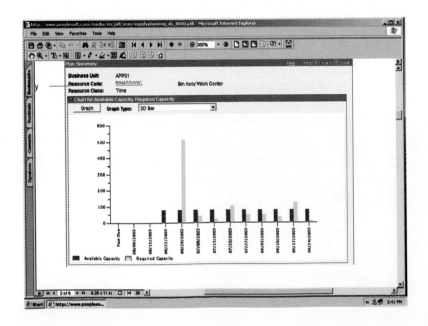

FIGURE 11-6   *Intranets and extranets for supply chain management.*

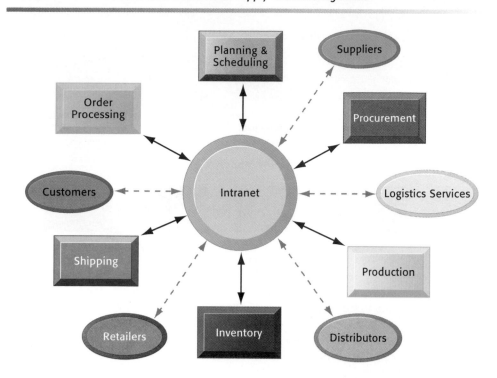

Intranets can be used to integrate information from isolated business processes within the firm to help them manage their internal supply chains. Access to these private intranets can also be extended to authorized suppliers, distributors, logistics services, and, sometimes, to retail customers to improve coordination of external supply chain processes.

determine whether inventory and production capabilities match demand for the firm's products. Business partners can use Web-based supply chain management tools to collaborate online on forecasts. Sales representatives can access suppliers' production schedules and logistics information to monitor customers' order status. The low cost of providing this information with Web-based tools instead of costly proprietary systems encourages companies to share critical business information with a greater number of suppliers.

GLOBAL SUPPLY CHAIN ISSUES

As more and more companies outsource manufacturing operations, obtain supplies from other countries, and sell abroad, they must operate supply chains extending across multiple countries and regions. Global supply chains typically span greater geographic distances and time differences than domestic supply chains, with participants from many different countries. The Internet provides a standard set of tools that can be used by companies all over the world to coordinate overseas sourcing, transportation, communications, financing, and compliance with customs regulations.

DEMAND-DRIVEN SUPPLY CHAINS: FROM PUSH TO PULL MANUFACTURING AND EFFICIENT CUSTOMER RESPONSE

Internet-based supply chain management applications are clearly changing the way businesses work internally and with each other. In addition to reducing costs, these supply chain management systems facilitate efficient customer response, enabling the workings of the business to be driven more by customer demand. (Efficient customer response systems were introduced in Chapter 3.)

Earlier supply chain management systems were driven by a push-based model (also known as *build-to-stock*). In a **push-based model**, production master schedules are based on forecasts or best guesses of demand for products, and products are "pushed" to customers. With new flows of information made possible by Web-based tools, supply chain management can more easily follow a **pull-based model**. In a pull-based model, also known as a *demand-driven model* or *build-to-order*, actual customer orders or purchases trigger events in the supply chain. Transactions to produce and deliver only what customers have ordered move up the supply chain from retailers to distributors to manufacturers and eventually to suppliers. Only products to fulfill these orders move back

FIGURE 11-7 *Push- versus pull-based supply chain models.*

The difference between push- and pull-based models is summarized by the slogan "Make what we sell, not sell what we make."

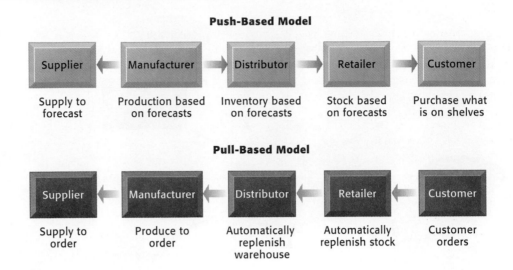

Push-Based Model

Supplier	Manufacturer	Distributor	Retailer	Customer
Supply to forecast	Production based on forecasts	Inventory based on forecasts	Stock based on forecasts	Purchase what is on shelves

Pull-Based Model

Supplier	Manufacturer	Distributor	Retailer	Customer
Supply to order	Produce to order	Automatically replenish warehouse	Automatically replenish stock	Customer orders

down the supply chain to the retailer. Manufacturers would use only actual order demand information to drive their production schedules and the procurement of components or raw materials, as illustrated in Figure 11-7. Wal-Mart's continuous replenishment system and Dell Computer's build-to-order system, both described in Chapter 3, are examples of the pull-based model.

The Internet and Internet technology make it possible to move from sequential supply chains, where information and materials flow sequentially from company to company, to concurrent supply chains, where information flows in many directions simultaneously among members of a supply chain network. Members of the network can immediately adjust to changes in schedules or orders. Ultimately, the Internet could create a "digital logistics nervous system" throughout the supply chain. This system would permit simultaneous, multidirectional communication of information about participants' inventories, orders, and capacities, and would work to optimize the activities of individual firms and groups of firms interacting in e-commerce marketplaces (see Figure 11-8).

FIGURE 11-8 *The future Internet-driven supply chain.*

The future Internet-driven supply chain operates like a digital logistics nervous system. It provides multidirectional communication among firms, networks of firms, and e-marketplaces so that entire networks of supply chain partners can immediately adjust inventories, orders, and capacities.

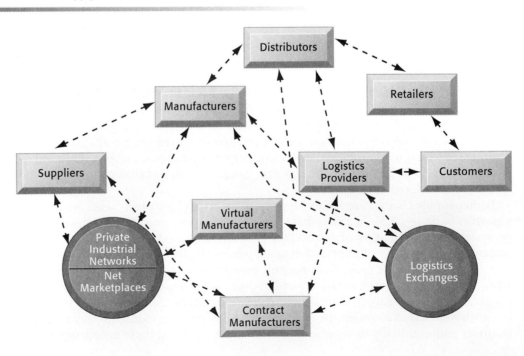

Business Value of Supply Chain Management Systems

Supply chain management systems enable firms to streamline both their internal and external supply chain processes and provide management with more accurate information about what to produce, store, and move. By implementing a networked and integrated supply chain management system, companies can match supply to demand, reduce inventory levels, improve delivery service, speed product time to market, and use assets more effectively. Companies that excel in supply chain management have been found to produce higher rates of growth in their market value than the average for their industries (D'Avanzo, von Lewinski, and Van Wassenhove, 2003). Effective supply chain management systems enhance organizational performance in the following areas:

1. *Improved customer service and responsiveness.* If a product is not available when a customer wants it, that customer will likely try to purchase it from someone else. Having the right product at the right place at the right time will increase sales.

2. *Cost reduction.* Supply chain management helps companies contain, and often reduce, some or all of the costs associated with moving a product through the supply chain. These costs include material acquisition, inventory carrying, transportation, and planning costs. (Inventory carrying costs may amount to 30 or 40 percent of the value of the entire inventory.) Total supply chain costs represent the majority of operating expenses for many businesses and in some industries approach 75 percent of the total operating budget (Handfield, 1999). Reducing supply chain costs can thus have a major impact on firm profitability.

3. *Cash utilization.* The sooner a company delivers a product, the sooner that company will get paid. Companies leading in supply chain efficiency have cash available two to three months faster than companies that do not have this capability.

11.3 CUSTOMER RELATIONSHIP MANAGEMENT SYSTEMS

Businesses have always valued their customers, but today there is much greater appreciation of the importance of customers for the profitability of the enterprise. Because competitive advantage based on an innovative new product or service can be very short lived, companies are realizing that their only enduring competitive strength may be their relationships with their customers. Some say that the basis of competition has switched from who sells the most products and services to who "owns" the customer, and that customer relationships represent the firm's most valuable asset.

Customer Relationship Management and Partner Relationship Management

Many firms are turning to **customer relationship management** (CRM) to maximize the benefits of their customer assets. Customer relationship management is both a business and technology discipline for managing customer relationships to optimize revenue, profitability, customer satisfaction, and customer retention. It uses information technology to track all of the ways in which a company interacts with its customers and to analyze these interactions to maximize the lifetime value of customers for the company while simultaneously maximizing satisfaction for the customers.

Different customers represent different levels of profit for the firm. Some customers cost a great deal to attract and to service, whereas others cost very little to service and to attract for large purchases. Customer relationship management helps organizations identify customers who cost little to attract and to keep and who provide the greatest revenues for every marketing or customer service dollar spent. These "good" customers represent about 80 to 90 percent of a company's profits, but they represent only 10 to 20 percent of the company's customer base.

CRM also focuses on ways of retaining profitable customers and maximizing lifetime revenue from them. It can cost up to six times as much to acquire a new customer as to keep an old customer. These figures vary by industry, but higher customer retention rates generally increase revenues and reduce costs for the firm.

Customer relationship management extends to a firm's business partners who are responsible for selling to customers. **Partner relationship management (PRM)** uses many of the same data, tools, and systems as customer relationship management to enhance collaboration between a company and its selling partners. If a company does not sell directly to customers but rather works through distributors or retailers, PRM helps these channels sell to customers directly. It provides a company and its selling partners with the ability to trade information and distribute leads and data about customers, integrating lead generation, pricing, promotions, order configurations, and availability. It also provides a firm with tools to assess its partners' performance so it can make sure its best partners receive the support they need to close more business.

Customer Relationship Management Applications

Although companies have always talked about putting customers first, until recently, their information systems could not help them do this. Pieces of customer data were often fragmented in isolated systems serving finance, distribution, sales, service, and marketing or organized around product line, line of business, or communication channel. E-commerce generated massive amounts of data about customers and prospects that could not be integrated with the data in compartmentalized information systems.

Customer relationship management (CRM) systems were designed to address these problems by providing information and tools to deliver superior customer experience and to maximize customer lifetime value for the firm. CRM systems capture and integrate customer data from all over the organization, consolidating the data, analyzing the data, and then distributing the results to various systems and customer touch points across the enterprise. A **touch point** (also known as a contact point) is a method of interaction with the customer, such as telephone, e-mail, customer service desk, conventional mail, Web site, or retail store.

Well-designed CRM systems can provide a single enterprise view of customers that can be used for improving both sales and customer service. Such systems can likewise provide customers with a single view of the company regardless of what touch point the customer uses.

CUSTOMER RELATIONSHIP MANAGEMENT (CRM) SOFTWARE

Commercial customer relationship management (CRM) software packages range from niche tools that perform limited functions, such as personalizing Web sites for specific customers, to large-scale enterprise applications that capture myriad interactions with customers, analyze them with sophisticated reporting tools, and link to other major enterprise applications, such as supply chain management and enterprise systems. The more comprehensive CRM packages contain modules for partner relationship management (PRM) and **employee relationship management (ERM).**

Employee relationship management software deals with employee issues that are closely related to CRM, such as setting objectives, employee performance management, performance-based compensation, and employee training. Major CRM application software vendors include Siebel Systems, Clarify, and Salesforce.com. Enterprise software vendors such as SAP, Oracle, and PeopleSoft are also active in customer relationship management and feature tools for integrating their enterprise system modules with their customer relationship management modules.

Customer relationship management systems typically provide software and online tools for sales, customer service, and marketing. Their capabilities include the following:

Sales force automation (SFA).   Sales force automation modules in CRM systems help sales staff increase their productivity by focusing sales efforts on the most profitable customers, those who are good candidates for sales and services. CRM systems provide sales prospect and contact information, product information, product configuration capabilities, and sales quote generation capabilities. Such software can assemble information about a particular customer's past purchases to help the salesperson make personalized recommendations. CRM software enables customer and prospect information to be shared easily among sales, marketing, and delivery departments. It increases each salesperson's efficiency in reducing the cost per sale as well as the cost of acquiring new customers and retaining old ones. CRM software also has capabilities for sales forecasting, territory management, and team selling.

Customer service. Customer service modules in CRM systems provide information and tools to make call centers, help desks, and customer support staff more efficient. They have capabilities for assigning and managing customer service requests.

One such capability is an appointment or advice telephone line: When a customer calls a standard phone number, the system routes the call to the correct service person, who inputs information about that customer into the system only once. Once the customer's data are in the system, any service representative can handle the customer relationship. Improved access to consistent and accurate customer information helps call centers handle more calls per day and decreases the duration of each call. Thus, call centers and customer service groups can achieve greater productivity, reduced transaction time, and higher quality of service at lower cost. The customer is happier because he or she spends less time on the phone restating his or her problem to customer service.

CRM systems may also include Web-based self-service capabilities: the company Web site can be set up to provide inquiring customers personalized support information as well as the option to contact customer service staff by phone for additional assistance.

Marketing. Customer relationship management systems support direct-marketing campaigns by providing capabilities for capturing prospect and customer data, for providing product and service information, for qualifying leads for targeted marketing, and for scheduling and tracking direct-marketing mailings or e-mail. Marketing modules would also include tools for analyzing marketing and customer data—identifying profitable and unprofitable customers, designing products and services to satisfy specific customer needs and interests, and identifying opportunities for cross-selling, up-selling, and bundling.

Cross-selling is the marketing of complementary products to customers. (For example, in financial services a customer with a checking account might be sold a money market account or a home improvement loan.) **Up-selling** is the marketing of higher-value products or services to new or existing customers. (An example might be a credit card company persuading a good customer to upgrade from a conventional credit card to a "platinum" card with a larger credit line, additional services—and a higher annual fee.)

Bundling is one kind of cross-selling in which a combination of products is sold as a bundle at a price lower than the total cost of the individual products. For example, Verizon sells bundled telephone services that include local and long-distance service, voice mail service, caller identification, and digital subscriber line (DSL) access to the Internet. CRM tools also help firms manage and execute marketing campaigns at all stages, from planning to determining the rate of success for each campaign.

Figure 11-9 illustrates the most important capabilities for sales, service, and marketing processes that would be found in major CRM software products. Like enterprise software, this software is business-process driven, incorporating hundreds of business processes thought to represent best practices in each of these areas.

Siebel Systems, the market-leading vendor of customer relationship management software, provides both generic and industry-specific best practices for its software. In addition to codifying best practices for sales, marketing, and service processes that are common across all industries, Siebel has identified and modeled business processes representing best practices for more than 20 specific industries and industry segments, including best practices in finance, consumer goods, and communication and media. To achieve maximum benefit from implementing Siebel software, companies would revise and model their business processes to correspond to the best practice business processes for CRM in the Siebel system.

FIGURE 11-9   *CRM software capabilities.*

The major CRM software products support business processes in sales, service, and marketing, integrating customer information from many different sources. Included are support for both the operational and analytic aspects of CRM.

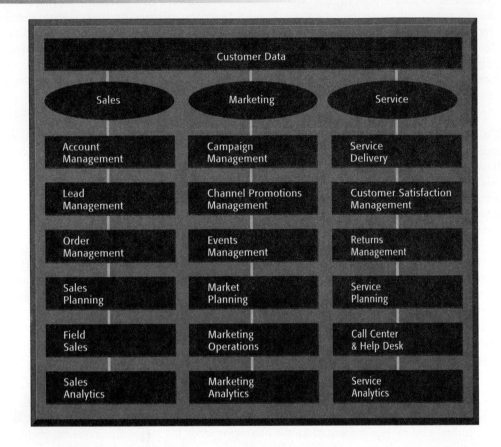

Figure 11-10 illustrates how a best practice for increasing customer loyalty through customer service might be modeled by CRM software. Directly servicing customers provides firms with opportunities to increase customer retention by singling out profitable long-term customers for preferential treatment. CRM software can assign each customer a score based on that person's value and loyalty to the company and provide that information to help call centers route each customer's service request to agents who

FIGURE 11-10   *Customer loyalty management process map.*

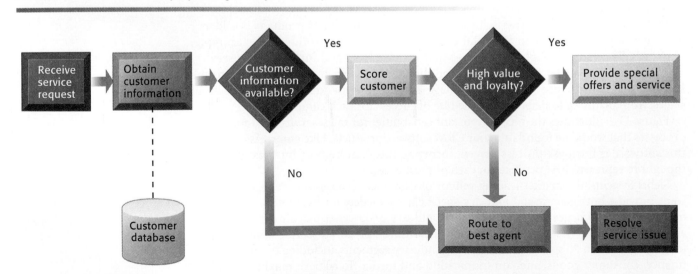

This process map shows how a best practice for promoting customer loyalty through customer service would be modeled by customer relationship management software. The CRM software helps firms identify high-value customers for preferential treatment.

can best handle that customer's needs. The system would automatically provide the service agent with a detailed profile of that customer that included his or her score for value and loyalty. The service agent could use this information to present special offers or additional service to the customer to encourage the customer to keep transacting business with the company. Table 11-3 describes other best practice business processes in the Siebel CRM system.

Operational and Analytical CRM

All of the applications we have just described support either the operational or analytical aspects of customer relationship management. **Operational CRM** includes customer-facing applications such as tools for sales force automation, call center and customer service support, and marketing automation. **Analytical CRM** includes applications that analyze customer data generated by operational CRM applications to provide information for improving business performance management. Table 11-4 provides more specific examples of operational and analytical CRM functions.

Analytical CRM applications are based on data warehouses that consolidate the data from operational CRM systems and customer touch points for use with online analytical processing (OLAP), data mining, and other data analysis techniques (see Chapters 7 and 13). Customer data collected by the organization might be combined with data from other sources, such as customer lists for direct marketing campaigns purchased from other companies or demographic data. Such data could be analyzed to identify buying patterns, to create segments for targeted marketing, and to pinpoint profitable and unprofitable customers (see Figure 11-11). Analytical CRM could also create individual customer profiles, showing each person's accounts, transactions with the business, and known interests.

Retailers could use the customer knowledge gleaned from analytical CRM to make recommendations across sales channels. Multichannel customers are known to have a higher lifetime value than single-channel customers. With multichannel customer data analysis, businesses can identify patterns, such as customers who like to use the Web to view products but then visit a retail store to purchase the product. To sell to this type of customer, businesses might e-mail a coupon to be redeemed at a physical store. Conversely, retailers could use knowledge of multichannel customers' offline purchases to tailor promotions that enhance their online shopping.

TABLE 11-3 *Examples of Best Practice Business Processes in the Siebel CRM System*

Business Process	Description
Priority-based lead qualification and distribution	Evaluates and scores leads, providing scripted assessment guides to enable sales agents to focus on the leads with the highest potential value.
Integrated customer order management	Automates the workflow for order management, including designing a customer solution, developing a detailed product configuration, applying correct pricing and contract terms, and entering and shipping the order.
Real-time offer optimization	Ensures that the optimal marketing offer is presented to a customer.
Value-based customer segmentation	Enables marketing organizations to deliver different offers and services based on current and potential customer value.
Contact strategy-based targeting	Enables marketing organizations to define and consistently enforce across the enterprise policies governing the types and frequencies of communications with customers. Ensures compliance with customer privacy and communication preferences.
Rules-based service order fulfillment	Ensures that service orders are fulfilled in an order based on the lifetime value of the customer and the specific details of that customer's service agreement.
Value-based service coverage	Ensures that an organization's highest-value customers are routed to the most-qualified customer service agents.

TABLE 11-4 *Examples of Operational Versus Analytical CRM*

Operational CRM	Analytical CRM
Campaign management	Develop customer segmentation strategies
E-marketing	Develop customer profiles
Account and contact management	Analyze customer profitability
Lead management	Analyze product profitability
Telemarketing	Identify cross-selling and up-selling opportunities
Teleselling	Select the best marketing, service, and sales channels for each customer group
E-selling	Identify trends in sales cycle length, win rate, and average deal size
Field sales	Analyze service resolution times, service levels based on communication channel, and service activity by product line and account
Field service dispatch	Analyze leads generated and conversion rates
Customer care and help desk	Analyze sales representative and customer service representative productivity
Contract management	Identify churn problems

FIGURE 11-11 *Analytical CRM data warehouse.*

Analytical CRM uses a customer data warehouse and tools to analyze customer data collected from the firm's customer touch points and from other sources.

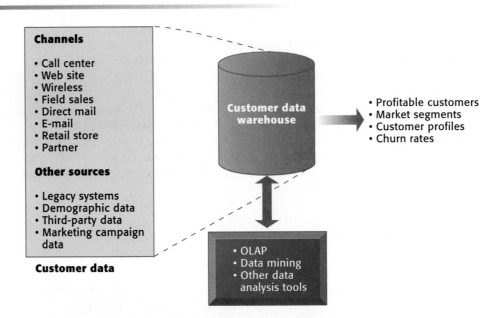

Business Value of Customer Relationship Management Systems

Companies with effective customer relationship management systems can realize many benefits, including increased customer satisfaction, reduced direct marketing costs, more effective marketing, and lower costs for customer acquisition and retention. Information from CRM systems can increase sales revenue by identifying the most profitable customers and segments for focused marketing, cross-selling, and up-selling.

Customer churn is reduced as sales, service, and marketing better respond to customer needs. The **churn rate** measures the number of customers who stop using or purchasing products or services from a company. It is an important indicator of the growth or decline of a firm's customer base.

The Window on Organizations illustrates how customer relationship systems have provided value for automotive dealers. Both Mercedes-Benz Canada and Saab Cars U.S.A. invested in customer relationship management systems to help them compete for cus-

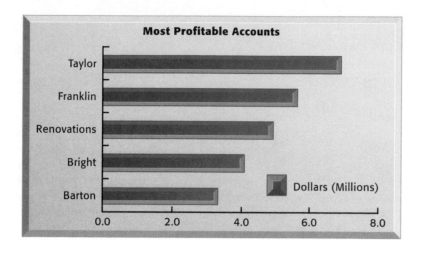

Most Profitable Accounts

Dollars (Millions)

Taylor, Franklin, Renovations, Bright, Barton
0.0 2.0 4.0 6.0 8.0

Customer relationship management software provides analytical tools to help firms identify their most important customers, predict future buying patterns, and position the correct resources to increase sales.

tomers in the crowded premium automotive market. Both had been hampered by fragmented customer data and uncoordinated processes for dealing with customers.

THE IMPORTANCE OF CRM PERFORMANCE MEASUREMENT

A company's decision about which customer-related activities to measure, how costs are assigned to the activities, and the manner in which the activities are assigned back to customers can have a huge impact on profitability calculations. Some companies that invest in CRM have little or no idea of their return on investment (ROI). They fail to create measurements of current performance or set targets for improved performance with the new CRM system. Successful CRM implementations require that financial and operational goals and the metrics to evaluate them be clearly defined at the beginning of the project. Metrics for customer relationship management might include the cost per lead, cost per sale, number of repeat customers, reduction of churn, or sales closing rate.

Another important metric is the **customer lifetime value (CLTV)**. CLTV is based on the relationship between the revenue produced by a specific customer, the expenses incurred in acquiring and servicing that customer, and the expected life of the relationship between the customer and the company (Sabri, 2003). CLTV represents the difference between revenues and expenses minus the cost of promotional marketing used to retain an account; the value of this amount is expressed in today's dollars. (See the discussion of net present value in Chapter 15.)

11.4 ENTERPRISE INTEGRATION TRENDS

Businesses are now pursuing even greater degrees of cross-functional process integration than that supplied by the traditional enterprise applications. They want to make customer relationship management, supply chain management, and enterprise systems work closely together with each other, and they want to link these systems tightly with those of customers, suppliers, and business partners. Businesses also want to obtain more value from enterprise applications, Web services, and other integration technologies by using them as platforms for new enterprise-wide services.

Extending Enterprise Software

Enterprise software has become more flexible and capable of integration with other systems. The major enterprise software vendors have developed Web-enabled software for customer relationship management, supply chain management, decision support, enterprise portals, and other business functions that integrate with their enterprise software to create what they call "enterprise solutions," "business suites," "enterprise suites," or "e-business suites." SAP's mySAP and Oracle's e-Business Suite are examples. The enterprise

WINDOW ON ORGANIZATIONS

CRM Drives Sales at Mercedes and Saab

Mercedes-Benz and Saab are both premium automobile brands, with large followings of loyal customers. However, both operate in a highly competitive market space with larger rivals launching aggressive marketing campaigns, price incentives, and inexpensive financing offers. Generating showroom traffic has proved a constant challenge. Instead of spending more on advertising, Mercedes-Benz Canada and Saab U.S.A. turned to customer relationship management to fight back.

Toronto-based Mercedes-Benz Canada, with a network of 55 dealers, believed it did not know enough about its customers. Dealers provided customer data to the automaker on an ad hoc basis. Mercedes did not force dealers to report this information, and its process for tracking dealers that failed to report was cumbersome.

Georgia-based Saab U.S.A., a subsidiary of the Swedish company Saab Automobile AB, imports and distributes more than 37,000 Saab sedans, wagons, and convertibles to 200 U.S. dealerships. Saab had been engaging customers through three channels: its dealer network, a customer assistance center dealing with service inquiries from Saab owners, and a lead management center handling marketing and information requests from prospective customers.

Each of these channels maintained customer data in its own database, leaving Saab with a splintered view of its customers. The customer assistance center relied on a SQL Server database to manage customer information; dealers kept customer data in their own lead management systems; and Saab stored lead data in other internal systems as well as in systems run by third-party vendors. The company had about 3 million records and 55 files at three different vendors.

Fragmentation of customer data meant that a prospective customer might receive a direct mail offer from Saab one week and an e-mail with an unrelated offer from a third-party marketing vendor the next week. The local dealer might not know about either of these offers and consequently delivered an ineffective pitch when the prospect visited the showroom.

Saab had no integrated lead management process. Saab salespeople received leads from Saab's lead management center by fax. The leads then had to be manually re-entered into the dealership's own lead management systems, a time-consuming and error-prone process. Lead quality was highly variable, so many dealers simply ignored the leads. Follow-up to leads was often slow and the company had no way of tracking leads faxed to its dealers.

Mercedes-Benz Canada sought a solution that would increase customer loyalty through personalized service and targeted marketing campaigns. The company chose Napoleon CRM software for automotive dealers sold by Strategic Connections.

Using its new CRM system, Mercedes-Benz Canada can determine, for example, which customers purchased earlier diesel cars and can send those buyers information about its new E Class diesel vehicle. The system helps salespeople at the dealerships create personalized brochures of vehicles for customers. If the customer does not want to purchase on the first showroom visit, that person can take home leasing, finance, and product specifications for the car that is of interest. The information is stored and made available on the Mercedes Web site for the prospective customer as well. The system also notifies salespeople to follow up with a potential customer in a set number of days or weeks.

Saab U.S.A. implemented three CRM applications from Siebel Systems' Automotive Dealer Integration Set. In January 2002 Saab implemented Siebel Call Center for 45 employees in a new Customer Interaction Center, which combines the former customer assistance center and lead management groups. This application provides Customer Interaction Center staff with a 360-degree view of each customer, including prior service-related questions and all the marketing communication they have received.

In July 2002 Saab rolled out Siebel Dealer to its 220 U.S. dealers. This application provides Saab dealers with a Web-based solution for coordinating sales and marketing activities. Sales leads generated by the Customer Interaction Center are delivered rapidly by this system to the right salespeople at the right dealerships. Saab salespeople now receive qualified leads through Siebel Dealer rather than from faxes.

The system provides detailed information to evaluate each lead more effectively. Saab can track the status of referred leads by monitoring events such as the salesperson's initial call to the customer and the scheduling and completion of a test drive. Saab can use this information to measure the sales results of specific leads, recommend better selling techniques, and target leads more precisely. Since the CRM system was implemented, Saab's follow-up rate on sales leads has increased from 38 to 50 percent and customer satisfaction has risen from 69 percent to 75 percent.

Sources: Lisa Picarille, "Planes, Trains, and Automobiles," *Customer Relationship Management Magazine*, February 2004; "Saab Cars USA Increases Lead Follow-Up from 38 Percent to 50 Percent with Siebel Automotive," www.siebel.com, accessed May 4, 2004; and Ginger Conlon, "Driving Sales," *Customer Relationship Management Magazine*, July 1, 2003.

To Think About: How did customer relationship management systems provide value for both of these companies? What management, organization, and technology issues had to be addressed when these companies implemented their CRM systems?

vendors also provide middleware and tools that use XML and Web services for integrating enterprise systems with older legacy applications and systems from other vendors (see Chapters 6 and 14).

Enterprise software vendors are refashioning their architectures to be more Web-centric so that core systems can work with the Internet, extended supply chains, CRM systems, and new business-to-business (B2B) and business-to-consumer (B2C) e-commerce models. This new generation of extended enterprise applications is sometimes referred to as *XRP* or *ERP II*.

Service Platforms and Business Process Management

Firms seeking better returns on their technology investments are focusing on ways to create entire services based on new or improved business processes that integrate information from multiple functional areas. These services are built on enterprise-wide service platforms that provide a greater degree of cross-functional integration than the traditional enterprise applications. A **service platform** integrates multiple applications from multiple business functions, business units, or business partners to deliver a seamless experience for the customer, employee, manager, or business partner.

For instance, the order-to-cash process involves receiving an order and seeing it all the way through obtaining payment for the order. This process begins with lead generation, marketing campaigns, and order entry, which are typically supported by CRM systems. Once the order is received, manufacturing is scheduled and parts availability is verified—processes that are usually supported by enterprise software. The order then is handled by processes for distribution planning, warehousing, order fulfillment, and shipping, which are usually supported by supply chain management systems. Finally, the order is billed to the customer, which is handled by either enterprise financial applications or accounts receivable. If the purchase at some point required customer service, customer relationship management systems would again be invoked.

A service such as order-to-cash requires data from enterprise applications and financial systems to be further integrated into an enterprise-wide composite process. To accomplish this, firms need a business process management plan and application integration software that ties the various pieces together. **Business process management** is a methodology for dealing with the organization's need to change its business processes continually to remain competitive. It includes tools for creating models of improved processes that can be translated into software systems. Because most companies are unlikely to jettison their existing customer relationship management, supply chain management, enterprise systems, and homegrown legacy systems, software tools that could use existing applications as building blocks for new cross-enterprise processes would also be required (see Figure 11-12).

The major enterprise application vendors now have tools for creating cross-application sets of services from existing systems. SAP's version of cross-application services is called xApps. xApps enables businesses to build and automate new cross-functional, end-to-end processes atop existing applications, regardless of the technology platform they use. xApps uses Web services standards to pull together data from the firm's SAP software suite, from internal legacy systems, or from external systems for use in new business processes that span multiple functions and application areas. The software synchronizes with the existing business processes embedded in these systems. (Chapters 6 and 14 provide more detail on Web services and how the technology supports enterprise integration.) SAP now has prepackaged xApps for mergers and acquisitions, new product launches, and resource and program management. Similar tools from other enterprise vendors include Siebel's Universal Application Network and PeopleSoft's AppConnect.

Increasingly, these new services will be delivered through portals. Today's portal products provide frameworks for building new composite services. Portal software can integrate information from enterprise applications and disparate in-house legacy systems, presenting it to users through a Web interface so that the information appears to be coming from a single source.

FIGURE 11-12   *Order-to-cash service.*

Order-to-cash is a composite process that integrates data from individual enterprise systems and legacy financial applications. The process must be modeled and translated into a software system using application integration tools.

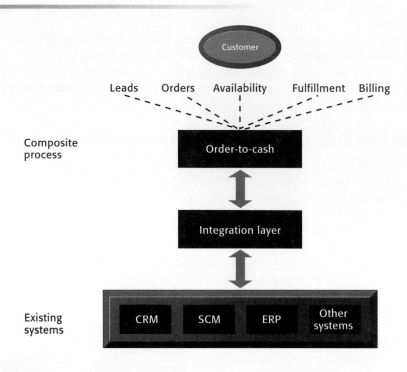

11.5 MANAGEMENT OPPORTUNITIES, CHALLENGES, AND SOLUTIONS

Implementing an enterprise application is above all a business decision rather than a technology decision. Companies need to be sure that they are defining a problem that a customer relationship management, supply chain management, or enterprise system can solve. It is also critical for organizations to know how much integration they want and what the organization will look and feel like when it is achieved. These systems can provide enormous value if managers understand—and can deal with—their challenges.

Opportunities

Both the promise and the peril of enterprise applications lie in their power to fundamentally change the way the organization works. Over time, most firms obtain extraordinary business value from enterprise applications because of their power to improve process coordination and management decision making. Promises of dramatic reductions in inventory costs, order-to-delivery time, as well as more efficient customer response and higher product and customer profitability make these applications very alluring. But to obtain this value, firms must clearly understand how their business has to change to use these systems effectively.

Management Challenges

Although enterprise applications can improve organizational coordination, efficiency, and decision making, they are difficult to build and use successfully. A very high percentage (as much as 70 percent) of companies investing in enterprise systems or systems for supply chain management or customer relationship management have not obtained the promised benefits on schedule or spend much more on these systems than originally anticipated. Enterprise applications involve complex pieces of software and large investments of time, money, and expertise. Such systems pose multiple challenges: high total cost of ownership (TCO), extensive organizational change, and difficulty realizing strategic value. Managers who are aware of these challenges at the outset can plan accordingly.

HIGH TOTAL COST OF OWNERSHIP

Enterprise systems, supply chain management, and customer relationship management systems are very expensive to purchase and implement. It might take a large company three years to fully implement all of the organizational and technology changes required by a large-scale enterprise system, supply chain management system, or customer relationship management system. The total implementation cost, including hardware, software, database tools, consulting fees, personnel costs, and training, might amount to five to six times the software package purchase price. Costs run even higher for organizations with global operations, which must manage organizational and technology changes in many different languages, time zones, currencies, and regulatory environments.

A Meta Group study of the total cost of ownership (TCO) of enterprise systems, including hardware, software, professional services, and internal staff costs, found that the average TCO was $15 million (the highest was $300 million and the lowest $400,000). The median initial investment in a CRM application is approximately $426,000, but the cost can run as high as $100 million for a large and complex CRM implementation, and many do not generate the financial returns that justify these expenditures (Schneider, 2004; Ebner, Hu, Levitt, and McCrory, 2002). Large supply chain management systems have similar costs.

ORGANIZATIONAL CHANGE REQUIREMENTS

Enterprise applications require not only deep-seated technological changes but also fundamental changes in the way the business operates. Business processes change dramatically, as do organizational structure and culture. Organizations that do not understand the need for these changes or that are unable to make them will have problems implementing enterprise applications and using them effectively (Agarwal, Harding, and Schumacher, 2004).

Employees must accept new job functions and responsibilities. They will have to learn how to perform a new set of processes and understand how the information they enter into the system can affect other parts of the company. New organizational learning is required for organizational members to acquire complex new knowledge about new business rules and business processes (Robey, Ross, and Boudreau, 2002).

Most firms embracing CRM systems need to transform their focus from a product-centric view to a customer-centric view in which retaining a customer is a priority. These changes require more interdepartmental cooperation. If a firm's sales, marketing, support systems, back-office systems, and data warehouses exist in isolation, the cross-functional information sharing, integration, and business intelligence to optimize the customer experience cannot occur. Companies typically underestimate the time and cost of cleaning up customer data from disparate sources and of organizing customer data in a company-wide format.

Supply chain management raises implementation hurdles because it extends beyond the walls of the company. Business managers have been accustomed to thinking about their firms, the best interests of their firms, and business process improvements that benefit the entire firm. But in an interorganizational supply chain, they may be asked to redesign the way they work to optimize the performance of the supply chain as a whole (Lee, 2004).

Unless enterprise application investments are accompanied by improvements in the firm's business processes, they are unlikely to improve the flow of information and goods. If enterprise application software is implemented atop flawed processes, the software could actually make matters worse (Day, 2003; Rigby, Reichheld, and Schefter, 2003).

The Window on Management addresses this issue. Novartis Pharmaceuticals was experiencing problems paying invoices on time because of incompatibilities between its SAP R/3 enterprise software and the company's business processes for initiating purchase requisitions and paying suppliers. It decided to simplify the process, but chose to use other software to support it instead of enterprise software.

WINDOW ON MANAGEMENT

WHY NOVARTIS BACKED OFF FROM ENTERPRISE SOFTWARE

Novartis A.G. is a leading global pharmaceutical and health care company headquartered in Basel, Switzerland. It operates in more than 140 countries around the world, employing about 77,200 people and producing nearly US$25 billion in revenue in 2003.

Novartis is replacing legacy systems at Novartis offices in more than 50 countries with SAP enterprise software for human resources, supplier relationship management, and supply chain management. Management believes the SAP software will help the company cut down system integration costs as well as standardize and streamline administrative processes, work flow, and reporting in its worldwide operations. The SAP software would also help the company comply with U.S. Food and Drug Administration regulations on electronic records and signatures for the pharmaceutical industry.

A research survey conducted by Frost & Sullivan, a global consulting company specializing in emerging high-technology and industrial markets, recognized SAP as the dominant enterprise resource planning and supply chain management vendor for the global pharmaceuticals industry. Pharmaceutical companies seeking a single system that could tie together their operations in various countries were impressed by SAP's ability to address their industry-specific business requirements as well as the vendor's superior global service and support network.

Novartis had already adopted SAP's R/3 enterprise resource planning and financial modules for many of its operating units. Given the company's enthusiasm for enterprise systems and SAP, it was surprising to learn that the accounts payable department at Novartis Pharmaceuticals, the U.S. arm of the company, was having problems with its SAP enterprise system. Somewhere in the process of paying invoices, payments were being held, and a backlog of overdue bills was building. A few vendors even withheld credit from the company.

The accounts payable and strategic sourcing departments fingered a recent upgrade to the SAP R/3 financial modules as the source of their financial crisis. Novartis had insisted that SAP be its global standard and the software just wasn't working for them. In frustration, these groups began meeting to figure out a way to redesign their requisition-to-pay process, even if it meant scrapping SAP modules that did not meet their needs. They did not want to work with the Novartis information systems department.

Novartis's information systems staff, on the other hand, believed the unpaid invoices were not entirely caused by the SAP software. The company's existing process for invoicing was inefficient, requiring manual approvals from many different managers. It was not a true integrated requisition-to-pay process. Work was still structured into silos and no one knew what was going on.

The information systems staff thought a recent implementation of the SAP R/3 software would solve the problem. It believed that if it let the SAP software handle as many business processes as possible, it would not have to deal with so many interfaces between different information systems. The information systems department had assigned special staff members to serve as business information managers (BIMs) who could work more closely with end user departments to clarify and support business goals. Nevertheless, because of tight deadlines and limited budget, information systems specialists scrimped on training and did not pay sufficient attention to the new system's impact on business processes.

Something had to be done to get user and information systems groups to cooperate. Ray Pawlicki, Novartis's vice president for information and chief information officer, invited accounts payable and information systems groups to a six-month program to foster joint leadership. The groups met many times. Eventually, both groups finally started listening to each other and committed to two outcomes.

One was to create a new way for the information systems, accounts payable, and strategic sourcing departments to work together to facilitate rapid business transformation. The other outcome was a proposal to improve the purchasing process for Novartis departments so that they would no longer make independent purchases. Instead, all requisitions would be channeled through the strategic sourcing department. By centralizing purchases, the company would be able to obtain larger discounts from suppliers because it was buying in larger quantities. About US$4 million to $5 million could be saved annually this way.

Business information managers (BIMs) from the information systems department emerged with a deeper appreciation of business requirements and how these matched up with SAP and other software providers. In the end, the information systems group agreed to what accounts payable and strategic sourcing had originally requested: a solution that was the "best of breed," irrespective of the software vendor, that would best support the company's redesigned purchasing process.

In May 2003 the information systems department agreed to update an old system from Ariba that would reduce late payments by automatically reconciling sourcing and accounts payable. The Ariba upgrade improved Novartis's purchasing process so much that US$4 to $5 million in savings were achieved within six months.

Sources: Stephanie Overby, "Can't We All Just Get Along?" *CIO Australia*, March 10, 2004 and "SAP Chosen by Novartis as a Major Building Block," *EETimes*, June 16, 2003.

To Think About: Why was Novartis having trouble with its requisition-to-pay process? What management, organization, and technology factors were involved? Was the solution to this problem a good one? Why or why not?

REALIZING STRATEGIC VALUE

Companies may fail to achieve strategic benefits from enterprise applications if the generic processes enforced by enterprise applications prevent the firm from using unique business processes that had been sources of advantage over competitors. Enterprise systems promote centralized organizational coordination and decision making, which may not be the best way for some firms to operate (Davenport, 2000, 1998). Enterprise applications that are state-of-the-art today could bind firms to outdated business processes and technologies tomorrow.

Solution Guidelines

Successful implementation of enterprise applications requires knowledge of how the business works today as well as how it wants to work tomorrow. Learning how enterprise applications work and how the business would have to change to use these systems effectively represents a major research and development effort. In a nutshell, it takes a lot of work to get enterprise applications to work properly. Everyone in the organization must be involved.

LOOK AT BUSINESS OBJECTIVES FIRST

A customer relationship management, supply chain management, or enterprise system isn't merely a technology change—it represents a fundamental change in the way the company conducts its business. Many managers contemplating such systems focus too much on the technology and not enough on business goals. Managers must understand the business objectives they want to achieve with enterprise applications before buying any software. They must determine whether an enterprise application will actually help the company meet these objectives. Identifying the key business processes the company is trying to improve and how much these processes must change with an enterprise application should always be the first step.

ATTENTION TO DATA AND DATA MANAGEMENT

Enterprise applications require that information that was previously maintained in different systems and different departments or functional areas be integrated and made available to the company as a whole. Firms implementing enterprise applications must develop organization-wide definitions of data. Understanding how the organization uses its data and how the data would be handled in a customer relationship management, supply chain management, or enterprise system is a large-scale research effort.

Managers and employees will have to study the enterprise application software very carefully to make sure they understand the definitions of the data elements in the system, how they relate, and how they can be used for decision making and operational support. They will need to examine their organization's existing data model and see how much it needs to be changed to work with the new software.

The firm must make sure that the data elements needed for decision making are in a form that can be used throughout the organization and that the data are accurate and complete. If, for instance, a firm has data available on product sales but the data cannot be linked back to data on sales promotions or to data on which retailer purchased which item, the system won't be able to link product sales to promotions. Analytic insights from the system will be limited.

SENIOR MANAGEMENT COMMITMENT AND EMPLOYEE SUPPORT

Support and backing from the CEO are critical for ensuring that all the changes required by enterprise applications will be adopted by the entire company. People are much more willing to take on different job responsibilities or change the way they work if senior management is firmly behind the effort.

Rank-and-file employees—the people who actually are going to use the system on a day-to-day basis—should not be overlooked. They need to be involved in some of the decisions about the system as well as implementation and training. Support for the system can be encouraged by clearly demonstrating the business value that comes with the enterprise application project and how all can contribute to its success.

EDUCATION AND TRAINING

Education and training are always essential for successful information system implementation, but even more so for enterprise applications. Managers must learn how the system can change key processes, organizational structure, and the information they use. Employees will need to learn exactly how the system supports the work they perform and how it affects the broader organization each time it is used.

MAKE IT YOUR BUSINESS

Finance and Accounting

Financial and accounting applications are usually the first enterprise software modules to be implemented because these systems provide firms with immediate online views of their financial status and more integrated financial information for management decision making. All of the enterprise applications provide financial information for measuring firm performance, including product costs and profitability, inventory turns, or customer profitability. You can find examples of finance and accounting applications on pages 379 and 404.

Human Resources

Enterprise systems support the human resources function by automating processes for personnel administration, benefits, workforce planning, compensation, and performance management. Sophisticated customer relationship management systems include modules for employee relationship management, supporting the aspects of the human resources function that deal with employee performance monitoring, training, and compensation that are also closely related to improving sales and customer service. Human resources plays a role in helping organizations resolve "people issues," such as the impact of changing job responsibilities, the need for training in new systems and business processes, and resistance to the change, that are critical to the successful implementation of enterprise applications.

Manufacturing and Production

Enterprise systems and supply chain management systems have made it possible for the manufacturing and production func-

tion to become more efficient and flexible so that it could get products and services to customers more rapidly and precisely at lower cost. Enterprise systems can drive the execution of many internal manufacturing processes, and supply chain management systems are increasingly driving the flow of materials in the organization's internal and external supply chains. You can find examples of manufacturing and production applications on pages 411–413.

Sales and Marketing

All of the enterprise applications described in this chapter support sales and marketing. Customer relationship management systems enhance the performance of sales and marketing by maximizing customer relationships. They provide tools for important sales functions for lead generation, order management, and customer service so that sales staff can focus on the most profitable customers. CRM systems assemble detailed data on customers and their interactions with the firm that are very useful to marketing for planning campaigns, advancing new products and services, or implementing cross-selling activities. Enterprise software supports some sales and marketing processes for ordering and sales planning, but it is not as focused on the customer as CRM systems are. Even supply chain systems support sales and marketing by helping firms get products to customers rapidly and by providing accurate information for customer service. You can find examples of sales and marketing applications on pages 400 and 411–413.

Summary

1. ***Assess how enterprise systems provide value for businesses and describe how they work.***

    Enterprise systems integrate the key business processes of a firm into a single software system so that information can flow seamlessly throughout the organi-

zation, improving coordination, efficiency, and decision making. Enterprise software is based on a suite of integrated software modules and a common central database. The database collects data from and feeds the data into numerous applications that can support nearly all of an organization's internal business activities. When new information is entered by one process, the information is made available immediately to other business processes. Organizations implementing enterprise software would have to adopt the business processes embedded in the software and, if necessary, change their business processes to conform to those in the software.

Enterprise systems support organizational centralization by enforcing uniform data standards and business processes throughout the company and a single unified technology platform. The firmwide data generated by enterprise systems can help managers monitor organizational performance. By integrating business processes in sales, production, finance, and logistics, the entire organization can more efficiently respond to customer requests for products or information, forecast new products, and build and deliver them as demand appears.

2. *Assess how supply chain management systems provide value for businesses and explain how they work.*

Supply chain management systems automate the flow of information between members of the supply chain so they can use it to make better decisions about when and how much to purchase, produce, or ship. More accurate information from supply chain management systems reduces uncertainty and the impact of the bullwhip effect. The correct movement of information makes it possible to time orders, shipments, and production properly to minimize inventory levels and expedite deliveries to customers.

Supply chain management software includes software for supply chain planning and for supply chain execution. Supply chain planning systems enable the firm to generate demand forecasts for a product and to develop sourcing, manufacturing, and distribution plans. Supply chain execution systems manage the flow of products through the final stages of production, distribution, and delivery. Supply chain management systems provide data such as fill rates, inventory turns, or source/make cycle time for evaluating the performance of supply chain processes. Firms can use intranets to improve coordination among their internal supply chain processes, and they can use extranets to coordinate supply chain processes shared with their business partners. Internet technology facilitates the management of global supply chains by providing the connectivity for organizations in different countries to share supply chain information. Improved communication among supply chain members also facilitates efficient customer response and movement toward a demand-driven model.

3. *Assess how customer relationship management systems provide value for businesses and describe how they work.*

Customer relationship management (CRM) systems integrate and automate many customer-facing processes in sales, marketing, and customer service, providing an enterprise-wide view of customers. These systems track all of the ways in which a company interacts with its customers and analyze these interactions to maximize customer lifetime value for the firm. CRM systems capture and integrate customer data from all over the organization, analyzing the data and distributing the results to customer-related systems and customer touch points across the enterprise. Companies can use this customer knowledge when they interact with customers to provide them with better service or to sell new products and services. These systems can also identify profitable or nonprofitable customers or opportunities to reduce the churn rate. The major customer relationship management software packages integrate customer-related processes in sales, marketing, and customer service and provide capabilities for both operational CRM and analytical CRM. They often include modules for managing relationships with selling partners (partner relationship management) and for employee relationship management.

If properly implemented, CRM systems help firms increase customer satisfaction, reduce direct marketing costs, and lower costs for customer acquisition and retention. Information from CRM systems can increase sales revenue by identifying the most profitable customers and segments for focused marketing, cross-selling, and up-selling. Customer churn can be reduced as sales, service, and marketing better respond to customer needs.

4. *Explain how enterprise applications can be used in platforms for new cross-functional services.*

Enterprise applications can serve as building blocks for new cross-functional services for customers, suppliers, or business partners based on enterprise-wide business processes by using service platforms and enterprise portals. Service platforms integrate data and processes from the various enterprise applications (customer relationship management, supply chain management, and enterprise systems), as well as from disparate legacy applications to create new composite processes. The new composite process is modeled using business process management tools, and application integration software ties various systems together. The new services are delivered through enterprise portals, which can integrate disparate applications so that information appears to be coming from a single source.

5. *Identify the challenges posed by enterprise applications and management solutions.*

Enterprise applications are very difficult to implement successfully. They require extensive organizational change, large new software investments, and careful assessment of how these systems will enhance organizational performance. Management vision and foresight are required to take a firm- and industry-wide view of problems and to find solutions that realize strategic value from the investment. Enterprise applications create new interconnections among myriad business processes and data flows inside the firm (and in the case of supply chain management systems, between the firm and its external supply chain partners) to streamline operations and to make better management decisions. Employees are often unprepared for new procedures and roles. Enterprise applications cannot provide value if they are implemented atop flawed processes or if firms do not know how to use these systems to measure performance improvements.

Companies can meet these challenges by putting business objectives first, securing top management support, paying attention to data and data management, and providing education and training.

Key Terms

Analytical CRM, 397
Best practices, 381
Bullwhip effect, 387
Bundling, 395
Business process management, 401
Churn rate, 398
Cross-selling, 395
Customer lifetime value (CLTV), 399
Customer relationship management (CRM), 393

Demand planning, 389
Employee relationship management (ERM), 394
Enterprise software, 380
Just-in-time, 387
Logistics, 387
Metric, 389
Operational CRM, 397
Partner relationship management (PRM), 394
Pull-based model, 391

Push-based model, 391
Service platform, 401
Supply chain, 385
Supply chain execution systems, 389
Supply chain management, 385
Supply chain planning systems, 388
Touch point, 394
Up-selling, 395

Review Questions

1. *What is an enterprise system? How does enterprise software work?*

2. *How do enterprise systems provide value for a business?*

3. *What is a supply chain? What entities does it comprise? What is supply chain management?*

4. *List and describe the five major supply chain processes.*

5. *What is the bullwhip effect? How can supply chain management systems deal with it?*

6. *What are supply chain planning systems and supply chain execution systems? What functions do they perform?*

7. *How can the Internet and Internet technology facilitate supply chain management?*

8. *How do supply chain management systems provide value for a business?*

9. *What is customer relationship management? Why are customer relationships so important today?*

10. *How is partner relationship management (PRM) related to customer relationship management (CRM)?*

11. *Describe the tools and capabilities of customer relationship management software for sales, marketing, and customer service.*

12. *Distinguish between operational and analytical CRM.*

13. *How do customer relationship management systems provide value for a business?*

14. *What are service platforms? How can they be used with enterprise applications to provide more cross-functional process integration?*

15. *What are the challenges posed by enterprise applications? How can these challenges be addressed?*

Discussion Questions

1. *Supply chain management is less about managing the physical movement of goods and more about managing information. Discuss the implications of this statement.*

2. *If a company wants to implement an enterprise application, it had better do its homework. Discuss the implications of this statement.*

Application Software Exercise:
Database Exercise: Managing Customer Service Requests

Prime Service is a large service company that provides maintenance and repair services for close to 1,200 commercial businesses in New York, New Jersey, and Connecticut. Its customers include businesses of all sizes. Customers with service needs call into its customer service department with requests for repairing heating ducts, broken windows, leaky roofs, broken water pipes, and other problems. The company manually tracks the date each service request was made and assigns each request a service request number. The service requests are handled on a first-come, first-served basis. After the service work has been completed, Prime calculates the cost of the work and bills the client.

Management is not happy with this arrangement because the most important and profitable clients—those with accounts over $70,000—are treated no differently from its clients with small accounts. It would like to find a way to provide its best customers with better service. Management would also like to know which types of service problems occur the most frequently so that it can make sure it has adequate resources to address them.

Prime Service has a small database with client account information, which can be found on the Laudon Web site for Chapter 11. It includes fields for the account ID, company (account) name, street address, state, zip code, account size (in dollars), contact last name, contact first name, contact telephone number, and contact fax number. The contact is the name of the person in each company who is responsible for contacting Prime about maintenance and repair work. Use your database software to design a solution that would enable Prime's customer service representatives to identify the most important customers so that they could receive priority service. Your solution will require more than one table. Populate your database with at least 20 service requests. Create several reports that would be of interest to management, such as a list of the highest- and lowest-priority accounts or a report showing the most frequently occurring service problems. Create another report showing customer service representatives which service calls they should respond to first on a specific date.

Identifying Supply Chain Management Solutions

Required software: Web browser software
Word processing software
Electronic presentation software (optional)

A growing number of Dirt Bikes orders cannot be fulfilled on time because of delays in obtaining some important components and parts for its motorcycles, especially their fuel tanks. Complaints are mounting from distributors who fear losing sales if the dirt bikes they have ordered are delayed too long. Dirt Bikes management has asked you to help it address some of its supply chain issues.

1. Use the Internet to locate alternative suppliers for motorcycle fuel tanks. Identify two or three suppliers. Find out the amount of time and cost to ship a fuel tank (weighing about 5 pounds) by ground (surface delivery) from each supplier to Dirt Bikes in Carbondale, Colorado. Which supplier is most likely to take the shortest amount of time and cost the least to ship the fuel tanks?

2. Dirt Bikes management would like to know if there is any supply chain management software for a small business that would be appropriate for Dirt Bikes. Use the Internet to locate two supply chain management software providers for companies such as Dirt Bikes. Briefly describe the capabilities of the two software applications and indicate how they could help Dirt Bikes. Which supply chain management software product would be more appropriate for Dirt Bikes? Why?

3. (Optional) Use electronic presentation software to summarize your findings for management.

Electronic Business Project: Evaluating Supply Chain Management Services

Trucking companies no longer merely carry goods from one place to another. They can also provide supply chain management services to their customers and help them manage their information. Investigate the Web sites of two companies, J. B. Hunt (www.jbhunt.com) and Schneider Logistics (www.schneiderlogistics.com) to see how these companies' services can be used for supply chain management. Then respond to the following questions:

1. What supply chain processes can each of these companies support for their clients?

2. How can customers use the Web site of each company to help with supply chain management?

3. Compare the supply chain management services provided by these companies. Which company would you select to help your firm manage its supply chain? Why?

Group Project: Analyzing Enterprise Process Integration

Management at your agricultural chemicals corporation has been dissatisfied with production planning. Production plans are created using best guesses of demand for each product, which are based on how much of each product has been ordered in the past. If a customer places an unexpected order or requests a change to an existing order after it has been placed, there is no way to adjust production plans. The company may have to tell customers it cannot fill their orders, or it may accumulate extra costs maintaining additional inventory to prevent stockouts.

At the end of each month, orders are totaled and manually keyed into the company's production planning system. Data from the past month's production and inventory systems are manually entered into the firm's order management system. Analysts from the sales department and from the production department analyze the data from their respective systems to determine what the sales targets and production targets should be for the next month. These estimates are usually different. The analysts then get together at a high-level planning meeting to revise the production and sales targets to take into account senior management's goals for market share, reve-

nues, and profits. The outcome of the meeting is a finalized production master schedule.

The entire production planning process takes 17 business days to complete. Nine of these days are required to enter and validate the data. The remaining days are spent developing and reconciling the production and sales targets and finalizing the production master schedule.

With a group of three or four students, prepare an analysis of this scenario:

1. Draw a diagram of the existing production planning process.

2. Analyze the problems this process creates for the company.

3. How could an enterprise system solve these problems? In what ways could it reduce costs? Diagram what the production planning process might look like if the company implemented enterprise software.

4. If possible, use electronic presentation software to present your findings to the class.

CASE STUDY
Can Information Systems Restore Profitability to Restoration Hardware?

Restoration Hardware is a retailer of furniture, hardware, and home accessories such as bathroom fixtures and decorative furnishings. The company is based in California; it started operations in 1979 and incorporated in 1987. The company sells through multiple channels: a network of 103 retail stores across the United States and Canada, a print mail-order catalog, and its RestorationHardware.com Web site. Restoration Hardware is a major player in an industry that includes competitors such as Pottery Barn, Pier 1, and Williams Sonoma. Restoration employs 3,500 workers, 1,400 of those full-time.

Restoration's business strategy puts the company in a unique sector of the marketplace. Restoration focused from the start on merchandise that honors classic America. The company's original furniture and fixtures were designed to match the décor and form of older houses. Today, when you walk into a Restoration Hardware store, the merchandise clearly evokes images of the past. Many products, such as portable record players or wooden toys, are intent on inspiring feelings of tradition, if not nostalgia, in older generations of customers. The younger generations may recognize these products from reruns of old television shows and movies set in the times of their parents and grandparents. Many of these products are difficult to find elsewhere and they are very appealing. Up front, the company knows what it wants to do and has maintained a consistent vision. According to Ed Weller, an analyst at ThinkEquity Partners, "When you go to the stores, it's clear that Restoration Hardware has something customers want." Many of Restoration's top executives come from merchandising backgrounds.

A significant portion of Restoration's revenue stream comes from its direct-to-customer ventures. Circulation of the mail-order catalog

surpassed 30 million in 2003, with 58 percent of the catalogs earmarked for past customers. Mail-order catalog and Web site operations saw substantial revenue gains both in the fourth quarter (51%) and annual (52%) numbers for 2003.

In recent years, the company has improved its e-commerce software, increasing its capacity to support simultaneous online shoppers by 8,000 percent. This upgrade to Art Technology Group's e-commerce software is just one of several technology investments that Restoration has made in its Web site. In late 2003, Restoration brought in iPhrase Technologies to implement its One Step natural language search and navigation software as a replacement for RestorationHardware.com's keyword-oriented product search facility. The new search technology has made the Web site more user-friendly.

In March 2004, Scene7, Inc., a provider of dynamic imaging software, announced that Restoration Hardware had adopted Scene7's eCatalog solution for its online print catalog. Restoration now outsources the entire process of publishing and hosting its print catalog on the Web. Restoration only has to provide Scene7 with the print catalog in Portable Document Format (PDF). The published Web catalog includes dynamic links from areas on each catalog page to corresponding product pages on the Restoration Hardware Web site. Scene7's eCatalog solution has also made it possible to implement advanced image-viewing features such as panning, zooming, and rollover product descriptions. Additionally, customers can now use a "colorizer" feature to change the fabric style on any upholstered product that they are viewing. Such technology saves Restoration from the enormous expenses that would accompany studio photography of all the different combinations of fabric and furniture. According to Scene7, its

eCatalog solution has resulted in the doubling of Restoration Hardware's conversion rate of browsers to buyers.

Despite a strong product line and upward growth in sales, Restoration has not been able to make money. By the end of 2003 the company posted a $2.9 million net loss, down from $3.9 million the previous year. The year 2003 was the fifth straight year the company did not turn a profit. Analysts point to the less-visible aspects of Restoration's business, specifically its supply chain management systems and technology infrastructure, as profit drains. Russell Hoss, a Roth Capital Partners analyst, states that Restoration simply does not "know how to make money." Good products alone do not guarantee success. Retail businesses need to juggle an extraordinarily complex system of variables to meet their expectations of success. The analysts contend that Restoration Hardware is failing to control these variables to the best of its ability. Among the greatest concerns is Restoration's ability to keep its inventory in line with customer demand.

Over the 2003 holiday shopping season, same-store sales figures for Restoration experienced a drop of 3.5 percent from the previous year's holiday season. One of the biggest culprits was a line of couches and chairs that shoppers can customize by choosing from a selection of 50 fabric styles, with delivery promised within 8 to 10 weeks. High demand of the most popular styles set off a chain reaction of profit-draining events. Customers had to wait longer than they had been told initially to receive their couches and chairs. In some cases, the customers simply canceled their orders. Other customers chose to purchase less-popular styles instead, with the incentive of a discounted price. Some of the orders that customers did not cancel could not be fulfilled in time to count in the holiday season sales figures.

In the last few years, Restoration has implemented a repositioning plan, which involves reducing the company's debt, upgrading management, weeding out poor products from the product line, and closing stores that aren't performing. Additionally, the company has introduced new products and remodeled its retail locations. The plan does not address improvements to the company's aging information technology (IT) infrastructure.

Restoration Hardware stores use point-of-sale equipment that is nearly 10 years old. The equipment lacks the capability to process debit card purchases without a physical signature, nor can it automate processes such as checking fabric stocks when a customer makes a request for a custom furniture order. Customers placing custom furniture orders must fill out a paper form that includes their fabric selection. Then a salesperson must call Michael's Furniture (which manufactures Restoration's furniture) in Sacramento, California, to see what is in stock.

A system polls Restoration stores nightly to aggregate sales, inventory, and pricing data to provide information that can help managers fine-tune the company's merchandise assortments. However, the system is not capable of providing demand forecasting. Restoration has systems to support "smooth warehouse operations in a multi-warehouse environment" consisting of three warehouses in California and one in Baltimore.

Restoration Hardware's most recent annual report on Form 10-K for the U.S. Securities and Exchange Commission states that the company relies on a single vendor for its point-of-sale, merchandise management, and warehouse management systems, along with the software support required to maintain these systems. Restoration purchased these systems and services from STS Systems, which has since become part of NSB Group, in the mid-1990s. NSB's most recent version of its warehouse-management system is far more advanced than the version that Restoration continues to use, with capabilities for XML-enabled processing of advance shipping notices and real-time task tracking. Upgrades to the older version of the system are covered by Restoration's service agreement with NSB, but Restoration has not taken advantage of the new technology. The company has also not improved its systems for restocking its products once they have been distributed from the various warehouses.

Statistics show that in areas such as frequency of inventory turnover and gross profit margin, Restoration trails its competitors. During the 12 months ending November 1, 2003, Restoration turned over its inventory only 1.9 times, compared to 3.2 times at Williams Sonoma. Restoration's gross profit margin is only 30 percent, putting it among the lowest-category performers for its industry even though same-store sales for 2003 averaged 7 percent higher than the previous year.

Restoration's annual report paints a picture of a complex business environment that is vulnerable to a host of trends, restrictions, and abnormalities. From a competition standpoint, Restoration's offerings place it in the same realm as specialty stores, traditional furniture stores, and department stores. At stake are customers, viable store locations, suppliers, and personnel. Restoration asserts that many of its competitors have greater financial, marketing, and operational resources for obtaining these assets, and that such hearty competition puts its financial performance and future success at risk. To stay in the race Restoration believes that the company should focus on fortifying its management, improving and increasing its product line, improving customer service, enhancing its presentation of merchandise, and maintaining competitive pricing and retail locations.

The report goes on to say, "Our success is highly dependent on improvements to our planning and supply chain process. . . . An important part of our efforts to achieve efficiencies, cost reductions and sales growth is the identification and implementation of improvements to our planning, logistical and distribution infrastructure and our supply chain. . . . An inability to improve our planning and supply chain processes or to take full advantage of supply chain opportunities could have a material adverse effect on our operating results." The company must also be able to better anticipate consumer trends. Restoration does not speculate on how successful it will be at implementing these improvements or offer any specific plans for doing so.

The one thing that Restoration Hardware does seem sure of is the litany of factors that could undermine its future success. These include seasonal fluctuations in revenue (including a dependence on peak sales and earnings from the fourth-quarter holiday season), dependence on vendors to supply merchandise and services, disruptions in distribution to stores from its warehouses, labor strife, dependence on external funding, trade restrictions and currency fluctuations associated with foreign imports and purchases, general economic conditions, and the negative impacts on business of war and threats of terrorism.

Each of these factors has its own set of variables that adds to the unpredictability of running a retail business. For example, Restoration acquires its merchandise from a pool of over 500 vendors. However, two vendors were the sources of nearly one-quarter of all merchandise purchases in 2003. Restoration does not have purchase contracts with these two vendors, or with any of their smaller vendors. Therefore, the company has no guarantee that it can continue to acquire the merchandise that it intends to market in the proper quantities, at the appropriate cost, or at all. Additionally, many vendors must have purchase orders submitted well in advance of when Restoration wants to move its inventory to the shelves of its stores. This long lead time leaves the company without the ability to respond to sales trends, which is especially risky during the holiday season, when Restoration also spends more money on marketing and personnel. The company expects to hit certain sales highs during the holidays. Failure to do so as a result of insufficient inventory or a miscalculation of what products will appeal to shoppers can have significant negative impact on the health of the business.

Restoration purchased nearly half of its merchandise from foreign vendors in 2003 and the company expects the percentage of foreign goods to rise in the future. Importing goods adds another layer of risk factors for the business. Tariffs, quotas, trade relations and restrictions, political unrest, shipping costs, exchange rates, and other variables all mitigate Restoration's ability to maximize the efficiency of its supply chain. The company must weigh the risks involved with importing merchandise against the benefits, such as cheaper goods and the availability of products that cannot be purchased anywhere else.

Restoration's report even points out that its thriving direct-to-customer operations may not sustain its current level of profitability. Decreased performance by those departments could be detrimental to the profitability of the business as a whole. Even though Restoration has placed great empha-

sis on upgrading the direct-to-customer operations, they remain as vulnerable to risk factors as the rest of the business.

Although a business such as Restoration Hardware faces numerous obstacles in operating to a profit, many of those outlined by the company are speculation or worst-case scenarios. Nevertheless, loss of revenue during the key selling period of the year is clear evidence of a problem that needs attention.

Sources: Larry Dignan, "Restoration Project," *Baseline Magazine*, February 2004; Restoration Hardware 10-K Report for the Fiscal Year Ending January 31, 2004, www.restorationhardware.com; "Restoration Hardware," Corporate Design Foundation, www.cdf.org, accessed April 20, 2004; "Restoration Hardware Increases Conversion Rates Using Scene7's eCatalog e-Merchandising Solutions," www.scene7.com/news, accessed March 23, 2004; "Restoration Hardware Reports Mixed Annual Results," Home Channel News, March 19, 2004; "Financial Reports: Direct Business Soars at Restoration Hardware," *Catalog Age*, March 24, 2004; "Hardware Chain Makes

Progress on Restoration," *San Francisco Business Times,* March 18, 2004; and "Restoration Hardware Utilizes iPhrase to Drive Sales and Provide Industry-Leading Self-Service Shopping Experience," *Internet Retailer,* December 1, 2003.

CASE STUDY QUESTIONS

1. Evaluate Restoration Hardware using the value chain and competitive forces models. How is the company responding to the forces that influence it?

2. What is Restoration Hardware's business strategy? How well do the company's information systems support that strategy?

3. What management, organization, and technology factors are responsible for the problems Restoration Hardware is encountering?

4. What role does supply chain management play at Restoration Hardware?

5. How can Restoration Hardware improve its information systems to solve its problems?

Chapter 12

Managing Knowledge in the Digital Firm

OBJECTIVES

After completing this chapter, you will be able to:

1. Assess the role of knowledge management and knowledge management programs in business.

2. Define and describe the types of systems used for enterprise-wide knowledge management and demonstrate how they provide value for organizations.

3. Define and describe the major types of knowledge work systems and assess how they provide value for firms.

4. Evaluate the business benefits of using intelligent techniques for knowledge management.

5. Identify the challenges posed by knowledge management systems and management solutions.

CHAPTER OUTLINE

12.1 THE KNOWLEDGE MANAGEMENT LANDSCAPE
Important Dimensions of Knowledge
Organizational Learning and Knowledge Management
The Knowledge Management Value Chain
Types of Knowledge Management Systems

12.2 ENTERPRISE-WIDE KNOWLEDGE MANAGEMENT SYSTEMS
Structured Knowledge Systems
Semistructured Knowledge Systems
Knowledge Network Systems
Supporting Technologies: Portals, Collaboration Tools, and Learning Management Systems

12.3 KNOWLEDGE WORK SYSTEMS
Knowledge Workers and Knowledge Work
Requirements of Knowledge Work Systems
Examples of Knowledge Work Systems

12.4 INTELLIGENT TECHNIQUES
Capturing Knowledge: Expert Systems
Organizational Intelligence: Case-Based Reasoning
Fuzzy Logic Systems
Neural Networks
Genetic Algorithms
Hybrid AI Systems
Intelligent Agents

12.5 MANAGEMENT OPPORTUNITIES, CHALLENGES, AND SOLUTIONS
Opportunities
Management Challenges
Solution Guidelines

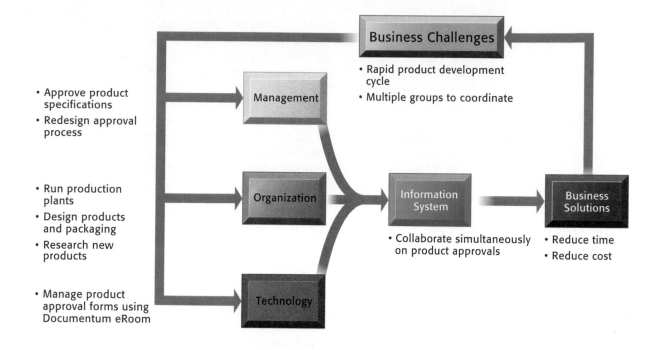

- Approve product specifications
- Redesign approval process

Management

Business Challenges
- Rapid product development cycle
- Multiple groups to coordinate

- Run production plants
- Design products and packaging
- Research new products

Organization

Information System
- Collaborate simultaneously on product approvals

Business Solutions
- Reduce time
- Reduce cost

- Manage product approval forms using Documentum eRoom

Technology

Opening Case: Cott Struggles to Manage Unstructured Information

Cott Corporation is the world's leading supplier of store-brand soft drinks and juices, with beverage manufacturing facilities in the United States, Canada, Mexico, and the United Kingdom and a concentrate production plant and research and development center in Columbus, Georgia. Like other companies in its industry, Cott is under pressure to bring out new products very quickly.

Cott had been using e-mail to route product approval forms with details such as a new product's flavor formula or the artwork for a bottle label to managers of various groups involved in the product development process. Difficulties controlling this unstructured information delayed efforts to get new soda and juice products onto store shelves. Because of time lags in routing e-mail from one person to another, it took an average of 60 days for a form to obtain all the necessary approvals. People would begin various production activities before the approval was finalized in order to avoid delaying production of new beverages. But changes were inevitably required. The art department might start working on a product label based on an approval form and later learn that they needed to modify the design because of a change in equipment that affected the label's dimensions. Production of the

new product might be moved to a different plant. As CIO Douglas Neary observed, "This was a major business problem that needed to be solved."

Cott solved this problem by adopting Documentum eRoom software to manage product approval forms. The software enables employees to set up online project work spaces to create and share documents. The documents are preserved in a company-wide document repository where they can be easily shared and accessed by everyone working on a new product. Each time a new product order triggers the creation of a new product approval form, the system sets up a work space for that product. Managers of various groups involved in product development can track the form, view any changes to the form, and work jointly with others on changes that affect multiple areas of production. By managing product approval information more effectively, Cott's product approval process takes only two to three days and production is much more efficient.

Sources: Tony Kontzer, "Content Overload," *Information Week*, January 19, 2004; "New Product Development," www.documentum.com, accessed June 12, 2004; and www.cott.com, accessed June 12, 2004.

Cott Corporation's experience shows how organizational performance can benefit by making organizational knowledge more easily available. Collaborating and communicating with practitioners and experts, creating new knowledge, facilitating access to knowledge, and using that knowledge to improve business processes and decision making have become vital to organizational innovation and survival. As a manager, you'll want to know how your firm can benefit from information systems for knowledge management.

In this chapter, we look at information systems that are specifically designed to help organizations create, capture, distribute, and apply knowledge and information. First, we discuss how knowledge has become such an important organizational asset and the series of processes that transform data into useful knowledge. Next, we describe the major types of systems for knowledge management. We conclude by discussing the steps that can be taken by managers to ensure knowledge management systems provide value for the firm.

12.1   THE KNOWLEDGE MANAGEMENT LANDSCAPE

There has been a surge of interest in knowledge management, and knowledge management systems have become one of the fastest-growing areas of corporate and government software investment. Figure 12-1 shows that sales of enterprise content management software for knowledge management are expected to grow 35 percent annually through 2006, even though overall software sales are projected to grow only 6 percent annually during the same period (eMarketer, 2003). The past decade has likewise shown an explosive growth in research on knowledge and knowledge management in the economics, management, and information systems fields (Alavi and Leidner, 2001; Cole, 1998; Spender, 1996).

Why all the interest in knowledge management? Chapter 1 describes the emergence of the information economy and the digital firm in which the major source of wealth and prosperity is the production and distribution of information and knowledge and how firms increasingly rely on digital technology to enable business processes. For example, 55 percent of the U.S. labor force consists of knowledge and information workers, and 60 percent of the gross domestic product of the United States comes from the knowledge and information sectors, such as finance and publishing. Knowledge management has become an important theme at many large business firms as managers realize that much of their firm's value depends on the firm's ability to create and manage knowledge. Studies have found that a substantial part of a firm's stock market value is related to its intangible assets, of which knowledge is one important component, along with brands, reputations, and unique business processes. (Lev, 2004; Gu and Lev, 2004). Well-executed knowledge-based projects have been known to produce extraordinary returns on investment, although knowledge-based investments are difficult to measure (Blair and Wallman, 2001).

Important Dimensions of Knowledge

There is an important distinction between data, information, knowledge, and wisdom. Chapter 1 defines *data* as a flow of events or transactions captured by an organization's systems that, by itself, is useful for transacting but little else. To turn data into useful *information,* a firm must expend resources to organize data into categories of understanding, such as monthly, daily, regional, or store-based reports of total sales. To transform information into **knowledge,** a firm must expend additional resources to discover patterns, rules, and contexts where the knowledge works. Finally, **wisdom** is thought to be the collective and individual experience of applying knowledge to the solution of problems. Wisdom involves where, when, and how to apply knowledge.

Knowledge is both an individual attribute and a collective attribute of the firm. Knowledge is a cognitive, even a physiological, event, that takes place inside peoples' heads, but it is also stored in libraries and records; shared in lectures; and stored by firms in the form of business processes and employee know-how. Knowledge residing in the minds of employees that has not been documented is called **tacit knowledge,** whereas knowledge that has been documented is called **explicit knowledge.** Knowledge can reside

FIGURE 12-1   *U.S. enterprise knowledge management software revenues, 2001–2006.*

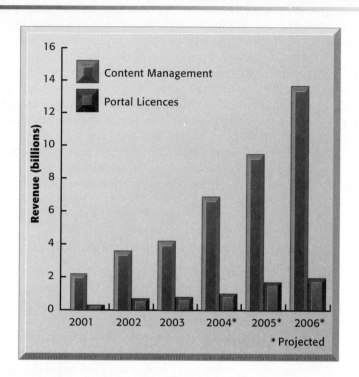

Enterprise knowledge management software includes sales of content management and portal licenses, which have been growing at a rate of 35 percent annually, making it among the fastest-growing software applications.

Source: Based on data in eMarketer, "Portals and Content Management Solutions," June 2003.

in e-mail, voice mail, graphics, and unstructured documents as well as structured documents. Knowledge is generally believed to have a location, either in the minds of humans or in specific business processes. Knowledge is "sticky" and not universally applicable or easily moved. Finally, knowledge is thought to be situational and contextual. For example, you must know when to perform a procedure as well as how to perform it. Table 12-1 reviews these dimensions of knowledge.

TABLE 12-1 *Important Dimensions of Knowledge*

Knowledge Is a Firm Asset

Knowledge is an intangible asset.

The transformation of data into useful information and knowledge requires organizational resources.

Knowledge is not subject to the law of diminishing returns as are physical assets, but instead experiences network effects (law of expanding returns) as its value increases as more people share it.

Knowledge Has Different Forms

Knowledge can be either tacit or explicit (codified).

Knowledge involves know-how, craft, and skill.

Knowledge involves knowing how to follow procedures.

Knowledge involves knowing why, not simply when, things happen (causality).

Knowledge Has a Location

Knowledge is a cognitive event involving mental models and maps of individuals.

There is both a social and an individual basis of knowledge.

Knowledge is "sticky" (hard to move), situated (enmeshed in a firm's culture), and contextual (works only in certain situations).

Knowledge Is Situational

Knowledge is conditional: Knowing when to apply a procedure is just as important as knowing the procedure (conditional).

Knowledge is related to context: You must know how to use a certain tool and under what circumstances.

We can see that knowledge is a different kind of firm asset from, say, buildings and financial assets; that knowledge is a complex phenomenon; and that there are many aspects to the process of managing knowledge. We can also recognize that knowledge-based core competencies of firms—the two or three things that an organization does best—are key organizational assets. Knowing how to do things effectively and efficiently in ways that other organizations cannot duplicate is a primary source of profit and competitive advantage that cannot be purchased easily by competitors in the marketplace.

For instance, having a unique build-to-order production system or customer relationship management system constitutes a form of knowledge and can be a unique asset that other firms cannot copy easily. With knowledge, firms become more efficient and effective in their use of scarce resources. Without knowledge, firms become less efficient and less effective in their use of resources and ultimately fail. Organizations differ in their abilities to apply knowledge, and firms that apply knowledge more effectively than competitors are more successful.

Organizational Learning and Knowledge Management

How do firms obtain knowledge and how do firms manage knowledge? Like humans, organizations create and gather knowledge using a variety of organizational learning mechanisms. Through collection of data, careful measurement of planned activities, trial and error (experiment), and feedback from customers and the environment in general, organizations gain experience. Organizations that learn then adjust their behavior to reflect that learning by creating new business processes and by changing patterns of management decision making. This process of change is called **organizational learning**. Arguably organizations that can sense and respond to their environments rapidly will survive longer than organizations that have poor learning mechanisms.

The Knowledge Management Value Chain

Knowledge management refers to the set of business processes developed in an organization to create, store, transfer, and apply knowledge. Knowledge management is, in this sense, an enabler of organizational learning. Knowledge management increases the ability of the organization to learn from its environment and to incorporate knowledge into its business processes. Figure 12-2 illustrates the five value-adding steps in the knowledge management value chain. Each stage in the value chain adds value to raw data and information as they are transformed into usable knowledge.

In Figure 12-2, a line divides information systems activities and related management and organizational activities, with information systems activities on the top of the graphic and organizational and management activities below. One apt slogan of the knowledge management field is, "Effective knowledge management is 80 percent managerial and organizational, and 20 percent technology."

In Chapter 1 we define *organizational and management capital* as the set of business processes, culture, and behavior required to obtain value from investments in information systems. In the case of knowledge management, as with other information systems investments, supportive values, structures, and behavior patterns must be built to maximize the return on investment in knowledge management projects. In Figure 12-2, the management and organizational activities in the lower half of the diagram represent the investment in organizational capital required to obtain substantial returns on the information technology (IT) investments and systems shown in the top half of the diagram.

KNOWLEDGE ACQUISITION

Organizations acquire knowledge in a number of ways, depending on the type of knowledge they seek. The first knowledge management systems sought to build corporate libraries of documents, reports, presentations, and best practices and encouraged employees to create documents based on their experiences. These efforts have been extended to include unstructured documents (such as e-mail). In other cases organiza-

FIGURE 12-2   *The knowledge management value chain.*

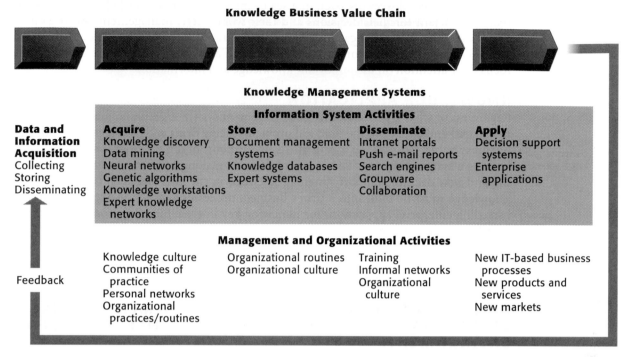

Knowledge management today involves both information systems activities and a host of enabling management and organizational activities.

tions acquire knowledge by developing online expert networks so that employees can "find the expert" in the company who has the knowledge in his or her head.

In still other cases firms must create new knowledge by discovering patterns in corporate data or by using knowledge workstations where engineers can discover new knowledge. These various efforts are described throughout this chapter. A coherent and organized knowledge system also requires systematic data from the firm's transaction processing systems that track sales, payments, inventory, customers, and other vital data, as well as data from external sources such as news feeds, industry reports, legal opinions, scientific research, and government statistics.

KNOWLEDGE STORAGE

Once they are discovered, documents, patterns, and expert rules must be stored so they can be retrieved and used by employees. Knowledge storage generally involves the creation of a database. **Document management systems** that digitize, index, and tag documents according to a coherent framework are large databases adept at storing collections of documents. Communities of expertise and expert systems also help corporations preserve the knowledge that is acquired by incorporating that knowledge into organizational processes and culture. Each of these is discussed later in this chapter and in the following chapter.

Management must support the development of planned knowledge storage systems, encourage the development of corporate-wide schemas for indexing documents, and reward employees for taking the time to update and store documents properly. For instance, it would reward the sales force for submitting names of prospects to a shared corporate database of prospects where all sales personnel can identify each prospect and review the stored knowledge.

KNOWLEDGE DISSEMINATION

Portal, e-mail, instant messaging, and search engine technology have resulted in an explosion of "knowledge" and information dissemination. These technologies have added to an existing array of groupware technologies and office systems for sharing calendars, documents, data, and graphics (see Chapter 8). Rather than a shortage of information and

FIGURE 12-7 *Hummingbird's integrated knowledge management system.*

Hummingbird's enterprise solution combines document management, knowledge management, business intelligence, and portal technologies and can be used for managing semistructured as well as structured knowledge.

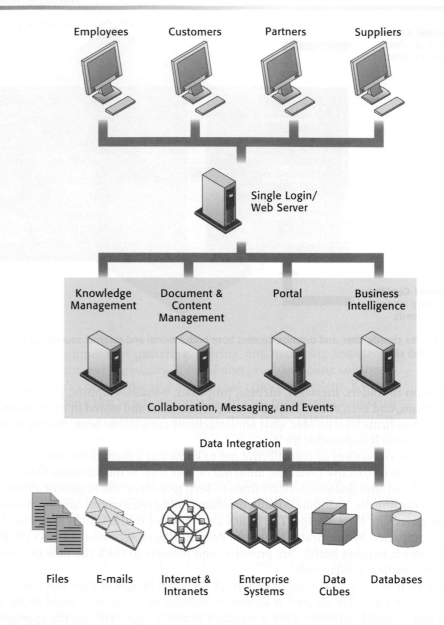

One user of Hummingbird's enterprise knowledge management system is Hennigan, Bennett and Dorman LLP, a Los Angeles-based law firm. The firm handles many big-name, multiparticipant lawsuits, such as government bankruptcies or institutional shareholder fraud cases. New requests for electronic discovery require a legal team to sift through thousands of electronic messages to search for potential evidence. The firm was inundated with backup tapes of hundreds of thousands of e-mail messages and needed a way to filter that information into something its attorneys could use more easily. The firm implemented Hummingbird's Enterprise document management system, which automates the capture, manipulation, and distribution of document-based knowledge embedded in e-mail. Instead of sifting through piles of printed copies of e-mails, attorneys can run powerful electronic searches, locating only the e-mails they need for a case and marking them up electronically. The system can also re-create all of the threads of an entire e-mail discussion for attorneys to follow and scan e-mail attachments. Using this system has cut the time to process e-mail in half (Hummingbird, 2003a).

Another Hummingbird user is Cuatrecasas, a leading Spanish law firm described in the Window on Management. Cuatrecasas implemented Hummingbird Enterprise to provide a standard platform for organizing and managing both structured and semistructured information. Cuatrecasas maintains many offices in many different locations, each previously with its own information systems. The only way information could be shared among offices was by e-mail, and that was also difficult to manage because of version control problems. These problems were solved by adopting a single platform for enterprise-wide knowledge management.

ORGANIZING KNOWLEDGE: TAXONOMIES AND TAGGING

One of the first challenges that firms face when building knowledge repositories of any kind is the problem of identifying the correct categories to use when classifying documents. It is, of course, possible simply to "dump" millions of documents into a large database and rely on search engine technology to produce results for users. However, a brute search engine approach produces far too many results for the user to cope with and evaluate.

Firms are increasingly using a combination of internally developed taxonomies and search engine techniques. A **taxonomy** is a scheme for classifying information and knowledge in such a way that it can be easily accessed. A taxonomy is like a table of contents in a book or like the Library of Congress system for classifying books and periodicals according to subject matter and author. A business firm can access information much more easily if it devises its own taxonomy for classifying information into logical categories. The more precise the taxonomy, the more relevant are the search results produced by search engines. Once a knowledge taxonomy is produced, documents are all *tagged* with the proper classification. Generally, Extensible Markup Language (XML) tags are used for this purpose so the documents can be easily retrieved in a Web-based system.

Products such as ActiveKnowledge (Autonomy Corporation) and Taxonomy (Semio Corporation) attempt to reduce the burden on users by categorizing documents using an existing corporate taxonomy. Such products consider the user's prior searches, the context of the search term in the document (the relationships between words in a document), related concepts the user may not have entered, as well as keyword frequency and the popularity of the document. The purpose of these newer tools is to increase the probability that the correct response will be in the first 10 results.

Several tools perform auto tagging and reduce the need for managers to develop their own unique taxonomies. Semio's Tagger software is a categorization and indexing engine that identifies key phrases in documents, assigns relevance factors to these phrases, and organizes the documents into categories, creating XML-based document tags using rules that users can see and modify. Tagger can access more than 200 different document types stored in legacy, enterprise, or other intranet databases. Users can integrate existing taxonomy categories and add, delete, or merge categories after examining how the system responds. Semio claims that its semiautomatic system can achieve 95 percent of the accuracy obtained by manually reviewing and tagging documents in a fraction of the time required for manual efforts (**www.semio.com**).

One user of Semio's auto-tagging tools is Stanford University's HighWire Press, which publishes 298 online journals containing more than 12 million articles. When the company expanded its collection in 2001 from 1 million to 12 million articles, it needed a way to automate and expand its indexing process. It also needed to provide researchers with better browsing and searching capabilities to support the discovery of unexpected relationships, to link articles from a variety of disciplines, to identify concepts in articles, and to link these concepts in logical categories. Currently, the system has developed 22,000 categories and more than 300,000 concepts. The system supports 84 million hits each week with a database of 6 terabytes (Semio, 2003). The system requires some active management. HighWire Press reviews its classification scheme every month and makes changes based on user feedback and management insight.

Knowledge Network Systems

Knowledge network systems address the problem that arises when the appropriate knowledge is not in the form of a digital document but instead resides in the memory of expert individuals in the firm. According to a survey by KPMG, 63 percent of employees in Fortune 500 firms complain of the difficulty in accessing undocumented knowledge as a

WINDOW ON MANAGEMENT

AN ENTERPRISE-WIDE KNOWLEDGE MANAGEMENT SYSTEM PAYS OFF FOR CUATRECASAS

Cuatrecasas is one of Spain's largest independent law firms, specializing in all areas of business law, including corporate and finance, litigation, tax, and labor. The firm was founded in 1917 and now has 600 attorneys and 17 offices in the principal cities of Spain and Portugal, New York City, Brussels, and Sao Paulo. Many Cuatrecasas clients are the largest businesses in Spain, and the firm is especially active in foreign investments in Spain and in counseling Spanish companies expanding abroad.

Cuatrecasas desperately needed to improve collaboration, information exchange, and reuse of knowledge assets among its far-flung employees. Each office had its own file system, so lawyers and other employees had no common medium other than e-mail for searching, accessing, or sharing the firm's collective knowledge assets. Even information in e-mail could not be used efficiently because of problems with version control. Very few internal announcements documents and other content were published on the firm's homegrown intranet because the available tools were too difficult to use. The existing infrastructure prevented Cuatrecasas from effectively creating online communities where attorneys could obtain information about best practices.

In May 2002, Cuatrecasas chose Hummingbird Enterprise portal and knowledge management solutions. Hummingbird provided a broad range of capabilities, could be implemented in a relatively short period of time, and allowed for ongoing customization. Cuatrecasas started with two pilot projects with a select group of end users in March 2002. The firm's information systems team spent the period from April through June defining user profiles and standardizing taxonomies for classifying information. By mid-January 2003, nearly 1,000 Cuatrecasas employees in 10 global offices had been trained to use the system.

Cuatrecasas used Hummingbird to create a standardized platform for centralized document management, collaboration, and information sharing using a single Web-based desktop interface. Employees across all global office locations—but especially attorneys and administrative assistants—can easily and rapidly locate and share information and reuse best practices, regardless of where they work. The new system helped Cuatrecasas reduce the time formerly spent on document management by 10 percent.

The firm can publish nearly three times as much content as in the past and it can publish this volume of content three to four times more rapidly than before. Publishing the same volume and quality of content with the same speed would have required one full-time dedicated information systems employee, so Cuatrecasas saved $50,000 annually with its new publishing capability.

Standardizing on a single knowledge management platform has reduced infrastructure costs. Current Cuatrecasas offices have been able to reuse file servers that were formerly required to support disparate file systems. Some of these file servers can be deployed in new offices that the firm expects to open over the next three years. Cuatrecasas can also save on its costs for information systems staff. Before Hummingbird was implemented, information systems personnel spent almost 10 percent of their time maintaining disparate file systems and infrastructures at individual offices. A standardized system reduced the time that information systems staff had to spend on all of Cuatrecasas's disconnected systems.

Cuatrecasas subsequently implemented a client extranet that permits its clients to access and retrieve documents related to their cases electronically without contacting their attorneys' administrative staff. As use of this extranet expands, the firm anticipates lower administrative costs for client support.

How much value did Cuatrecasas obtain from its new knowledge management system? Nucleus Research was assigned to find out. Nucleus quantified the benefits provided by the system and Cuatrecasas's total investment in software, hardware, consulting, personnel, training, and other expenditures over a three-year period. Software costs for the initial Hummingbird licenses and annual license maintenance fees amounted to 42 percent of overall costs. Consulting costs in the first year made up over one-fifth of total costs. Time spent by Cuatrecasas information systems staff on the initial implementation of the system amounted to 15 percent of costs, while hardware costs were only 7 percent of total costs. The remaining costs were for training. Direct and indirect benefits far outweighed the costs of the system, producing a net cash flow after taxes of nearly $700,000 each year.

Cuatrecasas was able to reduce infrastructure costs by deploying existing hardware and by using Hummingbird publishing capabilities to eliminate the need for a full-time information systems employee. Additional savings came from increased productivity of both users and information systems staff. Users did not need to spend as much time as in the past searching for and sharing documents. Information systems staff no longer had to maintain so many disparate systems. Nucleus did not put a price tag on the decreased administrative costs that the company expects to achieve in the future once its client extranet is widely adopted.

Nucleus used various capital budgeting models (see Chapter 15) to analyze Cuatrecasas's return on its Hummingbird knowledge system investment. It found that over a three-year period, the new system produced an annual rate of return on investment (ROI) of 84 percent and achieved a payback of the initial investment in only 1.2 years.

Sources: "A Law Firm's Nucleus of Knowledge," *KM World*, February 2004; and Nucleus Research, "ROI Case Study: Hummingbird Cuatrecasas," www.hummingbird.com, accessed June 10, 2004.

To Think About: Why would a knowledge management system be especially useful for a law firm such as Cuatrecasas? What problems did the Hummingbird system solve for this firm? How did the Hummingbird system provide value for this company?

FIGURE 12-8   *The problem of distributed knowledge.*

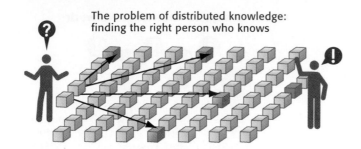

The problem of distributed knowledge: finding the right person who knows

In many organizations, essential knowledge is not available even though someone in the firm may have the information. The problem is finding the right person or group.

major problem. Because the knowledge cannot be conveniently found, employees expend significant resources rediscovering knowledge. An International Data Corporation (IDC) study estimated that the average cost of redundant effort in Fortune 500 companies exceeds $60 million per year per firm (AskMe, 2003a). Figure 12-8 illustrates the problem of "collective ignorance," a situation in which someone in a firm knows the answer, but that knowledge is not collectively shared.

Knowledge network systems seek to turn tacit, unstructured, and undocumented knowledge into explicit knowledge that can be stored in a database. Solutions that are developed by experts and others in the firm are added to the knowledge database. This new knowledge can be stored as recommended best business practices or as an answer in a database of frequently asked questions. Table 12-3 lists some of the key features of enterprise knowledge network systems.

AskMe, Inc., produces a widely adopted enterprise knowledge network system. Its users include Procter & Gamble and Intec Engineering Partnership, a project management company with more than 500 employees worldwide serving the global oil and gas industry. The software, AskMe Enterprise, enables firms to develop a database of employee expertise and know-how, documents, best practices, and FAQs, and then to share that information across the firm using whichever portal technology the firm has adopted.

Figure 12-9 illustrates how AskMe Enterprise works. An Intec engineer with a question, for instance, could access relevant documents, Web links, and answers to previous related questions by initiating a keyword search. If the answer could not be found, that person could post a general question on a Web page for categories such as Pipeline or Subsea for other engineers accessing that page to answer. Alternatively, the person could review the profiles of all company engineers with relevant expertise and send a detailed e-mail query to experts who might have the answer. All questions and answers are automatically incorporated into the knowledge database.

TABLE 12-3 *Key Features of Enterprise Knowledge Network Systems*

Features	Description
Knowledge exchange services	Support for interactive Q&A sessions
	Ability to identify qualified firm experts
	Publish and share documented knowledge with all employees
Community of practice support	Ability to connect experts across functions and units
	Ability to push information to communities
	Strong collaborative tools for communities, such as scheduling, document retrieval, and communication
Autoprofiling capabilities	Ability to profile employee experts automatically
	Ability to permit individuals to manage their own profiles
Knowledge management services	Automatically manage the nomination, approval, and dissemination of best practices and solutions
	Ensure business knowledge and rules conform to regulations and support business processes

FIGURE 12-9   *AskMe Enterprise knowledge network system.*

A knowledge network maintains a database of firm experts, as well as accepted solutions to known problems, and then facilitates the communication between employees looking for knowledge and experts who have that knowledge. Solutions created in this communication are then added to a database of solutions in the form of FAQs, best practices, or other documents.

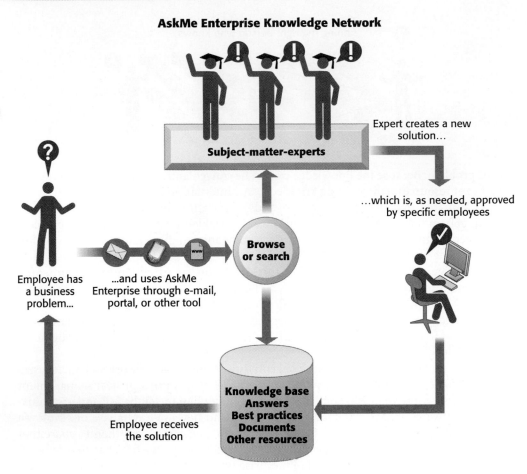

Supporting Technologies: Portals, Collaboration Tools, and Learning Management Systems

The major commercial knowledge management system vendors are integrating their content and document management capabilities with powerful portal and collaboration technologies. Enterprise knowledge portals provide access to external sources of information, such as news feeds and research, as well as to internal knowledge resources along with capabilities for e-mail, chat/instant messaging, discussion groups, and videoconferencing. Users can, for example, easily add a collection of documents obtained through a portal to a collaborative work space. The Gartner Group consulting firm uses the term *Smart Enterprise Suites* for this leading-edge knowledge management software.

LEARNING MANAGEMENT SYSTEMS

Companies need ways to keep track of and manage employee learning and to integrate it more fully into their knowledge management and other corporate systems. A **learning management system (LMS)** provides tools for the management, delivery, tracking, and assessment of various types of employee learning and training. A robust LMS integrates with systems from human resources, accounting, and sales so that the business impact of employee learning programs can be more easily identified and quantified.

The first learning management systems primarily automated record keeping in instructor-led training. These systems have been enhanced to support multiple modes of learning, including CD-ROM, downloadable videos, Web-based classes, live instruction in classes or online, and group learning in online forums and chat sessions. The LMS consolidates mixed-media training, automates the selection and administration of courses, assembles and delivers learning content, and measures learning effectiveness. If a company had a customer relationship management (CRM) system that kept track of call-handling time, for instance, a sophisticated learning management system might be able to correlate performance data with training data to see whether training correlated with on-the-job performance. Recent versions of learning management systems with open architectures have capabilities for exporting their data to other systems.

The Window on Organizations describes some of the benefits of learning management systems. Training for combat readiness and for job skills is an essential part of the U.S. Navy's mission, and it must be conducted on a very large scale in many different settings and locations. Trainees have many different aptitudes, skills, and career paths to be managed. Trainees must be tested before and after they take courses. The Naval Education Training Command was able to implement a single learning management system that could handle all of these requirements.

12.3 KNOWLEDGE WORK SYSTEMS

The enterprise-wide knowledge systems we have just described provide a wide range of capabilities that can be used by many if not all the workers and groups in an organization. Firms also have specialized systems for knowledge workers to help them create new knowledge for the firm.

Knowledge Workers and Knowledge Work

Knowledge workers, which we introduced in Chapter 1, include researchers, designers, architects, scientists, and engineers who primarily create knowledge and information for the organization. Knowledge workers usually have high levels of education and memberships in professional organizations and are often asked to exercise independent judgment as a routine aspect of their work. For example, knowledge workers create new products or find ways of improving existing ones. Knowledge workers perform three key roles that are critical to the organization and to the managers who work within the organization:

- Keeping the organization current in knowledge as it develops in the external world—in technology, science, social thought, and the arts
- Serving as internal consultants regarding the areas of their knowledge, the changes taking place, and opportunities
- Acting as change agents, evaluating, initiating, and promoting change projects

Most knowledge workers rely on office systems, such as word processors, voice mail, e-mail, videoconferencing, and scheduling systems, which are designed to increase worker productivity in the office. However, knowledge workers also require highly specialized knowledge work systems. These knowledge work systems (KWS) are specifically designed to promote the creation of knowledge and to ensure that new knowledge and technical expertise are properly integrated into the business. Moreover, knowledge work is segmented into many highly specialized fields, and each field has a different collection of knowledge work systems that are specialized to support workers in that field.

Internet Connection —

The Internet Connection for this chapter will take you to the National Aeronautics and Space Administration (NASA) Web site where you can complete an exercise showing how knowledge workers can use this Web site.

Requirements of Knowledge Work Systems

Knowledge work systems have characteristics that reflect the special needs of knowledge workers. First, knowledge work systems must give knowledge workers the specialized tools they need, such as powerful graphics, analytical tools, and communications and document management tools. These systems require great computing power to handle the sophisticated graphics or complex calculations necessary for such knowledge workers as scientific researchers, product designers, and financial analysts. Because knowledge workers are so focused on knowledge in the external world, these systems also must give the worker quick and easy access to external databases.

WINDOW ON ORGANIZATIONS

The U.S. Navy Creates the World's Largest Classroom

The Naval Education Training Command (NETC) operates the world's largest classroom. It is responsible for the development and delivery of training for 1.2 million active and retired Navy, Marine, and civilian personnel and their families. That's a daunting task: NETC must oversee 47,000 officers and enlisted students training in 3,600 different courses at training sites across the United States and at remote sites overseas, plus 69 Naval Reserve Officers Training Corps (NROTC) in colleges and 584 Naval Junior ROTC units at civilian high schools. What's more, the Navy must be able to deliver continuous and consistent online programs to sailors at sea or service people stationed around the world.

The NETC takes its mission very seriously. According to Sandra Drummer, director of NETC's learning strategies division, NETC has a vision of becoming the world's premier learning organization. A true learning organization is skilled in acquiring and transferring knowledge as well as developing and creating it. The NETC believes training is key to the military's current and future readiness for combat and the ability of Navy people to make contributions to civilian life when they leave military service. In 2001, NETC decided to enlist technology to power its learning programs. NETC wanted a learning management system that was capable of managing learning on a massive scale and that could be used at sea and other remote locations. Rather than introduce multiple training programs, the NETC opted for a unified approach in which all training would be conducted within a single framework. It selected THINQ Training Server Learning Management System as the foundation for its Navy Knowledge Online portal.

The THINQ Learning Management System is a multitier Web-based system for initiating, managing, and tracking all learning activities in one language or multiple languages across the organization. It launches and tracks e-learning courseware and supports instructor-led training. It provides tools for training administrators to assess individual skills and competencies, manage personalized learning plans, and track required certifications. The system provides comprehensive reports on resource and learner data and creates specific learner profiles for jobs, organizations, and locations, and it can administer pretesting and posttesting.

According to Saundra Drummer, Navy Knowledge Online creates "a dynamic learning environment, with the idea of increasing the learners' control and responsibility for their own learning." Learners can choose from an array of learning modalities, including instructor-led training, e-learning over the Internet, video, and self-paced CD-ROMs. Each learner can use the system to find out exactly what training he or she should receive, "where they are in this learning path, and where they need to go next," Drummer notes.

With Navy Knowledge Online, the Navy can now deliver and track training programs distributed worldwide in a variety of environments—from shore-based installations with Internet access to standalone installations on surface ships and submarines. Naval reservists can log on to the learning site and complete courses for both military training and civilian career skills.

The new system facilitates staffing new positions and filling positions that have been vacated. Navy Knowledge Online can collect data for each person, including that person's training records and skill sets, to help identify people who are qualified for specific operations and billets. Navy recruiters can use the system to map out a recruit's training and career path even before that person enters the service. By matching Navy and civilian job codes, recruitment officers can outline the appropriate knowledge and training required for a particular job. The e-learning system enables the Navy to apply metrics to analyze the effectiveness of training based on an individual's skill needs.

Implementing this system was not without challenges. The NETC had to find standards for creating content and for developing reusable learning objects that could be accessed across numerous technology platforms. It had to consolidate a number of different databases and mine the data to determine what kinds of learning each person needed. Organizational culture at the Navy had to undergo some transformation.

Investment in Navy Knowledge Online has delivered several types of returns. The most obvious savings have been on travel costs because the learning is now available from any location. Using the system saves the Navy about $40 million in travel costs per year. The system has also produced major savings by reducing the amount of time required for training. Because the technology enables NETC to create reusable "learning objects," the system is saving development costs. NETC is developing its courseware as reusable objects. That means it will be able to take small bits of courseware that have been developed in the past and combine them in new ways to create new training in the future. The Navy's online learning program won the E-Gov Explorer Award for exploring e-learning. In addition, the Navy was judged a top leader in e-learning practices in the United States.

Sources: Emily Hollis, "U.S. Navy: Smooth Sailing for Education," *Chief Learning Officer*, February 2004; www.thinq.com, accessed June 10, 2004; and Raymond Maskell, "Taking Learning to the Next Level," *Military Training Technology* 8, no. 2 (June 11, 2003).

To Think About: Why is learning management so important for the U.S. Navy? How does its learning management system provide value?

A user-friendly interface is very important to a knowledge worker's system. User-friendly interfaces save time by enabling the user to perform needed tasks and get to required information without having to spend a lot of time learning how to use the computer. Saving time is more important for knowledge workers than for most other employees because knowledge workers are highly paid—wasting a knowledge worker's time is simply too expensive, and knowledge workers can easily fall prey to information overload (Farhoomand and Drury, 2002). Figure 12-10 summarizes the requirements of knowledge work systems.

Knowledge workstations often are designed and optimized for the specific tasks to be performed; so, for example, a design engineer requires a different workstation setup than a financial analyst. Design engineers need graphics with enough power to handle three-dimensional computer-aided design (CAD) systems. However, financial analysts are more interested in access to a myriad of external databases and technology for efficiently storing and accessing massive amounts of financial data.

Examples of Knowledge Work Systems

Major knowledge work applications include computer-aided design (CAD) systems, virtual reality systems for simulation and modeling, and financial workstations. **Computer-aided design (CAD)** automates the creation and revision of designs, using computers and sophisticated graphics software. Using a more traditional physical design methodology, each design modification requires a mold to be made and a prototype to be tested physically. That process must be repeated many times, which is a very expensive and time-consuming process. Using a CAD workstation, the designer need only make a physical prototype toward the end of the design process because the design can be easily tested and changed on the computer. The ability of CAD software to provide design specifications for the tooling and the manufacturing processes also saves a great deal of time and money while producing a manufacturing process with far fewer problems.

For example, architects from Skidmore, Owings, & Merrill LLP used a 3D design program called Revit to work out the creative and technical details of the design for the Freedom Tower at the site of the former World Trade Center. The software enabled the architects to strip away the outer layer to manipulate the shape of the floors. Changes appeared immediately in the entire model, and the software automatically recalculated the technical details in the blueprints (Frangos, 2004).

Hawkes Ocean Technology used Autodesk's Inventor three-dimensional design and engineering program to create and manipulate flowing shapes when designing the revolutionary Deep Flight Aviator submarine for the U.S. Navy. The software allowed Hawkes to create and manipulate flowing shapes, test their stress points, and refine them without

FIGURE 12-10 *Requirements of knowledge work systems.*

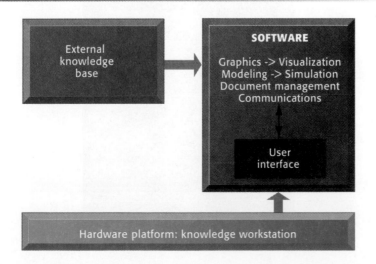

Knowledge work systems require strong links to external knowledge bases in addition to specialized hardware and software.

ever having to touch a lathe or mold. The system also enabled Hawkes to cut design costs by one-third, reduce engineering staff from 10 to 3, and bypass the prototyping stage when developing new products (Salkever, 2002).

Virtual reality systems have visualization, rendering, and simulation capabilities that go far beyond those of conventional CAD systems. They use interactive graphics software to create computer-generated simulations that are so close to reality that users almost believe they are participating in a real-world situation. In many virtual reality systems, the user dons special clothing, headgear, and equipment, depending on the application. The clothing contains sensors that record the user's movements and immediately transmit that information back to the computer. For instance, to walk through a virtual reality simulation of a house, you would need garb that monitors the movement of your feet, hands, and head. You also would need goggles containing video screens and sometimes audio attachments and feeling gloves so that you can be immersed in the computer feedback.

Virtual reality is starting to provide benefits in educational, scientific, and business work. For example, neuroradiologists at New York's Beth Israel Medical Center can use the Siemens Medical Systems 3D Virtuoso System to peek at the interplay of tiny blood vessels or take a fly-through of the aorta. Surgeons at New York University School of Medicine can use three-dimensional modeling to target brain tumors more precisely, thereby reducing bleeding and trauma during surgery.

Virtual reality applications developed for the Web use a standard called **Virtual Reality Modeling Language** (VRML). VRML is a set of specifications for interactive, three-dimensional modeling on the World Wide Web that can organize multiple media types, including animation, images, and audio to put users in a simulated real-world environment. VRML is platform independent, operates over a desktop computer, and requires little bandwidth. Over the Internet using their Web browsers users can download from a server a three-dimensional virtual world designed using VRML.

DuPont, the Wilmington, Delaware, chemical company, created a VRML application called HyperPlant, which enables users to access three-dimensional data over the Internet using Web browser software. Engineers can go through three-dimensional models as if they were physically walking through a plant, viewing objects at eye level. This level of detail reduces the number of mistakes they make during construction of oil rigs, oil plants, and other structures.

Computer-aided design (CAD) systems improve the quality and precision of product design by performing much of the design and testing work on the computer

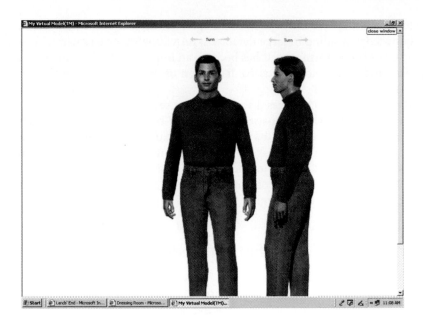

Users can create a VRML "virtual model" that approximates their physical proportions to help them visualize how they will look in clothing sold at the Lands' End Web site. This digitized image can be rotated to show how the outfits will look from all angles and users can click to change the clothes' color.

The financial industry is using specialized **investment workstations** to leverage the knowledge and time of its brokers, traders, and portfolio managers. Firms such as Merrill Lynch and UBS Financial Services have installed investment workstations that integrate a wide range of data from both internal and external sources, including contact management data, real-time and historical market data, and research reports. Previously, financial professionals had to spend considerable time accessing data from separate systems and piecing together the information they needed. By providing one-stop information faster and with fewer errors, the workstations streamline the entire investment process from stock selection to updating client records. Table 12-4 summarizes the major types of knowledge work systems.

12.4 INTELLIGENT TECHNIQUES

Artificial intelligence and database technology provide a number of intelligent techniques that organizations can use to capture individual and collective knowledge and to extend their knowledge base. Expert systems, case-based reasoning, and fuzzy logic are used for capturing tacit knowledge. Neural networks and data mining are used for **knowledge discovery.** They can discover underlying patterns, categories, and behaviors in large data sets that could not be discovered by managers alone or simply through experience. Genetic algorithms are used for generating solutions to problems that are too large and complex for human beings to analyze on their own. Intelligent agents can automate routine tasks to help firms search for and filter information for use in electronic commerce, supply chain management, and other activities.

TABLE 12-4 *Examples of Knowledge Work Systems*

Knowledge Work System	Function in Organization
CAD/CAM (computer-aided design/computer-aided manufacturing)	Provides engineers, designers, and factory managers with precise control over industrial design and manufacturing
Virtual reality systems	Provide drug designers, architects, engineers, and medical workers with precise, photorealistic simulations of objects
Investment workstations	High-end PCs used in financial sector to analyze trading situations instantaneously and facilitate portfolio management

Data mining, which we introduced in Chapter 7, helps organizations capture undiscovered knowledge residing in large databases, providing managers with new insight for improving business performance. It has become an important tool for management decision making, and we provide a detailed discussion of data mining for management decision support in Chapter 13.

The other intelligent techniques discussed in this section are based on **artificial intelligence (AI)** technology, which consists of computer-based systems (both hardware and software) that attempt to emulate human behavior. Such systems would be able to learn languages, accomplish physical tasks, use a perceptual apparatus, and emulate human expertise and decision making. Although AI applications do not exhibit the breadth, complexity, originality, and generality of human intelligence, they play an important role in contemporary knowledge management.

Capturing Knowledge: Expert Systems

Expert systems are an intelligent technique for capturing tacit knowledge in a very specific and limited domain of human expertise. These systems capture the knowledge of skilled employees in the form of a set of rules in a software system that can be used by others in the organization. The set of rules in the expert system adds to the memory, or stored learning, of the firm.

Expert systems lack the breadth of knowledge and the understanding of fundamental principles of a human expert. They typically perform very limited tasks that can be performed by professionals in a few minutes or hours, such as diagnosing a malfunctioning machine or determining whether to grant credit for a loan. Problems that cannot be solved by human experts in the same short period of time are far too difficult for an expert system. However, by capturing human expertise in limited areas, expert systems can provide benefits, helping organizations make high-quality decisions with fewer people. Today expert systems are widely used in business in discrete, highly structured decision-making situations.

HOW EXPERT SYSTEMS WORK

Human knowledge must be modeled or represented in a way that a computer can process. The model of human knowledge used by expert systems is called the **knowledge base**. A standard programming construct is the IF–THEN construct, in which a condition is evaluated. If the condition is true, an action is taken. For instance,

IF INCOME > $45,000 (condition)

THEN PRINT NAME AND ADDRESS (action)

A series of these rules can be a knowledge base. A software program for an expert system may have 200 to 10,000 of these rules, which are much more interconnected and nested than in a traditional software program (see Figure 12-11).

Could you represent the knowledge in the *Encyclopedia Britannica* this way? Probably not, because the **rule base** would be too large, and not all the knowledge in the encyclopedia can be represented in the form of IF–THEN rules. In general, expert systems can be efficiently used only in those situations in which the domain of knowledge is highly restricted (such as in granting credit) and involves no more than a few thousand rules.

The **AI shell** is the programming environment of an expert system. In the early years of expert systems, computer scientists used specialized artificial intelligence programming languages, such as LISP or Prolog, that could process lists of rules efficiently. Today, a growing number of expert systems use AI shells that are user-friendly development environments. AI shells can quickly generate user-interface screens, capture the knowledge base, and manage the strategies for searching the rule base.

The strategy used to search through the rule base is called the **inference engine**. Two strategies are commonly used: forward chaining and backward chaining (see Figure 12-12).

In **forward chaining** the inference engine begins with the information entered by the user and searches the rule base to arrive at a conclusion. The strategy is to fire, or carry

FIGURE 12-11 *Rules in an AI program.*

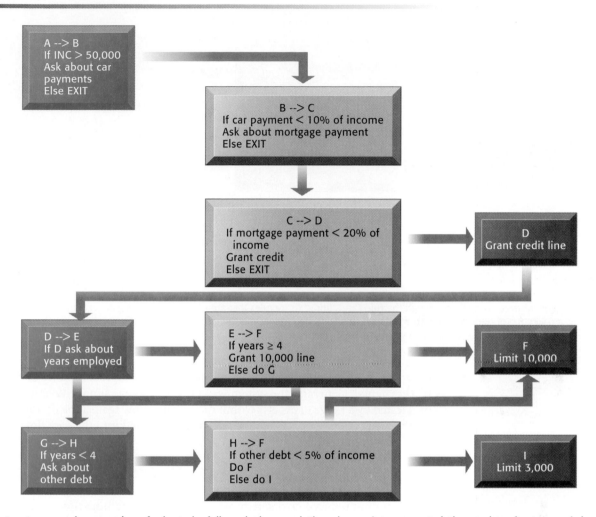

An expert system contains a number of rules to be followed when used. The rules are interconnected; the number of outcomes is known in advance and is limited; there are multiple paths to the same outcome; and the system can consider multiple rules at a single time. The rules illustrated are for simple credit-granting expert systems.

out, the action of the rule when a condition is true. In Figure 12-12, beginning on the left, if the user enters a client's name with income greater than $100,000, the engine will fire all rules in sequence from left to right. If the user then enters information indicating that the same client owns real estate, another pass of the rule base will occur and more rules will fire. Processing continues until no more rules can be fired.

In **backward chaining** the strategy for searching the rule base starts with a hypothesis and proceeds by asking the user questions about selected facts until the hypothesis is either confirmed or disproved. In our example, in Figure 12-12, ask the question, "Should we add this person to the prospect database?" Begin on the right of the diagram and work toward the left. You can see that the person should be added to the database if a sales representative is sent, term insurance is granted, or a financial adviser visits the client.

Developing an expert system requires input from one or more experts, who have a thorough command of the knowledge base, and one or more knowledge engineers, who can translate the knowledge (as described by the expert) into a set of rules. A **knowledge engineer** is similar to a traditional systems analyst but has special expertise in eliciting information and expertise from other professionals.

An expert systems development project balances potential savings from the proposed system against the cost. The team members develop a prototype system to test assumptions about how to encode the knowledge of experts. Next, they develop a full-scale system, focusing mainly on the addition of a very large number of rules. The complexity of

FIGURE 12-12   *Inference engines in expert systems.*

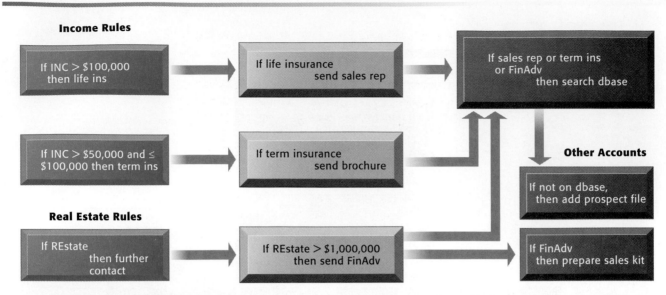

An inference engine works by searching through the rules and "firing" those rules that are triggered by facts gathered and entered by the user. Basically, a collection of rules is similar to a series of nested IF statements in a traditional software program; however, the magnitude of the statements and degree of nesting are much greater in an expert system.

the entire system grows with the number of rules, so the comprehensibility of the system may be threatened. Generally, the system is pruned to achieve simplicity and power. The system is tested by a range of experts within the organization against the performance criteria established earlier. Once tested, the system is integrated into the data flow and work patterns of the organization.

EXAMPLES OF SUCCESSFUL EXPERT SYSTEMS

The following are examples of expert systems that provide organizations with an array of benefits, including reduced errors, reduced costs, reduced training time, improved decisions, and improved quality and service.

Countrywide Funding Corporation in Pasadena, California, is a loan-underwriting firm with about 400 underwriters in 150 offices around the country. The company developed a PC-based expert system in 1992 to make preliminary creditworthiness decisions on loan requests. The company had experienced rapid, continuing growth and wanted the system to help ensure consistent, high-quality loan decisions. Countrywide's Loan Underwriting Expert System (CLUES) has about 400 rules. Countrywide tested the system by sending every loan application handled by a human underwriter to CLUES as well. The system was refined until it agreed with the underwriters in 95 percent of the cases.

Countrywide does not rely on CLUES to reject loans because the expert system cannot be programmed to handle exceptional situations, such as those involving a self-employed person or complex financial schemes. An underwriter must review all rejected loans and makes the final decision. CLUES has other benefits. Traditionally, an underwriter could handle six or seven applications a day. Using CLUES, the same underwriter can evaluate at least 16 per day. Countrywide now is using the rules in its expert system to answer inquiries from visitors to its Web site who want to know if they qualify for a loan.

Galeria Kaufhof, a German superstore chain, uses a rule-based system to help it manage more than 120,000 deliveries of goods that it receives each day, ranging from clothing to complex electronics and fine china. Inspecting each delivery is time consuming and expensive, but the company wants to make sure that it is receiving goods that are not damaged or defective. Kaufhof implemented a rule-based system that identifies high-risk deliveries and passes along lower-risk ones automatically. The system scans delivery labels and identifies each delivery in terms of its size, type of product, whether the product is a new product, and the supplier's past history of deliveries to Kaufhof. Deliveries of large numbers of complex products that are new or that have suppliers with unfavorable delivery histories are carefully inspected, whereas other deliveries are passed on without inspection (Booth and Buluswar, 2002).

The investment banking firm Goldman Sachs uses a rule-based expert system to keep unwanted stocks out of individual portfolios. Almost all of its client portfolios have restrictions specified by owners on which stocks or even entire sectors to exclude. Goldman wants to make sure its global network of financial advisers respect these restrictions so they do not make any purchases that clients do not want. Goldman's business managers, compliance officers, and private wealth managers all play roles in deciding which stocks to purchase for a portfolio. The company developed a rule-based system that maintains rules for keeping a particular stock from entering a client's portfolio. By creating a centralized portfolio-filtering system, Goldman is better able to catch mistakes before erroneous trades go through (Guerra, 2001).

Although expert systems lack the robust and general intelligence of human beings, they can provide benefits to organizations if their limitations are well understood. Only certain classes of problems can be solved using expert systems. Virtually all successful expert systems deal with problems of classification in which there are relatively few alternative outcomes and in which these possible outcomes are all known in advance. Many expert systems require large, lengthy, and expensive development efforts. Hiring or training more experts may be less expensive than building an expert system. Typically, the environment in which an expert system operates is continually changing so that the expert system must also continually change. Some expert systems, especially large ones, are so complex that in a few years the maintenance costs equal the development costs.

The applicability of expert systems to managerial problems is very limited. Managerial problems generally involve drawing facts and interpretations from divergent sources, evaluating the facts, and comparing one interpretation of the facts with another; they are not limited to simple classification. Expert systems based on the prior knowledge of a few known alternatives are unsuitable to the problems managers face on a daily basis.

Organizational Intelligence: Case-Based Reasoning

Expert systems primarily capture the tacit knowledge of individual experts, but organizations also have collective knowledge and expertise that they have built up over the years. This organizational knowledge can be captured and stored using case-based reasoning. In **case-based reasoning** (CBR), descriptions of past experiences of human specialists, represented as cases, are stored in a database for later retrieval when the user encounters a new case with similar parameters. The system searches for stored cases with problem characteristics similar to the new one, finds the closest fit, and applies the solutions of the old case to the new case. Successful solutions are tagged to the new case and both are stored together with the other cases in the knowledge base. Unsuccessful solutions also are appended to the case database along with explanations as to why the solutions did not work (see Figure 12-13).

Expert systems work by applying a set of IF–THEN–ELSE rules against a knowledge base, both of which are extracted from human experts. Case-based reasoning, in contrast, represents knowledge as a series of cases, and this knowledge base is continuously expanded and refined by users. One can find case-based reasoning in diagnostic systems in medicine or customer support where users can retrieve past cases whose characteristics are similar to the new case. The system suggests a solution or diagnosis based on the best-matching retrieved case.

Fuzzy Logic Systems

Most people do not think in terms of traditional IF–THEN rules or precise numbers. Humans tend to categorize things imprecisely using rules for making decisions that may have many shades of meaning. For example, a man or a woman can be *strong* or *intelligent*. A company can be *large, medium,* or *small* in size. Temperature can be *hot, cold, cool,* or *warm.* These categories represent a range of values.

FIGURE 12-13 *How case-based reasoning works.*

Case-based reasoning represents knowledge as a database of past cases and their solutions. The system uses a six-step process to generate solutions to new problems encountered by the user.

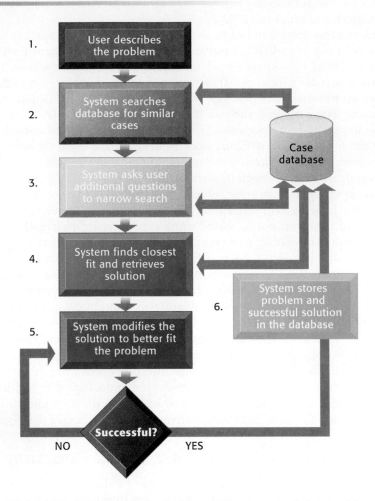

1. User describes the problem
2. System searches database for similar cases
3. System asks user additional questions to narrow search
4. System finds closest fit and retrieves solution
5. System modifies the solution to better fit the problem
6. System stores problem and successful solution in the database

Case database

Successful?

NO   YES

Fuzzy logic is a rule-based technology that can represent such imprecision by creating rules that use approximate or subjective values. It can describe a particular phenomenon or process linguistically and then represent that description in a small number of flexible rules. Organizations can use fuzzy logic to create software systems that capture tacit knowledge where there is linguistic ambiguity.

For example, Ford Motor Company developed a fuzzy logic application that backs a simulated tractor trailer into a parking space. The application uses the following three rules:

IF the truck is *near* jackknifing, THEN *reduce* the steering angle.

IF the truck is *far away* from the dock, THEN steer *toward* the dock.

IF the truck is *near* the dock, THEN point the trailer *directly* at the dock.

This logic makes sense to us as human beings because it represents how we think as we back that truck into its berth. To see how such logic would be translated into a software system, let us look at the way fuzzy logic would represent various temperatures in a computer application to control room temperature automatically. The terms (known as membership functions) are imprecisely defined so that, for example, in Figure 12-14, cool is between 50 degrees and 70 degrees, although the temperature is most clearly cool between about 60 degrees and 67 degrees. Note that cool is overlapped by cold or norm. To control the room environment using this logic, the programmer would develop similarly imprecise definitions for humidity and other factors, such as outdoor wind and temperature. The rules might include one that says: "If the temperature is cool or cold and the humidity is low while the outdoor wind is high and the outdoor temperature is low, raise the heat and humidity in the room." The computer would combine the membership function readings in a weighted manner and, using all the rules, raise and lower the temperature and humidity.

FIGURE 12-14   Implementing fuzzy logic rules in hardware.

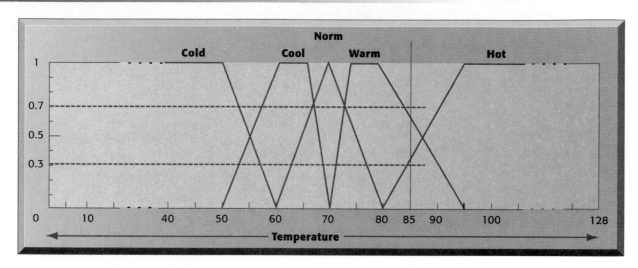

The membership functions for the input called temperature are in the logic of the thermostat to control the room temperature. Membership functions help translate linguistic expressions such as *warm* into numbers that the computer can manipulate.

Source: James M. Sibigtroth, "Implementing Fuzzy Expert Rules in Hardware," *AI Expert,* April 1992. © 1992 Miller Freeman, Inc. Reprinted with permission.

Fuzzy logic provides solutions to problems requiring expertise that is difficult to represent in the form of crisp IF–THEN rules. In Japan, Sendai's subway system uses fuzzy logic controls to accelerate so smoothly that standing passengers need not hold on. Mitsubishi Heavy Industries in Tokyo has been able to reduce the power consumption of its air conditioners by 20 percent by implementing control programs in fuzzy logic. The autofocus device in cameras is only possible because of fuzzy logic. Williams-Sonoma sells a rice steamer made in Japan that uses fuzzy logic. A variable heat setting detects the amount of grain, cooks it at the preferred temperature, and keeps the food warm up to 12 hours. In these instances, fuzzy logic allows incremental changes in inputs to produce smooth changes in outputs instead of discontinuous ones, making it useful for consumer electronics and engineering applications.

Fuzzy logic can be used to express relationships very generally and compactly, requiring fewer IF–THEN rules than traditional software programs. Compact software programs require less computer capacity, enabling, for example, Sanyo Fisher USA to implement fuzzy logic for camcorder controls without adding expensive memory to its product.

Management also has found fuzzy logic useful for decision making and organizational control. A Wall Street firm created a system that selects companies for potential acquisition, using the language stock traders understand. Recently, a system has been developed to detect possible fraud in medical claims submitted by health care providers anywhere in the United States.

Neural Networks

Neural networks are used for modeling complex, poorly understood problems for which large amounts of data have been collected. They are especially useful for finding patterns and relationships in massive amounts of data that would be too complicated and difficult for a human being to analyze. **Neural networks** discover this knowledge by using hardware and software that emulate the processing patterns of the biological brain. Neural networks "learn" patterns from large quantities of data by sifting through data, searching for relationships, building models, and correcting over and over again the model's own mistakes.

A neural net has a large number of sensing and processing nodes that continuously interact with each other. Figure 12-15 represents one type of neural network comprising an input layer, an output layer, and a hidden processing layer. Humans "train" the network by feeding it a set of training data for which the inputs produce a known set of outputs or conclusions. This helps the computer learn the correct solution by example. As the computer is fed more data, each case is compared with the known outcome. If it differs, a

FIGURE 12-15 *How a neural network works.*

A neural network uses rules it "learns" from patterns in data to construct a hidden layer of logic. The hidden layer then processes inputs, classifying them based on the experience of the model.

Source: Herb Edelstein, "Technology How-To: Mining Data Warehouses," *InformationWeek*, January 8, 1996. Copyright © 1996 CMP Media, Inc., 600 Community Drive, Manhasset, NY 12030. Reprinted with permission.

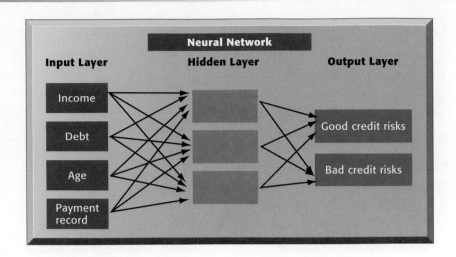

correction is calculated and applied to the nodes in the hidden processing layer. These steps are repeated until a condition, such as corrections being less than a certain amount, is reached. The neural network in Figure 12-15 has learned how to identify a good credit risk. Also, self-organizing neural networks can be trained by exposing them to large amounts of data and allowing them to discover the patterns and relationships in the data.

Whereas expert systems seek to emulate or model a human expert's way of solving problems, neural network builders claim that they do not model human intelligence, do not program solutions, and do not aim to solve specific problems per se. Instead, neural network designers seek to put intelligence into the hardware in the form of a generalized capability to learn. In contrast, the expert system is highly specific to a given problem and cannot be retrained easily.

Neural network applications are emerging in medicine, science, and business to address problems in pattern classification, prediction, financial analysis, and control and optimization. In medicine, neural networks applications are used for screening patients for coronary artery disease, for diagnosing patients with epilepsy and Alzheimer's disease, and for performing pattern recognition of pathology images. The financial industry uses neural networks to discern patterns in vast pools of data that might help investment firms predict the performance of equities, corporate bond ratings, or corporate bankruptcies. Visa International is using a neural network to help detect credit card fraud by monitoring all Visa transactions for sudden changes in the buying patterns of cardholders.

Unlike expert systems, which typically provide explanations for their solutions, neural networks cannot always explain why they arrived at a particular solution. Moreover, they cannot always guarantee a completely certain solution, arrive at the same solution again with the same input data, or always guarantee the best solution. They are very sensitive and may not perform well if their training covers too little or too much data. In most current applications, neural networks are best used as aids to human decision makers instead of substitutes for them.

Genetic Algorithms

Genetic algorithms (also referred to as adaptive computation) are used for finding the optimal solution for a specific problem by examining a very large number of possible solutions for that problem. Their problem-solving techniques are conceptually based on the method that living organisms use to adapt to their environments—the process of evolution. They are programmed to work the way populations solve problems—by changing and reorganizing their component parts using processes such as reproduction, mutation, and natural selection.

Thus, genetic algorithms promote the evolution of solutions to particular problems, controlling the generation, variation, adaptation, and selection of possible solutions using genetically based processes. As solutions alter and combine, the worst ones are discarded and the better ones survive to go on to produce even better solutions. Genetic algorithms breed programs that solve problems even when no person can fully understand their structure

A genetic algorithm works by representing information as a string of 0s and 1s. A possible solution can be represented by a long string of these digits. The genetic algorithm provides methods of searching all possible combinations of digits to identify the right string representing the best possible structure for the problem.

In one method, the programmer first randomly generates a population of strings consisting of combinations of binary digits (see Figure 12-16). Each string corresponds to one of the variables in the problem. One applies a test for fitness, ranking the strings in the population according to their level of desirability as possible solutions. After the initial population is evaluated for fitness, the algorithm then produces the next generation of strings, consisting of strings that survived the fitness test plus offspring strings produced from mating pairs of strings, and tests their fitness. The process continues until a solution is reached.

Many business problems require optimization because they deal with issues such as minimization of costs, maximization of profits, efficient scheduling, and use of resources. If these situations are very dynamic and complex, involving hundreds or thousands of variables or formulas, genetic algorithms can expedite the solution because they can evaluate many different solution alternatives quickly to find the best one.

For example, General Electric engineers used genetic algorithms to help optimize the design for jet turbine aircraft engines, where each design change required changes in up to 100 variables. The supply chain management software from i2 Technologies uses genetic algorithms to optimize production-scheduling models incorporating hundreds of thousands of details about customer orders, material and resource availability, manufacturing and distribution capability, and delivery dates. International Truck and Engine used this software to iron out snags in production, reducing costly schedule disruptions by 90 percent in five of its plants. Genetic algorithms have helped market researchers performing market segmentation analysis (Kuo, Chang, and Chien, 2004; Burtka, 1993; Wakefield, 2001).

Hybrid AI Systems

Genetic algorithms, fuzzy logic, neural networks, and expert systems can be integrated into a single application to take advantage of the best features of these technologies. Such systems are called **hybrid AI systems.** Hybrid applications in business are growing. In Japan, Hitachi, Mitsubishi, Ricoh, Sanyo, and others are starting to incorporate hybrid AI in products such as

FIGURE 12-16   *The components of a genetic algorithm.*

		Color	Speed	Intelligence	Fitness
	1	White	Medium	Dumb	40
	2	Black	Slow	Dumb	43
	3	White	Slow	Very dumb	22
	4	Black	Fast	Dumb	71
	5	White	Medium	Very smart	53
A population of chromosomes			**Decoding of chromosomes**		**Evaluation of chromosomes**

This example illustrates an initial population of "chromosomes," each representing a different solution. The genetic algorithm uses an iterative process to refine the initial solutions so that the better ones, those with the higher fitness, are more likely to emerge as the best solution.

Source: Dhar, Stein, SEVEN METHODS FOR TRANSFORMING CORPORATE DATA INTO BUSINESS INTELLIGENCE (Trade Version), 1st © 1997. Electronically reproduced by permission of Pearson Education, Inc., Upper Saddle River, New Jersey.

Illustrated here is a sample application from Ward Systems' Gene Hunter for optimizing a portfolio of securities by minimizing risk while simultaneously maximizing return. The trader picks a number of stocks that he or she believes will offer a high rate of return. The genetic algorithm is used to minimize the risk by helping to adjust the portfolio so that it behaves more like the Standard & Poors (S&P) 500 index. The S&P 500 portfolio is considered less risky because it is much larger and more diversified than just a handful of stocks.

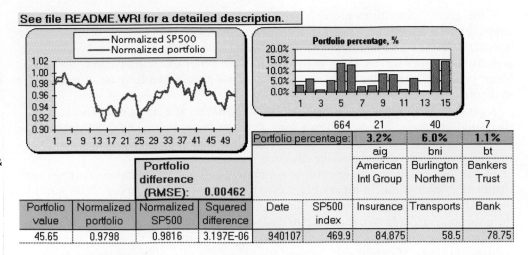

Portfolio value	Normalized portfolio	Normalized SP500	Squared difference	Date	SP500 index	aig American Intl Group Insurance	bni Burlington Northern Transports	bt Bankers Trust Bank
						664	21	40	7
		Portfolio difference (RMSE): 0.00462			Portfolio percentage:	3.2%	6.0%	1.1%
45.65	0.9798	0.9816	3.197E-06	940107	469.9	84.875	58.5	78.75

home appliances, factory machinery, and office equipment. Matsushita has developed a "neurofuzzy" washing machine that combines fuzzy logic with neural networks. Nikko Securities has been working on a neurofuzzy system to forecast convertible-bond ratings.

Intelligent Agents

Intelligent agent technology can help businesses navigate through large amounts of data to locate only information that is considered important and, in some cases, act on that information on behalf of the user. **Intelligent agents** are software programs that work in the background without direct human intervention to carry out specific, repetitive, and predictable tasks for an individual user, business process, or software application. The agent uses a limited built-in or learned knowledge base to accomplish tasks or make decisions on the user's behalf. Intelligent agents can be programmed to make decisions based on the user's personal preferences—for example, to delete junk e-mail, schedule appointments, or travel over interconnected networks to find the cheapest airfare to California. The agent can be likened to a personal digital assistant collaborating with the user in the same work environment. It can help the user by performing tasks on the user's behalf, training or teaching the user, hiding the complexity of difficult tasks, helping the user collaborate with other users, or monitoring events and procedures.

There are many intelligent agent applications today in operating systems, application software, e-mail systems, mobile computing software, and network tools. For example, the wizards found in Microsoft Office software tools have built-in capabilities to show users how to accomplish various tasks, such as formatting documents or creating graphs, and to anticipate when users need assistance.

Of special interest to business are intelligent agents for cruising networks, including the Internet, in search of information. Chapter 8 describes how these *shopping bots* can help consumers find products they want and assist them in comparing prices and other features. Because these mobile agents are personalized, semiautonomous, and continuously running, they can help automate several of the most time-consuming stages of the buying process and thus reduce transaction costs.

Agent technology is finding applications in supply chain management for improving coordination among different members of the supply chain in response to changing business conditions (Lee et al., 2004; Sadeh, Hildum, and Kjenstad, 2003; Cavalieri, Cesarotti, and Introna, 2003). Figure 12-17 illustrates the use of intelligent agents in Procter & Gamble's supply chain network. The network models a complex supply chain as a group of semiautonomous "agents" representing individual supply chain components, such as trucks, production facilities, distributors, or retail stores. The behavior of each agent is programmed to follow rules that mimic actual behavior, such as "dispatch a truck when it is full." Simulations using the agents enable the company to perform what-if analyses on inventory levels, in-store stockouts, and transportation costs.

FIGURE 12-17   *Intelligent agents in P&G's supply chain network.*

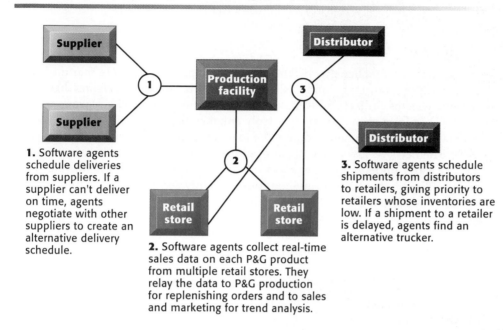

Intelligent agents are helping Procter & Gamble shorten the replenishment cycles for products such as a box of Tide.

1. Software agents schedule deliveries from suppliers. If a supplier can't deliver on time, agents negotiate with other suppliers to create an alternative delivery schedule.

2. Software agents collect real-time sales data on each P&G product from multiple retail stores. They relay the data to P&G production for replenishing orders and to sales and marketing for trend analysis.

3. Software agents schedule shipments from distributors to retailers, giving priority to retailers whose inventories are low. If a shipment to a retailer is delayed, agents find an alternative trucker.

Using intelligent agent models, P&G discovered that trucks should often be dispatched before being fully loaded. Although transportation costs would be higher using partially loaded trucks because of both driver time and fuel to deliver fewer goods, the simulation showed that retail store stockouts would occur less often, thus reducing the amount of lost sales, which would more than make up for the higher distribution costs. Agent-based modeling has saved P&G $300 million annually on an investment of less than 1 percent of that amount (Anthes, 2003). Table 12-5 shows how other companies are using intelligent agent technology.

12.5 MANAGEMENT OPPORTUNITIES, CHALLENGES, AND SOLUTIONS

Successful deployment of knowledge management systems requires a very clear understanding of how the firm creates and uses knowledge. Organizations need to determine precisely how they can benefit from knowledge management programs and whether the benefits are realistic.

Opportunities

Businesses armed with proprietary knowledge about their customers and operations have what could be called an "invisible competitive advantage" if this knowledge is not available to competitors and cannot be purchased by others in the marketplace. For that reason,

TABLE 12-5 *How Businesses Are Using Intelligent Agents*

Organization	Intelligent Agent Application
Merck & Co.	Agents help it find more efficient ways to distribute anti-HIV drugs in Zimbabwe.
Southwest Airlines	Agents help optimize cargo routing.
Ford Motor Co.	Agents are used to simulate buyer preferences to recommend packages of car options that optimize the trade-off between production costs and customer demands.
Edison Chouest Offshore LLC	Offshore service company in Galliano, Louisiana, uses agents to optimize its deployment of service and supply vessels in the Gulf of Mexico.

knowledge management systems can be a source of tremendous value if they enable firms to further leverage that knowledge.

Management Challenges

Proving the quantitative benefits of knowledge management projects that deal with intangibles such as "knowledge" and "collaboration" is often more challenging than other information systems projects (Davenport, DeLong, and Beers, 1998; Davenport and Prusak, 1998). Information systems that truly enhance the productivity of knowledge workers may be difficult to build because the manner in which information technology can enhance higher-level tasks, such as those performed by managers and professionals, is not always clearly understood. Some aspects of organizational knowledge are tacit, unstructured, and not easily captured or codified. Only certain kinds of information problems are appropriate for intelligent techniques.

Research conducted in the past five years on knowledge management projects has uncovered a number of difficulties in implementing knowledge management systems. Among these difficulties are the following:

- Insufficient resources are available to structure and update the content in repositories.
- Poor quality and high variability of content quality results from insufficient validating mechanisms.
- Content in repositories lacks context, making documents difficult to understand.
- Individual employees are not rewarded for contributing content, and many fear sharing knowledge with others on the job.
- Search engines return too much information, reflecting lack of knowledge structure or taxonomy.

Solution Guidelines

There are both managerial and technological solutions to these challenges. Communities of practice are useful in providing motivation to employees and help provide context to knowledge. Properly designed knowledge taxonomies are also helpful in organizing knowledge. Firms can revise their employee compensation systems to reward knowledge sharing.

Proper planning and rollout can increase the chances of success for knowledge management projects. There are five important steps in developing a successful knowledge management project that has measurable results:

- Develop in stages
- Choose a high-value business process
- Choose the right audience
- Measure ROI during initial implementation
- Use the preliminary ROI to project enterprise-wide values

Staged implementation and choice of business process or group to impact are perhaps the most critical decisions (see Figure 12-18). At each stage in the implementation process somewhat different metrics can be used to evaluate a project.

In general, pilot projects should have 30 to 500 people involved. Knowledge management projects produce value by sharing knowledge among a large number of users and developing a large, useful knowledge repository or knowledge network. Measures of value will change as the project moves from the pilot stage through the group and enterprise stages (see Table 12-6).

In the early stages, bottom-up reports and evaluations from users can be gathered. Users can be asked to assign a value (either a dollar value or minutes and hours saved during work) to the various uses they make of the knowledge management system:

- Number of conversations viewed
- Number of visits

FIGURE 12-18 *Implementing knowledge management projects in stages.*

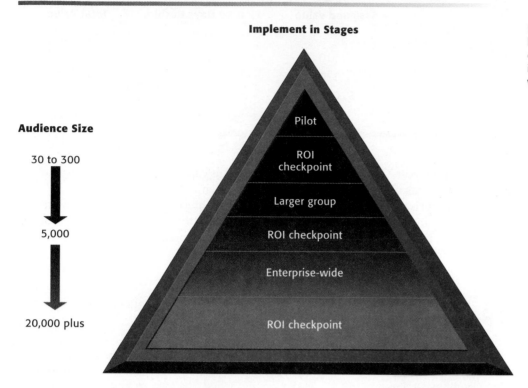

Knowledge management projects have a greater chance of succeeding if they are implemented in stages with clearly defined ways of measuring results.

- Number signed on to system
- Number of answers found in the knowledge base
- Number of answers received from expert providers
- Average rating of answers (on a scale of 1 to 5)
- Number of FAQs requested

In the group implementation stage, a different set of top-down measures can be used. Here, managers need to assign a value to answers viewed, improvements in business processes, new unexpected answers, the number of documents shared (as opposed to reinvented), and the number of FAQs accessed. The emphasis in these stages is on establishing a dollar value for the system's benefits based on reasonable assumptions and reports from users developed in the pilot stage.

Table 12-7 illustrates one set of results of using these measures for 1,000 users during a 90-day period. The total savings produced by all of these improvements during that period amounted to $225,010, or an average savings of $225.01 per user. If we projected these benefits for an entire year, total savings would amount to $900,040 (or $900.04 per user). If the system cost $700,000 to implement and $100,000 annually to maintain after the first year, the total benefits would amount to $200,040 in the first year and $800,040

TABLE 12-6 *Stages for Measuring Value of Knowledge Management Systems*

Stage	Approach	Required Time	Data Availability	Accuracy
Pilot project	Bottom up Evaluation metrics	Short	Usually available	Good
Group implementation	Group utilization data (e.g., demand)	Moderate	Easily gathered	Better
Enterprise-wide implementation	Process improvement	Lengthy	Requires effort	Best

TABLE 12-7 *Example of Savings from a Knowledge Management System*

Metric	Assigned Value	First 90 Days Results	Total Value
Documents shared	$450	172	$77,400
Answers viewed	$10	6,103	$61,030
New answers	$30	486	$14,580
Best practices	$3,000	18	$54,000
FAQs	$225	80	$18,000

each succeeding year. Chapter 15 describes the various capital budgeting models that can then be used to calculate the actual return on investment.

In the enterprise-wide implementation stage, other enterprise business process metrics become more important, such as response time to customers, speed of new product development, reductions in head count, reduction in procurement costs, and reductions in management decision-making intervals.

MAKE IT YOUR BUSINESS

Finance and Accounting

Many expert system, neural network, and hybrid AI applications as well as knowledge work systems have been developed for the finance and accounting function. Rule-based expert systems have been widely used tools for evaluating the credit risk of loan applicants and for investment portfolio selection. A number of financial services firms use neural networks for stock and bond trading strategies, commodity trading, and detecting credit card fraud. Financial professionals use investment workstations that integrate a wide range of financial data from internal and external sources as well as enterprise-wide knowledge management systems with structured and unstructured financial, accounting, and tax information.

Human Resources

The human resources function uses Web publishing tools and knowledge repositories to communicate company policies to employees and to provide online directories of human resources policies and training programs. Human resources specialists are also in charge of employee training programs to help employees use knowledge management systems and may also be responsible for operating the firm's learning management systems. The data from learning management systems often are exported to human resources systems so that they become part of each employee's permanent records. Human resources staff may be asked to help management develop policies and procedures to promote a "knowledge culture." Knowledge networks can help human resources with staffing by locating and identifying employees with the expertise for new job openings. You can find examples of human resources applications on pages 428 and 432.

Manufacturing and Production

The manufacturing and production function is replete with knowledge system applications. Many companies are using knowledge work and group collaboration tools for creating and sharing product design and manufacturing specifications and for project management. Expert systems have been used to guide the configuration of orders when products with many different parts or features are being assembled. Both expert systems and case-based reasoning systems are used for assisting diagnostic and repair work on malfunctioning products and equipment. Fuzzy logic helps improve the performance of products such as camcorders, air conditioners, washing machines, and subway cars. Genetic algorithms have generated solutions for problems in optimizing scheduling or design. Intelligent agents are starting to be used in supply chain management. You can find examples of manufacturing and production applications on pages 415 and 453–455.

Sales and Marketing

Specialized corporate portals and repositories for structured and unstructured knowledge have been created for sales and marketing staff to help them access and share information about customers, sales leads, competitors, and changes in product pricing and specifications. Virtual reality and VRML simulations can help customers experience the "look and feel" of products and even tailor some of these products more precisely to their needs. Case-based reasoning systems have been widely used for customer service and support. Many online intelligent agent tools and services have been developed to search the Web for products and services specified by users and to assist them in comparing prices and features.

Summary

1. **Assess the role of knowledge management and knowledge management programs in business.**

   Knowledge management is a set of processes to create, store, transfer, and apply knowledge in the organization. Businesses need knowledge management programs because knowledge has become a central productive and strategic asset in today's information economy and a potential source of competitive advantage. Much of a firm's value depends on its ability to create and manage knowledge. Knowledge management promotes organizational learning by increasing the ability of the organization to learn from its environment and to incorporate knowledge into its business processes. Effective knowledge management systems require organizational and management capital to promote a knowledge culture and programs for knowledge management, including the creation of a chief knowledge officer. There are three major types of knowledge management systems: enterprise-wide knowledge management systems, knowledge work systems, and intelligent techniques.

2. **Define and describe the types of systems used for enterprise-wide knowledge management and demonstrate how they provide value for organizations.**

   Enterprise-wide knowledge management systems are firmwide efforts to collect, store, distribute, and apply digital content and knowledge. Structured knowledge systems provide databases and tools for organizing and storing structured documents, whereas semistructured knowledge systems provide databases and tools for organizing and storing semistructured knowledge, such as e-mail or rich media. Knowledge network systems provide directories and tools for locating firm employees with special expertise who are important sources of tacit knowledge. Often these systems include group collaboration tools, portals to simplify information access, search tools, and tools for classifying information based on a taxonomy that is appropriate for the organization. Enterprise-wide knowledge management systems can provide considerable value if they are well designed and enable employees to locate, share, and use knowledge more efficiently.

3. **Define and describe the major types of knowledge work systems and assess how they provide value for firms.**

   Knowledge work systems (KWS) support the creation of new knowledge and its integration into the organization. KWS require easy access to an external knowledge base; powerful computer hardware that can support software with intensive graphics, analysis, document management, and communications capabilities; and a user-friendly interface. These capabilities can increase the productivity of highly paid knowledge workers. KWS often run on workstations that are cus-

tomized for the work they must perform. Computer-aided design (CAD) systems and virtual reality systems, which create interactive simulations that behave like the real world, require graphics and powerful modeling capabilities. KWS for financial professionals provide access to external databases and the ability to analyze massive amounts of financial data very quickly.

4. **Evaluate the business benefits of using intelligent techniques for knowledge management.**

   Artificial intelligence lacks the flexibility, breadth, and generality of human intelligence, but it can be used to capture, codify, and extend organizational knowledge. Businesses can use artificial intelligence to help them capture and preserve tacit knowledge; for knowledge discovery; to generate solutions to specific problems that are too massive and complex to be analyzed by human beings on their own; and to help firms search for and filter information.

   Expert systems capture tacit knowledge from a limited domain of human expertise and express that knowledge in the form of rules. The strategy to search through the knowledge base, called the inference engine, can use either forward or backward chaining. Expert systems are most useful for problems of classification or diagnosis. Case-based reasoning represents organizational knowledge as a database of cases that can be continually expanded and refined. When the user encounters a new case, the system searches for similar cases, finds the closest fit, and applies the solutions of the old case to the new case. The new case is stored with successful solutions in the case database.

   Fuzzy logic is a software technology for expressing knowledge in the form of rules that use approximate or subjective values. Fuzzy logic has been used for controlling physical devices and is starting to be used for limited decision-making applications.

   Neural networks consist of hardware and software that attempt to mimic the thought processes of the human brain. Neural networks are notable for their ability to learn without programming and to recognize patterns that cannot be easily described by humans. They are being used in science, medicine, and business primarily to discriminate patterns in massive amounts of data.

   Genetic algorithms develop solutions to particular problems using genetically based processes such as fitness, crossover, and mutation. Genetic algorithms are beginning to be applied to problems involving optimization, product design, and monitoring industrial systems where many alternatives or variables must be evaluated to generate an optimal solution.

   Intelligent agents are software programs with built-in or learned knowledge bases that carry out specific, repetitive, and predictable tasks for an individual user, business process, or software application. Intelligent agents can be programmed to navigate through large amounts of data to locate useful information and in some cases act on that information on behalf of the user.

5. *Identify the challenges posed by knowledge management systems and management solutions.*

Knowledge management systems are difficult to implement successfully and they do not always provide value after they are put in place. Firms can provide appro-

priate organizational and management capital to make these systems successful by rewarding knowledge sharing, promoting communities of practice and a knowledge culture, and designing appropriate taxonomies for organizing knowledge. Proper planning, development of appropriate measurements of benefits, and staged rollout can increase the chances of success for knowledge management projects. Key management decisions include identifying business processes for which knowledge management systems can provide the most value.

Key Terms

AI shell, 436	Hybrid AI systems, 443	Learning management system (LMS), 430
Artificial intelligence (AI), 436	Inference engine, 436	Neural networks, 441
Backward chaining, 437	Intelligent agent, 444	Organizational learning, 418
Case-based reasoning (CBR), 439	Intelligent techniques, 421	Rule base, 436
Chief knowledge officer (CKO), 420	Investment workstations, 435	Semistructured knowledge, 422
Communities of practice (COPs), 420	Knowledge, 416	Semistructured knowledge systems, 422
Computer-aided design (CAD), 433	Knowledge base, 436	Structured knowledge, 422
Document management systems, 419	Knowledge discovery, 435	Structured knowledge systems, 422
Expert systems, 436	Knowledge engineer, 437	Tacit knowledge, 416
Explicit knowledge, 416	Knowledge management, 418	Taxonomy, 427
Forward chaining, 436	Knowledge network systems, 423	Virtual Reality Modeling Language (VRML), 434
Fuzzy logic, 440	Knowledge repository, 422	Virtual reality systems, 434
Genetic algorithms, 442	Knowledge work systems (KWS), 421	Wisdom, 416

Review Questions

1. *What is knowledge management? How does it promote organizational learning? Why is it of great interest to business?*

2. *Describe the important dimensions of knowledge. Distinguish between data, knowledge, and wisdom and between explicit and tacit knowledge.*

3. *Describe the stages in the knowledge management value chain that add value as data and information are transformed into useful knowledge.*

4. *Describe the role played by organizational and management capital in knowledge management.*

5. *What are structured knowledge systems? Describe their capabilities.*

6. *What are semistructured knowledge systems? Describe their capabilities.*

7. *How do taxonomies and tools for tagging facilitate knowledge management?*

8. *Describe the capabilities of knowledge network systems.*

9. *Describe the role of the following in facilitating knowledge management: portals, collaboration tools, and learning management systems.*

10. *What are knowledge work systems? What role do they play in knowledge management? What are the generic requirements of knowledge work systems?*

11. *Describe how the following systems support knowledge work: computer-aided design (CAD), virtual reality, and investment workstations.*

12. *What are intelligent techniques? Why are they of interest to businesses for knowledge management? How does artificial intelligence differ from human intelligence?*

13. *Define an expert system, describe how it works, and explain how it can contribute to knowledge management.*

14. *What is case-based reasoning? How does it differ from an expert system? How does it support knowledge management?*

15. *What is a neural network? How can neural networks help companies with knowledge management?*

16. *Define and describe fuzzy logic. For what kinds of applications is it suited?*

17. *What are genetic algorithms? How can they help organizations solve problems? For what kinds of problems are they suited?*

18. *What are intelligent agents? How can they be used to benefit businesses?*

19. *What management challenges are raised by knowledge management systems? How can businesses obtain value from their knowledge management investments?*

Discussion Questions

1. *Knowledge management is a business process, not a technology. Discuss.*

2. *Describe various ways that knowledge management systems could help firms with sales and marketing or with manufacturing and production.*

Application Software Exercise:
Expert System Exercise: Building a Simple Expert System for Retirement Planning

When employees at your company retire, they are given cash bonuses. These cash bonuses are based on the length of employment and the retiree's age. To receive a bonus, an employee must be at least 50 years of age and have worked for the company for five years. The following table summarizes the criteria for determining bonuses.

LENGTH OF EMPLOYMENT	BONUS
< 5 years	No bonus
6–10 years	20 percent of current annual salary
11–15 years	30 percent of current annual salary
16–20 years	40 percent of current annual salary
20–25 years	50 percent of current annual salary
26 or more years	100 percent of current annual salary

Using the information provided, build a simple expert system. Find a demonstration copy of an expert system software tool on the Web that you can download (see the recommendations at www.prenhall.com/Laudon). Alternatively, use your spreadsheet software to build the expert system. (If you are using spreadsheet software, we suggest using the IF function so you can see how rules are created.)

Identifying Opportunities for Knowledge Management

Required software: Web browser software
Word processing software
Electronic presentation software (optional)

Senior management has started reading about knowledge management and has asked you to explore opportunities for improving knowledge management at Dirt Bikes. Write a report answering the following questions.

1. What are the most important knowledge assets at Dirt Bikes? What functions and employee positions are responsible for creating, distributing, and using these knowledge assets? Are all of these assets explicit knowledge?

2. What knowledge outside the organization is required by the company?

3. How could the following employee groups benefit from knowledge management:
   • Designers and engineers
   • Product development specialists
   • Marketing specialists
   • Sales department staff and representatives
   • Managers

   Describe the kinds of knowledge management systems that would be most valuable for each of these groups. What information would each of these systems provide?

4. Use the Web to research how the company could make better use of the Internet for knowledge management. What Internet information resources (specific Web sites or Usenet groups) would be most useful to Dirt Bikes?

5. Describe an enterprise portal for one of the employee groups listed in question 3. To which knowledge resources would it link? What would the homepage of this portal look like?

6. (Optional) Use electronic presentation software to summarize your findings for management.

Electronic Commerce Project: Using Intelligent Agents for Comparison Shopping

You have decided it is time to supplement your old film camera with a new digital camera, but you do not know what to purchase. So, prior to buying one, you want to find sites that review digital cameras and explain them. Begin your search using a popular search engine. Certain sites, such as Imaging Resource, also enable you to see the quality of the photographs, which is necessary for you to make your final choice. Several other sites, such as dpreview.com or dcresource.com enable you to compare features and prices. Having read material on the cameras and compared the quality of the photographs on these sites, select a digital camera you might want to purchase, such as the Canon PowerShot SD-10 or the Fuji FinePix S310.

You would like to purchase the camera as inexpensively as possible. Try several of the shopping bot sites, which do the price comparisons for you. Visit mySimon (www.mysimon.com), BizRate.com (www.bizrate.com), and CNET.com (www.cnet.com). Compare them in terms of their ease of use, number of offerings, speed in obtaining information, thoroughness of information offered about the product and seller, and price selection. Note that with some of the shopping bot sites, you are able to sort the results by model number or price by clicking the column title. Which site or sites would you use and why? Which camera would you select and why? How helpful were these sites for making your decision?

Group Project: Rating Knowledge Network Systems

With a group of classmates, select two knowledge network system products, such as AskMe, Tacit Knowledge Systems, Kamoon Connect, or Sopheon. Compare their features and capabilities. To prepare your analysis, use articles from computer magazines and the Web sites for the knowledge network software vendors. If possible, use electronic presentation software to present your findings to the class.

CASE STUDY
Can Knowledge Management Systems Help Pfizer?

Pharmaceutical companies are among the most intensive users of knowledge management systems, and you can easily see why. The drug discovery process is long and arduous. Researchers must first identify a biological target such as an enzyme or gene that appears related to a disease; fling hundreds of thousands of compounds at the target to see which interact with it; and conduct animal studies of toxicity, absorption, and the properties of the most promising molecules. If all still looks good, they would then test one of the compounds on humans.

Only one new chemical entity in 10,000 makes it through the U.S. Food and Drug Administration (FDA) approval process, and only half the drugs approved make it to market. The complete process costs $500 million to $700 million per drug, and each day of delay in a seven-year testing cycle for a hot new drug can cost $2.5 million.

Today the stakes are higher than ever. There are very few new drugs in the pipelines of major pharmaceutical companies. Despite steadily increasing expenditures on research and development, which now totals more than $25 billion annually in the United States alone, the U.S. FDA statistics show a steady decline in the approval of new drugs, or "new molecular entities."

The pharmaceutical companies are doing everything they can to develop new products and come up with new ideas—promoting a more innovative corporate culture, forging collaborative ties with university researchers, and acquiring young pharmaceutical and biotechnology firms to obtain new sources of expertise. Any knowledge from any source that can bring a new drug to market or expedite the drug development process is obviously very valuable.

Let us look at the role of knowledge management at one of these companies. Pfizer is the world's

largest research-based pharmaceutical firm. Its best-known products include Celebrex, Zoloft, Lipitor, and Viagra. In addition to prescription drugs, the firm makes over-the-counter remedies such as Bengay, Listerine, Benedryl, Visine, and animal health products. Pfizer is divided into three major business segments: pharmaceutical, health care, and animal health, with the pharmaceutical segment accounting for 88 percent of Pfizer's total revenue.

Among Pfizer's 122,000 employees, over 12,500 are scientists who work in research labs around the world. Pfizer Global Research and Development is the industry's largest pharmaceutical R&D organization, with a $7.1 billion budget for R&D in 2003. Pfizer's search for new drugs encompasses hundreds of research projects across 18 therapeutic areas—more than any other company. The company maintains links with more than 250 partners in academia and industry.

Like other major pharmaceutical companies, Pfizer relies heavily on knowledge management systems to drive its research and development work. It has systems to manage all of the documents and pieces of data involved in developing a new drug; expertise location systems to identify scientists and knowledge leaders within the company and outside experts who are involved in drug research and development; and searchable databases of information collected during clinical trials. Pfizer has Web-based portals to manage all of the documents and other pieces of knowledge associated with the product life cycle development process, including online discussions. A discussion list capability keeps track of discussion threads.

Pfizer's Global Research Division intranet has many dozens of applications organized both geographically and functionally for virtually every area and division of the com-

pany. They include an internal telephone directory, access to scientific publications, and sharing of research findings across international borders and time zones. Pfizer linked its intranet with an extranet for managing some 500 strategic alliances so its global teams can access legacy data and collaborate on projects more quickly. Researchers can link from the Pfizer intranet to the U.S. Food and Drug Administration Internet site. A tool called E-sub enables the company to access historical data to expedite preparation of the laborious new drug applications (NDAs) required by the FDA.

The company is moving toward a global approach to information management. In the past, each R&D library would look first in its own collection to locate requested articles. If the articles were not found there, public libraries and resources would be searched. If a requested article was still not found, an outside firm was commissioned to locate the article. Now Pfizer scientists can search the journal collections of each major Pfizer library from a single master list.

Pfizer adopted Oracle's Clinical application, which is designed to help pharmaceutical companies bring products to market faster. The software establishes standards and common working practices. Oracle Clinical has a capability for tracking who accesses each piece of data and how and why changes were made. It includes a subsystem for managing data definitions and can flag any data entered during a study that it cannot validate, so researchers can quickly identify problems with the data or the product under development. Definitions and amendments are automatically propagated to all locations.

Pfizer was one of the pioneers in using advanced information technology for combinatorial chemistry and high-throughput screening.

Combinatorial chemistry enables companies to design, screen, and test compounds very rapidly by using chemistry, molecular biology, and information technology to create and test thousands of chemical combinations at once. Previously, pharmaceutical companies had to evaluate thousands of compounds individually before finding one possible candidate for further development.

Combinatorial chemistry and high-throughput screening became popular in the early to mid-1990s as a way to accelerate this process. Rather than have chemists cook up each type of molecule by hand, which could take weeks, machines would create thousands of chemicals in a day by mixing and matching common building blocks. Then robots would drop bits of each chemical into tiny vials containing samples of a bodily substance involved in a disease, such as the protein that triggers cholesterol production. A "hit" occurred when the substance and the chemical produced a desired reaction. (The testing process is called high-throughput screening.)

Virtually all the major pharmaceutical companies embraced combinatorial chemistry and high-throughput screening, spending tens of millions of dollars forming alliances with smaller companies that specialized in this technology. Between 1995 and 2000, Pfizer entered into 36 alliances with 29 different companies in combinatorial chemistry alone, and the number rises to 50 if you include Pfizer's acquisitions of Warner-Lambert and Agouron.

Intelligent machines churned out chemical after chemical, but almost none produced useful results. Often the machines threw so many ingredients together that the resulting chemicals were too "large" from a molecular standpoint. They would work in a test tube but would get broken down too easily in the human stomach. In one case a drug that prevented infection showed promising results in a test tube, but could not dissolve in water, which is required for intravenous drips. When chemicals were made individually, chemists usually dealt with such issues during the initial stages of development.

According to Carl Decicco, head of discovery chemistry at Bristol-Myers, many chemists became fixated on creating thousands or millions of chemicals for testing without thinking about whether any of them had any real use. "You end up making things that you can make, rather than what you should make," he says. Countless combinations of potential druglike chemicals are theoretically possible, but most of these combinations are really useless to humans. Pfizer senior research fellow Carl Lipinski, who retired in 2002, compiled a list of complex technical traits that often make chemicals difficult for humans to absorb and persuaded Pfizer to reprogram its computers so chemists would be warned if chemicals violated the "Lipinski rule."

Critics of combinatorial chemistry and high-throughput screening point out that these methods lack human insight, intuition, and intellectual creativity. Opponents believe these methods eliminate opportunities for serendipitous discovery. For example, in 1991 Schering-Plough scientists were looking for a drug to block a certain cholesterol-producing enzyme in the body. During a test on hamsters, they noticed that one molecule failed to block the enzyme but nevertheless lowered cholesterol. Some additional hand-tweaking by chemists turned the molecule into the cholesterol-lowering drug Zetia, which was approved by the FDA in 2002. If a robot had tested the molecule in a test tube, it would have noted the failure but would have missed its serendipitous side effect.

Because robot screeners can work only with liquids, the huge chemical libraries created by combinatorial chemistry and high-throughput screening are often placed in dimethyl sulfoxide, a standard solution for storing chemicals. In some cases the chemicals settle as a solid at the bottom of the solution or the solution containing the chemical breaks down. The drug-testing robot reaching into such mixtures may only come up with a drop of useless soup. Traditional labs avoid this problem by storing chemicals that might break down in dimethyl sulfoxide as pow-

ders, which are put into solution just before screening.

Pfizer and the other major pharmaceutical companies are trying to rectify these problems. Pfizer spent over $600 million at labs around the world to ensure that the chemicals in its libraries are more druglike and diverse. It is using techniques other than combinatorial chemistry and making sure each chemical can meet Lipinski's test. Martin Mackay, a senior vice president at Pfizer's research labs, reports that a higher percentage of compounds at Pfizer are now making it through each stage of testing but that it will take 10 years to tell whether efforts to improve the technology are working. "We're very confident," he says.

Other scientists echo his belief that the industry has solved its early problems with combinatorial chemistry and high-throughput screening and that the pipelines will be filled with new drugs created by these methods a decade from now. "It took a while to learn how to use all these new technologies," says Richard Gregg, vice president of clinical discovery at Bristol-Myers research labs.

A study led by David Newman of the National Cancer Institute concluded that combinatorial chemistry and high-throughput screening had failed to create a single FDA-approved drug through the end of 2002. A separate study of 350 cancer drugs now in human trials found only one that had been created with these methods, although the technology did help improve some drugs that were created by more traditional means.

Some observers believe that pharmaceutical firms' widespread use of combinatorial chemistry and high-throughput screening is one reason why there is such a dearth of new drugs today. The number of new drugs approved by the FDA each year has declined since 1996. In 2003, the FDA approved only 21 new drugs (of which one was produced by Pfizer and one by Agouron), compared to 56 in 1996.

Sources: Peter Landers, "Drug Industry's Big Push into Technology Falls Short," *Wall Street Journal,* February 24, 2004;

Madanmohan Rao, "Leveraging Pharmaceutical Knowledge," *Knowledge Management*, March 2003; www.pfizer.com, accessed June 10, 2004; Kim Ann Zimmermann, "In Search of Experts: Pharmaceuticals Enter Next Phase of KM," *KWorld*, January 2003; Helene S. Gidley, "Hand in Hand," *PM Network*, August 2003; and Stephen S. Hall, "Revitalizing Drug Discovery," *Technology Review*, October 2003.

CASE STUDY QUESTIONS

1. Analyze Pfizer's business strategy using the competitive forces and value chain models.

2. How important are knowledge management systems at Pfizer? How do they provide value to the company? How do they support the company's business strategy?

3. Evaluate Pfizer's use of combinatorial chemistry and high-throughput screening in its business strategy? How effective has it been?

4. How successful do you think Pfizer will be in using its current knowledge management systems in the future?

Chapter 13

Enhancing Decision Making for the Digital Firm

OBJECTIVES

After completing this chapter, you will be able to:

1. Describe different types of decisions and the decision-making process.

2. Evaluate the role of information systems in helping people working individually and in a group make decisions more efficiently.

3. Demonstrate how executive support systems can help senior managers make better decisions.

4. Assess how systems that support decision making can provide value for the firm.

5. Identify the challenges posed by decision-support systems, group decision-support systems, and executive support systems and management solutions.

CHAPTER OUTLINE

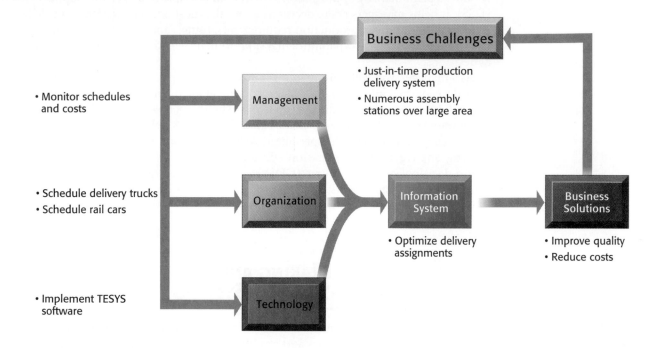

Monitor schedules and costs

Schedule delivery trucks
Schedule rail cars

Implement TESYS software

Management

Organization

Technology

Business Challenges
- Just-in-time production delivery system
- Numerous assembly stations over large area

Information System
- Optimize delivery assignments

Business Solutions
- Improve quality
- Reduce costs

Opening Case: Daimler's Bremen Plant Optimizes Deliveries with a DSS

The automotive plant of DaimlerChrysler in Bremen, Germany, has 13,000 employees and produces more than 800 cars per day. Each day, 70 rail cars and 500 trucks transport parts, components, and materials to the factory, which occupies an area of about 1 million square meters. This plant uses a just-in-time delivery system: All of the parts and components must be delivered to the plant's various assembly stations just at the moment when they are needed.

Nearly 20 years ago, Daimler management realized that the intraplant transport capacity was not utilized efficiently because there was no way to manage plant deliveries effectively. Once arriving at the plant, drivers moved their trucks to their loading points, not knowing if they would arrive there in the right order or if the loading point would be free. The trucks were not always able to deliver the required material during the agreed time frame. Material on the trucks might arrive too soon, or urgently needed material might not be available because the truck was waiting in line. Daimler needed a better way to make decisions about organizing its in-plant deliveries.

The company decided to use the Transportation Efficiency Support System (TESYS) to solve this problem. TESYS is a decision-support and optimization software system developed by INFORM GmbH of Aachen, Germany. It synchronizes deliveries with the capacities of loading points within the area of a plant and with the current needs of production. TESYS is currently used at multiple intermodal hubs, ports, and other logistic centers throughout the world.

When a delivery arrives at the DaimlerChrysler plant, requests for unloading are submitted to the plant's control board using either an automated order reception model or the telephone. The system optimizes the assignment, showing the shortest routes and quickest on-time completion of all transport orders. New delivery instructions are transmitted to the appropriate driver using two-way radio.

The system handles most time-critical operations automatically, although the software does allow human controllers to handle important special deliveries. Optimal use of resources cuts costs and increases the quality and productivity of the entire plant logistics system. The plant's logistics operations became much more efficient, with utilization of plant transport capacity increasing from 60 percent to 94 percent.

Sources: Hans Jurgen Zimmermann, "Online Optimization," *OR/MS Today*, April 2004; and www.inform-ac.com/tess/en/02_08.htm, accessed May 9, 2004.

Daimler's plant delivery optimization system is an example of a decision-support system (DSS). It helps managers make decisions about the most efficient way to stage deliveries to loading points given production requirements, routes, and time frames. Such systems have powerful analytical capabilities that support managers during the process of arriving at decisions.

As a manager, you will want to know how you can use information systems to improve your decision making, whether you are working alone or in a group. Just as important, you will be responsible for the decisions made by the people who work under you, and you'll want systems to help them make better decisions as well.

This chapter focuses on the specialized systems that firms use to achieve better decision making: management information systems (MIS), decision-support systems (DSS), group decision-support systems (GDSS), and executive support systems (ESS). You'll learn how these systems work, how they provide value for the business, and the challenges of building and using them wisely.

13.1   DECISION MAKING AND DECISION-SUPPORT SYSTEMS

Chapter 1 points out that information systems have business value when they enable more efficient business processes and improve management decision making. As organizations flatten and push decision making to lower levels to include non-management employees, information systems make significant contributions to the overall quality of decision making for the entire firm.

For instance, a service firm such as EchoStar Communications, one of the world's largest television satellite firms, receives millions of calls at the company's call centers each year. If a customer service representative has the right information about a customer calling into the call center, that employee can decide to offer the customer special services that could encourage the customer to stay with the company or perhaps purchase additional services, thus contributing to the firm's value.

On a larger scale, there are 142 million workers in the U.S. labor force producing $12.2 trillion in gross domestic product (GDP). If the decision-making quality of these employees could be improved by just 1 percent in a year, then the GDP might expand by a substantial amount, perhaps equivalent to 1 percent, or $122 billion, annually, perhaps far more. For both small and large firms the ability of managers and employees to make the right decision at the right time with the right information can have extraordinary business value.

Business Intelligence and Decision Support

Because of the importance of high-quality decision making, firms are investing heavily in **business intelligence** systems, which consist of technologies and applications designed to help users make better business decisions. When we think of *intelligence* as applied to humans, we typically think of people's ability to combine learned knowledge with new information and change their behavior in such a way that they succeed at their task or adapt to a new situation. Likewise, business intelligence provides firms with the capability to amass information, develop knowledge about operations, and change decision-making behavior to achieve profitability and other business goals.

Figure 13-1 illustrates the major applications and technologies used for business intelligence. They include the supply chain management, customer relationship management, and enterprise systems; systems for knowledge management; and technologies such as data mining and online analytical processing (OLAP) for obtaining knowledge and insight from analyzing large quantities of data. These systems work with specialized systems for management decision making (MIS, DSS, ESS) that focus on the specific decision needs of managers and employees.

FIGURE 13-1   *Systems and technologies for business intelligence.*

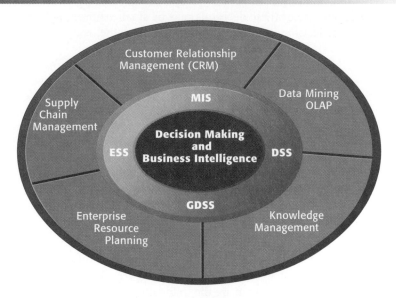

Each of the major enterprise applications provides support for decision making or "business intelligence" at all levels of the firm in addition to processing daily transactions. Specialized systems such as MIS, DSS, and ESS described in this chapter work with these systems and technologies for data mining and online analytical processing (OLAP) to focus on the specific decision needs of managers and employees.

Systems and Technologies for Business Intelligence

Business Value of Improved Decision Making

Let's try to measure the business benefits of improved decision making and link these improvements to firm profitability. Table 13-1 describes an example of a small manufacturing firm operating in the United States with $280 million annual revenue and 140 employees. The firm has identified a number of key decisions where new systems investments might improve the quality of decision making and produce value. Analysts have estimated the value to the firm of improving each decision. The table provides selected estimates of the annual value (either in cost savings or revenue enhancement) of improved decision making in selected areas of the firm.

TABLE 13-1 *Business Value of Enhanced Decision Making*

Example Decision	Decision Maker	Number of Annual Decisions	Estimated Value to Firm of a Single Improved Decision	Annual Value
CUSTOMER RELATIONSHIP MANAGEMENT (CRM)				
Allocate support to most valuable customers	Accounts manager	12	$100,000	$1,200,000
Predict call center quarterly demand	Call center management	4	$150,000	$600,000
SUPPLY CHAIN MANAGEMENT (SCM)				
Decide parts inventory levels daily	Inventory manager	365	$5,000	$1,825,000
Identify competitive bids from major vendors	Senior management	1	$2,000,000	$2,000,000
ENTERPRISE SYSTEM				
Schedule production to fill orders	Manufacturing manager	150	$10,000	$1,500,000
Allocate labor to complete a job	Production floor manager	100	$4,000	$400,000
KNOWLEDGE MANAGEMENT (KM)				
Determine testing procedure for a new chemical compound	Project team of scientists and engineers	3	$800,000	$2,400,000

Table 13-1 shows that decisions are made at all levels of the firm and that some decisions are very common and routine, but exceptionally valuable. Although the value of improving any single one of these decisions may be small, improving hundreds of thousands of these small decisions adds up to a large annual value.

Business Decision Making and the Decision-Making Process

Before making improvements in corporate decision making with system investments, you must understand more about the nature of decisions and the decision-making process. There are different information requirements at different levels of responsibility in the organization that affect the types of decisions made at each level.

DECISION-MAKING LEVELS

Chapter 2 shows that there are different levels in an organization. Each of these levels has different information requirements for decision support and different constituencies or groups that information systems need to serve (see Figure 13-2). The four different decision-making constituencies in a firm are the following:

* *Senior management.* Senior management is concerned with general yet timely information on changes in the industry and society at large that may affect both the long-term and near-term future of the firm, the firm's strategic goals, short-term and future per-

FIGURE 13-2   *Information requirements of key decision-making groups.*

Information Requirements of Key Decision-Making Groups in a Firm

Decision Characteristics		Information Requirements
Unstructured	Senior Management	General Broad scope Interactive External Internal Real-time Ad hoc
Semistructured	Middle Management	Focused Specified Interactive Internal Real-time Scheduled
Structured	Operational Management Individual Employees and Teams	Specified Scheduled Narrow Interactive Real-time Internal Detailed

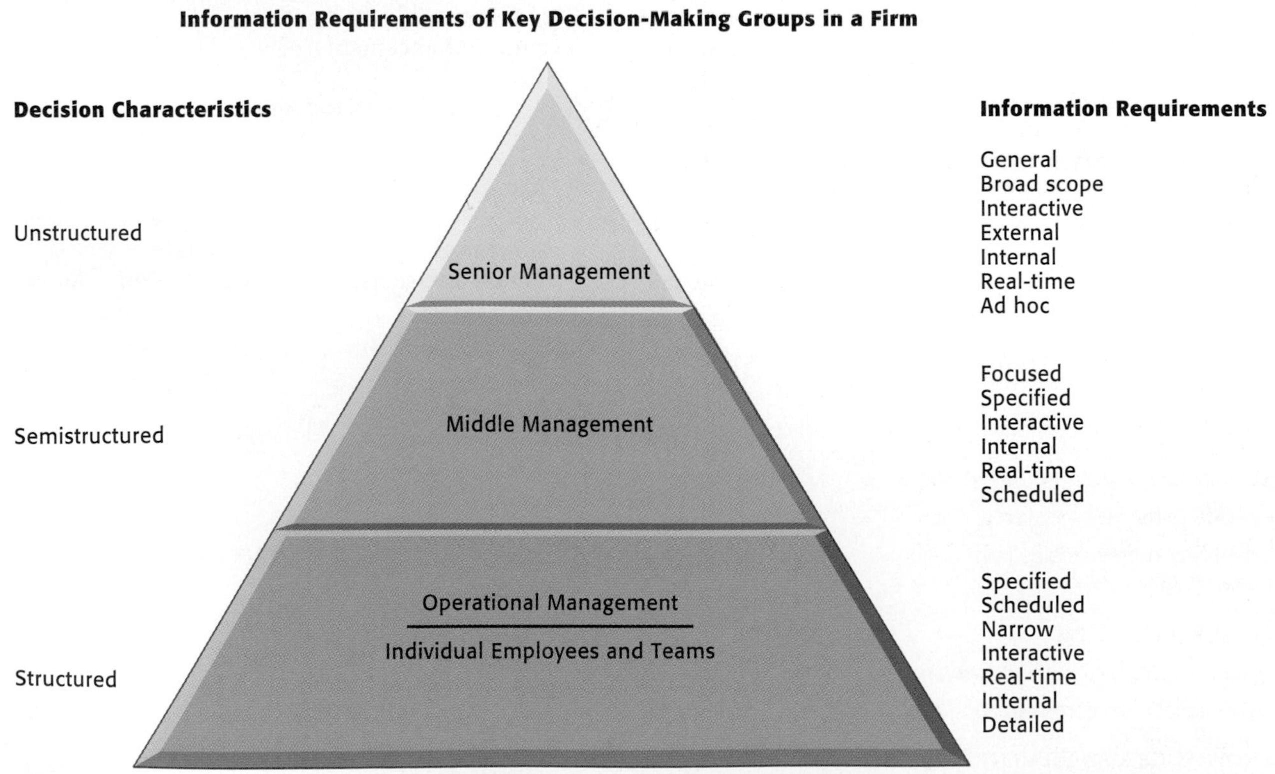

Various levels of management in the firm have differing information requirements for decision support because of their different job responsibilities and the nature of the decisions made at each level.

formance, specific bottlenecks and trouble affecting operational capabilities, and the overall ability of the firm to achieve its objectives.

- *Middle management and project teams.* Middle management is concerned with specific, timely information about firm performance, including revenue and cost reduction targets, and with developing plans and budgets to meet strategic goals established by senior management. This group needs to make important decisions about allocating resources, developing short-range plans, and monitoring the performance of departments, task forces, teams, and special project groups. Often the work of middle managers is accomplished in teams or small groups of managers working on a task.

- *Operational management and project teams.* Operational management monitors the performance of each subunit of the firm and manages individual employees. Operational managers are in charge of specific projects and allocate resources within the project budget, establish schedules, and make personnel decisions. Operational work may also be accomplished through teams.

- *Individual employees.* Employees try to fulfill the objectives of managers above them, following established rules and procedures for their routine activities. Increasingly, however, employees are granted much broader responsibilities and decision-making authority based on their own best judgment and information in corporate systems. Employees may be making decisions about specific vendors, customers, and other employees. Because employees interact directly with the public, how well they make their decisions can directly impact the firm's revenue streams.

TYPES OF DECISIONS

The characteristics of decisions faced by managers at different levels are quite different. Decisions can be classified as structured, semistructured, and unstructured. **Unstructured decisions** are those in which the decision maker must provide judgment, evaluation, and insights into the problem definition. Each of these decisions is novel, important, and non-routine, and there is no well-understood or agreed-on procedure for making them.

Structured decisions, by contrast, are repetitive and routine, and decision makers can follow a definite procedure for handling them to be efficient. Many decisions have elements of both and are considered **semistructured decisions**, in which only part of the problem has a clear-cut answer provided by an accepted procedure. In general, structured decisions are made more prevalently at lower organizational levels, whereas unstructured decision making is more common at higher levels of the firm.

Senior executives tend to be exposed to many unstructured decision situations that are open ended and evaluative and that require insight based on many sources of information and personal experience. For example, a CEO in today's music industry might ask, "Whom should we choose as a distribution partner for our online music catalog—Apple, Microsoft, or Sony?" Answering this question would require access to news, government reports, and industry views as well as high-level summaries of firm performance. However, the answer would also require senior managers to use their own best judgment and poll other managers for their opinions.

Middle management and operational management tend to face more structured decision scenarios, but their decisions may include unstructured components. A typical middle-level management decision might be "Why is the order fulfillment report showing a decline over the last six months at a distribution center in Minneapolis?" This middle manager could obtain a report from the firm's enterprise system or distribution management system on order activity and operational efficiency at the Minneapolis distribution center. This is the structured part of the decision. But before arriving at an answer, this middle manager will have to interview employees and gather more unstructured information from external sources about local economic conditions or sales trends.

Rank-and-file employees tend to make more structured decisions. For example, a sales account representative often has to make decisions about extending credit to customers by consulting the firm's customer database that contains credit information. In this case the decision is highly structured, it is a routine decision made thousands of times each day in most firms, and the answer has been preprogrammed into a corporate risk management or credit reporting system.

The types of decisions faced by project teams cannot be classified neatly by organizational level. Teams are small groups of middle and operational managers and perhaps employees assigned specific tasks that may last a few months to a few years. Their tasks may involve unstructured or semistructured decisions such as designing new products, devising new ways to enter the marketplace, or reorganizing sales territories and compensation systems.

SYSTEMS FOR DECISION SUPPORT

There are four kinds of systems used to support the different levels and types of decisions just described (see Table 13-2). We introduced some of these systems in Chapter 2. *Management information systems (MIS)* provide routine reports and summaries of transaction-level data to middle and operational-level managers to provide answers to structured and semistructured decision problems. *Decision-support systems (DSS)* are targeted systems that combine analytical models with operational data and supportive interactive queries and analysis for middle managers who face semistructured decision situations. *Executive support systems (ESS)* are specialized systems that provide senior management making primarily unstructured decisions with a broad array of both external information (news, stock analyses, industry trends) and high-level summaries of firm performance. Group decision-support systems (GDSS) are specialized systems that provide a group electronic environment in which managers and teams can collectively make decisions and design solutions for unstructured and semistructured problems.

STAGES IN THE DECISION-MAKING PROCESS

Making decisions consists of several different activities. Simon (1960) describes four different stages in decision making: intelligence, design, choice, and implementation (Figure 13-3).

Intelligence consists of discovering, identifying, and understanding the problems occurring in the organization—why is there a problem, where, and what effects is it having on the firm. Traditional MIS that deliver a wide variety of detailed information can help identify problems, especially if the systems report exceptions.

Design involves identifying and exploring various solutions to the problem. Decision-support systems (DSS) are ideal in this stage for exploring alternatives because they possess analytical tools for modeling data, enabling users to explore various options quickly.

Choice consists of choosing among solution alternatives. Here, DSS with access to extensive firm data can help managers choose the optimal solution. Also group decision-support systems can be used to bring groups of managers together in an electronic online environment to discuss different solutions and make a choice.

TABLE 13-2 *Organizational Level and Systems for Decision Support*

Organizational Level	Decision Type	Type of Decision-Support System	Examples
Senior management	Unstructured	Executive support systems (ESS)	Decide entrance or exit from markets Approve capital budget Decide long-term corporate objectives
Middle management/ project teams	Semistructured	Management information systems (MIS) Decision-support systems (DSS) Group decision-support systems (GDSS)	Allocate resources to managers and departments Design a new corporate Web site Develop a marketing plan Design a departmental budget
Operational management/ project teams Employees	Semistructured Structured	Decision-support systems (DSS) Management information systems (MIS) Group decision-support systems (GDSS)	Evaluate employee performance Restock inventory Routine credit decisions Determine special offers to customers

FIGURE 13-3   *Stages in decision making.*

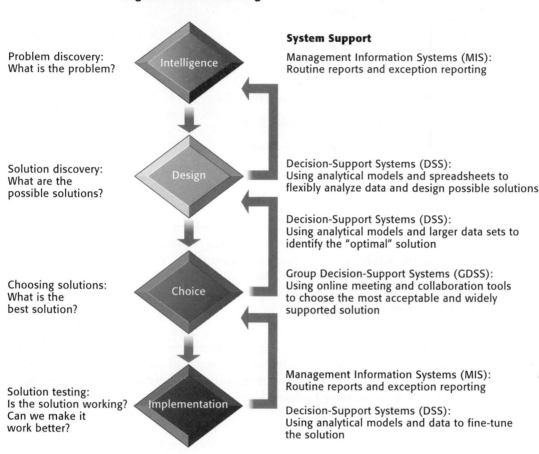

Stages in Decision Making

Problem discovery:
What is the problem?

Intelligence

System Support

Management Information Systems (MIS):
Routine reports and exception reporting

Solution discovery:
What are the
possible solutions?

Design

Decision-Support Systems (DSS):
Using analytical models and spreadsheets to
flexibly analyze data and design possible solutions

Decision-Support Systems (DSS):
Using analytical models and larger data sets to
identify the "optimal" solution

Choosing solutions:
What is the
best solution?

Choice

Group Decision-Support Systems (GDSS):
Using online meeting and collaboration tools
to choose the most acceptable and widely
supported solution

Solution testing:
Is the solution working?
Can we make it
work better?

Implementation

Management Information Systems (MIS):
Routine reports and exception reporting

Decision-Support Systems (DSS):
Using analytical models and data to fine-tune
the solution

The decision-making
process can be described
in four steps that follow
one another in a logical
order. In reality, decision
makers frequently circle
back to reconsider the
previous stages and
through a process of
iteration eventually arrive
at a solution that is
workable.

Implementation involves making the chosen alternative work and continuing to monitor how well the solution is working. Here, traditional MIS come back into play by providing managers with routine reports on the progress of a specific solution. Support systems can range from full-blown MIS to much smaller systems, as well as project-planning software operating on personal computers.

In the real world, the stages of decision making described here do not necessarily follow a linear path. You can be in the process of implementing a decision, only to discover that your solution is not working. In such cases, you will be forced to repeat the design, choice, or perhaps even the intelligence stage.

For instance, in the face of declining sales, a sales management team may strongly support a new sales incentive system to spur the sales force on to greater effort. If paying the sales force a higher commission for making more sales does not produce sales increases, managers would need to investigate whether the problem stems from poor product design, inadequate customer support, or a host of other causes, none of which would be "solved" by a new incentive system.

DECISION MAKING IN THE REAL WORLD

The premise of this book and this chapter is that investments in systems to support decision making produce better decision making by managers and employees in the firm, above average returns on investment for the firm, and ultimately higher profitability. Unfortunately, in the real world, for some firms, investments in decision-support systems do not always work out this way for three reasons: data quality, management filters, and organizational culture. Review the discussion on organizations in Chapter 3 as well.

Information Quality High-quality decisions require high-quality information regardless of information systems. You should consider seven dimensions of information quality when designing decision-support systems:

Accuracy: Do the data represent reality?

Integrity: Are the structure of data and relationships among the entities and attributes consistent?

Consistency: Are data elements consistently defined?

Completeness: Are all the necessary data present?

Validity: Do data values fall within defined ranges?

Timeliness: Are data available when needed?

Accessibility: Are the data accessible, comprehensible, and usable?

Chapter 7 has shown that corporate databases and files have varying levels of inaccuracy and incompleteness, which in turn can degrade the quality of decision making. When the underlying data are poor, the quality of decision making suffers. For instance, until recently, the United Kingdom's Royal Navy was plagued by inaccuracies and inconsistent data for the 510,770 items of supply in its inventory systems. It found 56,035 incorrect or missing entries for the attribute "Packaging Code" alone. Management could not make accurate decisions on what items needed to be ordered or how many items should be kept in inventory (Wrazen, 2004).

Management Filters Even with timely, accurate information, some managers make bad decisions. Managers (like all human beings) absorb information through a series of filters to make sense of the world around them. Managers have selective attention, focus on certain kinds of problems and solutions, and have a variety of biases that isolate them from reality. They filter by turning off information they do not want to hear because it does not conform to their prior conceptions.

For instance, Cisco Systems Corporation, one of the most advanced users of online decision-support systems, nevertheless was forced to write off as a loss $3.4 billion in excess inventory in 2001. Cisco's managers built inventory in response to the output from the company's online sales order entry system, which throughout 1999 and 2000 showed exceptionally strong orders. Unfortunately, Cisco managers did not pay attention to the quality of those orders. Customers, perceiving a shortage of routers and other networking equipment, were placing orders with multiple manufacturers, awarding the business to the first one who could deliver, and canceling other orders. Cisco's systems were recording high levels of order cancellation, but management ignored this "bad news" and emphasized the "good news": new orders were piling up (Laudon and Laudon, 2003).

Organizational Inertia Chapter 3 shows that organizations are bureaucracies with limited capabilities and competencies for acting decisively. When environments change and businesses need to adopt new business models to survive, strong forces within organizations resist making decisions calling for major change. Decisions taken by a firm often represent a balancing of the firm's various interest groups rather than the best solution to the problem.

Consider the record label industry. Despite declining sales since 2000 and the explosion of songs downloaded for free over the Internet, major recording companies did not move quickly into online music retailing. This required a much leaner business model. The recording companies resisted selling music over the Internet for years. Until very recently, nearly all executives and most employees at record label companies continued to believe that music should be distributed on physical devices (records, tapes, or CDs) and sold through retail record stores.

Studies of business restructuring find that firms tend to ignore poor performance until threatened by outside takeovers, and they systematically blame poor performance on external forces beyond their control such as economic conditions (the economy), foreign competition, and rising prices, rather than blaming senior or middle management for poor business judgment (Kose, Lang, Netter, et. al., 1992).

Trends in Decision Support and Business Intelligence

Systems supporting management decision making originated in the early 1960s as early MIS that created fixed, inflexible paper-based reports and distributed them to managers on a routine schedule. In the 1970s, the first DSS emerged as standalone applications with limited data and a few analytic models. ESS emerged during the 1980s to give senior managers an overview of corporate operations. Early ESS were expensive, based on custom technology, and suffered from limited data and flexibility.

The rise of client/server computing, the Internet, and Web technologies has made a major impact on systems that support decision making. Many decision-support applications are now delivered over corporate intranets. We see six major trends:

- *Detailed enterprise-wide data.* Enterprise systems create an explosion in firmwide, current, and relatively accurate information, supplying end users at their desktops with powerful analytic tools for analyzing and visualizing data.

- *Broadening decision rights and responsibilities.* As information becomes more widespread throughout the corporation, it is possible to reduce levels of hierarchy and grant more decision-making authority to lower-level employees.

- *Intranets and portals.* Intranet technologies create global, company-wide networks that ease the flow of information across divisions and regions and delivery of near real-time data to management and employee desktops.

- *Personalization and customization of information.* Web portal technologies provide great flexibility in determining what data each employee and manager sees on his or her desktop. Personalization of decision information can speed up decision making by enabling users to filter out irrelevant information.

- *Extranets and collaborative commerce.* Internet and Web technologies permit suppliers and logistics partners to access firm enterprise data and decision-support tools and work collaboratively with the firm.

- *Team support tools.* Web-based collaboration and meeting tools enable project teams, task forces, and small groups to meet online using corporate intranets or extranets. These new collaboration tools borrow from earlier GDSS and are used for both brainstorming and decision sessions.

13.2 SYSTEMS FOR DECISION SUPPORT

Exactly how have these trends affected systems for business decision making? What can today's decision-support systems do for the firm? Let's look more closely at how each major type of decision-support system works and provides value.

The Difference between MIS and DSS

Management information systems (MIS) provide information on the firm's performance to help managers monitor and control the business. They typically produce fixed, regularly scheduled reports based on data extracted and summarized from the firm's underlying transaction processing systems (TPS). The formats for these reports are often specified in advance. A typical MIS report might show a summary of monthly sales for each of the major sales territories of a company. Sometimes MIS reports are exception reports, highlighting only exceptional conditions, such as when the sales quotas for a specific territory fall below an anticipated level or employees have exceeded their spending limits in a dental care plan. Traditional MIS produced primarily hard-copy reports. Today, these

TABLE 13-3 Examples of MIS Applications

Company	MIS Application
California Pizza Kitchen	Inventory Express application "remembers" each restaurant's ordering patterns and compares the amount of ingredients used per menu item to predefined portion measurements established by management. The system identifies restaurants with out-of-line portions and notifies their managers so that corrective actions can be taken.
PharMark	Extranet MIS identifies patients with drug-use patterns that place them at risk for adverse outcomes.
Black & Veatch	Intranet MIS tracks construction costs for various projects across the United States.
Taco Bell	Total Automation of Company Operations (TACO) system provides information on food, labor, and period-to-date costs for each restaurant.

reports are available online through an intranet, and more MIS reports can be generated on demand. Table 13-3 provides some examples of MIS applications.

Decision-support systems support decisions in a different way. Whereas MIS primarily address structured problems, DSS support semistructured and unstructured problem analysis. An MIS provides managers with reports based on routine flows of data and assists in the general control of the business, whereas a DSS emphasizes change, flexibility, and a rapid response. With a DSS there is less of an effort to link users to structured information flows and a correspondingly greater emphasis on models, assumptions, ad hoc queries, and display graphics.

Types of Decision-Support Systems

The earliest DSS primarily used small subsets of corporate data and were heavily model driven. Recent advances in computer processing and database technology have expanded the definition of a DSS to include systems that can support decision making by analyzing vast quantities of data, including firmwide data from enterprise systems and transaction data from the Web.

Today, there are two basic types of decision-support systems, model driven and data driven (Dhar and Stein, 1997). **Model-driven DSS** were primarily standalone systems isolated from major corporate information systems that used some type of model to perform "what-if" and other kinds of analyses. Their analysis capabilities were based on a strong theory or model combined with a good user interface that made the model easy to use. The voyage-estimating DSS described in Chapter 2 and DaimlerChrysler's Transportation Efficiency Support System described in the chapter-opening case are examples of model-driven DSS.

The second type of DSS is a **data-driven DSS**. These systems analyze large pools of data found in major corporate systems. They support decision making by enabling users to extract useful information that was previously buried in large quantities of data. Often data from transaction processing systems are collected in data warehouses for this purpose. Online analytical processing (OLAP) and data mining can then be used to analyze the data. Companies are starting to build data-driven DSS to mine customer data gathered from their Web sites as well as data from enterprise systems.

Traditional database queries answer such questions as, "How many units of product number 403 were shipped in November 2004?" OLAP, or multidimensional analysis, supports much more complex requests for information, such as, "Compare sales of product 403 relative to plan by quarter and sales region for the past two years." We describe OLAP and multidimensional data analysis in Chapter 7. With OLAP and query-oriented data analysis, users need to have a good idea about the information for which they are looking.

Data mining, which we introduce in Chapter 7, is more discovery driven. Data mining provides insights into corporate data that cannot be obtained with OLAP by finding hidden patterns and relationships in large databases and inferring rules from them to predict future behavior. The patterns and rules then can be used to guide decision making and forecast the effect of those decisions. The types of information that can be obtained from data mining include associations, sequences, classifications, clusters, and forecasts:

- *Associations* are occurrences linked to a single event. For instance, a study of supermarket purchasing patterns might reveal that when corn chips are purchased, a cola drink is purchased 65 percent of the time, but when there is a promotion, cola is purchased 85 percent of the time. With this information, managers can make better decisions because they have learned the profitability of a promotion.

- In *sequences,* events are linked over time. We might find, for example, that if a house is purchased, a new refrigerator will be purchased within two weeks 65 percent of the time, and an oven will be bought within one month of the home purchase 45 percent of the time.

- *Classification* recognizes patterns that describe the group to which an item belongs by examining existing items that have been classified and by inferring a set of rules. For example, businesses such as credit card or telephone companies worry about the loss of steady customers. Classification can help discover the characteristics of customers who are likely to leave and can provide a model to help managers predict who they are so that they can devise special campaigns to retain such customers.

- *Clustering* works in a manner similar to classification when no groups have yet been defined. A data-mining tool can discover different groupings within data, such as finding affinity groups for bank cards or partitioning a database into groups of customers based on demographics and types of personal investments.

- Although these applications involve predictions, *forecasting* uses predictions in a different way. It uses a series of existing values to forecast what other values will be. For example, forecasting might find patterns in data to help managers estimate the future value of continuous variables such as sales figures.

Data mining uses statistical analysis tools as well as neural networks, fuzzy logic, genetic algorithms, and rule-based and other intelligent techniques (described in Chapter 12). It is an important aspect of *knowledge discovery*, which includes selection, preparation, and interpretation of the contents of large databases to identify novel and valuable patterns in the data.

The Window on Organizations describes a data-driven DSS used for analyzing customer data at Harrah's hotels and casinos. This massive DSS mines customer data gathered by Harrah's when people play its slot machines or use Harrah's casinos and hotels. Harrah's carefully analyzes these data to identify profitable customers and find ways to

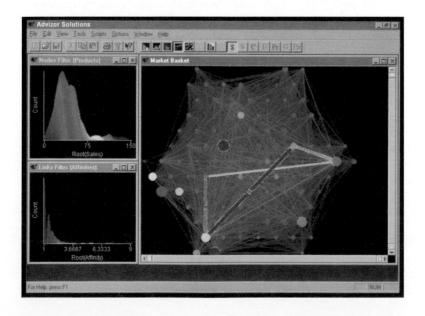

Advizor Solutions software can help businesses detect patterns in their data. Each dot in this example represents items purchased at one supermarket, with lines drawn between purchases of individual shoppers. The software shows links between different purchase items, such as cookies and milk.

WINDOW ON ORGANIZATIONS

HARRAH'S FINDS DIAMONDS IN THE DATA MINE

For decades Harrah's was a fairly small gambling company, but by 2001 it had become the second-largest in the industry, behind only MGM Entertainment. Harrah's is headquartered in Memphis, Tennessee, and has 26 casinos in 13 states. This company's success partially is a result of its understanding of the changing conditions of gambling in the United States, but it is also a result of Harrah's strategic use of information systems.

All the major casinos now use computers to track their customers' play on a real-time basis, and all issue loyalty cards, providing free rooms or shows to frequent customers. These companies focused most of their attention on building lavish casinos with imaginative attractions, whereas Harrah's spent on technology to help it learn more about its customers.

Harrah's COO, Gary Loveman, formerly a Harvard business professor, recognized an opportunity in the gambling industry to apply what he had been teaching about customer loyalty in the classroom. Loveman pointed out that Harrah's profited by 36 cents for every dollar its customers spent in casinos and that a rise to 40 cents would be a "monstrous" gain in profits.

By applying Loveman's strategy, Harrah's "wallet share" had actually risen to 42 cents in 2001, and for each percentage point gained, Harrah's had shown a profit increase of $125 million. Since then, by carefully analyzing its customer data, Harrah's has learned that 80 percent of its casino revenues comes from customers who spend only between $100 and $500 per visit. The data showed that many of Harrah's customers live relatively nearby and can visit Harrah's casinos more often without expensive plane fares or even hotel costs.

The centerpiece of the Harrah's strategy is its Total Rewards program. When gamblers arrive at Harrah's hotels or casinos, they are asked to apply for a Total Rewards card, although using it is voluntary. Total Rewards applicants must provide information on their gender, age, home location, and the games they like to play. If a gambler inserts the card into the slot machine he or she is playing (or other machines, such as poker), the machine records on the card the amount of money put into the machine, the total number of bets placed, the average size of bets, and the total amount of money deposited ("coin-in"). Gamblers are rewarded based on the amount spent on gambling. The reward amounts are saved on each customer's record, and gamblers can exchange their rewards for cash or other items. Each time a Total Rewards customer returns to a Harrah's hotel or casino, his or her record is updated.

These data are stored in a massive data warehouse. Harrah's combines its gambling data with data from other sources, such as its hotel reservation system, and demographic data. The company then analyzes these data using Cognos Impromptu, a CRM query tool from the Cognos Corporation, and modeling tools from SAS Institute to estimate how much the company can earn from an individual over time. The overall system Harrah's developed is called WINet (Winner's Information Network), and it is used in all Harrah's locations. Harrah's marketing department uses the information to build a detailed gambling profile on each customer. It then can create a personalized marketing program, including a plan to entice each gambler to the casinos.

Harrah's has established 90 demographic segments to identify customer value to the company. According to Harrah's profile studies, the "perfect" player is a 62-year-old woman who lives within 30 minutes of a casino and plays the dollar video poker. Harrah's analysts say such customers have time on their hands, ample disposable cash, and easy access to a casino. The more likely a customer is to return often and the more the customer is predicted to spend, the higher the demographic segment assigned to the customer.

Harrah's rewards depend on which segment the customer is in and include cash, complimentary trips, meals, hotel room upgrades, free hotel weekends, welcome gifts such as flowers or candy in the hotel room, tickets to sporting and entertainment events, and possibly even escorts from the airport and transportation to the hotel. Highly valued customers receive preferential service when they park their cars, eat in restaurants, or check in at the front desk. Those who return regularly receive enticing promotional mailings a month or two before they are expected to return, giving them perks that can be used when they arrive. By using this rewards system to entice customers, Harrah's has a 90 percent hit ratio in turning customers who are presently worth $500 into customers who are worth $5,000.

Sources: Tony Kontzer, "Big Bet on Customer Loyalty," *Information Week*, February 9, 2004; Gary Rivlin, "Bet on It," *New York Times Magazine*, May 9, 2004; Christina Binkley, "Harrah's Is Revamping Rewards Plan," *Wall Street Journal*, June 17, 2003; Gary Loveman, "Diamonds in the Data Mine," *Harvard Business Review*, May 2003; and Thomas Hoffman, "Casino Gambles on Customer Retention Technology," *Computerworld*, August 8, 2003.

To Think About: What kinds of decisions does WINet support? How is it related to Harrah's business strategy? Can Harrah's competitive advantage be sustained? Why or why not? Are there any ethical problems raised by these casinos' use of customer data? Explain your response.

encourage them to spend more. The system has been so successful that it has become the centerpiece of Harrah's business strategy.

Components of DSS

Figure 13-4 illustrates the components of a DSS. They include a database of data used for query and analysis; a software system with models, data mining, and other analytical tools; and a user interface.

The **DSS database** is a collection of current or historical data from a number of applications or groups. It may be a small database residing on a PC that contains a subset of corporate data that has been downloaded and possibly combined with external data. Alternatively, the DSS database may be a massive data warehouse that is continuously updated by major corporate TPS (including enterprise systems and data generated by Web site transactions). The data in DSS databases are generally extracts or copies of production databases so that using the DSS does not interfere with critical operational systems.

The **DSS software system** contains the software tools that are used for data analysis. It may contain various OLAP tools, data-mining tools, or a collection of mathematical and analytical models that easily can be made accessible to the DSS user. A **model** is an abstract representation that illustrates the components or relationships of a phenomenon. A model can be a physical model (such as a model airplane), a mathematical model (such as an equation), or a verbal model (such as a description of a procedure for writing an order). Each decision-support system is built for a specific set of purposes and makes different collections of models available depending on those purposes.

Perhaps the most common models are libraries of statistical models. Such libraries usually contain the full range of expected statistical functions, including means, medians, deviations, and scatter plots. The software has the ability to project future outcomes by analyzing a series of data. Statistical modeling software can be used to help establish relationships, such as relating product sales to differences in age, income, or other factors between communities. Optimization models, often using linear programming, determine optimal resource allocation to maximize or minimize specified variables, such as cost or time. A classic use of optimization models is to determine the proper mix of products within a given market to maximize profits.

Forecasting models often are used to forecast sales. The user of this type of model might supply a range of historical data to project future conditions and the sales that

FIGURE 13-4 *Overview of a decision-support system.*

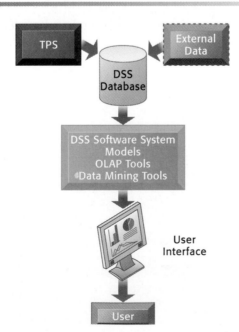

The main components of the DSS are the DSS database, the DSS software system, and the user interface. The DSS database may be a small database residing on a PC or a massive data warehouse.

might result from those conditions. The decision maker could vary those future conditions (entering, for example, a rise in raw materials costs or the entry of a new, low-priced competitor in the market) to determine how new conditions might affect sales. Companies often use this software to predict the actions of competitors. Model libraries exist for specific functions, such as financial and risk analysis models.

Among the most widely used models are **sensitivity analysis** models that ask "what-if" questions repeatedly to determine the impact on outcomes of changes in one or more factors. "What-if" analysis—working forward from known or assumed conditions—allows the user to vary certain values to test results to better predict outcomes if changes occur in those values. What happens if we raise the price by 5 percent or increase the advertising budget by $100,000? What happens if we keep the price and advertising budget the same? Desktop spreadsheet software, such as Microsoft Excel or Lotus 1-2-3, is often used for this purpose (see Figure 13-5). Backward sensitivity analysis software is used for goal seeking: If I want to sell 1 million product units next year, how much must I reduce the price of the product?

The DSS user interface permits easy interaction between users of the system and the DSS software tools. A graphic, easy-to-use, flexible user interface supports the dialogue between the user and the DSS. The DSS users can be managers or employees with no patience for learning a complex tool, so the interface must be relatively intuitive. Many DSS today are being built with Web-based interfaces to take advantage of the Web's ease of use, interactivity, and capabilities for personalization and customization. Building successful DSS requires a high level of user participation to make sure the system provides the information managers need.

Business Value of DSS

DSS can be used in many ways to support decision making. Table 13-4 lists examples of DSS in well-known companies. Both data-driven and model-driven DSS have become very powerful and sophisticated, providing fine-grained information for decisions that enable the firm to coordinate both internal and external business processes much more precisely. Some of these DSS are helping companies with decisions in supply chain management or customer relationship management. Some take advantage of the company-wide data provided by enterprise systems. DSS today can also harness the interactive capabilities of the Web to provide decision-support tools to both employees and customers.

To illustrate the range of capabilities of a DSS, the following sections describe some successful DSS applications. DaimlerChrysler's Transportation Efficiency Support System described in the chapter-opening case, ShopKo's pricing optimization system, and Sonoco's inventory management system are examples of model-driven DSS. The customer analysis systems used by Harrah's and the Dreyfus Corporation, as well as Parkway

---

FIGURE 13-5   *Sensitivity analysis.*

This table displays the results of a sensitivity analysis of the effect of changing the sales price of a necktie and the cost per unit on the product's break-even point. It answers the question, "What happens to the break-even point if the sales price and the cost to make each unit increase or decrease?"

Total fixed costs	19000					
Variable cost per unit	3					
Average sales price	17					
Contribution margin	14					
Breakeven point	1357					
				Variable Cost per Unit		
Sales	1357	2	3	4	5	6
Price	14	1583	1727	1900	2111	2375
	15	1462	1583	1727	1900	2111
	16	1357	1462	1583	1727	1900
	17	1267	1357	1462	1583	1727
	18	1188	1267	1357	1462	1583

TABLE 13-4 *Examples of Decision-Support Systems*

Organization	DSS Application
General Accident Insurance	Customer buying patterns and fraud detection
Canadian Pacific Railway	Train scheduling and routing
Frito-Lay, Inc.	Price, advertising, and promotion selection
Burlington Coat Factory	Store location and inventory mix
Intrawest	Targeting direct mail and e-mail marketing
National Gypsum	Corporate planning and forecasting
The Gap	Inventory stocking and merchandising
Texas Oil and Gas Corporation	Evaluation of potential drilling sites
United Airlines	Flight scheduling and passenger demand forecasting
U.S. Department of Defense	Defense contract analysis

Corporation's asset utilization system, are examples of data-driven DSS. Sweden's Laps Care system for managing elderly home care is an application of geographic information systems (GIS), a special category of DSS for visualizing data geographically.

SHOPKO: DSS FOR PRICING DECISIONS

Discount chain ShopKo Stores was losing millions of dollars because its price markdowns were "best guesses." If it waited too long to discount an item that wasn't selling well, it would be stuck with truckloads of inventory. If it discounted too early, it would lose profits because people rushed in to buy goods they might have bought at a higher price. ShopKo's retail operations encompass 162 ShopKo discount stores in large and midsized cities and 165 Pamida discount stores in smaller rural communities, so knowing the best price to charge for items at each store has an enormous impact on profits. ShopKo now uses Spotlight Markdown Optimizer software to determine the optimal time and price for marking down items. The software uses mathematical models and three years of ShopKo sales data to pinpoint exactly when and how much to mark down the price of an item to maximize gross profit margins. By analyzing several years of sales data for similar items, the software estimates a "seasonal demand curve" for each item and predicts how many units would sell each week at various prices. The software also uses sales history to predict how sensitive customer demand will be to price changes. Before using the software, ShopKo often marked down items three or four times. Now it needs to make only one or two markdowns to sell out items (Abate 2002; Levinson, 2002).

SONOCO PRODUCTS: DSS FOR SUPPLY CHAIN MANAGEMENT

Supply chain decisions involve determining "who, what, when, and where" from purchasing and transporting materials and parts through manufacturing products and distributing and delivering those products to customers. Supply chain management systems use data about inventory, supplier performance, logistics, production schedules, and costs to help managers search among a huge number of alternatives for the combinations that are most efficient and cost-effective for moving goods through the supply chain. The prime management goal might be to reduce overall costs while increasing the speed and accuracy of filling customer orders. Both model-driven and data-driven DSS can help managers make better supply chain decisions.

Model-driven DSS can help firms model alternative inventory stocking levels, production schedules, or transportation plans, and data-driven DSS can provide firms with information on key performance indicators such as lead time, cycle time, inventory turns, or total supply chain costs. We have already described some of the decision-support functionality of supply chain management systems in Chapter 11.

Sonoco Products, a global manufacturer of industrial and consumer packaging, maintains hundreds of manufacturing operations around the world and has a complex supply chain. It filled orders on time with its inventory on hand about 90 percent of the time. To fill the rest of its orders on time, Sonoco had to take costly steps, such as calling in extra shifts at its factories or shipping orders by air instead of using ground transportation. It started using Optiant's PowerChain 4.0 analysis and design software to set optimal inventory targets and explore alternative scenarios with various lead times, costs, raw materials inventory, and other factors. The software helps Sonoco have the right amount of inventory at the right location at the right time. It also shows Sonoco how it can postpone the conversion of metal into finished products until the last possible moment, reducing its finished goods inventory and producing additional savings. The new system has made it possible for Sonoco to fill orders on time with inventory on hand 95 percent of the time (Bacheldor, 2003).

PARKWAY CORPORATION: DSS FOR ASSET UTILIZATION

Parkway Corporation, headquartered in Philadelphia, owns and manages 30,000 parking spaces and 100 garages in East Coast cities stretching from Toronto, Canada, to Jacksonville, Florida. Its revenues surged during the late 1990s, but so did its costs, to the point where they were seriously eroding gains. Parkway was saddled by paper-based reporting systems that could not provide the information it needed to better manage its costs and revenues. For example, Parkway could measure the performance of individual lots but could not quickly obtain a unified company-wide view of how all its lots were performing in total or in relation to each other. Nor could management determine which lots, type of garage (automated, self-service, or valet parking), and customers were the most profitable or which employees were responsible for the most overtime claims or damage costs.

In 2001, Parkway implemented a data warehouse and analytics software to answer these questions. The new system enables Parkway to analyze revenue by type of garage, length of stay, rate structure, overtime costs, and utilization rates so that managers can make better decisions on prices and garage space allocation. Parkway can also use this system to determine the best mix of monthly, daily, and weekly parking in a particular city and to identify its most profitable customers. The system has helped Parkway management reduce overtime costs by 65 percent, increase the percentage of filled spaces per lot, and increase revenues between 5 and 10 percent. Car damage claims can be tracked by garage, employee, and time of day (Lindorff, 2003).

DREYFUS CORPORATION: DSS FOR CUSTOMER RELATIONSHIP MANAGEMENT

The analytical CRM applications described in Chapter 11 represent DSS for customer relationship management, using data mining to guide decisions about pricing, customer retention, market share, and new revenue streams. These systems typically consolidate customer information from a variety of systems into massive data warehouses and use various analytical tools to slice it into tiny segments for one-to-one marketing and predictive analysis. **Predictive analysis** uses data-mining techniques, historical data, and assumptions about future conditions to predict outcomes of events such as the probability a customer will respond to an offer or purchase a specific product (see Figure 13-6).

The Dreyfus Corporation, a leading mutual fund company that manages about $183 billion in more than 200 mutual fund portfolios nationwide, uses tools from SAS Institute to analyze its vast pool of customer data to identify profitable customers, to lower customer attrition rates, and to segment customers into smaller groups that could benefit from more targeted marketing. When Dreyfus examined its customer database, it found out that 20 percent of its customers were redeeming 80 percent of assets. Dreyfus wanted to know why they were redeeming assets and cashing out their mutual funds.

Segmenting Dreyfus clients into different life stages helped the company learn which age groups were redeeming assets at a high rate and which investments were of greatest interest. Dreyfus then approached customers with a high risk of attrition with new financial plans that were more appropriate to their age and interests to keep them investing in

FIGURE 13-6   A DSS for customer analysis and segmentation.

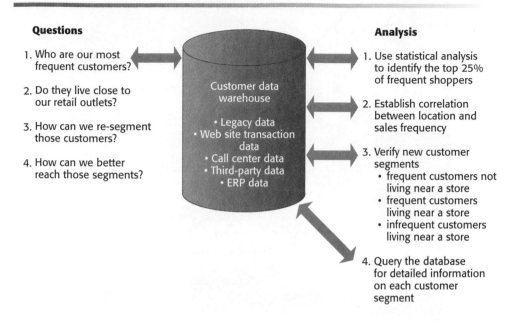

Questions

1. Who are our most frequent customers?

2. Do they live close to our retail outlets?

3. How can we re-segment those customers?

4. How can we better reach those segments?

Customer data warehouse

• Legacy data
• Web site transaction data
• Call center data
• Third-party data
• ERP data

Analysis

1. Use statistical analysis to identify the top 25% of frequent shoppers

2. Establish correlation between location and sales frequency

3. Verify new customer segments
   • frequent customers not living near a store
   • frequent customers living near a store
   • infrequent customers living near a store

4. Query the database for detailed information on each customer segment

This DSS enables companies to segment their customer database with a high level of precision where it can be used to drive a marketing campaign. Based on the results of data mining, a firm can develop specific marketing campaigns for each customer segment. For example, it could target frequent customers living near a store with coupons for products of interest and with rewards for frequent shoppers.

the company's mutual funds. Asset redemption rates dropped from 22 to 23 percent in 1997 to 7 percent, and customer attrition has been reduced by nearly 50 percent. Information from the customer database has also changed the way Dreyfus runs marketing campaigns. Instead of placing one generic ad in, for example, the *Wall Street Journal*, Dreyfus marketing staff now use ads targeted to smaller groups (Parlin, 2003).

Some of these DSS for customer relationship management use data gathered from the Web. Chapter 4 describes how each action a visitor takes when visiting a particular Web site can be captured on that Web site's log. Companies can mine these data to answer questions about what customers are purchasing and what promotions are generating the most traffic. The results can help companies tailor marketing programs effectively, redesign Web sites to optimize traffic, and create personalized buying experiences for Web site visitors. Other DSS combine Web site transaction data with data from enterprise systems.

DATA VISUALIZATION AND GEOGRAPHIC INFORMATION SYSTEMS

Data from information systems can be made easier for users to digest and act on by using graphics, charts, tables, maps, digital images, three-dimensional presentations, animations, and other data visualization technologies. By presenting data in graphical form, **data visualization** tools help users see patterns and relationships in large amounts of data that would be difficult to discern if the data were presented as traditional lists of text. Some data visualization tools are interactive, enabling users to manipulate data and see the graphical displays change in response to the changes they make.

Geographic information systems (GIS) are a special category of DSS that use data visualization technology to analyze and display data for planning and decision making in the form of digitized maps. The software can assemble, store, manipulate, and display geographically referenced information, tying data to points, lines, and areas on a map. GIS have modeling capabilities, enabling managers to change data and automatically revise business scenarios to find better solutions.

GIS can thus be used to support decisions that require knowledge about the geographic distribution of people or other resources in scientific research, resource management, and development planning. For example, GIS might be used to help state and local governments calculate emergency response times to natural disasters, retail chains identify profitable new store locations, or banks identify the best locations for installing new branches or automatic teller machine (ATM) terminals. GIS tools have become affordable even for small businesses, and some can be used on the Web.

HAZUS-MH Multi-Hazard risk assessment and loss estimation software for the Federal Emergency Management Agency (FEMA) maps and displays hazard data so that governments at all levels can plan for natural disaster response and recovery. Illustrated here is a map for earthquake planning displaying ground acceleration relative to the Newport-Inglewood fault in southern California. The GIS environment allows users to create geographic presentations, helping companies visualize and understand their hazard risks and solutions.

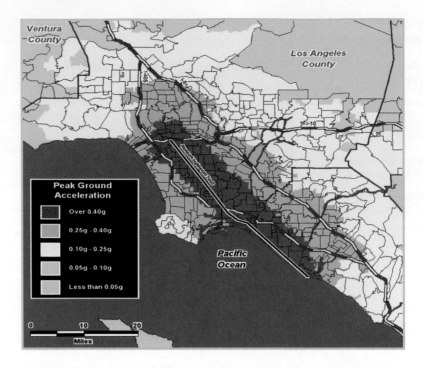

Internet Connection —
The Internet Connection for this chapter will take you to a series of Web sites where you can complete an exercise using Web-based DSS.

The Window on Management shows how GIS are being used in Sweden to help plan the assignment of home health aides that assist elderly people. Planners of elderly home care must deal with a complex set of variables that include multiple tasks, many different caregivers and clients, and limited time frames for both care giving and travel. This particular problem lends itself to geographic information system software because the locations of both elderly clients and home caregivers must be considered when planning daily schedules.

Web-Based Customer Decision-Support Systems

The growth of electronic commerce has encouraged many companies to develop DSS where customers and employees can take advantage of Internet information resources and Web capabilities for interactivity and personalization. DSS based on the Web and the Internet can support decision making by providing online access to various databases and information pools along with software for data analysis. Some of these DSS are targeted toward management, but many have been developed to attract customers by providing information and tools to assist their decision making as they select products and services. Companies are finding that deciding which products and services to purchase has become increasingly information intensive. People are now using more information from multiple sources to make purchasing decisions (such as purchasing a car or computer) before they interact with the product or sales staff. **Customer decision-support systems (CDSS)** support the decision-making process of an existing or potential customer.

People interested in purchasing a product or service can use Internet search engines, intelligent agents, online catalogs, Web directories, newsgroup discussions, e-mail, and other tools to help them locate the information they need to help with their decision. Information brokers, such as Edmunds.com, described in Chapter 4, are also sources of summarized, structured information for specific products or industries and may provide models for evaluating the information. Companies also have developed specific customer Web sites where all the information, models, or other analytical tools for evaluating alternatives are concentrated in one location. Web-based DSS have become especially popular in the financial services area because so many people are trying to manage their own assets and retirement savings. Table 13-5 lists some examples.

WINDOW ON MANAGEMENT

GIS HELP THE ELDERLY IN SWEDEN

Caring for elderly people when they are too old to care for themselves is a growing concern in the United States, Europe, Japan, and other countries. In Sweden, elderly people in need of daily care can be placed in retirement homes or they can remain in their own home with home assistance provided by the state. Today the trend is to encourage the elderly to say in their own homes as long as possible.

To bring support services into the home, an assessor working with Swedish local authorities determines what type and how much assistance the client needs. A typical care plan might call for two showers per week, weekly laundry, weekly cleaning, monthly doctor's visit, and 20 hours of additional care per month.

All of this information serves as input to a visit plan stating when and where each visit should be performed. The visit plan can either be administered by the local government or, more commonly, by a private contractor.

The schedule for home health aide visits is normally planned several days in advance. However, plans may need to be revised if staff members become ill or the clients have to be taken to the hospital. Some visits may need to be shortened or postponed or have extra staff allocated. Last-minute changes are made to the plan each morning. Making these last-minute changes might consume 30 to 45 minutes per day, delaying the departure of staff members until everyone's daily assignments are finalized.

Ideally, the planning for elderly care should be as efficient as possible, distributing the workload evenly among the staff. Each visit has a window of time and requires a set of skills that must be met by a staff member. Sufficient travel time between visits must be allocated and each staff member must be given planned breaks for meals. Each elderly client has one or several preferred staff members who visit and certain visits require multiple staff members.

This problem was similar to vehicle routing problems, which have been popular applications for geographic information systems. Planning must consider many different variables, including skills, time frame, locations, and the number of staff.

The Home Care Department of the Swedish city of Danderyd, Linkoping University, and the Linkoping software company Optimal Solutions AB came up with a solution. They created a staff planning system called Laps Care that enables rapid and efficient planning of home care staff schedules. Laps Care has been used daily for elderly home care planning since November 2002.

Here's how the system works. The user inputs data about home health care employees, their clients, and the visits that are to be performed, as well as data about the time staff members must spend in transit to reach each client. Maps are included based on map data from Navigation Technologies, which contains a detailed description of the local road network. Using address matching, the system positions each customer on the map. The system uses these data to calculate travel time between visits, generating a plan that represents an optimal solution where the right person with the right skills provides the right care at the right time.

The resulting solution can be viewed as a text grid, in a Gantt chart, or on a map displaying the route of each staff member and the assigned visits. It takes the system about two minutes to generate each alternative solution. Users often use the system to create alternative solutions to evaluate, so within half an hour, they can easily test 5 to 10 scenarios.

When the city of Danderyd started using Laps Care, it found that the system dramatically cut down the time to develop a daily visit plan. One person could create the plan within 15 minutes, and home health staff could leave for their assignments much earlier, saving about 7 percent of total working time. The system divides the workload much more evenly among caregivers than the earlier manual system and uses staff members' special skills more effectively. Although travel times have been reduced, the system is valued more for producing accurate travel time estimates and good working schedules that leave enough time for traveling. There is much less early morning chaos.

Did the system provide an answer for everything? Not quite. There were some cases for which the system could not come up with a feasible solution, even though there were manual plans for home health care. Some home health aides were combining several tasks into one (e.g., doing laundry for three people at once).

Senior staff members initially posed problems by trying to keep the more desirable tasks for themselves, leaving harder work for their newer colleagues. Laps Care eliminated this inequitable situation by creating the fairest possible schedule for everyone. Laps Care was so successful that it won the EURO Award 2003 for Excellence in Practice in Operations Research. Other organizations have adopted the system.

Sources: Patrik Eveborn, Patrik Flisberg, and Mikael Ronnqvist, "Home Care Operations," *OR/MS Today*, April 2004; www.math.liu.se, accessed May 5, 2004; www.optimalsolutions.com, accessed May 5, 2004; and Optimal Solutions, "Laps Care," 2002.

To Think About: How does Laps Care help home health care services make decisions? What problems does it solve? How does it provide value for these organizations and for their clients?

The Vanguard Group's Web site provides online tools to help users with investment planning decisions. Illustrated here is a proposed asset allocation strategy for a college savings plan, showing different proportions of stocks, bonds, and short-term reserves based on the child's age and the investor's tolerance for risk.

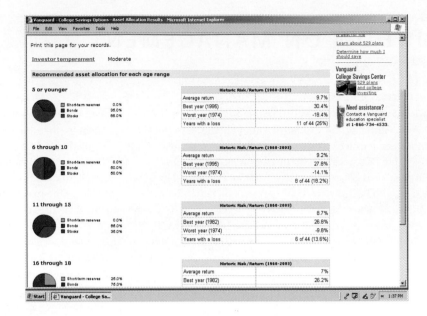

TABLE 13-5 *Examples of Web-Based DSS*

DSS	Description
General Electric Plastics	Web site provides a Design Solutions Center with a Web-based suite of online engineering tools for materials developers in the plastics industry. Visitors can select plastics materials, perform production cost estimates, search for product-specification information, and get online training.
T.D. Waterhouse	Web site features online, interactive tools application to help clients make decisions about bond investments. It provides information about bonds as investments and an interactive tool to show the effect of price and yield changes.
Homes.com	Provides a nationwide listing of homes for sale, apartments for rent, and mortgages available. Visitors can find out which mortgages they qualify for and calculate the maximum mortgage they can afford and alternative monthly mortgage payments. They can also use tools to help them determine whether they should rent or buy.
Autosite.com	Visitors to this Web site can compare prices and features of new and preowned vehicles and use an online tool to help them decide whether to purchase or lease a car.

13.3 GROUP DECISION-SUPPORT SYSTEMS

The DSS we have just described focus primarily on individual decision making. However, so much work is accomplished in groups within firms that a special category of systems called group decision-support systems (GDSS) has been developed to support group and organizational decision making.

What Is a GDSS?

A **group decision-support system (GDSS)** is an interactive computer-based system used to facilitate the solution of unstructured problems by a set of decision makers working together as a group (DeSanctis and Gallupe, 1987). Groupware and Web-based tools for videoconferencing and electronic meetings described earlier in this text can support some group decision processes, but their focus is primarily on communication. GDSS, however, provide tools and technologies geared explicitly toward group decision making and were developed in response to a growing concern over the quality and effectiveness of meetings. The underlying problems in group decision making have been the explosion of decision-maker meetings, the growing length of those meetings, and the increased number of attendees. Estimates on the amount of a manager's time spent in meetings range from 35 to 70 percent.

COMPONENTS OF GDSS

GDSS make meetings more productive by providing tools to facilitate planning, generating, organizing, and evaluating ideas; establishing priorities; and documenting meeting proceedings for others in the firm. GDSS consist of three basic elements: hardware, software tools, and people. *Hardware* refers to the conference facility itself, including the room, the tables, and the chairs. Such a facility must be physically laid out in a manner that supports group collaboration. It also must include some electronic hardware, such as electronic display boards, as well as audiovisual, computer, and networking equipment.

Chapters 8 and 12 describe groupware tools for collaborative work that can be used to support group decision making. In addition specific GDSS *software tools* support group meetings. These tools were originally developed for meetings in which all participants are in the same room, but they also can be used for networked meetings in which participants are in different locations. Specific GDSS software tools include the following:

- *Electronic questionnaires* aid the organizers in premeeting planning by identifying issues of concern and by helping to ensure that key planning information is not overlooked.
- *Electronic brainstorming tools* enable individuals, simultaneously and anonymously, to contribute ideas on the topics of the meeting.
- *Idea organizers* facilitate the organized integration and synthesis of ideas generated during brainstorming.
- *Questionnaire tools* support the facilitators and group leaders as they gather information before and during the process of setting priorities.
- *Tools for voting or setting priorities* make available a range of methods from simple voting, to ranking in order, to a range of weighted techniques for setting priorities or voting.
- *Stakeholder identification and analysis tools* use structured approaches to evaluate the impact of an emerging proposal on the organization and to identify stakeholders and evaluate the potential impact of those stakeholders on the proposed project.
- *Policy formation tools* provide structured support for developing agreement on the wording of policy statements.
- *Group dictionaries* document group agreement on definitions of words and terms central to the project.

People refers not only to the participants but also to a trained facilitator and often to a staff that supports the hardware and software. Together, these elements have led to the creation of a range of different kinds of GDSS, from simple electronic boardrooms to elaborate collaboration laboratories. In a collaboration laboratory, individuals work on their own desktop PCs or workstations. Their input is integrated on a file server and is viewable on a common screen at the front of the room; in most systems the integrated input is also viewable on the individual participant's screen.

Overview of a GDSS Meeting

In a GDSS electronic meeting, each attendee has a workstation. The workstations are networked and are connected to the facilitator's console, which serves as the facilitator's workstation and control panel, and to the meeting's file server. All data that the attendees forward from their workstations to the group are collected and saved on the file server. The facilitator is able to project computer images onto the projection screen at the front of the room. The facilitator also has an overhead projector available. Whiteboards are visible on either side of the projection screen. Many electronic meeting rooms have seating arrangements in semicircles and are tiered in legislative style to accommodate a large number of attendees. The facilitator controls the use of tools during the meeting.

Attendees have full control of their own desktop computers. An attendee is able to view the agenda (and other planning documents), look at the integrated screen (or screens, as the session progresses), use ordinary desktop PC tools (such as a word processor or a spreadsheet), tap into production data that have been made available, or work on the screen associated with the current meeting step and tool (such as a brainstorming screen).

During the meeting all input to the integrated screens is saved on the file server and participants' work is kept confidential. When the meeting is completed, a full record of the meeting (both raw material and resultant output) is available to the attendees and can be made available to anyone else with a need for access. Figure 13-7 illustrates the sequence of activities at a typical electronic meeting along with the types of tools used and the output of those tools.

Business Value of GDSS

Studies show that in traditional decision-making meetings without GDSS support the optimal meeting size is three to five attendees. Beyond that size, the meeting process begins to break down. Using GDSS software, studies show the number of attendees at a meeting can increase while productivity also increases. One reason for this is that attendees contribute simultaneously rather than one at a time, which makes more efficient use of meeting time.

A GDSS contributes to a more collaborative atmosphere by guaranteeing contributors' anonymity so that attendees can focus on evaluating the ideas themselves. Attendees can contribute without fear of personally being criticized or of having their ideas rejected because of the identity of the contributor. GDSS software tools follow structured methods for organizing and evaluating ideas and for preserving the results of meetings, enabling nonattendees to locate needed information after the meeting. The documentation of a meeting by one group at one site can also be used as input to another meeting on the same project at another site.

If properly designed and supported, GDSS meetings can increase the number of ideas generated and the quality of decisions while producing the desired results in fewer meetings in both face-to-face and distributed meeting environments (Anson and Munkvold, 2004). When used by project teams for frequent meetings, GDSS can lead to more participative and democratic decision making (Dennis and Garfield, 2003). However, GDSS outcomes are not necessarily better than face-to-face meetings, and electronic brain-

FIGURE 13-7   *Group system tools.*

The sequence of activities and collaborative support tools used in an electronic meeting system facilitate communication among attendees and generate a full record of the meeting.

Sources: From Nunamaker et al., "Electronic Meeting Systems to Support Group Work," *Communications of the ACM,* July 1991. Reprinted by permission.

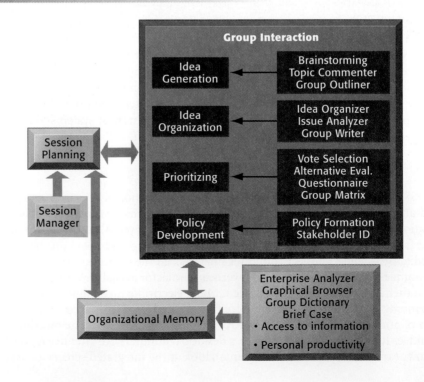

storming has not been widely adopted (Dennis and Reinicke, 2004). GDSS seem most useful for tasks involving idea generation, complex problems, and large groups (Fjermestad and Hiltz, 2000–2001, 1998–1999).

One problem with understanding the value of GDSS is their complexity. A GDSS can be configured in an almost infinite variety of ways, and the nature of electronic meeting technology is only one of a number of factors that affect meeting processes and output. The outcome of group meetings depends on the composition of the group, the manner in which the problem is presented to the group, the facilitator's effectiveness, the organization's culture and environment, the quality of the planning, the cooperation of the attendees, and the appropriateness of tools selected for different types of meetings and decision problems (Dennis and Wixom, 2001–2002; Dennis, Wixom, and Vandenberg, 2001; Hender, Dean, Rodgers, and Nunamaker, 2002).

13.4   EXECUTIVE SUPPORT IN THE ENTERPRISE

Executive support systems (ESS), which we introduce in Chapter 2, help managers with unstructured and semistructured problems by focusing on the information needs of senior management. Combining data from internal and external sources, ESS create a generalized computing and communications environment that can be focused and applied to a changing array of problems. ESS help senior executives monitor organizational performance, track activities of competitors, spot problems, identify opportunities, and forecast trends.

The Role of Executive Support Systems in the Firm

Contemporary ESS can bring together data from all parts of the firm and enable managers to select, access, and tailor them as needed using easy-to-use desktop analytical tools and online data displays. Use of the systems has migrated down several organizational levels so that the executive and any subordinates are able to look at the same data in the same way.

Today's systems try to avoid the problem of data overload so common in paper reports because the data can be filtered or viewed in graphic format (if the user so chooses). ESS have the ability to **drill down**, moving from a piece of summary data to lower and lower levels of detail. The ability to drill down is useful not only to senior executives but also to employees at lower levels of the firm who need to analyze data. OLAP tools for analyzing large databases provide this capability.

A major challenge of building executive support systems has been to integrate data from systems designed for very different purposes so that senior executives can review organizational performance from a firmwide perspective. In the traditional firm, which typically had hundreds or even thousands of incompatible systems, pulling such information together and making sense out of it was a major task. Today, properly configured and implemented enterprise systems can provide managers with timely, comprehensive, and accurate firmwide information. ESS based on such data can be considered logical extensions of enterprise system functionality.

External data, including data from the Web, are now more easily available in many ESS as well. Executives need a wide range of external data, from current stock market news to competitor information, industry trends, and even projected legislative action. Through their ESS, many managers have access to news services, financial market databases, economic information, and whatever other public data they may require.

Contemporary ESS include tools for modeling and analysis. With only a minimum of experience, most managers find they can use these tools to create graphic comparisons of data by time, region, product, price range, and so on. (Whereas DSS use such tools primarily for modeling and analysis in a fairly narrow range of decision situations, ESS use them primarily to provide status information about organizational performance.)

ESS must be designed so that high-level managers and others can use them without much training. One area that merits special attention is the determination of executive information requirements. ESS need to have some facility for environmental scanning. A key information requirement of managers at the strategic level is the ability to detect signals of problems in the organizational environment that indicate strategic threats and opportunities (Walls et al., 1992). The ESS need to be designed so that both external and internal sources of information can be used for environmental scanning purposes.

Business Value of Executive Support Systems

Much of the value of ESS is found in their flexibility. These systems put data and tools in the hands of executives without addressing specific problems or imposing solutions. Executives are free to shape the problems as necessary, using the system as an extension of their own thinking processes.

The most visible benefit of ESS is their ability to analyze, compare, and highlight trends. The easy use of graphics enables the user to look at more data in less time with greater clarity and insight than paper-based systems can provide. In the past, executives obtained the same information by taking up days and weeks of their staffs' valuable time. By using ESS, those staffs and the executives themselves are freed for the more creative analysis and decision making in their jobs. ESS capabilities for drilling down and highlighting trends also may enhance the quality of such analysis and can speed decision making (Leidner and Elam, 1993–1994).

Executives are using ESS to monitor performance more successfully in their own areas of responsibility. Some companies are using these systems to monitor key performance indicators for the entire firm and to measure firm performance against changes in the external environment. The timeliness and availability of the data result in needed actions being identified and carried out earlier than previously could have been done. Problems can be handled before they become too damaging; opportunities can also be identified earlier. These systems can thus help businesses move toward a "sense-and-respond" strategy.

A well-designed ESS could dramatically improve management performance and increase upper management's span of control. Immediate access to so much data enables executives to better monitor activities of lower units reporting to them. That very monitoring ability could enable decision making to be decentralized and to take place at lower operating levels. Executives are often willing to push decision making further down into the organization as long as they can be assured that all is going well. Alternatively, executive support systems based on enterprise-wide data could potentially increase management centralization, enabling senior executives to monitor the performance of subordinates across the company and direct them to take appropriate action when conditions change.

Executive Support Systems and the Digital Firm

To illustrate the different ways in which an ESS can enhance management decision making, we now describe important types of ESS applications for gathering business intelligence and monitoring corporate performance, including ESS based on enterprise systems.

FOUR STAR DISTRIBUTION: ESS FOR COMPETITIVE INTELLIGENCE

Today, customer expectations, Internet technology, and new business models can alter the competitive landscape so rapidly that managers need special capabilities for competitive intelligence gathering. ESS can help managers identify changing market conditions, formulate responses, track implementation efforts, and learn from feedback.

Four Star Distribution, a designer and distributor of innovative snowboarding and skateboarding equipment based in San Clemente, California, is considered a leader in new technologies and innovative products. It sells a wide variety of brands, including Forum Jeenyus Snowboards, C1 apparel, Special Blend and Foursquare Outerwear, and C1RVCA footwear. Four Star needs to stay abreast of the latest global buying trends in a volatile industry catering to teenagers and young adults. It relies on a hosted Oracle E-Business suite with Oracle 9i AS Discoverer ad hoc query, reporting, and analysis software to provide the most accurate, up-to-date information on the performance of Four Star's business and global buying trends. For instance, one report tracks C1RVCA footwear, showing which shoes are the most popular and where in the world they are selling the best. Four Star can immediately share this information with its manufacturers, distributors, and sales representatives to get the latest products to the customer before the new selling season begins (Joch, 2003).

VERIZON COMMUNICATIONS AND PHARMACIA CORPORATION: MONITORING CORPORATE PERFORMANCE WITH DIGITAL DASHBOARDS AND BALANCED SCORECARD SYSTEMS

ESS can be configured to summarize and report on key performance indicators for senior management in the form of a **digital dashboard** or "executive dashboard." The dashboard displays on a single screen all of the critical measurements for piloting a company, similar to the cockpit of an airplane or an automobile dashboard. The dashboard presents key performance indicators as graphs and charts in a Web browser format, providing a one-page overview of all the critical measurements necessary to make key executive decisions (Few, 2004).

For example, Paul Lacouture, president of network services for Verizon Communications, constantly reviews screens with live feeds of key performance statistics such as the number of customer complaints or the number or repairs needed. When he spots an unusually high number of line outages in a particular location, he can immediately contact the area manager to discuss the quickest way to solve the problem. Before this dashboard system was in place Lacouture could obtain information about problems only by going through several layers of managers, and the managers would rely on months-old data stored in thick binders (Latour, 2004).

Companies have traditionally measured value using financial metrics, such as return on investment (ROI), which we describe in Chapter 15. Many firms are now implementing a **balanced scorecard** model that supplements traditional financial measures with measurements from additional perspectives, such as customers, internal business processes, and learning and growth. Managers can use balanced scorecard systems to see how well the firm is meeting its strategic goals. The goals and measures for the balanced scorecard vary from company to company. Companies are setting up information systems to populate the scorecard for management.

Pharmacia Corporation, a subsidiary of Pfizer Inc., uses Oracle's Balanced Scorecard software and a data warehouse to ensure the entire organization is operating in a coordinated manner. Pharmacia develops and delivers innovative medicines and has 43,000 employees and more than $16 billion in annual revenues. Pharmacia's over-the-counter medications include Rogaine and Nicotrol, and its prescription medications include

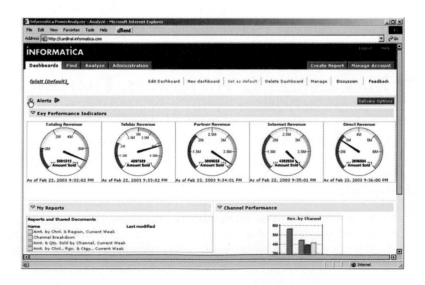

Informatica PowerAnalyzer is a robust data visualization solution designed for the rapid deployment of corporate data in real time through dashboards and custom applications. The digital dashboard helps transform data into immediate, accurate, and understandable information.

Celebrex for arthritis relief. Pharmacia spends about $2 billion annually on research and development, and the company wanted to make more effective use of the funds allocated for research. The balanced scorecard reports show, for example, how Pharmacia's U.S. or European clinical operations are performing in relation to corporate objectives and other parts of the company. Pharmacia can use the scorecard system to track the attrition rate of new compounds under study, to monitor the number of patents in clinical trials, and to see how funds allocated for research are being spent (Oracle, 2003).

ROADWAY EXPRESS: ENTERPRISE-WIDE REPORTING AND ANALYSIS

Enterprise application vendors are now providing capabilities to extend the usefulness of data captured in operational systems to give management a picture of the overall performance of the firm. Some provide reporting of metrics for balanced scorecard analysis as well as more traditional financial and operating metrics. For example, SAP offers a Web-enabled mySAP Strategic Enterprise Management module featuring corporate performance metrics, simulation, and planning tools. Managers can model and communicate key performance indicators for a balanced scorecard. Another measurement tool called the Management Cockpit can be used to monitor strategic performance indicators using internal and external benchmarks.

Companies can use these new enterprise-reporting capabilities to create measures of firm performance that were not previously available, including activity-based costing. **Activity-based costing** is a budgeting and analysis model that identifies all the resources, processes, and costs, including overhead and operating expenses, required to produce a specific product or service. It focuses on determining firm activities that create costs rather than on merely tracking what has been spent. It enables managers to ascertain which products or services—or customers—are profitable and those that are not profitable so they can determine the changes required to maximize firm profitability. Instead of reporting in terms of product and income, the system can focus on contribution margins and customer accounts, with the ability to calculate the current and lifetime value of each account.

Roadway Express, headquartered in Akron, Ohio, uses activity-based costing to analyze every step in the process of serving a customer. The company specializes in less-than-truckload freight hauling in North America, handling 50,000 to 60,000 shipments per day. Labor constitutes 60 percent of its operating expenses and average profit margins for the industry are only 2.5 percent. In 1997, Roadway built an Oracle data warehouse and installed Business Objects data analysis software to analyze information about the size, content, number of shipments, and the time and cost for each step in moving goods from source to destination. The system also captures time and cost data for activities associated with settling claims for damaged freight. This system calculates exactly how much each activity costs and even the actual costs of specific activities for a particular customer. It can identify which customer and which shipment types are the most and least profitable and which are associated with the most damage claims. Better understanding its costs helps Roadway reduce fixed costs, identify profitable customers, and price its services to maximize operating margins (Cone and Carr, 2002).

13.5 MANAGEMENT OPPORTUNITIES, CHALLENGES AND SOLUTIONS

DSS, GDSS, and ESS are systems for decision making, and they create a special set of challenges and opportunities.

Opportunities

Systems for decision support provide extraordinary opportunities for increasing the precision, accuracy, and rapidity of decisions made by both managers and employees. Imagine the total impact on the organization if these systems equip all decision makers in the firm to make better decisions!

Management Challenges

DSS, GDSS, and ESS can provide the information to help managers and employees make better decisions that will enhance organizational performance, but they do not necessarily create additional value. It is not always easy to understand a managerial decision problem if it is very unstructured. Managers may not be able to change their thinking to harness the power of these systems. Systems to support decision making raise the following challenges:

BUILDING SYSTEMS THAT CAN ACTUALLY FULFILL EXECUTIVE INFORMATION REQUIREMENTS

Even with the use of critical success factors and other information requirements determination methods, it may still be difficult to establish information requirements for ESS and DSS serving senior management. Many decisions made by high-level managers are unstructured or completely novel, and information systems may not be able to support them. Even if a problem can be addressed by an information system, senior management may not fully understand its actual information needs. For instance, senior managers may not agree on the firm's critical success factors, or the critical success factors they describe may be inappropriate or outdated if the firm is confronting a crisis requiring a major strategic change.

CHANGING MANAGEMENT THINKING TO MAKE BETTER USE OF SYSTEMS FOR DECISION SUPPORT

Enterprise systems and data warehouses have made it much easier to supply DSS and ESS with data from many different systems than in the past. The remaining challenge is changing management thinking to use the data that are available to maximum advantage, to develop better reporting categories for measuring firm performance, and to inform new types of decisions. Many managers use the new capabilities in DSS and ESS to obtain the same information as before. Major changes in management thinking will be required to encourage managers to ask better questions about the data.

ORGANIZATIONAL RESISTANCE

ESS potentially could give top executives the capability of examining other managers' work without their knowledge, so there may be some resistance to ESS at lower levels of the organization. Implementation of ESS should be carefully managed to neutralize such opposition (see Chapter 15).

Solution Guidelines

Users of DSS, GDSS, and ESS are middle and high-level managers and employees who are very pressed for time. The system must be one that the user can learn rapidly. Developers must be certain the system will work before they demonstrate it to high-level users or it will be rejected.

FLEXIBLE DESIGN AND DEVELOPMENT

Building a DSS, GDSS, or ESS is different from building a TPS or MIS, which are based on a specific set of information requirements. The information requirements for a DSS or ESS are more unstructured and fluid and require a much greater level of user participation to develop. Users must work with information systems specialists to identify a problem and a specific set of capabilities that will help them arrive at decisions about the problem. The system must be flexible, easy to use, and capable of supporting alternative decision options (Lilien et. al., 2004).

TRAINING AND MANAGEMENT SUPPORT

Several studies have noted that user training, involvement, and experience; top management support; and length of use are the most important factors in the success of management support systems. Success was measured as perceived improvement in decision making and overall satisfaction with the system (Alavi and Joachimsthaler, 1992). These success factors are not very different from those for other types of systems (see Chapter 15).

MAKE **IT** YOUR BUSINESS

Finance and Accounting

The finance and accounting function is replete with DSS and ESS applications. Many DSS are based on financial models for break-even analysis, profitability analysis, capital budgeting, and financial forecasting. Retail financial service firms depend on model-based DSS for client portfolio analysis and investment recommendations. ESS often provide overviews of firmwide financial performance, including activity-based costing and financial measures for balanced scorecard reporting. Reporting monthly or yearly cash flows and balances is a typical MIS function for the finance and accounting function.

Human Resources

The human resources function uses model-based decision-support systems for analysis of labor contract costs or alternative compensation plans for nonunion employees. Executive information systems are used for human resources planning to project a firm's long-term labor force requirements. Comparing employee salaries to budgeted compensation amounts is a typical MIS function for human resources. You can find examples of human resources applications on page 475.

Manufacturing and Production

The manufacturing and production function requires many decisions about the optimization of production, logistics, and maintenance that must evaluate many interrelated variables. Model-based DSS have been guiding decisions about supply chain management, including the development of optimal pro-

duction plans, delivery schedules, and inventory allocations. Recommending optimal plans for dispatching and routing vehicles and for facilities management are popular GIS applications. ESS can provide overviews of a firm's production resources. Comparing actual production amounts to targeted amounts for a monthly or yearly period is a typical MIS function for manufacturing and production. You can find examples of manufacturing and production applications on pages 457 and 489–491.

Sales and Marketing

DSS applications abound in sales and marketing. Model-driven DSS support decisions about product pricing, sales forecasting, and advertising and promotional campaigns. Companies increasingly use data-driven DSS for customer relationship management (CRM) to analyze customer purchasing patterns, detect customer retention problems, identify profitable customers, and develop targeted marketing campaigns. Some of these DSS for CRM combine customer data from Web transactions with customer transaction data from offline sources. Many Web-based DSS provide access to information and products to influence customer purchasing decisions. ESS can be used for competitor analysis and identification of opportunities for new products or sales channels. GIS can analyze sales patterns and market data by location, supporting decisions on where to locate retail outlets or target marketing campaigns. Listing the best- and worst-performing sales territories for a monthly or yearly period is a typical MIS function for sales and marketing. You can find examples of sales and marketing applications on page 468.

Summary

1. *Describe different types of decisions and the decision-making process.*

   The different levels in an organization (strategic, management, operational) have different decision-making requirements. Decisions can be structured, semistructured, or unstructured, with structured decisions clustering at the operational level of the organization and unstructured decisions at the strategic level. Decision making can be performed by individuals or groups and includes employees as well as operational, middle, and senior managers. There are four stages in decision making: intelligence, design, choice, and implementation. Systems to support decision making do not always produce better manager and employee decisions that improve firm performance because of problems with information quality, management filters, and organizational inertia.

2. *Evaluate the role of information systems in helping people working individually and in a group make decisions more efficiently.*

   Specialized systems for business intelligence are specifically designed to help managers and employees make better decisions. Business intelligence includes management information systems (MIS), decision-support systems (DSS), group decision-support systems (GDSS), and executive support systems (ESS) and makes use of data from enterprise applications and technologies such as data mining and online analytical processing (OLAP).

   Management information systems (MIS) provide information on firm performance to help managers monitor and control the business, often in the form of fixed, regularly scheduled reports based on data summarized from the firm's transaction processing systems. MIS support structured decisions and some semistructured decisions.

Decision-support systems (DSS) combine data, sophisticated analytical models and tools, and user-friendly software into a single powerful system that can support semistructured or unstructured decision making. The components of a DSS are the DSS database, the DSS software system, and the user interface. There are two kinds of DSS: model-driven DSS and data-driven DSS. DSS can help support decisions for pricing, asset utilization, supply chain management, and customer relationship management as well model alternative business scenarios. DSS targeted toward customers as well as managers are becoming available on the Web. A special category of DSS called geographic information systems (GIS) uses data visualization technology to analyze and display data for planning and decision making with digitized maps.

People working together in a group can use group decision-support systems to help them in the process of arriving at a decision. Group decision-support systems have hardware, software, and people components. Hardware components consist of the conference room facilities, including seating arrangements and computer and other electronic hardware. Software components include tools for organizing ideas, gathering information, ranking and setting priorities, and documenting meeting sessions. People components include participants, a trained facilitator, and staff to support the hardware and software.

A GDSS helps decision makers meeting together to arrive at a decision more efficiently and is especially useful for increasing the productivity of meetings of more than four or five people. However, the effectiveness of a GDSS is contingent on the composition of the group, the task, appropriate tool selection and meeting support, and the organizational context of the meeting.

3. ***Demonstrate how executive support systems can help senior managers make better decisions.***

Executive support systems (ESS) help senior managers with unstructured problems that occur at the strategic level of the firm. ESS provide data from both internal and external sources and provide a generalized computing and communications environment that can be focused and applied to a changing array of problems. ESS help senior executives monitor firm performance, spot problems, identify opportunities, and forecast trends. These systems can filter out extraneous details for high-level overviews, or they can drill down to pro-

vide senior managers with detailed transaction data if required. ESS are starting to take advantage of firmwide data provided by enterprise systems.

ESS help senior managers analyze, compare, and highlight trends so that the managers may more easily monitor organizational performance or identify strategic problems and opportunities. They are very useful for environmental scanning, providing business intelligence to help management detect strategic threats or opportunities from the organization's environment. ESS can increase the span of control of senior management, allowing them to oversee more people with fewer resources.

4. ***Assess how systems that support decision making can provide value for the firm.***

DSS, GDSS, and ESS are starting to take advantage of more accurate firmwide data provided by enterprise systems and the new information technology infrastructure to support very fine-grained decisions for guiding the firm, coordinating work activities across the enterprise, and responding rapidly to changing markets and customers. DSS can be used to guide company-wide decisions in supply chain management, customer relationship management, and business planning scenarios. ESS can be used to monitor company-wide performance using both traditional financial metrics and the balanced scorecard model. The ability to explore the outcomes of alternative organizational scenarios, use precise firmwide information, and provide tools to facilitate group decision processes can help managers make decisions that help the firm achieve its strategic objectives.

5. ***Identify the challenges posed by decision-support systems, group decision-support systems, and executive support systems and management solutions.***

Systems to support decision making do not always lead to better decisions or improved organizational performance. It is not always easy to understand a managerial decision problem if its very unstructured. Managers may not be able to change their thinking to harness the power of these systems, to ask better questions of their data, and to interpret system output accurately. There may be some resistance to ESS at lower levels of the organization if senior management is using them to monitor performance carefully. These systems are more likely to be successful if they are designed and built with flexibility and if they have adequate management support and training programs.

Key Terms

Activity-based costing, 482	Choice, 462	Data visualization, 473
Balanced scorecard, 481	Customer decision-support systems (CDSS), 474	Design, 462
Business intelligence, 458	Data-driven DSS, 466	Digital dashboard, 481

Review Questions

1. **What is business intelligence? What applications and technologies does it include?**

2. **What are the different decision-making levels and decision-making constituencies in organizations? How do their decision-making requirements differ?**

3. **What is the difference between an unstructured, semi-structured, and structured decision?**

4. **List and describe the stages in decision making.**

5. **What is the difference between a decision-support system (DSS) and a management information system (MIS)?**

6. **What is the difference between a data-driven DSS and a model-driven DSS? Give examples.**

7. **What are the three basic components of a DSS? Briefly describe each.**

8. **How can DSS help firms with supply chain management and customer relationship management? How do DSS provide value for a business?**

9. **What is a geographic information system (GIS)? How does it use data visualization technology? How can it support decision making?**

10. **What is a customer decision-support system? How can the Internet be used for this purpose?**

11. **What is a group decision-support system (GDSS)? How does it differ from a DSS? What underlying problems in group decision making led to the development of GDSS?**

12. **Describe the three elements of a GDSS and five GDSS software tools.**

13. **How can GDSS provide value for a business?**

14. **Define and describe the capabilities of an executive support system (ESS).**

15. **How can the Internet and enterprise systems provide capabilities for executive support systems?**

16. **How do ESS enhance managerial decision making? How do they provide value for a business?**

17. **What are the challenges posed by systems to support decision making? How can these challenges be addressed?**

Discussion Questions

1. *As a manager or user of information systems, what would you need to know to participate in the design and use of a DSS or an ESS? Why?*

2. *If businesses used DSS, GDSS, and ESS more widely, would they make better decisions? Do you agree? Why or why not?*

Application Software Exercise:
Spreadsheet Exercise: Performing Break-Even Analysis and Sensitivity Analysis

Selmore Collectible Toy Company (SCTC) makes toy sets consisting of collectible trucks, vans, and cars for the retail market. The firm is developing a new toy set that includes a battery-powered tractor trailer, complete with cab and trailer; a sports car; and a motorcycle. Each set sells for $100. Table 1 shows the major components of SCTC's annual fixed costs for the toy set. Each component includes the cost of purchases, depreciation, and operating expenses. Table 2 shows the major components of SCTC's variable costs.

Prepare a spreadsheet to support the decision-making needs of SCTC's managers. The spreadsheet should show the fixed costs, variable costs per unit, the contribution margin,

TABLE 1   SCTC Fixed Costs

Category	Amount
Land	$ 42,500
Buildings	332,500
Manufacturing machinery	532,000
Office equipment	212,800
Utilities	30,500
Insurance	99,700
Total	**$1,250,000**

TABLE 2 *SCTC Variable Costs*

Category	Amount
Labor	$15.00
Advertising	1.00
Shipping and receiving	5.00
Total	**$21.00**

and the break-even point for this product. How many sets does SCTC have to sell before it can start turning a profit? Include a data table to show alternative break-even points, assuming variations in insurance costs and labor costs. How would increasing the sale price to $125 affect the break-even point? The Laudon Web site for Chapter 13 provides more detail on the range of costs to include in your sensitivity analysis and on the calculations required for a simple break-even analysis.

Analyzing the Impact of Component Price Changes

Software requirements: Spreadsheet software

Dirt Bikes's management has asked you to explore the impact of changes in some of its parts components on production costs. Review the following bill of materials information for the brake system for Dirt Bikes's Moto 300 model. A bill of materials is used in manufacturing and production to show all of the parts and materials required to manufacture a specific item or for the sub-assembly of a finished product, such as a motorcycle. The information in the bill of materials is useful for determining product costs, coordinating orders, and managing inventory. It can also tell how product costs will be affected by price changes in components or raw materials. The bill of materials for this case has been simplified for instructional purposes.

Bill of Materials: Moto 300 Brake System

Component	Component No.	Source	Unit Cost	Quantity	Extended Cost
Brake cable	M0593	Nissin	28.81	1	
Brake pedal	M0546	Harrison Billet	5.03	2	
Brake pad	M3203	Russell	27.05	2	
Front brake pump	M0959	Brembo	66.05	1	
Rear brake pump	M4739	Brembo	54.00	1	
Front brake caliper	M5930	Nissin	106.20	1	
Rear brake caliper	M7942	Nissin	106.78	1	
Front brake disc	M3920	Russell	143.80	1	
Rear brake disc	M0588	Russell	56.42	1	
Brake pipe	M0943	Harrison Billet	29.52	1	
Brake lever cover	M1059	Brembo	2.62	1	

The bill of materials for this assignment should contain the description of the component, the identification number of each component, the source of the component, the unit cost of each component, the quantity of each component needed to make each finished brake system, the extended cost of each component, and the total materials cost. The extended cost is calculated by multiplying the quantity of each component needed to produce the finished brake system by the unit cost. The prices of components are constantly changing, and you will need to develop a spreadsheet application that can show management the impact of such price changes on the cost to produce each brake system and on total production costs for the Moto 300 model.

1. Complete the bill of materials by calculating the extended cost of each component and the total materials cost for each brake system.

2. Develop a sensitivity analysis to show the impact on total brake system materials costs if the front brake calipers unit cost ranges from $103 to $107 and if the brake pipe unit cost ranges from $27 to $31.

3. The brake system represents 30 percent of the total materials cost for one Moto 300 motorcycle. Use sensitivity analysis again to show the impact of the changes in front brake caliper unit costs and brake pipe unit costs described previously on total materials costs for this motorcycle model.

Electronic Commerce Project: Using a Web-Based DSS for Retirement Planning

The Web sites for Quicken and *SmartMoney Magazine* provide Web-based DSS for financial planning and decision making. Select either site to plan for retirement. Use your chosen site to determine how much you need to save to have enough income for your retirement. Assume that you are 50 years old and plan to retire in 16 years. You have one dependant and $100,000 in savings. Your current annual income is $85,000. Your goal is to be able to generate an annual retirement income of $60,000, including Social Security benefit payments. To calculate your estimated Social Security benefit, use the Quick Benefits Planner Calculator at the Social Security Administration Web site (www.ssa.gov/planners/calculators.htm). Use the Web site you have selected to determine how much money you need to put away to help you achieve your retirement goal. Then critique the site—its ease of use, its clarity, the value of any conclusions reached, and the extent to which the site helps investors understand their financial needs and the financial markets.

Group Project: Designing a University GDSS

With three or four of your classmates, identify several groups in your university that could benefit from a GDSS. Design a GDSS for one of those groups, describing its hardware, software, and people elements. Present your findings to the class.

CASE STUDY
Optimizing Operations at UPS

United Parcel Service (UPS) is the world's largest air and ground package-distribution company, with annual sales of about $34 billion. It is also a leading provider of specialized transportation and logistics services. Following its nearly 100-year promise of the "best service and lowest rates," this company currently delivers over 13.6 million parcels and documents every business day within the United States and in over 200 other countries and territories.

UPS's primary business is time-definite delivery of packages and documents worldwide. It has established a global transportation infrastructure and comprehensive set of guaranteed delivery services, including integrated supply chain solutions for major companies. UPS is the industry leader in the delivery of goods purchased over the Internet.

UPS operates a ground fleet of more than 88,000 vehicles, including its famous brown delivery trucks and large tractors and trailers. In the United States, UPS manages 27 large package operating facilities as well as over 1,000 additional smaller package operating facilities. The smaller facilities have vehicles and drivers stationed for the pickup of packages and for the sorting, transfer, and delivery of packages. UPS owns or leases nearly 600 facilities to support its international package operations and over 750 facilities that support non-package operations.

This vast ground delivery system is integrated with express air services that use 600 airplanes. UPS operates the ninth largest airline in North America and the eleventh largest in the world. UPS aircraft operate in a hub and spokes pattern in the United States with a primary air hub in Louisville, Kentucky, and six other regional air hubs in various cities throughout the United States. These hubs house facilities for the sorting, transfer, and delivery of packages. UPS estimates that this

integrated door-to-door delivery system carries goods worth more than 2 percent of the world's gross domestic product (GDP).

The company faces relentless competition from such other organizations as FedEx, DHL Worldwide Express, the United States Postal Service, Deutsche Post, and TNT Post Group. Although UPS is the overall leader, the company is not number one in every way. For example, FedEx, with about $34 billion in annual sales, leads the market in overnight deliveries, whereas DHL is the leader in cross-border (international) express deliveries.

To meet competitors head on, UPS long ago started investing heavily in advanced information systems. Technology powers virtually every service the company offers and every operation it performs. UPS offers many choices: overnight air versus low-cost ground delivery, simple shipping or a panoply of supply chain and warehousing services. Customers can choose the delivery option or service that is most cost-effective and appropriate for their requirements.

UPS has been using its automated package-tracking system to monitor all packages throughout the delivery process, collecting electronic data on 93 percent of the packages that move through U.S. systems each day. Its customers can track their own parcels and letters using the UPS Web site, and many customers can also track their items on their own computers using a UPS system that the customers embed into their own Web sites.

However, UPS's competition now uses much of this same tracking technology and is moving into areas where UPS has been dominant. FedEx, for instance, is trying to become a player in ground palletized-freight and international shipping. It wants to funnel package data from all of its operations into a single transparent system. Fierce competition has stimulated UPS to

find even more innovative ways of servicing customers while also reducing its own costs.

UPS management believes the company is still a leader in reliable package delivery and that its unmatched integrated air and ground network provide it with a level of service quality and economies of scale that differentiate it from competitors. The company's strategy emphasizes increasing core domestic revenues by cross-selling its existing and new services to a large and diverse customer base. It hopes to grow its package business by offering services for synchronized commerce, helping customers manage the flow of goods, information, and funds throughout their supply chains. For example, UPS developed Web-based software for DaimlerChrysler AG to manage centrally all parts moving to and from more than 4,500 dealerships. While expanding these services, UPS hopes to limit the rate at which expenses are growing. It is counting on information technology–driven efficiencies to increase its operating profit.

In 2003, UPS announced plans to invest $600 million to simplify and optimize its package-sorting and delivery systems. Management believes that this systems investment will produce significant gains in efficiency, reliability, and flexibility. Once fully deployed in 2007 in over 1,000 UPS package-sorting facilities, these systems are expected to reduce operating costs by approximately $600 million each year. In 2003, UPS domestic operating profit declined $304 million, caused by both slow growth in revenue coupled with higher operating expenses. Higher costs for fuel and higher rents both played major roles in expense increases. More efficient dispatching and loading of delivery trucks could reduce the distance covered by UPS drivers by about 100 million miles, saving as much as 14 million gallons of fuel per year.

The project began when, in the mid-1990s, the company recognized it needed a new software program to map its core operations in the United States, including its pickups and deliveries, its sorting facilities, and its delivery centers. In the past, distribution center delivery truck loaders had to remember which trucks were headed where, then take the package off the conveyor belt, see the street on the shipping label of the package, and place it on the correct truck. "It was very chaotic," said Bob Sylsbury, a Mount Olive loader.

Originally, to map every pickup and delivery option to select the best was thought to be impossible by Jack Levis, portfolio manager in the UPS industrial engineering division. There would be more than 15.5 trillion options for calculating every possible route using just 25 points. At that time (about 1995) UPS estimated that computing this would require 500,000 years with the fastest computers in existence. So, the project turned to developing optimization software to assess the most-feasible options for selecting the least-expensive and shortest delivery routes.

Meanwhile, during those years hardware and software also became more powerful, the necessary computing time fell from years to months, then to days, and then to hours, and it is still dropping today. UPS now has optimization software for both its ground and air delivery services. Systems use the real-time information produced by UPS's package-tracking system, including bar-code labels with all the data the company needs to deliver packages on time. Logistics software aggregates ZIP code information and uses the data supplied by the bar codes to map out how packages should be loaded onto trucks for the most efficient deliveries.

Lou Rivieccio, a UPS division manager, says the new system is improving delivery from its Mount Olive, New Jersey, delivery center, enabling drivers to increase their daily deliveries from 130 stops to 145 stops while reducing their average route by eight miles. Whereas in the past loaders could load only 2.5 trucks, with the new system each loader can load between 3 and 4 trucks. Moreover, the past confusion during loading resulted in an annual loader turnover rate of 45 percent. That has now been reduced to 8 percent at the 95 distribution centers where the new system is already operating.

The client/server system for optimizing hub operations and delivery fleets of the UPS ground network is called Hub and Feeder Network Optimization. Five full-time planners set up problems using data on package origination, destination, and volume; data on sorting facility location, capacity, and time and distance between sites; and data from a flow file that defines paths packages take between different sortings. Once the problem is set up, it is transmitted to a Unix server, which runs the computations and transmits the results in the form of reports back to the PCs.

Calculations for UPS hub and feeder network optimizations are performed only several times each year. The information they provide helps answer long-range questions such as when UPS will run out of capacity with its current network, where it should expand, or the impact of changing the service level for its ground operations.

By 2006, UPS wants to use software on wireless handhelds so that its drivers, each averaging more than 100 stops per day, can optimize their own routes. Early versions of the system are being tested on leading-edge custom handhelds with local and wide area wireless connectivity and the ability to communicate with peripheral devices, PCs, or global positioning satellites. The software on the handhelds will be synchronized with the dispatch planning optimization systems deployed at UPS delivery centers.

The system for optimizing UPS air operations at the UPS Worldport hub in Louisville is called Volcano (standing for Volume, Location, and Aircraft Network System). The system takes into account all UPS aircraft delivery routes to optimize fleet assignments, routes, and package allocations within days or hours. Company executives expect the system to save more than $200 million over the next 10 years by improving the planning and scheduling of air deliveries. The company also uses the system to help schedule the pilots and to help determine if UPS should lease or purchase more aircraft, particularly in high-volume periods such as in the Christmas season when required flights can jump by 45 percent. Preventing the company from leasing just one aircraft can save the company $3 million in costs.

UPS ran 1,500 optimizations to help determine where and how it should build sites as it expands its European operations. So, for example, it selected the site for a new sorting facility in Germany and it also calculated how large the facility should be. It actually had selected the Louisville, Kentucky, site for its Worldport air hub in 1999 and projected the price tag to be $1 billion. The software selected the Louisville site over many other possible sites because expanding that site rather than building a new one would be both quicker and less costly than other possibilities. In 1986, when UPS was considering a new facility in the Chicago area, it took four people three months to run a single optimization calculation. "Today you can make a much more fine-tuned decision with fewer people," Levis points out.

Optimization software has also helped so much in improving customer service, according to UPS, that the company has been able to cut at least a day from the guaranteed delivery time for certain shipments. For example, the company now can guarantee that shipment time between New York and Los Angeles will be no more than four business days rather than the five days it used to be.

Sources: Beth Bacheldor, "Breakthrough," *Information Week*, February 9, 2004; Anna Maria Virzi, "United Parcel Service: Sticky Fix," *Baseline Magazine*, February 5, 2004; United Parcel Service, "Annual Report for Fiscal Year Ending December 31, 2003," Form 10-K, U.S. Securities and Exchange Commission; Steve Berez and Chris Zook, "UPS Links to Customers," *Optimize Magazine*, February 2004; and Paul McDougall, "Load 'Em Up," *Information Week*, September 29, 2003.

CASE STUDY QUESTIONS

1. Analyze UPS using the competitive forces and value chain models.

2. What is UPS's business strategy? How do information systems support that strategy?

3. Why was a DSS to optimize delivery routes so important for UPS? What decisions did it support?

4. How successful are these DSS for helping UPS achieve a competitive advantage? Explain your answer.

PART THREE PROJECT
Designing an Enterprise Information Portal

You are the CIO of a major corporation that researches, develops, manufactures, and distributes pharmaceuticals. Your company, which is named United States Pharma Corp., is headquartered in the state of New Jersey in the United States, but it has sites in many countries around the world. Many of the research sites are in the United States, Germany, France, Great Britain, Australia, and Switzerland. Distribution sites are not only in the United States and Europe but also in a number of countries in East and South Asia, Africa, and the Middle East.

Your company is involved with much more than research and development of new drugs. For example, it owns two companies that produce and sell generic drugs (drugs that are no longer protected by a patent and so are copied and sold under other names). It also produces many over-the-counter drugs to combat such problems as headaches, pain, athlete's foot, and allergic reactions. The company also produces and sells some drugs that help to cure or improve some animal diseases such as heartworm and fleas.

The key to the ongoing profits of the company is the research and development of new pharmaceuticals. The company researches thousands of possible drugs in order to finally develop and patent just one that is successful and so becomes a widely sold pharmaceutical product. Such products take 8 to 15 years to research, develop, and test, followed by clinical trials and finally approval by the Food and Drug Administration (FDA). The staff must research both diseases and their treatments and the potential pharmaceuticals that could become innovative new drugs. Experts who are working on the cutting edge of medical, chemical, and other fields are carrying out research in order to develop possible new drugs and medical treatments.

To undertake the research, test the new products, and eventually obtain FDA approval, the researchers and other scientists must test all the possible pharmaceuticals. They must also turn to many places to obtain and share information with others both within and outside of the company. For example they will want to communicate with the World Health Organization, the FDA, and the Centers for Disease Control and Prevention. In addition they will need to connect to the pharmaceutical industry's organizations such as the International Federation of Pharmaceutical Manufacturers Associations (IFPMA). Health education and information sites are also critical, such as the U.S. National Library of Medicine and such private organizations as the Mayo Clinic.

As the CIO, you have concluded that your company needs a corporate knowledge portal that can provide many of the corporate employees with easy access to the information they need. The users of the portal would primarily be chemical, biological, and pharmaceutical researchers as well as medical personnel involved in research, tests, and eventually clinical trials.

1. Write a brief description of the company, its key functions, and systems.

2. Design the corporate portal, providing a description that can be reviewed and approved by your senior executive committee. Your design specifications should include:

   - Internal systems and databases that users of the portal would need to access

   - External sources researchers would need to access to further their research

   - Internal and external communication and collaboration facilities the researchers would need to develop their ideas, pursue their research, and share their research and ideas with others

   - Intranet and Internet search tools to support research

   - Sources for relevant news relating to the company and research

   - FDA rules and regulations regarding clinical programs, clinical trials, and patent applications

   - Connections to pharmaceutical conferences and forums as well as professional organizations and appropriate professional journals

   - Any additional sources of information that would prove helpful to users

   Use the Web to research these features. Your analysis should include the qualities of a good corporate portal and describe commercially available tools for building your portal.

3. Design a homepage for your portal that you can present to management.

Building and Managing Information Systems

Part Four Project: Redesigning
Business Processes for Healthlite
Yogurt Company

Part Four focuses on the process of building and managing systems in organizations. Chapters 14 and 15 describe how companies can use information systems to redesign their organizations and business processes, emphasizing the need to understand and measure a system's business value and to manage system-related organizational change. Chapter 16 describes the issues that must be addressed when building and managing international information systems, including the management of offshore software outsourcing and global teams.

Chapter 14

Redesigning the Organization with Information Systems

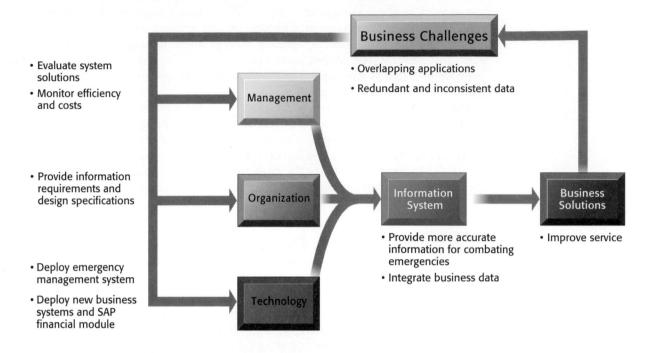

Evaluate system
- solutions
- Monitor efficiency and costs

Management

Business Challenges
- Overlapping applications
- Redundant and inconsistent data

Provide information requirements and design specifications

Organization

Information System
- Provide more accurate information for combating emergencies
- Integrate business data

Business Solutions
- Improve service

- Deploy emergency management system
- Deploy new business systems and SAP financial module

Technology

Opening Case: Australia's Victoria Country Fire Authority Responds with New Systems

The Victoria Country Fire Authority (CFA) is one of the world's largest volunteer emergency services, with 63,000 volunteer members, more than 1,200 fire stations, and 850 permanent support and administrative staff in the state of Victoria, Australia. It is responsible for 2.5 million people in 980,000 homes and 150,182 square kilometers of land. In 2001–2002, CFA brigades responded to 34,139 incidents. CFA's ability to communicate effectively with its volunteer force can be a matter of life and death.

Until recently CFA was struggling to manage multiple technologies and applications with overlapping processes and functionality. These systems were maintaining a great deal of redundant—and often inconsistent—data that were getting out of hand. The data in CFA systems could not be trusted and were affecting CFA's ability to provide emergency management and ensure community safety.

CFA management contracted with consultants to develop a Web site called Brigades Online that provides information for volunteers and to develop more integrated business systems. The most critical project was an emergency management system, which provides mission-critical management of people and equipment for combating fires, and a supporting locality information system. The locality information system contains information about a particular location, including local risks such as the existence of dangerous goods in industrial areas, operational pre-plans, and CFA educational activities in that area.

Other important projects include new systems for finance, asset management, and human resources; interactive portals for staff and volunteers and for the community; a portal for communicating with local government authorities, utilities, and other state agencies; a performance management system; and a multimedia corporate database. CFA was able to use finance modules of the SAP enterprise system developed for another agency, the Metropolitan Fire brigade.

For each project, CFA researched information requirements, evaluated alternative solutions, reviewed business processes, and developed a business case and implementation schedule to ensure they were aligned with its business goals. Brigade volunteers as well as information systems specialists provided input on how the systems should be designed. Although not all systems could be immediately implemented, CFA emerged with a clear idea of what it needed and a strategy to move forward.

Sources: Sue Bushell, "Blazing a Strategy Trail," *CIO Australia*, June 2, 2004; and www.cfa.vic.gov.au, accessed September 24, 2004.

The Victoria Country Fire Authority's system-building program illustrates the many factors at work in the development of a new information system. Building the new system entailed analyzing the organization's problems with existing information systems, assessing people's information needs, selecting appropriate technology, and redesigning business processes and jobs. Management had to monitor the system-building effort and to evaluate its benefits and costs. The new information system represented a process of planned organizational change.

During your career, you will undoubtedly look for ways to use new information systems to improve the performance of your firm. You may be asked to help your organization build a new information system. In this chapter, you'll learn how new information systems are conceived, built, and installed, and how they change the way the organization works. The chapter describes the core systems development activities, alternative approaches for building systems, and alternative methodologies for modeling systems.

14.1 SYSTEMS AS PLANNED ORGANIZATIONAL CHANGE

Building a new information system is one kind of planned organizational change. The introduction of a new information system involves much more than new hardware and software. It also includes changes in jobs, skills, management, and organization. When we design a new information system, we are redesigning the organization. System builders must understand how a system will affect the organization as a whole.

Linking Information Systems to the Business Plan

Deciding which new systems to build should be an essential part of the organizational planning process. Organizations need to develop an information systems plan that supports their overall business plan and in which strategic systems are incorporated into top-level planning. Once specific projects have been selected within the overall context of a strategic plan for the business and the systems area, an **information systems plan** can be developed. The plan serves as a road map indicating the direction of systems development (the purpose of the plan), the rationale, the current systems/situation, new developments to consider, the management strategy, the implementation plan, and the budget (see Table 14-1).

The plan contains a statement of corporate goals and specifies how information technology will support the attainment of those goals. The report shows how general goals will be achieved by specific systems projects. It identifies specific target dates and milestones that can be used later to evaluate the plan's progress in terms of how many objectives were actually attained in the time frame specified in the plan. The plan indicates the key management decisions concerning hardware acquisition; telecommunications; centralization/decentralization of authority, data, and hardware; and required organizational change. Organizational changes are also usually described, including management and employee training requirements; recruiting efforts; changes in business processes; and changes in authority, structure, or management practice.

Establishing Organizational Information Requirements

To develop an effective information systems plan, the organization must have a clear understanding of both its long- and short-term information requirements. Two principal methodologies for establishing the essential information requirements of the organization as a whole are enterprise analysis and critical success factors.

ENTERPRISE ANALYSIS (BUSINESS SYSTEMS PLANNING)

Enterprise analysis (also called business systems planning) argues that the firm's information requirements can be understood only by examining the entire organization in terms of organizational units, functions, processes, and data elements. Enterprise analysis can help identify the key entities and attributes of the organization's data.

TABLE 14-1 Information Systems Plan

1. Purpose of the Plan
   Overview of plan contents
   Current business organization and future organization
   Key business processes
   Management strategy

2. Strategic Business Plan Rationale
   Current situation
   Current business organization
   Changing environments
   Major goals of the business plan
   Firm's strategic plan

3. Current Systems
   Major systems supporting business functions and processes
   Current infrastructure capabilities
      Hardware
      Software
      Database
      Telecommunications and Internet
   Difficulties meeting business requirements
   Anticipated future demands

4. New Developments
   New system projects
      Project descriptions
      Business rationale
      Applications' role in strategy
   New infrastructure capabilities required
      Hardware
      Software
      Database
      Telecommunications and Internet

5. Management Strategy
   Acquisition plans
   Milestones and timing
   Organizational realignment
   Internal reorganization
   Management controls
   Major training initiatives
   Personnel strategy

6. Implementation Plan
   Anticipated difficulties in implementation
   Progress reports

7. Budget Requirements
   Requirements
   Potential savings
   Financing
   Acquisition cycle

The central method used in the enterprise analysis approach is to take a large sample of managers and ask them how they use information, where they get their information, what their objectives are, how they make decisions, and what their data needs are. The results of this large survey of managers are aggregated into subunits, functions, processes, and data matrices. Data elements are organized into logical application groups—groups of data elements that support related sets of organizational processes.

Figure 14-1 is an output of enterprise analysis conducted by the Social Security Administration as part of a massive systems redevelopment effort. It shows what information is required to support a particular process, which processes create the data, and which use them. The shaded boxes in the figure indicate a logical application group. In this case, actuarial estimates, agency plans, and budget data are created in the planning process, suggesting that an information system should be built to support planning.

The weakness of enterprise analysis is that it produces an enormous amount of data that is expensive to collect and difficult to analyze. The questions frequently focus not on management's critical objectives and where information is needed but rather on what existing information is used. The result is a tendency to automate whatever exists. But in

FIGURE 14-1   *Process/data class matrix.*

Group	Process	Actuarial estimates	Agency plans	Budget	Program regulations/policy	Administrative regulations/policy	Labor agreements	Data standards	Procedures	Automated systems documentation	Educational media	Public agreements	Intergovernmental agreements	Grants	External	Exchange control	Administrative accounts	Program expenditures	Audit reports	Organization/position	Employee identification	Recruitment/placement	Complaints/grievances	Training resources	Security	Equipment utilization	Space utilization	Supplies utilization	Workload schedules	Work measurement	Enumeration I.D.	Enumeration control	Earnings	Employer I.D.	Earnings control	Claims characteristics	Claims control	Decisions	Payment	Collection/waiver	Notice	Inquiries control	Quality appraisal
PLANNING	Develop agency plans	C	C	C	U	U									U																												
	Administer agency budget	C	C	C	U	U						U	U	U			U	U	U	U	U					U	U	U					U	U			U		U			U	U
	Formulate program policies	U	U		C			U							U			U		U				U															U				U
	Formulate administrative policies		U		U	C	C	U							U					U	U			U																			
	Formulate data policies		U	U		U		C	U	U																					U	U	U	U									
	Design work processes		U		U	U		C	C			U	U							U																			U				U
GENERAL MANAGEMENT	Manage public affairs		U		U	U		U		C	C	C																															
	Manage intrgovernment affairs	U	U		U	U		U			U		C	C	C											U	U		U	U			U		U								
	Exchange data		U					U				U	U	U	U	C	U	U														U											
	Maintain administrative accounts		U		U			U				U	U				C		U							U	U	U							U					U			
	Maintain program accounts	U	U					U				U	U	C																						U			U	U	U	U	U
	Conduct audits		U	U				U	U								U	U	C	U										U													
	Establish organizations		U		U			U												C	U					U	U																U
	Manage human resources		U		U	U		U												C	C	C	C	C																			
	Provide security				U	U		U	U	U															C	C	C	C	U														
	Manage equipment		U		U			U	U	U																C	C	C	C														
	Manage facilities		U		U			U																		U	U	C															
	Manage supplies		U		U			U																		C	U	U	C														
	Manage workloads	U	U	U	U			U							U											U	U	U	C	C			U		U		U					U	U
PROGRAM ADMINISTRATION	Issue Social Security numbers							U				U		U																	C	C											
	Maintain earnings							U				U	U	U																	U		C	C	C	C	U						
	Collect claims information				U	U		U						U																	U	U				C	C	U	U	U			
	Determine eligibility/entitlement							U																							U	U	U			U		C	U	U			
	Compute payments				U			U										U													U		U				U		U	C	C		
	Administer debt management				U			U										U																						U	C		
SUPPORT	Generate notices							U						U																	U		U				U		U	U	C		
	Respond to program inquiries				U			U	U																						U		U	U			U		U	U	U	U	C
	Provide quality assessment				U	U		U	U																						U		U				U						C

KEY: C = creators of data   U = users of data

This chart depicts which data classes are required to support particular organizational processes and which processes are the creators and users of data.

TABLE 14-2 *Critical Success Factors and Organizational Goals*

Example	Goals	CSF
Profit concern	Earnings/share Return on investment Market share New product Energy standards	Automotive industry Styling Quality dealer system Cost control
Nonprofit	Excellent health care Meeting government regulations Future health needs	Regional integration with other hospitals Improved monitoring of regulations Efficient use of resources

Source: Rockart (1979).

many instances, entirely new approaches to how business is conducted are needed, and these needs are not addressed.

STRATEGIC ANALYSIS OR CRITICAL SUCCESS FACTORS

The strategic analysis, or critical success factors, approach argues that an organization's information requirements are determined by a small number of **critical success factors** (**CSFs**) of managers. If these goals can be attained, success of the firm or organization is assured (Rockart 1979; Rockart and Treacy, 1982). CSFs are shaped by the industry, the firm, the manager, and the broader environment. New information systems should focus on providing information that helps the firm meet these goals.

The principal method used in CSF analysis is personal interviews—three or four—with a number of top managers identifying their goals and the resulting CSFs. These personal CSFs are aggregated to develop a picture of the firm's CSFs. Then systems are built to deliver information on these CSFs. (See Table 14-2 for an example of CSFs. For the method of developing CSFs in an organization, see Figure 14-2.)

The strength of the CSF method is that it produces less data to analyze than does enterprise analysis. Only top managers are interviewed, and the questions focus on a small

FIGURE 14-2 *Using CSFs to develop systems.*

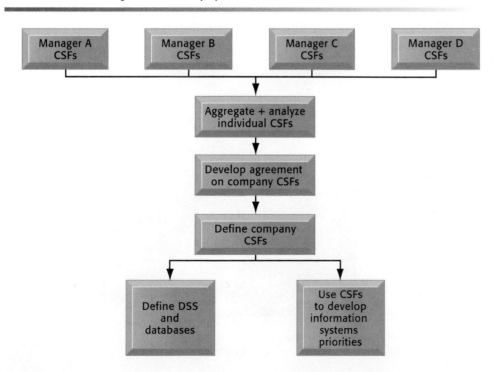

The CSF approach relies on interviews with key managers to identify their CSFs. Individual CSFs are aggregated to develop CSFs for the entire firm. Systems can then be built to deliver information on these CSFs.

number of CSFs rather than requiring a broad inquiry into what information is used in the organization. This method explicitly asks managers to examine their environments and consider how their analyses of them shapes their information needs. It is especially suitable for top management and for the development of decision-support systems (DSS) and executive support systems (ESS). Unlike enterprise analysis, the CSF method focuses organizational attention on how information should be handled.

The method's primary weakness is that the aggregation process and the analysis of the data are art forms. There is no particularly rigorous way in which individual CSFs can be aggregated into a clear company pattern. Second, interviewees (and interviewers) often become confused when distinguishing between *individual* and *organizational* CSFs. These types of CSFs are not necessarily the same. What may be considered critical to a manager may not be important for the organization as a whole. This method is clearly biased toward top managers, although it could be extended to elicit ideas for promising new systems from lower-level members of the organization (Peffers and Gengler, 2003).

Systems Development and Organizational Change

Information technology can promote various degrees of organizational change, ranging from incremental to far-reaching. Figure 14-3 shows four kinds of structural organizational change that are enabled by information technology: (1) automation, (2) rationalization, (3) reengineering, and (4) paradigm shifts. Each carries different rewards and risks.

The most common form of IT-enabled organizational change is **automation**. The first applications of information technology involved assisting employees with performing their tasks more efficiently and effectively. Calculating paychecks and payroll registers, giving bank tellers instant access to customer deposit records, and developing a nationwide network of airline reservation terminals for airline reservation agents are all examples of early automation.

A deeper form of organizational change—one that follows quickly from early automation—is **rationalization of procedures**. Automation frequently reveals new bottlenecks in production and makes the existing arrangement of procedures and structures painfully cumbersome. Rationalization of procedures is the streamlining of standard operating procedures. For example, the Victoria Country Fire Authority's new emergency

FIGURE 14-3   *Organizational change carries risks and rewards.*

The most common forms of organizational change are automation and rationalization. These relatively slow-moving and slow-changing strategies present modest returns but little risk. Faster and more comprehensive change—such as reengineering and paradigm shifts—carries high rewards but offers substantial chances of failure.

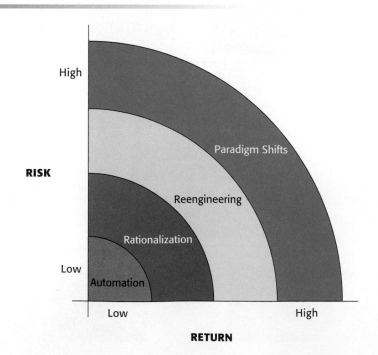

management system described in the chapter-opening case is effective not only because it uses computer technology but also because its design enables the organization to operate more efficiently. The procedures of the Victoria Country Fire Authority (CFA), or any organization, must be rationally structured to achieve this result. CFA had to have standard identification codes for emergency equipment, fire brigades, and localities and standard rules for routing brigades and equipment to the appropriate emergency location. Without a certain amount of rationalization in the CFA's organization, its computer technology would have been useless.

A more powerful type of organizational change is **business process reengineering**, in which business processes are analyzed, simplified, and redesigned. Using information technology, organizations can rethink and streamline their business processes to improve speed, service, and quality. Business reengineering reorganizes work flows, combining steps to cut waste and eliminating repetitive, paper-intensive tasks (sometimes the new design eliminates jobs as well). It is much more ambitious than rationalization of procedures, requiring a new vision of how the process is to be organized.

A widely cited example of business reengineering is Ford Motor Company's invoiceless processing, which reduced headcount in Ford's North American Accounts Payable organization of 500 people by 75 percent. Accounts payable clerks used to spend most of their time resolving discrepancies between purchase orders, receiving documents, and invoices. Ford reengineered its accounts payable process so that the purchasing department enters a purchase order into an online database that can be checked by the receiving department when the ordered items arrive. If the received goods match the purchase order, the system automatically generates a check for accounts payable to send to the vendor. There is no need for vendors to send invoices (Hammer and Champy, 1993).

Rationalizing procedures and redesigning business processes are limited to specific parts of a business. New information systems can ultimately affect the design of the entire organization by transforming how the organization carries out its business or even the nature of the business. For instance, the long-haul trucking and transportation firm Schneider National used new information systems to change its business model. Schneider created a new business managing the logistics for other companies. Baxter International's stockless inventory system (described in Chapter 3) transformed Baxter into a working partner with hospitals and into a manager of its customers' supplies. This more radical form of business change is called a **paradigm shift**. A paradigm shift involves rethinking the nature of the business and the nature of the organization.

Paradigm shifts and reengineering often fail because extensive organizational change is so difficult to orchestrate (see Chapter 15). Why, then, do so many corporations contemplate such radical change? Because the rewards are equally high (see Figure 14-3). In many instances firms seeking paradigm shifts and pursuing reengineering strategies achieve stunning, order-of-magnitude increases in their returns on investment (or productivity). Some of these success stories, and some failure stories, are included throughout this book.

14.2 BUSINESS PROCESS REENGINEERING AND PROCESS IMPROVEMENT

Many companies today are focusing on building new information systems that will improve their business processes. Some of these system projects represent radical restructuring of business processes, whereas others entail more incremental process change.

Business Process Reengineering

If organizations rethink and radically redesign their business processes before applying computing power, they can potentially obtain very large payoffs from their investments in information technology. Let's look at how the home mortgage industry in the United States accomplished this.

The application process for a home mortgage currently takes about six to eight weeks and costs about $3,000. The goal of many mortgage banks is to reduce that cost to $1,000 and the time to obtain a mortgage to about one week. Leading mortgage banks, such as FleetBoston, Countrywide Funding Corporation, and Bank One Corporation, have redesigned the mortgage application process to reduce the cost to $1,000 and the time to obtain a mortgage to about one week (see Figure 14-4).

In the past, a mortgage applicant filled out a paper loan application. The bank entered the application into its computer system. Specialists, such as credit analysts and underwriters from perhaps eight different departments, accessed and evaluated the application individually. If the loan application was approved, the closing was scheduled. After the closing, bank specialists dealing with insurance or funds in escrow serviced the loan. This "desk-to-desk" assembly-line approach might take up to 17 days.

The banks replaced the sequential desk-to-desk approach with a speedier "work cell" or team approach. Now, loan originators in the field enter the mortgage application directly into laptop computers. Software checks the application transaction to make sure that all of the information is correct and complete. The loan originators transmit the loan applications over a network to regional production centers. Instead of working on the application individually, the credit analysts, loan underwriters, and other specialists convene electronically, working as a team to approve the mortgage.

After closing, another team of specialists sets up the loan for servicing. The entire loan application process can take as little as two days. Loan information is easier to access than before, when the loan application could be in eight or nine different departments. Loan originators also can dial into the bank's network to obtain information on mortgage loan costs or to check the status of a loan for the customer.

By radically rethinking their approaches to mortgage processing, mortgage banks have achieved remarkable efficiencies. They have not focused on redesigning a single business process, but instead they have reexamined the entire set of logically connected processes required to obtain a mortgage.

To support the new mortgage application process, the banks have implemented work flow and document management software. **Work flow management** is the process of streamlining business procedures so that documents can be moved easily and efficiently. Work flow and document management software automates processes such as routing documents to different locations, securing approvals, scheduling, and generating reports. Two or more people can work simultaneously on the same document, allowing much quicker completion time. Work need not be delayed because a file is out or a document is in transit. And with a properly designed indexing system, users will be able to retrieve files in many different ways, based on the content of the document.

Steps in Effective Reengineering

One of the most important strategic decisions that a firm can make is not deciding how to use computers to improve business processes but rather understanding what business processes need improvement. When systems are used to strengthen the wrong business model or business processes, the business can become more efficient at doing what it should not do (Hammer, 2002). As a result, the firm becomes vulnerable to competitors who may have discovered the right business model. Considerable time and cost can also be spent improving business processes that have little impact on overall firm performance and revenue. Managers need to determine what business processes are the most important to focus on when applying new information technology and how improving these processes will help the firm execute its strategy.

Management must understand and measure the performance of existing processes as a baseline. If, for example, the objective of process redesign is to reduce time and cost in developing a new product or filling an order, the organization needs to measure the time and cost consumed by the unchanged process. For example, before reengineering, it cost C. R. England & Sons $5.10 to send an invoice; after processes were reengineered, the cost per invoice dropped to 15 cents (Davidson, 1993).

FIGURE 14-4 *Redesigning mortgage processing in the United States.*

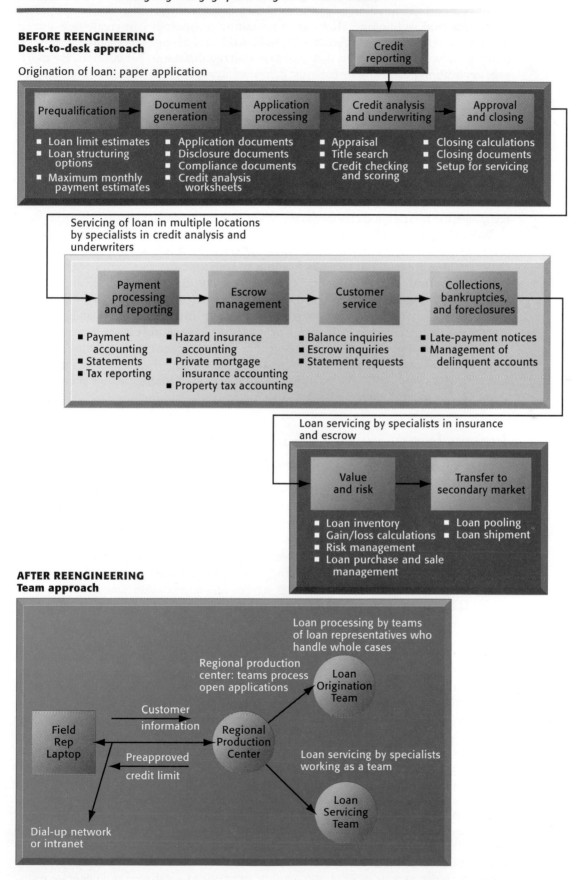

BEFORE REENGINEERING
Desk-to-desk approach

Origination of loan: paper application

Credit reporting

Prequalification	Document generation	Application processing	Credit analysis and underwriting	Approval and closing

- Loan limit estimates
- Loan structuring options
- Maximum monthly payment estimates

- Application documents
- Disclosure documents
- Compliance documents
- Credit analysis worksheets

- Appraisal
- Title search
- Credit checking and scoring

- Closing calculations
- Closing documents
- Setup for servicing

Servicing of loan in multiple locations by specialists in credit analysis and underwriters

Payment processing and reporting	Escrow management	Customer service	Collections, bankruptcies, and foreclosures

- Payment accounting
- Statements
- Tax reporting

- Hazard insurance accounting
- Private mortgage insurance accounting
- Property tax accounting

- Balance inquiries
- Escrow inquiries
- Statement requests

- Late-payment notices
- Management of delinquent accounts

Loan servicing by specialists in insurance and escrow

Value and risk	Transfer to secondary market

- Loan inventory
- Gain/loss calculations
- Risk management
- Loan purchase and sale management

- Loan pooling
- Loan shipment

AFTER REENGINEERING
Team approach

Loan processing by teams of loan representatives who handle whole cases

Regional production center: teams process open applications

Loan Origination Team

Field Rep Laptop

Customer information →

Regional Production Center

← Preapproved credit limit

Loan servicing by specialists working as a team

Loan Servicing Team

Dial-up network or intranet

By redesigning their mortgage processing systems and the mortgage application process, mortgage banks will be able to reduce the costs of processing the average mortgage from $3,000 to $1,000 and reduce the time of approval from six weeks to one week or less. Some banks are even preapproving mortgages and locking interest rates on the same day the customer applies.

The conventional method of designing systems establishes the information requirements of a business function or process and then determines how they can be supported by information technology. However, information technology can create new design options for various processes because it can be used to challenge long-standing assumptions about work arrangements that used to inhibit organizations. For example, the mortgage application processing we have just described shows that it is no longer necessary for people to be in the same physical location to work together on a document. Using networks and document management technology, people can access and work on the same document from many different locations. Information technology should be allowed to influence process design from the start.

Following these steps does not automatically guarantee that reengineering will always be successful. The majority of reengineering projects do not achieve breakthrough gains in business performance because the organizational changes are often very difficult to manage. Managing change is neither simple nor intuitive, and companies committed to reengineering need a good change management strategy (see Chapter 15).

Today's digital firm environment involves much closer coordination of a firm's business processes with those of customers, suppliers, and other business partners than in the past. Organizations are required to make business process changes that span organizational boundaries. These interorganizational processes, such as those for supply chain management, not only need to be streamlined but also coordinated and integrated with those of other business partners. In such cases, reengineering will involve many companies working together to jointly redesign their shared processes. Reengineering expert James Champy calls the joint redesign of interorganizational business processes *X-engineering,* and it is even more challenging to implement successfully than reengineering processes for a single company (Champy, 2002). We examine the organizational change issues surrounding reengineering more carefully in Chapter 15.

Process Improvement: Business Process Management, Total Quality Management, and Six Sigma

Business process reengineering (BPR) is primarily a one-time effort, focusing on identifying one or two strategic business processes that need radical change. BPR projects tend to be expensive and organizationally disruptive. But organizations have many business processes and support processes that must be constantly revised to keep the business competitive. Business process management and quality improvement programs provide opportunities for more incremental and ongoing types of business process change.

BUSINESS PROCESS MANAGEMENT

Mergers and acquisitions, changes in business models, new industry requirements, and changing customer expectations all pose multiple process-related problems that continually confront organizations. Business process management (BPM), which we introduce in Chapter 11, enables organizations to manage incremental process changes that are required simultaneously in many areas of the business. It provides a methodology and tools for dealing with the organization's ongoing need to revise—and ideally optimize—its numerous internal business processes and processes shared with other organizations. It enables organizations to make continual improvements to many business processes simultaneously and to use processes as the fundamental building blocks of corporate information systems.

BPM includes work flow management, business process modeling, quality management, change management, and tools for recasting the firm's business processes into a standardized form where they can be continually manipulated. Companies practicing business process management use process-mapping tools to identify and document existing processes and to create models of improved processes that can then be translated into software systems. The process models might require entirely new systems or could be based on existing systems and data. BPM software tools automatically manage processes across the business, extract data from various sources and databases, and generate transactions in multiple related systems.

FIGURE 14-5 *The*

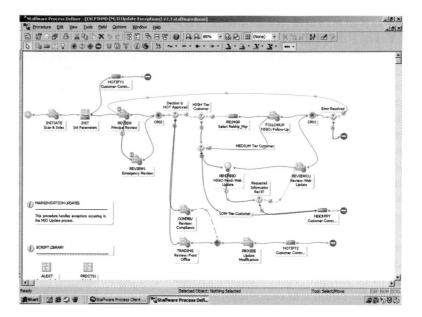

TIBCO Business Process Management software provides a graphical interface that lets users model, monitor, and modify process flows.

The feasibility study ment, whether the te by the firm's informa the changes introduc

Normally, the syst organization can pu tems proposal repor each alternative. It is nical features, and or

ESTABLISHING

Perhaps the most cha tion requirements th level, the **informatio** information, where, tives of the new or r that the new system i tems failure and hig around the wrong se performance or will tive approaches to eli

Some problems d adjustment in manag procedures. If the pr diagnose the problen

Systems Desig

Systems analysis des and **systems design** s mation system is the or house, it consists o

The systems desig identified during syst rial, organizational, a the types of specifica

BPM also includes process monitoring and analytics. Organizations must be able to verify that process performance has been improved and measure the impact of process changes on key business performance indicators. A number of commercial software vendors, including IBM, BEA Systems, Vitria, Intalio, FileNet, Tibco, and Fuego, supply business process management products.

Oil refiner Tesoro Petroleum set up a Business Process Office with six full-time employees to oversee process improvements. This group used Fuego BPM software to create in six weeks a sales order entry process that interacts with SAP enterprise software. It is also using the software to automate mission-critical processes, such as order-to-cash (sales and invoicing), purchase-to-pay (accounts receivable), and capital budgeting to asset retirement. Tesoro's management reports that business process management has helped the company improve cycle times and reduce non-value-added activities and errors. Transactions that previously took four days are instantaneous and more accurate because the data are verified. Employees who previously spent most of their time entering data can now devote themselves to analyzing data and handling exceptions. By making processes easier to perform, the company has also lowered support costs (Lunt, 2003).

TOTAL QUALITY MANAGEMENT AND SIX SIGMA
Quality management is another area of continuous process improvement. In addition to increasing organizational efficiency, companies must fine-tune their business processes to improve the quality in their products, services, and operations. Many are using the concept of **total quality management** (TQM) to make quality the responsibility of all people and functions within an organization. TQM holds that the achievement of quality control is an end in itself. Everyone is expected to contribute to the overall improvement of quality—the engineer who avoids design errors, the production worker who spots defects, the sales representative who presents the product properly to potential customers, and even the secretary who avoids typing mistakes. TQM derives from quality management concepts developed by American quality experts such as W. Edwards Deming and Joseph Juran, but it was popularized by the Japanese.

Another quality concept that is being widely implemented today is six sigma. **Six sigma** is a specific measure of quality, representing 3.4 defects per million opportunities. Most companies cannot achieve this level of quality but use six sigma as a goal to implement a set of methodologies and techniques for improving quality and reducing costs. Studies have repeatedly shown that the earlier in the business cycle a problem is eliminated, the less it costs the company. Thus, quality improvements not only raise the level of product and service quality, but they can also lower costs.

TABLE 14-3 *Design Specifications*

OUTPUT	CONTROLS
Medium	Input controls (characters, limit, reasonableness)
Content	Processing controls (consistency, record counts)
Timing	Output controls (totals, samples of output)
	Procedural controls (passwords, special forms)
INPUT	
Origins	**SECURITY**
Flow	Access controls
Data entry	Catastrophe plans
	Audit trails
USER INTERFACE	
Simplicity	**DOCUMENTATION**
Efficiency	Operations documentation
Logic	Systems documents
Feedback	User documentation
Errors	
	CONVERSION
DATABASE DESIGN	Transfer files
Logical data model	Initiate new procedures
Volume and speed requirements	Select testing method
File organization and design	Cut over to new system
Record specifications	
	TRAINING
PROCESSING	Select training techniques
Computations	Develop training modules
Program modules	Identify training facilities
Required reports	
Timing of outputs	**ORGANIZATIONAL CHANGES**
	Task redesign
MANUAL PROCEDURES	Job design
What activities	Process design
Who performs them	Organization structure design
When	Reporting relationships
How	
Where	

Like houses or buildings, information systems may have many possible designs. Each design represents a unique blend of all technical and organizational components. What makes one design superior to others is the ease and efficiency with which it fulfills user requirements within a specific set of technical, organizational, financial, and time constraints.

THE ROLE OF END USERS

User information requirements drive the entire system-building effort. Users must have sufficient control over the design process to ensure that the system reflects their business priorities and information needs, not the biases of the technical staff. Working on design increases users' understanding and acceptance of the system. As we describe in Chapter 15, insufficient user involvement in the design effort is a major cause of system failure. However, some systems require more user participation in design than others, and section 14.4 shows how alternative systems development methods address the user participation issue.

Completing the Systems Development Process

The remaining steps in the systems development process translate the solution specifications established during systems analysis and design into a fully operational information system. These concluding steps consist of programming, testing, conversion, production, and maintenance.

FIGURE 14-5   *The systems development process.*

Building a system can be broken down into six core activities.

The feasibility study would determine whether the proposed system was a good investment, whether the technology needed for the system was available and could be handled by the firm's information systems specialists, and whether the organization could handle the changes introduced by the system.

Normally, the systems analysis process identifies several alternative solutions that the organization can pursue. The process then assesses the feasibility of each. A written systems proposal report describes the costs and benefits, advantages and disadvantages of each alternative. It is up to management to determine which mix of costs, benefits, technical features, and organizational impacts represents the most desirable alternative.

ESTABLISHING INFORMATION REQUIREMENTS

Perhaps the most challenging task of the systems analyst is to define the specific information requirements that must be met by the system solution selected. At the most basic level, the **information requirements** of a new system involve identifying who needs what information, where, when, and how. Requirements analysis carefully defines the objectives of the new or modified system and develops a detailed description of the functions that the new system must perform. Faulty requirements analysis is a leading cause of systems failure and high systems development costs (see Chapter 15). A system designed around the wrong set of requirements will either have to be discarded because of poor performance or will need to undergo major modifications. Section 14.4 describes alternative approaches to eliciting requirements that help minimize this problem.

Some problems do not require an information system solution but instead need an adjustment in management, additional training, or refinement of existing organizational procedures. If the problem is information related, systems analysis still may be required to diagnose the problem and arrive at the proper solution.

Systems Design

Systems analysis describes what a system should do to meet information requirements, and **systems design** shows how the system will fulfill this objective. The design of an information system is the overall plan or model for that system. Like the blueprint of a building or house, it consists of all the specifications that give the system its form and structure.

The systems designer details the system specifications that will deliver the functions identified during systems analysis. These specifications should address all of the managerial, organizational, and technological components of the system solution. Table 14-3 lists the types of specifications that would be produced during systems design.

TABLE 14-3 Design Specifications

OUTPUT	CONTROLS
Medium	Input controls (characters, limit, reasonableness)
Content	Processing controls (consistency, record counts)
Timing	Output controls (totals, samples of output)
	Procedural controls (passwords, special forms)
INPUT	
Origins	**SECURITY**
Flow	Access controls
Data entry	Catastrophe plans
	Audit trails
USER INTERFACE	
Simplicity	**DOCUMENTATION**
Efficiency	Operations documentation
Logic	Systems documents
Feedback	User documentation
Errors	
	CONVERSION
DATABASE DESIGN	Transfer files
Logical data model	Initiate new procedures
Volume and speed requirements	Select testing method
File organization and design	Cut over to new system
Record specifications	
	TRAINING
PROCESSING	Select training techniques
Computations	Develop training modules
Program modules	Identify training facilities
Required reports	
Timing of outputs	**ORGANIZATIONAL CHANGES**
	Task redesign
MANUAL PROCEDURES	Job design
What activities	Process design
Who performs them	Organization structure design
When	Reporting relationships
How	
Where	

Like houses or buildings, information systems may have many possible designs. Each design represents a unique blend of all technical and organizational components. What makes one design superior to others is the ease and efficiency with which it fulfills user requirements within a specific set of technical, organizational, financial, and time constraints.

THE ROLE OF END USERS

User information requirements drive the entire system-building effort. Users must have sufficient control over the design process to ensure that the system reflects their business priorities and information needs, not the biases of the technical staff. Working on design increases users' understanding and acceptance of the system. As we describe in Chapter 15, insufficient user involvement in the design effort is a major cause of system failure. However, some systems require more user participation in design than others, and section 14.4 shows how alternative systems development methods address the user participation issue.

Completing the Systems Development Process

The remaining steps in the systems development process translate the solution specifications established during systems analysis and design into a fully operational information system. These concluding steps consist of programming, testing, conversion, production, and maintenance.

Building successful information systems requires close cooperation among end users and information systems specialists throughout the systems development process.

PROGRAMMING

During the **programming** stage, system specifications that were prepared during the design stage are translated into software program code. Today, many organizations no longer do their own programming for new systems. Instead, they purchase the software that meets the requirements for a new system from external sources such as software packages from a commercial software vendor, software services from an application service provider, or outsourcing firms that develop custom application software for their clients (see section 14.4).

TESTING

Exhaustive and thorough **testing** must be conducted to ascertain whether the system produces the right results. Testing answers the question, "Will the system produce the desired results under known conditions?"

The amount of time needed to answer this question has been traditionally underrated in systems project planning (see Chapter 15). Testing is time consuming: Test data must be carefully prepared, results reviewed, and corrections made in the system. In some instances parts of the system may have to be redesigned. The risks resulting from glossing over this step are enormous.

Testing an information system can be broken down into three types of activities: unit testing, system testing, and acceptance testing. **Unit testing**, or program testing, consists of testing each program separately in the system. It is widely believed that the purpose of such testing is to guarantee that programs are error free, but this goal is realistically impossible. Testing should be viewed instead as a means of locating errors in programs, focusing on finding all the ways to make a program fail. Once they are pinpointed, problems can be corrected.

System testing tests the functioning of the information system as a whole. It tries to determine whether discrete modules will function together as planned and whether discrepancies exist between the way the system actually works and the way it was conceived. Among the areas examined are performance time, capacity for file storage and handling peak loads, recovery and restart capabilities, and manual procedures.

Acceptance testing provides the final certification that the system is ready to be used in a production setting. Systems tests are evaluated by users and reviewed by management. When all parties are satisfied that the new system meets their standards, the system is formally accepted for installation.

The systems development team works with users to devise a systematic test plan. The **test plan** includes all of the preparations for the series of tests we have just described.

Figure 14-6 shows an example of a test plan. The general condition being tested is a record change. The documentation consists of a series of test-plan screens maintained on a database (perhaps a PC database) that is ideally suited to this kind of application.

CONVERSION

Conversion is the process of changing from the old system to the new system. Four main conversion strategies can be employed: the parallel strategy, the direct cutover strategy, the pilot study strategy, and the phased approach strategy.

In a **parallel strategy** both the old system and its potential replacement are run together for a time until everyone is assured that the new one functions correctly. This is the safest conversion approach because, in the event of errors or processing disruptions, the old system can still be used as a backup. However, this approach is very expensive, and additional staff or resources may be required to run the extra system.

The **direct cutover** strategy replaces the old system entirely with the new system on an appointed day. It is a very risky approach that can potentially be more costly than running two systems in parallel if serious problems with the new system are found. There is no other system to fall back on. Dislocations, disruptions, and the cost of corrections may be enormous.

The **pilot study** strategy introduces the new system to only a limited area of the organization, such as a single department or operating unit. When this pilot version is complete and working smoothly, it is installed throughout the rest of the organization, either simultaneously or in stages.

The **phased approach** strategy introduces the new system in stages, either by functions or by organizational units. If, for example, the system is introduced by functions, a new payroll system might begin with hourly workers who are paid weekly, followed six months later by adding salaried employees (who are paid monthly) to the system. If the system is introduced by organizational units, corporate headquarters might be converted first, followed by outlying operating units four months later.

Moving from an old system to a new one requires that end users be trained to use the new system. Detailed **documentation** showing how the system works from both a technical and end-user standpoint is finalized during conversion time for use in training and everyday operations. Lack of proper training and documentation contributes to system failure, so this portion of the systems development process is very important.

FIGURE 14-6   *A sample test plan to test a record change.*

When developing a test plan, it is imperative to include the various conditions to be tested, the requirements for each condition tested, and the expected results. Test plans require input from both end users and information systems specialists.

Procedure	Address and Maintenance "Record Change Series"		Test Series 2		
	Prepared By:		Date:	Version:	
Test Ref.	Condition Tested	Special Requirements	Expected Results	Output On	Next Screen
2.0	Change records				
2.1	Change existing record	Key field	Not allowed		
2.2	Change nonexistent record	Other fields	"Invalid key" message		
2.3	Change deleted record	Deleted record must be available	"Deleted" message		
2.4	Make second record	Change 2.1 above	OK if valid	Transaction file	V45
2.5	Insert record		OK if valid	Transaction file	V45
2.6	Abort during change	Abort 2.5	No change	Transaction file	V45

PRODUCTION AND MAINTENANCE

After the new system is installed and conversion is complete, the system is said to be in **production**. During this stage, the system will be reviewed by both users and technical specialists to determine how well it has met its original objectives and to decide whether any revisions or modifications are in order. In some instances, a formal **postimplementation audit** document is prepared. After the system has been fine-tuned, it must be maintained while it is in production to correct errors, meet requirements, or improve processing efficiency. Changes in hardware, software, documentation, or procedures to a production system to correct errors, meet new requirements, or improve processing efficiency are termed **maintenance**.

Studies of maintenance have examined the amount of time required for various maintenance tasks (Lientz and Swanson, 1980). Approximately 20 percent of the time is devoted to debugging or correcting emergency production problems; another 20 percent is concerned with changes in data, files, reports, hardware, or system software. But 60 percent of all maintenance work consists of making user enhancements, improving documentation, and recoding system components for greater processing efficiency. The amount of work in the third category of maintenance problems could be reduced significantly through better systems analysis and design practices. Table 14-4 summarizes the systems development activities.

Modeling and Designing Systems: Structured and Object-Oriented Methodologies

There are alternative methodologies for modeling and designing systems. Structured methodologies and object-oriented development are the most prominent.

STRUCTURED METHODOLOGIES

Structured methodologies have been used to document, analyze, and design information systems since the 1970s. **Structured** refers to the fact that the techniques are step by step, with each step building on the previous one. Structured methodologies are top-down, progressing from the highest, most abstract level to the lowest level of detail—from the general to the specific.

Structured development methods are process-oriented, focusing primarily on modeling the processes, or actions that capture, store, manipulate, and distribute data as the data flow through a system. These methods separate data from processes. A separate programming

TABLE 14-4 *Systems Development*

Core Activity	Description
Systems analysis	Identify problem(s) Specify solutions Establish information requirements
Systems design	Create design specifications
Programming	Translate design specifications into program code
Testing	Unit test Systems test Acceptance test
Conversion	Plan conversion Prepare documentation Train users and technical staff
Production and maintenance	Operate the system Evaluate the system Modify the system

procedure must be written every time someone wants to take an action on a particular piece of data. The procedures act on data that the program passes to them.

The primary tool for representing a system's component processes and the flow of data between them is the **data flow diagram** (DFD). The data flow diagram offers a logical graphic model of information flow, partitioning a system into modules that show manageable levels of detail. It rigorously specifies the processes or transformations that occur within each module and the interfaces that exist between them.

Figure 14-7 shows a simple data flow diagram for a mail-in university course registration system. The rounded boxes represent processes, which portray the transformation of data. The square box represents an external entity, which is an originator or receiver of data located outside the boundaries of the system being modeled. The open rectangles represent data stores, which are either manual or automated inventories of data. The arrows represent data flows, which show the movement between processes, external entities, and data stores. They always contain packets of data with the name or content of each data flow listed beside the arrow.

This data flow diagram shows that students submit registration forms with their name, identification number, and the numbers of the courses they wish to take. In process 1.0 the system verifies that each course selected is still open by referencing the university's course file. The file distinguishes courses that are open from those that have been canceled or filled. Process 1.0 then determines which of the student's selections can be accepted or rejected. Process 2.0 enrolls the student in the courses for which he or she has been accepted. It updates the university's course file with the student's name and identification number and recalculates the class size. If maximum enrollment has been reached, the course number is flagged as closed. Process 2.0 also updates the university's student master file with information about new students or changes in address. Process 3.0 then sends each student applicant a confirmation-of-registration letter listing the courses for which he or she is registered and noting the course selections that could not be fulfilled.

The diagrams can be used to depict higher-level processes as well as lower-level details. Through leveled data flow diagrams, a complex process can be broken down into successive levels of detail. An entire system can be divided into subsystems with a high-level data flow diagram. Each subsystem, in turn, can be divided into additional subsystems with second-level data flow diagrams, and the lower-level subsystems can be broken down again until the lowest level of detail has been reached.

Another tool for structured analysis is a data dictionary, which contains information about individual pieces of data and data groupings within a system (see Chapter 7). The

FIGURE 14-7 *Data flow diagram for mail-in university registration system.*

The system has three processes: Verify availability (1.0), Enroll student (2.0), and Confirm registration (3.0). The name and content of each of the data flows appear adjacent to each arrow. There is one external entity in this system: the student. There are two data stores: the student master file and the course file.

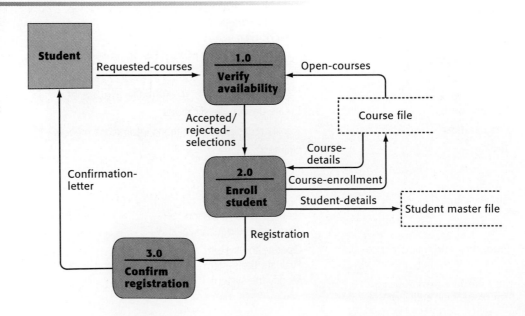

data dictionary defines the contents of data flows and data stores so that systems builders understand exactly what pieces of data they contain. **Process specifications** describe the transformation occurring within the lowest level of the data flow diagrams. They express the logic for each process.

In structured methodology, software design is modeled using hierarchical structure charts. The **structure chart** is a top-down chart, showing each level of design, its relationship to other levels, and its place in the overall design structure. The design first considers the main function of a program or system, then breaks this function into subfunctions, and decomposes each subfunction until the lowest level of detail has been reached. Figure 14-8 shows a high-level structure chart for a payroll system. If a design has too many levels to fit onto one structure chart, it can be broken down further on more detailed structure charts. A structure chart may document one program, one system (a set of programs), or part of one program.

OBJECT-ORIENTED DEVELOPMENT

Structured methods are useful for modeling processes, but do not handle the modeling of data well. They also treat data and processes as logically separate entities, whereas in the real world such separation seems unnatural. Different modeling conventions are used for analysis (the data flow diagram) and for design (the structure chart).

Object-oriented development tries to deal with these issues. Object-oriented development uses the **object** as the basic unit of systems analysis and design. An object combines data and the specific processes that operate on those data. Data encapsulated in an object can be accessed and modified only by the operations, or *methods*, associated with that object. Instead of passing data to procedures, programs send a message for an object to perform an operation that is already embedded in it. The system is modeled as a collection of objects and the relationships among them. Because processing logic resides within objects rather than in separate software programs, objects must collaborate with each other to make the system work.

Object-oriented modeling is based on the concepts of *class* and *inheritance*. Objects belonging to a certain class, or general categories of similar objects, have the features of that class. Classes of objects in turn can inherit all the structure and behaviors of a more general class and then add variables and behaviors unique to each object. New classes of objects are created by choosing an existing class and specifying how the new class differs from the existing class, instead of starting from scratch each time.

We can see how class and inheritance work in Figure 14-9, which illustrates the relationships among classes concerning employees and how they are paid. Employee is the common ancestor, or superclass, for the other three classes. Salaried, Hourly, and Temporary are subclasses of Employee. The class name is in the top compartment, the attributes for each class are in the middle portion of each box, and the list of operations is

FIGURE 14-8   *High-level structure chart for a payroll system.*

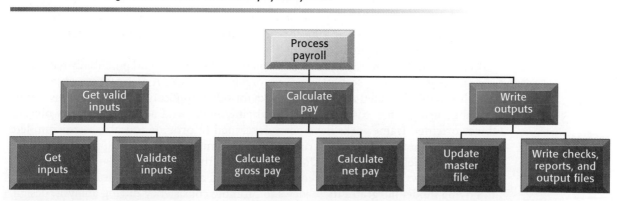

This structure chart shows the highest or most abstract level of design for a payroll system, providing an overview of the entire system.

FIGURE 14-9 *Class and inheritance.*

This figure illustrates how classes inherit the common features of their superclass.

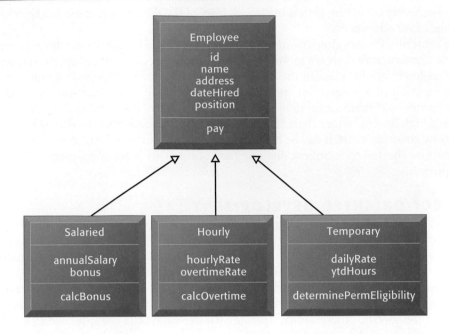

in the bottom portion of each box. The features that are shared by all employees (id, name, address, date hired, position, and pay) are stored in the Employee superclass, whereas each subclass stores features that are specific to that particular type of employee. Specific to Hourly employees, for example, are their hourly rates and overtime rates. A solid line from the subclass to the superclass is a generalization path showing that the subclasses Salaried, Hourly, and Temporary have common features that can be generalized into the superclass Employee.

The phases of object-oriented development are similar to those of conventional systems development, consisting of analysis, design, and implementation. However, object-oriented development is more iterative and incremental than traditional structured development. During analysis, systems builders document the functional requirements of the system, specifying its most important properties and what the proposed system must do. Interactions between the system and its users are analyzed to identify objects, which include both data and processes. The object-oriented design phase describes how the objects will behave and how they will interact with one other. Similar objects are grouped together to form a class, and classes are grouped into hierarchies in which a subclass inherits the attributes and methods from its superclass.

The information system is implemented by translating the design into program code, reusing classes that are already available in a library of reusable software objects and adding new ones created during the object-oriented design phase. Implementation may also involve the creation of an object-oriented database. The resulting system must be thoroughly tested and evaluated.

Because objects are reusable, object-oriented development could potentially reduce the time and cost of writing software because organizations can reuse software objects that have already been created as building blocks for other applications. New systems can be created by using some existing objects, changing others, and adding a few new objects. Object-oriented frameworks have been developed to provide reusable, semicomplete applications that the organization can further customize into finished applications.

Unified Modeling Language (UML) has become the industry standard for representing various views of an object-oriented system using a series of graphical diagrams. The underlying model integrates these views to promote consistency during analysis, design, and implementation. UML uses two principal types of diagrams: structural diagrams and behavioral diagrams.

Structural diagrams are used to describe the relationship between classes. Figure 14-9 is an example of one type of structural diagram called a class diagram. It shows classes of employees and the relationships between them. The terminators at the end of the relationship lines in this diagram indicate the nature of the relationship. The relationships depicted in Figure 14-9 are examples of *generalization*, which is a relationship between a general kind of thing and a more specific kind of thing. This type of relationship is sometimes described as an "is a" relationship. Generalization relationships are used for modeling class inheritance.

Behavioral diagrams are used to describe interactions in an object-oriented system. Figure 14-10 illustrates one type of behavioral diagram called a use case diagram. A use case diagram shows the relationship between an actor and a system. The actor (represented in the diagram as a stick man) is an external entity that interacts with the system, and the use case represents a series of related actions initiated by the actor to accomplish a specific goal. Several interrelated use cases are represented as ovals within a box. Use case modeling is used to specify the functional requirements of a system, focusing on what the system does rather than how it does it. The system's objects and their interactions with each other and with the users of the system are derived from the use case model.

COMPUTER-AIDED SOFTWARE ENGINEERING

Computer-aided software engineering (CASE)—sometimes called computer-aided systems engineering—provides software tools to automate the methodologies we have just described to reduce the amount of repetitive work the developer needs to do. CASE tools

FIGURE 14-10   A UML use case diagram.

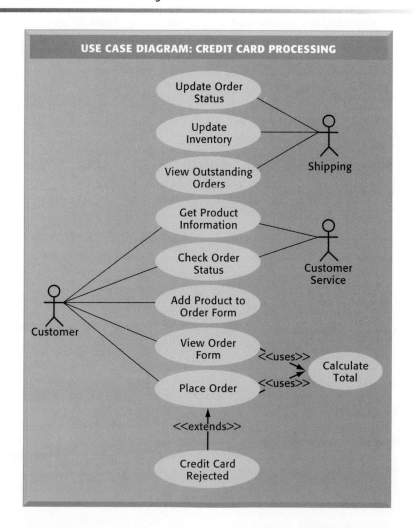

Use case diagrams model the functions of a system, showing how objects interact with each other and with the users of the system. Illustrated here is a use case diagram for credit card processing that was created with SmartDraw software.

also facilitate the creation of clear documentation and the coordination of team development efforts. Team members can share their work easily by accessing each other's files to review or modify what has been done. Modest productivity benefits can also be achieved if the tools are used properly. Many CASE tools are PC-based, with powerful graphical capabilities.

CASE tools provide automated graphics facilities for producing charts and diagrams, screen and report generators, data dictionaries, extensive reporting facilities, analysis and checking tools, code generators, and documentation generators. In general, CASE tools try to increase productivity and quality by doing the following:

- Enforce a standard development methodology and design discipline
- Improve communication between users and technical specialists
- Organize and correlate design components and provide rapid access to them using a design repository
- Automate tedious and error-prone portions of analysis and design
- Automate code generation and testing and control rollout

Many CASE tools have been classified in terms of whether they support activities at the front end or the back end of the systems development process. Front-end CASE tools focus on capturing analysis and design information in the early stages of systems development, whereas back-end CASE tools address coding, testing, and maintenance activities. Back-end tools help convert specifications automatically into program code.

CASE tools automatically tie data elements to the processes where they are used. If a data flow diagram is changed from one process to another, the elements in the data dictionary would be altered automatically to reflect the change in the diagram. CASE tools also contain features for validating design diagrams and specifications. CASE tools thus support iterative design by automating revisions and changes and providing prototyping facilities. A CASE information repository stores all the information defined by the analysts during the project. The repository includes data flow diagrams, structure charts, entity-relationship diagrams, UML diagrams, data definitions, process specifications, screen and report formats, notes and comments, and test results.

To be used effectively, CASE tools require organizational discipline, management support, and an organizational culture that appreciates the value of such tools (Limayem, Khalifa, and Chin, 2004). Every member of a development project must adhere to a common set of naming conventions and standards as well as to a development methodology. The best CASE tools enforce common methods and standards, which may discourage their use in situations where organizational discipline is lacking.

14.4 ALTERNATIVE SYSTEMS-BUILDING APPROACHES

Systems differ in terms of their size and technological complexity and in terms of the organizational problems they are meant to solve. A number of systems-building approaches have been developed to deal with these differences. This section describes these alternative methods: the traditional systems life cycle, prototyping, end-user development, application software packages, and outsourcing.

Traditional Systems Life Cycle

The **systems life cycle** is the oldest method for building information systems. The life cycle methodology is a phased approach to building a system, dividing systems development into formal stages. Systems development specialists have different opinions on how to partition the systems-building stages, but they roughly correspond to the stages of systems development that we have just described.

The systems life cycle methodology maintains a very formal division of labor between end users and information systems specialists. Technical specialists, such as system analysts and programmers, are responsible for much of the systems analysis, design, and implementation work; end users are limited to providing information requirements and reviewing the technical staff's work. The life cycle also emphasizes formal specifications and paperwork, so many documents are generated during the course of a systems project.

The systems life cycle is still used for building large complex systems that require a rigorous and formal requirements analysis, predefined specifications, and tight controls over the systems-building process. However, the systems life cycle approach can be costly, time consuming, and inflexible. Although systems builders can go back and forth among stages in the life cycle, the systems life cycle is predominantly a "waterfall" approach in which tasks in one stage are completed before work for the next stage begins. Activities can be repeated, but volumes of new documents must be generated and steps retraced if requirements and specifications need to be revised. This encourages freezing of specifications relatively early in the development process. The life cycle approach is also not suitable for many small desktop systems, which tend to be less structured and more individualized.

Prototyping

Prototyping consists of building an experimental system rapidly and inexpensively for end users to evaluate. By interacting with the prototype, users can get a better idea of their information requirements. The prototype endorsed by the users can be used as a template to create the final system.

The **prototype** is a working version of an information system or part of the system, but it is meant to be only a preliminary model. Once operational, the prototype will be further refined until it conforms precisely to users' requirements. Once the design has been finalized, the prototype can be converted to a polished production system.

The process of building a preliminary design, trying it out, refining it, and trying again has been called an **iterative** process of systems development because the steps required to build a system can be repeated over and over again. Prototyping is more explicitly iterative than the conventional life cycle, and it actively promotes system design changes. It has been said that prototyping replaces unplanned rework with planned iteration, with each version more accurately reflecting users' requirements.

STEPS IN PROTOTYPING

Figure 14-11 shows a four-step model of the prototyping process, which consists of the following:

1. **Step 1:** *Identify the user's basic requirements.* The system designer (usually an information systems specialist) works with the user only long enough to capture the user's basic information needs.

2. **Step 2:** *Develop an initial prototype.* The system designer creates a working prototype quickly, using tools for rapidly generating software.

3. **Step 3:** *Use the prototype.* The user is encouraged to work with the system to determine how well the prototype meets his or her needs and to make suggestions for improving the prototype.

4. **Step 4:** *Revise and enhance the prototype.* The system builder notes all changes the user requests and refines the prototype accordingly. After the prototype has been revised, the cycle returns to step 3. Steps 3 and 4 are repeated until the user is satisfied.

When no more iterations are required, the approved prototype then becomes an operational prototype that furnishes the final specifications for the application. Sometimes the prototype is adopted as the production version of the system.

ADVANTAGES AND DISADVANTAGES OF PROTOTYPING

Prototyping is most useful when there is some uncertainty about requirements or design solutions. Prototyping is especially useful in designing an information system's **end-user interface** (the part of the system with which end users interact, such as online display and

FIGURE 14-11   *The prototyping process.*

The process of developing a prototype can be broken down into four steps. Because a prototype can be developed quickly and inexpensively, systems builders can go through several iterations, repeating steps 3 and 4, to refine and enhance the prototype before arriving at the final operational one.

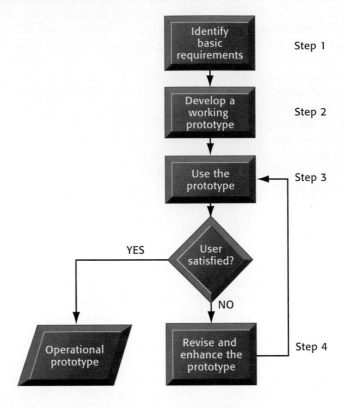

data-entry screens, reports, or Web pages). Because prototyping encourages intense end-user involvement throughout the systems development life cycle, it is more likely to produce systems that fulfill user requirements.

However, rapid prototyping can gloss over essential steps in systems development. If the completed prototype works reasonably well, management may not see the need for reprogramming, redesign, or full documentation and testing to build a polished production system. Some of these hastily constructed systems may not easily accommodate large quantities of data or a large number of users in a production environment.

End-User Development

Some types of information systems can be developed by end users with little or no formal assistance from technical specialists. This phenomenon is called **end-user development**. A series of software tools categorized as fourth-generation languages makes this possible. **Fourth-generation languages** are software tools that enable end users to create reports or develop software applications with minimal or no technical assistance. Some of these fourth-generation tools also enhance professional programmers' productivity.

Fourth-generation languages tend to be nonprocedural, or less procedural, than conventional programming languages. Procedural languages require specification of the sequence of steps, or procedures, that tell the computer what to do and how to do it. Nonprocedural languages need only specify what has to be accomplished rather than provide details about how to carry out the task.

Table 14-5 shows that there are seven categories of fourth-generation languages: PC software tools, query languages, report generators, graphics languages, application generators, application software packages, and very high level programming languages. The table shows the tools ordered in terms of ease of use by nonprogramming end users. End users are most likely to work with PC software tools and query languages. **Query languages** are software tools that provide immediate online answers to requests for information that are not predefined, such as "Who are the highest-performing sales representa-

TABLE 14-5 *Categories of Fourth-Generation Languages*

PC software tools	General-purpose application software packages for PCs.	WordPerfect Microsoft Access
Query language	Languages for retrieving data stored in databases or files. Capable of supporting requests for information that are not predefined.	SQL
Report generator	Extract data from files or databases to create customized reports in a wide range of formats not routinely produced by an information system. Generally provide more control over the way data are formatted, organized, and displayed than query languages.	Crystal Reports
Graphics language	Retrieve data from files or databases and display them in graphic format. Some graphics software can perform arithmetic or logical operations on data as well.	SAS Graph Systat
Application generator	Contain preprogrammed modules that can generate entire applications, including Web sites, greatly speeding development. A user can specify what needs to be done, and the application generator will create the appropriate program code for input, validation, update, processing, and reporting.	FOCUS PowerBuilder Microsoft FrontPage
Application software package	Software programs sold or leased by commercial vendors that eliminate the need for custom-written, in-house software.	PeopleSoft HRM SAP R/3
Very high-level programming language	Generate program code with fewer instructions than conventional languages such as COBOL or FORTRAN. Designed primarily as productivity tools for professional programmers.	APL Nomad2

tives?" Query languages are often tied to data management software and to database management systems (see Chapter 7).

On the whole, end-user-developed systems can be completed more rapidly than those developed through the conventional systems life cycle. Allowing users to specify their own business needs improves requirements gathering and often leads to a higher level of user involvement and satisfaction with the system. However, fourth-generation tools still cannot replace conventional tools for some business applications because they cannot easily handle the processing of large numbers of transactions or applications with extensive procedural logic and updating requirements.

End-user computing also poses organizational risks because it occurs outside of traditional mechanisms for information systems management and control. When systems are created rapidly, without a formal development methodology, testing and documentation may be inadequate. Control over data can be lost in systems outside the traditional information systems department (see Chapter 7).

To help organizations maximize the benefits of end-user applications development, management should control the development of end-user applications by requiring cost justification of end-user information system projects and by establishing hardware, software, and quality standards for user-developed applications.

Application Software Packages and Outsourcing

Chapter 6 points out that the software for most systems today is not developed in-house but is purchased from external sources. Firms can rent the software from an application service provider, they can purchase a software package from a commercial vendor, or they can have a custom application developed by an outside outsourcing firm.

The Window on Technology illustrates a company that is using multiple approaches to obtain better systems. Elie Tahari Limited is using software packages for business transaction systems and for end-user computing tools. The company outsourced the cleansing of its retail point-of-sale data to another company that could do the work more efficiently than Tahari's in-house staff. By combining all of these approaches, Tahari came up with a powerful set of systems and tools that increased operational efficiency and the ability to take advantage of market trends while allowing the firm to concentrate on its core competency—fashion design.

WINDOW ON TECHNOLOGY

NEW SYSTEMS KEEP ELIE TAHARI A TOP FASHION INNOVATOR

Elie Tahari Limited is a fashion pacesetter represented in all major upscale department stores. This company pioneered the "shop-in-shop" concept for presenting designer fashions. High-fashion department stores such as Neiman Marcus, Bloomingdales, and Saks Fifth Avenue each set aside a dedicated space within their stores to display the Elie Tahari Collection.

The Elie Tahari company tries to be equally innovative with its information systems. Tahari counts on information systems to help maintain operational efficiency, spot trends, and take advantage of new business opportunities.

New systems enable Tahari's managers to know exactly what's happening in its the company warehouses, factories, and in each store that sells its fashions—and to take action on that information. If, for instance, a reversible tweed jacket with contrasting trim starts being snapped up at the stores, the company can immediately recut that style and move it onto the sales floor within four to six weeks to keep the sales momentum going. Most clothing manufacturers can't react that quickly.

Until a few years ago, Tahari couldn't either. Mickey Klein, Tahari's vice president in charge of business processes and expansion, had little more than shipping notices to track goods from the company's manufacturers to its distribution centers and to its retailers. The quality of sales data Tahari received from retailers was "misleading." Sales reports from the retail chains selling Tahari clothing were compiled and transmitted to Tahari as Excel spreadsheets or Electronic Data Interchange (EDI) documents. The information transmitted was often incomplete, redundant, or inconsistent. Some retailers provided data showing the percentage of decrease or increase in sales; whereas others supplied actual dollar amounts. Two full-time Tahari staffers spent two full days at the beginning of each work week checking the retailers' sales reports for completeness and accuracy. As a result, Tahari managers could not see the sales reports until midweek, which left them very little time to use the information to improve that week's sales.

Klein developed a system that would collect sales data from retailers and deliver on-demand reports showing orders in the pipeline, sales by styles and stores, and the movement of merchandise into and out of its distribution center. Tahari contracted with Edifice and Kliger-Weiss Infosystems (KWI) to collect and cleanse weekly retail data from the stores before they enter Tahari's corporate data warehouse.

Tahari followed with a reporting and analysis system called InSeam based on a software package called WebFOCUS from Information Builders. InSeam enables authorized users to obtain self-service reports on orders, inventory, sales, and finance using the cleansed weekly retail data and shipment and inventory data from an industry-standard operations package called Apparel Computer Systems supplied by Computer Generated Solutions. Apparel Computer Systems runs on an IBM AS/400 midrange computer, and WebFOCUS runs on an HP ProLiant DL380 G3 server that accesses a data warehouse running on an AS/400 machine.

Sales executives can see their accounts, which merchandise is selling, and what customers have on order. They can also request specific pieces of information for ad-hoc reports. Many of the reports include pictures of the pertinent merchandise, and all are accessible using standard Web browsers. Users can further customize these reports by drilling down to more detail. A WebFOCUS tool called ReportCaster enables every report produced by InSeam to be sent by e-mail on a scheduled or ad hoc basis. Every day Klein automatically gets an e-mail message summarizing that day's financial and order status, and every sales executive receives weekly reports highlighting orders requiring immediate attention.

These WebFOCUS applications make information retrieval much less labor-intensive for end users. Users can export tables from InSeam to Microsoft Excel worksheets with a simple mouse click. For more complex financial and sales reports, Elie Tahari has WebFOCUS specialist Susannah Jones on staff to work with the software tools in the package. For example, Jones uses WebFOCUS to create a revenue versus cost report showing gross margins, year-to-date growth, and other relevant information.

The WebFOCUS reporting environment includes security features so that each user can access only the information needed for his or her job. For example, sales reports are segmented by division and only authorized accounting personnel can view financial reports.

Immediate access to such information has enabled Elie Tahari to reduce inventory in its warehouse and quickly deliver the sizes and styles that are selling to the appropriate stores. Costs at one key shipping-delivery process were reduced by 15 percent.

Sources: John McCormick, "Elie Tahari: Ready to Wear," *Baseline Magazine*, September 2004; and Information Builders, "Elie Tahari Ltd. Unveils New End-User Reporting Framework," www.informationbuilders.com, accessed September 21, 2004.

To Think About: How did Elie Tahari benefit from using software packages and end-user development tools? What management, organization, and technology issues had to be addressed to use these tools effectively?

APPLICATION SOFTWARE PACKAGES

During the past several decades, many systems have been built on an application software package foundation. Many applications are common to all business organizations—for example, payroll, accounts receivable, general ledger, or inventory control. For such universal functions with standard processes that do not change a great deal over time, a generalized system will fulfill the requirements of many organizations.

If a software package can fulfill most of an organization's requirements, the company does not have to write its own software. The company can save time and money by using the prewritten, predesigned, pretested software programs from the package. Package vendors supply much of the ongoing maintenance and support for the system, including enhancements to keep the system in line with ongoing technical and business developments.

If an organization has unique requirements that the package does not address, many packages include capabilities for customization. **Customization** features allow a software package to be modified to meet an organization's unique requirements without destroying the integrity of the package software. If a great deal of customization is required, additional programming and customization work may become so expensive and time consuming that they negate many of the advantages of software packages.

Figure 14-12 shows how package costs in relation to total implementation costs rise with the degree of customization. The initial purchase price of the package can be deceptive because of these hidden implementation costs. If the vendor releases new versions of the package, the overall costs of customization will be magnified because these changes will need to be synchronized with future versions of the software.

When a system is developed using an application software package, systems analysis will include a package evaluation effort. The most important evaluation criteria are the functions provided by the package, flexibility, user friendliness, hardware and software resources, database requirements, installation and maintenance efforts, documentation, vendor quality, and cost. The package evaluation process often is based on a **Request for Proposal** (RFP), which is a detailed list of questions submitted to packaged-software vendors.

When a software package solution is selected, the organization no longer has total control over the system design process. Instead of tailoring the system design specifications directly to user requirements, the design effort will consist of trying to mold user requirements to conform to the features of the package. If the organization's requirements conflict with the way the package works and the package cannot be customized, the organization will have to adapt to the package and change its procedures. Even if the organization's business processes seem compatible with those supported by a software package, the

Internet Connection ———

The Internet Connection for this chapter will direct you to the mySAP Web site where you can complete an exercise to evaluate the capabilities of this major multinational software package and learn more about enterprise applications.

FIGURE 14-12   *The effects on total implementation costs of customizing a software package.*

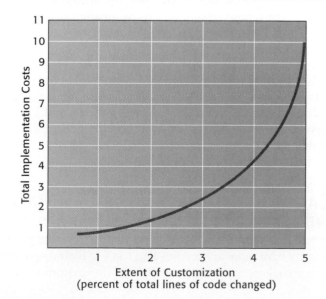

As the number of modifications to a software package rise, so does the cost of implementing the package. Savings promised by the package can be whittled away by excessive changes.

Extent of Customization
(percent of total lines of code changed)

package may be too constraining if these business processes are continually changing (Prahalad and Krishnan, 2002).

OUTSOURCING

If a firm does not want to use its internal resources to build or operate information systems, it can outsource the work to an external organization that specializes in providing these services. Application service providers (ASPs), which we describe in Chapter 6, are one form of outsourcing. Subscribing companies would use the software and computer hardware provided by the ASP as the technical platform for their systems. In another form of outsourcing, a company could hire an external vendor to design and create the software for its system, but that company would operate the system on its own computers. The outsourcing vendor might be domestic or in another country, and we discuss the special issues raised by offshore outsourcing in Chapter 16.

Outsourcing has become popular because some organizations perceive it as providing more value than an in-house computer center or information systems staff. The provider of outsourcing services benefits from economies of scale and complementary core competencies that would be difficult for a firm that does not specialize in information technology services to replicate (Levina and Ross, 2003). The vendor's specialized knowledge and skills can be shared with many different customers, and the experience of working with so many information systems projects further enhances the vendor's expertise. Outsourcing enables a company with fluctuating needs for computer processing to pay for only what it uses rather than build its own computer center, which would be underutilized when there is no peak load. Some firms outsource because their internal information systems staff cannot keep pace with technological change or innovative business practices or because they want to free up scarce and costly talent for activities with higher paybacks.

Not all organizations benefit from outsourcing, and the disadvantages of outsourcing can create serious problems for organizations if they are not well understood and managed (Lacity and Willocks, 1998; Earl, 1996). Many firms underestimate costs for identifying and evaluating vendors of information technology services, for transitioning to a new vendor, and for monitoring vendors to make sure they are fulfilling their contractual obligations. These hidden costs can easily undercut anticipated benefits from outsourcing (Barthelemy, 2001). When a firm allocates the responsibility for developing and operating its information systems to another organization, it can lose control over its information systems function. If the organization lacks the expertise to negotiate a sound contract, the firm's dependency on the vendor could result in high costs or loss of control over technological direction (Lacity, Willcocks, and Feeny, 1996).

Firms should be especially cautious when using an outsourcer to develop or to operate applications that give it some type of competitive advantage. A firm is most likely to benefit from outsourcing if it understands exactly how the outsourcing vendor will provide value and can manage the vendor relationship using an appropriate outsourcing strategy (Lee, Miranda, and Kim, 2004). Table 14-6 compares the advantages and disadvantages of each of the systems-building alternatives.

The Window on Organizations describes how some financial services firms deal with the issue of selecting systems-building alternatives. Some firms opt to purchase the technology for new wealth management systems from outside vendors because they believe their strategic advantage lays in their knowledge of clients and investment selection. Other firms believe that the technology is a source of competitive differentiation as well and choose to build their systems in-house.

14.5 MANAGEMENT OPPORTUNITIES, CHALLENGES, AND SOLUTIONS

System builders today have more alternatives and tools at their disposal than ever before as they confront new challenges posed by the digital firm environment.

TABLE 14-6 Comparison of Systems-Development Approaches

Approach	Features	Advantages	Disadvantages
Systems life cycle	Sequential step-by-step formal process Written specification and approvals Limited role of users	Useful for large, complex systems and projects	Slow and expensive Discourages changes Massive paperwork to manage
Prototyping	Requirements specified dynamically with experimental system Rapid, informal, and iterative process Users continually interact with the prototype	Rapid and relatively inexpensive Useful when requirements uncertain or when end-user interface is very important Promotes user participation	Inappropriate for large, complex systems Can gloss over steps in analysis, documentation, and testing
Application software package	Commercial software eliminates need for internally developed software programs	Design, programming, installation, and maintenance work reduced Can save time and cost when developing common business applications Reduces need for internal information systems resources	May not meet organization's unique requirements May not perform many business functions well Extensive customization raises development costs
End-user development	Systems created by end users using fourth-generation software tools Rapid and informal Minimal role of information systems specialists	Users control systems-building Saves development time and cost Reduces application backlog	Can lead to proliferation of uncontrolled information systems and data Systems do not always meet quality assurance standards
Outsourcing	Systems built and sometimes operated by external vendor	Can reduce or control costs Can produce systems when internal resources are not available or technically deficient	Loss of control over the information systems function Dependence on the technical direction and prosperity of external vendors

Opportunities

New information systems enable organizations to redesign their structure, scope, power relationships, work flows, products, and services. In many instances, building a new system creates an opportunity to redefine how the organization conducts its business, leading to higher levels of productivity and performance.

Management Challenges

Electronic commerce, electronic business, and the emerging digital firm intensify the challenges of systems building.

APPLICATION DEVELOPMENT IN THE DIGITAL FIRM ERA

There is greater demand than ever for information systems solutions under ever-tightening deadlines (Chiang and Mookerjee, 2004). Advances in computer software have not kept pace with the breathtaking productivity gains in computer hardware and networking. Despite the gains from fourth-generation languages, personal desktop software tools, object-oriented methods, and software tools for the Web, many businesses face backlogs in developing the information systems they need.

Technologies and business conditions are changing so rapidly that agility and scalability have become critical success factors and primary goals of systems design. Businesses

WINDOW ON ORGANIZATIONS

WALL STREET FIRMS GRAPPLE WITH BUILD VERSUS BUY

One of the big growth areas for financial services firms is the wealth management business, which specializes in high-end services to wealthy clients. A financial adviser works with clients to create individualized financial plans, suggest investments for achieving the client's goals, and discuss the likelihood of success. These affluent investors expect the highest level of services and sophisticated advice, so information systems serving these clients merit special scrutiny.

Typically, a financial services firm develops an overall plan for these clients on how to manage their various assets rather than just provide advice on stock and bond transactions. Most of the systems at these firms were built over the years for transaction-based businesses rather than a wealth management business model. At many financial services firms, new systems are required for wealth management.

Should these systems be built in-house or acquired from external vendors? Do wealth management businesses gain any competitive advantage from building their own in-house? Jaime Punishill, a senior analyst at Forrester Research, believes that they don't. "You don't gain any differentiation by running your own back office," he observers, and the same may be true of front-office applications dealing with clients. He believes that expertise, investment selection, and strategy differentiate one financial services firm from another, not the technology they use.

RBC Dominion Securities agrees. It decided in 2001 to focus on better front-office systems for dealing with its wealth management clients. This company had used off-the-shelf software for its back-office applications, and it sought similar tools for the front office. "The competitive advantage in wealth management is about product offerings and how you service the client, not necessarily being the best software in the world," said John Tracy, RBC Dominion's manager of strategic initiatives.

RBC Dominion replaced six different legacy systems serving 3,000 desktops with contact management and portfolio management software supplied by x.eye Inc. RBC did decide to keep the integration software linking its front- and back-office systems in-house, however, because it believed it had superior knowledge of its data.

Wachovia Securities likewise opted to use an external service provider. This company enlisted Thomson Financial to provide its 19,000 financial advisers with front- and back-office tools that would be useful for wealth management. About 6,000 of these advisers formerly worked for Prudential Securities (which recently merged with Wachovia).

The solution calls for replacing their desktop systems based on Reuters workstations with Thomson's new broker workstation using the Thomson ONE Advisor Financial Planning software. Thomson ONE features real-time market data, client portfolio management capabilities, and powerful decision-support applications that enable advisers to create concise financial plans and demonstrate the probability of success using various financial models. It also has powerful prospecting tools for advisers to open discussions with clients. Thomson also supplied Wachovia with back-office processing and software for integrating front- and back-office systems.

UBS, a leading global investment bank and provider of wealth management services, opted to keep its wealth management systems in-house. Several years ago. UBS decided it had too much invested in its own wealth management systems to discard them in favor of solutions from an external vendor and could more easily manage integration between the systems itself. It internally enhanced its systems to add the new functions it needed. UBS's 7,700 advisers can perform an array of functions, such as entering orders, conducting research, reviewing client accounts, and taking notes without having to navigate through separate applications. Information from UBS's back-office record keeping and transaction processing systems is immediately available to its front-office desktop systems for working with clients.

In addition to improving integration among multiple systems, UBS also built its own contact management system called Relationship Manager, which went live in March 2004. Normally, financial services firms use commercial contact management software packages, but UBS chief technology officer Scott Abbey believes that his firm's existing wealth management platform already has most of the functionality of commercial high-end customer relationship management (CRM) systems. The cost of adding a few missing CRM functions to UBS's own system was much less than implementing an off-the-shelf solution.

UBS also believes technology can provide a competitive edge in wealth management. Even if a third-party vendor was willing to create the right software for the company, UBS management would not want a vendor to build something it could resell to UBS rivals. According to Abbey, UBS has unique requirements and would not want to give its know-how to competitors.

Sources: Jessica Pallay, "Build versus Buy on Wall Street," *Information Week,* April 26, 2004; www.thomson.com, accessed September 23, 2004; and http://financialservicesinc.ubs.com, accessed September 23, 2004.

To Think About: What management, organization, and technology issues did these companies have to consider in determining whether to build their wealth management systems in-house or buy them from external software and service vendors?

need software components that can be added, modified, replaced, or reconfigured to enable the firm to respond rapidly to new opportunities. Systems must be scalable to accommodate growing numbers of users and to deliver data over multiple platforms— client/server networks, desktop computers with Web browsers, cell phones, and other mobile devices. E-commerce and e-business systems may also need to be designed so that they can run in hosted environments as well as on the company's own hardware and software platforms. To remain competitive, some firms feel pressured to design, develop, test, and deploy Internet or intranet applications in a matter of weeks or months (Earl and Khan, 2001).

The development methods we described earlier often take months or years and were ill suited to the pace and profile of Internet or intranet projects (Avison and Fitzgerald, 2003). Traditional methods do not address the new features of Internet-based applications, which might have multiple tiers of clients and servers with different operating systems linked to transaction processing systems, as well as business processes that have to be coordinated with those of customers or suppliers.

NEW INTERORGANIZATIONAL SYSTEM REQUIREMENTS

E-commerce and e-business also call for systems development based on a very broad view of the organization, one that encompasses business processes extended beyond firm boundaries (Fingar, 2000). Firms can no longer execute their business and system plans alone because they need to forge new electronic relationships with suppliers, distributors, and customers. Traditional IT infrastructures in which a single firm manages and owns its own infrastructure and applications are giving way to networks of applications that are owned and managed by many different business partners. Systems building will therefore need to address more interorganizational processes and requirements than in the past, with applications capable of integrating business processes within a single enterprise or across multiple enterprises.

Solution Guidelines

In the digital firm environment, organizations need to be able to add, change, and retire their technology capabilities very rapidly. Companies are adopting shorter, more informal development processes for many of their e-commerce and e-business applications, processes that provide fast solutions that do not disrupt their core transaction processing systems and organizational databases. In addition to using software packages, application service providers, and other outsourcing services, they are relying more heavily on fast-cycle techniques such as joint application design (JAD), prototypes, and reusable standardized software components that can be assembled into a complete set of services for e-commerce and e-business.

RAPID APPLICATION DEVELOPMENT (RAD)

Object-oriented software tools, reusable software, prototyping, and fourth-generation language tools are helping systems builders create working systems much more rapidly than they could using traditional systems-building methods and software tools. The term **rapid application development (RAD)** is used to describe this process of creating workable systems in a very short period of time. RAD can include the use of visual programming and other tools for building graphical user interfaces, iterative prototyping of key system elements, the automation of program code generation, and close teamwork among end users and information systems specialists. Simple systems often can be assembled from prebuilt components. The process does not have to be sequential, and key parts of development can occur simultaneously.

Sometimes a technique called **joint application design (JAD)** is used to accelerate the generation of information requirements and to develop the initial systems design. JAD brings end users and information systems specialists together in an interactive session to

ClearNova's ThinkCAP is a powerful RAD tool for simplifying and accelerating Web-based business application development. Illustrated here is a template for rapidly designing data entry forms and linking them to relational or non-relational data and objects. RAD tools enable businesses to create system solutions quickly without extensive programming.

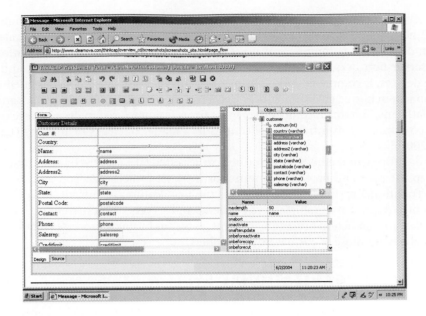

discuss the system's design. Properly prepared and facilitated, JAD sessions can significantly speed up the design phase and involve users at an intense level.

COMPONENT-BASED DEVELOPMENT

We have already described some of the benefits of object-oriented development for building systems that can respond to rapidly changing business environments, including Web applications. To further expedite software creation, groups of objects have been assembled to provide software components for common functions such as a graphical user interface or online ordering capability that can be combined to create large-scale business applications. This approach to software development is called **component-based development**, and it enables a system to be built by assembling and integrating existing software components. Businesses are using component-based development to create their e-commerce applications by combining commercially available components for shopping carts, user authentication, search engines, and catalogs with pieces of software for their own unique business requirements.

WEB SERVICES AND SERVICE-ORIENTED COMPUTING

Chapter 6 introduced Web services as loosely coupled, reusable software components deliverable using Extensible Markup Language (XML) and other open protocols and standards that enable one application to communicate with another with no custom programming required to share data and services. In addition to supporting internal and external integration of systems, Web services can be used as tools for building new information system applications or enhancing existing systems. Web services can create software components that are deliverable over the Internet and provide new functions for an organization's existing systems or create new systems that link an organization's systems to those of other organizations. Because these software services use a universal set of standards, they promise to be less expensive and less difficult to weave together than proprietary components.

Web services can perform certain functions on their own, and they can also engage other Web services to complete more complex transactions, such as checking credit, procurement, or ordering products. By creating software components that can communicate and share data regardless of the operating system, programming language, or client device, Web services can provide significant cost savings in systems building while opening up new opportunities for collaboration with other companies (Ferris and Farrell, 2003; Hagel and Brown, 2001; Patel and Saigal, 2002).

MAKE IT YOUR BUSINESS

Finance and Accounting

The finance and accounting function helps systems builders identify the costs and benefits of new information system projects and assess their economic feasibility. It also assists with the financial analysis of systems-building alternatives, comparing the costs of custom in-house development to the costs of development with application software packages or outsourcing to external vendors. You can find examples of finance and accounting applications on pages 524 and 532–533.

Human Resources

The human resources function assists with the analysis of changes in work flows and job responsibilities resulting from new information systems. Human resources specialists may also be involved with corporate programs to educate employees in total quality management (TQM) principles as well as efforts to train employees to use new information systems. You can find examples of human resources applications on page 495.

Manufacturing and Production

Manufacturing and production have been a focal point for process improvements to improve quality. Information systems have been used to identify defects and variances from quality standards, to reduce cycle time, and to increase precision in design and production. When firms install new enterprise systems, one of their major objectives is to improve coordination of business processes for manufacturing and production processes and between manufacturing and production and the other functional areas. You can find examples of manufacturing and production applications on pages 532–533.

Sales and Marketing

Information systems have supported quality improvements in sales and marketing that provide better customer service as well as products and sales experiences that increase customer satisfaction. Web-based information systems for online sales and marketing have become a high priority for corporate systems building during the past few years. You can find examples of sales and marketing applications on page 520.

Summary

1. **Demonstrate how building new systems produces organizational change.**

   Building a new information system is a form of planned organizational change that involves many different people in the organization. Because information systems are sociotechnical entities, a change in information systems involves changes in work, management, and the organization. Four kinds of technology-enabled change are (a) automation, (b) rationalization of procedures, (c) business process reengineering, and (d) paradigm shift, with far-reaching changes carrying the greatest risks and rewards. Many organizations are attempting business process reengineering to redesign work flows and business processes in the hope of achieving dramatic productivity breakthroughs. Information systems can also be used to support business process management, total quality management (TQM), six sigma, and other initiatives for incremental process improvement.

2. **Explain how a company can develop information systems that fit its business plan.**

   Organizations should develop information systems plans that describe how information technology supports the attainment of their business goals. The plans indicate the direction of systems development, the rationale, the implementation strategy, and the budget.

   Enterprise analysis and critical success factors (CSFs) can be used to elicit organization-wide information requirements that must be addressed by the plans.

3. **Identify and describe the core activities in the systems development process.**

   The core activities in systems development are systems analysis, systems design, programming, testing, conversion, production, and maintenance. Systems analysis is the study and analysis of problems of existing systems and the identification of requirements for their solutions. Systems design provides the specifications for an information system solution, showing how its technical and organizational components fit together.

4. **Evaluate alternative methods for building information systems and alternative methodologies for modeling systems.**

   There are a number of alternative methods for building information systems, each suited to different types of problems. The oldest method for building systems is the systems life cycle, which requires that information systems be developed in formal stages. The stages must proceed sequentially and have defined outputs; each requires formal approval before the next stage can commence. The system life cycle is useful for large projects that need formal specifications and tight management control over each stage of systems building. However, this approach is very rigid and costly and is not well suited for unstructured, decision-oriented applications for which requirements cannot be immediately visualized.

Prototyping consists of building an experimental system rapidly and inexpensively for end users to interact with and evaluate. The prototype is refined and enhanced until users are satisfied that it includes all of their requirements and can be used as a template to create the final system. Prototyping encourages end-user involvement in systems development and iteration of design until specifications are captured accurately. The rapid creation of prototypes can result in systems that have not been completely tested or documented or that are technically inadequate for a production environment.

Developing an information system using an application software package eliminates the need for writing software programs when developing an information system. Using a software package reduces the amount of design, testing, installation, and maintenance work required to build a system. Application software packages are helpful if a firm does not have the internal information systems staff or financial resources to custom develop a system. To meet an organization's unique requirements, packages may require extensive modifications that can substantially raise development costs.

End-user development is the development of information systems by end users, either alone or with minimal assistance from information systems specialists. End-user-developed systems can be created rapidly and informally using fourth-generation software tools. The primary benefits of end-user development are improved requirements determination; reduced application backlog; and increased end-user participation in, and control of, the systems development process. However, end-user development, in conjunction with distributed computing, has introduced new organizational risks by propagating information systems and data resources that do not necessarily meet quality assurance standards and that are not easily controlled by traditional means.

Outsourcing consists of using an external vendor to build (or operate) a firm's information systems. The work is done by the vendor rather than by the organization's internal information systems staff. Outsourcing can save application development costs or enable firms to develop applications without an internal information systems staff. However, firms risk losing control over their information systems and becoming too dependent on external vendors.

Structured methodologies and object-oriented development are alternative methodologies for designing and modeling systems. Structured methodologies are process-oriented, whereas object-oriented development models a system as a collection of objects that combine processes and data. Managers should be aware of the strengths and weaknesses of each systems-building approach and the types of problems for which each is best suited.

5. *Assess the challenges of building information systems and management solutions.*

Businesses today are often required to build e-commerce and e-business applications very rapidly to remain competitive. New systems are likely to have more interorganizational requirements and processes than in the past. Companies are turning to rapid application design, joint application design (JAD), and reusable software components to improve the systems development process. Rapid application development (RAD) uses object-oriented software, visual programming, prototyping, and fourth-generation tools for very rapid creation of systems. Component-based development expedites application development by grouping objects into suites of software components that can be combined to create large-scale business applications.

Web services enable firms to obtain software application components delivered over the Internet for building new systems or integrating existing systems. Web services provide a common set of standards that enable organizations to link their systems regardless of their technology platform through standard plug and play architecture.

Key Terms

Acceptance testing, 509
Automation, 500
Benchmarking, 506
Business process reengineering, 501
Component-based development, 526
Computer-aided software engineering (CASE), 515
Conversion, 510
Critical success factors (CSFs), 499
Customization, 521
Data flow diagram (DFD), 512
Direct cutover, 510
Documentation, 510
End-user development, 518

End-user interface, 517
Enterprise analysis, 496
Feasibility study, 506
Fourth-generation languages, 518
Information requirements, 507
Information systems plan, 496
Iterative, 517
Joint application design (JAD), 525
Maintenance, 511
Object 513
Object-oriented development, 513
Paradigm shift, 501
Parallel strategy, 510
Phased approach, 510

Pilot study, 510
Postimplementation audit, 511
Process specifications, 513
Production, 511
Programming, 509
Prototype, 517
Prototyping, 517
Query languages, 518
Rapid application development (RAD), 525
Rationalization of procedures, 500
Request for Proposal (RFP), 521
Six sigma, 505
Structure chart, 513
Structured, 511

Review Questions

1. *Why can an information system be considered planned organizational change?*

2. *What are the major categories of an information systems plan?*

3. *How can enterprise analysis and critical success factors be used to establish organization-wide information systems requirements?*

4. *Describe each of the four kinds of organizational change that can be promoted with information technology.*

5. *What is business process reengineering? What steps are required to make it effective? How does it differ from business process management?*

6. *How do information systems support process changes that promote quality in an organization?*

7. *What is the difference between systems analysis and systems design? What activities does each comprise?*

8. *What are information requirements? Why are they difficult to determine correctly?*

9. *Why is the testing stage of systems development so important? Name and describe the three stages of testing for an information system.*

10. *What role do programming, conversion, production, and maintenance play in systems development?*

11. *Compare object-oriented and traditional structured approaches for modeling and designing systems.*

12. *What is the traditional systems life cycle? Describe each of its steps and its advantages and disadvantages for systems building.*

13. *What do we mean by information system prototyping? What are its benefits and limitations? List and describe the steps in the prototyping process.*

14. *What is an application software package? What are the advantages and disadvantages of developing information systems based on software packages?*

15. *What is meant by end-user development? What are its advantages and disadvantages? Name some policies and procedures for managing end-user development.*

16. *What is outsourcing? Under what circumstances should it be used for building information systems?*

17. *Describe the management challenges posed by building systems and suggest some solutions.*

Discussion Questions

1. *Why is selecting a systems development approach an important business decision? Who should participate in the selection process?*

2. *Some have said that the best way to reduce systems development costs is to use application software packages or fourth-generation tools. Do you agree? Why or why not?*

Application Software Exercise
Database Exercise: Designing a Customer System for Auto Sales

Ace Auto Dealers specializes in selling new vehicles from Subaru. The company advertises in local newspapers and also is listed as an authorized dealer on the Subaru Web site and other major Web sites for auto buyers. The company benefits from a good local word-of-mouth reputation and name recognition and is a leading dealer for Subaru vehicles in the Portland, Oregon, area.

When a prospective customer enters the showroom, he or she is greeted by an Ace sales representative. The sales representative manually fills out a form with information such as the prospective customer's name, address, telephone number, date of visit, and model and make of the vehicle in which the customer is interested. The representative also asks where the prospect heard about Ace—whether it was from a newspaper ad, the Web, or word of mouth—and this information is noted on the form also.

If the customer decides to purchase an auto, the dealer fills out a bill of sale form and enters the following information into Ace's sales information system: the vehicle identification number, vehicle make and model, color, options selected, the list price, the final price, and the date of the sale, along with the purchaser's name, address, and telephone number. (The final price is the list price minus any dealer discounts.) Files for this system can be found on the Laudon Web site for Chapter 14.

Ace does not believe it has enough information about its customers. It cannot easily determine which prospects have made auto purchases or the percentage of prospects who have been converted into buyers. Nor can it identify which customer touch points have produced the greatest number of sales leads or actual sales so it can focus advertising and marketing more on the channels that generate the most revenue. Are purchasers discovering Ace from newspaper ads, from word of mouth, or from the Web? Additionally, the firm cannot tell whether its customers are more interested in no-frills cars or those with luxury options.

Prepare a systems analysis report detailing Ace's problem and a system solution that can be implemented using PC database management software. Then use database software to develop a simple system solution. Your systems analysis report should include the following:

1. Description of the problem and its organizational and business impact.
2. Proposed solution, solution objectives, and solution feasibility.

3. Costs and benefits of the solution you have selected. The company has a PC with Internet access and the full suite of Microsoft Office desktop productivity tools.
4. Information requirements to be addressed by the solution.
5. Management, organization, and technology issues to be addressed by the solution, including changes in business processes.

On the basis of the requirements you have identified, design the database and populate it with at least 10 records per table. Consider whether you can use or modify the existing customer database in your design. Print out the database design. Then use the system you have created to generate queries and reports that would be of most interest to management. Create several prototype data input forms for the system and review them with your instructor. Then revise the prototypes.

Designing an Employee Training and Skills Tracking System

Required software: Database software

Word processing software

Electronic presentation software (optional)

Dirt Bikes promotes itself as a "learning company"; it pays for employees to take training courses or college courses to help them advance in their careers. Its labor force is quite young and mobile. As employees move on, their job positions become vacant and Dirt Bikes must quickly fill them to maintain its pace of production. Dirt Bikes's human resources staff would like to find a way to quickly identify high-performing employees that have the training to fill vacant positions. Once the company knows who these employees are, it has a better chance of filling open positions internally rather than paying to recruit outsiders. Dirt Bikes would like to track each employee's years of education, performance ratings, and the title and date completed of training classes that each employee has attended. Dirt Bikes's performance rating codes are as follows:

1 = Exceptional performance

2 = Good performance

3 = Fair performance

4 = Unacceptable performance

Dirt Bikes currently cannot identify such employees. Its existing employee database is limited to basic human resources data, such as employee name, identification number, birth date, address, telephone number, marital status, job position, and salary. You can find some sample records from this database on the Laudon Web site for Chapter 14 and on the Laudon Multimedia Edition CD-ROM. Dirt Bikes's human resources staff keeps skills, performance evaluation, and training data in paper folders.

Prepare a systems analysis report describing Dirt Bikes's problem and a system solution that can be implemented using PC database software. Then use the database software to develop a simple system solution. Your report should include the following:

1. Description of the problem and its organizational and business impact.
2. Proposed solution and solution objectives.
3. Information requirements to be addressed by the solution.
4. Management, organization, and technology issues to be addressed by the solution, including changes in business processes.

On the basis of the requirements you have identified, design the solution using database software and populate it with at least 10 records per table. Consider whether you can use or modify the existing employee database in your design. Print out the design for each table in your new application. Use the system you have created to design queries and reports that would be of most interest to management (for instance, which employees have performance ratings of 1 or 2, or which employees have training in project management or advanced computer-aided design [CAD] tools).

If possible, use electronic presentation software to summarize your findings for management.

Electronic Business Project: Redesigning Business Processes for Web Procurement

You are in charge of purchasing for your firm and would like to use the Grainger.com (www.grainger.com) B2B e-commerce site for this purpose. Find out how to place an order for painting supplies by exploring the Catalog, Order Form, and Repair Parts Order capabilities of this site. Do not register at the site. Describe all the steps your firm would need to take to use this system to place orders online for 30 gallons of paint thinner. Include a diagram of what you think your firm's business process for purchasing should be and the pieces of information required by this process.

In a traditional purchase process, whoever is responsible for making the purchase fills out a requisition form and submits it for approval based on the company's business rules. When the requisition is approved, a purchase order with a

unique purchase order identification number is sent to the supplier. The purchaser might want to browse supplier catalogs to compare prices and features before placing the order. The purchaser might also want to determine whether the items to be purchased are available. If the purchasing firm were an approved customer, that company would be granted credit to make the purchase and would be billed for the total cost of the items purchased and shipped after the order was placed. Alternatively, the purchasing company might have to pay for the order in advance or pay for the order using a credit card. Multiple payment options might be possible. How might this process have to change to make purchases electronically from the Grainger site?

Group Project: Preparing Web Site Design Specifications

With three or four of your classmates, select a system described in this text that uses the Web. Review the Web site for the system you select. Use what you have learned from the Web site and the description in this book to prepare a

report describing some of the design specifications for the system you select. If possible, use electronic presentation software to present your findings to the class.

CASE STUDY
Blue Rhino Slows Down to Get Ahead

Blue Rhino is a publicly traded corporation based in Winston-Salem, North Carolina, that considers itself the national leader in propane cylinder exchange services. Owners of propane-fueled backyard grills can visit nearly 30,000 retail locations, including Home Depot, Wal-Mart, and Kmart, in 48 states and Puerto Rico to exchange their empty propane cylinders for full cylinders provided by Blue Rhino. The company employs 355 workers, 63 percent of whom fulfill distributor operations duties. The remaining employees serve in the departments of administration and finance, sales and marketing, information systems, and warehouse operations. In addition to its cylinder exchange services, Blue Rhino markets a number of propane-related products including grills, outdoor heaters, and pest control devices.

In operation for only a decade, Blue Rhino's business is growing rapidly. Its revenue for the fiscal year 2003 reached $258.2 million, which was an increase of 86 percent over two years. The company's operating income soared by over 500 percent during the same period. Much of this growth is a result of a relatively recent change in approach to propane cylinder transactions. Traditionally, propane grill owners would bring their empty propane cylinders to a retail outlet to be refilled. The Blue Rhino approach of exchanging empty cylinders for ones that have already been filled is more efficient and safer. Customers do not have to wait for a retail employee to fill their cylinders or be in the presence of a transaction involving the transfer of a flammable agent. Additionally, this exchange prevents customers from using the same cylinder over many years, which could lead to dangerous malfunctions or cylinder corrosion. Converting refill customers to the exchange approach and increasing the demand for, and awareness of, cylinder exchange are two of the key elements of Blue Rhino's business strategy.

Blue Rhino has implemented its business strategy in much the same way many new companies of the last decade have—with an entrepreneurial spirit. Under the leadership of CEO Billy Prim, Blue Rhino avoids micromanagement and bureaucracy, allowing its managers to act quickly and pursue business opportunities unabashedly. Prim extols not only the merits of his company's products and services, but the activities and lifestyles that make those products and services desirable as well. Prim went so far as to buy Winston-Salem's minor league baseball team, whose games serve as a perfect venue to promote outdoor activities such as summertime grilling.

In the last few years, however, Prim has had to grip the reins of the stampeding Blue Rhino a little tighter. In the wake of numerous egregious accounting scandals at major corporations that dominated news headlines for months, Congress passed the Sarbanes-Oxley Act in 2002. Section 404 of the Sarbanes-Oxley Act requires upper-level executives (CEOs, CFOs) of companies with market capitalization above $75 million to take greater responsibility for the income statements and balance sheets of their businesses. Specifically, after June 15, 2004, companies must prepare a management report that verifies the accuracy of their quarterly and annual financial statements at the close of the current fiscal year. The report must indicate that the company has taken appropriate measures to ensure the veracity of these statements. Additionally, the company's outside auditor must sign the report.

Penalties that can be imposed for fraudulent statements are severe, up to a maximum jail term of 20 years. As a result of this legislation, many companies have been compelled to examine and overhaul their business processes and systems, often at great expense. Many businesses employ distinct systems to manage different departments, such as accounting, inventory, and customers. Streamlining these systems into one reliable system for compliance reporting is a complex task.

For Blue Rhino, complying with Sarbanes-Oxley also requires a fundamental change in culture and operating procedures. Part of the company's rise was caused by its ability to make business decisions and enact deals almost at a moment's notice. Under the watch of Sarbanes-Oxley, every decision must pass through a series of checks and approvals to ensure the validity and legality of all business processes. Initially, this was an uncomfortable change for Blue Rhino employees, who were used to being trusted to act on their own.

Blue Rhino's executives do admit, somewhat grudgingly, that being subject to the Sarbanes-Oxley legislation does have some benefits. Prior to the passing of the legislation, Blue Rhino had begun revamping its financial practices. However, that effort had been wandering somewhat aimlessly until the requirements of Sarbanes-Oxley jump-started it.

One of the greatest issues facing the company was its degree of control over inventory. Distributors would submit accounts receivable and payable data piece by piece. These statements were collected at the end of the month by Blue Rhino employees who entered the figures manually into spreadsheets and integrated the spreadsheets into company-wide reports. The company had no method for automating the centralization of inventory data. It took a week or more to close the books, instead of a few days. The extra time required to consolidate the data manually resulted in frequent disconnects with inventory status throughout the country, often leaving Blue Rhino with profit-eating overstocks in its inventory.

The first step toward rectifying the inventory problem was implementing software that could automate delivery of inventory information to corporate headquarters. Blue Rhino turned to

Metastorm's E-work business process management (BPM) software for a solution. With inventory data now automated, Blue Rhino could ship cylinders to its distributors according to actual demand rather than estimations based on figures that might be outdated. However, revamping data and retraining employees to get the system to work properly took months.

Compliance with Sarbanes-Oxley required additional systems work. Blue Rhino had to document the company's direct and indirect financial operations. CIO Bob Travatello's team depicted each process—the flow of data, the movement of money, and personnel activities involved in accounting, ordering, inventory, supply chain management, and delivery. The team looked for places where there weren't sufficient controls to ensure that information could not be changed without appropriate permission. Additionally, the staff needed to ensure that data were presented in such a way that mistakes and inconsistencies would be obvious to managers who were reviewing the data. The information technology (IT) staff also looked for holes in the system that weren't readily apparent. In the process of examining the company's processes through these filters, Blue Rhino discovered security flaws such as IT staff having the ability to modify tax data.

Travatello's team found some processes that needed improvement even though they were not directly related to financial systems. For example, the Human Resources department had previously communicated the technology needs of new employees to the IT department through phone calls and e-mails. As a result, these needs often were not addressed until a new employee was actually on the job. It could take several days before a new employee received all of the equipment that was required to perform his or her duties, which was an unnecessary loss of productivity. Blue Rhino solved this problem by implementing a human resources application that automates the process of sending new hires' equipment requirements

to the IT department. The automated work flow enables the IT department to set up computers, phone numbers, accounts, passwords, and more as soon as a new employee is hired so that workers can begin fulfilling their responsibilities the first day on the job.

Other efforts include redesigning Blue Rhino's purchasing and customer service systems. Distributors had been filling out manual order forms for propane cylinders and faxing or e-mailing them to headquarters. It might take days until the orders were completed. A new system enables distributors to enter their requests into online forms that are automatically transmitted to central purchasing. Approved orders are filled instantly, making data immediately available to accounting, inventory, and supply chain management as well as company executives. The new system cuts days out of the order cycle.

To improve customer service, Blue Rhino developed an automated work flow system to handle customer requests such as checking on warranty information, ordering and shipping replacement parts, and providing repair instructions.

The seeds for these business improvements were planted before Sarbanes-Oxley entered the picture. However, Blue Rhino chief financial officer Mark Castaneda says, "Sarbanes-Oxley got us going faster down the path we were already on." The initial inventory management project taught the organization a great deal about redesigning information systems. When Sarbanes-Oxley became a reality, Blue Rhino dedicated $400,000 and 25 percent of its IT staff specifically to the task of meeting the requirements of the legislation. The staff determined that it could use the same E-work BPM software that it had already adopted for inventory management to implement Sarbanes-Oxley compliance procedures.

Blue Rhino's management expects all of these system changes to help it keep down the cost of staff, sales, and administration while the company continues to grow its revenues. If that

occurs, net earnings would rise about 25 percent each year for the next two to four years.

Without disavowing the benefits brought about by Sarbanes-Oxley, Blue Rhino executives remain steadfast in their belief that the legislation has been a hindrance. They feel that their own reengineering efforts would have led to the same positive results without compromising the company's aggressive spirit. CIO Travatello laments that Blue Rhino has been forced to develop unnecessary layers of bureaucracy. He doesn't feel that this bureaucracy will drag down the company's business; employees and clients will have to adjust to the idea that things will happen at a more deliberate pace. However, on the positive side, Travatello is confident that Blue Rhino will meet its compliance deadline and be able to finalize its financial statements in half the time that it used to take. The company also has newfound confidence in the accuracy and security of its data.

Sources: Jeffrey Rothfeder, "Better Safe Than Sorry: Blue Rhino Corp.," and "Thinking Out Loud: CIO Bob Travatello," *CIO Insight*, February 1, 2004; Sandra O'Laughlin, "Blue Rhino Shows the Joy of Swapping," *Brandweek*, April 6, 2004, www.brandweek.com; and "Blue Rhino Applies BPM to Sarbanes-Oxley," *Transform Magazine*, November 2003.

CASE STUDY QUESTIONS

1. What is Blue Rhino's business strategy? How well was that strategy supported by information systems?

2. Why did Blue Rhino have to revamp its systems and business processes?

3. What management, organization, and technology issues did the company have to deal with as it built its new systems?

4. Did Blue Rhino benefit from Sarbanes-Oxley? Explain your answer.

5. How successful has Blue Rhino been in responding to the requirements of the Sarbanes-Oxley legislation?

Chapter 15

Understanding the Business Value of Systems and Managing Change

OBJECTIVES

After reading this chapter, you will be able to:

1. Evaluate models for understanding the business value of information systems.

2. Analyze the principal causes of information system failure.

3. Assess the change management requirements for building successful systems.

4. Select appropriate strategies to manage the system implementation process.

5. Identify the challenges posed by implementing new systems and management solutions.

CHAPTER OUTLINE

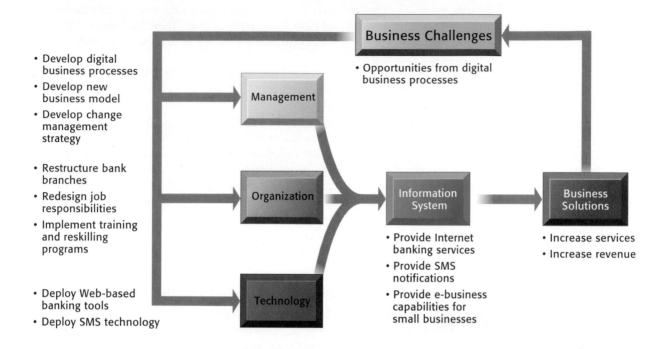

- Develop digital business processes
- Develop new business model
- Develop change management strategy

- Restructure bank branches
- Redesign job responsibilities
- Implement training and reskilling programs

- Deploy Web-based banking tools
- Deploy SMS technology

Business Challenges
- Opportunities from digital business processes

Management

Organization

Technology

Information System
- Provide Internet banking services
- Provide SMS notifications
- Provide e-business capabilities for small businesses

Business Solutions
- Increase services
- Increase revenue

Opening Case: HSBC Malaysia: Master of Change Management

HSBC Malaysia Bhd. is one of the oldest banks in the country of Malaysia. It is a wholly owned subsidiary of HSBC Holdings, headquartered in London, which is one of the largest financial services companies in the world.

This bank has been a leader in introducing Internet banking and Short Message Service (SMS)–based banking in Malaysia, as well as new value-added banking services for businesses. HSBC's V-Banking (Value Banking) provides new electronic services to retail customers, whereas its automate@ HSBCinitiative provides e-business and collaborative commerce technologies to local Malaysian small and medium-sized businesses.

V-Banking provides retail customers with over 30 telebanking and Internet banking services, consolidated portfolio summaries, and detailed account reconciliation. Customers can receive SMS Smart Alert notifications of returned checks, credit card payment details, and birthday greetings.

These initiatives have made the bank's business processes more digital, with 96 percent of its transactions now handled online. In changing the way the bank delivers services to both retail and corporate customers, these systems have naturally changed the way the bank works.

HSBC restructured bank branches across Malaysia to become Personal Financial Services (PFS) Centers. These PFS Centers offer 24-hour electronic banking machines with more self-service options and fewer counters manned by tellers. These counters focus more on providing personal customer service rather than traditional cash banking functions such as accepting checks and deposits. A portion of the HSBC Malaysia workforce had to change their job responsibilities from manual, labor-intensive tasks to working more closely with customers as "personal bankers." HSBC's customer relationship management systems and call centers were enhanced to handle the new customer demand for information across a variety of touch points.

CIO Chu Hong Keong and his staff had to sell this new way of doing business to the rest of the organization. They tried to enlist support for the new business processes through meetings, demonstrations, and strategy discussions. The team ran retraining and reskilling exercises to promote more customer-oriented attitudes among banking staff. To train customers in new banking habits, Chu's group stationed V-Banking ambassadors at key branches to demonstrate how the new electronic banking services and Internet banking kiosks would save customers time and money. V-Banking succeeded because Chu and his managers understood the importance of changing the organization along with the technology.

Sources: Raoul LeBlond, "Time as a Strategic Tool," *CIO Asia*, March 2004; and www.hsbc.com.my, accessed July 11, 2004.

One of the principal challenges posed by information systems is ensuring they can deliver genuine business benefits. There is a very high failure rate among information systems projects because organizations have incorrectly assessed their business value or because firms have failed to manage the organizational change process surrounding the introduction of new technology.

Chu Hong Keong and his team at HSBC Malaysia realized this and took special pains to prepare the bank and its customers for the changes brought about by its new systems and business processes for V-Banking.

At many points during your career, you will be involved in projects to build new information systems. You will need to know how to measure the business benefits of these investments and how to make sure that these systems work successfully in your organization. In this chapter you'll learn about alternative ways of measuring the business value provided by information systems. You'll also learn about the role of change management in successful system implementation and strategies for reducing the risks in systems projects.

15.1 UNDERSTANDING THE BUSINESS VALUE OF INFORMATION SYSTEMS

Before considering the business value of systems it is important to understand that firms make two kinds of information systems investments. Firms invest in information systems projects that have very specific objectives and that will be implemented in 12 to 24 months. Firms also invest in information technology (IT) infrastructure, and such investments often take place over longer periods of time. Infrastructure investments may include upgrading desktop client machines to the latest version of the Windows operating system, doubling the number of corporate servers, converting all telephones to Voice over IP (VoIP), or upgrading the firm's international bandwidth to speed up communication with offshore subsidiaries. Firms also make infrastructure investments by outsourcing.

Understanding the business value of information systems project investments is relatively straightforward and most system projects can be justified using traditional accounting methods. IT infrastructure investments are more difficult, but not impossible, to rationalize using newer techniques of valuation discussed later in this section.

All information technology investments—whether systems projects or infrastructure—produce value for firms primarily in two ways. The most obvious contribution to value is through improvement in existing business processes or the creation of entirely new business processes, the net result of which is to increase firm efficiency. Second, information systems contribute to improvements in management decision making by increasing the speed of decision making and by enhancing the accuracy of decision making. Both improvements in business processes and in management decision making can be measured using traditional capital budgeting methods described in this section.

Information systems can also create value by strengthening the firm strategically. The value to the firm may not be an immediate superior return on investment, but instead a longer-term return on investment that results from a better strategic position in the industry. Systems may help a firm achieve differentiable and sustainable advantages by, for instance, strengthening ties to customers and suppliers, differentiating products and services, and increasing flexibility and adaptability over longer periods.

First movers pay high costs for being the first to invest in a new technology, and they often fail, whereas fast followers can often imitate an innovation. But in the case of complex technology investments typical of firms such as Dell and Wal-Mart, it is unclear that imitators can follow, or follow quickly. For instance, Dell's efficient manufacturing capabilities and direct Internet marketing operation have helped it achieve record profits and growth in an industry where its competitors are struggling to break even. Wal-Mart appears to have achieved a long-lived logistics advantage through its investment in supply chain systems and related business processes. No other firms have yet copied Dell or Wal-Mart's business models.

A consistently strong information technology infrastructure can, over the long term, play an important strategic role in the life of the firm. In the long term of 5 to 10 years, IT infrastructure investments have option value by making it possible for the firm to implement new technologies (and launch new products) in the future. We discuss the real option value of information systems later in this section.

It is important also to realize that systems can have value but that the firm may not capture all or even some of the value. Although system projects can result in firm benefits, such as profitability and productivity, some or all of the benefits can go directly to the consumer in the form of lower prices or more reliable services and products (Hitt and Brynjolfsson, 1996). Society can acknowledge firms that enhance consumer surplus by allowing them to survive or by rewarding them with increases in business revenues. But from a management point of view, the challenge is to retain as much of the benefit of systems investments for the firm itself.

The value of systems from a financial perspective essentially revolves around the issue of return on invested capital. Does a particular information system (IS) investment produce sufficient returns to justify its costs?

Traditional Capital Budgeting Models

Capital budgeting models are one of several techniques used to measure the value of investing in long-term capital investment projects. The process of analyzing and selecting various proposals for capital expenditures is called **capital budgeting**. Firms invest in capital projects to expand production to meet anticipated demand or to modernize production equipment to reduce costs. Firms also invest in capital projects for many noneconomic reasons, such as installing pollution control equipment, converting to a human resources database to meet some government regulations, or satisfying nonmarket public demands. Information systems are considered long-term capital investment projects.

Six capital budgeting models are used to evaluate capital projects:

The payback method

The accounting rate of return on investment (ROI)

The net present value

The cost-benefit ratio

The profitability index

The internal rate of return (IRR)

Capital budgeting methods rely on measures of cash flows into and out of the firm. Capital projects generate cash flows into and out of the firm. The investment cost is an immediate cash outflow caused by the purchase of the capital equipment. In subsequent years, the investment may cause additional cash outflows that will be balanced by cash inflows resulting from the investment. Cash inflows take the form of increased sales of more products (for reasons such as new products, higher quality, or increasing market share) or reduced costs in production and operations. The difference between cash outflows and cash inflows is used for calculating the financial worth of an investment. Once the cash flows have been established, several alternative methods are available for comparing different projects and deciding about the investment.

Financial models assume that all relevant alternatives have been examined, that all costs and benefits are known, and that these costs and benefits can be expressed in a common metric, specifically, money. When one has to choose among many complex alternatives, these assumptions are rarely met in the real world, although they may be approximated. Table 15-1 lists some of the more common costs and benefits of systems. **Tangible benefits** can be quantified and assigned a monetary value. **Intangible benefits**, such as more efficient customer service or enhanced employee goodwill, cannot be immediately quantified but may lead to quantifiable gains in the long run.

Chapter 6 introduces the concept of total cost of ownership (TCO), which is designed to identify and measure the components of information technology expenditures beyond

TABLE 15-1 *Costs and Benefits of Information Systems*

COSTS

Hardware
Telecommunications
Software
Services
Personnel

TANGIBLE BENEFITS (COST SAVINGS)

Increased productivity
Lower operational costs
Reduced workforce
Lower computer expenses
Lower outside vendor costs
Lower clerical and professional costs
Reduced rate of growth in expenses
Reduced facility costs

INTANGIBLE BENEFITS

Improved asset utilization
Improved resource control
Improved organizational planning
Increased organizational flexibility
More timely information
More information
Increased organizational learning
Legal requirements attained
Enhanced employee goodwill
Increased job satisfaction
Improved decision making
Improved operations
Higher client satisfaction
Better corporate image

the initial cost of purchasing and installing hardware and software. However, TCO analysis provides only part of the information needed to evaluate an information technology investment because it does not typically deal with benefits, cost categories such as complexity costs, and "soft" and strategic factors discussed later in this section.

LIMITATIONS OF FINANCIAL MODELS

Many well-known problems emerge when financial analysis is applied to information systems. Financial models do not express the risks and uncertainty of their own costs and benefits estimates. Costs and benefits do not occur in the same time frame—costs tend to be up-front and tangible, whereas benefits tend to be back loaded and intangible. Inflation may affect costs and benefits differently. Technology—especially information technology—can change during the course of the project, causing estimates to vary greatly. Intangible benefits are difficult to quantify. These factors wreak havoc with financial models.

The difficulties of measuring intangible benefits give financial models an application bias: Transaction and clerical systems that displace labor and save space always produce more measurable, tangible benefits than management information systems, decision-support systems, and computer-supported collaborative work systems (see Chapters 12 and 13). Traditional approaches to valuing information systems investments tend to assess the profitability of individual systems projects for specific business functions. Theses approaches do not adequately address investments in IT infrastructure, testing new business models, or other enterprise-wide capabilities that could benefit the organization as a whole (Ross and Beath, 2002).

The traditional focus on the financial and technical aspects of an information system tends to overlook the social and organizational dimensions of information systems that may affect the true costs and benefits of the investment. Many companies' information systems investment decisions do not adequately consider costs from organizational disruptions created by a new system, such as the cost to train end users, the impact that users' learning curves for a new system have on productivity, or the time managers need to spend overseeing new system-related changes. Benefits, such as more timely decisions from a new system or enhanced employee learning and expertise, may also be overlooked in a traditional financial analysis (Ryan, Harrison, and Schkade, 2002).

There is some reason to believe that investment in information technology requires special consideration in financial modeling. Capital budgeting historically concerned itself with manufacturing equipment and other long-term investments, such as electrical generating facilities and telephone networks. These investments had expected lives of more than 1 year and up to 25 years. However, information systems differ from manufacturing systems in that their life expectancy is shorter. The very high rate of technological change in computer-based information systems means that most systems are seriously out of date in 5 to 8 years. The high rate of technological obsolescence in budgeting for systems means that the payback period must be shorter and the rates of return higher than typical capital projects with much longer useful lives. The bottom line with financial models is to use them cautiously and to put the results into a broader context of business analysis.

Case Example: Capital Budgeting for a New Supply Chain Management System

Let's look at how financial models would work in a real-world business scenario. Heartland Stores is a general merchandise retail chain operating in eight midwestern states. It has five regional distribution centers, 377 stores, and about 14,000 different products stocked in each store. The company is considering investing in new software and hardware modules to upgrade its existing supply chain management system to help it better manage the purchase and movement of goods from its suppliers to its retail outlets. Too many items in Heartland's stores are out of stock, even though many of these products are in the company's distribution center warehouses.

Management believes that the new system would help Heartland Stores reduce the amount of items that it must stock in inventory, and thus its inventory costs, because it would be able to track precisely the status of orders and the flow of items in and out of its distribution centers. The new system would reduce Heartland's labor costs because the company would not need so many people to manage inventory or to track shipments of goods from suppliers to distribution centers and from distribution centers to retail outlets. Telecommunications costs would be reduced because customer service representatives and shipping and receiving staff would not have to spend so much time on the telephone tracking shipments and orders. Heartland Stores expects the system to reduce transportation costs by providing information to help it consolidate shipments to retail stores and to create more efficient shipping schedules. If the new system project is approved, implementation would commence in January 2005 and the new system would become operational in early January 2006.

The solution builds on the existing IT infrastructure at the Heartland Stores but requires the purchase of additional server computers, PCs, database software, and networking technology, along with new supply chain planning and execution software. The solution also calls for new radio-frequency identification technology to track items more easily as they move from suppliers to distribution centers to retail outlets.

Figure 15-1 shows the estimated costs and benefits of the system. The system had an actual investment cost of $11,467,350 in the first year (year 0) and a total cost over six years of $19,017,350. The estimated benefits total $32,500,000 after six years. Was the

FIGURE 15-1 *Costs and benefits of the new supply chain management system.*

	A	B	C	D	E	F	G	H	I	J	K
						Estimated Costs and Benefits — New Supply Chain Management System					
1	Year :					0	1	2	3	4	5
2						2005	2006	2007	2008	2009	2010
3	**Costs: Hardware**										
4		Servers			7@ 80000	560,000					
5		Backup servers			4@ 80000	320,000					
6		PCs at loading dock			100@ 1250	125,000					
7		Radio-frequency devices			1000@ $1175	1,175,000					
8		Storage				800,000					
9											
10	**Network Infrastructure**										
11		Routers and hubs			300@ 4100	1,230,000					
12		Firewalls			2@ 6300	12,600					
13		Wireless RF network				1,750,000					
14		Backup network system				1,150,000					
15		Telecom links				74,250	225,000	225,000	225,000	225,000	225,000
16											
17	**Software**										
18		Database				475,000					
19		Web servers (Apache)				0					
20		Supply chain planning & execution modules				1,187,500					
21											
22	**Labor**										
23		Business staff				425,000	115,000	115,000	115,000	115,000	115,000
24		IS staff				1,225,000	525,000	525,000	525,000	525,000	525,000
25		External consultants				576,000	95,000	95,000	95,000	95,000	95,000
26		Training (end users)				382,000	35,000	35,000	35,000	35,000	35,000
27	**Subtotal**					11,467,350	995,000	995,000	995,000	995,000	995,000
28											
29	**Maintenance and Support**										
30		Hardware maintenance & upgrades					240,000	240,000	240,000	240,000	240,000
31		Software maintenance & upgrades					275,000	275,000	275,000	275,000	275,000
32		Subtotal					515,000	515,000	515,000	515,000	515,000
33	**Total by Year**					11,467,350	1,510,000	1,510,000	1,510,000	1,510,000	1,510,000
34											
35	**Total Costs**					19,017,350					
36	**Benefits**										
37		Reduced labor costs					1,650,000	1,400,000	1,400,000	1,400,000	1,400,000
38		Reduced inventory costs					3,500,000	3,500,000	3,500,000	3,500,000	3,500,000
39		Reduced transportation costs					1,300,000	1,300,000	1,300,000	1,300,000	1,300,000
40		Reduced telecommunications costs					250,000	250,000	250,000	250,000	250,000
41											
42	**Subtotal**					0	6,700,000	6,450,000	6,450,000	6,450,000	6,450,000
43											
44	**Net Cash Flow**					−11,467,350	5,190,000	4,940,000	4,940,000	4,940,000	4,940,000
45											
46	**Total Benefits**					32,500,000					

Sheet1 | Sheet2 | Sheet3

This spreadsheet analyzes the basic costs and benefits of implementing supply chain management system enhancements for a midsized midwestern U.S. retailer. The costs for hardware, telecommunications, software, services, and personnel are analyzed over a six-year period.

investment worthwhile? If so, in what sense? There are financial and nonfinancial answers to these questions. Let us look at the financial models first. They are depicted in Figure 15-2.

THE PAYBACK METHOD

The **payback method** is quite simple: It is a measure of the time required to pay back the initial investment of a project. The payback period is computed as follows:

$$\frac{\text{Original investment}}{\text{Annual net cash inflow}} = \text{Number of years to pay back}$$

In the case of Heartland Stores, it will take more than two years to pay back the initial investment. (Because cash flows are uneven, annual cash inflows are summed until they equal

FIGURE 15-2   *Financial models.*

	A	B	C	D	E	F	G	H	I	J	K	L	M
1	Year:							0	1	2	3	4	5
2	Net Cash Flow (not including original investment) for years 2005–2010								$5,190,000.00	$4,940,000.00	$4,940,000.00	$4,940,000.00	$4,940,000.00
3	Net Cash Flow (including original investment) for years 2005–2010							–$11,467,350.00	$5,190,000.00	$4,940,000.00	$4,940,000.00	$4,940,000.00	$4,940,000.00
4													
5	Payback Period = 2.5 years					Cumulative Cash Flow							
6	Initial Investment =			Year 0	–$11,467,350.00	–$11,467,350.00							
7				Year 1	$5,190,000.00	–$6,277,350.00							
8				Year 2	$4,940,000.00	$1,337,350.00							
9				Year 3	$4,940,000.00	$3,602,650.00							
10				Year 4	$4,940,000.00	$8,542,650.00							
11				Year 5	$4,940,000.00	$13,482,650.00							
12													
13	Accounting Rate of Return												
14	(Total Benefits – Total Costs – Depreciation)/Useful Life					Total Benefits $32,500,000.00							
15						Total Costs $19,017,350.00							
16	Total Initial Investment					Depreciation $11,467,350.00							
17					Total Benefits–Total Costs–Deprec.	$2,015,300.00							
18													
19						Life	6 years						
20	Return on Investment (ROI) = 2.93%												
21													
22													
23	Cost–Benefit Ratio =			Total Benefit $32,500,000.00		1.71							
24				Total Costs	$19,017,350.00								
25													
26	Net Present Value =												
27			=NPV(0.05,H2:M2)–11,467,350			$10,158,359.99							
28													
29	Profitability Index												
30			PV/Investment= NPV(0.05,H2:M2)/11,467,350			1.89							
31													
32	Internal Rate of Return												
33			= IRR(H3:M3)			33%							

Sheet1 Sheet2 Sheet3

To determine the financial basis for a project, a series of financial models helps determine the return on invested capital. These calculations include the payback period, the accounting rate of return on investment (ROI), the cost-benefit ratio, the net present value, the profitability index, and the internal rate of return (IRR).

the original investment to arrive at this number.) The payback method is a popular method because of its simplicity and power as an initial screening method. It is especially good for high-risk projects in which the useful life of a project is difficult to determine. If a project pays for itself in two years, then it matters less how long after two years the system lasts.

The weakness of this measure is its virtue: The method ignores the time value of money, the amount of cash flow after the payback period, the disposal value (usually zero with computer systems), and the profitability of the investment.

ACCOUNTING RATE OF RETURN ON INVESTMENT (ROI)

Firms make capital investments to earn a satisfactory rate of return. Determining a satisfactory rate of return depends on the cost of borrowing money, but other factors can enter into the equation. Such factors include the historic rates of return expected by the firm. In the long run, the desired rate of return must equal or exceed the cost of capital in the marketplace. Otherwise, no one will lend the firm money.

The **accounting rate of return on investment (ROI)** calculates the rate of return from an investment by adjusting the cash inflows produced by the investment for depreciation. It gives an approximation of the accounting income earned by the project.

To find the ROI, first calculate the average net benefit. The formula for the average net benefit is as follows:

$$\frac{\text{(Total benefits – Total cost – Depreciation)}}{\text{Useful life}} = \text{Net benefit}$$

This net benefit is divided by the total initial investment to arrive at ROI. The formula is as follows:

$$\frac{\text{Net benefit}}{\text{Total initial investment}} = \text{ROI}$$

In the case of Heartland Stores, the average rate of return on the investment is 2.93 percent.

The weakness of ROI is that it can ignore the time value of money. Future savings are simply not worth as much in today's dollars as are current savings. However, ROI can be modified (and usually is) so that future benefits and costs are calculated in today's dollars. (The present value function on most spreadsheets can perform this conversion.)

NET PRESENT VALUE

Evaluating a capital project requires that the cost of an investment (a cash outflow usually in year 0) be compared with the net cash inflows that occur many years later. But these two kinds of cash flows are not directly comparable because of the time value of money. Money you have been promised to receive three, four, and five years from now is not worth as much as money received today. Money received in the future has to be discounted by some appropriate percentage rate—usually the prevailing interest rate, or sometimes the cost of capital. **Present value** is the value in current dollars of a payment or stream of payments to be received in the future. It can be calculated by using the following formula:

$$\text{Payment} \times \frac{1 - (1 + \text{interest})^{-n}}{\text{Interest}} = \text{Present value}$$

Thus, to compare the investment (made in today's dollars) with future savings or earnings, you need to discount the earnings to their present value and then calculate the net present value of the investment. The **net present value** is the amount of money an investment is worth, taking into account its cost, earnings, and the time value of money. The formula for net present value is this:

Present value of expected cash flows – Initial investment cost = Net present value

In the case of Heartland Stores, the present value of the stream of benefits is $21,625,709, and the cost (in today's dollars) is $11,467,350, giving a net present value of $10,158,359. In other words, for a $21 million investment today, the firm will receive more than $10 million. This is a fairly good rate of return on an investment.

COST-BENEFIT RATIO

A simple method for calculating the returns from a capital expenditure is to calculate the **cost-benefit ratio**, which is the ratio of benefits to costs. The formula is

$$\frac{\text{Total benefits}}{\text{Total costs}} = \text{Cost-benefit ratio}$$

In the case of Heartland Stores, the cost-benefit ratio is 1.71, meaning that the benefits are 1.71 times greater than the costs. The cost-benefit ratio can be used to rank several projects for comparison. Some firms establish a minimum cost-benefit ratio that must be attained by capital projects. The cost-benefit ratio can, of course, be calculated using present values to account for the time value of money.

PROFITABILITY INDEX

One limitation of net present value is that it provides no measure of profitability. Neither does it provide a way to rank order different possible investments. One simple solution is provided by the profitability index. The **profitability index** is calculated by dividing the present value of the total cash inflow from an investment by the initial cost of the investment. The result can be used to compare the profitability of alternative investments.

$$\frac{\text{Present value of cash inflows}}{\text{Investment}} = \text{Profitability index}$$

In the case of Heartland Stores, the profitability index is 1.89. The project returns more than its cost. Projects can be rank ordered on this index, permitting firms to focus on only the most profitable projects.

INTERNAL RATE OF RETURN (IRR)

Internal rate of return (IRR) is defined as the rate of return or profit that an investment is expected to earn, taking into account the time value of money. IRR is the discount (interest) rate that will equate the present value of the project's future cash flows to the initial cost of the project (defined here as negative cash flow in year 0 of $11,467,350). In other words, the value of R (discount rate) is such that Present value − Initial cost = 0. In the case of Heartland Stores, the IRR is 33 percent.

RESULTS OF THE CAPITAL BUDGETING ANALYSIS

Using methods that take into account the time value of money, the Heartland Stores project is cash-flow positive over the time period under consideration and returns more benefits than it costs. Against this analysis, you might ask what other investments would be better from an efficiency and effectiveness standpoint. Also, you must ask if all the benefits have been calculated. It may be that this investment is necessary for the survival of the firm, or necessary to provide a level of service demanded by the firm's clients. What are competitors doing? In other words, there may be other intangible and strategic business factors to consider.

Strategic Considerations

Other methods of selecting and evaluating information systems investments involve strategic considerations that are not addressed by traditional capital budgeting methods. When the firm has several alternative investments from which to select, it can employ portfolio analysis and scoring models. It can apply real options pricing models to IT investments that are highly uncertain or use a knowledge value-added approach to measure the benefits of changes to business processes. Several of these methods can be used in combination.

PORTFOLIO ANALYSIS

Rather than using capital budgeting, a second way of selecting among alternative projects is to use portfolio analysis. **Portfolio analysis** helps the firm develop an overall understanding of where it is making information technology investments by inventorying all information systems projects and assets, including infrastructure, outsourcing contracts, and licenses. This portfolio of information systems investments can be described as having a certain profile of risk and benefit to the firm (see Figure 15-3) similar to a financial portfolio.

Each information systems project carries its own set of risks and benefits. (Section 15.2 describes the factors that increase the risks of systems projects.) Firms would try to

FIGURE 15-3 A system portfolio.

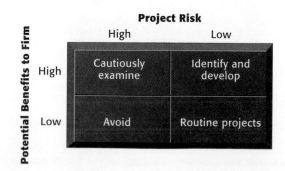

Companies should examine their portfolio of projects in terms of potential benefits and likely risks. Certain kinds of projects should be avoided altogether and others developed rapidly. There is no ideal mix. Companies in different industries have different profiles.

improve the return on their portfolios of IT assets by balancing the risk and return from their systems investments. Although there is no ideal profile for all firms, information-intensive industries (e.g., finance) should have a few high-risk, high-benefit projects to ensure that they stay current with technology. Firms in non-information-intensive industries should focus on high-benefit, low-risk projects.

Once strategic analyses have determined the overall direction of systems development, the portfolio analysis can be used to select alternatives. Obviously, you can begin by focusing on systems of high benefit and low risk. These promise early returns and low risks. Second, high-benefit, high-risk systems should be examined; low-benefit, high-risk systems should be totally avoided; and low-benefit, low-risk systems should be reexamined for the possibility of rebuilding and replacing them with more desirable systems having higher benefits. By using portfolio analysis, management can determine the optimal mix of investment risk and reward for their firms, balancing riskier high-reward projects with safer lower-reward ones. Firms where portfolio analysis is aligned with business strategy have been found to have a superior return on their IT assets, better alignment of information technology investments with business objectives, and better organization-wide coordination of IT investments (Jeffrey and Leliveld, 2004).

SCORING MODELS

A quick and sometimes compelling method for arriving at a decision on alternative systems is a **scoring model**. Scoring models give alternative systems a single score based on the extent to which they meet selected objectives. Using Table 15-2 the firm must decide

TABLE 15-2 *Example of a Scoring Model for an ERP System*

Criteria	Weight	ERP System A %	ERP System A Score	ERP System B %	ERP System B Score
1.0 Order Processing					
1.1 Online order entry	4	67	268	73	292
1.2 Online pricing	4	81	324	87	348
1.3 Inventory check	4	72	288	81	324
1.4 Customer credit check	3	66	198	59	177
1.5 Invoicing	4	73	292	82	328
Total Order Processing			1,370		1,469
2.0 Inventory Management					
2.1 Production forecasting	3	72	216	76	228
2.2 Production planning	4	79	316	81	324
2.3 Inventory control	4	68	272	80	320
2.4 Reports	3	71	213	69	207
Total Inventory Management			1,017		1,079
3.0 Warehousing					
3.1 Receiving	2	71	142	75	150
3.2 Picking/packing	3	77	231	82	246
3.3 Shipping	4	92	368	89	356
Total Warehousing			741		752
Grand Total			3,128		3,300

among two alternative enterprise resource planning (ERP) systems. The first column lists the criteria that decision makers will use to evaluate the systems. These criteria are usually the result of lengthy discussions among the decision-making group. Often the most important outcome of a scoring model is not the score but agreement on the criteria used to judge a system. Table 15-2 shows that this particular company attaches the most importance to capabilities for sales order processing, inventory management, and warehousing. The second column in Table 15-2 lists the weights that decision makers attached to the decision criteria. Columns 3 and 5 show the percentage of requirements for each function that each alternative ERP system can provide. Each vendor's score can be calculated by multiplying the percentage of requirements met for each function by the weight attached to that function. ERP System B has the highest total score.

As with all objective techniques, there are many qualitative judgments involved in using the scoring model. This model requires experts who understand the issues and the technology. It is appropriate to cycle through the scoring model several times, changing the criteria and weights, to see how sensitive the outcome is to reasonable changes in criteria. Scoring models are used most commonly to confirm, to rationalize, and to support decisions, rather than as the final arbiters of system selection. If Heartland Stores had other alternative systems projects from which to select, it could have used the portfolio and scoring models as well as financial models to establish the business value of its systems solution.

REAL OPTIONS PRICING MODELS

Some information systems projects are highly uncertain. Their future revenue streams are unclear and their up-front costs are high. Suppose, for instance, that a firm is considering a $20 million investment to upgrade its information technology infrastructure. If this upgraded infrastructure were available, the organization would have the technology capabilities to respond to future problems and opportunities. Although the costs of this investment can be calculated, not all of the benefits of making this investment can be established in advance. But if the firm waits a few years until the revenue potential becomes more obvious, it might be too late to make the infrastructure investment. In such cases, managers might benefit from using real options pricing models to evaluate information technology investments.

Real options pricing models (ROPM) use the concept of options valuation borrowed from the financial industry. An option is essentially the right, but not the obligation, to act at some future date. A typical call option, for instance, is a financial option in which a person buys the right (but not the obligation) to purchase an underlying asset (usually a stock) at a fixed price (strike price) on or before a given date.

For instance, on July 12, 2004, for $4.40 you could purchase the right (a call option) maturing in January 2006 to buy a share of Wal-Mart common stock for $55. If, by the end of January 2006, the price of Wal-Mart stock did not rise above $55, you would not exercise the option, and the value of the option would fall to zero on the strike date. If, however, the price of Wal-Mart common stock rose to, say, $100 per share, you could purchase the stock for the strike price of $55 and retain the profit of $45 per share minus the cost of the option. (Because the option is sold as a 100-share contract, the cost of the contract would be 100 × $4.40 before commissions, or $440, and you would be purchasing and obtaining a profit from 100 shares of Wal-Mart.) The stock option enables the owner to benefit from the upside potential of an opportunity while limiting the downside risk.

ROPMs value information systems projects similar to stock options, where an initial expenditure on technology creates the right, but not the obligation to obtain the benefits associated with further development and deployment of the technology as long as management has the freedom to cancel, defer, restart, or expand the project. Real options involving investments in capital projects are different from financial options in that they cannot be traded on a market and they differ in value based on the firm in which they are made. Thus, an investment in an enterprise system will have very different real option values in different firms because the ability to derive value from even identical enterprise systems depends on firm factors, for example, prior expertise, skilled labor force, market conditions, and other factors. Nevertheless, several scholars have argued that the real options theory can be useful when considering highly uncertain IT investments, and potentially the same techniques for valuing financial options can be used (Benaroch and Kauffman 2000; Taudes, Feurstein, and Mild, 2000).

ROPMs offer an approach to thinking about information technology projects that takes into account the value of management learning over time and the value of delaying investment. In real options theory, the value of the IT project (real option) is a function of the value of the underlying IT asset (present value of expected revenues from the IT project), the volatility of the value in the underlying asset, the cost of converting the option investment into the underlying asset (the exercise price), the risk-free interest rate, and the option time to maturity (length of time the project can be deferred).

The real options model addresses some of the limitations of the discounted cash flow models described earlier, which essentially call for investing in an information technology project only when the discounted cash value of the entire investment is greater than zero. The ROPM enables managers to consider systematically the volatility in the value of IT projects over time, the optimal timing of the investment, and the changing cost of implementation as technology prices or interest rates rise or fall over time.

This model gives managers the flexibility to stage their IT investment or test the waters with small pilot projects or prototypes to gain more knowledge about the risks of a project before investing in the entire implementation. Briefly, the ROPM places a value on management learning and the use of an unfolding investment technique (investing in chunks) based on learning over time.

The disadvantages of this model are primarily in estimating all the key variables affecting option value, including anticipated cash flows from the underlying asset and changes in the cost of implementation. Models for determining option value of information technology platforms are being developed (Fichman, 2004; McGrath and MacMillan, 2000). The ROPM can be useful when there is no experience with a technology and its future is highly uncertain.

KNOWLEDGE VALUE-ADDED APPROACH

A different approach to traditional capital budgeting involves focusing on the knowledge input into a business process as a way of determining the costs and benefits of changes in business processes from new information systems. Any program that uses information technology to change business processes requires knowledge input. The value of the knowledge used to produce improved outputs of the new process can be used as a measure of the value added. Knowledge inputs can be measured in terms of learning time to master a new process, and a return on knowledge can be estimated. This method makes certain assumptions that may not be valid in all situations, especially product design and research and development, where processes do not have predetermined outputs (Housel, El Sawy, Zhong, and Rodgers, 2001).

Information Technology Investments and Productivity

Information technology now accounts for about 35 to 50 percent of total business capital investment in the United States. Whether this investment has translated into genuine productivity gains remains open to debate, although most of the evidence suggests that the answer is positive. Productivity is a measure of the firm's efficiency in converting inputs to outputs. It refers to the amount of capital and labor required to produce a *unit of output.* For more than a decade, researchers have been trying to quantify the benefits from information technology investments by analyzing data collected at the economy level, industry level, firm level, and information systems application level. The results of these studies have been mixed and the term *productivity paradox* was coined to describe such findings.

Information technology has increased productivity in manufacturing, especially the manufacture of information technology products, as well as in retail. Wal-Mart, which dominates U.S. retailing, has experienced increases in both productivity and profitability during the past decade through managerial innovations and powerful supply chain management systems. Competitors, such as Sears, Kmart, and Costco, are trying to emulate these practices. A 2002 study estimated that Wal-Mart's improved productivity alone accounted for more than half of the productivity acceleration in U.S. general merchandise retailing (Johnson, 2002).

However, the extent to which computers have enhanced the productivity of the service sector remains unclear. Some studies show that investment in information technology has not led to any appreciable growth in productivity among office workers. The banking industry, which has been one of the most intensive users of information technology, did not experience any gains in productivity throughout the 1990s (Olazabal, 2002). Corporate downsizings and cost-reduction measures have increased worker efficiency but have not yet led to sustained enhancements signifying genuine productivity gains (Roach, 2003). Cell phones, home fax machines, laptop computers, and information appliances enable highly paid knowledge workers to get more work done by working longer hours and bringing their work home, but these workers are not necessarily getting more work done in a specified unit of time.

Researchers have not made a systematic effort to measure the impact of these devices on unit output or quality of product or service. For instance, university professors who answer their students' e-mail queries within set office hours are clearly communicating with their students more than in the past, and in that sense the service of higher education has improved. Measuring the value of this improvement is a challenge.

The contribution of information technology to productivity in information and knowledge industries may be difficult to measure because of the problems of identifying suitable units of output for information work (Panko, 1991). How do you measure the output of a law office? Should productivity be measured by examining the number of forms completed per employee (a measure of physical unit productivity) or by examining the amount of revenue produced per employee (a measure of financial unit productivity) in an information- and knowledge-intense industry?

Other studies have focused on the value of outputs (essentially revenues), profits, ROI, and stock market capitalization as the ultimate measures of firm efficiency. A number of researchers have found that information technology investments have resulted in increased productivity and better financial performance, including higher stock valuations (Banker, 2001; Brynjolfsson and Hitt, 1999, 1993; Brynjolfsson, Hitt, and Yang, 1999; Chatterjee, Pacini, and Sambamurthy, 2002; Davamanirajan, Mukhopadhyay, and Kriebel, 2002; Hitt, Wu, and Zhou, 2002).

Information technology investments are more likely to improve firm performance if they were accompanied by complementary investments in new business processes, organizational structures, and organizational learning that could unleash the potential of the new technology. In addition to this organizational and management capital, complementary resources, such as up-to-date IT infrastructures, have been found to make e-commerce investments more effective in improving firm performance (Zhu, 2004; Kraemer and Zhu, 2002). Firms that have built appropriate infrastructures—and view their infrastructures as sets of services providing strategic agility—have faster times to market, higher growth rates, and more sales from new products (Weill and Broadbent, 1998; Weill, Subramani, and Broadbent, 2002).

In addition to reducing costs, computers may increase the quality of products and services for consumers or may create entirely new products and revenue streams. These intangible benefits are difficult to measure and consequently are not addressed by conventional productivity measures. Moreover, because of competition, the value created by computers may primarily flow to customers rather than to the company making the investments (Brynjolfsson, 1996).

For instance, the investment in automatic teller machines (ATMs) by banks has not resulted in higher profitability for any single bank, although the industry as a whole has prospered and consumers enjoy the benefits without paying higher fees. Productivity gains may not necessarily increase firm profitability. Hence, the returns of information technology investments should be analyzed within the competitive context of the firm, the industry, and the specific way in which information technology is being applied.

15.2 THE IMPORTANCE OF CHANGE MANAGEMENT IN INFORMATION SYSTEMS SUCCESS AND FAILURE

Benefits from information technology investments are reduced if firms do not consider the costs of organizational change associated with a new system or make these changes effectively (Irani and Love 2000–2001; Ryan and Harrison, 2000). The introduction or alteration of an information system has a powerful behavioral and organizational impact. It transforms how various individuals and groups perform and interact. Changes in the way that information is defined, accessed, and used to manage the organization's resources often lead to new distributions of authority and power. This internal organizational change breeds resistance and opposition and can lead to the demise of an otherwise good system.

A very large percentage of information systems fail to deliver benefits or to solve the problems for which they were intended because the process of organizational change surrounding system building was not properly addressed. Successful system building requires careful change management.

Information Systems Problem Areas

The problems causing information **system failure** fall into multiple categories, as illustrated in Figure 15-4. The major problem areas are design, data, cost, and operations.

DESIGN

The actual design of the system may fail to capture essential business requirements or improve organizational performance. Information may not be provided quickly enough

FIGURE 15-4 *Information systems problem areas.*

Problems with an information system's design, data, cost, or operations can be evidence of a system failure.

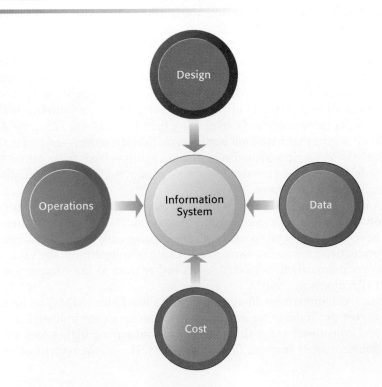

to be helpful; it may be in a format that is impossible to digest and use; or it may represent the wrong pieces of data.

The way in which nontechnical business users must interact with the system may be excessively complicated and discouraging. A system may be designed with a poor user interface. The **user interface** is the part of the system with which end users interact. For example, an input form or an online data entry screen may be so poorly arranged that no one wants to submit data. The procedures to request online information retrieval may be so unintelligible that users are too frustrated to make requests or the requested data may be displayed in a format that is too difficult to comprehend (Spier and Morris, 2003).

Web sites may discourage visitors from exploring further if the Web pages are cluttered and poorly arranged, if users cannot easily find the information they are seeking, or if it takes too long to access and display the Web page on the user's computer (Palmer, 2002). This is what happened to Quixtar.com, a major e-commerce sales channel for the Amway Corporation. This site is considered highly successful, but it is not providing as much value as it could because of poor design. The Window on Organizations explains how Quixtar.com's design affected its ability to convert Web site visitors to buyers and how Quixtar fixed these problems.

An information system can be deemed a failure if its design is not compatible with the structure, culture, and goals of the organization as a whole. Historically, information systems design has been preoccupied with technical issues at the expense of organizational concerns. The result has often been information systems that are technically excellent but incompatible with their organization's structure, culture, and goals. Without a close organizational fit, such systems create tensions, instability, and conflict.

Internet Connection —

The Internet Connection for this chapter will direct you to a series of Web sites where you can complete an exercise to evaluate user interfaces and user-system interactions.

DATA

The data in the system may have a high level of inaccuracy or inconsistency. The information in certain fields may be erroneous or ambiguous, or it may not be organized properly for business purposes. Information required for a specific business function may be inaccessible because the data are incomplete.

COST

Some systems operate quite smoothly, but their costs to implement and run on a production basis may be way over budget. Other system projects may be too costly to complete. In both cases, the excessive expenditures cannot be justified by the demonstrated business value of the information they provide.

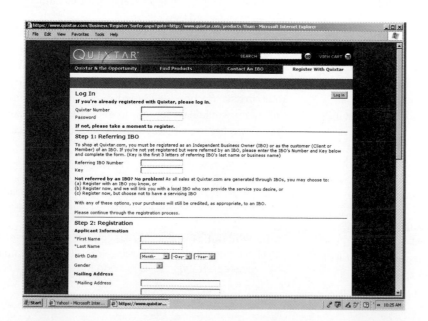

This registration form pops up when a visitor to the Quixtar.com Web site places his or her first item in the site's electronic shopping cart, interrupting the shopping process. This feature could discourage some potential buyers from completing their purchases.

WINDOW ON ORGANIZATIONS

WHAT'S WRONG WITH QUIXTAR.COM?

Amway is the largest multilevel marketing organization in the world, selling billions of dollars a year of products such as soap, water purifiers, vitamins, and cosmetics. Amway runs its business through a network of independent business owners, or IBOs. The IBOs sell Amway products to retail customers, recruit other sellers, and are paid a percentage of sales booked by newcomers.

Amway no longer sells face-to-face in the United States. In September 1999, it set up a Web site called Quixtar.com to enable its IBOs to sell over the Web to new IBOs or retail customers. IBOs earn income on sales to other IBOs, Members, and Clients they register at the site. IBOs participate in Quixtar's compensation plan, while Members pay an annual fee to order products at special pricing. Clients purchase products at full retail price. Quixtar's brands include Nutrilife nutritional supplements, Atristry skin care and cosmetics, XS Sports Nutrition, and eSpring water purifiers. Through its Store for More, Quixtar also offers products from leading brands such as Maytag, Adidas, and Calvin Klein. The site handles 2.5 million registered users and 930,000 unique users, reflecting the company's multiple levels of membership.

Sales at Quixtar.com have surpassed $1 billion during each of the last two years, making Quixtar one of the top online retailers in the United States. In June 2004, Internet Retailer ranked Quixtar.com first in its online Drug/Health and Beauty category and twelfth among all e-commerce sites in its annual *Top 300 Guide* to the Web.

Quixtar.com works hard at making its Web site available and reliable. It takes in about $3 million in sales each day, spiking to $10 million on the last day of each month. It uses RealiTea software from TeafLeaf Technology in San Francisco to monitor the activities of its visitors to help it pinpoint application failures or bottlenecks. RealiTea tracks every click and keystroke, and these data are captured in a 2-terabyte database that can store 10 days' worth of user activity. When a problem occurs, Quixtar staff can pinpoint the error by accessing the database to play back specified user sessions. The TeaLeaf replay highlights the visitor's session history to help Quixtar staff see every field a customer typed in or link that a customer clicked.

But something is not quite right. Quixtar's Web site is not as good as it could be because it has usability problems. Mark Hurst, president of Creative Good, an Internet consultancy, estimates that fixing Quixtar's design flaws could produce another $100 million annually.

Both IBOs and individual shoppers who are not part of the Quixtar network can use the site to place orders. Veteran IBOs were able to muddle through because they're very familiar with the Quixtar lingo and procedures. But most retail shoppers backed away, creating losses because Quixtar wants very much

to sell to the general public and the Web site's confusing interface thwarts sales. Let's see how.

Claudia Case, a usability consultant at Keynote Systems, a Web measurement company, found that Quixtar.com lacked a consistent look and was organized to reflect how Quixtar works rather than how customers shop. Quixtar itself encountered problems with its checkout procedure. In the fall of 2003, the site automatically filled out an incorrect shipping address for 14 online orders without customers' knowledge. Quixtar called the affected customers, and its technicians then fixed the software problem.

Keynote Systems found several design flaws in Quixtar.com's purchasing process that prevented the system from converting as many visitors as it could to buyers of its products. For instance, every time a customer puts his or her first item in a shopping cart, a registration form pops up, interrupting the shopping process before it is completed. The form does not acknowledge that the shopper has chosen any items and could annoy a visitor before that person has committed to spending money at that site. If a user makes a mistake while filling out this or other forms, there is no easy way to correct such errors during the checkout process. These problems could be avoided if Quixtar.com asked for registration or identification information when the customer was ready to pay and if it introduced a process to correct forms on the spot.

Quixtar.com assigns each customer a 9- to 11-digit account number that is required for shopping at the site. The account number is not meaningful to the customer and obviously is difficult to remember. Customers could only change their passwords by themselves but not their account numbers themselves. Hard-to-remember account numbers could slow down or even deter customers from shopping. Quixtar could remedy the situation by providing a capability for customers to personalize their passwords.

Quixtar.com's Order History page contains confusing language. Customers who want to view past and pending orders have to decipher unclear terminology. For example, the page contains a "hint" to the customer to "Select a display option. Your current selection is all orders in the current month." Customers would have to work to understand the meaning. If a drop-down bar was labeled "View open and past orders," a hint would not be necessary.

Sources: Kim S. Nash, "Cleaning Up," *Baseline Magazine*, June 2004; www.quixtar.com, accessed July 14, 2004; RSA Security, "Quixtar Accelerates Business with Identity and Access Management Solution from RSA Security," *PR Newswire*, December 6, 2004; and www.tealeaf.com, accessed July 14, 2004.

To Think About: How does the design of Quixtar.com's Web site affect the way it runs its business? Evaluate the features that both enhance and impede its performance.

OPERATIONS

The system does not run well. Information is not provided in a timely and efficient manner because the computer operations that handle information processing break down. Jobs that abort too often lead to excessive reruns and delayed or missed schedules for delivery of information. An online system may be operationally inadequate because the response time is too long.

Some of these problems can be attributed to technical features of information systems, but most stem from organizational factors (Keil, Cule, Lyytinen, and Schmidt, 1998). System builders need to understand these organizational issues and learn how to manage the change associated with a new information system.

Change Management and the Concept of Implementation

To manage the organizational change surrounding the introduction of a new information system effectively, you must examine the process of implementation. **Implementation** refers to all organizational activities working toward the adoption, management, and routinization of an innovation, such as a new information system. In the implementation process, the systems analyst is a **change agent**. The analyst not only develops technical solutions but also redefines the configurations, interactions, job activities, and power relationships of various organizational groups. The analyst is the catalyst for the entire change process and is responsible for ensuring that all parties involved accept the changes created by a new system. The change agent communicates with users, mediates between competing interest groups, and ensures that the organizational adjustment to such changes is complete.

One model of the implementation process is the Kolb/Frohman model of organizational change. This model divides the process of organizational change into a seven-stage relationship between an organizational *consultant* and his or her *client*. (The consultant corresponds to the information system designer, and the client to the user.) The success of the change effort is determined by how well the consultant and client deal with the key issues at each stage (Kolb and Frohman, 1970). Other models of implementation describe the relationship as one among designers, clients, and decision makers, who are responsible for managing the implementation effort to bridge the gap between design and utilization (Swanson, 1988).

Causes of Implementation Success and Failure

Implementation outcome can largely be determined by the following factors:

- The role of users in the implementation process
- The degree of management support for and commitment to the implementation effort
- The level of complexity and risk of the implementation project
- The quality of management of the implementation process

These are largely behavioral and organizational issues and are illustrated in Figure 15-5.

USER INVOLVEMENT AND INFLUENCE

User involvement in the design and operation of information systems has several positive results. First, if users are heavily involved in systems design, they have more opportunities to mold the system according to their priorities and business requirements, and more opportunities to control the outcome. Second, they are more likely to react positively to the completed system because they have been active participants in the change process. Incorporating user knowledge and expertise leads to better solutions.

Thanks to widespread use of the Internet and fourth-generation tools, today's users are assuming more of a leadership role in articulating the adoption, development, and implementation of information technology innovations (Kettinger and Lee, 2002). However, users often take a very narrow and limited view of the problem to be solved and may

FIGURE 15-5   *Information systems success or failure factors.*

The implementation outcome can be largely determined by the role of users, the degree of management support, the level of risk and complexity of the implementation project, and the quality of management of the implementation process. Evidence of the information system's success or failure can be found in the areas of design, cost, operations, and data.

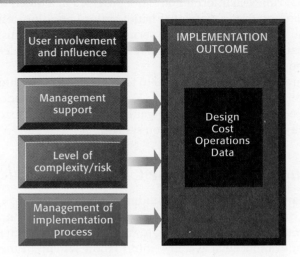

overlook important technology issues or alternative information systems solutions. The skills and vision of professional systems designers are still required much the same way that the services of an architect are required when building a new house (Markus and Keil, 1994).

The relationship between consultant and client has traditionally been a problem area for information systems implementation efforts. Users and information systems specialists tend to have different backgrounds, interests, and priorities. This is referred to as the **user-designer communications gap.** These differences lead to divergent organizational loyalties, approaches to problem solving, and vocabularies.

Information systems specialists, for example, often have a highly technical, or machine, orientation to problem solving. They look for elegant and sophisticated technical solutions in which hardware and software efficiency is optimized at the expense of ease of use or organizational effectiveness. Users prefer systems that are oriented toward solving business problems or facilitating organizational tasks. Often the orientations of both groups are so at odds that they appear to speak in different tongues.

These differences are illustrated in Table 15-3, which depicts the typical concerns of end users and technical specialists (information systems designers) regarding the development of a new information system. Communication problems between end users and designers are a major reason why user requirements are not properly incorporated into information systems and why users are driven out of the implementation process.

TABLE 15-3   *The User-Designer Communications Gap*

User Concerns	Designer Concerns
Will the system deliver the information I need for my work?	How much disk storage space will the master file consume?
How quickly can I access the data?	How many lines of program code will it take to perform this function?
How easily can I retrieve the data?	How can we cut down on CPU time when we run the system?
How much clerical support will I need to enter data into the system?	What is the most efficient way of storing these data?
How will the operation of the system fit into my daily business schedule?	What database management system should we use?

Systems development projects run a very high risk of failure when there is a pronounced gap between users and technicians and when these groups continue to pursue different goals. Under such conditions, users are often driven out of the implementation process. Because they cannot comprehend what the technicians are saying, users conclude that the entire project is best left in the hands of the information specialists alone. With so many implementation efforts guided by purely technical considerations, it is no wonder that many systems fail to serve organizational needs.

MANAGEMENT SUPPORT AND COMMITMENT

If an information systems project has the backing and commitment of management at various levels, it is more likely to be perceived positively by both users and the technical information services staff. Both groups will believe that their participation in the development process will receive higher-level attention and priority. They will be recognized and rewarded for the time and effort they devote to implementation. Management backing also ensures that a systems project receives sufficient funding and resources to be successful. Furthermore, to be enforced effectively, all the changes in work habits and procedures and any organizational realignments associated with a new system depend on management backing. If a manager considers a new system a priority, the system will more likely be treated that way by his or her subordinates (Doll 1985; Ein-Dor and Segev, 1978).

LEVEL OF COMPLEXITY AND RISK

Systems differ dramatically in their size, scope, level of complexity, and organizational and technical components. Some systems development projects are more likely to fail or suffer delays because they carry a much higher level of risk than others. The level of project risk is influenced by project size, project structure, and the level of technical expertise of the information systems staff and project team.

- *Project size.* The larger the project—as indicated by the dollars spent, the size of the implementation staff, the time allocated for implementation, and the number of organizational units affected—the greater the risk. Very large-scale systems projects have a failure rate that is 50 to 75 percent higher than that for other projects because such projects are complex and difficult to control. The organizational complexity of the system—how many units and groups use it and how much it influences business processes—contributes to the complexity of large-scale systems projects just as much as technical characteristics, such as the number of lines of program code, length of project, and budget (Xia and Lee, 2004; Concours Group, 2000; Laudon, 1989; U.S. General Services Administration, 1988).

- *Project structure.* Some projects are more highly structured than others. Their requirements are clear and straightforward so outputs and processes can be easily defined. Users know exactly what they want and what the system should do; there is almost no possibility of the users changing their minds. Such projects run a much lower risk than those with relatively undefined, fluid, and constantly changing requirements; with outputs that cannot be fixed easily because they are subject to users' changing ideas; or with users who cannot agree on what they want.

- *Experience with technology.* The project risk rises if the project team and the information system staff lack the required technical expertise. If the team is unfamiliar with the hardware, system software, application software, or database management system proposed for the project, it is highly likely that the project will experience technical problems or take more time to complete because of the need to master new skills.

The Navy/Marine Corps Intranet described in the Window on Management is an example of a very complex systems project—perhaps the largest outsourcing project ever contracted. It is much more than a private Web site, involving servers, computer centers, 4,000 locations, 345,000 personal computer "seats," and 100,000 legacy applications that must either be retired, converted, or maintained as is in separate systems. Navy and Electronic Data Systems (EDS) planners underestimated both the sheer amount work involved and the difficulties they would encounter during implementation.

WINDOW ON MANAGEMENT

THE NAVY/MARINE CORPS INTRANET TURNS INTO A BATTLEGROUND

The U.S. Navy/Marine Corps Intranet (NMCI) is a giant project for consolidating hundreds of disparate networks and 100,000 legacy applications into a single, integrated, secure architecture with standardized hardware and software linking 345,000 computers at 4,000 Navy and Marine Corps bases in the United States and abroad. (Tactical networks used aboard ships or in combat zones are not included.)

Desktop computers, servers, software, and networking equipment must all be consolidated and replaced with more up-to-date technology. When completed, the project is expected to reduce the total cost of ownership (TCO) from $3,851 to $3,741 per laptop or desktop.

In 2000, the military hired Electronic Data Systems (EDS) to head the project, which was considered the largest outsourcing project on record, with an initial price tag of $6.9 billion. (In 2002, the total cost was expanded to $8.8 billion.) EDS was responsible for overseeing the work of other vendors, including Microsoft, Dell, Cisco Systems, and Raytheon.

The project has been fraught with delays and implementation problems since its inception. Navy planners expected an upgraded and secure network in 2001, but may not have all of the Navy computers converted until 2005. EDS, which contracted to deliver the project at a fixed cost, has already lost $1.6 billion on the assignment and stands to lose much more over the next few years.

Congress held up work for 18 months so that EDS could provide new network performance tests. EDS appears to have underestimated the complexity of the project. Many Navy networks were established years ago by base commanders, who procured their own hardware and software, and the project had to replace or separately maintain those legacy applications. It turned out that there were about 100,000 applications to deal with instead of 9,000, as the Navy had originally estimated.

About 3,000 applications were approved for use with NMCI. Another 24,000 have been "quarantined," meaning that they can't be run on new NMCI systems but will continue to be used until they are replaced or retired. Because not all of the old applications could be immediately eliminated, sailors and officers were allowed to use both their old and new computers. This dramatically increased technical support and equipment costs. Moreover, the large number of legacy applications that had to be integrated into the intranet, combined with testing delays, caused implementation to fall further and further behind.

The project had to surmount serious cultural hurdles. Insiders describe the Navy as a conglomerate of hundreds of information technology fiefdoms that fiercely resist losing con-

trol over their systems and networks. Though organized as a branch of the Navy, the Marine Corps wanted to opt out of the project and continue managing its own networks. (Congress, which had been skeptical about the business value of the project, kept the Marines from being included.) Massive cultural change would be required to get the Navy to accept the intranet in the interests of the enterprise as a whole.

Critics charge that the initial implementation plans for the intranet were overly ambitious and mismanaged. Although EDS had met project targets during the initial testing and evaluation phase, the remainder of the project started to fall behind schedule. Until the Navy established a central project office in 2002, EDS had to work out implementation plans separately with different organizations within the Navy, including Naval Air Systems Command (NAVAIR) and NAVSUP (supply management).

Taking advantage of poor coordination among EDS managers, some naval commanders made their own deals with EDS teams. Ranking officers sometimes ordered security restrictions loosened for their own convenience, although everyone was supposed to adhere to the same standards.

The project called for Navy personnel to order customized computers from EDS, and EDS would configure and install them. However, EDS installers were sometimes turned away from bases because they lacked proper security clearance or because the users of these computers were busy or overseas. EDS's order-processing systems could not complete an order without a serviceperson's rank. EDS, however, neglected to tell the Navy to provide information about rank on orders. Boxes of computers for orders that could not be completed piled up in warehouses. Unfilled orders meant lost revenue for EDS, which had agreed to pay for the computers and not bill the Navy until after they were installed.

To deal with these problems, EDS decided to install computers at the largest Navy bases first instead of trying to work at many bases simultaneously. It has stopped individually customizing computers, providing the same computer configuration to servicepeople with similar jobs. It is reusing expensive hardware such as network firewalls and installing computers that are already in the warehouses before ordering new ones.

Sources: Gary McWilliams, "After Landing Huge Navy Pact, EDS Finds It's in Over Its Head," *Wall Street Journal*, April 6, 2004; David F. Carr, "Half Speed," *Baseline Magazine*, April 2004; and Dan Verton, "DOD IT Projects Come Under Fire," *Computerworld*, May 20, 2002.

To Think About: What management, organizational, and technology factors caused NMCI to have so many problems? How could these problems have been prevented?

MANAGEMENT OF THE IMPLEMENTATION PROCESS

The development of a new system must be carefully managed and orchestrated, and the way a project is executed is likely to be the most important factor influencing its outcome (Wallace and Keil, 2004). Often basic elements of success are forgotten. Training to ensure that end users are comfortable with the new system and fully understand its potential uses is often sacrificed or forgotten in systems development projects. If the budget is strained at the very beginning, toward the end of a project there will likely be insufficient funds for training and documentation (Bikson et al., 1985).

The conflicts and uncertainties inherent in any implementation effort are magnified when an implementation project is poorly managed and organized. As illustrated in Figure 15-6, a systems development project without proper management will most likely suffer these consequences:

- Costs that vastly exceed budgets

- Unexpected time slippage

- Technical shortfalls resulting in performance that is significantly below the estimated level

- Failure to obtain anticipated benefits

How badly are projects managed? On average, private sector projects are underestimated by one-half in terms of budget and time required to deliver the complete system promised in the system plan. A very large number of projects are delivered with missing functionality (promised for delivery in later versions). The Standish Group International found that only 9 percent of all technology investments were completed on time, on budget, or within scope. Between 30 and 40 percent of all software projects are "runaway" projects that far exceed the original schedule and budget projections and fail to perform as originally specified (Keil, Mann, and Rai, 2000). Why are projects managed so poorly and what can be done about it? Here we discuss some possibilities.

- *Ignorance and optimism.* The techniques for estimating the length of time required to analyze and design systems are poorly developed. Most applications are "first time" (i.e., there is no prior experience in the application area). The larger the scale of systems, the greater the role of ignorance and optimism. The net result of these factors is that estimates tend to be optimistic, "best case," and wrong. It is assumed that all will go well when in fact it rarely does.

- *The mythical man-month.* The traditional unit of measurement used by systems designers to project costs is the **man-month**. Projects are estimated in terms of how many man-months are required. However, adding more workers to projects does not necessarily reduce the elapsed time needed to complete a systems project (Brooks, 1974). Unlike cotton picking—when tasks can be rigidly partitioned, communication between participants is not required, and training is unnecessary—building systems often involves *tasks that are sequentially linked, that cannot be performed in isolation, and that require extensive communications and training.* Adding labor to software projects where there are many task interdependencies can often slow down delivery as the communication, learning, and coordination costs escalate and detract from the output of participants (Andres and Zmud, 2001–2002). For comparison, imagine what would happen if five amateur spectators were added to one team in a championship professional basketball game. The team composed of five professional basketball players

FIGURE 15-6   *Consequences of poor project management.*

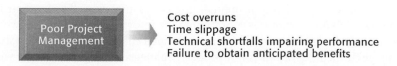

Cost overruns
Time slippage
Technical shortfalls impairing performance
Failure to obtain anticipated benefits

Without proper management, a systems development project takes longer to complete and most often exceeds the allocated budget. The resulting information system most likely is technically inferior and may not be able to demonstrate any benefits to the organization.

would probably do much better in the short run than the team with five professionals and five amateurs.

- *Falling behind: Bad news travels slowly upward.* Among projects in all fields, slippage in projects, failure, and doubts are often not reported to senior management until it is too late (Keil and Robey, 2001; Smith, Keil, and Depledge, 2001). The CONFIRM project, a very large-scale information systems project to integrate hotel, airline, and rental car reservations, is a classic example. It was sponsored by Hilton Hotels, Budget Rent-A-Car, and the Marriott Corporation and developed by AMR Information Services, a subsidiary of American Airlines Corporation. The project was very ambitious and technically complex, employing a staff of 500. Members of the CONFIRM project management team did not immediately come forward with accurate information when the project began encountering problems coordinating various transaction-processing activities. Clients continued to invest in a project that was faltering because they were not informed of its problems with database, decision-support, and integration technologies (Oz, 1994).

Change Management Challenges for Business Process Reengineering, Enterprise Applications, and Mergers and Acquisitions

Given the challenges of innovation and implementation, it is not surprising to find a very high failure rate among enterprise application and business process reengineering (BPR) projects, which typically require extensive organizational change and which may require replacing old technologies and legacy systems that are deeply rooted in many interrelated business processes. A number of studies have indicated that 70 percent of all business process reengineering projects fail to deliver promised benefits. Likewise, a high percentage of enterprise applications fail to be fully implemented or to meet the goals of their users even after three years of work.

Many enterprise application and reengineering projects have been undermined by poor implementation and change management practices that failed to address employees' concerns about change. Dealing with fear and anxiety throughout the organization; overcoming resistance by key managers; changing job functions, career paths, and recruitment practices; and managing training have posed greater threats to reengineering than the difficulties companies faced visualizing and designing breakthrough changes to business processes. All of the enterprise applications require tighter coordination among different functional groups as well as extensive business process change (see Chapter 14).

SYSTEM IMPLICATIONS OF MERGERS AND ACQUISITIONS

Mergers and acquisitions (M&As) have been proliferating because they are major growth engines for businesses. Potentially, firms can cut costs significantly by merging with competitors, reduce risks by expanding into different industries (e.g., conglomerating), and create larger pools of competitive knowledge and expertise by joining forces with other players. There are also economies of time: A firm can gain market share and expertise very quickly through acquisition rather than building over the long term.

Although some firms, such as General Electric, are quite successful in carrying out mergers and acquisitions, research has found that more than 70 percent of all M&As result in a decline in shareholder value and often lead to divestiture at a later time (Frank and Sidel, 2002; Lipin and Deogun 2000). Many deals suffer from poor planning and from unrealistic expectations about the synergies that could result from merging companies.

Architects of mergers and acquisitions often fail to appreciate the difficulty of integrating the systems of different companies. Mergers and acquisitions are deeply affected by the organizational characteristics of the merging companies as well as by their information technology (IT) infrastructures. Combining the information systems of two different companies usually requires considerable organizational change and complex systems projects to manage. If the integration is not properly managed, firms can emerge with a tangled hodgepodge of inherited legacy systems built by aggregating the systems of one firm after another. Without a successful systems integration, the benefits anticipated from the merger cannot be realized, or, worse, the merged entity cannot execute its business processes and loses customers.

Once a company targeted for acquisition has been identified, information systems managers need to identify the realistic costs of integration; the estimated benefits of economies in operation, scope, knowledge, and time; and any problematic systems that require major investments to integrate. In addition, IT managers can critically estimate any likely costs and organizational changes required to upgrade the IT infrastructure or make major system improvements to support the merged companies.

15.3 MANAGING IMPLEMENTATION

Not all aspects of the implementation process can be easily controlled or planned. However, anticipating potential implementation problems and applying appropriate corrective strategies can increase the chances for system success. Various project management, requirements gathering, and planning methodologies have been developed for specific categories of problems. Strategies have also been devised for ensuring that users play appropriate roles throughout the implementation period and for managing the organizational change process.

Controlling Risk Factors

The first step in managing project risk involves identifying the nature and level of risk confronting the project (Schmidt, Lyytinen, Keil, and Cule, 2001). Implementers can then handle each project with the tools, methodologies, and risk-management approaches geared to its level of risk (Iversen, Mathiassen, and Nielsen, 2004; Barki, Rivard, and Talbot, 2001; McFarlan, 1981).

MANAGING TECHNICAL COMPLEXITY

Projects with *challenging and complex technology* to master benefit from **internal integration tools**. The success of such projects depends on how well their technical complexity can be managed. Project leaders need both heavy technical and administrative experience. They must be able to anticipate problems and develop smooth working relationships among a predominantly technical team. The team should be under the leadership of a manager with a strong technical and project management background and team members should be highly experienced. Team meetings should take place frequently. Essential technical skills or expertise not available internally should be secured from outside the organization.

This project team of professionals is using computing tools to enhance communication, analysis, and decision making.

FORMAL PLANNING AND CONTROL TOOLS

Large projects benefit from appropriate use of **formal planning tools** and **formal control tools**. With project management techniques, such as Program Evaluation and Review Technique (PERT) or Gantt charts, a detailed plan can be developed. PERT lists the specific activities that make up a project, their duration, and the activities that must be completed before a specific activity can start. A Gantt chart such as that illustrated in Figure 15-7 visually represents the sequence and timing of different tasks in a development project as well as their resource requirements. Tasks can be defined and resources budgeted.

These project management techniques can help managers identify bottlenecks and determine the impact that problems will have on project completion times. They can also help systems developers partition implementation into smaller, more manageable segments with defined, measurable business results (Fichman and Moses, 1999). Standard control techniques can successfully chart the progress of the project against budgets and target dates, so deviations from the plan can be spotted.

INCREASING USER INVOLVEMENT AND OVERCOMING USER RESISTANCE

Projects with relatively *little structure and many undefined requirements* must involve users fully at all stages. Users must be mobilized to support one of many possible design options and to remain committed to a single design. **External integration tools** consist of ways to link the work of the implementation team to users at all organizational levels. For instance, users can become active members of the project team, take on leadership roles, and take charge of installation and training. The implementation team can demonstrate its responsiveness to users, promptly answering questions, incorporating user feedback, and showing their willingness to help (Gefen and Ridings, 2002). E-business initiatives that require rapid system responses to emerging opportunities may benefit from using special "organizational architects" with skills and expertise to bridge communication gaps between business users and technology specialists (Sauer and Willcocks, 2002).

Unfortunately, systems development is not an entirely rational process. Users leading design activities have sometimes used their positions to further private interests and to gain power rather than to promote organizational objectives (Franz and Robey, 1984). Users may not always be involved in systems projects in a productive way.

Participation in implementation activities may not be enough to overcome the problem of user resistance. The implementation process demands organizational change. Such change may be resisted because different users may be affected by the system in different ways. Whereas some users may welcome a new system because it brings changes they perceive as beneficial to them, others may resist these changes because they believe the shifts are detrimental to their interests (Joshi, 1991).

If the use of a system is voluntary, users may choose to avoid it; if use is mandatory, resistance will take the form of increased error rates, disruptions, turnover, and even sabotage. Therefore, the implementation strategy must not only encourage user participation and involvement, but it must also address the issue of counterimplementation (Keen, 1981). **Counterimplementation** is a deliberate strategy to thwart the implementation of an information system or an innovation in an organization.

Strategies to overcome user resistance include user participation (to elicit commitment as well as to improve design), user education and training, management edicts and policies, and better incentives for users who cooperate. The new system can be made more user friendly by improving the end-user interface. Users will be more cooperative if organizational problems are solved prior to introducing the new system.

Designing for the Organization

Because the purpose of a new system is to improve the organization's performance, the systems development process must explicitly address the ways in which the organization will change when the new system is installed, including installation of intranets, extranets,

FIGURE 15-7 *Formal planning and control tools help to manage information systems projects successfully.*

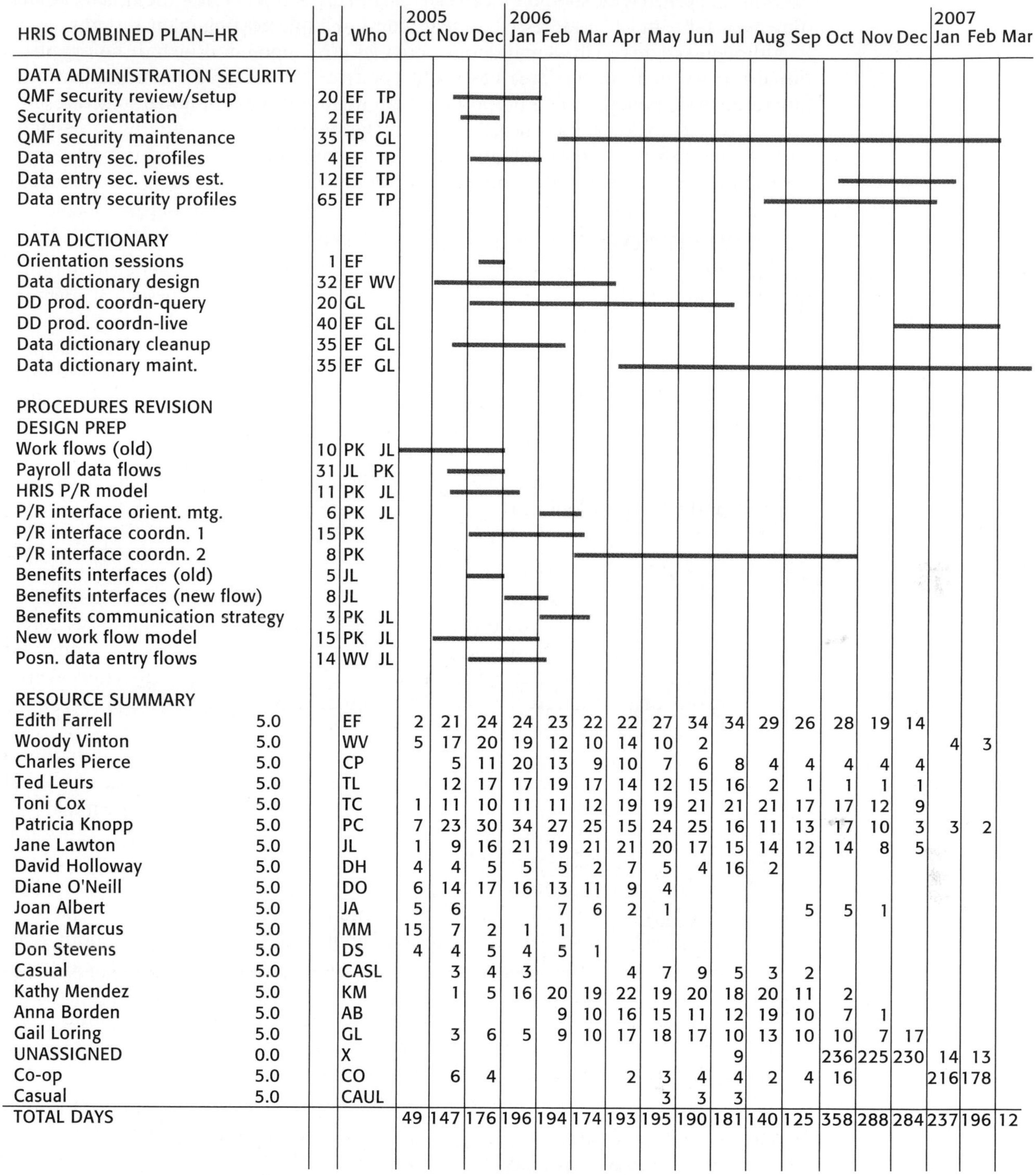

HRIS COMBINED PLAN–HR — Gantt chart (tasks with person-days "Da" and responsible initials "Who"; timeline across 2005 Oct – 2007 Mar)

HRIS COMBINED PLAN–HR	Da	Who
DATA ADMINISTRATION SECURITY		
QMF security review/setup	20	EF TP
Security orientation	2	EF JA
QMF security maintenance	35	TP GL
Data entry sec. profiles	4	EF TP
Data entry sec. views est.	12	EF TP
Data entry security profiles	65	EF TP
DATA DICTIONARY		
Orientation sessions	1	EF
Data dictionary design	32	EF WV
DD prod. coordn-query	20	GL
DD prod. coordn-live	40	EF GL
Data dictionary cleanup	35	EF GL
Data dictionary maint.	35	EF GL
PROCEDURES REVISION		
DESIGN PREP		
Work flows (old)	10	PK JL
Payroll data flows	31	JL PK
HRIS P/R model	11	PK JL
P/R interface orient. mtg.	6	PK JL
P/R interface coordn. 1	15	PK
P/R interface coordn. 2	8	PK
Benefits interfaces (old)	5	JL
Benefits interfaces (new flow)	8	JL
Benefits communication strategy	3	PK JL
New work flow model	15	PK JL
Posn. data entry flows	14	WV JL

RESOURCE SUMMARY

Name	Rate	Who	2005 Oct	Nov	Dec	2006 Jan	Feb	Mar	Apr	May	Jun	Jul	Aug	Sep	Oct	Nov	Dec	2007 Jan	Feb	Mar
Edith Farrell	5.0	EF	2	21	24	24	23	22	22	27	34	34	29	26	28	19	14			
Woody Vinton	5.0	WV	5	17	20	19	12	10	14	10	2								4	3
Charles Pierce	5.0	CP		5	11	20	13	9	10	7	6	8	4	4	4	4	4			
Ted Leurs	5.0	TL		12	17	17	19	17	14	12	15	16	2	1	1	1	1			
Toni Cox	5.0	TC	1	11	10	11	11	12	19	19	21	21	21	17	17	12	9			
Patricia Knopp	5.0	PC	7	23	30	34	27	25	15	24	25	16	11	13	17	10	3	3	2	
Jane Lawton	5.0	JL	1	9	16	21	19	21	21	20	17	15	14	12	14	8	5			
David Holloway	5.0	DH	4	4	5	5	5	2	7	5	4	16	2							
Diane O'Neill	5.0	DO	6	14	17	16	13	11	9	4										
Joan Albert	5.0	JA	5	6			7	6	2	1				5	5	1				
Marie Marcus	5.0	MM	15	7	2	1	1													
Don Stevens	5.0	DS	4	4	5	4	5	1												
Casual	5.0	CASL		3	4	3			4	7	9	5	3	2						
Kathy Mendez	5.0	KM			1	5	16	20	19	22	19	20	18	20	11	2				
Anna Borden	5.0	AB					9	10	16	15	11	12	19	10	7	1				
Gail Loring	5.0	GL		3	6	5	9	10	17	18	17	10	13	10	10	7	17			
UNASSIGNED	0.0	X												9	236	225	230	14	13	
Co-op	5.0	CO		6	4					2	3	4	4	2	4	16		216	178	
Casual	5.0	CAUL									3	3	3							
TOTAL DAYS			49	147	176	196	194	174	193	195	190	181	140	125	358	288	284	237	196	12

The Gantt chart in this figure was produced by a commercially available project management software package. It shows the task, person-days, and initials of each responsible person, as well as the start and finish dates for each task. The resource summary provides a good manager with the total person-days for each month and for each person working on the project to manage the project successfully. The project described here is a data administration project.

and Web applications (Chatterjee, Grewal, and Sambamurthy, 2002). In addition to procedural changes, transformations in job functions, organizational structure, power relationships, and behavior should be carefully planned. Table 15-4 lists the organizational dimensions that must be addressed for planning and implementing many systems.

Although systems analysis and design activities are supposed to include an organizational impact analysis, this area has traditionally been neglected. An **organizational impact analysis** explains how a proposed system will affect organizational structure, attitudes, decision making, and operations. To integrate information systems successfully with the organization, thorough and fully documented organizational impact assessments must be given more attention in the development effort.

ALLOWING FOR THE HUMAN FACTOR

The quality of information systems should be evaluated in terms of user criteria rather than the criteria of the information systems staff. In addition to targets such as memory size, access rates, and calculation times, systems objectives should include standards for user performance. For example, an objective might be that data entry clerks learn the procedures and codes for four new online data entry screens in a half-day training session.

Areas where users interface with the system should be carefully designed, with sensitivity to ergonomic issues. **Ergonomics** refers to the interaction of people and machines in the work environment. It considers the design of jobs, health issues, and the end-user interface of information systems. The impact of the application system on the work environment and job dimensions must be carefully assessed.

SOCIOTECHNICAL DESIGN

Most contemporary systems-building approaches tend to treat end users as essential to the systems-building process but as playing a largely passive role relative to other forces shaping the system, such as the specialist systems designers and management. A different tradition rooted in the European social democratic labor movement assigns users a more active role, one that empowers them to codetermine the role of information systems in their workplaces (Clement and Van den Besselaar, 1993).

This tradition of participatory design emphasizes participation by the individuals most affected by the new system. It is closely associated with the concept of sociotechnical design. A **sociotechnical design** plan establishes human objectives for the system that lead to increased job satisfaction. Designers set forth separate sets of technical and social design solutions. The social design plans explore different workgroup structures, allocation of tasks, and the design of individual jobs. The proposed technical solutions are compared with the proposed social solutions. Social and technical solutions that can be combined are proposed as sociotechnical solutions. The alternative that best meets both social and technical objectives is selected for the final design. The resulting sociotechnical design is expected to produce an information system that blends technical efficiency with sensitivity to organizational and human needs, leading to high job satisfaction (Mumford and Weir, 1979). Systems with compatible technical and organizational elements are expected to raise productivity without sacrificing human and social goals.

TABLE 15-4 *Organizational Factors in Systems Planning and Implementation*

Employee participation and involvement
Job design
Standards and performance monitoring
Ergonomics (including equipment, user interfaces, and the work environment)
Employee grievance resolution procedures
Health and safety
Government regulatory compliance

15.4 MANAGEMENT OPPORTUNITIES, CHALLENGES, AND SOLUTIONS

Given the relationship between systems and firm performance, investing in systems that provide the most benefit to the firm is one of the most important decisions managers can make—and perhaps one of the most difficult to execute successfully.

Opportunities

By changing business processes and the culture of management decision making, new information systems can produce extraordinarily high returns if system builders effectively manage the change process and accurately calculate the costs and benefits of their investments.

Management Challenges

Successful systems building requires the ability and the desire to measure the business value of systems and to pay serious attention to change management. You should be aware of the following management challenges:

DETERMINING SYSTEM BENEFITS AND COSTS WHEN THEY ARE DIFFICULT TO QUANTIFY

Many costs and benefits of information systems are difficult to quantify. The impact of a single technology investment may be difficult to ascertain if it is affected by other inter-related systems and multiple layers of hardware, software, and database and networking technology in the firm's information technology (IT) infrastructure. Managers may have difficulty measuring the social costs of implementing new technology in the organization.

As the sophistication of systems grows, the systems produce fewer tangible and more intangible benefits. By definition, there is no solid method for pricing intangible benefits. Organizations could lose important opportunities if they only use strict financial criteria for determining information systems benefits. However, organizations could make very poor investment decisions if they overestimate intangible benefits.

DEALING WITH THE COMPLEXITY OF LARGE-SCALE SYSTEMS PROJECTS

Large-scale systems, including enterprise applications that affect large numbers of organizational units and staff members and have extensive information requirements and business process changes, are difficult to oversee, coordinate, and plan for. Implementing such systems, which have multiyear development periods, is especially problematic because the systems are so complex. In addition, there are few reliable techniques for estimating the time and cost to develop large-scale information systems.

Solution Guidelines

To meet these challenges, organizations need to find ways of measuring the business value of their information systems and ensuring that systems actually deliver the benefits they promise. Here are some additional recommendations for obtaining more value from information technology investments and for managing large, complex projects.

OBTAINING MORE VALUE FROM INFORMATION TECHNOLOGY INVESTMENTS

A series of studies has shown that very few organizations are obtaining the full value of their systems investments. A sizable percentage of firms do not have central oversight over their IT budgets and lack a process for ranking and managing their technology investments. They typically chose their investments ad hoc, favoring pet projects of powerful managers. Many also lack criteria for defining project success or they fail to measure fully the returns on their projects after they have been completed. IT investments at these firms are not well integrated into corporate strategy, and senior management is not sufficiently involved in IT planning.

Firms can take a number of steps to obtain more benefits and returns from their systems investments. They can start by fully documenting the firm's applications and IT infrastructure and conducting periodic reviews of the firm's IT portfolio. They should make sure they have appropriate metrics for monitoring project outcomes and that information systems investments are closely linked to the most important business objectives of the firm. Project risks and returns should be clearly identified. Real options analysis should be conducted to identify projects that will enable future opportunities. Managers should be measuring business value throughout the duration of new system projects and should not hesitate to weed out underperforming projects if necessary.

For projects in which benefits involve improved decision making, managers should try to identify the decision improvements that would provide the greatest additional value to the firm. They should then develop a set of metrics to quantify the impact of more timely and precise information on the outcome of the decision (see Chapter 13 for more detail on this topic).

NEW APPROACHES TO PROJECT MANAGEMENT

Traditional techniques for managing projects deal with problems of size and complexity by breaking large projects into subprojects; assigning teams, schedules, and milestones to each; and focusing primarily on project mechanics rather than business results. These techniques are inadequate for enterprise systems and other large-scale systems projects with extremely complex problems of organizational coordination and change management, complex and sometimes unfamiliar technology, and continually changing business requirements. A new set of project management techniques is emerging to address these challenges.

In this model, project planning assumes an enterprise-wide focus, driven by the firm's strategic business vision and technology architecture. Project and subproject managers focus on solving problems and meeting challenges as they arise rather than simply meeting formal project milestones. They emphasize learning as well as planning, seeking ways to adapt to unforeseen uncertainties and chaos that, if properly handled, could provide additional opportunities and benefits (DeMeyer, Loch, and Pich, 2002; Markus and Benjamin, 1997; Orlikowski and Hofman, 1997). It may be useful for organizations to establish a separate program office to manage subprojects; coordinate the entire project effort with other ongoing projects; and coordinate the project with ongoing changes in the firm's business strategy, information technology infrastructure, and business processes (Concours Group, 2000).

MAKE IT YOUR BUSINESS

Finance and Accounting

A series of financial models is used to justify capital investments in new information systems. The finance and accounting function is responsible for supervising the financial analysis of information systems investments and for providing information on corporate cash flows used in capital budgeting calculations. You can find examples of finance and accounting applications on pages 535 and 567–569.

Human Resources

The human resources function can play a valuable role in systems implementation by helping with change management. When a new system is proposed, human resources staff can assist with the organizational impact analysis and locate new positions for employees whose jobs may be eliminated. Human resources could also arrange for employee training in the new system. You can find examples of human resources applications on page 554.

Manufacturing and Production

Supply chain management systems and enterprise resource planning systems can provide significant tangible benefits, such as reductions in inventory costs, and intangible benefits, such as faster response times to customer demands. However, both types of systems are among the most difficult systems to implement successfully because they require major business process changes as well as new technology.

Sales and Marketing

Customer relationship management systems can provide tangible benefits, such as reduced direct marketing costs, and intangible benefits, such as better customer service and support. These systems can be difficult to implement because they may require integrating customer information from multiple

sources and changes to the firm's business processes for interacting with customers and gathering customer data. User interface design is especially important for customer-facing Web applications. You can find examples of sales and marketing applications on pages 550 and 573–575.

Summary

1. **Evaluate models for understanding the business value of information systems.**

   Information systems can provide business value for a firm in many different ways, including increased profitability and productivity. Some, but not all, of these business benefits can be quantified and measured.

   Capital budgeting models are used to determine whether an investment in information technology produces sufficient returns to justify its costs. The principal capital budgeting models are the payback method, accounting rate of return on investment (ROI), net present value, cost-benefit ratio, profitability index, and internal rate of return (IRR).

   Other models for evaluating information systems investments involve nonfinancial and strategic considerations. Portfolio analysis and scoring models can be used to evaluate alternative information systems projects. Real options pricing models, which apply the same techniques for valuing financial options to systems investments, can be useful when considering highly uncertain IT investments.

   Although information technology has increased productivity in manufacturing, especially the manufacture of information technology products, the extent to which computers have enhanced the productivity of the service sector remains under debate. In addition to reducing costs, computers may increase the quality of products and services for consumers or may create entirely new products and revenue streams. These intangible benefits are difficult to measure and consequently are not addressed by conventional productivity measures.

2. **Analyze the principal causes of information system failure.**

   A very large percentage of information systems fail to deliver benefits or solve the problems for which they were intended because the process of organizational change surrounding system building was not properly addressed. The principal causes of information system failure are (1) insufficient or improper user participation in the systems development process, (2) lack of management support, (3) high levels of complexity and

   risk in the systems development process, and (4) poor management of the implementation process. There is a very high failure rate among business process reengineering and enterprise application projects because they require extensive organizational change that is often resisted by members of the organization. Enterprise applications as well as system changes resulting from mergers and acquisitions are also difficult to implement successfully because they usually require far-reaching changes to business processes.

3. **Assess the change management requirements for building successful systems.**

   Building an information system is a process of planned organizational change that must be carefully managed. The term *implementation* refers to the entire process of organizational change surrounding the introduction of a new information system. One can better understand system success and failure by examining different patterns of implementation. Especially important is the relationship between participants in the implementation process, notably the interactions between system designers and users. Conflicts between the technical orientation of system designers and the business orientation of end users must be resolved. The success of organizational change can be determined by how well information systems specialists, end users, and decision makers deal with key issues at various stages in implementation. Eliciting user support and maintaining an appropriate level of user involvement at all stages of system building are essential.

4. **Select appropriate strategies to manage the system implementation process.**

   Management support and control of the implementation process are essential, as are mechanisms for dealing with the level of risk in each new systems project. Some companies experience organizational resistance to change. Project risk factors can be brought under some control by a contingency approach to project management. The level of risk in a systems development project is determined by three key dimensions: (1) project size, (2) project structure, and (3) experience with technology. The risk level of each project determines the appropriate mix of external integration tools, internal integration tools, formal planning tools, and formal control tools to be applied.

Appropriate strategies can be applied to ensure the correct level of user participation in the systems development process and to minimize user resistance. Information systems design and the entire implementation process should be managed as planned organizational change. Participatory design emphasizes the participation of the individuals most affected by a new system. Sociotechnical design aims for an optimal blend of social and technical design solutions.

5. *Identify the challenges posed by implementing new systems and management solutions.*

Building successful systems is something of an art form. It is becoming increasingly difficult to determine the costs and benefits of systems, especially those in which benefits are primarily intangible or those that are interrelated with other systems and pieces of technology in the firm. Implementing large-scale systems and obtaining benefits from such investments are especially challenging. Management solutions include developing metrics and processes to make sure information systems investments provide business value and using more dynamic approaches to project management.

Key Terms

Accounting rate of return on investment (ROI), 541
Capital budgeting, 537
Change agent, 551
Cost-benefit ratio, 542
Counterimplementation, 558
Ergonomics, 560
External integration tools, 558
Formal control tools, 558
Formal planning tools, 558

Implementation, 551
Intangible benefits, 537
Internal integration tools, 557
Internal rate of return (IRR), 543
Man-month, 555
Net present value, 542
Organizational impact analysis, 560
Payback method, 540
Portfolio analysis, 543

Present value, 542
Profitability index, 542
Real options pricing models (ROPM), 545
Scoring model, 544
Sociotechnical design, 560
System failure, 548
Tangible benefits, 537
User-designer communications gap, 552
User interface, 549

Review Questions

1. *Name and describe the principal capital budgeting methods used to evaluate information system projects.*

2. *What are the limitations of financial models for establishing the value of information systems?*

3. *Describe how portfolio analysis and scoring models can be used to establish the worth of systems.*

4. *How can real options pricing models be used to help evaluate information technology investments?*

5. *Have information systems enhanced productivity in businesses? Explain your answer.*

6. *Why do builders of new information systems need to address change management?*

7. *What kinds of problems provide evidence of information systems failure?*

8. *Why is it necessary to understand the concept of implementation when managing the organizational change surrounding a new information system?*

9. *What are the major causes of implementation success or failure?*

10. *What is the user-designer communications gap? What kinds of implementation problems can it create?*

11. *Why is there such a high failure rate among enterprise application implementations and business process reengineering (BPR) projects? What role do information systems play in the success or failure of mergers and acquisitions?*

12. *What dimensions influence the level of risk in each systems development project?*

13. *What project management techniques can be used to control project risk?*

14. *What strategies can be used to overcome user resistance to systems development projects?*

15. *What organizational considerations should be addressed by information systems design?*

16. *What challenges are posed by trying to determine the business value of systems and manage system-related change? Suggest some solutions.*

Discussion Questions

1. *It has been said that when we design an information system we are redesigning the organization. What are the ramifications of this statement?*

2. *It has been said that most systems fail because systems builders ignore organizational behavior problems. Why might this be so?*

Application Software Exercise:
Spreadsheet Exercise: Capital Budgeting for a New CAD System

Your company would like to invest in a new computer-aided design (CAD) system that requires purchasing hardware, software, and networking technology, as well as expenditures for installation, training, and support. The Laudon Web site for Chapter 15 contains tables showing each cost component for the new system as well as annual maintenance costs over a five-year period. You believe the new system will produce annual savings by reducing the amount of labor required to generate designs and design specifications, thus increasing your firm's annual cash flow. Using the data provided and instructions at the Laudon Web site for this chapter, create a worksheet that calculates the costs and benefits of the investment over a five-year period and analyzes the investment using the six capital budgeting models presented in this chapter. Is this investment worthwhile? Why or why not?

Analyzing the Return on a New System Investment

Required software: Spreadsheet software
                        Word processing software
                        Electronic presentation software (optional)

Dirt Bikes's management would like to analyze the return on its investment in its employee training and skills tracking system described in the previous chapter. The system runs on the human resources specialists' PCs using PC database software. Because the entire corporate administrative staff recently received new desktop PC systems with database and other productivity software, there are no additional hardware and software purchase costs. The main costs include the initial cost of designing and implementing the database (business staff cost of $5,000; information systems staff cost of $15,000), gathering and adding employee skills and training data to the database ($5,500 initial data conversion cost plus $1,000 annual data entry costs), and ongoing maintenance and support ($3,000 annually). Human resources staff members believe the new application could save each of them two hours of work per week. (Their annual salaries are $37,000 and $42,000 each.) The company would also save about $11,000 annually in employee recruiting costs because it would be able to fill many vacant positions with existing employees, thereby reducing its costs for recruiting outside the company. The system would not be installed until the end of 2005 and would return benefits from 2006 to 2010.

1. Prepare a report for management analyzing the return on the investment for this system over a five-year period using the following capital budgeting models: net present value, accounting rate of return on investment (ROI), internal rate of return (IRR), cost-benefit ratio, profitability index, and payback method. Assume a 5 percent interest rate for your net present value calculations. Use spreadsheet software for your calculations.

2. (Optional) If possible use electronic presentation software to summarize your findings for management.

Electronic Business Project: Buying and Financing a Home

You have found a new job in Denver, Colorado, and would like to purchase a home in that area. Ideally, you would like to find a single-family house with at least three bedrooms and one bathroom that costs between $150,000 and $225,000 and finance it with a 30-year fixed rate mortgage. You can afford a down payment that is 20 percent of the value of the house. Before you purchase a house, you would like to find out what homes are available in your price range, find a mortgage, and determine the amount of your monthly payment. You would also like to see how much of your mortgage payment represents principal and how much represents interest. Use Yahoo!'s Real Estate site (realestate.yahoo.com/) to help you with the following tasks:

1. Locate homes in your price range in Denver, Colorado. Find out as much information as you can about the houses, including the real estate listing agent, condition of the house, number of rooms, and school district.

2. Find a mortgage for 80 percent of the list price of the home. Compare rates from at least three sites (use search engines to find sites other than Yahoo!).

3. After selecting a mortgage, calculate your closing costs.

4. Calculate the monthly payment for the mortgage you select.

5. Calculate how much of your monthly mortgage payment represents principal and how much represents interest, assuming you do not plan to make any extra payments on the mortgage.

When you are finished, evaluate the whole process. For example, assess the ease of use of the site and your ability to find information about houses and mortgages; the accuracy of the information you found; the breadth of choice of homes and mortgages; and how helpful the whole process would have been for you if you were actually in the situation described in this project.

Group Project: Identifying Implementation Problems

Form a group with two or three other students. Write a description of the implementation problems you might expect to encounter for the information system you designed for the business process redesign project that follows Chapter 14. Write an analysis of the steps you would take to solve or prevent these problems. Alternatively, you could describe the implementation problems that might be expected for one of the systems described in the Window boxes or chapter-ending cases in this text. If possible, use electronic presentation software to present your findings to the class.

CASE STUDY
Can the IRS Modernize Its Systems?

The United States Internal Revenue Service was one of the first organizations to use computer systems—and it may be one of the last to modernize. It is still running systems dating back to the 1960s with 62 million lines of program code that are so antiquated that young technicians can't read them. (The agency has to pay incentives to retain programmers who can.) The IRS Master Files, which store the taxpaying histories of 227 million individuals and corporations, are not based on contemporary database management software but on antiquated file management systems that make information very difficult to access and maintain.

These systems are massive, complex, and frustrating to use. More than 200 accounting, auditing, and research systems aren't integrated, so IRS agents cannot easily locate all the records on a taxpayer to answer certain types of questions or fix certain errors. Some experts believe the Master Files are poised for a fatal crash that would shut down the agency.

During the past 25 years, the IRS has tried multiple times to modernize its systems. Congress has been pressuring the IRS and other federal agencies to provide a higher level of service to citizens comparable to that of banks, credit card companies, and other private sector businesses. But the IRS systems were not capable of offering this level of service and convenience to taxpayers and they were highly inefficient: In 2002, it still cost 45 cents to collect every dollar of revenue, and this cost had not appreciably declined for two decades.

The first modernization effort to network the Master Files with IRS business applications was halted by the Carter administration because there were no reliable provisions in place to secure the privacy of taxpayers. In the mid-1990s, a second modernization campaign met its demise at the hands of Congress after a decade of work and a $2 billion investment resulted in insufficient progress.

With these failures still visible in history's rearview mirror, the IRS launched an $8 billion modernization program called Business Systems Modernization in 1999. The previous year, Congress had passed the IRS Restructuring and Reform Act, which reorganized the IRS so that its units were based not on geography, but on business function. In the past, IRS information systems employees did not report to its CIO but to the directors of the 10 regional service centers that administered tax returns. This organizational structure left gaps in accountability and inhibited the application of agency-wide standards. Under the Restructuring and Reform Act, IRS Commissioner Charles Rossotti put the IRS CIO in charge of the entire information systems budget and staff, which formerly had been dispersed among the old geographic units.

Business Systems Modernization allocated $8 billion to upgrade the IRS IT infrastructure and more than 100 business applications between 1999 and 2002. Fragile Master Files were to be replaced by a state-of-the-art centralized database called the Customer Account Data Engine (CADE) to provide faster processing of tax returns, speedier refunds, and more timely customer service. The first intended practical application of CADE was to streamline the processing of the 1040EZ tax return form, which more than 20 million taxpayers use. Other projects included integrated financial and accounting systems for IRS internal operations, a modernized e-file capability for online filing of tax returns, and online services for tax preparers.

To avoid repeating the past, the IRS tried to make sure that there were business sponsors for its projects, that vendors contracted to work on the systems had clear deliverables, and that both internal staff and contractors were held accountable for the results. For project consultants, it assembled a "dream team" headed by Computer Sciences Corporation (CSC) that included IBM, Lucent, Northrup Grumman, and Unisys. CSC, the prime contractor, would bear the major responsibility for program management and systems integration. The new systems modernization team was called the Business Systems Modernization Office, or BSMO (pronounced "Bizmo"), reporting directly to the CIO and Rossotti.

New policies required upper-level managers at the IRS to approve each phase of the project before the information systems team could start working. CSC and its subcontractors were to receive more detailed instructions and expectations for their work than had been delivered in the previous modernization efforts. Every proposed project also had a business sponsor, verifying that time and money were being spent on projects that had practical and useful applications.

Unfortunately, the path to success for the Business Systems Modernization project has been as treacherous as it was for previous modernization programs. As of April 2004, the schedule of software releases for CADE was three years late and over budget by a figure approaching $40 million. Eight other subprojects have missed their deadlines, with cost overruns amounting to $200 million.

The IRS did learn from past mistakes, but failed to follow through on many of the measures it implemented to avoid repeating them. Observers believe that the IRS succeeded in the planning stages of Business Systems Modernization, but failed in its execution. The IRS and its Oversight Board have placed much of the blame on CSC, saying that their main vendor was insufficiently equipped to handle such a large and complex project. Closer investigation reveals that in addition to CSC not living up to expectations, by missing deadlines, for example, the Bizmo team and CSC dream team had a poor working relationship.

Despite its best intentions, the IRS did not always follow through on its plan to provide CSC with detailed instructions and expectations for delivery. Furthermore, key players on the Bizmo team proved unwilling to yield their powers of decision to their dream team counterparts, who were supposed to have such powers. Neither Bizmo nor CSC communicated effectively with those in the IRS who would ultimately be using CADE and the other new systems in the field. IRS information systems staff in charge of maintaining existing systems resented the modernization project team, and CSC did not reach out to them or their managers. The lack of input from field workers and their managers resulted in important features and requirements being left out of design schemes.

No one within the IRS, including its CIO had enough stature to champion the business process changes that the new systems required. Business managers were involved in approving plans and resolving problems, but only as members of large committees, and were not sources of either authority or accountability. Business managers were not held accountable for ensuring that new systems were delivered—they assumed that was the responsibility of the information systems group. Neither Bizmo nor CSC had proper procedures in place for defining requirements, assessing project risks, or tracking project costs. It often took weeks to get approvals, even for purchasing equipment, creating delays that added to project costs.

Paul M. Cofoni, president of the CSC unit running the IRS project, admits, "In the early part of the program we did a poor job of defining" what needed to be done. But this was largely because the IRS lacked records of many changes to its legacy systems and was reluctant to approve specifications for its new system until it was sure that the system would be able to find and display the old information.

As the Business Systems Modernization Project proceeded, the IRS underwent a series of leadership changes. Shortly before the new IRS customer service–oriented call center routing system, the first new system to be completed, was to be deployed, Paul Cosgrave resigned as CIO. His replacement, John Reece, served from 2001 to 2003, when W. Todd Grams took the position. Transition hit once again in May 2003, when the IRS named Mark Everson the new commissioner, replacing Charles Rossotti, whose term had expired.

CSC's initial plan to deliver CADE by May 2002 came up well short. The production schedule that it established initially was based on thin information and resulted in cost overruns and inaccurate projections of feasibility and risk. Before CSC had finished designing the software code, Bizmo had approved a critical piece of middleware for CADE called "balance, control, and reconciliation," which ensures that the data processed by CADE was updated in the Master File. Moreover, neither the IRS nor CSC consulted with the IRS field office that would run CADE about integrating the two systems. The field office eventually added its input, but it conflicted with the information requirements CSC had obtained from Bizmo. CSC ignored both groups and came up with its own solution.

John Reece, then-CIO of the IRS, reacted angrily to the missed deadline, but set upon the task of assessing the project's shortcomings and figuring out how to fix them. Members of the dream team admitted that the team needed more experienced managers who also had expertise in taxes and accounting. For its part, Bizmo needed to fulfill its obligations of overseeing and controlling the dream team's progress. This would require an increase in the size and competence of the IRS staff in charge of monitoring the dream team.

Once it became clear that CSC would not deliver CADE on time, Reece took additional measures to stop the bleeding. He entertained thoughts of firing CSC outright, and then let it be known that a quick turnaround was expected or the IRS would find a new lead vendor. The IRS also set a maximum cost for the project, placing the burden of future cost overruns directly on CSC.

When Mark Everson took over as commissioner of the IRS in May 2003, he promoted W. Todd Grams from CFO to CIO. Together, they set about the task of moving Business Systems Modernization forward. The IRS and CSC revised their working agreement so that the cost of the project was fixed and could not balloon because of unforeseen delays. CSC staffed its dream team with people who were more familiar with the complexities of tax codes and administration. The IRS scaled back the number of modernization projects in the works and disqualified CSC from working on two systems so that the vendor could focus on CADE and the Integrated Financial System (IFS), which will enable the IRS to audit itself more effectively.

As of November 2004, an initial version of CADE and a modernized e-File system that enables large corporations to file their returns electronically had been deployed. The IFS went live during at that time, although the total cost for full deployment increased by $74 million.

The U.S. government will not perpetually support programs that fail to meet expectations and drain funds while they do so. At the same time, successful modernization of the IRS Master File is absolutely necessary for the continued viability of the American tax system. According to IRS CIO Grams, "We've tried to do too much over too short a time in the past. I believe everything we've taken on has exceeded CSC's capacity to deliver, as well as our capacity to manage." Larry Levitan, chairman of the IRS Oversight Board's Business Transformation Committee, asserts, "CSC's significant fault was accepting the status quo, accepting an environment that would not be successful." As for the modernization project itself, Levitan states that the welfare of the entire federal government rests on the success or failure of the program.

Sources: Elana Varon, "For the IRS There's No EZ Fix," *CIO Magazine*, April 1, 2004; Juan Carlos Perez, "IRS Commissioner Bars CSC from Upcoming Projects," *Computerworld*, February 13, 2004; Mary Mosquera, "IRS Modernization Program Makes Strides,"

Government Computer News, November 19, 2004; "IRS Holds Back Future CADE, Accounting System Releases," *Government Computer News*, January 9, 2004; "CADE Advances to Operational Testing," *Government Computer News*, April 4, 2004; Mary Mosquera, "CADE Release Depends on Employee Mastery," *Government Computer News*, January 16, 2004; "IRS, CSC Act to Right the Agency's IT Overhaul," *Government Computer News*, January 12, 2004; and "IRS to Pare Down Modernization Projects," *Government Computer News*, December 12, 2003; David Cay Johnston, "At I.R.S., a Systems Update Gone Awry," *New York Times*, December 11, 2003; Grant Gross, "IRS Database Upgrade Delayed Again," *Computerworld*, August 4, 2003; Juan Carlos Perez, "CSC, IRS Blasted for IT Project Work," *Computerworld*, December 11, 2003; and Eric Chabrow, "IRS Takes Contractors to Task for Lengthy Contract Delays," *Information Week*, July 28, 2003.

CASE STUDY QUESTIONS

1. How important are information systems for the Internal Revenue Service?

2. Classify and describe the problems the IRS faced in trying to modernize its systems, using the categories described in this chapter on the causes of system failure.

3. What management, organization, and technology factors caused those problems?

4. Evaluate the risks of the IRS systems modernization project and key risk factors.

5. Describe the steps you would have taken to control the risk in the IRS modernization project.

Chapter 16

Managing International Information Systems

- Set standards
- Design global business processes

- Standardize intercompany processes
- Standardize worldwide data model

- Implement Oracle 9i DBMS and Adapter
- Implement PointOut software for standard global interface

Business Challenges

- Rapid expansion through aquisitions
- Decentralized systems
- Localized order processes

Management

Organization

Technology

Information System

- Track orders automatically worldwide
- Manage global inventory

Business Solutions

- Reduce costs
- Increase revenue

Opening Case: Dräger Safety Creates a Global Supply Chain

Dräger Safety, based in Luebeck, Germany, develops and sells a wide range of safety products, including protective suits, breathing equipment, and gas detection systems. The company mushroomed from a two-person shop in 1889 to a network of more than 40 subsidiaries and is considered one of the world's most innovative safety-product companies.

As the number of Dräger subsidiaries grew during the last decade, the company was losing revenue and facing higher costs. Dräger could not rapidly take and fulfill orders among 40 companies spread across Europe, Asia, and North America. Every order had to be handled manually because each Dräger subsidiary maintained its own set of information systems. Dräger had no way to link sales, production, storage, and shipping automatically across all of its units worldwide.

For example, the company might take an order in Canada, generate a purchase order in Germany, source the product in the United States, and then ship it to Canada. The salesperson taking the order would create a purchase order on paper and mail it to a production hub. There the order would be input, assembled, stored, and shipped back to the originating sales office, which would then ship it out to the customer. This cumbersome manual system created delays and poorly managed inventory.

For a solution, Dräger selected Oracle9i Database and Oracle 9i Application Server (Oracle9iAS) Inter-

connect Adapter with standardized enterprise resource planning (ERP) interfaces. The Interconnect Adapter middleware enabled Dräger to link the systems from all its subsidiaries easily because it did not require programming point-to-point connections between the various systems and could connect a broad range of enterprise systems to the same data platform.

Dräger did have to standardize intercompany processes, including planning, reporting, and product and inventory management to use the common database effectively. The company also had to create a single worldwide data model with standard codes and definitions for customer items, vendor items, production orders, and bills of materials. A software program called PointOut developed by Munich software firm mSE provides a desktop data interface with the same look and functionality at each company.

Today, Dräger's entire order process is fully automated and can track orders worldwide. Dräger can centralize inventory in each region and ship products directly to customers from the closest regional warehouse. Orders that used to take weeks to fulfill can now be processed in minutes. Dräger has been able to reduce its global inventory by 40 percent, slash inventory at sales locations by 95 percent, and lower process costs by 30 percent.

Sources: Shari Caudron, "Safety in Numbers," *Profit Magazine*, February 2004; and www.drager-safety.com, accessed June 4, 2004.

Dräger Safety's efforts to create global supply chain processes are some of the changes in international information systems architecture—the basic systems needed to coordinate worldwide trade and other activities—that organizations need to consider if they want to operate across the globe.

As a manager, you'll want to know what special issues must be addressed when developing and managing international information systems. To be effective, you'll need a global perspective on business and an understanding of the information systems needed to conduct business on an international scale. This chapter shows you how to organize, manage, and control the development of international information systems.

16.1 THE GROWTH OF INTERNATIONAL INFORMATION SYSTEMS

In earlier chapters we describe the emergence of a global economic system and global world order driven by advanced networks and information systems. The new world order is sweeping away many national corporations, national industries, and national economies controlled by domestic politicians. Many localized firms will be replaced by fast-moving networked corporations that transcend national boundaries. The growth of international trade has radically altered domestic economies around the globe. Over $1 trillion worth of goods, services, and financial instruments changes hands each day in global trade.

Today, the production and design of many high-end electronic products is parceled out to a number of different countries. Consider the path to market for Hewlett-Packard's ProLiant ML150 server, which is illustrated in Figure 16-1. The idea for the product was hatched in Singapore, which did the initial design work. HP headquarters in Houston approved the concept. Contractors in Taiwan did the machine's engineering design and initial manufacture. Final assembly of the server takes place in Singapore, China, India, and Australia (Buckman, 2004). None of this would be possible without powerful international information and communication systems.

Developing an International Information Systems Architecture

This chapter describes how to go about building an international information systems architecture suitable for your international strategy. An **international information systems architecture** consists of the basic information systems required by organizations to coordinate worldwide trade and other activities. Figure 16-2 illustrates the reasoning we follow throughout the chapter and depicts the major dimensions of an international information systems architecture.

The basic strategy to follow when building an international system is to understand the global environment in which your firm is operating. This means understanding the overall market forces, or business drivers, that are pushing your industry toward global competition. A **business driver** is a force in the environment to which businesses must respond and that influences the direction of the business. Likewise, examine carefully the inhibitors or negative factors that create *management challenges*—factors that could scuttle the development of a global business. Once you have examined the global environment, you will need to consider a corporate strategy for competing in that environment. How will your firm respond? You could ignore the global market and focus on domestic competition only, sell to the globe from a domestic base, or organize production and distribution around the globe. There are many in-between choices.

After you have developed a strategy, it is time to consider how to structure your organization so it can pursue the strategy. How will you accomplish a division of labor across

FIGURE 16-1   *Global product development and production.*

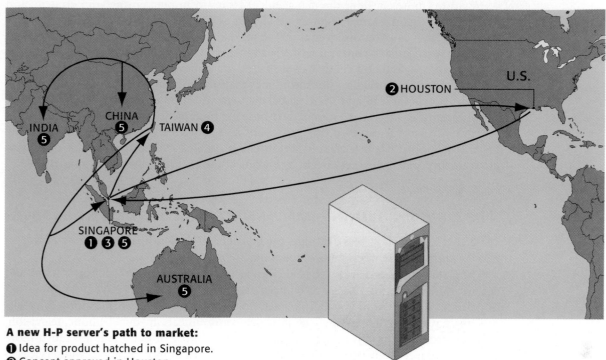

A new H-P server's path to market:

❶ Idea for product hatched in Singapore.

❷ Concept approved in Houston.

❸ Concept design done in Singapore.

❹ Engineering design in Taiwan, where many computer components are made;
  initial manufacture by a Taiwanese contractor.

❺ Final assembly in Singapore, Australia, China, and India. Products made in Australia,
  China, and India are primarily for those markets; machines made in Singapore go to all of Southeast Asia.

Hewlett-Packard and other electronics companies assign distribution and production of high-end products to a number of different countries.

Source: © *New York Times.* Used with permission.

FIGURE 16-2   *International information systems architecture.*

International Information Systems Architecture

The major dimensions for developing an international information systems architecture are the global environment, the corporate global strategies, the structure of the organization, the management and business processes, and the technology platform.

a global environment? Where will production, administration, accounting, marketing, and human resource functions be located? Who will handle the systems function?

Next, you must consider the management issues in implementing your strategy and making the organization design come alive. Key here will be the design of business processes. How can you discover and manage user requirements? How can you induce change in local units to conform to international requirements? How can you reengineer on a global scale, and how can you coordinate systems development?

The last issue to consider is the technology platform. Although changing technology is a key driving factor leading toward global markets, you need to have a corporate strategy and structure before you can rationally choose the right technology.

After you have completed this process of reasoning, you will be well on your way toward an appropriate international information systems architecture capable of achieving your corporate goals. Let's begin by looking at the overall global environment.

The Global Environment: Business Drivers and Challenges

Table 16-1 lists the business drivers in the global environment that are leading all industries toward global markets and competition.

The global business drivers can be divided into two groups: general cultural factors and specific business factors. Easily recognized general cultural factors have driven internationalization since World War II. Information, communication, and transportation technologies have created a *global village* in which communication (by telephone, television, radio, or computer network) around the globe is no more difficult and not much more expensive than communication down the block. The cost of moving goods and services to and from geographically dispersed locations has fallen dramatically.

The development of global communications has created a global village in a second sense: A **global culture** created by television and other globally shared media such as movies now permits different cultures and peoples to develop common expectations about right and wrong, desirable and undesirable, heroic and cowardly. The collapse of the Eastern bloc has speeded the growth of a world culture enormously, increased support for capitalism and business, and reduced the level of cultural conflict considerably.

A last factor to consider is the growth of a global knowledge base. At the end of World War II, knowledge, education, science, and industrial skills were highly concentrated in North America, western Europe, and Japan, with the rest of the world euphemistically called the *Third World*. This is no longer true. Latin America, China, southern Asia, and eastern Europe have developed powerful educational, industrial, and scientific centers, resulting in a much more democratically and widely dispersed knowledge base.

TABLE 16-1 *Global Business Drivers*

GENERAL CULTURAL FACTORS
Global communication and transportation technologies
Development of global culture
Emergence of global social norms
Political stability
Global knowledge base

SPECIFIC BUSINESS FACTORS
Global markets
Global production and operations
Global coordination
Global workforce
Global economies of scale

These general cultural factors leading toward internationalization result in specific business globalization factors that affect most industries. The growth of powerful communications technologies and the emergence of world cultures create the condition for *global markets*—global consumers interested in consuming similar products that are culturally approved. Coca-Cola, American sneakers (made in Korea but designed in Los Angeles), and Cable News Network (CNN) programming can now be sold in Latin America, Africa, and Asia.

Responding to this demand, global production and operations have emerged with precise online coordination between far-flung production facilities and central headquarters thousands of miles away. At Sealand Transportation, a major global shipping company based in Newark, New Jersey, shipping managers in Newark can watch the loading of ships in Rotterdam online, check trim and ballast, and trace packages to specific ship locations as the activity proceeds. This is all possible through an international satellite link.

The new global markets and pressure toward global production and operation have called forth whole new capabilities for global coordination of all factors of production. Not only production but also accounting, marketing and sales, human resources, and systems development (all the major business functions) can be coordinated on a global scale.

Frito Lay, for instance, can develop a marketing sales force automation system in the United States and, once provided, may try the same techniques and technologies in Spain. Micromarketing—marketing to very small geographic and social units—no longer means marketing to neighborhoods in the United States, but to neighborhoods throughout the world! These new levels of global coordination permit for the first time in history the location of business activity according to comparative advantage. Design should be located where it is best accomplished, as should marketing, production, and finance.

Finally, global markets, production, and administration create the conditions for powerful, sustained global economies of scale. Production driven by worldwide global demand can be concentrated where it can best be accomplished, fixed resources can be allocated over larger production runs, and production runs in larger plants can be scheduled more efficiently and precisely estimated. Lower cost factors of production can be exploited wherever they emerge. The result is a powerful strategic advantage to firms that can organize globally. These general and specific business drivers have greatly enlarged world trade and commerce.

Not all industries are similarly affected by these trends. Clearly, manufacturing has been much more affected than services that still tend to be domestic and highly inefficient. However, the localism of services is breaking down in telecommunications, entertainment, transportation, financial services, and general business services including law. Clearly, those firms within an industry that can understand the internationalization of the industry and respond appropriately will reap enormous gains in productivity and stability.

BUSINESS CHALLENGES

Although the possibilities of globalization for business success are significant, fundamental forces are operating to inhibit a global economy and to disrupt international business. Table 16-2 lists the most common and powerful challenges to the development of global systems.

At a cultural level, **particularism**, making judgments and taking action on the basis of narrow or personal characteristics, in all its forms (religious, nationalistic, ethnic, regionalism, geopolitical position) rejects the very concept of a shared global culture and rejects the penetration of domestic markets by foreign goods and services. Differences among cultures produce differences in social expectations, politics, and ultimately legal rules. In certain countries, such as the United States, consumers expect domestic name-brand products to be built domestically and are disappointed to learn that much of what they thought of as domestically produced is in fact foreign made.

Different cultures produce different political regimes. Among the many different countries of the world are different laws governing the movement of information, information

***TABLE 16-2** Challenges and Obstacles to Global Business Systems*

GENERAL

Cultural particularism: Regionalism, nationalism, language differences

Social expectations: Brand-name expectations, work hours

Political laws: Transborder data and privacy laws, commercial regulations

SPECIFIC

Standards: Different Electronic Data Interchange (EDI), e-mail, telecommunications standards

Reliability: Phone networks not uniformly reliable

Speed: Different data transfer speeds, many slower than United States

Personnel: Shortages of skilled consultants

privacy of their citizens, origins of software and hardware in systems, and radio and satellite telecommunications. Even the hours of business and the terms of business trade vary greatly across political cultures. These different legal regimes complicate global business and must be considered when building global systems.

For instance, European countries have very strict laws concerning transborder data flow and privacy. **Transborder data flow** is defined as the movement of information across international boundaries in any form. Some European countries prohibit the processing of financial information outside their boundaries or the movement of personal information to foreign countries. The European Union Data Protection Directive, which went into effect in October 1998, restricts the flow of any information to countries (such as the United States) that do not meet strict European laws on personal information. Financial services, travel, and health care companies could be directly affected. In response, most multinational firms develop information systems within each European country to avoid the cost and uncertainty of moving information across national boundaries.

Cultural and political differences profoundly affect organizations' business processes and applications of information technology. A host of specific barriers arise from the general cultural differences, everything from different reliability of phone networks to the shortage of skilled consultants (see Steinbart and Nath, 1992).

National laws and traditions have created disparate accounting practices in various countries, which impact the ways profits and losses are analyzed. German companies generally do not recognize the profit from a venture until the project is completely finished and they have been paid. Conversely, British firms begin posting profits before a project is completed, when they are reasonably certain they will get the money.

These accounting practices are tightly intertwined with each country's legal system, business philosophy, and tax code. British, U.S., and Dutch firms share a predominantly Anglo-Saxon outlook that separates tax calculations from reports to shareholders to focus on showing shareholders how fast profits are growing. Continental European accounting practices are less oriented toward impressing investors, focusing rather on demonstrating compliance with strict rules and minimizing tax liabilities. These diverging accounting practices make it difficult for large international companies with units in different countries to evaluate their performance.

Language remains a significant barrier. Although English has become a kind of standard business language, this is truer at higher levels of companies and not throughout the middle and lower ranks. Software may have to be built with local language interfaces before a new information system can be successfully implemented.

Currency fluctuations can play havoc with planning models and projections. A product that appears profitable in Mexico or Japan may actually produce a loss because of changes in foreign exchange rates. Some of these problems will diminish in parts of the world where the euro becomes more widely used.

These inhibiting factors must be taken into account when you are designing and building international systems for your business. For example, companies trying to implement "lean production" systems spanning national boundaries typically underestimate the time, expense, and logistical difficulties of making goods and information flow freely across different countries.

State of the Art

One might think, given the opportunities for achieving competitive advantages as outlined previously and the interest in future applications, that most international companies have rationally developed marvelous international systems architectures. Nothing could be further from the truth. Most companies have inherited patchwork international systems from the distant past, often based on concepts of information processing developed in the 1960s—batch-oriented reporting from independent foreign divisions to corporate headquarters, with little online control and communication. Corporations in this situation increasingly face powerful competitive challenges in the marketplace from firms that have rationally designed truly international systems. Still other companies have recently built technology platforms for international systems but have nowhere to go because they lack global strategy.

As it turns out, there are significant difficulties in building appropriate international architectures. The difficulties involve planning a system appropriate to the firm's global strategy, structuring the organization of systems and business units, solving implementation issues, and choosing the right technical platform. Let us examine these problems in greater detail.

16.2 ORGANIZING INTERNATIONAL INFORMATION SYSTEMS

Three organizational issues face corporations seeking a global position: choosing a strategy, organizing the business, and organizing the systems management area. The first two are closely connected, so we discuss them together.

Global Strategies and Business Organization

Four main global strategies form the basis for global firms' organizational structure. These are domestic exporter, multinational, franchiser, and transnational. Each of these strategies is pursued with a specific business organizational structure (see Table 16-3). For simplicity's sake, we describe three kinds of organizational structure or governance: centralized (in the home country), decentralized (to local foreign units), and coordinated (all

TABLE 16-3 Global Business Strategy and Structure

Business Function	Domestic Exporter	Multinational	Franchiser	Transnational
Production	Centralized	Dispersed	Coordinated	Coordinated
Finance/Accounting	Centralized	Centralized	Centralized	Coordinated
Sales/Marketing	Mixed	Dispersed	Coordinated	Coordinated
Human Resources	Centralized	Centralized	Coordinated	Coordinated
Strategic Management	Centralized	Centralized	Centralized	Coordinated

units participate as equals). Other types of governance patterns can be observed in specific companies (e.g., authoritarian dominance by one unit, a confederacy of equals, a federal structure balancing power among strategic units, and so forth; see Keen, 1991).

The **domestic exporter** strategy is characterized by heavy centralization of corporate activities in the home country of origin. Nearly all international companies begin this way, and some move on to other forms. Production, finance/accounting, sales/marketing, human resources, and strategic management are set up to optimize resources in the home country. International sales are sometimes dispersed using agency agreements or subsidiaries, but even here foreign marketing is totally reliant on the domestic home base for marketing themes and strategies. Caterpillar Corporation and other heavy capital-equipment manufacturers fall into this category of firm.

The **multinational** strategy concentrates financial management and control out of a central home base while decentralizing production, sales, and marketing operations to units in other countries. The products and services on sale in different countries are adapted to suit local market conditions. The organization becomes a far-flung confederation of production and marketing facilities in different countries. Many financial service firms, along with a host of manufacturers, such as General Motors, Chrysler, and Intel, fit this pattern.

Franchisers are an interesting mix of old and new. On the one hand, the product is created, designed, financed, and initially produced in the home country, but for product-specific reasons must rely heavily on foreign personnel for further production, marketing, and human resources. Food franchisers such as McDonald's, Mrs. Fields Cookies, and KFC fit this pattern. McDonald's created a new form of fast-food chain in the United States and continues to rely largely on the United States for inspiration of new products, strategic management, and financing. Nevertheless, because the product must be produced locally—it is perishable—extensive coordination and dispersal of production, local marketing, and local recruitment of personnel are required.

Generally, foreign franchisees are clones of the mother country units, but fully coordinated worldwide production that could optimize factors of production is not possible. For instance, potatoes and beef can generally not be bought where they are cheapest on world markets but must be produced reasonably close to the area of consumption.

Transnational firms are the stateless, truly globally managed firms that may represent a larger part of international business in the future. Transnational firms have no single national headquarters but instead have many regional headquarters and perhaps a world headquarters. In a **transnational** strategy, nearly all the value-adding activities are managed from a global perspective without reference to national borders, optimizing sources of supply and demand wherever they appear, and taking advantage of any local competitive advantages. Transnational firms take the globe, not the home country, as their management frame of reference. The governance of these firms has been likened to a federal structure in which there is a strong central management core of decision making, but considerable dispersal of power and financial muscle throughout the global divisions. Few companies have actually attained transnational status, but Citicorp, Sony, Ford, and others are attempting this transition.

Information technology and improvements in global telecommunications are giving international firms more flexibility to shape their global strategies. Protectionism and a need to serve local markets better encourage companies to disperse production facilities and at least become multinational. At the same time, the drive to achieve economies of scale across national boundaries moves transnationals toward a global management perspective and a concentration of power and authority. Hence, there are forces of decentralization and dispersal, as well as forces of centralization and global coordination.

Global Systems to Fit the Strategy

Information technology and improvements in global telecommunications are giving international firms more flexibility to shape their global strategies. The configuration, management, and development of systems tend to follow the global strategy chosen (Roche, 1992; Ives and Jarvenpaa, 1991). Figure 16-3 depicts the typical arrangements.

FIGURE 16-3   *Global strategy and systems configurations.*

SYSTEM CONFIGURATION	Strategy			
	Domestic Exporter	Multinational	Franchiser	Transnational
Centralized	X			
Duplicated			X	
Decentralized	x	X	x	
Networked		x		X

The large Xs show the dominant patterns, and the small Xs show the emerging patterns. For instance, domestic exporters rely predominantly on centralized systems, but there is continual pressure and some development of decentralized systems in local marketing regions.

By *systems* we mean the full range of activities involved in building information systems: conception and alignment with the strategic business plan, systems development, and ongoing operation. For the sake of simplicity, we consider four types of systems configuration. *Centralized systems* are those in which systems development and operation occur totally at the domestic home base. *Duplicated systems* are those in which development occurs at the home base but operations are handed over to autonomous units in foreign locations. *Decentralized systems* are those in which each foreign unit designs its own unique solutions and systems. *Networked systems* are those in which systems development and operations occur in an integrated and coordinated fashion across all units.

As can be seen in Figure 16-3, domestic exporters tend to have highly centralized systems in which a single domestic systems development staff develops worldwide applications. Multinationals offer a direct and striking contrast: Here, foreign units devise their own systems solutions based on local needs with few if any applications in common with headquarters (the exceptions being financial reporting and some telecommunications applications). Franchisers have the simplest systems structure: Like the products they sell, franchisers develop a single system usually at the home base and then replicate it around the world. Each unit, no matter where it is located, has identical applications. Last, the most ambitious form of systems development is found in the transnational: Networked systems are those in which there is a solid, singular global environment for developing and operating systems. This usually presupposes a powerful telecommunications backbone, a culture of shared applications development, and a shared management culture that crosses cultural barriers. The networked systems structure is the most visible in financial services where the homogeneity of the product—money and money instruments—seems to overcome cultural barriers.

Reorganizing the Business

How should a firm organize itself for doing business on an international scale? To develop a global company and information systems support structure, a firm needs to follow these principles:

1. Organize value-adding activities along lines of comparative advantage. For instance, marketing/sales functions should be located where they can best be performed, for least cost and maximum impact; likewise with production, finance, human resources, and information systems.

2. Develop and operate systems units at each level of corporate activity—regional, national, and international. To serve local needs, there should be *host country systems units* of some magnitude. *Regional systems units* should handle telecommunications and systems development across national boundaries that take place within major geographic regions (European, Asian, American). *Transnational systems units* should be

established to create the linkages across major regional areas and coordinate the development and operation of international telecommunications and systems development (Roche, 1992).

3. Establish at world headquarters a single office responsible for development of international systems, a global chief information officer (CIO) position.

Many successful companies have devised organizational systems structures along these principles. The success of these companies relies not only on the proper organization of activities, but also on a key ingredient—a management team that can understand the risks and benefits of international systems and that can devise strategies for overcoming the risks. We turn to these management topics next.

16.3 MANAGING GLOBAL SYSTEMS

Table 16-4 lists the principal management problems posed by developing international systems. It is interesting to note that these problems are the chief difficulties managers experience in developing ordinary domestic systems as well! But these are enormously complicated in the international environment.

A Typical Scenario: Disorganization on a Global Scale

Let's look at a common scenario. A traditional multinational consumer-goods company based in the United States and operating in Europe would like to expand into Asian markets and knows that it must develop a transnational strategy and a supportive information systems structure. Like most multinationals it has dispersed production and marketing to regional and national centers while maintaining a world headquarters and strategic management in the United States. Historically, it has allowed each of the subsidiary foreign divisions to develop its own systems. The only centrally coordinated system is financial controls and reporting. The central systems group in the United States focuses only on domestic functions and production.

The result is a hodgepodge of hardware, software, and telecommunications. The e-mail systems between Europe and the United States are incompatible. Each production facility uses a different manufacturing resources planning system (or a different version with local variations) and different marketing, sales, and human resource systems. Hardware and database platforms are wildly different. Communications between different sites are poor, given the high cost and low quality of European intercountry communications. The central systems group at headquarters recently was decimated and dispersed to the U.S. local sites in the hope of serving local needs better and reducing costs.

What do you recommend to the senior management leaders of this company, who now want to pursue a transnational strategy and develop an information systems architecture to support a highly coordinated global systems environment? Consider the problems you

TABLE 16-4 *Management Challenges in Developing Global Systems*

Agreeing on common user requirements
Introducing changes in business processes
Coordinating applications development
Coordinating software releases
Encouraging local users to support global systems

face by reexamining Table 16-4. The foreign divisions will resist efforts to agree on common user requirements; they have never thought about much other than their own units' needs. The systems groups in American local sites, which have been enlarged recently and told to focus on local needs, will not easily accept guidance from anyone recommending a transnational strategy. It will be difficult to convince local managers anywhere in the world that they should change their business processes to align with other units in the world, especially if this might interfere with their local performance. After all, local managers are rewarded in this company for meeting local objectives of their division or plant. Finally, it will be difficult to coordinate development of projects around the world in the absence of a powerful telecommunications network and, therefore, difficult to encourage local users to take on ownership in the systems developed.

Global Systems Strategy

Figure 16-4 lays out the main dimensions of a solution. First, consider that not all systems should be coordinated on a transnational basis; only some core systems are truly worth sharing from a cost and feasibility point of view. **Core systems** are systems that support functions that are absolutely critical to the organization. Other systems should be partially coordinated because they share key elements, but they do not have to be totally common across national boundaries. For such systems, a good deal of local variation is possible and desirable. A final group of systems is peripheral, truly provincial, and needed to suit local requirements only.

DEFINE THE CORE BUSINESS PROCESSES

How do you identify *core systems?* The first step is to define a short list of critical core business processes. Business processes are defined and described in Chapter 2, which you should review. Briefly, business processes are sets of logically related tasks to produce specific business results, such as shipping out correct orders to customers or delivering innovative products to the market. Each business process typically involves many functional areas, communicating and coordinating work, information, and knowledge.

FIGURE 16-4   *Local, regional, and global systems.*

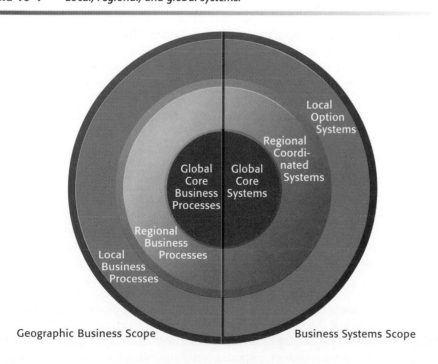

Agency and other coordination costs increase as the firm moves from local option systems toward regional and global systems. However, transaction costs of participating in global markets probably decrease as firms develop global systems. A sensible strategy is to reduce agency costs by developing only a few core global systems that are vital for global operations, leaving other systems in the hands of regional and local units.

Source: Adapted from *Managing Information Technology in Multinational Corporations* by Edward M. Roche, © 1993.

The way to identify these core business processes is to conduct a work-flow analysis. How are customer orders taken, what happens to them once they are taken, who fills the orders, how are they shipped to the customers? What about suppliers? Do they have access to manufacturing and production systems so that supply is automatic? You should be able to identify and set priorities in a short list of 10 business processes that are absolutely critical for the firm.

Next, can you identify centers of excellence for these processes? Is the customer order fulfillment superior in the United States, manufacturing process control superior in Germany, and human resources superior in Asia? You should be able to identify some areas of the company, for some lines of business, where a division or unit stands out in the performance of one or several business functions.

When you understand the business processes of a firm, you can rank-order them. You then can decide which processes should be core applications, centrally coordinated, designed, and implemented around the globe, and which should be regional and local. At the same time, by identifying the critical business processes, the really important ones, you have gone a long way to defining a vision of the future that you should be working toward.

IDENTIFY THE CORE SYSTEMS TO COORDINATE CENTRALLY

By identifying the critical core business processes, you begin to see opportunities for transnational systems. The second strategic step is to conquer the core systems and define these systems as truly transnational. The financial and political costs of defining and implementing transnational systems are extremely high. Therefore, keep the list to an absolute minimum, letting experience be the guide and erring on the side of minimalism. By dividing off a small group of systems as absolutely critical, you divide opposition to a transnational strategy. At the same time, you can appease those who oppose the central worldwide coordination implied by transnational systems by permitting peripheral systems development to progress unabated, with the exception of some technical platform requirements.

CHOOSE AN APPROACH: INCREMENTAL, GRAND DESIGN, EVOLUTIONARY

A third step is to choose an approach. Avoid piecemeal approaches. These surely will fail for lack of visibility, opposition from all who stand to lose from transnational development, and lack of power to convince senior management that the transnational systems are worth it. Likewise, avoid grand design approaches that try to do everything at once. These also tend to fail, because of an inability to focus resources. Nothing gets done properly, and opposition to organizational change is needlessly strengthened because the effort requires huge resources. An alternative approach is to evolve transnational applications from existing applications with a precise and clear vision of the transnational capabilities the organization should have in five years.

MAKE THE BENEFITS CLEAR

What is in it for the company? One of the worst situations to avoid is to build global systems for the sake of building global systems. From the beginning, it is crucial that senior management at headquarters and foreign division managers clearly understand the benefits that will come to the company as well as to individual units. Although each system offers unique benefits to a particular budget, the overall contribution of global systems lies in four areas.

Global systems—truly integrated, distributed, and transnational systems—contribute to superior management and coordination. A simple price tag cannot be put on the value of this contribution, and the benefit will not show up in any capital budgeting model. It is the ability to switch suppliers on a moment's notice from one region to another in a crisis, the ability to move production in response to natural disasters, and the ability to use excess capacity in one region to meet raging demand in another.

A second major contribution is vast improvement in production, operation, and supply and distribution. Imagine a global value chain, with global suppliers and a global distribution network. For the first time, senior managers can locate value-adding activities in regions where they are most economically performed.

Third, global systems mean global customers and global marketing. Fixed costs around the world can be amortized over a much larger customer base. This will unleash new economies of scale at production facilities.

Last, global systems mean the ability to optimize the use of corporate funds over a much larger capital base. This means, for instance, that capital in a surplus region can be moved efficiently to expand production of capital-starved regions; that cash can be managed more effectively within the company and put to use more effectively.

These strategies will not by themselves create global systems. You will have to implement what you strategize. The following two sections describe the challenges in implementing a global strategy.

16.4 TECHNOLOGY ISSUES AND OPPORTUNITIES FOR GLOBAL VALUE CHAINS

Once firms have defined a global business model and systems strategy they must select hardware, software, and networking standards along with key system applications to support global business processes. Many companies today are using teams in other countries to develop and run their software and hardware, so they'll need to address the challenges of managing global technology services as well.

Technology Challenges of Global Systems

Hardware, software, and networking pose special technical challenges in an international setting. One major challenge is finding some way to standardize a global computing platform when there is so much variation from operating unit to operating unit and from country to country. Another major challenge is finding specific software applications that are user friendly and that truly enhance the productivity of international work teams. The major networking challenge is making data flow seamlessly across networks shaped by disparate national standards. Overcoming these challenges requires systems integration and connectivity on a global basis.

COMPUTING PLATFORMS AND SYSTEMS INTEGRATION

The development of a transnational information systems architecture based on the concept of core systems raises questions about how the new core systems will fit in with the existing suite of applications developed around the globe by different divisions, different people, and for different kinds of computing hardware. The goal is to develop global, distributed, and integrated systems to support digital business processes spanning national boundaries. Briefly, these are the same problems faced by any large domestic systems development effort. However, the problems are magnified in an international environment. Just imagine the challenge of integrating systems based on Windows, Linux, Unix, or proprietary operating systems running on IBM, Sun, Hewlett-Packard, and other hardware in many different operating units in many different countries!

Moreover, having all sites use the same hardware and operating system does not guarantee integration. Some central authority in the firm must establish data, as well as other technical standards, with which sites are to comply. For instance, technical accounting terms such as the beginning and end of the fiscal year must be standardized (review the earlier discussion of the cultural challenges to building global businesses), as well as the acceptable interfaces between systems, communication speeds and architectures, and network software.

CONNECTIVITY

Truly integrated global systems must have connectivity—the ability to link together the systems and people of a global firm into a single integrated network just like the phone system but capable of voice, data, and image transmissions. However, integrated global networks are extremely difficult to create (Lai and Chung, 2002). For example, many countries cannot fulfill basic business telecommunications needs such as obtaining reliable circuits, coordinating among different carriers and the regional telecommunications authority, obtaining bills in a common currency standard, and obtaining standard agreements for the level of telecommunications service provided. Table 16-5 lists the major challenges posed by international networks.

Despite moves toward economic unity, Europe remains a hodgepodge of disparate national technical standards and service levels. Although most circuits leased by multinational corporations are fault-free more than 99.8 percent of the time, line quality and service vary widely from the north to the south of Europe. Network service is much more unreliable in southern Europe. Existing European standards for networking and Electronic Data Interchange (EDI) are very industry specific and country specific.

Firms can provide international connectivity by building their own international private network using proprietary standards or by using Internet technology. The firm can put together its own private network based on leased lines from each country's post, telegraph, and telephone (PTT) authorities and services from the major global telecommunications providers. Each country, however, has different restrictions on data exchange, technical standards, and acceptable vendors of equipment. These problems magnify in certain parts of the world.

An increasingly attractive alternative is to create global networks based on the Internet and Internet technology. Companies can create global intranets for internal communication or extranets to exchange information more rapidly with business partners in their supply chains. They can create global networks using virtual private networks (VPNs) from Internet service providers, which provide many features of a private network using the public Internet (see Chapter 8). However, VPNs may not provide the same level of quick and predictable response as private networks, especially during times of the day when Internet traffic is very congested, and they may not be able to support large numbers of remote users.

Moreover, the Internet is not yet a worldwide tool because many countries lack the communications infrastructure for extensive Internet use. Countries face high costs, government control, or government monitoring. Many countries also do not have the speedy and reliable postal and package delivery services that are essential for electronic commerce.

Western Europe faces both high transmission costs and lack of common technology because it is not politically unified and because European telecommunications systems are still in the process of shedding their government monopolies. The lack of an infrastructure and the high costs of installing one are even more widespread in the rest of the world. Only about one-third of the world's households has basic telephone services.

TABLE 16-5 *Problems of International Networks*

Costs and tariffs
Network management
Installation delays
Poor quality of international service
Regulatory constraints
Changing user requirements
Disparate standards
Network capacity

FIGURE 16-5   *Internet population in selected countries.*

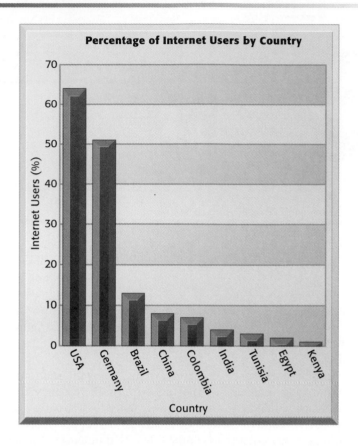

Percentage of Internet Users by Country

The percentage of the total population using the Internet in developing countries is much smaller than in the United States, Canada, and Europe.

Sources: *CIA World Factbook* 2003; *Computer Industry Almanac; and* www.cia.gov, accessed November 9, 2004.

Low penetration of PCs and widespread illiteracy limit demand for Internet service in India and other developing countries (see Figure 16-5). Where an infrastructure exists in less-developed countries, it is often outdated, lacks digital circuits, and has very noisy lines. The purchasing power of most people in developing countries makes access to Internet services very expensive. Many countries monitor transmissions. Governments in China, Singapore, Tunisia, Iran, and Saudi Arabia monitor Internet traffic and block access to Web sites considered morally or politically offensive (McFarquhar, 2004).

Global networking will benefit as wireless networking services described in Chapter 9 fall in price and gain in power. *Communicate and compute any time, anywhere* networks based on satellite systems, digital cell phones, and mobile handheld devices will make it even easier to coordinate work and information in many parts of the globe that cannot be reached by existing ground-based systems.

SOFTWARE

The development of core systems poses unique challenges for application software: How will the old systems interface with the new? Entirely new interfaces must be built and tested if old systems are kept in local areas (which is common). These interfaces can be costly and messy to build. If new software must be created, another challenge is to build software that can be realistically used by multiple business units from different countries given these business units are accustomed to their unique business processes and definitions of data.

Aside from integrating the new with the old systems, there are problems of human interface design and functionality of systems. For instance, to be truly useful for enhancing productivity of a global workforce, software interfaces must be easily understood and mastered quickly. Graphical user interfaces are ideal for this but presuppose a common language—often English. When international systems involve knowledge workers only,

This Web page from the Pearson Prentice Hall Web site for this text was translated into Russian using AltaVista's translation tools. Web sites and software interfaces for global systems may have to be translated into multiple languages to accommodate users in other parts of the world.

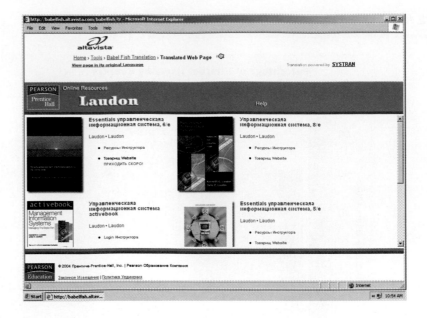

English may be the assumed international standard. But as international systems penetrate deeper into management and clerical groups, a common language may not be assumed and human interfaces must be built to accommodate different languages and even conventions.

What are the most important software applications? Many international systems focus on basic transaction and management reporting systems. Increasingly, firms are turning to supply chain management and enterprise systems to standardize their business processes on a global basis and to create coordinated global supply chains. However, these cross-functional systems are not always compatible with differences in languages, cultural heritages, and business processes in other countries (Martinsons, 2004; Liang et al., 2004; Davison 2002). Company units in countries that are not technically sophisticated may also encounter problems trying to manage the technical complexities of enterprise applications.

Electronic Data Interchange (EDI) systems and supply chain management systems are widely used by manufacturing and distribution firms to connect to suppliers on a global basis. Groupware systems, e-mail, and videoconferencing are especially important worldwide collaboration tools for knowledge- and data-based firms, such as advertising firms, research-based firms in medicine and engineering, and graphics and publishing firms. Internet-based tools will be increasingly employed for such purposes.

The Window on Management describes some of the challenges faced by global companies trying to implement software systems in China. China is a vast country that is modernizing very rapidly, with many growth opportunities for foreign firms. It welcomes advanced technology but it does not always have the appropriate business processes or infrastructure to support leading-edge system applications. Global companies doing business in China are finding that they must spend additional time on training and on helping Chinese companies modernize their business processes.

Internet Connection ——
The Internet Connection for this chapter will direct you to a series of Web sites where you can evaluate offshore software outsourcing services.

Managing Global Software Development

Both global and domestic firms increasingly are managing their hardware and software resources using global teams. Many companies now outsource some of their new systems development work or maintenance of existing systems to external vendors in another country. This practice is called **offshore software outsourcing** and it's becoming wildly popular. According to the Gartner Group consultants, by 2004, 8 out of 10 CIOs had already been instructed to outsource at least part of their firm's technology services offshore.

The reasons for offshore outsourcing are very compelling: A skilled programmer in India or Russia earns about US$10,000 per year, compared to $70,000 per year for a

WINDOW ON MANAGEMENT

GETTING SYSTEMS TO WORK IN CHINA—SLOWLY

China looks like the world's hottest market: It has nearly 1 billion consumers between the ages of 15 and 65, with more disposable income than any other time in the country's history. Economic growth is sizzling. By 2006, it will have more broadband Internet and mobile phone users than any nation on earth. But not so fast. Most of the Chinese population is still poor, and its transportation and technology infrastructures are still undeveloped. Companies seeking to grow their businesses in China must make special efforts to adapt.

General Motors (GM) found this out the hard way when it tried to implement a customer relationship management system using Siebel Systems software at its operational centers in Shanghai. GM is trying to overtake Volkswagen as the leading foreign auto brand in China, hoping to sell 1.3 billion vehicles by 2007. GM sells most of its vehicles in China through its joint venture partner Shanghai Automotive Industry Corporation. The company wanted to use the CRM system to develop a more sophisticated view of Chinese car buyers.

Unfortunately, local dealers had never heard of customer relationship management and had little incentive to provide GM with the sales data it needed to make the system work. To encourage dealer participation, GM built a portal that makes it easier for dealers to order vehicles. To use this portal, dealers must supply the customer data that GM needs. When GM receives a vehicle order, it gets the customer data at the same time.

GM is trying to control costs by replicating key aspects of its global technology platform within Shanghai Automotive. It is using SAP software to coordinate sales and shipping information between its factories and its warehouse and trading unit. GM is helping Shanghai Automotive adopt a consistent PC image of all of GM operations worldwide. GM provided Shanghai Automotive with the specifications, but is relying on its partner's information systems staff for implementation. Shanghai Automotive has the local knowledge and can implement new systems for GM at a much lower cost. "Moreover," says Addons Wu, CIO for GM China, "in China, we put more time into getting consensus. . . . You can order people to do things once or twice but you lose your influence after that."

United Parcel Service (UPS) has been able to profit from China's poor transportation infrastructure and complicated import and export requirements. Multinational companies operating in China are relying on UPS because it can provide integrated shipping and logistics services to deal with these challenges. UPS focuses on serving multinationals and local businesses partly through Sinotrans, its joint venture partner.

UPS is training its own and Sinotrans drivers to make sure they understand English and that they can upload the correct shipping information into UPS systems using tools such as its handheld Driver Information Acquisition and Delivery (DIAD) system. Equally important is the need to train Chinese small businesses to use automated shipping technology.

According to Edward Choi, UPS marketing director for China, "There's a huge group of mom-and-pop shops where business is still done by fax and phone." UPS cannot ignore this market segment because these small businesses supply the big distributors that in turn supply the big multinational companies.

UPS has deployed Chinese language versions of its WorldShip, QuantumVie, and CampusShip shipping-management systems and made them accessible to customers on the Web. UPS installs Web terminals at smaller companies that provide it with a large volume of business. Sometimes UPS even purchases the equipment for these businesses to make sure they will use its systems. UPS also runs seminars and conferences to educate business owners about how the technology works and the benefits it provides.

Making UPS systems work in China requires Chinese businesses to standardize their shipping data. In other countries, business clients might clean up their shipping data to verify addresses and avoid duplicates, but Chinese companies sometimes expect UPS to do this work for them.

Other companies operating in China have also found they must provide extensive training and collaboration to prepare their business partners for effective deployment. MasterCard trains its business partners in e-commerce. China still does not have central credit-rating agencies, but it does have regional credit bureaus that profile the banking and payment histories of residents in metropolitan areas such as Beijing and Guangzhou. MasterCard provides consulting services to regional banks to help them automate processes such as credit scoring and credit reviews.

Although about 60 million Chinese people have MasterCard debit cards, very few actually have true credit cards. MasterCard's goal is to have 100 million Chinese credit card customers by 2009. To reach this goal, MasterCard needs to persuade small merchants to accept credit cards. (It's primarily the large hotels and other businesses catering to international travelers that accept MasterCard in China right now.) Small merchants may need to wait years before they have the telecommunications capability and technology to link to MasterCard's payment network. So, MasterCard offers these small businesses offline transaction processing services. Merchants can send paper receipts to processing centers if they wish to use MasterCard.

Sources: Paul McDougall, "The Place to Be," *Information Week*, April 5, 2004; Bruce Einhorn, "China.Net," *BusinessWeek*, March 15, 2004; Keith Bradsher, "G.M. to Speed Up Expansion in China," *The New York Times*, June 8, 2004; Laurie Sullivan, "Road Work in China," *Information Week*, August 30, 2004; and Elaine Kurtenbach, "GM to Spend $3B in China Over Next 3 Yrs," Associated Press, June 7, 2004.

To Think About: What management, organization, and technology factors explain why global companies must make special efforts to implement their systems in China? Describe some of the steps companies can take to get their systems to work in China.

General Motors partners with Shanghai Automotive Industry Corporation to produce and sell automobiles for the Chinese market. It had to take special steps to implement its information systems in China.

comparable programmer in the United States. The Internet and low-cost communications technology have drastically reduced the expense and difficulty of coordinating the work of global teams in faraway locations. In addition to cost savings, outsourcing provides firms with access to world-class complementary technology assets and skills.

There is a very strong chance that at some point in your career, you'll be working with offshore outsourcers or global teams. Thus, it's very important to understand how offshore resources can best be managed. Not all work can be exported, special managerial and organizational issues must be addressed, and the savings are not as great as simple wage comparisons suggest (Krishna, Sahay, and Walsham, 2004).

Your firm is most likely to benefit from outsourcing if it takes the time to evaluate all the risks and to make sure outsourcing is appropriate for its particular needs. Any company that outsources its applications must thoroughly understand the project, including requirements, method of implementation, source of expected benefits, cost components, and metrics for measuring performance.

Offshore outsourcing can reduce software development costs but companies will not save as much as they initially think. There are hidden costs to offshore outsourcing, and these costs can increase the total cost of ownership (TCO) of offshore-developed software by over 50 percent. Here are the major cost components of offshore software development:

1. *Contract cost.* Most of this cost is for labor required by the project—programmers, software engineers, systems analysts, network specialists, project team managers.

2. *Vendor selection costs.* With any outsourced service, the expense of selecting a service provider can run from 0.2 percent to 2 percent above the cost of the contract. Companies will need to allocate resources for documenting requirements, sending out requests for proposal (RFPs), travel expenses, negotiating contracts, legal fees, and project management. A project leader may be assigned to work full time on this, with others contributing, and these are lost labor costs. The entire process can take three to six months to a year.

3. *Transition management and knowledge transfer costs.* It takes from three months to a full year to completely transfer work to an offshore partner and make sure the vendor thoroughly understands your business. Users should be prepared to spend even more time with the offshore team than an in-house group to make sure the team fully understands their requirements. A certain number of outsourcer staff have to travel to the client company to analyze the client's technology and applications before they can begin the actual work. The client company's systems and specifications have to be thoroughly documented. The offshore employees have to work in parallel with costly in-house employees, and neither can produce very much during the training period. If not included in the outsourcing contract, additional travel costs and visa costs must be figured in. Companies should expect to spend an additional 2 to 3 percent of their contracts on transition costs.

4. *Domestic human resources costs.* If your company has to lay off domestic employees as a result of the offshore outsourcing, you may have to pay laid-off workers severance pay and retention bonuses to keep them working long enough to share their knowledge with their offshore replacements. Layoffs can also adversely impact employee morale and productivity. The firm's staff may resist working with the outsourcer and resign, taking valuable knowledge with them. Layoffs and related costs can add an extra 3 to 5 percent.

5. *Costs of improving software development processes.* If a company doesn't have solid in-house processes for software development, it will take much longer to coordinate work with the vendor.

   Both parties should agree on the processes to be used. If the outsourcer has to follow your standards, make sure the offshore team thoroughly understands them.

   U.S. firms often use rather informal methods for documenting and analyzing software projects. They may need to formalize their software development processes and adopt the methodology used by the offshore vendor. (Many Indian companies use the Capability Maturity Model [CMM] developed by Carnegie-Mellon as their software development methodology, and their clients may need to come up to speed in CMM to work effectively with them.) Ability to write clear specifications is critical as well, and creating a good set of specifications is very time consuming.

   Quality assurance testing also must be beefed-up in an offshore arrangement. There must be a dedicated group of people in the client organization who are always available to develop test plans and review results as they are generated by the offshore team. Companies outsourcing software development to external vendors should anticipate spending an additional 1 to 10 percent on improving software development processes.

6. *Costs of adjusting to cultural differences.* Cultural differences can drain productivity. A seasoned U.S. employee cannot automatically be replaced by an offshore worker. Their values and attitudes are different. American workers tend to feel much more comfortable about speaking up and making suggestions. If something doesn't make sense or does not appear workable, they'll voice concerns. But offshore programmers may keep these feelings to themselves, believing that their aim is to please and this is what the client wants. The work then may take more time and money to complete and require extensive rework. Likewise, an application that makes sense to a U.S. worker such as automating consumer credit cards may be a foreign concept offshore. Lags in productivity can add as much as 20 percent of additional costs to the offshore contract during the first two years. There will probably be a need for more face-to-face interaction than originally anticipated because offshore workers don't interpret things the same way. Productivity lags and adjustments to cultural differences can add an extra 3 to 27 percent to total project costs.

7. *Cost of managing an offshore contract.* Managing the offshore relationship requires additional work—invoicing, auditing, additional telecommunications costs, ensuring work is billed correctly, making sure time is properly recorded. Maintaining security merits special attention. Offshoring partners must agree on common procedures for data security, data recovery, protection of intellectual property rights, network security, and access control. The EU Data Protection Directive could prohibit an outsourcing agreement from transferring personal data to non-EU countries unless both parties satisfy EU data protection standards. Companies should expect to pay an additional 6 to 10 percent on managing the offshore contract.

Figure 16-6 shows best- and worst-case scenarios for the total cost of ownership of an outsourcing project. It shows how much hidden costs can affect the total cost of an outsourcing project. The best case reflects the lowest estimates for additional costs and the worst case reflects the highest estimates for these costs. As you can see, hidden costs will increase the total cost of an outsourcing project by an extra 15 to 57 percent.

Even with these extra costs many firms will benefit from offshore outsourcing if they manage the work well. The total cost of doing the same software work in-house might run to $18 million, so even under the worst-case scenario, the firm would still save about 15 percent.

Although offshore software outsourcing might benefit individual firms, its broader social impact is less clear. Companies that outsource their software work may be eliminating

FIGURE 16-6 *Total cost of outsourcing.*

TOTAL COST OF OFFSHORE OUTSOURCING				
Cost of outsourcing contract			**$10, 000, 000**	
Hidden Costs	Best Case	Additional Cost ($)	Worst Case	Additional Cost ($)
1. Vendor selection	0.2%	20,000	2%	200,000
2. Transition costs	2%	200,000	3%	300,000
3. Layoffs & retention	3%	300,000	5%	500,000
4. Lost productivity/cultural issues	3%	300,000	27%	2,700,000
5. Improving development processes	1%	100,000	10%	1,000,000
6. Managing the contract	6%	600,000	10%	1,000,000
Total additional costs		**1,520,000**		**5,700,000**
	Outstanding Contract ($)	Additional Cost ($)	Total Cost ($)	Additional Cost
Total cost of outsourcing (TCO) best case	10,000,000	1,520,000	11,520,000	15.2%
Total cost of outsourcing (TCO) worst case	10,000,000	5,700,000	15,700,000	57.0%

If a firm spends $10 million on offshore outsourcing contracts, that company will actually spend 15.2 percent in additional costs even under the best-case scenario. In the worst-case scenario, where there is a dramatic drop in productivity along with exceptionally high transition and layoff costs, a firm can expect to pay up to 57 percent in extra costs on top of the $10 million outlay for an offshore contract.

jobs of their own employees or employees of the domestic software industry. As the practice becomes widespread, will countries whose jobs are going overseas wind up with mass unemployment or higher productivity and better jobs? The Window on Organizations looks at both sides of the debate.

16.5 MANAGEMENT OPPORTUNITIES, CHALLENGES, AND SOLUTIONS

When firms operate in many different countries, creating an appropriate organizational and technology infrastructure for conducting international business is very challenging.

Opportunities

Firms have extraordinary opportunities to lower costs through global scale economies by building international systems that enable them to produce as well as sell goods and services in different regions of the world.

Management Challenges

Building and managing global systems raise challenges about finding the right global business strategy, managing change in a multicultural enterprise, and achieving sufficient connectivity and integration.

FINDING THE RIGHT GLOBAL BUSINESS STRATEGY

If a company wishes to operate internationally, it's essential to determine the right global business model. Should some or all of the business be managed on a global basis using a transnational model? How much local autonomy should be allowed? Which way of organizing the business best fits the company's strategic direction? There are some lines of business in which local variations are slight, and the possibility exists to reap large rewards

WINDOW ON ORGANIZATIONS

OFFSHORE OUTSOURCING: GOOD OR BAD?

If you're a U.S. customer of E-Loan, an Internet company offering online loan services, you have a choice about where your loan application will be processed. You could have the application processed in India, or you can request to have the loan processed domestically in the United States. If you choose processing in India, you'll have the results two days earlier than if you had the work done in the United States. E-Loan farmed out loan processing work to Wipro Ltd., a giant Indian outsourcing company, because Indian labor costs are so much lower than in the United States.

E-Loan's contracting loan application processing to India is not an isolated phenomenon. It is part of a swelling movement toward *offshore outsourcing*, a term designating the movement of white-collar jobs abroad. Many other companies, including Delta Air Lines and American Express, have moved their call centers to India or the Philippines. The consulting firm Accenture doubled its staff in India to 10,000. Procter & Gamble has 7,000 workers handling payroll, travel, benefits administration, accounts payable, and invoice processing in offices in Costa Rica, the Philippines, and the United Kingdom. Mindcrest Incorporated of Chicago maintains a staff of 15 in Bombay to provide legal research for companies and law firms.

Call center jobs, telemarketing jobs, financial analysts, and jobs in banking and insurance have been steadily moving offshore. Also threatened are jobs in medical transcription, insurance applications and claims processing, and typesetting, as well as some jobs in accounting and tax preparation. Low-cost telecommunications networks and the Internet make it possible to communicate and exchange documents with people many thousands of miles away as inexpensively as if they were in the next town.

Forrester Research estimated that 3.3 million white-collar jobs will be transferred from the United States abroad by 2015. The impact of offshore outsourcing in the information technology industry could be especially severe: According to the Gartner Group, 1 out of 10 jobs in U.S. computer services may have already shifted to lower-cost countries such as Russia or India.

In mid-July 2003, IBM set off a firestorm when news of its plans to move more white-collar and programming jobs overseas was leaked to the press. Hewlett-Packard has 5,000 Indian employees in research, software development, and customer support. Many nontechnology companies now use offshore programmers for much of their routine programming work.

Critics claim that offshore outsourcing shifts jobs from high-wage countries to low-wage countries, taking jobs away from U.S. workers or pressuring them to take lower pay to remain working. These critics fear that highly trained and educated workers will be ground down by globalization, just as blue-collar workers were in the 1970s and 1980s. Several state legislatures in the United States are considering bills requiring state agencies and contractors to use employees based in the United States, and U.S. job losses to overseas companies became a hot button during the 2004 presidential campaign.

But other experts point out that offshore outsourcers often provide better quality work at lower costs. Firms also have a better chance of long-term survival if they can keep their prices competitive. Companies can pass these saving from outsourcing on to consumers or use them to expand the business and create new jobs that provide more value than those replaced. A study by the McKinsey Global Institute estimated that every dollar of costs moved from the U.S. to offshore yields a benefit of $1.12 to $1.14 to the U.S. economy.

Another study by economics consulting firm Global Insight commissioned by the pro-outsourcing Information Technology Association of America found that the productivity generated by U.S. companies sending computer services work abroad boosted domestic employment by 90,000 jobs in 2003. This study claimed that outsourcing created twice as many U.S. jobs as it displaced and would lead, by 2008, to the creation of 337,000 new jobs in construction, education, health care, and financial services.

The kinds of jobs that are moving overseas are those that can be most easily reduced to a series of rules and performed overseas by another person—or perhaps by a computer. Jobs that will most likely stay in the United States or that will be newly created in the next decade are those that require human contact or complex analytical skills. In the information systems field, jobs that will remain in the United States are those for high-level software designers and people who can apply technology to solve problems in specific businesses such as banking, retailing, or manufacturing. Most at risk are software jobs that involve straightforward coding of software programs, where technical specifications can be handed off to a programmer. These are exactly the technology jobs where wages have fallen since 2002.

Sources: David Wessel, "The Future of Jobs: New Ones Arise, Wage Gap Widens," *Wall Street Journal*, April 2, 2004; Michael Schroeder, "Outsourcing May Create U.S. Jobs," *Wall Street Journal*, March 30, 2004; Kris Maher, "Next on the Outsourcing List," *Wall Street Journal*, March 23, 2004; Stephen Baker and Manjeet Kripalani, "Software: Will Outsourcing Hurt America's Supremacy?" *BusinessWeek*, March 1, 2004; Jesse Drucker and Ken Brown, "Press 1 for Delhi, 2 for Dallas," *Wall Street Journal*, March 9, 2004; Reuters, "Offshore Outsourcing Set to Hit U.S. Job Market," www.itweb.co.za, accessed July 30, 2003; Stephanie Armour and Michelle Kessler, "USA's New Money-Saving Export: White-Collar Jobs," *USA Today*, August 9, 2003; and Bob Evans, "Business Technology: Offshore Outsourcing: A Means to an End," *InformationWeek*, July 28, 2003.

To Think About: Does offshore outsourcing create an ethical dilemma? Why or why not?

by organizing globally. It is likely that firms with many lines of business will have to maintain a mixed organizational structure.

DIFFICULTIES OF MANAGING CHANGE IN A MULTICULTURAL FIRM

Although engineering change in a single corporation in a single nation can be difficult, costly, and long term, bringing about significant change in very large scale global corporations can be daunting. Cultural, political, and language diversity magnifies differences in organizational culture and business processes when companies operate internationally in various countries. These differences create barriers to the development of global information systems that transcend national boundaries.

DIFFICULTIES OF ACHIEVING GLOBAL CONNECTIVITY AND INTEGRATION

Choices of technology, platforms, networks, hardware, and software are the final elements in building transnational information systems infrastructures. The Internet and Internet technology will increasingly be used to provide global connectivity and to serve as a foundation for global systems, but many companies will still need proprietary systems for certain functions, and therefore international standards. Even with the proper organizational structure and appropriate management choices, it is still possible to stumble over technological issues.

Solution Guidelines

We now can reconsider how to handle the most vexing problems facing managers developing the global information systems architectures that were described in Table 16-4.

AGREEING ON COMMON USER REQUIREMENTS

Establishing a short list of the core business processes and core support systems will begin a process of rational comparison across the many divisions of the company, develop a common language for discussing the business, and naturally lead to an understanding of common elements (as well as the unique qualities that must remain local).

INTRODUCING CHANGES IN BUSINESS PROCESSES

Your success as a change agent will depend on your legitimacy, your actual raw power, and your ability to involve users in the change design process. **Legitimacy** is defined as the extent to which your authority is accepted on grounds of competence, vision, or other qualities. The selection of a viable change strategy, which we have defined as evolutionary but with a vision, should assist you in convincing others that change is feasible and desirable. Involving people in change, assuring them that change is in the best interests of the company and their local units, is a key tactic.

COORDINATING APPLICATIONS DEVELOPMENT

Choice of change strategy is critical for this problem. At the global level there is far too much complexity to attempt a grand design strategy of change. It is far easier to coordinate change by making small incremental steps toward a larger vision. Imagine a five-year plan of action rather than a two-year plan of action, and reduce the set of transnational systems to a bare minimum to reduce coordination costs.

COORDINATING SOFTWARE RELEASES

Firms can institute procedures to ensure that all operating units convert to new software updates at the same time so that everyone's software is compatible.

ENCOURAGING LOCAL USERS TO SUPPORT GLOBAL SYSTEMS

The key to this problem is to involve users in the creation of the design without giving up control over the development of the project to parochial interests. Recruiting a wide range of local individuals to transnational centers of excellence helps send the message that all significant groups are involved in the design and will have an influence. These centers draw heavily from local national units, are based on multinational teams, and must report to worldwide management—their first line of responsibility is to the core applications.

The overall tactic for dealing with resistant local units in a transnational company is cooptation. **Cooptation** is defined as bringing the opposition into the process of designing and implementing the solution without giving up control over the direction and nature of the change. As much as possible, raw power should be avoided. Minimally, however, local units must agree on a short list of transnational systems, and raw power may be required to solidify the idea that transnational systems of some sort are truly required.

MAKE IT YOUR BUSINESS

Finance and Accounting

The most widespread use of international systems is to enable the flow of funds between corporate headquarters and operating units and to facilitate purchases in different countries. The core systems that firms operating internationally are most likely to build are financial reporting. You can find examples of finance and accounting applications on pages 597–598.

Human Resources

Language and cultural differences can affect the successful implementation and use of international systems. Human resources specialists will need to advise system builders on these issues and help ensure that employees receive the proper training and motivation to use international system tools. Human resources systems may be used to identify employees with the requisite language and other skills to serve as leaders in international systems projects or to work on assignments outside of their home country. You can find examples of human resources applications on pages 591 and 597–598.

Manufacturing and Production

Disparate local manufacturing and production systems make it difficult for companies to manage their inventories and supply chains as global entities. Companies aspiring to some form of global business organization are installing standard supply chain management software or enterprise software for this purpose. Extranets can also be used to develop private industrial networks for this purpose. You can find examples of manufacturing and production applications on page 571.

Sales and Marketing

Systems for selling and marketing internationally have mushroomed because of the low cost of doing business on the Web and the Internet's global reach. Companies of all sizes can set up Web sites to buy and sell on the world market instead of being limited to local markets. However, large-scale global e-commerce initiatives may require country-specific Web sites and large expenditures for customization and ongoing management. You can find examples of sales and marketing applications on pages 571 and 587.

Summary

1. *Identify the major factors driving the internationalization of business.*

    There are general cultural factors and specific business factors to consider. The growth of cheap international communication and transportation has created a world culture with stable expectations or norms. Political stability and a growing global knowledge base that is widely shared contribute also to the world culture. These general factors create the conditions for global markets, global production, coordination, distribution, and global economies of scale.

2. *Compare strategies for developing global businesses.*

    There are four basic international strategies: domestic exporter, multinational, franchiser, and transnational. In a transnational strategy, all factors of production are coordinated on a global scale. However, the choice of strategy is a function of the type of business and product.

3. *Demonstrate how information systems can support different global business strategies.*

    There is a connection between firm strategy and information systems design. Transnational firms must develop networked system configurations and permit considerable decentralization of development and operations. Franchisers almost always duplicate systems across many countries and use centralized financial controls. Multinationals typically rely on decentralized independence among foreign units with some movement toward development of networks. Domestic exporters typically are centralized in domestic headquarters with some decentralized operations permitted.

4. *Evaluate the issues and technical alternatives to be considered when developing international information systems.*

Implementing a global system requires an implementation strategy that considers both business design and technology platforms. Typically, global systems have evolved without a conscious plan. The remedy is to define a small subset of core business processes and focus on building systems that could support these processes. Tactically, you will have to co-opt widely dispersed foreign units to participate in the development and operation of these systems, being careful to maintain overall control.

The main hardware and telecommunications issues are systems integration and connectivity. The choices for integration are to go either with a proprietary architecture or with open systems technology. Global networks are extremely difficult to build and operate. Firms can build their own global networks or they can create global networks based on the Internet (intranets or virtual private networks). The main software issue concerns building interfaces to existing systems and selecting applications that can work with multiple cultural, language, and organizational frameworks.

5. *Identify the challenges posed by global information systems and management solutions.*

Global information systems pose challenges because cultural, political, and language diversity magnifies differences in organizational culture and business processes and encourages proliferation of disparate local information systems that are difficult to integrate. Businesses may have to struggle to find the right global business strategy. Management solutions include identifying a common set of user requirements for the entire global enterprise; coordinating applications development and software releases; and using legitimacy and cooptation to enlist user support in the change process.

Key Terms

Business driver, 572
Cooptation, 593
Core systems, 581
Domestic exporter, 578
Franchisers, 578

Global culture, 574
International information systems architecture, 572
Legitimacy, 592
Multinational, 578

Offshore software outsourcing, 586
Particularism, 575
Transborder data flow, 576
Transnational, 578

Review Questions

1. *What are the five major factors to consider when building an international information systems architecture?*

2. *Describe the five general cultural factors leading toward growth in global business and the four specific business factors. Describe the interconnection among these factors.*

3. *What is meant by a global culture?*

4. *What are the major challenges to the development of global systems?*

5. *Why have firms not planned for the development of international systems?*

6. *Describe the four main strategies for global business and organizational structure.*

7. *Describe the four different system configurations that can be used to support different global strategies.*

8. *What are the major management issues in developing international systems?*

9. *What are three principles to follow when organizing the firm for global business?*

10. *What are three steps of a management strategy for developing and implementing global systems?*

11. *What is meant by cooptation, and how can it be used in building global systems?*

12. *Describe the main technical issues facing global systems.*

13. *What is offshore software outsourcing? What challenges does it pose? What are the cost components of offshore software development?*

14. *What are the challenges posed by global systems? How can these challenges be addressed?*

Discussion Questions

1. *If you were a manager in a company that operates in many countries, what criteria would you use to determine whether an application should be developed as a global application or as a local application?*

2. *Describe ways the Internet can be used in international information systems.*

Application Software Exercise:
Database and Web Page Development Tool Exercise: Building a Job Database and Web Page
for an International Consulting Firm

KTP Consulting operates in various locations around the world. KTP specializes in designing, developing, and implementing enterprise systems for medium- to large-size companies. KTP offers its employees opportunities to travel, live, and work in various locations throughout the United States, Europe, and Asia. The firm's human resources department has a simple database that enables its staff to track job vacancies. When an employee is interested in relocating, she or he contacts the human resources department for a list of KTP job vacancies. KTP also posts its employment opportunities on the company Web site.

What type of data should be included in the KTP job vacancies database? What information should not be included in this database? Based on your answers to these questions, build a job vacancies database for KTP. Populate the database with at least 20 records. You should also build a simple Web page that incorporates job vacancy data from your newly created database. Submit a copy of the KTP database and Web page to your professor.

Expanding International Sales

Software requirements: Web browser software
Word processing software
Electronic presentation software (optional)

Management would like to expand international sales for Dirt Bikes. You have been asked to analyze opportunities for global business expansion of the company, using the Web to find the information you need. Prepare a report for management that answers the following questions:

1. Which countries would provide the best markets for Dirt Bikes's products? Your analysis should consider factors such as the following: In which countries are dirt bikes popular? What is the per capita income of these countries?

2. How could Dirt Bikes use the Web to increase international sales? What features should it place on its Web site to attract buyers from the countries it targets?

3. (Optional) If possible, use electronic presentation software to summarize your findings for management.

Electronic Business Project: Conducting International Marketing and Pricing Research

You are in charge of marketing for a U.S. manufacturer of office furniture that has decided to enter the international market. You have been given the name of Sorin SRL, a major Italian office furniture retailer, but your source had no other information. You want to test the market by contacting this firm to offer it a specific desk chair that you have to sell at about $125. Using the Web, locate the information needed to contact this firm and to find out how many European euros you would need to get for the chair in the current market. One source for locating European companies is the

Europages Business Directory (www.europages.com). In addition, consider using the Universal Currency Converter Web site (www.xe.net/ucc/), which determines the value of one currency expressed in other currencies. Obtain both the information needed to contact the firm and the price of your chair in their local currency. Then locate and obtain customs and legal restrictions on the products you will export from the United States and import into Italy. Finally, locate a company that will represent you as a customs agent and gather information on shipping costs.

Group Project: Identifying Information Technology for Global Business Strategies

With a group of students, identify an area of information technology and explore how this technology might be useful for supporting global business strategies. For instance, you might choose an area such as digital telecommunications (e.g., e-mail, wireless communications, value-added networks), enterprise systems, collaborative work group software, or the Internet. It will be necessary to choose a business scenario to discuss the technology. You might choose, for instance, an automobile parts franchise or a clothing franchise, such as the Limited Express, as example businesses. Which applications would you make global, which core business processes would you choose, and how would the technology be helpful? If possible, use electronic presentation software to present your findings to the class.

CASE STUDY
Celanese Recentralizes with a New Enterprise System

At the end of 2003, Celanese AG, a global chemical company, had about $5 billion in annual sales and about 9,500 employees. Celanese is headquartered in Kronberg, Germany, and has 30 facilities in 11 countries on 6 continents, although most of its facilities are located in North America. Celanese had been part of Hoechst AG pharmaceuticals since 1979. However, it was spun off in 1999 when Hoechst merged with Rhône-Poulenc to create a new pharmaceutical company, Aventis.

Celanese is a rather complex multinational organization with five main businesses: Celanese Chemicals, consisting of Acetyl Products, which processes natural gas and ethylene used in products for manufacturing industries, and Chemical Intermediates, which produces specialty chemicals for paints, coatings, agrochemicals, and textiles; Celanese Acetate Products, which manufactures cellulose acetate filament and tow; Ticona Technical Polymers, which makes chemical products for the electronics, telecommunications, automotive, and medical industries; Performance Products, which produces ingredients for food products, such as the Nutrinova sweetener used in Pepsi One; and Celanese Ventures, specializing in research and development, including artificial fibers and alternative energy.

Celanese, like many large corporations, had focused on decentralization during the 1980s and 1990s, and, as a result, its corporate headquarters operated largely like a holding company. Its highly independent units implemented enterprise systems from SAP, the leading enterprise software company. Each unit had its own separate system, and each felt free to modify the SAP package software to meet its own requirements. To complicate matters even further, Celanese had grown during those 20 years partly by purchasing smaller companies, many of which already had their own enterprise systems. Altogether,

Celanese enterprise systems totaled 13 in 2000 (reduced to 10 by 2002 when Celanese sold one of its business units) and were in five different computer centers.

By 2000, as the U.S. and world economies began weakening, many companies began looking for ways to reduce their expenses in the face of declining sales. Centralizing these companies became popular as a way to reduce costs once the expenses of centralization had been absorbed. This approach was very popular in the chemical industry, partly because its raw materials costs were rising at the same time that sales were dropping. When Celanese was spun off, its management set a formidable goal of doubling its sales in five years. To enable the company to achieve that goal, some of the increased sales would have to come from acquisitions, and that meant its stock price would have to go higher for it to afford such purchases.

How could centralization help Celanese reduce its costs? There were numerous ways. The most obvious one was to make the various units of Celanese use the same version of SAP. Versions of the software used by Celanese units varied from version 3.1 to version 4.6. It was expensive to obtain so many different versions. However, the expense was even higher when so many of the IT staff had first to learn and then to support all of these versions at different Celanese units. Having only one version running on one computer for the whole company would mean far smaller IT staffs within the various units.

But there also were other less obvious costs that could be significantly reduced. Under the decentralized approach, for corporate managers to collect all the financial information they needed was not only time consuming, and, therefore, expensive, but also it increased the likelihood of errors in that data. In addition, different units used different names for what were really the same

pieces of data. For example, *price* in one system might be *cost* or *purchase price* in another. Furthermore, many of the units often failed to take advantage of some of the useful new features of their SAP systems. For example, one new function in SAP in 2003 was its supply chain event management (SCEM), an ERP component that enables a company to better forecast its supply needs and so better manage its supply chain while reducing its inventory costs.

The problem in a decentralized environment is that some units adopt that feature, whereas others will not. And some that do adopt it might use it to benefit their own needs rather than using it to benefit the organization as a whole. Another hidden cost of separate ERP systems was that they prevented the company from obtaining a single companywide view of customers that might indicate opportunities to cross-sell and up-sell customers between business units.

In late 1999, when Hoechst spun off Celanese, the company management initiated a new project to recentralize the company, which it named One Celanese. They then began searching for a new global CIO who could reduce the company's costs by integrating many of its information systems. Karl Wachs was hired and given a simple instruction—cut costs. Wachs quickly decided to roll up all the units' disparate enterprise systems into a single system, and he named the project OneSAP. With the aid of 70 people, Wachs began the process of actually initiating the project, saying, "This is not a four-week decision cycle. It should take a year for approval." In fact, it took 11 months. The project was not cheap. According to Wachs, at the height of the project, it was costing Celanese between $100,000 and $200,000 a day. One of the project managers said the overall cost would be about $60 million. However, Celanese's management concluded OneSAP would pay for itself in two years once the project was completed.

How did Wachs and the Celanese information systems unit go about rolling up the various SAP systems into one? The technical aspects—installing new SAP software so that the various units could begin to use it—were far from the most difficult. Much greater challenges were posed by the organizational cultures of the disparate Celanese operating units. Employees were comfortable using enterprise systems, and they were not necessarily ready to change their way of working to fit a standard set of business processes. The various units were intensely independent; they were not used to thinking of Celanese first but rather of the needs of their own units. According to the employees' old way of thinking, if something went wrong with a transaction that was not in their own unit, it was someone else's responsibility. That thinking had to change.

Moreover, in the past the Celanese culture had been one of building consensus, an approach that cannot work in a situation where people are told to make changes they do not want to make. "If we tolerate business units explaining why their outputs are different so that they don't have to change their inputs," Wachs concluded, "then we have lost. The mistake of the past was trying to adapt software to the business." Now the company would have to adapt the business to the software. To accomplish these cultural changes required a lot of explanation, a lot of educa-

tion, and also clear and absolute orders from the very top.

The project was divided into seven tracks, including finance, supply chain management, manufacturing, "order-to-cash," business intelligence reporting, technology, and change management. Each track had several functional stakeholders who were given the responsibility for that track's progress. Each track also had one person responsible for working at a higher level. For example, the finance track had one person assigned to work with the chief financial officer and the controllers "to design the business processes for that organization," as Wachs explained. The project leadership also demanded that Celanese employees follow the six sigma philosophy of "total quality management," which meant that every person was responsible for quality.

The project certainly had its problems. The U.S. and German human resources systems (and several other small systems) were allowed to keep their own SAP systems for "legitimate business reasons." However, by the end of the project, 7 out of 10 of the old SAP systems, representing 90 percent of the business, were shut off. When OneSAP was ready to install the SCEM software, Wachs learned that SAP did not have the software ready. Another problem was that in early 2003 Celanese spent $150 million to purchase the emulsion businesses from Clariant, a very old Basle, Switzerland, chemistry company. That meant that

the Clariant unit had to be included in OneSAP. Another problem the project team had to face was cleaning and integrating the data from the various existing SAP systems into OneSAP so the new system is reliable and accurate.

Sources: www.celanese.com, accessed June 4, 2004; Rick Mullin, "The Age of Interoperability," www.e-chemmerce.com, accessed March 28, 2003; Scott Berinato, "A Day in the Life of Celanese's Big ERP Rollup," *CIO Magazine*, January 15, 2003; Celanese, "1000 Days in Five (Not So) Easy Steps," *CIO Magazine*, January 15, 2003; Celanese Project Team, "The Top Eight Risks to the OneSAP Project," *CIO Magazine*, January 15, 2003; Celanese, "A Brief Tale of a Long History," *CIO Magazine*, January 15, 2003; and OSISoft Case Study, "Celanese Corporation, "www.osisoft.com, accessed April 1, 2003.

CASE STUDY QUESTIONS

1. Analyze Celanese using the competitive forces and value chain models.

2. How important is Celanese's centralized enterprise system to its business strategy? Why? What is its business value to the company?

3. What management, organization, and technology challenges did Celanese face as it tried to implement OneSAP? Which were the most difficult?

4. How successful was Celanese in meeting these challenges? What problems did it solve? How? Which problems remained unsolved?

PART FOUR PROJECT

Redesigning Business Processes for Healthlite Yogurt Company

Healthlite Yogurt Company, a U.S. market leader in yogurt and related health products, is experiencing sharp growing pains. Healthlite's sales have tripled over the past five years. However, new local competitors, offering fast delivery from local production centers and lower prices, are challenging Healthlite for retail shelf space with a bevy of new products. Healthlite needs to justify its share of shelf space to grocers and is seeking additional shelf space for its new yogurt-based products such as frozen desserts and low-fat salad dressings. Yogurt has a very short shelf life measured in days, and must be moved very quickly.

Healthlite's corporate headquarters is in Danbury, Connecticut. Corporate headquarters has a central mainframe computer that maintains most of the major business databases. All production takes place in processing plants that are located in New Jersey, Massachusetts, Tennessee, Illinois, Colorado, Washington, and California. Each processing plant has its own minicomputer, which is connected to the corporate mainframe. Customer credit verification is maintained at corporate headquarters, where customer master files are maintained and order verification or rejection is determined. Once processed centrally, order data are then fed to the appropriate local processing plant minicomputer.

Healthlite has 20 sales regions, each with approximately 30 sales representatives and a regional sales manager. Healthlite has a 12-person marketing group at corporate headquarters. Each salesperson is able to store and retrieve data for assigned customer accounts using a terminal in the regional office linked to the corporate mainframe. Reports for individual salespeople (printouts of orders, rejection notices, customer account inquiries, etc.) and for sales offices are printed in the regional offices and mailed to them.

Sometimes, the only way to obtain up-to-date sales data is for managers to make telephone calls to subordinates and then piece the information together. Data about sales and advertising expenses, promotional campaigns, and customer shelf space devoted to Healthlite products are maintained manually at the regional offices. The central computer contains only consolidated, company-wide files for customer account data and order and billing data.

The existing order processing system requires sales representatives to write up hard-copy tickets to place orders through the mail or by fax. Each ticket lists the amount and kind of product ordered by the customer account. Approximately 20 workers at Healthlite corporate headquarters open, sort, and enter 500,000 order tickets per week into the system. Frequently orders are delayed when the fax machines break down. This order information is transmitted every evening from the mainframe to a minicomputer at each of Healthlite's processing sites. This daily order specifies the total yogurt and yogurt product demand for each processing center. The processing center then produces the amount and type of yogurt and yogurt-related products ordered and ships the orders out. Shipping managers at the processing centers assign the shipments to various transportation carriers, who deliver the product to receiving warehouses located in the regions.

A year ago, growth in new products and sales had reached a point where the firm was choking on paper. For each order, a salesperson filled out at least two forms per account. Some sales representatives have more than 80 customers. As it became bogged down in paper, Healthlite saw increased delays in the processing of its orders. Since yogurt is a fresh food product, it could not be held long in inventory. Yet Healthlite had trouble shipping the right goods to the right places in time. It was taking between 4 and 14 days to process and ship out an order, depending on mail delivery times. Healthlite also found accounting discrepancies of $1.5 million annually between the sales force and headquarters.

Communication between sales managers and sales representatives has been primarily through the mail or by telephone. For example, regional sales managers have to send representatives letters with announcements of promotional campaigns or pricing discounts. Sales representatives have to write up their monthly reports of sales calls and then mail this information to regional headquarters.

Healthlite is considering new information system solutions. First of all, the firm would like to solve the current order entry crisis and develop immediately a new order processing system. Management would also like to make better use of information systems to support sales and marketing activities and to take advantage of new Web-based information technologies. In particular, management wants a sales-oriented Web site to help market the products but is unsure how this will fit into the sales effort. In conjunction, management wants to know how these new technologies can assist the local groceries and large chains who sell the product to the actual consumer.

Senior management is looking for a modest reduction in employee head count as new, more effective systems come online to help pay for the investment in new systems. While senior management wants the company to deploy contemporary systems, they do not want to experiment with new technologies and are only comfortable using technology that has proven itself in real-world applications.

Sales and Marketing Information Systems: Background

Sales orders must be processed and related to production and inventory. Sales of products in existing markets must be monitored and new products must be developed for new markets. Firms need sales and marketing information in order to do product planning, make pricing decisions, devise advertising and other promotional campaigns, and forecast market potential for new and existing products. They must also monitor the efficiency of the distribution of their products and services. The sales function of a typical business captures and processes customer orders and produces invoices for customers and data for inventory and production. A typical invoice is illustrated here:

Healthlite Yogurt Inc.
Customer:
   Highview Supermarket
   223 Highland Avenue
   Ossining, New York 10562
Order Number: 679940
Customer Number: #00395
Date: 02/15/05

Quantity	SKU#	Description	Unit Price	Amount
100	V3392	8 oz Vanilla	.44	44.00
50	S4456	8 oz Strawberry	.44	22.00
65	L4492	8 oz Lemon	.44	28.60
Shipping:				10.00
Total Invoice:				$104.60

Data from order entry are also used by a firm's accounts receivable system and by the firm's inventory and production systems. The production planning system, for instance, builds its daily production plans based on the prior day's sales. The number and type of product sold will determine how many units to produce and when.

Sales managers need information to plan and monitor the performance of the sales force. Management also needs information on the performance of specific products, product lines, or brands. Price, revenue, cost, and growth information can be used for pricing decisions, for evaluating the performance of current products, and for predicting the performance of future products.

From basic sales and invoice data, a firm can produce a variety of reports with valuable information to guide sales and marketing work. For weekly, monthly, or annual time periods, information can be gathered on which outlets order the most, on what the average order amount is, on which

products move slowest and fastest, on which salespersons sell the most and least, on which geographic areas purchase the most of a given product, and on how current sales of a product compare to last year's product.

The Assignment

Either alone, or with a group of three or four of your classmates, develop a proposal for redesigning Healthlite's business processes for sales, marketing, and order processing that would make the company more competitive. Your report should include the following:

- An overview of the organization—its structure, products, and major business processes for sales, marketing, and order processing.

- An analysis of Healthlite's problems: What are Healthlite's problems? How are these problems related to existing business processes and systems? What management, organization, and technology factors contributed to these problems?

- An overall management plan for improving Healthlite's business and system situation. This would include a list of objectives, a time frame, major milestones, and an assessment of the costs and benefits of implementing this plan.

- Identification of the major changes in business processes required to achieve your plan.

- Identification of the major new technology components of your plan that are required to support the new business processes. If your solution requires a new system or set of systems, describe the functions of these systems, what pieces of information these systems should contain, and how this information should be captured, organized, and stored.

- A sample data entry screen or report for one of the new systems, if proposed.

- A description of the steps you would take as a manager to handle the conversion from the old system to the new.

- Quality assurance measures.

Your report should also describe the organizational impact of your solution. Consider human interface issues, the impact on jobs and interest groups, and any risks associated with implementing your solution. How will you implement your solution to take these issues into account?

It is important to establish the scope of the system project. It should be limited to order processing and related sales and marketing business processes. You do not have to redesign Healthlite's manufacturing, accounts receivable, distribution, or inventory control systems for this exercise.

CASE STUDY 1:

The Selection of the IT Platform: Enterprise System Implementation in the NZ Health Board

Maha Shakir, Zayed University, United Arab Emirates
Dennis Viehland, Massey University, New Zealand

Executive Summary

The Health Board[1] is one of the largest public health care providers in New Zealand (NZ). In early 1999, a supply chain optimization review recommended an enterprise system (ES) implementation to provide better control and reporting of organizational finances. The focus of this case is the IT platform decision made in conjunction with the ES implementation process. This decision was thoroughly considered by all Health Board stakeholders and the final choice was made in alignment with the Board's strategic IT policy. Nevertheless, initial testing two months prior to go-live revealed major performance problems with the new system. The case documents the events that led up to the selection of the original IT platform and the challenges the project team faced in deciding what to do when the platform did not meet contractual specifications.

Keywords: IS project risk management; IT decision process; IT platform; MIS implementation

ORGANIZATIONAL BACKGROUND

The Health Board is a non-profit public organization that is one of New Zealand's (NZ) largest providers of public hospital and health services. The Board has approximately two million patient contacts annually and provides regional services for 30% of NZ's population. The organization is structured around seven business units that include four specialist teaching hospitals and other facilities offering community health services, mental health services, and clinical support services. The Health Board vision focuses on patients' needs.

Being a non-profit organization, surplus funds are allocated to supporting patients, research, and education. Table 1 provides the organization's profile.

Health funding in NZ is disseminated through 21 district health boards (DHBs). Each DHB is responsible for improving, promoting, and protecting the health of the population it serves. For their catchment area, each DHB is delegated the responsibility for making decisions on the mix, the level, and the quality of the health services that are publicly funded. They are also responsible for entering into agreements with providers for health service delivery. DHB decisions are made on the basis of local needs, within national guidelines. Funding is based on the size and characteristics of the population of the district each DHB serves; however, a few nationally funded services still exist.

The Health Board is one of three DHBs in the same region that share a vision to promote close cooperation for the provision of health services. The Board is made up of 11 members: seven elected and four appointed. All Board members report directly to the Minister of Health.

SETTING THE STAGE

In 1999, ConsultCo, a big-five consultancy firm, was engaged to assess the strengths and weaknesses of the supply chain management function at the Health Board, with a view to provide recommendations for the improvement of that function. The product of that engagement was a supply chain optimization (SCO) review report. The SCO review identified problems in business operations and suggested a combination of an organizational restructure, business process reengineering (BPR), and ES (ERP) implementation to accomplish the change program.

The core financial modules of Oracle 10.7 ERP system had been implemented in 1997 and were operational at the time the SCO review was conducted. However, that implementation was heavily customized and could not provide for

TABLE 1   *Organization Profile*

Categories	Health Board Profile
Core business	The provision of public hospital and health services
Type of organization	Non-profit organization
Ownership	Public organization
Business units	Four specialist teaching hospitals and facilities offering community health services, mental health services, and clinical support services
Mission statement (1999–2000)	"The Health Board will provide New Zealand's finest comprehensive health service through excellence and innovation in patient care, education, research, and technology" (Health Board Annual Report, 1999–2000).
Customers	Patients (two million patient contacts annually)
Reach	Regional (within NZ)
Organization size	8,500 employees; $600 million budget for the year 2000/2001

realizing the new strategic vision that aimed to "standardize, consolidate, and integrate services ... and control finances" (Strategic Plan for the Health Board 2002–2007).

In addition to the recommendation of the SCO review, in early 1999 the Health Board was informed that Oracle 10.7 financials was going to be de-supported by Oracle by the end of 2000, leading to the realization that a major application upgrade was urgently needed. As a result, and in partnership with ConsultCo, an ES business case was developed with a view to rectify these problems. The business case included eight key objectives that were linked to the Health Board's strategic plan. These are summarized in Table 2.

Despite the problems the SCO review had identified with the Oracle 10.7 system, there was an agreement that the new implementation would still be an Oracle ES. The Health Board would have had to write off the huge investment in the Oracle 10.7 application if it chose to change to a different vendor. Therefore, the business case for the new system was written with a focus on an Oracle upgrade and implementation that was financially justifiable.

Organizational restructuring started by the end of 1999, with new job descriptions being written and advertised to fulfill the new organizational design. All new roles had a focus on system implementation experience in preparation for a re-implementation of ERP applications to support the change program. Table 3 presents a chronology of ES implementation events.

The final business case the Board considered in July 2000 compared two upgrade alternatives. These were an upgrade from Oracle 10.7 to either Oracle 11 or Oracle 11i ERP

TABLE 2   *ES Project Objectives*

Objective	Descriptions
1	To achieve the savings identified in the Health Board strategic business plan.
2	To account for savings through an appropriate standard costing mechanism within inventory.
3	To have reporting systems that enable management by exception and the control of rogue expenditure.
4	To implement procurement through a standard requisition process with a catalogue environment.
5	To implement processes for the delegation of authority and risk management of the procurement process.
6	To have a platform in place which: • positions the Health Board to enter into external shared services with other local health care providers • facilitates internal interconnectivity, which allows for the consolidation of accounts payable, inventory management, internal logistics, and enables external supply chain connectivity.
7	To implement the "Health Board Way" throughout the supply chain process, with a particular focus on standardization of processes, integration of systems, and consolidation of service.
8	To act as a catalyst for the change in business processes and work practices.

Note: Adapted from the Health Board ERP System Business Case (June 2000, p. 25)

TABLE 3   *Main ES Implementation Events (1997–2000)*

Date	Event(s)
1997	- Implementation of the heavily customized financial modules of Oracle 10.7 ES.
Early 1999	- Oracle users were informed that the Oracle 10.7 ES would be de-supported by the end of 2000. An upgrade was suggested to address the loss of future support.
Mid-1999	- The newly appointed CFO recruited a BPR Manager to project manage and review both the supply chain and the finance functions in partnership with ConsultCo, a big-five consultancy firm. The output of that partnership was the supply chain optimization (SCO) review.
End of 1999	- The ES business case was developed to resolve the majority of the SCO review recommendations, including a major system upgrade, with the CFO being the ES project sponsor.
March 2000	- In conjunction with the initiation of the ES project, new organizational roles were established, advertised, and filled by March 2000. All new recruits received training on the Oracle 10.7 applications.
March–May 2000	- A request for proposals for implementation consultancy services was issued. Bids were received and evaluated, with the winning bid going to ConsultCo.
June 2000	- The new version of the Internet-enabled Oracle 11i application was released.
July 2000	- The ES business case was submitted to the Board and approved.
August 2000	- The ES implementation project started, including core financials, fixed assets, and procurement modules.

applications. While Oracle 11 was in operation since 1999, Oracle 11i was a new release that was launched in NZ in June 2000. The Health Board chose the upgrade to the Web-enabled Oracle 11i application to avoid the need to undergo a further upgrade a short time later. A profile of the ES implementation project is included in Table 4.

CASE DESCRIPTION

It is October 2000. James Keen, the chief financial officer (CFO) of the Health Board and the business sponsor of the ES project, is faced with a difficult decision. The implemen-

tation of the Oracle 11i ERP system is scheduled to go live in mid-December. However, initial testing shows that there are some key performance problems with the system. In a meeting with the project team earlier that day, James was told that software testing on PCs that use the Windows NT platform showed substantial delays in data processing. Even worse, the tests were carried out using mockup data and the expectation was that these would be fairly manageable by the system.

James remembers that the IT platform issue was one of the issues the ES project team had spent considerable time on during the evaluation phase. The IT platform is the foundation for all business applications; hence it is key to any successful IS implementation. As shown in Figure 1, the base

TABLE 4   *ES Project Summary*

Categories	Descriptions
ES product name & version	Oracle 11i
ES core modules	Financials (upgrade), fixed assets (new implementation), and procurement (new implementation)
Number of users	8,500 users, including 120 power users
Cost of implementation in dollars	Approximately NZ$2.3 million that included NZ$1.7 million for hardware, software, consultancy, and internal costs; plus NZ$650,000 for operational costs, including backfill and change management.
Number of locations	One instance implementation on multiple sites (seven business units on two geographically distributed sites).
Implementation management/consultancy	Third-party implementer: ConsultCo, a big-five consultancy firm.

of the IT platform is the hardware (HW) and operating system (OS) layer. Although the components in this base layer are largely commodities and are readily available in the marketplace (Broadbent & Weill, 1997), the hardware and software architecture form the basis for the IT capability and functionality of the firm (Meyers & Oberndorf, 2001).

When purchasing any new, large application the organization must consider a number of criteria for a suitable IT platform. One obvious factor is the vendor's choice of platforms. For example, if a Linux-based version of the application is unavailable, then Linux is not an option. A second factor is the cost of the operating system and the hardware. For example, initial investment in Windows is generally considered to be a high-cost option, while Unix and Linux cost less (NetNation Communications, 2003). However, organizations must also look beyond acquisition costs to total cost of ownership (TCO), which also includes operations and control costs. TCO can be as much as 100% more than hardware acquisition costs (David, Schuff & Louis, 2002). A third factor is any hardware/software standard configuration policy in place, usually to solve operational problems (McNurlin & Sprague, 2002). Because of existing staff expertise, the need to integrate applications across a uniform platform, or attempts to reduce TCO, an IT department may prefer or require a standard IT platform for all applications. Other factors such as ease-of-use, portability, processing capability, track record, reliability, and scalability also influence the IT platform choice. See Table 5 for a more detailed comparison of the Windows NT and Unix operating systems platforms.

These general factors apply to enterprise systems implementations. TCO is a critically important component in determining the business value of an ERP initiative (Meta Group, 2000). Additionally, a new ES implementation or upgrade requires knowledge and expertise in areas of software functionality, systems configuration and integration, and other technical aspects of the IT platform (Ng, 2001). Other factors that are part of an IT platform decision for ES implementation include vendor customer support, lease versus buy options, and the working relationship, good or bad, that the IT vendor has with the organization (Hirt & Swanson, 1999).

Many of these criteria for the IT platform decision were considered by the NZ Health Board ES project team. Vendor 1 had proposed an IT platform consisting of Sun computers using the Unix operating system. Vendor 2's proposal was to support the ERP application on IBM computers running Windows NT. Michael Field, who has the conjoint role of ERP Project Director and BPR Manager, recalls how the initial IT platform decision was made:

We gave the opportunity to a number of hardware suppliers based on our statistics [that] we'd collected through the business case exercise. . . . ConsultCo was helping us write the business case. Also was Oracle. . . . We had already collected all of that information informally so we already had a view on what was possible and what wasn't.

Part of our strategy was preferably to go down an NT operating system route. That's why we went down the hardware route that we did because it was an NT operating system. . . . By the time it got to formally go out for RFP for the hardware, we knew what we wanted and how we would evaluate it. . . . We wanted to make sure we had the right guarantees. So contract negotiations with those hardware vendors was very much written into warranty—[we had a] strong focus on warranty provisions. . . . We again ended choosing objectively a hardware solution, which was based on the NT platform. . . .

Then it was up to the hardware vendor to guarantee that the Oracle software would work on their hardware. That was a large part of the negotiations because we knew we were going into a risky environment and that was the only way that we could seal it because we didn't have a relationship with a prime vendor. . . . We had to make very sure each one of the individual contracts we signed had good warranty clauses in them. . . .

The Board's IT department had favored the Windows NT platform because it was the standard IT platform for the organization. Furthermore, two years earlier, a review of information systems at the Health Board had concluded that business operations were disadvantaged because of an inconsistent approach in managing IT. A standard configuration policy was promoted and this had a strong influence in the selection of the IT platform. Finally, there were significant price savings in adopting the Windows NT platform over the Unix alternative due to lower TCO.

An issue that complicated the evaluation of the IT platform decision was that Oracle 11i had just been released at the time the IT platform was being considered. The proposed Health Board implementation was to be the first implementation of Oracle 11i in NZ. Additionally, the only planned implementation in Australia was in a for-profit business that was relatively smaller than the Health Board. As a result the Board lacked any concrete evidence of how the application would perform under either platform.

Theoretically, the Oracle 11i set of applications could be supported by both platforms, Windows NT or Unix. Andrew Smith, the Accounts Manager for Oracle at the time, had explained that "yes, both alternatives were possible," though he recommended the Unix platform. Experience in implementing ERP applications on the Unix platform showed that system performance was often more stable, especially for an implementation the size of the Health Board. Andrew, whose role was focused on sales and managing the client-Oracle relationship, left both options open for the Health Board project team to decide.

The other party involved in the IT platform decision was ConsultCo, the big-five consultancy firm that was the ES implementation partner. Like many public organizations in NZ, the Health Board was embarking on a big ERP project, but with a considerably low implementation budget for the size of the organization. To support the fast track project, the Health Board contracted with ConsultCo to manage both the evaluation and implementation processes.

TABLE 5   *Unix vs. Windows NT*

Platform features	Unix	Windows NT
Administrative support	Unix has advanced server and user management administrative functions. For example, Unix has a disk space allocation utility that can control disk space for any user.	A disk storage facility is not available with the NT platform.
Costs	Most Unix applications are free to use.	Most Microsoft's applications are proprietary; therefore companies pay for using them. Furthermore, compared with other hosting platforms, Windows often require more staff resources to maintain. Hence, the Windows total cost of ownership is relatively high.
Interface/Ease of use	Unix is text-based and uses a command line structure.	Windows uses a graphical user interface (GUI) and is the operating system of choice for many new users, with a reputation for ease of use and administration.
Portability	Unix is an open source platform; therefore, there is a wide variety of CGI scripts, PHP scripts, and MySQL applications that will work on nearly any Unix system. However, writing an application with a Shell script or Perl in a Unix environment needs a lot of programming experience. Also, not designed for Windows, many of these scripts will not work on a Windows platform. Unix is portable to numerous hardware platforms. However, different vendors of Unix have released different versions. As a result, an application loses its portability if it is not running on all versions.	The Windows platform is compatible with Microsoft applications, such as FrontPage, Access and MS SQL. It also offers the use of programming environments such as Active Server Pages (ASP), Visual Basic Scripts, MS Index Server, and ColdFusion. These server-scripting technologies are now becoming more popular because they are easy to use.
Processing capability	Unix is a multi-user, multitasking operating system that is text-based. As a result it can dedicate the full power of the server to applications. Hence, its powerful multiprocessing capabilities are still unparalleled.	The Windows NT platform is a multi-user and multitasking operating system.
Track record, reliability, and scalability	Unix has been in a state of constant refinement since its inception 30 years ago. The platform has a proven track record of performance, stability, and security. Furthermore, Unix can be used over networks that range in size from small servers to supercomputers.	Windows NT was a relatively new platform. Currently, the Windows 2000 Server is the newer hosting platform that completely replaced Windows NT.

Adapted from Alexander (2004), BroadSpire (2003), and NetNation Communications (2003)

FIGURE 1   *Business Applications & the IT Platform*

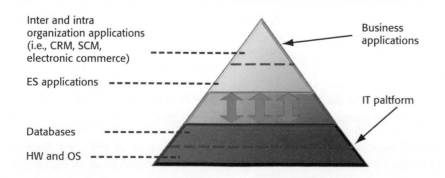

Inter and intra organization applications (i.e., CRM, SCM, electronic commerce)

ES applications

Databases

HW and OS

Business applications

IT paltform

Note: Adapted from Broadbent and Weill (1997)

In NZ, it is common practice that the client organization determines what the new IT platform should be. Most organizations in NZ are small and medium-sized enterprises (SME), especially when compared to organizations in North America or Europe. As a result, the resources allocated to these implementations are relatively small, even though the systems involved usually have the same amount of sophistication and complexity. As one means of cutting costs, the client organization generally takes more responsibility in implementation decisions. That was the case here—the Health Board was responsible for a large portion of the implementation risk and the IT platform was one of those risks.

After considering the advice offered by the Board's IT department, the Oracle Account Manager, and ConsultCo, the Health Board ES project team selected the Windows NT platform for the implementation of Oracle 11i ERP system. Knowing the risks involved, and to mitigate these risks, they put into the agreement with Vendor 2 a condition to ensure that the new system performed according to specification. If performance was not acceptable, the legal agreement allowed for the contract to be terminated. Vendor 2 accepted this condition and implementation began.

Coming back into the present, James was very disturbed to learn that the performance tests during the past week had shown unacceptable delays in data processing. He realized that a revisit of the earlier evaluation decision was imminent. James knew that this could represent a major setback to the project. If this problem were to delay the go-live date, even if only by a few months, then the whole project would collapse. Any delay, he thought, would require a huge boost in the implementation cost. Specialized ERP consultants were scarce and the ConsultCo consultants working on the Health Board project were being flown into NZ from the ConsultCo office in Australia every week. To consider extending the project, even for a few weeks, would mean a large increase in costs and the Health Board did not have a large contingency fund to cover this blowout. Furthermore, as part of new government regulations, the Health Board was to start implementing a new chart of accounts in December. Plans for implementing the new chart of accounts were embedded within the new ERP system, so statutory requirements, as well as cost considerations, were at risk.

James, as the business sponsor of this project, knows he needs to move on this issue very quickly. Going over both the earlier considerations of the IT platform decision and the contractual obligations with the hardware vendor, he wondered: Could he recommend that the contract be terminated and go for the alternative path of the Unix platform? Because of the size of the contract, organization policy necessitated that such a decision needed to go to the Board members for approval. Other questions that needed a careful assessment were: What if the hardware vendor decided to go the litigation path? What if the problems were not caused by the IT platform? What if the Board did not approve the change?

James knows that a decision needs to be made and to be made very quickly. It is one of those times when not making a decision is going to jeopardize the fate of the project any way. He picks up his phone and schedules an urgent meeting with his project team the next day.

CURRENT CHALLENGES/PROBLEMS FACING THE ORGANIZATION

One of the main problems that affected the choice of both the OS and the hardware platform was the relationship between the release version of the ES application and the IT platform. The Health Board had chosen to implement the new release of Oracle 11i; yet, experience in implementing different combinations of OS and hardware platforms with the new release was very limited. In the following, Michael Field, the ERP Project Director/BPR Manager), explains the implication this decision had on ES implementation:

One of the important areas in terms of a large ERP implementation is around the maturity of the software and its relationship with the operating system. This had quite a large impact on the issues which we had to manage for our project. For us, one of the biggest things in this particular implementation was the relationship of the application to an operating system. That triggered a whole lot of things for us. What we did on the project might have been different to some other ERP applications because this issue looked like it was going to have an impact on us being able to deliver the whole project on time.

When a lot of people do an implementation they bundle the whole implementation with no risk. They pass the risk onto the party implementer who supplies everything—the hardware, software, and implementation services. In our case we believed we didn't want to do that so we structured the project in a certain way and that was to get a third party to help us do the implementation. We'd buy our software from someone else and we would get the hardware from somewhere else. This in terms of managing a project of this size proved too challenging. But for us, that was the only way we could afford to do this project.

It [selection of the IT platform] had a major impact on the project. So . . . [it] went up through to the steering committee, even to the Board. . . . Even though we had used all the expertise from Oracle, all the expertise from the IT platform vendor in this case, plus ConsultCo's collective expertise, so-called best around the world, the decision ended up in hindsight not the right one. But at least we made a decision.

Although the initial IT platform decision was made at the project manager level, where Michael (ERP Project Director) and ConsultCo were key decision-makers, when performance deteriorated James (the CFO) stepped in in order to rescue the project. He says:

I didn't get involved in those [IT platform] decisions at all. That was driven out of the IS function working with the consultants. That's where we had major problems all around—around the hardware and the database. A decision had been taken to go down that path. As we got into the project, there were problems.

There are two different explanations to the software performance problems that caused the Board to consider a change in the IT platform decision. The Health Board attributed performance problems to the newly released Oracle 11i. Oracle, the ES vendor, attributed the problems to a combination of unrealistic expectations, limited vendor participation, and an immature implementation experience. A detailed explanation of these two views is provided next.

The Health Board based their conclusion that the Oracle 11i had not been thoroughly tested within an NT environment on their own experience, as well as the experience of others who were implementing Oracle 11i at the same time. Heated discussion in the online forum of the Oracle application user group (Hawaii Ebuzz, 2000; Songini, 2000) and a 2001 report from the Gartner Group ("Oracle calls Gartner Group biased," 2001) affirmed this explanation that Oracle 11i was not ready to go to the market in its initial release.

The ES vendor Oracle believed that the IT infrastructure problem was exaggerated for three reasons. First, neither the vendor nor any of its representatives were actively involved in the implementation. Therefore, critical issues did not come to their attention until a problem became significant and needed immediate action.

Second, although the implications of implementing a new release had not been clearly explained by Oracle in advance, the Health Board should have had realistic expectations when they chose the new 11i release. One fact most computer professionals are aware of is that new software releases are never bug free until they are validated by users. Therefore, problems inherent in the new software release could have complicated the diagnosis of performance problems.

Third, the ConsultCo implementation team did not have prior experience in implementing the Oracle 11i applications on an NT platform and had refused several suggestions to add an Oracle person to complement their team. The Oracle Accounts Manager best summarizes those three issues in the following statement:

IT were the people that were saying that you must use an NT system in the first place because "that's our standard." . . . They were more worried about the fact that they were trying to have an NT Microsoft type strategy. . . . We most assuredly suggested to them and recommended to them many times that they should go down a Unix path and they didn't listen to us there. . . . We [Oracle] concluded that [ConsultCo] had little experience with NT—very little experience with NT and with Oracle. Even less, [they] certainly had no experience for putting 11i onto it. They had no experience in putting 11i into a Sun box, which is why I always felt uncomfortable that they weren't taking Oracle people [as sub contractors on to the project].

In summary, the main challenge facing James Keen is how to resolve the IT platform problem within the two months before go-live. James knows that not resolving IT platform implications in a timely manner is likely to result in a failed project. Hence, a decision needs to be made and actioned quickly. Is it possible to work with Vendor 2 to resolve these problems, assuming these were only teething problems? Or need a change of IT platform be actioned as soon as possible with implications of a cost overrun and a legal suit?

REFERENCES

Alexander, B. (2004). Unix vs. Windows NT. *India Web Developers*. Retrieved January 30, 2004: http://www.indiawebdevelopers.com/technology/scripts/chapter1.asp.

Broadbent, M., & Weill, P. (1997). Management by maxim: How business and IT managers can create IT infrastructures. *Sloan Management Review*, 77–92.

BroadSpire. (2003). Windows vs. Linux: Choosing the right hosting platform. Retrieved January 30, 2004: http://www.broadspire.com/solutions/express/shared/linuxvswindows.html.

David, J.S., Schuff, D., & Louis, S. (2002). Managing your IT total cost of ownership. *Communications of the ACM, 45*(1), 101–106.

Hawaii Ebuzz. (2000, October 27). OAUG conference offers users chance to ask Oracle. *Hawaii Ventures Corporation*. Retrieved July 2003: http://www.hawaiiventures.com/news10023.html.

Hirt, S.G., & Swanson, E.B. (1999). Adopting SAP at Siemens Power Corporation. *Journal of Information Technology, 14*, 243–251.

McNurlin, B.C., & Sprague, R.H. (2002). *Information Systems Management in Practice* (5th ed.). Upper Saddle River, NJ: Prentice Hall.

Meta Group. (2000). ERP platform-related analysis total cost of ownership study: A platform-related cost analysis of ERP applications on-going support costs in the mid-tier. Retrieved April 21, 2004: http://www.verio.co.uk/powerplatform/library/erp_tco.pdf.

Meyers, B.C., & Oberndorf, P. (2001). *Managing Software Acquisition: Open Systems and COTS Products*. Boston: Addison-Wesley.

NetNation Communications. (2003, October 6). Unix versus Windows. Retrieved January 30, 2004: http://www.netnation.com/products/unix_or_nt.cfm.

Ng, C.S.P. (2001). A decision framework for enterprise resource planning maintenance and upgrade: A client perspective. *Journal of Software Maintenance and Evolution: Research and Practice, 13*, 431–468.

Oracle calls Gartner Group biased after consultant knocks operations. (2001, August 28). *CFO*. Retrieved July 31, 2003: http://www.cfo.com/article/1,5309,4748%7C%7CA%7C134%7C6,00.html.

Songini, M.L. (2000, October 20). Oracle applications users look for more help on upgrades. *Computerworld*. Retrieved July 2003: http://archive.infoworld.com/articles/hn/xml/00/10/20/001020hnorapps.xml.

ENDNOTES

[1] All organization and personal names have been disguised.

Maha Shakir (maha.shakir@zu.ac.ae) is an assistant professor of information systems at Zayed University. Her primary research areas are strategic IS implementations, management information systems and enterprise system applications where her publications appeared in the Journal of Decision Systems, ERP edited books, ACM Software Engineering Notes, and several international IS conferences.

Dennis Viehland (d.viehland@massey.ac.nz) is an associate professor of information systems at Massey University's

Auckland (New Zealand) campus. His primary research areas are information management, electronic commerce strategy, and ubiquitous computing. He has published widely, most recently as co-author of Electronic Commerce 2004: A Managerial Perspective.

CASE STUDY QUESTIONS

1. Describe the NZ Health Board and the environment in which it operates. Why did it need a new enterprise system?

2. Discuss the pros and the cons of selecting Oracle11i ERP applications and Windows NT for the operating system for the Health Board's new enterprise system.

3. Why were there performance problems with the new system? What management, technology, and organizational factors were involved?

4. What should James Keen do to solve these problems so that the new enterprise system is successful?

CASE STUDY 2:
A Knowledge Platform for the Customer Contact Center of Union Investment

WALTER BRENNER, LUTZ M. KOLBE, AND ADRIAN BUEREN
University of St. Gallen (Switzerland)

"Can you help me?"

"Hello, could you please tell me why the stock price of my bond fund dropped so steeply on November 23rd?" asks Mrs. Jones, customer of Union Investment. "Sure, Mrs. Jones, but it will take a few minutes. Can I call you back?" answers the Customer Contact Center (CCC) agent. She first checks out which funds the customer has in her account using a host application. Then she looks up information about the fund in a brochure on her desk. She figures out the solution of the enquiry and calls Mrs. Jones back. This is a typical customer enquiry of which Union Investment has to answer over 4,000 each day.

Founded in 1956, Union Investment is the third-largest German mutual fund company with assets exceeding USD 100 billion as of 2002. Union Investment offers public funds as well as restricted funds. The range of public funds encompasses equity funds, fixed income funds, money market funds, and mixed securities and property funds as well as open property funds. These products are distributed exclusively via partners in Germany in a co-operative of banks called the "Finanzverbund". The Finanzverbund consists of mostly medium-sized banks like the Sparda Bank or the Volks- und Raiffeisenbanken, which pool some of their resources in back-end processes but are otherwise independent of each other.

Besides investment funds, Union Investment also offers services concerning the administration of deposits for more than 3.5 million customers across Europe. Union Investment has its headquarters in Frankfurt, Germany. It also has affiliates and branch offices in Germany, Luxembourg, Switzerland, Spain, Italy, and Poland.[1]

Up to the late 1990s, Union Investment only provided customer service to bank representatives and had no dedicated service department. Rather, some employees from the department "Product Information" were available by phone for bank representatives and handled this traffic besides their regular jobs. With the booming stock markets of the

late 1990s, however, Union Investment experienced significant growth in the number of customers and deposits. As a consequence, the old structure couldn't cope with the increased volume of inquiries anymore. Management therefore decided to reorganize the company in 1999, not only to improve communication to banking representatives, but also to allow customers to contact Union Investment directly.

CUSTOMER SERVICE AT UNION INVESTMENT

The Customer Communication Center (CCC)—Interface to the Customer

Union Investment aims at sustaining its competitive position by providing high-value customer service as well as attractive financial products of all sorts. Customers typically have a long-term financial portfolio strategy and quite different levels of financial markets expertise. Therefore, they not only expect a broad spectrum of products and services that fit their investment strategies, but also superior service. This service demand exists regardless of whether the customers turn to their local bank representatives or contact Union Investment directly as their mutual funds specialist.

To achieve a high level of service without sacrificing economies of scale, the organization has been separated into two major units since the reorganization in 1999. One is concerned with the efficient execution of transactions ordered via the bank representatives while the other, the Customer Service unit, is concerned with providing superior service in the interaction with customers. Retail-customers can call Union Investment directly to resolve problems with their existing portfolio as well as to demand information on specialized products of Union Investment. The Customer

---

[1]Further information about the company can be obtained at http://www.union-investment.de.

FIGURE 1   *Organizational structure of customer service at Union Investment*

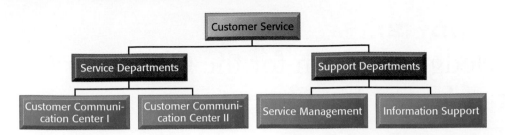

Service unit consists of the Customer Communication Center (CCC), which processes all customer communication and the supporting departments "Service Management" and "Information Support" (cf. Figure 1). In the beginning, the unit was made up mainly of employees of the former "Product Information" department.

It is the Customer Service unit that is responsible for applying concepts of *Customer Relationship Management (CRM)* in order to increase customer focus and strengthen the competitive position of the company. As a consequence, it is of significant strategic importance. This especially applies to the CCC, which serves as the only interface to the customers of Union Investment. The communication consists primarily of over one million inbound telephone calls a year. Furthermore, the CCC has to manage increasing numbers of enquiries via other channels such as fax, email, or letter. The services of the CCC consist of the provision of solutions for customers having problems or requiring information on their status and past transactions.

The CCC I consists of 80 employees who cover the first level of customer support. The 40 employees of the CCC II cover the second level of support with more complex topics

and process enquiries in the form of emails, letters, and faxes (about 6,000 a month). Most of the 90,000 monthly calls are received on the first level and can be escalated to the CCC II if necessary. Banking representatives may contact the second level directly with questions concerning specific topics. Service Management deals with reporting issues, complaint management and process design as well as application support to the CCC. Information Support provides knowledge to the CCC and resolves questions that agents can not resolve by themselves.

The CCC attempts to increase customer satisfaction by resolving as many enquiries as possible within the first contact (first call resolution rate), making it unnecessary for the customer to call again. If enquiries are resolved immediately, efficient means of escalation are used to reduce overall cycle time. This means that the required expertise needs to be located very quickly if the agent cannot answer the request herself. Keeping the service level constant is quite challenging as the call volume varies significantly during the day but also between different times of the year (cf. Figure 2, Figure 3). The high level of skills of the agents is helpful as each one can rapidly process questions concerning a wide

FIGURE 2   *CCC daily call volume in 2002*

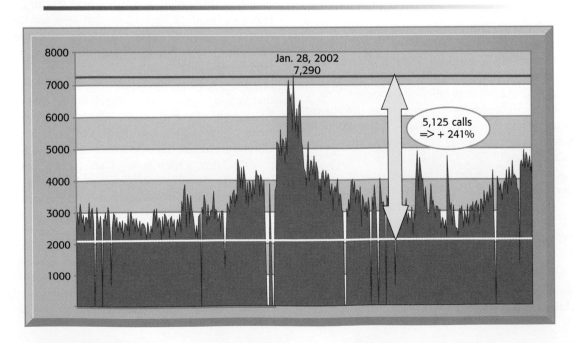

FIGURE 3   *CCC spread of call volume/half hour during the day*

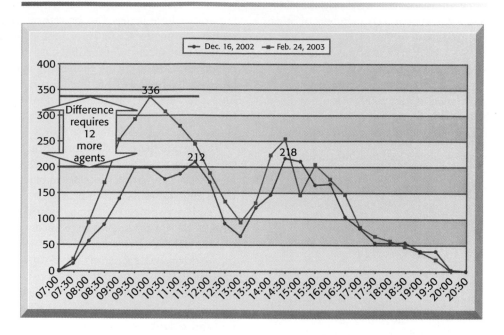

array of topics, making a first call resolution more probable. However, this high skill level needs to be constantly renewed by training measures. Ideally, these training measures are offered electronically to enable agents to study them in off-peak hours. This way, agents who are not busy can still use their time productively and generate benefits to Union Investment by better serving customers later due to their improved skill level.

Figure 4 illustrates the role of the CCC as a communication interface. Prospects or customers either get in touch personally or pose their enquiries to the representative of the local bank who forwards them to the CCC, usually by telephone.

Upon an enquiry, there are three possibilities for the CCC agent to answer:

1. If the request can be handled by the agent solely based on her expertise, she can directly respond to the customer, thereby not requiring any further information sources.

2. If the agent is unable to resolve the issue without further information resources, she can try to find the answer in "real-time" in the Web-based knowledge platform "HelpMe", in her email-file, or by escalating the call to a known expert within the CCC who is likely to know the answer. As in the previous case, the customer's issue is resolved instantly.

3. If the needed information cannot be retrieved in "real-time", the agent can engage in further research in "HelpMe". It not only offers short answers, but also information in the form of cases or background stories, which serve as training measures to further deepen one's expertise. If the needed information cannot be found there, the agents have the possibility

FIGURE 4   *Communication between Union Investment and its customers*

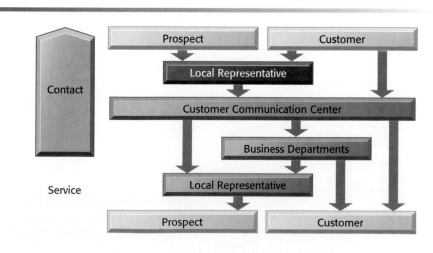

of calling the Information Support team, which will deliver the needed information. If necessary, the Information Support team contacts members of other parts of the organization, thereby serving as an interface between the CCC and the rest of the company. Once the answer is determined, it is forwarded directly to the requesting agent and included in "HelpMe" so that it can be accessed by the other agents. Finally, the agent forwards the answer to the customer or bank representative by phone or (e)mail.

Prior to the project described here, new information was usually sent first by email to deliver it as quickly as possible and create awareness for the news. In a second step, Information Support also published the information to "HelpMe" where it was available on demand. Therefore, CCC agents had two platforms from which to choose. This resulted in email becoming the preferred channel due to better functionality. For one, a full-text search could be applied to the email-file, which was not available in "HelpMe". And just as important was the ability to completely customize the information structure within the email file for faster retrieval. This made it more difficult for a central information repository to gain acceptance. When using email, however, each agent had a different level of information accessible depending on the time spent on the job. New agents started with no information and only developed their own collection slowly.

Supporting the Customer Communication Center with Knowledge

The CCC agents all have a banking background and can be considered highly qualified. Nevertheless, they still need an effective information system to supply them with the required relevant, credible, and timely information. Before the 1999 reorganization, only a small number of employees were involved in answering phone enquiries. They all knew each other and were also aware of where to find information that was stored in disparate locations. But with the experienced explosive growth, management of Customer Service realized that this need required an extra department and created Information Support in 2001. Most of the members of Information Support were initially recruited from the CCC. Its scope of responsibility is essentially *knowledge management* and training within the Customer Service unit:

1. To provide information of all kinds to the CCC.

2. To resolve enquiries which require information from other departments within Union Investment.

3. To evaluate and process knowledge from the customers in order to enable the organization to improve its processes.

Information Support consists of seven employees who are responsible for creating, editing, and publishing all content

(or information) available to the CCC. Usually, this content is forwarded from other departments to Information Support, where it needs to be reformatted. Upon urgent requests from the CCC, Information Support researches information specifically for that case. Such information is directly passed on to the requesting agent and later published in "HelpMe". As the CCC forms the communication interface between Union Investment and its customers, Information Support forms the communication interface between the CCC and other parts of the organization.

To provide the needed information to the agents of the CCC, the *users* of the knowledge platform "HelpMe", there needs to be supporting processes in place in the form of editorial and administrative processes. The *administrative process* is concerned with maintaining the technical infrastructure. Prior to the project, it encompassed such tasks as the manual administration of the navigational structure of the platform and the manual check of consistency concerning hyperlinks between different pieces of content.

The *editorial process* for Content Management for the CCC consisted of creating, formatting, publishing, modifying and deleting relevant content. These elements were designed as follows:

❏ *Content Creation and Formatting* Although most of the required content already existed in written and electronic form in the organization, it was edited to meet the needs of the CCC agents. This was done in Microsoft Office applications, which are the familiar working environments of the editors in the Information Support team. In a second step, all content was converted into the HTML-format (Hypertext Markup Language). For this, the editors used a special HTML-tool. Since they were not Web technology experts, they had to acquire deep insights into HTML first. The manual formatting and converting was a laborious process, especially for spreadsheets and tables. For emails, the documents were sent as Office files without any conversion.

❏ *Content Publication* The publication process did not require any further approval. The editor could save the content to the appropriate folder of the file-server in "HelpMe". In a second step, the new content was inserted into the navigational structure.

❏ *Content Modification* Modifications were carried out either in the HTML-tool or in the Office application, depending on the degree of revision necessary. New versions of content could not just be inserted into the old ones because there was no separation of content and layout. When a new version of a spreadsheet needed to be published, it was converted as if it were a new document.

❏ *Content Deletion* Outdated content was removed from the platform by deleting the file and manually adapting the navigational structure.

FIGURE 5 *Support of the service process at Union Investment*

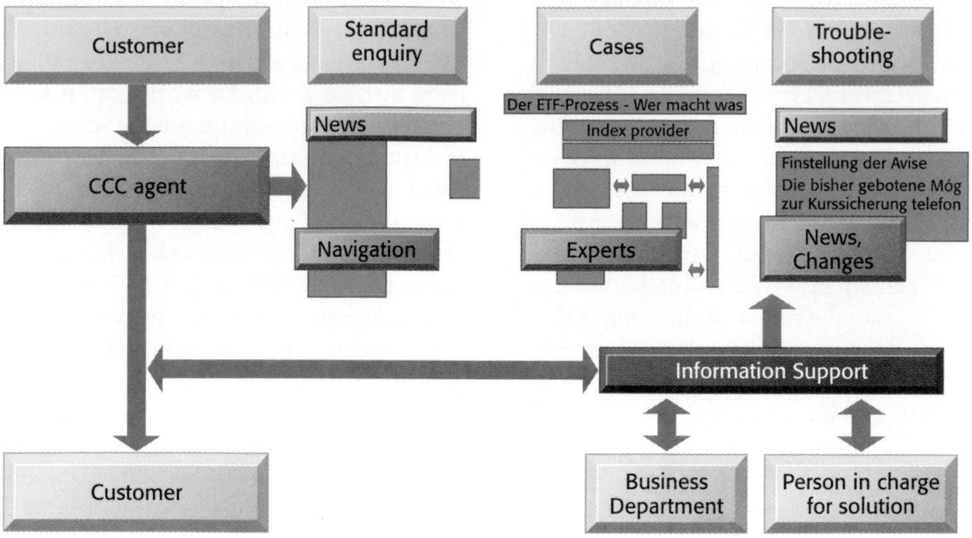

Information Systems Supporting Content Management for the CCC

With the creation of the Information Support department, management realized that adequate information systems would be crucial to support the knowledge flow to the CCC. Concerning the realization of Content Management Systems, a company-wide project was to provide a solution for different areas such as the intranet, the extranet and also the CCC knowledge platform. With this project in its early phase, all other developments on a departmental level were suspended. Yet, due to several organizational issues and rising pressure to reduce costs, the company-wide project was never completed. Since the problem of explosive growth in call volumes and CCC agents still persisted, Information Support decided to set up its own knowledge platform with very limited funds which became "HelpMe". As a consequence, this project did not have an official project status and because the IT department was not involved, they would not provide support in any way for this new solution.

"HelpMe" is a Web-based Content Management System (CMS) to deliver information to the agents in the CCC. This system provides opportunities for discovering information (navigation) as well as experts in certain topics (so-called yellow pages). Furthermore, it creates awareness for new items and changes in existing content by highlighting these at prominent positions on the platform (Figure 5). As a consequence, "HelpMe" is an important part of the service process at Union Investment.

Technically, "HelpMe" originally consisted of HTML-files stored on a local fileserver. From there, they could be retrieved with a standard Web-browser. In order to create and manage the navigational structure that linked those pages, a tool based on Microsoft Access was developed in-house. The HTML file corresponding to the navigational structure was recreated with this tool each time a document

was inserted, moved, or deleted. Furthermore, hyperlinks between the different documents had to be checked manually with each deletion or revision of existing content. In contrast to the email files, there was no search function available in "HelpMe". This hampered retrieval, especially because the navigational structure had grown historically and was difficult to understand. Security and user management did not have to be specifically administered for "HelpMe" as the system was based solely on a file-server to which everyone in the CCC had access. As a consequence though, it was not possible to restrict access to certain areas or to personalize content, for example by CCC-level.

The platform had been programmed by a single employee of the Customer Service unit who had left the organization when the redesign took place without leaving any documentation. Besides being published in "HelpMe", new information was always sent via email as well. These emails often including attachments of up to ten megabytes in size were sent to all CCC agents. This caused storage problems on one hand, as email files of all agents constantly grew and also caused significant traffic, which put a strain on network bandwith.

IMPROVING KNOWLEDGE FLOW— THE REDESIGNING OF "HELPME"

Why "HelpMe" Needed to Be Redesigned

While solving the challenge of providing the CCC with knowledge for the customer to some extent, the original version of "HelpMe" required some improvements which would significantly increase usability and efficiency of the content management processes. So the Head of Information

Support decided to launch a project to address these challenges of improving usability and retrieval in "HelpMe" as well as to streamline the costly content management processes. The project kick-off was in the summer of 2001. To improve the prior solution, the project team wanted to introduce a new technical infrastructure based on a standard software product which was implemented together with a conceptional redesign of "HelpMe". Since there were no experts in the field of knowledge management in the organization, some external consultants took part in the project to a lesser extent. For the most part, however, the members of Information Support gained expertise about knowledge management by themselves in the course of this project.

The redesign addressed the issue of complex structure by providing a new navigational structure based on the terminology of the CCC agents and implementing a search function. By concentrating the knowledge flow on the channel "HelpMe", redundancies to email were eliminated. For the editors and administrators, the redesign aimed at reducing the costs and time needed for the costly content management processes. The new system was to simplify conversion, publication and revision of existing content and provide tools to better manage the navigational structure in "HelpMe".

At the same time, budgetary and organizational constraints needed to be complied with, which meant that the software being selected should be one that was already used in-house, thereby reducing costs and integration efforts. By concentrating on the knowledge platform, the network infrastructure of Union Investment would also be relieved of a significant amount of traffic caused by emails with partially large file attachments.

To evaluate whether the goals had been achieved, the team proposed a system of performance indicators based on the user, editor, and administrator processes. This allowed an analysis of the changes achieved at the level of the CCC agents as well as the editors in Information Support. The most important criteria were high system performance to make content available quickly as well as high quality of content.

How "HelpMe" Was Redesigned

To properly align the new CMS to the processes it was to support, the project team started with a *process analysis*. After the project was delayed for several months, the project team met for a two-day workshop in late January 2002 to analyze the processes of the users, editors and administrators in using "HelpMe". During this workshop, the team also spent some time in the CCC, observing agents doing their work and checking on how they use the different information sources. Figure 6 shows how the different user processes can be supported by "HelpMe".

The process analysis was the foundation for deriving the requirements of the new technical solution in a *requirements analysis*. Each requirement was weighted to be "optional", "important" or "critical", depending on significance. Using metrics for each requirement, the team determined if the evaluated software solutions fulfilled these adequately, extensively or not at all. By aggregating the 29 requirements in a benefit analysis, the different products could be compared. For the comparison, points were assigned to the weights (1 point for optional, 5 points for important, 10 points for critical) and to the fulfillment of criteria (1 for "adequately fulfilled", 2 for "extensively fulfilled", 0 for "not fulfilled"). Figure 7 shows a snapshot of the benefit analysis for the part of the user processes. To avoid selecting a product which required extensive and costly customizing in order to fulfill the requirements, the project team created a benefit analysis for an "out-of-the-box" and a "customizing" scenario.

Besides the requirements analysis, members of the project team were also able to use a live system based on the evaluated products. This proved whether the products could live up to their promises and enabled the simulation of a typical working scenario. Within the simulation some additional factors came up which the team simply hadn't considered when doing the requirements analysis.

Because of the limited budget, only those products would be evaluated that were already in use in other parts of Union

FIGURE 6   *User processes are the basis for "HelpMe"*

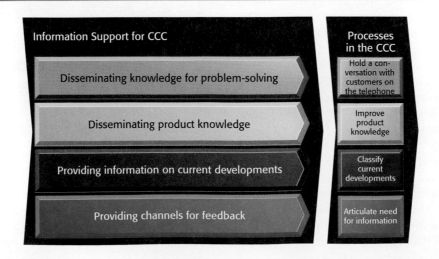

FIGURE 7   *Snapshot of the benefit analysis "Out-of-the-box"*

No.	Requirement	Importance	Arago DocMe	Pironet Pirobase	Lotus Quickplace
	Requirements based on processes of users				
1	High system performance	critical	10	10	20
2	Structured navigation	critical	10	20	10
3	Sitemap (Overview of structure of HelpMe)	important	5	5	0
4	High-capacity search	critical	0	10	0
5	What's new functionality	critical	0	0	0
6	Consolidated display of relevant content with possibility to delve into details	critical	10	10	10
7	. . .	. . .	. . .	. . .	. . .

Investment. The first system was Arago DocMe, a CMS which mainly focuses on supporting the editor in publishing information and administrating the navigational structure, while not integrating its own Web server and therefore not providing any functions to manage users or restrict access to the content via a Web browser. DocMe was already used to manage the extranet and the Internet Website of Union Investment. The second system was Pironet Pirobase. It too was already in use in the organization at a newly acquired subsidiary. It is a typical Web content management system, meaning that it integrates the back-end for the editors and the Web server that controls access for the users via a Web browser. The third product was Lotus Quickplace of IBM. It was recommended by the external consultants as it focuses on managing rather small amounts of content for users engaged in a common project and is easy to implement. This product, however, was not in use at Union Investment yet and would have caused significant costs since the IT out-sourcer of Union Investment did not have the expertise required for running this application yet.

Since the benefit analysis yielded very close results, some *Knock Out-criteria* were developed to better differentiate the products. A product that would not fulfill all these criteria would be ruled out immediately. Examples for these criteria were a reliable search function, no limit of the size of documents or the securing of integrity in hyperlinks within the CMS.

With the *requirements analysis* and the *K.O.-criteria* to back up the decision, as well as the financial restrictions and the integration aspect, the Union Investment team members chose Arago DocMe.

To ensure that the requirements were implemented adequately, the project team developed a *system design draft* based on the selected software that described in detail how the requirements were to be implemented. This document also served as a basis for the communication with the software supplier, Arago.

Besides selecting and customizing the software, the *structure* of the content needed to be determined to fit the preferences of the users when navigating. The project team developed a consistent three-level *navigational structure* that

defines the most relevant business terms in a way they are understood within the organization.

With the use of templates, the 39,000 documents already present in "HelpMe" were migrated to the new structure. In parallel, the project team created the documentation of the customized settings in "HelpMe" and provided training session for users and editors to ensure a smooth transition.

The project lasted for about one year. One important reason for this relatively long project duration was the fact that the team was not fully dedicated to the project.

HOW THE NEW "HELPME" CHANGED BUSINESS AND SUPPORT PROCESSES

The goal of the new "HelpMe" was to ease the work of CCC agents and thereby enable increased performance. This was achieved by reducing cycle times necessary for the editors to publish information and facilitating access and retrieval.

The *user process* of the CCC agent is now better supported through improvements in search and navigation. The revised navigational structure facilitates the use of "HelpMe". It consists of three levels, of which the first level can always be accessed on the top bar and the others on the left side, depending on the context (Figure 8). It helps the user find information where she assumes it can be found. If she cannot find the needed information in the navigational structure, the new search function offers an alternative to retrieve it quickly, for example, during a phone call. Since the new system also supports metadata for documents such as topic, author or publication date, agents can search specifically for these keywords in addition to just searching full text. This is quite crucial as agents only have a few seconds on the phone to find relevant answers. So in order to avoid impatient customers, the system needs to have a high performance but also provide a navigational structure that is intuitive to the users.

The knowledge flow now concentrates on "HelpMe", making it an important part of the working environment of

FIGURE 8   *User interface of "HelpMe"*

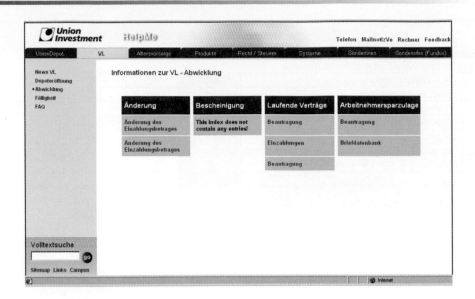

each CCC agent. Email is no longer used to publish information. This way, it can be ensured that every agent has access to all information, regardless of the time spent on the job. Furthermore, only the most up-to-date version is available. The "What's new" function reminds the agents of revised content that they would otherwise not notice because they have memorized the old version already.

Within the *editor* and *administrator processes,* some of the time-consuming manual steps are now carried out or at least facilitated by the system. *Templates* accelerate the conversion of content into a format that matches the need of the CCC agents and can be displayed in a Web browser. To support the editors, several templates for different types of documents (i.e., news, charts, reports, etc.) are available. These templates can be used in Microsoft Office applications and define the layout that helps to automatically convert the content into HTML. They improve the performance of the converter, which can be customized specifically for these templates. They also make the use of style sheets possible for a centrally-managed layout. Thus, the editors do not need to redefine the layout and formats each time a document is created. The templates help the editors realize how the final result of their work will look in "HelpMe". Editors are now able to *publish* and *disseminate* content directly from the office application, similar to the way a file is stored on a local disk drive. The conversion is accomplished fully automatically by the CMS, which also publishes the converted HTML files. This offers a great improvement in efficiency compared to the former system. The office applications are used to revise existing content as well, making the introduction of other applications unnecessary.

The *administrator* now uses a separate client. With this client, she can administer the navigational structure of the site to automatically include newly-added content. The administrator can also manage additional components like

indices, which automatically create tables of contents for documents fulfilling certain criteria. Finally, the client can be used to manage user groups among the editors, although not among the users in the CCC.

DIVIDE AND CONQUER

With worsening economic conditions, Union Investment was reluctant to initiate large, enterprise-wide projects in the area of knowledge management. In this regard, the new "HelpMe" can be considered as a pilot project to indicate potential benefits of such concepts. Although it was intended to effectively solve a problem within a specific business process, service management, the achievement was widely recognized upon completion. At the time of writing, other internal departments at Frankfurt, Germany, as well as subsidiaries of Union Investment in Switzerland and Luxembourg were eager to be shown how the solution works and to find out how they can use it for their own processes.

"We realize how important the provision of the right information to CCC agents is to keep customers satisfied and ultimately make Union Investment successful. Redesigning 'HelpMe' was an important step to provide this information to our agents. Combined with our CRM-System, all the information needed is now available at the touch of a button, improving service and the performance of our CCC agents alike," notes Giovanni G., Head of Customer Service.

"HelpMe" is also a first step to introduce other knowledge management tools in the future that not only focus on the retrieval of knowledge contained in documents. As a significant amount of knowledge cannot be explicated and remains in the heads of employees, a possible next step could be to establish a skill management system to further improve the access to experts on certain topics. This would also make the management of competencies of CCC agents possible and indicate gaps on the department level. Finally, a challenging issue is the topic of delivering knowledge directly to the customers on the Internet and to also integrate mechanisms to support the knowledge flow back from the customers to Union Investment to enable continuous improvement in the future.

"Of course, we can help you."

"Hello, could you please tell me why the stock price of my bond fund dropped so steeply on November 23rd?" asks Mrs. Jones, customer of Union Investment. "Sure, Mrs. Jones, just a second," replies the CCC agent. She first checks out which funds the customer has in her account using a host application. Then she looks up information about the fund in

"HelpMe". "Mrs. Jones, the stock price dropped because on the date you mentioned, there was the yearly disbursement." "Oh, I completely forgot. Thanks for the information."

CASE STUDY QUESTIONS

1. Evaluate the content management process before and after the project. What steps could be taken to improve knowledge flows besides the information supplied by the content management process?

2. Assess the change in information provided for the agent and the customer. What factors benefit Union Investment and how could they eventually affect its bottom line?

CASE STUDY 3:

Citigroup's CEEMEA Sales & Trading Unit: Rapid Business Improvement Through Effective Use of Information, People and IT

Research Associate Rebecca Chung prepared this case under the supervision of Professor Donald A. Marchand of IMD and Professor William J. Kettinger of the University of South Carolina as a basis for class discussion rather than to illustrate either effective or ineffective handling of a business situation.

Infocentricity cannot be compromised. I can negotiate on other things. But not this one!

Suneel Bakhshi, former head of CEEMEA Sales & Trading

In 2000, Suneel Bakhshi was appointed head of the CEEMEA[1] Sales & Trading Business at Citigroup. At the time, the company believed the CEEMEA region had a significant opportunity for improvement compared with Latin America and Asia, the company's two other major emerging market business regions. Bakhshi was determined to put CEEMEA on a sustainable growth path through increased client satisfaction. He decided to make significant changes in the business and to increase the client focus by offering a more extensive range of client products. To do so, Bakhshi decided he needed to employ top class trading and risk management talent and take a more direct and regional approach to the treasury business to tighten controls and reduce costs. Moreover, as information flow in emerging markets was highly imperfect and the speed of decision-making in the treasury business was high, Bakhshi sought to increase the use of relevant real-time information to improve trading results across his diverse region.

To implement these changes, Bakhshi needed to leverage information, people and IT capabilities in the unit. To do so he built IT applications for decision-making and product

[1]Central and Eastern Europe, Middle East, and Africa: an emerging market region.

innovation aimed at managing the fast-moving treasury business and changing the way his team sensed, shared and used information across the region.

By mid-2003, Bakhshi's team had become more effective in managing and using information. For example, the traders were more willing to share trading intelligence on a daily basis; and the salespeople focused time and attention on customer needs, designing new products to meet those needs. Over the three years, the profit of the business doubled (*refer to* **Exhibit 1**).

Could the positive results of building an infocentric approach to business be replicated in other Citigroup units? If so, what lessons could business managers learn about leveraging information, people and IT capabilities to improve business performance?

TAKING OVER CEEMEA SALES & TRADING

In April 2000, Suneel Bakhshi was named head of the CEEMEA Sales & Trading business. It had hundreds of customers, including corporations, governments, and institutional and individual customers in the CEEMEA markets. The CEEMEA region covered 31 countries grouped into the following geographic clusters: Central & Eastern Europe (CEE), Commonwealth of Independent States (CIS), Middle East & Egypt, Africa, Poland, Turkey, and South Africa (*refer to* **Exhibit 2** for breakdown of countries).

The unit generated revenue from two sources: 1) profit from trading financial instruments; and 2) spread revenue from customers for providing them with hedges for their exposures. It traded two types of financial instruments: 1) "simple" financial instruments, such as foreign currencies,

EXHIBIT 1   *CEEMEA Sales & Trading Unit: Financial Performance (Figures are indexed)*

	2000 Actual	**2001 Actual**	**2002 Actual**	**2003 Forecast**	**Change 2002/2000**
Revenue	206	277	323	347	+57%
Expense	100	107	105	103	+5%
EBIT[*]	106	170	218	244	+106%

[*]Earnings before interest and tax

Source: Company information

money market instruments[2] and fixed income instruments[3]; and 2) derivatives,[4] such as options[5] and forwards.[6]

Bakhshi's Assessment

Bakhshi used the few months before he officially took over the unit to assess the situation and gather best practices from other emerging market regions. He made the following findings:

The relationship between the hub and the countries in the CEEMEA region was different from that in the other two

[2]Money market instruments are short-term debts.

[3]Fixed income instruments pay a fixed interest rate—bonds are an example.

[4]A derivative is a financial instrument whose characteristics and value depend on those of an underlying instrument, such as currency or debt. Advanced investors sometimes buy or sell derivatives to manage risk associated with the underlying instrument by protecting against fluctuations in value, or to profit from periods of inactivity or decline.

[5]An option is the right, but not the obligation, to buy or sell a specific amount of a given currency or debt, at a specified price during a specified period of time.

[6]A forward is a contract obligating one party to buy and another party to sell a financial instrument, such as currency, at a specific future date.

EXHIBIT 2   *Countries in the CEEMEA Region Geographic Clusters*

Geographic Cluster	Countries
Central and Eastern Europe (CEE)	Bulgaria, Czech Republic, Hungary, Romania, Slovakia
Commonwealth of Independent States (CIS)	Russia, Kazakhstan, Ukraine
Middle East and Egypt	Bahrain, Jordan, Lebanon, Pakistan, United Arab Emirates, Egypt
Africa	Algeria, Cameroon, Congo, Côte d'Ivoire, Gabon, Kenya, Morocco, Nigeria, Senegal, Tanzania, Tunisia, Uganda, Zambia
Poland	
Turkey	
South Africa	
London	

Source: Company information

emerging market regions, where there was a very strong relationship between the hub and the countries. They shared common values and practices. Managing the CEEMEA region was more complicated because the countries were more diverse in size, culture, risk, financial market development, regulatory regime, and corporate governance. Countries in the CEEMEA region were managed in a more decentralized way, and rarely shared performance results, new ideas and best practices. Management reporting needed to become faster and more accurate. There were no comprehensive systems and processes for local markets to report profitability and risks. At every month end, it took too much time to reconcile the numbers and produce even high-level management reports.

In local markets, IT was sub-optimal and information was not used as effectively as Bakhshi wanted. There was no integrated risk management monitoring process due to the fragmentation of systems across the region. In most cases, the procedures were manual, using spreadsheets to control the business. People did not trust each other enough to share information and learn from each other's mistakes. Sales-people tended to push "simple" products into the market and take orders, rather than focus on client relationships and recommend alternatives to satisfy different client needs. There were no comprehensive systems and processes to collect and maintain customer information.

Bakhshi's direct superior, Dipak Rastogi, at the time CEO of CEEMEA, suggested that he participate in the Breakthrough Program for Senior Executives at IMD in Lausanne, Switzerland, in June 2000 to gain management insights. Bakhshi heard Professor Donald A. Marchand explaining the Information Orientation (IO) Framework[7] (*refer to* **Exhibit 3**). He agreed with the concept that an organization could improve business performance if it increased its IO Maturity, i.e., how well it effectively managed and used information, knowledge, people and IT capabilities. Bakhshi remarked:

> *Infocentricity is something that I thought about, but nobody ever put it on paper and explained it that way. This model is a science.*

Bakhshi's New Business Model

Bakhshi developed a new centralized business model consisting of a regional network with strong relationships between the hub in London and the countries. The model was put in place to promote regional operational efficiency, leveraged product expertise, pooled local market knowledge, trading expertise and intense customer focus. To make the model work, he needed world-class talent with high EQ (emotional quotient[8]) and a commitment to teamwork and infocentricity.

Building infocentricity was significant because the centralized model required timely, accurate and sufficient management reporting. Moreover, the price of financial instruments in emerging markets was particularly sensitive to political factors. To be able to profit, traders needed to have smart trading ideas and real-time information about political changes. And to improve customer relationships, sales-people needed sufficient customer information and tracking of their sales activities.

However, building infocentricity in the Sales & Trading unit would be a challenge: resources for IT investment were limited; market research and analysis on emerging markets were either not available or not reliable; and it would be difficult to change the ways people managed and used information. As Robert Lustberg, a trader at the London hub, commented:

> *If you are a trader, by definition, you are an information collector. It's not easy to get traders to share information because traders historically have been measured exclusively by how much money they make.*

Bakhshi's Intervention

Bakhshi discussed his ideas and challenges with his other direct superior, Y.S. Wong, Executive Vice President and global head—Emerging Markets Sales & Trading. Wong fully supported Bakhshi and asked his team in the New York headquarters to collaborate with Bakhshi on enhancing IT applications specific to the treasury business in the CEEMEA region.

Bakhshi recruited people whom he knew and trusted to become his direct reports, and invited Professor Marchand to present the IO Framework to them. He wanted his new management team to diffuse the concepts behind the IO Framework throughout the unit.

Professor Marchand also measured the IO Maturity of Bakhshi's team using the IO Diagnostic[™9] tool. The results (IO Dashboard[™10]) showed that the unit's IO Maturity was very low (*refer to* **Exhibit 4**). Professor Marchand helped the new management team develop an action plan. The key initiatives included adding IT applications, improving deal capturing and client contact processes, training staff to adopt the new applications and processes, and designing a scorecard to measure an employee's effectiveness in information use. In particular, Bakhshi recognized that Michael Page, MD—business management, had high EQ and good change management skills, and asked him to orchestrate the implementation process.

THE NEW MANAGEMENT TEAM BUILDS INFOCENTRICITY

The members of the management team faced different challenges. They implemented various change initiatives in parallel to contribute to building infocentricity and business capabilities.

---

[7]The IO Framework was developed and scientifically validated during a three-year study—carried out at IMD with the financial support of Accenture—involving 1,200 senior managers and over 200 senior management teams from 103 international companies. These companies formed the benchmark sample against which an organization could measure its IO Maturity. References: 1) Marchand, Donald A., William J. Kettinger, and John D. Rollins. *Making the Invisible Visible: How Companies Win with the Right Information, People and IT.* Chichester: J. Wiley & Sons, 2001: 24. 2) Marchand, Donald A., William J. Kettinger, and John D. Rollins. *Information Orientation: the Link to Business Performance.* Oxford: Oxford University Press, 2001.

[8]EQ is a measure of emotional intelligence—a person's psychological functioning and interpersonal skills. Source: Stein, Steven J. and Howard E. Book. *The EQ Edge: Emotional Intelligence and Your Success.* Stoddart Publishing, 2000.

[9]The IO Diagnostic™ tool is a trademarked product of enterpriseIQ® (see www.enterpriseIQ.com).

[10]The IO Dashboard™ is a trademarked product of enterpriseIQ©.

EXHIBIT 3   The *Information Orientation Framework: Leveraging Infocentricity*

Information Orientation (IO)
Measures the capabilities of a company to effectively manage and use information

Information Technology Practices (ITP) Capability
The capability of a company to effectively manage appropriate IT applications and infrastructure in support of operational decision-making, and communication processes.

IT for Management Support
includes the software, hardware, telecommunication networks and capabilities that **facilitate executive decision-making.**
It facilitates monitoring and analysis of internal and external business **issues** concerning
- knowledge sharing,
- market developments,
- general business situations,
- market positioning, future market direction,
- and business risk.

IT for Innovation Support
includes the software, hardware, telecommunication networks and capabilities that
- **facilitate people's creativity** and that
- **enable the exploration, development, and sharing of new ideas.**
It also includes the hardware and software support **to develop and introduce new products and services.**

IT for Business Process Support
focuses on the deployment of software, hardware, networks, and t echnical expertise to **facilitate the management of business processes and people**
- **across functions** within the company and
- **externally with suppliers and customers.**

IT for Operational Support
includes the software, hardware, telecommunication networks and technical expertise to
- **control business operations** ,
- **to ensure that lower-skilled workers perform** their responsibilities **consistently and with high quality** and
- **to improve the efficiency of operations** .

Information Management Practices (IMP) Capability
The capability of a company to manage information effectively over its life cycle.

Sensing
involves **how information is detected and identified concerning** :
- economic, social, and political changes;
- competitors' innovation so that might impact the business;
- market shifts and customer demands for new products;
- anticipated problems with suppliers and partners.

Processing
into useful knowledge **consists of accessing and analyzing appropriate information sources and databases before business decisions are made.**
- Hiring,
- training,
- evaluating and
- rewarding people with analytical skills
is essential for processing information into useful knowledge .

Maintaining
involves
- **reusing existing information** to avoid collecting the same information again,
- **updating information** databases so that they remain current and
- **refreshing data**
to ensure that people are using the best information available.

Organizing
includes
- **indexing, classifying and linking information and databases together** to provide access within and across business units and functions;
- **training and rewarding employees** for accurately and completely organizing information for which they are responsible.

Collecting
consists of the systematic process of
- **gathering relevant information** by profiling information needs of employees;
- **developing filter mechanisms** (computerized and non -computerized) to prevent information overload;
- **providing access to existing collective knowledge** ;
- and, training and rewarding employees for accurately and completely collecting information for which they are responsible .

Information Behaviors and Values (IBV) Capability
The capability of a company to instill and promote behaviors and values in its people for effective use of information.

Proactiveness
An organization is called "information proactive" when its members
- **actively seek out and respond to changes** in their competitive environment and
- **think about how to use this information** to enhance existing and create new products and services.

Sharing
is the free exchange of non -sensitive and sensitive information. Sharing occurs
- **between individuals in teams,**
- **across functional boundaries and**
- **across organizational boundaries** (i.e., with customers, suppliers and partners).

Transparency
An organization is "information transparent" when **its members trust each other enough to talk about failures, errors and mistakes in an open and constructive manner** and without fear of unfair repercussions.

Control
is the **disclosure of information about business performance to all employees** to influence and direct individual and, subsequently, company performance

Formality
refers to **the degree to which members of an organization use and trust formal sources of information** . Depending on the size, virtualness, and geographic dispersion of an organization, this balance shifts towards more formal or informal information behavior.

Integrity
is an organizational value manifested through individual behavior that is **characterized by the absence of manipulating information for personal gains** such as
- knowingly passing on inaccurate information,
- distributing information to justify decisions after the fact or
- keeping information to oneself.
Good information integrity results in effective sharing of sensitive information.

Source: Marchand, Donald A., William J. Kettinger, and John D. Rollins. *Making the "nvisible Visible: How Companies Win with the Right Information, People and IT.* Chichester: J. Wiley & Sons, 2001: 24.

EXHIBIT 4 Information Orientation Maturity Results of Citigroup's CEEMEA Sales & Trading Unit

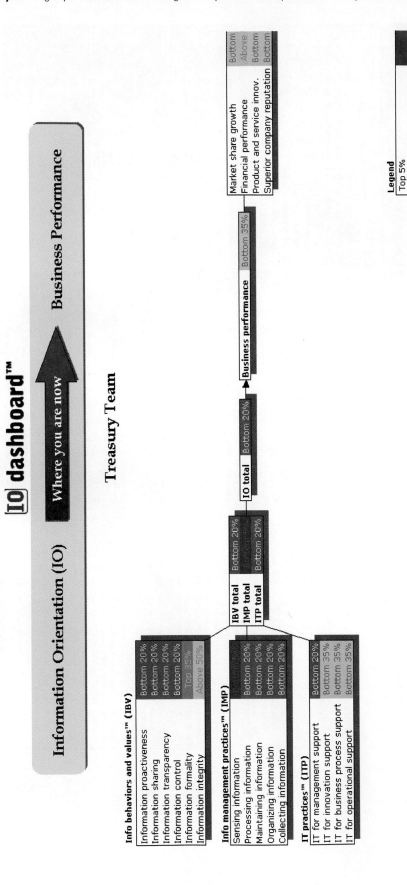

Acting as an Involved Change Agent

Bakhshi himself worked hard to drive the change. Initially, he traveled frequently to the countries to gain support for the new business model. He also initiated the distribution of messages and monthly newsletters to all staff, informing them of the progress of change and its impact on business performance. During the process, he held regular discussions with his direct reports to form a common understanding of what building higher IO Maturity in their unit was about and how it should evolve.

Adding IT Applications

In July 2000, Bakhshi appointed Umesh Jagtiani, MD, as regional head of eCommerce for the Sales & Trading business. (By the summer of 2003, the eCommerce unit had grown significantly with a team of business and technology professionals.) In addition to rolling out Treasury products to clients, the team had built a robust intranet platform for reporting, risk and credit management, trading information flow management, and a fully functional client relationship management (CRM) application.

Jagtiani worked closely with the Business Technology team, headed by Rakesh Joshi, and Citigroup's Operations & Technology unit to integrate front- and back-office technologies. Joshi had to ensure that CEEMEA had the applications and data specific to their business requirements.

TREASURY PORTAL

The eCommerce team first built a treasury portal showing such information as the latest market news, transaction details, and profit and loss. The portal's interactive component permitted traders to share information about markets and generic client flows, along with "behind the scenes" impact analysis they were having on the price of traded instruments. Jagtiani commented:

The inherent risk of contagion between different CEEMEA clusters meant that the implications of a market event were not isolated to a specific geography. A default on domestic debt in Russia and the devaluation of the currency, for example, would have a knock-on effect on other related economies and potentially impact oil prices. The dissemination of information and the collective behavior of traders were in the past difficult to gauge. Today, with the information tools and behaviors embedded into our business, the decision-making process is based on more sound analysis from the information.

Jagtiani and the business heads encouraged trading desks from other markets to join. Lustberg noted:

When traders in other CEEMEA countries, such as Jordan, saw the idea flow between London and Poland, they thought, "If they buy in why don't we?"

CUSTOMER RELATIONSHIP MANAGEMENT TOOL

In March 2001, the team launched an in-house solution for customer relationship management. The application tracked information on revenue—broken down into spread and volume by customer, product and country—and account management activities such as frequency of customer calls/visits.

ONLINE CREDIT ENGINE

The team launched an online credit engine in July 2001. This application provided information such as credit lines, utilization and quality metrics.

RISK ANALYSIS PORTAL

In October 2001, a risk analysis portal was released to help the management team assess the risk levels of different countries. The portal included information such as consolidated balance sheets and stress tests.

Previously, it had never been a priority for traders to record information about profitability and risk exposure and submit it to the hub at the end of each trading day. But reporting this information was important. Bakhshi stipulated, "Before you go home, you need to know this information and put it on the web-based template for submission." If someone did not submit the information, the space on the template would turn red and the system would automatically e-mail a reminder to that person. Bakhshi reflected,

Once I could see the Profit & Loss and risk exposure on the web, I traveled less as I was able to know what was going on in the countries every day.

WEB-BASED CENTRALIZED PLATFORM

Historically, operational activities like quoting prices, capturing deals, verifying credit, reconciliation with the back office, and reporting had been manual, inefficient and—usually—delayed. To increase operational efficiency, the team began a complex project in October 2001: to build a single centralized platform and a common database for automating and integrating the deal capturing processes for multiple products (*refer to **Exhibits 5a and 5b**). This platform acted as a core to bring all portals and applications developed earlier together.

During 2002, the team launched various features to capture:

❑ Foreign exchange deals—in March (rolled out to 30 countries by mid-2003)

❑ Fixed income deals—in September (rolled out to five countries by mid-2003)

❑ Money market deals—in October (rolled out to seven countries by mid-2003).

The feature for capturing derivative deals would be added later.

The platform offered huge benefits. Information that had previously been fragmented across multiple systems was

EXHIBIT 5a   *IT Applications*

TECHNICAL DESCRIPTION

The web-based centralized platform, linked to external systems—such as the Reuters and Citigroup's Money Market and Foreign Exchange online trading systems—to capture deals in real time. It also linked to the Global Credit Engine to obtain credit limits.

Transaction information was collected from the start, stored in a centralized database, organized and analyzed according to user requirements, and accessed through various applications or portals such as those described in the case study. In addition, the platform was connected to Citigroup's back-office systems for integration and reconciliation.

brought together to become real-time intelligence easily accessible by salespeople, traders and managers. Streamlined processing from the platform straight to the back office systems increased productivity. For example, in Russia, the treasurer was able to save 25% to 30% of his time per day, and then use the time saved for more proactive client services. It also allowed easier identification and speedier resolution of mismatches, and hence, solved the problem of delays in generating monthly management reports. The paperless workflow for deal booking and authorization also reduced costs. Finally, the platform facilitated the building of an infocentric culture. Jagtiani reflected:

In the past, traders saw information as proprietary and shared it strategically, if there was an underlying benefit to themselves, or if it reflected positively on their trading views and results. Today this information is no longer "personally" owned. A culture of transparency has transformed the way business is managed. Both good and bad results are shared within the team, and overall the impact on business has been extremely positive.

Strengthening the Trading Arm

Bakhshi hired Anil Prasad, MD and regional head of trading, to manage the trading team. Like all other department or cluster heads, Prasad had to build an infocentric culture within his team. At the outset, he faced a team of 18 trading desks split between two locations in London. Overall morale was low, and communication and collaboration between the two groups was limited. Prasad said of the situation, "On day one, they didn't even talk to each other, let alone share proprietary information."

When Prasad arrived, he put all the desks in a single location. He then organized team-building events to develop trust among traders. He hired trading talents only if they were team players and saw the value of infocentricity. He stressed:

We have star traders. But they need to fit our culture. . . To be the best, you have to share information and trade ideas.

Lustberg commented on his own appointment:

One of the considerations prior to joining this team was that both Bakhshi and Prasad subscribed to a view that we need to share and promote the flow of information.

Prasad encouraged such advocates of infocentricity to persuade their peers to share information and ideas by, for example, joining the chat on the treasury portal. He also improved his team's trading expertise by providing them with market research and analyst reports as well as training.

With all these efforts, the London hub became the center of sophisticated trading expertise. In addition to improving the trading expertise in countries, traders at the London hub also served as role models to encourage traders in local markets to share trading ideas and market information.

Prasad also started to provide intensive training to traders in local markets.

Improving the Sales Team's Product Expertise and Customer Focus

In 2001, Okan Pekin, MD—Sales and Structuring, engaged Greenwich Research to conduct a survey of more than 800 clients (corporate and institutional) across 12 key countries. The survey helped the unit understand market penetration, market share and client perceptions to help segment the market.

Pekin pushed his team to use the customer relationship management portal. Only three months after launch, it covered 5,000 clients (corporate and institutional) in 25 countries. In addition to allowing Pekin to understand customers' trading history and sales opportunities, the customer relationship management portal enabled him to review his team's client contact. For example, if a salesperson had not contacted his or her clients enough, an early warning indicator reminded the salesperson to visit the customers, as well as alerting Pekin, who would then ask the salesperson why he or

EXHIBIT 5b   IT Applications

eDealer

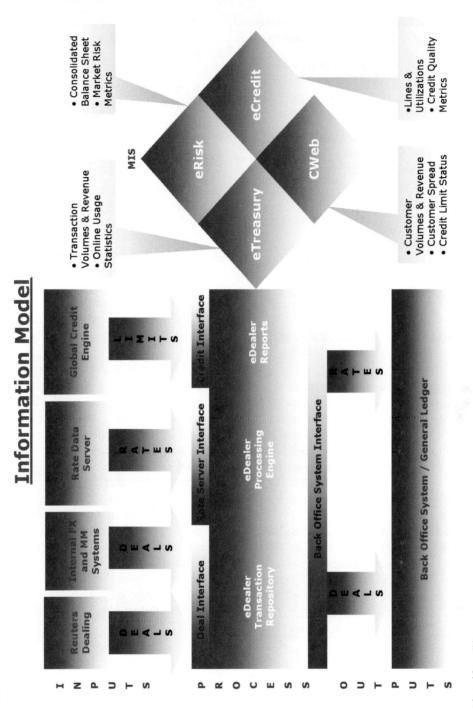

Source: Adapted from Citigroup

she had not contacted the clients. Pekin coached his team to develop the ability to sense customer needs. He commented:

> Opinions of customers always override revenue numbers. The latter is backward looking while the former is about the future. A salesperson has to ask himself or herself, "If I have to contact customers more often, what do I ask them?"

He also sent his team to an in-house School of Foreign Exchange and Derivatives to improve product knowledge and client contact skills (by mid-2003, the School had successfully trained 150 staff).

Pekin's team had become better at sharing sales and product development ideas and sensing customer needs. He noted:

> We had tools to communicate new concepts, disciplined processes to force new things to happen, and incentives to change behavior. Now, the challenge is to liberate people to proactively create and share new ideas, and take on initiatives.

Pushing Behavioral Changes with the IO Scorecard™11

While the other change initiatives were continuing, Page formed a cross-functional team of six to work with Professor Marchand on developing an IO Scorecard™. The team's challenge: to translate the IO Framework into a Scorecard that could be used to guide the staff and measure how they sensed, shared, and used information. Moreover, the Scorecard needed to address in practical terms the functional contexts in this particular industry. The scorecard had to be in a language that all staff could understand.

In February 2002, the team rolled out the online IO Scorecard™ (*refer to* **Exhibit 6**), which measured an employee on 20 information-sharing activities, including how frequently and how well he or she developed quality contact with clients; how much he or she contributed to product innovation; how much he or she contributed information and ideas to the treasury portal; how well he or she shared best practices and mistakes; and how much he or she used and updated the treasury portal.

On a quarterly basis, each unit head had to evaluate their team's performance. All managers had to review their team's performance against average scores by function, country and the entire region. Managers also worked with the unit heads to set improvement objectives. Staff were rewarded according to the evaluations.

Overcoming Barriers to Higher IO Maturity in Different Geographic Clusters

While the London hub continued to make progress in improving information, people and IT practices in the region, the diversity of the region required specific changes

[11]The IO Scorecard™ is a trademarked product of enterpriseIQ®.

in information use by local treasury employees. Every subregion faced a different set of challenges. A few examples are looked at in more detail below.

AFTER THE ACQUISITION IN POLAND: "HOW WAS THE DAY?"

In June 2000, Citigroup acquired a majority interest in Bank Handlowy, a leading state bank in Poland, Citigroup's Treasury unit in the country had 150 customers, whereas Bank Handlowy's had a customer base of 10,000 small and medium-sized enterprises. Bank Handlowy's Treasury unit operated out of a hub in Warsaw and six regional offices, where detailed knowledge of the unit's day-to-day activities and performance was limited.

Ted Dabrowski, treasurer in Poland, recalled:

> I remember when I first walked into one of Poland's regional offices and asked, "How was the day?" A trader just said, "Good." When I probed to find out the transaction volume and spread, the trader responded, "Not sure . . ."

Dabrowski decided that his team should first focus on integrating the IT platforms (three front office systems and three back office systems) and building a unified infocentric culture. Employees in the country's regional offices saw the acquisition and change initiatives as opportunities; they were open to change. Employees in the Warsaw hub, by contrast, saw themselves as professional enough to know what work to do—and how. They regarded these initiatives as infringements of their rights, and hence, resented them. Dabrowski made a point of communicating closely with them to gain their buy-in.

By mid-2001, dealers had changed their ways of sensing, sharing and using information. For example, dealers started to record trading results daily, participate in morning conference calls to share market information, and call customers. Dabrowski commented:

> You can feel the activity and life in the room, which is completely opposite to the scene shortly after the acquisition. Now, my traders can tell me details of how the day was!

After the global economic downturn in 2001, the operations in Poland experienced tough times. The country's future entry into the European Union had also reduced the foreign exchange spreads. The IO Scorecard™ helped push salespeople to make more customer contacts and to launch derivatives. By the end of 2002, the team was calling 600 customers a day, in addition to what they used to do in late 2000–answering 400 incoming calls a day. They gained 350 customers and introduced 40 derivatives. According to the 2002 Greenwich survey, they received high ratings for their service quality; and they increased their market shares in the foreign exchange market and the derivative market in the CEEMEA region to 20% and 35%, respectively, making them the leader in both markets. They increased revenue by

EXHIBIT 6   *Online IO Scorecard*™

Source: Company information; copy of actual screenshot

I/O REVIEW REPORTS

| Detail Report | Detail group Avg. Report | Country-wise Average Report | Region-wise Average Report |

SELF REVIEW ANALYSIS

Note: Choosing a review period and Review type displays the group list and member list belonging to that group.
Select a Group and it's member from "Review On" list and click "Go" to view his Review

Review Period	Jul 01, 2003 - Sep 30, 2003 ▼	Review Type	Self Review ▼		Treasurer ▼
				Group	

Treasurer Client

1. **Client satisfaction based on surveys**
      5   4   3   2   1   [N/A]

2. **Market share based on surveys**
      5   4   3   2   1   [N/A]

3. **Ensure active discussion and meetings with clients takes place on a regular basis**
      5   [4]   3   2   1   N/A

4. **Quality of Sales / Structuring team with regards to franchise development and client interaction**
      5   [4]   3   2   1   N/A
                         Question Type Total: 8.0

Treasurer Product

5. **Work in partnership with the Structuring team and London Hub on new product development**
     [5]   4   3   2   1   N/A

6. **Ability of group to generate new ideas**
     [5]   4   3   2   1   N/A

7. **Ability of group to sell new products**
      5   [4]   3   2   1   N/A

8. **Encourage the contribution into whiteboard, use of EMFlow, and update of daily flow on eTreasury**
      5   4   [3]   2   1   N/A

9. **Awareness of policies and procedures that relate to countries and function**
     [5]   4   3   2   1   N/A

10. **Attendance and participation in weekly trading conference calls**
      5   4   3   [1 - 3]   N/A
                         Question Type Total: 23.0

Treasurer Teamwork

11. **Staff exchanges between countries to be encouraged**
      5   [4]   3   2   1   N/A

12. **Regular debriefing with staff on winning/losing trades and missed deals to improve/learn from mistakes**
     [5]   4   3   2   1   N/A

13. **Peer reviews to be initiated and feedback given to participants**
      5   4   3   2   1   [N/A]

14. **Quarterly staff reviews to give them a sense of benchmark vs goals set.**
     [5]   4   3   2   1   N/A
                         Question Type Total: 14.0

Treasure Others

15. **Relationship with the Regulators / Central Bank**
     [5]   4   3   2   1   N/A

16. **Ensure controls and processes are being implemented and followed as per policy**
   - ensure Quarterly Self Assessments are complete and corrective actions / audit finds actioned
     [5]   4   3   2   1   N/A

17. **Attract talent and retain key personnel**
      5   [4]   3   2   1   N/A

18. **Increase the daily use of eTreasury within the team**
      5   4   3   2   1   [N/A]

19. **Implementation of any applicable technology solutions**
     [5]   4   3   2   1   N/A

20.1. **eTreasury to be updated (daily) for risk in a timely fashion**
   [5 - 137] 4   3   2   1   N/A

20.2. **eTreasury to be updated (daily) for P&L in a timely fashion**
   [5 - 232] 4   3   2   1   N/A
                         Question Type Total: 19.5

Review Analysis Summary

Question Classification	Question Type Total	
Treasurer Client	8.0	
Treasurer Product	23.0	
Treasurer Teamwork	14.0	
Treasurer Others	19.5	
Average Overall Grade is	**64.5 [80.60 %]**	

43% between the time of the acquisition and the end of 2002. Dabrowski commented:

We measure people's extent of information management and use more often than the rest of Citigroup. It's tiring and stressful . . . you feel like you are always being watched. But we offer very good compensation for performance.

CENTRAL & EASTERN EUROPE AND CIS: MANAGING DIVERSITY TO FACILITATE IMPROVED INFORMATION BEHAVIORS

Historically, management had focused on the largest market, Russia. After Misbah Shah took over as managing director in these clusters, he devoted more attention to other countries and used different techniques to make the whole team change the way they sensed, shared and used information.

For example, he turned country diversity from a management challenge into an execution advantage. Talents from the larger and more developed countries, such as the Czech Republic and Hungary, were more confident in themselves and less open to new ideas. By contrast, people from less developed countries, such as Ukraine, were eager to learn and deliver results. Therefore, Shah piloted new initiatives in less developed countries to create success stories to influence the more developed countries.

In addition, Shah sometimes sent employees to meet Bakhshi to let them understand the level of commitment he had to IO. Shah commented:

If you micro-manage, you can make a guy give you all the accurate information. But what's more important is whether the guy has learned how to use the information.

With all these efforts, the cluster's revenue had increased by 43% between 2000 and the end of 2002. Shah reflected:

You have to be very intense about this [the process of building infocentricity]. It's evolving . . . not just implemented once. The next step is to take infocentricity externally to the customers for value creation.

SOUTH AFRICA: LEVERAGING THE LONDON HUB'S PRODUCT EXPERTISE AND THE COUNTRY'S LOCAL KNOWLEDGE TO INTRODUCE DERIVATIVES

Four local banks dominated South Africa, accounting for 80% to 85% of the market. Citigroup was the largest and the only foreign full-scale corporate bank. Before Nadir Mahmud assumed the role of treasurer, the team had focused on "simple" foreign exchange and money market products. Mahmud wanted to serve clients better by offering more sophisticated products that satisfied local market needs. Therefore, Mahmud ensured that his team provided Pekin with the necessary inputs to develop new products, which were then localized by about 10 percent. The collaboration also allowed his team to gain product expertise from the London hub.

Traders needed to thoroughly understand these sophisticated products, so Mahmud hired trading talents with the necessary knowledge. He also trained his team and encouraged them to participate in the treasury portal to gain product knowledge.

By the end of 2002, the team had increased derivative revenues by 165%. According to the Greenwich survey, in the same year they increased their market share in the foreign exchange option market to 5 percent. And the team increased revenue by 180% between 2000 and the end of 2002.

MIDDLE EAST & EGYPT: ALIGNMENT OF MANAGEMENT MINDSET AND GOALS, AND FULL-SPEED TRANSFORMATION UNDER WAR CONDITIONS

Before Shujaat Nadeem became regional director, relationships between the cluster hub in Bahrain and the countries were weak. For example, managers in the hub did not pay enough visits to smaller countries such as Lebanon and Jordan. The cluster was fragmented, with no common management mindset or goals—management parameters, such as balance sheets, scale of measuring risk, and levels of acceptable risk, varied from one country to another.

Nadeem first had to focus on aligning goals and management mindset. He required managers in the Bahrain hub to visit all countries with the same frequency, and did so himself. He pushed his employees to use the new IT applications. For example, two months after the treasury portal was implemented, he made all his employees regularly log onto the portal.

He also initiated and encouraged more group discussions to instill the habit of information sharing. Nadeem commented:

It's not efficient and infocentric to have separate conversations with six country managers individually every day. I told them to communicate with me via SameTime so that all other country managers can participate in the discussion and know what has been discussed.

Nadeem believed that his team's performance and infocentricity would not be improved without his close involvement:

Following the lead of Suneel, it closely monitored the results of the IO Scorecard™. It allowed me to quickly monitor the performance of the group.

The cluster increased revenue by 160% between 2000 and the end of 2002. In addition, the information capabilities, product expertise and customer focus of the team created the strategic value of attracting joint venture opportunities.

IMPACT ON BUSINESS PERFORMANCE

With all these efforts, the unit's business performance improved in a number of ways. Profit increased by more than 100% from 2000 to 2002 (*refer to **Exhibit 1***). According to the 2002 Greenwich survey, the percentage of clients who regarded the unit as their "lead bank" in the foreign exchange market and the derivative market increased, respectively, to 61% (from 50% in 2001) and 38% (from 22% in 2001). Derivatives were introduced in a number of countries.

The team also received exceptional client satisfaction scores across the region. Finally, the unit won a number of *Euromoney* awards in 2002, including those for "Best in Emerging Market Currencies" and "Best at Risk Management."

THE FUTURE

Jagtiani summed up Bakhshi's influence:

The reason why the idea of improving information management and use didn't go away is because Bakhshi continuously drove it with a passion.

In mid-2003, Bakhshi was promoted to become Global Head of the newly formed Emerging Markets Local Finance unit and joined Citigroup's management committee (In early 2004, Bakhshi was named Executive Vice President of Citigroup and assumed responsibility for the Emerging Markets - Corporate Banking business). Despite Bakhshi's departure, people in the Sales & Trading unit were confident that they would continue with the new information behav-

iors and practices he had supported. However, moving up in Citigroup would expose Bakhshi to new challenges. Could he replicate his initiatives in strengthening information capabilities in another unit of Citigroup?

CASE STUDY QUESTIONS

1. Analyze Citigroup's CEEMEA Sales & Trading unit using the value chain and competitive forces models.
2. What is the role of information systems at this unit? How do information systems support its business strategy and provide value?
3. What management, organization, and technology factors affect the performance of the CEEMEA Sales & Trading unit?
4. How did applying the Information Orientation Framework solve the problems of the CEEMEA Sales & Trading Unit?
5. Could the positive results of using an infocentric approach be replicated at other Citigroup units? Explain your answer.

Hands-On Guide: How to Analyze a Case Study

Management Information Systems, Ninth Edition provides a number of case studies for you to analyze. Included in these cases are questions to help you understand and analyze the case. You may, however, be assigned other case studies that do not have questions. This Hands-On Guide presents a structured framework to help you analyze such cases as well as the case studies in this text. Knowing how to analyze a case will help you attack virtually any business problem.

A case study helps students learn by immersing them in a real-world business scenario where they can act as problem solvers and decision makers. The case presents facts about a particular organization. Students are asked to analyze the case by focusing on the most important facts and using this information to determine the opportunities and problems facing that organization. Students are then asked to identify alternative courses of action to deal with the problems they identify.

A case study analysis must not merely summarize the case. It should identify key issues and problems, outline and assess alternative courses of action, and draw appropriate conclusions. The case study analysis can be broken down into the following steps:

1. Identify the most important facts surrounding the case.
2. Identify the key issue or issues.
3. Specify alternative courses of action.
4. Evaluate each course of action.
5. Recommend the best course of action.

Let's look at what each step involves.

1. *Identify the most important facts surrounding the case.* Read the case several times to become familiar with the information it contains. Pay attention to the information in any accompanying exhibits, tables, or figures. Many case scenarios, as in real life, present a great deal of detailed information. Some of these facts are more relevant that others for problem identification. One can assume the facts and figures in the case are true, but statements, judgments, or decisions made by individuals should be questioned. Underline and then list the most important facts and figures that would help you define the central problem or issue. If key facts and numbers are not available, you can make assumptions, but these assumptions should be reasonable given the situation. The "correctness" of your conclusions may depend on the assumptions you make.

2. *Identify the key issue or issues.* Use the facts provided by the case to identify the key issue or issues facing the company you are studying. Many cases present multiple issues or problems. Identify the most important and separate them from more trivial issues. State the major problem or challenge facing the company. You should be able to describe the problem or challenge in one or two sentences. You should be able to explain how this problem affects the strategy or performance of the organization.

    You will need to explain why the problem occurred. Does the problem or challenge facing the company come from a changing environment, new opportunities, a declining market share, or inefficient internal or external business processes? In the case of information systems-related problems, you need to pay special attention to the role of technology as well as the behavior of the organization and its management.

    Information system problems in the business world typically present a combination of management, technology, and organizational issues. When identifying the key issue or problem, ask what kind of problem it is: Is it a management problem, a technology problem, an organizational problem, or a combination of these? What management, organizational, and technology factors contributed to the problem?

    ❏ To determine if a problem stems from management factors, consider whether managers are exerting appropriate leadership over the organization and monitoring organizational performance. Consider also the nature of management decision making: Do managers have sufficient information for performing this role, or do they fail to take advantage of the information that is available?

    ❏ To determine if a problem stems from technology factors, examine any issues arising from the organization's information technology infrastructure: its hardware, software, networks and telecommunications infrastructure, and the management of data in databases or traditional files. Consider also whether the appropriate management and organizational assets are in place to use this technology effectively.

    ❏ To determine the role of organizational factors, examine any issues arising from the organization's structure, culture, business processes, work groups, divisions among interest groups, and relationships with other organizations, as well as the impact of changes in the organization's external environment—changes in government regulations, economic conditions, or the actions of competitors, customers, and suppliers.

You will have to decide which of these factors—or a combination of factors—is most important in explaining why the problem occurred.

3. *Specify alternative courses of action.* List the courses of action the company can take to solve its problem or meet the challenge it faces. For information system-related problems, do these alternatives require a new information system or the modification of an existing system? Are new technologies, business processes, organizational structures, or management behavior required? What changes to organizational processes would be required by each alternative? What management policy would be required to implement each alternative?

Remember, there is a difference between what an organization "should do" and what that organization actually "can do." Some solutions are too expensive or operationally difficult to implement, and you should avoid solutions that are beyond the organization's resources. Identify the constraints that will limit the solutions available. Is each alternative executable given these constraints?

4. *Evaluate each course of action.* Evaluate each alternative using the facts and issues you identified earlier, given the conditions and information available. Identify the costs and benefits of each alternative. Ask yourself, "What would be the likely outcome of this course of action?" State the risks as well as the rewards associated with each course of action. Is your recommendation feasible from a technical, operational, and financial standpoint? Be sure to state any assumptions on which you have based your decision.

5. *Recommend the best course of action.* State your choice for the best course of action and provide a detailed explanation of why you made this selection. You may also want to provide an explanation of why other alternatives were not selected. Your final recommendation should flow logically from the rest of your case analysis and should clearly specify what assumptions were used to shape your conclusion. There is often no single "right" answer, and each option is likely to have risks as well as rewards.

Hands-On Guide to Database Design, Normalization, and Entity-Relationship Diagramming

This Hands-On Guide will show you how to design a relational database system for a small business using normalization and entity-relationship diagrams. The system we will be developing is for a small but growing barber shop/hair salon business. The shop, named HisNHers, is owned by Clarence and Clarissa. They have big plans to expand soon and believe their system of maintaining customer information on index cards can no longer support their business needs.

INFORMATION GATHERING

Your first step is to gather information about how the new system will be used, what information the user needs, how a new system can speed up and simplify operations, as well as how the system could help the business to grow. A database is a model not only of reality but also of the future. If there is a need to know information which is not yet stored anywhere or docs not currently exist, room for this data should be included in the system design.

Both Clarence and Clarissa want a system that can maintain information about their business with over 300 customers. Also, they want to be able to begin tailoring advertising to particular customers based on their profiles and to send birthday cards containing special offers.

DESIGNING THE DATABASE: A CONCEPTUAL SCHEMA

To begin developing a conceptual schema of the system, Clarence and Clarissa (and perhaps their employees) need to describe their business. You will need to look at any paperwork generated by the business, starting with those index cards, which contain a lot of information about each customer. But you'll also look at the phone log, the appointment book, any financial reports that are generated, and perhaps talk to their accountant and/or see if they are using a small accounting package such as QuickBooks, and study what they do with it. There is often informal written information that is also good to know about—do the staff at HisNHers keep their own notes about anything?

The HisNHers Salon now receives payment immediately after the service is performed. But with the proper design of a database, a billing system could be integrated. Targeted marketing could be performed whenever a new product (a new purple hair rinse for all the gray-haired customers) becomes available.

HisNHers is a small business where a personal computer running Microsoft Access would be an appropriate platform for its new system. Since you are most likely using Access in your course work, we will illustrate the design of the database as it would be implemented in Access.

After completing your information requirements analysis, your next task it to develop a conceptual schema of the database. One problem that can arise in this step is that the discussions with users may have shown multiple views of the system. These multiple views will need to be integrated into a single conceptual schema.

For example, at HisNHers, both Clarissa and Clarence often referred to "products." Only after Clarence said that they might like to keep a "product" inventory and Clarissa mentioned that a customer made an appointment for a "product" did you realize that Clarence meant items such as a package of hair-coloring and Clarissa meant services, (e.g., hair cuts). This sort of double meaning for a single term is called a homonym and needs to be resolved before an integrated view of the system can be developed. In a similar fashion, when Clarence referred to the "customers" and Clarissa referred to the "heads," it was clear that "heads" was a synonym for "customer." Unfortunately not all synonyms are so obvious.

In a large organization, personnel with different jobs often see the data in light of their own job function. For example to the colorist applying the hair-coloring, vendor is only an attribute of the product. To the person doing the ordering, vendor is an entity with attributes of its own such as address and phone number.

ENTITIES, RELATIONSHIPS, AND NORMALIZATION

Once a cohesive view of the system is established, the entity classes (tables) need to be defined along with their attributes (fields). Review the discussion of entities, attributes, and relational databases in Chapter 7. Your requirements analysis showed that two main documents are central to HisNHers' operation—Clarissa's index cards and the salon's appointment book.

Clarissa used the index cards to store information about the customers of the salon. They contain: the customer's name, sometimes the address, usually the home phone number and/or a cell phone number, a small number scribbled in the corner, a few notes about the customer's social life, plans, or children, and occasional comments about a particular appointment—(e.g., used Clairol #12 on 10/15).

The appointment book contains the date and time of the appointment, the customer's name, phone number, service requested (e.g., hair cut, beard trim, frosting) and staff member who will do the job.

These documents indicate the need for both a CUSTOMER Table and an APPOINTMENT Table. But, what other tables are needed? What information belongs in each table? How should the tables be linked together? It is important to start slowly and carefully, building on what is obvious. Sometimes it helps to visualize one instance of the data (e.g., one customer and his appointments). Begin sketching out a simplified entity-relationship (ER) diagram to help you visualize the system's tables and relationships. The verbs used for describing the relationships in the ER diagram are often helpful, (e.g., a customer *makes* an appointment, a service *uses* a product).

At HisNHers, Clarissa's index cards contain the beginnings of the Customer entity. The entity known as the CUSTOMER Table will contain demographic data about the person as well as a notes where special "conversational" or unusual items about the customer can be stored. An initial breakdown of the attributes of this entity (or putting it more simply, the fields for the CUSTOMER Table) along with their type (as represented in Access) and size are:

Field Name	Type	Size
CUSTID	Long Integer	4
FNAME	Text	20
MIDNAME	Text	15
LNAME	Text	20
ADDR1	Text	30
ADR2	Text	30
CITY	Text	20
STATE	Text	2
ZIP	Text	5
HOMEPHONE	Text	10
WORKPHONE	Text	10
CELLPHONE	Text	10
EMAIL	Text	50
DOB	Date/Time	8
SEX	Text	1
PERSONAL_INFO	Memo	–
OLDCUSTNUMBER	Integer	3

The customer name field should be broken into first name, middle, and last name. This will insure the ability to sort reports based on last name and allow for personalized reports which use just the first name. Breaking up data into its smallest usable elements is known as *atomization*.

While HisNHers doesn't currently have all of this customer demographic information, providing for these fields

will allow the system to grow and meet Clarence's desire for targeted marketing and a possible billing system. The last field in the CUSTOMER Table is the "old customer number." It is taken from Clarissa's index cards and will allow her to use both the old and new customer numbers until she is comfortable with the new system. This is often a good practice when converting manual or legacy systems (those done in an older computer program).

Discussions with the staff and studying the appointment book indicate that another entity would be the APPOINTMENT Table. It would include the following attributes (fields).

Field Name	Type	Size
CUSTID	Long Integer	4
SERVICE_ID	Long Integer	4
APPT_DATE	Date/Time	8
APPT_TIME	Date/Time	8
EMP_SS	Text	9
PROD_NUM	Long Integer	4
APPT_COMMENT	Memo	—

The Appointment Book shows that customers make appointments. In this sentence lies the beginning of the table relationships in the HisNHers database. The ER diagram which shows the relationship between these initial two tables is:

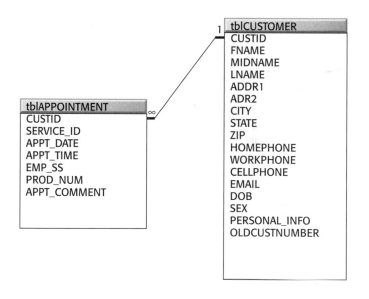

As the system develops, we will add entities and information to this ER diagram until the entire conceptual schema for the database is illustrated.

There are a number of different formats for entity-relationship diagrams. Figure 7-12 in Chapter 7 is one example. Since we are using Microsoft Access to build the database, we will use ER diagrams as they are shown in Microsoft Access's table relationship view. In these ER diagrams, tables are shown with all of their fields. Related tables are shown via lines which link their key fields together and show

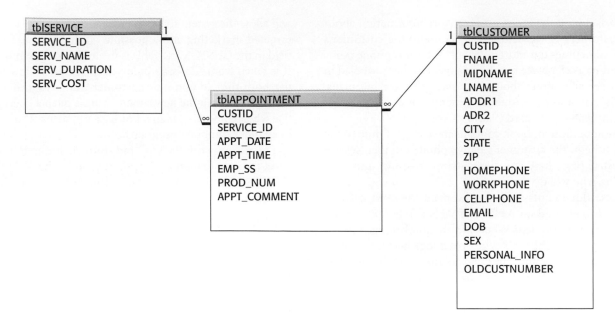

whether the entities have a one-to-one or one-to-many relationship. A small number 1 next to the key means that a table is on the one side of a relationship. A small ∞ symbol indicates that the table is on the many side of a relationship. For example, one customer makes many appointments.

Because the CUSTOMER Table will be linked to the APPOINTMENT Table, it will not be necessary to include either the customer name or phone number in the APPOINTMENT Table. The CUSTOMER Table and APPOINTMENT Table will be linked based on a key (which is not the customer's name). Thus, only the key field from the CUSTOMER Table needs to be included in the APPOINTMENT Table in order for all of the information about a customer to be available.

If a field from the CUSTOMER Table, like the phone number, were to be included in the APPOINTMENT Table, it would have to be entered each time an appointment was made. Also, if the phone number were to change, each record for that customer in the APPOINTMENT Table would have to modified. *No entity ever needs to include attributes from an entity to which it is linked.* Doing so would cause repeating information, which would violate the first rule of normalization, which states that there should be no repeating groups or many-to-many relationships among entity classes.

HisNHers appointment book includes the service provided. This could be an attribute of the CUSTOMER Entity since many customers have many services performed. However, this would create a many-to-many relationship. A many-to-many relationship requires a join or linking table (sometimes called an intersection relation) to prevent repeating data (similar to the table ORDERED_PART in Figure 7-11 of Chapter 7). The APPOINTMENT entity is, in fact such a join table. The APPOINTMENT entity joins the customer with the service provided on a particular date. Other details about a particular appointment such as the employee who performs the service and the product used are

also included. These details or attributes relate only to this particular appointment, not to the customer or service.

For any one CUSTOMER record there may be many related APPOINTMENT records. This is indicated on the ER diagram by the small 1 next the CUSTID field in the CUSTOMER Table and the ∞ symbol next to the CUSTID field in the APPOINTMENT Table. Similarly, the small 1 next to the SERVICE_ID field in the SERVICE Table is linked to the SERVICE_ID field in the APPOINTMENT Table with a ∞ symbol indicating that for any one type of service there may be many related records in the APPOINTMENT Table. Simply put, Justin Jumpup can make many appointments in the APPOINTMENT Table but there is only one Justin Jumpup in the CUSTOMER Table. (If there were two customers named Justin Jumpup each would have a separate CUSTID.) Hair Cuts can be given in many appointments but there is only one type of service called Hair Cut.

The service (Hair Cut, Perm, etc.) could have been an attribute (a field) of the APPOINTMENT Table but the SERVICE itself has an attribute of Duration (e.g., Hair Cut ½ hour, Coloring 2 hours). *Whenever an attribute itself has attributes, it must become an entity unto itself.* If it does not, it will violate the second rule of normalization, which says that each non-key field must relate to the entire primary key field, not to just one part of it. The key field of the SERVICE entity will be included in the APPOINTMENT entity as a foreign key in order to link the name of the service and its duration.

Each SERVICE may or may not include a Product (e.g., haircuts require no product, but a hair frosting requires a colorant). Once again, the attribute of Product itself has attributes (e.g., product type, product number, vendor etc.). Thus, PRODUCT becomes an entity. Its relationship differs slightly from that of APPOINTMENT to SERVICE since not every SERVICE requires a PRODUCT. This information is shown on the ER diagram by the line which links the tables with no small 1 or ∞ symbol present next to the joined fields.

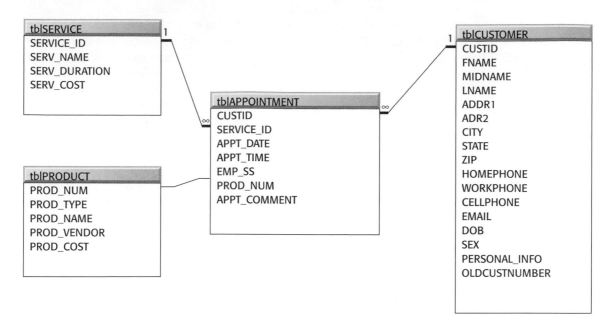

The APPOINTMENT entity could have as an attribute the employee who will provide the SERVICE. However, yet again the employee him/herself also has attributes such as first name and last name. So a separate entity for EMPLOYEE will be created and it will be linked to the APPOINTMENT entity by its key.

The attributes of the APPOINTMENT entity consist almost entirely of foreign keys which link it to information contained in other entities. It is on the many side of these relationships.

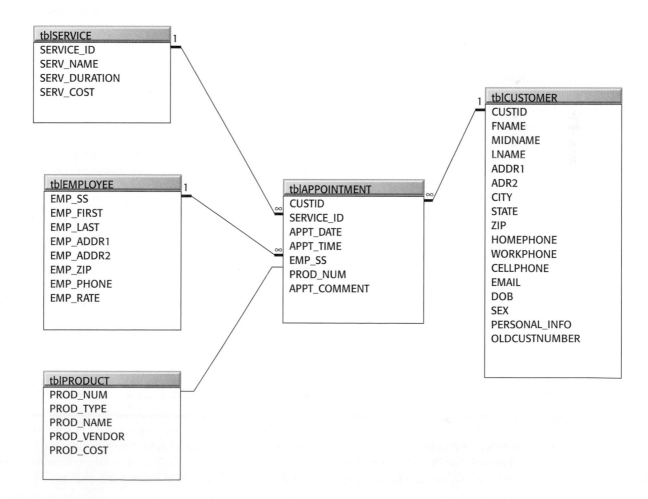

The conceptual schema for the HisNHers Salon now includes five separate entities: CUSTOMER, APPOINTMENT, SERVICE, EMPLOYEE, and PRODUCT.

DETERMINING KEY FIELDS

To ensure that each record of an entity class is unduplicated, it must contain a field which is its unique identifier or key. Often referred to as the primary key, this field becomes the link from one entity to another. When the primary key of one entity is used as a field in a table to which it links, it is called a foreign key. For example the field CUSTID in the CUSTOMER Table is its primary key. When the CUSTID field is used in the APPOINTMENT Table to link it to the CUSTOMER Table, it is called a foreign key. Within the physical database, keys are used also used as indexes to speed up record retrieval.

The value of a key field in a record should never change and much care should go into selecting it. Guidelines for selecting a key include simplicity and stability. For the EMPLOYEE Table, Social Security Number is an obvious choice for a key field. This number is known to the employer, is unique, and never changes.

You might be tempted to use the Social Security Number as the key in the CUSTOMER Table as well. However, many people are protective of this number and not inclined to give it out. Another possible choice for the CUSTOMER Table key is the last name but there are can be several customers with the same last name and women frequently change their last name. It is also possible to create a composite key of two or more fields in a table so that first name and last name could be joined into one field. But in this case such a composite key would not ensure a unique record (e.g., Maria Jones and her daughter, Maria Jones). The CUSTOMER entity requires the creation of a new attribute to be used as the primary key.

Often a composite key of date and time is a good choice for an entity that is time based, since it precludes duplicates. For the HisNHers database, the APPOINTMENT Table could use such a key if the service provider's ID were added. (Two staff members frequently have appointments at the same time.)

Often the user wants keys that are meaningful to him. For example, in the SERVICE Table, Clarence would like to create a key based on the name of the service, like HCM for male haircut. BT for beard trim, and CF for coloring female. However, in a large database it is easy to run into duplicates with schemes like this, and the keys can quickly become meaningless to all but the person who established them. In a small system, such as HisNHers these problems are minimal, and using familiar abbreviations might make learning to use the new system easier.

If you have the luxury of being able to set up a new primary key, one of the best choices is to allow the system to create an automatically numbering field for each record. The CUSTID field in the CUSTOMER entity is such a field. This will ensure that keys are unique and unduplicated. It is seldom necessary for the user to even be aware of the contents of a primary key field. The job of the primary key is to link tables. Today's database products include powerful look-up features so that you would not need to look up a customer by their ID number but could use their last name, then the first name, then the address, etc., until the requested record is located for use.

In many businesses some sort of key already exists for an entity. For example, Clarence and Clarissa had been using a small number that had been written in the corner of each customer's index card, which could become the key. When you are using existing numbers, gaps in a numbering scheme do not matter but care must be taken that the numbers to be used in the primary key field are both unique and not duplicated, which is often not the case with a key that is used in a manual system.

If a key has been in use for a while on an older system but is found to no longer be appropriate as a primary key, you may need to carry this information into the new system, to help the user identify the records. For example if Clarissa's index card numbers were inappropriate to use as a key field, but she had typed up notes about her personal customers using these numbers instead of names, you would carry the old key as a field (but not a key field) in the new database. When reports are printed from the new system they will include this old number so she can match the new reports to her old notes.

REVIEWING THE DESIGN

After the "final" conceptual schema has been developed and the ER diagram includes all of the entities with their keys, attributes, and relationships, it is time for a design review. All of the principal stakeholders in the system should study it to be sure that the necessary information is included and available. Also, provisions for possible expansion should be included. If the system expands to include inventory and ordering, a sixth entity, VENDOR, would have to be added. Allowance has been made for this growth in the PROD_VENDOR field of the PRODUCT entity. While it isn't impossible to redesign a system after data is entered, it is time consuming, error prone and requires serious skill in handling data via SQL commands.

DEVELOPING THE USER INTERFACE: FORMS AND REPORTS

The user interface includes menus, data entry forms, and reports. In short, despite your beautiful ER diagram, the interface is what the user will think of when he or she thinks of the database. The tools to create these objects vary signifi-

HisNHers Shop APPOINTMENTS: November 05, 2004

TIME	CUSTOMER	PROVIDER	SERVICE	PRODUCT NEEDED
8:30 AM	Malone, Patrick	Clarissa	Hair Cut	
8:30 AM	MacGregor, Mark	Clarence	Hair Cut	
9:00 AM	Smith, Mary Allen	Clarence	Coloring	Henna
9:30 AM	Greene, Jeanne	Clarissa	Blow Dry	Spray2Set
10:00 AM	Montague, Juliet	Clarence	Set	Spray2Set
10:30 AM	Brown, Thomas	Clarence	Consultation	
11:30 AM	Jumpup, Justin	Clarissa	Set	
12:00 PM	Smith, Mary Allen	Clarence	Coloring	EasyGlo Gold
1:00 PM	Nother, Zoe	Clarissa	Permanent Wave	
2:30 PM	Smith, Mary Ann	Clarence	Blow Dry	Spray2Set
3:00 PM	Smith, Mary Ellen	Clarissa	Hair Cut	
3:30 PM	Brown, Georgia	Clarence	Hair Cut	
4:30 PM	Jones, John Paul	Clarence	Hair Cut	

cantly among database packages. In Microsoft Access, the development of both entry forms and reports can be quickly accomplished via wizards that create basic objects and then allow them to be customized.

Development of reports for the system can teach you much about the design of the system, and it is critical to have sample reports examined by the user. If the owners of HisNHers wanted to see the customer's hair color on a report, you would soon realize that there is no field for this information. While it's possible to change the database to include a field for hair color, this type of oversight should have been caught at an earlier stage of the design process.

The owners of HisNHers wish to have a daily appointment list which shows not just the customer and appointment time but also the provider, the service requested, and any special product that will be needed. Above is a sample from this report. Creation of this report requires data from all five of the tables in the database. If tables are improperly related to each other, reports will be difficult if not impossible to create.

Since each table is related to another by a key field, records will be linked together based on matching data in the key fields. If a record in one table has no matching record in another table, it will not be included on the report. For example, only records from the tblAPPOINTMENT in which the appointment date = November 5, are selected for the 11/5 appointment list. If the group of records selected from the APPOINTMENT Table where appointment date = 11/5/04 contain no record with the customer ID for Jim Brown, Jim Brown will not show on the appointment list. Since Jim didn't have an appointment on 11/5, he shouldn't show!

Hands-On Guide to SQL

This Hands-On Guide is a brief introduction to Structured Query Language (SQL), the standard language for relational database management systems. SQL can be used for defining database structures, querying databases, and updating database data. If you are using Access, you will probably use its Query, Report, and Table-building tools rather than SQL for most of your querying and reporting work. However, you may want to use SQL to edit Access queries, and you can use your knowledge of SQL when you work with other database management systems. We will use tables from the HisNHers database developed in the previous appendix to illustrate how SQL works, focusing on the most important SQL commands for retrieving data. We will show you how to create SQL queries using sample data from the CUSTOMER Table and the APPOINTMENT Table illustrated here.

CUSTOMER Table with sample data

CUSTID	FNAME	MID NAME	LNAME	ADDR1	ADR2	CITY	STATE	ZIP	HOME PHONE	WORK PHONE	CELL PHONE	EMAIL	DOB	SEX	PERSONAL INFO	OLD CUSTN
1	Georgia	A	Brown	88 Main Street		Missoula	NY	10521	(914) 332-1234	(914) 222-8182	(912) 455-5555	gbrown@qqq.org	7/7/1951	F	WORKS AT M8	
2	Patrick		Malone	42 Sweetbriar L		Bocarain	NY	10598	(914) 333-4333	(211) 222-2121		PMAL@AOL.COM	6/12/1981	M		
3	Juliet	Q	Montague	11 Venice Plaza	Apt. 22	Bocarain	NY	10598	(914) 888-8181	(212) 921-0404	(212) 222-1221		12/25/1971	F		
4	Mary Ellen		Smith	Marian Lane		Catalan	NY	10520	(914) 821-3666				1/23/1959	F		
5	Mary Allen		Smith	22 September		Bocarain	NY	10598		(914) 999-1919		masmith@smith.com	4/25/1973	F		
6	Justin	J	Jumpup	6233 Ridgeview		Catalan	NY	10520				jjup@bigcompany.com	9/13/1966	M		
7	Thomas	E	Brown	7 Schiff Ave	Bldg. C	Bocarain	NY	10598		(212) 333-4567	(912) 456-7823		2/27/1981	M	LOVE THE ME	
8	Zoe		Nother	91 Glendale		Bocarain	NY	10598	(212) 345-6789				3/14/1968	F		
9	Mary Ann		Smith	8 Race Road		Catalin	NY	10520	(941) 222-1888	(941) 765-3424			5/30/1083	F	Early gray show	
10	John Paul		Jones	66 Ocean View		Bocarain	NY	10598		(212) 459-7878	(430) 686-8565			M	very quiet guy	
12	Jeannie	J	Greene	9499 Threws Le		Bocarain	NY	10598								
13	Mark		MacGregor	43 Schiff Ave		Catalan	NY	10520								
15	Jim	Q	Brown	9 Penland Park		Missoula	NY	10521	(518) 333-3311				6/10/1979	M	handsome!	

* Number)

APPOINTMENT Table with sample data

CUSTID	SERVICE_ID	APPT_DATE	APPT_TIME	EMP_SS	PROD_NUM	APPT_COMMENT
1	2	11/5/2004	3:30 PM	123456789		
1	2	11/7/2004	2:00 PM	123456789		
2	2	11/5/2004	8:30 AM	987654321		
2	3	11/7/2004	3:00 PM	123456789	4	
3	5	11/5/2004	10:00 AM	123456789	8	
3	5	11/7/2004	11:30 AM	987654321	8	
4	2	11/5/2004	3:00 PM	987654321		
4	1	11/7/2004	9:00 AM	123456789	6	
5	3	11/5/2004	12:00 PM	123456789	3	
5	3	11/5/2004	9:00 AM	123456789	2	
6	5	11/5/2004	11:30 AM	987654321		
7	6	11/5/2004	10:30 AM	123456789		
7	2	11/7/2004	4:30 PM	987654321		
8	1	11/5/2004	1:00 PM	987654321		
9	4	11/5/2004	2:30 PM	123456789	8	
10	2	11/5/2004	4:30 PM	123456789		
12	4	11/5/2004	9:30 AM	987654321	8	
13	2	11/5/2004	8:30 AM	123456789		

BASIC SQL SYNTAX RULES

SQL, like all computer languages has a particular syntax or grammar which must be followed in order for the commands to be understood and executed properly. Its most basic rules are:

1. Identifiers (names of tables, columns, and other objects) should contain between 1 and 30 characters. The identifiers can be upper or lower case, but no embedded spaces are allowed. For example, WORK PHONE would have to be written as WORKPHONE or WORK_PHONE.

2. SQL is not case sensitive, although SQL keywords such as SELECT or FROM are usually capitalized. Keywords have predefined meanings and cannot be used as identifiers.

3. SQL statements can take up more than one line (and there are no restrictions on the number of words per line or where to break a line). However, a new line is often started when a new clause in an SQL statement begins.

4. Commands begin with the SQL operator (e.g., CREATE or SELECT).

5. Field (column) names are separated from each other by a comma (e.g., SELECT FNAME, LNAME FROM tblCUSTOMER).

6. Field (column) names are separated from table names by a period (e.g., tblCUSTOMER.FNAME, tblCUSTOMER.LNAME). (Access uses this convention.) The name of the table does not have to be written before the name of the field from that table unless two tables used in the same SQL statement have identical field names (such as the CUSTID field in both the CUSTOMER and APPOINTMENT tables). Then the table name must be included (e.g., tblCUSTOMER.CUSTID and tblAPPOINTMENT.CUSTID).

7. Strings must be enclosed in quotation marks. A string is text for a collection of bits that is foreign to the database. The SQL statement to find the phone number for all of the customers whose last name is MacGregor would be written as:

```
SELECT HOMEPHONE
FROM tblCUSTOMER
WHERE LNAME = "MacGregor";
```

Remember too that a space is considered a character and must always be included in the quotation marks if it is needed for the comparison. "Mac Gregor" and "MacGregor" will not return the same Scotchman.

8. Nested operations must be enclosed in parentheses. One of the strengths of SQL is its ability to perform quite complex data manipulation. This is primarily due to its use of nesting. Commands within commands are enclosed in parentheses and the innermost ones are executed first.

USING THE SELECT STATEMENT

The most often used SQL command is SELECT, which returns rows of data from columns in the tables that the user would like to see in a result table. Following are a series of SELECT statements which demonstrate how to have all or specified columns returned in the result table. The names of the columns to be queried follow the keyword SELECT and the name of the table to use follows the keyword FROM.

SELECT every column and every row

```
SELECT *
FROM tblCUSTOMER;
```

The asterisk after SELECT causes every column to be included in the records from the table, tblCUSTOMER. The results show all the rows in the CUSTOMER Table as displayed earlier.

SELECT only some columns and every row

```
SELECT ADDR1, LNAME
FROM tblCUSTOMER;
```

Only the columns which are listed are returned from the CUSTOMER Table and they are presented in the order they are listed in the statement.

ADDR1	LNAME
88 Main Street	Brown
42 Sweetbriar Lane	Malone
11 Venice Plaza	Montague
Marian Lane	Smith
22 September Street	Smith
6233 Ridgeview	Jumpup
7 Schiff Ave	Brown
91 Glendale	Nother
8 Race Road	Smith
66 Ocean View	Jones
9499 Threws Le.	Greene
43 Schiff Ave	MacGregor
9 Penland Park	Brown

SORTING DATA: USING ORDER BY

The following examples show the ORDER BY statement which is used to sort the data returned by the SELECT statement.

Select only some columns and every row in sorted order by one field

```
SELECT LNAME, FNAME
FROM tblCUSTOMER
ORDER BY LNAME;
```

The ORDER BY command causes the records to be sorted in order by the contents of the column name following it.

LNAME	FNAME
Brown	Jim
Brown	Thomas
Brown	Georgia
Greene	Jeanne
Jones	John Paul
Jumpup	Justin
MacGregor	Mark
Malone	Patrick
Montague	Juliet
Nother	Zoe
Smith	Mary Ann
Smith	Mary Allen
Smith	Mary Ellen

Select only some columns and every row in sorted order by several fields

The returned records may be sorted in order by several fields. Each listed field after the ORDER BY clause is separated by a comma. First the records are sorted by last name, and if the last names are the same they are sorted by first name.

```
SELECT NAME, FNAME
FROM tblCUSTOMER
ORDER BY LNAME, FNAME;
```

LNAME	FNAME
Brown	Georgia
Brown	Jim
Brown	Thomas
Greene	Jeanne
Jones	John Paul
Jumpup	Justin
MacGregor	Mark
Malone	Patrick
Montague	Juliet
Nother	Zoe
Smith	Mary Allen
Smith	Mary Ann
Smith	Mary Ellen

SELECTING ONLY RECORDS THAT MEET SPECIFIED CRITERIA: USING WHERE

The WHERE clause determines which records are returned based on criteria described in the clause. It includes conditions for selecting specific rows in a table. Operators, such as = (equal), > (greater than), < (less than), and <> (not equal), as well as logical operators such as AND and OR are used to create the selection criteria. "IS NULL" is used to find fields that are empty (i.e., they contain no data). Remember that to a computer, a space is a character and a field into which only one space has been keyed is not considered NULL.

Select only records where the field SEX contains an F in sorted order by last name and first name.

```
SELECT LNAME, FNAME, SEX
FROM tblCUSTOMER
WHERE SEX = "F"
ORDER BY LNAME, FNAME;
```

Note that the letter F is a string and therefore must be enclosed in quotes.

LNAME	FNAME	SEX
Brown	Georgia	F
Montague	Juliet	F
Nother	Zoe	F
Smith	Mary Allen	F
Smith	Mary Ann	F
Smith	Mary Ellen	F

Select only the records where SEX does not contain an F in sorted order by last name and first name

```
SELECT FNAME, LNAME, SEX
FROM tblCUSTOMER
WHERE SEX <> "F"
ORDER BY LNAME, FNAME;
```

FNAME	LNAME	SEX
Jim	Brown	M
Thomas	Brown	M
John Paul	Jones	M
Justin	Jumpup	M
Patrick	Malone	M

Select only the records where SEX contains an F and the zip code is 10520 in sorted order by last name and first name.

```
SELECT LNAME, FNAME, SEX, ZIP
FROM tblCUSTOMER
WHERE SEX = "F" AND ZIP = "10520"
ORDER BY LNAME, FNAME;
```

The logical operator AND is used to select information that is contained within two different fields. Multiple AND and OR operators can be contained within one WHERE clause.

The zip code 10520 is enclosed in quotes because it is a string. The ZIP code field is a text field and even though its data may look numeric, it is stored as text characters and can only be found with a string. If the field had been defined as a numeric one, the quotes around 10520 would not be used.

LNAME	FNAME	SEX	ZIP
Smith	Mary Ann	F	10520
Smith	Mary Ellen	F	10520

Joining Multiple Tables

Data from two or more tables can be joined together to provide data from both tables where the contents of a field found in both tables matches. Both tblCUSTOMER and tblAPPOINTMENT are needed to see who has an appointment on a particular date. Since both tables contain the customer's ID, the contents of this field must match for the records to be returned.

Select the appointment date, time, and last name of all male customers with appointments.

```
SELECT APPT_DATE, APPT_TIME, LNAME
FROM tblCUSTOMER, tblAPPOINTMENT
WHERE tblCUSTOMER.CUSTID = tblAPPOINTMENT.CUSTID AND
SEX = "M";
```

The preceding SQL syntax that works with most DBMS products. Access, however, uses a slightly different syntax for this particular operation. It would be:

```
SELECT tblAPPOINTMENT.APPT_DATE,
tblAPPOINTMENT.APPT_TIME, tblCUSTOMER.LNAME
FROM.tblCUSTOMER
INNER JOIN tblAPPOINTMENT ON tblCUSTOMER.CUSTID =
tblAPPOINTMENT.CUSTID
WHERE (((tblCUSTOMER.SEX) = "M"));
```

APPT_DATE	APPT_TIME	LNAME
11/5/2004	8:30 AM	Malone
11/7/2004	3:00 PM	Malone
11/5/2004	11:30 AM	Jumpup
11/5/2004	4:30 PM	Jones

References

CHAPTER 1

Aldrich, H. E. "Technology and Organizational Structure: A Reexamination of the Findings of the Aston Group." *Administrative Science Quarterly* 17 (March 1972).

Allen, Brandt R., and Andrew C. Boynton. "Information Architecture: In Search of Efficient Flexibility." *MIS Quarterly* 15, no. 4 (December 1991).

Avison, David. "Information Systems in the MBA Curriculum: An International Perspective." *Communications of the Association for Information Systems* 11, Article 6 (January 2003).

Baily, Martin. "The U.S. Outlook: Capital Spending and Productivity Growth." *Institute for International Economics* (April 3, 2002).

Baskerville, Richard L. and Michael D. Myers. "Information Systems as a Reference Discipline." *MIS Quarterly* 26, no. 1 (March 2002).

Bautsch, Holly, et. al. "An Investigation of Mobile Phone Use: A Sociotechnical Approach." Department of Industrial Engineering, University of Wisconsin, Madison (2001).

Bebasat, Izak, and Robert W. Zmud. "The Identity Crisis Within the Discipline: Defining and Communicating the Discipline's Core Properties." *MIS Quarterly* 27, no. 2 (June 2003).

Brown, Ken, and Almar Latour. "Phone Industry Faces Upheaval as Ways of Calling Change Fast." *Wall Street Journal* (August 25, 2004).

Brynjolfsson, Erik. "The IT Productivity Gap." *Optimize Magazine* 21 (July 2003).

Brynjolfsson, Erik, and Lorin M. Hitt. "Beyond Computation: Information Technology, Organizational Transformation, and Business Performance." *Journal of Economic Perspectives* 14, no. 4 (2000).

Brynjolfsson, E. T., T. W. Malone, V. Gurbaxani, and A. Kambil. "Does Information Technology Lead to Smaller Firms?" *Management Science* 40, no. 12 (1994).

Bureau of the Census. *Statistical Abstract of the United States.* Washington, D.C.: Bureau of the Census (2003).

Carr, Nicholas. "IT Doesn't Matter." *Harvard Business Review* (May 2003).

Davis, Gordon B., and Margrethe H. Olson. *Management Information Systems: Conceptual Foundations, Structure, and Development,* 2nd ed. New York: McGraw-Hill (1985).

Dedrick, Jason, Vijay Gurbaxani, and Kenneth L. Kraemer. "Information Technology and Economic Performance: A Critical Review of the Empirical Evidence." Center for Research on Information Technology and Organizations, University of California, Irvine (December 2001).

eMarketer. "B2C E-Commerce in the U.S." eMarketer.com. www.emarketer.com/Report.aspx?b2c_us_jul04 (accessed July 2004).

Feeny, David E., and Leslie P. Willcocks. "Core IS Capabilities for Exploiting Information Technology." *Sloan Management Review* 39, no. 3 (Spring 1998).

Galliers, Robert D., and Maureen Meadows. "A Discipline Divided: Globalization and Parochialism in Information Systems Research." *Communications of the Association for Information Systems* 11, Article 5 (January 2003).

Gallupe, R. Brent. "Images of Information Systems in the Early 21st Century." *Communications of the Association for Information Systems* 3, no. 3 (February 2000).

Greenspan, Alan. "The Revolution in Information Technology." Boston College Conference on the New Economy (March 6, 2000).

Hacki, Remo, and Julian Lighton. "The Future of the Networked Company." *McKinsey Quarterly* 3 (2001).

Hartman, Amir. "Why Tech Falls Short of Expectations." *Optimize Magazine* (July 2002).

Hoffman, Donna L., Thomas P. Novak, and Alladi Venkatesh. "Has the Internet Become Indispensable?" *Communications of the ACM* 47, no. 7 (July 2004).

Ives, Blake, Joseph S. Valacich, Richard T. Watson, and Robert W. Zmud. "What Every Business Student Needs to Know about Information Systems." *Communications of the Association for Information Systems* 9, Article 30 (December 2002).

Jorgenson, Dale W. "Information Technology and Economic Performance: A Critical Review of Empirical Evidence." Center for Research on Information Technology and Organizations, University of California, Irvine (December 2001).

King, John. "Centralized vs. Decentralized Computing: Organizational Considerations and Management Options." *Computing Surveys* (October 1984).

Lamb, Roberta, Steve Sawyer, and Rob Kling. "A Social Informatics Perspective on Socio-Technical Networks." http://lamb.cba.hawaii.edu/pubs (2004).

Lee, H. "Broadband and Mobile Opportunities: A Socio-Technical Perspective." *Journal of Information Technology* 18 (2003).

Leonard-Barton, Dorothy. *Wellsprings of Knowledge.* Boston: Harvard Business School Press (1995).

Lev, Baruch. *Intangibles: Management, Measurement and Reporting.* Washington, D.C.: Brookings Institution Press (2001).

Marchand, Donald A. "Extracting the Business Value of IT: It Is Usage, Not Just Deployment That Counts!" *Copco Institute Journal of Financial Transformation* (2004).

Marchand, Donald A., William J. Kettinger, and John D. Rollins. *Making the Invisible Visible: How Companies Win with the Right Information, People and IT.* Chichester: Wiley (2001).

———. *Information Orientation: The Link to Business Performance.* Oxford: Oxford University Press (2001).

McFarlan, F. Warren, James L. McKenney, and Philip Pyburn. "The Information Archipelago—Plotting a Course." *Harvard Business Review* (January–February 1983).

———. "Governing the New World." *Harvard Business Review* (July–August 1983).

McKenney, James L., and F. Warren McFarlan. "The Information Archipelago—Maps and Bridges." *Harvard Business Review* (September–October 1982).

Mumford, Enid. "Socio Technical Design: An Unfulfilled Promise or a Future Opportunity." In *The Social and Organizational Perspective on Research and Practice in Information Technology,* edited by R. Baskerville, et al. London: Chapman-Hall (2000).

———. "Assisting Work Restructuring in Complex and Volatile Situations." In *Developing Organizational Consultancy,* edited by J. Neuman et al. London: Rutledge (1997).

Orlikowski, Wanda, and D. C. Gash. "Technological Frames: Making Sense of Information Technology in Organizations." *ACM Transactions in Information Systems* (April 1994).

Orlikowski, Wanda J., and Stephen R. Bailey. "Technology and Institutions: What Can Research on Information Technology and Research on Organizations Learn from Each Other?" *MIS Quarterly* 25, no. 2 (June 2001).

Orlikowski, Wanda J., and Jack J. Baroudi. "Studying Information Technology in Organizations: Research Approaches and Assumptions." *Information Systems Research* 2, no. 1 (March 1991).

Quinn, James Brian. "Strategic Outsourcing: Leveraging Knowledge Capabilities." *Sloan Management Review* 40, no. 4 (Summer 1999).

Roche, Edward M. "Planning for Competitive Use of Information Technology in Multinational Corporations." Paper presented at AIB UK Region Conference, Brighton Polytechnic, Brighton, U.K. (March 1992.) Edward M. Roche, W. Paul Stillman School of Business, Seton Hall University.

Ross, Jeanne W., and Peter Weill. "Six IT Decisions Your IT People Shouldn't Make." *Harvard Business Review* (November 2002).

Sambamurthy, V., and Robert W. Zmud. "Research Commentary: The Organizing Logic for an Enterprise's IT Activities in the Digital Era— A Prognosis of Practice and a Call to Research." *Information Systems Research* 11, no. 2 (June 2000).

Sawyer, S., and J. P. Allen. "Broadband and Mobile Opportunities: A Socio-Technical Perspective." *Journal of Information Technology* 18 (June 2003).

Slywotzky, Adrian J., and David J. Morrison. *How Digital Is Your Business?* New York: Crown Business (2001).

Stiroh, Kevin. "The Economic Impact of Information Technology." Federal Reserve Bank of New York (2001).

Teece, David. *Economic Performance and Theory of the Firm: The Selected Papers of David Teece.* London: Edward Elgar Publishing (1998).

Tornatsky, Louis G., J. D. Eveland, and David Wessel. "NASA Explores Future of Software." The Technological Innovation: Reviewing the Literature." Washington, D.C.: National Science Foundation (1983).

Triplett, Jack E., and Barry P. Bosworth. "Productivity in Services Industries: Trends and Measurement Issues." Washington D.C.: The Brookings Institution (2003).

Tuomi, Ilkka. "Data Is More Than Knowledge." *Journal of Management Information Systems* 16, no. 3 (Winter 1999–2000).

Williams, R., and D. Edge. "The Social Shaping of Technology." *Research Policy* 25 (1996).

Zhu, Kevin, Kenneth L. Kraemer, Sean Xu, and Jason Dedrick. "Information Technology Payoff in E-Business Environments: An International Perspective on Value Creation of E-business in the Financial Services Industry." *Journal of Management Information Systems* 21, no. 1 (Summer 2004).

CHAPTER 2

Anthony, R. N. *Planning and Control Systems: A Framework for Analysis.* Cambridge, Mass.: Harvard University Press (1965).

Barrett, Stephanie S. "Strategic Alternatives and Interorganizational System Implementations: An Overview." *Journal of Management Information Systems* (Winter 1986–1987).

Bensaou, M. "Portfolios of Buyer–Supplier Relationships." *Sloan Management Review* 40, no. 4 (Summer 1999).

Choi, Soon-Yong, and Andrew B. Whinston. "Communities of Collaboration." *IQ Magazine* (July–August 2001).

Concours Group. "ESII: Capitalizing on Enterprise Systems and Infrastructure." (1999).

Cox, Butler. *Globalization: The IT Challenge.* Sunnyvale, Calif.: Amdahl Executive Institute (1991).

Culnan, Mary J. "Transaction Processing Applications as Organizational Message Systems: Implications for the Intelligent Organization." Working paper no. 88-10, 22nd Hawaii International Conference on Systems Sciences (January 1989).

Davenport, Tom. *Mission Critical: Realizing the Promise of Enterprise Systems.* Boston: Harvard Business School Press (2000).

———. "Putting the Enterprise into Enterprise Systems." *Harvard Business Review* (July–August 1998).

Ferdows, Kasra, Michael A. Lewis, and Jose A. D. Machuca. "Rapid-Fire Fulfillment." *Harvard Business Review* (November 2004).

Houdeshel, George, and Hugh J. Watson. "The Management Information and Decision Support (MIDS) System at Lockheed Georgia." *MIS Quarterly* 11, no. 1 (March 1987).

Huber, George P. "Organizational Information Systems: Determinants of Their Performance and Behavior." *Management Science* 28, no. 2 (1984).

Johnston, Russell, and Michael J. Vitale. "Creating Competitive Advantage with Interorganizational Information Systems." *MIS Quarterly* 12, no. 2 (June 1988).

Kalakota, Ravi, and Marcia Robinson. *e-Business2.0: Roadmap for Success.* Reading, Mass.: Addison-Wesley (2001).

Keen, Peter G. W. *The Process Edge.* Boston: Harvard Business School Press (1997).

Keen, Peter G. W., and M. S. Morton. *Decision Support Systems: An Organizational Perspective.* Reading, Mass.: Addison-Wesley (1978).

Malone, Thomas M., Kevin Crowston, Jintae Lee, and Brian Pentland. "Tools for Inventing Organizations: Toward a Handbook of Organizational Processes." *Management Science* 45, no. 3 (March 1999).

McAfee, Andrew. "Do You Have Too Much IT?" *MIT Sloan Management Review* (Spring 2004).

O'Leary, Daniel E. *Enterprise Resource Planning Systems: Systems Life Cycle, Electronic Commerce, and Risk.* New York: Cambridge University Press (2000).

Rockart, John F., and Michael E. Treacy. "The CEO Goes On-line." *Harvard Business Review* (January–February 1982).

Sprague, Ralph H., Jr., and Eric D. Carlson. *Building Effective Decision Support Systems.* Englewood Cliffs, N.J.: Prentice Hall (1982).

CHAPTER 3

Allison, Graham T. *Essence of Decision—Explaining the Cuban Missile Crisis.* Boston: Little, Brown (1971).

Ancona, Deborah, Henrik Breaman, and Katrin Kaufer. "The Comparative Advantage of X-Teams." *Sloan Management Review* 43, no. 3 (Spring 2002).

Attewell, Paul, and James Rule. "Computing and Organizations: What We Know and What We Don't Know." *Communications of the ACM* 27, no. 12 (December 1984).

Bakos, J. Yannis, and Michael E. Treacy. "Information Technology and Corporate Strategy: A Research Perspective." *MIS Quarterly* (June 1986).

Beer, Michael, Russell A. Eisenstat, and Bert Spector. "Why Change Programs Don't Produce Change." *Harvard Business Review* (November–December 1990).

Bikson, T. K., and J. D. Eveland. "Integrating New Tools into Information Work." The Rand Corporation (1992). RAND/RP-106.

Blau, Peter, and W. Richard Scott. *Formal Organizations.* San Francisco: Chandler Press, 1962.

Brancheau, James C., Brian D. Janz, and James C. Wetherbe. "Key Issues in Information Systems Management: 1994–1995 SIM Delphi Results." *MIS Quarterly* 20, no. 2 (June 1996).

Bresnahan, Timothy F., Erik Brynjolfsson, and Lorin M. Hitt. "Information Technology, Workplace Organization, and the Demand for Skilled Labor." *Quarterly Journal of Economics* 117 (February 2002).

Camuffo, Arnaldo, Pietro Romano, and Andrea Vinellie. "Benetton Transforms Its Global Network." *Sloan Management Review* 43, no. 1 (Fall 2001).

Cash, J. I., and Benn R. Konsynski. "IS Redraws Competitive Boundaries." *Harvard Business Review* (March–April 1985).

Chan, Yolande E., Sid L. Huff, Donald W. Barclay, and Duncan G. Copeland. "Business Strategic Orientation, Information Systems Strategic Orientation, and Strategic Alignment." *Information Systems Research* 8, no. 2 (June 1997).

Chen, Pei-Yu (Sharon), and Lorin M. Hitt. "Measuring Switching Costs and the Determinants of Customer Retention in Internet-Enabled Businesses: A Study of the Online Brokerage Industry." *Information Systems Research* 13, no. 3 (September 2002).

Christensen, Clayton. "The Past and Future of Competitive Advantage." *Sloan Management Review* 42, no. 2 (Winter 2001).

Weber, Max. *The Theory of Social and Economic Organization.* Trans. by Talcott Parsons. New York: Free Press (1947).

Williamson, Oliver E. *The Economic Institutions of Capitalism.* New York: Free Press (1985).

Wiseman, Charles. *Strategic Information Systems.* Homewood, Ill.: Richard D. Irwin (1988).

Wrapp, H. Edward. "Good Managers Don't Make Policy Decisions." *Harvard Business Review* (July–August 1984).

Zipkin, Paul. "The Limits of Mass Customization." *Sloan Management Review* (Spring 2001).

CHAPTER 4

Akcura, M. Tolga, and Kemal Altinkemer. "Diffusion Models for B2B, B2C and P2P Exchanges and E-Speak." *Journal of Organizational Computing and Electronic Commerce* 12, no. 3 (2002).

Andal-Ancion, Angela, Philip A. Cartwright, and George S. Yip. "The Digital Transformation of Traditional Business." *MIT Sloan Management Review* 44, no. 4 (Summer 2003).

Anderson, Philip, and Erin Anderson. "The New E-Commerce Intermediaries." *Sloan Management Review* 43, no. 4 (Summer 2002).

Armstrong, Arthur, and John Hagel III. "The Real Value of On-line Communities." *Harvard Business Review* (May–June 1996).

Ba, Sulin, and Paul A. Pavlou. "Evidence of the Effect of Trust Building Technology in Electronic Markets: Price Premiums and Buyer Behavior." *MIS Quarterly* 26, no. 3 (September 2002).

Bakos, Yannis. "The Emerging Role of Electronic Marketplaces and the Internet." *Communications of the ACM* 41, no. 8 (August 1998).

Barua, Anitesh, Prabhudev Konana, Andrew B. Whinston, and Fang Yin. "Driving E-Business Excellence." *Sloan Management Review* 43, no. 1 (Fall 2001).

Bhargava, Hemant K., and Vidyanand Chourhary. "Economics of an Information Intermediary with Aggregation Benefits." *Information Systems Research* 15, no. 1 (March 2004).

Bhattacherjee, Anol. "Individual Trust in Online Firms: Scale Development and Initial Test." *Journal of Management Information Systems* 19, no. 1 (Summer 2002).

Brynjolfsson, Erik, Yu Hu, and Michael D. Smith. "Consumer Surplus in the Digital Economy: Estimating the Value of Increased Product Variety at Online Booksellers." *Management Science* 49, no. 11 (November 2003).

Chaudhury, Abhijit, Debasish Mallick, and H. Raghav Rao. "Web Channels in E-Commerce." *Communications of the ACM* 44, no. 1 (January 2001).

Christensen, Clayton M. *The Innovator's Dilemma.* New York: HarperCollins (2000).

Clemons, Eric K., Bin Gu, and Karl Reiner Lang. "Newly Vulnerable Markets in an Age of Pure Information Products: An Analysis of Online Music and Online News." *Journal of Management Information Systems* 19, no. 3 (Winter 2002–2003).

Devaraj, Sarv, Ming Fan, and Rajiv Kohli. "Antecedents of B2C Channel Satisfaction and Preference: Validating e-Commerce Metrics." *Information Systems Research* 13, no. 3 (September 2002).

Dewan, Rajiv M., Marshall L. Freimer, and Jie Zhang. "Management and Valuation of Advertisement-Supported Web Sites." *Journal of Management Information Systems* 19, no. 3 (Winter 2002–2003).

eMarketer. "B2C E-Commerce in the U.S." (July 2004).

Evans, Philip, and Thomas S. Wurster. *Blown to Bits: How the New Economics of Information Transforms Strategy.* Boston: Harvard Business School Press (2000).

———. "Getting Real about Virtual Commerce." *Harvard Business Review* (November–December 1999).

Fichman, Robert G., and Mary J. Cronin. "Information-Rich Commerce at a Crossroads: Business and Technology Adoption Requirements." *Communications of the ACM* 46, no. 9 (September 2003).

Gallaugher, John M. "E-Commerce and the Undulating Distribution Channel." *Communications of the ACM* 45, no. 7 (July 2002).

Gefen, David, Elena Karahanna, and Detmar W. Straub. "Trust and TAM in Online Shopping: An Integrated Model." *MIS Quarterly* 27, no. 1 (March 2003).

Grover, Varun, and Pradipkumar Ramanlal. "Six Myths of Information and Markets: Information Technology Networks, Electronic Commerce, and the Battle for Consumer Surplus." *MIS Quarterly* 23, no. 4 (December 1999).

Gulati, Ranjay, and Jason Garino. "Get the Right Mix of Bricks and Clicks." *Harvard Business Review* (May–June 2000).

Hagel, John, III, and Marc Singer. *Net Worth.* Boston: Harvard Business School Press (1999).

Haskell, Kari. "Do-It-Yourself Design: Just Point and Click." *New York Times,* October 24, 2004.

Huang, Gregory T. "The Web's New Currency." *Technology Review* (November 2003).

Hui, Kai Lung, and Patrick Y. K. Chau. "Classifying Digital Products." *Communications of the ACM* 45, no. 6 (June 2002).

Iansiti, Marco, F. Warren McFarlan, and George Wessterman. "Leveraging the Incumbent's Advantage." *MIT Sloan Management Review* 44, no. 4 (Summer 2003).

Jones, Sara, Marc Wilikens, Philip Morris, and Marcelo Masera. "Trust Requirements in E-Business." *Communications of the ACM* 43, no. 12 (December 2000).

Kanan, P. K., Ai-Mei Chang, and Andrew B. Whinston. "Marketing Information on the I-Way." *Communications of the ACM* 41, no. 3 (March 1998).

Kaplan, Steven, and Mohanbir Sawhney. "E-Hubs: the New B2B Marketplaces." *Harvard Business Review* (May–June 2000).

Kauffman, Robert J., and Bin Wang. "New Buyers' Arrival under Dynamic Pricing Market Microstructure: The Case of Group-Buying Discounts on the Internet." *Journal of Management Information Systems* 18, no. 2 (Fall 2001).

Kenny, David, and John F. Marshall. "Contextual Marketing." *Harvard Business Review* (November–December 2000).

Koufaris, Marios. "Applying the Technology Acceptance Model and Flow Theory to Online Consumer Behavior." *Information Systems Research* 13, no. 2 (2002).

Lai, Vincent S. "Intraorganizational Communication with Intranets." *Communications of the ACM* 44, no. 7 (July 2001).

Laudon, Kenneth C., and Carol Guercio Traver. *E-Commerce: Business, Technology, Society.* Boston: Addison-Wesley (2004).

Lee, Hau L., and Seungin Whang. "Winning the Last Mile of E-Commerce." *Sloan Management Review* 42, no. 4 (Summer 2001).

Lee, Ho Geun. "Do Electronic Marketplaces Lower the Price of Goods?" *Communications of the ACM* 41, no. 1 (January 1998).

Lee, Younghwa, Zoonky Lee, and Kai R. T. Larsen. "Coping with Internet Channel Conflict." *Communications of the ACM* 43, no.7 (July 2003).

Lightner, Nancy J. "Evaluating E-Commerce Functionality with a Focus on Customer Service." *Communications of the ACM* 47, no. 10 (October 2004).

Lim, Gyoo Gun, and Jae Kyu Lee. "Buyer-Carts for B2B EC: The b-Cart Approach." *Journal of Organizational Computing and Electronic Commerce* 13, nos. 3 and 4 (2003).

Looney, Clayton A., and Debabroto Chatterjee. "Web-Enabled Transformation of the Brokerage Industry." *Communications of the ACM* 45, no. 8 (August 2002).

Magretta, Joan. "Why Business Models Matter." *Harvard Business Review* (May 2002).

Markillie, Paul. "A Perfect Market." *The Economist* (May 15–21, 2004).

McKnight, D. Harrison, Vivek Choudhury, and Charlea Kacmar. "Developing and Validating Trust Measures for e-Commerce: An Integrative Typology." *Information Systems Research* 13, no. 3 (September 2002).

McWilliam, Gil. "Building Stronger Brands through Online Communities." *Sloan Management Review* 41, no. 3 (Spring 2000).

Mougayar, Walid. *Opening Digital Markets,* 2nd ed. New York: McGraw-Hill (1998).

Pavlou, Paul A., and David Gefen. "Building Effective Online Marketplaces with Institution-Based Trust." *Information Systems Research* 15, no. 1 (March 2004).

Pinker, Edieal, Abraham Seidmann, and Riginald C. Foster. "Strategies for Transitioning 'Old Economy' Firms to E-Business." *Communications of the ACM* 45, no. 5 (May 2002).

Prahalad, C. K., and Venkatram Ramaswamy. "Coopting Consumer Competence." *Harvard Business Review* (January–February 2000).

Rayport, J. F., and J. J. Sviokla. "Managing in the Marketspace." *Harvard Business Review* (November–December 1994).

Reichheld, Frederick E., and Phil Schefter. "E-Loyalty: Your Secret Weapon on the Web." *Harvard Business Review* (July–August 2000).

Rifkin, Glenn, and Joel Kurtzman. "Is Your E-Business Plan Radical Enough?" *Sloan Management Review* 43, no. 3 (Spring 2002).

Riggins, Frederic J. "Market Segmentation and Information Development Costs in a Two-Tiered Fee-Based and Sponsorship-Based Web Site." *Journal of Management Information Systems* 19, no. 3 (Winter 2002–2003).

Rust, Roland T., and P. K. Kannan. "E-Service: A New Paradigm for Business in the Electronic Environment." *Communications of the ACM* 46, no. 6 (June 2003).

Sawhney, Mohanbir, Emanuela Prandelli, and Gianmario Verona. "The Power of Innomediation." *MIT Sloan Management Review* (Winter 2003).

Schlueter-Langdon, Christoph, and Michael J. Shaw. "Emergent Patterns of Interaction in Electronic Channel Systems." *Communications of the ACM* 45, no. 12 (December 2002).

Schultze, Ulrike, and Wanda J. Orlikowski. "A Practice Perspective on Technology-Mediated Network Relations: The Use of Internet-Based Self-Serve Technologies." *Information Systems Research* 15, no. 1 (March 2004).

Shelfer, Katherine M., and J. Drew Procaccino. "Smart Card Evolution." *Communications of the ACM* 45, no. 7 (July 2002).

Shi, Xinping, and Philip C. Wright. "E-Commercializing Business Operations." *Communications of the ACM* 46, no. 2 (February 2003).

Smith, Michael Alan. "Portals: Toward an Application Framework for Interoperability." *Communications of the ACM* 47, no. 10 (October 2004).

Smith, Michael D., Joseph Bailey, and Erik Brynjolfsson. "Understanding Digital Markets: Review and Assessment." In *Understanding the Digital Economy*, edited by Erik Brynjolfsson and Brian Kahin. Cambridge, Mass.: MIT Press (1999).

Southard, Peter B., and Keng Siau. "A Survey of Online E-Banking Retail Initiatives." *Communications of the ACM* 47, no. 10 (October 2004).

Strader, Troy J., and Sridhar N. Ramaswami. "Investor Perceptions of Traditional and Online Channels." *Communications of the ACM* 47, no. 7 (July 2004).

Subramanian, Rangan, and Ron Adner. "Profits and the Internet: Seven Misconceptions." *Sloan Management Review* 42, no. 4 (Summer 2001).

Thomke, Stefan, and Eric von Hippel. "Customers as Innovators." *Harvard Business Review* (April 2002).

Torkzadeh, Gholamreza, and Gurpreet Dhillon. "Measuring Factors That Influence the Success of Internet Commerce." *Information Systems Research* 13, no. 2 (June 2002).

Urbaczewski, Andrew, Leonard M. Jessup, and Bradley Wheeler. "Electronic Commerce Research: A Taxonomy and Synthesis." *Journal of Organizational Computing and Electronic Commerce* 12, no. 2 (2002).

Venkatraman, N. "Five Steps to a Dot-Com Strategy: How to Find Your Footing on the Web." *Sloan Management Review* 41, no. 3 (Spring 2000).

Werbach, Kevin. "Syndication: The Emerging Model for Business in the Internet Era." *Harvard Business Review* (May–June 2000).

Westland, J. Christopher. "Preference Ordering Cash, Near-Cash and Electronic Cash." *Journal of Organizational Computing and Electronic Commerce* 12, no. 3 (2002).

Wigand, Rolf T., and Robert Benjamin. "Electronic Commerce: Effects on Electronic Markets." *JCMC* 1, no. 3 (December 1995).

Willcocks, Leslie, and Robert Plant. "Pathways to E-Business Leadership." *Sloan Management Review* (Spring 2001).

Wise, Richard, and David Morrison. "Beyond the Exchange: The Future of B2B." *Harvard Business Review* (November–December 2000).

Yen, Benjamin P.-C., and Elsie O. S. Ng. "The Impact of Electronic Commerce on Procurement." *Journal of Organizational Computing and Electronic Commerce* 13, nos. 3 and 4 (2003).

Yoo, Byungjoon, Vidyanand Choudhary, and Tridas Mukhopadhyay. "A Model of Neutral B2B Intermediaries." *Journal of Management Information Systems* 19, no. 3 (Winter 2002–2003).

CHAPTER 5

Association of Computing Machinery. "ACM's Code of Ethics and Professional Conduct." *Communications of the ACM* 36, no. 12 (December 1993).

Ball, Kirstie S. "Situating Workplace Surveillance: Ethics and Computer-Based Performance Monitoring." *Ethics and Information Technology* 3, no. 3 (2001).

Barrett, Larry, and Sean Gallagher. "What Sin City Can Teach Tom Ridge." *Baseline* (April 2004).

Bellman, Steven, Eric J. Johnson, and Gerald L. Lohse. "To Opt-in or Opt-out? It Depends on the Question." *Communications of the ACM* 44, no. 2 (February 2001).

Bennett, Colin J. "Cookies, Web Bugs, Webcams, and Cue Cats: Patterns of Surveillance on the World Wide Web." *Ethics and Information Technology* 3, no. 3 (2001).

Berdichevsky, Daniel, and Erik Neunschwander. "Toward an Ethics of Persuasive Technology." *Communications of the ACM* 42, no. 5 (May 1999).

Bhattacharjee, Sudip, Ram D. Gopal, and G. Lawrence Sanders. "Digital Music and Online Sharing: Software Piracy 2.0?" *Communications of the ACM* 46, no. 7 (July 2003).

Bowen, Jonathan. "The Ethics of Safety-Critical Systems." *Communications of the ACM* 43, no. 3 (April 2000).

Brod, Craig. *Techno Stress—The Human Cost of the Computer Revolution.* Reading, Mass.: Addison-Wesley (1982).

Brown Bag Software vs. Symantec Corp. 960 F2D 1465 (Ninth Circuit, 1992).

Burk, Dan L. "Copyrightable Functions and Patentable Speech." *Communications of the ACM* 44, no. 2 (February 2001).

Carr, David F., and Sean Gallagher. "BofA's Direct-Deposit Debacle." *Baseline* (May 15, 2002).

Cavazos, Edward A. "The Legal Risks of Setting Up Shop in Cyberspace." *Journal of Organizational Computing* 6, no. 1 (1996).

Clarke, Roger. "Internet Privacy Concerns Confirm the Case for Intervention." *Communications of the ACM* 42, no. 2 (February 1999).

Collins, W. Robert, Keith W. Miller, Bethany J. Spielman, and Phillip Wherry. "How Good Is Good Enough? An Ethical Analysis of Software Construction and Use." *Communications of the ACM* 37, no. 1 (January 1994).

Day, George S., Adam J. Fein, and Gregg Ruppersberger, "Shakeouts in Digital Markets." *California Management Review* 45, no. 3 (Winter 2003).

Earp, Julia B., and David Baumer. "Innovative Web Use to Learn About Consumer Behavior and Online Privacy." *Communications of the ACM* 46, no. 4 (April 2003).

Farmer, Dan, and Charles C. Mann. "Surveillance Nation." Pts. I and II. *Technology Review* (April 2003) and (May 2003).

Froomkin, A. Michael. "The Collision of Trademarks, Domain Names, and Due Process in Cyberspace." *Communications of the ACM* 44, no. 2 (February 2001).

Gattiker, Urs E., and Helen Kelley. "Morality and Computers: Attitudes and Differences in Judgments." *Information Systems Research* 10, no. 3 (September 1999).

Geitner, Paul. "Survey: 36 Percent of Software Pirated." Associated Press (July 7, 2004).

Gopal, Ram D., and G. Lawrence Sanders. "Preventive and Deterrent Controls for Software Piracy." *Journal of Management Information Systems* 13, no. 4 (Spring 1997).

Hagerty, James R., and Dennis K. Berman. "New Battleground in Web Privacy War: Ads That Snoop." *Wall Street Journal* (August 27, 2003).

Hansell, Saul. "The Internet Ad You Are About to See Has Already Read Your E-Mail." *New York Times* (June 21, 2004).

Harrington, Susan J. "The Effect of Codes of Ethics and Personal Denial of Responsibility on Computer Abuse Judgments and Intentions." *MIS Quarterly* 20, no. 2 (September 1996).

Heingartner, Douglas. "Software Piracy Is in Resurgence, with New Safeguards Eroded by File Sharing." *New York Times* (January 19, 2004).

Jackson, Linda A., Alexander von Eye, Gretchen Barbatsis, Frank Biocca, Hiram E. Fitzgerald, and Yong Zhao. "The Impact of Internet Use on the Other Side of the Digital Divide." *Communications of the ACM* 47, no. 7 (July 2004).

Jackson, Thomas W., Ray Dawson, and Darren Wilson. "Understanding Email Interaction Increases Organizational Productivity." *Communications of the ACM* 46, no. 8 (August 2003).

Johnson, Deborah G. "Ethics Online." *Communications of the ACM* 40, no. 1 (January 1997).

Johnson, Deborah G., and John M. Mulvey. "Accountability and Computer Decision Systems." *Communications of the ACM* 38, no. 12 (December 1995).

Kapner, Suzanne. "Internet Site, Fearing Suit over Content, Curbs Activity." *New York Times* (March 14, 2003).

Kling, Rob. "When Organizations Are Perpetrators: The Conditions of Computer Abuse and Computer Crime." In *Computerization and Controversy: Value Conflicts and Social Choices,* edited by Charles Dunlop and Rob Kling. New York: Academic Press (1991).

Kreie, Jennifer, and Timothy Paul Cronan. "Making Ethical Decisions." *Communications of the ACM* 43, no. 12 (December 2000).

Laudon, Kenneth C. *Dossier Society: Value Choices in the Design of National Information Systems.* New York: Columbia University Press (1986).

———. "Ethical Concepts and Information Technology." *Communications of the ACM* 38, no. 12 (December 1995).

Laudon, Kenneth C., and Carol Guercio Traver. *E-Commerce: Business, Technology, Society.* Boston: Addison-Wesley (2004).

Lee, Jintae. "An End-User Perspective on File-Sharing Systems." *Communications of the ACM* 46, no. 2 (February 2003).

Lenhart, Amanda, John Horrigan, Lee Rainie, Katherine Allen, Angie Boyce, Mary Madden, and Erin O'Grady. "The Ever-Shifting Internet Population." *Pew Internet and American Life Project* (April 16, 2003).

Lohr, Steve. "Software Group Enters Fray over Proposed Piracy Law." *New York Times* (July 19, 2004).

Maltz, Elliott, and Vincent Chiappetta. "Maximizing Value in the Digital World." *Sloan Management Review* 43, no. 3 (Spring 2002).

Mann, Catherine L. "What Global Sourcing Means for U.S. I.T. Workers and for the U.S. Economy." *Communications of the ACM* 47, no. 7 (July 2004).

Martin, David M., Jr., Richard M. Smith, Michael Brittain, Ivan Fetch, and Hailin Wu. "The Privacy Practices of Web Browser Extensions." *Communications of the ACM* 44, no. 2 (February 2001).

Mason, Richard O. "Applying Ethics to Information Technology Issues." *Communications of the ACM* 38, no. 12 (December 1995).

———. "Four Ethical Issues in the Information Age." *MIS Quarterly* 10, no. 1 (March 1986).

Moores, Trevor, and Gurpreet Dhillon. "Software Piracy: A View from Hong Kong." *Communications of the ACM* 43, no. 12 (December 2000).

Mykytyn, Kathleen, Peter P. Mykytyn Jr., and Craig W. Slinkman. "Expert Systems: A Question of Liability." *MIS Quarterly* 14, no. 1 (March 1990).

National Telecommunications and Information Administration, U.S. Department of Commerce. "Falling through the Net: Defining the Digital Divide" (July 8, 1999).

Nissenbaum, Helen. "Computing and Accountability." *Communications of the ACM* 37, no. 1 (January 1994).

Okerson, Ann. "Who Owns Digital Works?" *Scientific American* (July 1996).

Oz, Effy. "Ethical Standards for Information Systems Professionals." *MIS Quarterly* 16, no. 4 (December 1992).

———. *Ethics for the Information Age.* Dubuque, Iowa: W. C. Brown, 1994.

Payton, Fay Cobb. "Rethinking the Digital Divide." *Communications of the ACM* 46, no. 6 (June 2003).

Pear, Robert. "Survey Finds U.S. Agencies Engaged in 'Data Mining.'" *New York Times* (May 27, 2004).

Rainie, Lee, and Dan Packel. "More Online, Doing More." *Pew Internet and American Life Project* (February 18, 2001).

Reagle, Joseph, and Lorrie Faith Cranor. "The Platform for Privacy Preferences." *Communications of the ACM* 42, no. 2 (February 1999).

Redman, Thomas C. "The Impact of Poor Data Quality on the Typical Enterprise." *Communications of the ACM* 41, no. 2 (February 1998).

Rifkin, Jeremy. "Watch Out for Trickle-Down Technology." *New York Times* (March 16, 1993).

Rigdon, Joan E. "Frequent Glitches in New Software Bug Users." *Wall Street Journal* (January 18, 1995).

Rotenberg, Marc. "Communications Privacy: Implications for Network Design." *Communications of the ACM* 36, no. 8 (August 1993).

Samuelson, Pamela. "Computer Programs and Copyright's Fair Use Doctrine." *Communications of the ACM* 36, no. 9 (September 1993).

———. "The Ups and Downs of Look and Feel." *Communications of the ACM* 36, no. 4 (April 1993).

Sewell, Graham, and James R. Barker. "Neither Good, nor Bad, but Dangerous: Surveillance as an Ethical Paradox." *Ethics and Information Technology* 3, no. 3 (2001).

Sipior, Janice C., and Burke T. Ward. "The Dark Side of Employee Email." *Communications of the ACM* 42, no. 7 (July 1999).

Smith, H. Jeff. "The Shareholders vs. Stakeholders Debate." *MIT Sloan Management Review* 44, no. 4 (Summer 2003).

Smith, H. Jeff, and John Hasnas. "Ethics and Information Systems: The Corporate Domain." *MIS Quarterly* 23, no. 1 (March 1999).

Smith, H. Jeff, Sandra J. Milberg, and Sandra J. Burke. "Information Privacy: Measuring Individuals' Concerns about Organizational Practices." *MIS Quarterly* 20, no. 2 (June 1996).

Stone, Amey. "The Digital Divide That Wasn't." *BusinessWeek* (August 19, 2003).

Straub, Detmar W., Jr., and William D. Nance. "Discovering and Disciplining Computer Abuse in Organizations: A Field Study." *MIS Quarterly* 14, no. 1 (March 1990).

Straub, Detmar W., Jr., and Rosann Webb Collins. "Key Information Liability Issues Facing Managers: Software Piracy, Proprietary Databases, and Individual Rights to Privacy." *MIS Quarterly* 14, no. 2 (June 1990).

Tuttle, Brad, Adrian Harrell, and Paul Harrison. "Moral Hazard, Ethical Considerations, and the Decision to Implement an Information System." *Journal of Management Information Systems* 13, no. 4 (Spring 1997).

Urbaczewski, Andrew, and Leonard M. Jessup. "Does Electronic Monitoring of Employee Internet Usage Work?" *Communications of the ACM* 45, no. 1 (January 2002).

U.S. Department of Health, Education, and Welfare. *Records, Computers, and the Rights of Citizens.* Cambridge, Mass.: MIT Press (1973).

Volokh, Eugene. "Personalization and Privacy." *Communications of the ACM* 43, no. 8 (August 2000).

Wang, Huaiqing, Matthew K. O. Lee, and Chen Wang. "Consumer Privacy Concerns about Internet Marketing." *Communications of the ACM* 41, no. 3 (March 1998).

Wellman, Barry. "Designing the Internet for a Networked Society." *Communications of the ACM* 45, no. 5 (May 2002).

CHAPTER 6

Acharya, Ravi. "EAI: A Business Perspective." *EAI Journal* (April 2003).

Aries, James A., Subhankar Banerjee, Marc S. Brittan, Eric Dillon, Janusz S. Kowalik, and John P. Lixvar. "Capacity and Performance Analysis of Distributed Enterprise Systems." *Communications of the ACM* 45, no. 6 (June 2002).

Barry, Douglas K. *Web Services and Service-Oriented Architectures: The Savvy Manager's Guide.* New York: Morgan Kaufman (2003).

Bell, Gordon, and Jim Gray. "What's Next in High-Performance Computing?" *Communications of the ACM* 45, no. 1 (January 2002).

Benamati, John, and Albert L. Lederer. "Coping with Rapid Changes in IT." *Communications of the ACM* 44, no. 8 (August 2001).

Bulkeley, William M. "New IBM Service Will Test Vision of Computing Power as Utility." *Wall Street Journal* (July 1, 2002).

Butler, Steve. "Telecom Spending." *EMarketer* (April 2004).

Champy, James. "Re-examining the Infrastructure." *Optimize* 23 (September 2003).

Chari, Kaushal, and Saravanan Seshadri. "Demystifying Integration." *Communications of the ACM* 47, no. 7 (July 2004).

Conry-Murray, Andrew. "Grid Computing's Promises and Perils." Network Magazine.com (February 5, 2004).

Cuomo, Jerry, et al. "WebSphere Capacity—On Demand: Developing Edge Computing Applications." IBM Corporation and Akamai (2003). www.106.ibm.com/developerworks/websphere/library/techarticles/0310_haberkorn/haberkorn.html.

Da Cruz, Frank. *A Chronology of Computing at Columbia University.* Columbia University Computing History http://www.columbia.edu/acis/history/watsonlab.html (December 31, 2004).

David, Julie Smith, David Schuff, and Robert St. Louis. "Managing Your IT Total Cost of Ownership." *Communications of the ACM* 45, no. 1 (January 2002).

Dempsey, Bert J., Debra Weiss, Paul Jones, and Jane Greenberg. "What Is an Open Source Software Developer?" *Communications of the ACM* 45, no. 1 (January 2001).

Ganek, A. G., and T. A. Corbi. "The Dawning of the Autonomic Computing Era." *IBM Systems Journal* 42, no. 1 (2003).

Gerlach, James, Bruce Neumann, Edwin Moldauer, Martha Argo, and Daniel Frisby. "Determining the Cost of IT Services." *Communications of the ACM* 45, no. 9 (September 2002).

Hagel, John, III, and John Seeley Brown. "Your Next IT Strategy." *Harvard Business Review* (October 2001).

HP (Hewlett-Packard). "Success Stories: Canadian Imperial Bank of Commerce (CBC)—with HP Services." http://www.hp.com (accessed September 30, 2004).

IBM. "20th Century Disk Storage Technology." www-1.ibm.com/ibm/history/exhibits/storage/storage_chrono20.html (accessed July 2004).

———. "Gridlines: The Intersection of Technology and Business." IBM. www-1.ibm.com/grid/gridlines/January2004/feature/teamwork.shtml (accessed July 2004).

———. "How Customers Are Making On Demand Real." IBM. www.ibm.com/news/us/2003/11/on_demand_real.html (accessed July 2004).

———. "The Mainframe Family Tree and Chronology." IBM. www-1.ibm.com/ibm/history/exhibits/mainframe/mainframe_FT1.html (accessed July 2004).

Intel Corporation. "Expanding Moore's Law: The Exponential Opportunity." (Fall 2002).

———. "Microprocessor Quick Reference Guide." Intel. www.intel.com/pressroom/kits/quickreffam.htm (accessed July 2004).

International Technology Roadmap for Semiconductors Committee. "The International Technology Roadmap for Semiconductors 2003 Edition." http://public.itrs.net/ (accessed July 2004).

Kephart, Jeffrey O., and David M. Chess. "The Vision of Autonomic Computing," *Computer Magazine, IEEE* (2003).

Kern, Thomas, Leslie P. Willcocks, and Mary C. Lacity. "Application Service Provision: Risk Assessment and Mitigation." *MIS Quarterly Executive* 1, no. 2 (2002).

Kerstetter, Jim. "The Linux Uprising." *BusinessWeek Online* (March 2003).

King, John. "Centralized vs. Decentralized Computing: Organizational Considerations and Management Options." *Computing Surveys* (October 1984).

Kurzweil, Ray. "Exponential Growth an Illusion?: Response to Ilkka Tuomi." KurzweilAI.net (September 23, 2003).

Lee, Jinyoul, Keng Siau, and Soongoo Hong. "Enterprise Integration with ERP and EAI." *Communications of the ACM* 46, no. 2 (February 2003).

Lohr, Steve. "IBM Helps Promote Linux." *New York Times* (November 11, 2003).

Loo, Alfred W. "The Future of Peer-to-Peer Computing." *Communications of the ACM* 46, no. 9 (September 2003).

Lyman, Peter, and Hal R. Varian. "How Much Information? 2003." School of Management and Systems, University of California at Berkeley (2003).

Markoff, John, and Jennifer L. Schenker. "Europe Exceeds U.S. in Refining Grid Computing." *New York Times,* November 10, 2003.

Marks, Eric A., and Mark J. Werrell. *Executive's Guide to Web Services.* New York: Wiley (2003).

Marshak, David. "Charles Schwab Responds to Market Conditions and Customer Needs: Services-Oriented Architecture Improves Time to Market and Leverages Existing Investments." *Patricia Seybold Group* (December 2003).

McDougall, Paul. "Dow Hires IBM to Take VoIP Project over from EDS." *Information Week* (August 3, 2004).

Miller, Gerry. ".NET vs. J2EE." *Communications of the ACM* 46, no. 6 (June 2003).

Moore, Gordon. "Cramming More Components onto Integrated Circuits." *Electronics* 38, no. 8 (April 19, 1965).

Muscarella, Gregory, M. S. Krishnan, and Harry Ault. "Business Advantages Flow with XML." *Optimize Magazine* (November 2003).

National Science Foundation. "Revolutionizing Science and Engineering through Cyberinfrastructure: Report of the National Science Foundation Blue-Ribbon Advisory Panel on Cyberinfrastructure." Washington, D.C. (January, 2003).

Niemeyer, Alex, Misok H. Pak, and Sanjay E. Ramaswamy. "Smart Tags for Your Supply Chain." *McKinsey Quarterly* 4 (2003).

Noffsinger, W. B., Robert Niedbalski, Michael Blanks, and Niall Emmart. "Legacy Object Modeling Speeds Software Integration." *Communications of the ACM* 41, no. 12 (December 1998).

Open Source Development Lab. "The Linux Marketplace—Moving From Niche to Mainstream." Prepared by IDC for OSDL (December 14, 2004). http://www.osdl.org/docs/linux_market_overview.pdf.

Pancake, Cherri M., and Christian Lengauer. "High-Performance Java." *Communications of the ACM* 44, no. 10 (October 2001).

Patel, Samir, and Suneel Saigal. "When Computers Learn to Talk: A Web Services Primer." *McKinsey Quarterly,* no. 1 (2002).

Phillips, Charles. "Stemming the Software Spending Spree." *Optimize Magazine* (April 2002).

Ricadela, Aaron. "Living on the Grid." *Information Week* (June 17, 2002).

Salkever, Alex, with Olga Kharif. "Slowly Weaving Web Services Together." *BusinessWeek* (June 24, 2003).

Schmerken, Ivy. "Girding for Grid." *Wall Street and Technology* (April 2003).

Schuff, David, and Robert St. Louis. "Centralization vs. Decentralization of Application Software." *Communications of the ACM* 44, no. 6 (June 2001).

Shankland, Stephen. "IBM: On Demand Computing Has Arrived." CNET News.com (November 12, 2003). http://news.com.com/2100-7784-5106577.html.

———. "T-Rec Bites into Server Market." CNET News.com (February 27, 2004).

Stango, Victor. "The Economics of Standards Wars." *Review of Network Economics* 3, no. 1 (March 2004).

Susarla, Anjana, Anitesh Barua, and Andrew B. Whinston. "Understanding the Service Component of Application Service Provision: An Empirical Analysis of Satisfaction with ASP Services." *MIS Quarterly* 27, no. 1 (March 2003).

Tatemura, Junichi, et al. "Acceleration of Web Service Workflow Execution through Edge Computing." NEC Laboratories America, Inc. (2003).

Tuomi, Ilkka. "The Lives and Death of Moore's Law." *FirstMonday,* col 7, no. 11 (November 2002). www.firstmonday.org.

Walsh, Kenneth R. "Analyzing the Application ASP Concept: Technologies, Economies, and Strategies." *Communications of the ACM* 46, no. 8 (August 2003).

Weill, Peter, and Marianne Broadbent. *Leveraging the New Infrastructure.* Cambridge, Mass.: Harvard Business School Press, 1998.

———. "Management by Maxim: How Business and IT Managers Can Create IT Infrastructures." *Sloan Management Review* (Spring 1997).

Weill, Peter, Mani Subramani, and Marianne Broadbent. "Building IT Infrastructure for Strategic Agility." *Sloan Management Review* 44, no. 1 (Fall 2002).

Weitzel, Tim. *Economics of Standards in Information Networks.* Springer (2004).

CHAPTER 7

Cappiello, Cinzia, Chiara Francalanci, and Barbara Pernici. "Time-Related Factors of Data Quality in Multichannel Information Systems." *Journal of Management Information Systems* 20, no. 3 (Winter 2004).

Chen, Andrew N. K., Paulo B. Goes, and James R. Marsden. "A Query-Driven Approach to the Design and Management of Flexible Database Systems." *Journal of Management Information Systems* 19, no. 3 (Winter 2002–2003).

Clifford, James, Albert Croker, and Alex Tuzhilin. "On Data Representation and Use in a Temporal Relational DBMS." *Information Systems Research* 7, no. 3 (September 1996).

Cooper, Brian L., Hugh J. Watson, Barbara H. Wixom, and Dale L. Goodhue. "Data Warehousing Supports Corporate Strategy at First American Corporation." *MIS Quarterly* (December 2000).

Eckerson, Wayne W. "Data Quality and the Bottom Line." Data Warehousing Institute (2002).

Fayyad, Usama, Ramasamy Ramakrishnan, and Ramakrisnan Srikant. "Evolving Data Mining into Solutions for Insights." *Communications of the ACM* 45, no. 8 (August 2002).

Gardner, Stephen R. "Building the Data Warehouse." *Communications of the ACM* 41, no. 9 (September 1998).

Goldstein, R. C., and J. B. McCririck. "What Do Data Administrators Really Do?" *Datamation* 26 (August 1980).

Goodhue, Dale L., Judith A. Quillard, and John F. Rockart. "Managing the Data Resource: A Contingency Perspective." *MIS Quarterly* (September 1988).

Goodhue, Dale L., Michael D. Wybo, and Laurie J. Kirsch. "The Impact of Data Integration on the Costs and Benefits of Information Systems." *MIS Quarterly* 16, no. 3 (September 1992).

Goodhue, Dale L., Laurie J. Kirsch, Judith A. Quillard, and Michael D. Wybo. "Strategic Data Planning: Lessons from the Field." *MIS Quarterly* 16, no. 1 (March 1992).

Grover, Varun, and James Teng. "How Effective Is Data Resource Management?" *Journal of Information Systems Management* (Summer 1991).

Hirji, Karim K. "Exploring Data Mining Implementation." *Communications of the ACM* 44, no. 7 (July 2001).

Jukic, Boris, Nenad Jukic, and Manoj Parameswaran. "Data Models for Information Sharing in E-Partnerships: Analysis, Improvements, and Relevance." *Journal of Organizational Computing and Electronic Commerce* 12, no. 2 (2002).

Kahn, Beverly K. "Some Realities of Data Administration." *Communications of the ACM* 26 (October 1983).

King, John L., and Kenneth Kraemer. "Information Resource Management Cannot Work." *Information and Management* (1988).

Klau, Rick. "Data Quality and CRM." Line56.com (March 4, 2003).

Kroenke, David. *Database Processing: Fundamentals, Design, and Implementation,* 9th ed. Upper Saddle River, N.J.: Prentice Hall (2004).

Lee, Yang W., and Diane M. Strong. "Knowing-Why about Data Processes and Data Quality." *Journal of Management Information Systems* 20, no. 3 (Winter 2004).

March, Salvatore T., and Young-Gul Kim. "Information Resource Management: A Metadata Perspective." *Journal of Management Information Systems* 5, no. 3 (Winter 1988–1989).

McCarthy, John. "Phenomenal Data Mining." *Communications of the ACM* 43, no. 8 (August 2000).

McFadden, Fred R., Jeffrey A. Hoffer, and Mary B. Prescott. *Modern Database Management,* 6th ed. Upper Saddle River, N.J.: Prentice Hall (2002).

Morrison, Mike, Joline Morrison, and Anthony Keys. "Integrating Web Sites and Databases." *Communications of the ACM* 45, no. 9 (September 2002).

Pierce, Elizabeth M. "Assessing Data Quality with Control Matrices." *Communications of the ACM* 47, no. 2 (February 2004).

Rundensteiner, Elke A., Andreas Koeller, and Xin Zhang. "Maintaining Data Warehouses over Changing Information Sources." *Communications of the ACM* 43, no. 6 (June 2000).

Truman, Gregory E. "Integration in Electronic Exchange Environments." *Journal of Management Information Systems* 17, no. 1 (Summer 2000).

Watson, Hugh J., and Barbara J. Haley. "Managerial Considerations." *Communications of the ACM* 41, no. 9 (September 1998).

CHAPTER 8

Amor, Daniel. *The E-Business Revolution,* 2nd ed. Upper Saddle River, N.J.: Prentice Hall (2002).

Banerjee, Snehamay, and Ram L. Kumar. "Managing Electronic Interchange of Business Documents." *Communications of the ACM* 45, no. 7 (July 2002).

Ben Ameur, Walid, and Herve Kerivin. "New Economical Virtual Private Networks." *Communications of the ACM* 46, no 6 (June 2003).

Berners-Lee, Tim, Robert Cailliau, Ari Luotonen, Henrik Frystyk Nielsen, and Arthur Secret. "The World-Wide Web." *Communications of the ACM* 37, no. 8 (August 1994).

Billsus, Daniel, Clifford A. Brunk, Craig Evans, Brian Gladish, and Michael Pazzani. "Adaptive Interfaces for Ubiquitous Web Access." *Communications of the ACM* 45, no. 5 (May 2002).

Brandt, Richard. "Net Assets." *Stanford Magazine* (November–December 2004).

Chatterjee, Samir, and Suzanne Pawlowski. "All-Optical Networks." *Communications of the ACM* 42, no. 6 (June 1999).

Damsgaard Jan, and Kalle Lyytinen. "Building Electronic Trading Infrastructures: A Public or Private Responsibility?" *Journal of Organizational Computing and Electronic Commerce* 11, no. 2 (2001).

Dutta, Amitava, and Rahul Roy. "Anticipating Internet Diffusion." *Communications of the ACM* 46, no. 2 (February 2003).

Elgin, Ben, with Jay Greene. "Google." *BusinessWeek* (May 3, 2004).

Ewalt, David M. "The New Voice Choice." *Information Week* (March 1, 2004).

Farhoomand, Ali, Pauline S. P. Ng, and Justin K. H. Yue. "The Building of a New Business Ecosystem: Sustaining National Competitive Advantage through Electronic Commerce." *Journal of Organizational Computing and Electronic Commerce* 11, no. 4 (2001).

Federal Networking Council. "Definition of 'Internet.'" October 24, 1995. www.hpcc.gov/fnc/Internet res.html (accessed January 7, 2004).

Festa, Paul. "Point, Click and Swap—Digital Photos Go P2P." CNETNews.com (May 17, 2004).

Frauenfelder, Mark. "Sir Tim Berners-Lee." *Technology Review* (October 2004).

Glezer, Chanan, and Surya B. Yadav. "A Conceptual Model of an Intelligent Catalog Search System." *Journal of Organizational Computing and Electronic Commerce* 11, no. 1 (2001).

Glover, Eric J., Steve Lawrence, Michael D. Gordon, William P. Birmingham, and C. Lee Giles. "Web Search—Your Way." *Communications of the ACM* 44, no. 12 (December 2001).

Grant, Peter. "Ready for Prime Time." *Wall Street Journal* (January 12, 2004).

Grote, Brigitte, Thomas Rose, and Gerhard Peter. "Filter and Broker: An Integrated Architecture for Information Mediation of Dynamic Sources." *Journal of Organizational Computing and Electronic Commerce* 12, no. 2 (2002).

Grover, Varun, and Khawaja Saeed. "The Telecommunication Industry Revisited." *Communications of the ACM* 46, no. 7 (July 2003).

Hearst, Marti, Arne Elliott, Jennifer English, Rashmi Sinha, Kirsten Swearinge, and Ka-Ping Yee. "Finding the Flow in Web Search." *Communications of the ACM* 45, no. 9 (September 2002).

Hong, Weiyin, James Y. L. Thong, and Kar Yan Tam. "Does Animation Attract Online Users' Attention? The Effects of Flash on Information Search Performance and Perceptions." *Information Systems Research* 15, no. 1 (March 2004).

Housel, Tom, and Eric Skopec. *Global Telecommunication Revolution: The Business Perspective.* New York: McGraw-Hill, 2001.

Isakowitz, Tomas, Michael Bieber, and Fabio Vitali. "Web Information Systems." *Communications of the ACM* 41, no. 7 (July 1998).

Kanter, Rosabeth Moss. "The Ten Deadly Mistakes of Wanna-Dots." *Harvard Business Review* (January 2001).

Karahanna, Elena, and Moez Limayem. "E-Mail and V-Mail Usage: Generalizing across Technologies." *Journal of Organizational Computing and Electronic Commerce* 10, no. 1 (2000).

Kautz, Henry, Bart Selman, and Mehul Shah. "ReferralWeb: Combining Social Networks and Collaborative Filtering." *Communications of the ACM* 40, no. 3 (March 1997).

Keen, Peter. "Ready for the 'New' B2B?" *Computerworld* (September 11, 2000).

Keen, Peter G. W. *Competing in Time: Using Telecommunications for Competitive Advantage.* Cambridge, Mass.: Ballinger, 1986.

Kocas, Cenk. "Evolution of Prices in Electronic Markets under Diffusion of Price-Comparison Shopping." *Journal of Management Information Systems* 19, no. 3 (Winter 2002–2003).

Kuo, Geng-Sheng, and Jing-Pei Lin. "New Design Concepts for an Intelligent Internet." *Communications of the ACM* 41, no. 11 (November 1998).

Lieberman, Henry, Christopher Fry, and Louis Weitzman. "Exploring the Web with Reconnaissance Agents." *Communications of the ACM* 44, no. 8 (August 2001).

Madden, Mary, and Lee Rainie. "America's Online Pursuits." *Pew Internet and American Life Project* (April 25, 2004).

Maes, Patti, Robert H. Guttman, and Alexandros G. Moukas. "Agents That Buy and Sell." *Communications of the ACM* 42, no. 3 (March 1999).

Mangalindan, Mylene, Nick Wingfield, and Robert A. Guth. "Rising Clout of Google Prompts Rush by Internet Rivals to Adopt." *Wall Street Journal* (July 16, 2003).

Nasaw, Daniel. "Instant Messages Are Popping Up All Over." *Wall Street Journal* (June 12, 2003).

National Research Council. "The Internet's Coming of Age." Washington, D.C.: National Academy Press (2000).

Ngwenyama, Ojelanki, and Allen S. Lee. "Communication Richness in Electronic Mail: Critical Social Theory and the Contextuality of Meaning." *MIS Quarterly* 21, no. 2 (June 1997).

Papazoglou, Mike P. "Agent-Oriented Technology in Support of E-Business." *Communications of the ACM* 44, no. 4 (April 2001).

Pitkow, James, Hinrich Schutze, Todd Cass, Rob Cooley, Don Turnbull, Andy Edmonds, Eytan Adar, and Thomas Breuel. "Personalized Search." *Communications of the ACM* 45, no. 9 (September 2002).

Pogue, Dave. "Video Chat Software Reviewed." *New York Times Circuits* (June 26, 2003).

Ramstad, Evan, and Ken Brown. "China Expands Phone Service via Internet." *Wall Street Journal* (April 22, 2004).

Roush, Wade. "The Internet Reborn." *Technology Review* (October 2003).

Smith, Steve. "Push Back?" *eContent* (July 2003).

Spangler, Todd. "Voice on Data Networks: A Sound Move?" *Baseline* (March 2004).

Thompson, Marjorie Sarbough, and Martha S. Feldman. "Electronic Mail and Organizational Communication." *Organization Science* 9, no. 6 (November–December 1998).

Totty, Michael, and Mylene Mangalindan. "As Google Becomes Web's Gatekeeper, Sites Fight to Get In" *Wall Street Journal* (February 26, 2003).

Travis, Paul. "Present a United Front." *Information Week* (August 2, 2004).

Valera, Francisco, Jorge E. López de Vergara, José I. Moreno, Víctor A. Villagrá, and Julio Varshney, Upkar, Andy Snow, Matt McGivern, and Christi Howard, "Voice Over IP." *Communications of the ACM* 45, no. 12 (January 2002).

Vara, Vauhini. "High-Speed Surpasses Dial-Up as Top Home Web Access in U.S." *Wall Street Journal,* August 18, 2004.

Varshney, Upkar, Andy Snow, Matt McGivern, and Christi Howard. "Voice Over IP." *Communications of the ACM* 45, no. 1 (January 2002).

Weiser, Mark. "What Ever Happened to the Next-Generation Internet?" *Communications of the ACM* 44, no. 9 (September 2001).

Whitman, Michael E., Anthony M. Townsend, and Robert J. Aalberts. "Considerations for Effective Telecommunications-Use Policy." *Communications of the ACM* 42, no. 6 (June 1999).

Wilson, E. Vance. "Email Winners and Losers." *Communications of the ACM* 45, no. 10 (October 2002).

CHAPTER 9

Brandt, Richard. "Net Assets." *Stanford Magazine* (November–December 2004).

Brandt, Richard, and Ron Vetter. "Emerging Mobile and Wireless Networks." *Communications of the ACM* 42, no. 6 (June 2000).

Cho, Cynthia H. "For More Advertisers, the Medium Is the Text Message." *Wall Street Journal* (August 2, 2004).

Dignan, Larry. "RFID: Hit or Myth?" *Baseline* (February 2004).

Evans, Robert. "Mobile Phone Users Double Since 2000." Reuters (December 9, 2004).

Feder, Barnaby J. "Keeping Better Track from Factory to Checkout." *New York Times* (November 11, 2004).

Hellweg, Eric. "Tag—You're It." *Technology Review* (July 2004).

Imielinski, Tomasz, and B. R. Badrinath. "Mobile Wireless Computing: Challenges in Data Management." *Communications of the ACM* 37, no. 10 (October 1994).

Intel Corporation. "Wireless LAN Productivity Studies." Intel. www.intel.com/business/bss/infrastructure/wireless/roi/productivity_studies.htm (accessed July 23, 2004).

Kenny, David, and John F. Marshall. "Contextual Marketing." *Harvard Business Review* (November–December 2000).

Kontzer, Tony. "RFID Flies High with Airplane Makers." *Information Week* (June 14, 2004).

Lehr, William, and Lee W. McKnight. "Wireless Internet Access: 3G vs. WiFi?" Center for eBusiness@MIT (August 2002).

Mears, Rena, and Jason Salzetti. "The New Wireless Enterprise." *Information Week* (September 18, 2000).

Nicopolitidis, Petros, Georgios Papademitriou, Mohammad S. Obaidat, and Adreas S. Pomportsis. "The Economics of Wireless Networks." *Communications of the ACM* 47, no. 4 (April 2004).

Niemeyer, Alex, Minsok H. Pak, and Sanjay E. Ramaswamy. "Smart Tags for Your Supply Chain." *McKinsey Quarterly*, no. 4 (2003).

Overby, Christine Spivey. "RFID at What Cost?" *Forrester Research* (March 1, 2004).

Palen, Leysia. "Mobile Telephony in a Connected Life." *Communications of the ACM* 45, no. 3 (March 2003).

Pottie, G. J., and W. J. Kaiser. "Wireless Integrated Network Sensors." *Communications of the ACM* 43, no. 5 (May 2000).

Research in Motion. "BlackBerry Expands Leadership in the Legal Sector with Integrated Email, Phone, and Data Applications." (July 25, 2004).

Rothfeder, Jeffrey. "What's Wrong with RFID?" *CIO Insight* (August 1, 2004).

Sandsmark, Fred. "What You Need to Know about Wireless Networking." *CISCO IQ Magazine* (November–December 2002).

Songini, Marc L. "Wireless CRM Takes to the Field." *Computerworld* (July 12, 2004).

Varshney, Upkar. "Multicast Over Wireless Networks." *Communications of the ACM* 45, no. 12 (December 2002).

———. "Networking Support for Mobile Computing." *Communications of the Association for Information Systems* 1 (January 1999).

Vetter, Ron. "The Wireless Web." *Communications of the ACM* 44, no. 3 (March 2001).

Wareham, Jonathan, and Armando Levy. "Who Will Be the Adopters of 3G Mobile Computing Devices? A Profit Estimation of Mobile Telecom Diffusion." *Journal of Organizational Computing and Electronic Commerce* 12, no. 2 (2002).

Wingfield, Nick. "Tomorrow's Wi-Fi." *Wall Street Journal,* May 24, 2004.

CHAPTER 10

Alberts, David S. "The Economics of Software Quality Assurance." Washington, D.C.: National Computer Conference (1976).

Austin, Robert D., and Christopher A. R. Darby. "The Myth of Secure Computing." *Harvard Business Review* (June 2003).

Backhouse, James, Carol Hsu, and Aidan McDonnell. "Toward Public-Key Infrastructure Interoperability." *Communications of the ACM* 46, no. 6 (June 2003).

Bank, David. "Mydoom Worm Renews Debate on Cyber-Ethics." *Wall Street Journal* (November 11, 2004).

———. "Outbreak!" *Wall Street Journal* (November 15, 2004).

———. "What's That Sneaking into Your Computer?" *Wall Street Journal* (April 26, 2004).

Banker, Rajiv D., and Chris F. Kemerer. "Performance Evaluation Metrics in Information Systems Development: A Principal-Agent Model." *Information Systems Research* 3, no. 4 (December 1992).

Banker, Rajiv D., Robert J. Kaufmann, and Rachna Kumar. "An Empirical Test of Object-Based Output Measurement Metrics in a Computer-Aided Software Engineering (CASE) Environment." *Journal of Management Information Systems* 8, no. 3 (Winter 1991–1992).

Banker, Rajiv D., Srikant M. Datar, Chris F. Kemerer, and Dani Zweig. "Software Complexity and Maintenance Costs." *Communications of the ACM* 36, no. 11 (November 1993).

Barrett, Jennifer. "Phishing Fall-Out." *Newsweek* (April 15, 2004).

Berghel, Hal. "The Discipline of Internet Forensics." *Communications of the ACM* 46, no. 8 (August 2003).

Borzo, Jeannette. "Something's Phishy." *Wall Street Journal* (November 15, 2004).

Brenner, Susan W. "U.S. Cybercrime Law: Defining Offenses." *Information Systems Frontiers* 6, no. 2 (June 2004).

Byers, Simon, and Dave Kormann. "802.11b Access Point Mapping." *Communications of the ACM* 46, no. 5 (May 2003).

Cam Winget, Nancy, Russ Housley, David Wagner, and Jesse Walker. "Security Flaws in 802.11b Data Link Protocols." *Communications of the ACM* 46, no. 5 (May 2003).

Cavusoglu, Huseyin, Birendra Mishra, and Srinivasan Raghunathan. "A Model for Evaluating IT Security Investments." *Communications of the ACM* 47, no. 7 (July 2004).

Chipman, Andrea. "Stealing You." *Wall Street Journal* (April 26, 2004).

Choy, Manhoi, Hong Va Leong, and Man Hon Wong. "Disaster Recovery Techniques for Database Systems." *Communications of the ACM* 43, no. 11 (November 2000).

Darby, Christopher. "The Dollars and Cents of Security." *Optimize Magazine* 12 (October 2002).

Datz, Todd. "The Interactive Nightmare." *CSO Magazine* (April 2004).

Di Pietro, Roberto, and Luigi V. Mancini. "Security and Privacy Issues of Handheld and Wearable Wireless Devices." *Communications of the ACM* 46, no. 9 (September 2003).

Duffy, Daintry. "Body of Evidence." *CSO Magazine* (May 2004).

Durst, Robert, Terrence Champion, Brian Witten, Eric Miller, and Luigi Spagnuolo. "Testing and Evaluating Computer Intrusion Detection Systems." *Communications of the ACM* 42, no. 7 (July 1999).

Fitzgerald, Michael. "At Risk Offshore." *CIO Australia* (April 4, 2004).

Foley, John, and George V. Hulme. "Get Ready to Patch." *Information Week* (August 30, 2004).

Fox, Armando, and David Patterson. "Self-Repairing Computers." *Scientific American* (May 2003).

Ghosh, Anup K., and Tara M. Swaminatha. "Software Security and Privacy Risks in Mobile E-Commerce." *Communications of the ACM* 44, no. 2 (February 2001).

Giordano, Scott M. "Electronic Evidence and the Law." *Information Systems Frontiers* 6, no. 2 (June 2004).

Gordon, Lawrence A., Martin P. Loeb, and Tashfeen Sohail. "A Framework for Using Insurance for Cyber-Risk Management." *Communications of the ACM* 46, no. 3 (March 2003).

Gordon, Lawrence A., Martin P. Loeb, William Lucyshyn, and Robert Richardson. "2004 CSI/FBI Computer Crime and Security Survey." Computer Security Institute (2004).

Hansell, Saul. "Online Swindlers Called 'Phishers' Lure the Unwary." *New York Times* (March 24, 2004).

Horowitz, Alan S. "Biting Back." *Computerworld* (January 13, 2003).

Housley, Russ, and William Arbaugh. "Security Problems in 802.11b Networks." *Communications of the ACM* 46, no. 5 (May 2003).

Hulme, George V. "Under Attack." *Information Week* (July 5, 2004).

Hulme, George V., and Thomas Claburn. "Tiny Evil Things." *Information Week* (April 26, 2004).

Ives, Blake, Kenneth R. Walsh, and Helmut Schneider. "The Domino Effect of Password Reuse." *Communications of the ACM* 47, no. 4 (April 2004).

Jajoda, Sushil, Catherine D. McCollum, and Paul Ammann. "Trusted Recovery." *Communications of the ACM* 42, no. 7 (July 1999).

Joshi, James B. D., Walid G. Aref, Arif Ghafoor, and Eugene H. Spafford. "Security Models for Web-Based Applications." *Communications of the ACM* 44, no. 2 (February 2001).

Keizer, Gregg. "Trojan Horse Poses as Windows XP Update." *Information Week* (January 9, 2004).

Klein, Barbara D., Dale L. Goodhue, and Gordon B. Davis. "Can Humans Detect Errors in Data?" *MIS Quarterly* 21, no. 2 (June 1997).

Laudon, Kenneth C. "Data Quality and Due Process in Large Interorganizational Record Systems." *Communications of the ACM* 29 (January 1986).

Littlewood, Bev, and Lorenzo Strigini. "The Risks of Software." *Scientific American* 267, no. 5 (November 1992).

Marer, Eva, and Patrick Thibodeau. "Companies Confront Rising Network Threats." *Datamation* (July 2, 2001).

Mercuri, Rebecca T. "Analyzing Security Costs." *Communications of the ACM* 46, no. 6 (June 2003).

———. "The HIPAA-potamus in Health Care Data Security." *Communications of the ACM* 47, no. 7 (July 2004).

Neumann, Peter G. "Risks Considered Global(ly)." *Communications of the ACM* 35, no. 1 (January 1993).

Newman, Robert. *Enterprise Security.* Upper Saddle River, N.J.: Prentice Hall (2003).

Oppliger, Rolf. "Internet Security, Firewalls, and Beyond." *Communications of the ACM* 40, no. 7 (May 1997).

Orr, Kenneth. "Data Quality and Systems Theory." *Communications of the ACM* 41, no. 2 (February 1998).

Panko, Raymond R. *Corporate Computer and Network Security.* Upper Saddle River, N.J.: Pearson Prentice Hall (2004).

Rainer, Rex Kelley, Jr., Charles A. Snyder, and Houston H. Carr. "Risk Analysis for Information Technology." *Journal of Management Information Systems* 8, no. 1 (Summer 1991).

Ravichandran, T., and Arun Rai. "Total Quality Management in Information Systems Development." *Journal of Management Information Systems* 16, no. 3 (Winter 1999–2000).

Redman, Thomas. "The Impact of Poor Data Quality on the Typical Enterprise." *Communications of the ACM* 41, no. 2 (February 1998).

Roche, Edward M., and George Van Nostrand. *Information Systems, Computer Crime and Criminal Justice.* New York: Barraclough (2004).

Russell, Bruce, and Sangit Chatterjee. "Relationship Quality: The Undervalued Dimension of Software Quality." *Communications of the ACM* 46, no. 8 (August 2003).

Sarkar, Pushpak. "A Paragon of Quality." *Intelligent Enterprise* (October 2002).

Schmerken, Ivy. "Offshore Outsourcing: Is Your Data Safe?" *Wall Street and Technology* (May 2004).

Schwerha, Joseph J., IV. "Cybercrime: Legal Standards Governing the Collection of Digital Evidence." *Information Systems Frontiers* 6, no. 2 (June 2004).

Slaughter, Sandra A., Donald E. Harter, and Mayuram S. Krishnan. "Evaluating the Cost of Software Quality." *Communications of the ACM* 41, no. 8 (August 1998).

Stillerman, Matthew, Carla Marceau, and Maureen Stillman. "Intrusion Detection for Distributed Applications." *Communications of the ACM* 42, no. 7 (July 1999).

Straub, Detmar W., and Richard J. Welke. "Coping with Systems Risk: Security Planning Models for Management Decision Making." *MIS Quarterly* 22, no. 4 (December 1998).

Strong, Diane M., Yang W. Lee, and Richard Y. Wang. "Data Quality in Context." *Communications of the ACM* 40, no. 5 (May 1997).

Tayi, Giri Kumar, and Donald P. Ballou. "Examining Data Quality." *Communications of the ACM* 41, no. 2 (February 1998).

Thomson, Iain. "Akamai Investigates Denial of Service Attack." Personal Computer World. www.pcw.co.uk/news/1155955 (accessed June 17, 2004).

Totty, Michael. "Business Solutions: The Dangers in Outbound E-Mail" *Wall Street Journal* (April 26, 2003).

Tucker, Bill. "SoBig.F Breaks Virus Speed Records." CNN (August 22, 2003).

Tynan, Craig K., and Joey F. George. "Improving Software Inspections with Group Process Support." *Communications of the ACM* 45, no. 9 (September 2002).

Viega, John, Tadayoshi Koho, and Bruce Potter. "Trust (and Mistrust) in Secure Applications." *Communications of the ACM* 44, no. 2 (February 2001).

Volonino, Linda, and Stephen R. Robinson. *Principles and Practices of Information Security.* Upper Saddle River, N.J.: Prentice Hall (2004).

Wagstaff, Jeremy. "Gone Phishing: Web Scam Takes Dangerous Turns." *Wall Street Journal* (May 27, 2004).

Wand, Yair, and Richard Y. Wang. "Anchoring Data Quality Dimensions in Ontological Foundations." *Communications of the ACM* 39, no. 11 (November 1996).

Wang, Huaiqing, and Chen Wang. "Taxonomy of Security Considerations and Software Quality." *Communications of the ACM* 46, no. 6 (June 2003).

Wang, Richard. "A Product Perspective on Total Data Quality Management." *Communications of the ACM* 41, no. 2 (February 1998).

Wang, Richard Y., Yang W. Lee, Leo L. Pipino, and Diane M. Strong. "Manage Your Information as a Product." *Sloan Management Review* 39, no. 4 (Summer 1998).

Weber, Ron. *Information Systems Control and Audit.* New York: McGraw-Hill (1999).

Whitman, Michael E. "Enemy at the Gate: Threats to Information Security." *Communications of the ACM* 46, no. 8 (August 2003).

Ye, Nong, Joseph Giordano, and John Feldman. "A Process Control Approach to Cyber Attack Detection." *Communications of the ACM* 44, no. 8 (August 2001).

Zhou, Jianying. "Achieving Fair Nonrepudiation in Electronic Transactions." *Journal of Organizational Computing and Electronic Commerce* 11, no. 4 (2001).

Zviran, Moshe, and William J. Haga. "Password Security: An Empirical Study." *Journal of Management Information Systems* 15, no. 4 (Spring 1999).

CHAPTER 11

Agarwal, Anupam, David P. Harding, and Jeffrey R. Schumacher. "Organizing for CRM." *The McKinsey Quarterly* no. 3 (2004).

Anderson, James C., and James A. Narus. "Selectively Pursuing More of Your Customer's Business." *MIT Sloan Management Review* 44, no. 3 (Spring 2003).

Bacheldor, Beth. "Implementation Imperative." *Information Week* (April 28, 2003).

D'Avanzo, Robert, Hans von Lewinski, and Luk N. Van Wassenhove. "The Link between Supply Chain and Financial Performance." *Supply Chain Management Review* (November 1, 2003).

Davenport, Thomas H. *Mission Critical: Realizing the Promise of Enterprise Systems.* Boston: Harvard Business School Press (2000).

———. "Putting the Enterprise into Enterprise Systems." *Harvard Business Review* (July–August 1998).

Davison, Robert. "Cultural Complications of ERP." *Communications of the ACM* 45, no. 7 (July 2002).

Day, George S. "Creating a Superior Customer-Relating Capability." *MIT Sloan Management Review* 44, no. 3 (Spring 2003).

Dowling, Grahame. "Customer Relationship Management: In B2C Markets, Often Less Is More." *California Management Review* 44, no. 3 (Spring 2002).

Ebner, Manuel, Arthur Hu, Daniel Levitt, and Jim McCrory. "How to Rescue CRM." *McKinsey Quarterly* 4 (2002).

Fayyad, Usama. "Optimizing Customer Insight." *Intelligent Enterprise* (May 13, 2003).

Fisher, Marshall L. "What Is the Right Supply Chain for Your Product?" *Harvard Business Review* (March–April 1997).

Fleisch, Elgar, Hubert Oesterle, and Stephen Powell. "Rapid Implementation of Enterprise Resource Planning Systems." *Journal of Organizational Computing and Electronic Commerce* 14, no. 2 (2004).

Goldenberg, Barton. "Don't Put the Cart Before the Horse." *Customer Relationship Management* (September 2004).

Goodhue, Dale L., Barbara H. Wixom, and Hugh J. Watson. "Realizing Business Benefits through CRM: Hitting the Right Target in the Right Way." *MIS Quarterly Executive* 1, no. 2 (June 2002).

Greenbaum, Joshua. "Build vs. Buy in the 21st Century." *Intelligent Enterprise* (April 22, 2003).

Greenbaum, Joshua, and Peter Graf. "SAP xApps: Maximizing Return on Strategic Assets." White paper. www.sap.com (accessed August 1, 2003).

Guptill, Bruce. "Customer Metrics That Matter." *Optimize Magazine* 18 (April 2003).

Handfield, Robert B., and Ernest L. Nichols Jr. *Introduction to Supply Chain Management.* Upper Saddle River, N.J.: Prentice Hall (1999).

Havenstein, Heather. "SAP Aims to Bridge Suites." *InfoWorld* (January 17, 2003).

Hitt, Lorin, D. J. Wu, and Xiaoge Zhou. "Investment in Enterprise Resource Planning: Business Impact and Productivity Measures." *Journal of Management Information Systems* 19, no. 1 (Summer 2002).

Jaiswal. M. P. "Implementing ERP Systems." *Dataquest* (June 30, 2003).

Kalakota, Ravi, and Marcia Robinson. *E-Business 2.0.* Boston: Addison-Wesley (2001).

———. *Services Blueprint: Roadmap for Execution.* Boston: Addison-Wesley (2003).

Kanakamedala, Kishore, Glenn Ramsdell, and Vats Srivatsan. "Getting Supply Chain Software Right." *McKinsey Quarterly,* no. 1 (2003).

Koch, Christopher. "The ABCs of ERP." CIO Enterprise Resource Planning Research Center. www.cio.com/research/erp/edit/erpbasics.html (accessed August 1, 2003).

Kopczak, Laura Rock, and M. Eric Johnson. "The Supply-Chain Management Effect." *MIT Sloan Management Review* 44, no. 3 (Spring 2003).

Kumar, Kuldeep, and Jos Van Hillegersberg. "ERP Experiences and Revolution." *Communications of the ACM* 43, no. 4 (April 2000).

Laudon , Kenneth C., and Jane P. Laudon. *Management Information Systems: Managing the Digital Firm,* 7th and 8th ed. Upper Saddle River, N.J.: Prentice Hall (2002, 2004).

Lee, Hau. "The Triple-A Supply Chain." *Harvard Business Review* (October 2004).

Lee, Hau, L. V. Padmanabhan, and Seugin Whang. "The Bullwhip Effect in Supply Chains." *Sloan Management Review* (Spring 1997).

LoFrumento, Tony. "How Profitable Are Your Customers?" *Optimize Magazine* 18 (April 2003).

Markus, M. Lynne, Conelis Tanis, and Paul C. van Fenema. "Multisite ERP Implementations." *Communications of the ACM* 43, no. 3 (April 2000).

McKie, Stewart. "The Big BAM." *Intelligent Enterprise* (July 18, 2003).

Mearian, Lucas. "Canadian Supermarket Chain Abandons SAP's Retail Software." *Computerworld* (February 2, 2001).

Mello, Adrian. "Global Supply Links." *Cisco IQ Magazine* (May/June 2003).

Myron, David. "6 Barriers to CRM Success." *CRM Magazine* (August 2003).

Norris, Grant, James R. Hurley, Kenneth M. Hartley, John R. Dunleavy, and John D. Balls. *E-Business and ERP: Transforming the Enterprise.* New York: Wiley (2000).

Palaniswamy, Rajagopal, and Tyler Frank. "Enhancing Manufacturing Performance with ERP Systems." *Information Systems Management* (Summer 2000).

Pan, Shan L., and Jae-Nam Lee. "Using e-CRM for a Unified View of the Customer." *Communications of the ACM* 46, no. 4 (April 2003).

Ranganathan, C., Jasbir S. Dhaliwal, and Thompson S. H. Teo. "Assimilation and Diffusion of Web Technologies in Supply-Chain Management: An Examination of Key Drivers and Performance Impacts." *International Journal of Electronic Commerce* 9, no. 1 (Fall 2004).

Reinartz, Werner J., and Pankaj Chugh. "Learning from Experience: Making CRM a Success at Last." *Journal of Call Centre Management* (March–April 2002).

Richebacher, Thomas F. "The Money Shift." *Intelligent Enterprise* (March 20, 2003).

Robey, Daniel, Jeanne W. Ross, and Marie-Claude Boudreau. "Learning to Implement Enterprise Systems: An Exploratory Study of the Dialectics of Change." *Journal of Management Information Systems* 19, no. 1 (Summer 2002).

Sabri, Hussain. "CRM: The Power of Prediction." *Intelligent Enterprise* (July 18, 2003).

Schneider, Martin. "ROI Is Increasing among CRM Projects." Destination CRM.com. www.destinationcrm.com/articles/default.asp?ArticleID= 3829%20&TopicID=9 (accessed February 2, 2004).

Scott, Judy E., and Iris Vessey. "Managing Risks in Enterprise Systems Implementations." *Communications of the ACM* 45, no. 4 (April 2002).

Sinha, Sudhi. "'The Smartest Link." *Intelligent Enterprise* (August 10, 2003).

Slone, Reuben E. "Leading a Supply Chain Turnaround." *Harvard Business Review* (October 2004).

"Supply Chain Challenges: Building Relationships." *Harvard Business Review* (July 2003).

Toh, Ann. "Portal Power." *CIO Asia* (August 2003).

Varon, Elena. "Portals Get Down to Business." *CIO* (December 1, 2002).

Welty, Bill, and Irma Becerra-Fernandez. "Managing Trust and Commitment in Supply Chain Relationships." *Communications of the ACM* 44, no. 6 (June 2001).

Winer, Russell S. "A Framework for Customer Relationship Management." *California Management Review* 43, no. 4 (Summer 2001).

Yu, Larry. "Successful Customer Relationship Management." *Sloan Management Review* 42, no. 4 (Summer 2001).

CHAPTER 12

Alavi, Maryam, and Dorothy Leidner. "Knowledge Management and Knowledge Management Systems: Conceptual Foundations and Research Issues."" *MIS Quarterly* 25, no. 1 (March 2001).

Allen, Bradley P. "CASE-Based Reasoning: Business Applications." *Communications of the ACM* 37, no. 3 (March 1994).

Anandarajan, Murugan. "Profiling Web Usage in the Workplace: A Behavior-Based Artificial Intelligence Approach." *Journal of Management Information Systems* 19, no. 1 (Summer 2002).

Anthes, Gary H. "Agents Change." *Computerworld* (January 27, 2003).

AskMe Corporation. "Select Customers: P&G Case Study" (August 2003). www.askmecorp.com/customers/default.asp.

Awad, Elias, and Hassan M. Ghaziri. *Knowledge Management*. Upper Saddle River, N.J.: Prentice Hall (2004).

Balasubramanian, V., and Alf Bashian. "Document Management and Web Technologies: Alice Marries the Mad Hatter." *Communications of the ACM* 41, no. 7 (July 1998).

Bargeron, David, Jonathan Grudin, Anoop Gupta, Elizabeth Sanocki, Francis Li, and Scott Le Tiernan. "Asynchronous Collaboration Around Multimedia Applied to On-Demand Education." *Journal of Management Information Systems* 18, no. 4 (Spring 2002).

Barker, Virginia E., and Dennis E. O'Connor. "Expert Systems for Configuration at Digital: XCON and Beyond." *Communications of the ACM* (March 1989).

Becerra-Fernandez, Irma, Avelino Gonzalez, and Rajiv Sabherwal. *Knowledge Management*. Upper Saddle River, N.J.: Prentice Hall (2004).

Bieer, Michael, Douglas Englebart Richard Furuta, Starr Roxanne Hiltz, John Noll, Jennifer Preece, Edward A. Stohr, Murray Turoff, and Bartel Van de Walle. "Toward Virtual Community Knowledge Evolution." *Journal of Management Information Systems* 18, no. 4 (Spring 2002).

Birkinshaw, Julian, and Tony Sheehan. "Managing the Knowledge Life Cycle." *MIT Sloan Management Review* 44, no. 1 (Fall 2002).

Blair, Margaret M., Steven Wallman, and Brookings Task Force on Intangibles. *Unseen Wealth*. Washington, D.C.: Brookings Institution Press (2001).

Booth, Corey, and Shashi Buluswar. "The Return of Artificial Intelligence." *McKinsey Quarterly*, no. 2 (2002).

Burtka, Michael. "Generic Algorithms." *Stern Information Systems Review* 1, no. 1 (Spring 1993).

Busch, Elizabeth, Matti Hamalainen, Clyde W. Holsapple, Yongmoo Suh, and Andrew B. Whinston. "Issues and Obstacles in the Development of Team Support Systems." *Journal of Organizational Computing* 1, no. 2 (April–June 1991).

Cannataro, Mario, and Domenico Talia. "The Knowledge Grid." *Communications of the ACM* 46, no. 1 (January 2003).

Cavalieri, Sergio, Vittorio Cesarotti, and Vito Introna. "A Multiagent Model for Coordinated Distribution Chain Planning." *Journal of Organizational Computing and Electronic Commerce* 13, nos. 3 and 4 (2003).

Churchland, Paul M., and Patricia Smith Churchland. "Could a Machine Think?" *Scientific American* (January 1990).

Cole, R. E. "Introduction, Knowledge Management Special Issue." *California Management Review* (Spring 1998).

Cross, Rob, and Lloyd Baird. "Technology Is Not Enough: Improving Performance by Building Organizational Memory." *Sloan Management Review* 41, no. 3 (Spring 2000).

Cross, Rob, Nitin Nohria, and Andrew Parker. "Six Myths about Informal Networks—and How to Overcome Them." *Sloan Management Review* 43, no. 3 (Spring 2002).

Davenport, Thomas H., and Lawrence Prusak. *Working Knowledge: How Organizations Manage What They Know*. Boston: Harvard Business School Press (1997).

Davenport, Thomas H., David W. DeLong, and Michael C. Beers. "Successful Knowledge Management Projects." *Sloan Management Review* 39, no. 2 (Winter 1998).

Davenport, Thomas H., Robert J. Thomas, and Susan Cantrell. "The Mysterious Art and Science of Knowledge-Worker Performance." *MIT Sloan Management Review* 44, no. 1 (Fall 2002).

Davis, Gordon B. "Anytime/Anyplace Computing and the Future of Knowledge Work." *Communications of the ACM* 42, no. 12 (December 2002).

Desouza, Kevin C. "Facilitating Tacit Knowledge Exchange." *Communications of the ACM* 46, no. 6 (June 2003).

Desouza, Kevin C., and J. Roberto Evaristo. "Managing Knowledge in Distributed Projects." *Communications of the ACM* 47, no. 4 (April 2004).

Dhar, Vasant. "Plausibility and Scope of Expert Systems in Management." *Journal of Management Information Systems* (Summer 1987).

Dhar, Vasant, and Roger Stein. *Intelligent Decision Support Methods: The Science of Knowledge Work*. Upper Saddle River, N.J.: Prentice Hall (1997).

Du, Timon C., Eldon Y. Li, and An-pin Chang. "Mobile Agents in Distributed Network Management." *Communications of the ACM* 46, no. 7 (July 2003).

Earl, Michael. "Knowledge Management Strategies: Toward a Taxonomy." *Journal of Management Information Systems* 18, no. 1 (Summer 2001).

Earl, Michael J., and Ian A. Scott. "What Is a Chief Knowledge Officer?" *Sloan Management Review* 40, no. 2 (Winter 1999).

Easley, Robert F., Sarv Devaraj, and J. Michael Crant. "Relating Collaborative Technology Use to Teamwork Quality and Performance: An Empirical Analysis." *Journal of Management Information Systems* 19, no. 4 (Spring 2003).

El Najdawi, M. K., and Anthony C. Stylianou. "Expert Support Systems: Integrating AI Technologies." *Communications of the ACM* 36, no. 12 (December 1993).

Farhoomand, Ali, and Don H. Drury. "Managerial Information Overload." *Communications of the ACM* 45, no. 10 (October 2002).

Flash, Cynthia. "Who Is the CKO?" *Knowledge Management* (May 2001).

Frangos, Alex. "New Dimensions in Design." *Wall Street Journal* (July 7, 2004).

Gelernter, David. "The Metamorphosis of Information Management." *Scientific American* (August 1989).

Glushko, Robert J., Jay M. Tenenbaum, and Bart Meltzer. "An XML Framework for Agent-Based E-Commerce." *Communications of the ACM* 42, no. 3 (March 1999).

Goldberg, David E. "Genetic and Evolutionary Algorithms Come of Age." *Communications of the ACM* 37, no. 3 (March 1994).

Gregor, Shirley, and Izak Benbasat. "Explanations from Intelligent Systems: Theoretical Foundations and Implications for Practice." *MIS Quarterly* 23, no. 4 (December 1999).

Griffith, Terri L., John E. Sawyer, and Margaret A Neale. "Virtualness and Knowledge in Teams: Managing the Love Triangle of Organizations,

Individuals, and Information Technology." *MIS Quarterly* 27, no. 2 (June 2003).

Grover, Varun, and Thomas H. Davenport. "General Perspectives on Knowledge Management: Fostering a Research Agenda." *Journal of Management Information Systems* 18, no. 1 (Summer 2001).

Gu, Feng, and Baruch Lev. "Intangible Assets: Measurements, Drivers, Usefulness." Baruch Lev's Homepage. http://pages.stern.nyu.edu/~blev/.

Guerra, Anthony. "Goldman Sachs Embraces Rules-Based Solution." *Wall Street and Technology* (May 2001).

Hansen, Morton T., Nitin Nohria, and Thomas Tierney. "What's Your Strategy for Knowledge Management?" *Harvard Business Review* (March–April 1999).

Hayes-Roth, Frederick, and Neil Jacobstein. "The State of Knowledge-Based Systems." *Communications of the ACM* 37, no. 3 (March 1994).

Hinton, Gregory. "How Neural Networks Learn from Experience." *Scientific American* (September 1992).

Holland, John H. "Genetic Algorithms." *Scientific American* (July 1992).

Housel, Tom, and Arthur A. Bell. *Measuring and Managing Knowledge.* New York: McGraw-Hill, 2001.

Hummingbird Ltd. "Conoco Drills into Hummingbird Portal." www.hummingbird.com (accessed 2003).

———. "Intuit Builds Stakeholder Value with Hummingbird KM." Hummingbird. www.hummingbird.com (accessed 2003).

Jarvenpaa, Sirkka L., and D. Sandy Staples. "Exploring Perceptions of Organizational Ownership of Information and Expertise." *Journal of Management Information Systems* 18, no. 1 (Summer 2001).

Jeong, Woo Seok, Sun Gwan Han, and Geun Sik Jo. "Intelligent Cyber Logistics Using Reverse Auction." *Journal of Organizational Computing and Electronic Commerce* 13, nos. 3 and 4 (2003).

Jones, Quentin, Gilad Ravid, and Sheizaf Rafaeli. "Information Overload and the Message Dynamics of Online Interaction Spaces: A Theoretical Model and Empirical Exploration." *Information Systems Research* 15, no. 2 (June 2004).

Kankanhalli, Atreyi, Frasiska Tanudidjaja, Juliana Sutanto, and Bernard C. Y. Tan. "The Role of IT in Successful Knowledge Management Initiatives." *Communications of the ACM* 46, no. 9 (September 2003).

King, William R., Peter V. Marks Jr., and Scott McCoy. "The Most Important Issues in Knowledge Management." *Communications of the ACM* 45, no. 9 (September 2002).

KPMG. "Insights from KPMG's European Knowledge Management Survey 2002/2003." KPMG (2003).

———. "Who We Are—Sharing Knowledge." KPMG. www.kpmgcampus.com (accessed 2003).

Kuo, R. J., K. Chang, and S. Y. Chien. "Integration and Self-Organizing Feature Maps and Genetic-Algorithm-Based Clustering Method for Market Segmentation." *Journal of Organizational Computing and Electronic Commerce* 14, no. 1 (2004).

Lee, Kyoung Jun, Yong Sik Chang, Hyung Rim Choi, Hyun Soo Kim, Young Jae Park, and Byung Joo Park. "A Time-Bound Framework for Negotiation and Decision Making of Virtual Manufacturing Enterprise." *Journal of Organizational Computing and Electronic Commerce* 14, no. 1 (2004).

Leonard, Dorothy, and Walter Swap. "Deep Smarts." *Harvard Business Review* (September 1, 2004).

Leonard-Barton, Dorothy, and John J. Sviokla. "Putting Expert Systems to Work." *Harvard Business Review* (March–April 1988).

Lev, Baruch. "Sharpening the Intangibles Edge." *Harvard Business Review* (June 1, 2004).

Lev, Baruch, and Theodore Sougiannis. "Penetrating the Book-to-Market Black Box: The R&D Effect." *Journal of Business Finance and Accounting* (April/May 1999).

Lou, Hao, and Richard W. Scannell. "Acceptance of Groupware: The Relationships among Use, Satisfaction, and Outcomes." *Journal of Organizational Computing and Electronic Commerce* 6, no. 2 (1996).

Maes, Patti. "Agents That Reduce Work and Information Overload." *Communications of the ACM* 38, no. 7 (July 1994).

Maglio, Paul P., and Christopher S. Campbell. "Attentive Agents." *Communications of the ACM* 46, no. 3 (March 2003).

Markus, M. Lynne. "Toward a Theory of Knowledge Reuse: Types of Knowledge Reuse Situations and Factors in Reuse Success." *Journal of Management Information Systems* 18, no. 1 (Summer 2001).

Markus, M. Lynne, Ann Majchrzak, and Less Gasser. "A Design Theory for Systems That Support Emergent Knowledge Processes." *MIS Quarterly* 26, no. 3 (September 2002).

Maryam, Alavi, and Dorothy E. Leidner. "Knowledge Management and Knowledge Management Systems." *MIS Quarterly* 25, no. 1 (March 2001).

McCarthy, John. "Generality in Artificial Intelligence." *Communications of the ACM* (December 1987).

Microsoft Corporation. "KPMG Turns Knowledge into Value with KWorld." Microsoft.com Korea. www.microsoft.com/korea/business/downloads/km/kworld.doc (accessed 2003).

Moravec, Hans. "Robots, After All." *Communications of the ACM* 46, no. 10 (October 2003).

Munakata, Toshinori, and Yashvant Jani. "Fuzzy Systems: An Overview." *Communications of the ACM* 37, no. 3 (March 1994).

Nidumolu, Sarma R., Mani Subramani, and Alan Aldrich. "Situated Learning and the Situated Knowledge Web: Exploring the Ground Beneath Knowledge Management." *Journal of Management Information Systems* 18, no. 1 (Summer 2001).

O'Leary, Daniel, Daniel Kuokka, and Robert Plant. "Artificial Intelligence and Virtual Organizations." *Communications of the ACM* 40, no. 1 (January 1997).

Orlikowski, Wanda J. "Knowing in Practice: Enacting a Collective Capability in Distributed Organizing." *Organization Science* 13, no. 3 (May–June 2002).

Perry, Andrew. "KM in Review: Tracing the Value of Knowledge Assets." *KM World* (October 2002).

Piccoli, Gabriele, Rami Ahmad, and Blake Ives. "Web-Based Virtual Learning Environments: A Research Framework and a Preliminary Assessment of Effectiveness in Basic IT Skills Training." *MIS Quarterly* 25, no. 4 (December 2001).

Ranft, Annette L., and Michael D. Lord. "Acquiring New Technologies and Capabilities: A Grounded Model of Acquisition Implementation." *Organization Science* 13, no. 4 (July–August 2002).

Rumelhart, David E., Bernard Widrow, and Michael A. Lehr. "The Basic Ideas in Neural Networks." *Communications of the ACM* 37, no. 3 (March 1994).

Sadeh, Norman, David W. Hildum, and Dag Kjenstad. "Agent-Based E-Supply Chain Decision Support." *Journal of Organizational Computing and Electronic Commerce* 13, nos. 3 and 4 (2003).

Schultze, Ulrike, and Dorothy Leidner. "Studying Knowledge Management in Information Systems Research: Discourses and Theoretical Assumptions." *MIS Quarterly* 26, no. 3 (September 2002).

Selker, Ted. "Coach: A Teaching Agent That Learns." *Communications of the ACM* 37, no. 7 (July 1994).

Semio Corporation. "Case Study: Leveraging the World's Largest Repository of Life Science Research with Entrieva's Semio Technology." Entrieva. www.entrieva.com/entrieva/downloads/CustomerImplementation_HighwirePress_Entrieva.pdf (accessed September 5, 2003).

Spangler, Scott, Jeffrey T. Kreulen, and Justin Lessler. "Generating and Browsing Multiple Taxonomies over a Document Collection." *Journal of Management Information Systems* 19, no. 4 (Spring 2003).

Spender, J. C. "Organizational Knowledge, Learning and Memory: Three Concepts in Search of a Theory." *Journal of Organizational Change Management* 9 (1996).

Starbuck, William H. "Learning by Knowledge-Intensive Firms." *Journal of Management Studies* 29, no. 6 (November 1992).

Sukhatme, Gaurav S., and Maja J. Mataric. "Embedding Robots into the Internet." *Communications of the ACM* 43, no. 5 (May 2000).

Sviokla, John J. "An Examination of the Impact of Expert Systems on the Firm: The Case of XCON." *MIS Quarterly* 14, no. 5 (June 1990).

Tiwana, Amrit. "Affinity to Infinity in Peer-to-Peer Knowledge Platforms." *Communications of the ACM* 46, no. 5 (May 2003).

Trippi, Robert, and Efraim Turban. "The Impact of Parallel and Neural Computing on Managerial Decision Making." *Journal of Management Information Systems* 6, no. 3 (Winter 1989–1990).

Vandenbosch, Betty, and Michael J. Ginzberg. "Lotus Notes and Collaboration." *Journal of Management Information Systems* 13, no. 3 (Winter 1997).

Wakefield, Julie. "Complexity's Business Model." *Scientific American* (January 2001).

Walczak, Stephen. "An Empirical Analysis of Data Requirements for Financial Forecasting with Neural Networks." *Journal of Management Information Systems* 17, no. 4 (Spring 2001).

Walczak, Steven. "Gaining Competitive Advantage for Trading in Emerging Capital Markets with Neural Networks. " *Journal of Management Information Systems* 16, no. 2 (Fall 1999).

Wang, Huaiqing, John Mylopoulos, and Stephen Liao. "Intelligent Agents and Financial Risk Monitoring Systems." *Communications of the ACM* 45, no. 3 (March 2002).

Widrow, Bernard, David E. Rumelhart, and Michael A. Lehr. "Neural Networks: Applications in Industry, Business, and Science." *Communications of the ACM* 37, no. 3 (March 1994).

Wijnhoven, Fons. "Designing Organizational Memories: Concept and Method." *Journal of Organizational Computing and Electronic Commerce* 8, no. 1 (1998).

Wong, David, Noemi Paciorek, and Dana Moore. "Java-Based Mobile Agents." *Communications of the ACM* 42, no. 3 (March 1999).

Yimam-Seid, Dawit, and Alfred Kobsa. "Expert-Finding Systems for Organizations: Problem and Domain Analysis and the DEMOIR Approach." *Journal of Organizational Computing and Electronic Commerce* 13, no. 1 (2003).

Zack, Michael H. "Rethinking the Knowledge-Based Organization." *MIS Sloan Management Review* 44, no. 4 (Summer 2003).

Zadeh, Lotfi A. "Fuzzy Logic, Neural Networks, and Soft Computing." *Communications of the ACM* 37, no. 3 (March 1994).

———. "The Calculus of Fuzzy If/Then Rules." *AI Expert* (March 1992).

CHAPTER 13

Abate, Carolyn. "Going Once, Going Twice . . . Sold!" *Smart Business* (May 1, 2002).

Alavi, Maryam, and Erich A. Joachimsthaler. "Revisiting DSS Implementation Research: A Meta-Analysis of the Literature and Suggestions for Researchers." *MIS Quarterly* 16, no. 1 (March 1992).

Anson, Rob, and Bjorn Erik Munkvold. "Beyond Face-to-Face: A Field Study of Electronic Meetings in Different Time and Place Modes." *Journal of Organizational Computing and Electronic Commerce* 14, no. 2 (2004).

Apte, Chidanand, Bing Liu, Edwin P. D. Pednault, and Padhraic Smith. "Business Applications of Data Mining." *Communications of the ACM* 45, no. 8 (August 2002).

Bacheldor, Beth. "Beating Down Inventory Costs." *Information Week* (April 21, 2003).

———. "Nimble, Quick Supply Chains in Demand." *Information Week* (March 24, 2003).

Barkhi, Reza. "The Effects of Decision Guidance and Problem Modeling on Group Decision-Making." *Journal of Management Information Systems* 18, no. 3 (Winter 2001–2002).

Briggs, Robert O., Gert-Jan de Vreede, and Jay. F. Nunamaker Jr. "Collaboration Engineering with ThinkLets to Pursue Sustained Success with Group Support Systems." *Journal of Management Information Systems* 19, no. 4 (Spring 2003).

Chidambaram, Laku. "Relational Development in Computer-Supported Groups." *MIS Quarterly* 20, no. 2 (June 1996).

Cone, Edward, and David F. Carr. "Unloading on the Competition." *Baseline* (October 2002).

Dennis, Alan R. "Information Exchange and Use in Group Decision Making: You Can Lead a Group to Information, but You Can't Make It Think." *MIS Quarterly* 20, no. 4 (December 1996).

Dennis, Alan R., and Monica J. Garfield. "The Adoption and Use of GSS in Project Teams: Toward More Participative Processes and Outcomes." *MIS Quarterly* 27, no. 2 (June 2003).

Dennis, Alan R., and Bryan A. Reinicke. "Beta versus VHS and the Acceptance of Electronic Brainstorming Technology." *MIS Quarterly* 28, no. 1 (March 2004).

Dennis, Alan R., and Barbara H. Wixom. "Investigating the Moderators of the Group Support Systems Use with Meta-Analysis." *Journal of Management Information Systems* 18, no. 3 (Winter 2001–2002).

Dennis, Alan R., Jay F. Nunamaker Jr., and Douglas R. Vogel. "A Comparison of Laboratory and Field Research in the Study of Electronic Meeting Systems." *Journal of Management Information Systems* 7, no. 3 (Winter 1990–1991).

Dennis, Alan R., Barbara H. Wixom, and Robert J. Vandenberg. "Understanding Fit and Appropriation Effects in Group Support Systems via Meta-Analysis." *MIS Quarterly* 25, no. 2 (June 2001).

Dennis, Alan R., Jay E. Aronson, William G. Henriger, and Edward D. Walker III. "Structuring Time and Task in Electronic Brainstorming." *MIS Quarterly* 23, no. 1 (March 1999).

Dennis, Alan R., Craig K. Tyran, Douglas R. Vogel, and Jay Nunamaker Jr. "Group Support Systems for Strategic Planning." *Journal of Management Information Systems* 14, no. 1 (Summer 1997).

Dennis, Alan R., Joey F. George, Len M. Jessup, Jay F. Nunamaker, and Douglas R. Vogel. "Information Technology to Support Electronic Meetings." *MIS Quarterly* 12, no. 4 (December 1988).

DeSanctis, Geraldine, and R. Brent Gallupe. "A Foundation for the Study of Group Decision Support Systems." *Management Science* 33, no. 5 (May 1987).

De Vreede, Gert-Jan, Robert M. Daviso, and Robert O. Briggs. "How a Silvery Bullet May Lose Its Shine." *Communications of the ACM* 46, no. 8 (August 2003).

Dhar, Vasant, and Roger Stein. *Intelligent Decision Support Methods: The Science of Knowledge Work.* Upper Saddle River, N.J.: Prentice Hall (1997).

Dutta, Soumitra, Berend Wierenga, and Arco Dalebout. "Designing Management Support Systems Using an Integrative Perspective." *Communications of the ACM* 40, no. 6 (June 1997).

Edelstein, Herb. "Technology How To: Mining Data Warehouses." *Information Week* (January 8, 1996).

El Sawy, Omar. "Personal Information Systems for Strategic Scanning in Turbulent Environments." *MIS Quarterly* 9, no. 1 (March 1985).

El Sherif, Hisham, and Omar A. El Sawy. "Issue-Based Decision Support Systems for the Egyptian Cabinet." *MIS Quarterly* 12, no. 4 (December 1988).

Few, Stephen. "Dashboard Confusion." *Intelligent Enterprise* (March 20, 2004).

Fjermestad, Jerry. "An Integrated Framework for Group Support Systems." *Journal of Organizational Computing and Electronic Commerce* 8, no. 2 (1998).

Fjermestad, Jerry, and Starr Roxanne Hiltz. "An Assessment of Group Support Systems Experimental Research: Methodology and Results." *Journal of Management Information Systems* 15, no. 3 (Winter 1998–1999).

———. "Group Support Systems: A Descriptive Evaluation of Case and Field Studies." *Journal of Management Information Systems* 17, no. 3 (Winter 2000–2001).

Forgionne, Giuseppe. "Management Support System Effectiveness: Further Empirical Evidence." *Journal of the Association for Information Systems* 1 (May 2000).

Gallupe, R. Brent, Geraldine DeSanctis, and Gary W. Dickson. "Computer-Based Support for Group Problem-Finding: An Experimental Investigation." *MIS Quarterly* 12, no. 2 (June 1988).

George, Joey. "Organizational Decision Support Systems." *Journal of Management Information Systems* 8, no. 3 (Winter 1991–1992).

Ginzberg, Michael J., W. R. Reitman, and E. A. Stohr, eds. *Decision Support Systems.* New York: North Holland Publishing, 1982.

Gorry, G. Anthony, and Michael S. Scott Morton. "A Framework for Management Information Systems." *Sloan Management Review* 13, no. 1 (Fall 1971).

Hender, Jillian M., Douglas L. Dean, Thomas L. Rodgers, and Jay F. Nunamaker Jr. "An Examination of the Impact of Stimuli Type and GSS Structure on Creativity." *Journal of Management Information Systems* 18, no. 4 (Spring 2002).

Hilmer, Kelly M., and Alan R. Dennis. "Stimulating Thinking: Cultivating Better Decisions with Groupware through Categorization." *Journal of Management Information Systems* 17, no. 3 (Winter 2000–2001).

Hogue, Jack T. "A Framework for the Examination of Management Involvement in Decision Support Systems." *Journal of Management Information Systems* 4, no. 1 (Summer 1987).

Houdeshel, George, and Hugh J. Watson. "The Management Information and Decision Support (MIDS) System at Lockheed, Georgia." *MIS Quarterly* 11, no. 2 (March 1987).

Joch, Alan. "Instant Insight." *Oracle Magazine* (March–April 2003).

Kalakota, Ravi, Jan Stallaert, and Andrew B. Whinston. "Worldwide Real-Time Decision Support Systems for Electronic Commerce Applications." *Journal of Organizational Computing and Electronic Commerce* 6, no. 1 (1996).

Keen, Peter G. W., and M. S. Scott Morton. *Decision Support Systems: An Organizational Perspective.* Reading, Mass.: Addison-Wesley (1982).

Kohavi, Ron, Neal J. Rothleder, and Evangelos Simoudis. "Emerging Trends in Business Analytics." *Communications of the ACM* 45, no. 8 (August 2002).

Kose, John, Larry Lang, and Jeffry Netter. "The Voluntary Restructuring of Large Firms in Response to Performance Decline" *Journal of Finance* (July 1992).

Kwok, Ron Chi-Wai, Jian Ma, and Douglas R. Vogel. "Effects of Group Support Systems and Content Facilitation on Knowledge Acquisition." *Journal of Management Information Systems* 19, no. 3 (Winter 2002–2003).

LaCroix, Benoit, and Jacques Desrosiers. "Altitude Manpower Planning." *OR/MS Today* (April 2004).

Latour, Almar. "After 20 Years, Baby Bells Face Some Grown-Up Competition." *Wall Street Journal* (May 28, 2004).

Laudon, Kenneth C., and Jane P. Laudon. *Management Information Systems: Managing the Digital Firm,* 8th ed. Upper Saddle River, N.J.: Prentice Hall (2004).

Leidner, Dorothy E., and Joyce Elam. "Executive Information Systems: Their Impact on Executive Decision Making." *Journal of Management Information Systems* (Winter 1993–1994).

———. "The Impact of Executive Information Systems on Organizational Design, Intelligence, and Decision Making." *Organization Science* 6, no. 6 (November–December 1995).

Levinson, Meridith. "They Know What You'll Buy Next Summer (*They Hope*)." *CIO* (May 1, 2002).

Lilien, Gary L., Arvind Rangaswamy, Gerrit H. Van Bruggen, and Katrin Starke. "DSS Effectiveness in Marketing Resource Allocation Decisions: Reality vs. Perception." *Information Systems Research* 15, no. 3 (September 2004).

Lindorff, Dave. "How Data Fuels Parkway Corp." *CIO Insight* (February 14, 2003).

Niederman, Fred, Catherine M. Beise, and Peggy M. Beranek. "Issues and Concerns about Computer-Supported Meetings: The Facilitator's Perspective." *MIS Quarterly* 20, no. 1 (March 1996).

Nunamaker, Jay, Robert O. Briggs, Daniel D. Mittleman, Douglas R. Vogel, and Pierre A. Balthazard. "Lessons from a Dozen Years of Group Support Systems Research: A Discussion of Lab and Field Findings." *Journal of Management Information Systems* 13, no. 3 (Winter 1997).

Nunamaker, J. F., Alan R. Dennis, Joseph S. Valacich, Douglas R. Vogel, and Joey F. George. "Electronic Meeting Systems to Support Group Work." *Communications of the ACM* 34, no. 7 (July 1991).

O'Keefe, Robert M., and Tim McEachern. "Web-Based Customer Decision Support Systems." *Communications of the ACM* 41, no. 3 (March 1998).

Oracle Corporation. "Pharmacia Gains Discipline and Improves Corporate Performance Management Thanks to a Comprehensive, Strategic View of Research Operations." Oracle.

www.oracle.com/pls/cis/Profiles.print_html?p_profile_id=7463 (accessed August 31, 2003).

Parlin, Kara, with Jennifer Hawthorne. "Coaxing Additional Sales from Clients." *Internet World* (April 2003).

PeopleSoft. "Spotlight on Performance at Detroit Edison." PeopleSoft. (accessed November 3, 2002).

Pinsonneault, Alain, Henri Barki, R. Brent Gallupe, and Norberto Hoppen. "Electronic Brainstorming: The Illusion of Productivity." *Information Systems Research* 10, no. 2 (July 1999).

Reinig, Bruce A. "Toward an Understanding of Satisfaction with the Process and Outcomes of Teamwork." *Journal of Management Information Systems* 19, no. 4 (Spring 2003).

Rockart, John F., and David W. DeLong. *Executive Support Systems: The Emergence of Top Management Computer Use.* Homewood, Ill.: Dow-Jones Irwin, 1988.

Schwabe, Gerhard. "Providing for Organizational Memory in Computer-Supported Meetings." *Journal of Organizational Computing and Electronic Commerce* 9, nos. 2 and 3 (1999).

Silver, Mark S. "Decision Support Systems: Directed and Nondirected Change." *Information Systems Research* 1, no. 1 (March 1990).

Simon, H. A. *The New Science of Management Decision.* New York: Harper & Row, 1960.

Sprague, R. H., and E. D. Carlson. *Building Effective Decision Support Systems.* Englewood Cliffs, N.J.: Prentice Hall, 1982.

Stodder, David. "True Tales of Performance Management." *Intelligent Enterprise* (June 1, 2004).

Turban, Efraim, and Jay E. Aronson. *Decision Support Systems and Intelligent Systems,* 7th ed. Upper Saddle River, N.J.: Prentice Hall, 2005.

Volonino, Linda, and Hugh J. Watson. "The Strategic Business Objectives Method for EIS Development." *Journal of Management Information Systems* 7, no. 3 (Winter 1990–1991).

Walls, Joseph G., George R. Widmeyer, and Omar A. El Sawy. "Building an Information System Design Theory for Vigilant EIS." *Information Systems Research* 3, no. 1 (March 1992).

Watson, Hugh J., Astrid Lipp, Pamela Z. Jackson, Abdelhafid Dahmani, and William B. Fredenberger. "Organizational Support for Decision Support Systems." *Journal of Management Information Systems* 5, no. 4 (Spring 1989).

Watson, Hugh J., R. Kelly Rainer Jr., and Chang E. Koh. "Executive Information Systems: A Framework for Development and a Survey of Current Practices." *MIS Quarterly* 15, no. 1 (March 1991).

Wrazen, Ed. "UK Forces Cut Supply Chain Costs by $30 Million in 'Dirty Data' Cleanup." TDWI. www.tdwi.org/research/display.aspx?ID=7073 (accessed May 26, 2004).

Yoo, Youngjin, and Maryam Alavi. "Media and Group Cohesion: Relative Influences on Social Presence, Task Participation, and Group Consensus." *MIS Quarterly* 25, no. 3 (September 2001).

CHAPTER 14

Agarwal, Ritu, Prabudda De, Atish P. Sinha, and Mohan Tanniru. "On the Usability of OO Representations." *Communications of the ACM* 43, no. 10 (October 2000).

Agarwal, Ritu, Jayesh Prasad, Mohan Tanniru, and John Lynch. "Risks of Rapid Application Development." *Communications of the ACM* 43, no. 11 (November 2000).

Alavi, Maryam. "An Assessment of the Prototyping Approach to Information System Development." *Communications of the ACM* 27 (June 1984).

Alavi, Maryam, R. Ryan Nelson, and Ira R. Weiss. "Strategies for End-User Computing: An Integrative Framework." *Journal of Management Information Systems* 4, no. 3 (Winter 1987–1988).

Albert, Terri C., Paulo B. Goes, and Alok Gupta. "GIST: A Model for Design and Management of Content and Interactivity of Customer-Centric Web Sites." *MIS Quarterly* 28, no. 2 (June 2004).

Arinze, Bay, and Murugan Anandarajan. "A Framework for Using OO Mapping Methods to Rapidly Configure ERP Systems." *Communications of the ACM* 46, no. 2 (February 2003).

Avison, David E., and Guy Fitzgerald. "Where Now for Development Methodologies?" *Communications of the ACM* 41, no. 1 (January 2003).

Barthelemy, Jerome. "The Hidden Costs of IT Outsourcing." *Sloan Management Review* (Spring 2001).

Barua, Anitesh, Sophie C. H. Lee, and Andrew B. Whinston. "The Calculus of Reengineering." *Information Systems Research* 7, no. 4 (December 1996).

Baskerville, Richard L., and Jan Stage. "Controlling Prototype Development through Risk Analysis." *MIS Quarterly* 20, no. 4 (December 1996).

Boehm, Barry W. "Understanding and Controlling Software Costs." *IEEE Transactions on Software Engineering* 14, no. 10 (October 1988).

Broadbent, Marianne, Peter Weill, and Don St. Clair. "The Implications of Information Technology Infrastructure for Business Process Redesign." *MIS Quarterly* 23, no. 2 (June 1999).

Bullen, Christine, and John F. Rockart. "A Primer on Critical Success Factors." Cambridge, Mass.: Center for Information Systems Research, Sloan School of Management (1981).

Champy, James A. *X-Engineering the Corporation: Reinventing Your Business in the Digital Age.* New York: Warner Books (2002).

Chiang, I. Robert, and Vijay S. Mookerjee. "A Fault Threshold Policy to Manage Software Development Projects." *Information Systems Research* 15, no. 1 (March 2004).

Curbera, Francisco, Rania Khalaf, Nirmal Mukhi, Stefan Tai, and Sanjiva Weerawarana. "The Next Step in Web Services." *Communications of the ACM* 46, no. 10 (October 2003).

Davenport, Thomas H., and James E. Short. "The New Industrial Engineering: Information Technology and Business Process Redesign." *Sloan Management Review* 31, no. 4 (Summer 1990).

Davidson, Elisabeth J. "Technology Frames and Framing: A Socio-Cognitive Investigation of Requirements Determination." *MIS Quarterly* 26, no. 4 (December 2002).

Davidson, W. H. "Beyond Engineering: The Three Phases of Business Transformation." *IBM Systems Journal* 32, no. 1 (1993).

Davis, Gordon B. "Determining Management Information Needs: A Comparison of Methods." *MIS Quarterly* 1 (June 1977).

———. "Strategies for Information Requirements Determination." *IBM Systems Journal* 1 (1982).

DeMarco, Tom. *Structured Analysis and System Specification.* New York: Yourdon Press (1978).

Den Hengst, Marielle, and Gert-Jan DeVreede. "Collaborative Business Engineering: A Decade of Lessons from the Field." *Journal of Management Information Systems* 20, no. 4 (Spring 2004).

Earl, Michael, and Bushra Khan. "E-Commerce Is Changing the Face of IT." *Sloan Management Review* (Fall 2001).

Ein Dor, Philip, and Eli Segev. "Strategic Planning for Management Information Systems." *Management Science* 24, no. 15 (1978).

El Sawy, Omar A. *Redesigning Enterprise Processes for E-Business.* New York: McGraw-Hill (2001).

Fingar, Peter. "Component-Based Frameworks for E-Commerce." *Communications of the ACM* 43, no. 10 (October 2000).

Fischer, G., E. Giaccardi, Y. Ye, A. G. Sutcliffe, and N. Mehandjiev. "Meta-Design: A Manifesto for End-User Development." *Communications of the ACM* 47, no. 9 (September 2004).

Gane, Chris, and Trish Sarson. *Structured Systems Analysis: Tools and Techniques.* Englewood Cliffs, N.J.: Prentice Hall (1979).

Gefen, David, and Catherine M. Ridings. "Implementation Team Responsiveness and User Evaluation of Customer Relationship Management: A Quasi-Experimental Design Study of Social Exchange Theory." *Journal of Management Information Systems* 19, no. 1 (Summer 2002).

Gemino, Andrew, and Yair Wand. "Evaluating Modeling Techniques Based on Models of Learning." *Communications of the ACM* 46, no. 10 (October 2003).

Grant, Delvin. "A Wider View of Business Process Engineering." *Communications of the ACM* 45, no. 2 (February 2002).

Grunbacher, Paul, Michael Halling, Stefan Biffl, Hasan Kitapci, and Barry W. Boehm. "Integrating Collaborative Processes and Quality Assurance Techniques: Experiences from Requirements Negotiation." *Journal of Management Information Systems* 20, no. 4 (Spring 2004).

Hagel III, John, and John Seeley Brown. "Your Next IT Strategy." *Harvard Business Review* (October, 2001).

Hammer, Michael. "Process Management and the Future of Six Sigma." *Sloan Management Review* 43, no. 2 (Winter 2002).

———. "Reengineering Work: Don't Automate, Obliterate." *Harvard Business Review* (July–August 1990).

Hammer, Michael, and James Champy. *Reengineering the Corporation.* New York: HarperCollins (1993).

Hickey, Ann M., and Alan M. Davis. "A Unified Model of Requirements Elicitation." *Journal of Management Information Systems* 20, no. 4 (Spring 2004).

Hirscheim, Rudy, and Mary Lacity. "The Myths and Realities of Information Technology Insourcing." *Communications of the ACM* 43, no. 2 (February 2000).

Hoffer, Jeffrey, Joey George, and Joseph Valacich. *Modern Systems Analysis and Design,* 3rd ed. Upper Saddle River, N.J.: Prentice Hall (2002).

Hopkins, Jon. "Component Primer." *Communications of the ACM* 43, no. 10 (October 2000).

Huizing, Ard, Esther Koster, and Wim Bouman. "Balance in Business Process Reengineering: An Empirical Study of Fit and Performance." *Journal of Management Information Systems* 14, no. 1 (Summer 1997).

Irwin, Gretchen. "The Role of Similarity in the Reuse of Object-Oriented Analysis Models." *Journal of Management Information Systems* 19, no. 2 (Fall 2002).

Ivari, Juhani, Rudy Hirscheim, and Heinz K. Klein. "A Dynamic Framework for Classifying Information Systems Development Methodologies and Approaches." *Journal of Management Information Systems* 17, no. 3 (Winter 2000–2001).

Iyer, Bala, Jim Freedman, Mark Gaynor, and George Wyner. "Web Services: Enabling Dynamic Business Networks." *Communications of the Association for Information Systems* 11 (2003).

Johnson, Richard A. "The Ups and Downs of Object-Oriented Systems Development." *Communications of the ACM* 43, no. 10 (October 2000).

Keen, Peter G. W. *Shaping the Future: Business Design through Information Technology.* Cambridge, Mass.: Harvard Business School Press (1991).

Kendall, Kenneth E., and Julie E. Kendall. *Systems Analysis and Design,* 5th ed. Upper Saddle River, N.J.: Prentice Hall (2002).

Klein, Gary, James J. Jiang, and Debbie B. Tesch. "Wanted: Project Teams with a Blend of IS Professional Orientations." *Communications of the ACM* 45, no. 6 (June 2002).

Lacity, M. C., and Willcocks, L. P. "An Empirical Investigation of Information Technology Sourcing Practices: Lessons from Experience." *MIS Quarterly* 22, no. 3 (September 1998).

Lee, Jae Nam, and Young-Gul Kim. "Effect of Partnership Quality on IS Outsourcing Success." *Journal of Management Information Systems* 15, no. 4 (Spring 1999).

Lee, Jae Nam, Shaila M. Miranda, and Yong-Mi Kim. "IT Outsourcing Strategies: Universalistic, Contingency, and Configurational Explanations of Success." *Information Systems Research* 15, no. 2 (June 2004).

Lee, Jae-Nam, Minh Q. Huynh, Ron Chi-wai Kwok, and Shih-Ming Pi. "IT Outsourcing Evolution—Past, Present, and Future." *Communications of the ACM* 46, no. 5 (May 2003).

Levina, Natalia, and Jeanne W. Ross. "From the Vendor's Perspective: Exploring the Value Proposition in Information Technology Outsourcing." *MIS Quarterly* 27, no. 3 (September 2003).

Lientz, Bennett P., and E. Burton Swanson. *Software Maintenance Management.* Reading, Mass.: Addison-Wesley (1980).

Limayem, Moez, Mohamed Khalifa, and Wynne W. Chin. "Case Tools Usage and Impact on System Development Performance." *Journal of Organizational Computing and Electronic Commerce* 14, no. 3 (2004).

Lunt, Penny. "Well-Oiled Machines. BPM Projects Point to Success." *Transform Magazine* (April 2003).

Martin, James. *Application Development without Programmers.* Englewood Cliffs, N.J.: Prentice Hall (1982).

Martin, James, and Carma McClure. *Structured Techniques: The Basis of CASE.* Englewood Cliffs, N.J.: Prentice Hall (1988).

Mazzucchelli, Louis. "Structured Analysis Can Streamline Software Design." *Computerworld* (December 9, 1985).

Nerson, Jean-Marc. "Applying Object-Oriented Analysis and Design." *Communications of the ACM* 35, no. 9 (September 1992).

Nidumolu, Sarma R., and Mani Subramani. "The Matrix of Control: Combining Process and Structure Approaches to Managing Software Development." *Journal of Management Information Systems* 20, no. 4 (Winter 2004).

Nissen, Mark E. "Redesigning Reengineering through Measurement-Driven Inference." *MIS Quarterly* 22, no. 4 (December 1998).

Pancake, Cherri M. "The Promise and the Cost of Object Technology: A Five-Year Forecast." *Communications of the ACM* 38, no. 10 (October 1995).

Parker, M. M. "Enterprise Information Analysis: Cost-Benefit Analysis and the Data-Managed System." *IBM Systems Journal* 21 (1982).

Parsons, Jeffrey, and Yair Wand. "Using Objects for Systems Analysis." *Communications of the ACM* 40, no. 12 (December 1997).

Patel, Samir, and Suneel Saigal. "When Computers Learn to Talk: A Web Services Primer," *The McKinsey Quarterly* no. 1 (2002).

Peffers, Ken, and Charles E. Gengler. "How to Identify New High-Payoff Information Systems for the Organization." *Communications of the ACM* 41, no. 1 (January 2003).

Phillips, James, and Dan Foody. "Building a Foundation for Web Services." *EAI Journal* (March 2002).

Pitts, Mitzi G., and Glenn J. Browne. "Stopping Behavior of Systems Analysts During Information Requirements Elicitation." *Journal of Management Information Systems* 21, no. 1 (Summer 2004).

Prahalad, C. K., and M. S. Krishnan. "Synchronizing Strategy and Information Technology." *Sloan Management Review* 43, no. 4 (Summer 2002).

Ravichandran, T., and Marcus A. Rothenberger. "Software Reuse Strategies and Component Markets." *Communications of the ACM* 46, no. 8 (August 2003).

Rivard, Suzanne, and Sid L. Huff. "Factors of Success for End-User Computing." *Communications of the ACM* 31, no. 5 (May 1988).

Rockart, John F. "Chief Executives Define Their Own Data Needs." *Harvard Business Review* (March–April 1979).

Rockart, John F., and Lauren S. Flannery. "The Management of End-User Computing." *Communications of the ACM* 26, no. 10 (October 1983).

Rockart, John F., and Michael E. Treacy. "The CEO Goes On-Line." *Harvard Business Review* (January–February 1982).

Sabherwahl, Rajiv. "The Role of Trust in IS Outsourcing Development Projects." *Communications of the ACM* 42, no. 2 (February 1999).

Scott, Louise, Levente Horvath, and Donald Day. "Characterizing CASE Constraints." *Communications of the ACM* 43, no. 11 (November 2000).

Shank, Michael E., Andrew C. Boynton, and Robert W. Zmud. "Critical Success Factor Analysis as a Methodology for MIS Planning." *MIS Quarterly* (June 1985).

Sharma, Srinarayan, and Arun Rai. "CASE Deployment in IS Organizations." *Communications of the ACM* 43, no. 1 (January 2000).

Sircar, Sumit, Sridhar P. Nerur, and Radhakanta Mahapatra. "Revolution or Evolution? A Comparison of Object-Oriented and Structured Systems Development Methods." *MIS Quarterly* 25, no. 4 (December 2001).

Smith, Howard, and Peter Fingar. *Business Process Management: The Third Wave.* Tampa, Fla.: Meghan-Kiffer Press (2002).

Sprott, David. "Componentizing the Enterprise Application Packages." *Communications of the ACM* 43, no. 3 (April 2000).

Swanson, E. Burton, and Enrique Dans. "System Life Expectancy and the Maintenance Effort: Exploring their Equilibration." *MIS Quarterly* 24, no. 2 (June 2000).

Tam, Kar Yan, and Kai Lung Hui. "A Choice Model for the Selection of Computer Vendors and Its Empirical Estimation" *Journal of Management Information Systems* 17, no. 4 (Spring 2001).

Turetken, Ozgur, David Schuff, Ramesh Sharda, and Terence T. Ow. "Supporting Systems Analysis and Design through Fisheye Views." *Communications of the ACM* 47, no. 9 (September 2004).

Van Den Heuvel, Willem-Jan, and Zakaria Maamar. "Moving Toward a Framework to Compose Intelligent Web Services." *Communications of the ACM* 46, no. 10 (October 2003).

Venkatraman, N. "Beyond Outsourcing: Managing IT Resources as a Value Center." *Sloan Management Review* (Spring 1997).

Vessey, Iris, and Sue Conger. "Learning to Specify Information Requirements: The Relationship between Application and Methodology." *Journal of Management Information Systems* 10, no. 2 (Fall 1993).

Vitharana, Padmal. "Risks and Challenges of Component-Based Software Development." *Communications of the ACM* 46, no. 8 (August 2003).

Watad, Mahmoud M., and Frank J. DiSanzo. "Case Study: The Synergism of Telecommuting and Office Automation." *Sloan Management Review* 41, no. 2 (Winter 2000).

Wulf, Volker, and Matthias Jarke. "The Economics of End-User Development." *Communications of the ACM* 47, no. 9 (September 2004).

Yourdon, Edward, and L. L. Constantine. *Structured Design.* New York: Yourdon Press (1978).

Zachman, J. A. "Business Systems Planning and Business Information Control Study: A Comparison." *IBM Systems Journal* 21 (1982).

CHAPTER 15

Agarwal, Ritu, and Viswanath Venkatesnh. "Assessing a Firm's Web Presence: A Heuristic Evaluation Procedure for the Measurement of Usability." *Information Systems Research* 13, no. 3 (September 2002).

Aladwani, Adel M. "An Integrated Performance Model of Information Systems Projects." *Journal of Management Information Systems* 19, no. 1 (Summer 2002).

Alleman, James. "Real Options Real Opportunities." *Optimize Magazine* (January 2002).

Alter, Steven, and Michael Ginzberg. "Managing Uncertainty in MIS Implementation." *Sloan Management Review* 20 (Fall 1978).

Andres, Howard P., and Robert W. Zmud. "A Contingency Approach to Software Project Coordination." *Journal of Management Information Systems* 18, no. 3 (Winter 2001–2002).

Armstrong, Curtis P., and V. Sambamurthy. "Information Technology Assimilation in Firms: The Influence of Senior Leadership and IT Infrastructures." *Information Systems Research* 10, no. 4 (December 1999).

Attewell, Paul. "Technology Diffusion and Organizational Learning: The Case of Business Computing." *Organization Science*, no. 3 (1992).

Banker, Rajiv. "Value Implications of Relative Investments in Information Technology." Department of Information Systems and Center for Digital Economy Research, University of Texas at Dallas (January 23, 2001).

Barki, Henri, and Jon Hartwick. "Interpersonal Conflict and Its Management in Information Systems Development." *MIS Quarterly* 25, no. 2 (June 2001).

Barki, Henri, Suzanne Rivard, and Jean Talbot. "An Integrative Contingency Model of Software Project Risk Management." *Journal of Management Information Systems* 17, no. 4 (Spring 2001).

Baudisch, Patrick, Doug DeCarlo, Andrew T. Duchowski, and Wilson S. Geisler. "Focusing on the Essential: Considering Attention in Display Design." *Communications of the ACM* 46, no. 3 (March 2003).

Beath, Cynthia Mathis, and Wanda J. Orlikowski. "The Contradictory Structure of Systems Development Methodologies: Deconstructing the IS-User Relationship in Information Engineering." *Information Systems Research* 5, no. 4 (December 1994).

Benaroch, Michel. "Managing Information Technology Investment Risk: A Real Options Perspective." *Journal of Management Information Systems* 19, no. 2 (Fall 2002).

Benaroch, Michel, and Robert J. Kauffman. "Justifying Electronic Banking Network Expansion Using Real Options Analysis." *MIS Quarterly* 24, no. 2 (June 2000).

Bharadwaj, Anandhi. "A Resource-Based Perspective on Information Technology Capability and Firm Performance." *MIS Quarterly* 24, no. 1 (March 2000).

Bhattacherjee, Ano. "Understanding Information Systems Continuance: An Expectation-Confirmation Model." *MIS Quarterly* 25, no. 3 (September 2001).

Bhattacherjee, Anol, and G. Premkumar. "Understanding Changes in Belief and Attitude Toward Information Technology Usage: A Theoretical Model and Longitudinal Test." *MIS Quarterly* 28, no. 2 (June 2004).

Bikson, Tora K., Cathleen Stasz, and Donald A. Monkin. "Computer-Mediated Work: Individual and Organizational Impact on One Corporate Headquarters." The Rand Corporation (1985).

Boer, F. Peter. "Real Options: The IT Investment Risk Buster." *Optimize Magazine* (July 2002).

Bostrom, R. P., and J. S. Heinen. "MIS Problems and Failures: A Socio-Technical Perspective. Part I: The Causes." *MIS Quarterly* 1 (September 1977); "Part II: The Application of Socio-Technical Theory." *MIS Quarterly* 1 (December 1977).

Brooks, Frederick P. "The Mythical Man-Month." *Datamation* (December 1974).

Brynjolfsson, Erik. "The Contribution of Information Technology to Consumer Welfare." *Information Systems Research* 7, no. 3 (September 1996).

———. "The IT Productivity GAP." *Optimize* 21 (July 2003).

———. "The Productivity Paradox of Information Technology." *Communications of the ACM* 36, no. 12 (December 1993).

Brynjolfsson, Erik, and Lorin M. Hitt. "Beyond the Productivity Paradox." *Communications of the ACM* 41, no. 8 (August 1998).

———. "Information Technology and Organizational Design: Evidence from Micro Data." (January 1998).

Brynjolfsson, Erik, and S. Yang. "Intangible Assets: How the Interaction of Computers and Organizational Structure Affects Stock Markets." MIT Sloan School of Management (2000).

Buss, Martin D. J. "How to Rank Computer Projects." *Harvard Business Review* (January 1983).

Chatterjee, Debabroto, Rajdeep Grewal, and V. Sabamurthy. "Shaping Up for E-Commerce: Institutional Enablers of the Organizational Assimilation of Web Technologies." *MIS Quarterly* 26, no. 2 (June 2002).

Chatterjee, Debabroto, Carl Pacini, and V. Sambamurthy. "The Shareholder-Wealth and Trading Volume Effects of Information Technology Infrastructure Investments." *Journal of Management Information Systems* 19, no. 2 (Fall 2002).

Chau, Patrick Y. K., and Vincent S. K. Lai. "An Empirical Investigation of the Determinants of User Acceptance of Internet Banking." *Journal of Organizational Computing and Electronic Commerce* 13, no. 2 (2003).

Clement, Andrew, and Peter Van den Besselaar. "A Retrospective Look at PD Projects." *Communications of the ACM* 36, no. 4 (June 1993).

Concours Group. "Delivering Large-Scale System Projects." (2000).

Cooper, Randolph B. "Information Technology Development Creativity: A Case Study of Attempted Radical Change." *MIS Quarterly* 24, no. 2 (June 2000).

Datz, Todd. "Portfolio Management: How to Do It Right," *CIO* (May 1, 2003).

Davamanirajan, Prabu, Tridas Mukhopadhyay, and Charles Kriebel. "Assessing the Business Value of Information Technology in Global Wholesale Banking: The Case of Trade Services." *Journal of Organizational Computing and Electronic Commerce* 12, no. 1 (2002).

Davern, Michael J., and Robert J. Kauffman. "Discovering Potential and Realizing Value from Information Technology Investments." *Journal of Management Information Systems* 16, no. 4 (Spring 2000).

Davis, Fred R. "Perceived Usefulness, Ease of Use, and User Acceptance of Information Technology." *MIS Quarterly* 13, no. 3 (September 1989).

De Berranger, Pascal, David Tucker, and Laurie Jones. "Internet Diffusion in Creative Micro-Businesses: Identifying Change Agent Characteristics as Critical Success Factors." *Journal of Organizational Computing and Electronic Commerce* 11, no. 3 (2001).

Delone, William H., and Ephraim R. McLean. "The Delone and McLean Model of Information Systems Success: A Ten-Year Update." *Journal of Management Information Systems* 19, no. 4 (Spring 2003).

De Meyer, Arnoud, Christoph H. Loch, and Michael T. Pich. "Managing Project Uncertainty: From Variation to Chaos." *Sloan Management Review* 43, no. 2 (Winter 2002).

Dempsey, Jed, Robert E. Dvorak, Endre Holen, David Mark, and William F. Meehan III. "A Hard and Soft Look at IT Investments." *McKinsey Quarterly,* no. 1 (1998).

Doll, William J. "Avenues for Top Management Involvement in Successful MIS Development." *MIS Quarterly* (March 1985).

Doll, William J., Xiaodung Deng, T. S. Raghunathan, Gholamreza Torkzadeh, and Weidong Xia. "The Meaning and Measurement of User Satisfaction: A Multigroup Invariance Analysis of End-User Computing Satisfaction Instrument." *Journal of Management Information Systems* 21, no. 1 (Summer 2004).

Dos Santos, Brian. "Justifying Investments in New Information Technologies." *Journal of Management Information Systems* 7, no. 4 (Spring 1991).

Ein-Dor, Philip, and Eli Segev. "Organizational Context and the Success of Management Information Systems." *Management Science* 24 (June 1978).

El Sawy, Omar, and Burt Nanus. "Toward the Design of Robust Information Systems." *Journal of Management Information Systems* 5, no. 4 (Spring 1989).

Fichman, Robert G. "Real Options and IT Platforms Adoption: Implications for Theory and Practice." *Information Systems Research* 15, no. 2 (June 2004).

———. "The Role of Aggregation in the Measurement of IT-Related Organizational Innovation." *MIS Quarterly* 25, no. 4 (December 2001).

Fichman, Robert G., and Scott A. Moses. "An Incremental Process for Software Implementation." *Sloan Management Review* 40, no. 2 (Winter 1999).

Frank, Robert, and Robin Sidel. "Firms That Lived by the Deal in '90s Now Sink by the Dozens." *Wall Street Journal* (June 6, 2002).

Franz, Charles, and Daniel Robey. "An Investigation of User-Led System Design: Rational and Political Perspectives." *Communications of the ACM* 27 (December 1984).

Gefen, David, and Catherine M. Ridings. "Implementation Team Responsiveness and User Evaluation of Customer Relationship Management: A Quasi-Experimental Design Study of Social Exchange Theory." *Journal of Management Information Systems* 19, no. 1 (Summer 2002).

Giaglis, George. "Focus Issue on Legacy Information Systems and Business Process Change: On the Integrated Design and Evaluation of Business Processes and Information Systems." *Communications of the Association for Information Systems* 2 (July 1999).

Ginzberg, Michael J. "Early Diagnosis of MIS Implementation Failure: Promising Results and Unanswered Questions." *Management Science* 27 (April 1981).

Hitt, Lorin, D. J. Wu, and Xiaoge Zhou. "Investment in Enterprise Resource Planning: Business Impact and Productivity Measures." *Journal of Management Information Systems* 19, no. 1 (Summer 2002).

Housel, Thomas J., Omar El Sawy, Jianfang J. Zhong, and Waymond Rodgers. "Measuring the Return on e-Business Initiatives at the Process Level: The Knowledge Value-Added Approach." *ICIS* (2001).

Hunton, James E., and Beeler, Jesse D. "Effects of User Participation in Systems Development: A Longitudinal Field Study." *MIS Quarterly* 21, no. 4 (December 1997).

Irani, Zahir, and Peter E. D. Love. "The Propagation of Technology Management Taxonomies for Evaluating Investments in Information Systems." *Journal of Management Information Systems* 17, no. 3 (Winter 2000–2001).

Iversen, Jakob H., Lars Mathiassen, and Peter Axel Nielsen. "Managing Risk in Software Process Improvement: An Action Research Approach." *MIS Quarterly* 28, no. 3 (September 2004).

Jeffrey, Mark, and Ingmar Leliveld. "Best Practices in IT Portfolio Management." *MIT Sloan Management Review* 45, no. 3 (Spring 2004).

Jiang, James J., Gary Klein, Debbie Tesch, and Hong-Gee Chen. "Closing the User and Provider Service Quality Gap." *Communications of the ACM* 46, no. 2 (February 2003).

Joshi, Kailash. "A Model of Users' Perspective on Change: The Case of Information Systems Technology Implementation." *MIS Quarterly* 15, no. 2 (June 1991).

Keen, Peter W. "Information Systems and Organizational Change." *Communications of the ACM* 24 (January 1981).

Keil, Mark, and Ramiro Montealegre. "Cutting Your Losses: Extricating Your Organization When a Big Project Goes Awry." *Sloan Management Review* 41, no. 3 (Spring 2000).

Keil, Mark, and Daniel Robey. "Blowing the Whistle on Troubled Software Projects." *Communications of the ACM* 44, no. 4 (April 2001).

Keil, Mark, Joan Mann, and Arun Rai. "Why Software Projects Escalate: An Empirical Analysis and Test of Four Theoretical Models." *MIS Quarterly* 24, no. 4 (December 2000).

Keil, Mark, Paul E. Cule, Kalle Lyytinen, and Roy C. Schmidt. "A Framework for Identifying Software Project Risks." *Communications of the ACM* 41, no. 11 (November 1998).

Keil, Mark, Richard Mixon, Timo Saarinen, and Virpi Tuunairen. "Understanding Runaway IT Projects." *Journal of Management Information Systems* 11, no. 3 (Winter 1994–1995).

Keil, Mark, Bernard C. Y. Tan, Kwok-Kee Wei, Timo Saarinen, Virpi Tuunainen, and Arjen Waassenaar. "A Cross-Cultural Study on Escalation of Commitment Behavior in Software Projects." *MIS Quarterly* 24, no. 2 (June 2000).

Kettinger, William J., and Choong C. Lee. "Understanding the IS-User Divide in IT Innovation." *Communications of the ACM* 45, no. 2 (February 2002).

Klein, Gary, James J. Jiang, and Debbie B. Tesch. "Wanted: Project Teams with a Blend of IS Professional Orientations." *Communications of the ACM* 45, no. 6 (June 2002).

Kolb, D. A., and A. L. Frohman. "An Organization Development Approach to Consulting." *Sloan Management Review* 12 (Fall 1970).

Laudon, Kenneth C. "CIOs Beware: Very Large Scale Systems." Working paper, Center for Research on Information Systems, New York University Stern School of Business (1989).

Lientz, Bennett P., and E. Burton Swanson. *Software Maintenance Management.* Reading, Mass.: Addison-Wesley (1980).

Lipin, Steven, and Nikhil Deogun. "Big Mergers of 90s Prove Disappointing to Shareholders." *Wall Street Journal* (October 30, 2000).

Lohse, Gerald L., and Peter Spiller. "Internet Retail Store Design: How the User Interface Influences Traffic and Sales." *Journal of Computer-Mediated Communication* 5, no. 2 (December 1999).

Lucas, Henry C., Jr. *Implementation: The Key to Successful Information Systems.* New York: Columbia University Press (1981).

Mahmood, Mo Adam, Laura Hall, and Daniel Leonard Swanberg. "Factors Affecting Information Technology Usage: A Meta-Analysis of the Empirical Literature." *Journal of Organizational Computing and Electronic Commerce* 11, no. 2 (November 2, 2001).

Markus, M. Lynne, and Robert I. Benjamin. "Change Agentry—The Next IS Frontier." *MIS Quarterly* 20, no. 4 (December 1996).

———. "The Magic Bullet Theory of IT-Enabled Transformation." *Sloan Management Review* (Winter 1997).

Markus, M. Lynne, and Mark Keil. "If We Build It, They Will Come: Designing Information Systems That People Want to Use." *Sloan Management Review* (Summer 1994).

Matlin, Gerald. "What Is the Value of Investment in Information Systems?" *MIS Quarterly* 13, no. 3 (September 1989).

McFarlan, F. Warren. "Portfolio Approach to Information Systems." *Harvard Business Review* (September–October 1981).

McGrath, Rita Gunther, and Ian C. McMillan. "Assessing Technology Projects Using Real Options Reasoning." *Industrial Research Institute* (2000).

McKinney, Vicki, Kanghyun Yoon, and Fatemeh "Mariam" Zahedi. "The Measurement of Web-Customer Satisfaction: An Expectation and Disconfirmation Approach." *Information Systems Research* 13, no. 3 (September 2002).

Mumford, Enid, and Mary Weir. *Computer Systems in Work Design: The ETHICS Method.* New York: Wiley (1979).

Nambisan, Satish, and Yu-Ming Wang. "Web Technology Adoption and Knowledge Barriers." *Journal of Organizational Computing and Electronic Commerce* 10, no. 2 (2000).

Nedda, Gabriela G. Olazabal. "Banking: The IT Paradox." *McKinsey Quarterly,* no. 1 (2002).

Nolan, Richard. "Managing Information Systems by Committee." *Harvard Business Review* (July–August 1982).

Nidumolu, Sarma R., and Mani Subramani. "The Matrix of Control: Combining Process and Structure Approaches to Management Software Development." *Journal of Management Information Systems* 20, no. 3 (Winter 2004).

Orlikowski, Wanda J., and J. Debra Hofman. "An Improvisational Change Model for Change Management: The Case of Groupware Technologies." *Sloan Management Review* (Winter 1997).

Oz, Effy. "When Professional Standards are Lax: The CONFIRM Failure and Its Lessons." *Communications of the ACM* 37, no. 10 (October 1994).

Palmer, Jonathan W. "Web Site Usability, Design and Performance Metrics." *Information Systems Research* 13, no. 3 (September 2002).

Panko, Raymond R. "Is Office Productivity Stagnant?" *MIS Quarterly* 15, no. 2 (June 1991).

Peffers, Ken, and Timo Saarinen. "Measuring the Business Value of IT Investments: Inferences from a Study of Senior Bank Executives." *Journal of Organizational Computing and Electronic Commerce* 12, no. 1 (2002).

Premkumar, G. "A Meta-Analysis of Research on Information Technology Implementation in Small Business." *Journal of Organizational Computing and Electronic Commerce* 13, no. 2 (2003).

Quan, Jin "Jim," Quing Hu, and Paul J. Hart. "Information Technology Investments and Firms' Performance—A Duopoly Perspective." *Journal of Management Information Systems* 20, no. 3 (Winter 2004).

Rai, Arun, Sandra S. Lang, and Robert B. Welker. "Assessing the Validity of IS Success Models: An Empirical Test and Theoretical Analysis." *Information Systems Research* 13, no. 1 (March 2002).

Rai, Arun, Ravi Patnayakuni, and Nainika Patnayakuni. "Technology Investment and Business Performance." *Communications of the ACM* 40, no. 7 (July 1997).

Reichheld, Frederick E., and Phil Schefter. "E-Loyalty: Your Secret Weapon on the Web." *Harvard Business Review* (July–August 2000).

Roach, Stephen S. "The Hollow Ring of the Productivity Revival." *Harvard Business Review* (November–December 1996).

———. *Industrialization of the Information Economy.* New York: Morgan Stanley (1984).

———. "Services under Siege—The Restructuring Imperative." *Harvard Business Review* (September–October 1991).

Robey, Daniel, and M. Lynne Markus. "Rituals in Information System Design." *MIS Quarterly* (March 1984).

Robey, Daniel, Jeanne W. Ross, and Marie-Claude Boudreau. "Learning to Implement Enterprise Systems: An Exploratory Study of the Dialectics of Change." *Journal of Management Information Systems* 19, no. 1 (Summer 2002).

Ross, Jeanne W., and Cynthia M. Beath. "Beyond the Business Case: New Approaches to IT Investment." *Sloan Management Review* 43, no. 2 (Winter 2002).

Ryan, Sherry D., and David A. Harrison. "Considering Social Subsystem Costs and Benefits in Information Technology Investment Decisions: A View from the Field on Anticipated Payoffs." *Journal of Management Information Systems* 16, no. 4 (Spring 2000).

Ryan, Sherry D., David A. Harrison, and Lawrence L Schkade. "Information Technology Investment Decisions: When Do Cost and Benefits in the Social Subsystem Matter?" *Journal of Management Information Systems* 19, no. 2 (Fall 2002).

Sambamurthy, V., Anandhi Bharadwaj, and Varun Grover. "Shaping Agility through Digital Options: Reconceptualizing the Role of Information Technology in Contemporary Firms." *MIS Quarterly* 27, no. 2 (June 2003).

Santhanam, Radhika, and Edward Hartono. "Issues in Linking Information Technology Capability to Firm Performance." *MIS Quarterly* 27, no. 1 (March 2003).

Sarkar, Pushpak. "A Paragon of Quality." *Intelligent Enterprise* (October 2002).

Sauer, Chris, and Leslie P. Willcocks. "The Evolution of the Organizational Architect." *Sloan Management Review* 43, no. 3 (Spring 2002).

Schmidt, Roy, Kalle Lyytinen, Mark Keil, and Paul Cule. "Identifying Software Project Risks: An International Delphi Study." *Journal of Management Information Systems* 17, no. 4 (Spring 2001).

Schneiderman, Ben. "Universal Usability." *Communications of the ACM* 43, no. 5 (May 2000).

Siewiorek, Daniel P. "New Frontiers of Application Design." *Communications of the ACM* 45, no. 12 (December 2002).

Sircar, Sumit, Joe L. Turnbow, and Bijoy Bordoloi. "A Framework for Assessing the Relationship between Information Technology Investments and Firm Performance." *Journal of Management Information Systems* 16, no. 4 (Spring 2000).

Smith, H. Jeff, Mark Keil, and Gordon Depledge. "Keeping Mum as the Project Goes Under." *Journal of Management Information Systems* 18, no. 2 (Fall 2001).

Speier, Cheri, and Michael. G. Morris. "The Influence of Query Interface Design on Decision-Making Performance." *MIS Quarterly* 27, no. 3 (September 2003).

Straub, Detmar W., Arun Rai, and Richard Klein. "Measuring Firm Performance at the Network Level: A Nomology of the Business Impact of Digital Supply Networks." *Journal of Management Information Systems* 21, no. 1 (Summer 2004).

Swanson, E. Burton. *Information System Implementation.* Homewood, Ill.: Richard D. Irwin (1988).

Tallon, Paul P., Kenneth L. Kraemer, and Vijay Gurbaxani. "Executives' Perceptions of the Business Value of Information Technology: A Process-Oriented Approach." *Journal of Management Information Systems* 16, no. 4 (Spring 2000).

Taudes, Alfred, Markus Feurstein, and Andreas Mild. "Options Analysis of Software Platform Decisions: A Case Study." *MIS Quarterly* 24, no. 2 (June 2000).

Teng, James T. C., Seung Ryul Jeong, and Varun Grover. "Profiling Successful Reengineering Projects." *Communications of the ACM* 41, no. 6 (June 1998).

Thatcher, Matt E., and Jim R. Oliver. "The Impact of Technology Investments on a Firm's Production Efficiency, Product Quality, and Productivity." *Journal of Management Information Systems* 18, no. 2 (Fall 2001).

Tornatsky, Louis G., J. D. Eveland, M. G. Boylan, W. A. Hetzner, E. C. Johnson, D. Roitman, and J. Schneider. *The Process of Technological Innovation: Reviewing the Literature.* Washington, D.C.: National Science Foundation (1983).

Venkatesh, Viswanath, Michael G. Morris, Gordon B Davis, and Fred D. Davis. "User Acceptance of Information Technology: Toward a Unified View." *MIS Quarterly* 27, no. 3 (September 2003).

Wallace, Linda, and Mark Keil. "Software Project Risks and Their Effect on Outcomes." *Communications of the ACM* 47, no. 4 (April 2004).

Weill, Peter, Mani Subramani, and Marianne Broadbent. "Building IT Infrastructure for Strategic Agility." *Sloan Management Review* 44, no. 1 (Fall 2002).

Xia, Weidong, and Gwanhoo Lee. "Grasping the Complexity of IS Development Projects." *Communications of the ACM* 47, no. 5 (May 2004).

Yin, Robert K. "Life Histories of Innovations: How New Practices Become Routinized." *Public Administration Review* (January–February 1981).

Zhu, Kevin. "The Complementarity of Information Technology Infrastructure and E-Commerce Capability: A Resource-Based Assessment of Their Business Value." *Journal of Management Information Systems* 21, no. 1 (Summer 2004).

Zhu, Kevin, and Kenneth L. Kraemer. "E-Commerce Metrics for Net-Enhanced Organizations: Assessing the Value of e-Commerce to Firm Performance in the Manufacturing Sector." *Information Systems Research* 13, no. 3 (September 2002).

Zhu, Kevin, Kenneth L. Kraemer, Sean Xu, and Jason Dedrick. "Information Technology Payoff in E-Business Environments: An International Perspective on Value Creation of E-business in the Financial Services Industry." *Journal of Management Information Systems* 21, no. 1 (Summer 2004).

CHAPTER 16

Agarwal, P. K. "Building India's National Internet Backbone." *Communications of the ACM* 42, no. 6 (June 1999).

Baily, Martin N., and Diana Farrell. "Exploding the Myths of Offshoring." *McKinsey Quarterly* (July 2004).

Blanning, Robert W. "Establishing a Corporate Presence on the Internet in Singapore." *Journal of Organizational Computing and Electronic Commerce* 9, no. 1 (1999).

Buckman, Rebecca. "H-P Outsourcing: Beyond China." *Wall Street Journal* (February 23, 2004).

Burkhardt, Grey E., Seymour E. Goodman, Arun Mehta, and Larry Press. "The Internet in India: Better Times Ahead?" *Communications of the ACM* 41, no. 11 (November 1998).

Cox, Butler. *Globalization: The IT Challenge.* Sunnyvale, Calif.: Amdahl Executive Institute (1991).

Davison, Robert. "Cultural Complications of ERP." *Communications of the ACM* 45, no. 7 (July 2002).

Deans, Candace P., and Michael J. Kane. *International Dimensions of Information Systems and Technology.* Boston: PWS-Kent, 1992.

Deans, Candace P., Kirk R. Karwan, Martin D. Goslar, David A. Ricks, and Brian Toyne. "Key International Issues in U.S.-Based Multinational Corporations." *Journal of Management Information Systems* 7, no. 4 (Spring 1991).

Ein-Dor, Philip, Seymour E. Goodman, and Peter Wolcott. "From Via Maris to Electronic Highway: The Internet in Canaan." *Communications of the ACM* 43, no. 7 (July 2000).

Farhoomand, Ali, Virpi Kristiina Tuunainen, and Lester W. Yee. "Barrier to Global Electronic Commerce: A Cross-Country Study of Hong Kong and Finland." *Journal of Organizational Computing and Electronic Commerce* 10, no. 1 (2000).

Ives, Blake, and Sirkka Jarvenpaa. "Applications of Global Information Technology: Key Issues for Management." *MIS Quarterly* 15, no. 1 (March 1991).

———. "Global Business Drivers: Aligning Information Technology to Global Business Strategy." *IBM Systems Journal* 32, no. 1 (1993).

———. "Global Information Technology: Some Lessons from Practice." *International Information Systems* 1, no. 3 (July 1992).

Jarvenpaa, Sirkka L., Kathleen Knoll, and Dorothy Leidner. "Is Anybody Out There? Antecedents of Trust in Global Virtual Teams." *Journal of Management Information Systems* 14, no. 4 (Spring 1998).

Jarvenpaa, Sirkka L., Thomas R. Shaw, and D. Sandy Staples. "Toward Contextualized Theories of Trust: The Role of Trust in Global Virtual Teams." *Information Systems Research* 15, no. 3 (September 2004).

Keen, Peter. *Shaping the Future.* Cambridge, M.A.: Harvard Business School Press (1991).

King, William R., and Vikram Sethi. "An Empirical Analysis of the Organization of Transnational Information Systems." *Journal of Management Information Systems* 15, no. 4 (Spring 1999).

Krishna, S., Sundeep Sahay, and Geoff Walsham. "Managing Cross-Cultural Issues in Global Software Outsourcing." *Communications of the ACM* 47, no. 4 (April 2004).

Lai, Vincent S., and Wingyan Chung. "Managing International Data Communication." *Communications of the ACM* 45, no. 3 (March 2002).

Liang, Huigang, Yajiong Xue, William R. Boulton, and Terry Anthony Byrd. "Why Western Vendors Don't Dominate China's ERP Market." *Communications of the ACM* 47, no. 7 (July 2004).

MacFarquhar, Neil. "Tunisia's Tangled Web Is Sticking Point for Reform." *New York Times* (June 25, 2004).

Mann, Catherine L. "What Global Sourcing Means for U.S. I.T. Workers and for the U.S. Economy." *Communications of the ACM* 47, no. 7 (July 2004).

Martinsons, Maris G. "ERP in China: One Package, Two Profiles." *Communications of the ACM* 47, no. 7 (July 2004).

Overby, Stephanie. "The Hidden Costs of Offshore Outsourcing." *CIO* (September 1, 2003).

Petrazzini, Ben, and Mugo Kibati. "The Internet in Developing Countries." *Communications of the ACM* 42, no. 6 (June 1999).

Quelch, John A., and Lisa R. Klein. "The Internet and International Marketing." *Sloan Management Review* (Spring 1996).

Roche, Edward M. *Managing Information Technology in Multinational Corporations.* New York: Macmillan (1992).

Soh, Christina, Sia Siew Kien, and Joanne Tay-Yap. "Cultural Fits and Misfits: Is ERP a Universal Solution?" *Communications of the ACM* 43, no. 3 (April 2000).

Steinbart, Paul John, and Ravinder Nath. "Problems and Issues in the Management of International Data Networks." *MIS Quarterly* 16, no. 1 (March 1992).

Straub, Detmar W. "The Effect of Culture on IT Diffusion: E-Mail and FAX in Japan and the U.S." *Information Systems Research* 5, no. 1 (March 1994).

Tan, Zixiang, William Foster, and Seymour Goodman. "China's State-Coordinated Internet Infrastructure." *Communications of the ACM* 42, no. 6 (June 1999).

Tractinsky, Noam, and Sirkka L. Jarvenpaa. "Information Systems Design Decisions in a Global versus Domestic Context." *MIS Quarterly* 19, no. 4 (December 1995).

Watson, Richard T., Gigi G. Kelly, Robert D. Galliers, and James C. Brancheau. "Key Issues in Information Systems Management: An International Perspective." *Journal of Management Information Systems* 13, no. 4 (Spring 1997).

Glossary

2.5G networks Wireless digital cellular networks that provide higher-speed data transmission rates ranging from 50 to 144 kilobits per second (Kbps) using the existing cellular network infrastructure.

3G networks Cellular networks based on packet-switched technology with speeds ranging from 144 kilobits per second (Kbps) for mobile users to over 2 megabits per second (Mbps) for stationary users enabling users to transmit video, graphics, and other rich media, in addition to voice.

802.11b Wireless local area network (LAN) standard that can transmit up to 11 megabits per second (Mbps) in the unlicensed 2.4-GHz band and that has an effective distance of 30 to 50 meters.

acceptable use policy (AUP) Defines acceptable uses of the firm's information resources and computing equipment, including desktop and laptop computers, wireless devices, telephones, and the Internet, and specifies consequences for noncompliance.

acceptance testing Provides the final certification that the system is ready to be used in a production setting.

access control Policies and procedures a company uses to prevent improper access to systems by unauthorized insiders and outsiders.

access point Box in a wireless local area network (LAN) consisting of a radio receiver/transmitter and antennas that link to a wired network, router, or hub.

accountability The mechanisms for assessing responsibility for decisions made and actions taken.

accounting rate of return on investment (ROI) Calculation of the rate of return on an investment by adjusting cash inflows produced by the investment for depreciation. Approximates the accounting income earned by the investment.

accumulated balance digital payment systems Systems enabling users to make micropayments and purchases on the Web, accumulating a debit balance on their credit card or telephone bills.

activity-based costing Model for identifying all the company activities that cause costs to occur while producing a specific product or service so that managers can see which products or services are profitable or losing money and make changes to maximize firm profitability.

administrative controls Formalized standards, rules, procedures, and disciplines to ensure that the organization's controls are properly executed and enforced.

agency theory Economic theory that views the firm as a nexus of contracts among self-interested individuals who must be supervised and managed.

AI shell The programming environment of an expert system.

analog signal A continuous waveform that passes through a communications medium; used for voice communications.

analytical CRM Customer relationship management (CRM) applications dealing with the analysis of customer data to provide information for improving business performance.

antivirus software Software designed to detect, and often eliminate, computer viruses from an information system.

application controls Specific controls unique to each computerized application.

application proxy filtering Firewall screening technology that uses a proxy server to inspect and transmit data packets flowing into and out of the organization so that all the organization's internal applications communicate with the outside using a proxy application.

application server Software that handles all application operations between browser-based computers and a company's back-end business applications or databases.

application service provider (ASP) Company providing software that can be rented by other companies over the Web or a private network.

application software Programs written for a specific application to perform functions specified by end users.

application software package A set of prewritten, precoded application software programs that are commercially available for sale or lease.

artificial intelligence (AI) The effort to develop computer-based systems that can behave like humans, with the ability to learn languages, accomplish physical tasks, use a perceptual apparatus, and emulate human expertise and decision making.

asynchronous transfer mode (ATM) A networking technology that parcels information into 8-byte cells, enabling data to be transmitted between computers from different vendors at any speed.

attribute A piece of information describing a particular entity.

authentication The ability of each party in a transaction to ascertain the identity of the other party.

authorization management systems Systems for allowing each user access only to those portions of a system or the Web that person is permitted to enter, based on information established by a set of access rules.

authorization policies Policies that determine differing levels of access to information assets for different levels of users in an organization.

automation Using the computer to speed up the performance of existing tasks.

autonomic computing Effort to develop systems that can manage themselves without user intervention.

backbone Part of a network handling the major traffic and providing the primary path for traffic flowing to or from other networks.

backward chaining A strategy for searching the rule base in an expert system that acts like a problem solver by beginning with a hypothesis and seeking out more information until the hypothesis is either proved or disproved.

balanced scorecard Model for analyzing firm performance that supplements traditional financial measures with measurements from additional business perspectives, such as customers, internal business processes, and learning and growth.

bandwidth The capacity of a communications channel as measured by the difference between the highest and lowest frequencies that can be transmitted by that channel.

banner ad A graphic display on a Web page used for advertising. The banner is linked to the advertiser's Web site so that a person clicking the banner is transported to the advertiser's Web site.

batch processing A method of collecting and processing data in which transactions are accumulated and stored until a specified time when it is convenient or necessary to process them as a group.

baud A change in signal from positive to negative or vice versa that is used as a measure of transmission speed.

behavioral models Descriptions of management based on behavioral scientists' observations of what managers actually do in their jobs.

benchmarking Setting strict standards for products, services, or activities and measuring organizational performance against those standards.

best practices The most successful solutions or problem-solving methods that have been developed by a specific organization or industry.

biometric authentication   Technology for authenticating system users that compares a person's unique characteristics, such as fingerprints, face, or retinal image, against a stored set profile of these characteristics.

bit   A binary digit representing the smallest unit of data in a computer system. It can have only one of two states, representing 0 or 1.

blade server   Entire computer that fits on a single, thin card (or blade) and that is plugged into a single chassis to save space and power and reduce complexity.

blog   Popular term for Weblog, designating an informal yet structured Web site where individuals can publish stories, opinions, and links to other Web sites of interest.

Bluetooth   Standard for wireless personal area networks that can transmit up to 722 kilobits per second (Kbps) within a 10-meter area.

broadband   High-speed transmission technology. Also designates a single communications medium that can transmit multiple channels of data simultaneously.

bugs   Program code defects or errors.

bullwhip effect   Distortion of information about the demand for a product as it passes from one entity to the next across the supply chain.

bundling   Cross-selling in which a combination of products is sold as a bundle at a price lower than the total cost of the individual products.

bureaucracy   Formal organization with a clear-cut division of labor, abstract rules and procedures, and impartial decision making that uses technical qualifications and professionalism as a basis for promoting employees.

bureaucratic models of decision making   Models of decision making in which decisions are shaped by the organization's standard operating procedures (SOPs).

business continuity planning   Planning that focuses on how the company can restore business operations after a disaster strikes.

business driver   A force in the environment to which businesses must respond and that influences the direction of business.

business ecosystem   Loosely coupled but interdependent networks of suppliers, distributors, outsourcing firms, transportation service firms, and technology manufacturers.

business functions   Specialized tasks performed in a business organization, including manufacturing and production, sales and marketing, finance and accounting, and human resources.

business intelligence   Applications and technologies to help users make better business decisions.

business model   An abstraction of what an enterprise is and how the enterprise delivers a product or service, showing how the enterprise creates wealth.

business processes   The unique ways in which organizations coordinate and organize work activities, information, and knowledge to produce a product or service.

business process management   Methodology for revising the organization's business processes to use business processes as fundamental building blocks of corporate information systems.

business process reengineering   The radical redesign of business processes, combining steps to cut waste and eliminating repetitive, paper-intensive tasks to improve cost, quality, and service and to maximize the benefits of information technology.

business strategy   Set of activities and decisions that determines the products and services the firm produces, the industries in which the firm competes, firm competitors, suppliers, and customers, and the firm's long-term goals.

business-to-business (B2B) electronic commerce   Electronic sales of goods and services among businesses.

business-to-consumer (B2C) electronic commerce   Electronic retailing of products and services directly to individual consumers.

bus network   Network topology linking a number of computers by a single circuit with all messages broadcast to the entire network.

byte   A string of bits, usually eight, used to store one number or character in a computer system.

cable modem   Modem designed to operate over cable TV lines to provide high-speed access to the Internet or corporate intranets.

call center   An organizational department responsible for handling customer service issues by telephone and other channels.

campus area network (CAN)   An interconnected set of local area networks in a limited geographical area such as a college or corporate campus.

capacity planning   The process of predicting when a computer hardware system becomes saturated to ensure that adequate computing resources are available for work of different priorities and that the firm has enough computing power for its current and future needs.

capital budgeting   The process of analyzing and selecting various proposals for capital expenditures.

carpal tunnel syndrome (CTS)   Type of repetitive stress disorder (RSI) in which pressure on the median nerve through the wrist's bony carpal tunnel structure produces pain.

case-based reasoning (CBR)   Artificial intelligence technology that represents knowledge as a database of cases and solutions.

cellular telephone   A device that transmits voice or data, using radio waves to communicate with radio antennas placed within adjacent geographic areas called cells.

centralized processing   Processing that is accomplished by one large central computer.

change agent   In the context of implementation, the individual acting as the catalyst during the change process to ensure successful organizational adaptation to a new system or innovation.

channel   The link by which data or voice is transmitted between sending and receiving devices in a network.

channel conflict   Competition between two or more different distribution chains used to sell the products or services of the same company.

chat   Live, interactive conversations over a public network.

chief information officer (CIO)   Senior manager in charge of the information systems function in the firm.

chief knowledge officer (CKO)   Senior executive in charge of the organization's knowledge management program.

chief security officer (CSO)   Person who manages a formal security function for the organization and who is responsible for enforcing the firm's security policy.

choice   Simon's third stage of decision making, when the individual selects among the various solution alternatives.

churn rate   Measurement of the number of customers who stop using or purchasing products or services from a company. Used as an indicator of the growth or decline of a firm's customer base.

classical model of management   Traditional description of management that focused on its formal functions of planning, organizing, coordinating, deciding, and controlling.

clicks-and-mortar   Business model where the Web site is an extension of a traditional bricks-and-mortar business.

clickstream tracking   Tracking data about customer activities at Web sites and storing them in a log.

client   The user point of entry for the required function in client/server computing. Normally a desktop computer, workstation, or laptop computer.

client/server computing   A model for computing that splits processing between clients and servers on a network, assigning functions to the machine most able to perform the function.

clustering   Linking two computers together so that the second computer can act as a backup to the primary computer or speed up processing.

coaxial cable   A transmission medium consisting of thickly insulated copper wire; can transmit large volumes of data quickly.

Code Division Multiple Access (CDMA)   Major cellular transmission standard in the United States that transmits over several frequencies, occupies the entire spectrum, and randomly assigns users to a range of frequencies over time.

collaborative commerce   The use of digital technologies to enable multiple organizations to design, develop, build, and manage products collaboratively through product life cycles.

collaborative filtering Tracking users' movements on a Web site, comparing the information gleaned about a user's behavior against data about other customers with similar interests to predict what the user would like to see next.

collaborative planning, forecasting, and replenishment (CPFR) Firms collaborating with their suppliers and buyers to formulate demand forecasts, develop production plans, and coordinate shipping, warehousing, and stocking activities.

communications technology Physical devices and software that link various computer hardware components and transfer data from one physical location to another.

competitive forces model Model used to describe the interaction of external influences, specifically threats and opportunities, that affect an organization's strategy and ability to compete.

complementary assets Additional assets required to derive value from a primary investment.

component-based development Building large software systems by combining preexisting software components.

computer Physical device that takes data as an input, transforms the data by executing stored instructions, and outputs information to a number of devices.

computer abuse The commission of acts involving a computer that may not be illegal but are considered unethical.

computer-aided design (CAD) Information system that automates the creation and revision of designs using sophisticated graphics software.

computer-aided software engineering (CASE) Automation of step-by-step methodologies for software and systems development to reduce the amounts of repetitive work the developer must do.

computer-based information systems (CBIS) Information systems that rely on computer hardware and software for processing and disseminating information.

computer crime The commission of illegal acts through the use of a computer or against a computer system.

computer forensics The scientific collection, examination, authentication, preservation, and analysis of data held on or retrieved from computer storage media in such a way that the information can be used as evidence in a court of law.

computer hardware Physical equipment used for input, processing, and output activities in an information system.

computer literacy Knowledge about information technology, focusing on understanding how computer-based technologies work.

computer software Detailed, preprogrammed instructions that control and coordinate the work of computer hardware components in an information system.

computer virus Rogue software program that attaches itself to other software programs or data files in order to be executed, often causing hardware and software malfunctions.

computer vision syndrome (CVS) Eyestrain condition related to computer display screen use; symptoms include headaches, blurred vision, and dry and irritated eyes.

conceptual schema The logical description of the entire database showing all the data elements and relationships among them.

connectivity The ability of computers and computer-based devices to communicate with each other and share information in a meaningful way without human intervention.

consumer-to-consumer (C2C) electronic commerce Consumers selling goods and services electronically to other consumers.

controls All of the methods, policies, and procedures that ensure protection of the organization's assets, accuracy and reliability of its records, and operational adherence to management standards.

control unit Component of the central processing unit (CPU) that controls and coordinates the other parts of the computer system.

converged network Network with technology to enable voice and data to run over a single network.

conversion The process of changing from the old system to the new system.

cookie Tiny file deposited on a computer hard drive when an individual visits certain Web sites. Used to identify the visitor and track visits to the Web site.

cooptation Bringing the opposition into the process of designing and implementing a solution without giving up control of the direction and nature of the change.

copyright A statutory grant that protects creators of intellectual property against copying by others for any purpose for a minimum of 70 years.

core competency Activity at which a firm excels as a world-class leader.

core systems Systems that support functions that are absolutely critical to the organization.

cost-benefit ratio A method for calculating the returns from a capital expenditure by dividing total benefits by total costs.

counterimplementation A deliberate strategy to thwart the implementation of an information system or an innovation in an organization.

critical success factors (CSFs) A small number of easily identifiable operational goals shaped by the industry, the firm, the manager, and the broader environment that are believed to assure the success of an organization. Used to determine the information requirements of an organization.

cross-selling Marketing complementary products to customers.

customer-decision-support system (CDSS) System to support the decision-making process of an existing or potential customer.

customer lifetime value (CLTV) Difference between revenues produced by a specific customer and the expenses for acquiring and servicing that customer minus the cost of promotional marketing over the lifetime of the customer relationship, expressed in today's dollars.

customer relationship management (CRM) Business and technology discipline that uses information systems to coordinate all of the business processes surrounding the firm's interactions with its customers in sales, marketing, and service.

customer relationship management systems Information systems that track all the ways in which a company interacts with its customers and analyze these interactions to optimize revenue, profitability, customer satisfaction, and customer retention.

customization The modification of a software package to meet an organization's unique requirements without destroying the packaged software's integrity.

data Streams of raw facts representing events occurring in organizations or the physical environment before they have been organized and arranged into a form that people can understand and use.

data administration A special organizational function for managing the organization's data resources that is concerned with information policy, data planning, maintenance of data dictionaries, and data quality standards.

data cleansing Activities for detecting and correcting data in a database or file that are incorrect, incomplete, improperly formatted, or redundant. Also known as data scrubbing.

data definition language The component of a database management system that defines each data element as it appears in the database.

data dictionary An automated or manual tool for storing and organizing information about the data maintained in a database.

data element A field.

data flow diagram (DFD) Primary tool for structured analysis that graphically illustrates a system's component process and the flow of data between them.

data inconsistency The presence of different values for the same attribute when the same data are stored in multiple locations.

data management software Software used for creating and manipulating lists, creating files and databases to store data, and combining information for reports.

data manipulation language A language associated with a database management system that end users and programmers use to manipulate data in the database.

data mart   A small data warehouse containing only a portion of the organization's data for a specified function or population of users.

data mining   Analysis of large pools of data to find patterns and rules that can be used to guide decision making and predict future behavior.

data quality audit   A survey and/or sample of files to determine accuracy and completeness of data in an information system.

data redundancy   The presence of duplicate data in multiple data files.

data security controls   Controls to ensure that data files on either disk or tape are not subject to unauthorized access, change, or destruction.

data visualization   Technology for helping users see patterns and relationships in large amounts of data by presenting the data in graphical form.

data warehouse   A database with reporting and query tools that stores current and historical data extracted from various operational systems and consolidated for management reporting and analysis.

data workers   People such as secretaries or bookkeepers who process the organization's paperwork.

database   A group of related files.

database (rigorous definition)   A collection of data organized to service many applications at the same time by storing and managing data so that they appear to be in one location.

database administration   Refers to the more technical and operational aspects of managing data, including physical database design and maintenance.

database management system (DBMS)   Special software to create and maintain a database and enable individual business applications to extract the data they need without having to create separate files or data definitions in their computer programs.

database server   A computer in a client/server environment that is responsible for running a database management system (DBMS) to process structured query language (SQL) statements and perform database management tasks.

dataconferencing   Teleconferencing in which two or more users are able to edit and modify data files simultaneously.

data-driven DSS   A system that supports decision making by enabling users to extract and analyze useful information that was previously buried in large databases.

debugging   The process of discovering and eliminating the errors and defects—bugs—in program code.

decision-support systems (DSS)   Information systems at the organization's management level that combine data and sophisticated analytical models or data analysis tools to support semistructured and unstructured decision making.

decisional roles   Mintzberg's classification for managerial roles in which managers initiate activities, handle disturbances, allocate resources, and negotiate conflicts.

dedicated lines   Telephone lines that are continuously available for transmission by a lessee. Typically conditioned to transmit data at high speeds for high-volume applications.

demand planning   Determining how much product a business needs to make to satisfy all its customers' demands.

denial of service (DoS) attack   Flooding a network server or Web server with false communications or requests for services in order to crash the network.

dense wave division multiplexing (DWDM)   Technology for boosting transmission capacity of optical fiber by using many different wavelengths to carry separate streams of data over the same fiber strand at the same time.

Descartes' rule of change   A principle that states that if an action cannot be taken repeatedly, it is not right to be taken at any time.

design   Simon's second stage of decision making, when the individual conceives of possible alternative solutions to a problem.

development methodology   A collection of methods, one or more for every activity within every phase of a development project.

digital cash   Currency that is represented in electronic form that moves outside the normal network of money.

digital certificate   An attachment to an electronic message to verify the identity of the sender and to provide the receiver with the means to encode a reply.

digital checking   Systems that extend the functionality of existing checking accounts so they can be used for online shopping payments.

digital credit card payment system   Secure service for credit card payments on the Internet that protects information transmitted among users, merchant sites, and processing banks.

digital dashboard   Displays all of a firm's key performance indicators as graphs and charts on a single screen to provide a one-page overview of all the critical measurements necessary to make key executive decisions.

digital divide   Large disparities in access to computers and the Internet among different social groups and different locations.

digital firm   Organization in which nearly all significant business processes and relationships with customers, suppliers, and employees are digitally enabled and key corporate assets are managed through digital means.

digital market   A marketplace that is created by computer and communication technologies that link many buyers and sellers.

Digital Millennium Copyright Act (DMCA)   Legislation that adjusts copyright laws to the Internet Age by making it illegal to make, distribute, or use devices that circumvent technology-based protections of copyrighted materials.

digital signal   A discrete waveform that transmits data coded into two discrete states as 1-bits and 0-bits, which are represented as on-off electrical pulses; used for data communications.

digital signature   A digital code that can be attached to an electronically transmitted message to uniquely identify its contents and the sender.

Digital Subscriber Line (DSL)   A group of technologies providing high-capacity transmission over existing copper telephone lines.

digital wallet   Software that stores credit card, electronic cash, owner identification, and address information and provides this data automatically during electronic commerce purchase transactions.

direct cutover   A risky conversion approach in which the new system completely replaces the old one on an appointed day.

disaster recovery planning   Planning for the restoration of computing and communications services after they have been disrupted.

disintermediation   The removal of organizations or business process layers responsible for certain intermediary steps in a value chain.

distance learning   Education or training delivered over a distance to individuals in one or more locations.

distributed database   A database that is stored in more than one physical location. Parts or copies of the database are physically stored in one location, and other parts or copies are stored and maintained in other locations.

distributed processing   The distribution of computer processing work among multiple computers linked by a communications network.

documentation   Descriptions of how an information system works from either a technical or end-user standpoint.

domain name   English-like name that corresponds to the unique 32-bit numeric Internet Protocol (IP) address for each computer connected to the Internet.

Domain Name System (DNS)   A hierarchical system of servers maintaining a database enabling the conversion of domain names to their numeric IP addresses.

domestic exporter   Form of business organization characterized by heavy centralization of corporate activities in the home country of origin.

downsizing   The process of transferring applications from large computers to smaller ones.

downtime   Period of time in which an information system is not operational.

drill down   The ability to move from summary data to lower and lower levels of detail.

DSS database   A collection of current or historical data from a number of applications or groups. Can be a small PC database or a massive data warehouse.

DSS software system Collection of software tools that is used for data analysis, such as online analytical processing (OLAP) tools, data-mining tools, or a collection of mathematical and analytical models.

due process A process in which laws are well known and understood and there is an ability to appeal to higher authorities to ensure that laws are applied correctly.

dynamic page generation Technology for storing the contents of Web pages as objects in a database where they can be accessed and assembled to create constantly changing Web pages.

dynamic pricing Pricing of items based on real-time interactions between buyers and sellers that determine what an item is worth at any particular moment.

e-government Use of the Internet and related technologies to digitally enable government and public sector agencies' relationships with citizens, businesses, and other arms of government.

e-learning Instruction delivered through purely digital technology, such as CD-ROMs, the Internet, or private networks.

e-mail handheld Handheld device for wireless data transmission that includes a small display screen and a keypad for typing short e-mail messages.

edge computing Method for distributing the computing load (or work) across many layers of Internet computers to minimize response time.

efficient customer response system System that directly links consumer behavior to distribution, production, and supply chains.

electronic billing and payment presentation system A system used for paying routine monthly bills that enables users to view their bills electronically and pay them through electronic funds transfers from banks or credit card accounts.

electronic business (e-business) The use of the Internet and digital technology to execute all the business processes in the enterprise. Includes e-commerce as well as processes for the internal management of the firm and for coordination with suppliers and other business partners.

electronic commerce The process of buying and selling goods and services electronically, involving transactions using the Internet, networks, and other digital technologies.

electronic commerce server software Software that provides functions essential for running e-commerce Web sites, such as setting up electronic catalogs and storefronts, and mechanisms for processing customer purchases.

Electronic Data Interchange (EDI) The direct computer-to-computer exchange between two organizations of standard business transactions, such as orders, shipment instructions, or payments.

electronic mail (e-mail) The computer-to-computer exchange of messages.

electronic payment system The use of digital technologies, such as credit cards, smart cards, and Internet-based payment systems, to pay for products and services electronically.

Employee relationship management (ERM) Software dealing with employee issues that are closely related to customer relationship management (CRM), such as setting objectives, employee performance management, performance-based compensation, and employee training.

encryption The coding and scrambling of messages to prevent their being read or accessed without authorization.

end user Representative of departments outside the information systems group for whom applications are developed.

end-user development The development of information systems by end users with little or no formal assistance from technical specialists.

end-user interface The part of an information system through which the end user interacts with the system, such as online screens and commands.

enterprise analysis An analysis of organization-wide information requirements made by looking at the entire organization in terms of organizational units, functions, processes, and data elements; helps identify the key entities and attributes in the organization's data.

enterprise application A system that can coordinate activities, decisions, and knowledge across many different functions, levels, and business units in a firm. Includes enterprise systems, supply chain management systems, and knowledge management systems.

enterprise application integration (EAI) software Software that works with specific software platforms to tie together multiple applications to support enterprise integration.

enterprise networking An arrangement of the organization's hardware, software, network, and data resources to put more computing power on the desktop and create a company-wide network linking many smaller networks.

enterprise portal Web interface providing a single entry point for accessing organizational information and services, including information from various enterprise applications and in-house legacy systems, such that information appears to be coming from a single source.

enterprise software Set of integrated modules for applications such as sales and distribution, financial accounting, investment management, materials management, production planning, plant maintenance, and human resources that allows data to be used by multiple functions and business processes.

enterprise systems Integrated enterprise-wide information systems that coordinate key internal processes of the firm.

entity A person, place, thing, or event about which information must be kept.

entity-relationship diagram A methodology for documenting databases illustrating the relationship between various entities in the database.

ergonomics The interaction of people and machines in the work environment, including the design of jobs, health issues, and the end-user interface of information systems.

ethical "no free lunch" rule Assumption that all tangible and intangible objects are owned by someone else, unless there is a specific declaration otherwise, and that the creator wants compensation for this work.

ethics Principles of right and wrong that can be used by individuals acting as free moral agents to make choices to guide their behavior.

EV-DO Technology used in Verizon's cellular network service for providing anytime, anywhere broadband wireless Internet access for PCs and other devices at average speeds of 300 to 500 kilobits per second (Kbps). Stands for Evolution Data Optimized.

exchange Third-party Net marketplace that is primarily transaction oriented and that connects many buyers and suppliers for spot purchasing.

executive support systems (ESS) Information systems at the organization's strategic level designed to address unstructured decision making through advanced graphics and communications.

expert system Knowledge-intensive computer program that captures the expertise of a human in limited domains of knowledge.

explicit knowledge Knowledge that has been documented.

external integration tools Project management technique that links the work of the implementation team to that of users at all organizational levels.

extranet Private intranet that is accessible to authorized outsiders.

facsimile (fax) A machine that digitizes and transmits documents with both text and graphics over telephone lines.

Fair Information Practices (FIPs) A set of principles originally set forth in 1973 that governs the collection and use of information about individuals and that forms the basis of most U.S. and European privacy laws.

fault-tolerant computer systems Systems that contain extra hardware, software, and power supply components that can back up a system and keep it running to prevent system failure.

feasibility study As part of the systems analysis process, the way to determine whether the solution is achievable, given the organization's resources and constraints.

feedback Output that is returned to the appropriate members of the organization to help them evaluate or correct input.

fiber-optic cable   A fast, light, and durable transmission medium consisting of thin strands of clear glass fiber bound into cables. Data are transmitted as light pulses.

field   A grouping of characters into a word, a group of words, or a complete number, such as a person's name or age.

file   A group of records of the same type.

File Transfer Protocol (FTP)   Specification for retrieving and transferring files from a remote computer.

finance and accounting information systems   Systems used to keep track of the firm's financial assets and fund flows.

firewall   Hardware and software placed between an organization's internal network and an external network to prevent outsiders from invading private networks.

focused differentiation   Competitive strategy for developing new market niches for specialized products or services in which a business can compete in the target area better than its competitors.

formal control tools   Project management technique that helps monitor the progress toward completion of a task and fulfillment of goals.

formal planning tools   Project management technique that structures and sequences tasks, budgeting time, money, and technical resources required to complete the tasks.

formal system   System resting on accepted and fixed definitions of data and procedures, operating with predefined rules.

forward chaining   A strategy for searching the rule base in an expert system that begins with the information entered by the user and searches the rule base to arrive at a conclusion.

fourth-generation language   A programming language that can be employed directly by end users or less-skilled programmers to develop computer applications more rapidly than conventional programming languages.

frame relay   A shared network service technology that packages data into bundles for transmission but does not use error-correction routines. Cheaper and faster than packet switching.

framing   Displaying the content of another Web site inside one's own Web site within a frame or a window.

franchiser   Form of business organization in which a product is created, designed, financed, and initially produced in the home country, but for product-specific reasons relies heavily on foreign personnel for further production, marketing, and human resources.

fuzzy logic   Rule-based artificial intelligence (AI) that tolerates imprecision by using nonspecific terms called membership functions to solve problems.

"garbage can" model   Model of decision making that states that organizations are not rational and that decisions are solutions that become attached to problems for accidental reasons.

general controls   Overall controls that establish a framework for controlling the design, security, and use of computer programs throughout an organization.

General Packet Radio Service (GPRS)   2.5G service that transports data over Global System for Mobile Communications (GSM) wireless networks and improves wireless Internet access.

genetic algorithms   Problem-solving methods that promote the evolution of solutions to specified problems using the model of living organisms adapting to their environment.

geographic information system (GIS)   System with software that can analyze and display data using digitized maps to enhance planning and decision making.

global culture   The development of common expectations, shared artifacts, and social norms among different cultures and peoples.

Global Positioning System (GPS)   Worldwide satellite navigational system.

Global System for Mobile Communications (GSM)   Major cellular transmission standard outside the United States with strong international roaming capability that operates primarily in the 900-megahertz (MHz) and 1.8-gigahertz (GHz) frequency bands using Time Division Multiple Access (TDMA) in which each user is allocated a portion of time on the frequency.

graphical user interface (GUI)   The part of an operating system users interact with that uses graphic icons and the computer mouse to issue commands and make selections.

grid computing   Applying the resources of many computers in a network to a single problem.

group decision-support system (GDSS)   An interactive computer-based system to facilitate the solution of unstructured problems by a set of decision makers working together as a group.

groupware   Software that provides functions and services that support the collaborative activities of work groups.

hacker   A person who gains unauthorized access to a computer network for profit, criminal mischief, or personal pleasure.

Hertz   Measure of frequency of electrical impulses per second, with 1 Hertz equivalent to 1 cycle per second.

hierarchical DBMS   One type of logical database model that organizes data in a treelike structure. A record is subdivided into segments that are connected to each other in one-to-many parent-child relationships.

high-availability computing   Tools and technologies, including backup hardware resources, that enable a system to recover quickly from a crash.

hit   An entry into a Web server's log file generated by each request to the server for a file.

homepage   A World Wide Web text and graphical screen display that welcomes the user and explains the organization that has established the page.

hotspot   A specific geographic location in which an access point provides public Wi-Fi network service.

hubs   Very simple devices that connect network components, sending a packet of data to all other connected devices.

human resources information systems   Systems that maintain employee records; track employee skills, job performance, and training; and support planning for employee compensation and career development.

hybrid AI systems   Integration of multiple artificial intelligence (AI) technologies into a single application to take advantage of the best features of these technologies.

hypermedia database   An approach to data management that organizes data as a network of nodes linked in any pattern the user specifies; the nodes can contain text, graphics, sound, full-motion video, or executable programs.

Hypertext Markup Language (HTML)   Page description language for creating Web pages and other hypermedia documents.

Hypertext Transport Protocol   The communications standard used to transfer pages on the Internet. Defines how messages are formatted and transmitted.

identity theft   Theft of key pieces of personal information, such as credit card or Social Security numbers, to obtain merchandise and services in the name of the victim or to obtain false credentials.

I-mode   Standard developed by Japan's NTT DoCoMo mobile phone network for enabling cell phones to receive Web-based content and services.

Immanuel Kant's Categorical Imperative   A principle that states that if an action is not right for everyone to take, it is not right for anyone.

implementation   Simon's final stage of decision making, when the individual puts the decision into effect and reports on the progress of the solution.

industry structure   The nature of participants in an industry and their relative bargaining power. Derives from the competitive forces and establishes the general business environment in an industry and the overall profitability of doing business in that environment.

inference engine   The strategy used to search through the rule base in an expert system; can be forward or backward chaining.

information   Data that have been shaped into a form that is meaningful and useful to human beings.

information appliance Device that has been customized to perform well a few specialized computing tasks with minimal user effort.

information asymmetry Situation in which the relative bargaining power of two parties in a transaction is determined by one party in the transaction possessing more information essential to the transaction than the other party.

information center A special facility within an organization that provides training and support for end-user computing.

information partnership Cooperative alliance formed between two or more corporations for the purpose of sharing information to gain strategic advantage.

information policy Formal rules governing the maintenance, distribution, and use of information in an organization.

information requirements A detailed statement of the information needs that a new system must satisfy; identifies who needs what information, and when, where, and how the information is needed.

information rights The rights that individuals and organizations have with respect to information that pertains to themselves.

information system Interrelated components working together to collect, process, store, and disseminate information to support decision making, coordination, control, analysis, and visualization in an organization.

information systems department The formal organizational unit that is responsible for the information systems function in the organization.

information systems literacy Broad-based understanding of information systems that includes behavioral knowledge about organizations and individuals using information systems as well as technical knowledge about computers.

information systems managers Leaders of the various specialists in the information systems department.

information systems plan A road map indicating the direction of systems development: the rationale, the current situation, the management strategy, the implementation plan, and the budget.

information technology (IT) infrastructure Computer hardware, software, data, storage technology, and networks providing a portfolio of shared IT resources for the organization.

informational roles Mintzberg's classification for managerial roles in which managers act as the nerve centers of their organizations, receiving and disseminating critical information.

informed consent Consent given with knowledge of all the facts needed to make a rational decision.

input The capture or collection of raw data from within the organization or from its external environment for processing in an information system.

input controls The procedures to check data for accuracy and completeness when they enter the system.

instant messaging Chat service that enables participants to create their own private chat channels so that a person can be alerted whenever someone on his or her private list is online to initiate a chat session with that particular individual.

intangible benefits Benefits that are not easily quantified; they include more efficient customer service or enhanced decision making.

Integrated Services Digital Network (ISDN) International standard for transmitting voice, video, image, and data to support a wide range of services over the public telephone lines.

intellectual property Intangible property created by individuals or corporations that is subject to protections under trade secret, copyright, and patent law.

intelligence The first of Simon's four stages of decision making, when the individual collects information to identify problems occurring in the organization.

intelligent agent Software program that uses a built-in or learned knowledge base to carry out specific, repetitive, and predictable tasks for an individual user, business process, or software application.

internal integration tools Project management technique that ensures that the implementation team operates as a cohesive unit.

internal rate of return (IRR) The rate of return or profit that an investment is expected to earn.

international information systems architecture The basic information systems required by organizations to coordinate worldwide trade and other activities.

Internet International network of networks that is a collection of hundreds of thousands of private and public networks.

Internet Protocol (IP) address Four-part numeric address indicating a unique computer location on the Internet.

Internet service provider (ISP) A commercial organization with a permanent connection to the Internet that sells temporary connections to subscribers.

Internet telephony Technologies that use Internet Protocol packet-switched connections for voice service.

Internet2 Research network with new protocols and transmission speeds that provides an infrastructure for supporting high-bandwidth Internet applications.

internetworking The linking of separate networks, each of which retains its own identity, into an interconnected network.

interorganizational systems Information systems that automate the flow of information across organizational boundaries and link a company to its customers, distributors, or suppliers.

interpersonal roles Mintzberg's classification for managerial roles in which managers act as figureheads and leaders for the organization.

intranet An internal network based on Internet and World Wide Web technology and standards.

intrusion detection system Tools to monitor the most vulnerable points in a network to detect and deter unauthorized users.

investment workstation Powerful desktop computer for financial specialists that is optimized to access and manipulate massive amounts of financial data.

iterative A process of repeating over and over again the steps to build a system.

Java Programming language that can deliver only the software functionality needed for a particular task, such as a small applet downloaded from a network; it can run on any computer and operating system.

joint application design (JAD) Process to accelerate the generation of information requirements by having end users and information systems specialists work together in intensive interactive design sessions.

just-in-time Scheduling system for minimizing inventory by having components arrive exactly at the moment they are needed and finished goods shipped as soon as they leave the assembly line.

key field A field in a record that uniquely identifies instances of that record so that it can be retrieved, updated, or sorted.

knowledge Concepts, experience, and insight that provide a framework for creating, evaluating, and using information.

knowledge- and information-intense products Products that require a great deal of learning and knowledge to produce.

knowledge base Model of human knowledge that is used by expert systems.

knowledge discovery Identification of novel and valuable patterns in large databases.

knowledge engineer A specialist who elicits information and expertise from other professionals and translates it into a set of rules, or frames, for an expert system.

knowledge management The set of processes developed in an organization to create, gather, store, maintain, and disseminate the firm's knowledge.

knowledge management systems Systems that support the creation, capture, storage, and dissemination of firm expertise and knowledge.

knowledge network system Online directory for locating corporate experts in well-defined knowledge domains.

knowledge repository Collection of documented internal and external knowledge in a single location for more efficient management and utilization by the organization.

knowledge workers   People such as engineers or architects who design products or services and create knowledge for the organization.

learning management system (LMS)   Tools for the management, delivery, tracking, and assessment of various types of employee learning.

legacy system   A system that has been in existence for a long time and that continues to be used to avoid the high cost of replacing or redesigning it.

legitimacy   The extent to which one's authority is accepted on grounds of competence, vision, or other qualities. Making judgments and taking actions on the basis of narrow or personal characteristics.

liability   The existence of laws that permit individuals to recover the damages done to them by other actors, systems, or organizations.

Linux   Reliable and compactly designed operating system that is an offshoot of Unix, that can run on many different hardware platforms, and that is available for free or at very low cost. Used as an alternative to Unix and Microsoft Windows NT.

LISTSERV   Online discussion groups using e-mail broadcast from mailing list servers.

load balancing   Distribution of large numbers of requests for access among multiple servers so that no single device is overwhelmed.

local area network (LAN)   A telecommunications network that requires its own dedicated channels and that encompasses a limited distance, usually one building or several buildings in close proximity.

logistics   Planning and control of all factors that will have an impact on transporting a product or service.

mainframe   Largest category of computer, used for major business processing.

maintenance   Changes in hardware, software, documentation, or procedures to a production system to correct errors, meet new requirements, or improve processing efficiency.

managed security service provider (MSSP)   Company that provides security management services for subscribing clients.

management control   Monitoring how efficiently or effectively resources are utilized and how well operational units are performing.

management information systems (MIS)   The study of information systems focusing on their use in business and management.

management-level systems   Information systems that support the monitoring, controlling, decision-making, and administrative activities of middle managers.

managerial roles   Expectations of the activities that managers should perform in an organization.

man-month   The traditional unit of measurement used by systems designers to estimate the length of time to complete a project. Refers to the amount of work a person can be expected to complete in a month.

manufacturing and production information systems   Systems that deal with the planning, development, and production of products and services and with controlling the flow of production.

mass customization   The capacity to offer individually tailored products or services using mass production resources.

megahertz (MHz)   A measure of cycle speed, or the pacing of events in a computer; one megahertz equals one million cycles per second.

message integrity   The ability to ascertain whether a transmitted message has been copied or altered.

metric   A standard measurement of performance.

metropolitan area network (MAN)   Network that spans a metropolitan area, usually a city and its major suburbs. Its geographic scope falls between a wide area network (WAN) and a local area network (LAN).

microbrowser   Web browser software with a small file size that can work with low-memory constraints, tiny screens of handheld wireless devices, and low bandwidth of wireless networks.

micropayment   Payment for a very small sum of money, often less than $10.

microprocessor   Very large scale integrated circuit technology that integrates the computer's memory, logic, and control on a single chip.

microwave   A high-volume, long-distance, point-to-point transmission in which high-frequency radio signals are transmitted through the atmosphere from one terrestrial transmission station to another.

middle managers   People in the middle of the organizational hierarchy who are responsible for carrying out the plans and goals of senior management.

middleware   Software that connects two disparate applications, enabling them to communicate with each other and to exchange data.

midrange computer   Middle-size computer that is capable of supporting the computing needs of smaller organizations or of managing networks of other computers.

minicomputer   Middle-range computer used in systems for universities, factories, or research laboratories.

mirroring   Duplicating all the processes and transactions of a server on a backup server to prevent any interruption in service if the primary server fails.

MIS audit   Identifies all the controls that govern individual information systems and assesses their effectiveness.

mobile commerce (m-commerce)   The use of wireless devices, such as cell phones or handheld digital information appliances, to conduct both business-to-consumer and business-to-business e-commerce transactions over the Internet.

mobile computing   Wireless computing that enables Internet-enabled cell phones, personal digital assistants (PDAs), and other wireless computing devices to access digital information from the Internet and other sources from any location.

mobile data networks   Wireless networks that enable two-way transmission of data files cheaply and efficiently.

mobile wallets (m-wallets)   Software that stores m-commerce shoppers' personal information and credit card numbers to expedite the purchase process.

model   An abstract representation that illustrates the components or relationships of a phenomenon.

model-driven DSS   Primarily standalone system that uses some type of model to perform "what-if" and other kinds of analyses.

modem   A device for translating a computer's digital signals into analog form for transmission over ordinary telephone lines, or for translating analog signals back into digital form for reception by a computer.

module   A logical unit of a program that performs one or several functions.

Moore's Law   Assertion that the number of components on a chip doubles each year.

MP3 (MPEG3)   Compression standard that can compress audio files for transfer over the Internet with virtually no loss in quality.

multicasting   Transmission of data to a selected group of recipients.

multimedia   The integration of two or more types of media, such as text, graphics, sound, voice, full-motion video, or animation into a computer-based application.

multinational   Form of business organization that concentrates financial management and control out of a central home base while decentralizing.

multiplexing   Capability of a single communications channel to carry data transmissions from multiple sources simultaneously.

multitiered (n-tiered) client/server architecture   Client/server network in which the work of the entire network is balanced over several different levels of servers.

nanotechnology   Technology that builds structures and processes based on the manipulation of individual atoms and molecules.

natural language   Nonprocedural language that enables users to communicate with the computer using conversational commands resembling human speech.

net marketplace   A single digital marketplace based on Internet technology that links many buyers to many sellers.

net present value (NPV)   The amount of money an investment is worth, taking into account its cost, earnings, and the time value of money.

network   The linking of two or more computers to share data or resources, such as a printer.

network DBMS   Older logical database model that is useful for depicting many-to-many relationships.

network economics   Model of strategic systems at the industry level based on the concept of a network where adding another participant entails zero marginal costs but can create much larger marginal gains.

network interface card (NIC)   Expansion card inserted into a computer to enable it to connect to a network.

network operating system (NOS)   Special software that routes and manages communications on the network and coordinates network resources.

neural network   Hardware or software that attempts to emulate the processing patterns of the biological brain.

nomadic computing   Wireless computing where users move from wireless hot spot to wireless hot spot to gain network or Internet access.

nonobvious relationship awareness (NORA)   Technology that can find obscure hidden connections between people or other entities by analyzing information from many different sources to correlate relationships.

normalization   The process of creating small stable data structures from complex groups of data when designing a relational database.

object   Software building block that combines data and the procedures acting on the data.

object-oriented DBMS   An approach to data management that stores both data and the procedures acting on the data as objects that can be automatically retrieved and shared; the objects can contain multimedia.

object-oriented development   Approach to systems development that uses the object as the basic unit of systems analysis and design. The system is modeled as a collection of objects and the relationship between them.

object-oriented programming   An approach to software development that combines data and procedures into a single object.

object-relational DBMS   A database management system that combines the capabilities of a relational database management system (DBMS) for storing traditional information and the capabilities of an object-oriented DBMS for storing graphics and multimedia.

office systems   Systems such as word processing, desktop publishing, e-mail, electronic scheduling, and videoconferencing, designed to increase worker productivity in the office.

Office 2000, Office XP, and Office 2003   Integrated desktop productivity software suites with capabilities for supporting collaborative work on the Internet or incorporating information from the Internet into documents.

offshore software outsourcing   Outsourcing systems development work or maintenance of existing systems to external vendors in another country.

on-demand computing   Firms off-loading peak demand for computing power to remote, large-scale data processing centers, investing just enough to handle average processing loads and paying for only as much additional computing power as the market demands. Also called utility computing.

online analytical processing (OLAP)   Capability for manipulating and analyzing large volumes of data from multiple perspectives.

online processing   A method of collecting and processing data in which transactions are entered directly into the computer system and processed immediately.

online transaction processing   Transaction processing mode in which transactions entered online are immediately processed by the computer.

open-source software   Software that provides free access to its program code, allowing users to modify the program code to make improvements or fix errors.

Open Systems Interconnection (OSI) reference model   Less widely used network connectivity model developed by the International Organization for Standardization for linking different types of computers and networks.

operating system   The system software that manages and controls the activities of the computer.

operational CRM   Customer-facing applications, such as sales force automation, call center and customer service support, and marketing automation.

operational-level systems   Information systems that monitor the elementary activities and transactions of the organization.

operational managers   People who monitor the day-to-day activities of the organization.

optical network   High-speed networking technologies for transmitting data in the form of light pulses.

opt-in   Model of informed consent prohibiting an organization from collecting any personal information unless the individual specifically takes action to approve information collection and use.

opt-out   Model of informed consent permitting the collection of personal information until the consumer specifically requests that the data not be collected.

organization (behavioral definition)   A collection of rights, privileges, obligations, and responsibilities that are delicately balanced over a period of time through conflict and conflict resolution.

organization (technical definition)   A stable, formal, social structure that takes resources from the environment and processes them to produce outputs.

organizational and management capital   Investments in organization and management such as new business processes, management behavior, organizational culture, or training.

organizational culture   The set of fundamental assumptions about what products the organization should produce, how and where it should produce them, and for whom the products should be produced.

organizational impact analysis   Study of the way a proposed system will affect organizational structure, attitudes, decision making, and operations.

organizational learning   Creation of new standard operating procedures and business processes that reflect organizations' experience.

organizational memory   The stored learning from an organization's history that can be used for decision making and other purposes.

organizational models of decision making   Models of decision making that take into account the structural and political characteristics of an organization.

output   The distribution of processed information to the people who will use it or to the activities for which it will be used.

output controls   Measures that ensure that the results of computer processing are accurate, complete, and properly distributed.

outsourcing   The practice of contracting computer center operations, telecommunications networks, or applications development to external vendors.

packet switching   Technology that breaks messages into small bundles of data and routes them in the most economical way through any available communications channel.

paging system   A wireless transmission technology in which the pager beeps when the user receives a message; used to transmit short alphanumeric messages.

paradigm shift   Radical reconceptualization of the nature of the business and the nature of the organization.

parallel processing   Type of processing in which more than one instruction can be processed at a time by breaking down a problem into smaller parts and processing them simultaneously with multiple processors.

parallel strategy   A safe and conservative conversion approach where both the old system and its potential replacement are run together for a time until everyone is assured that the new one functions correctly.

particularism   Making judgments and taking action on the basis of narrow or personal characteristics, in all its forms (religious, nationalistic, ethnic, regionalism, geopolitical position).

partner relationship management (PRM) Automation of the firm's relationships with its selling partners using customer data and analytical tools to improve coordination and customer sales.

patent A legal document that grants the owner an exclusive monopoly on the ideas behind an invention for 17 years; designed to ensure that inventors of new machines or methods are rewarded for their labor while making widespread use of their inventions.

payback method A measure of the time required to pay back the initial investment on a project.

peer-to-peer Network architecture that gives equal power to all computers on the network; used primarily in small networks.

peer-to-peer computing Form of distributed processing that links computers via the Internet or private networks so that they can share processing tasks.

peer-to-peer payment system Electronic payment system for people who want to send money to vendors or individuals who are not set up to accept credit card payments.

personal area network (PAN) Computer network used for communication among digital devices (including telephones and personal digital assistants, or PDAs) that are close to one person.

Personal Communication Services (PCS) A wireless cellular technology that uses lower-power, higher-frequency radio waves than does cellular technology and so can be used with smaller-sized telephones.

personal digital assistants (PDAs) Small, pen-based, handheld computers with built-in wireless telecommunications capable of entirely digital communications transmission.

pervasive computing Ubiquitous use of computers in every facet of everyday life, including cars, homes, office buildings, tools, and factories, making computers increasingly embedded in people's natural movements and interactions with their environments.

phased approach Introduction of the new system in stages either by functions or by organizational units.

pilot study A strategy to introduce the new system to a limited area of the organization until it is proved to be fully functional; only then can the conversion to the new system take place across the entire organization.

political models of decision making Models of decision making in which decisions result from competition and bargaining among the organization's interest groups and key leaders.

pop-up ad Ad that opens automatically and does not disappear until the user clicks it.

portal Web interface for presenting integrated personalized content from a variety of sources. Also refers to a Web site service that provides an initial point of entry to the Web.

portfolio analysis An analysis of the portfolio of potential applications within a firm to determine the risks and benefits and to select among alternatives for information systems.

postimplementation audit Formal review process conducted after a system has been placed in production to determine how well the system has met its original objectives.

predictive analysis Use of data-mining techniques, historical data, and assumptions about future conditions to predict outcomes of events.

present value The value in current dollars of a payment or stream of payments to be received in the future.

primary activities Activities most directly related to the production and distribution of a firm's products or services.

privacy The claim of individuals to be left alone, free from surveillance or interference from other individuals, organizations, or the state.

private exchange Another term for a private industrial network.

private industrial networks Web-enabled networks linking systems of multiple firms in an industry for the coordination of transorganizational business processes.

processing The conversion, manipulation, and analysis of raw input into a form that is more meaningful to humans.

processing controls The routines for establishing that data are complete and accurate during updating.

process specifications Describe the logic of the processes occurring within the lowest levels of a data flow diagram.

procurement Sourcing goods and materials, negotiating with suppliers, paying for goods, and making delivery arrangements.

product differentiation Competitive strategy for creating brand loyalty by developing new and unique products and services that are not easily duplicated by competitors.

product life cycle management (PLM) Systems based on a data repository that organizes every piece of information that goes into making a particular product.

production The stage after the new system is installed and the conversion is complete; during this time the system is reviewed by users and technical specialists to determine how well it has met its original goals.

production or service workers People who actually produce the products or services of the organization.

profiling The use of computers to combine data from multiple sources and create electronic dossiers of detailed information on individuals.

profitability index Used to compare the profitability of alternative investments; it is calculated by dividing the present value of the total cash inflow from an investment by the initial cost of the investment.

program-data dependence The close relationship between data stored in files and the software programs that update and maintain those files. Any change in data organization or format requires a change in all the programs associated with those files.

programmers Highly trained technical specialists who write computer software instructions.

programming The process of translating the system specifications prepared during the design stage into program code.

protocol A set of rules and procedures that govern transmission between the components in a network.

prototype The preliminary working version of an information system for demonstration and evaluation purposes.

prototyping The process of building an experimental system quickly and inexpensively for demonstration and evaluation so that users can better determine information requirements.

P3P Industry standard designed to give users more control over personal information gathered on Web sites they visit. Stands for Platform for Privacy Preferences Project.

public key infrastructure System for creating public and private keys using a certificate authority (CA) and digital certificates for authentication.

pull-based model Supply chain driven by actual customer orders or purchases so that members of the supply chain produce and deliver only what customers have ordered.

pure-play Business models based purely on the Internet.

push-based model Supply chain driven by production master schedules based on forecasts or best guesses of demand for products, and products are "pushed" to customers.

push technology Method of obtaining relevant information on networks by having a computer broadcast information directly to the user based on prespecified interests.

query language Software tool that provides immediate online answers to requests for information that are not predefined.

radio-frequency identification (RFID) Technology using tiny tags with embedded microchips containing data about an item and its location to transmit short-distance radio signals to special RFID readers that then pass the data on to a computer for processing.

rapid application development (RAD) Process for developing systems in a very short time period by using prototyping, fourth-generation tools, and close teamwork among users and systems specialists.

rational model Model of human behavior based on the belief that people, organizations, and nations engage in basically consistent, value-maximizing calculations.

rationalization of procedures The streamlining of standard operating procedures, eliminating obvious bottlenecks, so that automation makes operating procedures more efficient.

reach Measurement of how many people a business can connect with and how many products it can offer those people.

real options pricing models Models for evaluating information technology investments with uncertain returns by using techniques for valuing financial options.

record A group of related fields.

recovery-oriented computing Computer systems designed to recover rapidly when mishaps occur.

redundant array of inexpensive disks (RAID) Disk storage technology to boost disk performance by packaging more than 100 smaller disk drives with a controller chip and specialized software in a single large unit to deliver data over multiple paths simultaneously.

reintermediation The shifting of the intermediary role in a value chain to a new source.

relational DBMS A type of logical database model that treats data as if they were stored in two-dimensional tables. It can relate data stored in one table to data in another as long as the two tables share a common data element.

repetitive stress injury (RSI) Occupational disease that occurs when muscle groups are forced through repetitive actions with high-impact loads or thousands of repetitions with low-impact loads.

Request for Proposal (RFP) A detailed list of questions submitted to vendors of software or other services to determine how well the vendor's product can meet the organization's specific requirements.

resource allocation The determination of how costs, time, and personnel are assigned to different phases of a systems development project.

responsibility Accepting the potential costs, duties, and obligations for the decisions one makes.

reverse logistics The return of items from buyers to sellers in a supply chain.

richness Measurement of the depth and detail of information that a business can supply to the customer as well as information the business collects about the customer.

ring network A network topology in which all computers are linked by a closed loop in a manner that passes data in one direction from one computer to another.

risk assessment Determining the potential frequency of the occurrence of a problem and the potential damage if the problem were to occur. Used to determine the cost-benefit of a control.

Risk Aversion Principle Principle that one should take the action that produces the least harm or incurs the least cost.

router Specialized communications processor that forwards packets of data from one network to another network.

routines Precise rules, procedures and practices that have been developed to cope with expected situations.

rule base The collection of knowledge in an artificial intelligence (AI) system that is represented in the form of IF-THEN rules.

safe harbor Private self-regulating policy and enforcement mechanism that meets the objectives of government regulations but does not involve government regulation or enforcement.

sales and marketing information systems Systems that help the firm identify customers for the firm's products or services, develop products and services to meet their needs, promote these products and services, sell the products and services, and provide ongoing customer support.

satellite The transmission of data using orbiting satellites that serve as relay stations for transmitting microwave signals over very long distances.

scalability The capability of a computer, product, or system to expand to serve a larger number of users without breaking down.

scoring model A quick method for deciding among alternative systems based on a system of ratings for selected objectives.

search-based advertising Payment to a search service to display a sponsored link to a company's Web site as a way of advertising that company.

search costs The time and money spent locating a suitable product and determining the best price for that product.

search engine A tool for locating specific sites or information on the Internet.

security Policies, procedures, and technical measures used to prevent unauthorized access, alteration, theft, or physical damage to information systems.

Semantic web Collaborative effort led by the World Wide Web Consortium to make Web searching more efficient by reducing the amount of human involvement in searching for and processing Web information.

semistructured decisions Decisions in which only part of the problem has a clear-cut answer provided by an accepted procedure.

semistructured knowledge Information in the form of less structured objects, such as e-mail, chat room exchanges, videos, graphics, brochures, or bulletin boards.

semistructured knowledge system System for organizing and storing less structured information, such as e-mail, voice mail, videos, graphics, brochures, or bulletin boards. Also known as digital asset management system.

senior managers People occupying the topmost hierarchy in an organization who are responsible for making long-range decisions.

sensitivity analysis Models that ask "what-if" questions repeatedly to determine the impact of changes in one or more factors on the outcomes.

sequence construct The sequential single steps or actions in the logic of a program that do not depend on the existence of any condition.

server Computer specifically optimized to provide software and other resources to other computers over a network.

server farm Large group of servers maintained by a commercial vendor and made available to subscribers for electronic commerce and other activities requiring heavy use of servers.

service-oriented architecture Software architecture of a firm built on a collection of software programs that communicate with each other to perform assigned tasks to create a working software application.

service platform Integration of multiple applications from multiple business functions, business units, or business partners to deliver a seamless experience for the customer, employee, manager, or business partner.

shopping bot Software with varying levels of built-in intelligence to help electronic commerce shoppers locate and evaluate products or services they might wish to purchase.

short message service (SMS) Text message service used by digital cell phone systems to send and receive short alphanumeric messages less than 160 characters in length.

Simple Object Access Protocol (SOAP) Set of rules that allows Web services applications to pass data and instructions to one another.

six sigma A specific measure of quality, representing 3.4 defects per million opportunities; used to designate a set of methodologies and techniques for improving quality and reducing costs.

smart card A credit-card-sized plastic card that stores digital information and that can be used for electronic payments in place of cash.

smart phone Wireless phone with voice, text, and Internet capabilities.

social engineering Tricking people into revealing their passwords by pretending to be legitimate users or members of a company in need of information.

social networking sites Online communities for expanding users' business or social contacts by making connections through their mutual business or personal connections.

sociotechnical design Design to produce information systems that blend technical efficiency with sensitivity to organizational and human needs.

software metrics The objective assessments of the software used in a system in the form of quantified measurements.

software package A prewritten, precoded, commercially available set of programs that eliminates the need to write software programs for certain functions.

source code Program instructions written in a high-level language that must be translated into machine language to be executed by the computer.

spam Unsolicited commercial e-mail.

spyware Technology that aids in gathering information about a person or organization without its knowledge.

standard operating procedures (SOPs) Formal rules for accomplishing tasks that have been developed to cope with expected situations.

star network A network topology in which all computers and other devices are connected to a central host computer. All communications between network devices must pass through the host computer.

storage area network (SAN) A high-speed network dedicated to storage that connects different kinds of storage devices, such as tape libraries and disk arrays, so they can be shared by multiple servers.

storage service provider (SSP) Third-party provider that rents out storage space to subscribers over the Internet, allowing customers to store and access their data without having to purchase and maintain their own storage technology.

storage technology Physical media and software governing the storage and organization of data for use in an information system.

stored-value payment systems Systems enabling consumers to make instant online payments to merchants and other individuals based on value stored in a digital account.

strategic information systems Computer systems at any level of the organization that change goals, operations, products, services, or environmental relationships to help the organization gain a competitive advantage.

strategic-level systems Information systems that support the long-range planning activities of senior management.

strategic transitions A movement from one level of sociotechnical system to another. Often required when adopting strategic systems that demand changes in the social and technical elements of an organization.

structure chart System documentation showing each level of design, the relationship among the levels, and the overall place in the design structure; can document one program, one system, or part of one program.

structured Refers to the fact that techniques are carefully drawn up, step by step, with each step building on a previous one.

structured analysis A method for defining system inputs, processes, and outputs and for partitioning systems into subsystems or modules that show a logical graphic model of information flow.

structured decisions Decisions that are repetitive, routine, and have a definite procedure for handling them.

structured design Software design discipline encompassing a set of design rules and techniques for designing systems from the top down in hierarchical fashion.

structured knowledge Knowledge in the form of structured documents and reports.

structured knowledge system System for organizing structured knowledge in a repository where it can be accessed throughout the organization. Also known as content management system.

structured programming Discipline for organizing and coding programs that simplifies the control paths so that the programs can be easily understood and modified; uses the basic control structures and modules that have only one entry point and one exit point.

structured query language (SQL) The standard data manipulation language for relational database management systems.

subschema The specific set of data from the database that is required by each user or application program.

supply chain Network of organizations and business processes for procuring materials, transforming raw materials into intermediate and finished products, and distributing the finished products to customers.

supply chain execution systems Systems to manage the flow of products through distribution centers and warehouses to ensure that products are delivered to the right locations in the most efficient manner.

supply chain management Integration of supplier, distributor, and customer logistics requirements into one cohesive process.

supply chain management systems Information systems that automate the flow of information between a firm and its suppliers to optimize the planning, sourcing, manufacturing, and delivery of products and services.

supply chain planning systems Systems that enable a firm to generate demand forecasts for a product and to develop sourcing and manufacturing plans for that product.

support activities Activities that make the delivery of a firm's primary activities possible. They consist of the organization's infrastructure, human resources, technology, and procurement.

switch Device to connect network components that has more intelligence than a hub and can filter and forward data to a specified destination.

switched lines Telephone lines that a person can access from a terminal to transmit data to another computer, with the call being routed or switched through paths to the designated destination.

switching costs The expense a customer or company incurs in lost time and expenditure of resources when changing from one supplier or system to a competing supplier or system.

syndicator A business that aggregates content or applications from multiple sources, packages them for distribution, and resells them to third-party Web sites.

system failure An information system that does not perform as expected, is not operational at a specified time, or cannot be used in the way it was intended.

system software Generalized programs that manage the computer's resources, such as the central processor, communications links, and peripheral devices.

system testing Tests the functioning of the information system as a whole to determine whether discrete modules will function together as planned.

systems analysis The analysis of a problem that the organization will try to solve with an information system.

systems analysts Specialists who translate business problems and requirements into information requirements and systems and who act as liaisons between the information systems department and the rest of the organization.

systems design Details how a system will meet the information requirements as determined by the systems analysis.

systems development The activities that go into producing an information systems solution for an organizational problem or opportunity.

systems life cycle A traditional methodology for developing an information system that partitions the systems development process into formal stages that must be completed sequentially with a very formal division of labor between end users and information systems specialists.

T lines High-speed data lines leased from communications providers, such as T-1 lines (with a transmission capacity of 1.544 megabits per second).

tacit knowledge Expertise and experience of organizational members that have not been formally documented.

tangible benefits Benefits that can be quantified and assigned a monetary value; they include lower operational costs and increased cash flows.

taxonomy Method of classifying things according to a predetermined system.

teamware Group collaboration software that is customized for teamwork.

technology standards Specifications that establish the compatibility of products and the ability to communicate in a network.

technostress Stress induced by computer use; symptoms include aggravation, hostility toward humans, impatience, and enervation.

telecommunications system A collection of compatible hardware and software arranged to communicate information from one location to another.

teleconferencing The ability to confer with a group of people simultaneously using the telephone or electronic mail group communication software.

telematics Wireless services that combine wireless communication with tracking capabilities from the Global Positioning System (GPS).

Telnet Network tool that enables someone to log on to one computer system while doing work on another.

test plan A plan prepared by the development team in conjunction with the users; it includes all of the preparations for the series of tests to be performed on the system.

testing The exhaustive and thorough process that determines whether the system produces the desired results under known conditions.

topology The way in which the components of a network are connected.

total cost of ownership (TCO) Designates the total cost of owning technology resources, including initial purchase costs, the cost of hardware and software upgrades, maintenance, technical support, and training.

Total Quality Management (TQM) A concept that makes quality control a responsibility to be shared by all people in an organization.

touch point Method of firm interaction with a customer, such as telephone, e-mail, customer service desk, conventional mail, or point-of-purchase.

trade secret Any intellectual work or product used for a business purpose that can be classified as belonging to that business, provided it is not based on information in the public domain.

transaction cost theory Economic theory stating that firms grow larger because they can conduct marketplace transactions internally more cheaply than they can with external firms in the marketplace.

transaction processing systems (TPS) Computerized systems that perform and record the daily routine transactions necessary to conduct the business; they serve the organization's operational level.

transborder data flow The movement of information across international boundaries in any form.

Transmission Control Protocol/Internet Protocol (TCP/IP) Dominant model for achieving connectivity among different networks. Provides a universally agreed-on method for breaking up digital messages into packets, routing them to the proper addresses, and then reassembling them into coherent messages.

transnational Truly global form of business organization with no national headquarters; value-added activities are managed from a global perspective without reference to national borders, optimizing sources of supply and demand and local competitive advantage.

Trojan horse A software program that appears legitimate but contains a second hidden function that may cause damage.

tuple A row or record in a relational database.

twisted wire A transmission medium consisting of pairs of twisted copper wires; used to transmit analog phone conversations but can be used for data transmission.

unified messaging System combining voice messages, e-mail, and fax so that all messages can all be obtained from a single system.

Unified Modeling Language (UML) Industry-standard methodology for analysis and design of an object-oriented software system.

Uniform Resource Locator (URL) The address of a specific resource on the Internet.

unit testing The process of testing each program separately in the system. Sometimes called program testing.

Universal Description, Discovery, and Integration (UDDI) A framework that enables a Web service to be listed in a directory of Web services so that it can be easily located by other organizations and systems.

Unix Operating system for all types of computers that is machine independent and supports multiuser processing, multitasking, and networking. Used in high-end workstations and servers.

unstructured decisions Nonroutine decisions in which the decision maker must provide judgment, evaluation, and insights into the problem definition; there is no agreed-upon procedure for making such decisions.

up-selling Marketing higher-value products or services to new or existing customers.

Usenet Forums in which people share information and ideas on a defined topic through large electronic bulletin boards where anyone can post messages on the topic for others to see and to which others can respond.

user-designer communications gap The difference in backgrounds, interests, and priorities that impede communication and problem solving among end users and information systems specialists.

user interface The part of the information system through which the end user interacts with the system; type of hardware and the series of on-screen commands and responses required for a user to work with the system.

Utilitarian Principle Principle that assumes one can put values in rank order and understand the consequences of various courses of action.

utility computing Model of computing in which companies pay only for the information technology resources they actually use during a specified time period. Also called on-demand computing or usage-based pricing.

value-added network (VAN) Private, multipath, data-only, third-party-managed network that multiple organizations use on a subscription basis.

value chain model Model that highlights the primary or support activities that add a margin of value to a firm's products or services where information systems can best be applied to achieve a competitive advantage.

value web Customer-driven network of independent firms that use information technology to coordinate their value chains to collectively produce a product or service for a market.

videoconferencing Teleconferencing in which participants see each other on video screens.

virtual organization An organization that uses networks to link people, assets, and ideas to create and distribute products and services without being limited to traditional organizational boundaries or physical locations.

virtual private network (VPN) A secure connection between two points across the Internet used to transmit corporate data. Provides a low-cost alternative to a private network.

Virtual Reality Modeling Language (VRML) A set of specifications for interactive three-dimensional modeling on the World Wide Web.

virtual reality systems Interactive graphics software and hardware that create computer-generated simulations that provide sensations that emulate real-world activities.

voice mail A system for digitizing a spoken message and transmitting it over a network.

Voice over IP (VoIP) Facilities for managing the delivery of voice information using the Internet Protocol (IP).

voice portal Capability for accepting voice commands for accessing Web content, e-mail, and other electronic applications from a cell phone or standard telephone and for translating responses to user requests for information into speech for the customer.

walkthrough A review of a specification or design document by a small group of people that has been carefully selected based on the skills needed for the particular objectives being tested.

Web browser An easy-to-use software tool for accessing the World Wide Web and the Internet.

Web bugs Tiny graphic files embedded in e-mail messages and Web pages that are designed to monitor online Internet user behavior.

Web content management tools Software used to facilitate the collection, assembly, and management of content on a Web site, intranet, or extranet.

Web hosting service Company with large Web server computers used to maintain the Web sites of fee-paying subscribers.

Web personalization The tailoring of Web content directly to a specific user.

Web server Software that manages requests for Web pages on the computer where they are stored and that delivers the page to the user's computer.

Web services Set of universal standards using Internet technology for integrating different applications from different sources without time-consuming custom coding. Used for linking systems of different organizations or for linking disparate systems within the same organization.

Web Services Description Language (WSDL)   Common framework for describing the tasks performed by a Web service so that the service can be used by other applications.

Web site   All of the World Wide Web pages maintained by an organization or an individual.

Web site performance monitoring tools   Software tools for monitoring the time to download Web pages, perform Web transactions, identify broken links between Web pages, and pinpoint other Web site problems and bottlenecks.

Webmaster   The person in charge of an organization's Web site.

wide area network (WAN)   Telecommunications network that spans a large geographical distance. May consist of a variety of cable, satellite, and microwave technologies.

Wi-Fi   Standards for Wireless Fidelity and refers to the Institute of Electrical and Electronics Engineers (IEEE) 802.11 family of wireless networking standards.

WiMax   Popular term for Institute of Electrical and Electronics Engineers (IEEE) Standard 802.16 for wireless networking over a range of up to 31 miles with a data transfer rate of up to 75 megabits per second (Mbps). Stands for Worldwide Interoperability for Microwave Access.

Windows   Microsoft family of operating systems for both network servers and client computers.

Windows 2000   Windows operating system for high-performance PCs and network servers. Supports networking, multitasking, multiprocessing, and Internet services.

Windows Server 2003   Recent Windows operating system for servers.

Windows XP   Powerful Windows operating system that provides reliability, robustness, and ease of use for both corporate and home PC users.

Wintel PC   Any computer that uses Intel microprocessors (or compatible processors) and a Windows operating system.

Wireless Application Protocol (WAP)   System of protocols and technologies that enables cell phones and other wireless devices with tiny displays, low-bandwidth connections, and minimal memory to access Web-based information and services.

Wireless Markup Language (WML)   Markup language for wireless Web sites; based on Extensible Markup Language (XML) and optimized for tiny displays.

wireless NIC   An add-in card (network interface card) that has a built-in radio and antenna to enable wireless transmission.

wireless portals   Portals with content and services optimized for mobile devices to steer users to the information they are most likely to need.

wireless sensor networks (WSNs)   Networks of interconnected wireless devices with built-in processing, storage, and radio-frequency sensors and antennas that are embedded into the physical environment to provide measurements of many points over large spaces.

wisdom   The collective and individual experience of applying knowledge to the solution of problems.

work-flow management   The process of streamlining business procedures so that documents can be moved easily and efficiently from one location to another.

workstation   Desktop computer with powerful graphics and mathematical capabilities and the ability to perform several complicated tasks at once.

World Wide Web (WWW)   A system with universally accepted standards for storing, retrieving, formatting, and displaying information in a networked environment.

worms   Independent software programs that propagate themselves to disrupt the operation of computer networks or destroy data and other programs.

XHTML (Extensible Hypertext Markup Language)   Hybrid of Hypertext Markup Language (HTML) and Extensible Markup Language (XML) that provides more flexibility than HTML.

XML (Extensible Markup Language)   General-purpose language that describes the structure of a document and supports links to multiple documents, enabling data to be manipulated by the computer. Used for both Web and non-Web applications.

ZigBee   Protocol that handles application-level communication between devices in a wireless sensor network. Determines the content of messages transmitted by each node in the network.

Photo and Screen Shot Credits

Organizations Index

Subject Index

Clemons, Eric K. "Evaluation of Strategic Investments in Information Technology." *Communications of the ACM* (January 1991).

Clemons, Eric K., and Michael Row. "McKesson Drug Co.: Case Study of a Strategic Information System." *Journal of Management Information Systems* (Summer 1988).

———. "Limits to Interfirm Coordination through IT." *Journal of Management Information Systems* 10, no. 1 (Summer 1993).

———. "Sustaining IT Advantage: The Role of Structural Differences." *MIS Quarterly* 15, no. 3 (September 1991).

Clemons, Eric K., and Bruce W. Weber. "Segmentation, Differentiation, and Flexible Pricing: Experience with Information Technology and Segment-Tailored Strategies." *Journal of Management Information Systems* 11, no. 2 (Fall 1994).

Coase, Ronald H. "The Nature of the Firm." 1937. In *The Economic Nature of the Firm: A Reader*, edited by Louis Putterman and Randall Kroszner. Cambridge University Press (1995).

Cohen, Michael, James March, and Johan Olsen. "A Garbage Can Model of Organizational Choice." *Administrative Science Quarterly* 17 (1972).

Davenport, Thomas H., and Keri Pearlson. "Two Cheers for the Virtual Office." *Sloan Management Review* 39, no. 4 (Summer 1998).

Davenport, Thomas H., Keri Pearlson, Jeanne G. Harris, and Ajay K. Kohli. "How Do They Know Their Customers So Well?" *Sloan Management Review* 42, no. 2 (Winter 2001).

Drucker, Peter. "The Coming of the New Organization." *Harvard Business Review* (January–February 1988).

Eisenhardt, Kathleen M. "Has Strategy Changed?" *Sloan Management Review* 43, no. 2 (Winter 2002).

Enns, Harvey G., Sid L. Huff, and Christopher A. Higgins. "CIO Lateral Influence Behaviors: Gaining Peer' Commitment to Strategic Information Systems." *MIS Quarterly* 27, no. 1 (March 2003).

Erasala, Naveen, and John "Skip" Benamati. "Understanding the Electronic Commerce Cycles of Change." *Journal of Organizational Computing and Electronic Commerce* 13, no. 1 (2003).

Etzioni, Amitai. *A Comparative Analysis of Complex Organizations.* New York: Free Press (1975).

Farhoomand, Ali, and Pauline S. P. Ng. "Creating Sustainable Competitive Advantage through Internetworked Communities." *Communications of the ACM* 46, no. 9 (September 2003).

Fayol, Henri. *Administration industrielle et generale.* Paris: Dunods (1950). First published 1916.

Feeny, David. "Making Business Sense of the E-Opportunity." *Sloan Management Review* 42, no. 2 (Winter 2001).

Feeny, David E., and Blake Ives. "In Search of Sustainability: Reaping Long-Term Advantage from Investments in Information Technology." *Journal of Management Information Systems* (Summer 1990).

Fine, Charles H., Roger Vardan, Robert Pethick, and Jamal E-Hout. "Rapid-Response Capability in Value-Chain Design." *Sloan Management Review* 43, no. 2 (Winter 2002).

Fisher, Marshall L., Ananth Raman, and Anne Sheen McClelland. "Rocket Science Retailing Is Almost Here: Are You Ready?" *Harvard Business Review* (July–August 2000).

Freeman, John, Glenn R. Carroll, and Michael T. Hannan. "The Liability of Newness: Age Dependence in Organizational Death Rates." *American Sociological Review* 48 (1983).

Fritz, Mary Beth Watson, Sridhar Narasimhan, and Hyeun-Suk Rhee. "Communication and Coordination in the Virtual Office." *Journal of Management Information Systems* 14, no. 4 (Spring 1998).

Fulk, Janet, and Geraldine DeSanctis. "Electronic Communication and Changing Organizational Forms." *Organization Science* 6, no. 4 (July–August 1995).

Gallaugher, John M., and Yu-Ming Wang. "Understanding Network Effects in Software Markets: Evidence from Web Server Pricing." *MIS Quarterly* 26, no. 4 (December 2002).

Garvin, David A. "The Processes of Organization and Management." *Sloan Management Review* 39, no. 4 (Summer 1998).

Gilbert, Clark, and Joseph L. Bower. "Disruptive Change." *Harvard Business Review* (May 2002).

Gurbaxani, V., and S. Whang. "The Impact of Information Systems on Organizations and Markets." *Communications of the ACM* 34, no. 1 (January 1991).

Hinds, Pamela, and Sara Kiesler. "Communication across Boundaries: Work, Structure, and Use of Communication Technologies in a Large Organization." *Organization Science* 6, no. 4 (July–August 1995).

Hitt, Lorin M. "Information Technology and Firm Boundaries: Evidence from Panel Data." *Information Systems Research* 10, no. 2 (June 1999).

Hitt, Lorin M., and Erik Brynjolfsson. "Information Technology and Internal Firm Organization: An Exploratory Analysis." *Journal of Management Information Systems* 14, no. 2 (Fall 1997).

Holweg, Matthias, and Frits K. Pil. "Successful Build-to-Order Strategies Start with the Customer." *Sloan Management Review* 43, no. 1 (Fall 2001).

Hopper, Max. "Rattling SABRE—New Ways to Compete on Information." *Harvard Business Review* (May–June 1990).

Huber, George P. "Cognitive Style as a Basis for MIS and DSS Designs: Much Ado About Nothing?" *Management Science* 29 (May 1983).

———. "The Nature and Design of Post-Industrial Organizations." *Management Science* 30, no. 8 (August 1984).

———. "Organizational Learning: The Contributing Processes and Literature." *Organization Science* 2 (1991): 88–115.

Iansiti, Marco, and Roy Levien. "Strategy as Ecology." *Harvard Business Review* (March 2004).

Isenberg, Daniel J. "How Senior Managers Think." *Harvard Business Review* (November–December 1984).

Ives, Blake, and Gabriele Piccoli. "Custom Made Apparel and Individualized Service at Land's End." *Communications of the Association for Information Systems* 11 (2003).

Jasperson, Jon (Sean), Traci A. Carte, Carol S. Saunders, Brian S. Butler, Henry J. P. Croes, and Weijun Zheng. "Review: Power and Information Technology Research: A Metatriangulation Review." *MIS Quarterly* 26, no. 4 (December 2002).

Jensen, M. C., and W. H. Meckling. "Specific and General Knowledge and Organizational Science." In *Contract Economics,* edited by L. Wetin and J. Wijkander. Oxford: Basil Blackwell (1992).

Jensen, Michael C., and William H. Meckling. "Theory of the Firm: Managerial Behavior, Agency Costs, and Ownership Structure." *Journal of Financial Economics* 3 (1976).

Kanter, Rosabeth Moss. "The New Managerial Work." *Harvard Business Review* (November–December 1989).

Kauffman, Robert J., and Yu-Ming Wang. "The Network Externalities Hypothesis and Competitive Network Growth." *Journal of Organizational Computing and Electronic Commerce* 12, no. 1 (2002).

Keen, Peter G. W. "Information Systems and Organizational Change." *Communications of the ACM* 24, no. 1 (January 1981).

Kettinger, William J., Varun Grover, Subashish Guhan, and Albert H. Segors. "Strategic Information Systems Revisited: A Study in Sustainability and Performance." *MIS Quarterly* 18, no. 1 (March 1994).

King, J. L., V. Gurbaxani, K. L. Kraemer, F. W. McFarlan, K. S. Raman, and C. S. Yap. "Institutional Factors in Information Technology Innovation." *Information Systems Research* 5, no. 2 (June 1994).

King, W. R. "Creating a Strategic Capabilities Architecture." *Information Systems Management* 12, no. 1 (Winter 1995).

Kling, Rob. "Social Analyses of Computing: Theoretical Perspectives in Recent Empirical Research." *Computing Survey* 12, no. 1 (March 1980).

Kolb, D. A., and A. L. Frohman. "An Organization Development Approach to Consulting." *Sloan Management Review* 12, no. 1 (Fall 1970).

Konsynski, Benn R., and F. Warren McFarlan. "Information Partnerships—Shared Data, Shared Scale." *Harvard Business Review* (September–October 1990).

Konsynski, Benn, John Sviokla, and Christopher L. Marshall. "Baxter International: OnCall as Soon as Possible?" *Harvard Business School* 9-195-103 (1994).

Kopczak, Laura Rock, and M. Eric Johnson. "The Supply-Chain Management Effect." *MIT Sloan Management Review* 44, no. 3 (Spring 2003).

Kotter, John T. "What Effective General Managers Really Do." *Harvard Business Review* (November–December 1982).

Kraemer, Kenneth, John King, Debora Dunkle, and Joe Lane. *Managing Information Systems.* Los Angeles: Jossey-Bass (1989).

Lamb, Roberta, and Rob Kling. "Reconceptualizing Users as Social Actors in Information Systems Research." *MIS Quarterly* 27, no. 2 (June 2003).

Laudon, Kenneth C. *Computers and Bureaucratic Reform.* New York: Wiley (1974).

———. *Dossier Society: Value Choices in the Design of National Information Systems.* New York: Columbia University Press (1986).

———. "Environmental and Institutional Models of Systems Development." *Communications of the ACM* 28, no. 7 (July 1985).

———. "A General Model of the Relationship between Information Technology and Organizations." Working paper, National Science Foundation, Center for Research on Information Systems, New York University (1989).

———. "The Promise and Potential of Enterprise Systems and Industrial Networks." Working paper, The Concours Group. Copyright Kenneth C. Laudon (1999).

Laudon, Kenneth C., and Kenneth L. Marr. "Information Technology and Occupational Structure." (April 1995).

Lawrence, Paul, and Jay Lorsch. *Organization and Environment.* Cambridge, Mass.: Harvard University Press (1969).

Leavitt, Harold J. "Applying Organizational Change in Industry: Structural, Technological, and Humanistic Approaches." In *Handbook of Organizations,* edited by James G. March. Chicago: Rand McNally (1965).

Leavitt, Harold J., and Thomas L. Whisler. "Management in the 1980s." *Harvard Business Review* (November–December 1958).

Levecq, Hugues, and Bruce W. Weber. "Electronic Trading Systems: Strategic Implication of Market Design Choices." *Journal of Organizational Computing and Electronic Commerce* 12, no. 1 (2002).

Lindblom, C. E. "The Science of Muddling Through." *Public Administration Review* 19 (1959).

Machlup, Fritz. *The Production and Distribution of Knowledge in the United States.* Princeton, N.J.: Princeton University Press (1962).

Maier, Jerry L., R. Kelly Rainer Jr., and Charles A. Snyder. "Environmental Scanning for Information Technology: An Empirical Investigation." *Journal of Management Information Systems* 14, no. 2 (Fall 1997).

Main, Thomas J., and James E. Short. "Managing the Merger: Building Partnership through IT Planning at the New Baxter." *MIS Quarterly* 13, no. 4 (December 1989).

Malone, Thomas W. "Is Empowerment Just a Fad? Control, Decision-Making, and IT." *Sloan Management Review* (Winter 1997).

Malone, Thomas W., JoAnne Yates, and Robert I. Benjamin. "Electronic Markets and Electronic Hierarchies." *Communications of the ACM* (June 1987).

March, James G., and G. Sevon. "Gossip, Information, and Decision Making." In *Advances in Information Processing in Organizations,* edited by Lee S. Sproull and J. P. Crecine. Vol. 1. Hillsdale, N.J.: Erlbaum (1984).

March, James G., and Herbert A. Simon. *Organizations.* New York: Wiley (1958).

Markus, M. L. "Power, Politics, and MIS Implementation." *Communications of the ACM* 26, no. 6 (June 1983).

McAfee, Andrew, and Francois-Xavier Oliveau. "Confronting the Limits of Networks." *Sloan Management Review* 43 no. 4 (Summer 2002).

McFarlan, F. Warren. "Information Technology Changes the Way You Compete." *Harvard Business Review* (May–June 1984).

McKenney, James L., and Peter G. W. Keen. "How Managers' Minds Work." *Harvard Business Review* (May–June 1974).

Mendelson, Haim, and Ravindra R. Pillai. "Clock Speed and Informational Response: Evidence from the Information Technology Industry." *Information Systems Research* 9, no. 4 (December 1998).

Mintzberg, Henry. "Managerial Work: Analysis from Observation." *Management Science* 18 (October 1971).

———. *The Nature of Managerial Work.* New York: Harper & Row (1973).

———. *The Structuring of Organizations.* Englewood Cliffs, N.J.: Prentice Hall (1979).

Mintzberg, Henry, and Frances Westley. "Decision Making: It's Not What You Think." *Sloan Management Review* (Spring 2001).

Orlikowski, Wanda J., and Daniel Robey. "Information Technology and the Structuring of Organizations." *Information Systems Research* 2, no. 2 (June 1991).

Pindyck, Robert S., and Daniel L. Rubinfeld. *Microeconomics,* 5th ed. Upper Saddle River, N.J.: Prentice Hall (2001).

Porter, Michael. *Competitive Strategy.* New York: Free Press, (1980.)

———. *Competitive Advantage.* New York: Free Press (1985).

———. "How Information Can Help You Compete." *Harvard Business Review* (August–September 1985).

———. "Strategy and the Internet." *Harvard Business Review* (March 2001).

Porter, Michael E., and Scott Stern. "Location Matters." *Sloan Management Review* 42, no. 4 (Summer 2001).

Prahalad, C. K., and Venkatram Ramaswamy. "The New Frontier of Experience Innovation." *MIS Sloan Management Review* 44, no. 4 (Summer 2003).

Reich, Blaize Horner, and Izak Benbasat. "Factors That Influence the Social Dimension of Alignment between Business and Information Technology Objectives." *MIS Quarterly* 24, no. 1 (March 2000).

Reinartz, Werner, and V. Kumar. "The Mismanagement of Customer Loyalty." *Harvard Business Review* (July 2002).

Robey, Daniel, and Marie-Claude Boudreau. "Accounting for the Contradictory Organizational Consequences of Information Technology: Theoretical Directions and Methodological Implications." *Information Systems Research* 10, no. 42 (June 1999).

Sauter, Vicki L. "Intuitive Decision-Making." *Communications of the ACM* 42, no. 6 (June 1999).

Schein, Edgar H. *Organizational Culture and Leadership.* San Francisco: Jossey-Bass (1985).

Schwenk, C. R. "Cognitive Simplification Processes in Strategic Decision Making." *Strategic Management Journal* 5 (1984).

Shapiro, Carl, and Hal R. Varian. *Information Rules.* Boston: Harvard Business School Press, 1999.

Shore, Edwin B. "Reshaping the IS Organization." *MIS Quarterly* (December 1983).

Short, James E., and N. Venkatraman. "Beyond Business Process Redesign: Redefining Baxter's Business Network." *Sloan Management Review* (Fall 1992).

Simon, Herbert A. "Applying Information Technology to Organization Design." *Public Administration Review* (May–June 1973).

Slywotzky, Adrian J., and Richard Wise. "The Growth Crisis, and How to Escape It." *Harvard Business Review* (July 2002).

Starbuck, William H. "Organizations as Action Generators." *American Sociological Review* 48 (1983).

Starbuck, William H., and Frances J. Milliken. "Executives' Perceptual Filters: What They Notice and How They Make Sense." In *The Executive Effect: Concepts and Methods for Studying Top Managers,* edited by D. C. Hambrick. Greenwich, Conn.: JAI Press (1988).

Teo, H. H., K. K. Wei, and I. Benbasat. "Predicting Intention to Adopt Interorganizational Linkages: An Institutional Perspective." *MIS Quarterly* 27, no. 1 (March 2003).

Turner, Jon A. "Computer Mediated Work: The Interplay between Technology and Structured Jobs." *Communications of the ACM* 27, no. 12 (December 1984).

Turner, Jon A., and Robert A. Karasek Jr. "Software Ergonomics: Effects of Computer Application Design Parameters on Operator Task Performance and Health." *Ergonomics* 27, no. 6 (1984).

Tushman, Michael L., and Philip Anderson. "Technological Discontinuities and Organizational Environments." *Administrative Science Quarterly* 31 (September 1986).

Tversky, A., and D. Kahneman. "The Framing of Decisions and the Psychology of Choice." *Science* 211 (January 1981).

Vandenbosch, Mark, and Niraj Dawar. "Beyond Better Products: Capturing Value in Customer Interactions." *Sloan Management Review* 43, no. 4 (Summer 2002).

Walker, Marlon A. "The Day the E-Mail Dies" *Wall Street Journal* (August 26, 2004).

Index

Name Index